Persianate Prose and the Making of Malay Muslim Literature

Persianate Prose and the Making of Malay Muslim Literature

Text, Translation and Commentary of the *Durr al-Majālis*

by Majid Daneshgar

EDINBURGH
University Press

THE E J W GIBB
MEMORIAL TRUST

Edinburgh University Press is one of the leading university presses in the UK. Publishing new research in the arts and humanities, EUP connects people and ideas to inspire creative thinking, open new perspectives and shape the world we live in. For more information, visit www.edinburghuniversitypress.com.

Edinburgh University Press Ltd
13 Infirmary Street, Edinburgh EH1 1LT

The E. J. W. Gibb Memorial Trust
79 Fairview Crescent
Rayners Lane
Harrow HA2 9UB

Typeset in Minion Pro and Omar Naskh by
Advent Publishing Services, Leeds

A CIP record for this book is available from the British Library

ISBN 978 1 3995 3757 5 (hardback)
ISBN 978 1 3995 3759 9 (webready PDF)
ISBN 978 1 3995 3760 5 (epub)

EU Authorised Representative:
Easy Access System Europe
Mustamäe tee 50, 10621 Tallinn, Estonia
gpsr.requests@easproject.com

DEDICATED TO

Dr. Jutta Schurig

Contents

Acknowledgments xi
Transliteration Format xv
Table of Figures xvii
List of Tables xix
Preface xxi

PART A: ON LITERATURE, CONTEXT AND TEXT 1

I. Introduction 3

Durr al-Majālis in Southeast Asia 6
The Persian-Malay Network: Historical Ties between Muslims 7
Persian Phonology in Malay Language 20
Persian Origin of Malay Islamic Literature 25

II. *Durr al-Majālis*: Origins and Identity 41

Reception of the Text 46
Bibliographical and Biographical Details 47

III. Transregional Circulation 61

Durr al-Majālis in Punjabi 63
Durr al-Majālis in Pushto 63
Durr al-Majālis in Bengali (and in Bengal) 64
Durr al-Majālis in Turkic Languages and Contexts 67
Durr al-Majālis in the Arabic Zone 72
Durr al-Majālis in Kurdish 73

IV. Islamic Themes and Novelty 75

Belief and Doctrine 75
Philosophical Theology 76
Occultism and Magic 76
About the Prophets 77
A Killing Story of Sunnis and Shīʿīs, and the idea of de-Shīʿitisation 79
Dialogue 82

V. Persianate-Malay Islamic Stories: A Comparative Analysis 87

On Persian-Malay Muslim Literature 88
Shared Islamic Stories in Persian and Malay 88
Close Similarities 96

VI. A Critical Persian Edition and Critically Edited Translation of *Durr al-Majālis* 125

Persian Edition 125
English Translation 129
Formation 130

PART B: PERSIAN EDITION AND ENGLISH TRANSLATION 131

Introduction 133
1. On the virtues of the creation of His Eminence Adam (pbuh) and further similar examples 141
2. On the virtue of Abraham's (pbuh) generosity and further similar examples 161
3. On the virtue of Jethro (pbuh) 173
4. On the virtue of His Eminence Moses 179
5. On the virtue of His Eminence Solomon (pbuh) 189
6. On the virtue of His Eminence Jesus (pbuh) and his miracle 199
7. On the virtue of our Prophet 211
8. The right of orphans 229
9. The story of the Prophet's (pbuh) injured teeth 239
10. An Entreaty 245
11. On the Virtue of the Hero, the Commander of Believers ʿAlī (pbuh) 253
12. The story of Mary the Copt, the servant of Muḥammad (pbuh) 261
13. On the virtue of the Joseph-like youth after he was treated for the sake of God 269
14. On the virtue of Khālid b. Walīd (pbuh) 279
15. On the virtue of Bilāl, and a king from the Arab region 293

16. The advice of Luqmān the Wise, ʿAbd al-Raḥmān, to his son 305
17. On the coming to faith of an idolater through Abraham 313
18. The story of Sultan Ibrāhīm Adham, may his grave be sanctified 321
19. The story of the generous husband and the miserly wife 329
20. The story of Āzar, the idol-maker 339
21. The story of the parrot speaking with the Prophet Solomon (pbuh) 349
22. The story of Khʷāja Ḥasan Baṣrī God's mercy be upon him 353
23. The story of the request of the outcast Satan who harassed the nation of the Prophet Muḥammad 361
24. The story of the King of Nishapur's treatment of the oppressed 369
25. The story of Khʷāja Rabīʿ Ḥusām 375
26. The story of Khʷāja Sufyān Thawrī with the outcast Satan, God's curse be upon him 385
27. The story of Khʷāja Ḥasan Nūrī, may God's mercy be upon him 393
28. The story of Shaykh Barsīsā 401
29. On the virtue of the holy month of Ramadan 411
30. The story of the Kaʿba 423
31a. The story of the killing of the commanders of believers Ḥasan and Ḥusayn (pbuh) 435
31b. The story of the killing of the commanders of believers Ḥasan and Ḥusayn (pbuh) 469
32. The story of our sovereign-master Abu Saʿīd Abū al-Khayr 525
33. The story of the inhabitants of paradise 533
34. Regarding Balʿam Bāʿūr 545
35. The tale of Moses 551
36. The story of the King of the Levant 587
Epilogue: *Nūr-nāma* 597
List of the Chapters 609

PART C: APPENDICES 613

Bibliography 657
Index 673
Persian Preface 690

Acknowledgments

I started writing this book in New Zealand in summer 2017. I will never forget those productive days at Auckland Libraries where I was working as their George Grey scholar. I was going to list and catalogue Arabic, Persian, Hindustani and Ottoman Turkish manuscripts of Grey and Henry Shaw, two prominent book collectors. In doing so, I came across a copy of the Persian text which is the focus of this present study. Due to my familiarity with Malay-Indonesian literature since 2011, I soon realized that the manuscript collected by Sir George Grey could be the main prototype of several Malay-Indonesian Muslim stories.

Reading and checking Persian and Malay-Indonesian texts alongside each other was not an easy task. It took me three years to complete my comparative study while writing other chapters. It would not have been possible for me to become a reader, and a modest expert of the Malay history and literature without the kind support and assistance I received from many nice people. First and foremost, I am indebted to Peter G. Riddell, an extremely knowledgeable and generous historian of Muslim history and literature, a polyglot competent in reading old and modern materials in a wide range of languages. He has been one of the most important Indonesian linguists and historians of Islam in Southeast Asia. His publications changed academic discourses for the better, instructing emerging scholars how to read, transcribe, romanize and translate old Jawi texts. From 2011–2014, Peter provided me and many others with invaluable information about the existence of a deeper form of relationship between the Middle East and South-East Asia. He was so kind to me by offering his detailed comments on earlier drafts of this work since 2017. Further, I would like to thank Edwin P. Wieringa, the gem of the world of philology, with precise eyes in detecting the link between letters, terms, texts. His works on classical and modern historical and literary works from Southeast Asia are exemplary. Edwin always provided me with his constructive feedback about the earlier drafts of this work since 2017. I am also indebted to those who helped me to develop my work significantly: Annabel Teh Gallop, Ronit Ricci, R. Michael Feener, Martin van Bruinessen, David S. Powers, and Nile Green.

I delivered several lectures pertaining to this book in Europe, especially at Freiburg Institute for Advanced Studies (FRIAS), where I was a Marie Curie Junior Fellow of the European Union in 2017–2018. Their support was timely and encouraging. One of the main parts of my previous research about the Persianate origin of Malay Muslim literature, based on my FRIAS project, were later published in *Archipel*, a journal dedicated to 'interdisciplinary studies on Insulindia', in 2018.[1] I thank *Archipel* for granting me permission to reproduce parts of that article entitled "New evidence on the origin of the *Hikayat Muhammad Hanafiyyah*".

My thanks also go to Jane Wild, Georgia Prince, and Kate de Courcy from the Auckland Libraries for providing me with a chance to examine and catalogue their rich collection of oriental manuscripts. The main part of my arguments is based on the Auckland Libraries Heritage Collections GMS-170 and GMS-173. I am also grateful to Oriental Research Library of Srinagar, Kashmir; Staatsbibliothek zu Berlin (Berlin State Library) and die Bayerische Staatsbibliothek (Bavarian State Library), Germany; Leiden University Library Special Collections, the Netherlands; Lund University Library, Sweden; Cambridge University Library, British Library, and SOAS Library, UK; and the Australian National Library and University, Australia, Iranology Foundation, Iran, for providing me with different copies of their manuscripts. I thank all other libraries from Indonesia, Malaysia, Iran, India and the USA for sharing the materials publicly. Their names and locations are found in the appendices. Fathi Saleh and Shoaib Malik provided me with different manuscript copies kept in Talaat Library (Egypt) and the Academy of Sciences of Tajikistan, respectively, for which I am grateful.

Remembering friends who have been with me for about a decade and through different stages of completing this volume is a duty of mine. I am deeply grateful to Mohsen Feyzbakhsh for his unceasing support, finding all sorts of rare or newly published materials from Africa to China. His comments on my various readings of the Persianate text were quite helpful. My thanks go to Radman Rasooli Mehrabani for his patience and important comments on my Persian edition. My thanks go to Fatemeh Sajjadi, a wonderful friend with extremely helpful advice. I am indebted to Said Fard for sharing his critical thoughts with me. Also, I thank Sajjad Aftabi who always listened to my stories. My special thanks go to Rowena Abdul Razak for her support and assistance providing me withs some scanned copies of different manuscripts.

I also thank Mohammad Khoonkari a great friend who is always there to listen and

[1] Some short articles were also published by *Mizan Online Platform* between 2017–2019.

support. We met each other in Freiburg, Germany in 2017, a green city in Europe; a proper place for starting a new friendship. My sincere gratitude to Shahrokh Raei and Leila Samadi Rendy for their friendship. Shahrokh and I had several discussions on the concept of Sufism and Sufi orders in the Oriental Studies Institute, University of Freiburg. There were other colleagues, including Rashid who provided me with several Turkic printed volumes from Kazan. I also thank Johanna Pink, Barbara Ihle, Tim Epkenhans, Olmo Gölz, Simon Wolfgang Fuchs (now at The Hebrew University of Jerusalem), and Mostafa Najafi (now at Luzern University), who shared their time and knowledge with me about different aspects of my research in Germany for more than five years. Living in Germany became much more beautiful due to my friendship with Elke, Marinna and Peter, who were always kind to me and my family.

My friends and former colleagues at the University of Cambridge and St John's College, where I was their first CUL Munby Fellow in global bibliography, have always been very kind. I am indebted to all of them, especially Suzanne Paul, Jill Whitelock, Mark Purcell, Jessica Gardner, Yasmin Faghihi, Yan He, Alessandro Bianchi, Kristine Rose-Beers, Orietta da Rold, Frank Bowles, Sally Kent.

My colleagues and friends at the University of Kyoto and the Kyoto city were extremely nice, always ready to help: Fumiharu Mieno, Tomohiro Machikita, Chika Obiya, Mostafa Khalili, Ryota Sakamoto, Chiaki Abe, Tomoko Kawai, and Naoko Nishiyama, among others. My thanks go also to Chiya and Ken and their daughter; Hitaf and Tomo and their daughter; Nubo and Sarah and their children; Ryuta and Kasumi and their children; Mari and her family.

I benefited from constructive comments from all anonymous reviewers. I also thank Andrew Peacock, the chair and one of the series editors of The Gibb Memorial Trust for welcoming my book project to be considered for a possible publication with their series in association with Edinburgh University Press (EUP). Andrew's works on Arabic, Persian, Turkish and Malay literature and history have been groundbreaking, encouraging me and many others to expand transregional study of Islamic literature. I thank Rachel Bridgewater, the EUP's Senior Commissioning Editor for her patience and support from the beginning. My thanks to Amir Dastmalchian who assisted me in making significant improvements to the English language of this work. He was also responsible for typesetting the work.

I would like to dedicate this study to Dr Schurig of Freiburg, a treasure in the heart of Europe, a wonderful person and medical doctor, passionate about world languages and history.

Last but not least, I owe my happiness in life and success in career to my family. First of all, my love and wife, AZAR...She has been a wise friend, great listener and patient partner...She was the main engine behind this project, providing me with everything I needed to finish the book. Her comments on previous drafts of this book were extremely constructive. Second, my sweet daughter, Shahd (*not* Shahad), whose name, literally 'nectar or honey', was mentioned in various copies of the Persianate text in different languages, from Africa to Turkistan and Siam... Shahd, like asal, has been a global name for centuries. Third, my son and sun...Mehr with his beautiful smile, who has been always passionate, gazing at me while completing this work.

***All errors are exclusively mine.

Transliteration Format

Arabic	Transliteration (EI³)	Arabic	Transliteration (EI³)
ء	ʾ	ظ	*ẓ*
آ\ا	*ā*	ع	ʿ
ب	*b*	غ	*gh*
ت	*t*	ف	*f*
ث	*th*	ق	*q*
ج	*j*	ک	*k*
ح	*ḥ*	ل	*l*
خ	*kh*	م	*m*
د	*d*	ن	*n*
ذ	*dh*	ه	*h*
ر	*r*	ة	*a; "-at in iḍāfa"*
ز	*z*	و	*ū; "-uww-; word final ū"*
س	*s*	ى\ي	*ī; "-iyy-; word final ī"*
ش	*sh*	Short vowels: *a; i; u*	
ص	*ṣ*		
ض	*ḍ*		
ط	*ṭ*		

Persian	Transliteration (EI^3)	Persian	Transliteration (EI^3)
ء	ʾ	ظ	*ẓ*
آ\ا	*ā*	ع	ʿ
ب	*b*	غ	*gh*
پ	*p*	ف	*f*
ت	*t*	ق	*q*
ث	*th*	ک	*k*
ج	*j*	گ	*g*
چ	*ch*	ل	*l*
ح	*ḥ*	م	*m*
خ	*kh*	ن	*n*
خو	*khw*	و	*w; ū*
د	*d*	ه	*h*
ذ	*dh*	ة	*at*
ر	*r*	ى\ي	*ī; "-iyy-; word final ī"*
ز	*z*	ـِى	*-yi*
ژ	*zh*	Short vowels: *a; i; u*	
س	*s*		
ش	*sh*		
ص	*ṣ*		
ض	*ḍ*		
ط	*ṭ*		

* For Indonesian, Javanese, Malay and Turkish, modern-day orthographies are used.

Table of Figures

Figure 1	The opening page (fl.1) of the Persian manuscript GMS-170. Courtesy of Auckland Libraries, New Zealand.	xxiii
Figure 2	Folio 119 [the colophon], MS Jarring.Prov.91. Turkic version of *Durr al-Majālis* from Xinjiang, China. Courtesy of Lund University, Sweden.	69
Figure 3	Folio 31, MS Or.565. Persian copy of *Durr al-Majālis* including the most obvious type of de-Shīʿitisation, replacing the names of Shīʿī figures with those of the first three Sunni caliphs. Courtesy of Leiden University Library, the Netherlands.	83
Figure 4	Pp.56-57. MS. 21045. A versified chivalrous account of ʿAlī, part of the *Jang-nāma-yi Muḥammad Ḥanafiyya*. Courtesy of the Parliamentary Library of Iran, Tehran, Iran.	102
Figure 5	Fl.13. MS 37082, item 7. The Malay *Hikayat Nur Muhammad*. SOAS Digital Library. Courtesy of SOAS Library, University of London, United Kingdom.	123

List of Tables

Table 1	Theme of Prophetic Miracles according to the Persian and Malay versions of 'the Tale of Splitting the Moon'.	99
Table 2	Abbreviations of Holy Scripture Titles.	620
Table 3	A list of the chapters in a Kurmanji adaptation of Sayf Ẓafar's *Durr al-Majālis* known as No. ГПБ, курд 40 and a comparison to the chapters standardly found in his work.	652

Preface

I started writing the outline of this volume during a short period of research spent at the Auckland Libraries in New Zealand in 2017. This collection of libraries houses several oriental manuscripts collected by Sir George Grey (1812–1898) and Henry Shaw (1850–1928). Upon studying the items these men collected it became obvious that not only were the physical features of the books and manuscripts rare but so too was the content.

Grey was a colonial officer and book collector born in Lisbon, Portugal to Anglo-Irish parents. As one of the most distinguished colonial administrators of the Victorian era, he served as Governor of South Australia (1840–1845), New Zealand (1845–1853), Cape Colony (1854–1861), and once more New Zealand (1861–1868). As a lifelong bibliophile, he donated his private library, which included Arabic (from the Middle East and Africa), Persian, and Urdu (also Hindustani) manuscripts to the city of Auckland in 1887.

As for Henry Shaw, he was born in England in 1850 and accompanied his parents on a move to New Zealand in 1859. It is said that Shaw started to become a book collector in 1884 after introducing a tenth/sixteenth-century printed copy of the Bible to New Zealand. He established a shop to sell his books and manuscripts in the 1880s. The Arabic, Persian, and Ottoman Turkish materials he collected are valuable in terms of the diversity of topics they cover.

At the end of my research trip, as I waited in Auckland Airport for my flight to Dunedin, Otago in New Zealand's Southern Island, I reviewed the manuscript images I had recently taken. Before departure I went through the whole Persian manuscript of *Durr al-Majālis* (GMS-170), copied in Masnabi, a port in Mozambique, by a scribe of Indian origin who was possibly a Twelver Khoja with strong connections with Muslims of Mombasa in Kenya. With thirty-six chapters on prophets, Imams, saints, and Sufis and broaching different themes and subjects, the thirteenth/nineteenth-century manuscript promised to be most rewarding. As I uncovered more and more of the work I began to see the clear connections with Malay Muslim literature.

Having studied, lived, and worked in Malaysia and having visited Indonesian traditional schools and colleges, I was well aware of the relationships, both direct and convoluted, between Persian and Malay speaking communities. Scholars studying the history of Southeast Asia have long since demonstrated the influence of Persian literature on the formation and development of Malay Islamic literature, both poetry and prose. It is agreed that Persian stories, with its chivalrous and didactic themes, had a lasting impact on Malay Muslim prose literature just a few centuries after the dawn of Islam in Southeast Asia. Various hypotheses have been offered as to whether Persian textual sources were available to Malays or simply that Malay people were exposed to different stories through oral transmission. Given the scarcity of old Malay manuscripts most scholars have been of the view that Malay Muslim literature (*hikayat*) were based on but a few Persian prose works. This consensus dettered scholars from investigating the Persian influences any further.

Let's return to the departure zone of Auckland Airport. As I waited for my flight I reflected that most of the content of GMS-170 has parallels in the Malay *hikayat* and, therefore, could have possibly been the source for them. It stuck me that I needed to collect more manuscript copies of *Durr al-Majālis* and read them alongside Malay *hikayat* to confirm the accuracy of my hypothesis. So began a long academic journey which spanned some years and saw a large number of Persian manuscripts collected from locations in Africa, Europe, North America, the Middle East, and Central and South-East Asia. I discovered that *Durr al-Majālis* was, interestingly, reproduced in both its entirety and piecemeal with sometimes only individual chapters being scribed to form standalone stories.

Each copy of *Durr al-Majālis* has its own interesting story. Some complete copies of the work are now found in Tehran but were scribed by Tamils residing in southern India. A limited copy, but a short standalone treatise, also now found in Tehran, was copied in eleventh/seventeenth-century Siam (modern-day Thailand and Burma). Its Persian lines are in places interspersed with Ottoman Turkish. The manuscript was bound in Istanbul and circulated between Muslims of the Balkans and kept in Cairo for centuries. Another version, now preserved in the Bavarian State Library in Munich, Germany, languished in Cairo for many years before being collected by French colonial officers in the thirteenth/nineteenth century. Furthermore, over the years I have also discovered tens of translations of *Durr al-Majālis* into various languages throughout the world. Not only Malay-Indonesian renditions, but also Turkic, Kurdish, Dakhni, Punjabi, Pushto (Pashto), Bengali, Tatar, Uzbek, and Russian copies, among others. Influence on Filipino material is also evident.

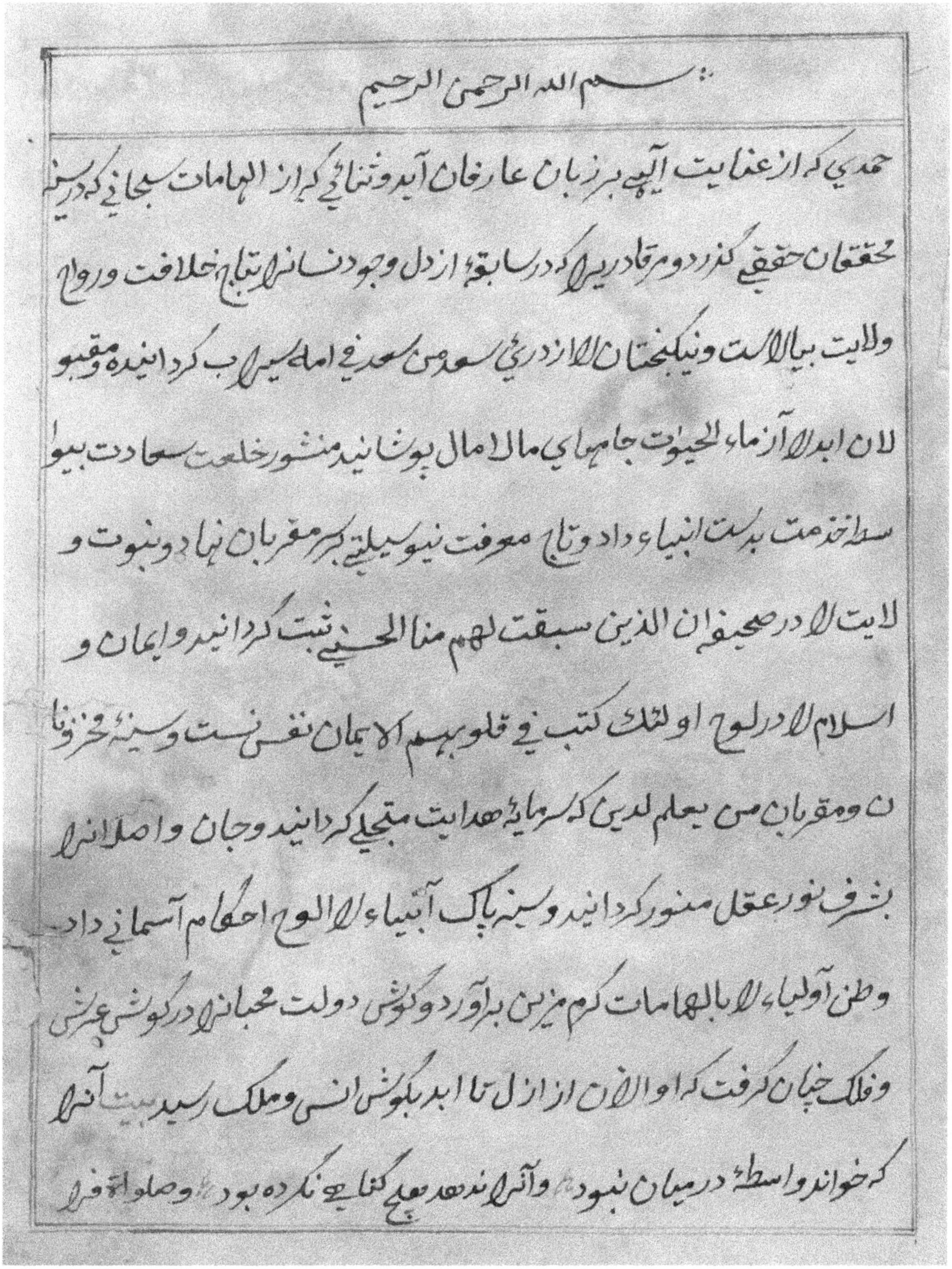

بسم الله الرحمن الرحیم

حمدی که از عنایت الهی بر زبان عارفان آید وثنائی که از الهامات سبحانی که در سینه
محققان حقیقی گذرد ومر قادریرا که درسابقهٔ ازل وجود نشان ابتاج خلافت ورواج
ولایت بیا الست ونیکبختان الازدری سعد من سعد فی امه سیراب کردانیده ومقبو
لان ابدالآزماء الحیوة جامهای مالامال پوشانید منشور خلعت سعادت بیو
سته خدمت بدست انبیاء داد وتاج معرفت نیوسیلتی بر سر مقربان نهاد ونبوت و
لایت را در صحیفهٔ ان الذین سبقت لهم منا الحسنی ثبت کردانید وایمان و
اسلام را در لوح اولئک کتب فی قلوبهم الایمان نقش بست وسینهٔ مخزونا
ن ومقربان من یعلم لدنی که سرمایهٔ هدایت متجلی کردانید وجان واصلانرا
بشرف نور عقل منور کردانید وسینهٔ پاک انبیاء را الوح احکام آسمانی داد
وطن اولیاء را بالهامات کرم مزین براورد وگوشی دولت محبانرا در گوشی عرشی
وفلک جهان گرفت که او الان از ازل تا ابد بگوش انس وملک رسید بیت آنرا
که خواند واسطهٔ درمیان نبود وآنرا ندهد هیچ گناهی نکرده بود وصلوات فرا

Figure 1. The opening page (fl.1) of the Persian manuscript GMS-170.
Courtesy of Auckland Libraries, New Zealand.

In this present study, therefore, we deal with a wonderful work which was welcomed in different Muslim communities for many years. The *Durr al-Majālis* has remained unknown in studies about Muslim literature and folk stories in general and Southeast Asia in particular and this volume is aimed at addressing this shortcoming. In order to provide an authentic and reliable comparative study between Persian and Malay texts I examined several original Malay, Indonesian, and other Southeast Asian manuscripts kept in Malaysia (Kuala Lumpur), Indonesia (Jakarta and Aceh), Germany (Berlin, Marburg, Munich), France (Paris and Strasbourg), the Netherlands (Amsterdam and Leiden), the United Kingdom (Cambridge, Oxford, London, and Edinburgh), among others.

PART A

ON LITERATURE, CONTEXT AND TEXT

I) Introduction

This volume is about a collection of short and long texts originally written in Persian somewhere between Bukhara and northern India in what was once the heart of the mediaeval Persianate world. The text was written during the late seventh and early eighth centuries of the Islamic calendar (thirteenth–fourteenth centuries CE) by Sayf Ẓafar and is titled *Durr al-Majālis* (Pearl of Gatherings). The author sought to provide both the learned and the illiterate with a sourcebook of Islamic learning. For the learned the book would be readable, easy to understand, and easy to memorise whereas for the illiterate the book would comprise inspirational stories that were easily transmitted. Sayf Ẓafar's text was produced during a period in which the Islamic religion and the Muslim territories were still expanding. It was a time that Muslim scholars were concerned to convert non-Muslims to the religion of Islam as well as to assure the Muslim masses that they were affiliated to the correct religion. The *Durr al-Majālis*, therefore, tells of numerous encounters between Muslims and non-Muslims and in a number of places compares Muslim and non-Muslim texts.

Sayf Ẓafar wrote using the eloquent language of his own time containing; a language replete with proverbs, couplets, Qurʾānic verses, and prophetic and mystical statements so as to entice readers to the 'pearl' that he believed to be 'Islam'. His text clearly shows that his target readers were people from across the world (*al-anām*). This is also evident through its transregional and global reception. Although elites and rulers showed a passion for reading Sayf Ẓafar's interpretation of Islam, there were often unknown scholars and ordinary Muslims who also paid to it close attention. After writing the *Durr al-Majālis*, a wide range of villagers, among whom were religious scholars and Sufi disciples, began to copy the text. Despite including more than thirty chapters about different aspects of classical Islamic sciences, the text's nature was inclusive of other cultures and traditions.

As was common during the period in which it was written, the *Durr al-Majālis* mixes various oriental themes and traditions with Islamic sources in the Persianate world. Readers would notice the way Sayf Ẓafar had added to his text Hindu qualities and characteristics alongside concepts from Islamic subjects such as the Qurʾānic sciences (*ʿulūm al-Qurʾān*), *tafsīr* (exegesis), Ḥadīth studies, jurisprudence (*fiqh*), morality (*adab*), poetry, language, and history – concepts that mainly originated in Arabia, Baghdad, the Levant, and Persia.

The *Durr al-Majālis* was circulated throughout the Persianate world, both in original form and in translation. The text also travelled beyond the so-called 'Balkans-to-Bengal' borders[1] and was both fully and partially copied, translated, and annotated virtually wherever Muslims were living. It was produced when the Persian language was a 'vibrant and prestigious literary language' and was a 'widely used medium in state bureaucracies, and the principal contact tongue for inter-regional diplomacy along the "Silk Road" between Anatolia and East Asia'.[2] Unsurprisingly, *Durr al-Majālis* made inroads into this whole area. But the point which contributes to the significance of this current study is the way the text moved beyond the already defined Persianate world. This text penetrated regions where the Persian language was used as but a foreign language for officials as opposed to a thriving indigenous language.[3] The original Persian text, as well as its translation, was reproduced beyond the Persianate heartlands in places such as Eastern Turkistan, Mongol-dominated China, Arabic-speaking Egypt, and throughout the Malay-Indonesian world.

The *Durr al-Majālis* owed its fame to not only its many translations. The text also benefitted from a renewed interest in Persian literarture in the late eighteenth to the early twentieth centuries. It is said that the Persianate regions had observed some decline in textual and cultural ties a few centuries earlier and this lead to textual

[1] Regarding Balkan to Bengal see, Marshall G. S. Hodgson, The Venture of Islam (Chicago: The University of Chicago Press, 1974) I: 96; and Shahab Ahmed, *What is Islam? The Importance of Being Islamic* (Princeton: Princeton University Press, 2016). Further studies on the Persianate regions, see Bert Fragner, *Die 'Persophonie': Regionalität, Identität und Sprachkontakt in der Geschichte Asiens* (Berlin: Das Arabische Buch, 1999). Abbas Amanat, and Assef Ashraf (eds). *The Persianate World: Rethinking a Shared Sphere* (Leiden: Brill, 2018). Nile Green (ed.) *The Persianate World: The Frontiers of a Eurasian Lingua Franca* (California: University of California Press, 2019).

[2] Richard M. Eaton, *India in the Persianate Age: 1000–1765* (London: Penguin UK, 2019), 13.

[3] '[…] from the tenth through the fourteenth centuries, new Muslim communities in Persianate lands of Iran and Tūrān (Central Asia) wrote themselves into Islamic histories dominated by Egyptian, Syrian, and Arabian places, persons, and lineages' see: Mana Kia, 'The Necessary Ornaments of Place: Similarity and Alterity in the Persianate Imaginary', *Comparative Islamic Studies* 13/1–2 (2017), 53; and also, Mimi Hanaoka, *Authority and Identity in Mediaeval Islamic Historiography: Persian Histories from the Peripheries* (Cambridge: Cambridge University Press, 2016).

disconnections from the Balkans to Bengal.[4] But Sayf Ẓafar's *Durr al-Majālis* was one of the few sources, which along with the Persian influential texts such as Saʿdī's (d. c. 690/1291) *Gulistān* (The Rose Garden), was widely circulated in imperial Russia where readers and translators of Persian materials were often in direct or indirect contact with the schools of Bukhara and Central Asia.[5] A large number of manuscript copies were either taken to Russia or copied in the Volga region. Russian universities, with both military and academic functions, taught and researched Persian, Tatar, and Arabic,[6] and Russian scholars of oriental sources were well-acquainted with Persian materials including the *Durr al-Majālis*. Even today works from Tataristan and by Siberian 'Bukharans' can be found in Russian libraries.

Moreover, some copies of *Durr al-Majālis* were circulated in Cairo or brought from North Africa to European libraries by book collectors and orientalists in the thirteenth/nineteenth century. This should not be surprising as both Turks and inhabitants of Greater Khurasan have for many centuries visited, studied, and lived in Arabic-speaking regions, in places such as Arabia and Egypt. Muslim scholars from Bukhara, Khwarazm, Balkh, Herat, Samarqand, and Turkistan used to exchange ideas frequently and were in communication with each other. Many of them chose to stay in Nishapur – as a hub for Islamic sciences – from where they could move out to the centre or northwest of Iran (e.g., Isfahan or Tabriz, respectively) and then to the Arabic zones of Baghdad, Damascus, Tartus, Aleppo, Mecca, Medina, and Egypt, and vice versa.[7] As will be shown, *Durr al-Majālis* was also highly influenced by thinkers of the school of Greater Khurasan – especially its celebrated Persian mystic and literary figure, Farīd al-Dīn ʿAṭṭār (d. c. 618/1221) – and was copied and read widely throughout this route.

4 For an introduction on the Persianate world, see Nile Green (ed.) *The Persianate World: The Frontiers of a Eurasian Lingua Franca* (Oakland: University of California Press, 2019), 4–5.

5 Alfrid Bustanov, 'Speaking 'Bukharan': The Circulation of Persian Texts in Imperial Russia', *The Persianate World: The Frontiers of a Eurasian Lingua Franca*, edited by Nile Green (Oakland: University of California Press, 2019), 193–194.

6 Denis V. Volkov, 'Persian Studies and the Military in Late Imperial Russia (1863–1917): State Power in the Service of Knowledge?' *Iranian Studies* 47/6 (2014): 918.

7 To see the list of Muslim scholars, their names and lifespans, who visited Nishapur to travel to the Arabic zone, see Muḥammad ʿAbdullāh Ḥakīm Nīshābūrī, *Tārīkh-i Nīshābūr*, trans. Muḥammad Ḥusayn Khalifa *Nīshāpūrī*, ed. Bahman Karīmī (Tehran: Ketāb-khāna Ibn Sīnā, n.d.), 13–116. On Persian inhabitants of Cairo see: Abdelkader Al Ghouz, *Brokers of Islamic Philosophy in Mamlūk Egypt: Shams ad-Dīn Maḥmūd b. ʿAbd ar-Raḥmān al-Iṣfahānī (d. 1348) as a Case Study in the Transmission of Philosophical Knowledge through Commentary Writing* [ASK Working Paper] (Bonn: Annemarie Schimmel Kolleg, 2015). It should be noted that some scholars and religious figures were sent by rulers to the Arabian Iraq and the Arabic zones, like Levant and Egypt. See al-Samarqandī, *Maṭlaʿ al-Saʿdayn*, Ms. 74695, Parliamentary Library of Iran, fl. 247.

The *Durr al-Majālis* was a primary source of religious instruction for different communities of the Middle East and transmitted both orally and in writing. We may mention the high status of *Durr al-Majālis* among Kurds in Iraq and Turkey, where many religious teachings are transferred orally. The oral tradition was instrumental in the rapid circulation and persistence of *Durr al-Majālis* among them. A very few copies in the Kurmanji language are kept in Russia and have attracted the attention of Kurdish scholars who found a strong tie between Sayf Ẓafar's text and their Sufi saints and thinkers from the late twelfth/eighteenth century onwards. As will be explained in the following chapters, their oral tradition and context affected the content and organisation of *Durr al-Majālis* to the extent that Kurds produced an indigenous version of it by removing some chapters and adding several more. Such redactions even occurred in early printed copies in Persian and Tatar at the turn of the fourteenth/twentieth century; both versions presenting a selective abridgement of Sayf Ẓafar's known original work.

As previously suggested, one of the main features of Sayf Ẓafar's *Durr al-Majālis* is that it could have been partially or thoroughly memorised, copied, or distributed in every stratum of society. Elites and villagers, both literate and illiterate, had some knowledge of its content, stories, and lessons. This may be a reason why more than two hundred copies, in different languages, forms, and styles are found across the world, in private and public libraries, in towns and villages, in courts and madrasas, dating from both times of peace and from times of war and military expedition. The reception of this text across the Persianate world and the Arabic zone, and among the abovementioned communities, will be examined in my next chapters. In so doing, original manuscript copies, early printed volumes, and catalogues in different languages will be referenced.

DURR AL-MAJĀLIS IN SOUTHEAST ASIA

The importance of *Durr al-Majālis* is confimed by it having been widely copied, rendered, annotated, and circulated in the Muslim world. In this study I would like to pay special attention to its reception in Southeast Asian contexts in general and in the Malay-Indonesian world in particular. The Malay-Indonesian world comprises the modern-day countries of Brunei, Burma (Myanmar), Cambodia, Indonesia, Malaysia, the Philippines, Singapore, Thailand, Laos, and Vietnam. It is a region where various groups from the Persianate and Arabic parts of the Muslim world used to visit and live. This volume demonstrates that *Durr al-Majālis* played a highly significant role in the 'Islamification' of Malay-Indonesian literature, and that this influence was not all of a sudden, but gradual. We already know that *Durr al-Majālis* was widely read in Western China as well as in South Asia and so it is not farfetched to expect that it also had an impact in other parts of the world. What we find is that *Durr al-Majālis* did indeed make a remarakable contribution to the Islamic literature of Southeast Asia, especially to Malaysia and Indonesia whose people began to convert to Islam during the formative period of Islam in Arabia but which only began to be known as Muslim territories from the seventh/thirteenth century onwards.[8]

It will be clear that the oriental nature of the *Durr al-Majālis*, including its Islamic and Hindu elements, was instrumental in its transregional success and its ability to connect the Persianate and Malay-Indonesian worlds. Through reading the text one may discover the extent to which the theological and mystical notions of the *Durr al-Majālis* contributed to traditional Muslim feasts, ceremonies, superstitions, occultism, and (most importantly) eschatological beliefs. A comparative study between the contents of Sayf Ẓafar's *Durr al-Majālis* and Malay *hikayat* makes clear that *Durr al-Majālis* was the main prototype of several Malay tales whose origins have thought to be undiscovered or uncertain. This present study, therefore, builds upon previous research which recognises an important link between between Persian and Malay literature.[9]

THE PERSIAN-MALAY NETWORK: HISTORICAL TIES BETWEEN MUSLIMS

At the time that Sayf Ẓafar wrote *Durr al-Majālis* around the thirteenth to fourteenth centuries CE (late seventh and early eighth centuries AH) the majority of people well acquainted with the Persian language lived in the region today known as the Middle East and Central Asia. Although the written form and orthography of Persian changed during the formative periods of Islam, its nature as an Indo-European language

[8] See Merle C. Ricklefs, *A History of Modern Indonesia Since c.1200*. (Hampshire: Palgrave, 2001), 3rd edn. xiv. [9] I learned a lot from the publications of four historians of Malay-Indonesian literature, including Richard Olaf Winstedt (d. 1966), Lode F. Brakel (d. 1981), Liaw Yock Fang (d. 2016), and the late Vladimir Braginsky (d. 2024). As will be seen in this part (A), the core elements of my arguments about the relationship between Persian and Malay hikayat are shaped on the basis of the intriguing works of these four scholars. In addition, recent studies conducted by several other scholars, and the present author, on different aspects of the Malay-Indonesian world have also shaped the arguments in this part of the book. To review the literature, see: Majid Daneshgar, 'The Study of Persian Shiʿism in the Malay-Indonesian World: A Review of Literature from the Nineteenth Century Onwards', *Journal of Shiʿa Islamic Studies* 7/2 (2014): 191–229.

remained fixed. Like other languages, Persian used to be a receiver as well as a giver: adopting and assimilating new foreign terms and phrases and lending its own to other communities. These cross-lingual exchanges occurred via commercial exchange, military expedition, and missionary activity in places like southern Iran (Siraf and Hormuz), southern India, as well as in the Far East. In this way, Persians used to have connections with the inhabitants of the Malay-Indonesian world. Naturally, this relationship was not one way, that is, from the so-called Muslim heartlands to Southeast Asia; rather, it was interactive and mutual. Persia was a noted stopover for foreign travellers from the Far East and, similarly, the lands of Southeast Asian were places with high significance for Persian traders. This interaction dates back to the pre-Islamic period when Malay-Indonesians were residing in southern Iran and after the emergence of Islam played a crucial role in Islamic armies, particularly in the 'Arab' Iraq, 'non-Arab' (*ʿIrāq-i ʿajam*), and the Levant. These groups, who were called Sayābija,

> would thus be in origin Indonesians who had emigrated to western India and who then, in the late Sāsānid period, found their way to the Persian Gulf shores in company with the Zuṭṭ. The famed seafaring expertise of the Malay-Indonesian peoples would have ensured their usefulness to the Middle Eastern powers in such matters as the policing of the Gulf and the protection of its trade against piracy, etc.[10]

The Persian Sasanids dealt with Malay-Indonesians not only in their own territories in the Middle East but also in diverse parts of Southeast Asia where they could have traded with them. Since the reign of Khusraw Anūshīrwān (r. 531–579 CE), Persians increased their trading through the Indian Ocean route to Southeast Asia and the Far East. The Persian Gulf became the main hub for global seafarers and merchants.[11] The Malay peninsula, Vietnam (Nam-Viet), and Cambodia were secure spots for Persians to stay, work, and share religious teachings.[12] This interaction lasted for centuries. The

[10] C. E. Bosworth, 'Sayābidja', in: *Encyclopaedia of Islam New Edition Online*; also see: Gabriel Ferrand, 'Sayābidja', in: *Encyclopaedia of Islam First Edition Online*. Regarding the name of Malay-Indonesians in classical Islamic literature see Ferrand, 'Zābag', in: *Encyclopaedia of Islam First Edition Online*.

[11] Masoud Keyhan, *Jughrāfi-yā-i Mufaṣṣal-i Irān* (Tehran: Maṭbaʿa Majlis, 1310/1931), I: 100; it is said that the coastal city of Siraf was one of the highly visited places in the Persian Gulf, which merchants from Sindh and southern India used to visit until its decline around 1200. Ibid., I: 101. For the link between Siraf and Southeast Asia, see Michael Laffan, *Finding Java: Muslim Nomenclature of Insular Southeast Asia from Śrivijaya to Snouck Hurgronje* (Singapore: Asia Research Institute, National University of Singapore, 2005).

[12] E.g., see Shahab Setudeh-Nejad, 'Cultural and Cosmological Impact of Iranian Civilization in Vietnam and Peninsular Areas of Southeast Asia,' Iran Chamber Society. Also, Tomaš

Maṭlaʿ al-Saʿdayn wa Majmaʿ al-Baḥrayn (The Rise of the Stars and the Junction of the Two Oceans), has a chapter titled 'The Story of the Hindustan Journey with Further Information on its Rarities and Wondrous Things' ('Dāstān-i Safar-i Hindūstān va Sharḥ-i Gharāyib va Bayān-i ʿAjāyib-i ān') in which ʿAbd al-Razzāq al-Samarqandī (d. c. 887/1482) describes the status of foreigners, especially the residents of Southeast Asia who were accommodated in the Persian Gulf port city of Hormuz in the 1440s CE, as follows:

[...] والی هرموز ملک فخرالدین تورانشاه کشتی روان فرمود وکشتی در شهرِ هرموز به سلامت بیرون آمد، وِثاق و مایحتاج مقرّر شده ملاقات پادشاه میسّر شد. و این هرموز که او را «جرون» گویند در میان دریا بندری است که در روی زمین بدل ندارد. تجّار اقالیم سبعه از مصر و شام و روم و آذربایجان و عراق عجم و عرب و ممالک فارس و خراسان و ماوراء النهر و ترکستان و مملکت دشت قبچاق و نواحی قلماق و تمام بلاد مشرق و چین و ماچین و خان بالیغ روی توجّه به آن بندر دارند. و مردم دریابار[۱۳] از حدودِ چین و جاوه و بنگاله و سیلان و شهرهای زیربادِ تناصری و سقوطره و شهرنو و جزایر دیوه محلّ، تا دیار ملیبار و حبشه و زنگبار و بندرهای بیجانگر و گلبرگه و گجرات و کنبات و سواحل برّ عرب تا عدن جدّه و ینبوع، نفایس و ظرائف که ماه و آفتاب و فیض سحاب آن را آب و تاب داده و بر روی دریا توان آوردن به آن بلده آورند. و مسافران عالم از هرجا که آیند و هرچه آرند، در برابر هر چه خواهند بی زیادت جست وجوی در آن شهر یابند. هم نقد و هم معاوضه کنند، و دیوانیان غیر زر و نقره عُشر ستانند، و اصحاب ادیان مختلفه بل کفّار در آن شهر بسیارند وبیرون از عدل با هیچ آفریده معامله ندارند وباین سبب آن بلده را «دارالامان» گویند و مردم آن بلده را تملق عراقیان و تعمق سندیان باشد و مدّت دوماه توقف واقع شد [...][۱۴]

[...] The ruler of Hormuz, Fakhr al-Dīn Turānshāh released the ship and it left this city of Hormuz safe and sound. The accommodation as well as all requirements to visit the king were prepared. And this Hormuz, which they also call Jarun, is a port on the open sea which has no equal on the face of the Earth. Merchants betake themselves from the seven climes; from Egypt, Syria, Asia Minor, Azerbaijan, Persian, and Arab Iraq, the provinces

Petrů, 'Lands below the Winds' as Part of the Persian Cosmopolis: An Inquiry into Linguistic and Cultural Borrowings from the Persianate societies in the Malay World', *Moussons* 27 (2016), 147–161.

[13] Daryā (ocean)+bār (coast). See *Farhang-i ʿAmid* (through www.vajehyab.com)

[14] I have edited the text according to various available copies of *Maṭlaʿ al-Saʿdayn*, including Ms. 813948 (fl. 609–610) kept in the National Library of Iran. Apparently, this copy was also used by ʿAlī Asghar Ḥekmat while translating Edward Browne's monograph in 1948. See Edward Browne, *Az Saʿdī tā Jāmī*, translation and commentary by ʿAlī Asghar Ḥekmat (Tehran: Bank Mellī Iran Printing House, 1327/1948), 433–434. For another translation of the full report, see, Thackston's translation in *A Century of Princes: Sources on Timurid History and Art* (London: Aga Khan Program for Islamic Architecture, 1989).

of Fars and Khurasan and Transoxiana and Turkistan and the territory of the Qipchaq plain [i.e., Kipchak or Cumania], the regions of the Calmucks [Kipchaks or Cumania] and all the realm of the East, and China and [its capital] Beijing (Khān Bālīgh; 元大都/汗八里). Coast-dwellers from the confines of China, Java, Bengal, Ceylon, and from the cities below the winds[15] of Tenasserim,[16] and Secotora, and Shahr-i Naw,[17] the Islands of Diwa-Mahall,[18] as far as Malabar, Abyssinia, and Zanzibar, the ports of Beejanuggur,[19] Gulbarga, Gujarat, and Khambhat,[20] the coasts of the Arabian peninsula as far as Aden, Jeddah, and Yanbu bring rare and precious things to which the Sun and Moon and the fertilising virtue of the clouds have given lustre and beauty, and which can be brought by sea to that country. To that land come travellers from all parts of the world, and whatever they bring they find in that city, without much searching, the equivalent value thereof in whatever form they desire, whether by sale or exchange. The officials levy a ten per cent *ad valorem* duty on everything except on gold and silver. In that city are many adherents of all manner of diverse religions, including heathens; yet they deal not otherwise than fairly with any creature, for which reason people call the city 'Dār al-Amān' (the Abode of Security). The people of that country combine the winning manner of the people of Iraq with the profound cunning of the Indians; and there stopped over for two months [...][21]

[15] Various meanings have been assigned to this. According to the *Burhān-i Qaṭiʿ*, also cited by the *Lughatnameh-yi Dehkhoda*, 'there is an Island known as Melakha (ملاخا) among the Islands of below the wind'. Here, Melakha should have been referred to as Malacca/Melaka, whose other spellings are found in Persian and Arabic sources like ملاقا، ملاقه، ملاککا، ملکا. Some refer to the regioins 'below the wind' as countries in the eastern side of India. [16] In Burma [17] Siam, Thailand. [18] 'Deo Mahal' or 'Dev Mahal' refers to the Maldives and Pandua or 'port of Deu in Gujarat'. See, Abdul Karim, *Social History of the Muslims in Bengal (Down to* A.D. *1538)* (Dacca: The Asiatic Society of Pakistan, 1959) citing Blochmann and Beveridge, 126. Also see the word in *Journal of the Pakistan Historical Society* (1959), 215. However, regarding the name of islands, including Maldives, and Muslims' [wrong] geographical calculations, there are a number of critical editions in French such as the work on Arab geographers by Abū al-Fidāʾ: 'Albyrouny , qui a recueilli sur la presqu'île de l'Inde des renseignements si précieux, s'exprime ainsi : « Les îles de la partie de la mer de l'Inde qui est tournée vers l'orient , et qui se rapproche de la Chine , sont les îles du Zabedj; les îles situées du côté de l'occident sont les îles des Zendj (Madagascar , etc.) ; les îles placées au centre sont les îles de Ram (Alramy) et les îles Dybadjat (Ceylan , les Maldives et les Laquedives) (Al-Bīrūnī, who has collected such valuable information on the Indian peninsula, expresses it as follows: 'The islands on the side of the Indian Sea which is turned towards the East and which is directed toward China, are those of Zabedj; the islands located on the western side are the Zendj islands (Madagascar, etc.); the central ones are the Ram Islands (al-Ramy) and the Dybadjat Islands (Ceylon, the Maldives and the Laccadive). See Abū l-Fidāʾ Ismāʿīl Ibn ʿAlī, *Géographie d'Aboulféda 1: Introduction générale à la géographie des Orientaux*, M. Reinaud (Paris: Imprimé par Autorisation du Gouvernement a L'imprimerie Nationale, 1846), 422. [19] Vijayanagara [20] Cambay

[21] The English translation is based on E. G. Browne's translation of the French text. As far as I edited the

It has been widely recorded that in the fourteenth and fifteenth centuries CE, Persian diplomatic delegations and military forces alike toured different parts of the world, from Turkey (Mardin), the Levant, Georgia, and Egypt to Sindh, Multan,[22] Delhi,[23] Baalbek[24] and the Eastern societies of China. It should, therefore, not be surprising to find a Persian folio from but a century earlier making its way to Japan from China.[25] As one of the first Persian documents to make its way to the Far East it includes a couplet ascribed to the famous Persian poet, Abū ʾl-Qāsim Firdawsī (d. c. 411/1020).

جهان یادگار است و ما رفتنی

زمردم نماند بجـــز مردمی

The world is a perpetual remembrance and we all leave it in the end

People will leave nothing behind but their good deed

Interestingly, this Persian couplet has also been found on a ninth/fifteenth-century inscription in Barus, Indonesia.[26]

Another example of early connectivity between the Persiante world and other regions can be seen in the expedition of a Persian delegation in the tenth/fifteenth century CE that left Herat and reached Beijing in China after a journey of one year and ten days.[27] In the same vein – according to Armenian reports from the seventh/thirteenth century preserved in the Mashots Matenadaran library in Yerevan, Armenia – Afghan merchants left Ghazna to reach the Indonesian cities of Lamrin or Aceh, Panchur or Barus, Krut or Lho' Kruet, Krudai or Daya (?), and so forth. On the way, they passed through India and 'Sarntip' or 'Sarandib' known today as Sri Lanka.[28]

original text in Persian (see above), the English was also slightly changed. Edward G. Browne, *A Literary History of Persia; Volume III: The Tartar Dominion (1265–1502)* (Cambridge: Cambridge University Press, 1928), III: 397–398. [22] Ibid., 273 [23] Ibid., 276 [24] Ibid., 312 [25] Paul Pelliot, 'Les plus anciens monuments de l'écriture arabe en Chine', *Journal Asiatique* 11/2 (1913): 181.

[26] For the new reading of this manuscript, see: Majid Daneshgar and R. Michael Feener, "'Discovering a Hidden Miraculous Grave': A Rare Persian Inscription of Ferdowsi's Shāhnāmah from Barus, Indonesia" (forthcoming).

[27] See Browne, *A Literary History of Persia*, III: 397–398. Scholars like Fatimi have argued that Islam might also have arrived in the Malay Archipelago through China, Arabia, Bengal and Persia. See page 185 in Liaw: S. Q. Fatimi, *Islam Comes to Malaysia* (Singapore: Malaysian Sociological Research Institute Ltd. 1963).

[28] R. Abramyan, 'Armyanskiy putevoditel' po Indii XII veka' [An Armenian itinerary to twelfth-century India], Vestnik Matenadarana, *Bulletin of Matenadaran* 4 (1958), 317–328, esp. 326–327. Also, Vladimir Braginsky, 'Two Eastern Christian Sources on Mediaeval Nusantara', *Bijdragen tot de Taal-, Land- en Volkenkunde* 154/3 (1998): 369.

Other reports also draw our attention to the Persian traders who visited Malay ports, including Malacca where they were also called the people of Pars or Parsees.[29] In addition, both archives and former studies demonstrate that, unlike Lode Frank Brakel's (1940–1981) claim that Persian influence on Malays used to be Islamic,[30] three groups of Persian communities visited the Malay Archipelago: Zoroastrians, Muslims, and Nestorian Christians who resided in Klang, on the western coast of Malaysia.[31] The eighth/fourteenth-century Christian European traveller Giovanni de' Marignolli had seen Persian Nestorians in Saba (Shabat)[32] and Mojopait (Majapahit) in Indonesia, who 'were the most energetic in evangelistic labours'.[33]

Some Persian names were already in use, according to Ibn Baṭṭūṭa (d. c. 770/1378), at the court of Pasai.[34] Persians were hired by the Acehnese sultanate to serve as warriors and contribute to military expeditions in the early tenth/sixteenth century. And these largely Persian communities were known as 'Khurasanian', referring to the Persian-speaking region of Greater Khurasan as well as to 'Muslims of non-Indian origin, emigrants from different countries in Asia and Africa'.[35] Perhaps, this may possibly refer to an account outlined in ʿAwfī's (d. 1242) *Jāmiʿ al-Ḥikāyāt* (the Collection of

[29] A number of reports about Persians of Malacca, Pasai and Barus were recorded by the Portuguese apothecary, Tomé Pires, *Suma Oriental*, 2 vols. (London: Hakluyt Society, 1944). Also see, G. E. Marrison, 'Persian Influences in Malay Life (1280–1650)', *Journal of the Malayan Branch of the Royal Asiatic Society* 28/1 (1955), 52; Braginsky 'Two Eastern Christian Sources' (1998), 382; Daneshgar, 'A Review Literature on Persian Shiʿism' (2014), and Peacock, 'Notes on Some Persian Documents from Early Modern Southeast Asia', *Sejarah* 27/1 (2018), 83. For more, see: Sanjay Subrahmanyam, 'Iranians abroad: Intra-Asian elite migration and early modern state formation', *The Journal of Asian Studies* 51/2 (1992): 340–363.

[30] Brakel says 'Persian Influence on the Malay world has always meant: Muslim influence'. L. F. Brakel, 'Persian Influence on Malay Literature', *Abr Nahrain* 9 (1969–1970): 1.

[31] See, Brian E. Colless, 'Persian Merchants and Missionaries in Mediaeval Malaya', *Journal of the Malaysian Branch of the Royal Asiatic Society* 2/2 (1969), 41.

[32] Whether Saba should be identified as Java has been debated among scholars. On this subject, Braginsky says that 'Modern scholars have identified Shabat with several different countries: Champa […], a region in Bengal […], and the island of Saba, which Henry Yule […], basing himself on the account of the fourteenth-century Italian traveller Marignolli, localised near either Java or Sumatra. In my opinion, Yule, and later I. P. Petrushevsky […] – who noted that the name Shabat resembles the Arab name for Java; Jawat – and Colless […]- who assumed that Shabat actually meant Java – were the closest to a plausible solution of the problem of the identification of Shabat. It appears that when Afanasiy Nikitin speaks of Shabat, he is referring not to Java, however, but to Sumatra, or, to be more exact, to the northern part of the island, which the Arabs and early European travellers called Jabat/Jawat/Java (Minor)'. Braginsky, 'Two Eastern Christian Sources', 375.

[33] Colless, 'Persian Merchants', 334.

[34] See H. K. J. Cowan, 'A Persian Inscription in North Sumatra'', *Tijdschrift voor Indische Taal-, Land- en Volkenkunde* 80/1 (1940), 21; Braginsky, 'Two Eastern Christian Sources', 382.

[35] Braginsky, 'Two Eastern Christian Sources', 382.

Stories), which informs the way various groups of Muslims left the heartlands of Islam, as well as Khurasan, and settled in the Far East.

> [...] [A]nd there is a land near the town of China, in which there is an island in the middle of it. On that island there is a stronghold (a fortified place) whose residents are *sādāt* [i.e., descendants of the Prophet Muḥammad] and Muslim ʿAlīds [...] And they had to reside in this land, because some of the descendants of the Prophet and the children of the Commander of Believers, ʿAlī, had already moved to Khurasan during the reign of Umayyad rulers. They were [eventually] able to settle there. They [again] realised that the Ummayads are seriously determined to take them, so they were afraid that they might be taken and be simply killed. As such, they moved towards the East [...].[36]

Many times the interaction between Persians and Malays took place in a third region such as southern India. Archives suggest that people from Hormuz, East Africa, northern Iran, and Khurasan, interacted with the inhabitants of Ceylon and Malacca in the kingdom of Cambay in Gujarat, in the Malabar regions and southern India. India was a meeting place for Persians and Malays.[37] In al-Samarqandī's *Maṭlaʿ al-Saʿdayn* under the section 'On the rest of the Hindustan journey and particular features of Beejanuggur [...]', there is an account of the popularity of Persian literature across southern India, where all these communities gathered. He calls the city of Beejanuggur 'an extremely large and prosperous place' in close connection with different communities from Ceylon, Gulberg, Bengal, and Khambhat where people are highly educated and view the stories from *Kalīla wa Dimna* as the best of Persian literature.

> The stories of the book of *Kalīla wa Dimna*, of which nothing better has been produced in the Persian language.[38]

The strong Persian maritime tradition and the fact that the Persian language was dominant across South Asia has [mis]led some scholars to conclude that in the interac-

[36] Based on the original manuscript copy of Bayerische Staatsbibliothek Cod. Pers. 184, fol. 308.
[...] و به نزدیک شهر چین، وادیست عظیم، و در میان آن وادی جزیره ایست، و در آن جزیره حصاری محکم و ساکنان آن حصار جماعتی اند از سادات و علویان مسلمانان [...] و سبب سکون علویان در آن زمین آن بود که جماعتی از سادات و فرزندان امیرالمؤمنین علی در ایام بنی امیّه به خراسان بودند و آنجا مقام ساختند و چون جد بنی امیه در طلب خود بدیدند، بترسیدند که مبادا که به دست ایشان افتند و به رایگان کشته شوند. پس روی به مشرق نهادند [...]

[37] Marrison, 'Persian Influences in Malay Life (1280–1650)', 52–53.

[38] The original text in Persian reads as follows: حکایات کتاب کلیله و دمنه که از زبان پارسی کتابی خوبتر از آن در بیان نیامده
See *Maṭlaʿ al-Saʿdayn*, Ms. 814239, fl. 612, National Library of Iran.

tion between Persians and Malays the influence would have been one way. Marrison points to 'Persianized Indian sources' from 'the Delhi Sultanate, Gujarat or the Deccan' and to travellers from the Persian empires of the Mongol Il-Khan dynasty (based in Tabriz, 1256–1336) and the Timurids (based in Samarqand, Khurasan and Herat, 1380–1506) as being influences on the Malay-Indonesian world.[39]

It is indeed true that a lot of direct Persian and Muslim Malay contact happened during the periods noted by Marison. This contact continued, albeit somewhat diminished, throughout the Safawid era (r. 1501–1736), when Shīʿism became the state religion of Iran. During this period, Persian Shīʿī and Shīʿī political figures visited different regions throughout Southeast Asia.[40] As a newly discovered manuscript, *Safina-yi Māzandarānī* (The Anthology [or Ship] of Mazandarni) alludes to the circulation of Persian stories and Shīʿī traditional accounts and anti-Sunni sentiments in Southeast Asia during the 1670s. According to a rare manuscript kept in the Parliamentary Library of Iran, Muḥammad Taqī Māzandarānī copied the Persian story of 'Rind wa Zāhid', originally by an Azeri scholar, Fuḍūlī Baghdādī (d. 1556), on the Tenasserim coast (Burma) on 11 Shawwāl 1083 (29 January 1673) when Burma was still a part of the kingdom of Siam.[41] Some years later in the 1680s, political delegations from Isfahan visited Thailand. The story of this encounter is known as the *Safina-yi Sulaymanī* ('Ship of Solomon').[42] Later, different groups from Moghul India continued their political and religious contribution to the northern side of the Malay-Indonesian world until the late thirteenth/nineteenth century.[43] By the 'northern side' of the Malay-Indonesian world, I refer to what Khazeni calls the 'Buddhist Southeast Asian mainland' where

[39] Marrison, 'Persian Influences'. The way Malay-Indonesians contributed to Persian literature and culture is the subject of my further studies.

[40] By 'Persian Shīʿī figures', I mean Shīʿī Persian speakers. And by 'Persian Shīʿī literature and customs', I mean the Shīʿī or Shīʿītised traditions largely promoted by Persians of Iran and Central Asia. See Daneshgar, 'The Study of Persian Shīʿism in the Malay-Indonesian World' (2014); regarding the traces of Persian-Shīʿism in Indonesia, see P. J. Veth, 'Opmerkingen naar aanleiding van het opstel, Hat Hasan-Hosein of Taboetfeest te Benkoelen', *Internationales Archivfür Ethnographie* I (1888), 230–233. For further developments of alid vs. Shīʿī customs in Indonesia, see R. Michael Feener, "ʿAlid Piety and State-sponsored Spectacle: Tabot Tradition in Bengkulu, Sumatra', In *Shiʿism in South-East Asia: 'Alid Piety and Sectarian Constructions*, edited by Chiara Formichi and R. Michael Feener (London: C. Hurst & Co. Ltd., 2015), 187–202.

[41] Majid Daneshgar, 'A Persian Shiʿi Anthology Circulating in Patna, Dhaka and Siam in the Seventeenth Century: A Lesser-known Ship of Persians to South-East Asia', In *Iran and Persianate Culture in the Indian Ocean World*, edited by A. C. S. Peacock (London: Bloomsbury, 2025), 249–260.

[42] See, Mohammad Ibrahim, *The Ship of Sulaiman*, ed. J. O'Kane (London: Routledge & Kegan Paul, 1972).

[43] There are some manuscripts in my possession regarding Persian Shīʿī religious activities across Southeast Asia from the late sixteenth until the late seventeenth century. This will be the subject of my forthcoming project.

Persian 'was a lingua franca of trade, diplomacy, and literature',[44] and where a large number of Persian Islamic sources were produced by native Persians.[45] However, the direct relationship between Persians and the Muslims of Malaysia and Indonesia gradually declined as the sectarian inclinations of the Middle East made inroads into the Malay-Indonesian world. Malay Muslims labelled Persians as heretical and works influenced by Persia were even censored. Such censorship can be seen in, for example, a rare Malay copy of the Malay *Hikayat Nabi Bercukur* (The Tale of the Prophet Shaving) kept in the Leiden University Library (Or.1953). The story is based on a Safawid chivalrous code for barbers, *Futuwwat-nāma-yi Salmāniyyān* and this appears to have been the reason for the disapproval of one graffitist who blackened several pages of the manuscript and wrote in the margin in Malay: 'Do not believe the Story of Shaving because it is the story of a heretic Rāfiḍī, do not believe the story of a Rāfiḍī'.[46]

Nonetheless, despite sectarianism, the two communities did not completely ignore one another's literature. Javanese Muslims showed interest in reading Persian legal texts, including Shīʿī accounts. A rare copy of the Persian legal text *Majmūʿih-yi Khānī* from the eleventh/seventeenth century with allusions to Shīʿī traditional, theological, and exegetical sources, including *al-Kāfī*, was found in Banten. This text was read, translated, and annotated by Javanese Muslims and was used as a reliable legal source since the late seventeenth century.[47] The manuscript Or.5658 at the Leiden University Library with Persian Shīʿī poetic verses regarding the leadership (*imāma*), infallibility (*ʿiṣma*) and divine authority of ʿAlī b. Abī Ṭālib has been copied in the late eleventh/seventeenth century in Banten, Indonesia.[48] Similiarly, the manuscript Or.5724 at Leiden University Library was copied in Central Java and contains several Persian and Shīʿī-oriented couplets.[49]

[44] Arash Khazeni, *The City and the Wilderness: Indo-Persian Encounters in Southeast Asia* (California: California University Press, 2020), 2 and 5. Also see, Peter Skilling, 'The Advent of Theravāda Buddhism to Mainland South-east Asia', *Journal of the International Association of Buddhist Studies* (1997): 93–107.

[45] Some parts of *Durr al-Majālis* were copied by Persians of Isfahan (originally from Mazandaran) in Thailand and Burma, and they are in my possession. I intend to make a separate study on this subject.

[46] See, Majid Daneshgar, 'The Prophet Shaving: Persians and the Origin of the Malay *Hikayat Nabi Bercukur*', *Der Islam* 98/2 (2021): 394–424.

[47] Majid Daneshgar, 'Persianate Fiqh in Indonesia: *Majmuʿih-yi Khani* as a Rare Legal Manuscript in a Cosmopolitan Context', *International Journal of Islam in Asia* 2/2 (2023): 144–169.

[48] Majid Daneshgar, 'Persianate Aspects of the Malay-Indonesian World: Some Rare Manuscripts in the Leiden niversity Library', *Dabir* 8 (2021) 51–78.

[49] Majid Daneshgar, 'Anthologies of Persian Poetry Inscribed in Indonesia: A Handlist of Rare Manuscripts', *Dabir* 10/1 (2024): 27–48.

On the other hand, for the Persian Safawids, Malay was an important language that was highly respected and that was used in official ceremonies and royal gatherings. On this subject, the French traveller-merchant, Jean-Baptiste Tavernier (1605–1689) provides a first-hand report about the status of foreign languages in Isfahan before 1650, during the reign of Shah Abbas II (1642–1666).[50]

> While we were eating, I wanted to see how many languages were spoken there, and counted thirteen Languages spoken [at the Table]. Latin, French, German,[51] English, Dutch,[52] Italian, Portuguese, Persian, Turkish, Arabic, Indian, Syriac, and Malay – which is the Language of the Learned, that is spoken from the River Indus to China and Japan, and in all Islands of the East – like Latin in Europe; not reckoning on the little Moresco or Gibberish of the country. So it is difficult to observe what is talked about in one's Company, where the discourse begins in one language, is persuaded in another, and finished in a third: and for the Turks and Armenians, they never speak above three or four languages at most.[53]

Europeans of the seventeenth century were aware of the relationship between Persia and the Malay-Indonesian world and of travel between the two regions.

> The greatest part of the kingdom of Siam lies between the Gulf of Siam and the Gulf of Bengal; bordering upon Pegu toward the North, and the Peninsula of Malacca toward the South. The shortest and nearest way for the Europeans to arrive in this kingdom, is to go to Isfahan, from Isfahan to Hormuz from Hormuz to Surat, from Surat to Golconda, from Golconda to Majlipatan [Masulipatam], there to embark for Denouserin [Tenasserim], which is one of the ports attached to the kingdom of Siam. From Denouserin to the capital city, which is also named 'Siam' is a thirty-five day journey, part by water, part over land, by wagon, or upon elephants. The way, whether land or water, is very troublesome; for by land you must always watch out for lions and tigers,[54] while through the water route, by reason of the many falls [and cascades] of the river, they are forced to equip their boats with engines.[55]

[50] Jean-Baptiste Tavernier, *Les six voyages de Jean-Baptiste Tavernier: Ecuyer, Baron D'aubonne, qu'il a fait en Turquie, en Perse et aux Indes, Pendant quarante Ans* (Paris: Gervais Clouzier [etc.] 1676), 188. There are also two English translations of this work by J Phillips in 1678 and by V. Ball 1889. The one also consulted by me is that of J. Phillips.

[51] In Phillips translation of 1687, it is translated as 'High-Dutch'. [52] 'Low-Dutch'.

[53] Jean-Baptiste Tavernier, *The Six Voyages of John Baptiste Tavernier*, trans. J. Phillips, 2 vols. (London: Printed for R. L. and *M. P.*, 1678), 76. [54] Perhaps, lions of India, and tigers of Thailand.

[55] 'Le Royaume de Siam pour la plus grande partie est entre le Golfe deméme nom & le Golfe de Bengala,

Malay people did not often use this route as the control of it was not in their hands. The seas were coming under the control of Sunni powers such as the Ottomans who were, along with Arabs, one of the main political and religious rivals of the Persian Safawids.

> [...] there were three struggles in the Persian Gulf: that between the two local powers of the Safawids and the Ottomans; that between the European powers of Portugal, Britain, and France; and that between all of these powers and the local Arab populations.[56]

During the period that the Ottomans controlled key Islamic territories, including the cities of Mecca and Medina, interaction between Malay-Indonesian and Arabs of the Middle East increased as Malay-Indonesians sought to perform the hajj pilgrimage and to pursue Islamic learning.[57] Safawid Persia, where Sunni's suffered discrimination and oppression,[58] could no longer have been the 'Abode of Security' for Sunni Malays as it once was. During this period, therefore, not only did Malay-Indonesians become more exposed to Sunni prejudice (which was on the increase) but neither were they as exposed to Shīʿī Persians as much as they had been before such that Sunni influence may have been counterbalanced.

Even after the fall of the Safawids in the 1720s, very little trading happened between Persians and Malays. Dutch ships were the main political and economic link between

touchant le Pegu au Septentrion, & la presqu'Ifle de Malacca au Midi. Le chemin le plus court & le meilleur que puissent tenir les Europeans pour se rendre en ce Royaume, est d'aller à Ispahan, d'Ispahan à Ormus, d'Ormus Surate, de Surate à Golconda, & de Golconda à Maslipatan, où l'on s'embarque pour Denouserin qui est un des ports du Royaume de Siam. De Denonserin à la ville capitale qui porte le méme nom du Royaume, il y a environ trente-cinq journées de chemin dont l'on fait une partie en remontant une riviere, & l'autre partie en charette ou sur des Elefans, Le chemin tant par terre que par eau est incommode; parce que par terre il faut toùjours estre en garde contre les lions & les tygres; & par eau, la riviere faisant des chutes en plusieurs endroits il est difficile de faire remonter les bateaux, de quoy toutefois on vien about avec des machines', Tavernier, *Les Six Voyages*, II: 431–432. Also, see Tavernier, *The Six Voyages*, 189.

[56] Aiza Khan, 'The Ottomans in the Arabian Peninsula', *Routledge Handbook of Persian Gulf Politics*, ed. Mehrdad Kamrava (London and New York: Routledge, 2020), 15. While travelling from Mesopotamia to Isfahan, Tavernier says, '*les Arabes ennemis des Perses*'(the Arabs, enemies to Persians). Tavernier, *Les Six Voyages*, 186. It should be noted some scholars do not agree that the influence of Ottomans were hugely dominant at sea.

[57] Regarding Ottoman-Malay relation, see, Andrew Peacock and Annabel Teh Gallop (ed.), *From Anatolia to Aceh Ottomans, Turks, and Southeast Asia* (Leiden and Boston: Brill, 2015).

[58] See Rudi Matthee, 'Safawid Dynasty', *Encyclopaedia Iranica* (2008).

Batavia and Persia.[59] As much as Persians had to reduce their direct relationship with Malays, Malay-Indonesians had to decrease their stopovers on the Persian coast while cautiously keeping open their diplomatic communications and negotiations. This political and geopolitical upheaval had widespread economic effects, to the extent that, according to available reports, in the late twelfth/eighteenth and early thirteenth/nineteenth centuries strong Malay-Indonesian agricultural ties existed with almost all key regions except Persia (such as China, India, Arabia, Europe, and even America).[60] This tragic loss of economic, political, and cultural interaction began to cease after the mid-thirteenth/nineteenth century, when, according to a recently discovered official document, the large Persian diaspora communities in Java and Burma began to increase their links with their homeland, Iran.[61]

Recent discoveries also suggest that while Persian seafarers had much less maritime liberty and security to visit Malay coasts, the Persian language was still viewed as the medium of diplomatic communication by Malay Muslims who used it to deal with foreigners such as the Portuguese. As Peacock has demonstrated, Persian letters were sent from Malacca, Aceh, and Burma from the tenth/sixteenth to the thirteenth/nineteenth century to different groups of foreign Europeans and Muslims, proving 'a considerable chronological and geographical spread in the use of Persian in Southeast Asia'.[62] Although a Persian letter from Malacca dated 2 Muharram 925 (5 January 1519) was apparently written by either a Jewish or Christian Persian speaker, other letters from Aceh from the twelfth/eighteenth century were possibly scribed – given the orthography – by people ('chanceries') with 'a limited to non-existent knowledge of Persian'. A letter sent out from Burma in 1869 that included both Persian and Ottoman Turkish phrases, 'was sent at King Mindon's request in response to previous attempts by the Ottomans to contact the Burmese'.[63] In addition, Peacock draws our attention to a list of Dutch translations of 'lost Persian letters' from the correspond-

[59] D. F. A. Hervey, 'Valentyn's Account of Malacca (Continued from p. 301 of No. 16 of the Society's Journal)', *Journal of the Straits Branch of the Royal Asiatic Society* 22 (1890), 234. Ismāʿīl Ranīn, *Daryā-navardī-yi Īrāniyyān* (Tehran: Jāvidān, 1356/1977), vol. 2, 903.

[60] John Crawfurd, F.R.S., *History of the Indian Archipelago Containing an Account of the Manners, Arts, Language, Religions, Institutions, and Commerce of its Inhabitants* (Edinburgh: Archibald Constable and Co. Edinburgh, 1820), I: 341.

[61] See, Majid Daneshgar, 'The Iranian Diaspora in Southeast Asia: Old Manuscript, New Perspectives', *Leiden Specialcollections Blog* (2024).

[62] Peacock, 'Notes on Some Persian Documents', 81. Regarding Persian letters from Malacca, also see, Jorge Dos Santos Alves and Nader Nasiri-Moghaddam, 'Une lettre en persan de 1519 sur la situation à Melaka', *Archipel* 75 (2008), 145–166.

[63] Peacock, 'Notes on Some Persian Documents', 90.

ence of the Dutch East India Company, kept in the National Archives of the Republic of Indonesia in Jakarta, sent from either Persia (e.g., Bandar Abbas) or India (e.g., Murshidabad) to Batavia, Indonesia, in the late twelfth/eighteenth century, making us more confident that Persian was a key language there.[64] Beyond its role as a common language of communication, Persian was also used in the Malay-Indonesian world for the study of Islamic sciences. The number of Persian manuscripts copied by local Malays increased. Western and Northern Sumatra, as well as Banten, were centres for producing melodies based on Persian musical modes and for reciting Persian Shīʿī and Persian Sufi poetry such as the poems of Shahbāz Qalandar.[65]

Besides, and far from the Malay-Indonesian world, there were still places like Mecca and Medina, or India where Persians and Malays could have influence on each other. This is also evident in several available manuscripts. The manuscript MS 515(1) kept in the National Library of Malaysia is a Qurʾānic divinatory treatise (*fāl*). The author of this manuscript is ʿAbd al-Majīd b. Ḥajj Ibrāhīm from Rembau (or Rimbu) near the village of Johol, Negeri Sembilan who was based in Mecca in the thirteenth/nineteenth century. Various features of his treatise are clearly influenced by Persian sources. Divinatory tables (sg., *jadwal*) and circles (sg., *dāʾira*) – through which one might seek an omen or to predict the future – were produced and disseminated in the Persianate world for centuries prior.[66]

Similarly, as I detail elsewhere, we find evidence of influence in the opposite direction, that is, of Malay-Indonesian influence on the Persianate world. For example, in a few underexamined Arabic manuscripts with Javanese interlinear translations brought to Iran before the fourteenth/twentieth century we see that Persian readers attempted to rewrite or copy the Javanese text in the margin of the manuscripts. Such attention to detail shows that these manuscripts were dealt with seriously and not just slipped on the top shelf to gather dust where nobody would notice them.[67]

In summary, we can say that Persian–Malay interactions were more complicated than we have ascertained so far, and (re)discovering unknown archives promises more surprising results in the future.[68] As a matter of fact, the more archives discovered, the more light is shed upon the less-examined side of the history of the two communities.

[64] Ibid., 92. [65] Daneshgar, 'Persianate Aspects of the Malay-Indonesian World'.

[66] Majid Daneshgar, 'The Divinatory Role of the Qurʾan in the Malay World', *Indonesia and the Malay World* 44/129 (2016), 123–144.

[67] Majid Daneshgar, 'Indonesian Manuscripts in Iran', *Indonesia and the Malay World* 49/143 (2021), 136.

[68] Although I agree that India was the main place of interaction for Persians and Malays, I do not agree with Brakel that 'Persian culture was in the main channelled, not by way of direct immediate contact, but through an India party converted to Islam' (Brakel, 'Persian Influence on Malay Literature', 2). Rather, as outlined above, there was significant contacts between the two peoples from the beginning.

As much as Persians and Arabs had employed Malay-Indonesians to bring security in the Persian Gulf or to contribute to military stability in Iraq during the formative period of Islam, Malays also hired Persians and Arabs in their sultanates for the sake of their military endeavours. In the same vein, to the extent that Persian islands and regions were previously quite safe for Southeast Asian merchants, Persian traders, missionaries, and sailors found security in western and central parts of the Malay Archipelago, too. And finally, to the extent that competing political Shīʿī, Sunni, and European agendas and interventions affected the Middle East, they also changed the direction of Persian–Malay ties after the tenth/sixteenth century.

PERSIAN PHONOLOGY IN MALAY LANGUAGE

One of the most significant outcomes of the Persian-Malay network is apparent in phonology and Islamic literature. The phonological-lexical effect can be seen even today in Malay-Indonesian society on a daily basis and there are hundreds of Persian words used in Malay literature. Early printed Dutch-Malay dictionaries are instrumental in drawing our attention to such lexical connections.[69] Bausani (d. 1988) listed 201 Persian loanwords in Malay-Indonesian languages,[70] and Brakel claimed that there should be about three hundred such words;[71] however, a number of Persian terms and phrases in Malay literature have either fallen from memory or not been recognised as being Persian in origin.[72] Bausani and Brakel address this issue yet their work is still incomplete.[73]

The phonological influence of Persian can be seen in both Jawi and Pegon, two modified forms of Arabic-Persian script for Malay and Javanese, respectively. As

[69] E.g., W. H. Ridderhof, *Nieuw Practisch Maleis-Nederlands Woordenboek* (Zutphen: W. J. Thieme & Cie, 1936); PH. S. Van Ronkel, *Maleis Woordenboek Maleis – Nederlands Nederlands – Malets In de Officiële Maleise Spelling, vierde druk* (s-Gravenhage: Batavia G. B. Van Goor Zonen's Uitgeversmij. N.V, 1939). There are also other Dutch dictionaries which show more than two hundred Persian words in Malay literature.

[70] Alessandro Bausani, 'Note sui vocaboli Persiani in Malese-Indonesiano', *Annali dell'Ist.Univ. Orientale di Napoli* 14 (1964), 1–32.

[71] Brakel, 'Persian Influence on Malay Literature', 1–2.

[72] Regarding the omitted Persian words (e.g., *ḥarām-zāda* meaning bastard) from Malay, see Majid Daneshgar, 'Persianate Aspects of the Malay-Indonesian World'.

[73] Also, see Russell Jones, *Loan-words in Indonesian and Malay* (Leiden: KITLV Press, 2007). On further analysis of Bausani's effort see, Antonia Soriente, 'I prestiti persiani in indonesiano. Bausani cinquant'anni dopo', *Iranian Studies in Honour of Adriano V. Rossi;* Part Two, Ed. Sabir Badalkhan, Gian Pietro Basello and Matteo de Chiara (Napoles: Università Degli Studi di Napoli 'L'Orientale'), 971–1031.

Bausani shows, the three vowels of *fatḥa* (ـَ), *kasra* (ـِ) and *ḍamma* (ـُ) in Malay Jawi are defined based on the Persian implications.

> [In] Persian *zebar* (= 'above', corresponding to the Arabic *fatḥa*)> [in Malay means] *baris atas* ('above the line'); Persian *zīr* ('below', [in] Arabic *kasra*)> [in Malay] *baris bawah* ('below the line'); Persian *pīsh* ('in front of', [in] Arabic *ḍamma*)> [in Malay] *baris hadapan* ('front line/front of the line').[74]

This influence is even more transparent in Javanese where the three short vowels are directly taken from Persian. They are known as *djabar, edjér, epés*[75] or, with a more modern spelling, as *jabar, jer,* and *pes.*[76] Wieringa contends that 'Jawi and Pegon did not merely borrow from the Persian-Arabic script [...], but those who developed the Pegon script must have been familiar with the Persian variant'.[77]

European scholars of the Orient were interested in a comparative study between these two influential languages: Persian in the Persianate world, and Malay as 'the Latin of the Orient'. One of the first known Persian-Malay philological analyses was conducted by George H. Wrendly[78] (d. 1744), who described the geographical names of Southeast Asia as follows:

> ([...] under the name of بالاباد *Bâlâbâd*, and the Eastern arm/side, on whose westside the island of Sumatra is laid, [and] under the name of زيرباد *Zirbâd*, these are both Persian names, which in Malay are داتس اڠين *Di atas angin* and دباوه اڠين *Di bawah angin*, that is,

[74] 'pers. zabar (=« sopra », corrispondente all'ar. fatha) > baris atas (= linea di sopra); pers. zér (« sotto », ar. kasra) > mal. baris bawah (linea di sotto); pers. pèš (« davanti » ar. ḍamma) > mal. baris hadapan (linea davanti).' Bausani, 'Note sui vocaboli Persiani in Malese-Indonesiano', 23. Interestingly, it came to my attention that while studying Arabic, Malays define *tanwin/nunation* (ـًـٍـٌ) on the basis of Persian definitions of *Tanwin*: *du-zabar* (two above), *du-zér* (two below) and *du-pésh* (two front). They are in Malay as *dua baris atas* (two above), *dua bawah* (two below), *dua depan* (two front). Regarding the Persian classification of vowels see: *Loghatnama Dehkhoda* through www.vajehyab.com.

[75] Bausani, 'Note sui vocaboli Persiani in Malese-Indonesiano', 23.

[76] Edwin Wieringa, 'Pegon', *Encyclopaedia of Islam*, third edition (Leiden and Boston: Brill, 2021), 139–140.

[77] Ibid. 139. Further, Arabic and Persian classical dictionaries and geographical works are replete with etymological and phonological information about the islands, cities, ports and inhabitants of Southeast Asia as well as the Far East. See *The Geographical Works of Sádik Isfaháni*. Translated by J. C. from Original Persian Mss. in the Collection of Sir William Ouseley (London, 1832). Also, see *Burhān-i Qāṭiʿ*. For comprehensive information about the modern status of Southeast Asia in Persian sources see, Arash Khazeni, *The City and the Wilderness: Indo-Persian Encounters in Southeast Asia*, 2020.

[78] There are disagreements about his birthplace as Switzerland or Germany. See Waruno Mahdi, 'The First Standard Grammar of Malay: George Werndly's 1736 Maleische spraakkunst', *Wacana* 19/2 (2018): 258.

> above the wind, and below the wind [respectively]; and in application in those countries mentioned they are called in Malay تانه داتس اغن *Tanah diatas' angin*, the land that is above wind, […]).[79]

For some orientalists, Persian and Malay were both a part of 'Oriental tongue' in general and 'Muslim language' in particular. This is despite the fact that Islamic manuscripts address the three languages of Arabic, Persian, and Ottoman Turkish as the main languages of Islam until the late twelfth/eighteenth century. One may refer to the manuscript *Kashf al-Rumūz* (Revealing the Secrets) ascribed to ʿUbaydallāh b. ʿAbdallāh, who introduces the three languages of Islam as Arabic, Persian, and Turkish,

> Believing in God [i.e., accepting Islam], according to what has been mentioned in the creeds, should be done in either Arabic, Persian, or Turkish; whatever the language […] of Islam, it should be considered.[80]

Nonetheless, orientalists expanded such linguistic notions and added Malay and Javanese to the main languages of Islam, that is, those languages which should be seen along with Arabic, Persian, and Turkish in being no less significant than the non-Islamic languages of the Orient such as Chinese. Thomas Erpenius (d. 1624) was one of the first orientalists who paid particular attention to philological connections between the Middle Eastern and Malay-Javanese languages. He collected many orien-

[79] '[…] onder den naam van بالاباد Bâlâbâd, en de Oostelyke arm, aan wiens Westkant 't eilandt Sumatra legt, onder den naam van زرباد Zirbâd voor, zynde zulks beide Persische namen, die in 't Maleisch luiden داتس اغن Di'âtas 'ângin en دباوه اغن Dibâwah 'ângin, dat is, boven den windt, en beneden den windt; en met toepassinge op deze gemelde landen worden die in 't Maleisch genoemd تانه داتس اغن Tanah diatas 'ângin, ' t landt dat boven wind is, […]' George Henrik Werndly, *Maleische Spraakkunst uit de eige schriften der Maleiers opgemacht met eene Voorreden* (Amsterdam: Wetstein, 1736), xxiii

[80] The original text in Persian reads as follows:

ایمان آوردن به خدا چنانچه در عقاید نوشته اند خواه بلفظ عربی، خواه بلفظ فارسی
خواه بلفظ ترکی؛ بهر لفظ که اعتقادن...ل اسلام است باید دانست

Manuscript 18745, fl. 66; Parliamentary Library of Iran. Such examples are found in the Persian legal text copied in Indonesia. See, Daneshgar, 'Persianate Fiqh in Indonesia'. A special issue *Le Lingue Islamiche: Forty Years Later*, edited by Simona Olivieri, Giuliano Lancioni and Michele Bernardini was published with the *Eurasian Studies* around the Bausani's 'Muslim/Islamic Language' theories, in which Versteegh, 'from a linguistic perspective', demonstrated his disagreement with the notion of 'Islamic language' and that 'Labels such as 'Islamic/Muslim' should therefore be applied to these speakers, rather than to their languages'. See, Kees Versteegh, 'Can a Language be Islamic?', *Eurasian Studies* 18/1 (2020), 5–25. Nonetheless, I think that the way Muslims classified their own languages should be considered.

tal manuscripts with the aim of finding a relationship between Arabic and other oriental languages. In so doing, he began practising and studying common phrases and alphabetical relationships between Arabic, Persian, Turkish, and Malay. His attempt to initiate a wide oriental language project is seen in his manuscript, Gg.6.40, kept at Cambridge University Library.[81] Subsequently, further scholars such as Adriaan Reland (d. 1718), Nikolaus Wilhelm Schröder (d. 1798), and Johann Wilhelm Schröder (d. 1793) brought more Malay-Indonesian literature to European academic discourse.[82] But it was L. Marcel Devic (d. 1888) who produced one of the first multilingual etymological sources for Oriental proverbs and idioms in French and 'langues musulmanes'. According to Devic,

> Under the name of oriental languages, we must comprehend all the languages/expressions [used in] Asia, from Arabic and Turkish that are spoken on the Mediterranean coasts, to Chinese and Japanese applied in the Pacific Ocean. We can attach them to the group of Oceanian languages, among which Malay is the most widespread type. Thanks to the traveling spirit of Europeans, driven by scientific curiosity or commercial needs, it was perhaps not one of these languages, even the most unknown dialect of the Altaic massif, which had not slipped some words into our vocabularies [...] The collected category in this book only contains Muslim languages, Arabic, Persian, Turkish and Malay (with Javanese).[83]

Devic's volume provides Arabic, Persian, Malay, Javanese, and Turkish equivalents in French based on *Sejarah Melayu* (the Malay Annals), one of the earliest Malay historical sources.[84] More orientalists showed interest to Malay-Indonesian philology and culture. Pieter Johannes Veth (d. 1895) produced fully developed studies on Indonesian culture and people, even though he never visited the East. In one of his short critical notes published in 1888, he reflected upon the origin of a common religious and traditional commemoration in Sumatra and Java.[85] The commemoration, known as

[81] Majid Daneshgar, *Reconstructing Erpenius' Library The First Collection of Oriental Manuscripts at Cambridge University Library* (Leiden: Brill, 2024). [82] Majid Daneshgar, 'An Old Malay Manuscript of *Tafsīr* and *Tajwīd*: Formative Islamic Sciences in Nusantara', in *Malay-Indonesian Islamic Studies: A Festschrift in Honor of Peter G. Riddell*, edited by Majid Daneshgar and Ervan Nurtawab (Leiden: Brill, 2023), 163–181. [83] L.-Marcel Devic, *Dictionnaire étymologique des mots français d'origine orientale* (arabe, persan, turc, malais) (Paris: Imprimerie nationale, 1876), i.

[84] Devic also used Favre's *Dictionnaire malais-français* (Vienne: Imprimerie imperiale et royale, 1875) and *Dictionnaire javanais-français* (Vienne: Imprimerie imperiale et royale, 1870).

[85] Pieter J. Veth, 'Opmerkingen naar aanleiding van het opstel, Hat Ḥassan-Ḥusayn of Taboetfeest te Benkoelen', 230–233.

Tabut,[86] was dedicated to remembering the martyrdoms of the second and third Shīʿī Imams, respectively, Ḥasan in Medina in 661 CE and Ḥusayn in Karbala in 680 CE. The feast day is interchangeably known as *het* ʻâsjoerâ- *of Ḥasan-Ḥusayn-feest* (the ʿĀshurā or Ḥasan-Ḥusayn feast), or, according to Hurgronje as *asan-usén* (Ḥasan-Ḥusayn) in Aceh.[87] To discuss the popularity of this commemoration, Veth relied on connections between Persian, Shīʿism, and Malay philology.

> It is not at all unlikely that in those times the ʿĀshurā celebration, under Persian influence, had more Shīʿī characteristics. We know very little about the earlier history and development of Islam in the Indian Archipelago; but that a Persian-Shīʿī vein running through it can be recognized in the many traces it has left behind [...] An interesting example is that on Java the common ablution before prayer is indicated equally with the Persian-derived *abdas* (for *ābdast*) as with the Arabic-derived *woeloe* [from *wuḍūʾ*].[88]

Geographical names in the Malay-Indonesian world are also derived from Persian classical literature.

> Kedah is sometimes called *Zamīn Turan*. In Persian *Zamīn* = ʻcountry' and Toran ʻTartary' or Turkistan. Probably the name is due to willful or unintelligent identification of Kedah with some place mentioned in an *Hikayat* [Islamic story]. Similarly, Perak is called *Kustan Zorīan*. Possibly Zorīan is a corruption of the word *Zuzan*, an ancient city in Khuzistan.[89]

A study of Persian manuscripts from the Malay-Indonesian world might suggest that the number of terms of Persian origin in Malay-Indonesian languages is in fact more than three hundred. Moreover, in order to better understand the relationship

86 See, Feener, ʻʿAlid Piety and State-sponsored Spectacle', 2015.

87 See, C. Snouck Hurgronje, *The Achehnese*, trans. A. W. S. O'Sullivan (Leiden: Brill, 1906). A manuscript kept in the Pedir Museum in Aceh introduces Muharram as *bulan Hasan-Husayn* (ʻthe Month of Ḥasan and Ḥusayn'). It contains alternative names for most of the months. For instance, the month of Ramadan and the month of Shawwal are also called *bulan puasa* (ʻthe Month of Fasting') and *bulan hari jadi* (ʻthe Month of Birthday'), respectively. My thanks go to Masykur Syafruddin for providing me with an image of this manuscript.

88 Veth, 233. Also, see Majid Daneshgar, ʻPieter J. Veth on the TabutFeast: Judaic and Persian-Shīʿī Traces of a Tradition in Java', *Berita* (Summer 2020), 4–9.

89 Richard O. Winstedt, ʻSome More Malay Words', *Journal of the Straits Branch of the Royal Asiatic Society* 80 (1919), 135. It is also said that Zuzan (or Zawazan) in Mamluk times referred to the region of Central Kurdistan. Thanks to Martin van Bruinsessen for letting me know about this point.

between the Persian and Malay worlds one should also consider the influence of Malay languages on Persian. As the 'Latin of the East' one might expect to see an influence on Persian from Malay that goes beyond a few internationally-used Malay-Indonesian terms such as *ikat*.[90]

PERSIAN ORIGIN OF MALAY ISLAMIC LITERATURE

Persian-Malay Evidence

In 1940, Hendrik Karel Jan Cowan was the first to show that Persian literary artefacts physically appeared in Sumatra through India. His essay is about an incomplete *ghazal* (love elegy) of the famous Persian poet Saʿdī engraved on the tomb of Nāʾinā Ḥusām al-Dīn (d. 823/1420) in Candi Uleeblang, Pasai,[91] whose tombstone was probably made in Cambay, India.[92] This inscription is the celebrated epigraph confirming the existence and/or devotional application of Persian in the Malay-Indonesian world before the tenth/sixteenth century. Another epigraphic evidence would be a tombstone from Teungku Sareh in Aceh dated 844/1440.[93] This one includes Persian phrases as well as the usual Arabic formulae used on tombstones. However, as indicated by Peacock,

> despite its greater distance from the Persophone heartlands of India and Iran, this Sumatran epigraphic evidence seems to predate that from Arakan, represented by a bilingual Persian-Arakanese inscription dated 900 Hijriyyah/1495, while Persian phrases appear on Arakan's idiosyncratic Arabic coinage around 1481–91.[94]

[90] There has been debates about the origin of the term "ikat", but I assume that it was commonly used (also pronounced differently) in the Archipelago for long time. The influence of Malay on the Persian language is the subject of my forthcoming study.

[91] Cowan, 'A Persian Inscription in North Sumatra', 15–21.

[92] Elizabeth Lambourn, 'From Cambay to Samudera-Pasai and Gresik: The Export of Gujarati Grave Memorials to Sumatra and Java in the Fifteenth Century CE', *Indonesia and the Malay World* 31/90 (2003), 221–289. On further Islamic tombstones coming from India, see a number of works by Winstedt in the *Journal of the Straits Branch of the Royal Asiatic Society*.

[93] Elizabeth Lambourn, 'The Formation of the Batu Aceh Tradition in Fifteenth-century Samudera-Pasai', *Indonesia and the Malay World* 32/93 (2004), 188–210. The information and transcription of the epigraph by Lambourn were not totally accurate, for which a correction was published: Majid Daneshgar, Gregorius Dwi Kuswanta, Masykur Syafruddin, and R. Michael Feener. 'A 15th-Century Persian Inscription from Bireuen, Aceh: An Early 'Flash'of Sufism before Fanṣūrī in Southeast Asia.' In *Malay-Indonesian Islamic Studies: A Festschrift in Honor of Peter G. Riddell*, edited by Majid Daneshgar and Ervan Nurtawab (Leiden: Brill, 2022), 86–105.

[94] Peacock, 'Notes on Some Persian Documents', 82.

Persian inscriptions dating from before 1500 CE have been found from throughout Sumatra. The poems of Rūmī (or: perhaps Kirmānī) and Firdawsī are engraved on some local Sumatran stones,[95] indicating that Persian poetry was common in Indonesia.[96] In addition to epigraphs, the existence of several bilingual Persian-Malay manuscripts demonstrate the circulation of Persian in Malay pedagogical environment.[97] One may mention the Persian manuscripts Or.7056 and Or.1666 in the Leiden University Library, with interlinear Malay translations.[98] The manuscript Or.7056 is an undated anthology of poems uncovered by Christiaan Snouck Hurgronje (d. 1936) from Lam Pisan in Aceh in 1896. It includes thirteen yellowish folios measuring 16 cm × 11 cm and was apparently taken as 'war booty'.[99] Some scholars including Voorhoeve, Bausani, and Braginsky have already discussed this manuscript in their studies, having examined it and identified some of its parts. As a follow up, in order to test and complete their findings, I went through the text again and examined the remaining unknown portions, identifiying some of the unknown poets and also the possible connections with the works of the famous Malay mystic and Sufi figure of the Archipelago, Ḥamza Fanṣūrī (from the tenth/sixteenth–eleventh/seventeenth centuries). I used Malay-style orthography (changing گ to ڬ and پ to ڤ) and identified localised Persian terms (i.e. 'Malayised' Persian). Studies of Or.7056 consider its age with Voorhoeve saying 'naar het mij voorkomt ook zeer oud' ('it seems very old to me').[100] This anthology includes the couplets of famous poets including Abū Tammām (804–845), Abū Saʿīd Abū al-Khayr (967–1049), Khayyām (1048–1131), Farīd al-Dīn ʿAṭṭār (1145–1221), Ibn al-ʿArabī (1165–1240), Rūzbihān Baqlī (1128–1209), Ibn al-Fāriḍ (1182–1235), Jalāl al-Dīn Rūmī (1207–1273), Saʿdī Shīrāzī (1210–1292), Fakhr al-Dīn ʿIrāqī (1213–1289), and Maḥmūd Shabistarī (1288–1340). However, particular elements which lead us to call it an old manuscript are nasalisation of the suffix *-ku* by means of *ng*, as inherited from Old Javanese, where it is the rule, or Old Malay, where it

[95] Daneshgar, Inscriptions [96] One of the main hubs could have been, as Feener has shown, Aceh, a Cosmopolis welcoming of various religious traditions. See, R. Michael Feener, Patrick Daly, Anthony Reed (eds.), *Mapping the Acehnese Past* (Leiden: KITLV Press, 2009)

[97] I have recently come across a number of rare Persian and Arabic manuscripts including Malay and Javanese glosses and interlinear translations in Germany. Those also seem quite old and are to be the subject of a forthcoming report. [98] For the edition and translation of Or.7056 see: Majid Daneshgar, 'An Old Persian-Malay Anthology of Poems from Aceh', *Dabir* 7 (2020), 61–90. A new study about the Ismaili nature of the last fragment of the manuscript Or.7056 will come out in the near future. And regarding Or.1666 see Majid Daneshgar, 'Persianate Aspects of the Malay-Indonesian World'.

[99] Jan J. Witkam, *Inventory of the Oriental Manuscripts of the Library of the University of Leiden* (Leiden: Ter Lugt Press, 2007), XIV: 46. [100] P. Voorhoeve, 'Kutaha, Ketah of Misschien Kutah?', *Bijdragen tot de Taal-, Land- en Volkenkunde* 140 (2/3): 333.

is optional. Advised by Annabel Gallop of the British Library, and with the assistance of Karin Scheper of the Leiden University Library, a sample of the manuscript was sent to the a laboratory at Groningen University for carbon dating. The result confirmed that Or.7056 was highly likely (70.5 per cent probability) produced between 1450 and 1521 CE with there being a small chance (24.9 per cent probability) that it was produced between 1586 and 1623 CE.[101]

The other bilingual manuscript, Or.1666, has been copied by a Malay-speaking person. This manuscript titled *Khulāṣa ʿIlm al-Ṣarf* (A Concise History of Arabic Grammar) shows that Malays used to learn Arabic through the Persian language. This manuscript was copied and owned (*kātibuh wa ṣāhibuh*) by ʿAbd al-Jamāl[102] and finished in September/October 1581 (Ramadan 990). Although the colophon is silent about the place of its writing, the manuscript's orthography, Javanese paper (dluang), and style all indicate that the author's Malay was far better than his Arabic as well as his Persian. A Latin note on early pages of the manuscript[103] demonstrates that it was in the possession of P. van der Vorm (1661–1731), 'the minister for the Malay-language congregation in Batavia, who lived more than forty-three years in Asia and who was competent in several Oriental languages'.[104] Van der Vorm had also translated *Mirʾāt al-Muʾminīn* by Shaykh Shams al-Dīn al-Samatrānī (d. 1630) into Dutch.[105] Bausani claimed that it is another proof of the remarkable contribution of Persian to the Malay 'Muslim' language.[106]

As I demonstrated earlier, Or.1666 is an abridged bilingual rendition (with minor commentary) of *Marāḥ* al-*Arwāḥ* (The Souls' Place of Rest), a renowned treatise on Arabic morphology and phonology by Aḥmad b. ʿAlī b. Masʿūd from the late seventh/thirteenth or early eighth/fourteenth century.[107] His work held influence on many Muslim and Christian Arabists and grammarians including al-Suyūṭī (d. c. 1505),[108]

[101] Majid Daneshgar, 'A Very Old Malay Islamic Manuscript: Carbon Dating and Further Analysis of a Persian-Malay Anthology', *Indonesia and the Malay World* 147 (2022).

[102] I assume that he is the famous poet of the late 16th century who was influenced by Ḥamza Fanṣūrī.

[103] The note reads, 'Grammatica sermonis Arabici, dicta تصريف, conscripta lingua Persica cum versione Malaïca interlineari. Transmissa est ad me de India Orientali per D. Van der Vorm, V. D. M. in Eccelesia Malaïca Bataviae Indorum.' [104] Wieringa, *Catalogue of Malay and Minangkabau Manuscripts*, 1998: 28. Jan Just Witkam, *Inventory of the Oriental Manuscripts of the Library of the University of Leiden* (Leiden: Ter Lugt Press, 2007), II: 212. [105] George H. Werndly, *Maleische Spraakkunst uit de eige schriften der Maleiers opgemacht met eene Voorreden* (Amsterdam: Wetstein, 1736), 354–355.; Wieringa, *Catalogue of Malay and Minangkabau Manuscripts*, 28. [106] Alessandro Bausani, "Un manoscritto Persiano-Malese di grammatica Araba del xvi secolo" *Annali dell'Ist.Univ. Orientale di Napoli* 19/29 (1969), 69–98. [107] Daneshgar, 'Persianate Aspects of the Malay-Indonesian World'.

[108] Joyce Åkesson, *Arabic Morphology and Phonology: Based on the Marāḥ al-arwāḥ by Aḥmad b. ʿAī b. Masʿūd* (Leiden and Boston: Brill, 2001), I: 3; II : 7.

and was widely explained and glossed by various scholars and lithographed in Egypt, Ottoman Turkey, India, and Iran.

Or.1666 provides evidence of 'Malayised' Persian throughout the text (e.g., ff. 7 and 30). This manuscript is dedicated to an anonymous ruler who 'defeated infidels' and 'revived the works of Afridūn' (i.e., the ancient Persian king Firīdūn).[109] One of its poetic fragments (fl. 3) is as follows.

شاهی که در زمان نه ندارد نظیر خویش   شکرانه واجب است که در روزگار است
راج يغ دلم زمانڽ تياد آد سمسماڽ   فرض شکر جوک سوات ڤد ماس کيت اين

raja yang dalam zaman-nya tiada ada sama-sama-nya
farad syukur juga suatu pada masa kita ini
The king who is unrivalled during his own time
it must be thanked that he is in our time[110]

Another intriguing manuscript, Gg.6.40(iii), was part of a collection kept at the Erpenius Library but is now kept in the Cambridge University Library. It is the earliest extant Malay rendition of *Akhlāq-i Muḥsinī*, a mirror for princes, by Ḥusayn Wāʿiẓ Kāshifī.[111] Being already a hub for reading, inscribing, and translating Persian, Indonesia welcomed scholars competent in Persian. Ḥamza Fanṣūrī was one of the most famous Malay-Indonesian scholars of the tenth/sixteenth century whose works were replete with Persian poems. His life, works, and disciples have been the subject of hundreds of studies in the fourteenth/twentieth century.[112] Almost all scholars agreed

[109] Similar couplet is found in another Persian manuscript *Kitāb Tawḍīḥ al-alḥān* (on Melodies), UPenn Oversize LJS 425, dedicated to the Sultan of Deccan, Mahmud of the Bahmanids (r. 887–915/1481–1509). See: http://dla.library.upenn.edu/dla/medren/detail.html?id=MEDREN_9951469233503681. Another copy is preserved in the private collection of Fakhr al-Dīn Nasirī, Iran. See: Rukn al-Dīn Humāyūn-Farrukh, 'Dasta-gulī Taqdīm bi-Dūstdārān-i Kitāb', *Hunar wa Mardum* 49 (1345/1966), 41–60.

[110] This couplet is also found in the Ottoman Turkish epic of 'Süleymannâme'.

[111] See Daneshgar, 'An Early 'Mirror for Princes' in Southeast Asia: The First Known Malay Translation of Akhlaq-i Mohseni', *Cambridge University Library Special Collection* (2022): https://specialcollections-blog.lib.cam.ac.uk/?p=23968

[112] E.g., H. Kraemer, *Een Javaansche Primbon uitde Zest iende Eeuw* (Leiden: Trap, 1921); J. Doorenbos, De *Geschriften van Hamzah Pansoeri*. Leiden: Batteljee & Terpst ra (Ph. D Thesis, Leiden State University, 1933); L. F. Brakel, 'The Birthplace of Hamzah Fanṣūrī', *Journal of the Malaysian Branch of the Royal Asiatic Society* 42/2 (1969), 206–212; L. F. Brakel, 'Hamza Fanṣūrī. Notes on: Yoga Pract ices, Lahir dan Zahir, the 'Taxallos', Punning, A Difffijicult Passage in the Kitab al-Muntahi, Hamzah's Likely Place of Birth and Hamza's Imagery', *Journal of the Malaysian Branch of the Royal Asiatic Society* 52/1 (1979), 73–98; Naquib al-Attas, *The Mysticism of Hamzah Fanṣūrī* (Kuala Lumpur: University of Malay Press,

upon his tendency to exhibit belief in *waḥdat al-wujūd* (the unity of existence), a mystical-metaphysical concept and trend ascribed to Ibn al-ʿArabī (d. 1240), also promoted through Persian poets like Rūmī, Shabistarī, Jāmī (d. 1492), and others. Fanṣūrī's belief in *waḥdat al-wujūd* began to be confronted by Muslim theologians from the late tenth/sixteenth century onwards, those who opened up a space for Islamic doctrinal sources like the *ʿAqāʾid* (Creeds) of Najm al-Dīn al-Nasafī (d. 536/1142), which outlined a legal-theological approach as a response to common Sufi currents in Aceh.[113] But the Fanṣūriyyān movement completely lost its life at the hands the Gujarati scholar, Nūr al-Dīn al-Ranīrī al-Sūratī (d. 1658), who was appointed as *shaykh al-islām* in Aceh.[114] Al-Ranīrī derogatively termed advocates of *waḥdat al-wujūd* as '*zindīq*' (dualists)[115] and disseminators of heresy.[116] With the hope of reforming Islam and the *sharʿīa* in Indonesia, the works of Fanṣūrī and Fanṣūrī-oriented literature were burned.

Although Persian experienced a considerable decline in the Malay-Indonesian world after the tenth/sixteenth century, there were still some Persian literary activity in Indonesia. Important evidences for this continued activity include Or.5656 (a legal text) and Or.5658 (a Sufi text) held at Leiden University Library. These texts are a mixture of Persian and Malay and provide further evidence about the circulation of Persian materials in central Indonesia.

Persian-Malay Islamic Stories

Less people showed interest in producing original Persian-Malay works after the eleventh/seventeenth century. During this period what was related to the Persian language was often taken from the Persian-Malay works of a previous era. Several Malay Muslim stories (*hikayat*; Ar. & Pers., pl. *ḥikāyāt*, sg., *ḥikāyat*) were produced based on Persian prototypes. Carrying various forms of tradition and presenting 'a tissue of quotations

1970); Vladimir I. Braginsky, 'Towards the biography of Hamzah Fanṣūrī. When did Hamzah live? Data from his poems and early European accounts', *Archipel* 57/2 (1999), 135–175. G. W. J. Drewes and L. F. Brakel, *The Poems of Hamzah Fanṣūrī/edited with an introduction, a translation, and commentaries, accompanied by the Javanese translations of two of his prose works* (Dordrecht-Holland and Cinnaminson, U.S.A.: Foris Publications, 1986), among others.

113 Peter G. Riddell, *Malay Court Religion, Culture and Language Interpreting the Qurʾān in 17th Century Aceh* (Leiden and Boston: Brill, 2017), 39.

114 For more see, Riddell, *Malay Court Religion*, 34.

115 Regarding controversies around Fanṣūrī's 'heretical' or 'heterodoxy-dualist' image in Raniri's works see, Syed Muḥammad Naquib al-Attas, 'Al-Raniri and the Wujudiyyah of 17th Century Acheh', (MA thesis, McGill University, 1962), 243. Also, Riddell, *Malay Court Religion*, 36.

116 al-Attas, 'Al-Raniri and the Wujudiyyah of 17th Century Acheh', 186.

drawn from the innumerable centres of culture',[117] Malay *hikayat* were instrumental in preserving and sharing Malay oral and written Islamic traditions. They are often placed in the *kitāb* category, serving religious teachings.[118] Several Malay *hikayat* are influenced by Hindu traditions[119] or shaped by the literature of Muslim India. Although some were introduced by Indian-born scholars of the Malay Archipelago,[120] a large corpus of *hikayat* literature developed based on common translation movements in various corners of India. The geographical closeness of India and the Malay Archipelago made this easier for their inhabitants to discover one another's literature and culture. The main part of this story-making period was affected by sociopolitical upheavals in Central and South Asia.

Persians of Iran and Central Asia, especially from Bukhara and Samarqand, continued their progress in various classical categories of Islamic sciences, philosophy, and poetry from the Samanid empire (r. 819–999) onwards. This intellectual movement spread to neighbouring lands. The major element that developed Islamic literature in Southern Asia was Persianism; a transregional intellectual trend transformed through the Ghaznawid Turks. They developed science, horsemanship, and survival and combat skills, about which Indians had less competence at that time. During the fifth/eleventh century, they raided North India for precious metals. By plundering Indian gold and silver mines, they could make their own coins to pay for their 'campaigns in Central Asia and Iran [...to purchase] war-horses, slaves and manufactured goods [...]'.[121] As Eaton clarifies,

> the transregional circulation of wealth through Central Asia, the Iranian plateau and north India was the material counterpart to a growing canon of Persian texts that spread through those same regions. By elaborating distinctive norms of kingship, governance, courtly etiquette, social comportment, Sufi piety, poetry, art, architecture and so on, these texts provided the ideological scaffolding that sustained an emerging Persianate World.[122]

[117] See Braginsky's argument around H. M. J. Maier's 'Fragments of Reading: The Malay Hikayat Merong Mahawangsa. (Ph.D. Thesis, Leiden University, 1985), 59. Vladimir Braginsky, 'Jalinan dan Khazanah Kutipan: Terjemaham dari Bahasa Parsi dalam Kesusasteraan Melayu, Khususnya yang berkaitan dengan 'Cerita-Cerita Parsi''. *Sadur: Sejarah Terjamahan di Indonesia dan Malaysia*, ed. Henri Chambert-Loir (Jakarta: Ecole Francaise de Extreme Orient, 2009), 59–117 [also translated into English by Braginsky]. [118] Brakel, 'Persian Influence', 7–9. [119] The contribution of Hindu elements in *Durr al-Majālis* as well as in Malay *hikayat* will be discussed in the next parts. [120] e.g., al-Raniri who came from India and became a leading Muslim figure in Aceh. Also, see Sir Richard Winstedt, *A History of Classical Malay Literature* (Kuala Lumpur: Oxford University Press, 1969), v, 7–8.
[121] Eaton, India in the Persianate Age, 32. [122] Ibid., 33.

In this vein, celebrated Persian texts were received by Indians. The works of, for example, Firdawsī were cited in different sources, and new mystical and theological trends were developing in South Asia. Even though the Ghaznawid Turks lost their power and influence – along with the Seljuq empire – Persian elements were still exchanged between Western and Central parts of Iran as far as northern India, through the Central Asian cosmopolitan cities like Herat and Balkh. The subsequent rulers also contributed to circulation of Persianism in India. Maḥmūd Ghūrī (d. 1206 CE) of the Ghurid empire commanded armies to plunder Multan (known as the 'Golden House')[123] and Gujarat, and to attack Hindu temples. Soon they altered the remit of their forces and seized and colonised northern India, mainly Peshawar in 1176 CE.[124] Through this military occupation, both Persian Sufis and Islamic texts from Khurasan and Central Asia moved to India. The Mongol invasion of the seventh/thirteenth century also led many Persian speaking communities to leave Iran and Central Asia and to start a new life in Indian in pursuit of security. While carrying their Persian legacy and literary treatises, the newcomers actively participated in the Delhi Sultanate (1206–1526). During this period Sufi figures achieved a significant status and they found new opportunities to present several Persian works, because 'Persian rather than Arabic, served as a means of dissemination of Islam, and as the lingua franca among the educated Muslims of South Asia'[125] in the Delhi Sultanate.

In the meantime, the influence of Persian in the Malay-Indonesian Muslim literature becomes more obvious. Since the late seventh/thirteenth century, northern Sumatra, especially Pasai, was turning into a region that was Muslim dominated. The first known prototypes of Malay *hikayat* were produced at this time and here we will mention two of the earliest stories taken from Persian sources.

First, the *Hikayat Muhammad Hanafiyya/Hanafiah* (The Tale of Muḥammad Ḥanafiyya), regarding Muḥammad Ḥanafiyya's revenge for the sake of his half-brothers, Ḥasan and Ḥusayn (the second and third Imams of Shīʿa Islam, respectively).

[123] 'The city of مولتان *Moultan* is about half the size of Mansoureh. It is called the "Golden House", for there is in the city a certain idol, to which the Indians of the country come as on a religious pilgrimage, every year, and bring great riches with them; and those who pray in the temple of this idol must pay a tribute. This temple is situated in the centre of Moultan; and in the middle of the temple there is a great cupola or dome. All round this building are various houses, in which the servants and attendants of the idol reside. Moultan is not reckoned as belonging to Hindoostan; but there is in it a race of idolaters who worship in this temple. See, 'The Oriental Geography of Ebn Haukal (*Masālik wa-Mamālik*), An Arabian Traveller of the Tenth Century', translated by Sir Wilian Ouseley (London: Orietnal Press, 1800), 148.

[124] Ibid. [125] Christoph Marcinkowski, 'Shiʿism in Thailand from the Ayutthaya Period to the Present', *Shīʿism in South East Asia: Alid Piety and Sectarian Constructions*, eds. Chiara Formichi and Michael Feener (London: C. Hurst & Co. Ltd., 2015), 32.

Both Van Ronkel and Brakel are of the view that this *hikayat* may have been a direct translation of a Persian story from the eighth/fourteenth century. Addressing Persian accounts, this story was also a Malay translation of a Persian prototype. Van Ronkel first expanded his hypothesis about the Persian origin of this story by referring to the manuscript Add.8149 listed in Charles Rieu's catalogue of the Persian manuscripts in the British Museum (now held in the British Library).[126] This Persian manuscript was copied in the Murshidabad region of Bengal in 1134–5/1721 and is composed of two parts. Van Ronkel concluded that the Malay *Hikayat Muhammad Hanafiyya* is a rendering of *Qiṣṣa-yi Amīr al-Muʿminīn Ḥasan wa Ḥusayn* (The Tale of the Commander of Believers Ḥasan and Ḥusayn) (ff. 1–28) and *Ḥikāyat-i Muḥammad Ḥanafiyya* (ff. 29–82). Winstedt agreed, stating that 'though in Arabic there are biographies of Muḥammad Ḥanafiyya, only in Persian is there a special *hikayat*'.[127] Later on, Brakel completed his PhD thesis examining various versions of this story, which concluded with an extensive analysis of the Malay texts in the light of the Persian manuscript Add.8149 originally from Bengal.[128] Through his investigation, he demonstrated that a large part of Add.8149 is found in the Malay version. He, suggests that Add.8149 is actually the prototype of the oldest known Malay *hikayat*. Despite this resemblance, there were still some portions of the *Hikayat Muhammad Hanafiyya* which studies have been unable to trace in Add.8149. An examination of all available sources dealing with *Hikayat Muhammad Hanafiyya* in fact revealed that *Durr al-Majālis*, the subject of this present volume, is the immediate source for the Malay version of this tale and also of another epic, the *Hikayat Nur Muhammad*.[129] I will return to this observation in the following chapters.

Second, is the *Hikayat Amir Hamza* (The Tale of Amīr Ḥamza), also a mixture of historical and fictional accounts about the chivalrous characteristics of Ḥamza, the Prophet's uncle. Van Ronkel examined two manuscripts relating to *Hikayat Amir Hamza* – Or.1697 and Or.1698 – both held in the Leiden University Library.[130] He demonstrated that the Malay version is a direct translation of a Persian work circulated in western- and South Asia. All known versions of this manuscript at the Leiden University Library (that is, including Or.7360, which I examined) contain Persian

[126] Charles Rieu, *Catalogue of the Persian Manuscripts in the British Museum* (London, The British Museum, 1881), II: 819; Vladimir Braginsky, *The Heritage of Traditional Malay Literature: A Historical Survey of Genres, Writings and Literary Views* (Leiden, KITLV Press, 2005), 181–182.

[127] Winstedt, *A History of Classical Malay Literature*, 106–107.

[128] L. F. Brakel, *The Story of Muḥammad Ḥanafiyya* (Leiden, Koninklijk Instituut Voor Taal-, Land- en Volkenkunde, 1977) and L. F. Brakel, *The Hikayat Muhammad Hanafiyyah: A Mediaeval Muslim-Malay Romance* (Berlin: Springer, 1981).

[129] Majid Daneshgar, 'New evidence on the origin of the Hikayat Muhammad Hanafiyyah', *Archipel* 96 (2018): 69–102.

[130] Ph. S. van Ronkel, De Roman van Amīr Hamza (Leiden: E. J. Brill, 1895).

sentences and terms and prove the competence of eighth/fourteenth-century Malays in Persian grammar and terminology.[131] This story is often placed in the category of romantic works rather than religious ones.[132] The estimated date for the compilation of *Hikayat Amir Hamza* is around 1390 CE. This story was known to the author of another important Malay work, *Hikayat Raja Pasai*, 'which was composed no later than the beginning of the ninth/fifteenth century'.[133]

One of the first sources indicating the name of these two classical stories is *Sejarah Melayu* (The Malay Annals) with sections about Malacca before the siege of the Portuguese Afonso d'Albuquerque in 1511.[134] According to the *Sejarah Melayu* (e.g., Ms. RAS Farquhar Malay 5, ff. 255–256), the royal court as well as Malay warriors were aware of the chivalrous qualities of *Hikayat Muhammad Hanafiyya* and *Hikayat Amir Hamza*:

> [...] the young nobles said, 'Why do we sit here idly. It would be well for us to read a tale of war that we may profit from'. Tun Muḥammad Unta said, 'That is very true, sir. Let us ask [the Raja] to give us the *Story of Muhammad Hanafiah*. Then the young nobles said to Tun Aria, 'Go, sir, and take this message to the Ruler, that all of us crave from him the Story of Muhammad Hanafiah, in the hope that we may obtain profit from it, for the Franks are attacking tomorrow'. Tun Aria accordingly went into the palace and presented himself before Sultan Ahmad, to whom he addressed the young nobles' request. And Sultan Ahmad gave him the *Story of Hamza* [...].[135]

[131] See: Daneshgar, 'Persinate Aspects of the Malay-Indonesian World'. [132] Braginsky, 'Jalinan dan Khazanah Kutipan', 6. [133] Ibid., 7. [134] Further evidence confirms that it was compiled in the late fifteenth century. Winstedt, *A History of Classical Malay Literature*, 158–159.

[135] C. C. Brown, 'The Malay Annals', *Journal of the Malayan Branch of the Royal Asiatic Society*, October 1952, Vol. 25, No. 2/3 (159), *Sějarah Mělayu or 'Malay Annals'* (October 1952), 168. This part in the MS. No. 18 of the Raffles collection was written differently and also transcribed and translated differently by Winstedt and Brown, respectively: [...]*Maka kata anak tuan-tuan itu, 'Apa kěrja dudok sahaja? Baik kita měmbacha hikayat, supaya kita běroleh fa'idah'. Maka kata Tun Muḥammad Unta, ' Běnar-lah kata tuan itu. Baik mohonkan Hikayat Muḥammad Hanafiahê' Maka anak tuan-tuan itu pun běrkata pada Tun Aria, ' Pěrgi-lah tuan hamba pěrsěmbah- kan pada yang di-pěrtuan, patek ini sakalian hěndak měmohonkan Hikayat Muḥammad Hanafiah, mudah-mudahan kalau patek itu měngambil fa'idah dari-pada-nya, karna Fěringgi akan mělanggar esok hari'. Maka Tun Aria pun masok-lah měngadap ka-pada Sultan Ahmad, maka sěmbah orang itu sěmua-nya di-pěrsěmbahkan ka-pada baginda. Maka oleh Sultan Ahmad Shah di-anugěrahkan Hikayat Hamzah* [...] Winstedt, *the Malay Annals or Sejarah Melayu*, 191.

[...] مک کات سکل تون ۲ «اف کیت [اتو کرج] بوة دودق ساج [؟] این بایک کیت ممباچ حکایة ڤرغ سڤای کیت براوله فائده [درفداڽ].
مک کات تن محمد انت «بنرله سڤرة کات تون ۲ ایت. بائیقله تن اندرسکار ڤرکی موهنکن «حکایة محمد حنفیه» مدهن ۲ داڤت ڤاتک ۲ ایة
مغمبل فائده درڤداڽ، کران فرغکی اکن ملغکر ایسق هاری». مک تن اندرسگارا فون ماسقله مغادق [کفد] سلطان احمد، مک [سکل]
سمبه اورغیت سمواڽ دڤرسمبهکن کباوه دلی سلطان احمد. مک اوله سلطان احمد دنکراه بکند «حکایة حمزه» [...]

According to Winstedt, 'the request of the Malay warriors to their Sultan to lend them the romance of Muhammad Hanafiah to read one night during the Portuguese attack on Malacca may be a reminiscence of Krishna reciting the Bhagavad-Gita to Arjuna before the great battle between the Pandavas and Kauravas began'.[136] Apart from reflecting upon the importance of the two stories with Persian origin, the *Sejarah Melayu* contains allusions to further Persian classical literature.[137] Winstedt also states that,

> [...] the evidence points to the first draft of the *Sejarah Melayu* being written by a scholar, possibly of mixed blood, who was interested in history and in such languages as Javanese and Arabic and even Persian, an observer who could note and mimic the foreigners of a cosmopolitan port, a man who knew and could describe intimately the court and nobility of the last Sultan of Malacca.[138]

Another old Malay story is *Hikayat Bayan Budiman* (Tale of the Parrot), which is based on the celebrated Persian work *Ṭūṭī-nāma* (Tale of the Parrot), originally from the Sanskrit source of Śukasaptati or the seventy tales of the parrot. According to Winstedt and Braginsky, this story would have been popular in the Archipelago in the tenth/sixteenth century, albeit sometimes only in part:

> which stories the work included at that time is uncertain, as the first of its old manuscripts contains only two and a half stories and ends abruptly, and the second one contains only ten stories.[139]

The colophons of some manuscripts introduce Qāḍī Ḥasan as the main narrator of the story in 773/1371. The identity of Qāḍī Ḥasan[140] has not been established and it remains uncertain as to whether he was (as advised by Winstedt) the main Persian storyteller or (as suggested by T. Iskandar) a Malay scribe. Braginsky, in line with Winstedt, also agreed that *Hikayat Bayan Budiman* was based on a Persian prototype written by Qāḍī Ḥasan.[141] They both reached the conclusion by examining the Or.3208 kept in Leiden University Library, in which the preface indicates that the text had already been trans-

[136] Winstedt, *A History of Classical Malay Literature*, 160. [137] E.g., foreigners are called 'فرغکی' or 'فرغکی' taken from 'فرنگی'; a term already found in Persian poetic literature (e.g., those of Saʿdī), also see مخدوم، سفال. [138] Richard Winstedt, 'the Malay Annals or Sejarah Melayu', *Journal of the Malayan Branch of the Royal Asiatic Society*, December, 1938, Vol. 16, No. 3 (132), *The Malay Annals of Sejarah Melayu* (December, 1938), 30. [139] Ibid., 27. [140] E.g., fl. 220, Ms. Malay B 7 (also John Leyden collection (285), acquired by the India Office Library in 1824) [141] Braginsky, 'Jalinan dan Khazanah Kutipan', 417.

lated from Persian and the colophon mentions the authorship as being 'by Qāḍī Ḥasan'.[142] Although their assertions seem inconclusive[143] the antiquity of the text is not in doubt.

Some more *hikayat* were written based on Persian translations of Sanskrit works. One such tale is the *Ḥikāyat-i Kalīla wa Dimna*,[144] which is based on the Sanskrit *Pañcatantra*, or the *Ḥikāyat-i Bakhtiyār*,[145] a framed-tale, 'traceable to a group of Persian literary works that tell of Prince Bakhtiyār [...] Abandoned in a desert by his royal parents, he was found and adopted by a gang of robbers and then rescued by a merchant who brought him to the presence of King Āzādbakht, his father'.[146]

Also, the *Marong Mahawangsa*, include some episodes influenced by Persian mateirals: '[...] in this Kedah legend we meet another instance of Malay indebtedness to Persian models, such as is seen in the introduction to the *Sejarah Mélayu* [...] and in the introduction of the same type to the "Kedah Annals"'.[147]

Apart from the abovementioned stories, most of which are placed in the category of 'religious works' or '*kitāb*' with the purpose of private or public recitation, a number of Malay works were positioned in the *adab* literaturere[148] also related to 'court literature'.[149] Here, the role of Persian literature is also obvious, as can be seen in *Tāj al-Salāṭīn* (The Crown of Kings) produced in Aceh in 1603 by Jawharī Bukhārī; and in the first extant Malay version of *Akhlāq-i Muḥsinī*, a mirror for princes by Ḥusayn Wāʿiẓ Kāshifī (d. c. 1504) kept in the Cambridge University Library (Gg.6.40iii).[150] Another work in the same literary genre is that of al-Ranīrī known as *Būstān al-Salāṭīn* (The Garden of Kings) compiled in Aceh between 1638 and 1641. The work is clearly inspired by Persian

142 That the text has been translated from Persian is mentioned in other copies, including the Malay B 7 of the Singapore National Library.

143 A copy of *Bayan Budiman* in the Dewan Bahasa dan Pustaka, Kuala Lumpur, deserves to be examined seriously, as it may lead us to a conclusion that Qāḍī Ḥassan was perhaps from the ʿAjam region (Eastern regions of Persian Iran). However, some still deem this text as the oldest known Malay *Hikayat*. See A. Jehngoh, *Arabic Elements in* Hikayat Bayan Budiman, *the Oldest Classical Malay Text* (Lund University, Sweden, 2003). Also, Hermann states that a concise version of the Persian *Ṭūṭī-nāma* was produced by Muḥammad Qādirī in the seventeenth century; whether this could have affected Malay *Bayan Budiman* should be discussed in the future. Hermann, 225.

144 *Ḥikāyat-i Kalīla wa Dimna* was also revised, updated and modified by Wāʿiẓ Kāshifī to give rise to the work titled *Anwār-i Suhaylī*. The standing of this work in different regions saw it translated into Ottoman Turkish, Hindustani, Chagatai and other languages. See my discussion of Hermann's work below.

145 Brakel, Persian Influence, 10.

146 Braginsky, 'Jalinan dan Khazanah Kutipan', 29.

147 Richard O. Winstedt, 'Perak the Arrow-Chosen', *Journal of the Straits Branch of the Royal Asiatic Society* 82 (1920), 137.

148 Brakel, 'Persian Influence', 8.

149 Ibid., 8–9.

150 Regarding Kāshifī's possible contribution to Malay commentaries on the Qurʾān see, my review Majid Daneshgar, 'Peter G. Riddell, Malay Court Religion, Culture and Language: Interpreting the Qurʾān in 17th Century Aceh', *Der Islam* 98(1), 293–296.

stories albeit through Arabic sources.[151] The influence of Persian, along with Arabic, in Malay *hikayat* should not be limited to these texts,[152] however, these are the key sources that received direct influence from Persian texts.

Hikayat Muhammad Hanafiyya, *Hikayat Amir Hamza*, and *Hikayat Bayan Budiman*[153] were introduced to the Malay-Indonesian world when Malays were engaged with making interlinear translations of original Persian texts (e.g., Or.7056). This could not have happened accidently as they all belonged to a period ranging from the late fourteenth to the early eleventh/seventeenth century, when Malays were in close contact with Persians and Persian sources. The formal reception of Islam in Sumatra in the late seventh/thirteenth century helped Persian to play an important role in the island up until the ninth/fifteenth century and to later become disseminated in Pasai, Malacca, and Aceh until the early decades of the eleventh/seventeenth century.[154] This happened during the Delhi Sultanate until early Mongol India when Persian was elevated as a literary and diplomatic language and offered to wider audiences despite its amalgamation with Hindu and other local works.[155]

Some scholars distinguish between Persian and Shīʿī *hikayat* with the latter covering themes such as ʿAlī b. Abī Ṭālib's leadership and and the disgrace of Umayyad rulers. Current epigraphic and manuscript information does not allow us to say with certainty how Shīʿism first arrived in the Malay-Indonesian world. As Zulkifli says,

> The first theory, widely accepted among historians, social scientists, and Indonesian Muslim scholars, such as Hamka, and Azyumardi Azra, neglects the existence of Shīʿism and generally affirms that Sunnism was the first branch of Islam to arrive in Indonesia and continues to predominant [*sic*] the Muslim community today. In contrast, the proponents of 'Shīʿī theory' such as Fatimi, Jamil, Hasymi, Azmi, Aceh, and Sunyoto, believe that the Shīʿīs have been present in Indonesia since the early days of Islamisation of the region and that, in fact, its adherents have played an important part in this process [...] Proponents of this theory generally admits [*sic*] that most Shīʿī traces have vanished over the course of time and as a result of the huge impact of Sunnism has had on the country.[156]

Despite such disagreements, the Indonesian scholar Baried (d. 1999) lists the Malay

[151] Jelani bin Harun, Nuruddin al-Raniri's Bustan al-Salatin: A Universal History and Adab Work from Seventeenth Century Aceh (Unpublished Ph.D. thesis, SOAS, University of London, 1999), 86–95. Also, Braginsky, 'Jalinan dan Khazanah Kutipan', 36. [152] E.g., *Hikayat Iskandar Zulkarnayn*.
[153] Also the old *Hikayat Pasai* was influenced by the *Hikayat Muhammad Hanafiyya*. Winstedt, 'The Malay Annals of Sejarah Melayu', preface. [154] Winstedt, 'the Malay Annals of Sejarah Melayu', 34.
[155] Marrison, 'Persian Influence'. [156] Zulkifli, The Struggle of the Shīʿīs in Indonesia (PhD Thesis, University of Leiden, 2009), 1–12.

hikayat which relate to personalities venerated by Shīʿī Islam, such *as Hikayat Nabi Muhammad Mengajar Anaknya Bibi Fatimah* (The Tale of Prophet Muḥammad Training his Daughter Fāṭima); *Hikayat Dhu al-Faqar* (The Tale of Dhū al-Faqār); *Hikayat Fatimah Berswami* (The Tale of Fāṭima's Marriage and Wedding); *Hikayat Wafat Nabi Muhammad* (The Tale of Prophet Muḥammad's Death); *Hikayat Raja Khandak* (The Tale of the King of the Trench); *Hikayat Bulan berbelah* (The Tale of the Splitting of the Moon); *Hikayat Muhammad Hanafiyya* (The Tale of Muḥammad al-Ḥanafiyya); *Hikayat Hasan dan Husain* (The Tale of Ḥasan and Ḥusayn); and *Cerita Tabut* (The History of Tabut).[157]

Some of these stories used to be bound and read along with some old Malay Islamic stories. For instance, as Ding Ch. Ming says, '*Hikayat Bayan Budiman, Hikayat Mu'jizat Nabi, Hikayat Nabi Mengajar Anaknya Fatimah*, or *Hikayat Nabi Wafat*, which are all bound together with the *Hikayat Muḥammad Hanafiah*' or 'similarly, the *Hikayat Amir Hamza, Hikayat Tatkal Fatimah Bertanya kepada Dzulfakar*, or *Cerita Umar Maya*'.[158] One may wonder if these sources, largely known as 'Persian' and/or 'Shīʿī' sources could have been connected in terms of either origin, date, content, or genre.[159] Cataloguers and historians of Malay literature have divided these Persian and/or Shīʿī sources into various categories. In 1899, Juynboll placed them in 'Mohammedaansche Legenden' (Islamic legends about Muḥammad), listing them as *Hikayat Nur Muhammad* (The Tale of the Light of Muḥammad), *Hikayat Bulan Berbelah, Hikayat Nabi Wafat* as well as *Hikayat Muhammad Hanafiyya*.[160] Subsequently, Winstedt categorised *Hikayat Nur Muhammad, Hikayat Bulan Berbelah, Hikayat Nabi Bercukur* (The Tale of the Shaving of the Prophet) and *Hikayat Nabi Allah Wafat* as 'relics of the Indo-Persian phase of Islamic culture'. On the other hand, Liaw Y. Fang added *Hikayat Muhammad Hanafiyya* to these four stories listed by Winsdedt and categorised them as 'stories of Prophet Muḥammad'.[161] According to him, the first part of *Hikayat Muhammad Hanafiyya* provides a sketch of Muḥammad's life, as such it can be related to prophetic stories.

Braginsky also presents a detailed analysis of the stories related to Muḥammad. His idea revolves around 'Hagiographic tales about the Prophet Muhammad', which

[157] Baroroh Baried, 'Le Shiʿisme en Indonésie', *Archipel* 15 (1978), 65-84. [158] Ding Ch. Ming, 'Access to Malay manuscripts', *Bijdragen tot de Taal-, Land- en Volkenkunde* 143/4 (1987), 444.

[159] This is a point also identified by Van Ronkel and Brakel when they found the *Hikayat Muhammad Hanafiyya* bound with *Hikayat Nur Muhammad*.

[160] H. Juynboll, *Catalogus van de Maleische en Sundaneesche handschriften der Leidsche universiteitsbibliotheek* (Leiden: Brill, 1899), 187.

[161] Liaw Y. Fang, *A History of Classical Malay Literature*, trans. Razif Bahari and Harry Aveling (Singapore and Jakarta: Institute of Southeast Asian Studies and Yayasan Pustaka Obor Indonesia, 2013), 215.

all aim to 'educate the reader in the spirit of piety and moral values of Islam'.[162] These *hikayat*, however, have various subsets. The major ones are *Hikayat Nabi Wafat*, *Hikayat Nur Muhammad/Hikayat kejadian Nur Muhammad* (The Tale of how the Light of Muḥammad was Created) also accompanied by the physical creation of Muḥammad, *Hikayat Kejadian Baginda Rasulullah* (The Tale of the Origin of God's Blessed Messenger) and *Hikayat Nabi Lahir* (The Tale of the Birth of the Prophet),[163] *Hikayat Nabi Miraj* (The Tale of the Prophet's Ascent), *Hikayat Bulan Berbelah/ Hikayat Bulan Berbelah Dua*. And all these stories, according to Braginsky, could have been produced in the sixteenth and seventeenth centuries – when Persian is still a main contributor in Malay literature.[164] Another subset of his classification is 'war stories' dealing with the enemies of Islam, such as *Hikayat Raja Khandak* (The Tale of the King of the Trench), *Hikayat Raja Lahad* (The Tale of King Laḥad), and *Hikayat Raja Khaibar* (The Tale of the King of Khaybar). Some other stories represent 'didactic' elements. Given that they are not found in earlier catalogues of Malay literature (e.g., those of Wrendly) or that available copies are quite recent, it is hard for scholars to date its reception in the Malay Archipelago. In this regard, there are *Hikayat Nabi Mengajar Anaknya Fatimah*, and *Hikayat Nabi Mengajar Ali*, dealing with the way the Prophet instructed Fāṭima and ʿAlī, respectively;[165] and each is delivered by different recensions.[166] Another addition to this instructional genre of Malay *hikayat* is *Hikayat Nabi dan orang Miskin* (The Tale of the Prophet and a Pauper). Braginsky's last category concerns the stories dealing with 'the Prophet's exhortations about the duties of humans in their worldly and religious life', like *Hikayat Nabi dan Iblis* (The Tale of the Prophet and Satan) – already a famous story in Persian and Ottoman Turkish literature.[167] As Edwin Wieringa demonstrated, some of these stories were scribed frequently until the late nineteenth century. They were affected by textual censorship to remove or substitute certain Shīʿī elements with those of Sunnis.[168]

Since many years ago, I have been developing my studies to figure out to what extent Malay *hikayat* are connected to the Persianate world, where Persian literature and Shīʿī

[162] Braginsky, *The Heritage of Traditional Malay Literature*, 608. [163] Ibid., 603.

[164] Ibid., 600–604. [165] Ibid., 608. [166] For instance, the *Hikayat Fatimah berkata-kata dengan pedang Ali* (The Tale of how Fāṭimah talked to ʿAlī's Sword). See, Braginsky, *The Heritage of Traditional Malay Literature*, 609. [167] Braginsky, *The Heritage*, 611. More or less similar approaches can be found in the book of Ismail Hamid, *The Malay Islamic Hikayat* (Bangi: Institut Bahasa, Kesusasteraan dan Kebudayaan Melayu, 1983); and in Jumsari Jusuf, Aisyah Ibrahim, Nikmah A. Soenardjo and Hani'ah (eds.) *Sastra Indonesia lama pengaruh Islam* (Jakarta: Pusat Pembinaan dan Pengembangan Bahasa. Departemen Pendidikan dan Kebudayaan, 1984).

[168] See Edwin Wieringa, 'Does Traditional Islamic Malay Literature Contain Shiitic Elements? Alî and Fâtimah in Malay Hikayat Literature', *Studia Islamika* 3/4 (1996), 93–111.

teachings moved together and continuously fed each other. And through this rather long journey, proving the origin of *Hikayat Muhammad Hanafiyya* in Sayf Ẓafar's *Durr al-Majālis* was the main starting point.[169] Not only are some of the abovementioned stories about Muḥammad and his household detectable in *Durr al-Majālis*, but other Malay *hikayat* on Sufi saints such as Ḥasan al-Baṣrī, Bāyazīd Basṭāmī, Sufyān al-Thawrī, and Ibrāhīm b. Adham, among others, are also to be found in this Persian source. *Durr al-Majālis* was a key text through which Malays shaped stories from the Qurʾān containing hagiographical works on prophets (*qiṣaṣ al-anbiyāʾ*) and about the Prophet's Companions.[170]

As I will demonstrate, *Durr al-Majālis*, as both an oral tradition and textual source, moved beyond the Balkans-to-Bengal paradigm and made inroads into the Arab world, the Far East, and the Malay-Indonesian world. Not only was it read but it was also translated into all known languages of the East from the time it was authored right up until the early fourteenth/twentieth century.

[169] Daneshgar, 'On the Origin of *Hikayat Muhamamd Hanafiyyah*' (2018).

[170] On Malay Islamic stories from the Qurʾān and the Prophet's Companion, see Liaw, *A History of Classical Malay Literature*, 191.

II) *Durr al-Majālis*: Origins and Identity

It seems bizarre that several hundred manuscript copies of *Durr al-Majālis* in different languages can be found in every corner of the world yet the text receives scant attention with scholars hardly mentioning it. While the text remains largely unknown – let alone thoroughly examined – both old and new manuscript copies are found in private and public collections in the East and West. While the text at one time enjoyed popularity its current relative anonymity may be the consequence of uncertainties about the author and disparities between extant copies.

Most known copies of *Durr al-Majālis* include thirty-three chapters, some resembling stories, some similar to lengthy supplications, and some that appear to be treatises on Islamic creed and doctrine. The longer copies have one or two more chapters (thirty-four or thirty-five chapters in total) accompanied by closing remarks. The chapters cover themes such as pre-creation, God, the lives of the prophets, and the Day of Judgement. Various admonitions are voiced by Sufi saints and tend to fall into a number of areas, such as the conflict between good and evil, conversion and confession, generosity and miserliness, killing and revenge, death and afterlife, and love for God. Persian literary collections with such content are numerous but what distinguishes *Durr al-Majālis* is the interconnection it displays between all chapters, despite them being independent of each other at the same time. Each chapter can be read and understood along with other chapters while being self contained and while conveying its own distinct message. Being aware of this structural significance, scribes were sometimes commissioned to reproduce *Durr al-Majālis* based only on one or two of its chapters. For instance, the chapters on Moses' conversation with God have been reproduced as *Mūsā-nāma* or *Munājāt-nāma*. Jesus' conversation with the skull of King Jumjuma and the story of Ḥasan and Ḥusayn's death are also parts that have been separated from the main text and circulated across the Muslim world for centuries. For example, the manuscript N.137 of the Shirani Collection in Pakistan titled *Maqtal-nāma* and which relates the 'martyrdom of Imam Ḥasan and Ḥusayn' is a chapter from *Durr al-Majālis*.[1]

Persianists and orientalists like Carl Hermann Ethé (d. 1917) places *Durr al-Majālis* in the category of a particular prose collection whose contents are interrelated and states that a limited number of classical works have such literary qualities.[2] One of the first Persian works having a similar thematic approach is that of Ḥusayn b. Asᶜad al-Dihistānī (sixth/twelfth century) based on the *Kitāb al-Faraj baᶜd al-Shidda* (Book of Relief after Adversity) of al-Tanūkhī (d. 384/939–994), containing thirteen chapters with various forms of stories, 'in which God grants relief to someone who finds himself in a difficult situation'.[3] Another similar work is *Gushāyish-nāma* (Book of Richness) (early twelfth/seventeenth century), based on Arabic and Indian literature, and co-authored by Radsehkran and Chayath. This collection is introduced as a source for 'praising God and the master of all prophets, Muḥammad', who like a Sun will shine upon elites and lay people.[4] The authors of *Gushāyish-nāma* followed Saᶜdī's style in his *Gulistān*. The *Majmaᶜ al-Nuqūl* (A Set of Narratives) by Muḥammad b. ᶜAlī b. Muḥammad Ḥasan Hindī is another example from the eighteenth century.[5] His volume covers the stories of 'Shīᶜī saints and their dedication to Imam Ḥusayn' whose content is fashioned on Prophetic statements, or *ḥadīth*, fictional stories, and reports from, and about, the caliphs of Islam.[6] The common point about these collection of stories is their resemblance to prophetic hagiography (*qiṣaṣ al-anbiyāʾ*).[7] One of the pioneering Persian sources on prophetic hagiography is that of Manṣūr b. Khalaf from Nishapur known as *Qiṣaṣ al-Anbiyāʾ-i Nayshāpūrī*, in the eleventh century. Manṣūr b. Khalaf's work covers reports of accounts about prophets from Adam to Muḥammad,

1 Moḥammad Bashīr Ḥosein, *Fihrist-i Makhṭūṭāt-i Shīrānī* (Lahore: Punjab Library, 1968), 26. Also, the manuscript 811/4 copied in Central Asia kept in the Oriental Institute of Tajikistan.

2 Carl H. Ethé, *Neupersische Literatur*, vol. II (Strassburg: Grundriss der iranischen Philologie Seperat-Abdruck, 1897) 212–368. I also use the Persian translation of this monograph, as Hermann Ethé, *Tārikh-i Adabiyāt-i Fārsī*, trans. and ed. Reḍā Zādeh Shafaq (Tehran: Bungāh-i Tarjumih va Nashr-i Kitāb 1337/1958).

3 On influence of Judeo-Arabic literature, see Arie Schippers, 'Stories about Women in the collections of Nissim ibn Shāhīn, Petrus Alphonsi, and Yosef ibn Zabāra, and their Relation to Mediaeval European Narratives', *Frankfurter Judaistische Beiträge* 37 (2012), 123–135, and on the Judeo-Persian, see Shervin Farridnejad, 'The Jewish Ḥāfeẓ: Classical New Persian Literature in the Judeo-Persian Garšūni Literary Tradition', *Journal of the Royal Asiatic Society* 31/3 (2021): 515–534.

4 Radsehkran, *Gushāyish-nāmah* (Lucknow: Nawal Kishore, 1287/1871), 86. This title should not be confused with that of Khājih Naṣīr al-Dīn al-Ṭūsī.

5 Ethé, 231.

6 Ibid.

7 See, Hermann Ethé, *Catalogue of Persian Manuscripts in the Library of the India Office* (Oxford: Printed for the India Office, 1903), I: 240–245.

and also the four rightly caliphs (Abū Bakr, ʿUmar, ʿUthman, and ʿAlī) until the death of Muʿāwiya (d. c. 60/680), the founder of Umayyad dynasty. Another important source is *Tāj al-Qiṣaṣ* (The Crown of Stories) by Abū Naṣr Aḥmad al-Bukhārī from the eleventh century relating to the history of Persia, from the birth of creation until the killing of Ḥusayn. *Tāj al-Qiṣaṣ* is known as one of the first comprehensive sources on the history of prophets and saints which was written in Persian, and collected according to the statements of Abū al-Qāsim Maḥmūd Jayhānī (mentor of Abū Naṣr Aḥmad al-Bukhārī) in Balkh. Being influenced by the Qurʾān and its exegetical works, *Tāj al-Qiṣaṣ* is divided into three parts, chronologically; 'The first part deals with a detailed introduction and the story of prophets (from Adam to Jacob); the second part includes the story of Joseph in forty sections [...]; The third part starts with the story of Moses and ends with the history of the formative period of Islam and its caliphs and narrates some incidents that happened after the emigration of Muḥammad from Mecca to Medina'.[8] The work of ʿAbd al-Waḥīd b. Muḥammad Muftī entitled *ʿAjāʾib al-Qiṣaṣ* (Wonders of Stories) from the tenth/sixteenth century, in twenty chapters, is another example. *Afṣah al-Aḥwāl* regarding the Biblical and Qurʾānic story of the People of the Cave and Shamʿūn and Khālid is worthy of attention.[9] *Durr al-Majālis* is placed, according to Ethé, in this category of prose works. He describes *Durr al-Majālis* as follows:

> [it] is a complex of different stories made of Jewish, early Arab, and formative elements of Islam and pays particular attention to early Sufi thinkers like Ḥasan Baṣrī, Sufyān Thūrī [Thawrī], Ibrāhīm Adham, and also Shaykh or Sultan Abū Saʿīd Abū al-Khayr, including thirty-three chapters about mystical principles for the sake of guiding Sufi disciples and seekers.[10]

Ethé believes that *Durr al-Majālis* and similar stories with interconnected narrations should be distinguished from other story-based prose works using several fictional figures to tell didactic stories about Muslim thinkers and scholars, such as

[8] Aḥmad b. Muḥammad Bukhārī, *Tāj al-Qiṣaṣ*, ed. Sayyid ʿAlī Āl-i Dāwūd (Tehran: Farhangistān-i Adab wa Zabān-i Fārsī, 1387/2009), vol. 1, 18.

[9] Ms. or. fol. 297 in Staatsbibliothek zu Berlin – Preußischer Kulturbesitz is from the eighteenth century, which also addresses the beginning of the creation and the story of Adam and Eve and their children Cain and Abel. Although this text has obviously been written on the basis of former stories of prophets in addition to *Durr al-Majālis*, one wonders whether it could be a prototype of the famous Malay stories known as *Hikayat Samaʿun* and whether studies which consider the origin of this *hikayat* to be Arabic could be questioned. This matter is discussed in my comparative section but is also a matter which I intend to study more fully elsewhere.

[10] Ethé, 233.

Jawāmiʿ al-Ḥikāyāt (A Collection of Tales) by Muḥammad ʿAwfī and *Zīnat al-Majālis* (The Embellishment of Assemblies) by Majd al-Dīn Muḥammad al-Ḥusaynī.

Durr al-Majālis should also, according to Ethé, be distinguished from framed/steered collections like *Kalīla wa Dimna*, or its updated and revised version known as *Anwār-i Suhaylī* by Wāʿiẓ Kāshifī, or those like *Bakhtiyār-nāma* and *Ṭūṭī-nāma*.[11]

It is not easy to accept all of Ethé's views about the genre and structure of *Durr al-Majālis*, because it was to a large extent influenced by several written and oral traditions (such as the previously mentioned ones). *Durr al-Majālis* was also written for a wide range of communities, engaging audiences from different social classes. In contrast to almost all classical prose works, *Durr al-Majālis* found its place in religious, mystical, political, and theological circles, and people showed an interest to *memorise* it in order to serve their oral traditions as well as translating it in order to serve their *written* cultures. Ethé also overlooked the remarkable contribution of *Durr al-Majālis* to theological, philosophical, and eschatological discussions meaning that the work was not only literary in nature. Perhaps Ethé's incomplete assessment of *Durr al-Majālis* was due to him having access to only two of its manuscript copies kept in the India Office (now in the British Library).

Less attention has been paid to *Durr al-Majālis in* relation to other medieval and premodern celebrated works of Islamic literature such as those written in Arabic by Jarīr al-Ṭabarī (d. c. 923), al-Zamakhsharī (d. c. 1144), and Fakhr al-Dīn al-Rāzī (d. c. 1210), and such as those written in Persian by Saʿdī (d. c. 1210), ʿAṭṭār (d. 1221), Rūmī (d. 1273), Jāmī (d. 1492), and Wāʿiẓ Kāshifī. These works were well received in their day and were widely recognised in royal courts, religious gatherings, and Sufi assemblies alike. Similarly, as will be shown below, *Durr al-Majālis* penetrated every corner of the Islamic world and was very soon indigenised by means of translation and structural modification.

The author of *Durr al-Majālis* had heard different narratives in various places and religious gatherings (*majālis-i tadhkīr*).[12] He received the gist of his stories from both earlier thinkers and from literary works in different languages and extended them to larger pieces or even into different forms. In the compilation of his work, the author of *Durr al-Majālis* followed a common tradition in listening to, and taking from, Sufi masters and religious figures. For example, as mentioned, the first known comprehensive story of prophets, written by Abū Naṣr Aḥmad al-Bukhārī, was produced based on the lectures of his teacher in Balkh.

The author of *Durr al-Majālis* borrowed from his predecessors both theme and

[11] Ethé, 228–229. [12] *Majālis-i tadhkīr*, literally, 'remembrance sessions', were mystical and religious assemblies often organised in the Delhi Sultanate and parts of Khurasan. They may also have been held by Sufi orders in Iran and Turkey.

content. His chapter 15 is comparable with what is found in Rūmī's *Mathnawī*. The role of ʿAṭṭār's literature is evident in chapters twenty-two, twenty-three, and twenty-six. The traces of narratives from al-Ṭabarī's history and his Qurʾānic commentary is seen in the story of Adam and Eve in chapter 1. *Durr al-Majālis* is enriched with direct quotations from both earlier and contemporaneous poets (e.g., Saʿdī). His strategy to borrow from others is mixed with his own strong imaginary taste to create different, new, and sometimes fictional stories and instructive chapters. The innovation of *Durr al-Majālis* is, contrary to the discussion of Ethé, found in its usage of various sources besides hagiographic works. *Durr al-Majālis* offers a combination of orientalised elements which usually did not exist in similar religious and literary works in Arabic and Persian. Integrating Asian-Islamic elements (e.g., Kuyūthā as an Islamised-Vedic Akuperat in chapter 28 of *Durr al-Majālis*), elevating women's status in society on various occasions, and ignoring the prophets' infallibility, are among its unusual features.

The author of *Durr al-Majālis* takes the reader to different worlds starting from the birth of Adam and Eve in paradise and their descent to Serendib (the Island of Sri Lanka). He brings together all forms of living and non-living beings and transports readers to their future. He allows his audience to imagine the joy, pain, and fear of life after death such as the moments after a corpse is placed into a dark and tiny grave; decomposition of the body by worms; being interrogated by the angels of the grave; and being associated with heavenly cherubs who hold bowls of wine.

Durr al-Majālis also gives a new impetus to the human imagination for interpreting the Qurʾān and the Prophetic statements. The reader is placed in a position whereby he can derive answers to his own legal, theological, mystical, and eschatological questions. For instance, in chapter 14 many of the issues of Islamic philosophy and theology are covered in the work, such as the creation of human beings, life after death, and prophetic miracles and infallibility. The author of *Durr al-Majālis* employs occultism and magical formulae to narrate an ethical lesson (e.g., chapter 16). Likewise, he is highly likely inspired by Hindu and Buddhist literature when he invites his readership to gain piety, chastity, and bravery by reading, listening, or holding the text.

> If one reads it nightly or daily, one acquires the merit of those who die in holy war. One is reminded of the indulgences of the Catholic Church and one is reminded of the introduction to the *Mahabharatas* – 'whoever presents a learned Brahmin with one hundred cows with gilded horns and whoever listens daily to the sacred stories of the Bharatas, these two acquire equal religious merit.'[13]

[13] Winstedt, *A History of Classical Malay Literature*, 102. However, such perscriptions are recently found on early Arabic inscriptions.

The author of *Durr al-Majālis* provides adequate information about all forms of the Islamic sciences (*ʿulūm al-dīn*), sciences which flourished in madrasas as well as in imperial courts. Yet the *Durr al-Majālis* was also accessible and, through the use of an intriguing linguistic style and beneficial content, it was used by those with less education and literacy such as those dwelling in rural communities and the warrior classes.

RECEPTION OF THE TEXT

Today the text of *Durr al-Majālis* is found in various locations with each copy produced in a different region of the world, strongly suggesting that it had been a well known and widely read text for several centuries. Some of its manuscript copies say that it informed the basis of an oral tradition among warriors and villagers and was part of a time-honoured Muslim tradition in which religious texts were not just read but recited. The manuscript M.82 in the Indian Council for Cultural Relations was scribed for 'the sake of bravery and the courage of the sovereign's forces' (*barā-yi shujāʿat va shahāmat-i dastgāh*; fl. 151). The Manuscript No.14248 (fl. 2) in the Parliamentary Library of Iran tells of the inscribing process of the text.

> The book of *Durr al-Majālis*, in the library of the shaykh of all of shaykhs and religious figures, Shaykh Bihaʾ al-Dīn and Shaykh Naṣr al-Dīn [?] [...] dated[?] 1094, was thoroughly copied and read. Written on 10 Rajab 1180/12 December 1776.

For some scribes *Durr al-Majālis* is seen as a sacred and auspicious work. At the end of manuscript Ms.5–24303 of the National Library of Iran (fl. 401), dated 1320/1902, we read that 'the noble and fortunate copy of the book of *Durr al-Majālis* [is] finished'.

Other scribes copied the text for instructing their children, as we see in the manuscript Lewis O.189 in the Special Collections of the Free Library of Philadelphia.

> I have finished this copy, and the miserable Satan has been ashamed. This valuable book has been written with the assistance of the All-Giving King, the treatise *Durr al-Majālis*, by the least and worthless man, Mawlānā ʿUmar, the son of Dūst Muḥammad, may God forgive them both. I have copied it for my children in the holy month of Ramadan on the ninth day, being a Tuesday of the year 1307 after the *ḥijra* of the Prophet peace be upon him [1890 CE].

Moreover, the manuscripts N.5991 and N.5994 in the Collection of Oriental Manuscripts of the Academy of Sciences of the Uzbek SSR (Uzbikestan) were copied in the local madrasa.[14] The Pushto versions of *Durr al-Majālis* were read along with legal works (e.g., *Fawāʾid al-Sharīʿa*) in Central Asian villages.[15]

Other copies of *Durr al-Majālis* were dedicated or offered to colonial officers and orientalists. Offering works to Europeans was not uncommon, but the dedicated works were usually the so-called 'classics'. For instance, a copy of Saʿdī's *Gulistān* in the Auckland Libraries of New Zealand (EASTMS:S310) was copied by Sayyid Aḥmad Ḥusayn for J. B. Jones on 4 April 1868.[16] Similarly, the French book collector, orientalist, and author Claudius James Rich (d. 1821) had a personal copy of the *Dīwān-i Ḥāfiẓ*, now kept in the Alexander Turnbull Library in Wellington, New Zealand (MSR-36), but which was placed on his grave in the Armenian cathedral at Julfa, Isfahan.[17] The *Durr al-Majālis* manuscript N.1886 of the India Office was dedicated to the officer Mr. Johnson. That *Durr al-Majālis* is found in European collections suggests that it was a highly regarded text, if not somewhat forgotten nowadays. As Semenov and Voronovsky say, *Durr al-Majālis* was 'A sort of widespread collection of anecdotes, [... which] later gained popularity among storytellers'.[18]

BIBLIOGRAPHICAL AND BIOGRAPHICAL DETAILS

Title of the Work and the Name of its Author

The preface of *Durr al-Majālis* contains information about its author, but the information varies from manuscript to manuscript. The name of the author and the book's title has been given in the following ways.

[14] Semenov and Voronovsky, *Собрание восточных рукописей Академии наук Узбекской ССР* (Tashkent: Издательство: 'Фан' Узбекской ССР, 1967), 435–436.

[15] H. G. Raverty, 'Account of Upper and Lower Suwat, and the Kohistan, to the Source of the Suwat River; with an Account of the Tribes Inhabiting Those Valleys', *Journal of the Asiatic Society of Bengal* 31(1862), 227–281 (esp. 248)

[16] Majid Daneshgar, *Middle Eastern & Islamic Manuscripts Sir George Grey Special Collections; Auckland Libraries New Zealand* (Auckland: Auckland Libraries, 2018), 29.

[17] Majid Daneshgar, and Anthony Tedeschi, *Middle Eastern and Islamic Manuscripts Alexander Turnbull Library Collections; The National Library of New Zealand* (Wellington: National Library, 2019),13; Regarding Rich's profile and his collection see Thompson Fawcett. 'The Rich Manuscripts', *The British Museum Quarterly* (1963): 18–23.

[18] Semenov and Voronovsky, *Собрание восточных рукописей Академии наук Узбекской СС* (Tashkent: Издательство: 'Фан' Узбекской ССР, 1967), 433.

- Sayf al-Dīn Ẓafar Nawbahārī; *Durar al-Majālis*
- Sayf al-Muẓaffar b. Burhān; *Durr al-Majālis*
- Sayf Ẓafar Burhān; *Durr al-Majālis*
- Sayf al-Dīn Ẓafar Nawbahārī; *Durr al-Majālis*
- Sayf Khiḍr Bukhārī; *Durr-i Majālis*
- Sayf Ẓafar Bukhārī; *Durr al-Majālis*
- Sayf al-Ẓafar Nawbahārī; *Dur al-Majālis*
- Sayyid Muẓaffar Abū Bahārī; *Dard al-Majālis*
- Sayyid Ẓafar Nūrbahārī; *Durr al-Majālis*
- Sayf al-Ẓafar b. Burhān al-Dīn Nawbahārī; *Durr al-Majālis*
- Sayf Ẓafar Būtahārī; *Durr al-Majālis*
- Sayf Muẓaffar Būtahārī; *Durr al-Majālis*
- Sayf Ẓafar Tūtahārī; *Durr al-Majālis*
- Sayf al-Naẓar Nawbahārī; *Durr al-Majālis*
- Yūsuf b. Muẓaffar Nawnahrī; *Durr al-Majālis*[19]
- Nawbukhārī; *Durr al-Majālis*[20]

Some copies are registered with another title. For instance, a copy in the Hazrat Pir Mohammed Shah Dargah Library of Ahmedabad, India (Ms.1395) is entitled *Durr al-Majālis al-Anām*, while another copy, N.1884, in the India Office is known as *Sullam al-Anbiya'* (The Latter of Prophets).[21] The author's name also differs in a few copies. The manuscript M.84 in the Indian Council for Cultural Relations introduces the author as Khʷāja Yaʿqūb Muṣliḥ Sayf Ẓafar Bahārī. In the manuscripts 5–6465 in the National Library of Iran and N.5989 of the Academy of Sciences in Uzbek SSR, he is introduced as Sayf Ẓafar Būstānī. Two other copies in the Uzbek SSR collection have mentioned the author's name differently: in N. 5991 as Sayyid Muẓaffar b. Burhān ʿUmrī [not ʿUmarī]; and in N. 5992 as al-Qārī Sayyid Naẓar Bukhārī. Also, in some unknown biographical sources he is known as Yūsuf Ẓafar Abū Ṭāhir.[22] Such diversity is found even in its early printed editions. A thirteenth/nineteenth-century [early]

[19] Only one available copy with this name, according to the information given by [Anonymous], [untitled] *Bayaz (Anjuman-i Fārsī)* 4/1–2 (1984): n.p.

[20] Only in one of the available copies at the Tipu Sultan's library, India.

[21] Ethé, Catalogue of India Office.

[22] On the diversity of his names, also see Ethé's *Catalogue of India Office* (N. 1882–1890; N. 1762), 1045–1050; also 960. See: Sayyid Maḥmūd Marʿashī Najafī, *Fihrist-i Nuskha-hā-yi Khaṭṭi-yi Kitāb-khāna-yi Buzurg-i Āyatullāh Marʿashī Najafī* (Qum: Kitāb-khāna-yi Buzurg-i Āyatullāh Marʿashī Najafī, 1383/2004), vol. 1, 32, no. 12750, and no. 10680, page 405; Muḥammad Ḥussein Nūrī-niyā et al. *Fihrist-i Nuskha-hā-yi Khaṭṭī* (Mashhad: Sāzmān-i Kitāb-khāna-hā, Mūza-hā, wa Markaz-i Asnād-i Āstān-i Quds-i Raḍawī, 1388/2009), manuscript no. 40539, page 75.

printed volume from Lahore introduces the author as Sayf al-Dīn Ẓafar Ūtahārī, or in the Tatar version, frequently produced in Kazan from 1898 to the 1910s, as Sayf Ẓafar Bukhārī.

A silent disagreement is seen about the original background and family of the author in both manuscript and early printed copies; being either someone from Central Asia or from South Asia. However, in some Kurdish, Pushto, Turkic, and Bengali versions the name of the author was replaced with the name of translators and commentators (see, e.g., the SOAS copy) or totally removed altogether. However, Sayf Ẓafar is the most frequent first name given for the author, and the one I adopt throughout this book.

We may now map a wide geographical area for the origin of the author of *Durr al-Majālis*. In Khurasan and Multan several regions are named as Nawbahar and the author may have originated in one of them.[23] On the other hand, perhaps the author originated in Bukhara whose scholars used to be known as Bukhārī or Bukhārāʾī. It is also possible, given the way the author has been named, that he originated from Butahar, Punjab or Etahar, Bihar State, India. Given the popularity that Persian literature and Islamic teachings enjoyed in all these areas, each of them could plausibly have been the home of the author.

Very few works have examined the biography of Sayf Ẓafar. Thomas William Beale's (d. 1875)[24] 'The Oriental Biographical Dictionary' provides valuable information based on 'Mohamadan Histories of India' and listed hundreds of works of Muslim scholars in the 'Orient', in general, and in India, in particular. According to Beale,

> Saif-uz-zafar Naubahari, سیف الظفر بنچر نوبهار, author of a work called 'Durr-ul-Majalis', containing anecdotes of various persons from the earliest ages to the time of Abu Sa'id Abu'l Khair who died in 1048 A.D., 440 A.H., together with a description of heaven and hell. He is also called Sayuf Zafar Naubahari.[25]

[23] The name of Nawbahār is found in various corners of central Iran, too. On this name, see Muḥammad Ḥusayn Pāpulī Yazdī, *Farhang-i Ābādīhā wa Makān-hā-yi Madhhabī-yi Kishwar* (Mashhad: Bunyād-i Pazhūhish-hā-yi Islāmī-yi Āstān-i Quds-i Raḍawī, 1367/1988), 566; also Richard W. Bulliet, 'Naw Bahār and the Survival of Iranian Buddhism', *Iran* 14 (1976), 140–145.

[24] Beale was 'formerly a clerk in the office of the Board of Revenue, N. W. P. at a time when the Secretary was Henry Myers Elliot'. Thomas W. Beale, *The Oriental Biographical Dictionary*, ed. the Asiatic Society of Bengal under the Supervision of Henry George Keene (Calcutta: J. W. Thomas, Baptist Mission Press, 1881), iii. He was probably the son of Captain William and Elizabeth Beale. Landon Carter, 'Extracts from Diary of Col. Landon Carter', *The William and Mary Quarterly* 13/1 (1904), 46.

[25] Beale, *The Oriental Biographical Dictionary*, 239.

The term, Banchar (بنچر) can refer to an area with the same name in the district of Bihar, India. However, this claim would probably not be quite right. Not only is it not found in any available copies of the text, but also Beale's preface indicates his limited access to materials,

> [i]n preparing a work of this nature, intended to be used as a work of reference on matters connected with Oriental History, it is proper to state that the greatest care has been taken to ensure the accuracy in the narrative, as also in the dates of births, deaths, and other events recorded [...] [T]he material collected in this Biography are only from those works which were within the reach of the author, and therefore it is to be considered as a nucleus to which those who have access to other sources may add new materials.[26]

Another short entry about the author of *Durr al-Majālis* is indicated in the *Kamus-ül alâm: tariḫ ve cografya lûġati ve ta'bir-i eṣâhhiyle kâffe-yi esma-yi ḫassa-yi camidir* (A Comprehensive Turkish Dictionary on History, Geography, Geographical Names, Figures and Regions) by Turkish (and Albanian) scholar, Şemseddin Sami Frashëriri/Fraşeri[27] (1850–1904). This dictionary includes the following relevant note: 'Sayf al-Ẓafar Nawbahārī, from the fifth century AH. His authored volume is *Durr al-Majālis*.'[28]

This claim seems inaccurate, too, as the text only includes direct references to people who died after the fifth/eleventh century (see below). Another source is *Histoire de la Littérature Hindoui et Hindoustani* (History of Hindu and Hindustani Literature) by Joseph Héliodore Garcin de Tassy (d. 1878) in which *Durr al-Majālis* is introduced under the biography of Abdullah Deccan who produced a poetic version of *Durr al-Majālis*,

> To this Hindustani writer, we have a *masnavi* entitled *Durr al-Majális*, 'The Pearl of the Assemblies'. This poem contains the life of the prophets mentioned in the Qur'an. There

[26] Ibid., iii–iv.

[27] Also written as 'Ch. Samy-Bey Fraschery' in French literature of the nineteenth century, who called the book *Dictionnaire universel d'histoire et de géographie*. He was known as "Sami Frashëri' in Albania and 'Şemseddin (or Şemsettin) Sami' in Turkey'. For more on his contribution to Turkey and Albania see, Bülent Bilmez, 'Shemseddin Sami Frashëri (1850–1904): Contributing to the Construction of Albanian and Turkish Identities', Centre for Advanced studies Sofia (CAS Sofia Working Papers 2011), 1–27.

[28] Şemseddin Sami, *Kamus-ül Alâm: Tarih ve Coğrafya Lûgati ve Tabir-i Esahhiyle Kâffe-yi Esma-yi Hassa-yi Camidir* (Istanbul: Mihran Matbaası, 1311/1894), vol. 4, 2766. However, the author of *Durr al-Majālis* should not be confused with others (including poets) bearing the name of Sayfī Bukhārī and Sayfī Bukhārā'ī from the late ninth and early tenth century. See: Sami, *Kamus*, 2767.

is a copy – 8th in the library of the East India House. There are works in Hindustani prose on the same subject. See the article on 'Miran'.[29] Among the Persian books in the library of the unfortunate Tippou, there is one which also bears the title of *Durr Majālis*. It is a collection of anecdotes on different characters, from the most ancient times to Khʷāja Sūfyān Thūrī[?], of heaven and hell. Its author is Sayf al-Ẓafar Nawbahārī. It seems that this work has been translated into Hindustani; because, among the number of Hindustani books of the Minister of Nizam in Hyderabad, there is a volume entitled *Tarjama-i Durr-i Majālis*, that is, the translation of the *Durr-i Majālis*.[30]

Between Uch and Bukhara

Durr al-Majālis not only includes well-known prophetic stories passed down from a previous era but also relates the names of individuals from previous generations. For instance, where the story of Sufi saints is narrated, similar names to those of ʿAṭṭār's *Tadhkirat al-Awliyāʾ* can be seen.[31] Moreover, traces of Niẓāmī Ganjawī's (d. 1209) lover and beloved, Laylī and Majnūn,[32] are addressed in two of *Durr al-Majālis*' chapters (6 and 17). More importantly, and more helpfully, direct references to the poems of Saʿdī (d. c. 1291) and his name are found (chapters 31 and 33). In some copies of the text, phrases such as *marḥūm* (deceased, late; lit., 'recipient of mercy'), or *raḥmat Allāh*, and *ʿalayh al-raḥma* (may God's mercy be upon him) are found even though these phrases are not usually used for Saʿdī. Rather, until the early seventh/thirteenth century Saʿdī

29 This name refers to 'Shaykh Wali Muhamamd bin Hafiz Miran the author of *Qissa-yi Payrambaran*'. See, Tassy, *Histoire*, 345–347.

30 'On doit à cet écrivain hindoustani un masnawi intitulé Durr almajális ', la Perle des Assemblées. Ce poëme contient la vie des prophètes mentionnés dans le Coran. Il y en a un exemplaire in – 8° à la bibliothèque de l'East- India House. Il existe des ouvrages en prose hindoustani sur le même sujet. Il existe des ouvrages en prose hindoustani sur le même sujet. Voyez l'article sur Miran. Parmi les livres persans de la bibliothèque de l'infortuné Tippou, il y en a un qui porte aussi le titre de Durr majális. C'est un recueil d'anecdotes sur différents personnages, depuis les temps les plus anciens jusqu'à Khâja Sûfián Sùri du ciel et de l'enfer. Saif ulzafar Nobehari en est l'au- on y trouve aussi une description teur. Il parait que cet ouvrage a été traduit en hindoustani; car, au nombre des livres hindoustani du ministre du Nizám, à Haiderábád, il y a un volume intitulé Tar jama i durr-i majális, c'est-à-dire traduction du Durr-i majális.' Garcin de Tassy, *Histoire de la littérature hindouie et hindoustanie*, 2nd ed. (Paris: Adolphe Labitte, 1870), 9–10.

31 It is believed that this is the only prose work of ʿAṭṭār which has survived. He has also borrowed from former thinkers while completing this source. See, Aṭṭār, *Tadhkira al-Awliyāʾ*, ed. Shafīʿī Kadkanī (Tehran: Sokhan, 1397/2018), xxxii–xxxiii.

32 Other Persian thinkers have also indicated the name of Laylī and Majnūn in their poems and collections.

is referred to as the 'Master of Poets' (*shaykh al-shuʿarā*),[33] or 'King of Poets' (*malik al-shuʿarā*).[34] This may possibly suggest that *Durr al-Majālis* was produced after the death of Saʿdī.

The last part of almost every complete manuscript copy includes two couplets, the composer of which was identified only in some of the available copies.

دریغا جمالش سیری ندیدم   من مست و مدهوش دیوانه بودم
نبودم لایق دیدار لیکن   بکرد لطف تو شایان دیدار

Alas, I could not fully see His Beauty,
as I was drunk and perplexed and mad
I was not actually qualified for the Vision, however,
due to Your kindness, I was able.

These couplets are attributed to Sayyid Jalāl al-Dīn, also a popular name in Central and South Asia. The manuscript Or.877, in Leiden University Library, introduces the poet of these verses as 'Jalāl al-Dīn Rūmī', which is wrong on two counts: firstly, its style is different to that of Rūmī and, secondly, it cannot be found in any Rūmī collections. The manuscript N.1222 of the Academy of Sciences of Tajikistan, dated 1454 CE, also bears the name Sayyid Jalāl al-Dīn.[35] The manuscript No.1375 in the Khudabakhsh Library in Patna, Bihar State, India,[36] dated 1571 CE, and M.82 in the Indian Council dated 1670 CE introduce the poet as Sayyid Jalāl al-Dīn Bukhārī.[37] No.1375, copied by Ibrāhīm Aḥmad Quṭbī, introduces the poet as Sayyid Jalāl Bukhārī, while M.82 copied by Shaykh Abū Layth Chishtī from Lucknow introduces the verses with 'Makhdūm-i Jahāniyyān, Sayyid Jalāl Bukhārī, may God sanctify his soul, says here regarding this point […]'.[38]

Sayyid Jalāl al-Dīn of Bukhara (707–785/1307–1383), widely known as Makhdūm-i Jahāniyyan, was a Sufi figure born in Uch, Punjab. His name is taken from his grandfather Sayyid Jalāl al-Dīn Surkh Bukhārī, who left Bukhara and became a disciple of Shaykh Bahāʾ al-Dīn Zakariyyā of Multan, who was a disciple of Shaykh Shihāb al-Dīn

[33] See the manuscript M.82 in the Indian Council for Cultural Relations of New Delhi. Also, Ms. 5–27641 in the National Library of Iran, introducing Saʿdī as the blazing flame of Shiraz (*shuʿla-yi shīrāzī*; fl. 124).

[34] Domenico Ingenito, *Beholding Beauty: Saʿdi of Shiraz and the Aesthetics of Desire in Mediaeval Persian Poetry* (Leiden and Boston: Brill, 2021), 1 and 34.

[35] This manuscript introduces Rūmī as Mawlawī.

[36] For the Khudabakhsh Sufi collection in the Persian language, see: https://kblibrary.bih.nic.in

[37] In some manuscripts (such as Ms. 33429 in the National Library of Iran) the name of the poet is not mentioned but their words are introduced as the words of a notable person (*buzurgī dar īn maḥal gūyad…*).

[38] See, fl. 151.

Suhrawardī, after whom the Suhrawardiyya Sufi order was named. In this regard, the followers or devotees of this Sufi order settled in two regions of India, Multan, and Uch.[39] Later on, Uch 'became permanently associated with Sayyid Jalāl Surkh and became known as Uch-i Bukhārī'.[40] The people of the region also carried the title of Bukhārī, the people were genealogically or, perhaps, mythically connected with the city of Bukhara, including Sayyid Jalāl Surkh Bukhārī and his grandson Sayyid Jalāl al-Dīn Bukhārī.

There are different ideas about the religious and sectarian inclinations of the people of Uch. However, available sources (e.g., *Malfūẓāt*) remaining from Sayyid Jalāl al-Dīn Bukhārī suggest that they practised Islam in accordance with Sunni law while nonetheless venerating the *ahl al-bayt* (the household of Muḥammad). Apart from being a shaykh of the Suhrawardiyya order, Sayyid Jalāl al-Dīn developed his connection with other Sufi trends. For instance, he 'sought an audience with Shaykh Naṣīr al-Dīn Maḥmūd Chirāgh Dihlawī (d. 757/1356) and became his disciple in turn; the latter bestowed upon him the Chishtī *khirqa* of deputyship'.[41] He was admired by Muḥammad b. Ṭughluq, the Sultan of Delhi (r. 1325–1351), and '[M]any inhabitants of the Punjab converted to Islam at his hand, and people flocked to Uch from all over India to become his disciples'.[42] Both the Makhdūmiyya and Jalāliyya (as well as the Jalāliyya Khāksāriyya) are connected to his grandfather and to himself.[43]

Due to the regional importance of Uch-i Bukhārī, it would not be farfetched to believe that the author of *Durr al-Majālis* was someone who arrived at the city seeking discipleship and devotion to the local branch of Sufism and who would end his lengthy volume - over the course of several decades - with a couplet by the well-known regional figure 'Makhdūm-i Jahāniyyān' Sayyid Jalāl Bukhārī. Moreover, the style of *Durr al-Majālis* resonates with the form of Islam that was prominent in Uch-i Bukhārī, a form which fused both Shīʿī and Sunni elements. For example, the author of *Durr al-Majālis* narrates stories concerning the Shīʿī Imams, especially Ḥasan and Ḥusayn, who were said to be the ancestors of Jalāl al-Dīn Surkh Bukhārī.[44] On the one hand, the text gives special attention to the teaching of the Sunni legal schools

[39] Clifford E. Bosworth, M. S. Asimov, *History of Civilizations of Central Asia: The Age of Achievement, A. D. 750 to the End of the Fifteenth Century. pt. 1. The Historical, Social and Economic Setting. pt. 2. The Achievements* (Paris: UNESCO, 1992), 378. [40] Gholam-Ali Arya, and Matthew Melvin-Koushki, 'Bukhārī, Sayyid Jalāl al-Dīn', *Encyclopaedia Islamica Online*, eds. Wilferd Madelung and Farhad Daftary (Leiden: Brill, 2011) http://dx.doi.org/10.1163/1875-9831_isla_COM_05000024 [41] Ibid.
[42] Ibid. [43] Ibid. [44] Ibid. Nonetheless, paying a particular attention to Muḥammad ibn al-Ḥanafiyya as an immortal Imam, and also exclusion of other Shīʿī Imams, suggests that *Durr al-Majālis* should have been influecned by the Shīʿī sect of Kaysāniyyah. Further argumetns will be present in the future.

(*madhāhib*; sg. *madhhab*), especially the Ḥanafī and Ḥanbalī school, on such issues as hajj, alms (*zakāt*), and farming. The theology found in *Durr al-Majālis* is quite compatible with what would have been found in Uch-i Bukhārī during the eighth/fourteenth century, as is comprehensively outlined in the *Malfūẓāt* of Jalāl al-Dīn Bukhārī, a work comprising a series of conversations and statements in different gatherings (i.e., *majālis*). Works in this gathering (or assembly) genre of Islamic literature, in which various forms of religious and mystical teachings and anecdotes from Sufi saints are purposefully imparted, were systematically produced from Sind to Bihar in the seventh/thirteenth and eighth/fourteenth centuries. Some Sufi orders aimed to produce very good instructive collections for which they would use superlatives in the titles, such as, *khayr* (best; as in *Khayr al-Majālis*; The Best of Assemblies), or *anwār* (lights; as in *Anwār al-Majālis*; The Lights of Assemblies).

After the collection of statements by the 'Sultan al-Mashaʾikh' (king of the Sufi masters), Shaykh Niẓām al-Dīn Awliyāʾ (d. 725/1325),[45] was compiled by a member of the Chishtī Sufi order, Ḥasan Dihlawī (d. 737/1328),[46] circles connected to Jalāl al-Dīn Bukhārī began to do the same. Three lengthy works were produced by the followers of Jalāl al-Dīn Bukhārī, namely, *Jāmiʿ al-ʿUlūm*, *Sirāj al-Hidāya*, and *Manāqib-i Makhdūm-i Jahāniyyān*.[47] All of these three works show a level of similarity in terms of theme, language, and content. It was in such as context that *Durr al-Majālis* was composed. To some extent its content is comparable with that of the *Malfūẓāt*. For instance, the length of the days and nights in heaven and the Day of Judgement are outlined in several parts of *Durr al-Majālis* (e.g., chapter 33) as well as in the *Malfūẓāt*.[48] Even the approach of *Durr al-Majālis* to the Companions of the Prophet is very similar to that of Bukhārī's *Malfūẓāt*. Both sources consider the first four caliphs as the 'commanders of the believers' (sg. *amīr al-muʾminīn*). ʿUmar is introduced as an accomplice of Satan or as one tempted by infidels to kill Muḥammad before converting to Islam and eventually becoming the second caliph. He is depicted as an important authority figure from the dawn of Islam. Although sometimes special attention is given to ʿAlī, the fourth caliph, due to his kinship with Muḥammad, *Durr al-Majālis* generally considers all caliphs equal in status and in their moral and political probity. While the status of Muḥammad's household, especially of Ḥasan and Ḥusayn, are elevated

[45] Nizam Ad-din Awliya *Morals for the Heart: Conversations of Shaykh Nizam Ad-din Awliya Recorded by Amir Hasan Sijzi*, translated and annotated by Bruce B. Lawrence, Introduction by Khaliq Ahmad Nizami, Preface by Simon Digby (New York and Mahwah: Paulist Press, 1992), 3. [46] *Hasan Dehlavi: Life & Poems*, translated and Introduction by Paul Smith (Victoria: Book Heaven, 2006).

[47] Nasir-u'd-din Chiragh of Delhi and Hamid Qalandar, *Khair-u'l-Mjaalis*, ed. Khaliq Ahmad Nizami (Aligarh: Department of History-Muslim University, 1959), 1–3.

[48] Manuscript 17811, Parliamentary Library of Iran, fl. 14.

in both texts, the devotees of ʿAlī are strongly criticised in *Malfūẓāt* (see chapter iv for further explanations).

> A story has been reported that 'I was invited to a party in those regions. I noticed that the wife/mother of the family came and sat next to me and said "I am forbidden upon my husband, while being permitted upon you as long as you are the guest at our house". Then I realised that they are heretics (*rāfiḍiyya*). So, I ran out from there. There were some fellows with me. We entered in to a mosque, began to take sanctuary and seclusion in order to get free from that misfortune, and then we pondered "where could be as good as here?"[49] Subsequently, he said that "they are deniers, they believe in the superiority of ʿAlī over other Companions, thank God that they are not in our land otherwise it would have become a custom" [...]'[50]

Reading this phrase about the devotees of ʿAlī in Bukhārī's *Malfūẓāt* gives the impression that this approach is also found in some copies of *Durr al-Majālis*, where no one from the Companions of the Prophet should be seen as superior to others.

One may also note common references to Khiḍr, as someone carrying the Sufi mantle (*khirqa*)[51] among Jalāl al-Dīn Bukhārī's circle, with Khiḍr indicated in *Durr al-Majālis*, who is elevated in some copies to 'king of the oceans' (*malak al-baḥr*; chapter 16). Similar figures such as Bāyazīd are mentioned in both *Malfūẓāt* and *Durr al-Majālis*.

Integrating the teachings of the Islamic sciences in the bounds of one volume was a practice found in the Delhi Sultanate, particularly in the circle of the Bukhārī family that settled in Uch and surrounding areas. The *Malfūẓāt* of Bukhārī also tries to be as inclusive as possible by not only having mystical accounts but also theological and legal arguments, which were used against 'ignorant Sufis',[52] with little knowledge of the Arabic language or of legal teachings. This integrated approach is also found in *Durr al-Majālis*.

In addition to the couplets of Saʿdī and Jalāl al-Dīn Bukhārī, the couplet of Amīr Ḥusaynī or Amīr Sādāt Ḥusaynī Hirawī (d. c. 718/1318), the famous poet of Herat, is found in chapter one of *Durr al-Majālis*, where the Throne, the Seat, the Heaven, and

49 Manuscript 17811, fl. 87.

50 The original text reads as follows:

حکایت فرمودند که «روزی آن طرفها مهمان خانه شدم، دیدم زن خانه نزدیک من آمد، نشست و گفت «حرمت علی زوجي وحللت لك مادمت في البيت» یعنی گفت من بر شوهر حرام شدم، و بر تو حلال، مادام که درین خانه مهمان هستی. دریافتم که این رافضیه است، پس ازینجا گریختم و با من چندیاری دیگر بودند. مسجدی درآمدم و نیت اعتکاف کردیم تا از آن علت خلاص یافتیم و گفتیم «بِه از این مقام کجا یابم؟»» بعد از آن فرمودند که «ایشان منکران اند، مفضله اند علی را بر اصحاب دیگر، الحمدلله در دیارِ ما نه اند که این رسم باشد» [...]».

51 Ibid., fl. 6. 52 Ms. 17811, fl. 84.

the Earth are all tested by God and the angels. With the Earth displaying a down beat mood, God decides to create Adam in the Earth and not from the arrogant Throne, Seat, or Heaven.[53] Such is the setting from which the couplet of Amīr Ḥusaynī emerges.

شاخی که بلند شد تبر خورد
نِی گفت که من نیم شکر خورد

A branch that grew tall received a blow from an axe
the sugarcane said, 'I am merely a reed; therefore, it was filled with sugar'[54]

Amīr Ḥusaynī was a Sufi of the Suhrawardiyya order, and had already visited Multan where he was a disciple of Shaykh Bahāʾ al-Dīn Zakariyyā of Multan.[55] This may also demonstrate that the author of *Durr al-Majālis* had close ties with the circle of the Suhrawardiyya order in northern and western India where such Sufi poets frequented. Another verse found in a number of manuscript copies of *Durr al-Majālis* (e.g., chapter 12) is ascribed to Ḥasan Dihlawī of the Chishtī order, also in contact with the Sufis of Multan.

Durr al-Majālis includes references to names and regions which support the idea that it was produced in the medieval Persianate world. In chapter 31, for instance, the Chinese empire (*khāqān-i chīn*) is referred to as an enemy; the military use of various animals, especially elephants, is mentioned; and names such as Turan, Tugha, and Tughan are also given. These references imply that the text was produced in a period when India and the ideology or customs of the Delhi Sultanate were shaping and penetrating other parts of the East. It was a period in which there were still non-Muslim communities around the Delhi Sultanate and in which there were people with Turkish/Turkic names active in the Delhi Sultanate and Central Asia.[56]

[53] Being dusty, a notion largely popular in the Sufism branch of *Khāksāriyya*, might have been taken from this story, through which the one who is the most modest and poorest will receive extra or especial attention from God.

[54] For the translation see, Thomas Roebuck, *A Collection of Proverbs, and Proverbial Phrases, in the Persian and Hindoostanee Languages* (Calcutta: Hindoostanee Press, 1824), 278.

[55] About him, see Leonard Lewisohn, 'Haravī, Amīr Ḥusaynī', *Encyclopaedia of Islam* III, Eds. Kate Fleet, Gudrun Krämer, Denis Matringe, John Nawas, Everett Rowson http://dx.doi.org/10.1163/1573-3912_ei3_COM_25692; also Moḥammad Javad Shams, 'Amīr Ḥusaynī' *Centre for the Great Islamic Encyclopaedia* (1399/2020) https://www.cgie.org.ir/fa/article/225765/امیر-حسینی

[56] All these are historical features are outlined in Samarqandī's reports of the northern India and the China. Ms. 813948.

ʿAbd al-Razzāq al-Samarqandī's historical report from 800/1398 indicates that a Timurid ruler had planned to move against the idolaters of Khitāyāy[57] and Khutan[58] and he learned about widespread heresy after the death of Sulṭān Fīrūz Shāh Tughlūq in 1388.

> [...] They camped near the borders of Turkistan [in winter]. The opinion of the world conqueror was to move their army against the idolaters of Khitāy and Khutan. Nonetheless, it was heard by His Excellency that Sulṭān Fīrūz Shāh in the land of Hindustan had already died. And although the signs and symbols of *tawḥīd* (Islamic monotheism) has been engraved on coins (dirhams) and dinars in some provinces, a number of transgressors have raised the banner of rebellion and antagonism and the country's surroundings had been affected by the wickedness of infidels [...][59]

An indication of enmity between China and the Muslims of Central and South Asia in the eighth/fourteenth and ninth/fifteenth centuries is also found in a report by al-Samarqandī.

> Given the graceful favour of the praise-worthy sultan, God, the power has been bestowed upon us to conquer the world with the sword and to topple the kings of the Earth by conquest and rage, and to take the lands free from rulers and tribal and regional chiefs, and the sovereignty of rulers, and with what divine decree granted upon us, very few kings had dreamed of. And the conquest of the world would not be possible without encouraging the warriors: if you wish to bring ease and stability in your kingdom, you should release the sword's blade [...] We have now thought of doing something [...] for which we need a lot of support and power. [That is] to eradicate the infidels and battle with China and Khitā[y], where are the dwellings of the infidels. That is the right thing to do [...] We would destroy idol houses and fire temples and build in their place mosques and assembly halls [...] Just as Rome [i.e., Byzantium] was conquered and the caesar was enslaved, the Chinese empire will, too, be seized in China.[60]

57 Northern areas of China, Mongolia and Eastern Turkistan including parts of Siberia. *Dehkhodā*.

58 Viz., Tataristan.

59 Ms. 813948, fl. 266:

[...] در حدّ ترکستان قشلاق فرمود. رای جهانگشای عازم آن بود که رایات همایون بدفع بُت پرستان ختای و ختن حرکت نماید. امّا سابقا بمسامع جلال رسیده بود که در ممالک هندستان سلطان فیروزشاه نمانده، اگر چه در بعضی بلاد نقش توحید بر درم و دینار نگاشته‌اند، امّا جمعی متغلب در هرگوشه رایت عناد برافراخته، و اطراف ممالک بخَبَث وجودِ کفّار ملوّث است [...]

60 Ms. 813948, fl. 377:

عنایت پروردگار عز سلطان ما را اقتدار آن داد که جهانرا به شمشیر مسخر ساختیم و پادشاهان روی زمین را به غلبه و قهر برانداختیم و ممالک را از تصرف ملوک طوایف و مسالک و از تحکم حکام مختلف باز پرداختیم و آنچه تایید الهی ما را کرامت فرمود، کم پادشاهی را در آیینه خیال

In terms of dating *Durr al-Majālis* we can also note that the Khuda-bakhsh manuscript was copied in a Bihārī (or Bahārī) script which was an Islamic calligraphy used in India.[61] The Bihārī script 'was mainly employed for the writing of the Qur'ans'[62] and it is,

> [a] stiff Indian script which continued to be used occasionally in Qurans until a comparatively recent period (late 8th century) and which is distinguished by a general clumsiness of effect by the thickness of its horizontal strokes [...] the thinness and approximately horizontality of the vowel marks and other peculiarities [...][63]

Of the Bihārī script it has also been said that,

> [...] the general effect of this style is not always clumsy. This style, which is commonly known as *Khatt-i-Bihar* or *Khatt-i-Bahar*, may look pleasant as well, as can be seen in the manuscript of the Qur'an, traditionally believed to be in the handwriting of Sultan Fīrūz Shah Tughluq [1309–1388] [...] this style of calligraphy was once popular and widely used in India. This purely Indian style, because there is no evidence of its use anywhere outside India, continued to be used, at least occasionally, for the transcription of the Qur'an until comparatively recently, as shown by a Qur'an in the India Office, transcribed in 990/1582.[64]

As such, it can be said that *Durr al-Majālis* must have been was well known in India, scribes copying it with a prestigious calligraphic hand, the same as was often used for copying the Qur'ān.

The theological themes of *Durr al-Majālis* and its strong emphasis on the disparity between Muslims and non-Muslims as well as of several conversion stories of non-Muslims who embraced Islam may lead us to conclude that it would have been produced in a period when there were still many non-Muslims being encountered by the Muslims of Asia.

That *Durr al-Majālis* is closely linked with the Bukhara region of Central Asia is

---

جمال نمود و چون تسخیر جهان بی تحریک تیغ دستان دست نمیدهد: ملک را اگر قرار خواهی داد، تیغ را بیقرار باید کرد...اکنون در خاطر چنان است که بکاری قیام نماییم...و آن را قوتی تمام می باید. قلع و قمع کفارست و غزو چین و ختا[ی] که دیار کفر است صواب است... بتخانه و آتشکده ها را خراب سازیم و به جای آن مساجد و معابد بنا کنیم ... که چون روم شد فتح و قیصر غلام، بچین نیز خاقان درآید بدام.

[61] *Maḥbūb al-Albāb fi ta'rīf al-Kutub wa l-Kuttāb* (Khoda-Bakhsh Oriental Public Library, 1991), 274.

[62] G. S. Farid, 'Khatt-i-Bihari, the Indian Style of Arabic Writing', *Indo-Iranica: The Quarterly Organ of the Iran society* 1–4/29 (1976), 102–112 (see p. 104)

[63] Ibid.

[64] Pares Islam Syed Mustafizur Rahman, *Islamic Calligraphy in Mediaeval India* (Bangladesh: University Press Limited, 1979), 47. This work is based on his PhD thesis written at the University of Cambridge.

evidenced in some of its early manuscripts. The Academy of Sciences of Tajikistan houses N.1222, dated 28 October 1454 and copied by Muḥammad b. Dūst Muḥammad al-Bukhārī who is possibly connected with other famous Bukhārī scholars and calligraphers such as Darwīsh Muḥammad b. Dūst Muḥammad Bukhārī (d. 970/1562 or 995/1587) and Muḥammad b. Aḥmad b. Ḥasan al-Bukhārī (d. 978) who wrote a gloss on *Tafsīr al-Bayḍāwī*.[65] A mention of a prison sentry named Qurbān Muḥammad Bāy Yār is made in this manuscript, possibly a reference to a person from Khwarazm (folio 151). This early manuscript also appears to have been produced sometime in the eighth/fourteenth century.[66] It should be of no surprise to us that a good number of copies of *Durr al-Majālis* were produced in Bukhara and Samarqand using local styles of calligraphy by scribes who also copied Sufi Naqshbandi treatises.

Finally, with respect to features which help us to confirm our view of *Durr al-Majālis*, we can note a number of philological features in the text that suggest that the author was indeed closely linked to Bukhara and Central Asia. Although the writing style of sentences vary in manuscript copies, a term which was fixed in almost all copies is the Persian verb *ghalṭīdan*, literally, 'rolling'. In classical and modern Central Asian dialects of Persian, including those used in Bukhara, this term means 'to fall', 'to lie down', or 'to fall down', which are similiarly used in *Durr al-Majālis*.[67] The term used for 'rolling' in Bukhara is usually *ghīlāndan* or *ghīlṭāndan*.[68] Moreover, the term *ghalghal*, referring to 'riot' and 'turbulence', is also found in some copies of *Durr al-Majālis*. This is a term that has often been used in Dari by Hazaras.[69]

All in all, I avoid using a full name for the author, and only introduce him as Sayf Ẓafar, a Muslim Sufi thinker attached to the Bukhārī families of Uch, who lived from the late seventh/thirteenth century and died in the mid-eighth/fourteenth century. Whether having resided in Uch since birth or having adopted as his home later in life, Sayf Ẓafar was apparently lived in the Delhi Sultanate at a time when the Persian language was widely used and spreading to southern parts of India where translation circles were launching their activities. It is also interesting to mention that the possible connection of the author with the Bukhārīs of Uch may justify why *Durr al-Majālis* moved very fast across India and different parts of the world. This Sufi family was

[65] On the calligraphy of Muḥammad bin Dūst Muḥammad al-Bukhārī see *Сокровищница восточных рукописей Института востоковедения имени Абу Райхана Бируни Академии Наук Республики Узбекистан*, 102. [66] Muslims from Bukhara used to visit India, Sindh and Multan for the sake of life, Islamic sciences and education. E.g., 'Nawab Murtaza Ahmad Bukhari', see Qazi Muhammad Zahidul Husaini, *Commentators of the Holy Quran*, trans. S. Naseer-ud-Din (Lahore: Ferozsons (Pvt.) LTD. 1992), 76. [67] Aḥmad A. Rajāʾī, *Yād-dāshtī darbāra Lahja Bukhārāʾī / Le Dialecte de Bukhārā* (Mashhad: Mashhad University, 1342–3/1964), 407. [68] Ibid., 410. [69] Shāh ʿAlī Akbar Shahristānī, *Qāmūs-i Lahja Dari-yi Hazāra-gī* (Kabul: Kabul University, Dalwa 1358/February 1980), 122 and 166.

highly regarded by the rulers and sultans of Delhi, especially Sultan Fīrūz Shāh Ṭughluq,[70] and had good connections with other groups of Sufis across the world, including the Malay-Indonesian Sufi thinkers in the tenth/sixteenth and eleventh/seventeenth centuries.

[70] Gholam-Ali Arya, and Matthew Melvin-Koushki, 'Bukhārī, Sayyid Jalāl al-Dīn'.

III) Transregional Circulation

Durr al-Majālis was produced at a time when all forms of Islamic and religious scholarship were undergoing formidable development. The most celebrated works were often sent to other parts of the world. For centuries *Durr al-Majālis* was copied frequently and its content was discussed in all Islamic disciplines. Were *Durr al-Majālis* not a unique work one would hardly expect it to have received close attention across the Muslim world for up to eight centuries, especially given its origins in the newly converted Islamic context of India. *Durr al-Majālis* was copied, translated, glossed, interpreted, and studied in both South and Central Asia and in every corner of the world where Islam had taken root. The reception of *Durr al-Majālis* is especially remarkable when we consider that it would have had plenty of competition from other works of Islamic science and literature. Throughout the Muslim world libraries and marketplaces alike would have been full of handwritten manuscripts and printed books by figures such as al-Zamakhsharī, al-Ṭabarī, and al-Bayḍāwī, on the one hand, and ʿAṭṭār, Rūmī, and Saʿdī, on the other. Yet despite the competition *Durr al-Majālis* persisted as a widely read work until the twentieth century

For a text to have produced in South Asia in the eighth/fourteenth century would have been particularly challenging as it was a time that coincided with the promotion of a huge number of Arabic and Persian works in India. For instance, the first known Arabic commentary on the Qurʾān in India was authored by the famous Persian Shīʿī polymath Niẓām al-Dīn al-Nīshābūrī (d. c. 730/1329)[1] who had settled in Dawlatabad, India.[2] From the ninth/fifteenth century, non-Arab speakers of Islam became one of the main agents of its teachings, spreading Islam to other corners

[1] On his lifespan and date of death, see: Robert Gordon Morrison, *Islam and Science: The Intellectual Career of Nizam al-Din al-Nisaburi* (London: Routledge, 2007).

[2] Husaini, *Commentators of the Holy Quran*, 51.

of the world. For instance, Sayyid Muḥammad b. Sayyid Yūsuf Ḥusaynī Shāh Rajū Qattāl known as Banda Nawāz (d. c. 825/1422) from Delhi produced the first gloss in India of al-Zamakhsharī's Qurʾānic commentary written in Arabic, *al-Kashshāf*,[3] and authored his own *tafsīr* known as *Durar Multaqiṭ* (Collected Pearls), also written in Arabic.[4] Other non-Arabs who helped to spread Islam include Shaykh ʿAlī b. Aḥmad b. ʿAlī Mahaymī (d. c. 835/1432) from Bombay and Qāḍī Shihāb al-Dīn Dawlatābādī al-Dihlawī (d. c. 849/1446) who produced both Arabic and Persian works on Islamic scriptures in line with previous commentaries.[5] In this period scholarly exchanges between Iran and India increased and these two communities greatly affected each other as they learned of one another's cultures and together helped to globalise Islamic teachings. Persian literary works by Saʿdī, ʿIrāqī, Jāmī, and others were widely circulated in the Delhi Sultanate. These works had a remarkable impact on Southeast Asian literature in general and the Malay-Indonesian world in particular. One can say with confidence that works which were circulated beyond their location of origin were those authored by elites and prolific religious thinkers who commanded attention in *madrasa*, *ḥawza*, mosque, *khānqāh*, and court settings. Yet despite this expectation *Durr al-Majālis* achieved widespread recognition and fame. Some copies of *Durr al-Majālis* were decorated and some copies were annotated, demonstrating the significance of the text. Lewis.O.189 serves as an example of an annotated manuscript that was prepared for the sake of religious teaching. *Durr al-Majālis* was copied by all Muslim denominations – Sufis, Shīʿīs, and Sunnis – who nevertheless each left their characteristic marks on the text. For instance, the manuscript from the Auckland library, GMS-170, ends with the genealogy of the twelve Shīʿī Imams (fl. 163).[6]

[3] For Sufis of seventh/thirteenth and eighth/fourteenth-century India, *al-Kashshāf* was incorporated into mystical rituals. See: Nasir-u'd-din Chiragh of Delhi and Hamid Qalandar, *Khair-u'l-Mjaalis*, 65.

[4] Ibid., 59.

[5] Ibid., 60–61.

[6] Medieval Shīʿī figures included information about the lineage of the Imams in Islamic treatises in order to document the blood relation between the Prophet and the descendants of ʿAlī and Fāṭima. The practice also flourished during the Safawid period.

دوازده امام اینان اند. امام را چند فرزند است: اوّل به مرتضی علی کرّم الله وجهه را هفده فرزند است. فاضل ترین ایشان امام حسن و امام حسین از جهت آنکه ایشان نزدیک تر به نبوّت و به ولایت اند. از واسطه مادر به نبوّت و از جهت پدر به ولایت. و امیرالمؤمنین حسین رضي الله عنه را سی فرزند بود یکی علی اکبر و دوم علی اصغر، سیّوم زین العابدین. امامت به زین العابدین رسید و امام زین العابدین را دو پسر بودند. یکی قاسم، دوم محمّد باقر. امام به محمّد باقر رسید و امام محمّد باقر را دو پسر بودند: عبدالله، دوم جعفر صادق. امامت به جعفر صادق رسید و امام جعفر صادق را سی فرزند بودند. یکی محمّد و دوم موسی (موسا) کاظم، سیّوم اسماعیل. امامت به موسی کاظم رسید و امام موسی کاظم را سی و نه فرزند بودند. امامت به موسی (موسا) رضا رسید و امام موسا رضا را دو پسر بودند یکی حسن. دوم محمّدن التقی. امامت به محمّدن التقی رسید و امام محمّدن تقی را سه پسر بودند یکی حسن، دوم حسین، سیّوم علی اکبر النقی. امامت علی النقی را رسید و امام علی النقی را دو پسر بودند یکی محمّد، دوم حسن عسکری. امامت به حسن عسکری رسید. و امام حسن عسکری را سه پسر بود یکی ابراهیم، دویّم قاسم، سیّوم محمّد مهدی. امامت محمّد مهدی را رسید «والله أعلم بالصواب».

DURR AL-MAJĀLIS IN PUNJABI

The audiences of *Durr al-Majālis* were keen to change its form from prose to verse, harmonising it in a literal context, making it easier to read and memorise; a form of creativity and indigenisation used by locals for foreign material. For instance, the manuscript 2489 in the India Office is a poetic version of *Durr al-Majālis* in Dakhni, a Hindustani spoken language from the Deccan region of India. Also, its chapter 31, 'The Killing of Ḥasan and Ḥusayn', one of the most popular parts of *Durr al-Majālis* which was widely translated and reproduced, was versified in different contexts. One worthy example is a copy of *Jang-nāma* (battle tale) bound with the prose version of *Durr al-Majālis*, coded Isl.Ms.853 in the Library of the University of Michigan. The *Jang-nāma* is in Punjabi with Shahmukhi script and is introduced as a sacred book[7] and was produced by the Indian Punjabi poet, Ḥāmida Shāha Abbāsī from the mid-seventeenth century. It starts with the story of Muḥammad, from his creation to his death and then discusses the virtues of the four 'rightly-guided' caliphs and moves on to the death of Muʿāwiya, Yazīd's killing of Ḥasan[8] and Ḥusayn, and the revenge taken by Muḥammad Ḥanafiyya. In some versions, this story has been titled as *maqtal-nāma* (killing tale). An episode of this story, which is found in all Malay versions, is the moment in which Shamir (also read as 'Shimr') attempts to behead Ḥusayn, the grandson of Muḥammad. During this episode, Ḥusayn asked Shamir to show his breast as he was given a prophecy by Muḥammad that 'your killer has the sign of leprosy on his breast'.

In Isl.Ms.853 we see these sentences, from the Prophet to Ḥusayn about "your killer" translated into Punjabi and related in verse.[9]

DURR AL-MAJĀLIS IN PUSHTO

The birth of Muḥammad outlined in some chapters of *Durr al-Majālis* was versified in Pushto (also, Pashto) by Ghulām Muḥammad Qādirī and was known as a separate treatise, *Tawallud-nāma* (Birth Tale).[10] Two other Pushto works about the births, lives,

[7] Isl. Ms. 853, fl. 232. [8] Most Shīʿī traditions do not blame Yazīd for killing Ḥasan, but his father Muʿāwiya. This modification should have been related to some mediaeval attempts to exonerate Muʿāwiya, as one of the scribes of the Revelation, from commiting sins. [9] See Isl. Ms. 853, fl. 164: سینہ اندر کھول (؟) وا ہوسے داغ ضرور ; it should be noted that the term "داغ" also used in Persian and Urdu, refers to the sign of leprosy on Shamir's breast. [10] Ms. 138 in the Collection of Prof. Muḥammad Iqbal Mujaddidi in the Punjab University Library. Also, see Akhtar Rāhī, *Tarjuma-hā-yi Mutūn-i Fārsī bi Zabān-hā-yi Pākistānī* (Islamabad: Markaz-i Taḥqīqāt-i Fārsi-yi Irān va Pākistān, 1986), 355.

and deaths of Ḥasan and Ḥusayn – *Tawallud-nāma* (Birth Tale) and *Jang-nāma* (Battle Tale) – were produced by Ghulām Muḥammad Gagyānī in the late twelfth/eighteenth and early thirteenth/nineteenth centuries, which were 'on the basis of the account in the Persian *Durr-i Majālis* by Sayf al-Ẓafar Nawbahārī'.[11]

DURR AL-MAJĀLIS IN BENGALI (AND IN BENGAL)

One may find several similarities between the Bengali version of *Nūr-namā*, regarding the creation of the universe from the light of Muḥammad, and the one outlined in *Durr al-Majālis*. The Bengali *Nūr-namā* was written by ʿAbd al-Ḥakīm (d. c. 1080/1670) from Bābūpūr, in the kingdom of Bhulua, southeastern Bangladesh,[12] whose magnum opus, according to d'Hubert 'is a Bengali adaptation of the narrative didactic Persian work *Durr-i majālis* [...] a collection of material about prophets and saints written by Sayf al-Ẓafar Nawbahārī (c. eighth/thirteenth)'.[13] However, d'Hubert, a scholar of Bengali literature, assumes that ʿAbd al-Ḥakīm's '*Nūr-nāma* (Book of Light, c. 1070/1660), [...] was likewise translated from an anonymous Persian'. The Auckland copy of *Durr al-Majālis* (GMS 170), which is the most comprehensive extant version, has the story of the light of Muḥammad at its end. A textual comparison can demonstrate that in both Persian and Bengali versions, the famous Persian thinker, al-Ghazālī (d. 505/1111) had interactions with Maḥmūd of Ghazna about a copy of *Nūr-nāma* and that the work is introduced as having particular spiritual, medical, magical, and occultic qualities. Such forms of recommendation to the audience to read, listen, and hold manuscripts themselves, come from Indian Hindu and Buddhist traditions, by which one may conjecture that the production and circulation of *Durr al-Majālis* in India could be one of the main engines behind Indian-Punjabi and Bengali Islamic literature from the eleventh/seventeenth century onwards, when most of its copies were made. As d'Hubert says, 'It goes without saying that even if the Persian *Nur-nama* is claimed to be the direct source of the Bengali versions, this does not imply that the original text came from outside South Asia.'[14]

ʿAbd al-Ḥakīm's Bengali treatise pertaining to the killing of Ḥasan and Ḥusayn

[11] See James Fuller Blumhardt and D. N. MacKenzie, *Catalogue of Pashto Manuscripts in the Libraries of the British Isles* (London: The Trustees of the British Museum and the Commonwealth Relations Office, 1965), 108–114. [12] See Thibaut d'Hubert, 'ʿAbd al-Ḥakīm', *Encyclopaedia of Islam III* edited by Kate Fleet, Gudrun Krämer, et al. (Leiden: Brill, 2021), 2–3. [13] Ibid.

[14] Thibaut d'Hubert, 'Persian at the Court or in the Village? The Elusive Presence of Persian in Bengal', in *The Persianate World* edited by Nile Green (California: University of California Press, 2019), 103.

and the aftermath of the battle of Karbala (61/680), titled *Hāniphāra Laṛāī* (Ḥānifa's Battle), is based on chapter 31 of *Durr al-Majālis* in which the story of Muhamamd Ḥanafiyya is portrayed as avenging the killing of Ḥasan and Ḥusayn. Besides being adapted by ʿAbd al-Ḥakīm, the original version by Sayf Ẓafar was also circulated in Bengal as an independent Persian language treatise. For example, the Persian copy of this story from Murshidabad, Bengal, now kept in the British Library, was highly likely one of the main prototypes of the Malay *Hikayat Muhammad Hanafiyya* from before the ninth/fifteenth century.[15] This might explain why one of the Malay copies of *Hikayat Muhammad Hanafiyya* in the Cambridge University Library, L.I.6.5., replaces the Arabic-origin terms *ḥikāyat* and *qiṣṣa* with the Sanskrit-origin term *mukti*.[16]

The contribution of *Durr al-Majālis* to Bengali Islamic languages is considerable to the extent that similarities can be seen between the themes of the Bengali *Nabīvaṃśa*, a hagiographical work on the prophets by Sayyad Sulṭān from the early decades of the eleventh/seventeenth century. Although being influenced by various works on the lineage of the prophets, it includes sections the identity and origin of which have neither been discussed nor identified. Irani's study of *Nabīvaṃśa*, in which a number of its chapters are listed, helps us to reveal origins in the Persian *Durr al-Majālis*. Comparable sections in the two works, for example, include 'Hāsāna Basorī [Ḥasan al-Baṣri] and his conversation with Iblisa [Iblīs]', 'Phiroyānera kerāmati' (Pharaoh's miracle), 'Cām̐da dvikhaṇḍīkaraṇa' (The Splitting of the Moon), 'Sādhaka Balaām Vāura' (The Sage Balam Bāʿūr), among others.[17] Of course, much of the *Nabīvaṃśa* can be said to have Persian origins as can be seen from a comparison with the Arabic works of Persian speakers such as Thaʿlabī and Kisāʾī or the Persian literature by Nīshābūrī and Juwayrī.[18] Nevertheless, the contribution of the *Durr al-Majālis* to *Nabīvaṃśa* can be plausibly imagined. As Irani says,

> [...] with regard to the sixteenth-century illustrated manuscripts of the Persian trio – Nīshābūrī, Juwayrī, and Daydūzamī – scribes would copy sections of one author into the work of another, rendering these manuscripts composite works. One possibility, therefore, is that Saiyad Sultān worked with one such composite manuscript, which itself bore

[15] See, Brakel, *Hikayat Muhammad Hanafiyyah*.

[16] Regarding the Sanskrit and Javanese application of Mukti, see P. S. Van Ronkel, 'Account of Six Malay Manuscripts of the Cambridge University Library', *Bijdragen tot de taal-, land-en volkenkunde/Journal of the Humanities and Social Sciences of Southeast Asia* 46(1): 43.

[17] See, Ayesha A. Irani, 'Sacred Biography, Translation, and Conversion: The Nabivamsa of Saiyad Sultan and the Making of Bengali Islam, 1600-present' (PhD Thesis: University of Pennsylvania, 2011), 488–497.

[18] Ayesha A. Irani, *The Muhammad Avatāra: Salvation History, Translation, and the Making of Bengali Islam* (Oxford: Oxford University Press, 2021), 77–78.

> an intertextual relationship with Nīshābūrī and Juwayrī, and also with Kisāʾī, Balʿamī, and Ṭabarī, unmediated by the former two Persian authors but perhaps by another unidentified Persian source. Alternatively, Sultān could have shared with the Persian authors a model of translation in which the author felt at liberty to choose tales from the full range of Arabic and Persian *qiṣaṣ al-anbiyāʾ* texts available to him, embroidering these, as they did, with his own imagination.[19]

Durr al-Majālis has broken the link between its stories and the concerns of historical accuracy and authenticity and has instead intertwined its content into a seamless narrative. This can be seen, for instance, in the way the miracle of Muḥammad attested in the Qurʾān is treated in *Durr al-Majālis* as compared to works of exegesis. So, commenting on the first few verses of *Sūra al-Qamar* (The Moon), chapter 54 of the Qurʾān, which apparently refer to the Prophet splitting the Moon in half,[20] al-Ṭabarī, among others, examines reports of the event and their chains of narrators.

In *Durr al-Majālis*, however, the historicity of the event is not considered but rather embellished with important figures from the early period of Islam such as Abū Jahl, Abū Bakr, and ʿUmar together with details about the pregnancy of Muḥammad's wife Khadīja. Such embellishments make their way into the *Nabīvaṃśa* and subsequently into the Malay *Hikayat Bulan Berbelah*.

Another copy of *Durr al-Majālis* is kept in the London School of Oriental and African Studies (SOAS). This manuscript, no.46429, was collected and stamped by James O'Kinealy (1837–1903), an imperial officer in Bengal and also a member of the Philological and Physical Science Committees of the Asiatic Society of Bengal who had a scientific and cultural relationship with Batavia, Indonesia.[21] Although being copied in Persian, some notes on the first two folios of the manuscript suggest that it was in the possession of someone practising Persian. The notes introduce the former owner of the text as Ḥājjī Nūr Muḥammad or Nūr Muḥammad the son of Ḥājjī. Legible notes about the identity of the text can be found.

Kitab Dur li-Majālis | *Kitab Durr Majālis* | *Kitab Durr-l-Majālish*[22]
(fl. 1)

[19] Ibid, 78.

[20] Some scholars believe that it has not happened and will be done later. Uri Rubin, 'Muḥammad's Message in Mecca: Warnings, Signs, and Miracles' in *The Cambridge Companion to Muḥammad*, edited by Jonathan E. Brockopp (Cambridge: Cambridge University Press, 2010), 39–60.

[21] See, The Honorary Secretaries (eds). the *Proceedings of the Asiatic Society of Bengal* (Calcutta: Printed by G. II. Rouse, Baptist Mission Press, and Published by Tile Asiatic Society, 1879).

[22] According to the manuscript no.46429: کتاب در لِ مجالس | کتاب درمجالس | کتاب درلمجالش

The first folio shows three attempts of the reader or second owner to transcribe the title of *Durr al-Majālis*. Changing the Persian letter *sīn* to *shīn* is something that was done in Sanskrit-influenced Malay Jawi.[23]

Ini kitab Durr Machālis
E(l)ka'i ini Nūr Muḥammad (?)
This is the Book of *Durr Machālis*
It is same as *Nūr-Muḥammad*
(fl. 2)

In the second folio (above) we see that the Persian letter *jīm* was changed to *cheh*, also apparent in the transcription of Sanskrit using Arabic letters.[24] The demonstrative *īnī*, meaning 'this', used in both Persian and Malay, is also seen. I do not mean to suggest at this point that *Durr al-Majālis* was in the possession of Malays residing in Bengal or surrounding areas but rather I intend to draw attention to how various forms of culture shaped different biographical and bibliographical identities for *Durr al-Majālis* in Bengal.

DURR AL-MAJĀLIS IN TURKIC LANGUAGES AND CONTEXTS

The influence of *Durr al-Majālis* in the Turkic world is evident from a review of Lund University's Jarring Collection alone. Gunnar Jarring (1907–2002), a Swedish diplomat and scholar of Turkic languages, donated 560 manuscripts from Eastern Turkistan to Lund University Library. The collection is a priceless treasure trove of Turkic manuscript copies of *Durr al-Majālis* produced on the eastern side of Russia and Eastern Turkistan. For instance, Jarring.Prov.383 includes a lengthy version of the *Killing Story of Ḥasan and Ḥusayn*. This story is introduced as *Ghazāt-nāma*, which is an equivalent term for *jang-nāma* in which Muḥammad Ḥanafiyya emerges as the

[23] In some old Malay literature, different spellings of original Sanskrit terms (e.g., *aksyara* instead of *aksara*) can be found. For more example, see, Syed Muhammad Naquib al-Attas, *The Oldest Known Malay Manuscript: A sixteenth Century Malay Translation of the 'Aqa'id of al-Nasafi* (Kuala Lumpur: Department of Publication, University of Malaya, 1988), 45.

[24] There is a long way to go to complete our knowledge about the contribution of Sanskrit to Arabic-Persian scripts.

chivalrous son of ʿAlī b. Abī Ṭālib.[25] In this story, references to Prophet Muḥammad, Abū Jahl, and the miracles of Muḥammad are found (fl. 196).

The Jarring.Prov.111 is also a complete Turkic version of *Durr al-Majālis.* Scribed by Raḥmān Qulī b. Mullā Yāghmurjī, this copy was translated from Persian, "as most inhabitants of Mongolia (Mughulistan) were only able to communicate in the Turkic languages".[26]

Raḥmān Qulī added extra stories, poems, and religious stories into his translation of *Durr al-Majālis.* Such additions bring to mind the Turkic translation of the Persian *Tārīkh-i Rashīdī* on the Mongols of Central Asia by Muḥammad Ṣādiq Kāshgarī who was commissioned by Yūnus b. Iskandar '*hakim beg* of Yarkand in 1805–1811',[27] for which the reason of the translation is outlined in a short passage,

> [...] this book was composed in Persian, with delicate expressions and subtle wording, and much obscure vocabulary. It relies on allusions and similes, and is full of rhyming prose. Because of this, the historical narratives in this book were hidden from the people of Mughulistan like a veiled virgin. Thus, it is necessary for you to render this into the Turkic speech that is current in Kashgar, so that the common people can understand it and gain insight into its secrets.[28]

Another manuscript worthy of note in the Lund University Library is Jarring. Prov.342 copied in Kashgar (Qäshqär), Xinjiang, China. This Turkic copy of *Durr al-Majālis* was apparently scribed by someone known as ʿAbd al-Laṭīf Khatāyanī (?), who belonged to the region of Khitāy, historically known as 'Turkistan'. It is dedicated to Abū al-Muẓaffar Muʿīn al-Dīn Khʷarāzm Shāh Bahādur Sulṭān, 'a prince' of Kbiva or Khiva in Central Asia, a Chagatai-dominated Turkic community that also had a degree of familiarity with Persian.

Jarring.Prov.91 is also from Xinjiang and dedicated to the prince of Khiva. Its colophon is as follows:

> The book *Durr al-Majālis* has been finished in the region of Kashgar in the month of

[25] The content of this story of Ḥanafiyya is different from other versions, which I will address it in the following sections.

[26] Fl. 4. Jarring Prov. 111: Probably during the time of ʿAbdul Raḥmān Beig:

ما انداغ عرض قیلورکم بو فقرالحقر اکثرالتقصر رحمن قلی ابن ملا یامغورجی بوکتاب دارالمجالس نی فارسی الفاظ تپلکان ایردی [...] و لیکن بو مغولستان ادلوسی نینک الفاضی ترکِ و اکثری می دورلار بوکتاب نی ترکی الفاض برله ترجمه قیلناتا کیم خاص عام موندین مستفید و بهرمند بوی لار خوب الدی [...]

[27] David Brophy, 'A Lingua Franca in Decline? The Place of Persian in Qing China', in *The Persianate World*, edited by Nile Green (California: California University Press, 2019), 187. [28] Ibid.

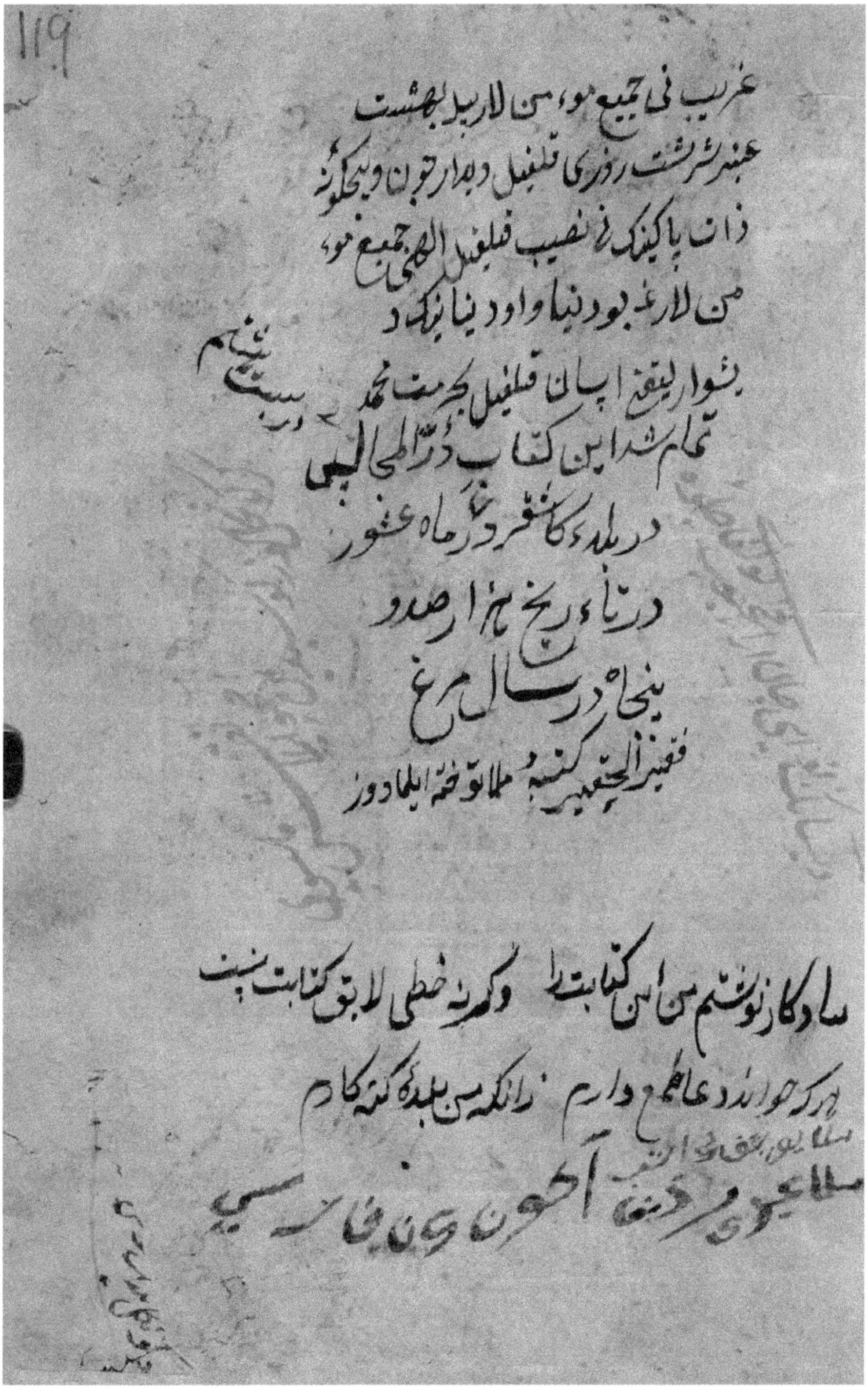

Figure 2. Folio 119 [the colophon], MS Jarring.Prov.91. Turkic version of *Durr al-Majālis* from Xinjiang, China. Courtesy of Lund University, Sweden.

ʿAshūr in 1150 [Muḥarram 1150/May 1737], the Year of the Rooster. Copied by the humble Mullā Tūkhta Īlmādūz.[29]

Turkic communities of Western China and Turkistan would mention both the Islamic lunar and local calendars while inscribing Persian works to specify their origin and identity.[30]

Several Turkic translations of *Durr al-Majālis* and further Persian works were done in the Chinese Qing dynasty from the early eleventh/seventeenth century until the early fourteenth/twentieth century. During this period, Persian sources were received differently in various contexts. As David Brophy says,

> [...] the picture that emerges is of a limited role for Persian in a series of disconnected spheres. From the viewpoint of the court, the 'Muslim language' of the empire was Turkic, not Persian or Arabic. From the second half of the eighteenth century onward, Turkic served as Xinjiang's interface with the cosmopolitan linguistic culture of the high Qing. For Qing officials, Persian was the language of a set of relatively insignificant tributary polities to the west of Xinjiang. Although the Manchus inherited translation capacity in Persian from the Ming, it was never utilized, and Persian correspondence was filtered at the frontier. The court had little to no knowledge of Iran as a distinct political actor, nor did it have direct diplomatic contact with Mughal India, and it therefore saw no need to enhance its ability to communicate with the outside world in Persian. Among the empire's Muslims, Persian texts were collected, read, and valued, although the language never became a popular vehicle for original literary or scholarly expression. The trajectories in this period of Persian in Qing China and further west in Central Eurasia, for example – particularly in a place like Khiva, where there was little or no native Persian-speaking population, in contrast to Khoqand and Bukhara – had much

[29] The original text in Persian reads as follows:

تمام شد این کتاب درّالمجالس در بلده کاشغر\ کاشقر در ماه عشور در تاریخ هزار صد و پنجاه در سال مرغ. فقیر الحقیر کتبهُ ملا توخته ایلمادوز.

[30] The Year of the Chicken/Rooster proves their geographical origin; and the month of Muḥarram proves their religious background as Muslims. Their years were divided into twelve parts of *Gāv* (Cow), *Mūsh* (Mouse), *Pūzīna* (Ape), *Gūsfand* (Sheep), *Asp* (Horse), *Mār* (Snake), *Nahang* (Wale), *Khargūsh* (Rabbit), *Palang* (Leopard), *Khūk* (Pig), *Sag* (Dog) and *Murgh* (Chicken/Rooster). The manuscript no.327 of the Staatsbibliothek zu Berlin (Königliche Bibliothek) is a treatise on the Calendars of Turkic Communities from Khāṭā and Khotan (in Turkistan and Tatarstan). Also see: Wilhelm Pertsch, *Verzeichniss der persischen Handschriften der Königlichen Bibliothek zu Berlin* (Berlin: A. Asher & Company, 1888), iv: 348. Regarding the form of Turkic Calendar along with the Lunar ones, see: Rashīd al-Dīn Faḍlullāh Hamadānī, *Tawārīkh: Taʾrīkh-i Mobārak-i Ghazānī*, edited and annotated by Muḥammad Roushan and Muṣṭafā Mūsawī (Tehran: Miras-i Maktoob, 1394/2015), i: 125–126.

> in common. While Sufi circles and madrasas kept up the tradition of reading Persian texts, considerable intellectual energy was expended during the Qing on translation from Persian into Chinese and Turkic.[31]

Nonetheless, a Persian copy of *Durr al-Majālis* in the Ganjbakhsh collection of Pakistan (No. PAK-001-1471, fl. 503)[32] shows that it was copied in Kashgar, inviting us rethink to what extent Persian was used in China.

> The manuscript has been completed on Tuesday 22 Ramadan 1257 [7 November 1841] [...] and Mullā Muḥammad Rāziq, the scribe from Kashgar.[33]

A further Turkic copy of *Durr al-Majālis* is kept in the Āstān-i Quds Raḍavī Library, Mashhad, Iran (N. 54165), apparently after having been circulated in Central Asia for several years. The original translation from Persian to Turkic was made by Naqīb b. Jaʿfar and the scribe was Qurbān b. ʿAlī in the thirteenth/nineteenth century.

The popularity that *Durr al-Majālis* enjoyed in Central Asia and parts of Russia was comparable with its popularity in Punjab, Bengal, and Kashgar. The Jarring.Prov.108 including 35 chapters, apparently based on Prov.342, by Mullā ʿAbd al-Sattār was copied in Russia on 21 Dhū al-Qaʿda 1286/22 February 1870. This copy used to be studied in Uzbek families with competence in Chagatai. The owners and readers of this text, who from a note in the manuscript apparently studied it in its entirety in 1347/1928, were Maḥmūd Ākhund and ʿAbd Walī Ākhund.

The popularity of *Durr al-Majālis* (in both manuscript copies and early printed volumes) in Central Asia may be due to the relationship between Bukhara (Uzbekistan) and Sayf. As DeWeese has demonstrated, Persian texts like *Durr al-Majālis* were copied in the village of Baraskai (Tatarstan) and Qïzïl Chapchak (Bashkurtustan) in c. 1748 and 1812, respectively.[34] Being located on the eastern side of the Soviet Union, Tatarstan and Kazan welcomed various Persian texts and their Turkic (and Russian) languages, 'from Kazan to Tobolsk people appear to have read Persian and to have sought out materials in Persian, keeping Persian manuscript culture alive until well toward the end of the thirteenth/nineteenth century.'[35]

31 Brophy, 'A Lingua Franca in Decline?', 188.

32 This copy ends with additional short notes in Turkic.

33 The original text in Persian reads as follows:

تمام شدنی این نسخه روز سه شنبه دوصد هزار تاریخ [؟] پنجاه هفت ماه شریف رمضان بیست دو [...] و کاتب کاشقر راقه ملاّ محمّد رازیق

34 See, Devin DeWeese, 'Persian and Turkic from Kazan to Tobolsk: Literary Frontiers in Muslim Inner Asia', *The Persianate World*, edited by Nile Green (California: California University Press, 2019), 152.

35 Ibid., 149.

DURR AL-MAJĀLIS IN THE ARABIC ZONE

Even for Arabs, Persian was an important language of study for a complete Islamic education with some Arabs, as a consequence of their study of Persian, managing to flourish under Ottoman rule.[36] The Talaat Library of Cairo houses a Persian copy of *Durr al-Majālis* (Ms.53). With partial interlinear notes and translation in Ottoman Turkish, this manuscript was copied by Ḥusayn b. Sayfullāh Yamliḥā b. Raḥmān-Qulī in 1825. The first folio includes an inscription mentioning that it was in the possession of refugees in Turkey:

> In the city of Constantinople and the Blissful Land, that is, Istanbul, the refugees of Hagia Sophia from [...] resided with [...] written by Molla [Yar-]Mehmed Oğlu Tahir Efendi.[37]

Molla Mehmed Oğlu Tahir Efendi would have been a Kosovan religious scholar who resided in Istanbul until his death in 1888.[38]

Further copies of *Durr al-Majālis* were in the possession of book collectors in Egypt in the thirteenth/nineteenth century. The manuscript Or.187, now kept in the Bayerische Staatsbibliothek in Munich, Germany, was in Cairo until it was brought to Europe by Jean-Joseph Marcel (d. 1845) the French scholar, philologist, and printer who accompanied Napoleon Bonaparte during his invasion of Egypt. *Durr al-Majālis* was one of the three thousand manuscripts Marcel collected from North Africa.[39] Further

[36] Majid Daneshgar, and Sajjad Rizvi, 'Inscribing Persian in the Arabic Cosmopolis: Case Study of Qur'ānic Exegesis from Khorasan', *Australian Journal of Islamic Studies* 7/1 (2022): 5–28.

[37] The original text in Ottoman Turkish reads as follows:

در شهر قسطنطنية و دارسعاداة يعنى ايصطامبولده قرمان مهاجرلرندان آياى صوفيه دن آشاغا [...] سنده

اقامت [...] بوزار ايلندا ملاّ يار محمّد اوغلى طاهر افندى ديو مكتوب طستينه يازولدى

The term يازو/yāzū used to be written as yāzī/يازى, meaning an inscription or a written text. See, J. W. Redhouse, *A Lexicon, English and Turkish; Shewing, in Turkish, the Literal, Incidental, Figurative, Colloquial, and Technical Significations of the English Terms, Indicating Their Pronunciation in a New and Systematic Manner and Preceded by a Sketch of English Etymology, to Faculitate to Turkish Students the Acquisition of the English Language*, 3rd ed. (Constantinople: A. H. Boyajian, 1884), 2185

[38] A number of other Persian copies of *Durr al-Majālis*, like those of the Leiden University Library (e.g., Or.565) were making a longer journey, moving back-and-forth between Muslim communities, Persians, and Turks, and then ended up in the collection of Levinus Warner (c.1618–1665), who lived in Istanbul for several years.

[39] „die Hs. wurde von J. J. Marcel aus Cairo gebracht". Joseph Aumer, *Die persischen Handschriften der Hof- und. Staatsbibliothek in München* (München: Commission der Palm'schen Hofbuchhandlung, 1866), 59.

Persian manuscripts were studied in Egypt at that time; the two manuscript copies of Saʿdī's *Gulistān* in Bayerische Staatsbibliothek, Or.147 and Or.148, coming from Egypt, both confirm that Arabs and Ottoman Turks (in both Egypt and the Levant) alike, as well as French officers, were all interested to study Persian.

DURR AL-MAJĀLIS IN KURDISH

A copy of Sayf Ẓafar's *Durr al-Majālis* was introduced among the Kurds of Iraq and Turkey by Mullā Mūsā Hikkārī. The Kurdish text of Hikkārī survived in Kurmanji and is largely different from its Persian prototype in terms of structure and content. There are fifty-eight chapters in the Kurdish version with some of the original chapters omitted. The Kurdish text was shared orally and parts of it were memorised by local people.

The Kurmanji translation of *Durr al-Majālis* was (re)produced at the behest of Auguste de Jaba/Żaba (d. 1894), an orientalist originally from Krasław and a Russian envoy and translator in Turkey. This copy, No.ГПБ, курд 40, in the USSR Academy of Sciences, Institute of the Peoples of Asia, includes the handwriting of Mela Mahmût Beyazîdî (d. 1858 or 1868), a famous Kurdish scholar and diplomat in Ottoman Tukey who used to work for de Jaba.[40] Apart from the first three chapters which bear titles such as 'Ḥikāyat Shaykh Barsīsa', 'Ḥikāyat Ṭūṭī', and 'Ḥikāyat Ghanim', the remaining chapters are indicated with short phrases, for example, chapter 10 is 'about Anūshīrvān the Just'.[41]

[40] See, Michiel Leezenberg, 'Between Islamic Learning and Philological Nationalism: Mullah Mahmûdê Bayazîdî's Auto-ethnography of the Kurds', *Die Welt des Islams* 60 (2020): 433–472.

[41] Apparently, some of these chapters were later translated into French by de Jaba/Żaba. For details of the manuscript, see M. B. Rudenko, *Описание курдских рукописей Ленинградских собраний* (Moscow: Izdatelstvo Vostochnoi Literatury, 1961), 14–15. Hêmin Omar Ahmad paid attention to some aspects of this copy in a conference in 2018. I have learned about this, and saw only a cover image, that the Kurmanji version with fifty-eight chapters was printed in Iraq a few years ago while I was writing this part of the book. Hêmin Omar Ahmad, 'Molla Musa Hakkari'nin Dürrü'l-Mecalis İsimli Yazma Eseri', *1st International Zap Basin Scholars Symposium* (Hakkari: Hakkari University, 2018), II: 320–334.

IV) Islamic Themes and Novelty

An examination of different manuscript copies of *Durr al-Majālis* shows that it comprises thirty-six major stories although often manuscript copies comprise only thirty-three chapters. Its chapters cover different Islamic themes some of which are taken from other sources. Notwithstanding a degree of 'borrowing' from other sources, *Durr al-Majālis* also includes a good deal of original content.

BELIEF AND DOCTRINE

Judaism, Christianity, and Islam are all discussed both in terms of their similarities and their differences (e.g., chapters 4, 6, 7, 20, 34, 36). The concept and function of prophetic miracles is also discussed. Sayf Ẓafar explains how Moses parted the Nile river with his cane, Jesus brought to life a corpse dead for 400 years, and Muḥammad split the Moon without touching it. Further theological themes with emphasis on inter-religious dialogue can be found. Chapter 14, for example, is about the concept of conversion to Islam, in which Muslims are referred to as 'Muḥammadi' (Muhammadan).

Durr al-Majālis provided readers from all social classes with a concise interpretation of Qurʾānic verses. Discussion stems from the citation of a Qurʾānic verse or passage and becomes the focus for the further citation of relevant narrations from the Prophet (sg., *ḥadīth*) and reports on the occasion of revelation (*shaʾn al-nuzūl*). Chapter 1 – with its references to the creation of Adam, the Universe, and its dialogues with Satan – is replete with Qurʾānic verses. In line with former exegetical works, Sayf Ẓafar interprets these verses as he mentions them. However, a second more innovative method for presenting and interpreting the Qurʾān is also apparent in *Durr al-Majālis*. In chapter 22, for example, Qurʾānic verses are used by a Muslim female traveller as an exegetical and theological tool through which she answers the questions of a stranger, ʿAbdallāh Mubārak. It appears Sayf Ẓafar intended to instruct his female readers not just with regard to the interpretation of the Qurʾān but also how to interact with strange men.

Statements related from Muḥammad also receive attention in *Durr al-Majālis* in their own right, and not just as explanations of Qurʾānic verses, as do matters of Islamic law (*aḥkām*) and jurisprudence (*fiqh*). For example, in terms of law, chapter 2 advises readers about the consumption of carrion (*mayta*) in times of deperation. Also, chapter 15 discusses the treatment of individuals in the mosque who lack mental capacity or, in the outdated term used by *Durr al-Majālis*, are 'insane' (*dīwāna*). As for ritual, the discussion of which is an important topic of Islamic law, in chapter 35, when Moses asks about the main features of Muḥammad's community (*umma*), God lists some of the main practices of the community such as prayer, fasting, ḥajj, and alms giving (*zakāt*).

PHILOSOPHICAL THEOLOGY

Themes of a philosophical nature are also explored in *Durr al-Majālis*. Chapter 14 is about the story of Khālid b. Walīd who converted many people to Islam. In most Islamic stories, the conversion of non-Muslims to Islam occurred after witnessing the glory of God, Muḥammad's miracles, or after powerful dreams. In chapter 14, however, Khālid provides philosophical answers to questions posed by a Christian monk. Another example of theological philosophy is depicted in chapter 35, where the justice and mercy of God are demonstrated to Moses by means of nature and natural phenomena.

OCCULTISM AND MAGIC

Perhaps unsurprisingly, traces of occultism can be found in *Durr al-Majālis* and some copies of *Durr al-Majālis*, such as Lucknow, no. M82, were even written to promote bravery among its readers.[1] In chapter 16 a curious practice to promote feminine hygiene is mentioned, one which may possibly have a scientific origin in

[1] As explained by Winstedt (see above), the Muslim idea of reading, listening, and/or holding a treatise for the blessings of health and happiness derives from a South Asian context and, ultimately, from Hindu and Buddhist traditions.

Ibn Sīnā (d. 428/1037)[2] but which may also be grounded in the occult.[3] According to *Durr al-Majālis* if a snake's head is burnt beneath the genital area of a women it can have the effect of removing both physical and spiritual ailments. This is not unlike a more recent practice that was found in Iran in recent history, according to anecdotal evidence from apothecaries and from female testimonies, whereby the dry dung of an ass (*ʿanbar-i niṣārā*) would be prescribed for female genital infections.

Apart from elevating the status of Muslim women as being pious, supportive, ambitious, and passionate, *Durr al-Majālis* also contains stories depicting women as untrustworthy (e.g., chapter 6) or as witches who ensure marriage proposals by using magic to eliminate rivals for a suitor's attention (e.g., chapter 31).

ABOUT THE PROPHETS

From a mere glance at the story of the creation of Adam in *Durr al-Majālis* the influence of hagiographocal works, especially those by al-Ṭabarī and al-Thaʿlabī, is clear. From the fourth/tenth century, tales (*qiṣaṣ*) of prophets and the lives of saints became an important way for Muslims to understand Islam and the Islamic sciences. Through the reading of such tales one would become acquainted with different aspects of the Islamic tradition. As Pregill, Klar, and Tottoli say,

> One of the most open frontiers of *qiṣaṣ* studies is thus surely the examination of the pre-Islamic prophets and their manifold significations in philosophy and theology, *adab* (especially post-classical literary arts in Persian and Turkish), the visual arts, and other realms of Muslim meaning-making.[4]

The Auckland copy of *Durr al-Majālis* includes an episode about Adam and Eve which is similar to that found in previous works in that Adam, tempted by Eve, eats from a forbidden 'tree' (which is actually said to be wheat) and is cast down to Serendib (i.e., Sri Lanka). However, *Durr al-Majālis* provides an incomplete account in that

[2] Regarding the medical application of *ʿanbar-i niṣārā*: Hasan Ali Shafiee and Elham Moravej-Salehi, 'Anbarnesa: The Past Tradition, the Future Medicine', *Iran Red Crescent Med Journal* 17(12) (2015), e29536.

[3] See, Matthew Melvin-Koushki, 'Is (Islamic) Occult Science Science?' *Theology and Science* 18/2 (2020): 303–324.

[4] Michael Pregill, Marianna Klar, Roberto Tottoli, 'Qiṣaṣ al-Anbiyāʾ as Genre and Discourse: From the Qurʾān to Elijah Muhammad' *Mizan: Journal for the Study of Muslim Societies and Civilizations* 2/1 (2017), 25 [1–28].

it does not give information about the fate of Eve or the Devil (Iblīs) neither does it acknowledge its sources.[5]

In another episode involving Adam, and this time featuring a fig tree, al-Thaʿlabī has Adam covering his nakedness.

> It is related that when Adam's evil became apparent and his nakedness appeared, he went about among the trees of the Garden asking them for a leaf with which to cover his pudenda. The trees of the Garden rebuffed him until the fig tree had pity on him and gave him a leaf. The two of them – meaning Adam and Eve – began at once sewing (clothes) for themselves from the leaves of the Garden. God rewarded the fig by making its outside and inside equally sweet and useful, and every year God gave him the fruit of the fig tree.[6]

This episode is retold in *Durr al-Majālis* in Persian with only a slight difference and the removal of the chain of narrators.

> No tree agreed to give its leaf to Adam to cover his nakedness, until he reached the Fig tree. He said to the Fig, 'Give me your leaf so that I may cover myself'. The Fig replied, 'I'll be pleased, take a leaf of mine'. Adam took some leaves and covered himself. Soon a message was sent to the Fig tree, 'None of the trees gave their leaves to Adam. What happened that you disobeyed Us and gave him your leaf?' The Fig replied, 'O God, I looked at and treated Adam [as] that day you wanted to create him and said, "I want to make a servant who will be my qualified successor, and will create children from him who will be Our friends". O God, one that you have taken as your friend due to your dignity, how soon would you like him to be discredited?' The divine command arrived, 'O Fig, you have cherished our beloved. Whatever fruits we have so far created in the world has seeds inside. As such, there will be none seen in you, so whoever takes you will benefit and be rewarded highly'.

While receiving most of his narratives from previous Arabic and Persian sources, Sayf Ẓafar enriches them, as well as simplifies them, with his own imaginary, fictional,

[5] Al-Ṭabarī reports that Eve was sent down to Jeddah and Iblis to Maysan. Al-Ṭabarī, *The History of al-Ṭabarī, General Introduction and from Creation to the Flood*, translated and annotated by Franz Rosenthal (New York: State University of New York Press, 1989), I: 292.

[6] Al-Thaʿlabī, *ʿArāʾis al-Majālis fī Qiṣaṣ al-Anbiyāʾ*, *Lives of the Prophets*, translated and annotated by William M. Brinner (Leiden, Boston and Köln: Brill, 2002), 52–53. Different versions of this episode, mentioning the role of the Fig tree in providing a garment for Adam and Eve is found in Christian literature and other Islamic genres produced by Sufis and Qalandars.

and traditional elements. Sayf Ẓafar was selective in using different sources. His episodes on Adam are hardly found in any other celebrated Persian hagiographical work although al-Nīsābūrī, who also bases his narrative on that given by al-Thaʿlabī, does have something to say on Adam and the beginning of the world,

> '[...] did not I tell you not to eat from this tree? Now, cast out from the Paradise.' Adam and Eve and Iblis and Peacock and Serpent all became enemies of each other [...] then Adam came and took the Fig's leaves and covered himself and Eve did the same, and all fell on Earth. Adam was cast down to Serendib, and Eve to Jeddah, and Peacock in India, and the Serpent in Serendib. All were crying and wailing.[7]

As can be seen, al-Nīsābūrī, in contrast to al-Thaʿlabī, gives roles in the story not just to Adam but also Eve, Iblīs, the serpent, and the peacock.

A KILLING STORY OF SUNNIS AND SHĪʿĪS, AND THE IDEA OF DE-SHĪʿITISATION

The account of *Durr al-Majālis* on the killing of Ḥasan and Ḥusayn is quite different from the historical account given by al-Ṭabarī. The long version of the story of Sayf Ẓafar (chapter 31b) is divided into two main parts. The first part is about Muḥammad and his death as well as the 'martyrdom' of the first four caliphs. This part sheds light on the relationship between Muḥammad and his grandsons Ḥasan and Ḥusayn, by which readers may realise the closeness and warmth of the relationship. Both Ḥasan and Ḥusayn, we are told, were killed by Yazīd. He appoints a witch to poison Ḥasan and orders his officers to behead Ḥusayn. The second part of the account begins with the rise of their half brother, Muḥammad Ḥanafiyya as an avenger. After hearing news of the martyrdom of Ḥusayn, and seeing the Prophet Muḥammad in his dream, Muḥammad Ḥanafiyya is deteremined to first stop Yazīd, then kill him and appoint Ḥusayn's sons as rulers of Muslim regions. In former accounts, being influenced by al-Ṭabarī – whose presentation was based on three older reports from Abū Jaʿfar al-Bāqir (d. 114/732–733), al-Ḥusayn b. ʿAbd al-Raḥmān (d. 136/753–754), and Abū Mikhnaf (d. 157/773–774) – Ḥusayn's martyrdom is not accompanied by an account of Ḥasan's death.[8] Also, the name of the people killed in the abovesaid Arabic reports are

[7] al-Nīsābūrī, *Qiṣaṣ al-Anbiyāʾ*, *Dāstān-hā-yi Peyghambarān*, edited by Ḥabīb Yaghmāī (Tehran: Sherkat-i Enteshārāt-i Elmī va Farhangī, 1340/1961), 20.

[8] The important contributions of Torsten Hylén should be taken into account. E.g., Torsten Hylén,

either incomplete or limited to a small group. In contrast, Sayf Ẓafar's story mentions a number of individuals and groups by name. It presents unique forms of prophecy in outlining the birth story of Yazīd from the loin of Muʿāwiya. Even, the celebrated work of Wāʿiẓ Kāshifī, *Rawḍat al-Shuhadā*ʾ (The Garden of Martyrs), does not particularly relate Yazīd to Ḥasan nor mentions the ill-omened birth of Yazīd.

Sayf Ẓafar's story of Ḥasan and Ḥusayn is tied with romantic moments. Both young men are in search of pretty women who are married and then divorced. This contrasts with the popular Shīʿī image of Ḥasan and Ḥusayn in the medieval era when, according to Hylén, they were viewed as 'superheroes'[9] innocent of blame.

Unlike the majority of Shīʿī sources, Muḥammad Ḥanafiyya is depicted as an immortal Imam – widely promoted in Kaysāniyya – although, as with the other Imams, he is not biologically related to Fāṭima, who is Muḥammad's daughter and the mother of Ḥasan and Ḥusayn. This suggests that *Durr al-Majālis* was produced in a critical period, when Muslims of the Persianate regions were still unsure how to define the concept of Shīʿism. They faced a dilemma of how to commemorate the death of Ḥasan and Ḥusayn, on the one hand, and express their love and kindness for the Companions of the Prophet, like Muʿāwiya, on the other. For them, only Muḥammad Ḥanafiyya could resolve this. He is depicted as chivalrous as his father, ʿAlī, and was as eligible to lead Shīʿism as his half-brothers, Ḥasan and Ḥusayn. Muḥammad Ḥanafiyya's aim is to please the Prophet by taking revenge on the killers of his grandchildren, and then to withdraw from the political stage.

Although the early caliphs of Islam are admired throughout the *Durr al-Majālis*, two caliphs in particular receive disapproval. The first is ʿUmar who is not cursed in the text but who is nevertheless depicted as someone who attempted to assassinate Muḥammad (chapter 7; also see below). The second is Yazīd who, we are told, was even cursed by Muḥammad before his birth (see the short and long versions, chapter 31a and 31b, respectively). In this regard the observation of Lieut-Colonel D. C. Phillott is important to note. Phillott says that Indian and Persian Shīʿīs would ritualistically curse the enemies of the Prophet's household (e.g., some caliphs) and their followers and would remember their names while relieving themselves.[10] In contrast, they commemorated Ḥusayn as the one who was killed while being thirsty.[11] It appears that *Durr al-Majālis* is one of the most prominent pre-Safawid resources which links the 'enemies' of Muḥammad's household with latrines and tells of a humiliatingly filthy death for

'Ḥusayn, the Mediator: A structural Analysis of the Karbalāʾ Drama according to Abū Ja'far Muḥammad b. Jarīr al-Ṭabarī (d. 310/923)', (PhD Thesis., Uppsala University, 2007). [9] Ibid.

[10] D. C. Phillott, 'Note on a Shi'a Imprecation', *Journal and Proceedings of the Asiatic Society of Bengal* 7/10 (1911), 691. [11] Ibid.

them. In the second part of chapter 31b the story of Muḥammad Ḥanafiyya has it that,

> Muḥammad Ḥanafiyya left all his people and went after Yazīd. Yazīd fled to the palace. When he saw Muḥammad Ḥanafiyya, he got off his horse and hid in the toilet, becoming covered in filth. Muḥammad Ḥanafiyya ordered a fire to be lit [around him], and some say that he [Yazīd] became like a black stone and would run around the mountain of Qaf, and be unclean until the Day of Judgement.[12]

Durr al-Majālis was produced in a cosmopolitan context where both Sunnis and Shīʿis lived, worshipped, and studied alongside each other. While elevating all four caliphs, calling them martyrs, Sayf Ẓafar lauds the martyrdom of Ḥusayn by relating it to Qurʾān 37:107, 'And We ransomed his son with a great sacrifice', obviously a Shīʿī exegetical doctrine put forward by Ibn Bābawayh al-Qummī (d. c. 3381/991).

Here, and given that *Durr al-Majālis* is the main source used in Southeast Asian Muslim stories, I would like to highlight former hypotheses dealing with Sunni and Shīʿī context of the Malay-Indonesian world. In line with Brakel, Edwin Wieringa has noted the representation of Shīʿī elements in Malay literature and the way in which ʿUmar b. al-Khaṭṭāb, the second caliph, is somewhat downgraded and marginalised as compared to what one might expect in Sunni literature.[13] A lowly portrayal of ʿUmar is found in almost all available copies of *Durr al-Majālis*, particularly in (i) chapter seven in which ʿUmar is tempted to kill Muḥammad; (ii) in chapter twelve in which ʿUmar is an impatient person; and (iii) in chapter twenty-six in which ʿUmar is unable to respond to the question of Satan. This may suggest that the whole concept of de-Shīʿitisation of the Malay Islamic literature, widely referred to by Brakel and Wieringa, should be viewed through the lense of Persianism. Here, *Durr al-Majālis* contains obvious traces of Shīʿitisation and de-Shīʿitisation. On the one hand, it elevates the Prophet's household – demonstrating the ʿAlid piety, referring to the widespread reverence for *ahl al-bayt* –[14] and humiliates some Companions and their children (e.g., ʿUmar, Muʿāwiya and his son Yazīd) on the other. The manuscript GMS-170 portrays all Companions as free from guilt and committing great sins. It is replete with ʿAlid piety elements. Also, an old copy of *Durr al-Majālis* kept in the Leiden University Library (Or.565) dated 972 (c.1564 CE) encompasses the most obvious type of de-Shīʿitisation; it clearly demonstrates that readers of this particular manuscript have replaced the names of

[12] References about throwing the enemies' head into the latrines is also found in the *Malay Hikayat Muhammad Hanafiyya*. See Brakel, *Hikayat Muhammad Hanafiyyah*, 56.

[13] Edwin Wieringa, 'Does Traditional Islamic Malay Literature Contain Shiitic Elements? Alî and Fâtimah in Malay Hikayat Literature', *Studia Islamika* 3/4 (1996), 93–111.

[14] Formichi and Feener, 2015.

Shīʿī figures (ʿAlī and the other Imams) with those of the first three Sunni caliphs, thus canonizing their preferred vision of history and effacing the alternative. Thus, the current proposal is that the de-Shīʿitisation was widely practised by Muslims throughout the world while reading Persian materials, and was not limited to Southeast Asian contexts. It first emerged in the Middle East and Central Asia, *especially* since the tenth/sixteenth century and upon the rise of the Safawid Persia when Shīʿism became the State religion of Iran and Sunnism was vilified.[15] Religious controversy between Sunnism and Shīʿism in western Asia spread eastward, making inroads to the Malay-Indonesian World. I would like to undertake an extensive review of literature in the future to determine why Persianate materials present a mixture of praise and blame regarding the Companions of the Prophet. Although requiring further investigation, there has always been a vigorous debate surrounding Muḥammad's Companions. This is embodied in the ʿĀshūrā of Ḥusayn. How the author, for example, described the Muslim account of the assassination of Ḥusayn, giving voice to his followers and assassins in different episodes, points to factors underpinning the eastward movement of Islam from West and Southeast Asia. This is an ongoing project and I shall be able to elaborate further over coming years.[16]

DIALOGUE

Durr al-Majālis offers several forms of dialogue and conversation throughout the text. Two dialogue-based chapters have been especially well received. One of them is the conversation of Moses with God that deals with various theological, eschatological, and legal issues (*masāʾil*) and is usually titled 'Munājāt-nāma-yi Mūsā' (The

[15] Another example is a Persian treatise on the genealogy of Shīʿa Imāms, the manuscript BSB Cod.pers. 167a. preserved at Bayerische Staatsbibliothek, Munich. This manuscript is replete with curses against Umayyads and Abbasids by its Shīʿī scribe, which are crossed out by its Ottoman (Sunni) reader.

[16] Peacock has recently published on transregional translation and circulation of Jamāl al-Ḥusaynī's *Rawżat al-Aḥbāb*, from the Middle East to Southeast Asia. According to Peacock, "The text attempted to reconcile Sunni and Shia views of the Prophet and early Islamic history". Thus, the idea of Shīʿtisation or de-Shīʿtisation should also be examined through the lens of translaton movements. One may wonder why the original Persian text of *Rawżat al-Aḥbāb* could not made inroads to Southeast Asia. Now, the role of *Durr al-Majālis* and *Rawżat al-Aḥbāb* in shaping Muslim literature in the Malay-Indonesian world should be seen alongside each other. See, A.C.S. Peacock, "Jamāl al-Ḥusaynī's *Rawżat al-Aḥbāb* between Herat, Istanbul and Sumatra: The transformations of a Timurid Persian history of the Prophet and early Islam," In *Authorship and Textual Transmission in the Manuscript Age: Contextualising Ideological Variants*, edited by Sacha Alsancakli and Philip Bockholt (Leuven Peeters Publishers, 2023), 21–57.

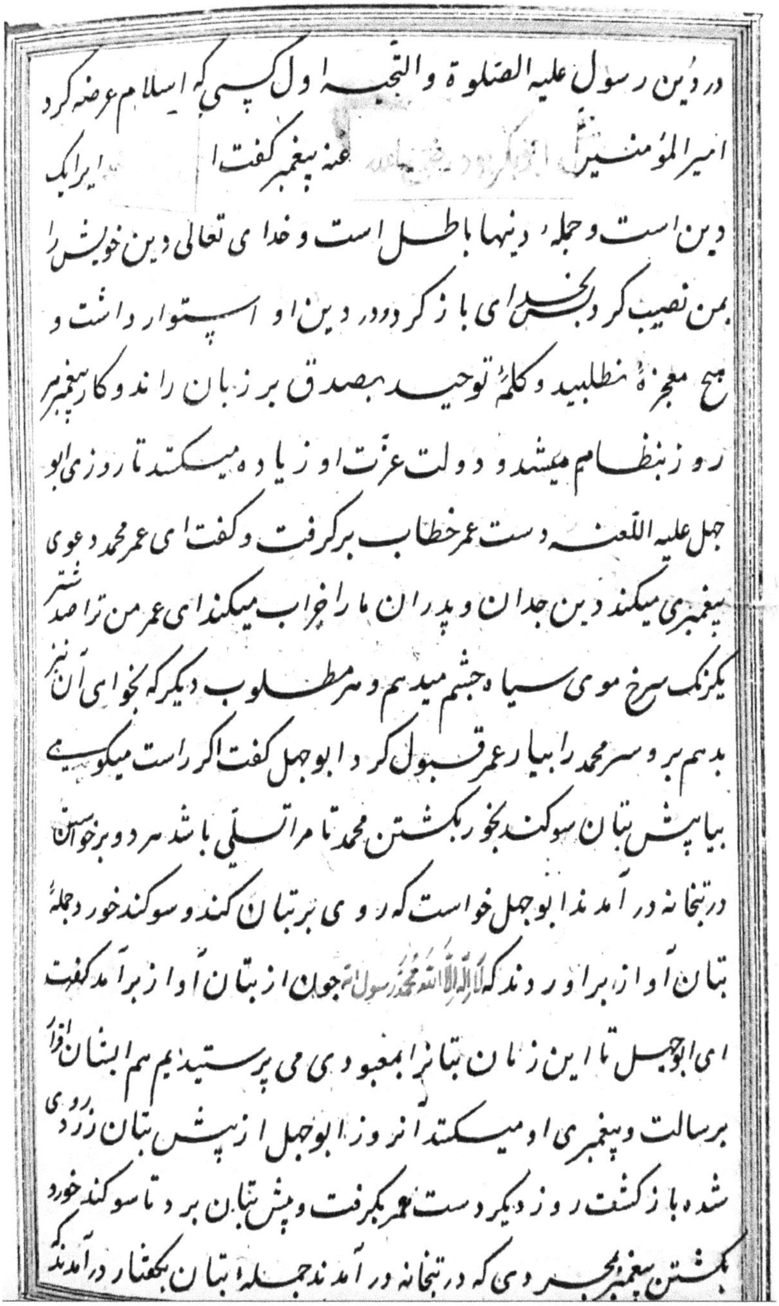
در دین رسول علیه الصلوة والتحیة اول کسی که اسلام عرضه کرد
امیر المؤمنین ابو بکر رضی الله عنه پیغمبر گفت ا[illegible] را یک
دین است وجمله دینها باطل است وخدای تعالی دین خویش را
بمن نصیب کرد بخدای باز گردو در دین او استوار داشت و
هیچ معجزه نطلبید وکلمه توحید بصدق بر زبان راند وکار پیغمبر
روز بنظام میشد ودولت عزت او زیاده میگشت تا روزی ابو
جهل علیه اللعنه دست عمر خطاب برگرفت وگفت ای عمر محمد دعوی
پیغمبری میکند دین جدان وپدران ما را خراب میکند ای عمر من ترا صد شتر
یکرنگ سرخ موی سیاه چشم میدهم و هر مطلوب دیگر که بخواهی آن نیز
بدهم برو سر محمد را بیار عمر قبول کرد ابو جهل گفت اگر راست میگویی
بیا پیش بتان سوگند بخور بگشتن محمد تا مرا تسلی باشد سر دو برخواستن
در بتخانه در آمدند ابو جهل خواست که روی بر بتان کند و سوگند خورد جمله
بتان آواز برآوردند که لا اله الا الله محمد رسول الله چون از بتان آواز برآمد گفت
ای ابو جهل تا این زمان بتان را بمعبودی می پرستیدیم هم ایشان اقرار
برسالت وپیغمبری او میکنند آن روز ابو جهل از پیش بتان زرد روی
شده باز گشت روز دیگر دست عمر بگرفت وپیش بتان برد تا سوگند خورد
بکشتن پیغمبر محمد که در بتخانه در آمدند جمله بتان بگفتار در آمدند که

Figure 3. Folio 31, MS Or.565. Persian copy of *Durr al-Majālis* including the most obvious type of de-Shīʿitisation, replacing the names of Shīʿī figures with those of the first three Sunni caliphs. Courtesy of Leiden University Library, the Netherlands.

Tale of Moses' Private Conversation with God) or 'Mūsā-nāma' (The Tale of Moses).[17] In an Uyghur version the same chapter is titled 'Rāḍī-nāma' (The Tale of Mystical Satisfaction). In his discussion of the meaning of the Arabic word *munājāt* Bosworth makes special reference to the conversation of Moses with the Almighty.

> [T]he verbal noun of the form III verb nā<u>dj</u>ā 'to whisper to, talk confidentially with someone', which is used in Ḳurʾān, LVIII, 13, in this sense, and in the reciprocal form VI in LVIII, 9, 10, of the murmurs of discontent amongst the Prophet's followers, probably after the Uḥud reverse [...]. Munā<u>dj</u>āt becomes, however, a technical term of Muslim piety and mystical experience in the sense of 'extempore prayer', as opposed to the corporate addressing of the deity in the *ṣalāt* [...], and of the Ṣūfīs' communion with God; the meanings here were perhaps influenced by Ḳurʾān, XIX, 53/52, where Moses engages in confidential talk (na<u>dj</u>iyy an) with God on Mount Sinai.[18]

The other noted dialogue-based chapter relates to the conversation between Jesus and the skull of a king named as Jumjuma (lit. 'skull'). Being Islamised, Jesus' conversation with the skull ended up with his imploration to bring the king back to life, who later becomes an adherent of God's Unity. Although there are various ideas about the origin of this story (see part VI in this current work), our attention is drawn to ʿAṭṭār although such an attribution is perhaps somewhat speculative.[19] Whatever the origins, a prose version, interconnected with other conversations, can be found in *Durr al-Majālis* and has been reproduced as an independent treatise.[20]

Apart from standard human–human and human–God conversations, found throughout *Durr al-Majālis*, other forms of conversation can also be found. Unconventional forms of conversation include conversations between animals (e.g., chapter 35); between animals and humans (e.g., chapters 4, 7, 14, 21, 27, 31, 35); between inanimate objects and humans (e.g., chapter 9, 13, 17, 29, 35 and the 'Nūr-nāma' *epi-*

[17] This should not be confused with a Judeo-Persian epic with the same name.

[18] C. E. Bosworth, 'Munā<u>dj</u>āt', in: *Encyclopaedia of Islam*, Second Edition, Edited by: P. Bearman, Th. Bianquis, C. E. Bosworth, E. van Donzel, W. P. Heinrichs. Consulted online on 18 June 2021 http://dx.doi.org/10.1163/1573-3912_islam_SIM_5499

[19] See, George Morrison, *History of Persian Literature from the Beginning of the Islamic Period to the Present Day* (Leiden and Köln: Brill, 1981) 57; also, Jes P. Assmussen, *Studies in Judeo-Persian Literature* (Leiden: Brill, E. J. Brill, 1973), 67.

[20] References to a conversation between human and a skull is also found in South-West African folkstories. One may, for example, refer to Loreto Todd, *Tortoise the Trickster, and Other Folktales from Cameroon* (London: Routledge & Kegan Paul, 1979). For the Persian translation, see: Loreto Todd, *Muzd-i Khirad*, trans. ʿAlī Khākbāz (Tehran: Daftar-i Nashr-i Farhang-i Islāmī, 1373/1994).

logue); between body limbs (e.g., chapter 1 and 'Nūr-nāma'); between the dead and humans (e.g., chapters 6, 8, 15, 17, 36); between angels and humans (e.g., chapters 1, 4, 7, 21, 24, 25, 30, 33, 36); between jinn and between jinn and humans (e.g., chapter 5); between Satan and humans (e.g., chapters 23, 26, 28, 30, 34); between nymphs and cherubs and humans (e.g., chapters 15, 19, 33); between God and the angels (e.g., chapters 1, 11, 15, 22, 23); and between God and the cosmos (e.g., chapter 1).

Beside such forms of conversation, *Durr al-Majālis* takes its readers into the imagination of key interlocutors by exploring interior dialogues where one speaks to oneself pensively. It also displays the personification of inanimate objects who speak with themselves, with a person, or with God. Each dialogue or monologue is positioned in a larger category; each can be viewed as an independent genre of religious literature. Some are replete with accounts of spiritual and material poverty, accounts which can be termed as *faqr-nāma* (poverty tales). One copy of *Durr al-Majālis* in the National Library of Iran is even accompanied by another short treatise that receives this title, that is, 'Faqr-nāma'. Some chapters of *Durr al-Majālis* address orphans and termed *yatīm-nāma* (orphan tales), or address dreams and dream interpretation and may be termed *khᵛāb-nāma* (dream tales). Every chapter has a lesson and/or instruction which is termed *naṣīḥat-nāma*, *pand-nāma*, or *andarz-nāma* (admonition tale).[21] Each of these categories represents the author's and seekers' eschatological, theological, sexual, and physical concerns.

[21] Traces of 'Tavahhum-nāma' referring to illusions and fictional stories can also be found.

V) Persianate-Malay Islamic Stories: A Comparative Analysis

Concise versions and select parts of *Durr al-Majālis* were circulated in regions such as the Indian subcontinent which is where the main body of Malay Islamic stories, or *hikayat*, were shaped. It appears that only one chapter from the Persian copy of *Durr al-Majālis* was written in Southeast Asia in the eleventh/seventeenth century, specifically, the eighth chapter about Mālik Dīnār and his journeying to Mecca for the purpose of hajj as reproduced by a group of Persian Shīʿī travellers in Siam and Burma , as described in *Safīna-yi Māzandarānī* in the seventeenth century. The story of Mālik Dīnār is accompanied with further Persian works which had influence on Malay literature. For example, some accounts from Khʷāja Niẓām al-Mulk (fl. 82) with influences on Malay ethical teachings, or parts of Ḥusayn Wāʿiẓ Kāshifī's *Akhlāq-i Muḥsinī* (ff. 141–142), already translated into the Malay language,[1] and cited in further ethical sources like Jahurī/Jawharī Bukhārī's *Tāj al-Salāṭīn* (Crown of the Kings) can be seen. Further East, one may observe the influence, both direct and indirect, of *Durr al-Majālis* on the Islamic tales of the Philippines and eschatological treatises such as the *Kabarol Akirat* (Reports of the Hereafter) of Panggaga Micky or the folktale *Dog Goes to Sue Humans* in the Chams.[2]

[1] Daneshgar, 'An Early 'Mirror for Princes' in Southeast Asia: The First Known Malay Translation of Akhlaq-i Mohseni' *Cambridge University Library Special Collection* 2022.

[2] I have referred to the influence of *Durr al-Majālis* in the Philippines and Cambodia, mainly on the basis of Sophia University's special issue of their 'Comparative Study of Southeast Asian Kitabs (6)' edited by Sugahara Yumi in 2021, which will be the subject of my forthcoming research.

ON PERSIAN-MALAY MUSLIM LITERATURE

The Persian origins of Malay Islamic tales have received some attention in academic literature with the work of Brakel in the 1970s being noteworthy. For example, the Malay *Hikayat Muhammad Hanafiyya*, one of the oldest known Islamic stories of the Archipelago, was considered by Van Ronkel to have been based on a Persian text by an unknown author from Murshidabad, Bengal. However, upon examination, it becomes clear that this Persianate Bengali text is in turn a selection from *Durr al-Majālis* which is usually titled in South Asia and Central Asia as *Jang-nāma*, *Qiṣṣa-yi Muḥammad Ḥanafiyya*, *Maqtal-nāma*, or similar. Following Van Ronkel, Brakel paid particular attention to this story. However, both of them were unable to detect some episodes of the Malay story in the Persian one but I have demonstrated that what Brakel could not find is in fact outlined in different copies of *Durr al-Majālis*. Given that *Hikayat Muhammad Hanafiyya* is among the most ancient Muslim tales in Southeast Asia, and that this story is part of the *Durr al-Majālis* text, I was prompted to explore whether this Persian collection of Islamic stories could also be the origin of other Malay Muslim literature. I do not suppose that the origin of every Malay Islamic story or *hikayat* can be found in *Durr al-Majālis* but, nevertheless, some important Malay *hikayat* do find their origins in this work and some chapters of *Durr al-Majālis* were fully translated into Malay-Indonesian languages.

SHARED ISLAMIC STORIES IN PERSIAN AND MALAY

The stories in *Durr al-Majālis* were read in both gatherings of the powerful and learned and of the lay masses. These stories fall into a number of categories: some resemble the stories of the prophets (*qiṣaṣ al-anbiyāʾ*) or Qurʾānic stories (*qiṣaṣ al-Qurʾān*) while some deal with historical figures and Sufi saints and other impart lessons for parents and children or broach the topic of the afterlife. Each story reflects upon both a central issue and a number of peripheral issues as is also evident in Malay Muslim literature.

The initial parts of *Durr al-Majālis* present an amalgamation of prose and short poetic notes praising God, Muḥammad, and other prophets mixed with Arabic couplets and Qurʾānic verses. Then the title of each chapter is listed. Each chapter has an exterior and interior implication. For example, the interior implication of the first chapter about the creation of Adam is that Muḥammad is superior to all other prophets in the sight of God.

The Creation of Adam

The story of Adam is told in the first chapter of *Durr al-Majālis*. The story is divided into different episodes, each of which are interconnected, as can be seen in the chapter's somewhat unwieldy overview.

> Running a dialogue in the Universe about the creation of Adam – God's representative in Heaven but not on Earth – the representative should be someone humble and unpretentious, for which the Earth is nominated among other divine titans to be the original essence of Adam's body; the task of taking soil from the Earth is tough and attempted by several divine angels; only one angel is successful in taking soil from the Earth, no one but ʿIzrāʾīl; given his courage and candid essence, ʿIzrāʾīl is chosen by God as the 'Angel of Death' (*malik al-mawt*); another form of dialogue is then presented in the fingers of the Prophet Solomon – the humbleness of the Earth is paralleled with this episode; the fingers converse about which from among them is qualified to wear the signet ring of Solomon and for what reason; it transpires that no finger is qualified to bear the signet ring except the little finger which remained silent due to its humbleness and down-to-Earth characteristic and its being favoured by God; the bodily conversations are changed now to other conversations between humans (e.g., Bāyazīd) and God; then the story of welcoming Adam in the Universe progresses, through which angels are ordered to prostrate before him, an act rejected by Satan (Iblīs); the complaints of angels are put forward; not only Satan but also other angels raised objections about the creation of Adam and his descendants 'who would slaughter on Earth'; the answers are provided by God; former prophets before Muḥammad have clearly shown their affection and great respect to God and Muḥammad; again the story turns towards Adam and Eve; again a shift towards the first night of the grave and the angels of the grave is found; the name of the [forbidden] wheat in heaven is indicated, which is eaten by Adam – through Eve's devilish temptation; the Fig tree emerges as self-giving and sacrifices itself to cover the naked Adam with its leaves; the Fig is now granted divine blessing and becomes a seedless and healthy fruit; Adam's descent to Serendib is the next part; he begins to cry on Earth and the birds drink from his tears; now God again speaks with Adam on Earth; then Adam encounters the name of Muḥammad written along with the name of 'Allah' on the divine Throne; it is said that the sins of human beings are forgiven just because of Muḥammad's name; the story of Muḥammad and his uncle who died as an infidel is present; Adam wishes to return to Heaven and God gives him a response; Adam begins another conversation with God about the aftermath of his death and the status of his body in the grave; the way a sinner would die and decompose in the grave is also discussed.

The overview gives an example of how various theological and historical accounts are placed in the first chapter of *Durr al-Majālis*. The back-and-forth between different parts of the story is obvious, which often revolves around the primary purpose of the creation of Adam, that is, the pre-existence of the biological Muḥammad. Other key figures and elements of this story including Eve, other prophets, Satan, angels, wheat, fig tree, and birds, all of which are used to lead the reader to the conclusion that Muḥammad is the final prophet of God. Through this story, religious teachings on eschatology, ethics, temptation, and the devil are imparted.

The approach of *Durr al-Majālis*, with its linking various themes to impart an overall message, is evident in Malay *hikayat* too. That this approach is found in Malay Islamic stories should be no surprise as Malay prophetic stories are highly influenced by the Persian work of Abū Isḥāq Nīsāpūrī which had already pervaded the whole of South Asia.[3] In Malay classical literature the story of the creation of the Universe and of Adam is placed under the category of Qurʾānic and prophetic stories and are didactic in nature. It is part of the Malay *Kisah al-anbiyāʾ* literature which is named differently in various Malay and Javanese collections like *Kitab Ahlu Tafsir, Hikayat Firawn, Anbiya, Serat Anbiya, Tapel Adam*.[4] The origins of some stories are yet unclear but they are more or less inspired or influenced by the famous Persian and Arabic hagiographical works. An examination of different copies of the Malay stories of prophets reveals the huge influence of *Taʾrīkh al-Ṭabarī* in the story of Adam, whether direct or indirect. However, it is also clear that some episodes and stories are taken from unidentified sources. Here, our *Durr al-Majālis* finds an opportunity to play a role. For instance, the Malay manuscript Cohen Stuart 122 (*Suratul Anbiya*), includes a section in which God created 'a gigantic bull with vast horns [that] sat on the back of the fish. And Allah placed the seven layers of the world on top of the bull's horns'.[5] Apart from narrated statements (*ḥadīth*) and exegetical accounts,[6] two sources from the thirteenth/nineteenth century have clearly mentioned this story, one is al-Qazwīnī's *ʿAjāʾib al-Makhlūqāt wa Gharāʾib al-Mawjūdāt* (The Marvels of Creation and the Oddities of Existence) and the other is the twenty-eighth chapter of *Durr al-Majālis* about Shaykh Barsīsa (and other parts of the chapter are also found in Malay).

Also, in the Malay version, when God created animals as the initial inhabitants of the Earth one of the first animals to be created was the bird. Later on, a bird was cre-

[3] Brakel, *Hikayat Muhammad Ḥanafiyya* (1979b), 23–24; Braginsky (2004), 358.

[4] Liaw, *A History of Classical Malay Literature*, 188 and 212.

[5] Liaw, 189.

[6] One may refer to the famous *Ḥadīth al-Ḥūt* and its traces in some Malay-Indonesian manuscripts at Cambridge University Library, Gg.6.40 and Ii.6.45.

ated which eats mustard seeds and would die upon finishing them.[7] This is also evident in two stories from *Durr al-Majālis*. First, when Adam is sent down from Heaven to Earth his first interlocutors are birds, who were on Earth before him. Then, it is outlined in the story of the private conversation of Moses with God, chapter thirty-four, in which a bird eats seeds but holds the last seed before consuming it as it knew it would die. As will be shown below, the story of Moses' private conversation with God is quite similar to the Malay *Hikayat Musa Munajat*.[8] Further parts of the account of *Durr al-Majālis* of the creation of the Universe and Adam are also found in the Malay *Kisah al-Anbiyāʾ*. One of the most obvious references is about the unsuccessful attempt of divine angels to take soil from the Earth to make Adam's physical body. The successful one was Izrāʾīl who is then granted permission to seize the soul of human beings. On another occasion, God informs Adam of the Islamic profession of faith (*shahāda*) in the Throne, by which Adam learned about Muḥammad's superiority for the first time. Other parts of the Malay story of Adam are found in other Arabic and Persian sources, too, some of which also had an influence on *Durr al-Majālis*.

The Javanese version of the story of Adam, widely known as *Tapel Adam* (Adam's Dough'), contains passages which are found in our Persian text. In contrast to Steenbrink's claim that *Tapel Adam* 'show the more typical Javanese style of the storyteller as different from the specific historian, theologian or mystical teacher,'[9] one may clearly notice the relationship between the Javanese and Persian story of Adam:

Adam's nakedness in Javanese and Persian versions

> When the fruit entered with some difficulty into Adam's throat, he experienced its savour and also immediately forgot God. [...] But soon afterwards he felt ashamed, because his clothes fell down, his magnificent crown disappeared, as also hisroyal attire and even this undershirt and Eve's long skirt and the covering of her upper parts. Adam wanted to take leaves from trees, but they all resisted. In a way, resembling the insurgency of the earth to be transformed into the material for the creation of Adam, the trees and leaves also protest: "We will not be taken by you for fear of God, that we shall later be reprimanded. The prescribed prayer is to believe always in God, in this world and until

7 Liaw, 189.

8 Indicating the names of Adam and Moses alongside each other in some Malay Muslim texts may be related to Q 20:115–124; 7:11–25; 2:30–39. See, Karel Steenbrink, *Adam Redivivus: Muslim Elaboration of the Adam Saga with Special Reference to the Indonesian Literary Traditions* (Zoetermeer: Meinema, 1998), 8.

9 Steenbrink, *Adam Redivivus*, 108.

> the coming world will arrive. God may provide, that we abstain from sins against God, that we shall not trespass his command, but refrain from heresy (*bidangah*) and insincerity (*munapek*).[10] (Javanese version)

> [...] [Adam] put a grain into his mouth. The grain was still there and did not properly go down his throat but the crown was overturned from his head and his dress was taken from his body. He became shattered and naked. He ran towards heaven. He approached every single palace and tree. All of them said to him, 'Get away from us as you have disobeyed, while we are obedient. Why do we want someone disobedient among us?' (Chapter One, *Durr al-Majālis*, Persian version)

Both Javanese and Persian sources also inform readers that the *Anjīr* or Fig tree agreed to grant a leaf to Adam to cover his 'shameful parts'.[11] They also indicate that Adam was expelled to Ceylon.[12]

Biblical Prophets

Stories of prophets and other revered figures such as Shayth (Seth) and Jethro, Abraham, Abraham and Ishmael, Joseph and Jacob, Joseph and Zulaykha, Moses, Jonah, Solomon, Jesus, and Muḥammad are found in both *Durr al-Majālis* and Malay tales. For instance, the Malay version of the story of Solomon has a Qurʾānic episode about a jinn who took the ring of Solomon. As a result, Solomon loses his kingdom and kingship...due to poverty, he has to work for a fisherman. The fisherman has a daughter who ends up becoming the wife of Solomon.[13] This story is taken from the fifth chapter of *Durr al-Majālis* concerning the virtues of Solomon. As Liaw mentions, 'apart from the *Kisasul Al-anbiyāʾ*, which tells the stories of all the prophets, there are also chronicles which recount the lives of individual prophets'.[14] This is also apparent in *Durr al-Majālis*, in which there are independent stories about the Prophets. Regarding the stories or episodes about Moses, one is identical to classical *qiṣaṣ al-anbiyāʾ* literature and others are more independent treatises or short episodes of other larger stories. For instance, the account of the death of Moses which is found in the Malay *Hikayat Nabi Musa* is identified in the fourth part of *Durr al-Majālis*.

[10] Steenbrink, 119. [11] It should be noted that the Persian term *Anjīr* was used in the Javanese *Tapel Adam*. Steenbrink, 119. [12] "Adam was expelled to the gunung selan, the Mountain of Ceylon, popularly also known as Adam's Peak." Steenbrink, 120. [13] Liaw, 208; Winstedt, *A History of Classical Malay Literature*, 108. [14] Liaw, 212.

Muḥammad and His Companions

The names and stories of the Prophet's Companions (*ṣahāba*) are also mentioned throughout Malay Islamic literature. One of the most important is *Hikayat Muhammad Hanafiyya*, the longer version of the killing story of Ḥasan and Ḥusayn in *Durr al-Majālis* (see my full discussion below). Among the names of the Companions we may note Māriya al-Qibṭiya (Mary the Copt), who is the subject of the twelfth chapter of *Durr al-Majālis*. Some episodes of this story are found in the Malay *Hikayat Samaun* in which Muḥammad married an Egyptian slave, Māriya or Dewi Mariah.[15] The role of Dewi Mariah is as one who fell in love with Muḥammad, and that the other wife of the Prophet, ʿĀʾisha, suggested Muḥammad should bring 'Dewi Mariah by force'.[16]

References to Khālid b. Walīd in chapter fourteen of *Durr al-Majālis* are seen in the Malay *Hikayat Samaun*, as well. Although the origin of this Malay story has been long debated, Samaun as the son of Khālid, and his role as a promoter of the faith of Islam, are very similar to those of Khālid in *Durr al-Majālis*. The Malay episode in which Samaun went out to convert King Bakti to Islam but ended up being killed by Samaun is similar to the last part of the story of Khālid b. Walīd in *Durr al-Majālis*. In this story Khālid fights and kills an Arab king, named King Muḥammad, who claimed to be the Muḥammad of the end times, and that he submitted a letter to the Prophet Muḥammad referring to him as 'the ruler of the rest of the Arabian zone'. Interestingly, this episode answers a doubt about the origin of the Malay story. Regarding *Hikayat Samaun*, Winstedt, among others, says that '[...] making Muḥammad king of Medinah, [is] evidence that it was written not in Arabic but in the Malay archipelago'.[17] However, given the existence of a direct reference in *Durr al-Majālis* to Muḥammad's kingship of the Arab world, it is clear that the Malay *Hikayat Samaun* was originally written outside of the Malay-Indonesian world, and that it is NOT necessarily, as Millie would have it, to be read as 'a locally specific interpretation of a martial hero in the service of the Prophet'.[18]

Another common element in Malay Muslim literature which is influenced by our Persian prototype is the tooth of Muḥammad which was broken. Overall, three Malay stories address Muḥammad's teeth. The first of them is mentioned in *Hikayat Amir*

15 Ibid., 233. 16 Ibid., 235. This episode outlined in Malay version may also be a canonisation of ʿĀʾisha who, in chapter twelve of *Durr al-Majālis*, is unhappy with Muḥammad's interaction with Māriya.

17 Winstedt, *A History of Classical Malay Literature*, 111.

18 Julian Millie, 'Three Books on the Literary Tradition of West Java', *Bijdragen tot de Taal-, Land-en Volkenkunde/Journal of the Humanities and Social Sciences of Southeast Asia* 160/2 (2004): 416–423.

Hamza, where 'Ali was hit in the leg by an arrow, and Muḥammad himself lost two teeth'.[19] Another Malay story talking about the teeth of Muḥammad is *Hikayat Lahad*, in which Muḥammad's tooth 'was hit by a stone thrown at him by an enemy'.[20] These episodes are found in chapter nine of *Durr al-Majālis*. However, the most direct Malay version is an anonymous treatise on the loss of Prophet Muḥammad's teeth, which is compatible with the first part of the chapter nine. According to Liaw,

> One night while Aisyah was sewing, she dropped her needle on her bed. She looked for the needle but could not find it. The Prophet Muhammad entered the room, and his teeth were so white that they shone a light on the missing needle, revealing where it had fallen. Muhammad, thought, 'What excellent teeth I have!' Immediately, two of his teeth broke.[21]

The way the needle of ʿĀʾisha was lost and Muḥammad lost his teeth due to being proud of his teeth is clearly based on the following episode of *Durr al-Majālis*.

> در حجرهٔ عایشه رضی‌الله‌عنها چراغ نبود و عایشه را پیراهن پاره شده بود و پیراهن را می دوخت. ناگاه سوزن در پیراهن گم شد و هر چه طلب کرد نیافت. چون پیغمبر ﷺ نزدیک خود دید در خاطرش گذشت که مبادا سوزن به اندام پیغمبر ﷺ رسد. در تجسّس و تفحّص سوزن مضطرب بود. رسول علیه‌السلام پرسید «یا عایشه، دل تو نگران است. در پیراهن خود چه می‌طلبی؟» گفت: «یا رسول الله، پیراهن من پاره شده بود وآن را می‌دوختم. سوزن گم شد. خوف می‌کنم که مبادا به اندام مبارک شما رسد. هرچند می جویم نیابم!» حضرت پیغمبر ﷺ در تبسّم شدند. چو لبها از یکدیگر گشاده شد نوری از دندان مبارک ایشان پیدا شد که تمام حجره منوّر گردید. سوزن را در روشنی آن نور یافت. پیغمبر علیه‌السلام رو به عایشه کرد و گفت: «دیدی روشنی دندان مرا». این سخن پیغمبر در نزد حقّ تعالی عزّوجلّ پسندیده نیفتاد. جبرئیل علیه‌السلام رسید و گفت: «یا محمّد، خدای تعالی می فرماید که «نظر به دندان خود کردی امّا نگفتی که دندان تو را که آفریده است؟ تا روز انصاف این سخن از دندان تو بستانم»».

In the Malay version of the *Wafāt-nāma* (Death Tale) of Muḥammad, it is indicated that 'the Prophet told his family that he would die, bidding them not to beat their breasts or tear their hair, as this was sinful'.[22] This episode is found in chapter four of *Durr al-Majālis* which addressed the death of Moses. Moreover, similarities between the Malay *Hikayat Nabi dan Iblis* (The Tale of the Prophet and Satan) and various episodes of *Durr al-Majālis* in general, and its chapter twenty-three dedicated to Satan in particular, are found.

[19] Liaw, 252. [20] Ibid., 253. [21] Ibid., 252. [22] Winstedt, 105.

Power and Poverty

The stories about material and spiritual poverty versus material richness are parts of both Persian and Malay Islamic stories. A number of Malay *hikayat* revolve around the poverty of ʿAlī and Fāṭima: *Hikayat Ali Kawin dengan Fatimah* (The Tale of the Marriage Ceremony of ʿAlī and Fāṭima), parts of the Malay *Hikayat Sultan Ibrahim* [*Adham*], and *Hikayat Nabi dan Orang Miskin* (The Tale of the Prophet and a Poor Man); their narrations are identified in *Durr al-Majālis*, particularly in chapter eleven on the Story of ʿAlī and Fāṭima.[23]

Further stories dealing with generosity and parsimony in *Durr al-Majālis* are found in *Hikayat Nabi dan Orang Miskin* and parts of the Malay *Bayan Budiman* or *Ṭūṭī-nāma* (Tale of the Parrot). Interestingly, some parts of the *Bayan Budiman*, whose 'counterparts' are not identified in the Persian *Ṭūṭī-nāma*[24] are traceable in *Durr al-Majālis*. The eighteenth chapter of *Bayan Budiman* on 'a husband who gave half of his lifetime to his wife'[25] is comparable with chapter six of *Durr al-Majālis*.

Sufi Saints

A couple of the well-known stories from Islamic literature about Sufi saints and figures can be found in *Durr al-Majālis*. Not only are the names and titles of the stories similar but so too are their contents. We may name the Persian *Story of Sultan Ibrāhīm Adham* whose genre resembles various Malay versions of this figure.[26] Moreover, a well-known story among Malay-Indonesians is *Hikayat Nasiha Lukman al-Hakim*[27] also known as *Hikayat Wasiat Lukman al-Hakim*. Although there are very few manuscript copies of this story available, it would have reached the Malay-speaking world several centuries ago.[28] The manuscript Wall 125[29] of Indonesia presents the fourfold advice or *empat perkara* that Luqmān gives to his son. Such forms of fourfold instructions are outlined in the Persian prototype, being the sixteenth chapter of *Durr al-Majālis*. Further, the stories of saints like Ḥasan al-Baṣrī (known as Bosri in some Malay materials), Sufyān

[23] Edwin Wieringa, 'Does Traditional Islamic Malay Literature Contain Shi 'itic Elements? 'Ali and Fātimah in Malay Hikayat Literature', *Studia Islamika* 3/4 (1996): 93–111 [103–104].

[24] Bragisnky, 418–419. [25] Ibid, and Liaw, 288 [26] Russell Jones has paid a particular attention to various short and long version of the *Hikayat Sultan Ibrahim ibn Adham*.

[27] In the Wall Collection N. 125 it is written as نصيح لقمان [28] Liaw, 333–334. [29] It refers to the collection of Hermann von de Wall (d. 1873). Regarding this collection, see T. E. Behrend (ed.) *Perpustakaan Nasional Republik Indonesia*. Jakarta: Yayasan Obor Indonesia & EFEO. (Katalog induk naskah-naskah Nusantara; Jil.4, 1998).

Thawrī, Ḥasan Nūrī, and Shaykh Barsīsā, are among the Persian chapters of *Durr al-Majālis* whose content are somehow found in Malay versions.

CLOSE SIMILARITIES

The greatest similarities with *Durr al-Majālis* in Malay literature can be found in *Hikayat Bulan Berbelah*, *Hikayat Muhammad Hanafiyya*, *Hikayat Musa Munajat*, *Hikayat Raja Jumjuma*, and the *Nūr-nāma* of Muḥammad. It is to these well-known tales that I now turn.

Hikayat Bulan Berbelah

The *Hikayat Bulan Berbelah* (The Tale of Splitting the Moon) is taken fully from the seventh chapter of the Persian *Durr al-Majālis*, which was widely circulated and reproduced in various Indian regions. This story is based on Qurʾān 54:1–2 by which it has been understood that Muḥammad split the Moon in half. Although some exegetical sources deem that act has not yet happened but would rather be something to occur in the future, the Qurʾānic verses have influenced how Muslims have remembered Muḥammad encountering the unbelievers of his time. Traces of this story are found in hagiographical works, commentaries on the Qurʾān, and traditional and prophetic biographical sources. A very short account of this miracle is found in the *ḥadīth* collections of al-Bukhārī, al-Tirmidhī, al-Muslim, and al-Nasāʾī.[30]

A manuscript in the Parliamentary Library of Iran, Ms.13674, includes the story of Muḥammad splitting the Moon, among others, in both Persian and Arabic. The Persian story is quite short, not more than 'a brief note on the story of splitting the Moon' (fl. 76). The manuscript was once possessed by the famous Persian poet and thinker Muḥammad Taqī Bahār (d. 1951) and includes a note that says 'on the basis of Bahār's examinations this is a unique manuscript'. Similarities between this concise Persian version and that given in *Durr al-Majālis* suggests that it may even have been a source for Sayf Ẓafar. The Arabic version in Ms.13674 (fl. 79) is clearly taken from the famous sixth/twelfth century Shīʿī exegetical work *Tafsīr Majmaʿ al-Bayān* by al-Ṭabrisī. However, none of the sources presents a story-like version of this narration without addressing references or naming the chain of reporters. The only exception, to my knowledge, would be that of *Durr al-Majālis* through which one may read the work

[30] Ismail Hamid, *The Malay Islāmic Ḥikāyat*, 172.

as an eloquent and rather long story without allusions to former Muslim traditional sources and accounts. The Malay version, according to Winstedt, would probably have come to the Archipelago around the early period of its Islamisation, although some contend that it is a twelfth/eighteenth-century importation to the Malay-Indonesian regions. But Braginsky points out that 'we do not know the exact date of composition of its Malay version'.[31]

Apart from being widely known as the *Hikayat Bulan Berbelah* in Malay, it is also variously named as *Hikayat Mujizat Nabi* (The Tale of the Prophet's Miracle), *Hikayat Bulan Belah Dua* (The Tale of the Split Moon), and *Hikayat Rasul Allah Memenggal Bulan* (The Tale of the Prophet's Splitting of the Moon).[32] In the Persian version of *Durr al-Majālis* the story appears in the chapter on the virtues of the Prophet as the Prophet's ability to convert non-Muslims to Islam by this miracle. Figures common to both the Persian and Malay versions are Muḥammad, Abū Jahl, the ruler of Mecca named Ḥabīb b. Mālik, also known as Janu Malik (in Malay copies), and his daughter who was born without hands and legs, and Abū Bakr.

Both the Persian and Malay versions begin with the story of the conversion of Muḥammad's Companions to Islam. However, the differences between the Persian and Malay versions are noticed when a few names in the Malay version are omitted. Where in the Persian copies the name of Abū Bakr is mentioned as the first one accepting the religion of Muḥammad – except in the Leiden copy (Ms Or.565) where the name of Abū Bakr is intentionally replaced with the name of ᶜAlī – the Malay copies note 'all his Companions' (*segala sahabat-nya*) learned the profession of faith (*syahadat atau kalima*).[33]

Abū Jahl, the enemy of Muḥammad, is determined to ruin Muḥammad's prophetic mission. As such, his purpose is to find someone who can defeat Muḥammad. Here, a distinct difference is found between the Persian and Malay copies. In almost every Persian copy Abū Jahl first approaches ᶜUmar, who is not yet Muslim, to assassinate Muḥammad. Unsuccessful, Abū Jahl next approaches the ruler of Mecca. The Malay version omits the episode dealing with ᶜUmar and his temptation to kill Muḥammad and the process of his conversion to Islam. Two more obvious omissions lead me to assume that the Malay story was edited so as to 'tone down' the sectarian element of the story. In line with the initial part of the work which replaces the name of 'Abū Bakr' and 'ᶜAlī' with 'Companions' as the first converts to Islam, the rest of the Malay story – contrary to the Persian prototype – removes the focus on the name of Abū Bakr and pays special attention to ᶜAlī as the hero. Some copies of *Durr al-Majalis*[34]

[31] Braginsky, 604. [32] Winstedt 100–103; also, see, Witkam, *Inventory of the Oriental Manuscripts of the Library of the University of Leiden*, II: 219 (Or.1691); Liaw, 218–219 [33] Wall.No.96, fl. 1.

[34] as well as Ms.13674 of the Parliamentary Library of Iran

includes an additional paragraph at the end of the Moon splitting story about the pregnancy of Khadīja by Muḥammad, of a girl who is introduced as the intercessor of the women of the worlds by the angel Gabriel.

Apart from a few instances, then, the rest of the Moon splitting story is largely similar in both its Persian and Malay versions. In both versions Muḥammad is the one who is claimed before his enemies to be the Prophet of the end times.

in Persian[...] شما میگویید «من پیغمبر آخر زمان مانم» [...]
in Jawi and romanised Malay مقتاکن ديري نبي اخرالزمان
mengatakan diri Nabi Akhir al-zaman

The ruler of Mecca wanted to ascertain the accuracy of Muḥammad's claim. He raises some fundamental theological questions about the miracles of former prophets. A list of miracles performed by Abraham, Moses, and Jesus is presented in both Persian and Malay copies: 'Abraham escaped unscathed from Nimrod's fire, Moses used his shape shifting staff, and Jesus brought people back to life' (see table 1.). However, the names of other Prophets, including Noah, David, and Solomon and their miracles are only found in the Malay version.

The episode about the ruler of Mecca's disabled daughter who is cured by Muḥammad is identical in both versions. The process of performing the miracle based on the request of the ruler and ordering the Moon to be split, is quite similar in Persian and Malay. Even references to making ablution and performing a two-unit (*rakʿa*) prayer is similar in both the Persian and Malay versions.

In the Persian version Muḥammad is first asked to order the sky to be dark: "the Sun sets and the Moon rises", which is identical in Malay version:

درڤد ايت مک متهاري فون ماسق مک بولن فون تربتله
Daripada itu maka matahari pun masuk maka bulan pun terbitlah

Apart from being split and moving towards the orient and occident of the Universe, the Moon's halves are supposed to be united and separated again and again and "then circumambulate around the Kaʿba seven times":

In Persian: ماه هفت کرّت طواف کعبه کرد
In Jawi and romanised Malay: بولن ايت برکليڠ توجه کل مڠليلڠ کفد کعبة الله
Bulan itu berkali yang (berkeliling) tujuh kali menggaliyang (menggeliling/mengelingi) kepada Ka'batullah

Persian	Malay	Theme of the Miracles
معجزهٔ ابراهیم عليه السلام آن بود که نمرود از بهر عقوبت او هفتاد فرسنگ زمین آتشی افکند. ابراهیم را آن آتش بر وی گلستان شد	ابراهیم تتکال دماسکن اوله نمرد کدالم اقی تیاده هاغوس ایتله تنداڽ [...]	Abraham escaped unscathed from Nimrod's fire
ومعجزهٔ موسی عليه السلام آن بود که عصائی داشت اژدها می شد	نبی الله موسی تتکال ممبوغکن توغکت مک منجدي الر [...] ایتله اکن [...]	Moses used his shape shifting staff
و معجزهٔ عیسی عليه السلام آن بود که مردهٔ چهارصد پانصد ساله را زنده کردی	[...] نبي الله عیسی ایت اورڠ يڠ مات بوله دباؤن برکت ٢ داغن دي ایتله اکن تندا معجزتڽ [...]	Jesus brought people back to life

Table 1. Theme of Prophetic Miracles according to the Persian and Malay versions of 'the Tale of Splitting the Moon'.

Finally, the miracle seems sufficient in the eyes of the ruler of Mecca. He then becomes a Muslim and embraces the religion of Muḥammad.[35] The theme and the lesson of the story is similar in both Persian and Malay copies; both demonstrating (a) the proofs of Muḥammad's prophecy, while being associated with his Companions against Abū Jahl and suchlike; and (b) Muḥammad's extraordinary capability granted by God to perform physical miracles like Moses and Jesus to convert non-Muslims to Islam. Presenting the lessons about conversion to Islam and defeating Muslim enemies allow researchers to speculate that this story should have arrived in the Malay-Indonesian world during its early phase of Islamisation, when a large number of residents were still non-Muslims. However, given the particular emphasis of the story on the role of ʿAlī, as the hero and saviour of Muḥammad and Abū Bakr, from being killed by Meccan enemies, Winstedt and Baried concluded that *Hikayat Bulan Berbelah* is a Shīʿī story.[36] This is also apparent from the end part of the shorter Persian

35 Although in some versions, another extra episode is mentioned that the ruler is not convinced and begins a war with Muḥammad. Also, see Liaw.

36 See my former discussion above.

version in Ms.13674, which includes verses (*rubāʿī*) by the scribe dedicated to the twelve Imams of the Shīʿa (fl. 79).

Hikayat Muḥammad Ḥanafiyya

Another story which has been fully taken from *Durr al-Majālis* is *Hikayat Muhammad Hanafiyya*.[37] It is usually a two or three part story beginning with (a) the killing of Ḥasan and Ḥusyan by Yazīd the son of Muʿāwiya the founder of the Ummayyad dynasty, and (b) turns to become a revenge tale in the second part in which Muḥammad al-Ḥanafiyya (also known as Muḥammad Ḥanīfa in some Persian and South - and Southeast Asian sources), the half-brother of Ḥasan and Ḥusayn, emerges as the saviour of the household of Muḥammad and of the oppressed. Muḥammad Ḥanafiyya is present as an Imam and a political leader who is not seeking worldly power but wishes to ease the suffering of the family of the Prophet and to free those members captured by Yazīd; (c) the third part in some Malay copies is the *Nūr-nāma* of Muḥammad. There are different Persian stories about Muḥammad Ḥanafiyya, each one surviving in both prose and verse. The version in *Durr al-Majālis* is one of the most popular and revolves around the messianic aspects of Muḥammad Ḥanafiyya, whose importance becomes apparent through his strategy towards, and attack against, the army of Yazīd. Another story about Muḥammad Ḥanafiyya pertains to his birth from a Roman princess. She is named Ḥanīfa Bānū, the daughter of a Roman emperor who is brought by ʿAlī. Upon seeing Ḥanīfa Bānū, Muḥammad asks her to convert to Islam. Then, she states that she would accept becoming a Muslim subject to three conditions.

> My first request is that upon my conversion to Islam you then marry me with ʿAlī; second that you tell your daughter Fāṭima, peace be upon her, to respect me and consider me as her sister and serve me properly; and third that if I got a son from ʿAlī, you name him [also] Muḥammad.[38]

Several versions of this particular story are kept in various libraries. The battles in which ʿAlī engaged are depicted along with the battles in which Muḥammad Ḥanafiyya

[37] The main parts of the analysis of the *Hikayat Muhammad Hanafiyya* in this section are based on my earlier article published with the *Archipel Journal* in 2018. The permission has kindly been granted by the respected journal.

[38] Fl. 45, Ms. 17641 in the Parliamentary Library of Iran.

engaged, the latter always introducing himself as the son of the brave ʿAlī and the one who carries the name of the Prophet.[39]

منم ابن حیدر محمّد بنام؛ وصیّ محمّد علیه‌السلام

I am the son of Ḥaydar (ʿAlī) carrying the name of Muḥammad;
[I am]the Successor of Muḥammad peace be upon him.

Another story, having commonalities with the previous one, emphasises the chivalry of Muḥammad Ḥanafiyya and his connection with Amīr Ḥamza. His brothers, the 'princes' (*shāhzadigān*) Ḥasan and Ḥusayn would like to accompany him hunting in the desert, but they first need to take permission from their father. ʿAlī is confident that they will all be safe as long as they are with the 'king' (*sulṭān*) Muḥammad Ḥanafiyya'. Then the story continues with Muḥammad Ḥanafiyya, his brothers, Mālik Azhdar (not Ashtar), and their confrontations with disbelievers.[40]

Lastly, there is a story about Muḥammad Ḥanafiyya, perhaps influenced by Firdawsī's *Shāhnāma*, which deals with his interaction with Zīfnūn (also, Zīghnūn/Zīghanūn), the daughter of the King of Iram, who was a valliant woman always ready to fight in battle. Muḥammad Ḥanafiyya and Zīfnūn fall in love and are met with a number of challenges that test their love. In this story Zīfnūn is called *bībī* and is the lady of the era and the matron of the epoch. As with the first of the Muḥammad Ḥanafiyya stories mentioned above, this version is also styled as a battle tale, such as the *Jangnāma Muḥammad Ḥanafiyya*, *Jangnāma-yi ʿAlī*, and *Jang-nāma-yi ʿAlī va Muḥammad Ḥanafiyya*.[41]

All these stories were circulated in South Asia and Eastern Turkistan. All of them show Muḥammad Ḥanafiyya as the chivalrous figure trained in the circles of Muḥammad and ʿAlī and who grew up with Ḥasan and Ḥusayn and their companions. He is always able to defeat the enemies in whichever form they appear, whether inside or outside of Muslim territories. We might imagine, from reading into a report in the *Sejarah Melayu*, that any one of these tales concerning Muḥammad Ḥanafiyya could have been read by Malay warriors in Malacca in 1515 before confrontation with their

[39] Referring to fl. 29, the manuscript 21045 of the Parliamentary Library of Iran. This story which pays a lot of attention to ʿAlī and fictional figures and enemies seems to be related to the Malay *Hikayat Raja Khandaq* which will be the subject of future studies.

[40] This is based on the manuscript 1327 of the National Library of Iran.

[41] I have examined the manuscript 5–9337 in the National Library of Iran. This copy is accompanied with another treatise about Sultan Ibrāhīm Adham.

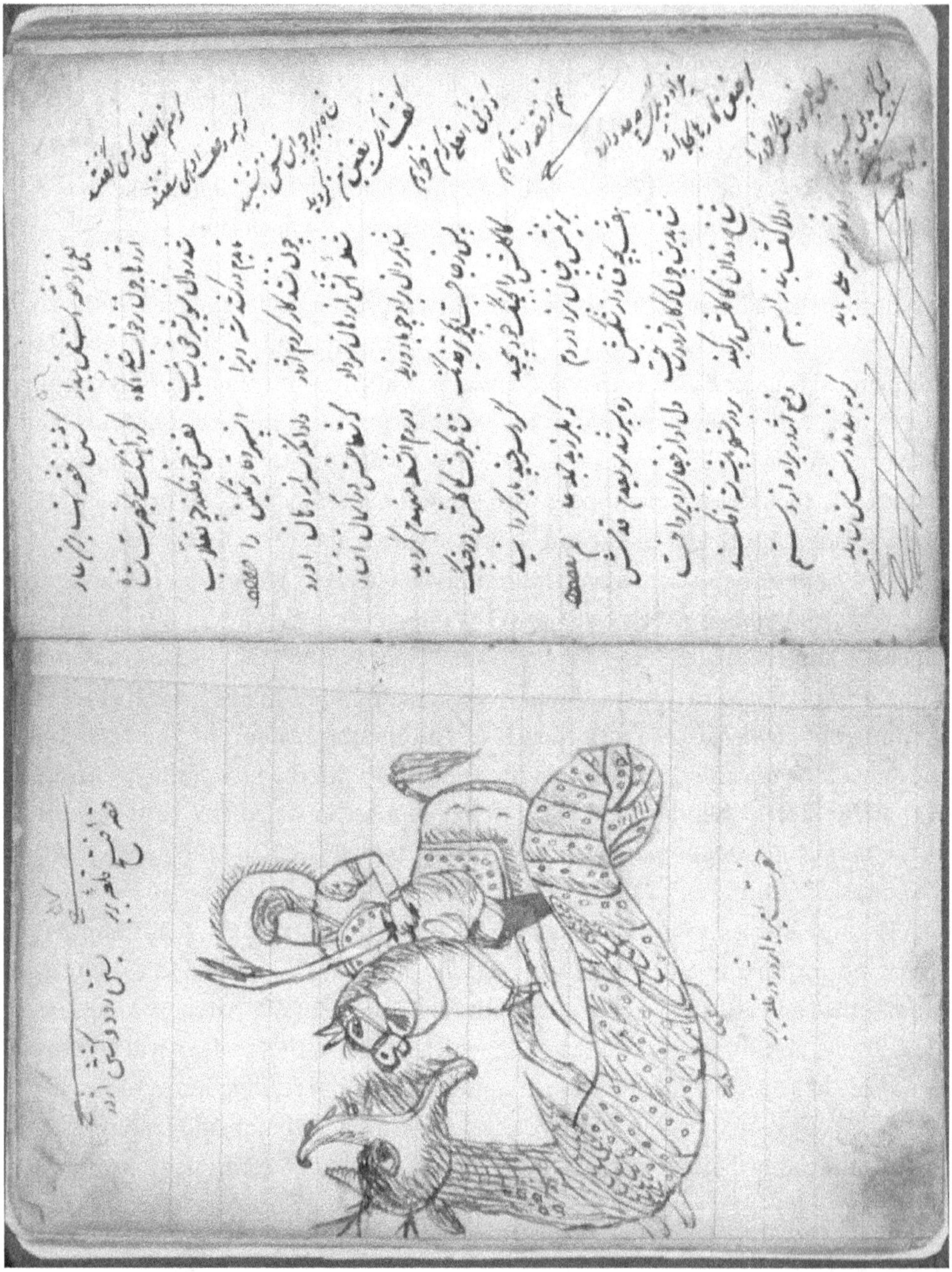

Figure 4. Pp.56-57. MS. 21045. A versified chivalrous account of ʿAlī, as part of the *Jang-nāma-yi Muḥammad Ḥanafiyya*. Courtesy of the Parliamentary Library of Iran, Tehran, Iran.

enemies.[42] Although the *Sejarah Melayu* is not explicit about this, given that the only Malay story known to have survived is the one dealing with the rise of Muḥammad Ḥanafiyya after the death of Ḥasan and Ḥusayn, we may conclude that the story which was read by the warriors was from *Durr al-Majālis*, in which he is displayed as an immortal Imam, a terminator, saviour, and guardian.[43]

As mentioned earlier, some Malay copies of *Durr al-Majālis* are accompanied by the *Nūr-nāma* of Muḥammad. Van Ronkel, Winstedt, and Brakel have already mentioned that this was originally based on a Persian prototype. The Persian manuscript that was available to them was a copy of the *Story of Muḥammad Ḥanafiyya* (Add.8149) kept in the British Museum (now in the British Library), which was copied in Bengal in the early eighteenth century. Brakel's full analysis of the Malay story in the light of the Persian Add.8149 – which had a tremendous impact on the history of Islam in Southeast Asia – provides us with a philological and historical analysis of the text by which we may be assured about the Persian origin of this Malay story. *Hikayat Muhammad Hanafiyya* has a particular status in the history of Malay-Indonesia, as it gives us first-hand information – as I explained earlier – about the popularity of this story among Malays before the tenth/sixteenth century and the Portuguese siege of Malacca. As such, the more one learns about the origin of this story, the more clues there are about the essential role of foreign Islamised materials in the region. Nonetheless, there were some episodes in the Malay *Hikayat Muhammad Hanafiyya* whose parallel Brakel and Braginsky, among others, were not able to find in Add.8149. Such ambiguities about the origin of a number of episodes as well as the whole story led some scholars, including Marcinkowski, to consider it as a work with an 'anonymous' and 'unknown' author.[44] However, as I have argued elsewhere,[45] I suggest that the story of *Hikayat Muhammad Hanafiyya* is actually taken from chapter thirty-one of *Durr al-Majālis*. This observation is made all the more clear upon examination of Add.8194 which shows that the story is actually taken from the longer version of *Hikayat Muhammad Hanafiyya* in *Durr al-Majālis* which is found in the eleventh/seventeenth century McGill copy, the twelfth/eighteenth century Ganjbaksh copy, and the thirteenth/nineteenth century Auckland copy. In this regard, Charles P. H. Rieu (d. 1902) was correct to note that Add.8194 could have been part of another collection,

[42] See my former discussion in part one. [43] Braginsky demonstrated that this story reached the Malay Archipelago through the Turkic communities of Central and South Asia since the seventh/thirteenth century. Vladimir Braginsky, *The Turkic-Turkish Theme in Traditional Malay Literature: Imagining the Other to Empower the Self* (Leiden: Brill, 2015). [44] Marcinkowski, From Isfahan to Ayutthaya, 13. [45] Majid Daneshgar, "New evidence on the origin of the Hikayat Muhammad Hanafiyyah," *Archipel. Études interdisciplinaires sur le monde insulindien* 96 (2018): 69–102.

'[...] [The] stories are apparently detached portions of a late composition exhibiting the Shiʿah legend in its most exuberant growth.'[46]

The point which deserves to be considered here is that the available copies of Sayf Ẓafar's *Durr al-Majālis* present two versions of the stories of Ḥasan and Ḥusayn. The first one is shorter, beginning with the death of Muʿāwiya and highlights the significance of Ḥasan and Ḥusayn, and their 'martyrdom' by the Ummayds. While in the second and larger version, the story begins with Muḥammad, caliphs, then the childhood of Ḥasan and Ḥusayn, their marriage, Ḥasan's interest in polygamy and divorcing, the killing of Ḥasan and Ḥusayn, and the emergence of Muḥammad Ḥanafiyya, and his defeat of Yazīd and installing the sons of Ḥusayn on ruling seats, without being dead, injured, or hurt...Muḥammad Ḥanafiyya is displayed as an immortal Imam. This form of ending is clearly found in Malay versions. In MS Malay B 6 (f. 93v) and MS Malay D 5 (f. 49v), both preserved in the British Library, Muḥammad Ḥanafiyya is said to have been from Bunīra which, according to Snouck Hurgronje, is 'a subdivision of the Kingdom of Medina'.[47] According to him, Muḥammad Ḥanafiyya of Bunīra was able to kill Yadib (Yazīd). Then, 'a small remnant of Yadib's followers took refuge in a cave. At this moment the cave closed of its own accord, and the holy man and his horse are still there, awaiting patiently the day appointed for their resurrection'.[48]

Apart from the immortality of Muḥammad Ḥanafiyya in both Persian and Malay stories, his popularity led Muslims to indigenise him for the sake of their own literature and history. When Hurgronje refers to his residence in Bunīra he does not provide any reference. We are almost sure that Bunīra is not identified as either a subdivision of Medina or the residence of Muḥammad Ḥanafiyya. Likewise, the earliest Islamic historical sources, such as Aḥmad b. Yaḥyā al-Balādhurī (d. c. 279/892 CE), do not have Bunīra as either a neighbourhood of Medina or Muḥammad Ḥanafiyya's place of residence. In his *Ansāb al-Ashrāf* (Genealogies of the Nobles), al-Balādhurī opens up new sections dealing with Muḥammad Ḥanafiyya after the story of the killing of Ḥusayn (*maqtal al-Ḥusayn b. ʿAlī*). In these sections, which also include references from Muḥammad b. ʿUmar al-Wāqidī (d. c. 823 CE), a well-known early Arab historian, the main regions related to Muḥammad Ḥanafiyya are Medina, which is also his place of death, and al-Baqīʿ, where his grave is located.[49] Nonetheless, there is a place in Medina called al-Buwayra that, according to Lecker, is related to the 'Jewish

[46] Charles Rieu, *Catalogue of the Persian Manuscripts in the British Museum* (London: The British Museum, 1881), II: 819. [47] C. Snouck Hurgronje, De Atjehers, Leiden & Batavia, E. J. Brill & Landsdrukkerij, 1894, vol. 2, p. 180. [48] Ibid. [49] See, al-Balādhurī, *Kitāb Jumal min Ansāb al-Ashrāf* (Beirut: Dār al-Fikr, n.d.) III: 395–487.

Naḍīr'.[50] Apart from the obvious difference between the orthography of al-Buwayra and Bunīra, a map of the markets of Medina on the eve of Islam created by Lecker as well as the reference by ʿAlī b. Aḥmad al-Samhūdī's (d. c.1505) *Wafāʾ al-Wafāʾ* to the house of Muḥammad Ḥanafiyya clearly demonstrate that he was living near 'Baqīʿ al-Gharqad, the cemetery of Medina', close to the Prophet's mosque, and far from al-Buwayra.[51]

However, we should bear in mind that the name of Muḥammad Ḥanafiyya's residence figures prominently in part two of the story, which, according to Brakel, is purely legendary. Thus, it is highly likely that its name will not be found in any historical or traditional sources of Islam. Instead, more attention should be paid to how his residence is introduced in other versions of this story, in different languages. Islamic epics present a lion-hearted and chivalric image of Muḥammad Ḥanafiyya (see above), who is displayed as the bravest of his age as well as a messiah. Traces of stories (Persian: *Qiṣaṣ wa ḥikāyāt*) dedicated to him can be found in various corners of western Asia, particularly in the Middle East, in places such as Kharg Island, in Bushehr province or Guilan, Iran, where a tomb ascribed to him (*Buqʿa-yi Mīr Muḥammad-i Ḥanafiyya* and *Imāmzāda-yi Muḥammad-i Ḥanafiyya*, respectively) is located. It is said that sailors from South Asia used to visit his tomb on Kharg Island in the Persian Gulf as well. The messianic facet of Muḥammad Ḥanafiyya has been underscored for many years in the Bamyan Valley of northern Afghanistan, where an area is dedicated to the 'dragon slayer' ʿAlī.[52] Local people believe that Emir (*Shahzāda*) Ḥanafiyya, the son of ʿAlī, is waiting in an underground passageway to reappear and will fight for peace, along with his horse and his beloved wife, Bībī Ḥanīfa.[53] Indeed, the legends of this region present Muḥammad Ḥanafiyya as the awaited *mahdī*, akin to a central tenet of Twelver Shiʿīsm. Calling Muḥammad Ḥanafiyya the *mahdī* 'was initiated by some Shīʿī groups which claimed that he had not died but was only hiding in mountains and which expected his immanent second coming.[54]

Following Marc Gaborieau, Calmard says:

> the cult and legendary accounts of Muḥammad b. Ḥanafiyya seem to have penetrated

[50] Michael Lecker, 'On the Markets of Medina (Yathrib) in Pre-Islamic and Early Islamic Times', *Jerusalem Studies in Arabic and Islam* 8 (1986), 133–147.

[51] Thanks to Michael Lecker for drawing my attention to this point.

[52] Jean Calmard, 'Mohammad b. al-Hanafiyya dans la religion populaire, le folklore, les légendes dans le monde turco-persan et indo-persan', *Cahiers d'Asie centrale* 5/6 (1998): 201–220.

[53] Ibid.

[54] The followers of the Kaysāniyya took Muḥammad b. Ḥanafiyya as their Imam and believed that he was alive but hidden in the mountains of Raḍwā, near Medina. See, W. Madelung, 'Kuraybiyya', *Encyclopaedia of Islam*, 2nd ed., ed. P. Bearman et al. (Leiden: Brill, 1979) V: 433–434. Braginsky 2004, 181.

> into India following the Ghaznawid expedition in the Panjab. A legend centred on Ghāzī Miyān (identified as a certain Sālār Masʿūd, a nephew of Maḥmūd of Ghazna) became very popular in Northern India. Ghāzī Miyān becomes a sort of avatar of the 'twin' brothers Ḥasan and Ḥusayn. Muḥammad Ḥanafiyya (or rather Ḥanīfah or Ḥanīf or Ḥambiya Muḥammad) appears as avenging his brothers killed by a Hindu raja.[55]

Perhaps, unsurprisingly, every author or copyist of the saga of Muḥammad Ḥanafiyya tried to present the hero according to local preferences, for example, as a South Asian, Indian, or Malay Muslim. So, for example, in the Auckland copy of *Durr al-Majālis* when the servant of Ḥusayn leaves Medina in order to inform Muḥammad Ḥanafiyya of the death of his half brother in Karbala, he is said to have travelled for three months in order to reach the city of Bamyan.[56] In the Ganjbakhsh version the servant is said to set off for the city of Banil, which refers to the region of Banil Kalle in Pakhtunkhwa, which had been conquered earlier by the Ghaznawids. The McGill copy introduces Muḥammad Ḥanafiyya's residence as being in the city of Banyaz, which is a district of the Nimruz Province of Afghanistan. More importantly, in the Persian manuscript of the British Library, Add.8149 (a manuscript that has received scholarly attention) the servant travelled to Anbaz(i), a city outside the Arabian Peninsula. These points clearly demonstrate the resemblance of the Malay story of Muḥammad Ḥanafiyya (mainly those introduced by Hurgronje) with those of Central and South Asia, and particularly of the Bamyan valley. Furthermore, another Malay version of this story, Ms.12377, also preserved in the British Library, suggests the residence of Muḥammad Ḥanafiyya was not Bunīra but another city, the name of which is derived from the root letters *b-n-t-y-a-r*.

> *pergi membawa surat kepada saudaranya ke benua b-n-t-y-a-r.*

Whether the name of the city reads as Bentara, Bentiar, or Bentyar, it is appears that the scribe of this version of *Hikayat Muhammad Hanafiyya* did not identify Bunīra as the residence of Muḥammad Ḥanafiyya, instead preferring to indigenise the story as did other scribes and authors before him. It could also be possible that the reference to 'Boeniara' in some Malay copies refers rather to a district in Southeast Asia rather than

[55] Marc Gaborieau, 'Légende et culte du saint musulman Ghâzî Miyân au Népal occidental et en Inde du Nord', *Objets et Mondes* 15/3 (1975) 289–310. Jean Calmard, 'Popular Literature under the Safawids', in *Society and Culture in the Early Modern Middle East: Studies on Iran in the Safawid Period*, edited by Andrew J. Newman, (Leiden & Boston: Brill, 2003), 316–339. [56] Or 'Banyan', which is a title used for Indian merchants who traded between India and the central and southern parts of Persia.

to a neighbourhood in Medina, Arabia. Conversely, perhaps the 'Boeniara' that is in Java derived its name from *Hikayat Muḥammad Ḥanafiyya* and is not an indigenous name.[57]

As the Safawids (r. 907–1148/1501–1736) established the Twelver Shīʿī school of Islam as the religion of their empire, storytellers tended or were compelled to produce more works that would decrease and marginalise the messianic and leadership significance of Muḥammad Ḥanafiyya more systematically – This is also evident through the manuscript No.1222 which is our oldest known copy produced in the ninth/fifteenth century. On the other hand, Sunni communities aimed to confront the Safawids' elevation of the household of Muḥammad in general, and Ḥasan and Ḥusayn in particular, by placing them along with their Sunni Imams and leaders. Thus, various forms of stories about Karbala or chivalrous aspects of Muḥammad's grandsons and his Companions were produced in different Shīʿī and Sunni contexts, in which the importance of Muḥammad Ḥanafiyya is understated. For instance, the Shīʿīs paid a lot of attention to [re]producing or revising older 'Epico-religious' texts such as the *Junayd-nāma*, and *Mukhtār-nāma*, among others, in which Muḥammad Ḥanafiyya is just a warrior while Zayn al-ʿĀbidīn instead is the main figure of the story, one who is presented as the only Imām of his age, the one who, according to the Safawids, can transfer the genes of ʿAlī and Fāṭima to the next Shīʿa Imām.[58] As such, we may say that the more comprehensive version of the story of Muḥammad Ḥanafiyya reached the Malay-Indonesian world through the Indian subcontinent or Central Asia – and not from Safawid Persia – owing to narratives about the immortality and chivalry of Ḥanafiyya still being acceptable to the Muslim communities in these regions during the tenth/sixteenth century and onwards.

The number of similarities between our Persian prototype and the Malay copy are numerous. I present a number of these similarities below so as to give readers a better idea about the textual relationship between the Persian and the Malay versions. In both copies, the story begins with Muḥammad, and then gradually is connected to his grandsons, Ḥasan and Ḥusayn, imparting to the reader an idea about the blood-connection between Muḥammad and his grandsons.[59] This close relationship is outlined on different occasions in the story. For example, an episode deals with the interest of Ḥasan and Ḥusayn in the fruits brought to them by Diḥyah al-Kalbī, also seen in both the Persian and Malay texts.

In Persian,

[57] Personal communication with Edwin Wieringa on 30 January 2018.

[58] Calmard, 'Popular Literature under the Safawids', 316–339.

[59] Thanks to David S. Powers for drawing my attention to this point.

رسول ﷺ گفت[...] هربار که دهیه قلبی\وحیة کلبی بر من می آید بجهت این چیزی می‌آرد

In Jawi and romanised Malay,

مک سبد رسول الله تونهمب این دسقکن حیاة الکلبی درفد قوم نبی...بارغکالی داتغ اداله سسواة بوه ۲ هن دباوان اکن حسن دان حسین

Maka sabda Rasul Allah tuan hamba ini disangyanka Hayat al-Kalbi dari pada qaum nabi...barang kali ia dating adalah suatu buah-buahan dibawanya akan Hasan dan Husayn[60]

English Translation,

The Messenger of God said that whenever Diḥyah al-Kalbī comes, he brings something [viz., fruits] for Ḥasan and Ḥusayn.

It should be noted that Diḥyah al-Kalbī's name is misspelt in the Persian texts and in the Malay version. Gabriel then brings them heavenly fruit – only a pomegranate (*anār*) in the Persian version but both a pomegranate (*delima*) and a grape (*anggur*) in the Malay. There are also references to Ḥasan and Ḥusayn's demand for a special garment. Ḥasan received a green one, symbolising his death with poison, while Ḥusayn had the blood red one, symbolising his murder in Karbala.

In Persian,

جامۀ سبز بیرون آورده به «حسن» دادند [...] جامۀ سرخ بیرون آورده به «حسین» دادند.

In Jawi and romanised Malay,

مک دامبل اوله حسن فکاین یغ هیجو[...]کمدین مک دامبل اوله حسین فکاین یغ میره[...]

Maka diambil oleh Hasan pakayan yang hijau [...] kemudian maka diambil oleh Husayn pakayan yang merah

English Translation,

The green garment was given to Ḥasan, then the red one was given to Ḥusayn.

60 Also, Brakel.

In another episode, the Malay story includes an account about an angel whose wing was burnt due to ignoring God's order. Upon the intervention of Gabriel, who requested that Ḥasan and Ḥusayn place their hands upon the injury of the angel, the angel was healed and flew away. This episode is clearly found in the Persian prototype – although in the majority of available Persian copies, only the hand of Ḥusayn touches the angel's wing. Upon seeing the injured wing of the angel, Muḥammad asked Gabriel for the reason.

In Persian,

پیغمبر علیه السلام پرسید که «ای برادر جبرئیل، حکمت چیست که آن فرشته را در بازوی خود نشانده آورده ای؟» جبرئیل گفت «یا نبیّ الله، این فرشته در جمیع عمر خود یک بار در فرمان خدای تعالی تقصیر کرده. از شومی آن گناه هر دو بازوی این فرشته سوخته گشته. اکنون از خدای تعالی التماس کرده است که «مرا نزدیک پیغمبر خدای بوبرید» تا تو را مبارک باد کند و مرا فرمان شده است که «او را نزدیک محمّد ببر و بگو که هر دو دست حسین بر هر دو بازوی فرشته نهد، نیکو شود»». پیغمبر علیه السلام هر دو دست امیرالمؤمنین حسین را بر هر دو بازوی وی فرود آورد. هر دو بازوی فرشته نیکو شد و در زمان این فرشته در هوا پرید.

In Malay,

[M]aka bertanya nabi Allah: 'Hay saudaraku Jibrail! Malaikat mana?' Maka kata Jibrail: 'Ya nabi Allah! Malaikat inilah yang taksir pada berbuat bakti kepada Allah ta'ala! Daripada sebab inilah sayapnya tertunu!' Adapun sekarang hendaklah tangan amir Hasan dan amir Husain disapukan kepada bahu malaikat itu! Maka nabi Allah menyapukan tangan amir Hasan dan amir Husain kepada bahu malaikat itu. Dengan takdir Allah ta'ala[61] *sayapnya itu baiklah pulang seperti dahulukala, maka malaikat inipun terbanglah keudara.*[62]

Brakel's translation of the Malay phrase,

Hereupon the angel went to the Prophet. He saw that there was an angel, seated on Gabriel's shoulder whose wings had been burnt, which according to Gabriel was due to an act of negligence shown in the service of God. Gabriel requested that the hands of Hasan and Husain rub against the shoulders of the angel. Upon this the wings were healed and the angel flew away. The Envoy, very happy himself, perceived that Gabriel was dispirited. The latter informed him that this angel would only descend to Earth again at the time that amir Husain's head would be separated from his body.[63]

[61] In the Wall. 72, 'Dengan takdir Allah ta'ala' is written as 'Dengan kudrat Rabb al-'Alamin.'

[62] Brakel I: 121.

[63] Brakel II: 3.

In both the Persian and Malay story, not only is Gabriel called a brother by Muḥammad but the term used for the negligence of the stricken angel is also equivalient, that is, *taqṣīr* in Persian and *taksir* (in some texts as *teksir*) *in* Malay. Some of the similarities found in both the shorter and longer Persian versions of the *Killing Story of Ḥasan and Ḥusayn* in *Durr al-Majālis* as compared to the Malay version are listed below. These similarities have also been noted by Brakel.

- Gabriel went to the plain of Karbala and picked up some of its Earth, gave it to the Prophet, and said that when this Earth turns red, the killing of Ḥusayn is close. And the Prophet told his wife Umm Salama to put the Earth into a bottle and keep it.
- Muʿāwiya's unsuccessful attempt not to have intercourse with a woman and 'to remain childless', as per Muḥammad's recommendation, is seen after he was bitten by a scorpion. To be cured, Muʿāwiya is advised by physicians to have intercourse to get rid of the poison. Nonetheless, due to having sexual intercourse with a bondwoman, Yazīd is born from her.
- Yazīd's desire to marry ʿAbdallāh Zubayr's wife who was 'particularly beautiful'.
- Muʿāwiya's offer to ʿAbdallāh Zubayr of his daughter's hand in marriage and the governership of Egypt.
- Muʿāwiya sent Mūsā Ashʿarī to the wife of ʿAbdallāh Zubayr, to propose his son to her. The wife of ʿAbdallāh Zubayr rejected Yazīd and instead accepted Ḥusayn's proposal, who, according to Mūsā Ashʿarī, also desired her.
- Yazīd asks the leader of Medina to kill Ḥasan and Ḥusayn; he replied that he was not capable of fighting openly against Ḥusayn.
- Yazīd persuades Ḥasan's wife to kill him with poison with the promise that he would marry her and make her a ruler. Ḥasan is killed with poisoned water. Before his death, Ḥasan asks Ḥusayn to bury him by the tomb of the Prophet, a request refused by Yazīd. ʿAbdallāh Masʿūd intervenes and does not allow Ḥusayn to attack Yazīd, because Ḥusayn was the only surviving descendant of the Prophet.
- Shamir (Shimr) went forward to behead Ḥusayn; Ḥusayn asked him to show his chest before doing his job. He noticed that Shamir's chest was black and he had the nipples of a dog. Ḥusayn recalled that the Prophet's statement had come true about his killer's physical features.
- Upon the death of Ḥusayn, Muḥammad Jaʿfar Ṣādiq (in Persian versions) or Muḥammad b. Abū Bakr (in Malay versions) stayed in Mecca where he performed the *ṭawāf.* There he saw a masked man who was seeking God's forgiveness as he had wanted to take the jewel on the belt of Ḥusayn's corpse.

When the man cut off both Ḥusayn's hands he heard a voice. Angels washed Ḥusayn's corpse and it became the time for the appearance of Noah, Abraham, Ishmael, Mary, Eve, Sarah, Hagar, and Isaac.

- Angels, along with Adam, Khadīja, Fāṭima, and Mary paid their respects to Ḥusayn's corpse.
- The women in Ḥusayn's army were captured by Yazīd's army.
- A believer in Damascus left the city and saw the women of the Prophet's family having their veils removed. The believer introduced himself as Sāliḥ.
- Muḥammad Ḥanafiyya sent messages to his brothers who were living in various parts of the world.
- Marwān and ʿUtbah b. Walīd come as allies of Yazīd.

Some of these episodes have a special significance. Firstly, the episode about the creation of Yazīd after his father had intercourse with a bondwoman was not identified by Brakel nor Braginsky, as they thought that it might be the innovation of Malay scribes. Nonetheless, it is now clear to what extent the Malay translators and scribes were faithful to the original Persian text of *Durr al-Majālis*. Moreover, after the death of Ḥusayn, both the Persian and Malay versions address a fictional treatise which could be the innovation of Sayf Ẓafar, through which a fellow named [Muḥammad] Jaʿfar Ṣādiq comes across a man with a half-concealed face in Mecca, who used to be the servant of Ḥusayn, but cut Ḥusayn's hands in order to take his jewels. In all available Malay copies, the name of Jaʿfar Ṣādiq is changed to Jaʿfar b. Abū Bakr;[64] a textual alteration leading Brakel and then Wieringa to conclude that the text was de-Shīʿitised by Malay readers. Moreover, this episode about the servant of Ḥusayn was later to become the backbone of another Malay story, entitled *Hikayat Tabut*, which revolves around this servant and his repentance. This fellow is usually called 'Nastal' or 'Nastala', and his repentance would be accepted as long as his descendants continued to commemorate Ḥusayn's death. The Tabut festival is still commemorated in Indonesia and the legend about the servant's conditional forgiveness receive wider assent until the early twentieth century.[65] Moreover, the letters written by Muḥammad Ḥanafiyya to his brothers in the Persian version are sent to Mashīb bi-Kāqah (a misspelling of Musayyib Qaʿqaʿ) in Iraq, one letter to Tughān Turk, the ruler of Tabriz, and one letter he sent to ʿUmar ʿAlī, Ṭālib ʿAlī, and ʿAqīl ʿAlī in Shām. Although slightly

[64] For example, it is written in the manuscript D 5 in the British Library as جعفر ابن ابوبكرنصديق (Ja'far ibn Abubakirini-Siddik) [65] For more about this figure, see: L., Helfrich, W. R. Winter, and D. M. J. Schiff, 'Het Hasan-Hosein of Taboet-feest te Bengkoelen', in *Internationales Archivfür Ethnographie* I (1888), 191–196. Also, Feener, 2015.

different, most of Muḥammad Ḥanafiyya's brothers in the Malay versions resided in the abovementioned geographical regions.

Further to the above list a number of similarities between the Persian and Malay versions of the the *Killing Story of Ḥasan and Ḥusayn* which Brakel was NOT able to find in his Persian prototype, Add.8149, can be discerned.

- Muḥammad is unable to recite but Gabriel instructs him to do so. It is expressed that Gabriel is henceforth as a brother to the Prophet.
- Muḥammad becomes ill; his close companions understand that his death is approaching.
- The death of Fāṭima after seeing her father, Muḥammad, in a dream; how ʿAlī and his sons buried Fāṭima; the Companion's demand for the body; how ʿAlī became furious and put on battle-dress; the Prophet's counselling Abū Bakr that all of mankind was no match for ʿAlī when he donned his battle garb.
- Shahrbānū desired to choose a husband but she rejected Ḥasan on account of him having other wives.
- Tughan Turk and Mughan Turk had set out to intercept the army of the Zanggi.
- A mighty battle between Yazīd and Muḥammad Ḥanafiyya ensues and the fighting became still more violent.

Muḥammad's illiteracy is clearly depicted in the Auckland version of *Durr al-Majālis*, when Ḥasan and Ḥusayn show their handwriting to Muḥammad to check it. Also, throughout the Ganjbakhsh copy, Muḥammad frequently addresses Gabriel as his brother. Although *Durr al-Majālis* talks about the death of Muḥammad, its quality differs from that of *Hikayat Muhammad Hanafiyya*. However, the Auckland copy starts with a Qurʾānic verse about martyrdom: 'And do not say about those who are killed in the way of Allah, "They are dead". Rather, they are alive, but you perceive [it] not'. Later, it talks about the death and/or killing of the Companions and the first four caliphs, whose names and deaths are mentioned in the sixth, ninth, thirteenth, fourteenth, fifteenth, and other chapters of the Malay *Hikayat Muhammad Hanafiyya*, as categorised by Brakel. Nonetheless, different stories about the death of Muḥammad and the Companions' roles are found in other chapters of *Durr al-Majālis*. Although the death of Fāṭima and her funeral are not discussed in this chapter of *Durr al-Majālis*, the story is found in another chapter of it entitled 'On the Story of ʿAlī and Fāṭima'. In this part, Fāṭima first dreamed about her father and then she died. However, interestingly, all the Companions were allowed to carry the coffin of Fāṭima, a point which is mentioned in Brakel's commentary. The only prophetic *ḥadīth* in the Auckland copy regarding ʿAlī relates to his knowledge, which is expressed by Muʿāwiya to his associates. Although *Durr al-Majālis*' chapter does not refer to Ḥasan's interest in Shahrbānū, there are several obvious references to his having more than one wife, which caused one of his wifves to poison him.

Brakel, based on a quote from al-Ranīrī, noticed that only an Acehnese manuscript, Or.8667 at Leiden University Library, mentions Muʿāwiya and Yazīd as fellow Muslims.[66] However, there is a point worth mentioning regarding the Auckland copy of *Durr al-Majālis*: 'when Muʿāwiya learned about the pregnancy of his female bondwoman he wanted her to terminate her pregnancy because Yazīd was cursed, however, the opinion of Sunnis is not to curse Yazīd, and this is the true opinion.' This clearly signifies the father and son as 'fellow Muslims'.

Hikayat Mūsā Munājāt

Another story from *Durr al-Majālis* which has been translated into Malay is *Musa Munajat* also known as *Hikayat Nabi Musa Munajat* or *Hikayat Musa Munajat dibukit Tur Sina* (The Tale of Moses' Private Conversation on Mount Sinai). Arabic, Persian, and Hindustani dialects in manuscript form and as early printed volumes have been found. The origin of this story lies in the Pentateuch as well as in the Qurʾān.

> [I]n the Jewish tradition, the books known as apocrypha and pseudoepygrapha contain legends on episodes like 'The Burning Bush', 'The Ascension (or Assumption) of Moses', 'Moses' visit to Paradise and Hell', 'The Revelation on Mount Sinai' and 'Moses receiving the Torah'. There is also an Ethiopian text on the 'Death of Moses'.[67]

All versions of the story contain information about a dialogue between God and Moses which include a series of questions from Moses and responses from the Almighty. The Qurʾānic story is found in concise form in 4:164 and 19:52 but receives further elaboration in various genres of Islamic literature such as *ḥadīth*, *tafsīr*, *kalām*, and *qiṣaṣ al-anbiyāʾ*. As Ali-de-Unzaga explains, this traditional account made inroads into various Islamic denominations.

[66] Brakel, 1975, 107.

[67] Umar Ali-de-Unzaga, 'The Conversation between Moses and God (Munājāt Mūsa) in the Epistles of the Pure Brethren (Rasa'il Ikhwan al-Safa')', *Al-Kitab: La Sacralité du Texte Dans Le Monde de l'Islam. Actes du Symposium International Tenu à Leuven et Louvain-la-Neuve du 29 Mai au 1 Juin 2002*, edited by Daniel De Smet, Godefroyde Callataÿ, and Jan van Reeth (Brussels, Louvain-la-Neuve; Leuven: Acta Orientalia Belgica, Subsidia III, 2004): 371–387.

> [I]n Shīʿī circles, Ibn Shuʿba al-Ḥarrānī ([d.] 380/990) transmits an anonymous version of 'Munājāt Allah li-Mūsā b. ʿImrān', which is in fact a long monologue addressed from God to Moses. Majlisī's (d.1110/1699) collection of Shīʿī *ḥadīth*, *Biḥār al-Anwār*, provides an excellent source of information. It includes some exegetical traditions of Qurʾānic verses referring to Moses, traditions on and pseudo-quotes from the Torah, and fragments from the *Munājāt*, some of which are not found anywhere else.[68]

An important aspect of all Islamic accounts of Moses' communication with God is the foretelling of the emergence of Muḥammad.[69]

In Persian Sufism, the concept of *munājāt* and private conversation has a particular status, in so far as Sufis seek to converse with both the 'self' and 'God'.[70] The Persian versions are few but have been reproduced frequently. The Persian story is also called *Dāstān-i Mūsā* (The Tale of Moses),[71] *Mūsā-nāma* (The Tale of Moses),[72] or *Munājāt-i Khudā bā Mūsā* (God's Private Conversation with Moses).[73] The majority of its Persian copies are from the eighteenth and nineteenth centuries whose origin remains unclear. While being largely similar to each other, the references introduced for them varies. Some are ascribed to a Shīʿī scholar, Fakhr al-Dīn Tarīḥī from the eleventh/seventeenth century, and his production of *Mūsā-nāma*. Interestingly, this version was already translated along with the full version of *Durr al-Majālis* into Uyghur, which is a Turkic language. The Uyghur version of the Moses tale is called *Rāḍī-nāma*.

Themes discussed in the story of Moses such as the Day of Judgement and the inhabitants of paradise are also mentioned in other chapters of *Durr al-Majālis*. The Persian manuscript MS.17641 held in the Parliamentary Library of Iran has a *Munājāt-i Mūsā* accompanied by a *tawallud-nāma* and *wafāt-nāma of* Muḥammad and a *jang-nāma* of Muḥammad Ḥanafiyya and ʿAlī. Moving towards Eastern Turkistan where it was translated into Turkic confirms its reputation among other new Muslim communities in the East. However, the details and origin of this story in the Malay context have not been seriously considered. The Malay story used to be copied along with *Hikayat bulan berbelah*, also from *Durr al-Majālis*[74](see above).

Two helpful works on the Malay version of the Moses story were produced by L'Abbe P. Favre and J. Nasikhun. Favre provided one of the first Jawi editions and French

[68] Ibid., 373–374. [69] Ibid. [70] On further information about theological aspects of this conversation, see: Ibid. 371–387, and about the conversation details, see the relevant story in this book.

[71] E.g., Ms. 5–28348/2 of the National Library of Iran

[72] E.g., Ms. 5–17454 of the National Library of Iran

[73] E.g., MS. 879 of the Parliamentary Library of Iran

[74] See the manuscript RAS Raffles Malay 62.

translations of the story in 1886 based on an undated and anonymous manuscript found in England in 1863. According to Favre, the Malay version must have been based on Arabic version with the Qurʾān as the main prototype. But the formation of sentences and the structure of questions and answers between God and Moses are compatible with our Persian prototype, and more importantly, the Persian version represents it in the form of the *qiṣṣa* or *ḥikāyat* which, unlike the traditional source, is free from Arabic or Persian *ḥadīth* accounts.

Nasikhun completed the romanisation of the Leiden University Library manuscript copy, Or.1744a, the *Hikayat Ceritera Nabi Musa Munadjat* under the supervision of the department of Agama, Sunan Kalijaga Yogyakarta in 1985. In the analytical part of his study Nasikhun mentions that fifty-five questions and answers are exchanged between God and Moses, of which forty-five are asked by Moses and ten are asked by God and answered by Moses.[75] In both Persian and Malay copies some questions are repeated frequently. Further particularities like God's unity and the name of Muḥammad (the weight of which is said to be more than the entire universe) is seen in both Persian and Malay copies.

In Persian,

اگر آسمانها و زمینها و آنچه در وی است، همه را در یک پلّه ترازو نهند
و این کلمه را در یک پلّه گذارند، هموَرانی کلمه گران آید

In Malay,

Maka pahala seberat bumi dan langit laut dan darat dan segala isi keduanya[76]

Moses also wonders with whom God has privately spoken before him:

In Persian,

موسیٰ گفت «خداوندا! از من پیشتر سخن با که گفتی و بعد از من با که گوئی؟»

In Malay,

Maka sembah nabi Mūsā: Ya Rabbie, ya Sayyidie ya Maula, Ya Tuhanku: 'adakah engkau berkata-kata kepada nabi yang lain-lain daripada aku dan yang dahulu-dahulu daripada hambamu seperti Nabi [...] dan nabi yang kemudian daripada hambamu ini?'

[75] *Hikayat Ceritera Nabi Musa Munadjat*, edited by Nasikhun (Yogyakarta: Sunan Kalijaga, 1985), 19. But the Persian version includes more queries from Moses and more responses by God.

[76] Transliteration of or. 1744a, fl. 1

Then God responded that the first one God had spoken with was Adam and the last one would be Muḥammad:

In Persian,

فرمان حضرت عزّت در رسید که «ای موسیٰ، اوّل سخن با آدم صفي
الله علیه‌السلام، بعده به محمّد مصطفی علیه‌السلام گویم و بشنوم»

In Malay,

> *maka firman Allah Taala: 'Ya Mūsā, adapun aku berkata-kata kepada nabi Allah [...] Adam dan nabi Muḥammad Rasul Allah Salli Allah 'alayh wa-sallam'*[77]

Parts of the dialogue that are similar in both the Persian and Malay versions include the rewards and punishments mentioned for the Day of Judgement, the features given of Muḥammad's community as compared to the community of Moses, and the rituals listed for Muḥammad's community. Even the origin and particularities of God as well as the age of Adam is discussed in both Persian and Malay versions albeit with differing values mentioned. The Malay version is shorter in comparison with the Persian one but the main themes and topics are similar and the Persian version is replete with repetitions of the same questions and answers and also an additional part coming after the first round of the conversation on theological and legal issues, a part which is rarely found in Malay copies.

Hikayat Raja Jumjuma

Another story which could have been directly translated from Persian and which has been widely discussed in the academic literature is *Hikayat Raja Jumjuma* (lit., 'The Story of King Skull') in which the skull of the king speaks with an Islamised Jesus on the hellfire and its torments.[78] According to Orum,

> The earliest written source of this story seems to be a version written by Abū Nuʿaym al-ʾIṣfāhānī (d. 1038 [CE]). It was first mentioned by Isḥāq b. Bishr (d. 821), who attributed the story to Abū Isḥāq al-Ḥimyarī al-ʾAḥbār, also known as Kaʿb al-ʾAḥbār, a Yemenite rabbi from the times of the Prophet Muḥammad.[79]

[77] Based on the RAS Raffles Malay 62, fl. 243. [78] For more, see: Roberto Tottoli, *Biblical Prophets in the Qur'an and Muslim Literature* (London: Routledge, 2002).

[79] Olav G. Orum, *ʾUṣṣit il-gumguma, or, 'The Story of the Skull': With Parallel Versions, Translation and*

Orums assertion may explain why the majority of prose versions of the story begin with the name of Kaʿb al-Aḥbār, a Jewish convert to Islam. It is also said that the story could have been derived from the literature of prophetic stories. Another popular version in Arabic – the content of which is largely like the Persian and Malay versions – was authored by ʿAbdallāh al-Kafīf (eleventh/seventeenth century).[80]

Another Arabic version resembling our Persian version is kept in the Malik museum of Iran; it is titled *Qiṣṣat al-Jumjuma wa-mā-jarā lahā maʿa nabī Allāh ʿĪsā ʿalayhi l-salām* (The Tale of Jumjuma and what happened to him with the Prophet of God, Jesus, peace be upon him) and catalogued as Ms.011.1.[81] One may find similarities between this manuscript and that of al-Kafīf. Marginal handwritten notes in Ottoman Turkish suggest that it was already in the possession of Turkish readers. It was produced along with other stories in Arabic during the early periods of the Safawid dynasty in Ramadan 917/1511, a few centuries after Sayf Ẓafar's *Durr al-Majālis*. It was copied from a Persian prototype as other Persian copies of this story – including the *Qiṣaṣ al-Qurʾān*, Ms.5–25045, of the National Library of Iran – are compatible with this one.

Having roots in non-Islamic traditions, the *Story of King Jumjuma* was soon adopted by various communities for meeting their religious or pedagogical needs. Although many copies are found in various languages across the Muslim world the best known manuscript copies are the versified ones.[82] The Islamised versions of the story explore the dynamic between Christianity and Islam and include narratives on conversion to Islam. The story has received the attention of both Christian missionaries and orientalists. For example, Or.3183 held in the Leiden University Library was 'made as a study copy for a European, and provided with numerous notes by J. J. Meinsma [d. 1886]'.[83] An English translation of the story was printed in the *Asiatic Journal* in 1823.

Winstedt contends that this story would have reached the Archipelago after the thirteenth/nineteenth century. However, Brakel-Papenhuyze says that 'the absence of a written version of *Hikayat Raja Jumjumah* prior to the late eighteenth or early nineteenth century does not necessarily mean that the legend was entirely unknown to the Malay-speaking world before that time."[84] Since the thirteenth/nineteenth and

Linguistic Analysis of Three 19th-century Judaeo-Arabic Manuscripts from Egypt. Supplemented with Arabic Transliteration (Leiden and Boston: Brill, 2017), 15. [80] Ibid.

[81] The full registration number is 1393.04.03630/011. [82] See, Kristof D'hulster, 'A 19th-century Chaghatay-Kazakh Version of the Story of Jesus and the Skull', *Turcologica Upsaliensia, An Illustrated Collection of Essays*, edited by Éva Á. Csató, Gunilla Gren-Eklund, Lars Johanson, Birsel Karakoç (Leiden and Boston, Brill, 2020), 198–208. [83] Witkam, *Inventory of the Oriental manuscripts in Leiden University Library* (Leiden: Ter Lugt Press, 2007), IV: 62 [84] Clara, Brakel-Papenhuyzen, 'The Tale of the Skull: An Islamic Description of Hell in Javanese', *Bijdragen tot de Taal-, Land-en Volkenkunde* 158/1 (2002), 3.

fourteenth/twentieth centuries polemical works that emphasise differences between Muslims and non-Muslims have been widely available in Central and South Asia and it seems unlikely that such a work would be actively selected by the Malay-Indonesian world for adoption. It is also worth noting a commonly held view that the poetic version of the King Jumjuma narrative was produced by the Persian poet Farīd al-Dīn ʿAṭṭār and that this version had already penetrated every corner of the Muslim world before the thirteenth/nineteenth century.

Manuscripts for the Persian version of the story are mainly to be found in the libraries of Pakistan and India. Many of the scribes of these manuscripts were from South Asia. This story used to be copied along with various treatises about Muḥammad and other prophets in different regions, including the Malay Archipelago.[85] The idea that Malays were unfamiliar with the story before the late nineteenth century seems somewhat farfetched. Having said this it is nevertheless unclear as to when exactly the Persian prose version of the King Jumjuma story was produced after being versified by ʿAṭṭār. Perhaps our best clue is *Durr al-Majālis*, the most complete copy of which includes the story of King Jumjuma.

There are various names for the Persian prototype of this story. It is usually known as *Qiṣṣa-yi Sulṭān Jumjuma* (The Tale of Sultan Jumjuma) but also known as *Ḥikāyat Jumjuma* or, more fully, *Ḥikāyat Jumjuma kih dar ʿAhd-i ʿĪsā ʿalayhi al-salām zinda shud* (The Tale of Jumjuma who was brought to Life during the Time of Jesus, peace be upon him). In *Durr al-Majālis* the story is titled *Ḥikāyat-i Pādshāh-i Shām* (The Tale of the King of the Levant). It was also variously titled in Malay-Indonesian languages. The Wall 109 manuscript of Indonesia is titled *Ceritera Akan Raja Jumjuman* (The Tale of Raja Jumjuma). The Malay version held at SOAS Library (MS 37082) is titled *Hikayat Ceritera Nabi Allah 'Isa dan Raja Jumjuma.*[86] The Javanese version is titled *Suluk Pathak* (translated by Brakel-Papenhuyze as Skull Song) or, in a version that is somewhat different in terms of content, as *Serat Raja Kepala* (The Tale of the Skull Shah) or *Serat Pathak utawi Serat Kabar Naraka* or (translated by Brakel-Papenhuyze as The Tale of Tidings from Hell).[87]

The story of King Jumjuma was read in different settings. Just as the story was of interest to Dutch teachers (Meinsma) and Malayists it was also of interest to Iranian teachers of the Qajar period in the late twelfth/eighteenth and thirteenth/nineteenth centuries.[88] It is clear that Sayf Ẓafar would have taken the story from the work of

[85] E.g., see the manuscripts Or.3213 and Or.3306 in the Leiden University Library.

[86] The original title of the manuscript 37082 حکاية چرترا نبي الله عيسى روح الله دان راج جمجمه

[87] Brakel-Papenhuyze, 'The Tale of the Skull', 4–7.

[88] See the Ms. 5–6428 in the National Library of Iran.

ʿAṭṭār al-Nisābūrī or al-Iṣfāhānī, or suchlike, with his contribution being the conversion of poetic and hagiographic sources into fluent Persian prose.

Some South Asian manuscripts suggest that Indians were familiar with both Sanskrit and Islamised traditions of speaking skulls. Manuscript 1109 of the University of Tehran Library titled *Mufarraḥ al-Qulūb* is the direct Persian translation of a Sanskrit collection of fables known as *Hitopadesha*. This translation was done in Bandar Surat, India in Rabīʿ al-Awwal 1062/February 1652. It ends with an additional poetic story, which is the story of Pādshāh Jumjuma (King Jumjuma) ascribed to ʿAṭṭār.[89] Furthermore, a Persian version of the *Mahabharata* in the Ganj-Baksh collection of Pakistan, Ms. 1602, addresses Raja Jumjuma, while its content is different from that of *Durr al-Majālis* and Malay copies. Some anonymous Persian stories of the prophets and stories of the Qurʾān like Mss.5–6428, 5–23796, and 5–25045 in the National Library of Iran have listed the *Story of Sultan Jumjuma* along with other prophetic tales which were already outlined in different Arabic and Persian hagiographic works.

It is noteworthy that the story of King Jumjuma has not been so popular in central Iran or in Shīʿī religious circles, as evidenced by fewer copies being produced in these contexts. A notable exception to this observation is the use of the story in the Qajar period for the teaching of Persian folk stories. Perhaps the reason for this unpopularity is explained by the fact that the first Shīʿī Imam, ʿAlī b. Abī Ṭālib, was believed to have spoken with the skulls of ancient kings and so the King Jumjuma tale might have appeared to be encroaching upon his status.[90] A number of scholars including Braginsky believe that some episodes from the Malay *Hikayat Maharaja Ali* could have been borrowed from the *Story of Raja Jumjuma*.[91] However, further investigation is required to establish this and to establish the similarity of those stories with other versions of the King Jumjuma narrative and of narratives regarding ʿAlī when he spoke with the skulls of Anushirvan and the King of Abyssinia. Again, it must be noted that *Durr al-Majālis*, including one of the earliest extant copies of this story, may offer clues as to its differing versions.

The Persian story of King Jumjuma in *Durr al-Majālis* has significant similarities with Malay versions of the King Jumjuma story. It has been my contention throughout

[89] Although this version of the *Story of Jumjuma* does not include some couplets and does not mention the name of ʿAṭṭār, its content is quite similar with the Ms. 818174 (5144/1) of the National Library of Iran, addressing ʿAṭṭār as the one who versified this story.

[90] Further references can be found here: https://www.haydarya.com/maktaba_moktasah/03/book_42/41/a22.html Accessed 10 May 2020

[91] For more see, Braginsky, The Heritage of Traditional Malay Literature.

this study that Malays became acquainted with various stories of *Durr al-Majālis*. That Persian and Malay versions of the King Jumjuma story share important similarities further confirms the contention. One of the main commonalities of the Persian and Malay versions is that Jesus asks God to allow him to have a conversation with the skull upon which the skull speaks to declare the unity of God and to recognise Jesus as the Spirit of God.

[أشهد أن] لآ إلهَ إلَّا الله، عيسىٰ رُوحِ الله

[I declare that] there is no god but God and that Jesus is the Spirit of God.

Jesus asked Jumjuma about his stance in the world, that is, what sort of human being he was. One of the first questions which is found in both Persian and Malay texts (i.e., Wall 109), and *not* in the Arabic version, is about his gender.

In Persian (with English translation),

مرد بودی یا زن؟

were you a man or a woman?

In Jawi and romanised Malay (with English translation),

ا ڤاكه اڠكوا لاک اتو ڤرمڤوان؟

Apakah? engkau laki atau permpuan

what were you, man or woman?

Then, sociable questions, also found in the Arabic version, are mentioned.

In Persian (with English translation),

جوانمرد بودی یا بخیل؟

were you chivalrous or a stingy?

In Jawi and romanised Malay (with English translation),

بودک اتو مرديکا

Budak atau merdeka?

were you a slave or a free man?

In Arabic (with English translation),

حُرًّا أم عَبداً
free or slave?

In the Malay version (as with the Persian version) King Jumjuma explains about his characteristics and authority in the world and how many soldiers and bondswomen were in his possession and that he helped orphans and the poor. Subsequently, Jesus asks him about the moment of his death (*tatkala sakrat al-maut*). This scenario is also clearly found in the Persian *Durr al-Majālis* and the Arabic version in the Malik museum. The main body of story begins from this point when the skull – in all three copies, Persian, Arabic and Malay – explains about a sudden illness and that no courtier nor physician was able to heal him and prevent the Angel of Death visiting. The rest of the story revolves around the manner in which he was treated by the Angel of Death and the angels of the grave, Munkar and Nakīr. The story ends with Jesus imploring the skull to return to life and the king lived for a couple of years or so depending on the manuscript.

The full story of King Jumjuma in *Durr al-Majālis* reveals more similarities with the Malay version. Either the Malay *Hikayat Jumjuma* is taken from *Durr al-Majālis* which itself is based on earlier Arabic and Persian works of prose and poetry or it is based on more recent Arabic works which are influenced by sources that include *Durr al-Majālis*. I suspect that the former is the case and one evidence that supports this view is that the Malay *Hikayat Jumjuma* in SOAS (MS 37082) includes other stories which are also from *Durr al-Majālis as* will be discussed below.

Nūr-nāma

One of the SOAS Malay manuscripts (Fig 5) includes *Nūr-nāma* (The Tale of Light) or *Nūr-Muḥammad* (The Light of Muḥammad).[92] There used to be various copies of *Nūr-nāma* in different languages. However, the main feature which distinguishes various copies of *Durr al-Majālis* is the form of its ending. Most versions of the *Nūr-nāma* begin with a dialogue between Gabriel and Muḥammad following a question raised by Muḥammad's daughter, Fāṭima. The creation of the light of Muḥammad is then mentioned, for which God has created seven oceans. Then the universe and 124,000 prophets are created from the drops of light from Muḥammad when it shook. Later, the spirit of beings is made as are the four crucial elements (in Malay: 'unasor yang empat')

[92] It should be noted that the SOAS' *Hikayat Nur Muhammad* MS 37082, item 7 is clearly translated from Persian, and has the highest level of similiarity with our Persian version.

of wind, soil, water, and fire with which Muḥammad converses. Among all of them, it is the soil which is finally chosen by Muḥammad and to which he shows great admiration. Muḥammad's interest in soil, taken from the Earth, is because of its humility, as already seen in the first chapter where God made Adam from the Earth due to its humbleness. The *Nūr-nāma* of *Durr al-Majālis* includes a note about the rewards of reading it. In the Persian copy, it is said that the reward of reading the *Nūr-nāma* is as the reward of reading the 'four scriptures' (i.e., the Torah, Gospels, Psalms, and Qurʾān).

In Persian

اوّل ثواب تورات موسی ﷷ، دوم ثواب انجیل که بر عیسی ﷷ فرود آمده بود، سیوم ثواب زبور که بر
داود ﷷ فرود آمده بود، چهارم ثواب فرقان که بر حضرت محمّد مصطفی ﷺ نازل شده بود[...]

In Jawi and romanised Malay (fl. 18, MS 37082/SOAS)

مك الله ﷻ ممبري [...] اكندي امفت كتاب ڤرتام توريت دان
كدوا انجيل دان كتيک زبور كا امفت قرأن [...]

Maka Allah Subhanahu wa-ta'ala memberi [...] akan-dia empat kitab pertama Taurat dan kedua Injil dan ketiga Zabur ke-empat al-Qoran

The Persian version begins with the story of the celebrated Muslim scholar Abū Ḥāmid Ghazālī (d. 505/1111) who takes a copy of 'this' *Nūr-nāma* to Sulṭān Maḥmūd of Ghazna, after which Sulṭān Maḥmūd dreams of the Prophet Muḥammad. This episode, which is also found in the Bengali rendition of *Durr al-Majālis*,[93] is a part of the Malay version.[94] The only obvious difference is that the name of 'Ghazālī' is replaced with 'a poor dervish' (درویس ڤقیر) (fl. 18), otherwise, even the way Sulṭān Maḥmūd of Ghazna (سلطان محمود عزناوى) "dreamed of the Prophet" is same (fl. 19).

In Jawi and romanised Malay

مک ڤد ملم اية جو اي برممڤي سلطان محمود دغن [...] برتمواكن چهيا رسول الله ﷺ

Maka pada malam itu jua ia ber-mempi(a) Sultan Mahmud dengan [...] bertemuakan cahaya Rasul Allah salli Allah alayh wa-sallam

This Malay story comes after the *Wafāt-nāma* in Ms.37082 in which various epi-

[93] See my parts 2 and 3. [94] Edwin Wieringa also detected similarities between Malay and Bengali *Nūr Muḥammad* literature. Wieringa, 'Does Traditional Islamic Malay Literature Contain Shiʿitic Elements?', 99.

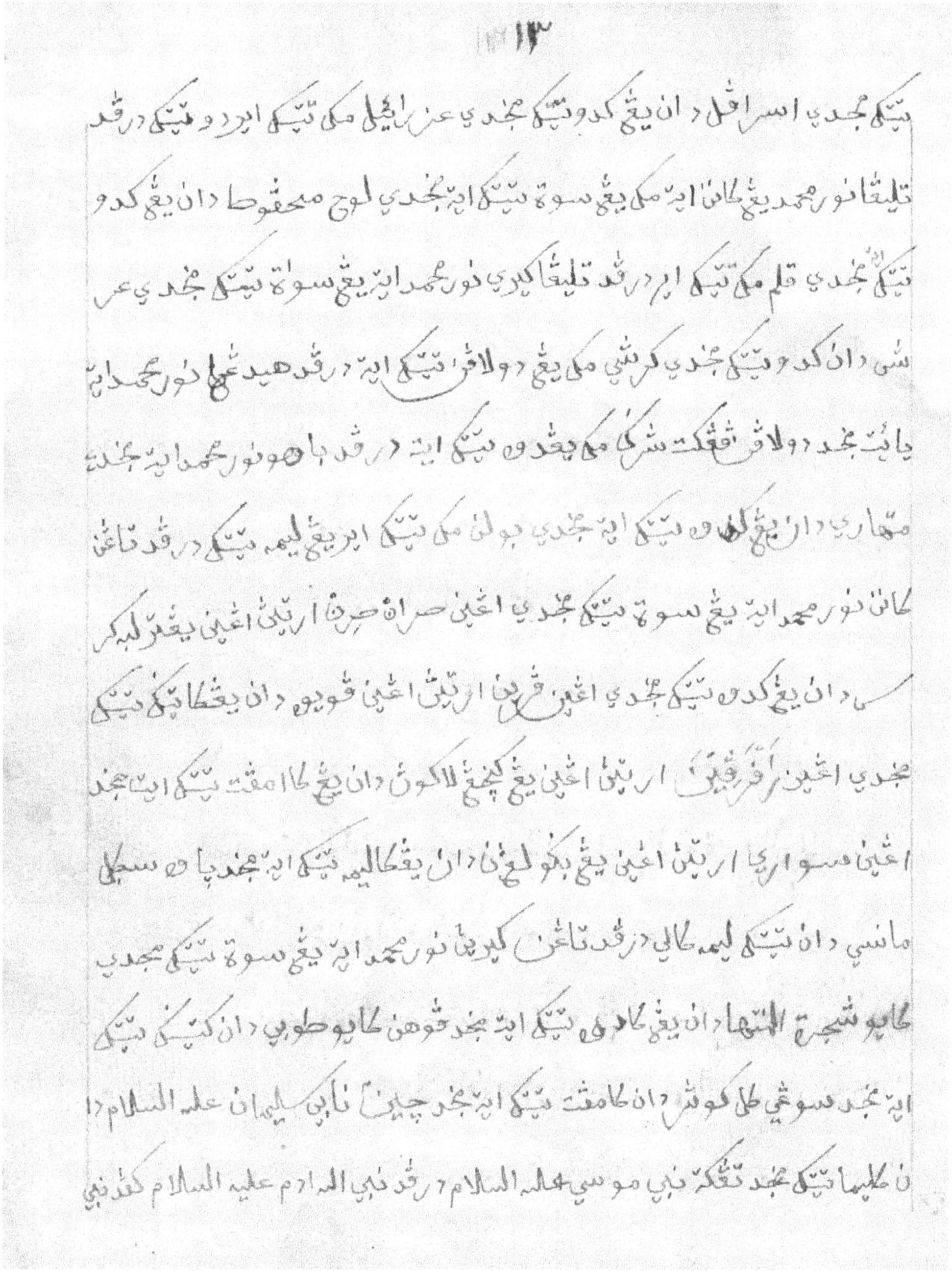

Figure 5. Fl.13. MS 37082, item 7. The Malay *Hikayat Nur Muhammad*. SOAS Digital Library. Courtesy of SOAS Library, University of London, United Kingdom.

sodes are similar to some stories from *Durr al-Majālis*. Traces of Maḥmūd of Ghazna in the Malay *Nūr-nāma* were also detected by Brakel,[95] suggesting to us that the whole work of *Durr al-Majālis* was probably in the possession of Malay readers or scribes.[96]

[95] Brakel, *Hikayat Muhammad Hanafiyyah*. [96] Another part of the SOAS MS 37082 collection, which is taken from *Durr al-Majālis*, is the description of hell and heaven. This description revolves around the role of the owner (*mālik*) of hell, Zabāniyya, the appointed angel for managing the hellfire, above which there is a sharp and thin rope (تاليڽ يڠ امت تاجم) (f. 21). Similar stories about the hellfire and that this angel is also known as Mālik (lit., 'owner') is obviously found in chapter eleven on the virtue of ʿAlī and Fāṭima and chapter thirty-three about the inhabitants of paradise.

VI) A Critical Persian Edition and Critically Edited Translation of *Durr al-Majālis*

PERSIAN EDITION

To edit the Persian text, I examined a large number of manuscripts and printed volumes, more than that listed in the Appendice. Manuscripts were either fully or partially examined. Given the popularity of the text in different Muslim societies – whether in translation or original form, whether handwritten or printed, and whether as a complete or incomplete text – it has not been possible to produce a critical apparatus based on a few key manuscript copies. Thus it resembles Brakel's study of the *Hikayat Muhammad Hanafiyyah*; he did not intend to reconstruct a stemma or represent its final archetype due to the existence of a wide range of different manuscripts and editorial efforts on the part of their copyists.[1] My attempt is to reconstruct and translate the text based on a precise scrutiny of different copies of *Durr al-Majālis*, through which I can also find the most accurate and relevant copies for each story. The manuscript copies are selected based on their thematic coverage, comprehensiveness, relevance to the Malay Muslim stories, and their availability. I worked with three main manuscripts: *GMS-170*; *PAK-001-1498*; *Or.565*. Together they contain all the relevant stories that are available in the Malay-Indonesian literature. But they are also read along with four important copies (*No.33(408)*; *53*; *Isl.Ms.853*; *No.1222*) whose particular features prompted me to consult them while editing the work. Although I have explained them in the Appendice, they are listed briefly here:

[1] Brakel, *Hikayat Muhammad Hanafiyyah*, 83 and 90.

- MS GMS-170: The longest version of *Durr al-Majālis*, also our first key manuscript, is held in the Auckland Libraries, New Zealand. According to the scribe, Khalīfa Shaykh Dāwūd, who also copied other stories like that of *Tamīm Anṣārī* and the *Tawallud-nāma* and *Wafāt-nāma* of Muḥammad (GMS-173), the *Durr al-Majālis* of Sayf Ẓafar is found in two versions; (a) a shorter one with thirty-three chapters as listed in most catalogues; and (b) the longer one with a complete version of chapter thirty-one on the killing of Ḥasan and Ḥusayn, plus two more stories on Moses and Jesus, and an ending section entitled the *Nūr-nāma* of Muḥammad which are found in Malay classical works. Having the most similarity and textual connection with Malay-Indonesian stories prompted me to place this manuscript on top of my list. Its scribe, Khalīfa Shaykh Dāwūd, reproduced both versions in the early thirteenth/nineteenth century, adding two colophons for each. Elsewhere, I have attested to the accuracy of his classification, arguing through a phrase-by-phrase comparison that the prototype of the Malay story of Muḥammad Ḥanafiyya is found in *Durr al-Majālis*' longer version of the killing of Ḥasan and Ḥusayn.[2] Given that the Malay story was already quite well known in the Malay Archipelago from the late ninth/fifteenth century, we may be confident that the Persian text's content and structure is as old as its creation and cannot be from the post-eleventh/seventeenth century Bengali versions and its content was subjected to serious textual censorship leading to the removal and reduction of the size of the Persian work.[3]
- MS PAK–001–1498: another Persian copy of *Durr al-Majālis* in the Ganjbakhsh collection of Pakistan contains the long version of the killing story of Ḥasan and Ḥusayn, also compatible with GMS-170. In both versions, the name of Muḥammad Ḥanafiyya is written as 'Muḥammad Ḥanīfa', as with some Bengali and Malay copies.
- MS Or.565: An old copy of *Durr al-Majālis*, being censored by both Sunni and Shīʿī figures over the course of history. It is held in Leiden University Library. It includes thirty-four chapters. Its last chapter is the *Story of Balʿam Bāʿūr*, also known as the *Story of Banū Isrāʾīl*, whose name and genre is traceable in Bengali editions, too.[4]

[2] Majid Daneshgar, 'New Evidence on the Origin of the Hikayat Muhammad Hanafiyyah', 69–102.

[3] Ibid.

[4] The influence of *Durr al-Majālis* may be detected in subsequent works of Islamic literature in work such as *Rawḍat al-Shuhadāʾ* (the Garden of Martyrs), *Tadhkirat Haft-Iqlīm* (Treatise of the Seven-Geographical Regions) by Amīn Aḥmad Rāzī (tenth-eleventh/sixteenth-seventeenth century). For instance, 27th chapter of *Durr al-Majālis* about Khājeh Ḥassan Nūrī is clearly found in *Haft-Eqlīm*.

- MS No.33 (408): already from the mausoleum of Shaykh Ṣafī al-Dīn Ardabīlī was copied and kept in Iran in 985/c.1577 CE. We are in possession of a few copies of *Durr al-Majālis* from Iran. As I mentioned in the appendices, the collection of this mausoleum is mainly owed to the patronage of the Safawid kings of Persia, which explains the significance of this copy.
- MS 53: kept at Talaat Library, Egypt was copied in Ottoman Turkey and circulated in the Balkans region. It was transported to Egypt and read by Egyptians, Ottomans and European colonial officers.
- MS Isl.Ms.853: The University of Michigan's manuscript was reproduced in nineteenth-century Punjab. It comes along with a Punjabi version of *Jang-nāma*, and in contrast to most available copies, ends with *The Killing Story of Ḥasan and Ḥusayn.*
- MS No.1222: While the manuscript kept in the Academy of Sciences of Tajikistan, dating from the ninth/fifteenth century, is the oldest of the texts that has been examined for this study, it does not cover all the chapters whose renditions are found in classical Malay-Indonesian literature. Besides, this early manuscript presents only a short version of chapter thirty-one on the killing of Ḥasan and Ḥusayn, which is not compatible with the content of its South Asian and Malay versions. It is replete with annotations and marginal accounts which were obviously made by a Shīʿī believer sometimes before the emergence of the Safawid empire. Due to its production date and Central Asian background, it will also be used to highlight some differences and uncommon additions.

This edition is mainly a reproduction of GMS-170 and, where this was not available, of PAK-001-1498 and Or.565. Where the information and texts of these items are not similar to what is identified in a large number of other manuscripts (also, in other languages), then I rely on common chapters/words/sentences used in the other four manuscripts. Also, for the sake of accuracy and assurance, the whole Persian edition has been checked against the following additional manuscripts:

1. *MS. 2940 (Oriental Research Library of Srinagar, Kashmir)*
2. *MS.863 (Oriental Research Library of Srinagar, Kashmir)*
3. *MS.14248 (The Parliamentary Library, Iran)*
4. *MS.5-22910 (Iranian National Library, Iran)*
5. *MS.5-7341 (Iranian National Library, Iran)*
6. *MS.5-33429 (Iranian National Library, Iran)*
7. *MS.5-34451(Iranian National Library, Iran)*

8. *MS.M82 (Indian Council for Cultural Relations, India)*
9. *MS.M84 (Indian Council for Cultural Relations, India)*
10. *MS.PAK-001-1180 (Ganjbakhsh, Pakistan)*
11. *MS.PAK–001-1043 (Ganjbakhsh, Pakistan)*
12. *MS.PAK–001-0770 (Ganjbakhsh, Pakistan)*
13. *MS.PAK–001-1471(Ganjbakhsh, Pakistan)*
14. *MS.6618 (Lahore University Library, Pakistan)*
15. *MS.BSB.Pers.Or.187 (Bayerische Staatsbibliothek, Germany)*
16. *MS.Pers.Or.188 (Bayerische Staatsbibliothek, Germany)*
17. *MS.Pers.Or.193 (Bayerische Staatsbibliothek, Germany)*
18. *MS.Or.Fol.3112 (Staatsbibliothek zu Berlin, Germany)*
19. *MS.Delhi Persian 917 (The British Library, UK)*
20. *MS.Or.565 (Leiden University Library, the Netherlands)*
21. *MS.MS BW IVANOW 0100 (McGill University Library, Canada)*
22. *MS.MS BW IVANOW 0101(McGill University Library, Canada)*
23. *MS.RBD LEWIS O 189 (Free Library of Philadelphia, USA)*
24. *MS.Isl. Ms. 853 (Special Collections Library, University of Michigan)*
25. *MS.GMS-173 (Auckland Libraries, New Zealand)*
26. *MS.Daneshgar.Durr.1. (Personal Digital Collection)*

Although I have based my edition of *Durr al-Majālis* on the above said main and additional manuscripts, there are some parts of the text where this has not been the case. Firstly, the longer version of the *killing story of Ḥasan and Ḥusayn* (chapter thirty-one) has been edited based on manuscripts *GMS-170* (Auckland Libraries), *PAK–001–1498* (Ganjbakhsh), *Ms BW Ivanow 0100* (McGill University Library), and a number of independent treatises (e.g., MS Add.8149 at the British Library) whose details are found in the Appendices. The edition of the story of Balʿam Bāʿūr (chapter thirty-four) is based on MSs *PAK–001–1043* and *Or.565*. The edition of the episode involving Moses (chapter four) is based on MS *GMS-170* and its Turkish version. The story of the King of the Levant (i.e., the Skull King, or Jumjuma; chapter thirty-six) is based on MS *GMS-170* and further independent treatises. Finally, the translation of the *Nūr-nāma* is based on MSs *GMS-170*, *GMS-173*, *Add.8149*, and other independent treatises and translation copies (see Appendices).

Secondly, and for the sake of consistency, I compared my edition with other manuscripts that were either incomplete or only partially available. This group of manuscripts numbered twenty-six altogether: *No.478*; *No.5988*; *No.5996*; *No.5–7992*; *No.5–21172*; *No.5–22341*; *No.5-27641*; *No.5-9182*; *No.5–28575*; *No.5–6465*; *No.5–29446*; *No.10680*; *No.813*;

No.2030; No.1395; No.1396; No.311; No.452; PAK–001-1666; PAK–001–1506; PAK–001–2123; No.128; No.137; No. 2273; No.H–125; No. b3126838.

ENGLISH TRANSLATION

I considered other early (non-English) translations of *Durr al-Majālis* in different 'Muslim' languages to gather insights as to the context of each story, its full rendition, and its reception. Twelve translations received particular attention:

1. *No. Prove.91 (Turkic) (The Jarring collection of Lund University, Sweden)*
2. *No. Prove.108 (Turkic) (The Jarring collection of Lund University, Sweden)*
3. *No. Prov.342 (Turkic) (The Jarring collection of Lund University, Sweden*
4. *No. Prov.383 (Turkic) (The Jarring collection of Lund University, Sweden)*
5. *No. Prov.111 (Turkic) (The Jarring collection of Lund University, Sweden)*
6. *No. Isl.Ms.853 (Punjabi) (The University of Michigan's Special Collections, United States of America)*
7. *No.323 (Bengali) (University of Dacca Library, Bengladesh; microfilm: Australian National University, Australia)*
8. *No. Afghan 4 (Pushto) (Rylands Library, Manchester, United Kindom)*
9. *No.Afghan 2 (Rylands Library, Manchester, United Kindom)*
10. *No. Afghan 13b (Rylands Library, Manchester, United Kindom)*
11. *No. Afghan 12 (Rylands Library, Manchester, United Kindom)*
12. *No. ГПБ, курд 40 (Institute of the Peoples of Asia of the former USSR Academy of Sciences, Russia)*

Some Malay materials whose names and contents were also described in the last part are also taken into account.

I compared a number of volumes printed in different languages, mostly from the late thirteenth/nineteenth century: Lahore 1876 (incomplete Persian version); Lahore 1884 (incomplete Persian version); Kazan 1898 (incomplete Turkic version); Kazan 1909 (incomplete Turkic version); Tashkent 1991 (incomplete Uzbek version); Soran 2019 (modified Kurmanji version).

In the translation of *Durr al-Majālis* that follows I have added explanations in the notes where I have found it necessary. For uncommon or classical terms, phrases, and poetical phrases a number of print and online Persian dictionaries have been consulted.[5] Arabic, Bengali, Punjabi, Malay, Turkish, and Urdu glossaries were also consulted, the references for which have been provided in footnotes where necessary. Unless otherwise noted, for translations of the Qurʾān and [Sunni] *ḥadīths* I consulted www.quran.com and www.Sunnah.com.

While translating the text into English, I chose biblical names for biblical prophets and figures. As such, 'Ibrāhīm' is written as 'Abraham' and 'Maryam' as 'Mary'. The Islamised or Islamic names of these figures are found in the Persian edition.

Throughout the following Persian text, numerals and *abjad* (الف-ب-ج-...ظ) are used for the commentary and editorial notes, respectively. The *abjad* sequence on every page is restarted.

FORMATION

Each chapter of *Durr al-Majālis* has a more or less similar structure. First, a story with a moral or didactic message is outlined. Sometimes the main story (x) is interrupted by relevant stories or "samples" (*naẓīr*) (y) which may even pertain to a different era. The main narrative (x) resumes with the term '*al-gharaḍ*' – often written in red – to mean 'anyway, now to return to the story', suggesting that the whole interrupted story was a vehicle by which the author wanted to convey the core message of the text (z):

$$x + y + y + \ldots + x = z$$

The length of the stories is not equal. Chapter three, on the virtue of Jethro for example, is very short whereas chapter thirty-one, on the killing of Ḥasan and Ḥusayn, is quite lengthy. Some stories, such as the story about King Jumjuma (chapter thirty-five), are of medium length. It is not unknown for Malay Islamic stories to be also of considerably different lengths, the varying lengths of *Hikayat Raja Jumjuma* and *Ḥasan and Ḥusayn* (also, *Muhammad Ḥanafiyyah*) serve to illustrate this point.

[5] Also, refer to: https://www.vajehyab.com/

PART B

PERSIAN EDITION AND ENGLISH TRANSLATION

مقدّمه

بِسۡمِ ٱللَّهِ ٱلرَّحۡمَٰنِ ٱلرَّحِيمِ

{۱} حمدی که از عنایت إلهي بر زبان عارفان رود و ثنایی که از الهامات سبحانی نامتناهی در سینهٔ محقّقان حقّیقی گذرد و هر آن قادری[الف] را که وجود شریف مُصْطَفَی را از سابقهٔ ازل موجود انبیاء ساخت، و انسان[ب] را به تاج خلافت و رواج ولایت بیاراست و نیک بختان را از د ریای سعادت «السَّعيدُ مَنْ سُعِدَ فِي بَطْنِ أُمِّه»[۱] سیراب گردانیده، و مقبولان ابد[ج] را از ماءالحیاتْ جام‌های مالامال نوشانیده، و منشورِ[۲] سعادت بی‌واسطهٔ خدمتْ به دستِ انبیاء داد، و تاجِ معرفت بی‌وسیلتْ[د] بر سرِ مُقرّبان نهاد، و ثبوت ولایت را در صحیفهٔ «إِنَّ الَّذِينَ سَبَقَتْ لَهُم مِّنَّا الْحُسْنَىٰ»[۳] ثبت گردانید، و ایمان و اسلام را در لوح «أُولَٰئِكَ كَتَبَ فِي قُلُوبِهِمُ الْإِيمَانَ»[۴] نقش بست، و سینهٔ محزونان و محرومان و مقرّبان را به علم لدُنّی که سرمایهٔ هدایت است مُتجلّی گردانیده، و جانِ واصلانِ رسیدْ را به شَرَفِ نورِعقل منوّر گردانید، و سینهٔ پاک انبیاء را لوح احکام آسمانی[ه] داد، و باطن اولیاء را با الهامات کَرَم مُزیّن[و] برآورد. و کوس[۵] دولت محبّان را در گوش و عیونِ عرش و فلک چنان کوفتند که آواز آن از اَزَل تا ابد به گوش اِنس و ملک دررسید.

{۲} بیت[۶]: آن را که خواند واسطه‌ای در میان نبود؛ وان را که راند هیچ گناهی نکرده بود.

[۱] مرتبط است به تعدادی از احادیث منسوب به پیامبر اسلام که در کتب حدیثی اهل سنّت و تشیّع ذکر شده است. یکی از این احادیث به نقل از ابوهریره چنین است: «السعیدُ من سعِد في بطنِ أمِّه والشقيُّ من شقيَّ في بطنِ أمِّه». [۲] اجازه و فرمان.
[۳] آیهٔ ۱۰۱ سورهٔ انبیاء. [۴] آیهٔ ۲۲ سورهٔ مجادلة. [۵] طبل. [۶] در برخی نسخ از واژهٔ «نظم» استفاده شده است. امّا به دلیل کاربرد مکرّر کلمهٔ «بیت» در ادبیات مالایی-اندونزیایی از به کار بردن «نظم» پرهیز می‌کنم.

[الف] پادشاهی. احتمالا «قادریست». [ب] اولیاء [ج] برلین «مقبولان آبدار». [د] قرب بی‌وسیلی
[ه] احکام اسلام [و] مزید

Introduction

In the Name of God, the Compassionate, the Merciful

{1} The praise expressed by gnostics is a divine providence and an adoration from unlimited pure divine inspiration. [This praise] touches the breast of the true seekers [of] the All-Powerful, who created the excellent substance of Muṣṭafā as the Prophet from pre-eternity, and made the human proud with the crown of His caliphate, fostered leadership, enriched the blessed people by the ocean of felicity, 'The blessed one was blessed once he was in the mother's womb', and served the eternally accepted ones with a cup brimful of the water of life. He granted the immediate blessed command of service to the prophets, placed the crown of knowledge barehanded and directly on the head of those who are near to Him, recorded the affirmation of leadership in the divine scroll: 'Truly, those for whom the best has preceded from Us' (Q. 21:101); inscribed the faith and the religion of Islam on the tablet, 'He has inscribed faith on their hearts' (Q. 58:22), and glorified the hearts of the heartbroken, the resigned and those who are close to Him with divine knowledge, which guarantees the path of guidance; illuminated the soul of those who have arrived at union with Him, radiating the exaltation of the intellect; sent the divine legal commands and tablets upon the purified breast of the prophets, and embellished the esoteric sense of the prophets with divine beneficence. So long as the drum of the lovers of happiness and the blessed state beats in the ears and eyes of the divine Throne and heavens its sound will remain in the ears of mankind and sovereignty forever.

{2} Poem: The one He has called upon, for whom there was no go-between;
And the one He has rejected who had not committed a sin

{۳} و صلوات فراوان و تحیّات بی‌پایان به روح مقدّس و منوّر و مطهّر افضل موجودات. قال الله تَعَالَی فِي حقّه: «إِنَّ اللَّهَ وَ مَلائِكَتَهُ يُصَلُّونَ عَلَى النَّبِيِّ يا أَيُّهَا الَّذِينَ آمَنُوا صَلُّوا عَلَيْهِ وَسَلِّمُوا تَسْلِيماً».[۷] آن پیغمبر که خلقت در عالم علوی و سفلی طفیل عظمت وجود اوست «لَوْلَاكَ مَا خَلَقْتُ الأَفْلَاكُ».[۸] آن رسولی که مَقَرّ انبیاء در زیر رأیت[۹] اوست و مَقَرّ اولیاء به هدایت اوست. واسطهٔ محبّت دوستان [است] كما قال الله تَعَالَى «فَاتَّبِعُونِي يُحْبِبْكُمُ اللَّه».[۱۰] زهی محبوب ازل که امان‌نامهٔ عذاب عامهٔ امّت را به وجودِ میمونِ اوست، در قرآن که مکتوبِ ذُوالجَلالِ اوست به سوی بندگان بشارت داد که «وَمَا أَرْسَلْنَاكَ إِلَّا رَحْمَةً لِّلْعَالَمِين»[۱۱].

{۴} و بر صحابهٔ کرام و خلفاء عظام خصوصاً بر آن چهارگانهٔ[ز] یگانه که چهار رکن کعبهٔ دین و قصر یقین‌اند، یعنی: أَمیر المُؤمِنین ابوبکر صدّیق، و عمر و عثمان و علی[۱۲] رضي الله تعالی عنهم أجمعین و بر سیّد شباب اهل الجنّة: الحسن و الحسین وعلی صحبه اجمعین.[۱۳]

{۵} فَرد[۱۴]: تا آل مُصْطَفَی را از حقّ درود باشد؛ از من درود باد[ا] بر مُصْطَفَی و آلش[۱۵]

{۶} و بعد حمد خدایْ و درود بر مُصْطَفَی و ثنای یارانِ مجتبی و نور دیدگان مرتضی رَضِيَ ٱللَّهُ تَعَالَىٰ عَنْهُمْ، می گوید بندهٔ گنه‌کارِ امیدوارِ به رحمتِ پروردگار، المستغفر إلی الله الباري، «سیف ظفر»، که عمر بنده در مجلس بندگان[ح] دین خداوندگان یقین گذشته، و از دقایق جواهر نبوی معانی سماط[ط] را اقتباس نموده و به توفیق الله تَعَالَی جمع آورده[ی] و آن‌را «درّالمجالس»[۱۶] نام نهاده تا طالبی و دردمندی به مطالعهٔ این دل بگشاید و در شنیدن اوصاف پاکشان جان او بیاساید. و در آن حال شریف این مسکین را از سر فاتحه[۱۷] مَدد بِدهد تا غفر و عفو گناهان گردد «وَذَلِكَ عَلَى الله يَسِيرٌ»[۱۸].

[۷] آیهٔ ۵۶ سورهٔ احزاب. [۸] صحّت این روایت قرنها مورد بحث بوده است. امّا علاوه بر مجموعه داستان‌های اسلامی، ردّپای آن را می‌توان در تفاسیر و حواشی تفسیری-کلامی یافت. [۹] پرچم. [۱۰] آیهٔ ۳۱ سورهٔ آل عمران. [۱۱] آیهٔ ۱۰۷ سورهٔ انبیاء.
[۱۲] لایدن ۵۶۵ «امیرالمونین شاه مردان علی». [۱۳] در نسخهٔ شیخ صفی‌الدین اردبیلی تمجید خلفای راشدین به چشم نمی‌خورد.
[۱۴] بنابر دهخدا: «یک بیت شعر که معنی و غرض در آن تمام شده باشد».
[۱۵] در برخی نسخه‌ها چنین آمده است «تا آل مُصْطَفَی را از حقّ درود باشد؛ از ما درود بی‌حدّ بر مُصْطَفَی و آلش». مثلاً برلین «برآل مُصْطَفَی از حقّ درود باشد؛ از من درورد بادا بر مُصْطَفَی و آلش». شبیه این بیت در دیوان اشعار خاقانی موجود است :«تا آل مُصْطَفَی را ز ایزد درود باشد؛ بر تو درود بادا از مُصْطَفَی و آلش». [۱۶] (درّ مجالس). برای دیگر اسامی به‌کاررفته برای این اثر به مقدّمه رجوع شود.
[۱۷] به برکت سورهٔ فاتحه. [۱۸] آیهٔ ۷ سورهٔ تغابن.

[ز] چهار یاران [ح] بزرگان [ط] بی‌شمار [ی] از فراختهٔ نبوی جواهر بی‌شمار جمع نموده

{3} Copious praise for, and unlimited greetings upon, the holy illuminated spirit and the manifestation of the best of beings, about whom God says: 'Truly, God and His angels hail blessings upon the Prophet. O those of you who have believed, request blessing and peace on him' (Q. 33:56). He is the Prophet for whom the creation of the upper and lower universe is host to his existence 'If not for you, I would not have created the creation'; the Prophet under whose banner and guidance is the assembly of prophets. He is the mediator of the love of [God's] friends, as God says in the Qurʾān: '...follow me, and God will love you...' (Q. 3:31). Blessings upon the eternal beloved whose existence – because of his auspicious existence there is a word for protecting the people from punishment – has been announced to mankind in the Qurʾān, which is the written [book] of the Lord of Majesty: 'And nothing has been sent to you, except as a mercy for the peoples' (Q. 21:107).

{4} [Praise be] upon the noble Companions and great caliphs, especially upon those four unique individuals who are the four pillars of the religious arena and are the castle of certainty, namely, the Commander of Believers Abū Bakr al-Ṣiddīq, the Commander of Believers ʿUmar, the Commander of Believers ʿUthmān, and the Commander of Believers ʿAlī, may God be pleased with all of them, and upon the lords of the youth of paradise, Ḥasan and Ḥusayn, and their followers and fellows.

{5} Poem: As God greets the descendants of Muḥammad;
I, too, greet him and his descendants[1]

{6} After praising God and sending greetings to Muḥammad and commending the selected friends and favoured children of ʿAlī , writes the guilty servant, Sayf Ẓafar, who is hopeful of God's mercy, one who seeks forgiveness from the Supreme Being, who has spent his life in the sessions and gatherings of the servants of God's religion, and has taken the spiritual realities of the [divine] feast from the detailed and precious prophetic gems, and due to divinely given success collected and called them *Durr al-Majālis*.[2] May the seeker and the one who suffers open his heart to read it and polish his soul by hearing their [i.e., the saints] pure stories; and, while in that unique state of feeling, assist this beggar [i.e., the author] by reciting *Sūrat al-Fātiḥa* in order to vanquish his sins and guilt: 'that is easy for God' (Q. 22:70).

[1] Similar couplets are found in *Dīwān Kāqānī*.

[2] Also, *Durr-i Majālis*. For more about its title, see the Inroduction.

{۷} و ترتیب ابواب: **باب اوّل** در فضیلتِ آفرینشِ مهتر آدم صَلَوَاتُ اللّٰهِ عَلَیْهِ وَسَلَامُه و نظیرها. **باب دوم** در فضیلتِ سخاوت ابراهیم علیه‌السلام و نظیرها. **باب سوم** در فضیلتِ مهتر شعیب[19] صَلَوَاتُ اللّٰهِ عَلَیْه. **باب چهارم** در فضیلتِ مهتر موسیٰ علیه‌السلام که بر کوه طور به وعدهٔ خدای تَعَالَی رفته بود و بعداز آن به حکم فرمان به دعوت فرعون رفته، خرامیدن موسیٰ از دارِ فنا به دارالبقا؛ **باب پنجم** در فضیلتِ مهتر سلیمان علیه‌السلام و انگشتری مملکت چگونه از دست ایشان رفته بود؛ چه سبب بود و چگونه باز به دست آمد. **باب ششم** در فضیلتِ مهتر عیسیٰ علیه‌السلام و معجزهٔ آن. **باب هفتم** در فضیلتِ پیغمبر ما در هدایت یافتن دوستان دین، و زردرویی دشمنان پیغمبر ﷺ. **باب هشتم** حقّ یتیمان در نیکوئی کردن در حقّ مادر و پدر ایشان و خشنودی و نظیرها. **باب نهم** حکایتِ مجروح شدن دندان مبارک پیغمبر ﷺ، چه حکمت بود؟ **باب دهم** در التماس و در فضیلتِ خواجهٔ عالم، محمّد مُصْطَفَی ﷺ و ملائم آن. **باب یازدهم** در فضیلتِ شاه مردان أمیرالمُؤمنین علی رضی‌الله‌عنه با خاتون قیامت فاطمهٔ زهرا رضی‌الله‌عنها.[20] **باب دوازدهم** حکایتِ ماریه قبطیه[ک] خدمتکار محمّد مُصْطَفَی ﷺ. **باب سیزدهم** فضیلتِ جوانانِ یوسف‌صِفَتان، آن‌گه در رضای خداوند چگونه بودند. **باب چهاردهم** فضیلتِ خالد بن‌ولید رضی‌الله‌عنه؛ چند کسان از دست او به دولت ایمان مشرّف شدند. **باب پانزدهم** فضیلتِ بلال و پادشاهی از اقلیم عرب.[ل] **باب شانزدهم** در نصیحت کردن لقمان حکیم عبدالرحمن بر پسر خویش. **باب هفدهم** در ایمان آوردن بت‌پرستی با ابراهیم. **باب هجدهم** حکایتِ سلطان ابراهیم ادهم قُدِّس سِرُّه. **باب نوزدهم** حکایتِ مرد سخی و زن بخیل. **باب بیستم** حکایتِ آزر بت‌تراش.[م] **باب بیست و یکم** حکایتِ طوطی به حضرت سلیمان بن‌داود علیه‌السلام.[ن] **باب بیست و دوم** حکایتِ آرزوی خواجه حسن بصری. **باب بیست و سوم** حکایتِ خواهش شیطان مردود که فردا بر امّت پیغمبر دعوی خواهد کرد. **باب بیست و چهارم** حکایتِ پادشاه نیشاپور با مظلومی. **باب بیست و پنجم** حکایتِ خواجه ربیع حسام با دختر خود سؤال و جواب کردن. **باب بیست و ششم** حکایتِ خواجه سفیان ثوری[21] با شیطان مردود عَلَیْه اللَعنَة. **باب بیست و هفتم** حکایتِ خواجه حسن نوری[س] رحمة الله. **باب بیست و هشتم** حکایتِ شیخ برسیسا که چگونه بود و چه کسی بود و سبب چه بود که ایمان کم کرد و مؤمن را از آن هُشیار باید بود؟ **باب بیست و نهم** در فضیلتِ ماه مبارک رمضان. **باب سی‌ام**[ع] حکایتِ خانهٔ کعبهٔ الله. **باب سی و یکم** [شامل روایت های کوتاه و بلند: الف و ب] مقتل أمیر المُؤمِنین امام حسن و حسین شهید کربلا رضی‌الله‌عنهما. **باب سی و دوم** حکایتِ سلطان ابوسعید ابوالخیر که حقّ مرید بر پیر چیست و حقّ پیر بر مرید چیست. **باب سی و سوم** حکایتِ اهل بهشت که به دیدار حقّ سُبْحَانَهُ وَتَعَالَی مشرّف خواهند شد و آخرین

[19] برلین «فضیلتِ مهتر شیث».
[20] در برخی نسخ فصل دهم و یازدهم جابه‌جا شده اند.
[21] برلین «خواجه سنعان».

[ک] ماریه قبطی
[ل] در حکایتِ بلال و هلال
[م] در حکایتِ بت‌پرست آزر
[ن] حکایتِ طوطی و مردی
[س] در حکایتِ خواجه ربیع جام
[ع] بیست و دهم

{7} And the chapters are as follows. **Chapter One:** On the virtues of the creation of His Eminence Adam (pbuh) and further similar examples; **Chapter Two:** On the virtue of Abraham's (pbuh) generosity and further similar examples; **Chapter Three:** On the virtue of Jethro (pbuh); **Chapter Four:** On the virtue of His Eminence Moses who had gone on Mount Sinai in order to see God; and who later went to Pharaoh based on a divine command; the elegant transition of Moses from the perishable abode to the eternal abode; **Chapter Five:** On the virtue of His Eminence Solomon (pbuh) and the way his signet ring disappeared from his hand; what was the reason and how it was brought back to him; **Chapter Six:** On the virtue of His Eminence Jesus (pbuh) and his miracle; **Chapter Seven:** On the virtue of our Prophet in guiding the friends of religion; and the embarrassment of Muḥammad's (pbuh) enemies; **Chapter Eight:** The right of orphans; on the proper behaviour of parents and their satisfaction, and further examples; **Chapter Nine:** The story of the Prophet's (pbuh) injured teeth; and why this should have happened; **Chapter Ten:** Entreating and on the virtue of the Master of the Worlds, Muḥammad (pbuh); **Chapter Eleven:** On the Virtue of the Hero, the Commander of Believers ʿAlī (pbuh), with the Lady of the Day of Judgement, Fāṭima al-Zahrāʾ (pbuh); **Chapter Twelve:** The story of Mary the Copt, the servant of Muḥammad (pbuh); **Chapter Thirteen:** On the virtue of the Joseph-like youth after he was treated for the sake of God; **Chapter Fourteen:** On the virtue of Khālid b. Walīd (pbuh); and how many people converted to the delight of faith through him; **Chapter Fifteen:** On the virtue of Bilāl, and a king from the Arab region; **Chapter Sixteen:** The advice of Luqmān the Wise, ʿAbd al-Raḥmān, to his son; **Chapter Seventeen:** On the coming to faith of an idolater through Abraham; **Chapter Eighteen:** The story of Sultan Ibrāhīm Adham, may his grave be sanctified; **Chapter Nineteen:** The story of the generous husband and the miserly wife; **Chapter Twenty:** The story of Āzar, the idol-maker; **Chapter Twenty-One:** The story of the parrot speaking with the Prophet Solomon (pbuh); **Chapter Twenty-Two:** The story of Khʷāja Ḥasan Baṣrī's desire; **Chapter Twenty-Three:** The story of the request of the outcast Satan who harassed the nation of Muḥammad; **Chapter Twenty-Four:** The story of the King of Nishapur's treatment of the oppressed; **Chapter Twenty-Five:** The story of Khʷāja Rabīʿ Ḥusām with his daughter; the question and the answer; **Chapter Twenty-Six:** The story of Khʷāja Sufyān Thawrī with the outcast Satan, God's curse be upon him; **Chapter Twenty-Seven:** The story of Khʷāja Ḥasan Nūrī, God's mercy be upon him; **Chapter Twenty-Eight:** The story of Shaykh Barsīsā, who he was, what type of person he was, and the reason that he lost his faith – believers should take heed!; **Chapter Twenty-Nine:** On the virtue of the holy month of Ramadan; **Chapter Thirty:** The story of the Kaʿba; **Chapter Thirty-One** (short and long versions: a and b): The story of the killing of the commanders of believers Imam Ḥasan and Imam Ḥusayn the Martyr of Karbala

از امّت محمّد مُصطَفَی ﷺ که از دوزخ بیرون آید. **باب سی و چهارم** در کیفیت بلعم باعور. **باب سی و پنجم** موسیٰ‌نامه. **باب سی و ششم** حکایتِ پادشاه شام. **[پایان]** نورنامه.[۲۲]

[۲۲] روایاتی در مورد «شرایط بانگ نماز» در حواشی فهرست فصول در نسخهٔ ۱۲۲۲ تاجیکستان نگاشته شده است.

(pbuh); **Chapter Thirty-Two:** The story of our sovereign-master Abu Saʿīd Abū al-Khayr regarding the right of the disciple upon the spiritual master, and the right of the spiritual master upon the disciple; **Chapter Thirty-Three:** The story of the inhabitants of paradise, who will be blessed with a meeting with God, and the last person from the community of Muḥammad to leave hell; **Chapter Thirty-Four:** Regarding Balʿam Bāʿūr; **Chapter Thirty-Five:** The tale of Moses; **Chapter Thirty-Six:** The story of the King of the Levant; and [the Epilogue] ***Nūr-nāma.***

درفضیلتِ آفرینش مهتر آدم صَلَوَاتُ اللّٰهِ عَلَیْهِ وسَلاَمُه ونظیرها

{۱} خداوند تَعَالَیٰ عَزَّوَجَلَّ خواست که آدم را بیافریند. ندای إِلٰهِي درهفت آسمان و زمین رسید که «ما می‌خواهیم بنده‌ای را پیدا کنیم که ایشان از دوستان حضرتِ پاکِ ما باشد و خلیفهٔ حضرتِ ما باشد و آرزوی بنده را دهد. از او بندگان پیدا کنیم که ایشان دوستان حضرت ما - جَلَّ وَعَلَا - باشند، و ما به کَرَمْ ایشان را دوست داریم وایشان مرا دوست دارند». چون ندای لطف يُحِبُّهُمْ وَ يُحِبُّونَهُۥ[1] دردادند، عَرشْ سربرآورد و گفت «بار خدایا، چون می‌خواهی که بندهٔ نیکبخت را پیدا گردانی و در کلام خود مرا عظیم خواندی که رَبُّ الْعَرْشِ الْعَظِيمِ.[2] آرزوی من آن است که این خلیفهٔ حضرتِ خویش را از من پیدا گردانی»؛ که کُرسی سر برآورد و گفت «إِلٰهِيّ، تو مرا وسیع خوانده و در کلام مجید خود فرمودی وَسِعَ كُرْسِيُّهُ السَّمَوَاتِ وَالأَرْضَ.[3] این بندهٔ نیکبخت را از من پیدا گردانی». آسمان سر برآورد و گفت «إِلٰهِيّ، تو مرا به ماه و آفتاب و کواکب و ستاره آراستی و در کلام خود فرمودی وَلَقَدْ زَيَّنَّا السَّمَاءَ الدُّنْيَا بِمَصَابِيحَ.[4] این بنده که در محبّت خود می‌آفرینی از من پیدا کن».

{۲} در آفرینش مهتر آدم صَلَوَاتُ اللّٰهِ هرکسی را به خودگمانی بود. امّا زمین هیچ سخن نمی‌گفت و سرِ خود به شکستگی فرود افکنده بود. فرمان آمد «ای زمین، هریکی را در آفرینش آدم به خودگمانی برده‌اند. چرا خاموشی و هیچ نمی‌گویی؟» گفت «إِلٰهِيّ، تو دانای سِرّهایی. عرش در عظمت خود نازیده، و کرسی به مسافت خود نازیده، آسمان به رفعت و کواکب خود نازیده. من که باشم که پایمالِ چهارپایان دنیایم. چگونه در آفرینش دوستِ تو به خودگمانی برم؟» فرمان شد که «چون تو در حضرت ما خود را چنین دانستی و شکستگی و

[1] آیهٔ ۵۴ سورهٔ مائده. [2] آیهٔ ۱۲۹ سورهٔ توبه. [3] آیهٔ ۲۵۵ سورهٔ بقره. [4] آیهٔ ۵ سورهٔ ملک.

CHAPTER 1

On the virtues of the creation of His Eminence Adam (pbuh) and further similar examples

{1} The Almighty and Glorious God decided to create Adam. The divine proclamation reached the seven layers of heaven and Earth, 'We want to create a servant who will be Our close friend, be Our successor, and meet Our expectations. We will make other servants out of him who will also be Our friends and We will love them with Our loving kindness and they will love Us, too'. As the compassionate proclamation of '…who love Him and are loved by Him…' (Q. 5:54) was announced, the Throne rose and said, 'O God! As You want to create an auspicious servant, and that You called me "the mighty" in Your own words: "He is the Lord of the Mighty Throne" (Q. 9:129), so my desire is that You make Your caliph from me'. The Seat stood and said, 'O God! You called me "the extended one" and in your glorious words stated, "His Seat extends over the heavens and the Earth' (Q. 2: 255); create this auspicious servant from me.' The Heaven rose and said, 'O God! You have adorned me with the Moon, Sun, planets, and stars and in Your own words said, "And We have verily embellished the heaven with lamps" (Q. 67:5). Create this servant, who You would make in Your love, from me.'

{2} Each was thinking differently regarding the creation of Adam (pbuh). But the Earth was silent, and humbly held its head down. The divine command asked, 'O Earth! Each of them thought differently about the creation of Adam from them, why are you silent and not expressing anything?' The Earth said, 'You are the Knower of all secrets. The Throne is proud of his mightiness, the Seat is honoured with his expanded dimension, the Heaven is proud of his height and stars and planets. So, who am I, as I am an animal pasture?! How dare I think about the creation of your friend from

بیچارگی آوردی ما دوستِ خود را از تو خواهیم پیدا گردانید تا بدانی که [ای] فرزندِ آدم، از آغاز کار تو [با؟] شکستگی برآمده است».

{۳} بیت: ای هرکه غرور کرد تبر خورد — خود را شکسته دیده برخورد
شاخی که بلند شد تبر خورد — نِی گفت که من نیم شکر خورد[۵]

{۴} نظیر دیگر بشنو. چون انگشترین خاتمِ به دست مهتر سلیمان علیه‌السلام رسید، هر پنج انگشت مهتر سلیمان با یکدیگر در سخن آمدند. انگشت شهادت بر انگشتان دیگر آغاز کرد که «انگشترین در من خواهند پوشانید زیرا که من از شما شرف دارم که انگشت شهادت هستم». و انگشت میانه نیز آغاز کرد که «من در میان شما بزرگتر هستم. در من خواهند پوشانید». وانگشت بِنْصِر[۶] آغاز کرد که «اگر انگشترین در میان شما نپوشانید، بعداز شما من بزرگ هستم [و] در من خواهد پوشانید».[۷]

{۵} و انگشت خُردُ مسکینْ و ساکنْ بماند و هیچ سخن نگفت. فرمان شد که «ای سلیمان، [از] انگشت خُرد بپرس که هر چهار انگشت. میان خود در آرزوی پوشیدن انگشتری بودند. تو چرا خاموش مانده‌ای و سخن نمی‌گویی؟» انگشت خُردُ گفت که «ای پیغمبر خدا، ایشان هریکی در بزرگی خود نازیدند و من در میان ایشان خُرد و ضعیف و ناتوانم. مرا باید که میان قومِ بزرگ بیچاره باشم. پس انگشترین در من چگونه خواهید پوشانید؟» فرمان شد که «ای سلیمانِ پیغمبر، خاتم مملکت در این انگشتِ خُردُ پوشان که خود را چیزی ندانسته».

{۶} نظیر دیگر هم بشنو. که شبی از شب‌ها بایزید را – قُدِّس سِرُّه – وقت خوش شده بود. گفت «إلهِيّ، لایقِ حضرت تو چیست که بایزید خدمت کند؟» فرمان شد که «سه چیز در خزانهٔ ما نیست. اگر تو داری بیار، ما خریداریم». گفت «آن سه چیز چه را است؟» ندا آمد «یکی شکستگی،[الف] دوم عذرِ تقصیرِ زبان، سوم بیچارگی تن».[۸]

[۵] . این ابیات منسوب به امیرحسینی سادات (هروی) است. در اکثر نسخ و دست‌نوشته‌های خاورشناسان به عنوان ضرب‌المثلی رایج در ادبیات فارسی مطرح شده است، و در کتب آموزش زبان فارسی تا اوایل قرن بیستم در جنوب آسیا به‌کار می‌رفته است. همچنین، عبارت «شاخی که بلند رفت به سر می‌خورد» به عنوان ضرب‌المثلی رایج در افغانستان شناخته می‌شود. مراجعه نمایید به: عنایت‌الله شهرانی، ضرب‌المثل‌های دری افغانستان (تهران: بنیاد موقوفات دکتر محمود افشار، ۲۰۰۳)، ۱۲۶. عبارتی با همین مضمون به سعدی شیرازی، کتاب بوستان، نیز منسوب است: «نهد شاخ پرمیوه سر بر زمین».

[۶] انگشت چهارم از سمت انگشت شست. در برخی محافل و منابع به عنوان «انگشت حلقه» شناخته می‌شود.

[۷] در نسخهٔ دانشگاه تهران «انگشت شرعیه» نیز به سخن می‌آید و آرزوی پوشیدن انگشتر را ابراز می‌کند.

[۸] در برخی نسخ ترتیب و چینش این سه مورد متفاوت است.

[الف] عجز

myself?' Then a divine proclamation was made, 'As you considered yourself so humble before Us, and that shows your abject and modesty, We would like to create Our friend from you in order to know that, [O] the child of Adam, your journey has begun with modesty and humbleness from the beginning.'

{3} Poem: Whoever is self-deluded, received a blow from an axe
Found himself forlorn;
A branch that grew tall, received a blow from an axe
The sugarcane said, I am merely a reed [viz. nothing]
therefore, it was filled with sugar[1]

{4} Here is another story. Once the signet ring had been given to Solomon (pbuh), his five fingers began conversing with each other. The index finger said, 'The ring will be worn on me, as I am superior to all of you, because I am the finger of the *shahāda*' [by which one indicates the profession of faith]. The middle finger asserted, 'I am longer than any of you. It will be worn on me.' Next the ring finger said, 'If he will not bestow the ring on either of you, it will be worn on me, as after you, I am greatest.'

{5} The little finger remained desolate and silent, and said nothing. God commanded Solomon, 'Ask your little finger why did it remain silent and not express its idea while other fingers stated their desire to wear the ring?' The little finger replied [to Solomon], 'O Messenger of God, each of these fingers has magnified himself and I am the weak and poor one among them. I must be desolate and and abject among the great ones. So, how could it be that your ring would be worn on me!?' God ordered, 'O Prophet Solomon, wear your signet ring on this little finger as it is humble and considers itself nothing.'

{6} And listen to another story. Once upon a night, Bāyazīd, may his grave be sanctified, was cheerful. He said, 'O God, what could be Your desire so that Bāyazīd can serve accordingly?' God commanded, 'There are three things not in Our treasury. If you have them, then bring them to Us as We are the Buyer.' Bāyazīd said, 'What are those three things?' A divine voice issued forth, 'One is humility, second is an apology for the tongue, third is desolation and abjection of the body'.

[1] This poem is ascribed to Amīr Ḥusaynī Harawī. The second couplet has been translated based on Thomas Roebuck, *A Collection of Proverbs, and Proverbial Phrases, in the Persian and Hindoostanee Languages* (Calcutta: Printed at the Hindustanee Press, 1824), 278. Also, see N. A. Hajib and E. Shahi, *Readings from Persian Prose and Poetry for High Schools* (Surat: I. P. Mission Press, 1899).

{۷} الغرض. چون اللّٰه تَعَالَی خواست تا آدم علیه‌السلام را در وجود آرد فرشتگان گفتند: «ما در لوح محفوظ نوشته دیدیم که آدم را بی‌فرمانی تو کند، و فرزندان او گنه‌کار و خونریز و زانی باشند. ما تو را به پاکی ثنا و بندگی می‌کنیم. با وجود ما این چنین کسانی را بیافرینی؟» فرمان شد که «دَمْ دَرکشید. آنچه[۹] ما دانیم شما ندانید». قال اللّٰه تَعَالَی «إِنِّي أَعْلَمُ مَا لاَ تَعْلَمُونَ»[۱۰].

{۸} آنگاه فرمان شد که «جبرئیل نزدیک زمین برو و یک مشت خاک بیار». جبرئیل نزدیک زمین شد. زمین به زبان حال آغاز کرد «ای مَلِک، به عزّت آن خدای که تو را آفریده از زمینِ گِل برنگیر». جبرئیل بازگشت. گفت: «إِلٰهِيّ، تو داناتری که مرا سوگند به تو می‌دهد که «از من چیزی برمگیر»».

{۹} میکائیل را فرمان شد که «تو برو و از زمین یک مشت خاک بیارید». باز زمین سوگند داد و زاری کرد. میکائیل بازگشت. گفت: «إِلٰهِيّ، تو می‌دانی که زمین ما را سوگند به تو می دهد».

{۱۰} اسرافیل را فرمان شد که «بروید و از زمین یک مشت خاک بیارید». باز زمین سوگند داد و زاری کرد.[۱۱] ایشان بازگشت و گفت: «إِلٰهِيّ، تو می‌دانی».

{۱۱} فرمان شد که «عزائیل تو برو و از زمین یک مشت خاک بیار». عزرائیل نزدیک زمین شد. باز زمین سوگند داد. عزرائیل گفت که «ای زمین! خاموش باش». و سپس خاک برداشت و بُرد. از حضرت عزّت ندا شنید که «ای عزائیل، تو را سوگند به من داد، چرا از او خاک برگرفتی؟» گفت «إِلٰهِيّ، اگرچه زمین سوگند تو داد، امّا من فرمان‌بُرداری تو از سوگند او مهتر[ب] دانستم». فرمان شد: «ای عزرائیل، امروز مرا فرمان‌بُرداری کردی و بر خاکِ مسکین رحم نکردی. چون از این خاک آدمیزادی پیدا کنیم، قابضِ ارواحِ ایشان تو باشی».

{۱۲} این چه حکمت بود که زمین خاک نمی‌داد؟ چون فرمان شد [که] «آدم را از تو پیدا خواهم کرد»، زمین از هیبت خدای تَعَالَی در لرزه افتاد. یعنی اینکه «نباید که از من کسی آفریده شود که بی‌فرمانی حقّ سبحانه وتَعَالَی کند».

{۱۳} الغرض. چون خاک از زمین بیاوردند، هفتادهزار سال قالب آدم علیه‌السلام حقّ سبحانه وتعالی به ید قدرت خود موجود گردانید. بعداز آن جان در قالب آدم درآورد.[۱۲] برخاست و بنشست و عطسه آمد. في الحال گفت «أَلْحَمْدُ للّٰه رَبِّ الْعَالَمِين»[۱۳]. از حضرت پاک جواب آمد «يَرْحَمُكَ اللّٰه».

{۱۴} فرشتگان گفتند «إِلٰهِيّ، هنوز آدم تو را نیکو نشناخته و لذّت[۱۴] بندگی تو درنیافته. چیست که

[۹] تاجیکستان ۱۲۲۲، «آنچه» به صورت «آنج» نگاشته شده است. [۱۰] آیهٔ ۳۰ سورهٔ بقره.
[۱۱] براساس سه نسخهٔ اردبیل، دانشگاه تهران و طلعت مصر، دو فرشتهٔ میکائیل و اسرافیل به همراه یکدیگر به سوی زمین فرستاده می‌شوند.
[۱۲] اشاره به آیهٔ ۲۹ سورهٔ حجر. [۱۳] آیهٔ ۲ سورهٔ فاتحه. [۱۴] در برخی نسخ به صورت «ذلّت» آمده است.

[ب] بهتر

{7} To go back to the story. When God wanted to create Adam (pbuh), the angels said, 'We have noticed in the Guarded Tablet that Adam will disobey You, and his descendants will be sinful, bloodthirsty, and adulterous. We worship and obey You purely. You have us and You still want to create him?' God commanded, 'Be silent! What We know, you would never know'. God said, 'I know what you do not know' (Q. 2:30).

{8} Then the angel Gabriel was ordered, 'O Gabriel get close to the Earth and bring us a fist of its soil'. Gabriel went to the Earth. The Earth found speech and said, 'O angel, by the glory of the God who has created you, do not take soil from Earth'. Gabriel returned and said, 'O God, You know why I have not brought soil as the Earth swore by You, "Do not take anything from me!"'

{9} Later, [the angel] Michael was ordered, 'Go take a portion of soil from the Earth'. Again, the Earth took oath and wailed. Michael returned and said, 'O God, You are aware of the Earth swore by You!'

{10} An order was revealed to [the angel] Isrāfīl , 'Go take a portion of soil from the Earth'. Again, the Earth took oath and wailed. Isrāfīl retruned and said, 'O God, You are aware of the Earth swore by You!'

{11} An order was revealed to [the angel] ʿIzrāʾīl, 'O ʿIzrāʾīl, go take soil from the Earth!' ʿIzrāʾīl went to the Earth. Again, the Earth swore by God. ʿIzrāʾīl exclaimed, 'O Earth! be silent.' Then, ʿIzrāʾīl took soil and returned. He heard a call from the Almighty, 'O ʿIzrāʾīl, the Earth took oath before you by Me. Why, nonetheless, did you ignore it and take the soil?' ʿIzrāʾīl responded, 'O God, although the Earth took oath by You, I considered your command more important than the Earth's oath'. It was then proclaimed, 'O ʿIzrāʾīl, today you have obeyed My order and did not take pity on the poor Earth. As mankind is made of this soil, then you are appointed as their Angel of Death, grabbing their souls upon Our order.'

{12} What could have been the reason for the Earth not granting soil? Once it heard the order that 'Adam would be made of you', the Earth feared the glory of God. It means that 'somebody must not be made out of me who will disobey God.'

{13} Again, returning to the story. Once the Earth's soil was brought, God created the shape of Adam (pbuh) within seventy thousand years, then breathed spirit into him.[2] Adam was born, sat, and sneezed. Immediately afterwards he said, 'Praise be to God, the Lord of the Universe' (Q. 1:2). A response was sent from the purified divine dominion: 'God Bless you'.

{14} The angels said, 'O God, Adam has no knowledge of You yet, and does not know about the joy of service to you.[3] How come that you responded with "bless you"? We have been at your service and praised you for a thousand years and no such warm

[2] Referring to Q. 15:29. [3] '[...] and does not know about prostrating to You.'

اجابت «یَرحَم بِكَ» در کار وی شد؟ ما چندین هزارسال در بندگی و تسبیح تو به سر می بریم، وقتی[۱۵] اجابتِ کَرَم در حقّ ما نشد. آدم یک ثنای تو بگفت فی‌الحال اجابت فرمودی و بنواختی». فرمان رسید که «مرا با این خاکیان چیزی بُوَد که با دیگران نَبُوَد. فرشتگان، همهٔ شما می گویید که آدم هنوز لذّت بندگی درنیافته. [امّا] کسی که در اوّل‌مرتبه پروردگارِ خود را بشناخت و حمد و ثنا گفت، من چگونه خلعت اِجابت در کار او نکنم»؟ اگرچه فرشتگان در حقّ او و فرزندان او به سختی گفتند که «بی فرمان، زانی و خون‌ریز باشند»، امّا یکی نظر کن که حقّ سُبحانَهُ وتَعالیٰ برگزیدگان خویش را بر فرشتگان چگونه کرامت می کند. حقّ سبحانه وتَعالَی بر فرشتگان عتاب کرد که «شما در حقّ بندگان ما چیزی دیگر می گفتید. اکنون ببینید چگونه فرمان‌بُرداری می کنند.

{۱۵} چون از مردم گناهی به وجود آید هم باری تَعَالَی می‌فرماید که «ای فرشتگان، نظر بر بدی بندگان ما مکنید که چندین چیز در آدمی پیدا کردم که در شما نیست. اوّل خوردن و آشامیدن، دوم شهوت نفسانی، سوم هوا و حرص، چهارم وسواس شیطانی، پنجم دنیای مکّار دادم ایشان را؛ دام ایشان ساختم. ای فرشتگان، اگر این چیزها در ذات شما مِی‌نهادم، هرآینه[۱۶] شما نیز گناه می کردید. دیگر، ای فرشتگان، عرش و کرسی و بهشت مرا معاینه می‌بینید و عبرت از دیدن دوزخ می گیرید. و بندگان ما هیچ از اینها نمی‌بینند و درغیبتْ ایمان به من آوردند».

{۱۶} نظیر دیگر بشنو که ازجهت تو فرشتگان را عتاب شده است. چون حضرت ابراهیم صَلَوَاتُ اللّٰهِ عَلَیْه را در خواب نمودند که «برخیز و فرزند خود را در راه ما قربانی کن». فی‌الحال کارد گرفت و اسماعیل عليه‌السلام را در مقام قربانی برد و گفت «ای فرزند، مرا در خواب نمودند که تو را در راه خدای تَعَالَی عَزَّوَجَلَّ قربان کنم». اسماعیل عليه‌السلام گفت: «ای پدر، زود باش به آنچه تو را امر کرده‌اند. اِنْشَاءَاللّٰه تَعَالَی مرا یکی از صابران یابی. یک جان چه باشد؟ اگر هفتادهزار جان بوده باشد به فرمودهٔ او قربانی کنم».

{۱۷} چون ابراهیم عليه‌السلام کارد بر گلوی اسماعیل عليه‌السلام راند، حقّ سُبحانَهُ وتَعالیٰ بر فرشتگان عتاب کرد که «شما گفتید که فرزندان آدم خون‌ریزان باشند، یک نظر کنید که اگر خون ریزند، آن را در راه ما ریزند. چنانچه ابراهیم عليه‌السلام خونِ فرزند خود را در رضای ما آورده».

{۱۸} دیگر در آن وقت که زلیخا یوسف را در قصر درآورد و گفت «اگر خلوتْ بایدْ هست و اگر خانهٔ خوبْ بایدْ هست و اگر جمالِ کمالْ بایدْ هست؛ اکنون من تو را هرگز نخواهم گذاشت تا مُرادِ من حاصل نکنی». مهتر یوسف گفت: «این سخن مگوی که خدای تَعَالَی می‌بینید. با تو زنا نکنم».

{۱۹} زلیخا گفت که «عشق تو بر من غلبه کرده است و مرا طاقت نمانده». یوسف عليه‌السلام گفت «در من چه دیدی که دل تو مایل شده؟» گفت «ای یوسف، اوّل موی سر زلف تو». گفت: «ای زلیخا، در گور اوّل چیزی که بریزد موی سر بوَد». زلیخا گفت «ای یوسف، چون نظر در نرگس چشم تو می کنم، این چشم من نمی‌خواهد که روی غیر ببیند». گفت «ای زلیخا، اوّل در گور چشم از خانهٔ چشم جدا خواهند کرد». «ای

[۱۵] لحظه‌ای. [۱۶] قطعا.

response was given to us. Adam praises You only once, and You have quickly responded and appeased him?!' God responded, 'There will be something between these earthly people and I that will not be with others. You angels agree that Adam does not know about the joy of service before Us. But one who has learned about his God from the beginning and praised his God, how can I not to respond to him?' Although the angels protested harshly about him and his descendants saying that 'he will be disobedient, an adulterer, and bloodthirsty,' observe how God respected His chosen ones rather than the angels.God shouted to the angels, 'You have said something different about Our servants. Now see how they obey Us'.

{15} When the people sin God says, 'O angels, do not take into account the badness of our servants, because we have put several things in humans which are not found in you. First, eating and drinking; second, lust; third, sensual desire and greediness; fourth, satanic temptation; and fifth, an alluring world; I gave these to temp them. O angels, if I had put such things in your essence, you would certainly have sinned. Also, O angels, you observe my Throne, Seat, and paradise and learnt a lesson after seeing hell. But my servants do not see any of these yet believed in me while being away from them.'

{16} Hear another story that the angels were shouted at, because of you. Once the Prophet Abraham (pbuh) dreamed: 'Hasten, wake up, and sacrifice your child in Our path!' He soon grabbed a knife and took Ishmael to the place of sacrifice and said, 'O my child, I slept and dreamed, based on the God's order, that I must sacrifice you in the path of God'. Ishmael (pbuh) said, 'Be as quick as possible to perform what you have been ordered to do. God willing, you will find me patient. One life is nothing, if I had seventy thousand lives, I would sacrifice them for His sake.'

{17} While Abraham (pbuh) was rubbing the knife against Ishmael's (pbuh) throat, God proclaimed to the angels, 'You had said that Adam's children are bloodthirsty! Now have a look and see if they are so bloodthirsty, they do it in our path. As Abraham (pbuh) sacrifices his child for Our satisfaction.'

{18} Also, once Zulaykha brought Joseph to the castle and told him, 'If privacy is required, so be it, and if there should be a proper house, so be it, and if beautiful perfection is needed, so be it; I will not let you go free until you make my dream true.' His Eminence Joseph said to her, 'Do not say this to me as God sees. I will not commit adultery with you.'

{19} Zulaykha replied, 'Your love has penetrated deep within me and I have no more tolerance.' Joseph (pbuh) asked, 'What have you seen in me that made you fall in love with me?' Zulaykha replied, 'O Joseph, first your charming hair'. Joseph responded, 'O Zulaykha, the first thing [after death] to be razed to the ground is the head's hair.' Zulaykha said, 'O Joseph, when I gaze at your beautiful eyes, my eyes do not want to see anyone else.' He said, 'The eyes will be taken out from the eye socket at first in the grave'.

یوسف، منِ گفتار تو را دوست دارم». یوسف گفت «مگر خبر نداری چون آدمی بمیرد مُهرِ خاموش چُنان نَهَنْد که از گفتار بازمانَد». زلیخا گفت «ای یوسف، از سرْ تا قَدَمْ جمیعِ اعضاء تو را دوست مِی‌دارم». گفت «ای زلیخا، مگر خبر نداری که در گور بند از بند جدا خواهند کرد».

{۲۰} چنین آورده‌اند که هرچند مهتر یوسف از حقّ باری تَعَالَی می‌ترسانْدْ، نصحیت را زلیخا قبول نمی‌کرد. دست به جانب یوسف دراز کرد. یوسف از خوفِ زِنا از پیش او بُگریخت. از عقب پیراهنِ یوسف را زلیخا پاره کرد. حقّ سُبْحَانَهُ وَتَعَالَى به فرشتگان خطاب کرد که «شما گفته بودید که فرزندان آدم زانیان باشد، اکنون بندهٔ من چگونه خود را از زنا نگاه آورد».

{۲۱} نظیر دیگر. یونسِ پیغمبرْ عَلَيْهِ السَّلَام را لقمهٔ ماهی گردانید. او را سه حال پیش آمد: یکی شکمِ ماهی، دوم هول دریا، سوم تاریکی به مجرّدی که در شکمِ ماهی رفت. درین حال تحریمِ نماز[17] بست و به ثنای حقّ تَعَالَی بگشاد و گفت اللّٰهُ أَكْبَر.

{۲۲} حقّ سُبْحَانَهُ وَتَعَالَى خطاب کرد که «ای فرشتگان، شما می‌گویید که «ما تو را ثنای می‌گوییم. این خاکیان را برای چه پیدا می‌کنی؟» یک نظر در کار این یونسِ خاکی کنید که در تنگی و تاریکی مبتلا گشته به ذکر و ثناء ما مشغول است. ای فرشتگان، شما را راحتِ عرش و کرسی و سِدْرَةِ الْمُنْتَهَی می‌رسد و هیچ غم و مشقّت به شما نمی‌رسد. و اگر چنین سختی که آن به آدم می‌رسید به شما رسید، یکی از فراموشکاران باشید».

{۲۳} بعداز آن فرمان شد: «ای فرشتگان، تخت آدم را بیارید و بر عرش نشانید و بانگ طرقو[18] بردارید و او را سجده کنید».[19] به حکمِ فرمان جمله ملائکه سجده کردند. و آنانی که آدم را سجده نکردند به قعر آتش خدای تَعَالَی سوخته گشتند.

{۲۴} و شیطان ایستاده مانده بود. چون فرشتگان سر از سجده برداشتند دیدند که شیطان استاده مانده بود و سجده نکرده. خود را فرمانبردار حقّ سبحانه تَعَالَی یافتند و دوم کرّت سجدهٔ شکر پیش آدم کردند. و این سنّتِ ایشان در میان فرزندان آدم بماند. فرمان رسید که «ای فرزندان آدم، فرشتگان دو نوبت پیش پدر شما سجده کردند، شما هم در نماز دو بار سجده کنید».[20]

{۲۵} الغرض. چون شیطان سجده نکرد فرمان شد که «ای ملعون، چرا بی‌فرمانی کردی و پیش برگزیدهٔ حضرت پاک سجده نبردی و خودبینی کردی. و ما خودبینان را دوست نداریم. و تو را ازجهتی که آدم را سجده نکردی و اِنکار ورزیدی از درِ خود براندیم و بر جبینِ ناپاکِ تو نهادیم و همیشه در لعنت ما باشی».[21]

[17] تکبیرة الاحرام. [18] بانگِ راه دهید. [19] اشاره به آیهٔ ۱۱ سورهٔ اعراف دارد.

[20] چنین خوانشی از دلیل سجدهٔ دوم در نماز مسلمانان با آنچه در کتب حدیثی سنّی و شیعی آمده تا حدّی متفاوت است.

[21] اشاره دارد به آیهٔ ۱۸ سورهٔ لقمان.

She said, 'I love your speech'. Joseph said, 'Do you not know that once mankind dies, the seal of silence is put on the mouth so that he is unable to speak?' Zulaykha said, 'I love you from head to toe; I love every limb of your body.' Joseph replied, 'O Zulaykha, are you not aware that every single part of the body will be decomposed in the grave?'

{20} It is reported that howsoever His Eminence Joseph warned her about God, Zulaykha did not accept. She reached out to him. In order not to commit adultery, Joseph ran away from her. Zulaykha tore Joseph's shirt from behind. Here God addressed the angels, 'You had said that Adam's children will be adulterous. See how my servant kept himself away from adultery!'

{21} Another story. Jonah (pbuh) was eaten by a fish. Three things happened to him in succession: first, falling into the fish's belly; second, thalassophobia;[4] third, darkness which he found once he fell into the fish's belly. Then, he began to pray and praised God and said, 'God is Great'.

{22} God then said, 'O angels, you contend that 'we praise You. What do You want to make these earthly people?' See the plight of this earthly Jonah, how he is trapped in tightness and darkness but remembers to praise Us. You are provided with joy and ease in the Throne and the Seat and the Sidrat al-Muntahā (i.e., heavenly lote tree) without sorrow and pain. And if such hardship that had been put on Adam's shoulder, was on yours, you would have been of the forgetful.'

{23} Subsequently, a command was given: 'O angels, bring the seat of Adam and put on the Throne, proclaim "Make way!" and prostrate before him.'[5] On account of the divine order the angels prostrated and those who did not prostrate before Adam burned at the bottom of hell.

{24} Satan had stood there. When the angels finished their prostration they noticed that Satan stayed there and did not prostrate. Then, they understood how obedient of God they were and they performed a second prostration before Adam, that is, a prostration for thanksgiving. This tradition invented by angels remained among the children of Adam [i.e., prostrating two times]. God commanded, 'O children of Adam, angels prostrated before Adam two times, you, too, prostrate two times in your prayers.'

{25} To go back to the story. As Satan did not prostrate before Adam, a divine announcement was made: 'O accursed, why did you disobey and not prostrate before the chosen of Our sanctified Throne, and acted arrogantly, and We do not like arrogant boasters.[6] We cast you out of Our presence due to not prostrating before Adam and denying, and We put a seal of curse on your impure forehead, and you will be cursed by Us forever'.

[4] i.e., fear of the ocean. [5] Referring to Q. 7:11. [6] Referring to Q. 31:18.

{۲۶} آنگاه شیطان گفت «إِلٰهِيّ، چندین هزارسال تو را بندگی کردم. ازجهت آدمِ خاکی مرا از درِ خود بِراندی. اکنون مُزْدِ چندین هزارسال مرا بده». فرمان شد «چه فرمایی و چه می‌خواهی»؟ گفت: «مرا ازجهت خاکیان این روز پیش آمد. اکنون مرا بر ایشان مسلّط کن تا انتقام خود از ایشان بکشم».

{۲۷} فرمان شد که «خواست تو به تو دادیم. امّا بگو بر ایشان چه کنی؟» [شیطان] گفت «إِلٰهِيّ، بَر دلِ هر مؤمنی هر روز سیصد و شصت بار حمله کنم». فرمان شد که «بر دل هر مؤمنی به کَرَم خود سیصد و شصت بار به نظرِ رحمتْ بنگریم».

{۲۸} باز گفت «إِلٰهِيّ، ایشان را چندین گناه بدارم که وقت مُردن گویم «این بنده همیشه بی‌فرمانی کرده. از چشمْ نادیدنی دیده، و از گوشْ ناشنیدنی شنیده، و در دهنْ ناخوردنی خورده، و در دستْ ناگرفتنی بگرفته، و از پایْ نارفتنی رفته. با چندین گناه تو را با حضرت سبحانه تَعَالَیٰ چه کار؟»» فرمان شد که «ای مردودِ بدبخت، چون بنده را عطای ایمان برابر باشد به کرم خود فرمان فرستیم که «ای بنده، لَا تَخَفْ وَلَا تَحْزَنْ،[22] هیچ مترس و اندوهگین مشو».» و گفت «دشمن قدیم[23] را اعتبار مکن[24] که به لطف خود به شما وعده کرده‌ایم إِنَّ اللَّهَ يَغْفِرُ الذُّنُوبَ جَمِيعًا،[25] به درستی و راستی خدای تَعَالَیٰ عَزَّوَجَلَّ آمرزیده گناهان است».

{۲۹} «دیگر ای مردود، در حضرت ما می‌گویی که هرعضوی گناهی کرده‌اند. چون بندهٔ مرا در گور دفن کنند چشم او بریزد. گویم «ای بنده، کفّارت چشم تو این بود. هر گناه که در چشم کرده بودی بیامرزیدم». چون زبان بریزد «گویم هر گناهی که به زبان و دهان کرده بودی بیامرزیدم». و چون دست و پای از بند جدای شود، گویم «ای بنده، مکافات گناهان تو همه در خاک ریخت و هر گناهی که از سر تا قدم تو بود آمرزیدم».

{۳۰} . دیگر چون بندهٔ ما بمیرد و در خاک دفن کنند دو فرشته فرستیم که «بندهٔ مرا از روزه و نماز و چیزهای دیگر بپرسید که نقصان دارد و از وحدانیّت ما بپرسید». شُکرْ خدایِ عَزَّوَجَلَّ که فرزندِ آدم را در وجودِ آدم بیاورده بود که شیطان را نومید گردانیَد.

{۳۱} الغرض. فرمان رسید که «آدم، تو با زوجهٔ خود در بهشت ساکن شو و از جمیع نعمت‌های بهشت بخور و بیاشام. و امّا گِرد شَجَرِ گندم نگرد و نخوری که اگر از این درخت بخوری فَتَكُونَ مِنَ الظَّالِمِينَ، تو یکی از ظالمان باشی».[۲۶، ج]

{۳۲} سُبحان الله، حکم براین رفته بود که آدم گندم بخورد تا بدان سبب به دنیا فرستند واز فرزندان او دوستان و دشمنان را از یکدیگر جدا گرداند و گروهی دوستان حضرت پاک او باشند، و گروهی لایق عذاب وعید گردند.

[22] آیهٔ ۳۳ سورهٔ عنکبوت. [23] شیطان. [24] «اعتبار کردن» اشاره به «اعتماد نمودن» دارد.
[25] آیهٔ ۵۳ سورهٔ زمر. [26] این جمله بر اساس آیهٔ ۳۵ سورهٔ بقره بیان شده است.

ج در خاطر مگیر

{26} Then Satan replied, 'O God, I have worshipped you for a thousand years, then you throw me out because of an earthly human! Now, give me my wage for these thousand years'. God said, 'What do you say and what do you want?' Satan replied, 'This has happened to me because of these earthly people. Command that I control them until I take my revenge.'

{27} A divine proclamation was made, 'Your request has been given to you by Us. But did you say what you wanted done with them?' Satan said, 'O God, I would attack the heart of each believer 360 times each day.' God said, 'Then, we would, because of Our kindness, shed our merciful light upon the heart of every believer.'

{28} Satan, again, replied, 'I would tempt them to sin repeatedly, so I can tell you during their death that "This servant of yours has always disobeyed, has seen with eyes the things that must not be seen, has heard with ears the things that must not be heard, and has received things by hand that must not be touched, and has walked a path by foot that must not be passed. What is your relationship with God with such a heavy burden of sin?' God said, 'O miserable and outcast! To the extent that the servant's bestowal of faith is weighty We, out of kindness, have revealed an order: "Fear not, nor grieve!" (Q. 29:33). And We said, "Do not trust the old enemy as we promised you mercifully that, "Truly, God forgives all your sins" (Q. 39:53).

{29} Also, outcast Satan, you have stated in Our presence that every part of the body has committed sin. Once My servant is buried in the grave, his eyes rot. I say to him, "My servant this was expiation of your eye. Whatever sin you have committed with this eye has been remitted and forgiven." When the tongue rots, I would say that "whatever sin is committed by the tongue and mouth has been forgiven." And when the hand and leg dissociate from the body, I would say, "O My servant, the retribution for all your sins has fallen on the soil of the grave and I have forgiven all your vice from head to toe".

{30} Also, once Our servant dies, We send two angels to him who are ordered to 'ask whether Our servant neglected fasting and saying prayer, among other things, and to ask about Our unity.' Praise be to God who places the children of Adam in the essence of Adam by which He disappointed Satan.'[7]

{31} Back to the story. A divine proclamation was made: '[O] Adam! reside in paradise along with your wife and eat and drink all sorts of heavenly graces and favour, but do not approach the Wheat tree. Do not eat from this tree, "Lest you be among the wrongdoers"' (Q. 2:35).[8]

{32} Glory be to God. It was predestined that Adam should eat the wheat for which

[7] The translation of this sentnece may be revised in the future.

[8] The entire paragraph is based on Q. 2:35.

{۳۳} نظیر دیگر. صبر از آدم برگرفتند و گندم را در نظر او چنان جلوه دادند که به چشم آدم هیچ درختی به جمال گندم نرسید تا خود را دلالت کند. و قُوت آدم گردانیدند تا هر دمی و هر زمانی آدم را بخوردن دهند تا نفس آرام گیرد. و شیطان مسخّر وسواس گشت. آدم عاجز چه کند؟ گندم بِخُورَد.

{۳۴} تا روزی حوّا نزدیک درخت گندم رفته بود که از وی دانه بخورد. و نزدیک آدم علیه‌السلام آمد و گفت که «من چُنین بر درخت گندم رفته بودم و از وی بخوردم. در حقّ من هیچ فرمان صادر نشد. تو را که گفته بود[د] از این درخت گندم که مقابل تخت تو است دانه نخور و از جنس دیگر بخور».[ه]

{۳۵} از گفتارِ حوّا، آدم علیه‌السلام را سهو افتاد و نزدیک شجرهٔ گندم برفت و دانه در دهان بکرد. هنوز دانه در حلقْ نیکو نرفته بود که تاج از سر وی پرید و حلّه از او برفته، مفلس و برهنه شد. به سوی بهشت می دوید.[و] و به هر کوشکی و درختی که شدی ایشان می گفتند که «از ما بُگذر که تو بی‌فرمانی کردی و ما فرمان‌بُرداریم. بی‌فرمانی در میان ما چه کند؟» آدم هر جانب رُخ بکردی[۲۷] هیچ نزدیک خود راه نمی‌داد. سرگردان و متحیّر گشت.

{۳۶} بیت: حُسن رخ تو ملک دو عالم فروگرفت؛ بیچاره‌ای که از تو گریزد کجا رود[۲۸]

{۳۷} هیچ درختی برگ خود مهتر آدم را نمی‌داد[ز] تا ستر خود بپوشد. تا آنکه گذر بر درخت انجیر افتاد.[۲۹] درخت انجیر را گفت «مرا برگ خود بده تا ستر خود بپوشم». انجیر گفت «منّت دارم؛ برگ از من بستان». چند برگ گرفت و خود را بپوشید. درزمانْ[۳۰] فرمان رسید بر درختِ انجیر که «هیچ درخت آدم را برگِ خود نداد و تو چرا بی‌فرمانی ما کردی و برگ خود دادی؟» انجیر گفت «إلٰهِيّ، من در آن حال در آدم نظر کردم. آن روز که خواستی آدم را آفریدن، ندا فرمودی که «می‌خواهم بنده(ای) را پیدا گردانیَم که او خلیفهٔ شایان ما باشد و از وی فرزندان پیدا آریَم که دوستان حضرت ما باشند». إلٰهِيّ، کسی را تو به عزّت خود و به دوستی گرفته باشی، او را چگونه زود ضایع خواهی کردی؟» فرمان شد که «ای انجیر، تو عزیزکردهٔ ما را عزیز کردی، هرمیوه که در دنیا پیدا کرده‌ایم او را در میان دانه باشد. امّا در تو دانه نباشد. هر که تو را بخورد او را نفع و ثواب بسیار باشد».[۳۱]

۲۷ به گمان من بعید است که «رخ بگردی» باشد.   ۲۸ احتمالا در نوشته‌های «بنده نواز» یافت شود.

۲۹ واژهٔ فارسی «انجیر» در نسخهٔ جاوه‌ای داستان حضرت آدم استفاده شده‌است. چنانچه در بخش انگلیسی مقدّمه بیان کرده‌ام، این قسمت از داستان حضرت آدم، با الهام از عبارات فارسی، در متن جاوه‌ای دیده می‌شود.

۳۰ معادل عبارت عربی «في الحال» است که به وفور در این کتاب دیده می‌شود.

۳۱ این نکته دلالت دارد بر اینکه اکثر متون اسلام در آسیا تا قرون میانه تحت تاثیر ادبیات رایج در خاورمیانه و خراسان نگاشته می‌شده‌اند. والّا در جنوب و جنوب‌شرق آسیا تعداد میوه‌های بدون دانه و بدون هسته کم نیست. به‌طور مثال می‌توان به اکثر گونه‌های موز و دراگن فروت اشاره کرد.

د منع کرده بود   ه امّا از جنس دیگر چرا بخوری؟   و در بهشت هر سو می‌دوید   ز هیچ درختی برگ خود را به مهتر آدم نمی‌داد

he is sent to Earth, and his children be divided into friends and enemies. One group is the friend of God, and the other deserves the promised punishment.

{33} Another story. Patience deserted Adam and the wheat before his eyes was the most beautiful tree ever. And it was given to him as his food, until his despotic soul was enriched every moment of time. And Satan gained control and became a whisperer. What can poor Adam do, unless eat wheat.

{34} Once upon a time, Eve had approached the Wheat tree to eat from it. She went to Adam (pbuh) and said to him, 'I approached the Wheat tree and tasted it. There was no verdict against me. Who may have alerted you not to take grain from the Wheat tree that is near your seat, but from other species?'

{35} Through Eve's utterance, Adam (pbuh) was tempted and went to the Wheat tree and put a grain into his mouth. The grain was still there and did not properly go down his throat but the crown was overturned from his head and his dress was taken from his body. He became shattered and naked. He ran towards heaven. He approached every single palace and tree. All of them said to him, 'Get away from us as you have disobeyed, while we are obedient. Why do we want someone disobedient among us?' Adam turned in every direction but nobody housed him. He remained astray and dumbstruck.

{36} Poem: The beauty of your side/the sight of your beauty conquers the two kingdoms;
the poor who gets away from you where would he go

{37} No tree agreed to give its leaf to Adam to cover his nakedness until he reached the Fig Tree. He asked the Fig, 'Give me your leaf so that I may cover myself'. The Fig replied, 'I'll be pleased, take a leaf of mine.' Adam took some leaves and covered himself. Soon a message was sent to the Fig Tree, 'None of the trees gave their leaves to Adam. What happened that you disobeyed Us and gave him your leaf?' The Fig replied, 'O God, I looked upon Adam as if it was that day you wanted to create him and proclaimed "I want to make a servant who will be my qualified successor, and will create children from him who will be Our friends". O God, one that you have taken as your friend due to your dignity, how soon would you like him to be discredited?' A divine proclamation descend, 'O Fig, you have cherished our beloved. Whatever fruits we have so far created in the world has seeds inside. As such, there will be none seen in you, so whoever takes you will benefit and be rewarded highly.'[9]

[9] This episode is found in the Javanese story of *Tapel Adam*, also including the Persian term, *Anjīr* ('Fig'). See the introduction.

{۳۸} الغرض. بعداز آن فرمان رسید که «آدم، بهشت جای بی‌فرمانی نیست. از بهشت بیرون شو و در دنیا برو». به حکم و فرمان خدای تَعَالَی مهتر آدم در سرندیب افتاد[۳۲] و حوّا بر کوه عرفات افتاد. و مهتر آدم پانصد سال بگریست و توبه و ندامت می‌کرد. دراین مدّت از شرم و ذلّتِ خودْ سر بالا نکردی و به جانب آسمان ندیدی. و روز و شب از گریه نیاسودی. تا روزی چندان گریستی که از هر دو چشم او چشمهٔ آب روان شدی و بر زمین جاری گشت.

{۳۹} پرندگان چون آب بر زمین دیدند از هوا فرود آمدند و به آب خوردن مشغول شدند. و با یکدیگر می‌گفتند: «هرگز چنین آب خوشبوی و شیرین نخورده‌ایم». این سخن پرندگان به سَمع آدم رسید. در خاطر گذرانید که «مگر این پرندگانِ هوا بر آب دیدهٔ من می‌خندند». فرمان آمد که «ای آدم، پرندگان راست می‌گویند. آبِ چشمِ شکستگی و ندامت در حضرت ما خوشبوی‌تر از مُشْکْ است و شیرین‌تر از شهد است».

{۴۰} چون این فرمان رسید دل آدم عليه السلام قرار گرفت و ساکِن گشت. بعداز پانصدسال آدم نظر سوی آسمان کرد. تا عرش در نظر مبارک او هیچ حجابی نبودی. در عرش عظیم نوشته است که لَآ إِلٰهَ إِلَّا اللّٰه، مُحَمَّدٌ رَسُولُ اللّٰه. آدم عليه السلام در حیرت این نام افتاد که «این کدام نیکبخت بنده است که نام او با نام حقّ سبحانه وتَعَالَی مشرّف شده است؟» که فرمان آمد: «ای آدم، در حیرت چه مانده‌ای که آن فرزندی از فرزندان تو است. اگر این فرزند در میان تو نبودی، تو آفریده نمی‌شدی، و هجده‌هزار[ح] عالم را خدای آشکار نمی‌گردانید و وحدانیّت خود را اظهار نکردی».

{۴۱} چون آدم عظمت فرزند خود بشنید در خاطر گذرانید که «مرا در حضرت ذوالجلال بهتر از این کلمه چیزی دیگر نیست». گفت «إِلٰهِیّ، به حرمت این کلمه که نام فرزند ما با نام پاک تو مشرّف گشته، مذلّت مرا در گذر». فرمان شد «نیکو شفیعی تو در حضرتِ ما آوردی. ذلّت تو را آمرزیدم و گناهان فرزندان تو به برکت این کلمه درگذرانیدم».

{۴۲} پس مؤمن باید همیشه، در نشستن و برخاستن و غلطیدن، با این کلمهٔ طیّبه مداومت می‌کرده باشد و فراموش نکند و بداند که این عطائْ کردهٔ پروردگار است که به کَرَمِ خود ارزانی کرده است.[ط]

{۴۳} در ملایم این حکایت بشنو. روزی که عمّ پیغمبر، ابوطالب، از جهان برفت، شیطان در صحرا شد نعره با درد زد؛ چنانچه آواز از شرق تا غرب عالم شنیدند. جملهٔ شیاطین که فرزندان اویند همه نزدیک او جمع آمدند و گفتند که «ای بزرگترین‌ها، تو را چه افتاد که نعره با درد زدی؟» جواب داد که «ابوطالب بِمُرد». شیاطین گفتند که «مگر او از جهان با ایمان برفت؟» گفت: «نی، در کُفر بمُرد». باز پرسیدند که «نعرهٔ غم از

[۳۲] مراد از «سرندیب» همان «سریلانکا» است. این قسمت با آنچه در داستان جاوه‌ای حضرت آدم آمده نیز هماهنگی محتوایی دارد.

[ح] هژده هزار

[ط] پس مؤمن را باید که زمان‌زمان در نشستن و برخاستن و غلطیدن این کلمه را از خاطر خود فراموش نکند

{38} Returning to the story. A divine pronouncement was made: 'Adam! Paradise is not the place of disobedience. Get out of paradise and go to the world'. On the basis of this divine order, His Eminence Adam was expelled to Serendib (Ceylon)[10] and Eve to the Mount of *Arafat*. His Eminence Adam cried for five hundred years, and repented and was full of remorse. During this period, he did not hold his head up and nor did he see the sky, due to his intense feelings of shame and degradation. And he did not stop crying day and night, insofar as a river flowed from his tearful eyes.

{39} Birds noticed water below and descended to drink it. They said to each other, 'We have never drunk such fragrant and fresh water'. The birds' conversation was heard by Adam. He wondered whether these birds are cheerful because of his tears. God said, 'O Adam, the birds are right. Tears of remorse before Us are more fragrant than musk and nectar'.

{40} Adam (pbuh) was relieved to hear this message and settled. After five hundred years, Adam [finally] looked at the sky. There was no veil in front of his holy eyes and he sighted the Throne. There, on the magnificent Throne, was written the phrase 'There is not god but God, Muḥammad is the Messenger of God'. Adam (pbuh) was amazed and in awe of this name and wondered as to the identity of this fortunate person 'whose name appears along with that of God?!' Then, God said, 'O Adam, why are you awed when his is one of your own children. If you were not to have this progeny you would not have been created, and God would not have manifested eighteen thousand worlds, and would not have demonstrated His unity'.

{41} As Adam heard about the dignity of his offspring he told himself that 'nothing would be better than this phrase in the presence of the Lord of Majesty.' Then he said, 'O God, by the dignity of this phrase in which the name of my offspring comes along with that of yours, please forgive my ignominy'. God responded, 'You requested through a nice intercessor. I have forgiven your ignominy as well as the sins of your descendants because of this phrase'.

{42} The believer should, therefore, be mindful of this pure and sacred phrase while sitting, standing, and sleeping and not forget it, and be aware that it has been granted through God, and has been offered as a mercy.

{43} In line with the previous story, hear that: when the Prophet Muḥammad's uncle, Abū Ṭālib, died, Satan went to the desert and wailed, to such an extent that his voice was heard from East to West. All devils that are his offspring gathered around him and said, 'O the greatest, what has happened that you wailed?' Satan responded, 'Abū Ṭālib has died'. The devils asked, 'Was he faithful when he died?' Satan said, 'No. He died as an infidel'. The devils, again, asked, 'So for what was your sorrowful

[10] Sri Lanka. This part is also identical in the Javanese version.

بهر چه بود؟» گفت که «نعرهٔ من از بهر دو واقعهٔ دیگر است». گفتند که «ما را نیز معلوم کن که درین میانْ واقعه چیست».

{۴۴} گفت شیطان «راست بگویید که محمّد کیست؟» همه گفتند که «بهترین همهٔ آفریدگان است». شیطان گفت که «مادامی که ابوطالب در حیات بود مَعونت محمّد برین بود که او ایمان آرد. امّا خواست حقّ تَعَالَی نبود که او را ایمان روزی کند. پس کوشش محمّدعَلَيْهِ ٱلسَّلَامُ هیچ سود نداشت که او بهترین عالمیان بود. ابوطالب را ایمان ندادند. من که راندهٔ درگاه خداوندم مَعونت من برین است که از هر مؤمنی ایمان بِرُبایم؛ به کوشش، و حضرت ایزد تَعَالَی عطای ایمان در حقّ مؤمنان ارزانی داشته است. پس چگونه بستانم؟»

{۴۵} و دیگر بر پیغمبر علیه‌السلام فرمان می‌شود: «فَعَّالٌ لِّمَا يُرِيد.[۳۳] ای محمّد، خواستْ خواستِ ماست. هرچه خواهیم آن کنیم. یکی را از خرابات بیرون آریم و نامِ دوستی بر او نهیم، و یکی را از مناجات در خرابات آوریم و اسم بیگانگی بر او نهیم. یکی را گوییم که تو مقبولی، و یکی را گوییم که تو ما را نمی‌شناسی و خراباتی.

{۴۶} و شیطان مردود را برانیم و بلعم باعور را برانیم، و سگ اصحاب کهف را شایان جنّت خود گردانیم.[۳۴] ابوطالب قریشی را ازعطای ایمان محروم گردانیم، و بلال حبشی را در صدر جنّت بِنْشانیم و آن کنیم که ما خواهیم. دیگر، ای محمّد، آدم را از مشت خاک بیافریدیم و یک‌نظرِ رحمتِ خود به وی کردیم، خلیفهٔ حضرتِ ما شد. ای محمّد، ابراهیم پسر آزر بت‌تراش بود. یک‌نظر در کار او کردیم، روح‌الله شد. دیگر، ای محمّد، چی بودی؟ یتیم ابوطالب بودی. یک‌نظر در کار تو کردیم حبیب حضرتِ ما شدی و سرور اولاد آدم گشتی. و امّتان تو از همهٔ امّتانْ گناه‌کارتر آمدند. یک‌نظر در کار ایشان کردیم، بهترینِ همهٔ امّتان شدند».

{۴۷} الغرض. آدم را چون از بهشت در دنیا آورده بودند، زمان‌زمانْ دل او به سوی بهشت نگران بودی. تا روزی مناجات کرد و گفت: «إِلٰهِيّ، از زندان دنیا به مقام جاوید بهشت چگونه خواهم رسید؟» فرمان شد «چون جان بدهی به بهشت رسی». گفت: «إِلٰهِيّ، چون من جان بدهم، جان من کجا باشد؟» فرمان رسید که «جان درعرش ما و تن تو به موافق فرزندان تو در دنیا باشد. آن روز که از بهشت به دنیا رسیدی تنها بودی. چون قیامت قایم شود با فرزندان خود در بهشت روی».

[۳۳] آیهٔ ۱۶ سورهٔ بروج. [۳۴] شاید دلیلی بر وجود داستان بلعم باعور و سگ اصحاب کهف در نسخهٔ ۵۶۵ لایدن باشد.

wailing?' Satan responded, 'My wail was because of two other incidents'. The devils said, 'So tell us the story'.

{44} Satan asked, 'Be honest, and tell me who is Muḥammad?' All of them mentioned that 'he is the best of creatures.' Satan said, 'While Abū Ṭālib was alive, Muḥammad wished him to convert to Islam. However, it was not according to God's will that he became faithful. As such, Muḥammad's effort was fruitless, although he is the best of creatures. Abū Ṭālib was not given faith. I, who am the one rejected from the divine Throne, attempted to grab their faith, expending a great deal of effort. Nonetheless, God provided believers with the favour of faith. So, how can I win back their faith?

{45} Also, it has been revealed upon the Prophet, "He executes whatever he will", "O Muḥammad, the will is Our will. Whatever We want, We will do. We will drag someone out from desolation, and call him a friend, while taking someone from worship down to desolation and labelling him as a stranger; tell someone that you are the accepted one, and tell the others than you are incognizant of Us and are desolated.

{46} And kick out the outcast Satan as well as Balʿam the son of Bāʿūr, while the dog of the Seven Sleepers deserves Our paradise. We have abdicated Abū Ṭālib of the Quraysh (the tribe of Mecca) from granting faith, while placing Bilāl al-Ḥabashī (i.e., the Abyssinian) at the forefront of paradise, and do whatever We would like to do. O Muḥammad, we have made Adam from a portion of the Earth's soil, and looked at him mercifully. Then he became Our successor. O Muḥammad, Abraham was son of Āzar, an idol-maker. We only paid kind attention to Abraham's affairs and he became Rūḥ Allāh (the Spirit of God). And what about you Muḥammad? You were the orphan of Abū Ṭālib's offspring, and We only paid kind attention to your affair and you became the close friend in Our presence and also the master of Adam's offspring. And your community committed sin more than other communities; We paid kind attention to them and they changed into the best community."'

{47} The rest of the story. When Adam was sent from paradise to the world, he frequently remembered it. He supplicated one day and said, 'O God, how can I reach my immortal heavenly position from the prison of this world?' God said, 'Once you die, you will reach paradise'. Adam said, 'O God, when I die, where will my spirit go?' God replied, 'Your spirit will be on Our Throne and your body, like those of your children, will remain in Earth. You were alone once you arrived on Earth from paradise. You will go to paradise once the world ends and the Judgement Day arrives'.

{۴۸} باز مناجات کرد و گفت: «إِلهِيّ، چون من بمیرم و مرا به خاک دفن کنند، باید که اندام مرا از آماسیدن نگاه داری». فرمان شد «آدم، بسی گناه است که از آماسیدن عفو می‌کنیم». گفت «إِلهِيّ، از کِرْمْ افتادن نگاه داری؟» فرمان شد که «بسی گناه است که از کِرْمْ افتادن عفو می‌شود». باز گفت «إِلهِيّ، چون کِرْمْ اُفتد از ریزیدن اندام نگاه داری؟» فرمان شد که «بسی گناه است که از ریزیدن اندام‌ها عفو می‌شوند، امّا اندام‌های پیغمبران در گور نریزَد و این معامله با امّتان گنه‌کار است».

{۴۹} إِلهِيّ، به حرمت خلیفهٔ عزیزکردهٔ خویش که ما را در هر دو جهان عزیز و باعزّت داری و جمیع مؤمنان را از شرّ شیطان مردود نگاه‌داری و همه را به مغفرت مقرون گردانی. بِمِنَّه وکَرمه.

{48} Again, he prayed and said, 'O God, I hope that my body will not swell once I die and they burried me'. God replied, 'O Adam, although you have committed many sins,[11] We will not allow your body to be swollen.' Adam said, 'O God, I hope that my body will not be eaten by worms'. God responded, 'It is excused from being eaten by worms'. Adam, again, requested, 'If it is going to be eaten by worms, keep the body's shape from decomposition.' God responded, 'It is excused from decomposition. The body of prophets will not decompose as it only exchanges with sinful communities.'

{49} *O God, may it be by your dearest successor that honours us in both worlds and protects all believers from the outcast Satan and grants forgiveness to all of them. By your undeserved favour and kindness. [Amen.]*

[11] This sentence may be rendered differently.

در فضیلتِ سخاوت ابراهیم علیه‌السلام و نظیرها[1]

{۱} آورده‌اند که حقّ سبحانه تَعَالَی مهتر ابراهیم علیه‌السلام را در سخاوت چنان آراسته بود که هرگز بی مهمان طعام نخوردی. تا روزی مردی[2] پیش در ایشان آمد و گفت «یا ابراهیم گرسنه ام. مرا طعامی ده». ابراهیم در روی او نظر کرد. دریافت که از دین بیگانه است.[الف] ابراهیم گفت «تو از دین بیگانه ای.[ب] طعام برای بیگانه نیست». چون آن مرد این سخن از زبان مهتر ابراهیم شنید شکسته‌دل بازگشت.

{۲} درزمانْ مهتر جبرئیل علیه‌السلام دررسید و گفت «یا ابراهیم، خدای تَعَالَی عَزَّوَجَلَّ می‌فرماید که هفتاد سال است که این مرد را رزق می دهم. وقتی[3] به او نگفته‌ایم که «تو بیگانه‌ای». تو یک وقت طعام نمی‌دهی و می‌گوی «تو بیگانه ای و طعام لایق تو نیست»».[ج]

{۳} چون ابراهیم این عتاب شنید بر عَقب آن مَرد دوید. چون نزدیک آن مرد رسید گفت «ای مرد، بازگرد و ایستاده شو که هر نعمتی که می‌خواهی بیارم». مهتر ابراهیم معذرت بسیار کردن[4] گرفت. آن مرد گفت « این‌زمان[5] تو مرا از پیش خود دورکردی، این دَمْ چرا می‌خوانی و چندین معذرت؟!»

{۴} سبب را ابراهیم علیه‌السلام گفت «باریتَعَالَی ازجهت تو با من عتاب کرد که «چرا بنده مرا طعام ندادی

[1] در ۱۲۲۲ تاجیکستان، در ذیل و و در حواشی این داستان واژه «خواص» و عبارت «بسم الله الرحمن الرحیم» و داستان های مرتبط با آن بیان شده است. همچنین، اشاراتی به نام «امام جعفر صادق» دیده می شود. [2] در برخی نسخ به عنوان «جهودی» معرفی شده است.
[3] هیچ‌گاه. [4] گردن؟ [5] همین چند لحظه پیش.

[الف] اثر بیگانگی در روی وی دید [ب] تو بیگانه مینمایی [ج] اگر یک وقت از تو طعام طلبید وبر او طعن می‌کنی که تو بیگانه‌ای و طعام من لایق تو نیست

CHAPTER 2

On the virtue of Abraham's (pbuh) generosity and further similar examples

{1} It has been reported that God had bestowed the virtue of generosity on His Eminence Abraham to the extent that he would never eat a meal without a guest. Once upon a time, a man went to Abraham's house and said, 'O Abraham, I am hungry, give me something to eat'. When Abraham saw his face, he realised that he was irreligious and said to him, 'You have no religion and the food is not served to such people'. The man returned with a broken heart when he heard this from His Eminence Abraham.

{2} Meanwhile, His Eminence Gabriel (pbuh) descended and said, 'O Abraham, God says, "We have sustained this man for seventy years and never ever told him that 'you are abandoned.' You haven't even served him with a meal and then told him that he abandoned and unqualified to have food?!"'

{3} When Abraham heard this exclamation, he ran after the man. When he got close to him, he said, 'O sir, return and wait that I should bring all sorts of favours that you would like to have'. His Eminence Abraham apologised profusely. The man said, 'You rejected me just a few moments ago, what has happened that you now call me and apologise?!'

{4} Abraham explained the reason for his action: 'God rebuked me because of you, asking "Why did you not serve Our servant with a meal even though We served him for seventy years and never told him that he was forsaken. Why did you offend him?"' Once the disbeliever[1] heard this from Abraham he began to cry and said, 'What

[1] i.e. a Jew, a Zoroastrian, or other non-Muslims.

و ما وی را هفتاد سال رزق دادیم، و نگفتیم تو بیگانه دلی. او را چرا آزار دادی؟»» چون گِبر[۶] این سخن از ابراهیم شنید چشم پُرآب کرد و گفت «نیکو خدایْ که تو داری که از بهر دشمنی با همچو تو دوستی عتاب کرد. پس از چنین رازقی چند توان بیگانه بود؟ ایمان عرضه کن[د] تا در دین تو درآیم». ابراهیم کلمه عرضه کرد و آن مرد به شرف ایمان مشرّف گشت.

{۵} روزی دیگر جماعتی از گِبران[ه] پیش ابراهیم آمدند وگفتند «ما گرسنه ایم». تعظیم ایشان بسیار کردند و طعام فراوان کشیدند. ایشان گفتند «یا ابراهیم، ما بیگانه‌ایم. چندین احسان در حقّ ما از کجا است؟» گفت «این مکارمِ اخلاق من از پروردگار خود آموخته‌ام که از بهرِ یک بنده بر من عتاب کرده بود». چون از طعام خوردن فارغ شدند مهتر ابراهیم گفت «نعمت پروردگار من بخوردید، یکبار خدای عَزَّوَجَلَّ مرا سجده کنید».

{۶} ایشان شرمنده شدند و گفتند «ای ابراهیم، از بهر خوشی خاطر تو سر سجده بریم». پس همه سر سجده بُردند. مهتر ابراهیم دست به دعا برد و گفت «إِلٰهِيْ، من سرهای ایشان را به سجده آورده‌ام، تو سرِ دل ایشان را[و] به شرف ایمان مشرّف گردانی».

{۷} هنوز دست به دعا فرو نیاورده بود که ایشان سرخویش برداشتند و گفتند «یا ابراهیم، روی سوی آسمان کن که قُفل‌های دل ما باز شده است. اکنون زود کلمه بگو تا در دین پاک تو در آیم». ابراهیم عَلَيْهِ السَّلَام کلمه عرضه کرد، جمله[۷] به شرف ایمان رسیدند.

{۸} الغرض. همّت مهتر ابراهیم عَلَيْهِ السَّلَام برین بود که بی مهمانْ طعام نخورد. دیگر روز تمام گذشت[ز] که مهمان نرسید.[ح] آن روز مهتر ابراهیم گرسنه بماند. روز دیگر نیز منتظر بودْ نیامد. روز سوم شد. در خاطر گذرانید که «خدای تَعَالَی را همچو من بنده باشد که سه روز بی مهمان طعام نخورَد». همان‌ساعت جبرئیل صَلَوَاتُ اللّٰه رسید و گفت «ابراهیم، فرمان شد که آنچه در خاطر تو گذشت از علم ما خالی[۸] نیست. اکنون بیرون شو تا بندگان مرا ببینی که در راه ما خود را چگونه می‌دارند».

{۹} ابراهیم از شهر برآمد. در بیابان رسید، صومعه بدید. و در آن صومعه جمع کثیری بودند که عبادت می‌کردند. آوازی شنید که «آوازۀ من در زُهد و تقوی زیاده است». روی جانب ایشان گردید[۹] که دید بنده‌ای از بندگان خدای تَعَالَی برابر قبله نشسته و هر دو چشمْ در هوا.[۱۰] نزدیک او رفت. سلام کرد.

{۱۰} زاهد جواب سلام داد و گفت «بیا ای مهمان که خوش آمدی که منتظر مهمان بودم». و هر دو دست برداشتند و حمد و ثنای حقّ تَعَالَی بر زبان راندند. و گفت «أَلْحَمْدُ لِلّٰه که توفیق صوم دادی،[ط] و هم

[۶] همچنین به صورت گَبر (با فتحه) خوانده می‌شود. به معنی کافر، مجوس، زرتشتی و همچنین گاها به معنی غیر مسلمان به کار می‌رود.
[۷] همگی. [۸] واژۀ «خالی» در ادبیات اسلامی منثور و منظوم مالایی دیده می‌شود. مثلاً به Or.7056 لایدن، Ll.6.5 و Gg.6.40 کیمبریج رجوع کنید. [۹] گردانید. [۱۰] به آسمان زل زده بود.

[د] کلمه عرضه کن [ه] یهودان [و] تو قلوب ایشان را [ز] یک روز تا شب شد [ح] که مهمان از حکم خدای تَعَالَی نرسید [ط] گفت که «شکر می‌گویم خدای را که امروز مهلت روزۀ من نزدیک رسیده بود و تنها افطار نکردم»

a nice God you have, one who berated such friend as you on account of such an enemy as me. How could it be that I became distant from such a Sustainer? Teach to us the declaration of faith (*kalama*) until I submit to your religion.' Abraham expressed the phrase and that man converted to the faith.

{5} Another day, a group of disbelievers went to Abraham and stated that 'we are hungry.' They were highly respected and served abundantly with food. They said, 'O Abraham, we are foreign to your religion, we wonder why are you so kind to us?' Abraham replied, 'I learned such good morals from my God, as He once berated me because of one of his servants'. Once they finished their food, Abraham said, 'You have eaten from my God's favour, now bow down and prostrate to him at once.'

{6} They were embarrassed and said, 'O Abraham, we prostrate just to satisfy you.' They all prostrated. Abraham then lifted up his hands in supplication and said, 'O God, I have bowed their heads in prostration. May You now convert their hearts to faith.'

{7} No sooner did he lower his hands but the guests began to lift their heads and said, 'O Abraham, look to the sky[2] now that our hearts are now unlocked! Teach to us the declaration of faith so that we can convert to your pure religion.' Abraham (pbuh) taught them the phrase and they all converted to the faith.

{8} To go back to the story. Abraham (pbuh) was determined not to eat without the company of guests. Another day passed and no guest arrived. His Eminence Abraham remained hungry the whole day. He waited another day and no one arrived again! On the third day, he told himself, 'God has such a servant who does not have a meal without guests for three days'. At that moment, Gabriel (pbuh) appeared and said, 'Abraham, the divine command has arrived, saying, "What has come to your mind is not hidden from Our knowledge. Now go out and see what Our servants do in Our path."'

{9} Abraham left the city and went into the desert. He noticed a monastery. There were many people who had been worshipping. He heard a voice saying, 'I am renowned because of my piety and piousness.' Abraham went towards the voice, and observed that a servant from the servants of God sat facing the qibla[3] while gazing up at the sky. He went to him and said, 'Greetings!'

{10} The pious person replied, 'Greetings!' and added, 'Come on in and be my guest. Welcome! I am eager for guests'. Both of them then lifted up their hands in supplication and expressed some form of invocation. The pious man said, 'All praise is for God, as He revealed that we should fast and also sent for us guests.' Abraham asked, 'O servant of God, tell me as to when you break your fast.' He replied, 'O guest,

[2] i.e., praise God [3] i.e. prayer direction

سعادت مهمانْ روزی کردی». ابراهیم پرسید که «ای بندهٔ خدای، مرا بگوی که مهلت روزهٔ تو چه مقدار بود؟» گفت «ای مهمان، نذْر کرده بودم به درگاه خدای تَعَالَی که چون بعداز سی‌روز روزه گشایم. امروز سی روز تمام گشته است و دولتِ مهمانْ روزی من گردانید تا افطار با تو کنم».[ی]

{۱۱} آنگاه نان از زنبیل برآورده و باهم افطار کردند. چون از طعام خوردند فارغ شدند ابراهیم گفت «از تو کسی در زهد و ریاضت زیاده است؟» گفت «آری. در فلان غار زاهدی که مرتبهٔ آن از مرتبهٔ من از زمین تا آسمان است». ابراهیم چون خبر بزرگی آن زاهد را شنید قصد دیدن او کرد.

{۱۲} چون رسید او را سلام داد. او [زاهد] گفت «مرحبا، خوش آمدی که من منتظر قدم مهمان بودم». في الحال، زاهد دست بر دعای حقّ سُبْحَانَهُ وَتَعَالَىٰ برداشت. ثنا و حمد گفتن آغاز کرد که «توفیق نذْر به آخر رسید و مهمان هم روزی کرد». ابراهیم گفت «چه نذْر کرده بودید؟» گفت «نذْر کرده بودم که چون نود روز بگذرد روزه گُشایم. امروز آخر شد[11] و خدای تَعَالَی شما را رسانید تا با شما افطار شود».

{۱۳} در میانِ گُفتنْ وقتِ افطار درآمد. نماز ادا کردند.[12] بعداز نماز دیدند رَمهٔ آهوان[13] پیدا شدند. زاهد نظر بر آن رمه کرد و گفت «بیا». یک آهو از رمه جدا شد و نزدیک زاهد آمد. زاهد گفت «بِسمِل شو».[14] همان دَم خون از حلق وی ریخت و از پوست جدا شد.[ک] باز زاهد گفت «بریان شو». آتش بی واسطه پیدا شد و بریان گردانید. باز زاهد گفت «در خوان[15] شو، پیش ما بیار». خوانی از هوا پیدا شد، آهوی بریان را گرفته نزدیک ایشان آمد. زاهد گفت «ای مهمان بخور».

{۱۴} هردو می‌خوردند و در خاطر ابراهیم گذشت «سبحان الله، پروردگارِ مرا چنین بندگانند که نود روز روزه دارند و از سخن ایشان آهویْ بِسمل شود و آتشی به غیر واسطه آن را بریان کند، و خوانی از عالم غیب آن را به نزدیکِ ما بیارَد». چون از طعام خوردن فارغ شدند ابراهیم عَلَيْهِ السَّلَام گفت «ای بزرگوار، چون به درگاه حقّ سُبْحَانَهُ وَتَعَالَىٰ مشغول شوی مرا به دعا یاد آری؟» زاهد گفت «ای مهمان، مدّت چهل سال باشد که دعای من قبول نمی‌شود». ابراهیم گفت «چرا چنین می گویی که به دعای تو آهوان صحرا بِسمل و بریان شوند. کسی را که به درگاه حقّ سُبْحَانَهُ وَتَعَالَىٰ چنین آبرویی باشد دعای او چگونه رد شود؟»

{۱۵} زاهد گفت «آنچه اراده می کُنیَم - هنوز دست از خواست باز نمی داشتم - که او را خدای عَزَّوَجَلَّ به من می‌رسانْد، و بعضی دعای چنین تاخیر گرداند. چهل سال است که مطلوبی دارم و میسّر نمی‌شود». مهتر ابراهیم پرسید که «چه مطلوب داری؟» گفت «ای مهمان، روزی در صحرا می‌گذشتم. دیدم شَبانْ[16] رمه می‌چرانید.

[11] سرانجام رسید. [12] ادای نماز پیش‌از خوردن غذا و افطار نمودن در بین شیعیان رایج‌تر است. [13] گله یا دستهٔ آهوها.
[14] ذبح نمودن به طریق حلال که با ذکر «بِسْمِ اللهِ» همراه است. نویسنده برآنست که کلمهٔ مالایی *sembelih* (سمبلیه) به معنای «ذبح نمودن» - که در متون مرتبط به حجّ به‌چشم میخورد - احتمالًا برگرفته شده از واژهٔ «بسمل» باشد. [15] سفره، بساط مهمانی. [16] چوپان.

[ی] امروز خدای تَعَالَی عَزَّوَجَلَّ مرا رساند تا به شما افطار شود [ک] درزمانْ خون از حلق آهو روان شد وبیفتاد

I vowed in the presence of God that I would only break my fast after thirty days. The thirtieth day will end today, and fate has offered a guest, so I break the fast with you.'

{11} He then took bread out of a basket and they broke their fast together. Once they finished the food, Abraham said, 'Is there anyone superior to you in piousness and abstinence? He replied, 'Yes, there is a pious person in a cave whose rank in comparison with mine is as the sky compared to the earth.' Once Abraham heard about the greatness of that ascetic he decided to visit him.

{12} When Abraham arrived, he said to him, 'Greetings!' The ascetic replied, 'Welcome, come in, I was waiting for a guest!' The ascetic lifted up his hands in supplication, and praised God the Glorious and said, 'The vow has ended successfully and also the guest has arrived.' Abraham asked, 'What was your vow?' He replied, 'I had vow not to break my fast until ninety days. The vow ends today and God has sent you so that I may break my fast with you.'

{13} As they spoke the time for breaking the fast arrived. They began to pray.[4] After saying their prayers, they noticed a herd of deer. The ascetic looked at the herd and said imperatively, 'Come here!' One deer left the group and approached the ascetic. The ascetic said, 'Be slaughtered in the name of God!' Immediately, blood flew from its throat and it was skinned. Then the ascetic said, 'Be grilled!' A fire was made out of nothing and it was grilled. Again, the ascetic said, 'Go to the table and bring it before us!' A spread appeared from the sky, grabbed the grilled deer, and came to them. The ascetic said, 'O guest, eat!'

{14} As both were eating, Abraham said to himself, 'God is Glorious! My God has such servants who fast for ninety days, through their word a deer is slaughtered and an immediate fire is made to grill it and a spread from the unseen world is brought to us.' After they finished their food, Abraham said, 'O gracious host, could you remember me whenever you worship in the presence of God?' The ascetic said, 'O guest, it has been forty years since my requests and prayers were accepted'. Abraham said, 'Why do you say this?! A deer from the desert was slaughtered and grilled just because of your prayer. For one who has such a dignity before God's presence, how is it possible that his request is rejected?!'

{15} The ascetic replied, 'Sometimes a request is approved by God while still begging. However, some requests are left unanswered. It is for forty years now that I have had a request that has not been accepted.' His Eminence Abraham asked, 'What is your request?' He replied, 'O guest, I was passing through the desert one day. I came across a herdsman who was pasturing a herd. I asked the herdsman, "To whom does this herd belong?" He said, "The herd is owned by the prophet of God." I asked the

[4] Performing prayer before breaking the fast is commonly practised by Shīʿī communities.

پرسیدم «این رمه از کیست؟» [شبان] گفت «ازانِ پیغمبر خدای عَزَّوَجَلَّ است». گفتم «آن چه نام دارد؟» گفت «خَلیل الرَّحمان». چون از وی این نام شنیدم، به خود گفتم «سبحان الله، زهی نیک‌بخت بنده که وی را خلیل الله[ل] می‌خوانند». ازآن روز که شنیدم، شب و روز دعایٔ می‌کنم که «ای پروردگار، مرا از جهان نَبَری تا پیغمبر تو را مُلازَمَت نکنم. این آرزو چهل سال برآمده است»».

{۱۶} چون ابراهیم علیه‌السلام این سخن شنید گفت «ای زاهد، خوش و خرّم باش که آن ابراهیم خلیل الله منم و دعای تو مستجاب شد». زاهد را وقت خوش شد. از جای خود برخاست، و ابراهیم نیز برخاست. یکدیگر را در بَغل[۱۷] گرفتند. اوّل کناری که در جهان گرفتند از بهر خدای عَزَّوَجَلَّ [کنار گرفتن] ابراهیم و آن زاهد بود. زاهد گفت «ای پیغمبر خدای، زمانی نزدیک من قرارگیر تا دو رکعت نماز شکرانه از ملاقات تو به جای آرم و [سپاس] خداوندی که مرا به مقصود چهل ساله رسانید». سر سجده نهاد، مناجات کرد و گفت «إلهیّ، در این جهان دیگر هیچ آروزی ندارم مگر از روی حضرتِ پاک تو که به تو می‌رسم». این گفت، و جان به حقّ تسلیم کرد.

{۱۷} نظیر دیگر. آورده‌اند که عبدالله مبارک رحمة الله علیه‌السلام اتّفاق حجّ افتاد. چون نزدیک دریا رسید، در کشتی سوار شد. زمانی نگذشت که عورتی[۱۸] نزدیک دجله،[۱۹] ژِنده[۲۰] دَرسَر کَشیده، پیدا شد. و نزدیک آن دجله مرغِ مُرداری افتاده بود. دید آن عورت آن مرغ را از زمین برداشت و روان شد. عبدالله مبارک از پیِ او روان شد و گفت «ای ضعیفه،[۲۱] این مرغ مُردار است، چه خواهی کرد؟» جواب داد که «این نزد من مُباح است. زیرا که در شرع حضرت محمّد مُصْطَفَی ﷺ، بعداز سه روز مُردار را مباح گفته اند. و امروز سه روز باشد که من با فرزندان هیچ چیز نخورده‌ام. حالت فرزندان دشوار شده است». چون عبدالله این سخن شنید به خود گفت «به حجّ چه می روی که حجّ تو همین‌جا است». هرآنچه زاد و راحله داشت به آن زن داد و خود در بغداد ماند.[۲۲]

{۱۸} چون حاجیان از حجّ بازگشتند، آوازه در شهر بغداد افتاد که «قافله حاجیان فردا می رسند». عبدالله مبارک گفت «اگر امسال به حجّ نرفتم، به استقبال حاجیان بروم و دریابم».[۲]

{۱۹} چون بیرون بغداد شد، دید چند نفر حاجیان از پیش بیامدند. و ملاقات کردند. دو حاجیان گفتند «ای عبدالله، در حجّ یک‌جا بودیم و تمام منزل همراه بودیم. امروز چه بوده باشد که پیش‌از ما به شهر آمدی؟» عبدالله در فکر شد و به خود گفت «مگر در این حکمت إلهیّ رفته است؟» در این اندیشه به خواب رفته و در خواب جوابش نمودند «ای عبدالله، در چه فکر مانده‌ای؟ حاجیان راست می‌گویند. چون

[۱۷] آغوش، در کنار گرفتن. [۱۸] بانو، زن. [۱۹] نهر آب، نزدیک ساحل. [۲۰] پارچه و پیراهن کهنه. [۲۱] زن.

[۲۲] بخشی از این داستان توسط شیعیان پارسی‌زبان عهد صفویه در مناطق جنوب شرقی آسیا از جمله سیام (تایلند) ذکر شده است: Majid Daneshgar, 'A Persian Shiʿi Anthology Circulating in Patna, Dhaka and Siam in the Seventeenth Century'.

[ل] ابراهیم خلیل الله [۲] پای و دست حاجیان را ببوسم

herdsman, “What is his name?” He replied, “Khalīl al-Raḥmān[5].” Once I heard this name from him, I said, “O God, congratulations to your auspicious servant who is called Khalīl Allāh[6]”. Since I heard this name, I have been demanding night and day, “O God, do not take my life if I am not yet accompanied by Your prophet”. It is now forty years since this request.’

{16} Once Abraham (pbuh) heard this statement, he said, ‘O ascetic, be cheerful that Abraham, the friend of God, is me, and your request has been approved.’ The ascetic became happy and stood up. Abraham, also, stood up. They embraced each other. And so, the first embrace ever in the world for the sake of God, was the embrace of Abraham and the ascetic. The ascetic said, ‘O Prophet of God, stay a few moments next to me while I perform two units (*rakʿas*) of prayer for thanksgiving on account of your visit, and that God accepted my forty-year request.’ He prostrated and praised and said, ‘O God, I have no more desire in this world, unless a vision of You and reaching Your sanctified presence.’ He expressed this and, then, submitted his soul to God.

{17} Another story. It is reported that ʿAbdallāh Mubārak, may God’s mercy be upon him, journeyed for hajj.[7] When he arrived at the sea he boarded a ship. After a while, a woman who wore a torn cloak was seen near the river. Beside the river was the corpse of a bird. ʿAbdallāh Mubārak noticed that the woman picked at the dead bird and left it there. He went behind her and said, ‘O woman,[8] what do you want to do with this dead bird?’ She replied, ‘This dead bird is permissible for me, because in the legal rule of the Prophet Muḥammad (pbuh), a carcass is permissible and today is the third day that my children have not eaten anything. They are not well and suffer.’ When ʿAbdallāh heard this he said to himself, ‘Why do you go to hajj, this is your real hajj!’ He then gave whatever was in his possession to that woman and went back to Baghdad.

{18} As the pilgrims returned from the hajj it was announced in the city of Baghdad that the caravan of pilgrims would arrive tomorrow. ʿAbdallāh Mubārak said, ‘Although I did not go to the hajj this year, I can go to welcome them’.

{19} When he left Baghdad a number of pilgrims approached and greeted him. Two of them said, ‘O ʿAbdallāh, we have been together during hajj and all moved along together. How many days earlier than us did you arrive in the city?’ ʿAbdallāh was thinking and said to himself, ‘Is there any divine wisdom behind this?’ While thinking about this matter his mind wandered[9] and he found an answer: ‘O ʿAbdallāh, what are you thinking about? The pilgrims are right. As you had given all your possessions to that woman and stayed for the sake of Us, We sent an angel on your behalf to the hajj

[5] lit., ‘friend of the Merciful’ [6] lit., ‘friend of God’ [7] Pilgrimage to Mecca

[8] In the original text, she is called by ʿAbdallāh Mubārak as *‘ḍaʿīfa’* meaning ‘one of the weak sex’, addressing women in traditional contexts. [9] He dreamed

تو از جهت ما زاد و راحلهٔ خود را بدان ضعیفه دادی و ماندی، ما به نیابت تو فرشته به صورت تو[۲۳] فرستادیم تا حجّ کند. و تمامِ منزل‌ها با ایشان روان شود، با ایشان حجّ بُگُذارد. و حجِّ اوّل کسی که او را قبول افتاد از آنِ تو بُود. حاجیان که امسال حجّ کردند، به برکت حجِ تو حجِ ایشان را قبول کردیم، تا بدانی که سخاوت در حضرت سبحانه وتَعَالَی چنین عزّت دارد».[۲۴]

{۲۰} نظیر دیگر. زنی مسلمان با فرزندان در همسایهٔ جهودی می‌بودند، و به قُوتِ بیوه‌گی اوقات گذارنیدن.[ن] هرچند سعی می‌کرد قُوت فرزندان و خودش هم نمی‌رسید. یک روز به فاقه[۲۵] گذشت. روز دیگر هم تردّد کرد، چیزی هم نرسید. فرزندان بی‌طاقت شدند و گفتند «ای مادر، چه کنیم. طاقت گرسنگی نمانده. در خانهٔ همسایهٔ جهود برو شاید چیزی دهد». مادر چون حالت فرزندان دشوار دید، پاره کهنه درسر کشید و پیشِ درِ جهود بیامد. اِستاده شد. نظر جهود بر عورت افتاد. در خاطر گذرانید که «این عورت برای دزدی آمده است. زمانی ببینم که این عورت چه می‌کند».[س]

{۲۱} لحظه ایستاد. باز پس گشت و در خانه بیامد. فرزندان گفتند «ای مادر، چیزی آوردی؟» گفت «رفته بودم زمانی مکث کردم. آن مرد جهود دید امّا چیزی نداد. به مرد بیگانه چه گویم؟» باز فرزندان فرمودند که «باز برو تا شاید که چیزی دهد». باز رفت. چون به در جهود رسید ایستاد. باز نظر جهود بر وی افتاد و با خود گفت «این به دزدی آمده». ضعیفه دید که چیزی نمی‌دهد؛ بازگشت.

{۲۲} و جهود از عقب او روان شد که بداند به چه کار آمده بود. چون به خانه درآمد، فرزندان دویدند و گفتند «ای مادر، چیزی آوردی؟» گفت «ای فرزندان، صبر و تحمّل کنید به درگاه حقّ سبحانه وتَعَالَی؛ در آن جهان بدهد نعمت‌های اَلوان[۲۶]». چون جهود[چنین] شنید دانست که بهر دزدی نیامده بود. جهود به خانه خود آمد و طعامی فکر کرد وفي الحال پُخت و نزدیک زن و فرزندان بُرد و بسیار عذر خواست که «من از حال فقر شما واقف نبودم. اکنون این طعام بخورید». چون طعام خوردند، مادر فرزندان گفت «در حقّ این مرد دعا کنیم». مادر و فرزندان سر بر سجده بردند و می‌گفتند «إِلٰهِيّ، این مرد جهود ما را نان داد. تو به کرم خویش او را ایمان ده». هنوز سر از سجده بر نداشته بودند که این مرد جهود گفت «سر از سجده بردارید که دعای شما مستجاب شد. زود کلمه عرضه کنید تا به شرف ایمان مشرّف گردم». کلمه گفتند که بگو «لَآ إِلٰهَ إِلَّا اللّٰه، مُحَمَّدٌ رَسُولُ اللّٰه».

{۲۳} چون [جهود] خلعت ایمان پوشید به خانهٔ خود رفت. نظر زن[۲۷] به رویش افتاد. زن گفت «هیچ وقت چنین نوری در روی تو ندیدم». گفت «ای زن، مُژده باد تو را که امروز خلعت ایمان در پوشیده‌ام و این نور ایمان است که [به] روی من می‌تابد». زن گفت «ای شوهر، من چرا از این سعادت محروم مانم؟ بر

[۲۳] شبیه تو. [۲۴] شباهت هایی بین این قسمت از داستان در مورد عبدالله مبارک و آنچه در «تذکرة الاولیاء» عطّار آمده وجود دارد.
[۲۵] نداری و تنگدستی. [۲۶] رنگارنگ. [۲۷] همسر.

[ن] بی‌غایت بی قوت بود [س] زمانی در کمین او باشم تا چه کند عورت

who accompanied other pilgrims in every place and performed hajj with them. And the first person accepted at the hajj was you. The pilgrims who also performed hajj this year, their hajj has been accepted because of yours, in order that you know how significant is generosity in the presence of God.'

{20} Another story. A Muslim woman and her children were neighbours of a Jew. They lived in poverty and she suffered the loneliness and poverty of widowhood. Whatever she tried, she was unable to provide food for her children and herself. A day of hardship passed. Another day, too, and still no relief arrived. The children could no longer bear it and said, 'O mother, what shall we do as we cannot tolerate the hunger. Go to the Jewish neighbour, perhaps he will give you something.' As their mother noticed their plight she put on her torn cloak and went to the Jew's house. She approached the door. The Jewish man saw her around and thought, 'She is coming to steal something. I need to wait and see what she wants to do'.

{21} She stopped there for a while and then returned home. The children said, 'O mother, did you bring something?' She said, 'I went there, and stayed for a while. That Jewish man saw me, but did not give me anything! What can I say to a strange man?' Her children, again, said, 'Go one more time, perhaps he will give you something'. She went again, and when she arrived near the Jew's house, stayed there. The Jewish man saw her again, and told himself, 'She comes to steal'. She saw that he did not give her anything, and returned.

{22} The Jew ran after her to see why she came to his door. When the woman arrived home her children ran out and said, 'O mother, did you bring something?' She replied, 'O my children, be patient and tolerate this for the sake of God. He will offer colourful favours in the next world'. When the Jew heard this, he realised that she did not come to steal from him. He returned to his house and thought about a meal. He prepared the meal and passed it on to that woman and her children. And he apologised profusely, 'I did not know about your poverty. Now enjoy this meal'. Once they finish the food, the mother told her children, 'Pray for this man'. The mother and her children prostrated and said, 'O God, this Jewish man fed us. By your kind love, may you offer to him faith'. While they were in prostration the Jewish man said, 'Take your head from prostration as your request has been accepted'. Keep expressing the declaration of faith to me until I convert to faith. They expressed the phrase, 'There is no god but God, Muḥammad is the Messenger of God'.

{23} Once he converted he went to his house. His wife saw his face and said, 'I have never seen such light in your face'. He said, 'O wife, Good news! I converted to faith and this is faith's radiation that shines on me'. The wife said, 'Why should I not have the advantage of this favour?! Express the creedal formula of Islam to me, too'.

من نیز اسلام عرض کن». گفت «ای عورت بگو «لآ إِلٰهَ إِلَّا اللّٰه، مُحَمَّدٌ رَسُولُ اللّٰه». زن هم مسلمان شد، و در شرف اسلام در آمد.

{۲۴} پس مؤمن باید که سخاوت را پیشه خود سازد که سعادت هر دو جهان روزی گردد، بِمِنَّة وکَمَال کَرَمه. وَاللّٰهُ أَعْلَمَ.

He said, 'O wife, say, "There is no god but God, Muḥammad is the Messenger of God."' She also became Muslim and entered under the illumination of Islam.

{24} *And the believer must consistently be generous, so that happiness in both worlds will be granted. By your undeserved favour and kindness. [Amen.]*

در فضیلتِ مهتر شعیب صَلَوَاتُ اللّٰهِ عَلَیْه[۱]

{۱} آورده‌اند که مهتر شعیب صَلَوَاتُ اللّٰهِ عَلَیْه از خوف خدای تَعَالَیٰ چندان گریست که چشمهایش پوشیده شد.[الف] از حضرت ربّ العزّت فرمان رسید که «ای شعیب، چرا گریه می کنی؟» گفت «خداوندا، از خوف تو و خوف دوزخِ تو و از عذابِ مرا گریه می‌دارد». فرمان شد که «آتش دوزخ بر جمیع پیغمبران حرام کرده‌ام، که ایشان با دوزخ کار ندارند.[ب] باز تو را چشم می‌دهم، بعداز این گریه نکنی». جبرئیل را فرمان داد «دو چشمِ شعیب فرو دار».[ج] به حکم فرمان خدای تَعَالَیٰ هر دو چشم شعیب بینا شد. و مدّتی بینا بود. باز بعداز چند روز چندان گریست که چشم های شعیب فتور گرفت.[د] باز مهترجبرئیل نازل شد و گفت «ای شعیب، فرمان شد که «از خوف دوزخ می گریستی؛ امان یافتی و چشمت بینا شد. اکنون چرا گریه می کنی؟»» شعیب گفت «ای جبرئیل، در تمنّای بهشت می گریم؛ که از دنیا فانی[ه] به مقام جاویدِ باقی کِی خواهم رسید؟» فرمان شد که «دَرِ بهشتْ اوّل پیغمبران درآیند. بعداز آن مردمِ دِگر آیند. بعد این گریه نکنی که بهشت به تو کرامت کردیم».[و] باز جبرئیل پرّ خویش را بر چشم شعیب کشید، چشم‌های او بینا شد».

{۲} چندگاه دیگر برین بگذشت. باز گریه کرد. باز جبرئیل دررسید که «یا پیغمبر خدای عَزَّوَجَلَّ، چه چیز تو را به گریه ماند؟»[ز] گفت «آرزوی جمال حضرت إِلٰهِيّ؛ کی باشد که این چشمِ فانی من به دیدار باقی او مشرّف شود؟» باز فرمان آمد که «بعداز این از گریه میاسایی که جزای دیدار ما گریهٔ چشم است».[ح]

[۱] در برخی نسخ «در فضیلتِ مهتر شیث» ذکر شده است.

[الف] که هر دو چشم او نابینا شد [ب] که ایشان را با دوزخ کاری نیست [ج] پس جبرئیل علیه‌السلام را فرمان شد که پرِّ خویش را بر چشم شعیب بمال [د] بعداز آن چندان گریست که باز هر دو چشم او نقصانی یافت [ه] از زندان دنیا به مقام باقی جاوید [و] بعداز این گریه نکنی که بهشت خویش را به تو ارزانی داشتیم [ز] چرا باز گریه آغاز کردی؟ [ح] باز فرمان شد که «ای شعیب\شیث، چشمی که گریانست از دیدار ما محروم نیست. دائم در گریه باش که جزای دیدار ما گریه است و آب چشم محزونان در نزد ما به غایت عزیز است».

CHAPTER 3

On the virtue of Jethro (pbuh)

{1} It is reported that His Eminence Jethro (pbuh) cried so much for fear of God that his eyes became blind. A message was revealed from God the Glorious, 'O Jethro, why do you cry?' Jethro replied, 'O God, I cry out of fear for You, Your hell, and the final punishment.'God proclaimed, 'I have forbidden the hellfire to all prophets, so they are removed from hell. I'll give your sight back. Cry no more after this.' God ordered Gabriel, 'Give back Jethro's sight.' By God's decree, both of Jethro's eyes became sighted. He was clear sighted for a while. Again, he cried so much that after a few days his eyes became fatigued. The angel Gabriel was sent down to tell him, 'O Jethro, this is a divine message: "You already cried as you feared hellfire. We protected you and you regained your sight. Why are you crying again?"' Jethro replied, 'O Gabriel, I am crying for the sake of paradise, wondering when I will reach the everlasting place after this mortal world.' A divine message was sent down, 'It is the prophets who enter paradise first. Later on, other people will enter. Cry no more as we have granted you paradise.' Again, Gabriel touched upon Jethro's eyes with his feathers and his eyes became sighted.

{2} After a while, he cried again. The angel Gabriel, again, arrived and said, 'O Messenger of God, what are you crying about?' Jethro replied, 'I wish for a vision of God. When will it be possible for my perishable eyes to become eligible to see Him and His eternal vision?' Again, a divine message was sent, 'Do not stop crying if that is your wish as Our vision will be rewarded through the tears of your eyes.'

{۳} نظیر دیگر. در زمانِ حضرت رسالت پناه محمّد مُصطَفَی ﷺ مؤمنی بود که چشم نداشت.[۲] به خدمت رسول آمد و گفت «یا نبي اَللّٰه، من کسی ندارم[ط] که مرا در مسجد آرد تا سعادت نماز با جماعتِ شما حاصل شود».[ی] پیغمبر فرمودند «از خانه آن شخص تا درِ مسجدِ حضرتِ رسول ریسمان بربندند[ک] تا آن را گرفته بیاید و بِرَود». همچنان کردند.[ل]

{۴} مدّتی براین طریق در مسجد می‌آمد ومی‌رفت. تا روزی منافقان و کافران بگفتند «جاییکه این کور از صحبت محمّد مُصطَفَی ﷺ نمی‌ماند، دگران چگونه مانند؛ [بلکه] بیایند. کاردها در رسن بربندیم تا او را عبرت شود، و از ثواب محمّد بماند».[م] کاردها بیاوردند و در رسن مقابل وی بستند. وقت نماز شد. چون متوجّه مسجد شد دست بر رسن بُرد. چون قدمی چند رفت، کارد بر روی او رسید. و تا مسجد رفتن چند کارد بر روی او خورد. خون‌چکان در مسجد درآمد.

{۵} نظر پیغمبر بر روی او افتاد. حضرت رسول اللّٰه ﷺ پرسید که «واقعه چیست؟[ن]» گفت «دشمنان تو با من این کردند تا از سعادت جماعت محروم مانم». حضرت مهتر چون گفتار او شنید و او را خون‌چکان بدید مِهر در کار او شد.[س] خواست تا دست بردارد و از حقّ ﷾ از جهت او روشنایی چشم خواهد. مهتر جبرئیل ﵇ آمد وگفت «یا محمّد، از خدای تَعَالَی فرمان می‌شود که ما در اَزَل حُکم کردیم که در شکم مادر نابینا باشد و در دنیا نابینا باشد و چون بمیرد نابینا بمیرد و چون جواب گور دهد نابینا دهد، و در قیامت و در عَرصات[۳] نابینا حاضر گردد. نامهٔ اعمال خود را نابینا بِخوانَد و پل صراط را نابینا بُگذرد. چون در بهشت رسد[ع] در آن وقت او را چشم دهیم. هم اوّلی که چشم بگشاید دیدار همچون و هیچگونه ما را ببیند.[ف] یا محمّد، تو این دوست خود را بگوی تا چه اختیار می کند. اگر در دنیا چشم می‌خواهد فردا از دیدار ما محروم خواهد ماند. و اگر نابینایی اختیار می کند فردا دیدار خدای تَعَالَی را خواهد دید».

{۶} چون پیغمبر ﵇ از جبرئیل ﵇ این سخنان شنید به وی گفتند که «ای دوست، تو را مقصود کدام است؟» آن مرد گفت «یا رسول اللّٰه، نخواهم که از بهر چشمان من دعا کنی که حیاتِ دنیا چندگاهی بیش نیست. و سعادت و دولتِ دیدارِ اَبَد کجا یابم که در شرف دیدار حقّ تَعَالَی به اوّل نظر مشرّف شود؟»[ص]

[۲] مردی محجوب. [۳] صحرای محشر.

[ط] من دست‌کش ندارم [ی] تا سعادت جماعت تو حاصل توانم کرد [ک] رَسنی بربندند [ل] همچنان گردید [م] از مسجد محمّد مُصطَفَی صلی اللّٰه علیه وسلم [ن] نظر پیغمبر بر روی اوفتاد از وی پرسید «این چه ماجراست که با تو کرد؟» [س] در دل افتاد؛ دل مبارکش بر وی مهربان شد [ع] قدم در بهشت نهد [ف] که در اوّل نظر دیدار ما را ببینید [ص] که حیات دنیا چه اندازه‌ای. چشمی که اوّل نظر به دیدار حقّ ﷾ مشرّف گردد

{3} Another story. During the time of the Prophet Muḥammad (pbuh) there was a believer who was blind. He came to the Prophet and said, 'O Prophet of God, I have no one to bring me to the mosque so I can enjoy your congregational prayer .' The Prophet ordered that a rope be fixed from the man's house to the Prophet's mosque so that he may take the rope and go to the mosque. They did so.

{4} He went to the mosque in this way for a while until hypocrites and disbelievers said among themselves one day, 'When this blind person is not away from Muḥammad's (pbuh) preaching just imagine what could be done for others. We will attach blades to the rope so that he gets a lesson from this punishment, and misses the reward of visiting Muḥammad.' They had gathered blades and attached them to his rope. The time of prayer arrived. To go towards the mosque, the blind man took the rope. After a few steps, the blades cut him. Several blades cut him on his way to the mosque. He entered the mosque blood soaked.

{5} The Prophet saw him and asked, 'What has happened?' He replied, 'Your enemies did this to me so that I should miss the reward of congregational prayer.' As His Eminence the Prophet heard this from him and saw him blood soaked he took pity on him and was about to lift up his hands in supplication and ask God to restore his sight. At the same time Gabriel arrived and said, 'O Muḥammad, a proclamation comes from God, "When this man was in his mother's womb We decreed that he remain blind in this world and when he dies and responds to the question in the grave We will present his blindness onn the Day of Judgement and in the Gathering of Resurrection. He will recite the record of his deeds blind and pass the bridge of Ṣirāṭ blind. When he enters paradise We will grant him sight. As he opens his eyes he will immediately see Our unparalleled and unique vision. O Muḥammad, tell your companion about this and see what he prefers; if he desires sight for this world, he will be unable to see Our vision. And if he prefers to remain blind, he will attain God's vision in the hereafter."'

{6} When Muḥammad (pbuh) heard this from Gabriel (pbuh), he asked the man, 'O companion, what is your preference?' That man replied, 'O Messenger of God, I do not want you to pray for the sake of my eyesight as the duration of this world is too short; instead may it be that I have everlasting sight and be honoured with the vision of God, my eyes will at the outset visit Him.'

{۷} نظیر دیگر. آورده‌اند که زنی صاحب‌جمال بود. در آرزوی حقّ سبحانه وتَعَالَی چندان گریه کرد که هر دو چشم نابینا شد. مردم[ق] نصیحت کردند که «تو، زن صاحب‌جمال بودی؛ چرا چندین گریستی که چشم‌های خود ضایع کردی؟»[ر] گفت «فردای قیامت از دو حال بیرون نیست: اگر این چشمْ دیدارِ خدای عَزَّوَجَلَّ بخواهد دید یا نخواهد دید. اگر خواهد دید، زهی دولت من که از بهرِ دیدارِ باقیْ چشم خود را باخته باشم؛ و اگر نخواهد دید بس چشمی که از سعادت دیدار حقّ تَعَالَی محروم مانَد هم در دنیا بِهْ که نَظَرِ ما بر نامحرم نیفتد».

{۸} إِلٰهِیْ، به حرمت آن نیک‌بختان که جان و تن خود را در راه رضای تو باخته‌اند و رضای تو حاصل کرده چشم همهٔ مؤمنان را به دیدار خویش منوّر گردان. بِمِنَّةٍ وَکَرَمِه.

[ق] قرابتان [ر] تو را چندین که گریانند که هر دو چشم به باد دادی

{7} Another story. It is reported that there was a pretty woman who was waiting for God's vision. She cried so much that she lost her eyesight. The people asked her, 'You, as a pretty woman! Why have your cried so much and lost your eyes?' She replied, 'There will only be two possibilities on the Resurrection Day: either this eye will see God or it will not. If it will see Him, then how lucky I am that I lose my eyesight for the rest of my life for the sake of His vision. And if it will not visit Him, then it is better that an eye which does not deserve to view God be like this in this world so it will not see strangers.'

{8} *O God, by those auspicious people who lost their soul and body for the sake of Your satisfaction and met Your expectations, illuminate the eyes of all believers to Your own vision. By your undeserved favour and kindness. [Amen.]*

در فضیلتِ موسیٰ علیه‌السلام
که در کوه طور به وعدهٔ خدای عزّوجلّ رفته بود؛ بعداز آن به حکم و فرمانْ به دعوت فرعون رفت، و خرامیدن او از دار فانی به دار البقا

{۱} آورده‌اند چون موسیٰ علیه‌السلام به کوه طور برآمد، فرمان رسید که «ثنای بگوی خدای تعَالَی را به چهارصد نام». ثنا گفت. بعداز آن دم در کشید. در خاطر گذشت که «در لحظه خدای عزّوجلّ را به چهار صد نام ثنا گفتم».[الف] هنوز این فکر در خاطر موسیٰ بود که فرمان آمد که «ای موسیٰ علیه‌السلام، بازگرد. به زیر کوه طور درآی که اندیشه خاطرِ تو ما را خالی نیست».

{۲} موسیٰ علیه‌السلام بازگشت. در پای کوه‌طور غاری بدید. در آن غار درآمد. چون پیشتر شد، صحرایی دید بامساحت[۱] و جویی در وی روان. و برسوی جویْ درخت لطیف[ب] سایه انداخته. در خاطر موسیٰ گذشت که «یک‌زمان زیر این درخت قرار گیرم [و] به فراغت مشغول». دید مرغی در شاخ آن درخت نشسته و خدای عزّوجلّ را ثنا می‌گوید.[ج] سخن آن جانور در گوش نهاد و شنید که در ساعتی خدای تعَالَی را به چهارهزار[د] نام بخوانْد. مهتر موسیٰ در فکر ماند و با خود گفت که «تو خدای را به چهارصد نام خواندی و مباهات کردی.[ه]

[۱] یعنی وسیع و مسافت.

[الف] زهی دولت من که خدای را به چهارصد نام خواندم [ب] درخت عظیم [ج] چون به پای درخت آمد دید که جانوری برشاخ درخت نشسته است و خدای را عزّوجلّ ثنا می‌گوید. [د] چهارصد هزار [ه] مهتر موسیٰ با خود گفت که «تو خدای را به چهارصد نام خواندی و گفتی که زهی روشنی خاطر من که حضرت حقّ را در یک‌ساعت به چهارصد نام خواندی.

CHAPTER 4

On the virtue of His Eminence Moses

who had gone on Mount Sinai in order to see God; and who later went to Pharaoh based on a divine command; the elegant transition of Moses from the perishable abode to the eternal abode

{1} It is reported that once Moses (pbuh) went to the top of Mount Sinai, a divine message was revealed, 'Praise God with His four hundred names'. Moses praised accordingly. Later, he stopped and remained silent. He said to himself, 'Behold! I have now praised God with four hundred names!' While he was thinking of this, God's command arrived, 'O Moses, go back down to the bottom of the mountain as we know what you have been thinking'.

{2} Moses (pbuh) went down. He noticed a cave at the bottom of the mountain. He went into the cave. After a few steps, he saw a wide desert through which a river flowed. And there was a lovely tree near the creek, casting shadows. Moses imagined 'how nice it would be to sit under this tree for a while.' [As he relaxed] he noticed a bird sitting on a branch, praising God. Moses listened carefully to the bird's speech and realised that the bird invoked God with four thousand names within a moment. His Eminence Moses pondered, 'You remembered God with four hundred names, for which you were proud. O Moses! Now you see how this bird remembers God with four thousand names within a short moment.' Later, Moses (pbuh) gave praise and entreated, 'O God, enable this bird to speak with me, so I can ask questions from it.'

اکنون ای موسیٰ تماشایِ این مرغ کن. درساعتی خدای را به چهارهزار نام بِخوانْد». آنگاه موسیٰ علیه‌السلام مناجات کرد و گفت «إلٰهِيّ، این مرغ را با من به سخن آر تا من از این چیزی پُرسم».[۲]

{۳} فرمان شد که موسیٰ «از زمانی که این مرغ آفریده شد به هیچ‌کس حرف نزده است؛ به جز ذکر ما سخن نگفته است. امّا دعای تو مستجاب کردیم. پُرس از او هر چه می‌پرسی». موسیٰ گفت «ای بندهٔ خدای عَزَّوَجَلَّ، با من به سخن درآی و هرچه بپرسم جواب گوی». مرغ گفت «سلام علیکم ای پیغمبر خدای عَزَّوَجَلَّ، آنچه مقصود تو است بپرس». موسیٰ گفت «ای جانور، چندگاه شد که درین شاخِ درختی هستی؟» گفت «مدّت چهار هزار سال باشد که من برین درخت نشسته ام و رزق من[د] ذکر حقّ است». موسیٰ گفت «در این مدّت هیچ چیز آرزو کرده ای؟» گفت «ای موسیٰ، سه هزار سال هیچ آرزوی نداشتم. امروز هزار سال برآمده است که گاهی دل من می‌خواهد که سَرِ مِنقارِ خود را در آب تَرْ کنم».

{۴} موسیٰ گفت «ای پرنده، زیر این درخت جوی آب می گُذرد. چرا نخوردی؟» مرغ سوی زمین دیدنْ گرفته و قسم یاد کرد و گفت «ای موسیٰ، به عظمت آن خدای عَزَّوَجَلَّ که غیر از او خدای نیست،[۳] در این چهار هزارسال چنان در ذکر حقّ سُبْحَانَهُ وَتَعَالَىٰ مشغول بودم که هیچ ندانستم در زیر این درخت[ذ] آب می‌رفت یا نه.» و روایت دیگر این است [که پرنده گفت] «اگرچه زیر این درخت آب می‌رود، و اندیشه کردم [اگر] در آب‌خوردن مشغول شوم ساعتی عزیز از من به غیرِ ذکرِ دوست رود، و ناگاه در آب خوردن تقدیرِ من برسد [و] جانم در این قبض شود. و از ذکر معبود خود محروم مانم». چون مهتر موسیٰ این سخن از آن جانور بِشُنید، زبان خود به ثنا بگشاد و می گفت که «ای کسی که از ذکر بندگان هفت آسمان و زمین مستغنی، و تو را هیچ احتیاج نی».[۴]

{۵} الغرض. چون موسیٰ علیه‌السلام به شرف معراج مشرّف گشت، به‌غیرِواسطه[۵] بِشُنید آنچه شَنید و آنچه دید،[۶] فرمان شد که «بازگرد و فرعون را به سوی ما دعوت کن».[۷] چون موسیٰ بازگشت پیش فرعون رفت و گفت «چند از پروردگار بیگانه باشی و نمی بینی که آسمان بی‌ستون بِداشْت و ستارگان در وی پدید آورْد[۸] و کوه ها بر زمین پیدا کرد و در زمین آب جاری گردانید و انواع نعمتها از آن رویانید. و نعمتهای[ح] او می‌خورید و چند دل سیاه داری؟ اکنون، ای فرعون، ایمان آر». فرعون گفت «اگر خدای تو مُلکِ آخَر[ط] دارد، من مُلکِ دنیا دارم. هر چه به قدرت خود بفرمایم آن شود».

{۶} موسیٰ علیه‌السلام گفت «تو عاجزی. کِی تو را به قدرت کاری کردن».[ی] فرعون گفت «ای موسیٰ، این رود نیل که خشک شده است را گویم باز گرد، زود روان شو تا قدرت مرا معلوم کنی که چگونه [قدرت]

[۲] این داستان مرتبط است با آیهٔ ۶۰ سورهٔ بقره.

[۳] اشاره به «لآ إِلٰهَ إِلَّا اللّٰه» دارد. [۴] بخش پایانی آیهٔ ۹۷ سورهٔ آل عمران. [۵] بدون واسطه.

[۶] اشاره به آیهٔ ۱۴۳ سورهٔ اعراف، مشهور به آیهٔ تجلّی. [۷] اشاره به آیات ۱۹-۱۷ سورهٔ نازعات و آیات ۴۴-۴۳ سورهٔ طه.

[۸] اشاره به آیهٔ ۲ سورهٔ رعد.

[د] غذای من [ذ] در فرود من [ح] میوه‌های [ط] مُلک آخرت

[ی] ای بیچارهٔ عاجز، تو کی توانی که کاری به قدرت خود بکنی؟

{3} God said, 'O Moses, this bird has not spoken with anybody since its creation, and the only thing the bird has said so far is Our remembrance. Nonetheless, we accept your request. Ask the bird whatever you wish to ask.' Moses said, 'O Worshipper of God! Come to speak and answer whatever I ask.' The bird said, 'Peace be upon you Prophet of God! Ask whatever you want.' Moses asked, 'O creature, for how long have you been on the branch of this tree?' The bird replied, 'I have been sitting on this tree for four thousand years, and my food is God's remembrance.' Moses asked, 'Have you wished for anything during this period?' The bird responded, 'O Moses, I had no desire for three thousand years. However, it has been my desire for one thousand years to soak my beak in water.'

{4} Moses then said, 'O bird, there is a river under this tree. Why have you not tried it yet?' The bird looked down and took oath, 'O Moses, by the Greatness of God there is no god except Him, to the extent that I have been engaged with remembering God during these four thousand years I have not noticed there is a river under this tree!' According to another report, [the bird responded thus,] 'Although there is a river under this tree, I thought that if I start drinking water from it I may lose my golden moments of the remembrance of the Friend. I do not want to die, being away from God's worship, just because of drinking water.' Once Moses heard this from the creature, his mouth began praising and remembering God and stated, 'O the One who does not need to be remembered by the creatures of the Seven Spheres and Climes, You do not need anything.'[1]

{5} To get back to the story. After Moses was honoured with drawing close and directly hearing and seeing God, a divine message was revealed to him, 'Return and go to Pharaoh and direct him to Us.' When Moses returned, he went to Pharaoh, and said, 'How long do you want be away from God? And do not you see that He raised up heavens without pillars and He has made stars therein, and placed mountains on Earth and flowed water thereon and grown favours and blessings from it so you can eat them; and how blackened is your heart?! Now, O Pharaoh, is it time to accept my call for faith?' Pharaoh replied, 'If your God holds the celestial sovereignty, I have this world in my possession. Whatever I wish in it will happen.'

{6} Moses (pbuh) said, 'You are powerless. How on Earth might you have power to make miracles?' Pharaoh replied, 'O Moses, see this Nile river that has been dry. I will tell the river to fill with water so you may witness my power and how the power and control of the world is in my possession.' Moses was surprised by his claim and said, 'Divinity is for He who created the heavens and Earth, no one was, nor will be, able to do so except Him. O Pharaoh, I really wonder how the Nile river fills with water

[1] Based on the last part of Q. 3:97.

خدایی دنیا دارم». از گفتار او موسیٰ را تعجّب آمد و گفت «خدایی او را سزاست که آسمان و زمین پیدا کرده[۹] و جز وی کسی نبوده و نباشد. ای فرعون، از تو مرا این عجب نمود که رود نیل به گفتهٔ تو چگونه روان گردد؟» فرعون گفت «ای موسیٰ، فردا بیا تا خدایی من تماشا کنی». موسیٰ این سخن از فرعون شنید [و] باز گشت.

{۷} بعداز آن چون شب شد فرعون در حُجْره درآمد و غُل در گردن کرد، و زنجیر دست و پای خود نهاد. و خود را سرپائین و بالا بیاویخت[ک] و به درگاه حقّ سُبْحَانَهُ وَتَعَالیٰ می نالید و می گفت «إلٰهِيّ، من با عیب بسیار به درگاه شاه بی‌عیب آمده‌ام. یاربّ، عیب آن دارم که بر سر من شاخ برآمده است. دوم آنکه بالای من کوتاه است و نزدیک[۱۰] و مثالِ سگ دُم دارم. و دیگر آنکه عنی‌ام[۱۱] و مردی ندارم.[۱۲] و هر عیب که درد بود شمرد.[۱۳]

{۸} و گفت که «یَا أَرْحَمَ الرّاحِمِينْ، مُلک عقبی که باقیست در باخته‌ام، و ملک فانی دنیا خریده‌ام. اکنون موسیٰ و خلق او بر سر نیل حاضر خواهند شد؛ مرا شرمنده نکنی. رود نیل را به فرمان من روان گردانی». ندایی از عالم غیب آمد که «رود نیل را به فرمان تو روان گردانیدیم». فرعون شادان از حُجْره بیرون آمد. دیار عالم در داد.[۱۴]

{۹} بعداز ساعتی به جانب رود نیل رفت و موسیٰ عَلَيْهِ السَّلَام آمد و خلقِ بسیار آمدند. فرعون گفت «ای موسیٰ، اکنون قدرت ما را تماشا کن». این بِگُفت و رو به طرف رود نیل کرد. گفت «ای رود نیل، روان شو، باز گرد و هرچه بگویم آن کن». درزمانْ رود نیل روان شد. فرعون از عقب او رفت. خلق در تعجّب ماندند. آنچه قوم فرعون بودند[ل] گفتند «اگر این فرعون خدا نباشد، رود نیل چگونه به فرمان او روان شود؟»

{۱۰} چون موسیٰ عَلَيْهِ السَّلَام این را بدید، به هم بَرآمد[۱۵] و دست به مناجات برداشت و گفت «إلٰهِيّ، مرا به دعوت فرعون فرستاده بودی. هر چه او گفت همان شد. پس آبروی بندهٔ تو چه باشد؟» جبرئیل عَلَيْهِ السَّلَام حاضر شد و فرمان رسانید «ای موسیٰ، در ذات پاک ما بخل روا نیست. و دوست و دشمن هر که از درگاه ما چیزی خواهد. ما چگونه او را ضایع کنیم؟ او تمامِ شب غل و زنجیر در دست و پای کرده می نالید و می گفت «إلٰهِيّ، مرا از روی موسیٰ و خلق شرمنده نکنی که لافی زده ام». ای موسیٰ، اگر امروز گفتهٔ فرعون رد نکردیم امّا تو خاطر جمع باش[م] که به دعای تو او را در این رود نیل غرق خواهم گردانید، با حَشَم و خَدَمی[۱۶، ن] که دارد».

[۹] اشاره به سورهٔ سجده آیهٔ ۴.

[۱۰] (بالای من یک گز و نیم است)؛ تشبیهی برای بیان مشخّصات جسمی غیرمتعارف دیوها و جانوران ناشناخته. احتمالا تحت تاثیر متونی همچون «عجائب المخلوقات وغرائب الموجودات» از زکریّا قزوینی بوده‌است.

[۱۱] نجاستم.

[۱۲] (عیب دیگر آنکه حیض هستم) این متن اشاره دارد به زنانگی پایین‌تنهٔ فرعون و اینکه او ویژگی‌های بیولوژیکی یک زن را دارا است.

[۱۳] (و هرعیبی که در وجود او بود همه را به درگاه خدای عَزَّوَجَلّ عرضه کرد).

[۱۴] (فرعون شادان و خوشدل از در حُجْره بیرون آمد و خلق مصر را باز [؟] داد). «دردادن» به معنی «عطا نمودن» است. هرچند معنای این عبارت در این جمله چندان روشن نیست.

[۱۵] در غضب شد.

[۱۶] خویشان و همراهان.

[ک] سرنگون بیاویخت [ل] بعضی که قوم او بودند [م] خاطر جمیع دار [ن] خدم و حشم

on your command!' Pharaoh replied, 'O Moses, come tomorrow in order to see my divinity'. Moses heard this from Pharaoh and returned.

{7} Later, when it was night, Pharaoh went to his chamber and put an iron collar around his neck, chained his hands and legs, hung himself upside down, and wailed in the presence of God and said, 'O my God! I came with much deficiency to the threshold of the innocent King; O Lord! Among my deficiencies are that I have two horns on my head. Second is that my upper body is short and pressed and has a tail like a dog, and also that I am as impure[2] as excrement and have no virility.' He expressed all his deficiencies, one by one.

{8} Pharaoh added, 'O the most Merciful of all those that are always merciful, I have lost the other eternal world, and purchased this temporary world, in return. Moses and his people will now come to the Nile river soon; do not embarrass me and make the Nile flow upon my order.' A voice arrived from the unseen world, 'We have commanded the Nile to flow upon your order'. Pharaoh became cheerful and left the chamber and rewarded the people.

{9} After a few hours he went to the Nile river and Moses (pbuh) arrived and a large number of people gathered there. Pharaoh said, 'O Moses, now witness our power!' Pharaoh said this and looked at the Nile river. He said, 'O Nile river! Flow and recede, and do what I tell you!' Immediately, the Nile flowed, and Pharaoh went after it. All the people were surprised. Those of Pharaoh's entourage said, 'If this Pharaoh is not the God, how come the Nile flowed after his order?'

{10} When Moses saw this, he became angry and lifted his hand in supplication, saying, 'O God, You sent me to invite Pharaoh. But whatever he ordered happened. What is going to happen to Your servant's [i.e., Moses'] dignity?' Gabriel descended and conveyed to him a divine message, 'O Moses! In Our sacred essence there is no place for stinginess. And if either friend or enemy asks something from us, how is it possible for Us to reject their request? Pharaoh had chained his hands and legs the whole night, wailing and asking, "O God, do not embarrass me before Moses as well as the people that I have bluffed." O Moses! Although We have not turned down Pharaoh's request, be assured that We will drown him and his followers and advocates in the Nile river on the basis of your supplication.'

[2] In some manuscripts, he stated that he is 'menstruated'.

{۱۱} الغرض. و غرق شدن فرعون مشهور است که حقّ تَعَالَی به دعای مهتر موسیٰ فرعون را با همهٔ لشگر در رود نیل غرق گردانید.

{۱۲} نظیر دیگر. آورده‌اند که روزی موسیٰ علیه‌السلام در بیابان می‌گذشت که ملک الموت رسید و گفت «ای موسیٰ، مرا فرمان شده است که جان شما را قبض کنم». مهتر موسیٰ گفت «ای قابض ارواح، حقّ تَعَالَی مرا دوست خود خوانده و [آیا] هیچ دوستی خواهد که دوست خو را بی‌جان کند؟» عزرائیل علیه‌السلام رفت و باز آمد و گفت «ای موسیٰ، فرمان می شود که «هیچ دوستی خواهد که به غیر دوست قرار گیرد؟»» و موسیٰ گفت «ای ملک الموت، جان مرا چگونه قبض می کنی؟» گفت «اگر بگویی در دهن درآیم».[س] گفت «در دهن چگونه درآیی که به آن دهن در کوه طور با پروردگار خود هم سخن شده ام.» گفت «در چشم درآیم». موسیٰ گفت «با این چشم در کوه طور نور تجلّی دیده‌ام». عزرائیل گفت «از جانب گوش درآیم». گفت «هرچه خدای تَعَالَی در طور با من گفت بدین شنیده‌ام». مهتر عزرائیل گفت «به جانب دست راست درآیم». موسیٰ گفت «بدین دست تورات می گیرم و می‌گشایم». عزرائیل گفت «اگر بگویی به جانب پا درآیم». موسیٰ گفت «بدین قَدَم به وعده خدا تَعَالَی به کوه طور بر آمده ام». هر عضوی که ملک الموت بگفتی موسیٰ چنین جواب گفتی. ملک الموت عاجز ماند. باز پیش حقّ سبحانه وتعالی رفته و گفت «إلٰهِيّ، پیغمبر تو چنین جواب می‌گوید».

{۱۳} موسیٰ علیه‌السلام دانست که وقت رسیدن و جان دادن می‌باید. به جانب خانه آمد. مادرش گفت «ای جگرگوشهٔ من، امروز روی تو چرا زرد است؟» گفت «ای مادر، الوداع که ما را سفر قیامت پیش آمده». مادرش گریان شد و حَرَم[۱۷] موسیٰ در گریه شد.[ع] چون فرزندان شنیدند همه جمع شده و در گریه شدند که «پیغمبر خدای از میان ما می‌رود». حرم موسیٰ گفت «ای موسیٰ، از دار فنا به دار بقا می‌روی؛ فرزندان را به که می‌سپاری؟»

{۱۴} دل مبارک مهتر موسیٰ از برای فرزندان تنگ شد. فرمان رسید «ای موسیٰ، عصایٰ که به دست داری به این سنگ که در صَحنِ خانهٔ[۱۸] تو افتاده است، بِزَن». موسیٰ عصا بر سنگ زد؛ دوپاره شد. از وی سنگ دیگر بیرون آمد. فرمان آمد که «برین سنگ هم عصا بزن». سنگ دوپاره شد. کِرْمی از آن سنگ بیرون آمد. برگ سبزی در دهن داشت و درزمانْ به ثنای حقّ سبحانه وتعالی درآمد. فرمان شد که «ای موسیٰ، ما کِرْمی را در بستر تاریکی ضایع نگذاشتیم و رزق دادیم. هرگز بنده زاده‌هایِ خود ضایع نگذاریم». چون مادر و فرزندان موسیٰ علیه‌السلام آن حال بدیدند – این ندا شنید – تسلّی خاطرِ ایشان شد.

[۱۷] همسر (همسران) و اهل خانه. [۱۸] میان حیاط خانه.

[س] گفت جان تو را از راه دهن تو قبض کنم [ع] و دختر شعیب علیه‌السلام که حرم موسیٰ بود بر روی شوهر خود نگاه کرده می‌گریست

{11} Returning to the story. The story of Pharaoh's drowning is quite well-known as God drowned Pharaoh and his army in the Nile due to Moses' request.

{12} Another story. It is reported that once upon a time, as Moses (pbuh) was passing through a desert the Angel of Death[3] arrived and told him, 'O Moses, I am ordered to seize your soul!' His Eminence Moses replied, 'O the Seizer of Souls! God has called me His own friend. I wonder if there is any friend who wants to extinguish his friend!?' ʿIzrāʾīl (pbuh) left and returned. He said, 'O Moses, it is commanded, "Are there friends who want to be apart from their friends?"' Moses asked, 'O Angel of Death, how would you take my soul?' The Angel of Death replied, 'If you wish, I'll go through your mouth to take your soul.' Moses asked, 'How would you come to my mouth as I spoke with it to my God on Mount Sinai.' ʿIzrāʾīl said, 'I'll take it through your eyes.' Moses said, 'I have witnessed the manifestation of light on Mount Sinai.' ʿIzrāʾīl said, 'I'll go through the ear.' Moses responded, 'Whatever God told me on top of Mount Sinai, I heard through this ear.' His Eminence ʿIzrāʾīl said, 'Through your right hand?' Moses replied, 'I hold the Torah and open it with this hand.' ʿIzrāʾīl asked, 'If you wish, I can take the soul from your leg?' Moses said, 'I took steps with it to meet God on Mount Sinai.' About taking the soul through every single limb questioned by ʿIzrāʾīl, Moses answered similarly. The Angel of Death became desperate. He went to God one more time and stated, 'O God, Your prophet talks like this.'

{13} Moses (pbuh) realised that his departure time and death had arrived. He went home. His mother said, 'O my darling, why do you seem distracted?' Moses replied, 'O mother, farewell! As I am about to die.' Moses' mother and entire household[4] began crying. Once his children heard about this, they gathered and cried, 'The prophet of God is going to leave us'. The women of his household[5] said, 'O Moses, you are going to go to the Everlasting Abode from this Fleeting Abode. Whom would you ask to care for your children?'

{14} Moses now missed the children. A divine message arrived, 'O Moses, hit the stone which is in the courtyard of the house using your staff.' Moses, hit the stone with his staff and it split in two; another stone lay in between. God ordered him, 'Hit this stone, too!' Moses did so, and it was split into two parts. A worm came out of it, holding a small green leaf, and began to praise God. Another divine message was sent down, 'O Moses, We would not leave a worm in such a dark place alone and would feed it. We will never forget Our children.' When the mother and children witnessed what Moses heard, they became relieved.

[3] i.e., ʿIzrāʾīl [4] Also, female members. [5] His wife (?)

{۱۵} موسیٰ با اهل بیت و اقوام خود وداع کرد و به جانب بیابان مِیل کرد[۱۹]. دید در صحرا دو کس قَبر[ف] می کنند. نزدیک ایشان رفت و پرسید «این قَبر کیست؟»[ص] ایشان گفتند که «این گور کسی است که خداوند او را دوست می‌دارد و او نیز خداوند تَعَالَی را دوست می‌دارد». موسیٰ گفت «زهی نیک‌بخت بنده! اگر رخصت باشد من برای تعظیم در قَبر بغلطم». ایشان رخصت کردند، و موسیٰ عليه‌السلام در قَبر درآمد بغلطیدن.

{۱۶} همان ساعت فرمان شد «عزرائیل عليه‌السلام، سیبی از حضرت ما بر دست موسیٰ ده».[ق] درحال مهتر عزرائیل دررسید و سیب به دست موسیٰ بداد. سیب را از دست عزرائیل ستد و بوی کرد، و در بوی کردن بود که همان لحظه جان به حقّ تسلیم کرد. فی الحال تربت[ر] گِرْد آمد. و قَبر ایشان همان شد.[ش] و آن دو کس که قَبر می کَنْدَنْد جبرئیل و میکائیل عليهما‌السلام بودند.

{۱۷} إِلٰهِیّ، به حرمت موسیٰ عليه‌السلام، فقیر را و جمیع مؤمنان را خشنودی رضای خود حاصل گردانی و کرم خویش را انیس جان ما گردانی. بِمِنَّة وکَرَمه.

[۱۹] حرکت کرد.

[ف] گور [ص] این گور کیست که مرده نمی نماید [ق] همان ساعت مهتر عزرائیل را فرمان رسید که سیبی از بهشت ببر و به دست موسیٰ بده [ر] قبر [ش] و ناپیدا شد

{15} Moses bid farewell to his family and relatives and left for the desert. He saw that there were two people digging graves. He approached them and asked, 'For whom is this grave?' They replied, 'This grave belongs to someone who is favoured by God and who also loves God.' Moses said, 'How fortunate is this servant of God! If it is possible, I will go down to the grave to bow and pay respect.' They allowed him to enter and Moses (pbuh) went and lay down.

{16} A divine message soon arrived, "ʿIzrāʾīl (pbuh)! take an apple from Our threshold and pass it on to Moses' hand'. Subsequently, His Eminence ʿIzrāʾīl arrived and passed an apple to Moses' hand. Moses took the apple from ʿIzrāʾīl's hand and smelled it. While smelling it, he died. Then, the soil covered the grave, and it became his tomb. And those two who were digging the grave were the angels Gabriel and Michael (pbuh).

{17} *O God, by the dignity of Moses (pbuh), provide this poor servant and all other believers with your satisfaction and bestow on us Your generosity. By Your undeserved favour and kindness. [Amen.]*

در فضیلتِ مهتر سلیمان صلوات الله علیه[۱]

که انگشترین مملکت چگونه از دست وی بیرون رفت، و سبب چه بود که باز به وی رسید[۱]

{۱} آورده‌اند که روزی سلیمان علیه‌السلام بر تخت نشسته بود، و تخت ایشان را باد به هوا می‌برد تا نزدیک دِهی رسید.[الف] دختری چندی بر لب آب با هم بودند و بازی می‌کردند. چون تخت برآن بدیدند دختران حیران شدند که چون تختِ کیست. گفتند «تخت سلیمانِ پیغمبر علیه‌السلام». دختری ماهی‌گیر در میان ایشان بود. روی به جانب دختران کرد و گفت «چه نیک بودی اگر این سلیمان شوهر من می‌بودی».

{۲} چون دختران این شنیدند گفتند که «دختر ماهی‌گیر به اندازهٔ خود سخن‌گوی». و او را چندان ملامت کردند که او شرمنده گشت و سر به شکستگی فروانداخت. رو به دختران گفت «مرا بدین گفتهٔ من ملامت مَکنید که هرچه آدمی‌زاد می‌کند و می‌گوییَد در آن حکم خداوند تَعَالَی رفته است؛ من و دیگری چه توانیم کرد؟ امّا هرچه در حقّ من می‌گویید بگویید که خدای تَعَالَی می‌داند که چه خواهد کرد. من چه کنم او در زبانِ من انداخت».

{۳} الغرض. تخت سلیمان علیه‌السلام در شهری رسید. نزدیک شهر مرد پیری پشتارهٔ[ب] هیزم بر سر داشت. اُفتان‌وخیزان می‌رفت. سلیمان علیه‌السلام را بر وی رحم آمد. پیشتر شد و پرسید که «ای پیر، چه نام داری؟» گفت

[۱] براساس ۱۲۲۲ تاجیکستان، ابیاتی منسوب به «مولوی» پیرامون این داستان دیده می‌شود.

[الف] روزی باد سخت تخت سلیمان را برگرفته بود و می‌برد تا نزدیک دهی برسید [ب] پشتواره

CHAPTER 5

On the virtue of His Eminence Solomon (pbuh)

and the way his signet ring disappeared from his hand; what was the reason and how it was brought back to him

{1} It is reported that once upon a time Prophet Solomon had been sitting on his throne[1] which was flying in the wind over the skies until it reached a village. A number of girls were near the river, playing together. When they noticed the throne, they wondered to whom the throne belonged. They said, 'This is Solomon's throne'. There was a fisherman's daughter among them. She looked at the other girls and expressed, 'How nice it would be if this Solomon was my husband!'

{2} When the girls heard this they said to her, 'O fisherman's daughter, know your limits!' and they rebuked her to such an extent that she was embarrassed. She told them, 'Do not rebuke me on the basis of my desire; whatever mankind does and says has been predestined by God's verdict. Neither I, nor anyone else, can do otherwise. Certainly, feel free to say whatever you want about me, however, it is God who knows what he will do. It was not my fault, as this was what God wanted me to say.'

{3} The rest of the story. Solomon's throne arrived in a city. There was an old man near the city who was walking slowly, carrying a sack of firewood propped on his head. Solomon approached him and asked, 'Old man, what is your name?' He replied, 'My name is Solomon.' Solomon the prophet pondered, 'Glory be to God! One Solomon becomes like me who has been given sovereignty of the whole world, and another

[1] Flying carpet.

«نامِ سلیمان است». در خاطر سلیمان گذشت «سُبحَانَ الله! یک سلیمان منم که مُلک تمام دنیا به من داده‌اند، ویک سلیمان اوست که وقت پیری هم از هیزم کشی خلاصی نمی‌یابد». چون این در خاطر مهتر سلیمان گذشت دستِ خود را بر سر دراز کرد. از تاج خود یک لعل خوب و زیبا جدا کرده به پیر داد، و گفت «ای پیر، هیزم‌کشیِ باقیِ عُمرِ تو را و فرزندانِ تو را بَس خواهد بود؛ دیگر هیزم‌کشی مکن». پس لعل را برگرفت، دستِ خود نهاده رو به خانه کرد.

{۴} درزمانْ در لعل نظر کرد و با خود گفت «زهی قادر خدای عَزَّوَجَلَّ که پاره‌سنگ را چنین آب‌ورنگی داده که قیمت او از هزارهزار[۲] بیشتر است». ناگاه غلیوازی[۳] در هوا نظر بر کفِ آن پیر کرد. پنداشت که پَرْگالَه[۴] گوشت است. فرودآمد آن لعل را از کف آن پیر خارکَش به‌رُبود. پیر حیران ماند. با خود در فکر شد که «لعل از دست رفت و امروز فرزندان چه خواهند خورد، بیا تا همان هیزم که در صحرا از پشت انداخته‌ام بیارم و بفروشم و قُوت فرزندان خود سازم». چون بدان مقام رسید دید که هیزم نیست، و دیگری بُرده بود. از شرمندگی عیال آن شب به خانه نرفت. هم در بیابان بماند.

{۵} چون روز شد به هیزم‌چیدن مشغول شد. تخت سلیمان در هوا بود. نظرش بر پیر افتاد و گفت «زهی حرص که فرزندان آدم را داده اند. که من آن پیر را لعلی داده‌ام که خراج مملکت می‌شود و آنکه باز هیزم‌کشی نکند تا فرزندان او را بَسَند باشد». در خاطرش گذشت «بروم از وی پرسم که چه حالست که باز مشغول هیزم‌کشی شده است؟» پس نزدیک پیر آمد و از وی سوال کرد.

{۶} پیر جواب داد که «ای سلیمان، آن لعل که داده بودی غلیوازی از کف دست من ربود، و من از شرمندگی عیال شب به خانه نرفتم. اکنون می چینم تا بفروشم و نفقهٔ عیال سازم». چون سلیمان دانست که راست می گوید رحمت آمد. باز از تاج مبارک خود لعل خوبی جدا کرده به دست آن پیر داد. پیر لعل محکم گرفته بر دستِ خودْ به سوی خانه روان شد.

{۷} نزدیک خانهٔ او چشمهٔ آب می‌رفت. خواست که بگذرد در آب افتاد و غوطه خورد. به هزار حیله[۵] از آن آب بیرون آمد و لعل از دست او رفت. باز غم فرزندان خورد که «چه خواهند خورد؟» به خود گفت «بروم و پشتارهٔ هیزم بیارم». به هیزم چیندن مشغول شد.

{۸} مهتر سلیمان از مقامی کوچ کرده بود، دید آن پیر هیزم بر سر کرده پیدا شد. نظر سلیمان بر وی افتاد. گفت «باز حال چیست که هیزم برداشته‌ای؟» گفت «حال این بود. سه روز شد که نمی‌دانم حال

[۲] هزار برابرِ هزار که معادل یک‌میلیون است. [۳] همچنین بصورت غیلواژ،غلیواج، خلواج و خلیواج. به معنی «مرغ مُردارخوار و زغن» و «مرغ گوشت‌ربا» به‌کار می‌رود. به منبع ذیل مراجعه شود:
Ioannis Augusti Vullers, *Lexicon persico-latinum etymologicum* (Bonnae ad Rhenum: Impensis Adolphi Marci, 1855), 718.

[۴] همچنین «پرگاله» به معنی «پاره‌ای از چیزی» و «یک‌تکه» به‌کار می‌رود. [۵] به سختی فراوان.

Solomon becomes this man who is destined to working and gathering firewood!' After this, Prophet Solomon lifted up his hands and took a ruby from his crown which he gave to the old man. He said, 'Old man, [this ruby] should suffice and make you and your children free from gathering firewood for the rest of your lives. There is no need to cut firewood anymore.' The old man held the ruby tightly and went homewards.

{4} In the meantime, he looked at the ruby and pondered, 'Compliments to the All-Powerful God who has coloured a stone beautifully that it is more valuable than one million. Suddenly, a falcon[2] arrived and saw what the old man had in his hand. The bird thought that it might be a piece of meat. It came and grabbed the ruby from his hand. The old man was bewildered. He pondered, 'The ruby was grabbed, so what will my children have to eat today? It is better to return to the desert and bring back the sack of firewood that I left there, and sell it to provide food for my children.' When he arrived where he had left the sack of firewood, he could not find them. Someone else took them. Feeling upset and extremely embarrassed, he did not go home that night, and stayed in desert overnight.

{5} In the morning, he went gathering firewood. Prophet Solomon's throne was nearby and again he noticed the old man. Prophet Solomon pondered, 'See the greed of human nature; I gave him a pricy ruby by which a nation can be satisfied so that he no longer needs to carry sacks and can provide for his children!' He said, 'I will go to him and ask him the reason for gathering firewood.' He approached the old man and asked him.

{6} He replied, 'O Solomon, that ruby you gave me was grabbed by a falcon. As I was then so embarrassed I did not go home last night. Now, I am engaged with gathering firewood in order to sell it and have money to spend on my household.' When Prophet Solomon realised that he was telling the truth, he took pity and gave him another beautiful ruby from his crown. The old man held it tightly and left for home.

{7} There was a water spring near his house. While crossing the spring, he fell down and became adrift, floating. He barely pulled himself out of the water. And the ruby was gone! He grieved again, 'What would the children have to eat?' He reflected that it was better to go back and bring a sack of firewood. The old man became busy with gathering firewood.

{8} His Eminence Solomon passed by and noticed that he had put a sack of firewood on his head again. He pondered, 'What could have happened this time that he returned for this sack?' Solomon asked, 'what has happened this time that you have gathered firewood?' The old man explained, continuing 'It is now about three days that I have not known how my children pass their lives.' Prophet Solomon

[2] Or a particular type of bird.

فرزندان چون گذشته باشد».[6،ج] حضرت سلیمان باز شفقّت کرد. لعل زیبای جدا کرد و به دست پیر داد.

{۹} دستار از سر خود گرفت و محکم بست و در سر نهاد. و به‌جانب خانه خود روان شد. قدری راه رفته بود که سواری پیدا شد و دید که نور و روشنایی از سر پیر می‌تابد. دستار از سر او برده و غایب شد. پیر نالان و زاری‌کنان نزدیک مهتر سلیمان آمد. قصّه را عرض کرد[د] و گفت «ای پیغمبر خدای عَزَّوَجَلَّ، شما منع کار من کردید بدانچه خدای تَعَالَی می‌داشت. واسطه شدی که مرا از فقر برهانی. چون خواستِ معبود نبود، خواستِ تو انگاری به من روی نکرد. و سه روز شد که من و فرزندان به فاقه گذارندیم». سلیمان گفت «من از جهت تو تقصیر نکردم. چون حقّ سُبْحَانَهُ وَتَعَالَی ندهد، سلیمان چه تواند کرد». پیر از پیش سلیمان رفت به هیزم مشغول شد. قصّه این پیر در آخر این حکایت تمام خواهد شد.[7]

{۱۰} نظیر دیگر. چون سلیمان از آنجا روان شد به کنارهٔ دریا رسید. خواست غسل کند، انگشترین کشید[8] و بر تخت نهاد، و به غسل کردن مشغول شد. دیوی بدبخت فرصت یافته بود به دیوان[9] دیگر گفت «چند خدمتِ مخلوقی کنم؟ تا زمانی که این انگشترین با او خواهد بود، ما را خدمت او باید کرد. این بگفت و انگشترین را برداشت و رفت به دریا انداخت». چون انگشترین رفت، تاج‌وتخت و هر چه در اَمر سلیمان بود در یک‌ساعت[10] گویی هیچ نبود.

{۱۱} [سلیمان] از آب بیرون آمد. همه رفته، [و] تنها ماند. نظر به خود کرد و قُوتِ یک روز نداشت. تا سه روز گرسنه بود. قصد مُزدوری کرد. نزدیک دریا ماهی‌گیری بود؛ ماهی پر کرده استاده بود. نزدیک او رفت که «مرا کاری فرمانی و مزدی ده». گفت «این سبد ماهی را به خانه رسان و تو را یک ماهی بدهم».

{۱۲} سلیمان آن سبد ماهی را گرفت و به خانهٔ پیر ماهی‌گیر آمد. مزدوری ماهی‌گیر کردی و یک ماهی گرفتی و هم در خانهٔ ماهی‌گیر بودی! مدّتی براین بگذشت. ماهی‌گیر دید که این جوان به غایت امین و راست و به‌طاعت است.[ه] به زن خود گفت که «این مردْ عجب خوش خُلق و بِهْ دیانت است. اگر بگویی دختر خود تسلیم او کنیم». زن گفت که «در جهان کس نمانده که دختر خود را به کسی دهیم که او در خانهٔ ما مزدوری می کند؟» مرد گفت که «نظر در مزدوری وی مکن. نظر در خُلق و امانت و دیانت وی کن. مادامی که بر ماست هرگز دروغ در ذات او ندیده‌ایم. و در خُلق و جمال او نظر کن که همه چیزِ پسندیده دارد. بهتراز‌این که خواهد بود که به وی خواهی داد؟» آخر[11] زن برین متّفق شد.[12] دختر را به حضرت سلیمان دادند.

{۱۳} دخترکان شنیدند که دخترِ ماهی‌گیر را به مزدوری دادند که او نامِ سلیمان دارد. همه جمع شدند و

[6] عبارتی که برآن تأکید نموده‌ام در برخی نسخ چنین نوشته شده‌است «امروز دوم شد».
[7] این عبارت در برخی نسخ موجود نیست. [8] از انگشت بیرون آورد. [9] دیوها. [10] یک لحظه، یک آن.
[11] به هر جهت، در انتها. [12] قبول کرد.

[ج] گفت «ای پیغمبر خدای، من در آب گذشتن بودم که پایم بلغزید و از خوف جان دست رها کردم. [لعل] از دست بیفتاد و امروز روز دوم شد که نمی‌دانم حال فرزندان من چون شد». [د] گفت ای پیغمبر خدای رهزنی در کار من کردی [ه] ایشان مزاج مهتر سلیمان دریافتند

again showed sympathy. He took another fine ruby and passed it to the old man.

{9} The latter took his turban and put the ruby inside, tied it tightly and put it on his head. He left towards home. After a few steps, a horseman arrived who saw something shining from the old man's head. He grabbed the old man's turban and disappeared. The old man went to Prophet Solomon, wailing profusely, and told him the story. He said, 'O Prophet of God, you stopped me from doing what God had ordained. You mediated to help and save me from poverty. As it was not in accordance with God's will, your will apparently did not work. And now it has been three days that my children and I have passed miserably.' Prophet Solomon said, 'So, in your case this is not my fault; once God does not want this, what can I do?' Solomon left the old man to continue gathering firewood. This tale of the old man will be finished at the end of this story.

{10} Another story. When Solomon left there, he arrived near the sea shore. In order to wash himself, he took off his ring and left it on his throne. While he was washing himself, a desperate demon found the moment opportune and asked the other demons, 'How much do you want to serve him? As long as he has this ring, we must be at his service'. The demon who said this, took the ring and threw it into the sea. Once the ring was gone, Solomon's kingdom and whatever was under his control disappeared.

{11} He came out of the sea, saw no one and he left alone. One day he looked at himself and found that he had nothing left to eat. He had been hungry for three days. He decided to work and earn money. He approached a fisherman near the sea who caught many fish. He went after him saying, 'I want to work and be paid'. The fisherman said, 'Take this basket of fish and deliver it to my home. In return, you will get one fish.'

{12} Solomon took the basket and went to the old fisherman's house. One worked for a fisherman, he received a fish, and now he is in their house! Some time passed in this manner. The fisherman understood that this young man was quite faithful, honest, and obedient. He said to his wife, how well mannered and faithful this man is. 'If you agree, we will give him our daughter.' His wife said, 'Is there nobody else on Earth that we could give our daughter to, but just to someone serving in our home?' The husband replied, 'Do not consider that he has been hired to work for us; see his behaviour, faithfulness, and piety. We have never seen him lie as long as he has been with us. See how nice his behaviour is and his gracefulness. Who better than him to give our daughter to?' At last, the wife agreed. The daughter married Solomon.

{13} Other girls heard that the fisherman's daughter had married their worker, whose name was Solomon. All of them gathered, and told her, 'Remember when Solomon's throne was passing over the skies, and you wished, "How nice would be if this Solomon was my husband!" Anyway, although you could not marry that Solomon, with

آمده، گفتند «یاد داری که روزی تخت سلیمان پیغمبر علیه‌السلام بر هوا می‌گذشت، تو گفتی چه نیکوی می‌بود که این شوهر می‌شد. باری اگر او سلیمانِ با جاه نیافتی، هم‌نام او یافتی». دخترِ ماهی‌گیر گفت «آنچه حُکمِ خدای مَنْ عَزَّوَجَلَّ رفته‌است در حقّ من خواهد شد».

{۱۴} بعداز چند روز ماهی‌گیر برای مزدوری این جوان دو ماهی داد. یک روز سلیمان دو ماهی راه پیش زن آوردی وگفت که بِپَزَد. دخترک رفت و در مقام پاک کردن شد. وشکم ماهی پاک می‌کرد که انگشترین بَرآمد. دختر در حیرت شد، و در فکر رفت که «این انگشترین به پدر و یا به مادر دهم؟» باز اندیشه کرد که «شوهر من چیزی ندارد. همان بهتر که به او دهم». انگشترین را نزدیک حضرت سلیمان آورد.

{۱۵} چون نظر مبارک حضرت سلیمان بر انگشترین افتاد شناخت و شادمان شد و شُکر به جای آورد. در انگشت مبارک کرد. همان‌ساعت تاج‌وتخت و دیوان و پریان و اسبابِ پادشاهی – که سُبحانَهُ وَتَعالیٰ آورده بود – همه جمیع آمدن[۱۳] و به فرمان گشتند. ماهی‌گیر و زن و خَلقِ شهر در حیرت ماندند. آنگاه دختر پُرسید «ای شوهر! در این چه حکمت که فی الحال بدین دولت دَررسیدی؟» سلیمان گفت «من پیغمبر خدای عَزَّوَجَلَّ بودم.[د] و انگشترین مرا دیوِ بدبخت به دریا انداخته بود. امروز خدای عَزَّوَجَلَّ از دست تو روزی کرد و جمیع مخلوقاتْ مسخّرِ من گردانید».

{۱۶} زن گفت «ای سلیمان، اکنون حکمت این واقعه را از من پُرس که چندگاه مملکت از تو رفته بود. سبب چه بود؟ روزی شما بر تخت خود درین ره می‌گذشتی. من با دخترکان بازی می‌کردم. چون تخت سلیمان پیدا شد، گفتم چه نیکو بُود اگر این سلیمانِ پیغمبر شوهرِ من بودی. به‌مجرّدِ گفتنِ این سخن همهٔ دخترکان مرا ملامت کردند که «به حدّ خود سخن گوی». من شکسته‌دل ماندم. و گفتم «ای پروردگارِ من، اگر این سخن نزد همه دشوارست نزد تو آسان است». پس ازجهت منِ شکسته چندگاه مُلکْ از شما بستانْدند. باز مملکت به شما روزی گشت». آنگاه دخترِ ماهی‌گیر دخترکان را طلب کرد و گفت «اکنون ببینید آنچه از خدای عَزَّوَجَلَّ خواسته‌ام چگونه به مقصود رساند. سخن من نزد شما دشوار نمود. حق سُبحانَهُ وَتَعالیٰ به من چه آسان داد که تا بدانید که هر که از روی صِدق از باری عَزَّوَجَلَّ جوید چُنین یابد».[۱۴]

{۱۷} بعداز آن سلیمان روان شد و به شهر آن هیزم‌کش رسید. در خاطرش آمد که از او خبر گیرد که وی چگونه است. شخصی را طلبید و گفت «درین مقام مرد پیری هیزم کشی می‌کرد و هم‌نامِ من بود. او را بگو «تو را پیغمبر می‌طلبد»».[ذ] چون [آن مرد] خبر یافت، جامه‌های قیمتی در بَرکرد و تحفه‌های خوب برداشتند.

[۱۳] آمدند. [۱۴] اشاره دارد به آیهٔ ۲۶ سورهٔ آل عمران.

[د] بدآن‌که من پیغمبر خدایم و نام من سلیمان بن داود است [ذ] آن مرد آمد و آواز داد. آن مرد نیز بیرون آمد و گفت که «خدمت من بر مهتر سلیمان برسان و بگو که من آسوده شده ام و نمی‌توانم آمدن». آن کس پیغام بیاورد و گفت [آن پیر] «چنین می گوید». مهتر سلیمان را از گفتار او عجب آمد که «از بارکشی خالی نبودی؛ اکنون چگونه است که نزد من نتُواند آمدن؟» [سلیمان] فرمود که «اسب بَرید و او را بیارید»». او را سوار کردند و بیاوردند و مهتر سلیمان از حال او پرسید.

such wealth and power, you married someone carrying the same name!' The fisherman's daughter responded, 'Whatever is the Almighty God's decree, it will happen to me.'

{14} After a few days, the fisherman brought two fish to the young man [i.e., Solomon] as his wage. Then Solomon took both fish home to his wife and asked her to cook them. The fisherman's daughter[3] went to clean the fish. While cleaning the fish's bellies, a ring appeared. She was surprised and pondered, 'It will be better to give this ring to my parents.' She then pondered again, 'My husband has nothing and it would be better to give it to him.' She brought the ring to Prophet Solomon.

{15} Once his pure eyes observed the ring, he recognised it and became happy, and thanked God. He put on the ring. Immediately, all his kingdoms, demons, fairies, and regalia brought by God gathered there, to be under Solomon's control. The fisherman, his wife, and the people were shocked. The fisherman's daughter asked her husband, 'O, Man! why has it happened that you have reached this glorious status?' Solomon replied, 'I used to be the prophet of God. And my ring was thrown into the sea by a desperate demon. Today, God gave it back to me through your hands and all creatures are under my control again.'

{16} Solomon's wife then said, 'Now you ask me about my own story why you have lost your sovereignty! While sitting on your throne, you were passing this way. I was playing with my friends. Once your throne appeared, I said how nice it would be if the Prophet Solomon was my husband. After this, my friends rebuked me, "Know your limits!" they said. My heart was broken and I said, "O my God, although it is hard for others to believe this desire of mine, whatever the hardship it is easy before You. Therefore, because of my broken heart, God took your sovereignty for a while and then brought it back to you."' Then, the fisherman's daughter gathered all her friends and told them, 'Now you can see how what I asked from God has been bestowed upon me! My desire seemed unbelievably farfetched to you. See how God granted it to me easily; when you believe that whoever purely requests something from God, he will acquire it.'

{17} Later, Solomon travelled and reached the city of that [old] man who gathered firewood. He thought, 'It might be good to greet him and see how he is doing.' He called to someone, enquiring, 'There used to be an old man who collected firewood and his name was the same as mine. Tell him that the Prophet wants to see you.' When the old man was informed, he put on expensive clothes and took nice gifts. He came to Prophet Solomon. Once the Prophet Solomon saw him he said, 'Tell me how difficult you have found the world.' He replied, 'O prophet of God, once you left, I wailed and cried so much in the presence of God and said to Him, 'O God, You are the Knower of everything. Your prophet's decision was to save me from poverty! However, no one can

[3] i.e. Solomon's wife

نزد سلیمان علیه‌السلام آمد. چون نظر سلیمان بر پیر افتاد گفت «بگو اسباب دنیا از چه زَجر یافتی؟» گفت «ای پیغمبر خدای عزّوجلّ، چون شما از سرِّوقتِ من گذشتید، به زجر و بیچارگی خود در حضرت معبود بنالیدم و گفتم «إلٰهي، تو داناتری به همه چیز. و خواستِ پیغمبرِ تو بر این بود که [مرا] از فقر برهاند. [امّا] تا تو ندهی هیچ‌کس نتَواند داد. اکنون تو می‌دانی آنچه پیغمبر تو داده بود از من رفته است. باز آنها را به من رسان». این بگفتم و در یکی درختی درآمدم برای هیزم؛ در نَظَرْ آشیانِ غلیوازی آمد. در آن نظر کردم، هر سه لعلی را که شما داده بودید آنجا دیدم. حمد و ثنای حقّ سبحانه وتعالی بر زبان راندم و در تصرّف خود آوردم».

{۱۸} پس بنده[ح] باید که دل در غیری نبندد جزء به حضرت پروردگار تا همهٔ کارهای دین و دنیای او ساخته کرده.

{۱۹} بیت: چون دل بر خلق بندی خسته گردی؛ چون دل بر حقّ بندی رسته گردی[۱۵]

{۲۰} إلٰهي، کارهای من بیچاره و جمیع مؤمنان را برآوردهٔ خیر گردانی. بِمِنَّة وَكَرَمه.

[۱۵] در «الهی نامه» منسوب به عطّار بیتی مشابه، البتّه با اندک جابه‌جایی وجود دارد «تو در حقّ بند دل تا رسته گردی، چو دل در خلق بندی خسته گردی».

ح مؤمن

give except You! Now You know whatever Your prophet had given me has been lost. [I ask] that You return them back to me. After this, I reached a tree to gather firewood, therein I noticed a falcon's nest. I looked inside and found all three rubies that you had given to me. I praised God and took them all.'

{18} As such, the servant of God should not believe in anyone else except God; so all his religious and worldly affairs will be made.

{19} Poem: Once you rely on people, you will be exhausted; Once you rely on God, you will be saved[4]

{20} *O God, make good the affair of this humble pauper and that of other believers. By Your unmerited favour and kindness. [Amen.]*

[4] A similar couplet with slight changes is found in the *Ilāhī-nāma* of ʿAṭṭār.

در فضیلتِ مهتر عیسیٰ پیغمبر علیه‌السلام و معجزهٔ ایشان

{۱} آورده‌اند که معجزهٔ ایشان این بود که مُردهٔ چهارصد ساله به دعای ایشان زنده[الف] گشتی، و هرچه ایشان پرسیدی جواب شنیدی.[ب] التماس مردگان این بود که «یا عیسیٰ، اکنون دعا کن همچنان شویم که بُود که حیاتِ دنیا نمی‌باید. که یک نوبت جان داده‌ایم و عذابِ جان‌دادن نمی‌توانیم».[۱،ج] عیسیٰ باز دعا کرد به حالِ اوّل شد.[د] چون کافران چنین معجزه می‌دیدند آن بدبختان با یکدیگر می‌گفتند که «عیسیٰ خدا است، و یا پسر خداست؟»[۲] خاک در دهن ایشان باد.[۳] چون عیسیٰ سخن ایشان شنیدی ترک شهر کرد و در بیابانها خدای تَعَالَی را بندگی می‌کرد.

{۲} روزی گذر ایشان در صحرایی افتاد و هفت شبانه‌روز باران بارید. هرچند عیسیٰ تردّد کرد پناه نیافت.[ه] شُغالی[و] سر خود از خانه بیرون کرده. نظر عیسیٰ بر شُغال افتاد. آب در چشم گردانید و روی سوی آسمان کرد، و گفت «بار خدایا، شغال را پناهی می‌دهی و پسر مریم را از باد و باران پناهی نمی‌دهی؟» باز [با] خود گفت «شکر و صبر در حضرت ذوالجلال خود کن که هرچه به تو رسد از پروردگار تو رسد. و چنین سختی خدای عَزَّوَجَلَّ

[۱] ارتباط معناداری بین این قسمت و داستان سی وششم پیرامون گفت‌وگوی عیسیٰ با جمجمه وجود دارد.

[۲] اشاره به باور بخش اعظمی از جامعه مسیحیت دارد که گاها در کنار باور «تثلیث» قرار می‌گیرد. بعدها این باور توسط مسیحیانی چون میکاییل سروتوس (کشته شده در سال ۱۵۵۳) به چالش کشیده شد.

[۳] ترجمهٔ عینی این نفرین در ادبیات مالایی و براساس متون فارسی چون درّالمجالس دیده می‌شود. معادل مالایی آن چنین است « تانه ایت مسقن کدالم ملوتم». شرح بیشتر در بخش ترجمهٔ انگلیسی این داستان بیان شده‌است.

[الف] زندگی [ب] و سؤالی که از ایشان کردی، آن‌را جواب دادی [ج] بعضی را التماس این بود که «یا عیسیٰ، اکنون دعا کن تا باز زنده نشویم که ما را حیات دنیا نمی باید. که یک‌بار تلخیِ جان‌کندن چشیدیم، بار دیگر چشیدن نمی‌توانیم [د] مهتر عیسیٰ دعا کردی تا مُرده و ناچیز شدی [ه] هرچند که مهتر عیسیٰ پناه جُست در هیچ محلّی پناه نیافت [و] شکاری

CHAPTER 6

On the virtue of His Eminence Jesus (pbuh) and his miracle

{1} It is reported that Jesus' miracle was that of a four hundred year-old dead person returned to life following supplication, and that whatever Jesus asked him, he responded. Those revived implored of Jesus, 'O Jesus, now pray for us to return to our former circumstance as we do not wish to be alive, as we have already died once and cannot tolerate the torment of death again.'[1] Jesus did so and they died again. As the unbelievers witnessed such miracles, the desperate ones were asking each other, 'Is Jesus God or the Son of God?' – and O God, they should be choked with dust.[2] When Jesus heard their words, he left the town and wandered in the desert to serve God.

{2} In time, he arrived in a desert where it had been raining for seven days and nights. Despite his efforts, Jesus was unable to find a shelter. A jackal raised its head from its lair. Jesus saw it. His eyes became tearful and looked at the sky and said, 'O God, You provide a jackal with shelter, but You do not protect the son of Mary from wind and rain?!' Then, he continued while contemplating, 'Praise your God and be patient in his presence as whatever reaches you comes from your God. And God does not go to such trouble unless it is to His own friends.' In the meantime, Gabriel arrived and said, 'O Jesus, God has said, "Because of your patience and the praise expressed by your tongue, God will offer you seventy thousand maidens with large black eyes,

[1] This may be related to the theme of the chapter thirty-six on the conversation between Jesus and the King Jumjuma.

[2] i.e., God's curse upon them, stop speaking like that. This phrase was directly translated into Malay and is found in the Malay *Hikayat Muhammad Hanafiyya*. Brakel has translated it as 'put dirt in his mouth and not to mention such matters', which is a verbatim translation of *tanah itu masukkan kedalam mulutmu*. For more, see: Brakel, *The Story of Muhammad Hanafiyyah* (1977), 48 and 115.

ندهد، مگر دوستان خود را». همان‌زمان[۴] جبرئیل رسید و گفت «ای عیسیٰ، فرمان شود که به همین صبر و شکر که بر زبان راندی فردای قیامت حق سُبْحَانَهُ وَتَعَالَىٰ تو را هفتادهزار[ز] حورٌعین بدهد و با هر حوری هفتادهزارِ دیگر پیشْ‌اِستاده خدمت کنند.[ح] امّا، ای عیسیٰ، مشقّت دنیا بُگذرد و به نعمت عقبی و ابدی برسی».

{۳} نظیر دیگر. روزی گذر عیسیٰ عَلَيْهِ السَّلَامُ در گورستان افتاد. دید مردی نزدیک گور نشسته است. پرسید «در این گور چه کس دادی؟»[ط] آن مرد گفت «ای پیغمبر خدای، در این خاک زن من است. و مدّت سی‌سال[ی] است که وی درین خاک مانده. و با یکدیگر عُمرها به سربردیم و میان من و این زن عهد کرده بودیم که «اگر تو پیش‌از من بمیری مجاور تو کنم». او نیز همین عهد کرده بود.[ک] حکم خدای تَعَالَی رسیده و این زن پیش‌از من بمرد. امروز مدّت سی‌سال است که وفای عهد به سر می‌برم».

{۴} از گفتار این مرد حضرت عیسیٰ را شفقّت آمد و گفت «اگر دراین ساعت او از این تربت زنده بیرون آید چه گویی؟» گفت «ای پیغمبر خدای تَعَالَی، آنچه از عمر من باقی مانده است نیمی به او بخشم». عیسیٰ را رحم آمد و دست به دعا برد و گفت «إِلٰهِيّ، این بندهٔ تو از غایت محبّت که بر زنِ خود دارد نصف از عمر خویش به این زن می‌بخشد. تو به کرم خود این مرده را زنده گردان». في الحال دعا مستجاب شد و تربت بشکافُت. زنی همچون ماهِ چهارده از تربت برآمد. و میان زن و شوهر ملاقات شد. و عیسیٰ عَلَيْهِ السَّلَامُ از سروقت ایشان رفت. واین زن و شوهر روزگار در بیابان به سر می‌بردند.

{۵} تا روزی پادشاده‌زاده در شکار به سروقتِ ایشان رسید. دید مرد در خواب و نزدیک او عورتِ صاحب‌جمال نشسته. نظر عورت به جمال پادشاه‌زاده افتاد. پرسید «تو کیستی؟» گفت «پادشاه‌زاده‌ام». زن شیفتهٔ پادشاه‌زاده شد. پادشاه‌زاده هم عاشق او شد. پادشاه‌زاده عورت را به جانب خود خواند. زن شوهر را خُفته گذاشت و نزد پادشاه‌زاده رفت.

{۶} پرسید «این مرد کیست که خفته است؟» زن گفت «این دزد است که مرا به حیله و مکر از شهر برون آورده است». پادشاه‌زاده گفت که «من فریفتهٔ جمال تو شده‌ام. مرا قبول داری، یا نه؟» زن گفت «اگر این مدّعی که خفته است، او را بکشی، به تو می‌رسم».[ل] پادشاه‌زاده گفت «چون این دزد است، من او را زنده نمی‌گذارم». به‌مجرّد همچین سخن، پادشاه‌زاده روان شد و باز پشیمان شد و قصد او نکرد. و شوهر را خفته گذاشت. و زن را گرفته به همراه خود به شهر آورد، و در پیش مادر خود بُرد و قصّه را با مادر گفت.

[۴] معادلی است که برای «في الحال» و «درزمانْ» به‌کار رفته‌است.

[ز] هفتاد [ح] و دنبال هر حوری هفتاد حور دیگر که خدمتکار ایشان باشد [ط] مهتر عیسیٰ پرسید که «تو را چه حالست که از سر این گور توده‌خاک بر نمی‌خیزی؟ در این خاک تو را کیست؟» [ی] سه‌سال [ک] مجاور خاک هم باشیم [ل] با تو راضی شوم

for whom there are another seven thousand cherubs in attendance, after the Day of Judgement. But O Jesus, the worldly difficulty will be gone and you will gain immortal favour and grace!"'

{3} Another story. Once upon a time, Jesus came across a graveyard. And a man sat near a grave. Jesus asked him, 'Who from your relatives is in this grave?' The man said, 'O Prophet of God! My wife is in there, and it is now around thirty years that she has been in this soil. We lived together for a long time. I had promised, "If you die earlier than me, I will stay next to your grave", and she promised similarly. As God destined, my wife died earlier. Now, I have been carrying out this promise for thirty years.'

{4} Prophet Jesus took pity on the man after hearing his statement, and said to him, 'If your wife came out of this grave alive, then what would you tell her?' He said, 'O, Prophet of God, I would give her half the rest of my life.' Jesus became emotional and lifted his hand in supplication and said, 'O God! This servant of Yours would like to offer half of his life to his wife due to his extreme love. Make this dead person alive due to Your kindness.' Jesus' request was soon accepted and the grave was opened. A pretty woman whose face was as illuminated as the full moon came out of the grave. And the wife and husband were reunited. Jesus left them alone. The couple spent time together in the desert.

{5} But some time later, a prince, while hunting, saw them. He noticed that the husband slept and there was a pretty woman sitting next to him. The wife looked at the prince's appearance and asked him, 'Who are you?' He replied, 'I am a prince'. The woman fell in love with that prince. The prince also fell in love with her. The prince asked the woman to join him. She left her husband asleep and alone and went to the prince.

{6} The prince asked her, 'Who is the man who slept?' The woman replied, 'This is a thief who brought me out of my town with cunning.' That prince said, 'I fell in love with your beautiful face. Will you accept me [i.e., as your husband]?' The woman said, 'If you kill this claimant who slept, I will surely be able to be with you.' He said, 'He is a thief and I will not leave him alive.' Soon he went to kill him but was full of regret and then decided not to kill him, and left the man asleep. He took the woman and brought her to his city and put her next to his mother. And he told the mother the story.

{۷} [سپس] مادرِ پادشاه را طلب کرد و این قصّه را با پدرِ شاه‌زاده بیان کرد. پدرْ پسرْ را ملامت کرد و گفت «چنین چرا کردی؟» شاه‌زاده گفت که «ای پدر؛ فریفتهٔ این زن شده‌ام و او را در عقد می‌آرم». و میان پدر و پسر گفت‌وگوی شده بود.[۵] چون مرد از خواب بیدار شد، دید زن نیست. آهی کشید؛ بیچارهٔ حقّ به هرجانب می‌دوید. فریاد و فغان می‌کرد و اثری از زن نبود. او گمان نیک می‌برد و با خود می‌گفت «مگر کسی تو را به زور برده باشد». سرِ چشمه آمد. ناگاه دید که پیِ اسپی آمده و باز پس‌رفته. مرد با خود گفت «نمی‌گفتم که قُوّتی به زور می‌برد؟».

{۸} او راستِ راه گرفته نیز روان شد تا به شهر رسید. از پیری سراغ کرد. آن پیر گفت «پادشاه‌زادهٔ این شهر را دیدم که زنی را به شهر درآورد». آن مرد نزد پادشاه‌زاده شد. دید که زن با او نشسته.[۴] مرد رسید و گفت «از خدای تَعَالَی نمی‌ترسی! و زن مرا به زور می‌بری؟» پادشاه‌زاده گفت «زنِ تو نیست. و تو این را به دزدی می‌بری». مرد گفت «زن من است و بر من افترا می‌کنی». زن گفت «ای پادشاه‌زاده، پیش‌از این گفتم که این دزد دست از من برندارد تا او را نکشی». پادشاه‌زاده ملازمان را فرمود بگیرند، و دست‌های او را محکم بربندند، وکشاله‌کنان بیارند به شهر.

{۹} و پادشاه‌زاده روان شد و پیش پدر آمد و واقعه که روی داده بود گفت. و تعریف بسیار کرد که «عجب حُسن خوب دارد این زن». پادشاه فرمود «هر دو را پیش من بیارید». از مرد پرسید «این عورت تو را چه باشد؟» گفت «زن من است». بعداز آن از زن پرسید «زن گفت این دزد است که مرا به مکر و حیله برآورد». پادشاه گفت «ای مرد، تو می‌گویی «زن من است»، و زن می گوید «مرا به دزدی و به مکر آورده»». مرد گفت «سُبْحَانَ اللهِ ای پادشاه! که در حقّ من چنین می‌گوید. امّا، از احوال ما عیسیٰ پیغمبر خبردار است و گواه من است».

{۱۰} پادشاه روی به وزیر کرد.[۶] وزیر گفت «ای پادشاه، محل دم‌زدن نیست که این مرد پیغمبر خدای را به گواهی می‌خواند». وزیر گفت «ای مرد، مهتر عیسیٰ را کی می‌آری؟» مرد گفت «فردا بیارم». پادشاه گفت «برو و بیار». مرد از پیش پادشاه روان شد و رفت. زن گفت «ای پادشاه، مرد بدین حیله و مکر خود را خلاص کرد. باز او را کجا یابید؟» پادشاه به وزیر گفت «اگر به این بهانه رفته و فردا نیاید چه کنیم؟» وزیر گفت «از عقب او چند نفر بروند و او را بیارند».

{۱۱} این مرد اندک راه رفته بود که در خاطرش رسید که عیسیٰ پیغمبر عليه السلام در بیابان مقام معینّی ندارد «کجا خواهم یافت؟» در این اندیشه در زیر درخت سر به زانو گرفته و در خواب رفته. در خواب جمال عیسیٰ عليه السلام را دید، و گفت «ای مرد، باز گرد و اندوه مکن که فردا نزد پادشاه خواهم آمد». در خواب بود که

[۵] قسمت مربوط به گفتگوی بین پدر و مادر و پادشاه‌زاده در برخی نسخ موجود نیست. [۶] نظر وزیر را جویا شد.

[۴] چون به سرعت تمام روان شد و فریاد کرد. پادشاه‌زاده عنان کشیده استاد.

{7} The mother then called the king and told him the story of their son. The king rebuked his son asking, 'Why did you do that?' The prince responded, 'O father, I fell in love with this woman and I want to marry her.' A discussion ensued between father and son. When the husband woke up he understood that his wife was no longer around. He, the poor servant of God, sighed. He ran everywhere and shouted and wailed, but could not find his wife! He was quite positive, pondering, 'She could have been forced to go.' He went to the water spring and suddenly noticed a hoof print suggesting that a horse came for water and then returned. The man thought, 'Did I not say that she has been kidnaped?'

{8} He then left there and followed the road. He arrived in a city. He asked a question from an old man. He replied, 'I saw the city's prince who brought a woman with him.' The man went to the prince, and saw his wife with him. The man said, 'Are you not afraid of God that you have kidnaped my wife?!' The prince said, 'She is not your wife, and you had kidnaped her!' The man said, 'She is my wife and you are accusing me.' The woman said, 'O prince, as I told you before, this thief will not leave me alone until you kill him.' The prince called to his retinue to seize the man, tie his hands, and drag him through the town.

{9} The prince went to the king and explained what had happened and imparted how well mannered the woman was. The king said, 'Bring both of them to me.' Then king asked the man, 'What is this woman's relationship with you?' He replied, 'She is my wife.' The king then asked the woman. She said, 'He is a thief who kidnaped me with cunning.' The king said, 'O man! You say that "she is my wife," and she says that "he kidnaped me with cunning".' The man said, 'O king! Glorious is God, why is she speaking like this about me! Nonetheless, Prophet Jesus knows everything about us, and he is my witness.'

{10} The king discussed the situation with his vizier. His vizier said, 'O king, we should not wait anymore as the man claims that God's prophet is his witness.' The vizier added, 'O man! When can you bring His Eminence Jesus?' The man said, 'I will bring him tomorrow.' The king said, 'Go and bring him.'The man left the king and went out. The woman then said, 'O king! This man has released himself with cunning! How are you going to find him again?' The king asked his vizier, 'What shall we do if he has lied and will not come back tomorrow?' The vizier said, 'I will send a few people after him to bring him back'.

{11} After a few steps, the man pondered, 'Prophet Jesus (pbuh) does not have a specific place in the desert. Where can I find him?' While thinking, he squatted down under a tree and slept. He saw Jesus (pbuh) in his dream and Jesus told him, 'O man, return and do not worry as I will come to the king tomorrow.' While sleeping, the king's people arrived and woke him up. They shouted at him, 'You were allowed to go

ملازمان پادشاه رسیده و بیدار کردند. و زبانِ تعرّض دراز کردند که «تو برای آوردن عیسیٰ عليه السلام رفته‌ای و در خواب شده‌ای و بی‌غم شده‌ای!»؛ گرفته نزدیک پادشاه آوردند، و گفتند «در خواب بود». مرد گفت «ای پادشاه، چون از خدمت شما رفتم آنچه اندیشه کردم که «عیسیٰ نبی مقام معیّنی ندارد، کجا خواهم یافت» که ناگاه در تپّه در خواب رفتم. ایشان را در خواب دیدم که گفت «غم و اندوه مخور که به خدمت پادشاه خواهم آمد»».

{۱۲} پادشاه به وزیر گفت «چه می‌گویی؟» وزیر گفت «تا فردا دیر نخواهد بود. چون فردا شود مهتر عیسیٰ عليه السلام نیاید همهٔ گفته‌های مرد دروغ باشد و هرچه سزای او باشد چنان کنید». مرد را سپردند و فردا گذشت. مهتر عیسیٰ نیامد. دوم روز پادشاه پسر خود را طلبید و گفت «این مرد دزد را سزا دهم».[ن] درین سخن بودن که دید نوری از جانب صحرا برآمد و رو به شهر می‌آمد. وزیر گفت «ای پادشاه، بنگر که عیسیٰ عليه السلام رسید». پادشاه از کرسی خود برخاست، و به استقبال مهتر عیسیٰ رفت و ملاقات کرد.[س] بعداز لحظه پادشاه کیفیت این مرد و زن را گفت به‌تمام.[ع]

{۱۳} عیسیٰ عليه السلام گفت «مرد را و زن را نزدیک من بیارید».[۷] چون آنها را آوردند عیسیٰ به زن گفت «قصّه دراز مکن و هر عطایی که این مرد به تو کرده است آن عطای او را باز دِه». زن به شوخی گفت «نیکو باشد». عیسیٰ به زن گفت «مستقبل[۸] قبله نشین و بگوی «إِلٰهِيّ، هر عطایی این مرد از عُمر خود به من کرده است من‌را نمی‌باید»». چون زن این سخن تمام گفت[۹] بر زمین افتادْ تودهٔ خاک شد.[ف]

{۱۴} پادشاه، و وزیران و پادشاه‌زاده و جملهٔ ارکان و مقرّبان دولت در حیرت افتادند که درزمانْ آدمی خاکستر شد. پادشاه گفت «یا پیغمبر خدای عزّوجلّ، سرّ این معلوم ما نیست. بعداز آن واقعهٔ گذشته را به تمامْ پیغمبر گفت».[ص]

{۱۵} نظیر دیگر. آورده‌اند که روزی عیسیٰ عليه السلام در بیابان سه نفر را دید؛ دو مرد و یک زن. پرسید که «شما چه کسانید؟» گفتند «ای پیغمبر خدای، ما زن و شوهریم و این چون پسرمان است. از غایت بی‌نوایی شهر را ترک دادیم. و میان ما سه نفر یک جامه بیش نیست و به نوبت پوشیم». در شهر از برای گدایی می‌رویم. اکنون حق سبحانه وتعالی شما را به سروقت ما رسانید. دعا کنید تا از این تنگی نجات یابیم». پیغمبر گفت «امشب احوال شما را عرض کنم. هر چه فرمان شود فردا به شما بگویم».

[۷] در برخی نسخ شرح ماجرای بین مرد و زن بار دیگر تکرار شده است. [۸] روی به. [۹] هنوز حرفش تمام نشده بود.

[ن] گفت «اکنون دزد را پیش آرید تا او را سیاست کنیم» [س] و قدم او ببوسید [ع] قصّه آن مرد و زن را در میان آورد [ف] آن عورت سخن تمام نگفته بود که بر زمین افتاد و بمرد [ص] مهتر عیسیٰ گفت «میان ایشان عهد و محبّتی بود که نه تو شوهر کنی و نه من زن عهد کرده. و حکم خدای تَعَالَی شد که این زن نقل کرد و این مرد مدّت سی‌سال است که به وفای زن بر سر تربت او عمر گذرانید تا روزی گذر من بر سر تربت افتاد. القصّه. هر چه که احوال آن زن و مرد بود به تمامی گفت. بعداز آن نیمهٔ عمر خود به زن داد و من دعا کردم، خدای تَعَالَی وی را زنده گردانید. امروز این عورت عطایی که این مرد بدو بخشیده بود باز داد. او هرآینه چنانکه بود در گور شد. درین وقت نیز خاک شد». درین بود که از عالم غیب آوازی آمد که «ای عیسیٰ، هر که به جز از ما دل به غیری بندد، همباز بی‌وفایی بینند»

only to bring Jesus (pbuh), now you sleep and do not care anymore?' They arrested him and brought him to the king, and said, 'He was asleep.' The man said, 'O king, when I left you, I could not recall "where Jesus could be or where I should go". I reached a hill where I slept and dreamed of Jesus and he said to me, "Do not worry as I will come to the king."'

{12} The king asked his vizier, 'What do you think?' The vizier said, 'Waiting until tomorrow will not hurt. If His Eminence Jesus (pbuh) does not come tomorrow, we will consider all the man's claims as lies and punish him accordingly.' They held the man, and the morrow passed and His Eminence Jesus did not come. On the second day, the king called for his son and told him, 'I will punish this thief.' While speaking with his son, he noticed a light coming towards the city from the desert. The vizier said, 'O king! See that Jesus (pbuh) is coming.' The king left his throne and went to welcome Jesus and they met. After a while, the king related the whole story of this man and woman.

{13} Jesus (pbuh) said, 'Bring to me both man and woman'. When they brought them, Jesus told the woman, 'No need to speak! Just give whatever this man gifted you back to him.' The woman did not take it seriously and said, 'Sure, let's take it back'. Jesus told her, 'Sit towards the direction of prayer and say, "O God, I do not want whatever this man has given to me from his life"'. Upon finishing her statement, she felt down and changed to a heap of soil.

{14} The king, viziers, princes, and all the entourage were surprised how quickly a person was turned to ashes! The king said, 'O Prophet of Almighty God, what has happened as we do not understand the secret.' The Prophet told the whole story.

{15} Another story. It is reported that Jesus (pbuh) saw three people in the desert – two men and one woman. Jesus asked them, 'Who are you?' They said, 'O Prophet of God, we are a couple and this is our son. We left our city due to our abject poverty. We have only one garment and we wear it in rotation. And we go to the city to beg. Now, God has sent you to us. Please pray for us to save us from this poverty.' The Prophet told them, 'I will mention your condition tonight. Whatever is decided by God, I will inform you.'

{١۶} عیسیٰ علیه‌السلام در وقتِ مناجاتِ خود احوال ایشان را عرض کرد. فرمان شد «بگو ایشان را بعداز صبح‌دم هریک از ایشان آنچه اوّل چیزی بخواهد به ایشان دهم». پیغمبر شادان نزدیک ایشان رفت، و گفت که «ای مردمان، از تنگی روزگار خلاص شدید. هرکدام از شما در اوّل صبح‌دم هرچه بخواهد از حق سبحانه و تعالی همان یابید». زن از شوهر پرسید «چون خواسته به مطلوب ما داده‌اند تو بگو چه خواهی طلبی؟» مرد گفت «پادشاهی». شوهر از زن پرسید «تو چه خواهی طلبید؟» گفت «من جوانی خواستن تا تو به جز من به غیر دل نبندی». در این حکایت بودند که شب به آخر رسید و صبح دمیدن گرفت.

{١٧} زن گفت «اوّل من بخواهم. بعداز آن شما بخواهید». زن برخاست، و به چشمهٔ آب نزدیک بود. در او وضو ساخت، و گفت که «یا بار خدایا، مرا جمال و جوانی ده که در این عصر هیچ عورتی را نباشد». به‌مجرّد گفتن حقّ سبحانه و تعالی چنان جمال داد که تمام وجود او منوّر جمال او گشت». درحال، پادشاهِ مملکت می‌گذشت که جمال زن دید و حیران ماند. گفت «تو حوری، یا پری؟»[ق] زن گفت «من آدمی‌زاده‌ام». پادشاه گفت که «اگر تو مرا قبول کنی، از همهٔ حَرَمانِ من بزرگتر باشی.[ر] و آنچه دارم در ملک تو گردانم».

{١٨} زن این سخن از پادشاه بشنید، راضی شُد، و اندیشید که «شوهر من پادشاهی خواهد خواست امّا او پیر است و من جوانِ صاحب جمال. این پادشاه که به سروقت من رسید، جوانست و عاشق من شده‌است. با این[١٠] بودن بهتر است». درحال راضی شد [و] همراه رفت. پادشاه زن را در کجاوه[ش] نشاند و با خود بُرد. و زن هیچ از پسر و شوهر یاد نکرد.

{١٩} پدر روی پسر می‌دید و پسر روی پدر می‌دید. عاقبت غیرت و غَضَب مردی درکار شد. به پسر گفت که «مادر تو با من بی‌وفائی کرد. من انتقام از او می‌کشم». مرد نزدیک چشمه رفت و وضو ساخت و دست به مناجات برد، و گفت «إِلٰهِيّ، التماس دارم که تمام اندام این زنِ من جنس آدمی باشد، امّا روی او همچون روی خوک باشد». چون پادشاه کجاوه را در حرم بُرد خواست که بیرون آرد، دید که صورت خوک گشته. پادشاه بترسید و گفت «من گفتم این‌چنین صورتِ آدمی در جهان نباشد. مبادا از این صورت مرا آسیب رسد». ملازمان را فرمود تا او را در آن کجاوه انداخته بر سر آن چشمه رسانند و گذاشته بیایند.

{٢٠} پدر و پسر نشسته بودند که ملازمانِ پادشاه زن را آورده، کناره چشمه گذاشته و رفتند. نظر پسر بر صورت مادر افتاد. گفت «ای پدر، دعای تو به درگاه حقّ تَعَالَیٰ مستجاب شده و صورت مادر من این‌چنین شده». آنگاه پسر برخاست و بر سر چشمه آمد و وضو ساخت، و دست به مناجات برداشته [و] گفته «مَلکا پادشاها، اگر مادر من خطا کرده است، اکنون من در حضرت پاک تو این درخواست دارم که چنانچه‌صورتْ

[١٠] با پادشاه.

[ق] نزدیک آن عورت آمده و گفت «ای ماهِ تابان، از آسمانِ کیستی؟ و ای دسته‌گل، از گلستانِ کیستی که از جمال تو بیابان منوّر است؟ چنین دانم مگر حوری یا پری؟» [ر] خاتون حرم من باشی [ش] محفه

{16} During his prayer, Jesus (pbuh) prayed for this family and their straightened circumstances.God's command arrived, 'Tell them that the first thing each of them requests during dawn, I will answer and accept.' The Prophet joyfully went to them and said, 'O people! You are free from poverty. Whatever each of you requests from God at dawn, he will be given.' The wife asked her husband, 'As they have given us what we really wanted, you tell me what you want to request?' The husband said, 'I will demand kingship'. He asked his wife, 'What about you?' His wife said, 'I will demand youthfulness so you will not fall in love with anybody except me.' While speaking about their wishes, the night ended and the morning was about to come.

{17} The wife said, 'I will go first, then you two go.' She stood. There was a water spring there. She performed ablution from it and said, 'O God, give me beauty and youthfulness as You have not given any other woman.' As soon as she said this, God beautified her so her body became illuminated with divine light. In the meantime, a king was passing and he saw the woman's beauty by which he was surprised. He asked her, 'Are you a heavenly angel or a fairy?' She said, 'I am just a human.' The king said, 'If you accept me, you will be superior to the other women of my court[3]. And whatever I have, I will give to you.'

{18} When she heard this from the king, she agreed. She contemplated, 'My husband would also like to become a king. But he is an old man and I am a young beautiful woman. This king, coming to me, is young and loves me. Being with the latter is much better.' She agreed and accompanied the king. He put the woman into the howdah and off she went, saying nothing of her husband and child.

{19} The father looked at the son and the son looked at the father. The man's jealousy and anger took hold. The man told his son, 'Your mother was unfaithful to me. I will take revenge on her.' He went near the water spring and performed ablution and lifted up his hand and entreated, 'O God, I wish that the whole body of my wife should be like a human but that her face changes to that of a pig.' The King took the howdah to his royal court but when he came to take the woman out he saw a pigs-head.[4] He was afraid and said to himself, 'I mused whether there could be such a beautiful face on Earth.' Then he said, 'Lest, I will be hurt by this head'. He asked his entourage to take her back to the howdah and send her back to that water spring.

{20} The father and son were there when the king's entourage brought the woman and left her by the spring. The son saw his mother's face. He said, 'O father, your request before the presence of God has been accepted and mother's face has changed, accordingly.' Then, the son stood, came to the spring and performed ablution. He lifted up his hand in supplication, saying, 'O the Ruler and King! If my mother has made

[3] *ḥaram* [4] Pig-face.

مادرِ منْ در قدیم داشت چنانْ بده». حقّ جَلَّ وَعَلَا دعای او را مستجاب کرد. في الحال به‌صورت قدیم شد.

{۲۱} غرض از این سخن آنست که دل بر هرچه غیر از خدای تَعَالَی بندی بی‌وفایی بینی و ثبات نیابی.

{۲۲} چون لیلی وفات کرد، خبر به مجنون رسید. به‌مجرّد شنیدن، مشت خاک گرفت و در دهن خود انداخت.[ت] پرسیدند «چرا خاک در دهن می کنی؟» گفت «به جز خدای تَعَالَی، کسی را چرا دوست داشتم که آخر زوال به دررفت؟»[ث]

{۲۳} إِلٰهِيّ، به حرمت کریمی خویش که جملهٔ یگانه‌گویان را بر حکم خویش صابر و راضی گردان. یَستمع لإجَابَة. وَاللّٰهُ أَعْلَمْ.

[ت] دست برخاک بکرد و بر سر خاک می‌افکند [ث] آخر او را زوال بوده است

a mistake, now I want to ask from Your sanctified throne to give my mother her first face.' God accepted his prayer and the face immediately changed to the former one.

{21} The purpose of this account is that if you rely on anyone except God, you will see disloyalty from them and will not experience wellbeing.

{22} When Laylī died the news reached Majnūn. Once he heard about this loss he took a fist of soil and ate it. He was asked, 'Why do you put soil in your mouth?'[5] Majnūn replied, 'Why! Why should I have, except God, loved someone who would die in the end?!'

{23} *O God, by your kindness offer patience to, and satisfy, all monotheists. He listens to put it into practice, and God Knows Best. [Amen.]*

[5] i.e. don't do this with yourself, man!

در فضیلتِ پیغمبر ما

در هدایت یافتن دوستان دین، و زردرویی دشمنان پیغمبر ﷺ[1، الف]

{۱} آورده‌اند که رسول ؑ که برای أَمیر المُؤمِنین ابوبکر تلقین کرد في الحال قبول کرد[ب] و هیچ از پیغمبر معجزه نطلبید و کلمهٔ طیبه[ج] به صدق دل بر زبان راند. و روزگار پیغمبر ﷺ به نظام شد، و دولت و عزّت و نصرت او زیاده می‌گشت.[د]

{۲} تا روزی ابوجهل عَلَيْه ٱللَّعْنَة[۲] دست أَمیر المُؤمِنین عمر را گرفت و می‌گفت «اینکه دعوی نبوّت می‌کند، و می‌خواهد که دین اجداد و پدران ما را خراب کند، اگر سر او را بیاری من تو را صد شتر یک‌رنگ سرخ بدهم، و هر مطلوب که داری برآرم». عمر خطّاب قبول کرد.

{۳} ابوجهل گفت «اگر تو راست می‌گویی بیا پیشِ بُتان سوگند خور تا مرا تسلّی دل شود». هر دو برخاسته در بُتخانه رفتند. ابوجهل می‌خواست سوگند دهد که جملهٔ بُتان آواز برآوردند «لآ إِلٰهَ إِلَّا الله، مُحَمَّدٌ رَسُولُ الله». چون أَمیر المُؤمِنین عمر از بُتان چنین اقرار شنید، گفت «ای ابوجهل، ما این بُتان را به معبودی می‌پرستیم. همْ ایشان اِقرار به رسالت پیغمبری محمّد ﷺ می‌کنند». ابوجهل روسیاه و زردروی از بُتان پیش برخاسته، رفت.

[۱] در بسیاری از منابع شرقی، ازجمله ادبیات مالایی-اندونزیایی و بنگالی، این داستان به عنوان «حکایت شقّ القمر» شناخته می‌شود.
[۲] نسخهٔ مالایی ۲۱۳ کتابخانهٔ کالج امانوئل دانشگاه کیمبریج سرشار از دشنام و لعنت علیه ابوجهل است.

[الف] در فضیلتِ پیغمبر ما مشرّف گردانید. چگونه دوستان را در هدایت دین می‌خواهد و دشمنان او چگونه زردروی می‌گشتند. [ب] آورده‌اند که رسول ؑ اوّل بار که اسلام عرضه کرد بر أَمیر المُؤمِنین ابوبکر صدّیق عرضه کرد و گفت «ای ابوبکر، خدای را عَزَّوَجَلَّ یک دین است و جمله دین‌های دیگر باطل است. و خدای تَعَالَی دین خود را به من بربسته است. پس به خدای عَزَّوَجَلَّ بِگرد و دین مرا استوار داری و کلمهٔ شهادت را بگوی و توحید یگانه‌گویان بر زبان بران» [ج] کلمهٔ توحید [د] و روز به روزگار حضرت در ترقّی

CHAPTER 7

On the virtue of our Prophet

in guiding the friends of religion; and the embarrassment of Muḥammad's (pbuh) enemies

{1} It is reported that when the Prophet (pbuh) recited the fundamentals of faith to the Commander of Believers, Abū Bakr, he then accepted the faith quickly, and did not demand any miracle or any word of purity [from the Prophet]; given his sincere heart, he declared his faith. And as the Prophet's situation was becoming stable, his blessed estate, dignity, and success were increased.

{2} Once upon a time, Abū Jahl, God's curse be upon him, took the hand of the Commander of Believers, ʿUmar, and said, 'This fellow who claims prophecy and wants to ruin the religion of our ancestors, I want you to bring his head to me[1] and I will give you one hundred red camels at once, and whatever you wish to have I will provide it for you.' ʿUmar Khaṭṭāb accepted the offer.

{3} Abū Jahl told ʿUmar, 'In order to believe what you have said and to be confident, come along with me to the idols and take a vow.' Both left for the temple. Abū Jahl was about to say, 'Stick to your word' to ʿUmar that all the idols said, 'There is no god but God, and Muḥammad is the Messenger of God'. When the Commander of Believers, ʿUmar, heard such statement from the idols, he said, 'O Abū Jahl, we worship these idols as a God; they have also expressed their faith in Muḥammad's (pbuh) Prophecy.' Abū Jahl, ashamed and humiliated, left there.

{4} Again, Abū Jahl took the hand of the Commander of Believers, ʿUmar, the next day, taking him to the temple in order to make a vow that he would 'bring the head of Muḥammad.' Once they arrived at the temple, all the idols stated together,

[1] i.e., to kill him

{۴} باز روز دیگر دست أَمیر المُؤمِنین عمر را ابوجهل گرفته به بُتخانه[۳] برد تا سوگند دهد که «سر محمّد بیاری». به‌مجرّدی که در بُتخانه درآمدند، جملهٔ بُتان در سخن آمدند که «پیغمبر برحقّ مردی است امین؛ خدای عَزَّوَجَلَّ بر شما فرستاد و شما را در دین می‌دارد و شما قصد کشتن او می‌کنید! اما یک تار موی از اندام او جدا نَتُوانید کرد». چون أَمیر المُؤمِنین عمر کرّت دوم از بُتان چنین شنید، در فکر شد. ابوجهل دست عمر را گرفته در بُتخانه برآمد و گفت «آنچه [از] بُتان شنیدی بر خلق مکّه نگوی که مبادا ایمان به محمّد آرند، و خواجه‌گی مکّه از دست ما برود».

{۵} روزی دیگر أَمیر المُؤمِنین عمر را در خانه طلبید وشراب[ه] در میان آورد و باهم می‌خوردند و تعریف شجاعت عمر می‌کرد که «همچو تو مرد مبارز و دلاور کجاست؟ و مرا غمِ محمّد بسیار سخت گرفته‌است؛ وی را از میان بردار». خاک در دهنش، عمر از سرمستی سوگند یاد کرد و تیغ از میان کشید و گفت «تا سر محمّد نیارم تیغ در نیام نکنم». این بگفت و روی به قریش کرد.

{۶} قدری راه رفته بود، دید که دو مرد گوساله را پیش انداخته از پی آن می‌دوند . هرچند می‌کُنند بگیرند نمی‌توانند. عمر گفت «من بگیرم». به قُوَّتی که داشت دوید و نتوانست گرفت. عاجز گشت و اِستاده شد. گوساله روی گردانید و گفت «ای عمر، به گرفتن من عاجز گشتی، به کدام قُوَّت[د] سَر محمّد را خواهی آورد؟ به‌خدای که جز آن خدایِ نیست، که یک سرِ موی از سر محمّد نتوانی جدا کردن». چون عمر از گوساله و بُتان چنین شنید جملهٔ اعضای او سست شد و آهسته رفتن گرفت.

{۷} چون پیشتر شد دو کس را دید. عمر را سلام کردند. و عمر گفت «از کجا می‌آیید و کجا خواهید رفت؟» ایشان گفتند «از قریش می‌آییم». و گفتند «یا عمر کجا می‌روی؟» گفت «می‌روم تا سر محمّد بیارم». گفتند «ای عمر، مگر معلومِ تو نیست که مادر و خواهر تو در دین محمّد درآمده‌اند». گفت «چگونه دانم؟» گفتند «اگر می‌خواهی آزمایش کنی مُرغی را بکش؛ ایشان کشتهٔ تو را نخواهند خورد».

{۸} چون به خانه آمد دید که مرغی می‌گردد.[۴] او را گرفته و بکشت. به خواهر گفت «زود این را بریان کن تا بخوریم». خواهر گفت «این را در دین خدای تَعَالَی حرام گفته‌اند و این را نخورند مگر مردارخور». مادر این شنید، اشارت کرد[ذ] که «چنین مگوی که معلوم خواهد کرد که ما مسلمان شده‌ایم». دختر گفت «ای

[۳] واژهٔ «بُتخانه» در ادبیات ترکی استانبولی و ترکی ترکستانی هم دیده می‌شود. استعمال آن در برخی مقالات و ویراست های متون اسلامی در *Journal of the Asiatic Society of Bengal* (ج۴۶، ۱۸۷۷) به چشم می‌خورد.

[۴] براساس برخی نسخ موجود، زمانی که عمر نزدیک خانه می‌شود با صحنه‌ای متفاوت روبه‌رو می‌شود (از درون خانه آواز قرآن خواندن می‌آید. عمر را جزم شد که ایشان در دین محمّد درآمده‌اند. عمر دست بر در زد و خواهرش گفت «کیست؟» عمر گفت «در را بگشای که منم عمر». خواهرش بیامد و در را بگشاد و مرغی را ذبح کرد).

[ه] شراب و کباب [د] به قوّت و جرأت [ذ] انگشت بر لب نهاد

'The Prophet is verily a faithful man. God has sent him to you and he want to bring you all to the religion [of Islam], but your aim is to kill him! But you will not actually be able to do it.'[2] When the Commander of Believers, ʿUmar, heard this from the idols for the second time, he pondered. Abū Jahl took ʿUmar's hand and led him out of the temple, telling him, 'Do not say anything about what happened in the temple to the people of Mecca, as they will then all convert to Muḥammad, and we will lose our authority and power'

{5} Another day, he invited the Commander of Believers, ʿUmar, to his house and served wine. They drank with each other. Abū Jahl praised ʿUmar's bravery, musing, 'Where can one find such a warrior and brave man?' And added, 'I am distressed by Muḥammad. Kill him!' Choked with earth,[3] ʿUmar was drunk and made the vow and took his sword out and said, 'I will not put this sword back in to its scabbard until I bring Muḥammad's head.' He said this and went towards the Quraysh clan.

{6} After a few steps, ʿUmar saw two men running after a calf. They could not catch the calf despite all their efforts. ʿUmar said, 'I will take it'. He ran as fast as possible but he could not take it. He became tired and stopped. The calf then looked at ʿUmar and told him, 'O ʿUmar, you are unable to catch me, how do you expect to bring Muḥammad's head?! By God, for whom there is no god except Him, you will not be able to hurt Muḥammad.' As ʿUmar had heard this from the calf as well as the idols, he felt weak and walked slowly.

{7} After a few steps, he noticed two other persons. They greeted ʿUmar and ʿUmar asked, 'Where have you come from and where are you going?' They replied, 'We are from the Quraysh clan'. And they asked, 'O ʿUmar, where are you going?' He said, 'I am going to bring Muḥammad's head.' They said, 'O ʿUmar, are you not aware that your mother and sister converted to the religion of Muḥammad.' He asked, 'How can I be sure about this?!' They said, 'If you want to be sure about their conversion, slaughter a chicken. They will not eat your sacrifice!'

{8} When ʿUmar came home, he saw a chicken. He caught it and slaughtered it. He asked his sister, 'Grill this chicken as quickly as possible so we can eat it'. The sister said, 'It is considered forbidden in the religion of God, and no one eats it unless carrion eater[4].' When his mother heard this, she signalled to her daughter, 'Do not say things like that as it will be clear that we are Muslims now'. The daughter said, 'O mother, be quiet! the musk's fragrance cannot be hidden!' Once ʿUmar heard this from his sister he hit her with his sword, and her head began bleeding. His mother then came to ʿUmar,

[2] But you will not be able to cut a hair from his body let alone his head.

[3] Curse upon them [4] i.e., desperate

مادر، دم درکش که مُشک پنهان نتوان کرد».[۵] عمر چون این سخن از خواهر شنید تیغ بر خواهر انداخت و از سر او خون روان شد. مادر بیامد او را نیز بِزَد. پشت تیغ به او رسید.[۶] آن دو بیچاره صبر کردند و گفتند «ای عمر، با تو چه بگوییم که تو لشگر شیطانی و ما کنیز[ح] رحمانیم. اکنون به درگاه او صبر کردیم تا خداوند در حقّ تو چه پیدا آرد».

{۹} عمر در خشم بود و هم مست بود. به خیالات شراب در خواب شد. زمانی گذشت. دختر به مادر گفت «بیا تا چیزی از کلام دوست[ط] برخوانیم». هر دو قرآن به یاد کردند که عمر در خواب بود. پهلو به پهلو می‌گشت. آواز خواندن قرآن در گوش وی آمد، و لذّت شنیدن قرآن در خاطر او افزوده. برخاست و گفت «ای خواهر، برخوان که به شنیدن این کلام قفل خاطرِ من باز می‌شود». خواهر گفت «ای برادر، تو آلودهٔ کفری، و کلام دوست پاک‌تر. در دریای ایمان غوطه بخور تا من بخوانم و تو بشنوی». آنگاه عمر گفت «ای خواهر، قفل دلم بشکست و دلم طالب محمّد ﷺ شد».

{۱۰} گفت «بگوی تا رسنی بیارند و مرا برببندند. و همچو گریزپایی کشاله‌کنان[ی] سوی حضرت محمّد ﷺ برند». خواهر گفت «ای برادر، حاجت بر این نیست. ازبرای‌آنکه هرچند کس تصوّر کند، حِکَمِ و خُلق ایشان زیاده از آن است».[ک] عمر گفت «ای خواهر، من شرمندهٔ روی ایشانم. به هر طریقی که می‌دانی مرا به نزدیک محمّد ببر». دستِ برادر گرفت و به جانب پیغمبر روان شد.

{۱۱} در ره بودند که جبرئیل عليه السلام به خدمت پیغمبر آمد، و گفت «ای محمّد، فرمان می‌شود که روزی عمر در نظر مبارک تو می‌گذشت و تو دعا کردی. دعای تو هم درآن روز قبول کرده بودیم. این‌زمان بیرون‌شو، عمر را استقبال کن که او در دین تو می‌آید». رسول الله ﷺ بیرون دوید. عمر و خواهرش از در مسجد درآمدند. چون نظر أَمیر المُؤمِنین عمر در روی پاک سرور دو عالم افتاد، بر زمین غَلطان شد و در زیر پای پیغمبر آمد و بوسه داد[ل] و گفت «ای برگزیدهٔ حضرت رحمان، پیش‌از این دشمنی از من بدتر نداشتی، این‌زمان بهتر از من به تو دوستی نیست. یا نبي اَللّٰه، کلمه بگو تا در دین پاک تو درآیم و مشرّف گردم. پیغمبر عليه السلام گفت بگوی «لآ إلهَ إلّا الله، مُحَمَّدٌ رَسُولُ الله».

[۵] در «پنج گنج» نظامی گنجوی این اصطلاح دیده می شود «براین مشک خاشاک نتوان فشاند، که بوی خوش مشک پنهان نماند». همچنین در «کشف الحقائق» اثر نسفی عبارتی با این مضمون دیده می‌شود: « مشک آنجا که باشد خود بوی دهد، مشک را پنهان نتوان داشت و آفتاب را در انبان نتوان کرد [...]». عزیزالدین بن محمّد نسفی، کشف الحقّائق، ویراست احمد مهدوی دامغانی (تهران: شرکت انتشارات علمی و فرهنگی، ۱۳۸۴/۲۰۰۵)، ص ۱۶۸. همچنین به عنوان ضرب‌المثل در مناطق آسیای مرکزی به کار می‌رود.

[۶] بیانگر اینکه به مادر آسیبی نرسید. در برخی نسخ، عمر تنها بر خواهرش حمله می‌کند. برای من نویسنده «پشت تیغ» یادآور بیتی منسوب به صائب تبریزی است: از دم تیغ است پشت تیغ بی‌آزارتر؛ هرکه می‌گرداند از ما روی، ممنونیم ما.

[ح] بنده [ط] کلام الله [ی] کشان کشان [ک] زیرا که محمّد به غایت حلیم است [ل] روی بر کف پای حضرت می مالید

and he hit her with the back of his sword,[5] too. Those two poor ladies stopped where they were and said, 'O ʿUmar what can we tell you as you are from the army of Satan and we are the slaves of the Merciful. We are patient now for the sake of God, and He will do the right thing by you'.

{9} ʿUmar was angry and drunk. Due to his drunkenness, he slept. After a while, the daughter told her mother, 'Let's recite something from the Word of our Friend'. Both recited the Qurʾān, and ʿUmar changed his sleeping position. Their recitation reached his ear, and he enjoyed listening to it. He woke up and said, 'O sister, recite it as my mind becomes open and unlocked, through listening to it'. The sister said, 'O brother, you are infected with unbelief,[6] and the Friend's Word is pure. Convert to the ocean of faith so I will recite and you will listen.' Then, ʿUmar said, 'O sister, my heart has become unlocked and I wish to visit Muḥammad (pbuh).'

{10} He said, 'Ask someone to bring a rope and tie me up and drag me like an escapee to the Prophet (pbuh).' The sister said, 'There is no need to do this. Because his wisdom and manner are more balanced than you have thought.' ʿUmar said, 'O sister, I am ashamed before Muḥammad. Just take me to him in any way that suits.' She took her brother's hand and went towards the Prophet.

{11} On the way, Gabriel (pbuh) came to Muḥammad and said, 'O Muḥammad, it is commanded, "You had seen ʿUmar one day and you prayed for him. Your prayer was accepted that day. Now go out and welcome ʿUmar as he will convert to your religion."' The Prophet (pbuh) ran out. ʿUmar and his sister came into the mosque. When the Commander of Believers observed the face of the Master of the Worlds, he fell down at the feet of the Prophet and kissed them and said, 'O you have been selected by the Merciful, you have not had a worse enemy than me! Now you have no better friend than me! O Prophet of God, now tell me the declaration of faith so I can convert to your purified religion and become a Muslim. The Prophet (pbuh) said, 'Now express, "There is not god but God, and Muḥammad is the Messenger of God."'

[5] i.e., mune or non-bladed side of the sword

[6] You are impure.

{۱۲} بعداز گفتن کلمهٔ طیّبه التماس کرد که «ابوجهل و خلق مکّه همه پیش در کعبه استاده‌اند، که عمر سر محمّد خواهد آورد. بیا تا به جای سر مبارک تو سر دشمنان تو را بیارم». همراه پیغمبر آمد و تیغ برکشید و حمله کرد. کفّار بسیار کشته شدند، و بعضی گریخته در کعبه رفته‌اند.[م] أَمیر المُؤمِنین عمر گفت «یا نبي اللّه، درون کعبه درآمدند». و بدبختان درون کعبه بُتان را داشته بودند. عمر نزدیک بُتان شد و گفت «ای بُتان نازل شوید[۷] و در عهد دولت او نگون‌سار گردید».[۸] جملهٔ بُتان نگون‌سار شدند و بر زمین افتادند.

{۱۳} چون ابوجهل لعین دید که عمر در دین محمّد ﷺ درآمده زردروی شد و اندیشهٔ کفر که در دل داشت زیاد گشت. بر پادشاه-عزیز[ن] و در قبیله‌ها کسان فرستاد که با جمعیّت تمام بیایند که «محمّد دعوی نبوّت می‌کند، و دین پدران و اجدادان ما را خراب می‌کند و خلق را در دین خود می‌آرد». پادشاه-عزیز چون بشنید، فرمود تا لشگرها ساخته گردد، و لشگر بسیار از قبیله‌ها جمع شدند؛ همراه پادشاه در مکّه درآمدند. ابوجهل[س] به استقبال ایشان رفت و ایشان را درون مکّه فرود آورد. پادشاه-عزیز حاجب[۹] خود را فرمود «برو محمّد را بیار».

{۱۴} حضرت محمّد با خدیجهٔ کبری، و أَمیر المُؤمِنین ابوبکر[ع] هر سه یکجا نشسته بودند. ابوبکر و خدیجه و مرد دیگر در گریه شدند که «ای پیغمبر، دشمنان خدای قصد کشتن تو کرده اند، و هیچ معلوم نیست که این‌زمان چه خواهند کرد». پیغمبر ﷺ گفت «ای ابوبکر و خدیجه،[ف] هیچ نگران نباشید که حافظ و ناصر محمّد پروردگار است، و آنچه خواست و رضای پروردگار من است در حقّ من همان خواهد شد، و من بدان راضیم». در این سخن بودند که شخصی طلبِ پیغمبر آمد، گفت «پادشاه شما را می‌طلبد». حضرت ابوبکر را خواست و روان شد.[۱۰] خدیجهٔ کبری دید که روان شدند به جانب دشمنان چشم پُرآب کرد و روی آسمان کرد، و دست برداشت و گفت «إِلٰهِيّ، پیغمبر را به تو سپردم».

{۱۵} ابوجهل بدبخت نزد پادشاه-عزیز و سران قبیله نشسته بود گفت «چون محمّد بیاید از جای خود هیچ‌کس نجنبد» و هرچه محمّد گوید سخن در حقارت او گویند. چون پیغمبر ﷺ از خانه بیرون آمد، حقّ سبحانه وتعالی از جبین مبارک او نوری پیدا کرد، تا آسمان رسید و روشنی آفتاب را مغلوب گردانید. و نوری در جهان پیدا شد که هیچ [کس] ندیده بود. از عالم غیب آوازی شنیدند که «این نور جبین مبارک حضرت محمّد مُصطَفَی ﷺ است که در جهان تابان گشته است». چون این سخن شنیدند در میان خود با یکدیگر گفتند که «محمّد می‌آید». درین بودند که حضرت محمّد مُصطَفَی ﷺ پیدا شد.

[۷] فرود آیید؛ بر زمین خورید. [۸] در برخی نسخ مانند نسخهٔ دانشگاه تهران این پیامبر است که به بُتان دستور می‌دهد تا فرو ریزند.
[۹] نگهبان و دربان. [۱۰] در برخی نسخ، محمّد همراه با حاجبِ پادشاه می‌رود.

[م] بعضی از کفّار کشته شدند. عمر با حضرت رسول در حرم کعبه درآمدند [ن] پادشاه عرب
[س] و دیگر جاهلان [ع] ابابکر [ف] ای دوستان

{12} After expressing the pure phrase,[7] ʿUmar broached a matter, 'Abū Jahl and the people of Mecca stood before the Kaʿba saying that "ʿUmar will bring the head of Muḥammad." Let's now bring your enemy's head instead of your head!' He accompanied the Prophet, took his sword, and attacked. A large number of infidels were killed, and some ran away and moved inside the Kaʿba. The Commander of Believers, ʿUmar, said, 'O Prophet of God, they went to the Kaʿba building.' Those desperate people were inside the Kaʿba with the idols. ʿUmar approached the idols, and said, 'O idols, fall down in respect and pledge to his estate.' All idols bowed down to the earth.

{13} When Abū Jahl, God's curse be upon him, noticed that ʿUmar has been converted to the religion of Muḥammad (pbuh), he was ashamed; his heretical thoughts increased. He sent a letter to ʿAzīz King[8] as well as other clans to come with their largest armies, saying that 'Muḥammad has begun his propaganda and is ruining the religion of the forefathers and is bringing the masses to his religion.' When the ʿAzīz King learned about this, he ordered his troops to prepare. A huge number of troops gathered. All came along to the King in Mecca. Abū Jahl welcomed them and took them into the city of Mecca. The ʿAzīz King ordered his servant, 'Go and bring Muḥammad along'.

{14} Prophet Muḥammad, along with Khadīja Kubra, and the Commander of Believers, Abū Bakr, had been sitting in one place. Abū Bakr, Khadīja, and another man [?], cried and said, 'O Prophet, God's enemies wish to kill you, and it is unclear what they really want to do now'. The Prophet (pbuh) said, 'O Abū Bakr and Khadīja, do not be worried at all as my protector and helper is God, and whatever He wants and what my God is satisfied with, that will be upon me and I will be happy with it'. While conversing, a man arrived asking for the Prophet: 'The king wants to see you'. The Prophet, asked Abū Bakr to accompany him. Once Khadīja saw that they had gone towards the enemies, her eyes became full of tears. She looked at the sky and lifted her hand imploring, 'O God, I left the Prophet with You'.

{15} The despicable Abū Jahl was before the ʿAzīz King and the leader of the clans. He stated, 'Once Muḥammad arrives, nobody should move', and whatever Muḥammad said they should humiliate him. When the Prophet (pbuh) left his house, a light shone from his holy forehead which went up to the sky and overcome the sunlight. A light emerged in the world, which no one had ever seen before. They heard a voice from the unseen world say, 'This is the light of the holy forehead of Muḥammad (pbuh) which has illuminated the world'. When they heard this voice they said to each other, 'Muḥammad is coming'. While speaking with each other, Prophet Muḥammad (pbuh) arrived.

[7] i.e., profession of faith [8] Arab King.

{۱۶} چون نظر پادشاه-عزیز و سرانِ قبیله بر جمالِ باکمالِ خواجهٔ کائنات و سپهر، صفّهٔ صفا و بدر خطّهٔ وفا، آن ماه‌رویِ وَالضُّحَی و آن سیاه‌مویِ وَاللَّیْلِ إِذَا سَجَی، و آن برگزیدهٔ بارگاه کبریا، و آن افتخار آلِ طه وَیَس، یعنی حضرت محمّد مُصْطَفَی ﷺ کردند، هیچ‌کدام را قدرت آن نبود که بر جای خود نشسته مانند. به تمامی[۱۱] از جای برخاستند و ایستاده ماندند. پادشاه-عزیز از کرسی خود فرود آمد و با خود گفت که «از چنین رویْ و مویْ دعوی پیغمبری هرگز دروغ نباشد».[ص] و دست پیغمبر را گرفته در کرسی خود نشاند. کرسی دیگر آوردند و پادشاه برآن کرسی نشست.

{۱۷} ابوجهل چون چنین دید زردروی شد، و می‌گفت که «ما را مطلوب حاصل نشد». آنگاه به پادشاه-عزیز گفت «تو از بهر این آمده‌ای تا محمّد را از میان برداری. حالا تعظیم و اکرام می‌کنی؟» پادشاه روی به جانب حضرت کرد و گفت «شما می‌گویید «من پیغمبر آخرِ زمان‌مانم»». رسول ﷺ فرمود « حق سبحانه و تعالی مرا به پیغمبری مبعوث گردانیده است». پادشاه گفت «پیش‌از شما پیغمبران بودند و هرکدام معجزه نمودند. معجزهٔ ابراهیم علیه‌السلام آن بود که نمرود از بهر عقوبت او هفتادفرسنگ[۱۲] زمین آتشی افکند. ابراهیم را آن آتش بر وی گلستان شد. جمله بند و سلاسل و اغلالی که بر دست و گردن داشت همه ناچیز شد و یک تار موی از اندام مبارک او نسوخت. و معجزهٔ موسیٰ علیه‌السلام آن بود که عصایی داشت؛ اژدها می‌شد و هر کار که به او می‌فرمود همان می‌شد. آن عصا بر سنگ زدی آب از سنگ جاری شدی. و اگر دشمنی قصد او کردی آن عصا مار شدی و او را هلاک کردی و اگر در آفتاب بودی آن عصا بر سر او سایه کردی، و به دعای او فرعون و لشگرش در رود نیل غرق شد. و معجزهٔ عیسیٰ علیه‌السلام آن بود که مُردهٔ چهارصد-پانصد ساله را زنده کردی. این‌زمانْ شما هم معجزه نمایید».

{۱۸} حضرت رسالت پناه فرمودند «و معجزه می‌طلبی پادشاه-عزیز؟» دیرینه بود[۱۳] و پادشاه گفت «وقت شام شود و تاریکی در جهان پیدا گردد. بعد آن چون من بگویم دعا کن تا تاریکی به نور مبدّل گردد. آنگه بگو تا ماه خود را بنماید و بر بام کعبه بایستد. و هفت‌بار گِرد کعبه طواف کند. بعداز آن بر شما سلام کند و ثنایی ذات پاک شما گوید، چنانکه ما همه را بشنویم. دگر بر ماه اشارت کن تا دوپاره شود. یک پاره در گریبان تو در آید، و در جانب دامن بیرون آید. دوم پاره در آستین راست شما درآید و از آستین چپ بیرون آید.[۱۴] باز هم دوپاره در آسمان یک‌جا شوند. باز ماه را بگو جانب مغرب فرو رود. باز بگو تا از جانب مغرب برآید. چون به میان آسمان رسید دو پاره گردد. یک پاره به جنوب رود، دوم پارهٔ دیگر به شمال رود، و تمام آسمان را در روشنی خود بَرَد. باز بگو چنانچه که قرص بود، چُنان شود. تا ما بدانیم که تو پیغمبری و به تو گردیم.»

[۱۱] تمام قد. [۱۲] بنابر فرهنگ معین، هر فرسنگ (یا فرسخ) معادل شش کیلومتر است.
[۱۳] احتمالا این چنین نیز خوانده می‌شود که حضرت رسالت پناهی فرمودند «و معجزه می‌طلبی پادشاه-عزیز؟ دیرینه بوَد»
[۱۴] در برخی نسخ در مورد پارهٔ دوم مطلبی وجود ندارد.

[ص] چون ندا شنیدند به یکدیگر گفتند «حضرت رسالت پناه محمّد ﷺ می‌آید، آن ماه شب چهارده طلوع کرد». پادشاه و سران قبیله چون نظر برپیغمبر ﷺ کردند همه برخاستند. و پادشاه بسیار اعزاز و اکرام کرد و با خود گفت «از چنین رویی دعوی نبوّت هرگز دروغ نباشد»

{16} When the king and leader of the clans saw the perfected beauty of the Master of the Worlds and heaven, the one from the throne of purity and delight and the Moon of the land of devotion, and the Moon faced one, 'The morning sunlight' (Q. 93:1), and the black hair one and, 'The night when it falls still' (Q. 93:2), and the one chosen by the Divine Majesty and honoured by 'Ṭāhā' and 'Yāsīn', that is, the Prophet Muḥamamd (pbuh), none of them were able to sit still. They stood up and remained standing. The king came down from his throne and pondered, 'From one with such a face and hair prophecy does not seem implausible'. ʿAzīz King took the hand of the Prophet and sat him on his own throne. They brought another throne and the king sat on it.

{17} When Abū Jahl saw this, he was humiliated and pondered, 'This is not what we wanted to happen'. He said to the king said, 'You have come to destroy Muḥammad, and now you are bowing and respecting him?!' ʿAzīz King looked at Muḥammad and said, 'You claim that you are the Prophet of the Last Day!?' The Prophet (pbuh) replied, 'God has appointed me as a Prophet'. ʿAzīz King said, 'There were prophets before you, and each of them had their own miracles. Abraham's miracle was that Nimrod wanted to punish Abraham by putting him into a huge fire and then the fire became as a garden to Abraham. All chains and shackles around his hands and neck were removed and not a hair on his body was burnt. And the miracle of Moses (pbuh) was that his staff could be changed to a dragon/serpent, and do whatever Moses ordered. When Moses touched a stone with his staff, water gushed from the stone. And when an enemy wanted to kill him, the staff was transformed into a snake that killed the enemy. Once Moses was under the scorching Sun, the staff was transformed into a canopy, and according to his supplication, Pharaoh and his army drowned in the Nile river. The miracle of Jesus (pbuh) was that he returned a four or five hundred year-old dead person to life. As such, you must also demonstrate your miracle.'

{18} The Prophet (pbuh) replied, 'You, ʿAzīz King, are asking me to prove my miracle?' It was late at night and the king said, 'Once the evening has passed and everywhere is dark you should pray that darkness changes to light when I say, and then you should ask the Moon to show itself and come above the Kaʿba and circumambulate the Kaʿba seven times, and then greet you and praise your pure essence such that we can all hear. Then order the Moon to split into two parts. One half goes to your collar and comes out from your lap. The second half comes in your right sleeve and comes out of your left sleeve. Then both halves come together in the sky. Again, order the Moon to set in the West. Then tell it to rise from the East. When it comes to the middle of the sky, then it splits into two parts. One half goes towards the South and the second half goes towards the North and sheds light on the whole sky. Then tell it to return to its original shape like a full moon. So, we can be assured that you are the Prophet and we will convert to you'.

{۱۹} چون ابوجهل از پادشاه این‌ها را شنید، شادمان گشت و گفت «ای پادشاه، تو معجزه [ای] طلبیدی که هیچ‌کس نطلبیده، و این چنین معجزه که می‌تواند نمود که محمّد بنماید. زیرا که سِحر محمّد در زمین کار می‌کند؛ در آسمان چه کار تواند کرد». ابوجهل در جامه نگنجید.

{۲۰} پادشاه-عزیز گفت «ای محمّد، من این دو معجزه از تو از شام تا دوپاس شب بگذرد طلبیده‌ام. امّا درین وقت چیزی در خاطر من گذشت، می‌باید که آن را بگویی و درزمانْ این معجزه بنمایی که در خاطر من چیست؟ و مرا چه مقصود است؟» پیغمبر ﵇ سر مبارک فرود برد و خاطر به حضرت حقّ سبحانه و تعالی متوجّه گردانید. درزمانْ وحی نازل شد «یا محمّد، هیچ می‌دانی پادشاه چه اندیشه کرده؟» گفت «إلٰهِيّ، احوال اندیشهٔ قلوب خلائق به جز تو کسی نداند». جبرئیل ﵇ آمد، و گفت «اندیشهٔ پادشاه این است که دختری دارد. چشم‌ها و گوش و دست و پای ندارد، و او را با خود همراه آورده است. و در خاطر قرار داده است که اگر محمّد پیغمبر برحقّ است اندیشه من بداند.[ق] اکنون دعا کردن از تو، چشم و گوش و دست و پای از کرَم طلب‌دار».

{۲۱} پیغمبر ﷺ روی سوی پادشاه کرد، و گفت «دختر تو چشم و گوش و دست و پای ندارد». پادشاه گفت «آری، ندارد». پیغمبر ﷺ دعا کرد، و گفت «إلٰهِيّ، اگر او را چنین آفریده، هر عضوی که نقصان دارد هم تو درست گردان». فرمان آمد که «ای محمّد، دعای تو قبول کردیم. پادشاه را بگو تا در منزل خود رود تا قدرت ما را ببیند». پیغمبر ﷺ رو به پادشاه کرد و گفت «ای عزیز، برخیز و به خانه خودْ رَوید تا قدرت آفریدگار مشاهده کنی». پادشاه رو به پسران و قبیله کرد و گفت «شب معجزه را می‌خواهیم، امّا اکنون بیایید تا حال از دختر من معلوم کنید».

{۲۲} جملهٔ اهل مجلس به خانهٔ پادشاه درآمدند. چون به خانه درآمدند، دیدند جمع اعضای او درست شد و چشم‌ها در کمال لطافت است.[ر] پادشاه را خوشحالی تمام روی داد و سران قبیله‌ها این را دیدند. پادشاه به خدمت پیغمبر آمد و گفت «یا محمّد، هر چه گفته بودی مشاهده کردیم». در مجلس اوّل ابوجهل رو سیاه[ش] شد.

{۲۳} أَمیر المُؤمِنین ابوبکر این معجزه بدید و دست مبارک آن حضرت گرفت، و به جانب خانه روان شد. ابوجهل بدبخت گفت «ای محمّد، سِحر تو در زمین کار می‌کند و نه در آسمان. چون شب درآید، به نمودن معجزهٔ ما درمانی. پیش‌از آن از جان خود دست بشوی که نتْوانی در آسمان آنچه از تو طلبیده‌اند بنْمایی». پیغمبر ﷺ ابوجهل را هیچ جواب نداد و به‌سوی خانه رفت.[ت] چون شب درآمد، أَمیر المُؤمِنین ابوبکرصدّیق نزد رسول ﷺ آمد و گفت «یا رسول الله، جملهٔ دشمنان یک‌جا جمع شده‌اند و معجزه می‌طلبند که «آنچه ما از محمّد طلبیده‌ایم اگر ما را ننماید درزمانْ وی را هلاک کنیم»». چون ابوبکر این سخن بگفت با خدیجهٔ کبری در گریه شد. رسول ﷺ گفت «ای دوستان، چرا گریه می‌کنید؟» گفتند «ای رسول خدا، می‌ترسیم مبادا از

[ق] او را با خود آورده‌است که این اعضای دختر من نیک شود [ر] دختر می‌گفت «پدرِ مرا بگویید تا بیاید و مرا ببیند که چه نیکو شده‌ام» [ش] زردروی [ت] متوجّه خانه شدند

{19} When Abū Jahl heard this from ʿAzīz King, he became happy and said, 'O king, you have demanded a particular miracle that no one has ever asked for. And who will be able to perform this miracle that is asked of Muḥammad? Because Muḥammad's sorcery works on Earth; how may his sorcery work in the sky?' Abū Jahl was extremely happy.

{20} ʿAzīz King said, 'O Muḥammad, I have asked you to perform these two miracles from sunset to midnight. In the meantime, something came to my mind. You must foretell what I have in mind and show the miracle that I was pondering and what I really wanted.' The Prophet (pbuh) pondered and turned his own attention to God. Soon a revelation was sent down, 'O Muḥammad, do you know everything of which the king thinks?' Muḥammad replied, 'O God, no one, except You, knows about whatever is thought in people's minds.' Gabriel (pbuh) came and said, 'The king's thought was about his daughter. She is without sight, hearing, hands, and legs, and he brought his daughter with him. And he was thinking, if Muḥammad is a true prophet then he must know what I am thinking. Now you must pray for his daughter and demand from our kindness the restoration of her sight, hearing, hands, and legs.'

{21} The Prophet (pbuh) looked at the king and said, 'Your daughter does not have sight, hearing, hands, and legs'. The king said, 'Right, she does not have these'. The Prophet (pbuh) lifted his hand in supplication asking, 'O God, as You have created her disabled, You also can enable all the disabled limbs of her body'. The Prophet (pbuh) then looked at the king and said, 'O ʿAzīz, stand up and go to your residence in order to witness the power of God.' The king gathered his sons and the clans and said, 'Although I wanted to witness [Muḥammad's] miracle during the night, let's now see what has happened to my daughter.'

{22} All members of the court went towards the king's residence. When they arrived at his residence all her limbs were healed and her eyes were dazzling. The king was overjoyed and the leaders of the clans witnessed what had happened. The king sent for the Prophet and said, 'O Muḥammad, we observed whatever you had said.' During the first round, Abū Jahl became humiliated.

{23} The Commander of Believers, Abū Bakr, noticed this miracle and took the hand of the Prophet and went towards his house. Abū Jahl said, 'O Muḥammad, your sorcery only works on Earth and not in the sky. When night comes, you will be unable to show your miracle. Before that happens prepare to die as you will not be able to perform [your miracle] in the sky, as requested'. The Prophet (pbuh) did not respond. Abū Jahl went home. When night time fell, the Commander of Believers, Abū Bakr the Veracious, came to the Prophet (pbuh) and said, 'O Messenger of God, all your enemies are assembled and want to see your miracle saying, "We will soon kill Muḥammad if he does not show us what we demanded from him."' After telling this to the Prophet, Abū

چشم بد گزندت رسد».[ث] رسول الله گفت «ای ابوبکر و خدیجه، از جهت من نگران مباشید. نگهبان محمّد هم اوست که محمّد را پیدا کرده است».

{۲۴} آنگاه وضو ساخت، و دو رکعت نماز گذارد،[خ] و سر سجده نهاد و در حضرت معبود خویش در عرض و عجز و زاری شد. و می گفت «إلٰهيٓ، معجزه که دشمنان از من طلبیدند تو را معلوم است. بندهٔ خود را اگر تو عزیز نگردانی، دیگر ننواز.»[ذ] در سجده بود که جبرئیل علیه‌السلام رسید، و گفت «ای محمّد، سرِ مبارک از سجده بردار». محمّد سر از سجده برداشت دید که جبرئیل نیزه در دست دارد و نیزه دو سر دارد؛[ض] یکی در مشرق و یکی در مغرب. و در پیش جبرئیل هفتاد هزار فرشتهٔ اسلحه‌پوشیده استاده‌اند. رسول گفت «یا أخي جبرئیل، این نیزه دو شاخ چیست؟ و این هفتادهزار فرشته از بهر چه آمده‌اند؟» گفت «یا رسول الله، مرا فرمان شده‌است که «اگر محمّد بگوید، همین نیمی از دشمنان را به یک شاخ نیزه در مشرق اندازد، نیمی دیگر را به شاخ دیگر در مغرب اندازد». دیگر فرمان شد «با هفتاد هزار فرشته برو. محمّد را بگوی که پادشاه با لشگر خود آمده و مردمانِ قبیله آورده. خدای تَعَالَی از بهر تو لشگر از آسمان فرستاده تا هرچه فرمانی همان کنند». دیگر ایشان از تو معجزه طلبیده اند، و ما به علم قدیم خود می‌دانستیم. و ماه را منوّر آفریده‌ایم،[15] و این معجزه در ماه نهاده بودیم که هر چه محمّد تو را بگوید همچنان شوی».»

{۲۵} رسول الله شُکر حضرت حقّ سبحانه وتعالی به جای آورده، روی به معرکهٔ دشمنان کرد. خدیجهٔ کبری تا در خانه بیامد و به جانب پیغمبر می دوید و زار گریست. و با خود می‌گفتد «نمی دانم این زمان دشمنان با پیغمبر چه خواهند کرد؟» هم درین اندیشه بود که آواز شنید که «نگرانی مکن! که حافظِ پیغمبر صلی الله علیه وسلم خداوند تَعَالَی عزّوجلّ است. اگر چه تنها رفته‌است، پادشاه با جمیع توابع و لشگر اسیر گردند».[غ]

{۲۶} چون پیغمبر صلی الله علیه وسلم نزد ایشان رفت، پادشاه-عزیز گفت «اکنون بگو تا جهان تاریک شود». رسول گفت «إلٰهيٓ، جهان تاریک گردد». همان لحظه جهان تاریک گشت.[ظ] چنانچه بیش طاقت نیاوردند دست‌های یکدیگر گرفتند و گفتند «ای محمّد، بگو تا این تاریکی به نور روشنی بدل گردد». پیغمبر علیه‌السلام گفت «إلٰهيٓ، این تاریکی به روشنایی مبدّل گردد». همان‌ساعت، به فرمان خدای تَعَالَی، جهان منوّر شد. گفتند «یا محمّد، بگو تا مَه خود را پیدا گرداند» – آن شب بیست وهشتم ماه بود و ماه در غایت نقصان که ایشان معجزه

[15] این عبارت در برخی نسخ نیست.

[ث] گفتند که «ای رسولِ خدای، مبادا که ذات پاک تو را اَلَمی رسد از چشم بد» [خ] آنگاه فرمود که «ای خدیجه، قدری آب بیار تا وضو سازم». خدیجه خاتون آب آورد و پیغمبر علیه‌السلام وضو ساخت، و دو رکعت نماز حاجت ادا کرد [ذ] می گفت «إلٰهيٓ، آنچه دشمنان از من طلب می‌کنند بر تو معلوم است. اگر تو بندهٔ مسکین شکستهٔ خود را عزیز نگردانی، دیگر که تواند گردانید؟» [ض] بر آن نیزه دوشاخ است [غ] خدیجه خاتون تا آستانهٔ در خانه بیامد و با خود می‌گفت که «ندانم این زمان دشمنان با پیغمبر چه خواهند کرد». هم درزمانْ از شکم خدیجه آوازی برآمد که «ای مادر هیچ نگرانی نکنی که حافظ و ناصر محمّد خداییست جلّ جلاله. اگر چه تنهاست امّا پادشاه-عزیز و سران قبیله پیش او اسیر گردند». [ظ] بر فرشته که بر تاریکی های دوزخ موکّل بود فرمان شد که «برمثالِ چشم سوزنی رها کن». همان‌زمانْ همهٔ جهان تاریک شد

Bakr as well as Khadīja, began to cry.The Prophet (pbuh) said, 'O my friends, why are you crying?' They said, 'O Messenger of God, we are concerned that you will be hurt by the evil eye.' The Messenger of God said, 'O Abū Bakr and Khadīja, do not worry about me. Muḥammad's protector is the One who has created him.'

{24} Then he performed ablution and a two *rakʿa* prayer, and then prostrated and wailed and expressed his own powerlessness before God. While Muḥammad prostrated, Gabriel (pbuh) arrived and said, 'O Muḥammad, lift up your head from prostration.' Muḥammad left his prostration and saw that Gabriel carried a halberd which had two horns; one horn in the East, and the other in the West, and that seventy thousand weaponised angels stood before Gabriel.The Messenger said, 'O brother Gabriel, what is this two-horned halberd? And why did these seventy thousand angels arrive?' Gabriel replied, 'O Messenger of God, I am ordered thus: "On Muḥammad's word dispatch half of the enemies to the East by one horn of this halberd and dispatch the other half to the West." Also, another order was received: "Go with seventy thousand angels. Inform Muḥammad that the king has come with his own army and brought people from different clans. God has brought an army from heaven for you and they do whatever you command of them. Moreover, they have asked you to perform miracle(s), and we know this due to Our eternal's knowledge. And we created the shining Moon, and had [from the beginning] told the Moon to follow whatever Muḥammad asks you."'

{25} The Messenger of God praised God and went to meet the enemies. Khadīja came to the doorstep, ran after the Prophet, and cried. She thought to herself, 'I do not know what the enemies want to do with the Prophet.' While thinking, she heard a voice say, 'Do not worry as God is the Protector of the Prophet (pbuh). Although he went alone, the king and his entourage and army will in the end be seized.'

{26} When the Prophet (pbuh) went to them, ʿAzīz King said, 'Now [Muḥammad] ask the world to become dark.' The Messenger said, 'O God, may the world grows dark now.' Immediately, the world became dark. As they were not able to tolerate this, they all took each other's hand and said, 'O Muḥammad, now say that this darkness converts to brightness and light.' The Prophet (pbuh) said, 'O God, change this darkness to light'. Right after this, the world became bright according to God's command. They said, 'O Muḥammad, now ask the Moon to come out.' The night on which they had asked for a miracle was the twenty-eighth of the month when the Moon has waned – the Prophet (pbuh) lifted his hand in imploration asking, 'O Bringer of moon and twilight, order the Moon to appear!' Soon the Moon rose up until it was stationed above the Kaʿba. They said, 'Muḥammad, tell the Moon to circumambulate the Kaʿba seven times!' The Prophet (pbuh) said, 'O Moon, circumambulate the chosen place of God seven times!' They were about to begin counting when the Moon finished its seventh circumambulation. They said, 'O Muḥammad, now order the Moon to praise you.' The Moon began

طلبیدند[الف‌الف] – پیغمبر ﷺ دست به دعا برآورد و گفت «آرندهٔ ماه و شفق، ماه را فرمان ده تا برآید». همانْ‌زمانْ ماه برآمد، و خود را بالا کشید و بیامد بر بام کعبه. گفتند «بگو تا هفت کرّت طواف کعبه کند». پیغمبر علیه‌السلام گفت که «ای ماه، مقام برگزیده حقّ را هفت کرّت طواف کن». ایشان در شمار بودند که ماه هفت کرّت طواف کعبه کرد. بعداز آن گفتند «اکنون ماه را بگوی در ثنایِ درآید». ماه در ثنای پیغمبر ﷺ درآمد.[ب‌ب] ماه گفت «السَّلَامُ عَلَيْكُمْ یا نبي ٱللّٰهْ.[ج‌ج] من بیچاره چه باشم که ثنای ذات پاک تو بگویم؟ اگر خلایق هفت آسمان و زمین و جمیع ایشان ثنای تو بگویند، حقّ سبحانه وتعالی بزرگیِ که در ذات تو آفریده یکی را هزاران نگفتند باشند».

{۲۷} باز گفتند «بگو ماه را دوپاره شود. یکی را در گریبان تو درآید، از جانب دامن برآید، و یکی در آستین راست درآید و از آستین چپ برآید». پیغمبر ﷺ با انگشت جانبِ ماه اشارت کرد؛ از میان دوپاره شد. یک‌پاره در گریبان درآمد و به جانب دامن بیرون شد. پارهٔ دیگر به آستین راست درآید و از آستین چپ بیرون شد. باز هر دوپاره در آسمان رفتند و یک‌جا شدند. آن‌ها باز گفتند «بگوی تا از جانب مغرب فرو رود». پیغمبر علیه‌السلام گفت «[خدایا] فرمان داد تا ماه فرو رود». ماه به جانب مغرب رفت. باز گفتند «بگوی تا از جانب مغرب برآید و جانب مشرق روان شود، چون میانهٔ آسمان رسد باز دونیم شود و خود را چنان وسیع گرداند که تمام آسمان در کنار هر دو پاره او درآید». پیغمبر دست به دعا برد، و گفت «إِلٰهِيْ، بر همه چیزها قادری و آنچه ایشان می گویند تو دانی».[۱۶] في الحال ماه از مغرب برآمده به مشرق رفت. چون به میان آسمان رسید باز دوپاره شد و خود را وسیع گردانید که تمام آسمان در کنار هر دوپاره ماه درآمد. و باز یک‌پاره به جانب جنوب رفت و یک‌پاره به جانب شمال. باز ماه جمیع شد چنانچه ماه آفریده‌اند.[د‌د]

{۲۸} پادشاه را طاقت نماند. روی سوی سران قبیله و لشگر کرد، و گفت «ای مردمان، چند دل خود را سخت کنیم و از دولت ایمان محروم مانیم؟» في الحال پیش حضرت رسالت پناهی استاده و با سیصد و چندکس به شرف اسلام مشرّف گشت.[ه‌ه] و خاک در دهن ابوجهل شد، و زردرویِ دین و آخرت شد. در آن حالت – با زردرویی – هنوز با خویش می گفت «زهی سِحری که محمّد دارد. من دانستم که سِحر او در آسمان کار خواهد آمد». سبحان الله، آن‌را که خدای تَعَالَی بخواهد از اقالیم بیارد و عطای ایمان روزی گرداند، و آن‌را که نخواهد گفتار او جز چنین نباشد.[۱۷]

{۲۹} القصّه. چون حضرت پیغمبر ﷺ با نصرت یزدانی بازگشت، رو به خانه نهاد و خدیجهٔ کبری را دید که پیش در خانه استاده. خدیجه گفت «ازجهت شما استاده‌ام». [پیغمبر] گفت «ای خدیجه، آنچه من از خدای تَعَالَی می‌خواستم، همان شد». خدیجهٔ کبری گفت «یا نبي ٱللّٰه، آنچه ماه در ثنای شما گفت من اینجا

[۱۶] این دعا در برخی نسخ موجود نیست. [۱۷] این نتیجه گیری از گفتار ابوجهل در برخی نسخ موجود نیست.

[الف‌الف] آن‌شب بیست و هفتم ماه بود [ب‌ب] ماه را بگوی تا در ثنای تو درآید. گفت «ای ماه، در ثنای من شو» [ج‌ج] اَلْسلام علیکَ یَارسُول اللّٰه [د‌د] چنانچه قرص قدیم بود [ه‌ه] درزمانْ پادشاه-عزیز و سران قبیله در دست و پای حضرت پیغمبر ﷺ افتادند و سیصد وهفتاد کس به شرف اسلام مشرّف شدند

to praise the Prophet (pbuh). The Moon said, 'Peace be upon you, O Prophet of God! Who am I but humble to praise you?! Even if the creatures of the seven heavens and earths together praise you, they will not able to praise a thousandth of the greatness that God has put in your essence.'

{27} They told Muḥammad, 'Now, order the Moon to split into two parts, one half goes to your collar and comes out of your lap, and the other half goes to your right sleeve and comes out from your left sleeve.' The Prophet ordered the Moon with his finger. Soon it split into two parts. One half went to his collar and came out of his lap, and the other half went to the right sleeve and came out of the left one. Then both joined each other in the sky. They, again, said, 'Now ask the Moon to go down in the West.' The Prophet (pbuh) said, '[O God] command the Moon to come down [in the West].' The Moon set towards the West. Then, they said, 'Now say to rise up from the West and come towards the East. When it arrives in the middle of sky, split into two halves and enlarge each half to the extent that they cover the whole sky.' The Prophet lifted his hand in supplication and said, 'O God, You are All-Powerful and have power over all things, and You are able to do what they are saying'. Soon, the Moon came out from the West and moved towards the East. When it arrived in the middle of the sky, it again split into two halves and enlarged itself to the extent that the whole sky was covered by both halves. And then, one half went towards the South and the other towards the North. Then, they joined each other, as when the Moon was created from the beginning.

{28} The king could not help it, he said to the leaders of the clans and his troops, 'O people, to what extent should we be hard-hearted and be away from the estate of faith?' Then, he along with the three hundred or so of his army stood before the Prophet (pbuh) and converted to Islam. And Abū Jahl was humiliated in religion and in the hereafter. Although humiliated, Abū Jahl still thought to himself, 'Bravo! what good sorcery Muḥammad is acquainted with. I have now realised that Muḥammad's sorcery works in the sky, too'. Glory to God who, upon His decision, brings people from other nations and grants them faith, and the ones that He does not want say such things as this statement!

{29} To get back to the story. When the Prophet (pbuh) became successful and victorious, he went home. He noticed that Khadīja stood there waiting. Khadīja said, 'I was waiting for you'. The Prophet said, 'O Khadīja, what I had asked from God happened.' Khadīja said, 'O Prophet of God, when the Moon praised you I heard while waiting here. But, Messenger of God, once you left, I was walking while being hesitant and worried. Suddenly, I heard a voice from my stomach saying, "God is the helper of Muḥammad". I did not realise who said this.' The Prophet (pbuh) thought, '"She heard a voice from her stomach!' What could Khadīja be meaning?' As the Prophet reflected,

استاده تمام می‌شنیدم. امّا، یا رسول اللهٰ، چون شما برفتید، از بهر شما در تردّد بودم و خاطر بسیار پریشان بودم. و ناگاه آوزای از شکم خود شنیدم که «نصرت‌دهندهٔ محمّد خدای تَعَالَی است».[dd] مرا معلوم نشد که این آواز که کرد».[zz] پیغمبر ﷺ در حیرت ماند که این چه سخن است خدیجه می‌گوید که «از شکم خود آوازی شنید». همان‌ساعت پیک حضرت رَبِّ الْعَالَمِین جبرئیل امین رسید و گفت «ای محمّد، تو را از خدیجهٔ کبری دختری می‌دهم که فردای قیامتْ شفیعِ[cc] زنان امّت تو باشد. چون دید که مادرش نگران شده از بهر شما [و] از برای تسکین دل مادر این آواز کرد».[18] چون پیغمبر ﷺ این مژده بشارت شنید، به غایت شادمان گشت، و حمد و ثنای حضرت حقّ سُبْحَانَهُ وَتَعَالَى بر زبان راند که «مرا فرزندی روزی خواهد کرد که او شفیع زنان امّت من خواهد بود».

{۳۰} إِلٰهِيْ، به حرمت آن بندهٔ نیک‌بخت که در دنیا و عقبی مِن بیچاره را و کاتب این قصّه را با جمیع مؤمنان عزیز و با عزّت داری، و سختی هر دو جهان آسانی گردانی. بِمِنَّةٖ وَكَرَمِه.

[18] عبارتی که در اکثر نسخ موجود نیست، و تنها در نسخهٔ دانشگاه تهران دیده می شود («و می فرماید که هر پیغمبری را نسل او در پشت او قرار دادیم، و نسل تو در پشت علی قرار دادیم».) این نکته اشاره به پذیرش داستان‌های درّالمجالس در بین گروه‌های متفاوت دینی دارد.

[dd] «ناگاه آوازی از شکم من برآمد و گفت «ای مادر، اندوهگین مباش که نصرت دهندهٔ وی خدایست عَزَّوَجَلَّ»» [zz] «یا رسول اللهٰ، هیچ مرا معلوم نشد که آن چه آواز بود که از شکم من برآمد؟» [cc] شفاعت خواه

the herald of the Lord of the Worlds, Gabriel the trustworthy, descended and said, 'O Muḥammad, God will give you and Khadīja a daughter who will be the intercessor of all women of your community in the hereafter. When she saw that her mother has been worried because of you, she said made that voice in order to relieve the mother's concern.' When the Prophet (pbuh) heard this great news, he was overjoyed and praised God and said, 'You will grant me a child who will be the intercessor of all women in my community.'

{30} *O God, by the fortunate servant of Yours, dignify me, a humble pauper, as well as the scribe of this story along with all of your believers, ease the difficulties of both worlds upon us. By Your unmerited favour and kindness. [Amen.]*

حقّ یتیمان

در نیکوئی کردن در حقّ مادر و پدر ایشان و خشنودی و نظیرها

{۱} آورده‌اند که حقّ سُبْحَانَهُ وَتَعَالَیٰ می‌فرماید که «مرا پرستید که آفریدگار شمایم[۱] تا از عذاب من نجات یابید، و در حقّ مادر و پدر نیکوئی بسیار باید کرد تا در بهشت رسید. و عاصی نشوید تا از مرگ مفاجات[۲] امان یابید. چنانچه که فرمونده‌اند[الف] «لَا یَدْخُلُونَ الْجَنَّةَ عَاقُّ لِوَالِدَیْنِ، آری! آزار کنندهٔ مادر و پدر از رحمت خدای تَعَالَیٰ بی‌نصیب‌اند». خوش آن نیک‌بختان که مادر و پدر در زمان حیات و ممات از ایشان خشنود باشد. و نَعُوذُ بِاللهِ مِنْهَا که مادر و پدر از وی ناخشنود باشند که هر کاری ناشایسته در زندگی ایشان می‌کرده و ایشان‌را ناخوشی می‌آید. ازآن کار توبه کند، تا از برکت توبهٔ او خدای تَعَالَیٰ بیامرزد. زنهار، زنهار، مادر و پدر خود را برنجانی جان دادن بر تو سخت گردد و گور نیز تنگ و تاریک گردد.[۳]

{۲} الغرض.[۴] آورده‌اند که جوانی مُرد او را در گور کردند. همان‌ساعت از گور آواز خر شنیدند. مردمان بر سر قَبر او بودند. حیران ماندند که این چه آواز است که از این گور می‌آید. چون تحقیق کردند گفتند که روزی با مادر خود سخت گفته بوده است؛ مادر را رنجانیده بود. و مادر گفت که «همچون خر فریاد می‌کنی».[ب] از شومی آن سخن «او را خر گردانیده تا بدانی که به یک سخت گفتن در روی مادر، آن معامله پیش می‌آید». پس [ای] جوان نیک‌بخت، اگر خواهی که در دین و دنیا خوشی و خرّمی بیابی، زینهار، که با مادر و پدر با ادب باشی.[۵]

[۱] شما هستم. [۲] همچنین مفاجاة؛ مرگ ناگهانی. [۳] این پاراگراف مربوط به آیات ۲۳ و ۲۴ سورهٔ اسراء است.
[۴] در اینجا مراد از «الغرض» شروع داستان است. [۵] این نتیجه‌گیری در برخی نسخ نیست.

[الف] چنانچه خدای تَعَالَیٰ در حدیث قدسی می فرماید
[ب] با مادر خود سخن سخت گفته بوده است و مادر در حقّ وی دعا کرده بود که آواز خر کنی

CHAPTER 8

The right of orphans

on the proper behaviour regarding parents and their satisfaction, and further examples

{1} It is reported that God said, 'Worship me as I am your Creator so that you will be saved from torment. And do a lot of good deeds for your mother and father in order that you may enter paradise. And avoid turbulence until you are safe from unexpected death.' As has been stated, 'They will not enter paradise, who have been disobedient to their parents'. Indeed, those who annoy their mother and father will be deprived of God's mercy. Fortunate are those good people whose mother and father – whether alive or deceased – were satisfied with them. And we seek refuge in God for those whose mothers and fathers are not happy, that whatever wrong they have done in their lives has brought them difficulty. They must repent of that sin until they are forgiven by God on account of the repentance. Beware! Becareful! If you annoy and irritate your mother and father, dying will be harsh for you and the grave will become tight and dark.[1]

{2} And now the story. It is reported that a young man died and was buried. After his burial, everyone heard a donkey's bray from his grave. People listened closely to his grave. They wondered, why is the bray coming from this grave? Then, after some investigation they realised that he did wrong one day and annoyed his mother. And his mother said, 'You will bray like a donkey!!' Due to this ominous phrase, 'As a retaliation, We turned him into a donkey, until he knew whatever he impolitely said had annoyed his mother.' O fortunate youth! If you want to become happy in religion and in the world, bear in mind that you should respect your parents.

[1] This paragraph may be related to Q. 17:23–24.

{۳} الغرض. آورده‌اند که جوانی بود. او را آرزوی حجّ شد،[ج] و مادر او را رخصت نمی‌داد. تا روزی حاجیان می‌رفتند.[د] روی به راه نهاد و رفت. تا شبی در بیابان از قافلهٔ کاروان دور افتاد و دزدان از عقب در آمدند و آن جوان را بگرفتند، و زاد و راحله و هرچه داشت بردند. وهر دو دست و پای او را جدا کردند و در راه گذاشتند.[۶] مؤذّن بیت المقدس را در خواب نمودند که «برخیز و در فلان بیابان رو و حال جوان را دریاب». مؤذّنِ بیت المقدس روی به راه نهاد. چون به سروقت او رسید گفت «ای جوان، حالت چیست؟» او گفت «چه باشد، بی‌دستور مادر روی به راه نهادم و به این حالت شدم».[ه] چون آن جوان از مؤذّن درخواست کرد که «مرا به خانهٔ مادر برسان تا دل مادر بدست آرم. چنانچه از دست و پای جدا شدم باری در دم آخر از شرف ایمان جدا نشوم»، مؤذّن او را به در خانه آورد و رفت. جوان آوازی از درون خانه می‌شنید که مادر می‌گفت «إلٰهِيّ، هیچ فرزندی دیگر ندارم. و نمی‌دانم که در غربتْ حالِ او چیست که او ناگفتهٔ من رفته است. اکنون او را به من رسان، ای دانای راز، که خاطرم از برای او نگرانست». جوانْ دستِ بریده را بر در خانه بزد.[۷] مادرش آغاز کرد که «کیست درِ بیوه‌گان و غم‌زده‌گان می‌کوبد؟ مگر کسی هست که خبر از غریب من دارد؟» نزدیک در آمد، دید غریبی نشسته‌است.

{۴} گفت «نانت دهم؟» جوان گفت «نان چگونه گیرم که دست ندارم». پیرزن گفت «پیش‌تر آی» . گفت «پای ندارم» . پیرزن گفت «آواز او به آواز فرزند من می‌ماند» . رفت و چراغ آورد. بر روی آن جوان بداشت. از پسرش یاد آمد. گریان شد و گفت «من نیز همچون تو پسری داشتم. امّا نمی‌دانم که در غریبی حال او چگونه باشد». پسر را صبر نماند. فریاد و زاری برآورد که «ای مادر، پسر تو منم». چون مادر نعره زد و بیهوش[۸] افتاد. بعداز ساعتی بهوش آمد، و روی به قبله کرد[و] و گفت «إلٰهِيّ، اگر چه ادبش کردی امّا هلاکش مگردان. و از سعادت و ایمان محروم نکن». که ناخشنودی مادر و پدر بی‌غایت دشوار است.[۹]

{۵} الغرض.[ز] روزی حضرت سید عالم حضرت مصطفی ﷺ به گورستان رسید. از گور ناله و زاری شنیدند که می‌گوید: «النَار مِنْ فَوقِي وَالنَار مِنْ تَحْتِي وَالنَارعَنْ يَمِينِي وَالنَارعَنْ يَساري،[۱۰] معنی وی آنست که «بالای من آتش، زیر من آتش، و بر راست من آتش است و بر چپ من آتش است». رسول ﷺ فرمودند که «منادی کنند که هر که درین گورستان مرده باشد بر سر گور او بیایند». هرکه مرده داشت آمد.

[۶] رهایش کردند. [۷] جوان سَرْدَر را جنبانید. [۸] واژهٔ «بیهوش» و «بهوش» به‌وفور در ادبیات اسلامی مالایی دیده می‌شود.
[۹] این عبارت پایانی در خیلی نسخ وجود ندارد.
[۱۰] در روایات اسلامی عموماً چنین آمده «النَارمِن فَوْقِي والنَار مِنْ تَحْتِي والنَار عَنْ يَمِيني والنَار عَنْ شِمَالي»

[ج] آورده‌اند که در مصر جوانی بود و او را هوای زیارت حرم محترم و مکّهٔ معظّم شد [د] و به غیر گفت [ه] تا برجوانان دیگر معلوم باشد که با وجود نیّت حج، بی‌اجازت مادر اینچنین رنج می‌رساند و تا آخر حالش چگونه است [و] روی به آسمان [ز] حکایت

{3} And back to another story. It is reported that there was a young man. He wished to perform the hajj. And his mother would not allow him to go. In the meantime, other pilgrims were about to begin their journey. Eventually, he left and travelled to perform the hajj. One night he lost sight of his caravan and bandits went after him and seized him, grabbing all his property. They cut his hands and legs and left him there. The *muʾadhdhin*[2] of Jerusalem had been summoned with a dream, 'Go to that desert and find that young man'. The *muʾadhdhin* went towards the desert. When he found the young man he said, 'What has happened to you, O young man?' He replied, 'What do you expect!? Disobeying my mother, I went out and this happened to me.' The young man then asked the *muʾadhdhin* to carry him to his mother's house, so that he could soothe his mother's heart, [saying] 'Although I am apart from my hands and legs, do not let me be apart from my faith at the end of my life', The *muʾadhdhin* took him to his house and left. The young man heard his mother's voice from the house, 'O God, I have no more children and do not know how he is in a foreign land, as he left me without telling me. Now, bring him back to me, O You who are the Knower of secrets, as I am very worried about him!' The young man took his severed hand and knocked on the door. His mother said, 'Who is there? Who is knocking on the door of widows and sad people? Is there even anybody who knows about my loneliness?' She came to the door and noticed a strange person sitting there.

{4} She asked him, 'Do you want me to feed you with bread?' The young man said, 'How can I take your bread as I have no hand.' The old woman said, 'Come closer'. The young man said, 'I have no leg.' The old woman pondered, 'His voice is similar to that of my son.' She went and brought a lantern near to the young man's face. He resembled her son. She cried and said, 'I have a son similar to you, and I do not know what he is doing far from here in a foreign land.' The young man was not able to wait any longer and wailed, 'O mother, I am your own son.' Then, his mother screamed and fainted. After a while, she regained consciousness and sat towards the direction of prayer and said, 'O God, although you have punished him, do not kill him, and do not deprive him from the realm of faith.' The dissatisfaction of the mother and father is difficult and complicated.

{5} Returning to the story. Once upon a time, the Prophet (pbuh) arrived in a cemetery. He heard a wailing from a grave, saying, 'The fire is above, beneath, and to the right and left of me.' It means that there is fire above my body, there is fire below me, there is fire to the right and left of my body. The Prophet (pbuh) said, 'Annouce that all people should attend the graves of their deceased in this cemetery'. The people, who had lost someone, came.

[2] the person who calls for prayer

{۶} بر سر این گور پیرزنی عصایٔ در دست بیامد. از او پرسیدند «در این گور تو را کیست؟» گفت «پسر منست، ولیکن از وی بیزارم».[ج] پیغمبر ﷺ گفت «چرا خشنود نمی‌گردی؟» گفت «من هرگز خشنود نشوم که مرا سخت رنجانیده». هرچه رسول خدا می‌گفتند خشنود نشد و قبول نکرد. حضرت دعا کردند و گفتند «إِلٰهِيّ، این حجاب از میان دور شود تا مادر عذاب او را با این حال ببیند». حجاب از میان دور شد. چون مادر دید فرزندش به این حال گرفتار است[ط] بی‌خود گشت و خود را بر تربت پسر افکند و گفت «یا بارخدایا، من خشنود شدم. تو هم خشنود شو و او را عفو کن و عذاب از وی دور کن». بمجرّد همین‌که مادر خشنود شد فرزند از عذاب خلاص شد. تا بدانی که دعای مادر و پدر در حقّ فرزندان چنین مستجاب می‌شود.

{۷} نظیر دیگر. در عهد حضرت رسالت‌پناه، جوانی در حال مستی طپانچه[11] بر روی مادر زد و چشم مادر از چشم‌خانه بیرون افتاد. مادر چشم را گرفت و پیش حضرت بُرد و گفت «که پسرم مرا به این حال کرده است». پسر در حال مستی به‌خواب رفته بود. چون بیدار شد مردمان وی را ملامت کردند و گفتند که «تو چشم مادر خود را در حال مستی کنده‌ای». پسر گفت «به کدام دست چنین گستاخی کرده‌ام؟» گفتند «بدین دست»[ی]. درساعت کارد گرفت و با دست خود گفت «چرا در حقّ مادر من این حرکت کردی!» و آن دست را از بند جدا کرد. به دستِ دیگر آن دستِ بریده را بگرفت و خون‌چکان نزد آن حضرت آمد.

{۸} نظر مادر بر دست پسر افتاد. درد چشم خود را فراموش کرد و دوان نزدیک پسر آمد، و گفت «ای جان مادر، دست تو را که بریده‌است؟» پسر گفت «خودم بریده‌ام. این دست چشم مبارک شما را بی‌نور کرد. به‌جزای خود رسید». مادر را از گفتار او شفقّت آمد و دست بریدهٔ او را گرفت و بوسه داد. حضرت را از حال ایشان تعجّب آمد. جبرئیل علیه‌السلام آمد و گفت «یا سیّدا، فرمان می‌شود که وقت فکر کردن نیست و وقت شفقّت است. در حقّ هر دو دعا کردن از تو و اجابت کردن از ما».

{۹} حضرت ضعیفه را نزدیک خود خواند و فرمود «دیده را برجای خود بِنه». مهتر عالم علیه‌السلام دست به دعا برآورد. درزمانْ مستجاب شد و چشم از آن که بود بهتر شد. زن در دست و پای آن حضرت افتاد که دست فرزندم را هم دعای کنید که از او خشنود شدم. فرمودند «ای جوان، آن دست بر جایِ خود بَنْد و به دست دیگر بگیر». چون حضرت دعای کرد في الحال درست و نیکو گشت.[12]

{۱۰} نظیر دیگر. آورده‌اند که جوانی را آرزوی کعبه شد. پیش مادر بسیار عجز و زاری کرد. مادر رخصت داد. چون عزم رفتن کرد مادر گفت «إِلٰهِيّ، فرزند خود را به تو می‌سپارم؛ سلامت بَری و سلامت بازرسانی». جوان را به خدا سپرد. و جوان مادر خود را وداع کرد. و روی به راه نهاد. تا روزی از قافله پس مانده بود. دزدی

[11] همچنین طبانچه یا تپانچه، به معنی سیلی زدن.
[12] براساس برخی نسخ، این قسمت با توصیهٔ اخلاق به جوانان پیرامون احترام به والدین خاتمه می‌یابد.

[ج] ناخشنودم [ط] گورِ فرزند پرآتش دید و پسرش در میان آتش می سوخت و ناله می کرد [ی] گفتند به دست راست

{6} An old woman with a cane came to this grave. She was asked, 'Who is in this grave?' She replied, 'My son is in there and I detest him.' The Prophet (pbuh) asked, 'Why are you not satisfied with him?' She said, 'I will never be happy as he annoyed me extremely.' Whatever the Prophet of God urged, she remained unhappy and did not agree. The Prophet prayed and stated, 'O God, remove this veil so the mother can see his torment [and punishment] there.' The veil was gone. When the mother noticed her son's situation, she became numb and threw herself on the grave, saying, 'O God! I am satisfied with him. Will you now be happy with him and forgive him and stop the torment!?' As soon as the mother was satisfied, the son was freed from torment, so you know that the prayers of mothers and fathers for their children will be responded to like this.

{7} Another story. During the period of the Prophet (pbuh), there was a young man who had punched his mother's face while being drunk and his mother's eye was dislodged. The mother took her eye and went to the Prophet and said, 'This is what my son did to me.' The son slept while being drunk. When he woke up people rebuked him and said to him, 'You gouged your mother's eye when you were drunk!' The son asked them, 'I did this with which hand of mine?' They said, 'With this hand.' Then, he quickly took the knife and asked his own hand, 'Why did you do this to my mother?' and then cut it off. Then, he took the chopped hand with his other hand and went to the Prophet while being blood soaked.

{8} The mother noticed her son's hand. She forgot the pain of her eye and ran towards her son and said, 'O my darling, who has cut your hand?' The son said, 'I did so. This hand has taken the light from your lovely eye. It has been punished accordingly.' The mother became emotional and tender-hearted after hearing his statement and took his severed hand and kissed it. The Prophet was surprised when he saw their interaction. Gabriel (pbuh) descended and said, 'O Prophet! It is now commanded that you should wait no more, now is the time for kindness. You pray for both of them and they then would receive a quick response from Us.'

{9} The Prophet asked the woman to approach him and told her put her eye back in its place. The Master of the Worlds (pbuh) lifted his hand in supplication. Immediately, his prayer was answered and her eye healed and became better than it was before. The woman fell to the ground and requested from the Prophet, 'Pray for the hand of my son, too, as I am happy with him now.' The Prophet said, 'O young man, return the severed hand back in its place and hold it with the other hand.' When the Prophet prayed for it the hand became fixed.

{10} Another story. It is reported that there was a young man desiring to visit the Kaʿba. He was insolent and moaned a lot to his mother. The mother then allowed him. When he was about to go, his mother said, 'O God, I have entrusted my son to

قصد کشتن او کرد. جوان به درگاه خدای تعالی بنالید و گفت «ای قریب از همه قریبان!» آواز «لبَّیك» آمد.

{۱۱} دزد متحیّر شد. چپ و راست خود را نگاه کرد و کسی را ندید. باز قصد کشتن جوان کرد. باز جوان گفت «ای کسی که از بنده ها دور نباشی!» بار دوم آواز آمد که «لبَّیك لبَّیك». همچنین، سه‌کرّت دزد قصد کشتن او کرد. جوان می‌نالید و از حضرتْ ندای اجابت می‌شنید. ناگاه سواری شمشیرْبرهنه بر سرِ[۱۳] دزد رسید. و چنان تیغ بزد سر از تن او جدا گردانید.

{۱۲} جوان پرسید که «تو کیستی که دشمن مرا هلاک کردی، و منّت جانی بر من نهادی؟» آن سوار گفت که «چندسالست که خدای تَعَالَی را در این بیابان طاعت می‌کنم. و این اسب[۱۴] و تیغ را خدای تَعَالَی به من داده‌است. و امروز دیدم که این اسب هیچ قرار نمی‌گیرد. فکر کردم که خالی از واقعه نیست.[۱۵] چون این دزد قصد کشتن تو کرده بود، فرمان رسید که «اسب را سوار شو و تیغ بردار و بندهٔ مرا از دزد خلاص کن. و به آن بندهٔ ما بگوی که «در آن وقت وداعِ مادر کرده بودی، او تو را به ما سپرده بود تا تو را نگاه داریم. چون به مادر رسی، سلام ما بگوی که خدای تَعَالَی عَزَّوَجَلَّ امانت تو را هم به تو رسانید»». پس رضای مادر و پدر سبب بقای ایمانست. إِلٰهِيْ، ایمان را از دزد شیطان در حفظ و امانِ خویش داری.

{۱۳} نظیر دیگر. آورده‌اند که مالک دینار رحمت الله علیه در کعبه بود. وی را در خواب نمودند که «برو و آن جوان که در حُجرهٔ تنگ و تاریک است، بگوی که تو را از رحمت خدای عَزَّوَجَلَّ نصیبی نیست». از خواب بیدار شد و روی به جانب حرم[۱۶] آورد. چون رسید دید که جوانی در یک حُجرهٔ تاریک زارزار می‌گرید. چون نظر جوان بر مالک افتاد گفت «ای مالک دینار، پیغام آورده‌ای؟» مالک گفت «تو چه دانی که من پیغام آورده‌ام؟» گفت «یا مالک، پنج سالیست که این سخن بر من می‌گویند که «تو را از رحمت خدای تَعَالَی نصیبی نیست» و لیکن من از رحمت او ناامیدم»». مالک گفت «چه گناه کرده‌ای؟» گفت «در حال مستی بر پدر مشت زدم و یک دندان ایشان شکسته شد. پنج سال باشد که گریهٔ آن گناه می‌کنم. تا فردای قیامت بر من چه‌ها رَود».[۱۷]

{۱۴} مالک دینار گفت «ای جوان، پدر تو کجاست؟» گفت «در فلان قبیله است و امسال در حجّ نیامده». مالک دینار گفت[۱۸] «به نشانی از پیش او رفتم و پدر او را دیدم که سرْبرهنه کرده بود، و دندان بر کف دست گرفته و می‌گفت «إِلٰهِيْ، بر دندان نَنِگر. بر من ظلم رسیده‌است و تو می‌دانی و می‌بینی». مالک گفت که «گریه در من افتاد». گفتم «ای پیر، اگر فرزند تو را مشت زد ازغایت شراب عجب نبود. بر وی رحم کن و حال فرزند با وی به تمامی بگفت».

[۱۳] سروقت. [۱۴] اسپ. [۱۵] بی‌دلیل نیست. [۱۶] احتمالا وی در حجره‌ای نزدیک کعبه بوده‌است.

[۱۷] این قسمت از داستان ارتباط معنایی با داستان رکابدار حسین در کربلا دارد زمانی که وی به دلیل قطع دستان حسین احساس شرمساری نمود.

[۱۸] در برخی نسخ این جمله اضافه شده است «به نشان وی رفتم. پدرش پس کعبه استاده دیدم».

you; take him in safety and bring him back in safety.' She entrusted the young man to God. And the young man bid farewell to his mother. As he went towards the road he fell behind the caravan. A bandit aimed to kill him. The young man wailed before God, 'O the one who is nearer than all other kinsmen!' A divine voice came, 'I am here.'

{11} The bandit was surprised. He looked to his left and right and did not notice anyone. Then he tried to kill the young man. The young man, again, wailed, 'O the one who will not leave His servants!' The divine voice was heard for a second time, 'I am here, I am here for you.' The bandit, nevertheless, tried to kill him three times. The young man, also, wailed and still heard approving messages from God. Suddenly, a horseman with an unsheathed sword arrived. He approached the bandit and beheaded him.

{12} The young man said, 'Who are you that killed my enemy, and did this favour to save my life?' The horseman replied, 'For several years I have been worshipping God in this desert. And God has granted me this horse and sword. And I noticed today that this horse is nervous. I thought that the horse's restlessness should not be without reason. When this bandit wanted to kill you, a command was sent down, "Ride the horse and take your sword and free My servant from the bandit. And let Our servant know that when he was saying goodbye to his mother she had entrusted him to Us. When he returns to his mother he should convey Our best greetings to her, saying that God sent him back safely."' As such, the mother's and father's satisfaction ensures faith. O God, preserve and save the faith from the [main] bandit, Satan!

{13} The next story. It has been reported that Mālik Dīnār,[3] God's mercy be upon him, was close to the Kaʿba. He fell asleep and dreamed. In his dream, he was ordered to go and tell the young man sitting in a tiny and dark chamber, 'You will not be rewarded with God's mercy.' Mālik woke up and went towards the house. When he arrived, he noticed that a young man was crying lamentably in a dark chamber. When the young man saw Mālik, he said, 'O Mālik Dīnār, have you brought news?' Mālik said, 'How do you know that I have news for you?' He replied, 'O Mālik, it has been five years since I was informed that I will not be rewarded with God's mercy and so I am disappointed not to receive His reward.'Mālik said, 'What is the matter?' He replied, 'I punched my father while I was drunk, and broke one of his teeth. For five years I have been crying over this fault, as what is going to happen to me after the Day of Judgement?'[4]

{14} Mālik Dīnār said, 'O young man, where is your father?' He replied, 'He is in that clan and he did not come for hajj this year.' Mālik Dīnār said, 'I looked for his father and found his father bareheaded[5] and holding his tooth in his hand. He was saying, "O God, You know the story of my teeth. Do not ask me about it! I was oppressed and You

[3] Mālik b. Dīnār. [4] This episode may be related to the regret feeling of the servant of Ḥusayn who attempted to cut the latter's hands in Karbala. [5] Shaved head/bald.

{۱۵} شفقّت پدری پیدا شد و رحمتش آمد. دعای خیر کرد. مالک شادمان نزدیک جوان رفت. و از دعای پدرش خبر داد. گریهٔ جوان زیاده گشت و آنگه گفت «یا مالک دینار، التماسی دارم». گفت «بگوی». گفت «اگر امروز پدر از من خشنود نمی‌شد، فردا مرا فرشتگان با غُل و زنجیر به‌سوی دوزخ می‌بردند. شما امروز بر من همان کنید. رَسنی بیارید و در گردن من بندید، و کشالی‌کنان پیش پدر برید و گویید که «گنه‌کار را آورده‌ایم»». ایشان همچنان کردند. چون پدرِ وی را برابر آن حال دید رسن از گردن او دور کرد و وی را کنار گرفت، و گفت که «ای جان پدر، از تو خشنود شدم. خدای تَعَالَی از تو خشنود باد».

{۱۶} إِلهِیَ، خشنودی خود در حقّ جملهٔ مادران و پدران روزی کنی، و جملهٔ فرزندان مؤمنان را خشنودی مادران و پدران روزی کنی. بِمِنَّة وَکَرَمه.

are All-Knowing and All-Seeing."' Mālik said, 'I began to cry. Then I said, "O old man, if your son punched you, which is not unexpected from a drunk person. Forgive him."' Then Mālik told him the whole of the young man's story.

{15} Paternal affection took hold and he forgave his son, and wished him well. Mālik went to the young man cheerfully and informed him of his father's good prayer. The son continued to cry more and more, and said, 'O Mālik Dīnār, I have a request.' Mālik said, 'Go ahead.' He replied, 'If my father had not been satisfied with me today, then angels would have taken me in shackles towards hell. Now you do the same to me today. Bring a rope to tie around my neck, and drag me towards my father and announce, "We have brought the sinner." They did so. Once the father saw his son in such a condition, he released the rope from his neck and hugged him tightly. And said, 'O beloved of your father, I am satisfied with you. God will be happy with you.'

{16} *O God, grant Your satisfaction to all mothers and fathers, and grant all children of the believers the satisfaction of their mothers and fathers. By Your unmerited favour and kindness. [Amen.]*

حکایتِ مجروح شدن دندان مبارک پیغمبر ﷺ چه حکمت بود

{۱} آورده‌اند که شبی وقت خفتن بود که حضرت رسول الله ﷺ از میان یاران به خانه آمد. در حُجره عایشه رضی الله عنها چراغ نبود.[الف] و عایشه را پیراهن پاره شده بود و پیراهن را می‌دوخت. ناگاه سوزن در پیراهن گم شد و هرچه طلب کرد نیافت. چون پیغمبر ﷺ نزدیک خود دید در خاطرش گذشت که مبادا سوزن به اندام پیغمبر ﷺ رسد. در تجسّس و تفحّص سوزن مضطرب بود. رسول علیه السلام پرسید «یا عایشه دل تو نگران است. در پیراهن خود چه می‌طلبی؟»

{۲} گفت «یا رسول الله، پیراهن من پاره شده بود و آن را می‌دوختم. سوزن گم شد. خوف می‌کنم که مبادا به اندام مبارک شما رسد. هرچند می‌جویم نیابم». حضرت پیغمبر ﷺ در تبسّم شدند. چو لبها از یکدیگر گشاده شد نوری از دندان مبارک ایشان پیدا شد که تمام حُجره منوّر گردید. سوزن را در روشنی آن نور یافت. پیغمبر علیه السلام رو به عایشه کرد و گفت «دیدی روشنی دندان مرا».

{۳} این سخن پیغمبر در نزد حقّ تَعَالَی عزّوجلّ پسندیده نیفتاد. جبرئیل علیه السلام رسید و گفت «یا محمّد، خدای تَعَالَی می‌فرماید که نظر به دندان خود کردی، امّا نگفتی که دندان تو را که آفریده است؟ تا روز[ی] انصافِ[1] این سخن از دندان تو بستانم».[ب] چون پیغمبر علیه السلام به جنگ اُحد رفت. یاران خودبینی کردند و نظر

[1] بعید است که منظور آن «روزِ انصاف»، که اشاره به قیامت دارد، بوده باشد.

[الف] روزی از مجلس صحابه بازگشتند و در حُجرهٔ عایشه رضی الله عنها درآمدند

[ب] و شکر پروردگار خود نیاوردی که دندان تو که نگاه داشت، تا روز انصاف این سخن از تو بستانم

CHAPTER 9

The story of the Prophet's (pbuh) injured teeth

and why this should have happened

{1} It is reported that the Prophet (pbuh) left his Companions and went home at bedtime. There was no light in ʿĀʾisha's chamber. Her dress was torn and she was sewing it. The needle became lost in the dress and she was unable to find it. When she noticed the Prophet (pbuh), she worried lest the needle hurt the Prophet's body. She was trying hard to find the needle. The Messenger said, 'O ʿĀʾisha, you are worried. What are you searching for in her dress?'

{2} She replied, 'O Messenger of God, my dress was torn and I was sewing it. The needle got lost. I am afraid it could hurt your sacred body. Try as I might, I cannot find it.' The Prophet (pbuh) smiled. As his lips parted, a light shone from his sacred tooth which illuminated the whole chamber. ʿĀʾisha found the needle by this light. The Prophet (pbuh) looked at ʿĀʾisha and said, 'You noticed the light of my teeth, right?'

{3} This statement from the Prophet did not meet God's expectations. Gabriel (pbuh) descended and said, 'O Muḥammad, God said, "You proudly admired your teeth, while you did not mention who had created them? So, We treat you with justice; we will take this tooth from you."' When the Prophet (pbuh) went to the Battle of Uḥud. His followers were full of complacency and were content with their might and power. During that battle, a stone hit the sacred tooth of the Prophet. Another story is that once upon a time, his sacred leg was painful. He heated up a stone and put it on his leg. The stone complained before God and said, 'O God, You observe how Your prophet has made me suffer with the fire's heat for the sake of himself!' It was commanded, 'O

بر مردی[۲] و قوّت خود کردند. در آن جنگ[ج] سنگی بر دندان مبارک ایشان رسید. و روایت دیگر آنست که روزی پای مبارک ایشان درد می‌کرد.[د] سنگی را گرم کرده بر پای نهاد.[ه] سنگ در حضرت حقّ سبحانه وتعالی بنالید و گفت «إِلٰهِيّ، تو می‌بینی که پیغمبر تو از برای نفعِ خودُ رنجِ گرمیِ آتش به من رساند». فرمان شد «ای سنگ، تو هم صبر کن تا روز[ی] انصاف از محمّد بستانی». فرشته را حکم شد که «آن سنگ را برده در میان سنگ‌های کوه اُحد انداز».

{۴} [ال]غرض. که در آن جنگ یاران گفتند «یا رسول الله، چندین جنگ‌ها کردیم و کفّار را از میان برداشتیم. اینها چه چیز باشد که پیش ما آیند؟!» این سخن پسندیدهٔ[۳] باری تَعَالَی نیامد که فرمان آمد که «ای محمّد، یاران به قوّت خود می نازند. با ایشان بیرون شو و با لشگر کفّار اُحد جنگ کن». بنیاد جنگ شد و حربی عظیم واقع شد. چون یاران نظر بر جوانی خود کردند در هزیمت شدند، وهفتادکس از صحابه شهادت یافتند. درآن میان حبشی بود. همان سنگ که در آتش گرم کرده بودند؛ برداشته بر دندان مبارک ایشان زد و مجروح گشت. به روایتی دو دندان مجروح شد.[و]

{۵} پس ای مؤمن! یک‌سخن پیغمبر در ستایش دندان خود گفت، و یا سنگ به‌واسطهٔ دردِ پا گرم کرد؛ آن هر دو انتقام کشیدند. هرگاه سرور اولاد آدم علیه السلام را چنین معامله کنند، با دیگران چه‌ها خواهند کرد. پس نظر بر افعال و کردار خود باید کردن، و غم آن باید خورد که ما روزی در پیش داریم که از آن ذرّه[ای] فروگذاشت نخواهد شد. و در آن نیک کرداران در حیرت و وحشت خود فرومانند.[۴]

{۶} نظیر دیگر. روزی پیغمبر ﷺ به غزایی رفته بود و گرمائی به غایت سخت بود. ابن‌مسعود به خدمت رسول بیامد و گفت «ای پیغمبر خدای عَزَّوَجَلَّ، از تشنگی هلاک شدم». آن حضرت در آن صحرا نظر کرد و از دور کوهی دید. پیغمبر گفت «ابن‌مسعود نزدیک آن کوه برو و بگو «مرا پیغمبر خدای تَعَالَی فرستاده است که تشنه ام؛ مرا آب ده»» . به‌موجبِ فرموده، ابن‌مسعود رفت پیشِ کوه و گفت که «مرا حضرتُ نزد تو فرستاده که آب دهی». کوه به سخن در آمد و گفت «ای ابن‌مسعود، از آن روز که این آیت نازل شده که «فَاتَّقُوا النَّارَ الَّتِي وَقُودُهَا النَّاسُ وَالْحِجَارَةُ،[۵] یعنی هیزم آتشِ دوزخِ آدمیان وسنگ‌ها باشند، از خوف حقّ تَعَالَی چندان گریسته‌ام که ذرّه آب در من نمانده است». چون ابن‌مسعود چنین شنید، تشنگی او سربه‌در رفت و از پیش کوه رفت. و کوه گفت «ای پسرِ مسعود، زمین‌بوسی[ز] مرا به خدمت پیغمبر ﷺ برسان و بگوی که «ای رحمت عالمیان، این سعادت من بود که نظر مبارک شما بر من افتاد. در حقّ من دعا کنید یا رسول الله، که خدای تَعَالَی

[۲] قدرت بدنی و دلیری. [۳] در اصل به‌صورت «پسندیده‌ی» نوشته شده‌است.
[۴] این جمله در برخی نسخ موجود نیست. [۵] آیهٔ ۲۴ سورهٔ بقره.

[ج] در آن روز [د] که روزی پای مبارک حضرت رسول علیه السلام آماس کرده بود [ه] سنگی برگرفت و در آتش انداخت. چون گرم شد بر پای خود بداشت [و] و به روایتی چهار دندان [ز] سلام مرا

stone, be patient until we deal with Muḥammad justly.' An angel was ordered to pick up this stone and put it among other stones on Mount Uḥud.'

{4} Rest of the story. the Companions said in a derogatory way during the battle, 'O Messenger of God! We have undertaken several battles and have vanquished the infidels. Who are these people now wishing to confront us?!' God did not like this statement and a proclamation was made: 'O Muḥammad, the Companions are proud of their power. Move alongside them and fight with the infidels of Uḥud. The huge battle began and there was a great fight. When the Companions looked to their youth, their plan turned into a fiasco, and seventy of the Companions were martyred. There was an Ethiopian there. He picked up that stone which had already been heated in the fire [by Muḥammad] and hit the Prophet's sacred tooth, injuring it. Another tradition mentions that two of his teeth were injured.

{5} So, O believer! The Prophet said one word in favour of his own tooth, or he put a stone into a fire for the sake of the pain in his leg; both actions received reprimands. When the master of Adam's children is reproached, what will be the case for others? Thus, one should review his own deeds and behaviour, and should always be concerned about the coming day on which nothing will be neglected and even the well mannered will be fearful and trembling.

{6} Another story. Once upon a time, the Prophet (pbuh) had gone into battle with infidels and the weather was extremely hot. Ibn Masʿūd came to the Messenger and said, 'O Prophet of God, I am about to die of thirst.' The Prophet looked around the desert and noticed a mountain far away. The Prophet said, 'Ibn Masʿūd, go near that mountain and say, "I am sent by the Prophet of God, as I am thirsty. Give me some water!"' Ibn Masʿūd then went to the mountain and said, 'The Prophet has sent me to you to give me water.' The mountain spoke and said, 'O Ibn Masʿūd, since this verse of the Qurʾān was revealed, "Then fear the fire fuelled with people and stones" (Q. 2:24), which means the fuel of hellfire is from human beings and stone, I fear God and have cried so much so that I have no more water.' When Ibn Masʿūd heard this, his thirst increased and he left the mountain. And the mountain said, 'O Ibn Masʿūd, convey my greetings to the Prophet (pbuh) and say to him, "O the Mercy of the Worlds! It was my honour that your sacred eyes viewed me. Pray for me, O Messenger of God, that God does not burn me among other stones [in hell]."' Ibn Masʿūd went to the Prophet and explained everything. The Prophet cried and lifted his hands in supplication saying, 'O God, the mountain seeks refuge from your torment. Do not burn him in the hellfire!'

مرا در میان آن سنگ‌ها نسوزانَد»». ابن‌مسعود نزد پیغمبر بیامد و احوال و التماس کوه بگفت. حضرت در گریه شد و دست به دعا برداشت و گفت «إلهِيّ، کوه از عذاب تو امان می‌طلبد. او را در میان دوزخ نسوزی».

{۷} پس مؤمن باید که به خود فکر کند که همچون حضرت محمّدی که مطلوب جمیع موجودات اوست از ایشان انصاف بستند،[۶] و دندان مبارک ایشان را مجروح کردند. و کوه بی‌گناه از ترس خدای تَعَالَی چندان گریسته که آب در او نمانده. و تو امروز از بهرِ متاعِ فانی، عقبیٰ فراموش کرده ای.[ح] امّا در عرصات قیامت ندامت‌ها و حسرت‌ها بَری.

{۸} إلهِيّ، من بیچارهٔ شکسته را و کاتب این قصّه را با جمیع مؤمنانِ دل‌حزین وچشم تمکین دهی و آب چشم را نجات آن جهان روزی گردانی. به حقّ محمّد وآله أجْمَعِین.

[۶] بستانند؟

[ح] در برخی نسخ این عبارات پایانی اضافه می شود (آورده‌اند که در روز قیامت «أمَنَّا به وَصدَّقنا» هریکی گناه‌کار چندان بگریند که از گریه او سیلها روان شود. اگر کشتی به‌رانی (برانی) از آبِ چشمِ هریکی کشتی‌ها روانِ روان شود. بعداز آن فرشتگان گویند که امروز گریه شما سود ندارد).

{7} Thus, a believer should reflect that even someone like Prophet Muḥammad, who is the most favoured of all creatures, has been treated with justice and his sacred tooth was damaged; and that the strange and faraway mountain cried to the extent that he had no more water. And you have forgotten the hereafter just for the sake of the world! But you will be filled with remorse and regret one the Day of Judgement!

{8} *O God, accept me, a humble pauper, and the scribe of this story along with all believers who have concerned hearts and eyes, and grant tears to save us in the next world. By Muḥammad and his household, together. [Amen.]*

در التماس
و در فضیلتِ خواجهٔ عالم، محمّد مُصطَفَی ﷺ

{۱} چنین آورده‌اند که روزی دل پیغمبر ﷺ در حضرت ذوالجلال خوش بود. دست به مناجات برد و می‌گفت «إِلٰهِيّ، ابراهیم پیغمبر ؈ را چندان ملک دادی که دنبال رمهٔ چهارپایانِ او هفتادهزار سگ با قلّاده‌های زرّین بیرون می‌شدندی. و برادرم مهتر سلیمان ؈ را چندان ملک دادی که نه پیش‌از وی و نه بعداز وی کسی را داده بودی. برادرم یوسف را در خواب وعدهٔ مُلک کردی و به آن رسانیدی».[الف] عطای هریکی از پیغمبران را در حضرت ذوالجلال عرض می‌کرد. آنگه گفت «إِلٰهِيّ، مرا و امّت مرا چه می‌دهی؟»

{۲} فرمان آمد که «ای محمّد، چیزی که تو را دادیم به هیچ پیغمبری ندادیم. و چیزی که امّت تو را دادیم به هیچ امّتی ندادیم. زیرا که شاه أنبیا تو را گردانیدم و بهترین امّت‌ها امّت تو را گردانیدیم. و هیچ چیز در آسمان‌ها و زمین آفریده نشد تا آنکه نور تو پیدا شد. و قسم به تو خوردیم که ای محمّد اگر در میان مطلوب تو نمی‌بودی هجده‌هزار[ب] عالم نمی‌آفریدیم و خدایی[ج] خود آشکار نمی‌کردیم. و چون تو را در شبِ معراج به قابِ قوسین رسانیدیم بعداز آن فرمان دادیم که عرض هفت آسمان و زمین پیش محمّد کنند. و با تو گفتیم ای حبیبِ حضرتِ ما دنیا وعقبی در خدمتِ تو آفریدیم. و گفتیم که ای محمّد! بِستان که با تو هیچ حساب و عقاب نباشد. و تو به گوشهٔ چشمی به آنها نظر نکردی، و گفتی: «فقر فخر منست، و من به جز لقا با بقای دوست به هیچ چیز دیگر خرسند نباشم».

[الف] برادرم مهتر یوسف را وعده، ملک در خواب کردی، و به ملک مصر رسانیدی [ب] هجده‌هزار [ج] قدرت

CHAPTER 10

An Entreaty

and on the virtue of the Master of the Worlds, Muḥammad (pbuh)

{1} It is reported that once upon a time, Muḥammad's heart was cherished by the love of God. He lifted his hands in supplication saying, 'O God, You granted Prophet Abraham (pbuh) power and sovereignty so that seventy thousand dogs with golden collars ran after his herd. And You granted sovereignty to my brother, His Eminence Solomon (pbuh) and had never given in such a way to anybody else before or after him. You promised my brother Joseph, while he was asleep, to grant him sovereignty, and you did so.' He [Muḥammad] was expounding before God the divine favours upon each prophet. He then said, 'O God, what will you grant me and my community?'

{2} A proclamation was made: 'O Muḥammad, what We have granted you, We have never granted to anyone else. And what We have granted to your community, we have never granted to other communities. We made you the king of prophets and determined your community to be the best of communities. And nothing was made in heaven nor Earth until your light first emerged. And We have sworn, "O Muḥammad, if you were not among the favoured ones, We would not have created eighteen thousand cosmoses nor demonstrated Our divinity." And once We brought you near to Us during the Night of Ascension, We then commanded the seven heavens and Earth should be shown before you. And We told you, "O friend of Our Throne, We have created this world and the other world at your service." And We said, "O Muḥammad, take it as there is no reckoning and punishment for you." But you did not take them into account and replied, "Poverty is my pride and I am not happy with anything other than being in the presence of my Friend."

{۳} «چون تو، ای محمّد، دلت دیدار ما اختیار کردی از این دولت زیادت[d] چیست که به تو دهم. دیگر امّت تو را مُلکی دادیم که ملک سلیمان و ملک یوسف به ملک ایشان نرسد. اگرچه ملک سلیمان مُلْكًا لَا يَنْبَغِي[۱] است، امروز سلیمان کجا و ملک او کجا؟ و اگرچه یوسف ملک رَبِّ قَدْ آتَيْتَنِي[۲] داشت، امروز یوسف کجا و ملک مصر او کجا؟ امّا امّت تو را ملک وفا دادند».

{۴} که پیغمبر علیه‌السلام گفت «إلهيّ، آن ملک کجاست؟» فرمان شد « وَإِذَا رَأَيْتَ ثَمَّ رَأَيْتَ نَعِيمًا وَمُلْكًا كَبِيرًا،[۳] یعنی در بهشت ایشان را ملک بزرگ دهیم که هیچ ملک دنیا بدان نرسد و زوال نپذیرد. امّا فردای قیامت ازجهت ملک دنیا، سلیمان و یوسف ندامت‌ها خورند که چرا دنیا خواستیم؛ آن مبغوضه[۴] حقّ تعَالَی بود». چون پیغمبر صلی‌الله‌علیه‌وسلم لطف و کرم خداوند تعَالَی را در حقّ امّت خود بسیار دید گفت «إلهيّ، حساب امّت من به دست من ده».[e] فرمان شد «بندگان ما در عرصات تا دیرگاه مانند، و سال‌ها باید تا از حساب خلاصی یابند. و ما نخواهیم تا نازنینانِ حضرت را در عرصات تا دیری در عقاب بداریم. و ما به کرم خود چنان حساب بر ایشان کنیم که نزدیک بر بنده یک‌ساعت نماید که فارغ شده باشند».

{۵} و دیگر. «ای محمّد، کافران و منافقان بر عایشه تهمت دروغ بکردند. تو دل از عایشه برگرفتی. تا[۵] هفتاد آیت در پاکی عایشه به تو فرستادیم. آنگاه با عایشه آشتی کردی. امّا در خاطر می‌گذرانیدی که «خدای تعَالَی کریم است، پردهٔ عایشه می‌پوشد».

{۶} تا همان‌روز که از همان‌کس که در گمان بودی، تو را بر خرمایستان[۶] بیرون آوردیم. تو وی را فرمودی که «بر درخت خرما بری و خرما فرود آر». ما هم درآن‌ساعت باد را فرمان دادیم که در وزیدن آید و عورت او را از میان بردار.[۷] چون باد در وزیدن آمد تو نظر خود بالا کردی تا جانب خود او را خوانی. نظر تو بر عورت او افتاد و آلت مردان ندیدی. در حیرت افتادی. آنگاه جبرئیل بیامد و گفت «ای محمّد، ما به علم خود دانسته بودیم که کافران و منافقان همچنین دروغ بر عایشه خواهند گفت. ازجهت این معنی امروز او را بی‌آلت آفریده بودیم. آنگاه دل تو از خیالات عایشه قرار گرفت».[۸]

{۷} و دیگر. «[ای محمّد،] شخصی به نزدیک تو آمد، و گفت «ای پیغمبر خدای، گناهی کرده‌ام بس عظیم». و تو فرمودی که «بگوی تا چه گناه کرده‌ای؟» او گفت «من عاشق دختر ملکی بودم. ناگاه او وفات کرد و وی را دفن کردند. چون شب آمد، من برفتم و تربت او را بشکافتم و او را در گور برگرفتم و بیرون کشیدم. و

[۱] آیهٔ ۳۵ سورهٔ ص. [۲] آیهٔ ۱۰۱ سورهٔ یوسف. [۳] آیهٔ ۲۰ سورهٔ انسان. [۴] در اصل، «مبغوضِ حقّ تعَالَی بوَد»

[۵] احتمالاً مراد اینست که «مرا در جریان حساب و کتاب پیروان دینم قرار بده». [۶] نخلستان.

[۷] در اینجا، عورت اشاره به ستر و پوشش دارد. [۸] مرتبط است به بحث‌های اعتقادی و روایی پیرامون «تهمت یا نسبت فحشا به عایشه» که در متون اسلامی اهل سنّت و تشیّع دیده می‌شود.

---

[d] بهتر [e] ما

{3} O Muḥammad! As your heart has requested to commune with Us, tell me, what is superior to this wealth so that I can give it to you? We have given your community a power which neither Solomon nor Joseph would be able to rival. Yet Solomon's power and authority is such that it 'will never be matched' (Q. 38:25) but now your power and Solomon's power are not comparable. And although Joseph has a power such that he said, 'My Lord! You have surely granted me [...]' (Q. 12:101), but now your power is not comparable with that of Joseph and his Egyptian authority. But your community has been granted the kingdom of faith!'

{4} Then the Prophet (pbuh) said, 'O God, where is that kingdom?' A response was revealed, '"And if you looked, you would see indescribable bliss and a vast kingdom" (Q. 76:20), which means that We have given them a large kingdom in paradise, that no earthly kingdom is comparable with, and which is everlasting. However, on the Day of Judgement, both Solomon and Joseph will be regretful, asking, "Why did we demand this world that is exteremly hated by God?"' When the Prophet (pbuh) became aware of such grace and kindness from God regarding his community, he said, 'O God, let me know how my community will be treated for their deeds on the Day of Judgement'. A proclamation was revealed, 'Our servants will wait on the Resurrection Plain for a very long time, and years must pass until they go through the final reckoning. But We do not like to torment the favourites of Our prophet on the Resurrection Plain. As such, We, as a kindness, will consider their cases without delay, a mere hour or so in the view of Our servants, so that they may be released.'

{5} Another story. 'O Muḥammad, both infidels and hypocrites accused ʿĀʾisha wrongly. You became disappointed. Then We sent down to you seventy signs[1] regarding the purity and chastity of ʿĀʾisha. Then you reproached ʿĀʾisha. Nonetheless, you were still thinking, "God is kind and will support ʿĀʾisha and not reveal the secret."

{6} Then, one day, We sent you out to the palm-grove with a fellow, the one you were already suspicious of. You asked him to go up the palm tree and bring down dates. We, in the meantime, ordered the wind to blow and remove the fellow's underwear. When the wind blew, you lifted up your head to call him to come down. You saw his private parts but did not see his penis. You were surprised. Then Gabriel arrived and said, "O Muḥammad, we knew through our eternal knowledge that infidels and hypocrites would accuse ʿĀʾisha. Hereby, we created this fellow without a penis." Then your heart was relieved about ʿĀʾisha.'

{7} Another story. A man came to the Prophet and said, 'O Prophet of God! I have committed a sin which is unbelievably great.' The Prophet asked, 'Tell me what you have done?' The man said, 'I was in love with a king's daughter. Suddenly, she died

[1] *āyāt*

خواستم که تا با وی نزدیکی کنم. او دست راست خود را جنبانید و بر شرمگاه خود نهاد. هرچند کردم که دست او را از شرمگاه او بردارم، نتوانستم؛ دست بریدم. او دست چپ پیش آورد. آن‌را هم ببریدم، و کار ناپسند کردم.

{۸} و از سر تربت خواستم که باز گردم او با من در سخن آمد. و گفت «ای نابکار، گناه عظیم کردی و مرا در میان لشگر مردگان جُنُب کردی». اکنون، ای پیغمبر خدای، پشیمان شده‌ام و نزد تو آمده‌ام. نمی‌دانم که در کدام درگه دوزخ عذاب من خواهد بود».

{۹} چون این سخن از وی بشنیدی، فی الحال از وی روی گردانیدی، وگفتی که «رو از پیش من. نباید که از نکبتِ گناه تو از آسمانْ عذابْ نازل شود. او گریان و ناامید رو به بیابان نهاد، و گفت «ای صَمَد و ای أَحَد، پیغمبر مرا از پیش خود رانْد. اگر تو هم مرا برانی، همچون منِ مردود را که راه دهد آخر؟» جبرئیل را به‌تو فرستادیم که او را از پیش خود مَران که آفریدگار ایشان نرانَد»».

{۱۰} و دیگر. «ای محمّد، امّتان جمیع پیغمبران همان‌قدر گناه کنند و امّتان تو همین‌قدر گناه کنند. امّا، در حقّ امّت تو به کرم خود گفته‌ایم که هي أُمَّة مذنبة ورَبّ غفور»[۹]. آنگاه، پیغمبر عليه السلام گفت «إلٰهيٓ، حساب امّتان خودِ تو خواستیم که با پیغمبرانِ دیگر فضحت نشود». فرمان آمد که «ای محمّد، چنانچه تو نمی‌خواهی که پیشِ پیغمبران دیگر فضیحت نشود، لطف [ما] نمی‌خواهد که پیش تو همه فضیحت شوند».

{۱۱} دیگر. «ای محمّد، موسیٰ به درگاه ما مناجات کرد که «إلٰهيٓ، به امّتِ محمّد چه معامله خواهی کرد؟»[۱۰] گفتیم «ای موسیٰ، چون محمّدیان را وقتِ جان دادن رسد در میان خود با یکدیگر گویند که هر جفایی که کرده بود همه را بِهٔ حلّ کردیم. آنگاه، فرمان شود که «ای فرشتگان، تفرّج کنید که امّت حبیب ما با یکدیگر مصالحت می‌کنند. به من شما نیز گواه باشید که من آفریدگار ایشانم». با ایشان مصالحت کردم و گناه ایشان را آمرزیدم».[۱۱]

[۹] عبارتی که در بسیاری از کتب روایی دیده می‌شود.

[۱۰] اشاره به داستان سی‌وپنجم یا «موسی‌نامه» دارد. چنین ارجاعاتی به داستان‌های پیش‌رو اثبات کنندهٔ این است که درّالمجالس از ابتدا حاوی بیش از سی‌وسه داستان بوده است.

[۱۱] احتمال اینکه این عبارت به موضوع کلامی-فقهی «مصالحة المیت» ربط داشته باشد وجود دارد.

and they buried her. When night arrived, I went to her and opened up her grave and took her out of the grave and was determined to be intimate with her. She moved her right hand and put it on her pudenda. Whenever I tried to remove her hand from her pudenda, I couldn't. I severed her hand. Then she raised her left hand. I severed it, too. And then I did the wrong thing.[2]

{8} When I wanted to leave the grave, she spoke to me and said, "O wicked one! You have committed a great sin and you put me in a state of impurity among the rest of the deceased." O Prophet of God! I am regretful and came to you. I do not know in what threshold of hell I will be punished.'

{9} When the Prophet heard this he turned away from him and said, 'Get away from me and hope that punishment and torment be not meted down on the Earth from heaven on account of your sin.' The man cried and went towards the desert, broken, and said, 'O the Everlasting Refuge! O the One! The Prophet rejected me! If You want also to reject me, then who would accept one as forsaken as me?' God sent Gabriel to Muḥammad, saying, 'Do not reject him as your Creator does not reject him.'

{10} And bear this 'O Muḥammad, the communities of other prophets have committed sins equal to your community. But We have kindly said regarding your community, "The community is guilty yet God is Forgiving."' Then the Prophet (pbuh) said, 'O God, I asked about the reckoning of my own community's affairs so that their failure should not be uncovered before other prophets.' A proclamation was revealed, 'O Muḥammad, as much as you do not want to be denounced before other prophets, our kindness does not desire for this to happen for others who went before you.'

{11} And another story. [God spoke] 'O Muḥammad, Moses had prayed in the presence of Our Throne, "O God, how will you treat Muḥammad's community?"'[3] [God replied,] 'O Moses, when Muslims near death, they tell each other that whatever one has done previously will be forgiven. Then a command is sent, "O angels, observe how the community of My friend is peacefully shaking hands. Take me as your witness that I am their Creator. I shall also shake hands with them and forgive their sins."'

[2] i.e., adultery [3] This is related to the theme and questions of Moses from God outlined in chapter thirty-five. This also demonstrates that *Durr al-Majālis* used to have more than thirty-three chapters.

{۱۲} و دیگر. مردی به خدمت رسول ﷺ آمد، و پرسید که «ای محمّد، مرا خبر کن که حسابِ امّت تو در دست که خواهد بود؟» گفت «ای پرسنده، چندان‌که خواستم که [...] فرمان شود». حقّ تَعَالَی می گوید که «حساب امّت تو ما خواهیم کرد». آن سائل به‌مجرّد شنیدنْ دست و پایش در جنبش درآمد و ثنای حقّ گفتن گرفت. و آنگاه سه کرّت گفت «رَضَیتُ رَضَیتُ رَضَیتُ». یاران پرسیدند که «چه دیدی که رضا شدی؟» بگفت «خدای را. یک نام او کریم است. زود سرِ گناه مشتی خاک می گذارد».

{۱۳} إلٰهِيّ، لطف تو قدیم است. من بیچاره را و کاتب این قصّه را با جمیع مؤمنان در آن روز شِمار [۱۲] آسان گردانی. بمِنَّة وَكَمَال كَرَمه.

[۱۲] روز حساب.

{12} And yet another story. A man came to the Prophet (pbuh) and asked, 'O Muḥammad, tell me who will be the master of your community's reckoning?'He said, 'O questioner! I have asked God […].' God says that 'We will reckon your community's account.' Upon hearing this, the questioner's hands and legs[4] began to shake and he praised God. And then said three times, 'I am satisfied! I am satisfied! I am satisfied!' The Companions asked him, 'What have you seen and realized that makes you satisfied?' He said, 'The God! One of his main attributions is Mercy. Soon he covers one's mistake with a small portion of soil.'

{13} *O God, you have been merciful since the beginning. Take ease on me, a poor fellow, and the scribe of this story, as well as all other believers on the Day of Reckoning. By Your unmerited favour and kindness. [Amen.]*

[4] i.e., became happy

در فضیلتِ شاه مردان أَمیر المُؤمِنین علی رَضِیَ اللهُ عَنهُ
با خاتون قیامت فاطمهٔ زهرا رَضِیَ اللهُ عَنهَا

{۱} آورده‌اند که روزی أَمیر المُؤمِنین علی رَضِیَ اللهُ عَنهُ با فاطمهٔ زهرا نشسته بودند. حضرت امیر حکایت سلیمان پیغمبر عَلَیهِ السَّلَام می‌کرد که «خدای او را چندان ملک داده بود در دنیا که هیچ‌کس را نداده بود. و چون مهتر سلیمان کار خیر دختر را پیش گرفت فرمود که تا به‌جهتِ داماد تاجی سازند که هفتصد جواهر درآن تاج باشد. هر جواهری ازآن خراجِ مملکتی بود.[الف] و قیمت دیگر گوهران هم، ای فاطمه، بدین قیاس باید دانست».[۱]

{۲} چون أَمیر المُؤمِنین علی کَرَّمَ اللهُ وَجهَه این حکایت گفت، در خاطر خاتون قیامت گذشت که «مگر حضرت امیر به‌جهت این می‌گوید که من هیچ چیز نیاوردم». و با شکستگیِ خاطر این اندیشه به دل می‌کرد و صبر می‌کرد. تا روزی خاتون قیامت به زیارت روضهٔ مقدّس حضرت رسول صَلَّی اللهُ عَلَیهِ وَسَلَّم رفت، و تربت را در کنار گرفت. می‌گفت که «ای پدر بزرگوار، در آرزوی جمال جهان‌آرای شما جهانِ روشن بر من تاریک شده‌است». و روی [بر؟] مرقد سیّد عالم نهاده بود و زارزار می‌گریست. بر تربت بود که به خواب رفت. و جمال جهان‌آرای پدر را در خواب دید. حضرت رسول عَلَیهِ السَّلَام می‌گفت «ای جگرگوشهٔ پدر، امروز فرمان شده‌است که «افطار با فاطمه رَضِیَ اللهُ عَنهَا بکنید». اکنون با مادر تو در انتظار آمدن تو می‌پریم[۲]».

[۱] به‌گمان من، جملهٔ پایانی اشاره دارد به توقع علی از توجه خانوادهٔ عروس به داماد. [۲] می‌پزیم؟

[الف] که تا به‌جهت داماد کلاهی راست کردند که هیچ‌کس آن را ندیده بود و هفتصد گوهر در آن کلاه مرتب کردند که هر گوهری خراج ولایتی بود.

CHAPTER 11

On the Virtue of the Hero, the Commander of Believers ʿAlī (pbuh)

with the Lady of the Day of Judgement Fāṭima al-Zahrāʾ (pbuh)

{1} It is reported that once upon a time, the Commander of Believers, ʿAlī (pbuh), sat with Fāṭima Zahrā. ʿAlī was explaining the story of Prophet Solomon in that 'God had granted him a kingdom that no one had before been given. When His Eminence Solomon wanted to prepare his daughter's wedding ceremony, he ordered that a crown be made for the groom on which there should be seven hundred gems. Every single gem on the crown could cover the expenses of a nation. O Fāṭima, other good grooms deserves to be admired, similiarly!'

{2} When the Commander of Believers ʿAlī (pbuh) told this story, it crossed the mind of the Lady of the Day of Judgement, 'Does ʿAlī tell this story because I did not bring anything into this life?' Sadly, she pondered this thought and tried to be patient. Then one day, the Lady of the Day of Judgement went to visit the holy tomb of the Messenger (pbuh). She fell and hugged the grave and said, 'O my honourable father, as I wait again to visit your beautiful face, by which the world is adorned, the world seems dark to me.' And she had put her face on the grave of the Master the Universe and lamented. Lying on the grave, she fell asleep. And she saw the beautiful face with which the world was adorned. The Messenger (pbuh) said, 'O darling of your father, an order arrived today, "You should break your fast with Fāṭima (pbuh)." Now I and your mother are excited that you are going to come to us.'

{۳} فاطمهٔ زهرا رَضِيَ اللهُ عَنْهَا درزمانْ از خواب بیدار شد و به خانه آمد. أَمیر المُؤمِنین حسن و حسین را نزدیک خود نشاند، و در روی ایشان نظر کرد و می‌گریست و می‌گریست و زمانی باز شادی می‌کرد. حضرت أَمیر المُؤمِنین علی از آن حالت عجب آمد. پرسید که «یا فاطمه، گریهٔ تو چیست و شادی تو از بهر چیست؟» گفت «یا علی، مرا سفر قیامت پیش آمده‌است. چون بی‌مادری فرزندان، حسن و حسین، به‌خاطرم می‌رسد گریه می‌آید.[۳] و چون آروزی آن جهان می‌کنم، که به خدمت معبود خود خواهم رفت و جمال پدر و مادر خواهم دید، شادی روی می‌دهد». آنگاه سخن چند دیگر گفت و کلمهٔ توحید بر زبان راند، و جان به حضرت حق سُبْحَانَهُ وَتَعَالَى تسلیم کرد.[ب]

{۴} فغان از اهل مدینه برخاست؛ گویی که آن روز قیامت شده بود. ابوبکر و یاران خود نماز جنازه گذاردند. یکی پایهٔ[ج] محفه ابوبکر برداشت، و پایهٔ دیگر عمر، و پایهٔ دیگر عثمان و علی کَرَّمَ اللهُ وجْهَه برگرفت. به گورستان روان شدند. سلمان فارسی رَضِيَ اللهُ عَنْهُ پیش‌از جنازه روی به گورستان آورد و روان شد و در آن موضع که به‌جهت حضرت فاطمه رَضِيَ اللهُ عَنْهَا اختیار کرده بودند نزدیک آن مقام رفت، و گفت «ای زمین، هیچ می‌دانی نزد تو که را می‌آرند؟ فاطمهٔ زهرا، جگرگوشهٔ حضرت محمّد مُصْطَفَى صَلَّى اللهُ عَلَيْهِ وَسَلَّمَ و مادرش خدیجهٔ کبری و حرم[د] علی مرتضی و مادر حسن و حسینِ شهیدِ کربلا، و شفیع زنان در روز قضا.» از زمین آوازی برآمد که «ای سلمان، از آن زیاده‌تر است که کس خیال کند».

{۵} چون خاتون قیامت را دفن کردند، حضرت امیر شب اوّل به خواب می‌بیند که فاطمهٔ زهرا پیش در بهشت استاده. دربان نمی‌گذارد که درآید. حضرت امیر گفت «یا فاطمه، حالت چیست که در پیشِ در استاده‌ای؟» گفت «فرمان به رضوان بهشت شده‌است که «فاطمه را درون بهشت نگذارند، که امانتی در گردن خود دارد»». و [فاطمه] گفت «یا علی، من سوزن همسایه آورده بودم تا پیرهن خود بدوزم. مرا از خاطر فراموش شده بود. اکنون بشتاب و برو، در فلان محلِّ دیوار خانه گذاشته‌ام؛ گرفته به صاحب ده».[ه] امیر چون از خواب بیدار شد نزدیک آن دیوار رفته و سوزن را یافته، به صاحبش برسانید.

{۶} شب دوم حضرت امیر به خواب دید که فاطمه در صدر بهشت بر تختی نشسته و حوران بر گِرد او صف زده‌اند و ایستاده‌اند؛ و بر دست هریک طبقی از موز.[۴،و] و بر هر طرف نظر کرد دید که حوران هفتاد هزار و پیشتر با حلّه‌های رنگ‌برنگ بر دست گرفته، نشسته و منتظر تا که‌را[۵] نزدیک خود خواند. حضرت امیر دختری را نزدیک فاطمه رَضِيَ اللهُ عَنْهُ دید که طبقی از پیرایه‌های گوهر و یاقوت بر دست گرفته و منتظر استاده است تا کِی خاتون قیامت آن‌را از دستِ او بسْتاند.

[۳] این قسمت را می‌توان در راستای داستان سی ویکم پیرامون شهادت حسن و حسین تفسیر نمود.
[۴] اشاره به «موز» در این متن دلالت به آشنایی مولّف و یا کاتب با این میوه دارد.
[۵] چه‌کسی‌را.

[ب] آنگاه وصیّت چندی که مشهور است در میان هردو بگذشت. بعداز آن جان بحقّ تسلیم کرد [ج] پایِ [د] جفت
[ه] بگیر و به خداوندش برسان [و] بر دست هریکی طبق‌های گوناگون و نعمت‌ها درآن و شربت‌ها

{3} Right after this, Fāṭima Zahrā (pbuh) woke up and went home. She drew the commanders of believers Ḥasan and Ḥusayn to her and looked at their faces and cried, and again looked at their faces and became cheerful. The Commander of Believers, ʿAlī, was surprised when he saw her behaviour. He asked her, 'O Fāṭima, what do you cry for and what causes your happiness?' She replied, 'O ʿAlī, I am about to leave this world, travel to the hereafter. When I thought of my children, Ḥasan and Ḥusayn, being motherless I began to cry, and when I thought of my desire for the next world and that I would go before my God and see the beautiful faces of my father and mother, then I became cheerful.' Then she said a few more words and expressed her belief in the divine unity and submitted her soul to God.

{4} The people of Medina gathered and wailed so much it seemed as though the Day of Judgement had arrived.[1] Abū Bakr and his companions began to pray over her corpse. One side of the coffin was taken by Abū Bakr, another side by ʿUmar, and the remaining sides by ʿUthmān and ʿAlī. They went towards the cemetery. Salmān the Persian (pbuh) proceeded in advance to the cemetery and went to the place that had already been prepared for Fāṭima (pbuh). He said, 'O Earth, do you know whom they bring to you?! Fāṭima Zahrā, darling of the Prophet Muḥammad (pbuh) and her mother, the great Khadīja, and the wife of ʿAlī, the one well approved by God, and the mother of Ḥasan and Ḥusayn, the martyrs of Karbala, and the intercessors of women on the Day of Judgement.' A voice came out of the Earth, 'O Salmān, this is much more than one could ever imagine!'

{5} When they buried the Lady of the Day of Judgement, ʿAlī dreamed the first night that Fāṭima stood before the gate of paradise, and the gatekeeper did not allow her to enter. ʿAlī then said, 'O Fāṭima, what has happened that you have had to wait before the gate?' She said, 'The gatekeeper of paradise has been ordered "not to permit Fāṭima to enter paradise, as there is a trusted item to return".' She said, 'O ʿAlī, my neighbour gave me a sewing needle in order to sew my cloth. I had totally forgotten to return it to the neighbour. Go as fast as possible to that place on the wall at home. Take it and give it back to its owner.' When ʿAlī woke up, he went to that wall and found the needle and took it back to the owner.

{6} On the second night, ʿAlī slept and dreamed that Fāṭima sat on a throne at the top of paradise and houris lined up and stood around her. And in the hands of each there was a tray of bananas. And wherever he looked, there were seventy thousand houris with many colourful garments, sitting and waiting for Fāṭima's order to see which of them would be asked to come close. ʿAlī saw a girl near Fāṭima (pbuh) who

[1] Referring to crying and lamenting after the death of a special person

{۷} حضرت امیر گفت «یا فاطمه، عظمت و بزرگی تو معلوم شد.[۶] امّا این دختر که طبقی بر دست جواهر گرفته کیست؟» فاطمه گفت «یا علی، شما روزی با من حکایت می کردید که سلیمان پیغمبر ؑ چون دختر خود را به داماد سپرد، و از هرجنس نفیس تاجی مرصّع که هفتصد جواهر در آن بود که هر جواهر خراج مملکتی بود بهرِ داماد داد. چون به من این حکایت کردی، در خاطر من گذشت مگر در خاطر علی می‌آید که «به دامادی حضرت محمّد چیز نیافتم».[ز] صبر وشکستگی به‌حضرت خداوند عزّوجلّ کردم. چون فرمان شد که مرا در بهشت آوردند، خطاب رسید که دختر سلیمان را حاضر کنند تا طبقی از برای فاطمه بر دست گیرد و به‌خدمت او مشرّف گردد. این آن دختر است که پیش من استاده‌است».

{۸} نظیر دیگر. چون قیامت قایم شود، خلق اوّلین و آخرین حاضر گردانند. و لِوای محمّدی بیآرند و در عرصات بدارند.[ح] و صفت عَلَم پیغمبر ﷺ بسیار است. اما مختصر بشنو که هفتاد هزارساله راه‌درازی عَلَم[ط] حضرت محمّد ﷺ بود و زلازلها در وی آویخته، در هر زلزله قبّه از نور باشد، و درون هر قبّه حوریِ باجمال نشسته باشد، و بر دست هر حوری براتی داده باشند که فلان بن فلان جفت گشت.[ی]

{۹} حوران نظر در نوشته‌های خود می کنند و دست دراز می کنند؛ هریکی را بر عَلَم بر [...] آرند. چون اینچنین دولت خداوند تَعَالَی نصیب بندگان خود می کند. فرمان شود که «ای فرشتگان، پیش روید و دست بر عَلَم زنید و از پل صراط بگذرانید». هرچند زور کنند از جای نتوانند جنباند؛ بس عاجز شوند. فرمان شود که «ای فرشتگان، از عَلَم محمّد دور شوید، و أسدالله را حاضر کنید».

{۱۰} به حکم فرمانْ أَمیر المُؤمِنین علی رضی‌الله‌عنه حاضر شود. خطاب ذوالجلال در رسید که «ای شیرخواندهٔ حضرت ما، تو قوّت خود در دنیا نیازموده‌ای که ببینی چه مقدار قوّت به تو داده‌ایم. این عَلَم که تمام فرشتگان از جای نتوانستند جنبانید تو بردار، و از پل صراط بگذر». به‌مجرّد شنیدن فرمان، حضرت امیر پیش رفت و دست در عَلَم زد و همچو گلدسته برگیرد و پل صراط بگذراند. همان ساعت حقّ سبحانه‌وتعالی باد را فرمان داد که «علی را بردار و از پل صراط بگذران». باز فرمان شود که «یا علی، عَلَم را برگیر و به سوی هوا کن». در آن وقت عَلَم بر سر علی مثال تاج باشد، و بندگان مؤمن گوهر آن تاج باشند.

[۶] در برخی نسخ چنین اضافه می‌شود (که تو را به کرامات بهشت رسانید)

[ز] در خاطر من این گذشت که مگر در فکر علی این می‌گذرد که «او به داماد خود این مقدار چیزی بداد»، به دامادی پیغمبر ؑ چیزی نیافت [ح] در عرصات نصب کنند [ط] لوای [ی] و بر دست هر حوری براتی باشد که فلان بن فلان جفت نیست، و فلان عورت شدهٔ توست

held a tray of ornaments made of gems and was waiting until the Lady of the Day of Judgement took the tray from her hand.

{7} ʿAlī said, 'O Fāṭima, your greatness and glory is already apparent. But who is this girl, holding the tray of gems?' Fāṭima said, 'O ʿAlī, you had already told me the story of Solomon and how he gave his daughter to the groom and that a crown was made for him, adorned with seven hundred gems, that every gem could cover the expenses of a nation. Once you told this story I wondered whether you thought had been given nothing after becoming the son-in-law of the Prophet." I tried to be patient and waited before God. When an order arrived bringing me to paradise, a voice was heard calling for the daughter of Solomon to prepare a tray for Fāṭima and come to her service. This girl who stands before me is that daughter of Solomon.'

{8} Another story. When the Day of Judgement begins, the first and last people will appear. And a Muḥammadan standard will be brought, and raised on the plain. And the attributions of the Prophet's (pbuh) standard are numerous. But listen! To be brief, seventy thousand years were represented by the length of the standard of the Prophet Muḥammad (pbuh) on which were hangers and on every hanger was a cupola of light and inside every cupola was a beautiful houri, and a note had to be placed in their hand regarding the man[2] they married with.

{9} The houris looked at the notes and extended their hands.[3] They get closer to the standard [...]. This glory is only granted to the servants by God. Then a command arrived: 'O angels, move forward and take the standard and take it across Ṣirāṭ[4].' Whatever they tried, they could not move the standard. Then they became exhausted. A divine command was given: 'O angels, stay away from the standard of Muḥammad. And bring the Lion of God.'

{10} After the divine order was given the Commander of Believers, ʿAlī, arrived. The statement of the Glorified One comes, 'O the one we call the Lion; you have not yet seen power in the world until you observe how much power we have given to you. Pick up this standard, the one that all the angels were unable to move, and cross with it over the bridge of Ṣirāṭ.' God ordered the wind to carry ʿAlī across the bridge of Ṣirāṭ. Then, again, a command was given: 'O ʿAlī take the standard and raise it.' At that moment, the standard placed on ʿAlī's head like a crowne and the believing servants resembled the gems of the crown.

[2] i.e., Muḥammad(?) [3] i.e., they are concerned and waited to be chosen

[4] i.e., the bridge over hell leading to paradise

{۱۱} فرمان شود که «ای علی، پیش فاطمه حدیث تاج‌دادن داماد سلیمان می‌کردی؟» حالا، یک‌نظر در سر خود کن که تاج دادیم؛ که عَلَم محمّد تاجِ سر تو گشته و بندگان مطیع ما گوهر آن تاج شده‌اند». این مرتبه و درجهٔ شفیع زنان امّت را باشد و عظمت او در حضرت خداوند چنین بود.

{۱۲} و دیگر. چون بهشتیان به بهشت برسد، ناگاه نوری در بهشت پیدا گردد که اهل بهشت پندارند که نور تجلّیست. جمله سرها به سجده برند. فرمان شود «ای بندگان ما، سر از سجده بردارید که این نور دیدار ما نیست. علی و فاطمه میان خود حکایت می‌کنند؛ این نور دیدار ایشان است که روشنی بهشت را معلوم کرد. و به نور دندان خویش منوّر گردانیده‌اند».

{۱۳} إِلٰهِيّ، به حرمت خاتون بهشت[ک] منِ شکسته را و کاتب این قصّه را و جمیع مؤمنان را بهشت روزی گردان. به حقّ مُحَمَّد وَ آلِهِ أَجْمَعِين.

[ک] إِلٰهِيّ، به حرمت ساقی بهشت که علی مرتضی است و به حقّ خاتون جنّت که فاطمه است

{11} Then a command came: 'O ʿAlī, did you tell Fāṭima about the coronation of Solomon's groom?! Now have a look at your own head. We gave you a crown; the standard of Muḥammad is your crown and our obedient servants are its gems.' This is the level and dignity of the intercessor of the women of the nation, and this is her high status before God.

{12} And another story. When the people of paradise reach paradise, a light appears suddenly, a light which the people of paradise assume is the light of God's theophanic manifestation. They all prostrate. Then a command comes: 'O servants! Arise from prostration as this is not Our light. ʿAlī and Fāṭima are speaking with each other; it is the light of their meeting that illuminates paradise. And [everywhere] is illuminated with the light of their teeth.'

{13} *O God, by the infallibility of the Lady of Paradise, grant paradise to this humble pauper together with the scribe of this story and all believers. By Muḥammad, and all his family. [Amen.]*

حکایتِ ماریه قبطیه، خدمتکار محمّد مُصطَفی ﷺ[1]

{۱} آورده‌اند که ماریه را از مُلک حبش[۲] به خدمت پیغمبر ﷺ فرستاده بودند. حضرت فرمودند که ماریه را در حجرهٔ حَفصَه، که دختر أَمیر المُؤمِنین عُمر باشد، برند. بعداز آن حضرت به حجرهٔ حَفصَه تشریف آوردند و فرمودند «ای دختر عمر، هیچ چیز داری از خوردنی؟» حَفصَه گفت «ندارم». پیغمبر گفت «برو شاید در خانهٔ پدرت چیزی باشد، بیار». امّا حَفصَه و ماریه هر دو در یک حُجره می‌بودند. حَفصَه روی به‌جانب [خانهٔ] پدر کرد.[الف] حضرت حجره خالی یافت و ماریه را نزدیک خود خواند. با وی خلوت کرد.[۳]

{۲} و در راه حَفصَه را به خاطر رسید که «حجره خالیست و ماریه در آن حجره است و مرا به این تقرب فرستاده که می‌خواهد امروز با وی خلوت کند».[۴] این اندیشه کرد و از راه خانهٔ پدر برگشت و به شتاب می‌آمد. چون بیامد دید که درِ خانه بسته است. چون رسول علیه‌السلام آواز پای شنید، درحال حضرت درِ حجره را باز کرد. چشم پیغمبر علیه‌السلام با چشم حَفصَه چهارشد. حَفصَه در آمد[ب] و گفت «یا نبي اَللّٰه، امروز نوبت من بودی و با ماریه خلوت کردید!» پیغمبر ﷺ حَفصَه را در کنار گرفته[ج] و گفت «از بهر خاطر تو بعداز این ماریه را بر خود حرام کردم. امّا این سخن[د] بر عایشه نگویی و با خود داری».

[1] در برخی نسخ عنوان دیگری به چشم می‌خورد: باب دوازدهم در حکایتِ ماریه قبطیه و حَفصَه که خدمتکار پیغمبر علیه‌السلام بودند. بنابر گزارش‌های منابع اسلامی، این داستان مرتبط است به آیهٔ اوّل سورهٔ تحریم و تفاسیر مرتبط با آن. در بسیاری از تفاسیر، بویژه تفاسیر دوران میانهٔ اسلامی، این آیه در رابطه با حضرت محمّد و سه همسر وی، عایشه، حَفصَه و ماریه قبطیه (بنابر تفسیر طبری: «مارية مملوكته القبطية») معرّفی شده است. با این وجود، شباهت این داستان به آنچه در تفسیر کَشفُ الأَسرَار از رشید الدین میبدی دیده می‌شود بیشتر است. رجوع کنید به رشید الدین میبدی، کشف الاسرار و عدة الابرار، به اهتمام علی اصغر حکمت (تهران: امیرکبیر، ۱۳۷۱/۱۹۹۲)، ج ۱۰، ص ۱۵۵.

[۲] سرزمین حبشه. [۳] براساس دهخدا، این واژه هم معنی «مجامعت کردن» نیز است. [۴] امّا در راه رفتن، در دل حَفصَه بگذشت که حجرهٔ من خالیست و ماریه در آن حجره است. و مرا هرگز پیغمبر علیه‌السلام به‌جهت طعام به خانهٔ پدرم نفرستاده بود. امروز مکرّراً با ماریه خلوت می‌کند.

[الف] به حکم و فرمان پیغمبر علیه‌السلام روی به خانهٔ پدر کرد و می‌رفت [ب] حَفصَه زبان بگشاد
[ج] پیغمبر به غایت از روی حَفصَه شرمنده شد [د] سرّ مرا

CHAPTER 12

The story of Mary the Copt, the servant of Muḥammad (pbuh)[1]

{1} It is reported that Mary[2] had been sent to the Prophet (pbuh) from the Kingdom of Ethiopia. The Prophet said that he led Mary to the house of Ḥafṣa, the daughter of the Commander of Believers, ʿUmar. Later on, the Prophet also went to Ḥafṣa's house. He asked, 'O daughter of ʿUmar, do you have anything to eat?' Ḥafṣa replied, 'No, I do not.' The Prophet said, 'Go out and check whether there is something in your father's house that you can bring.' But Ḥafṣa and Mary shared the same chamber so when Ḥafṣa went towards her father's house the Prophet felt alone in the chamber with no one around except Mary. He called Mary to him. And he had lay with her.

{2} On her way Ḥafṣa thought, 'No one was in the chamber except Mary, and [the Prophet] sent me out just as if he wished to get close to and lay with her.' She reflected on this and turned back quickly. When she arrived she noticed that the door to the house was closed. When the Messenger (pbuh) heard her coming he swiftly opened the door. The Prophet's (pbuh) eye locked with Ḥafṣa's eye. Ḥafṣa came in and said, 'O Prophet of God, you were supposed to be with me today but you instead laid with Mary.' The Prophet (pbuh) hugged Ḥafṣa and said, 'I have now forbidden Mary to lay with me just because of you, but do not say what I have now told you to ʿĀʾisha; treat it confidentially.'

[1] Classical Islamic exegetical works and Qurʾānic commentaries include references to Muḥammad and his three wives, ʿĀʾisha, Ḥafṣa, and Mary the Copt on the basis of the first verse (and other verses) of Q. 66. However, the closest resemblance to this story of *Durr al-Majālis* is the commentary of Rashīd al-Dīn Maybudī, *Kashf al-Asrār.*

[2] i.e., Mary the Copt (Māriya al-Qibṭiya)

{۳} و دیگر. حَفْصَه از برای پیغمبر علیه‌السلام شهد[۵] موجود کرده داشتی. چون پیغمبر ﷺ از صحبت اصحاب بازگشتی در حُجرهٔ حَفْصَه[۶] آمدی و گفتی که «چیزی هست تا بخوریم؟» او در زمانْ شهد را پیش آوردی. حضرت عایشه شنیدند که حضرت در حُجرهٔ حَفْصَه شهد و نان خورده‌اند. ناخوش آمد که رسول از جهت خوردنِ شهد دائم به حجرهٔ حَفْصَه درآید. چون رسول از حجره حَفْصَه درآمد و به حجرهٔ عایشه آمدند، عایشه پرسید «یا رسول الله، چه خورده‌اید که بوی دهن شما تبدیل شده است؟» رسول علیه‌السلام فرمودند که «شهد خورده‌ام». گفت «یا رسول الله، شهید پَس‌ماندهٔ مگس[۷] است». [ه] رسول گفت «اگر چنین است بر خود حرام کردم».

{۴} تا روزی حَفْصَه و عایشه هر دو نشسته بودند و حکایت می‌کردند. ناگاه از زبان عایشه بیرون آمد که «ای حَفْصَه، می‌بینی که حضرت را با ماریه آمیزش نیست؟»[د] حَفْصَه گفت «او را رسول از جهت من بر خود حرام کرده‌است». و تمام قصّه را پیش عایشه گفت. تا روزی عایشه در خدمت پیغمبر ﷺ نشسته بود. ناگاه بر زبان عایشه آمد که «نبي الله، چرا ماریه را بر خود حرام کرده‌ای؟» رسول گفت «تو از کجا دانستی؟» عایشه گفت «حَفْصَه با من گفت». حضرت فرمودند «چنانچه حَفْصَه سِر مرا، که با او منع کرده بودم، پیش تو گفت، من حَفْصَه را هم بر خود حرام کردم».

{۵} و پیغمبر ﷺ به غایت منقوض[۸] که مهتر جبرئیل در رسید و گفت «ای محمّد، فرمان شد که ماریه بی‌گناه و غریب است. تو چرا بر خود حرام کرده‌ای؟ به‌موجبِ فرمودهٔ ما، هم‌در[۹] آن حجرهٔ حَفْصَه یک ماه با ماریه خلوت کن و از حجره بیرون میای و در مسجد بهر جماعت هم نروی». به‌موجبِ فرموده رسول علیه‌السلام عمل می‌نمودند و از حجره بیرون نمی‌آمدند. یاران از بهر لقای مبارک پیغمبر ﷺ اضطراب[ذ] داشتند.

{۶} چون أَمیر المُؤمِنین ابوبکر و عمر را معلوم شد که به‌سبب دخترانشان از دیدار پیغمبر محروم شده‌اند، أَمیر المُؤمِنین عمر خطّاب را طاقت نمانْد. دست به تیغ برد و روی به حجرهٔ حَفْصَه کرد. چون نزدیک دختر رسید گفت «چرا چنین سخن گفتی که دل مبارک ایشان از تو رنجیده شده است، و ما از دیدار آن حضرت محروم ماندیم؟ اکنون سر تو از تنِ تو جدا کنم». حَفْصَه آب در چشم آورد و گفت «ای پدر، پیغمبر به کشتن من تو را رضا داده است یا نه؟» از این سخن أَمیر المُؤمِنین عمر رضی‌الله‌عنه اندیشه کرد که «اگر چه حَفْصَه دختر من است امّا الآن به حوالهٔ پیغمبر ﷺ است. چون او را کشته باشم، جواب پیغمبر چه گویم؟ باری بر در آن حُجره که حضرت آنجاست روم و بپرسم که احوال چیست».

[۵] در متون ترکی و پنجابی این داستان هم از کلمهٔ «شهد» استفاده شده است. ولی باور عامیانه اینست که مراد از «شهد» همان «شیره» یا «عسل» می‌باشد که با نان صرف می‌شود.
[۶] در برخی نسخ، محمّد در حُجرهٔ قبطیه وارد می‌شود.
[۷] بنابر دهخدا، زنبور عسل در برخی متون گذشته با عنوان «مگس»، «مگس انگبین» یا «مگس شهد» شناخته می‌شده است. با این وجود، گویا این متن «مگس» را نشان آلودگی در نظر گرفته است. لذا آن را به‌صورت flies ترجمه می‌کنم.
[۸] (منقض)؛(منقضب). «منقوض» به معنی «شکسته» هم به‌کار می‌رود.
[۹] هم‌اکنون.

[ه] عایشه گفت «یا رسول الله چگونه بوی نباید و تبدیل نشود»
[د] «ای حَفْصَه، می‌بینی که رسول علیه‌السلام را با ماریه میلش نیست؟»
[ذ] خسته خاطر

{3} And the other story. Ḥafṣa had made a honey syrup for the Prophet (pbuh). When the Prophet arrived in Ḥafṣa's house after his discussion with his Companions, he said, 'Is there anything for us to eat?' She hastily brought forward the dish. The lady ʿĀʾisha understood that the Prophet had been eating honey syrup and bread in Ḥafṣa's house. She became upset that the Prophet frequently went to Ḥafṣa's house to eat honey syrup and bread. When the Prophet left Ḥafṣa's house and arrived in ʿĀʾisha's house, ʿĀʾisha asked, 'O Messenger of God, what have you eaten that your mouth smells differently?' The Messenger (pbuh) replied, 'I have eaten honey syrup.' She replied, 'O Messenger of God, this honey syrup has been made of flies.' The Messenger (pbuh) said, 'If it is as you say, then I forbid myself from eating it.'

{4} One time, Ḥafṣa and ʿĀʾisha sat together, chatting. Suddenly, ʿĀʾisha exclaimed, 'O Ḥafṣa, did you notice that the Prophet has not laid with Mary?' Ḥafṣa said, 'The Prophet has forbidden himself from her just because of me.' Then she told the whole story to ʿĀʾisha. One day, ʿĀʾisha was sitting near the Prophet. Suddenly, she exclaimed, 'O Prophet of God, why have you forbidden yourself from Mary?' The Prophet asked, 'How did you know?' ʿĀʾisha said, 'Ḥafṣa told me the story.' The Prophet said, 'As Ḥafṣa revealed my secret to you, which I had asked her not to do, I now forbid myself from Ḥafṣa, too.'

{5} Thus, the Prophet's (pbuh) heart sank. In the meantime, His Eminence Gabriel arrived and said, 'O Muḥammad, a divine proclamation has arrived indicating that Mary is not guilty and she is alone. Why did you forbid yourself from her?! Follow Our command, go to that chamber beloning to Ḥafṣa and stay with Mary and lay with her for one month and do not leave the house and do not go to the mosque for congregational prayer.' The Prophet acted accordingly, and did not leave the house. The Companions were concerned by not being able to meet the Prophet.'

{6} When the commanders of believers Abū Bakr and ʿUmar realised that they had been deprived from meeting the Prophet because of their daughters, ʿUmar Khaṭṭāb could not tolerate it. He took his sword and went towards the house of Ḥafṣa. When he arrived, he said to his daughter, 'Why did you say this to break the Prophet's heart and upset him, and prevent us from meeting him? I will behead you now.' Ḥafṣa began to cry and said, 'O father, would the Prophet allow you to kill me or not?' Upon hearing Ḥafṣa's question, ʿUmar reflected, 'Although Ḥafṣa is my daughter, now she is under the Prophet's authority. If I kill her, how would I answer to the Prophet? Anyway, I shall go to that house in which the Prophet lives and see what he says.'

{٧} أَمیر المُؤمِنین عمر رَضِیَ‌اللهُ‌عَنهُ پیش در رسید و مهتر جبرئیل پیش‌از آن به خدمت پیغمبر صَلَّی‌اللهُ‌عَلَیهِ‌وَسَلَّم آمد و گفت «یا محمّد، عمر پیش در رسیده است. او را درون نطلبی و با او سخن نگویی». و أَمیر المُؤمِنین عمر پیش در استاده، زاری و ناله می‌کرد و می‌گفت «یا رسول اللّه، جان حَفْصَه با جان پدر و مادر من نثار قدم تو باد. چیست که بیرون نمی‌آیی؛ جمله جهانِ روشن بر ما تاریک گشته». هرچند پیشِ در سخن می‌گفت درِ حجره را نگشودند. آنگاه گفت «ای پیغمبر خدای تَعَالَی، عُمرِ بیچاره شکسته‌دل و پرخون بازمی‌گردد». فرمان شد که «در حجره بگشا امّا با عُمر سخن نگویی». به‌موجبِ فرموده پیغمبر در را باز کرد و عُمر درآمد. هرچند خواست که حضرت با او سخن گوید، پیغمبر عَلَیهِ‌السَّلَام با وی سخن نگفتند.

{٨} عُمر برخاست و بیرون آمد و پیش دختر خود رفت و گفت «هرچند خواستم که حضرت با من سخن کند نکرد. اکنون برو تا از تو خشنود شوند. و گرنه ما از تو راضی نشویم و دست از جان خود بِشُوی که سر از تن تو جدا کنم».

{٩} حَفْصَه برخاست و پیش عایشه رفت و گفت «اگر گناه کردیم هر دو کرده‌ایم. اکنون، بیا ای عایشه تا هر دو پیش رسول عَلَیهِ‌السَّلَام رویم». عایشه و حَفْصَه گریان هر دو رو به حجرهٔ پیغمبر صَلَّی‌اللهُ‌عَلَیهِ‌وَسَلَّم کردند. [گفتند] «شاید که از ما خشنود شود». باز گفتند «به درگاه حقّ سُبحَانَهُ‌وَتَعَالَی برویم و عجز و بیچارگی کنیم». هر دو سر سجده نهادند و زاری می‌کردند و می‌گفتند «إِلٰهِيّ، پیغمبر تو از ما روی گردانیده است. چون به کَرَمِ تدبیرِ ما نکنی، بر درِ کی رویم؟ و به جز تو ندامت‌زدگان را دستگیری که کند؟ هم تو را معلوم است که از فراقِ جمال پیغمبر صَلَّی‌اللهُ‌عَلَیهِ‌وَسَلَّم، نزدیک آمده‌است که جان ما از کالبد برآید».

{١٠} درزمانْ جبرئیل عَلَیهِ‌السَّلَام رسید و این آیه وحی آورد «يَا أَيُّهَا النَّبِيُّ لِمَ تُحَرِّمُ مَا أَحَلَّ اللَّهُ لَكَ تَبْتَغِي مَرْضَاتَ أَزْوَاجِكَ وَاللَّهُ غَفُورٌ رَّحِيمٌ»[١٠] یعنی ای محمّد حلال کرده ماریه را بر تو که حرام گرداند، با عایشه و حَفْصَه صلح کن»[ح] و این آیه بر ایشان برخوان «ضَرَبَ اللَّهُ مَثَلًا لِّلَّذِينَ كَفَرُوا امْرَأَتَ نُوحٍ وَامْرَأَتَ لُوطٍ كَانَتَا تَحْتَ عَبْدَيْنِ مِنْ عِبَادِنَا»[١١] یعنی فردای قیامت زن نوح و زن لوط پیغمبر را هر دو در آتش دوزخ فرستیم. ای جفتان محمّد نباید که شما در خاطر آورید که «اهل و عیال محمّدیم». اگر این معنی نفع کردی، زن نوح و زن لوط را نفع کردی. باید سخنی نگویید که دل محمّد صَلَّی‌اللهُ‌عَلَیهِ‌وَسَلَّم از شما رنجیده شود».

{١١} آنگه پیغمبر گفت «إِلٰهِيّ، فرمان چنین بود که یک ماه از حجره بیرون نیائی. امروز بیست و نه روز است. دیگر روز باقیست تا ماه تمام شود»[ط]. فرمان شد که «ای محمّد، اگرچه ازماهْ بیست ونهم است، فرمان

[١٠] آیهٔ ١ سورهٔ تحریم. [١١] آیهٔ ١٠ سورهٔ تحریم.

[ح] «یعنی ای محمّد شهد بر تو حلال کردیم، و تو از گفته عایشه برخود حرام کردی. و ماریه را برتو حلال کردیم و تو از بهتر حَفْصَه بر خود حرام کردی. و شهد بر تو حلال، و ماریه بر تو حلال، و حَفْصَه بر تو حلال گرداندیم ای محمّد، و حلال گردانیدهٔ ما را که تواند که بر تو حرام گرداند. اکنون ای محمّد برو به عایشه و حَفْصَه آشتی کن».

[ط] تا ماه راست شود

{7} The Commander of Believers, ʿUmar (pbuh) reached the door. His Eminence Gabriel had gone to the Prophet in advance and said, 'O Muḥammad, ʿUmar is approaching your house. Do not let him in and do not speak with him.' The Commander of Believers, ʿUmar was standing in front of the door. He was crying and wailing and said, 'O Messenger of God, Ḥafṣa's life as well as my father's and mother's lives will be sacrificed for you. Why do you not come out? Our whole bright world has turned gloomy.' Whatever he said, no one opened the door. Then he said, 'O Prophet of God, ʿUmar now leaves rejected and with his heartbroken.' A command arrived [to Muḥammad], 'Open the door, but do not speak to ʿUmar.' On the basis of this divine command, the Prophet opened the door and ʿUmar went in. However he tried to make the Prophet speak, the Prophet did not.

{8} ʿUmar stood up and went towards his daughter, and said, 'Whatever I tried to make the Prophet speak with me, he did not. Now you go to him, so he may satisfy himself with you. Otherwise, I will not be happy with you again, and you should prepare to die as I will behead you.'

{9} Ḥafṣa stood and went to ʿĀʾisha, and said, 'If we have made a mistake, we have done it together, jointly. Now ʿĀʾisha let's go to the Messenger (pbuh).' Both ʿĀʾisha and Ḥafṣa went towards the house of the Prophet (pbuh), crying [and saying], 'Let's hope that he forgives us'. Then they said, 'We will go to the presence of God and show our powerlessness and frustration.' Both prostrated and cried and said, 'O God, Your prophet has turned away from us. If you do not solve our problem with your kindness, then to whom should we refer? Would no one except You be able to help those who are remorseful? You are fully aware that our souls are going to leave our bodies[3] because we have fallen from the grace and beautiful face of the Prophet.'

{10} Gabriel (pbuh) arrived and revealed this verse, '"O Prophet! Why do you ban yourself from what Allah has made lawful to you, seeking to please your wives? And Allah is All-Forgiving, most Merciful" (Q. 66:1), meaning, O Muḥammad, who can keep you from Mary whom We have made lawful to you? Make peace with ʿĀʾisha and Ḥafṣa and recite this verse upon them: "Allah sets forth an example for the disbelievers: the wife of Noah and the wife of Lot. Each was married to one of Our righteous servants" (Q. 66:10), meaning, God will send the wives of Noah and Lot to hell after the Day of Judgement. The wives of Muḥammad should not take pride in being the married to Muḥammad otherwise they will have followed the wives of Noah and Lot. They should not speak words that break the Prophet's heart.'

{11} Then the Prophet said, 'O God, the divine order was that I should not leave my house for one month. Today is the twenty-ninth day of the month. One day is left

[3] i.e. we are going to die

دادیم که امروز ماهِ بیست و نهم شب برآید تا عایشه و حَفْصَه از درِ ما خالی نروند» . چون حضرت نظر بالا کرد ماهِ نو در نظر مبارکش درآمد. درزمانْ از حجره بیرون و با عایشه و حَفْصَه آشتی کرد. و هر دو شکر گویان دست پیغمبر گرفتند در حجره درآمدند، و به غایت خشنود شدند.

{۱۲} بیت «هم بار بدست آمد؛ هم کار فراهم شد»[۱۲]

{۱۳} المنّة الله که این هم شد و آن هم شد.

{۱۴} إلهِيّ، به‌حرمت پیغمبر تو و به برکت اهل بیت پیغمبر ﷺ، گناهان این بیچاره را و کاتب را با جمیع مؤمنان بیامرزی. بمِنَّة وکَرَمه یا أَرْحَم الرّاحِمین.

[۱۲] منسوب به حسن سجزی دهلوی از شاعران پارسی زبان هندوستان است. با این وجود، این بیت در برخی نسخ موجود نیست.

to complete this month.' A divine message arrived, 'O Muḥammad, although today is the twenty-ninth day of the month, we ordered that the crescent moon be visible tonight[4] so that ʿĀʾisha and Ḥafṣa do not leave Our Throne in disappointment.' When the Prophet looked up to the sky he noticed the new crescent moon. Soon, he left his house and made peace with ʿĀʾisha and Ḥafṣa. And both took the Prophet's hand while praising God, and went to the house together, and they were extremely happy.

{12} Poem: the load and the work both have been made[5]

{13} Praising God that both this and that ended up successfully.

{14} *O God, by Your prophet and by the bliss of the household of the Prophet (pbuh) forgive the sin of the poor scribe of this story as well as all believers. By Your unmerited favour and kindness, O the most Merciful of those who have mercy. [Amen.]*

[4] i.e., the old month ends and the new month starts

[5] Ascribed to Ḥasan Sijzī Dihlawī.

در فضیلتِ جوانانِ یوسف صِفَتان، آن‌گه در رضای خداوند چگونه بودند

{۱} آورده‌اند که در عهد محمّد مصطفی ﷺ جوانی بود و شتر داشت. و شتر را با خود به شهر برد به‌جهت غلّه خریدن. و جوان زر برداشت و به بازار رفت. زن صاحب‌جمالی در بام خانه بود. چون نظرش بر جوان افتاد عاشق او گشت. کنیزک را طلبید و گفت «نزدیک آن جوان برو که شتر سوار است. و بگو [به] چه کار به بازار آمده‌ای. آنچه او بگوید و مطلوب خود عرضه دارد، تو بگو که این چیز در خانهٔ ما موجود است. بدین طریق وی را طلب، و بیار».

{۲} کنیزک رفت و از جوان پرسید. جوان گفت «به غلّه خریدن آمده‌ام». کنیزک گفت که «در خانهٔ ما غلّه موجود است. بیا و بستان». جوان با کنیزک روان شد. چون پیشِ درآمد، کنیزک گفت «ای بی‌بی، جوان را پیشِ درآورده‌ام». زن به کنیزک گفت «هرگاه به خانه درآید من این جوان را به حکایت مشغول کنم. تو در خانه را قفل کن». همچنان کردند.

{۳} چون جوان به خانه درآمد زن پرسید «چه مقدار غلّه در کار داری؟» جوان گفت «یک شتر غلّه». زن رو به جوان کرد و گفت «یک شتر بار غلّه به تومی‌دهم، و از تو زر نمی‌گیرم. و دل من عاشق تو گشته و مُراد من حاصل کن. دیگر هم هرچه خواهی به تو بدهم». جوان گفت «این سخن مگو که حاکم می‌بینید و دو گواه حاضرند».[الف] زن گفت «حاکم و دو گواه کیست؟» جوان گفت «حاکم أَحْکَمُ الْحَاکِمِین[1] است، که هیچ چیز

[1] آیهٔ ۸ سورهٔ تین.

[الف] حاضراند

CHAPTER 13

On the virtue of the Joseph-like youth after he was treated for the sake of God

{1} It is reported that there was a young man during the time of the Prophet Muḥammad (pbuh) who had a camel. He went to town on the camel in order to purchase grain. The young man took gold coins and went to the bazaar. A beautiful lady was on the roof of her house. When she saw this young man, she fell in love with him. She called her maid and instructed, 'Go to that young man who is riding the camel and find out why he came to the bazaar. Whatever he says and whatever he is looking for, then you tell him that he can find it in our house. In this way, call him and bring him in.'

{2} The maid went out and asked the young man and the young man replied, 'I came to purchase grain.' The maid said, 'There is grain in our house. Come and take it.' The young man accompanied the maid. When they arrived at the door, the maid said, 'O lady, I brought the young man to the door.'The lady said to the maid, 'When he enters the house, I'll speak to him, engage and distract him. You lock the door.' This they did.

{3} When the young man came to the house, the woman asked him, 'How much grain do you need ?' The young man replied, 'To the extent that it can be carried by my camel.' The woman looked at the young man and said, 'I will give you grain as much as your camel can carry, and I will not take gold from you. However, I fell in love with you and you should meet my expectation and carnal desire. Whatever else you also want, I'll give it to you.' The young man said, 'Do not say such a thing as the Ruler will become aware and two witnesses are present.'The woman asked, 'Who is the ruler and who are the two witnesses?' The young man said, 'The ruler is, "The most just

از وی پوشیده نیست، و دوگواه کِرَامًا کاتِبِینَ[۲] هستند؛ یکی دست راست ایستاده و دیگری بر دست چپ، حاضرند که تا امروز هرچه بندگان می‌کنند در نامهٔ عمل نویسند، و فردای قیامت بر کردارها گواهی می‌دهند».

{۴} زن گفت «ای جوان، مرا بدین ها مترسان و به بهتان فریفته مکن. من تو را نگذارم تا مُراد من حاصل نکنی. وگرنه تو را در هلاکت می‌افکنم، و می‌گویم که «این دزد است که به خانهٔ من به دزدی درآمده است»».[ب] جوان گفت «اگر مرا پاره کنی، من گِرد تو نگردم. هرچه تو را خوش آمد، بر جان من بکن. من فضیحت دنیا اختیار کردم نه فضیحت آخرت که در عرصات در میان خلق اوّلین و آخرین روی‌سیاه و شرمنده باشم». هرچند جوان نصیحت می‌کرد زن قبول نمی‌کرد.

{۵} زن با خود گفت که «این جوان به کار بد رغبت نمی‌کند. دست دراز کرد و دامن جوان را محکم بگرفت. آنگاه گفت «ای جوان، گمان نبری که تو را از دست بگذارم تا آنکه مقصود مرا حاصل کنی». جوان دید که او را سخت گرفته است گفت که «مرا بگذار تا به فراغت‌گاه بروم و خود را فارغ سازم». زن محلّ قدم‌جای[۳] در درون خانه بنُمود و جوان به قدم‌جای درآمد». [جوان] در کیسه اُستره[۴] داشت. آن را برآورد و نظر به‌سوی آسمان کرد، و گفت «إِلٰهِيّ، تو می‌دانی که این زن مرا از بهر زنا گرفته است، و من از قهر تو و از خوف آتش دوزخ می‌ترسم. اگر مراد او اینست که با او شهوت نفسانی برانم، اکنون همین‌زمان آلت نفسانی خود را از میان دور کنم تا طمع او از من بریده شود». بگفت و اُستره بر آلت مردی خود بِراند. هرچند که زور می‌کرد ذرّه بریده نمی‌شد. جوان روی به آسمان کرد و گفت «إِلٰهِيّ، آنچه سزای نفس خود بود کردم. امّا نمی‌دانم که اُستره از برای چه کارگر نمی‌آید. درین چه حکمت باشد؟»

{۶} دراین حیرت مانده بود که ناگاه دیوار قدم‌جای از میان رفت و راهی پدید آمد. جوان حمد و ثناگویان از آن رخنه برون رفت. دید که شترش پُربار ایستاده‌است. چون جوان در حیرت افتاد که «که شتر مرا پربار کرده باشد و این غلّه حقّ که باشد؟» باز به خاطر آمد که «پیغمبر در میان ماست. پیش ایشان بروم و معلوم کنم که این غلّه حقّ کیست». این بگفت و مهار شتر را گرفته به خانهٔ پیغمبر عليه‌السلام روان شد. ازآن جانب مهتر جبرئیل عليه‌السلام به خدمت پیغمبر صلى‌الله‌عليه‌وسلم حاضر آمده، و گفت «یا محمّد، احوال کیفیت جوان با زن بدین موجبِ است و این آیت آورد «وَمَنْ يَتَّقِ اللَّهَ يَجْعَلْ لَهُ مَخْرَجا؛ وَيَرْزُقْهُ مِنْ حَيْثُ لا يَحْتَسِبُ وَمَنْ يَتَوَكَّلْ عَلَى اللَّهِ فَهُوَ حَسْبُهُ إِنَّ اللَّهَ بالِغُ أَمْرِهِ قَدْ جَعَلَ اللَّهُ لِكُلِّ شَيْءٍ قَدْرا،[۵] یعنی بگوی محمّد این جوان را چون تو در حضرت

[۲] آیهٔ ۱۱ سورهٔ انفطار. [۳] قدم‌گاه یا طهارت‌خانه. [۴] تیغ تیز. بنابر برگ ۱۴، نسخهٔ خطی Cod. Pers. ۳۰۹ در کتابخانهٔ باوریا، مونیخ، «استره» از «اُسُتَرِه» در زبان ترکی عثمانی برگرفته‌شده، که ترجمه‌ای از کلمهٔ فارسی «سُتُرِه» است.[۵] آیات ۲ و ۳ سورهٔ طلاق.

[ب] زن گفت «اگر تو گِرد من نگردی، من این‌زمان فریاد کنم که «این مرد بیگانه در خانهٔ من بهر دزدی درآمده»، و شتر و احوال و زر هم تلف شود. و خود در بند مانی. همان بهتر که مراد مرا حاصل کنی و غلّه و زر بستانی و بروی».

of all judges" (Q. 95:8) from whom nothing is hidden, and the two witnesses are the "venerable scribes [of deeds]" (Q. 82:11); one is on the right hand and the other one on the left hand in order to write whatever the servants have done to date on their record of deeds, and they will testify regarding the servants' deeds on the Day of Judgement.'

{4} The woman said, 'O young man, do not scare me with such stories and do not trick me with such accusations. I will not allow you to go until you do what I want you to do. Otherwise, I will destroy you, and say, "This fellow is a thief who came to rob my house."' The young man said, 'Even if you whip me, I will not touch you. You can do whatever you like against me. I have no problem with infamy in this world, but in the hereafter, where I will be present among the first and last beings,[1] I should not want to be disgraced and embarrassed.' Howsoever the young man tried to persuade the woman she would not desist.

{5} She reflected, 'This young man is not interested in a sordid affair.' She grabbed the man's waist tightly, and then said, 'O young man, do not think that I will leave you alone until you meet my desire.' The young man noticed that she has taken him forcefully. Then he told her, 'Allow me to go to the toilet and relieve myself.' She showed him the place and the young man went there. He had a blade in his bag. He took it out and looked up and said, 'O God, you know that this woman captured me for the sake of adultery, and I am afraid of your rage and wrath. If she really wants me to fulfil her carnal desires I will right now cut off my penis so she will have to give up on me.' He said this and put the blade to his penis. But despite his efforts he was unable to cut. The young man looked up and said, 'O God, whatever justice I performed was regarding my own self. But I do not know why this blade does not work. What could be the reason?'

{6} While he was thinking about his situation the toilet's wall crumbled and a path out appeared. The young man, while praising God, got out of that crack. He noticed that his camel was ready and had been loaded. The young man was surprised: 'Who has loaded my camel and who is the owner of this grain?' He thought, 'The Prophet is among us. I will go to him and will ask who might be the owner of this grain.' As he said this he took the camel's bridle and went towards the house of the Prophet. From the other side of the house, His Eminence Gabriel (pbuh) went to the Prophet and said, 'O Muḥammad, this is the story of this young man with a woman' and Gabriel revealed a verse of the Qurʾān, 'And whoever fears God, for him He brings a way out; and gives him provision from where he does not even imagine. And whoever places his trust in God, He is sufficient for him. Certainly, God is to accomplish His purpose. God has a measure for everything' (Q. 65:2–3), meaning, 'Muḥammad, tell this young man, "As you have practised piety before Us, then we saved you and opened up a way

[1] Mainly referring to the Muslim community

ما تقوی ورزیدی ما تو را نجات دادیم و راه پیدا کردیم. از کارد امان دادیم، تا از دیوار بیرون شدی و از دست او بجُستی». بعداز آن، پیغمبر ﷺ، بر وی این آیت بخوان».

{۷} جوان مهار شتر را گرفته به نزدیک پیغمبر ؑ آمد و گفت «یا رسول الله، مرا این چنین واقعه پیش آمده». و آن واقعه را بیان کرد و بعداز آن گفت «نمی‌دانم که این غلّه را در شتر من که بار کرده باشد، وحقّ کیست؟» پیغمبر ؑ بدید، تبسّم کرد، و این آیت بخواند. و گفت ای جوان خدای تَعَالَی می گوید که «چون در حضرت ما تقوی ورزیدی این شترغلّه مژدهٔ صلاحیت تو داده است، و هرکه به درگاه خدای تَعَالَی صلاحیت ورزد چنان رزق رساند که گمان ندارد که از کجا می‌رسد». و چنین نقل است که آن جوان دِحْيَة كَلْبِيّ بوده.

{۸} چون جوان از قدم‌گاه بیرون شد، و چنین مژدهٔ بشارت شنید شادمان شد، و حمد و ثنا گویان روی به خانهٔ خود کرد. از آن جانب زن زمانی بر آن منتظر بود. دید که آن جوان از قدم‌جای بیرون نشد. درآمد و نظر کرد بر قدم‌جای. دیدْ نیستْ، دویده.[۶] در[۷] را ملاحظه کرد که قفل کرده‌است. در حیرت افتاد و نعره در برآورد و گفت «إِلٰهِيّ، تو را چنین بندگانند که از خوف تو جان و تن در می‌بازند، و رضای تو حاصل می‌کنند. چنانچه بندهٔ نیک‌کردار تو را دیدم که در حضرت پاک تو چست و چالاکی نمود، به صلاحیّت او را خلاص کردی. ای پروردگارا، اگر همچو من بدکرداری به‌سوی تو بازگردد بخوانی یا نی؟» ندایی شنید که «ای بیچاره، چون تو به حضرت ما بازگردی، اجابت کنیم. کَرَم ما بیش از آن است. چون زن شنید توبه چنان به صدقِ دل کرد که یکی از خاصّان حضرت الهی شد».

{۹} نظیر دیگر. جوانی در کشتی بود، ناگاه آوازی از دریا شنید «کیست که ده‌هزار دینار دهد که او را چیزی بیاموزم که در دنیا و عقبی مرد را سودمند باشد». تمام اهل کشتی آواز شنیدند. هرچند چپ و راست نگاه کردند کسی ندیدند. دیگر مرتبی[۸] باز هم ندا شنیدند. اهل کشتی جواب ندانند. بار سوم ندا شنیدند که «کسی هست که ده‌هزار بدهد تا او را چیزی بیاموزیم که مقصود دو جهان حاصل کند».

{۱۰} جوانی گفت که «از اسباب دنیا ده هزار دینار دارم. آن را در می‌بازم؛ بیاموز تاچه آموزی». آوازی آمد که «اوّل ده‌هزار را در دریا انداز». جوان ده‌هزار دینار در دریا انداخت. ندا شنید «اکنون برخوان وَمَن يَتَّقِ اللَّهَ يَجْعَل لَّهُ مَخْرَجًا وَيَرْزُقْهُ مِنْ حَيْثُ لَا يَحْتَسِبُ وَمَن يَتَوَكَّلْ عَلَى اللَّهِ فَهُوَ حَسْبُهُ إِنَّ اللَّهَ بَالِغُ أَمْرِهِ قَدْ جَعَلَ اللَّهُ لِكُلِّ شَيْءٍ قَدْرًا».[۹] امّا سوداگران[۱۰] که بر جهاز سوار بودند به نزدیک جوان آمدند و گفتند که «هیچ کسی هرگز این چنین نکرده‌است که تو کردی؛ که به آوازی ده‌هزار دینار را به دریا انداختی، اگر تو را مطلوب این آیت بود، از قرآن مجید یاد می‌گرفتی و ملازمت در خواندن این آیت می‌کردی». هنوز درین عتاب بودند که

[۶] گریخته. [۷] درب. [۸] باردیگر. [۹] آیهٔ ۲ و ۳ سورهٔ طلاق. [۱۰] واژه «سوداگر» به معنای «تاجر و تجّار مسافرِ دریانورد» به وفور در ادبیات مالایی و با رسم الخط «سودکر» یا «سودکر» به چشم می‌خورد. در ادبیات مدرن مالایی به دو شیوه saudagar و sodagar نگاشته می‌شود. قابل توجّه که این واژه در ادبیات اسلامی-صوفیانهٔ هندوستان بسیار به کار می‌رفته است.

out. We saved you from the blade, so you could get out through the wall and get away from the woman", and then recite the verse to the young man.'

{7} The young man took the camel's bridle and came to the Prophet (pbuh) and said, 'O Messenger of God, this incident has happened to me', and he was detailed in his account, and then said, 'I do not know who has loaded this grain on my camel, and to whom it belongs'. The Prophet (pbuh) saw this, smiled, and recited the verse and said, 'O young man, God has said that as you have practised piety before Him this fully loaded camel with grain confirms Our approval and whoever qualifies in the presence of God receives such a provision and he will not even realise from where it came.' And it is also reported that that the young man was Diḥya al-Kalbī.

{8} When the young man escaped from the toilet, and then noticed God's confirmation, he became so happy, and went towards his house while praising God. However, on the other side,[2] the woman was still waiting as she noticed the young man did not leave the toilet. She went in to check. She saw that he was not there and ran out. She saw that the door was still locked. She was shocked and shouted, 'O God, you have such servants who will sacrifice their soul and body for the sake of your rage, and will attempt to meet your satisfaction. I have noticed how righteous your servant was before Your presence, and how he acted with speed [to find a way out], and You released him. O God! If an immoral person like me comes back to you, will you respond or not?' She heard a voice saying, 'O lowly one! As you have repented in Our presence, We will accept. Our kindness is beyond this.' When the woman heard this, she profoundly and honestly repented so much she became one of God's elite servants.

{9} Another story. A young man was on a ship. He suddenly heard a voice from the ocean saying, 'Who dares to give ten thousand dinars, so I will teach him something that would be of benefit in this world and the next.' Everyone on the ship heard this voice. They looked to the left and to the right but saw nothing. Again, they heard this voice. The people on board did not answer. They heard for a third time, 'Is there anyone who wants to give ten thousand dinars so we can teach him something by which he can possess both worlds?'

{10} The young man said, 'My entire wealth in this world is ten thousand dinars. I will sacrifice it. Sure, teach what you want to teach me!' A voice arrived, 'First, throw the ten thousand dinars into the ocean.' The young man threw his ten thousand dinars into the ocean and he heard the voice, 'Now recite, "And whoever fears God, for him He brings a way out; and gives him provision from where he does not even imagine. And whoever places his trust in God, He is sufficient for him. Certainly, God is to accomplish His purpose. God has a measure for everything"' (Q. 65:2–3). The merchants

[2] i.e., inside house

کشتی از میان دو پاره شد. گویندگان در دریا هلاک شدند و آن [جوان] بر تخته‌پارهٔ جهاز مانده، و بعد باد آن تخته را در جزیره انداخت.

{۱۱} جوان دید در کنار جزیره دختری صاحب‌جمال نشسته‌است. از وی پرسید «تو کیستی؟ و چگونه درین مقام افتادی؟» دختر گفت «پدر من سوداگری بود و مرا به غایت دوست داشتی، و هرجا که رفتی مرا با خود بردی. در کشتی بودیم که ناگاه کشتی بشکست و من بر تخته‌پاره ماندم. بعد باد آن تخته‌پاره را به این جزیره رساند». جوان گفت «ای دختر، واقعهٔ من و تو یکیست. امّا باید که دل به‌خدای عَزَّوَجَلَّ بندیم، تا چه آید». پس جوان پرسید «چند روز باشد که درین مقام افتادی؟» دختر گفت که «سه ۳[11] روز باشد که درین جزیره افتاده‌ام». جوان پرسید که «هیچ کشتی در نظر تو نیامده؟» دختر گفت «چهار کشتی دیدم. خواستم تا آواز دهم، همان‌ساعت پرده در نظرم آمد، برمثالِ کوهی در میان من و جهاز حائل شد، و از پیش من ناپدید گشت».

{۱۲} هم درین سخن بودند که سه[ب] جهاز دیگر پیدا شد. جوان خواست تا بانگ کند، همان ساعت پردهٔ کوهی در نظر آمد. جوان درزمانْ در خاطر گذرانید که «از دریا ندایی شنیده بودم که هر که بدین آیت مداومت کند مرادات[12] دنیا و عقبی بدو دهند». و این آیت را بنیاد کرد که « وَمَن يَتَّقِ اللَّهَ يَجْعَل لَّهُ مَخْرَجًا وَيَرْزُقْهُ مِنْ حَيْثُ لَا يَحْتَسِبُ وَمَن يَتَوَكَّلْ عَلَى اللَّهِ فَهُوَ حَسْبُهُ إِنَّ اللَّهَ بَالِغُ أَمْرِهِ قَدْ جَعَلَ اللَّهُ لِكُلِّ شَيْءٍ قَدْرًا».[13] چون این آیت را بخواند، پردهٔ کوه به طریق آب نمک بگداخت و پردهٔ کوه ناپیدا شد. اهل کشتی را بانگ کرد، پیش آمدند. جوان به دختر گفت «خاطر تو نگران نباشد که تو خواهر منی. بر تو به نظر خیانت نگاه نکنم. و تو را به خواست خدای تَعَالَی به پدرت رسانم».

{۱۳} آن‌گه هر دو بر کشتی نشستند، و دختر صدف بسیار جمع کرده بازی کرد؛ خود را مشغول می‌داشت. جوان روی به دختر کرد و گفت «صدف‌ها را در گوشهٔ چادر بند شاید یک‌بار به‌کار آمد». چنان کرد و از دریا به سلامت برآمدند و دختر را به شهر پدر رساند.[ج] چون به شهر مصر رسیدند در گوشه[ای] گذاشت دختر را، و جوان رفت تا از پدر دختر خبر کند.

{۱۴} جوان به در خانهٔ ایشان رسید، آواز گریه شنید. پرسید «گریه از برای چیست؟» گفتند «سوداگری بود همیشه سفر دریا می‌کرد و دختری داشت که او را به غایت دوست می‌داشت. با خود می‌برد. در کشتی بود که کشتی شکسته و آن دختر به دریا رفت. حالا پدر به خانه آمد. از برای دختر گریه می‌کنند».

[11] در برخی نسخ اعداد به‌صورت حروفی و عربی کنار یکدیگر نگاشته شده‌اند، چنانچه در ادبیات مالایی هم ریشه دوانده است.
[12] مرادهای. [13] آیهٔ ۲ و ۳ سورهٔ طلاق.

[ب] چهار [ج] و روی به راه مصر نهادند که خانهٔ آن دختر در شهر مصر بود

who were on board came to the young man and said, 'No one has ever done as you did. On hearing a voice you threw ten thousand dinars into the ocean! If you were to learn this verse you could have simply learned it from the Glorious Qurʾān and have regularly recited it.' While they were still busy remonstrating the ship was split in half. Those who were speaking [to that young man] drowned in the ocean yet he remained on a timber from the ship. And the wind blew the timber to an island.

{11} The young man noticed that there was a pretty girl on the island. He asked her, 'Who are you and how did you arrive here?' The girl said, 'My father was a merchant and loved me a lot. And wherever he went he allowed me to accompany him. We were on board a ship that suddenly broke and only I remained on a piece of timber. Then the wind brought the timber to this island.' The young man said, 'O girl, the same incident has happened to both of us. But we should trust in God, to see what happens.' Then he asked the girl, 'How long have you been here?' The girl said, 'Now I have been on this island for three days.' The young man asked, 'Have you not seen any ships yet?' The girl said, 'I saw four ships. As soon as I wanted to call them, a veil resembling a mountain appeared between me and the ship, and then the ship disappeared.'

{12} While speaking, three other ships appeared. The young man wanted to call them, but soon a mountain-like veil appeared. The young man then recalled, 'I heard a voice from the ocean that whoever recites and trusts in this verse regularly, the desire of this world and the hereafter will be given to him.' He began reciting, 'And whoever fears God, for him He brings a way out; and gives him provision from where he does not even imagine. And whoever places his trust in God, He is sufficient for him. Certainly, God is to accomplish His purpose. God has a measure for everything' (Q. 65:2–3). When he finished reciting this verse, the mountainous veil dissolved like salt in water. He called to the people on the ship. They came. The young man said, 'Do not worry as you are my sister. I will not betray you, and God willing, I will get you back to your father.'

{13} Then both went on board. The girl had collected many shells; she began playing with them to occupy herself. The young man looked at the girl and said, 'Hold these shells in your veil, perhaps, they will be of use sometime'. She did so, and they finished the journey safe and sound. And the girl reached her father's city. When they arrived in the Egyptian city, he left the girl somewhere. And the young man went to find the girl's father.

{14} He arrived at the father's door. He heard someone crying. He asked the people around, 'Why are they crying?' They said, 'There is a merchant who was always travelling over oceans, and he had a daughter whom he liked so much. He always took his daughter with him on his travels. They were on a ship that sank, and the girl drowned in the ocean and the father came home in this state. Now he is crying for his daughter.'

{۱۵} جوان گفت «دختر را آورده‌ام». سوداگر را خبر کردند. بیرون آمد و احوال دختر را معلوم کرد. رفته و دختر را دید، بسیار خوشحال شد.[۱۴] و سرش بوسه داد[۱۵] و گرفته به خانه برد و کیفیت دریا و همه را از جوان پرسید. سوداگر گفت «ای جوان، تو فرزند منی و این دختر را به نکاح به تو دادم». و دختر را نکاح بسته به جوان تسلیم کرد.

{۱۶} تا روزی زن و شوهر حکایت دریا می‌کردند، و شکر حضرت سبحانه وتعالی می‌کردند که «ما را نجات داد». بعد از آن جوان گفت «آن صدف‌ها که در گوشهٔ جامه بسته بودی، بیار تا ببینم». بیاورد چون یکی را پاره کردند پر از مروارید بود. و مرواریدی که از آن یک صدف برآمده بود در بازار ده‌هزار دینار قیمت کردند. و هر صدفی که بشکستی ده هزار دینار شدی. تا چندان مال شد که از حساب بگذشت. آنگه جوان ندایی شنید که «به‌جهت آیت کریمه وعده این بود که در دنیا و عقبی پسندیده باشد. در دنیا چندان دادیم که در حساب نمی‌آید، و در عقبی چندان دهیم که تمام مخلوقات جمع شوند در حساب آن عاجزند». باشد که مؤمن در خواندن این آیت کریمه مداومت و مبالغت کند که عزّت و شرف هر دو جهان حاصل گردد.

{۱۷} و إِلٰهِيّ، به حرمت این آیت کریمه که جمیع مؤمنان را با ایمان داری. بِرَحْمَتِكَ يَا أَرْحَمَ الرَّاحِمِينَ.

[۱۴] در برخی نسخ شرح ماجرا از زبان جوان بار دیگر تکرار می‌شود. [۱۵] اشاره به بوسیدن پیشانی مرد جوان دارد.

{15} The young man said, 'I brought the girl.' They called upon the merchant. He came out and learned about his daughter. He was shown where she was and he went to his daughter and was so happy. He kissed the young man's forehead and brought him to the house. And the father asked to hear the whole story of the ocean and all other things from the young man. The merchant said, 'O young man, you are my son and I will offer my daughter in marriage to you.' The young man married the girl.

{16} Once upon a time, the couple were both talking about the ocean, and praising God, and reflected on how they were 'saved by God'. Then the young man said, 'Bring those sea shells that you have kept in your garment and let me see them'. She brought them. When they split one of them, they found it replete with pearls. And the pearls of that shell were equal to ten thousand dinars in the bazaar. Every single shell that they split, was valued at ten thousand dinars. The amount of wealth was so large that it seemed impossible to calculate. Then the young man heard a voice saying, 'Due to reciting that sacred verse, the promise was to provide satisfaction in this world and the next. We have granted in this world to an extent that cannot be calculated, and we will grant even more in the hereafter that even if all creatures gather, they will be unable to calculate it.' Should a believer consistently and closely pay attention to reading this verse, his dignity and glory will be achieved in both worlds.

{17} *O God, by this sacred verse that you grant faith to all believers. By your mercy, O the most Merciful of those who have mercy. [Amen.]*

در فضیلتِ خالد بن ولید رَضِیَ‌اللهُ‌عَنهُ چند کسان از دست او به دولت ایمان مشرّف شدند

{۱} آورده‌اند که پدر خالد، ولید، پیغمبر صَلَّى‌اللهُ‌عَلَيهِ‌وَسَلَّم را در رنج می‌داشت. تا روزی پیغمبر روی سوی آسمان کرد، و گفت «إلٰهِيّ، تو می‌بینی که ولید مرا در رنج داشته‌است». همان‌ساعت جبرئیل عَلَيهِ‌السَّلَام دررسید و گفت «ای محمّد، فرمان می‌شود هرچه تو گویی در حقّ ولید همان کنیم. امّا چه کنیم که حکم ما برآن رفته که از پشت ولید پسری پیدا گردانیم که نام او «خالد» باشد، و از دست او هفتادهزار کس از شهر[ی] با پادشاه آن شهر باهم مسلمان شوند و ایمان آرند. و چندین هزارکسِ دیگر در شهرهای دیگر بر دست او مسلمان شوند». پیغمبر گفت «إلٰهِيّ، اگر چه محمّد را ولید در رنج می‌دارد، اکنون رنج او اختیار کردم که مشقّت دنیا بر محمّد بگذارد. امّا ولید را در دنیا چندان بدار تا آن گوهر در جهان پدید آید».

{۲} الغرض. چون حقّ سُبحَانَهُ‌وَتَعَالَى خالد را در جهان پیدا کرد. و خُرد بود که به دست پیغمبر عَلَيهِ‌السَّلَام به شرف ایمان مشرّف شد. و روزبه‌روز در کار او ترقّی بود تا روزی غزای پیش‌آمد و حضرت با جملهٔ یاران روان شد و خالد نیز روان شد. و لشگر بر بالای کوهی می‌رفت و شب و روز می‌رفتند. تا شبی لشگر پیغمبر صَلَّى‌اللهُ‌عَلَيهِ‌وَسَلَّم بر دامن کوهی رسید و می‌گذشت که خالد رَضِیَ‌اللهُ‌عَنهُ را خواب غلبه کرد. عنان اسب از دست رفت و اسب در راه دیگر افتاد. چون خالد بیدار شد دید از لشگر جدا افتاده. درزمانْ گفت «إِنَّا لِلّٰهِ وَإِنَّا إِلَيْهِ رَاجِعُونَ»[۱]. و تا سه روز در میان کوه‌ها می‌گشت و هیچ‌کس را در میان کوه نمی‌دید.

[۱] آیهٔ ۱۵۶ سورهٔ بقره.

CHAPTER 14

On the virtue of Khālid b. Walīd (pbuh)

and how many people converted to the delight of faith through him

{1} It is reported that Walīd, the father of Khālid, harassed the Prophet (pbuh). Once upon a time, the Prophet looked at the sky and said, 'O God, You observe how Walīd harasses me.' Thereafter, Gabriel (pbuh) arrived and said, 'O Muḥammad, it is reported that whatever you wish, we will inflict it upon Walīd. Nonetheless, God has destined to bring a son from Walīd's loin whose name will be Khālid; through him seventy thousand people in a town, as well as the town's king, will convert to Islam and accept the religion. And more thousands of people from other cities will convert to Islam through him.' The Prophet said, 'O God, I can tolerate Walīd's harassment as the hardships of the world will weigh on Muḥammad. But please keep Walīd in this world until his gem of a son is born.'

{2} A new story. God brought Khālid into the world. He was just a child when he became a Muslim by means of the Prophet (pbuh). He progressed day-by-day until one day a battle broke out and the Prophet along with his Companions moved towards the battle. Khālid, also, followed. Their army arrived on top of a mountain, and they continued their way, night and day, until one night the Prophet's (pbuh) army arrived on the mountainside. They continued on their way but Khālid (pbuh) was overcome by drowsiness. He dropped his horse's bridle and the horse took another road. When Khālid woke up he noticed that he had separated from the army. Then he said, 'Indeed,

{۳} بعد از سه روز بر کوهی برآمد. در پای کوه صحرایی دید به غایت خوش و خرّم؛ سایه‌بان‌ها و سراپردهٔ ابریشمین نصب کرده‌اند. و پادشاهی در آن صحرا فرود آمد و لشگر او تا نظرکار می‌کند صحرا را فرو گرفته بود. خالد رضي الله عنه شکر خدای تَعَالَی به جای آورد، و اسب را بر سنگ بست و به خدای تَعَالَی سپرد و در میان ایشان در آمد. بعد از زمانی دید که منبر نهاده‌اند و نزدیک منبر تختی بیاراسته و چپ و راست منبر کرسی‌های زرّین نصب کرده‌اند.

{۴} چون پادشاه رسید بر تخت خود بنشست. و معلّمِ دینِ ایشان ترسائی[۲] بود. بر منبر آمد و نزدیک پادشاه بر کرسی‌های زرّین بنشست. آنگاه معلّم ترسا خواست که ترغیب دین خود بر پادشاه و نزدیکان پادشاه کند. نظر خالد رضي الله عنه بر معلّم ترسا افتاد، و گفت «إِلٰهِيٓ، این‌زمان این معلّم ترسا در راهِ باطل ایشان را ترغیب خواهد کرد. اما تو قادری و بر همهٔ چیزها قدرت داری. می‌توانی که درساعتُ زبانِ این معلّمِ ترسا بسته گردانی تا به جز راستی و سخن حقّ چیزی دیگر نگوید». دعای خالد درحال مستجاب شد؛ هرچند که معلّم خواست تا سخن از دین خود بگوید، زبانش به گفتار نمی‌گردید. معلّم ترسا رو به پادشاه کرد و گفت که «ای پادشاه، بدانید که محمّدی در میان آمده است. از این جهت زبان من بپیچید. اکنون در میان خود تفحّص کنید و او را پیدا سازید».

{۵} هرچند ملاحظه کردند هیچ‌یک خالد را نیافتند. زیرا که در جامهٔ ایشان هفتاد پیوند بود.[۳، الف] چون معلّم دید که یافته نمی‌شود از منبر برخاست و گفت «ای محمّدی، تو را سوگند می‌دهم به آن خدایی که او را یکی می‌خوانی و یکی می‌دانی، و سوگند به آن محمّد که دین او اختیار کرده‌ای، از مجمع ما برخیز تا چند مسئله از دین تو پرسم». خالد با خود گفت «جان و تن من فدای سوگند پروردگار و رسول خدای عَزَّوَجَلَّ باد. من خلاف سوگند خدا و رسول خدا چگونه کنم؟»

{۶} خالد رضي الله عنه برپا خواست. معلّم ترسا او را نزدیک خود خواند، و گفت «ای محمّدی، راست گوی بر من چه سِحر خوانده‌ای که زبان بسته شده؟»[۴] خالد گفت «سِحر نکرده‌ام. امّا چون تو را بر منبر دیدم، از خداوند عَزَّوَجَلَّ خود خواستم و گفتم «این کافر چندین هزارکس را به کفر خواهد تلقین کرد. إِلٰهِيٓ، به جز راستی او را توفیقی دیگر ندهی»».[۵، ب] معلّم ترسا گفت «دین شما چگونه راست شد که دین ما باطل باشد؟! اکنون چند چیز از دین تو می‌پرسم. اگر جوابِ تسلّی دل بگویی نیکو باشد، و اگر نه پادشاه را بگویم تا تو را هفت‌پاره کند». خالد گفت «آنچه حکم الهی در حقّ من شده همان خواهد شد.[ج] امّا، اکنون هر سخنِ مشکلی که از دین مسلمانی داری بپرس».

[۲] در برخی نسخ معلّمِ دینِ پادشاه فردی جهود است. [۳] می‌تواند به خرقه پوشی وی اشاره داشته باشد.
[۴] در برخی نسخ این عبارت نیز اضافه شده (...اگر راست گفتی از عمر خود امان یافتی. و اگر نه دست از جان خود بشوی. خالد رضي الله عنه گفت «جان‌ده و جان‌ستان خداییست عَزَّوَجَلَّ، و در دین آفریده‌گار من و ملّت پیغمبرمن سحر حرامست»
[۵] این بخش می‌تواند به آخرین آیهٔ سورهٔ فاتحه نیز اشاره داشته باشد.

[الف] زیرا که در جامه مبارک او هفتاد دَربه داشت [ب] خواستم که «إِلٰهِي، این‌زمان معلّم چندین کسان را در راه باطل ترغیب خواهد نمود. به کرم عمیم خود، به جز از کلمهٔ حقّ بر زبان او جاری نگردانی. [ج] آنچه حکم الهی در حقّ من رفته‌است از آن کم و بیش نخواهد شد

to God we belong and to Him we will return' (Q. 2:156). And he wandered among mountains for three days, and he saw no one.

{3} After three days, he arrived on a mountain. He saw that at the bottom of the mountain there was a verdant plain. [He noticed that] encampments and canopies made of silk had been set up. And a king arrived and his army covered the plain as far as one's eye could see. Khālid (pbuh) praised God, and tied the horse to a stone and left it to God and went towards them. After a while, he noticed that they had placed a pulpit, and put a throne near the pulpit, and set up golden chairs to the left and right of the pulpit.

{4} When the king arrived, he sat on his own throne. And the king's minister of religion was Christian. He went towards the pulpit, too, and sat on one of the golden chairs near the king. Then the Christian minister began to preach among the king and his entourage. Khālid saw the Christian minister, and pondered, 'O God, this Christian minister wants to lead them towards an invalid and erroneous path. But You are Omnipotent and have control over everything. You can instantly close the mouth of this Christian minister unless he is able to speak only true and rightful statements.' Khālid's request was instantly approved; whatever the Christian minister tried to speak about his own religion, his tongue did not work. The Christian minister looked at the king and said, 'O king, be aware that there is a Muḥammadan here. This is why that I am not able to speak. Now investigate and find him among yourselves.'

{5} Wherever they looked, no one was able to find Khālid because his cloth had seventy patches.[1] When it became clear to the minister that he could not be found he went up the pulpit and announced, 'O Muḥammadan, I swear to you on the One you call God, and consider Him God, and swear to you on Muḥammad whose religion you have taken, rise up in our assembly so that I may ask a number of questions about your religion.' Khālid pondered, 'I would surely devote my soul and body for the sake of God and if the oath is taken on the Messenger of God. How I can overlook this and act contrary to swearing by God and the Messenger of God?!'

{6} Khālid (pbuh) stood up. The Christian minister called him nearer to himself and said, 'O Muḥammadan, be honest and tell me what magical spell you have read upon me that closed my mouth?' Khālid said, 'I have done no magic, but once I saw you on the pulpit I beseeched God, "This infidel has indoctrinated thousands of people with unbelief. O God! Do not make him successful except in the right path."'[2] The Christian minister asked, 'Why is your religion the right one and ours the wrong one? I will ask you a number of questions about your religion. If you provide satisfactory responses, that's fine, otherwise, I would ask the king to tear you into seven parts.' Khālid said,

[1] Looked poor? [2] This may be related to classical commentaries on the last verse of Q. 1.

{۷} ترسا گفت «من در تورات نوشته دیدم که در بهشت درختی است که خدای تَعَالَی او را آفریده‌است، و نام آن درختِ با میوه طوبیٰ است. و هیچ بهشتی نباشد که شاخی از آن درخت در خانهٔ او نباشد. و دیگر در تورات نوشته دیدم که هر بهشتیِ را در آنجا خانه باشد که ده مقدارِ دنیا باشد. چگونه این سخن در عقل گنجد که هیچ خانه نخواهد بود که از آن درخت شاخه‌ها و میوه‌های او را خدای تَعَالَی درآن خانه نیفتاده باشد و آن را روزی مسلمانان گردانیده است؟ و دیگر شما می‌گویید که «خدای ما قدرت بر همهٔ چیزها دارد. اگر سخن شما و خدای شما راست است، تمثیل آن درختِ طوبیٰ در جهان بنمای».

{۸} [خالد گفت] «معلّم شما تمثیل درخت طوبیٰ هم درین جهان می‌خواهد. اکنون بدانید که تمثیل آن درخت طوبیٰ را پروردگار عَزَّوَجَلَّ وعالی در آسمان پیدا گردانیده است، و اظهار آن در همهٔ سَموات وأَرض داشته. و مرا بگویید در آسمان یک ماه است یا بسیار؟» همه گفتند «یک ماه است». خالد رَضِيَ اللهُ عَنْهُ گفت «روشنی در قصر سلاطین و در کلبهٔ سالکین و همه [یکسان] می‌تابد. آفریدگاری که ماه خود را چنان نور داده است که به یدِ قدرت خود جملهٔ جهانیان به شعاع او منوّر می‌گردد، همان آفریدگار عَزَّوَجَلَّ عالی به قدرت خود درختی در بهشت آفریده‌است که شاخه‌ها و میوه‌های او به همهٔ بهشتیان می‌رسد، و نعمت او می‌خورند».

{۹} سؤال دیگر که «در تورات نبشته دیده‌ام که بهشتیان این نعمت‌هایی که می‌خورند، بول و غایط نکنند. این عجب می‌آید. مثل این در جهان بنما». خالد رَضِيَ اللهُ عَنْهُ گفت که «تمثیل آن حقّ تَعَالَی در بطن عورات[د] نهاده‌است. عورات بارِ حمل می‌گیرند، چون کودک چهارماه می‌شود، جان در قالبش در می‌دهند[۶] و در شکم مادر می‌گردد و رزق‌ها می‌خورد و پنج‌ماه دیگر برین طریق می‌گردد. اگر در شکم مادر بول و غایط کند، شکم مادر کنده شود و مادر بمیرد و قیام[۷] جهان نباشد. چون از مادر فرزند متولّد شود درحال بول و غایط از وی ظاهر گردد. در آن ساعت فرشته ندا می‌کند که «ای بندگان حقّ! ببینید قدرتِ آفریدگارِ خویش را که در شکم مادر چگونه می‌دارد». چون در جهان رسد از مقام حکمت بیرون آمده بود، بول و غایط برون گشته. پس ای معلّم ترسا، آفریدگاری که در شکمِ مادرْ فرزندِ رزق‌خورنده را چندین ماه پاک داشته است، اگر در بهشتْ بهشتیان را که نعمت‌های بهشتی می‌خورند پاک نگه دارد هیچ عیب[ه] نباشد».

{۱۰} معلّم ترسا باز آغاز کرد، و گفت «در تورات نوشته دیده‌ام که آدم را از خاک ناچیز و فرزندانش از نطفهٔ آب گنده پیدا کرده، و همه را بمی‌راند و باز زنده گرداند؛ تا مرده که زنده شود. عجب است، مثال آن در جهان چیست؟» خالد گفت «این مَثَلْ آفریدگار در پرندگان نهاده‌است. چون پرندگان با هم جفت می‌شوند و بیضه می‌نهند، اگر نظر در بیضه کنی، حیات زندگی ندارد جز اینکه در بیضه آب سفید و زردی بیش نباشد. امّا اظهار قدرت خداوند عَزَّوَجَلَّ این است که چند روز جانور بیضهٔ خود در زیر سینهٔ خود داشته، همان جانوران از

۶ می‌دمند؟ ۷ قایم؟ اشاره به زنده نماندن جنین دارد.

د در رحم زنان ه عجیب

'Whatever has been recorded in my destiny according to divine order, that is what will happen. But now ask whatever questions you have about the Muslim religion.'

{7} The Christian said, 'I have seen in the Torah that there is a tree in paradise that God has created. And the name of that fruitful tree is Ṭūbā. And there will be no paradise in which a branch of this tree cannot be found. And I also read notes in the Torah that every inhabitant of paradise has a house whose size is ten times bigger than the world. How does this statement match with our reason that in every single house there is a branch and fruits of that tree. How has He provisioned Muslims? And that you always say, "Our God has power over everything". If your statement as well as your God is true, then show us an example of the Ṭūbā tree in this world.'

{8} [Khālid addressed the assembly,] 'Your minister wants [a tangible] example of the Ṭūbā tree in this world. Now know that God has shown us an example of the Ṭūbā tree through heaven and Earth. Now answer me, is there one moon in the sky or more?' All responded, 'There is one moon.' Khālid (pbuh) said, 'The moonlight is illuminated [equally] upon the castles of the rulers as well as the huts of the paupers and beggars. The Creator has given light to His moon, through His powerful hand and the whole universe will be illuminated with it, the same God has created a tree in paradise with His power, whose branches and fruit reach all inhabitants of paradise, and they will eat of its bounty.'

{9} The minister posed another question, 'I have seen in the Torah that the inhabitants of paradise will not have urine or excrement after eating of the bounties. This seems wondrous. Show us its tangible example in this world.' Khālid (pbuh) said, 'God has placed this example in the womb of women. Women become pregnant. At four months the embryo will stir to life and move in its mother's womb and consume food. And the same occurs during the next five months. If the embryo urinates and defecates in the mother's womb her womb will be damaged and she and her baby will die. But once the child is born, then the urine and excrement will come out from the child. Then an angel calls, "O servants of God, behold the power of your God, who holds the child in a mother's womb like this." When it comes into the world, on the basis of divine wisdom, the child begins to urinate and defecate. Thus, O Christian minister, if the Creator keeps the fed child clean in the mother's womb for several months, then there should be no wonder that He keeps the people of paradise clean when they eat of the heavenly bounties.'

{10} Again, the Christian minister asked, 'I have seen in the Torah that Adam has been made of an inferior soil and his children from sperm, a nasty fluid, and takes all of their souls and animates them again; thus all the dead come to life. Very surprising. What could be an example in this world?' Khālid said, 'God has put this example in birds. Once birds perform a cloacal kiss, they lay eggs. Once you see the egg, it seems that

بیضه بیرون می‌آید. اگر مردم را از گل آفریده است، بعداز آن که بمیرد و در گل پوشیده شود، آن روز حق سبحانه وتعالی خواهد همچو جوجه‌گان[د] مرغ از زمین بیرون آید».

{۱۱} سؤال دیگر دارم «کدام پیغمبر بود که جانوری او را نصحیت کرد؟ و آن کدامین زمین است که آفتاب یک‌بار پیش آن نرفته‌است؟» خالد رضی‌الله‌عنه فرمود که «مورچه بود که سلیمان را نصیحت کرده‌است. تا روزی مهتر سلیمان علیه‌السلام با خیل و خشم خود بر زمین فرود آمده بود و مورچه‌گان از بهر طعمهٔ خود از سوراخ‌ها برون آمده بودند. چون لشکر مهتر سلیمان علیه‌السلام بدیدند صاحب خود را گفتند که «ولیِ ما توئی. برو مهتر سلیمان را خبر کن تا لشگر ما را زیر پای خود هلاک نکنند». مهتر مورچه‌گان نزدیک مهتر سلیمان آمد، و گفت که «ای پیغمبر خدای، لشگر خود را بگوی تا مورانِ ما را زیر پای نکنند، که ما همه مخلوقیم از مخلوقات، و فردای قیامت هر جانی که از جانی رنجیده شود اندر عرصات قیامت دعوی آن‌کس باشد». مهتر سلیمان علیه‌السلام از سخن مورچه ایستاده شد. همهٔ لشگر خود را خبر کرد که با احتیاط باشید. مبادا که مورچه آزرده شود.[8]

{۱۲} و دیگر، ای معلّم ترسا، ازجهت آفتاب و زمین پرسیدی؟ آن زمین که آفتاب یک‌بار بیش ندید آن قعرِ رودِ نیل است. چون مهتر موسیٰ علیه‌السلام را فرمان شد که «با امّت خود بیرون آی که تا ببینی که حکم ما در حقّ فرعون رفته‌است»، مهتر موسیٰ با جملهٔ امّت بیرون آمد. چون به رود نیل رسیدند، قوم او گفتند که «ای پیغمبر خدای، فرعون از عقبْ قصدِ ما کرده می‌آید. ما از این رود نیل چگونه گذر کنیم؟» مهتر موسیٰ علیه‌السلام دست به دعا برآوردند و گفتند که «إلٰهِيّ، تو دانایی. موسیٰ را با قوم حیرانی[9] ازجهت گذشتن رود نیل پیش آمده‌است که دشمن تو از عقب می‌رسد. تو به کرم خویش آسان گردان». فرمان آمد که «ای موسیٰ، تو با قوم خود خاطرجمع‌دار که رود نیل را فرمان دادیم که تا شقّ[10] شود و قوم تو را راه دهد تا بگذرید». مهتر موسیٰ با قوم دید که به قدرت خدای تَعَالَی آب شقّ شد و راهی پدید آمد. خواستند که بگذرند، ته دریا گِل بود، گذشتن نمی‌شد. همان‌ساعت ایستاده شدند. فرشتگان را امر شد که آفتاب را یک نیزه بالا به قعر رود نیل بگذاشتند.[ذ] به یک‌ساعت آن راهِ دریا خشک شد. مهتر موسیٰ و امّت او به سلامت بیرون آمد. همان‌روز آفتاب به قعر رود نیل تافته بود. تا قیامت دیگر نتابد. چون حکم الهی دررسید که فرعون غرق شد، دیگر آن زمین روی آفتاب را ندید».[11]

[8] در برخی نسخ شرح گفتگوی بین مورچه و سلیمان حذف شده و بطور خلاصه چنین بیان شده است «و این حکایت مشهور است».

[9] اگر به‌صورت «قومْ حیرانی از جهت» بخوانیم، سپس واژهٔ حیرانی را می‌توان «بلاتکلیفی» ترجمه کرد. امّا، اگر به‌صورت «قومِ حیرانی» بخوانیم، واژه حیرانی به عنوان صفتی برای قوم موسیٰ به‌کار می‌رود.

[10] دو قسمت؛ دو تکه. [11] ردّپای چنین سؤالاتی را در داستان‌های مالایی برگرفته از ادبیات آسیای جنوبی می‌توان مشاهده کرد. بارزترین نمونه داستان «ماهاشدها[ک]» است.
Winstedt, *A History of Classical Malay Literature*, 22–24.

[د] جوژه‌گان [ذ] و آفتاب را فرشتگان یک نیزه وار به قعر رود نیل داشتند

it is inanimate, and there is only clear fluid and yolk inside the egg. But God's manifestation of power is when the bird incubates the egg after a few days and similar animals come out of those eggs. If He created people from the soil, after they die they are buried in soil. On the Judgement Day, God brings them out from the soil like the hen's chicks.'

{11} 'I have another question', said the minister, 'Who was the prophet that was advised by an animal? And what is that piece of earth on which the Sun has shone only once?' Khālid (pbuh) said, 'It was an ant that advised Solomon. One day, when with his army, His Eminence Solomon was full of wrath and unmounted his horse. Ants had left their anthills in search of food. Once they saw the army of His Eminence Solomon (pbuh), they went to their leader, requesting, "You are our leader. Go and inform His Eminence Solomon that his army should not crush and kill us under their feet." 'The king of the ants went to His Eminence Solomon and said, "O prophet of God, tell your army not to walk on our ants, as we are all God's creatures, and on the Day of Judgement, every soul which is annoyed by another one will be recompensed on the Resurrection Plain." On account of the ant's statement, His Eminence Solomon (pbuh) stopped. He called upon his whole army, warning them that they should be cautious and not disturb the ants.

{12} 'And, O Christian minister, you asked about the Sun and a piece of earth. That piece of earth on which the Sun shone only once is the bed of the river Nile. When His Eminence Moses (pbuh) was ordered to flee with his community so that he may see what God had decreed for Pharaoh. His Eminence Moses left along with his community. When they arrived near the river Nile his community said, "O prophet of God, Pharaoh is coming after us. How can we cross this river Nile?" His Eminence Moses (pbuh) lifted his hand in supplication and said, "O God, You are Omniscient. Moses and his community are wondering how to cross the river Nile as now Your enemy is coming after us. Due to Your kindness, please make this easy." A command was revealed: "O Moses, you and your community may rest assured that We have ordered the river Nile to be parted to give way to your community so you can cross it.' His Eminence Moses and his community noticed that the water had parted due to God's power and a path appeared. Once they began to cross, the riverbed was full of mud, so crossing became impossible. They stopped there. Angels were commanded to shine the Sun on top of the riverbed. Soon the path through the river dried. His Eminence Moses and his community traversed safe and sound. Only on that day, did the Sun shine upon the bed of the river Nile, and it will not shine again until the Day of Judgement. When God's decree was determined, Pharaoh drowned and that piece of earth never saw the Sun again.[3]

[3] Such forms of questions can be found in the Malay story of the *Hikayat Mahashodhak* influenced by South Asian literature. Winstedt, *A History of Classical Malay Literature*, 22–24.

{۱۳} چون ترسا سؤال‌ها را جواب خوب شنید سر فرود افکند. آنگاه خالد آغاز کرد «آنچه مشکل در دین ما داشتی پرسیدی. من هم یک چیز از تو پرسم. باید که راست بگویی». معلم ترسا گفت «ای محمّدی، من بسیار خواستم که نوع دیگر سؤال کنم. چون تو پیش‌از آن در حقّ من دعا کرده بودی، به جز راستی سخن دیگر بر زبان من نمی‌آید». خالد رضی الله عنه گفت «بگو که در تورات[ح] چه نوشته دیده‌ای و بر در بهشت چه نوشته‌اند؟» معلم ترسا رو به جانب پادشاه کرد، و گفت که «ای مردمان، بدانید که این محمّدی سؤال به‌راستی از من می‌پرسد. اکنون رضای شما چیست؟» پادشاه و نزدیکان همه گفتند «تو هر سؤال این محمّدی کردی جواب به راستی و تسلّی دل تو و تسکین دل ما بگفت. و اگر محمّدی یک سؤال می‌کند تو هم به‌راستی جواب بده».

{۱۴} معلّم ترسا گفت «در تورات نوشته دیده‌ام که بر در بهشت نوشته‌اند هر که به صدق دل بگوید «لآ إِلٰهَ إِلَّا الله، مُحَمَّدٌ رَسُولُ الله» بهشت پرنعمتِ جاودانْ جای اوست. و خداوند تَعَالَی دوست اوست و او دوست خداوند تَعَالَی است».

{۱۵} چون معلّم ترسا این بگفت خود کلمهٔ شهادتین عرض کرد. پادشاه گفت «با معلم ترسا که سال‌ها ما را ترغیب دین خود می‌کردی و آنچه می‌فرمودی ما همان می‌کردیم. امروز تو دین محمّد صلی الله علیه وسلم اختیار کردی. پس ما چرا از این دولت دینِ حقّ محروم مانیم». معلّم گفت «ای مردمان، چرا تأخیر می‌کنید که حیات دنیا برباد است و حیات جاویدان در پیش است». درزمان پادشاه، نزدیکان و هفتاد هزارکس[ط] به شرف کلمهٔ توحید مشرّف شدند و بر دست خالد رضی الله عنه مسلمان شدند.

{۱۶} بعداز ایمان آوردن، پادشاه از خالد پرسید «ای کس، بر دین محمّد صلی الله علیه وسلم جان و تن خود باخته بودی و از ما نترسیدی، چگونه درین مقام افتادی؟» خالد گفت «حکم خدای تَعَالَی بدین رفته بود. من با لشگر پیغمبر صلی الله علیه وسلم همراه بودم. حق سبحانه وتعالی مرا از لشگر جدا گردانید تا بدین سبب خلعت ایمان در بر شما کنم». پادشاه پرسید «پیغمبر کجا است؟» خالد گفت «امروز سه‌روز باشد که از صحبت ایشان جدا شده‌ام. در فلان دامنِ کوه حضرت با یاران خود گذشتند که ناگاه خواب بر من غلبه کرد. تا به‌حکم الهی به شما رسیدم». پادشاه گفت «من قرار نگیرم تا دولتِ پای‌بوس محمّد را در نیابم».

ح اوّل ط غیره

{13} The Christian minister became embarrassed when he heard the eloquent responses to his questions. Then Khālid said, 'You have asked whatever questions you had regarding our religion. Now I want to ask you something; and you should tell the truth.' The Christian minister said, 'O Muḥammadan, I wanted to ask my questions differently. However, as you have earlier prayed for me, nothing, except truth, comes to my mouth.' Khālid (pbuh) said, 'Tell me what you have seen in the Torah and what has been written on the entrance gate to paradise?' The Christian minister looked at the king and said, 'O people, be aware that this Muḥammadan asked me an honest question. What do you want me to do now?Together the king and his entourage said, 'Whatever you asked from this Muḥammadan, he responded honestly and brought peace upon your and our hearts. And if the Muḥammadan asks one question also answer honestly.'

{14} The Christian minister said, 'I have seen in the Torah that whoever purely expresses, 'There is no god but God, Muḥammad is the Messenger of God', then his immortal place will be paradise, full of blessing. And that God is his friend and he is the friend of God.'

{15} When the Christian minister said this he himself witnessed to faith. The king said to the Christian minister, 'You have been encouraging us to join your own religion for years, and we have done whatever you said. Today, you have converted to the religion of Muḥammad (pbuh). Why should we be deprived of the blessing of the religion of truth.' The minister said, 'O people, why do you delay as the worldly life is fleeting, and the everlasting life is near.' Right after this the king, his entourage, and seventy thousand people were honoured to proclaim the faith and they became Muslim by means of Khālid (pbuh).

{16} After becoming a Muslim, the king asked Khālid, 'O you who has thoroughly devoted his soul and body to the religion of Muḥammad (pbuh), and were not afraid of us, how did you reach this status?' Khālid responded, 'It has been God's decree. I was in the Prophet's (pbuh) army. God separated me from the army in order to clothe you with the garment of faith.'[4] The king asked, 'Where is the Prophet?' Khālid replied, 'Today is the third day that I am separated from his companionship. While the Prophet and his Companions were passing that hillside, I fell asleep, until, on the basis of God's decree, I came to you.' The king said, 'I will not be at ease if I do not take the chance of kissing the Prophet's foot.'[5]

[4] i.e., to covert you to the religion of Islam.

[5] i.e. to show my respect and devotion

{۱۷} درآن وقت جبرئیل علیه‌السلام به خدمت حضرت رسید، و فرمان رسانید که «ای محمّد، هیچ تفحّص می‌کنی و می‌دانی که خالد تو کجاست؟» از یاران تفحّص کرد و پرسید «خالد کجاست؟» یاران گفتند «یا نبي اَللّٰه، سه‌روز شد که نمی‌نُماید». پیغمبر صلی الله علیه وسلم گفت «یا أخیَ جبرئیل، زود مرا خبر خالد بگو که واقعه چیست؟» جبرئیل گفت «تو را خبر نیست که حقّ جَلّ وَعَلا مرا به سوی تو فرستاده تا مژده و بشارت خالد به شما رسانم. امّا فرمان می‌شود که «ای محمّد، هیچ وعدهٔ ما یاد داری که گفته بودیم که از پشت ولید پسری پیدا گردانیم که هفتادهزارکس پیش او مسلمان خواهند شد؟ آن وعده وفا شد»». و تمام احوال خالد و معلّم ترسا، پادشاه و توابع که واقع شده بود گفت. و بعداز آن مهتر جبرئیل گفت «خالد و معلّم ترسا و پادشاه و تمام لشگر ایستاده، و در حیرت مانده‌اند که حضرت پیغمبر صلی الله علیه وسلم کجا طلب کنیم. شما پیک خود را روان کنید تا ایشان را بیارد».

{۱۸} در میان لشگر یکی بود وی را بادپای[۱۲] نام بود، که هفت‌روزه را به یک‌روز رفتی. پیغمبر آن‌کس را بخواند و کیفیت خالد را با وی گفت. پیک گفت «یا رسول الله، مرا راه بنمای؟» پیغمبر علیه‌السلام گفت «بدین طریق برو».[ی] پیک از غایت شادی چند-روزه-راه را همان‌روز رفت. نظر خالد بر پیک افتاد، اِستاد، و کنارش گرفت و می‌پرسید که «حضرت پیغمبر خدای عَزَّوَجَلَّ کجاست؟ و تو کجا بودی؟» پیک گفت «جبرئیل را حقّ سبحانه وتعالی پیش پیغمبر صلی الله علیه وسلم فرستاد، و واقعهٔ شما را و پادشاه و معلّم ترسا را به تمام گفت. و مرا پیغمبر صلی الله علیه وسلم فرستاده تا ره‌بری شما کنم. تا به خدمت آن حضرت مشرّف شوید».

{۱۹} پادشاه و معلّم و همهٔ مردمِ لشگر پیک را دیدند، و این اخبار از وی شنیدند. همه خوشحال شدند و گفتند «مرحبا، خوش آمدی! اکنون زودباش و ما را ره‌بری کن که از بهر جمال جهان‌آرای حضرت محمّد صلی الله علیه وسلم آمده‌ایم». پیک ره‌بری کرده همهٔ ایشان را به خدمت حضرت آورد. و حضرتُ پادشاه و معّلم و همهٔ مردم را کنار گرفته و بشارت بهشت دادند. بعداز آن روی به جانب خالد کرد و گفت «وعدهٔ خدای تَعَالَی بر محمّد اینست که چندین هزارکس از شهرهای دیگر پیش خالد مسلمان خواهند شد. از آن، یکی به سعادت رسید».

[۱۲] این واژه در اشعار فردوسی نیز دیده می‌شود.

[ی] از جبرئیل پرسید «کدام جانب رود؟» و جبرئیل راه را به حضرت نمود، و حضرت پیک را نمودند.

{17} Then, Gabriel (pbuh) went to the Prophet and conveyed a command: 'O Muḥammad, have you checked on Khālid and do you know where he is?' He turned to his Companions and asked, 'Where is Khālid?' A Companion said, 'O Prophet of God, it has been three days since he has not shown himself.' The Prophet (pbuh) said, 'O brother Gabriel, quickly tell me about Khālid and what has happened to him?' Gabriel said, 'You know that God has sent me to you in order to bring good news about Khālid.' A proclamation was conveyed: 'O Muḥammad, do you remember Our promise that We will bring a son from Walīd's loin by whom seventy thousand people will become Muslim? That promised is now fulfilled.' And the whole story was told about Khālid and the Christian minister, the king, and all the relevant things that had happened. After that, His Eminence Gabriel said, 'Khālid and the Christian minister, and the king and all his army are wondering where they should find you. Send your emissary to bring them.'

{18} There was someone among [the Prophet's] army known as, 'Speedy', who was able to cover a seven-day route in one day. The Prophet told him about Khālid. The emissary said, 'O Messenger of God, you just show me the route.' The Prophet (pbuh) said, 'Go through this way.' The emissary, while being extremely happy, completed a route of a few days in a single day. Khālid saw the emissary. He went close to him, hugged him and asked, 'Where is the Prophet of God? And from where have you come?' The emissary said, 'Gabriel was sent to the Prophet (pbuh) by God, and he explained the entire story about you, the king, and the Christian minister. And the Prophet (pbuh) has sent me to you in order to lead you, so you can reach the Prophet.'

{19} The king, the minister, and the entire army saw the emissary and heard this news from him. All became cheerful and said, 'Welcome! Now be quick and lead us, as we are here for the sake of the beautiful face of Muḥammad by whom the world is adorned.' The emissary led them all to the Prophet. And the Prophet welcomed and hugged the king, the minister, and all the people and promised them paradise. Then he looked at Khālid and said, 'God's promise upon Muḥammad is that thousands of people will become Muslim by Khālid. A group of those thousands successfully converted to Islam.'

{۲۰} نظیر دیگر. در وقتِ وفاتِ حضرت، پادشاهی[ک] پیش پیغمبر نامه فرستاد که «من پادشاهم و محمّد نام دارم. و محمّد آخرالزمانم. نیمِ مُلکِ عرب مرا باشد و نیم دیگر تو را باشد، تا درمیان ما صلح باشد. والاّ به خصومت انجامد». بعداز چند روز حضرت پیغمبر ﷺ به جوار رحمت حق سبحانه وتعالی رفت و أَمیر المُؤمِنین ابوبکر صدّیق رضی الله عنه به‌خلافت نشست. فرمود خالد را تا ساخته شود و رفته از آن پادشاه انتقام کشد. چون خالد به حکم خلیفه ساخته شد و با لشگر اسلام بیرون رفت، و به شهر پادشاده[ل] رسید. او هم آن روز مستعد شده به جنگ بیرون آمد. در اوّل جنگ پادشاه کشته شد.[۱۳] و شش هزار کس از آن شهر به‌دست خالد رضی الله عنه مسلمان شدند.

{۲۱} معلوم خوانندگان و نویسندگان باشد که هر قصّه که درین کتاب نوشته شده‌است و جمع گردیده شده به اخبار صحیح و درست نوشته‌ایم تا ثواب دو جهان حاصل شود.

{۲۲} إلٰهِیَ، اهل کفر را به کرم و لطف خویش اهل هدایت و توحید گردانی. و کاتب شکستهٔ بیچاره را بر معرفت توحید آراسته و مستقیم داری. به حرمت نبیّ و اصحاب محمّد.

[۱۳] در برخی نسخ اشاره شده که پادشاه اوّل فردی بود که به دست خالد به اسلام ایمان آورد.

[ک] پادشاه شام [ل] شهر بی‌باکان

{20} Another story. At the time of the death of the Prophet, a ruler sent a letter to the Prophet saying, 'I am a king and my name is Muḥammad. And I am the Muḥammad of the End Times. One half of the Arab land is mine, and the other half is yours. We should peacefully agree upon this. Otherwise, it will end up with enmity.' After a few days, the Prophet (pbuh) passed away and the Commander of Believers, Abū Bakr (pbuh), became the caliph. He ordered Khālid to prepare to exact revenge on that ruler. When Khālid was ready, based on the caliph's order, he moved out with the army of Islam and reached the city of that ruler. Also, the ruler prepared for battle but upon commencement of the battle the ruler was killed. And then six thousand people from that city became Muslim by means of Khālid.

{21} It should be evident to readers and scribes that every story which is written in this book has been compiled and based on sound traditions in order to gain the reward of both worlds.

{22} *O God, turn disbelievers into believers in divine unity due to Your kindness. And grant the knowledge of unity upon the poor author of this story and put him on the straight path. By the glory of the Prophet and the Companion of Muḥammad. [Amen.]*

فضیلتِ بلال و پادشاهی از اقلیم عرب[۱]

{۱} آورده‌اند که چون پیغمبر ﷺ در شب معراج بر عرش مجید برآمد، در خاطر مبارکشان گذشت که «برادرم موسیٰ علیه‌السلام به معراج کوه طور[۲] برآمده بود. و نعلین در پای داشت. فرمان شد که یا موسیٰ نعلین از پای بکش. ای محمّد، تا آنکه تو را نگفته‌اند که نعلین از پای کشی، رعایت آداب کن و نعلین از پای بیرون کش». خواست تا نعلین بیرون کند فرمان رسید «ای محمّد، آنچه در خاطر تو گذشته از علم ما خالی نیست، و ما نخواهیم که نعلین از پای بِکَنی. اشارت به نعلین کندن موسیٰ آن بود که گَردِ کوه طور بر پای موسیٰ رسد تا مستغفِر[۳] تو گردد.

{۲} و امّا، ای محمّد، او موسیٰ بود و تو محمّد. دولت و عظمت تو از آن بزرگ‌تر است که تو خیال می‌کنی. از آن روز باز که عرشِ مجید خود را بیافریده‌ام از جنبش قرار نمی‌گیرد. و چون سعادت قدم تو بدین عرش رسیده‌است آن قرار یافت. اکنون نعلین از پای خود بجنبان تا گَردِ نعلین تو بر تارَک[۴] عرش ما رسد. و ما فرماییم تا این گَردِ نعلین تو جمیع کنند، تا حوران بهشت سرمهٔ چشم سازند تا بَرکت قدم تو جمال چَشم ایشان گردد. ای محمّد، اگر قدم موسیٰ بر کوه طور رسید [به] برکت قدم او که در حضرت ما آمد ذرّه از پرتو جمال ما بر کوه تافت تا نیز سرمه اهل دنیا گشت. و گرد نعلین تو توتیای چشم حوران بهشت شود».[۵]

[۱] در برخی نسخ چنین آمده «در فضیلتِ بلال وهلال و پادشاه-عزیز». علاوه‌بر منابع روایی و ادبی متعدّد، احتمالا دفتر سوم مثنوی معنوی مولانا «وفات یافتن بلال رضی‌الله‌عنه با شادی» درون‌مایهٔ اصلی این داستان بوده است: «چون بلال از ضعف شد همچون هلال؛ رنگ مرگ افتاد بر روی بلال».
[۲] در برخی نسخ کوه سینا معرّفی شده است.
[۳] آمرزش خواهنده. به دهخدا مراجعه شود.
[۴] نوک، رأس.
[۵] در «موسیٰ نامه»، داستان سی‌وپنجم، اشاره به این واقعه مشهود است. دلیلی دیگر که چرا تعداد داستان‌های درّالمجالس بیش از سی‌وسه عدد می‌باشد.

CHAPTER 15

On the virtue of Bilāl, and a king from the Arab region[1]

{1} It is reported that when the Prophet (pbuh) reached the glorious Throne on the Night of Ascension he pondered, 'My brother Moses (pbuh) ascended Mount Sinai. He wore sandals. A divine command arrived, "O Moses take of your sandals." So, Muḥammad, behave properly and take off your sandals before you are commanded.' As he began to take off his sandals, a divine message arrived, 'O Muḥammad, We are not unaware of what has come into your mind, but We do not want you to take off your sandals. If We asked Moses to take off his sandals it was because We wanted the dust of the Mount Sinai to reach his foot in order to seek your forgiveness.

{2} But, O Muḥammad, he was Moses, and you are Muḥammad. Your dignity and greatness is more than his and more than what you think. Since the day that I created my glorious Throne, it has risen and fallen. Now your blessed step has reached this Throne, it has become comfortable and settled. Now take your sandals from your foot, so the dust of your sandal can touch upon the tip of Our Throne. And We order that the dust of your sandals be collected so the heavenly cherubs can use it as kohl. Thus, the blessing of your steps can provide beauty to their eyes. O Muḥammad, when Moses' steps reached Mount Sinai, from the blessing of his step in Our presence, a twinkle of the illumination of Our grace shed light on the mountain such that it made kohl[2] for the inhabitants of the Earth. Yet the dust of your sandals is kohl for the eyes of the heavenly cherubs.'

[1] Also, 'On the virtue of Bilāl and Hilāl'. Apart from traditional and literary sources, the gist of this story may be related to Book 3 of Rūmī's *Mathnawī*, 'The story of Bilāl, who embraced death with joy'.

[2] i.e., traditional mascara

{۳} الغرض. چون خداوند تَعَالَى پیغمبر ﷺ را از حضرتِ پاکِ خود باز گردانید، فرمان شد که «ای محمّد، تو باز می‌گردی امّا در اِقطاع بهشت خود برآیی و تصرّف گردانی». پیغمبر ﷺ فرمودند که «إِلٰهِيّ، هنوز جهان باقیست و بهشتیان در بهشت در نیامده‌اند، قسمت بر کیان کنم؟» ندا آمد که «آن‌روز که مجمع امّتانِ تو در بهشت درآیند، قسمت ایشان در بهشت خواهیم کرد. امروز چون تو نزدیک ابوبکر و عمر و عثمان و علی[۶] و صحابه خود می‌روی، ایشان خواهند گفت «سیّدا، تو را سعادت آنچنان روزی شد. برای ما چه تحفه آوردی؟» تو امروز در بهشت برو، و منزل ایشان را قسمت کن و مژدهٔ بشارت برایشان برسان، و بگو «بهر شما چنین در بهشت قسمت کرده‌ام. و پروردگار شما به کرم خود آن را به شما ارزانی داشت»».

{۴} نظیر دیگر. چون پیغمبر ﷺ در میان بهشت درآمد و به نام هر یاری قصرها و جوی‌ها و باغ‌ها و أنهار و أشجار و غلمان و حوران قسمت می‌کردند. ناگاه نظر مبارک پیغمبر ﷺ بر حوری درآمد. حضرت آن را به نام بلال رَضِيَ اللهُ عَنْهُ تعیین کرد. و این حور در کرشمه درآمد و گفت «یا رسول الله، منصف شو[۷]؛ بلال رَضِيَ اللهُ عَنْهُ سیاه است و سیاهیِ نسبت به شب دارد. و من زعفرانی‌ام و زعفران به روزِ روشن ماند». پیغمبر ﷺ گفت «ای حور، اگر نسبت خود به زعفران و روزِ روشن می‌کنی، بلالِ من به نسبت مشکِ سیاه ماند. و دیگر گفتی که سیاهی او به تاریکی شب مانَد. آخر نشنیده‌ای که روز خلیفهٔ شب است و شب خلیفهٔ روز؛[۸] در روز غوغای عالم است و شب رازدار دوستان حقّ است؟»

{۵} هنوز پیغمبر در سخن بود که فرمان رسید «ای محمّد، اکنون تو بر حور سخن مگوی تا من از جهت بلالِ خود با این حور سخن بگویم». آنگاه فرمان رسید «ای حور، تو را با جملهٔ حوران بهشت بی‌خال آفریده‌ایم، و فردای قیامت فرمان دهیم تا سیاهی بلال را جمع کنند و یکان یکان نقطهٔ سیاهی خال به رخسارهٔ حوران بکشند تا به برکت نقطهٔ سیاهی او هر روز جمال شمایان زیادت گردد». زهی! به برکت نقطهٔ سیاهی او که زینت جمال ایشان خواهد بود.

{۶} نظیر دیگر. آورده‌اند که حضرت پیغمبر ﷺ در شب معراج نزدیک درِ بهشت رسید. آواز بانگ نماز به سمع ایشان رسید. متحیّر شدند، و گفت «إِلٰهِيّ، وعدهٔ تو با محمّد این بود که پیش‌از من در بهشت کسی نیاید. این کیست که پیش‌از من در بهشت درآمده؟» فرمان آمد «ای محمّد، خادمِ دولت‌سرایِ تو، بلال، است که پیش‌از آنکه به ملازمت تو مشرّف شود اوّل در بهشت بانگ نماز می‌گوید، و بعداز آن مؤذّنان دیگر بانگ نماز می‌گویند». زهی مرتبهٔ بلال که در بهشت بانگ نماز به نام اوست، و فردای قیامت جملهٔ مؤذّنان زیر سایه عَلَم بلال باشند.

[۶] در برخی نسخ به غیر از «صحابه» نام خلفاء راشدین دیده نمی‌شود.
[۷] دادور و داور باش؛ به‌حقّ داوری کن!
[۸] اشاره به آیهٔ ۲۹ سورهٔ لقمان دارد.

{3} The rest of the story. When God sent Muḥammad back from His purified presence, a command was sent, 'O Muḥammad, return to paradise and allocate shares of heaven and acquire them.' The Prophet (pbuh) said, 'O God, the world remains, and the people of paradise have not yet come to paradise. To whom should I allocate shares of heaven?' A voice was heard, 'The day that the assembly of your community enters paradise, We will allocate to them in paradise. As you are today going back to Abū Bakr, ʿUmar, ʿUthmān, and ʿAlī as well as your Companions, they will request, "O master, you have been granted such a remarkable blessing. What have you brought us as a bounty?" Today, you should go to paradise and divide their land there and take good news to them and tell them that "I have allocated lands in paradise for you. And your God, due to His kindness, granted them to you".'

{4} Another story. Regarding the time when the Prophet (pbuh) arrived in paradise and divided and allocated castles, streams, gardens, brooks, trees, and handsome/youthful lads and heavenly cherubs for each of his Companions. Suddenly, the Prophet's (pbuh) sacred eye noticed a houri. The Prophet named the houri, 'Bilāl' (pbuh). And the houri coquettishly said, 'Be just, O Messenger of God! Bilāl (pbuh) was black, and blackness is a reminder of night. While I am a saffronish-colour,[3] and saffron resembles the day.' The Prophet (pbuh) replied, 'O houri, if you are comparing yourself with saffron and day, my Bilāl looks like a black musk. And you also said that his black colour is like the darkness of the night. Did you not know that day is the successor of night and night is the successor of day?[4] During the day the world is embroiled in a scuffle and the night is secret keeper and is entrusted to God's friends?'

{5} While the Prophet was speaking, a command arrived, 'O Muḥammad, do not speak to that houri any more, as I want to talk to the houri in defense of Bilāl.' Then God said, 'O houri, We created you as well as our heavenly cherubs without a beauty mark/spot. Upon the Day of Judgement, We order for all the blackness of Bilāl to be collected and for a beauty mark to be drawn on the faces of the cherubs, one by one. The blessing of the dark spots will increase your beauty every day.' Hooray for the blessing of that black spot from Bilāl for it becomes the beauty of their faces!

{6} Another story. It is reported that the Prophet (pbuh) arrived at the gates of paradise. He heard the sound of the call to prayer. He was surprised and said, 'O God, You had promised me that no one would enter paradise before me. Who is this man who entered paradise before me?!' A proclamation was made: 'O Muḥammad, this is the servant of your court, Bilāl, who has announced a call to prayer in paradise, before serving you. And after him, other *muʾadhdhin* will begin to call for prayer.' Huzzah!

[3] Also, referring to "cheerfulness". [4] This part referes to Q. 31:29.

{۷} نظیر دیگر. هلال[۹] نام غلامی بود و او پیش‌تر به شرف مسلمانی مشرّف شده‌بود. و هیچ‌کس او را نمی‌دانست تا روزی پیغمبر ﷺ در مسجد با اصحاب نشسته بود و فرمود «ای یاران، بدانید که این‌زمان نزدیکِ محمّد کسی خواهد آمد که بهشت مشتاق دیدار اوست». چون یاران چنین شنیدند بیرون آمدند تا به استقبال آن شخص روند. حضرت فرمود «ای یاران، کجا می‌روید که مردانِ خدای عزّوجلّ را نشناسند». یاران جانب در مسجد آمدند و منتظر بودند که ناگاه «مرد سیاهی اندر مسجد درآمد. هر دو چشم سوی هوا دوخته و حضرت پیغمبر ﷺ را سلام کرد. رسول او را به تعظیم تمام پیش خود آورد و نزدیک خود نشاند. و به نظر مبارک جانب روی هلال می‌دید که به غایت گرسنه است و چشم در حدقه فرو رفته است؛ چند روز باشد که خوردنی نخورده.

{۸} پیغمبر ﷺ گفت «اگر بگوئی چیزی بیارم تا افطار کنی». گفت «یا رسول الله، نذر کردم به درگاه مولا چون سعادت دیدار شما روزی شود، سه روز شکرانهٔ آن روزه دارم». پیغمبر ﷺ گفت «چون این سه روز بگذرد وقت افطار محمّد را به دعا یاد داری؟» گفت «یا رسول الله، تو برگزیدهٔ حضرت رحمانی؛ به دعای من تو را حاجت نیست. اما هیچ نمی‌دانم تا سه روز حیات من وفا خواهد کرد یا نه». این‌قدر گفت و از خدمت رسول رفت.

{۹} بعداز سه‌روز جبرئیل عليه‌السلام بیامد، و گفت «ای محمّد، خدای تبارک‌وتعالی در جهان مژدهٔ بشارت می‌دهد به وفاتِ هلال که از جهان رحلت نمود». جبرئیل این سخن بگفت و به تعجیل بازگشت. حضرت گفت «یا أخي، چرا به شتاب باز می‌گردی؟» گفت «سیّدا، مرا فرمان شد که این خبر به محمّد رسانم و سر بالین هلال حاضر شوم، و سر مبارک هلال را در کنار گیرم. مگس را نی کنم[۱۰] تا آنکه محمّد بر سر بالین او برسد». پیغمبر عليه‌السلام گفت «ای برادر جبرئیل، هلال کجا نقل کرده است؟»[۱۱] جبرئیل گفت که «او غلام مغیره است، و در خانهٔ مغیره نقل کرده است». پیغمبر ﷺ روی سوی یاران کرد و گفت «بدانید که بهشت مشتاق دیدارهلال بود. به‌دیدار او رسید. اکنون بیایید تا تجهیز، تکفین و تلقین او کنیم».

{۱۰} روی به خانهٔ مغیره کردند. چون به در خانهٔ مغیره رسیدند او را خبر کردند که حضرت محمّد پیش در خانهٔ استاده است. مغیره پرغصّه و از روی غضب بر در خانه آمد،[الف] و گفت «ای محمّد، چه خواهی که بر در خانهٔ ما آمده‌ای؟» حضرت گفت «من از برای تو نیامده‌ام. امّا، درخانهٔ تو کسی نقل کرده‌است که به‌جهت او آمده‌ام». مغیره گفت «جملهٔ اهل خانهٔ من به سلامتند و کسی نقل نکرده است. از کجا می‌گوئی؟» پیغمبر ﷺ فرمود «من از خود نمی‌گویم، و مرا پروردگار عزّ وعَلا فرستاده‌است. هرگز نوعی دیگر نگویم. و پروردگار من هرگز دروغ نگوید».

[۹] چندین تن از صحابهٔ پیامبر با نام «هلال» شناخته می شوند (مثل هلال بن أمية)

[۱۰] دور کنم.

[۱۱] اشاره به محلّ درگذشت هلال دارد.

[الف] مغیره متغیّر شد که «آیا او به چه کار آمده باشد به در خانهٔ من؟»

Hooray for Bilāl[5] for the call to prayer in paradise comes after his name and, on the Day of Judgement, all *mu'adhdhins* are under the flag of Bilāl!

{7} Another story. Hilāl was the name of a slave, who was earlier converted to Islam. But no one knew him. One day, when the Prophet (pbuh) was with his Companions in the mosque, he said, 'O Companions, be aware that someone will come to Muḥammad very soon; one for whom paradise is waiting.' When the Companions heard this they left the mosque to get ready to welcome him. The Prophet said, 'O Companions! Where are you heading, as the men of God are not known?' The Companions returned to the mosque and waited until a black man entered. He looked up and greeted the Prophet (pbuh). The Messenger took him and treated him with a lot of respect and led him to a place near himself. He kindly looked at Hilāl who was extremely hungry with his eyes sunken into their sockets. It had been a couple of days since he had eaten anything.

{8} The Prophet (pbuh) said, 'If you wish, I'll bring something with which to break your fast.' He replied, 'O Prophet of God, I have made a vow to God that when I visit you, I will fast for three days on account of the grace and blessing.' The Prophet (pbuh) said, 'Would you remember, Muḥammad, during the breaking of fast, when these three days pass?' He said, 'O Messenger of God, you are the chosen one of the merciful Lord; you do not need my prayer. However, I am not sure whether I will be alive for the next three days or not.' He said this and left the Prophet.

{9} After three days Gabriel came and said, 'O Muḥammad! God conveys good news that Hilāl has left this world.' Gabriel said this and promptly went back. The Prophet said, 'O brother, why do you return so fast?' He said, 'O my master, I was ordered to convey this message to you and go to the corpse of Hilāl, hold his sacred head, and scare away flies until you go to his corpse.'The Prophet (pbuh) said, 'O brother Gabriel, where did Hilāl die?' Gabriel said, 'He was the slave of Mughīra and he died in Mughīra's house.' The Prophet (pbuh) looked at his Companions and said, 'Truly, we knew that paradise was looking forward to receiving Hilāl. Now paradise has gained. Join me to prepare him, shroud him, and conduct his funeral rites.'

{10} They went to the house of Mughīra. When they arrived at his door, they informed him that Prophet Muḥammad was at the door of the house. Mughīra, while being sad and angry, came out and said, 'O Muḥammad, what do you want from my house?' The Prophet said, 'I did not come for you, but there is someone who has died in your house. I came for him.' Mughīra said, 'All my household is safe and sound and no one has died. What makes you think this?' The Prophet (pbuh) said, 'I do not say this from my own self. And Almighty God has sent me here. I never say an untruth and my God never lies.'

[5] i.e., how lucky he is

{۱۱} مغیره به درون خانه درآمد و تمامی اهل و بیت خود را تفحّص کرد. همه را سلامت دید. شادمان برون آمد تا سخن رسول ﷺ را تغییر دهد. درین زمان غلامی از پیش برآمد و گفت «ای خواجه، هلال که نگهبان اشتران بود نقل کرده‌است». مغیره گفت «ای محمّد، جملهٔ خانهٔ من سلامت‌اند. مگر آنکه غلامی بود کمترینِ غلامان، شتربانی کردی و سرگین کشیدی. او نقل کرده‌است». پیغمبر گفت «اگر بر تو کمینه است امّا در حضرتِ پادشاهِ هر دو عالم[ب] مقرّب است». آنگاه مغیره گفت «ای محمّد، او نزدیک ستوران و در میان سرگین‌ها افتاده‌است».

{۱۲} پیغمبر ﷺ با صحابه خود برآن محلّ رسیدند. دیدند که در جای ستوران افتاده است، و جبرئیل علیه‌السلام سر او را به زانو گرفته، و مگس از روی او می‌راند. آنگه پیغمبر به دست مبارک خود او را غسل داد. هرچند که امیر المؤمنین عُمر گفت «من غسل بدهم»[ج] رسول فرمود «ای عُمر، شستن هلال کار محمّد است. زیرا که محمّد غریب و هلال هم غریب است».[۱۲]

{۱۳} الغرض. بعداز شستن به کفن پیچیدند و جنازه نهادند[۱۳] و به گورستان بردند. پیغمبر ﷺ به جانب لحد می‌دید و تبسّم می‌کرد. یاران گفتند «یا رسول الله، شما فرموده بودید که گورستان مقام حیرت و عبرت است؛ خنده و تبسّم شما از کجاست؟» فرمود که «ای یاران، چون تختهٔ لحد و خاک بر هلال پوشیدند، چهار حوری در آمدند و بر دست یکی شراب بهشت و بر دست دیگر طعام بهشت. و یکی حوری می‌گوید «از دنیا تشنه برآمده است، اوّل شراب بهشت من دهم»، و یکی می‌گوید «اوّل عقد من برخوان و دیگری می‌گوید «از آنِ من برخوان»».[د] هلال در لحد از پهلو بگردید[ه] و حوران را گفت «لاَ أُرِیدُ إلاّ هُو، یعنی نخواهم شما را تا آنکه اوّل دیدار پروردگار خود را نبینم». صحابه چون این خبر شنیدند از سر تربت شادان و خرّم بازگشتند.

{۱۴} نظیر دیگر. چون پیغمبر ﷺ به شرف پیغمبری مبعوث شد و کوس مراتب پیغمبر و دولت او در هفت آسمان و زمین بکوفتند، و عَلَم اسلام او بر جملهٔ جهانیان تابان گشت، پادشاهی از اقلیم عرب تَرکِ پادشاهی کرد و جامهٔ کهنه دربرکرد. روی به شهر مدینه کرد. آن‌روز که در مدینهٔ مبارکه رسید از یکی پرسید «محمّد که دعوی پیغمبری می‌کند کجا باشد؟»[و] گفتند «در مسجد با یاران خود نشسته است». آن پادشاه در خاطر گذرانید که من در تورات و انجیل صفت او بسیار شنیده‌ام که او رحمت عالمیان باشد و خُلق او دامِ دل‌ها باشد. اکنون خُلق او را بیازمایم که چگونه است و چه صفا دارد».

[۱۲] در برخی نسخ این جمله اضافه می شود (پیغمبر غسل دادند و یاران آب ریختند) [۱۳] در تابوت نهادند.

[ب] در نظر ما [ج] هرچند که صحابه خواستند که از دست رسول علیه‌السلام بستانند [د] جماعتی از حوران بهشت آمده و بردست یکی شراب بهشت، و در دست یکی طعام بهشت. آن یکی می گوید که «تشنه آمده باشی، بگیر شراب بهشتی بخور»، دیگری می گوید «گرسنه آمده، بگیر طعام بخور» و یک حور می گوید که «یا رسول الله، اوّل عقد من بر هلال برخوان» و دیگری می گوید که «ازآنِ من برخوان»
[ه] بر پهلوی دگر گشت [و] و می گوید که ««من پیغمبر آخرالزّمانم» کجا باشد؟»

{11} Mughīra went back into the house and checked his whole family and house. He found all of them safe. Happily, he returned to question the Prophet's (pbuh) statement – but lo and behold – a servant came forward and said, 'O sir, Hilāl, who looked after the camels, has died.' Mughīra said, 'O Muḥammad, my whole family is healthy, with the exception of one servant, who was the most inferior, and who looked after camels and cleaned out their dung. He has died.' The Prophet said, 'He may be inferior in your eyes, but he is the one nearest to the Lord of the two worlds.' Mughīra said, 'O Muḥammad, he has been left near the livestock and among the dung.'

{12} The Prophet (pbuh), along with his Companions, reached that place. They noticed that he had fallen in the stable of livestock, and that Gabriel (pbuh) held his head on his knee and waved away flies. Then the Prophet washed him with his own sacred hands. Whenever the Commander of Believers ʿUmar insisted to wash him instead, the Messenger replied, 'O ʿUmar, washing Hilāl is the task of Muḥammad, because both Muḥammad and Hilāl are both lonely[6].'

{13} To return to the story. After washing him they wrapped him in a shroud and prepared the corpse and went towards the cemetery. The Prophet (pbuh) looked at the niche and vault in the side of the grave and smiled. The Companions asked, 'O Messenger of God, you have stated that the cemetery is the place of reflection and of learning lessons. What is the reason for your smiling?' [The Prophet] said, 'O Companions, once Hilāl was covered by the laḥad board and soil, four houris arrived. One of them held wine from heaven, another heavenly food, and one houri said, "He has just come from the world while being thirsty; I will serve him first with the wine of paradise." The remaining houri said, "[O Prophet] first marry me to him" and the other said, "Read the marriage sermon upon me." Hilāl was side-by-side[7] in the grave[8] and said to them, "I do not desire anyone except Him", meaning that I did not desire any of you until I first met my Lord.' When the Companions heard this story, they left the grave cheerfully.

{14} Another story. After the Prophet (pbuh) was appointed as a prophet and the drum of his prophecy and his status was beaten in the seven heavens and earths, and the standard of Islam was raised over all beings, a king from the Arabian zone left and renounced his kingship and wore old clothes and travelled towards Medina. When he arrived in the holy city of Medina, he asked someone, 'Where is Muḥammad, who claims to be the Prophet?' He said, 'He is sitting in the mosque with his Companions.' That king pondered, 'I have heard a lot about his attributions in the Torah and the Gospel, that he is the mercy of creatures, and that his behaviour entraps people's hearts. Now I want to witness his behaviour for myself to see if this is true and to see how pleasant it is.'

[6] [and special] [7] He changed his side [8] [with the houris?]

{۱۵} پادشاه خود را مجنون ساخت و در مسجد درآمد. و هر فحش که بر زبان جاری شد گفتی. یاران تند شدند و گفتند «او را ادب کنیم». حضرت فرمودند «ای یاران، نخواهم که کسی مجنون را برنجاند. از بدگفتن کسی نمی‌باید رنجید که کار او از حدّ و حُکم شرع گذشته باشد». چون یاران از زبان مبارک حضرت ﷺ این سخن شندیدند همه خاموش شدند. باز آن مرد جامه از شرمگاه خود جدا کرد و در میان مسجد بول[۱۴] کردن گرفت. یاران گفتند «یا رسول الله، بیت الله را به نجاست پلید ساخت». پیغمبر فرمود «این به برداشتن قدری خاک از مسجد پاک گردد، امّا آزار دل بندهٔ خدای تَعَالَی هرگز محمّد نخواهد». چون پادشاه از زبان پیغمبر دو کرّت چنین شنید در خاطر گفت «از چنین روی و گفتاری هرگز دعوی نبوّت دروغ نباشد».

{۱۶} آنگاه پادشاه گفت «کسی که در دین تو درآید چه مقدار درجه باشد؟» پیغمبر ﷺ فرمود «هرکه در دین من درآید حقّ سُبْحَانَهُ وَتَعَالَىٰ او را بهشت روزی کند». و صفت بهشت بیان کردند که کوشک‌ها و شهرستان‌ها و جویبارها و انهار و اشجار و حوران و قصرها چنین باشد. پادشاه آغاز کرد که «ای محمّد، من هم پادشاه بودم. کوشک‌ها و شهرستان‌ها و کنیزکان زیبا داشتم. اکنون بدین‌ها حاجت ندارم». پیغمبر ﷺ چون دید که رغبت بهشت نمی‌کند گفت «وی را از آتش دوزخ بترسانم».

{۱۷} آغاز کرد که «هرکه به دین من در نیاید خدای تَعَالَی او را در زندان دوزخ دارد» و سپس عذاب‌های دوزخ بیان می‌کرد. آنگاه پادشاه گفت «ای محمّد، قصّهٔ آن دراز مکن. اگر خدای عَزَّ وَجَلَّ خواهد بنده را عذاب کند توفیق عذاب کشیدن هم به او خواهد داد». پیغمبر ﷺ دید که نه رغبت بهشت می‌کند و نه بیم دوزخ دارد. پس فرمود که «مطلوبِ چه داری؟» گفت «ای محمّد، من به یک شرط به تو ایمان می‌آرم. اگر ضامن شوی و خط بدهی[۱۵] که حقّ سُبْحَانَهُ وَتَعَالَىٰ مرا فردای قیامت به دیدار خود روزی گرداند». پیغمبر ﷺ گفت «محمّد کجا تواند که ضامن دیدار حقّ شود؟»

{۱۸} چون پیغمبر ﷺ او را این جواب داد، درهمان ساعت جبرئیل عَلَيْهِ ٱلسَّلَامُ رسید. و خطّی بر کاغذ حریر نوشته بیاورد[ذ] و گفت «ای محمّد، فرمان می‌شود که بیا. به یدِ قدرت خود این خطّ به ضامنی تو نوشته‌ایم. به دست عرب بده». آن پادشاه اعرابی چون آن خطّ حضرت صمدیّت رَبِّ الْعَالَمِين بدید از غایت شوق گفت «ای بهترینِ عالمیان، زود کلمه عرض کن تا در دین پاک تو در آیم». حضرت فرمود بگو «لآ إِلٰهَ إِلَّا الله، مُحَمَّدٌ رَسُولُ الله».

[۱۴] ادرار. [۱۵] گواهی دادن، تضمین نمودن.

[ذ] و خطّ سبزی بر حریر نوشته آورد

{15} Like a madman he went to the mosque and whatever bad words came [to his mind] he expressed. The Companions were angry and said, 'We'll teach him a lesson.' The Prophet said, 'O Companions, I do not want anyone to disturb one who is mad. One should not be annoyed by his swear words as his acts are not liable for Islamic punishment nor sentence.' When the Companions heard this from the sacred mouth of the Prophet (pbuh) they became silent. Later on, the man uncovered himself and urinated in the mosque. The Companions said, 'O Messenger of God, he made the house of God impure with urine!' The Prophet said, 'This [impurity] may simply be cleansed by portions of soil, but Muḥammad never wishes to see the suffering of God's servant.' Once the king heard such things from the Prophet twice, he pondered, 'From a person with such a nice character and behaviour, the claim of prophecy will never be false.'

{16} Then the king said, 'What would be the rank of the one who coverts to your religion?' The Prophet (pbuh) said, 'Whoever comes to my religion, God will provide for him in paradise', and then he explained the features of paradise, 'Palaces, regions, brooks, rivers, trees, cherubs, and castles.' The king said, 'O Muḥammad, I was a king, too. I was in possession of palaces, regions, and fair maidens. Now I do not need these anymore.' When the Prophet (pbuh) noticed that he was not interested in paradise, he thought, 'I will scare him with hellfire.'

{17} [The Prophet] said, 'Whoever does not convert to my religion, God will place him in a hellish prison', and then he explained the torments of hell. The king said, 'O Muḥammad, say no more! If God wants to punish a servant, He would give him full measure.' The Prophet (pbuh) noticed that he was not interested in paradise nor afraid of hell. Then he asked, 'What you are seeking?' He said, 'O Muḥammad, I accept your religion subject to one condition; that you guarantee and provide me with a recognition that God will grant that I will meet Him on the Day of Judgement.' The Prophet (pbuh) said, 'How can Muḥammad guarantee that you will meet God?'

{18} When Muḥammad responded with this answer, Gabriel (pbuh) soon descended. He brought a note written on silky paper and said, 'O Muḥammad, it is commanded, "Take it. By Our powerful hand, we have written this, on behalf of you as guarantor. Pass it into the Arab's hand."' When that Arab king noticed the handwriting of the Lord of all worlds, with great happiness he said, 'O the best of the worlds, recite to me the declaration of faith in order to convert me to your pure religion.' The Prophet said, 'Say, "I bear witness that there is not god but God; Muḥammad is the Messenger of God."'

{۱۹} چون اعرابی به سعادت ایمان مشرّف گشت، گفت «ای سرور اولاد آدم، شکرانهٔ ملاقات شما دو رکعت به درگاه خدای تَعَالَی بگذارم». حضرت ترغیب نماز کرد. اعرابی برخاست و دو رکعت نماز گذارد. سر به سجده نهاد و گفت «ای خالق، مقصودی که در حضرت پاک تو داشتم بدان رسانیدی. دیگر هیچ مطلوب ندارم به‌جز دیدار ذات پاکت». و در سجده بود که جان به حق سبحانه وتعالی سپرد. پیغمبر صلی الله علیه وسلم فرمود تا غسل دادند[۱۶] و در گورستان بردند.

{۲۰} پیغمبر صلی الله علیه وسلم همراه بود. چون دفن کردند حضرت در تبسّم آمد. یاران پرسیدند که «سبب تبسّم چیست؟» فرمود «ای یاران، چون اعرابی را در لحد درآوردیم، دیدم دو دست به ید قدرت خدای تَعَالَی در لحدِ اعرابی پیدا شد و اعرابی را در کنار گرفت و معذرت بسیار می‌کرد[۱۷] و می‌گفت «ای بلندهمّت، نه طمع در بهشت کردی و نه از خوف دوزخ ترسیدی. به جز دیدار ما هیچ چیز نپرداختی»» .

{۲۱} إِلٰهِيَ، به حرمت هزار و یک نام تو، همه را ایمان و دیدار خود روزی گردانی. بِمِنَّة وَکَرَمه.

[۱۶] که غسل دهند. [۱۷] احتمالا اشاره به پذیرفتن عذر وی دارد.

{19} When the Arab was honoured by converting to the faith, he said, 'O the master of Adam's children, due to the privilege of meeting you, I would like to prostrate and worship.' The Prophet also encouraged him to perform prayer. The Arab stood up and performed a two-unit prayer. He prostrated and said, 'O Creator, You gave me what I wanted before Your pure presence. Now I want nothing more except to witness Your pure essence.' While being in prostration he left his life to God. The Prophet (pbuh) ordered for him to be washed and carried him to the cemetery.

{20} The Prophet (pbuh) also accompanied them. When they had buried him, the Prophet smiled. The Companions asked, 'What is the reason for your smile?' He replied, 'O Companions, when we put the Arab into the grave, I noticed that two hands, by the power of God, went to the Arab's grave and hugged the Arab and forgave everything,[9] and said, 'O ambitious one, you were not greedy for paradise, nor afraid of hell. You did not pay attention to anything but experiencing Our vision.'

{21} *O God, by the holiness of your one thousand and one names, grant everyone the faith and Your vision. By Your unmerited favour and kindness. [Amen.]*

[9] Or: accepted his request?

نصیحت کردن لقمان حکیم عبدالرحمن بر پسر خویش را[الف]

{۱} چنین آورده‌اند که خواجه لقمان حکیم علیه الرحمة در کتاب نوشته دیده‌بود که «هر که ثواب بسیار از ما طمع دارد باید که در حضرت ما قرض حسنه بدهد. که در سخاوت ده نیکی است، و در دادن قرضِ حسنه هجده نیکی است». برین نیّت هر حاجت‌مندی که پیش وی رفتی، خواجه لقمان قرض حسنه بدادی. مردمان از شهرها برای او می‌رفتند و از وی قرض حسنه می‌ستاندند. تا آنکه روزی سوداگری قصد دیار خواجه لقمان کرد. در خاطر ایشان اندیشه کرد که «خواجه بی‌ضمان[۱] مال می‌دهد. بیا تا پاره‌زر بگیرم. اگر مرا خوش آید زر او را خواهم داد، و الّا از من چگونه مال بستاند».

{۲} این مرد نزد خواجه لقمان آمد، و گفت «من سوداگر بودم، و مال من به غارت رفته‌است و از دست من کار دیگر نمی‌آید به جز سوداگری». خواجه لقمان چون این حکایت شنید، خط قرضی بست و مبلغ مالی به وی داد. و آن مرد مال‌ها را از خواجه بستاند و در شهر خود درآمد. و سوداگری می‌کرد. و از مال خواجه او را چندان مال شد که هیچ‌کس حساب آن را ندانستی.

{۳} تا روزی خواجه لقمان پسر خود را گفت «چندین مال من در ذمّهٔ فلان سوداگر است که از فلان شهر آمده بود. برو، و مال را از وی بیار». پسر به حکم پدر ساخته شد تا روان شود. خواجه لقمان گفت «ای فرزند، تو را چهار وصیّت می‌کنم. باید که بدان عمل کنی». فرزند گفت «قبول کردم».

[۱] ضمانت.

[الف] نصیحت خواجه لقمان حکیم بر پسر خویش علیه الرحمة والغفران

CHAPTER 16

The advice of Luqmān the Wise, ʿAbd al-Raḥmān, to his son

{1} It is reported that Khʷāja Luqmān Ḥakīm (may God's mercy be upon him) had seen in the Book that 'whoever wishes to receive more reward from God should give a goodly loan, as there are seven blessings and rewards for generosity while there are eighteen blessings and rewards for a goodly loan.' As a result, whenever the poor went to him for something, Khʷāja Luqmān gave them a goodly loan. People from other cities went to him, too, and received a goodly loan from him. One day a merchant planned to visit Khʷāja Luqmān. He pondered, 'Khʷāja gives loans without security. Let's go and get some gold from him. If I like I will give his gold back, otherwise, how else will he get it back from me?'

{2} This man went to Khʷāja Luqmān and said, 'I used to be a merchant, and my property has been stolen and I cannot do anything, except trading.' When Khʷāja Luqmān heard this story he decided to lend him money. And the man took the money from Khʷāja and went to his hometown. And he began to continue his trading. Through Khʷāja's money, his wealth was multiplied to the extent that no one was able to imagine how much so.

{3} One day, Khʷāja Luqmān said to his son, 'A particular amount of my wealth is for long time in the possession of that merchant who came from that city. Go, and bring that money.' Following his father's order, the son prepared to go. Khʷāja Luqmān said, 'O my son, I have four pieces of advice for you. You should follow them.' The son said, 'Of course, I agree.'

{۴} «اوّل: آنگه که از این شهر بیرون روی باید که با مرد پیرِ صالح صحبت کنی.[۲] و هرچه پیر بگوید بشنوی و همان کنی؛ دوم: آنکه زیر درخت خواب نکنی[ب]؛ سوم: آنکه چون در شهرِ سوداگر رسی با او مخالفت نکنی و هر چه بگوید بشنوی؛ چهارم: آنکه اگر زن صاحب جمال تو را به خود فریفته کند، فریفته نشوی و وی را نخواهی». پس خواجه لقمان این چهار وصیّت به فرزند بکرد و فرزند را به خدای تَعَالَی سپرد. پسر از پدر وداع کرد و از شهر برآمد.

{۵} پاره راه رفته بود دیدی مرد پیر خوش لقائی[۳] پیدا گردید. جوان با او ملاقات کرد. پیر پرسید «ای جوان، کجا خواهی رفت؟» جوان گفت «در فلان شهرِ فلان سوداگر خواهم رفت». پیر گفت «من هم همراهم». جوان گفت «زهی سعادت من که در قدم شما باشم». از نصیحت پدر یادش آمد، و همراه پیر روان شد. چند فرسنگ رفته بودند که درخت بلند، در کمال خوبی سایه‌انداخته، دید. پیر را خوش آمد و در پای درخت بنشست. جوان در آفتاب نشسته. پیرگفت «در آفتاب حرّا می‌نشینی؟» فرمود که «پدر من نصیحت کرده که در پای درخت خواب نکنی». پیر گفت «اگر پدر منع کرده امّا گفته که سخن پیر شنوی؟» فی الحال قبول کرد و زیر درخت آمد.

{۶} پیر به جوان گفت «زمانْ بِخُسب[۴] تا اندام سبک گردد، و تا منزلی پیش‌تر توانی رفت». و سخن پیر قبول کرده در خواب شد. در آن درخت ماری بود عظیم و بزرگ. هرگاه بوی آدمی شنیدی از درخت فرود آمدی، و در دم به نیش خود هلاک کردی. چون پیر مار را دیده بود به عصای خود مار را کشت. چون جوان بیدار شد مار عظیمی نزد خود کشته دید. روی به جانب پیر کرد و پرسید که «واقعه چه بود؟» پیر گفت «این مار قصد تو کرده بود، تا تو را هلاک کند. او را کشتم. امّا، ای جوان، اکنون سر این مار را بِبُر، و در کیسهٔ خود نگاه‌دار». پسر چنان کرد و از آنجا روان شدند و به شهر سوداگر رسیدند.

{۷} چون سوداگر پسر خواجه را دید بشناخت. و معذرتِ زبانی به نفاق[۵] نمود. و تمام روز مهمان‌داری کرد. چون شب شد، با پسر خواجه گفت «در کنارهٔ دریا مقام مزوج[۶] است. امشب آنجا خفتن بهتر است. و من جای خواب خود و شما را آنجا فرستاده‌ام». این بگفت و دست پیر و پسر خواجه لقمان را گرفته به کنار دریا برد، و گفت «شما هر دو درین مقام باشید تا فردا مال‌های شما را در آن محلّ بدهم».

[۲] اشاره به همراهی و هم‌صحبتی دارد.
[۳] خوش‌لقایی؛ به معنی خوب‌رویی و یا نیک‌رویی که در اشعار فرّخی سیستانی دیده می‌شود.
[۴] چُرتی بزن.
[۵] به ریا و ظاهری.
[۶] اشاره به «تخت‌خواب دونفره دارد»

[ب] آنکه در زیر درخت تنها خواب نکنی

{4} [Luqmān said,] 'First, once you leave this city, should you speak with and to accompany a pious old man, you listen carefully to whatever he tells you and act accordingly. Second, do not sleep under a tree. Three, once you arrive in the merchant's city do not disobey him and do whatever he says. Four, when a pretty woman tries to seduce you, do not be seduced by her and do not desire her.' In this way, Kh^{w}āja advised his son with these four points and bid farewell to him while entrusting him to God. The son bid farewell to his father and went out of the city.

{5} After a few steps, he saw a friendly old man. The young man greeted him. The old man said, 'O young man, where are you heading to?' The young man said, 'I am off to that city where that merchant lives.' The old man said, 'I will accompany you, Ok?' The young man said, 'How I am blessed to walk along with you.' He was reminded of his father's advice and moved along with the old man. After passing some distance along the road, he noticed a tall tree which had a perfect shady area. The old man liked it and sat under the tree. The son sat in the sunshine. The old man said, 'Why do you sit under the scorching Sun?!' He replied, 'My father has advised me not to lie down under the tree.' The old man said, 'Although your father has prohibited you, he told you to listen to the old man's statement, right?!' The young man, then, agreed upon this and sat under the tree.

{6} The old man told the young man, 'Take a nap until your body is rested and you can proceed to the next place.' He accepted the old man's idea and fell sleep. There was a snake in that tree; a huge, thick snake. Once the snake noticed the smell of human it came down the tree to kill them with its venom. As the old man had earlier noticed the snake, he killed it with his own cane. Once the young man woke up, he saw a huge snake near him which had been killed. He looked at the old man and said, 'What has happened?' The old man said, 'This snake wanted to bite you in order to kill you. So, I killed it. But, O young man, now you must cut the snake's head off and put it into your bag.' The young man did so and they left there until they arrived in the merchant's city.

{7} When the merchant saw Kh^{w}āja's son he recognised him and insincerely made an excuse [for not having repaid the loan]. The merchant hosted him for the whole day. During the night, the merchant said to Kh^{w}āja's son, 'there is a place for two people near the sea. It is better there for sleeping and I have arranged to have our bedding prepared there.' He said this and took the hands of the old man as well as Kh^{w}āja's son to lead them near the sea. 'You, two, stay here, and I will bring your money back sometime tomorrow.'

{۸} و حال آنکه هر شبی درآن موضع دریا موج زدی و هرچه در کنارهٔ دریا بودی همه را ربودی. پیر گفت «ای جوان، این سوداگر قصد تو و ما کرده، می‌خواهد ما را در دریا تلف کند. امّا، تو با این مرد بگو که ما را در صحرا ضرور است.[۷] شما زمانی اینجا باشید تا ما بیائیم». پس سوداگر آنجا بایستاد. پیر گفت «ای جوان، بیا تا بر بلندی برآییم و تماشا کنیم تا چه خواهد شد».

{۹} هر دو برفتند. آن مرد سوداگر در آن مقام انتظاری ایشان می‌کشید که «تا ایشان کی بیایند و من بروم». در ین فکر بود که دریا موجی زد و سوداگر هلاک شد. و هر دو ایشان سلامت ماندند. و بر تمام این شهر معلوم بود که مال سوداگر از زرِ خواجه لقمان پیدا گشته و ارث هم ندارد. آنگاه پادشاه آن شهر تمامی مال آن سوادگر را تسلیم پسر خواجه کردند.

{۱۰} و در آن شهر زنی بود به غایت صاحب‌جمال. به طلب پسر خواجه کس فرستاد که «بروید و پسر خواجه طلب کنید». آن‌کس بیامد و خبر گفت. جوان جانب پیر دید تا چه فرماید. پیر گفت «برو! ببین چه می‌گوید». جوان به اشارت پیر برفت. چون نزدیک آن عورت رسید و در جمال و صورت وی نظر کرد، به خوبی او هرگز ندیده بود. زن گفت «ای جوان، بدان‌که به جمال من درین شهر و عصر نیست، و از مال چندان دارم که مال پدر تو، و مال سوداگر، از چهار حصه[۸] مال من یکی هم نباشد. و من عاشق جمال تو گشته‌ام.[۹] اگر مرا بخواهی نیکو باشد و تمام مال خود را نثار تو کنم». پسر نصیحت پدرش را یاد آمد که «اگر زنی صاحب‌جمالی تو را بخواهد که فریب دهد فریفته نشوی». امّا این جوان دل فریفتهٔ آن جمال گشته بود.

{۱۱} اندیشه کنان به‌خاطر حزین و دل‌غمناک به جانب پیر روان شد.[۱۰] و قصّه را با پیر گفت. پیر از بشرهٔ جوان معلوم کرد که فریفته شده‌است. پیر گفت «اندیشه مکن. برو و وی را بخواه». جوان شادان شد، و حمد و ثنای خدای تَعَالَی به جا آورده نزد آن عورت رفته و عقد بسته. پیر آغاز کرد، و گفت «جوان، زنهار تا من نگویم به او نزدیکی نکنی و هر شبی که با او خواب کنی، پشت جانب او کرده خواب روی».

{۱۲} جوان هر شب چنین کردی تا آنکه عورت را طاقت نماند. گفت «این چه حالت است که گِرد من نمی‌آیی؟» پسر آمد و به پیر گفت «زن چنین می‌گوید». پیر گفت «تو او را بگوی به یک شرط با تو نزدیکی می‌کنم. عودسوزی بیاری و زیر پای و پیراهن خود بکشی، و من چیزی در آن عود دود کنم. چنان کنم که دود در اندام نهانی تو رود و بعداز آن با تو نزدیکی کنم». زن گفت «این سهلست. منّت دارم». پسر به خدمت پیر آمد و گفت «آنچه فرموده بودید قبول کرد».

[۷] برای قضای حاجت؟ [۸] قسمت. [۹] این جملهٔ ستایشی در برخی نسخ موجود نیست.
[۱۰] وصف حال جوان از دلدا گی او به آن زن در برخی نسخ موجود نیست.

{8} This [the merchant said] despite the fact that the tide comes in that place every night and takes whatever is close to the sea. The old man said, 'O young man, this merchant has plans to kill you and me, he wants to drown us in the sea. Now, you tell the merchant, "We need to go to inland[1] and you stay here, until we get back."' The merchant went and stopped there. The old man said, 'O young man, let's go to the high ground and see from above what will happen.'

{9} They both went to the high ground. The merchant was waiting for them down below, and thought, 'Let's wait until they come,[2] and I will go then.' While pondering this, a wave came from the sea and killed the merchant. And both [the old and young men] remained safe. And it was already apparent to all the people of city that the merchant's wealth was produced because of Khʷāja's gold[3], and it was not inherited,[4] so the ruler of the city gave all of the merchant's wealth to Khʷāja's son.

{10} And there was a woman in the city who was very pretty. She sent someone to call Khʷāja's son: 'Go and bring Khʷāja's son.' That emissary arrived with the message. The young man asked the old man what to do. The old man said, 'Go, and see what she says.' The young man followed the order of the old man. When he arrived before her, he saw her beautiful face; he had never seen such beauty before. The woman said, 'O young man, be aware that there is no prettier woman than me in this city and in this period of time, and I have so much wealth that the wealth of your father and of that merchant will not be even a quarter of it. And I have fallen in love with your handsomeness. If you want me it will be wonderful and I will dedicate all my wealth to you.' The son remembered his father's advice that 'when a beautiful woman attempts to seduce you, you should be careful not to be seduced.' But the young man had already fallen in love with the beautiful woman.

{11} While in thought, and being upset and remorseful, he went towards the old man. And he shared the story with him. The old man realised from his manner that he had fallen in love with her. The old man said, 'Do not worry. Go and propose to her.' The young man was so happy and praised God. He went to the woman and married her. The old man then gave a warning, 'O young man, just avoid consummating the marriage until I tell you to do so. And turn your back on her before you go to sleep every night.'

{12} The young man complied with everything until the woman could no longer bear it. She said, 'What does this mean, that you do not come to me?' The young man related the situation to the old man. The old man said, 'You tell her, "I will consummate our marriage on one condition: you must find an incense burner and put it under your skirt, I will then burn something in that burner. I will burn something so its smoke

[1] to relieve themselves? [2] i.e., God knows when they will come [3] i.e., coin
[4] i.e., is not a type of inheritance

{۱۳} پیر گفت «چون آتش در عودسوز انداختی، سرِ ماری را که در کیسهٔ توست آنجا انداز، و بگو در اندام نهانی خود دارد و حاضر باشی تا چه پیدا گردد. و بعداز آن با وی خلوت کنی». چون زن عودسوز را نزدیک اندام نهائی خود داشت، جوان سر مار را در عودسوز انداخت.

{۱۴} القصّه.[۱۱] در شکم آن عورت ماری بود که هر که بدان شهر رسیدی به جمال آن زن فریفته شدی. و به خواستی به‌مجرّدی که با وی جمع شود آن مار از شکم بیرون آید و آلت آن‌کس را نیش زدی و بعداز چند روزی بمردی. و تمام مال را به‌جهت مَهر خود گرفتی. بدین طریق آن مال را بسیار بود.[۱۲]

{۱۵} القصّه.[۱۳] چون سر مار را در عودسوز انداخت بوی او به آن مار که در شکم زن بود رسید. مار به خود شورید که «در مقام من مار دیگر چه کند». درزمانْ از جانب فرج[۱۴] به جنگ برآمد. جوان به اشارت پیر ملاحظه می‌کرد و فی الحال مار را بکشت.[۱۵] زن در حیرت ماند و از غایت وَهْم بیهوش شد. چون بهوش آمد سر خود را به پای جوان نهاد و روی خود بر کف پای او مالید، و می‌گفت «از این بلای عظیم به دولت تو نجات یافتم. مرا به کنیزگی قبول کن. و تمام مال خود را در قدم تو نثار گردانم که مرا از بلای عظیم خلاص کردی. مال چه باشد که جان و تن من فدای تو باد».

{۱۶} جوان دست زن را بگرفت و نزد پیر آورد. و هر دو سر در قدم پیر نهادند. پیر گفت «ای جوان، من در حقّ تو چندین نیکی کردم: از مارِ درخت نجات یافتی؛ دگر از مکر آن سوداگر جستی؛ و دیگر چنین زن صاحب‌جمال با مال بسیار روزی شدی. اکنون به ما چه می‌دهی؟» پسر خواجه لقمان گفت «زن و مال و همه در مُلک شما گردانیدم». پیر تبسّم کرد و گفت «من مال چه خواهم کرد، امّا شما را آزمودم. چون به شهر خود روی پدر خود را سلام من برسانی، و بگویی «مرا با خواجهٔ خضر ملاقات شده‌بود»».

{۱۷} إِلٰهِيّ، به حرمت خواجه خضر[۱۶] و حضرت لقمان حکیم عَلَیْهِمَا ٱلسَلام جملهٔ حاجتِ حاجت‌مندان را برآوردهٔ خیر گردانی. به حقّ محمّد وآله أجمعین.

[۱۱] قصّه کوتاه کنیم. [۱۲] این پاراگراف در برخی نسخ موجود نیست. [۱۳] ادامهٔ داستان. [۱۴] آلت تناسلی. همچنین شرمگاه.

[۱۵] ارتباط دارد به باوری در میان جامعهٔ زنان (بویژه در ایران کنونی) مبنی بر سوزاندن عنبرنسارا\عنبرنصارا در زیر دامن برای از بین بردن بیماری‌ها و یا حساسیت‌های پوستیِ ناحیهٔ آلت تناسلی، بطوری‌که دود حاصل از سوزاندن نبایستی از زیر دامن به بیرون پخش شود. به بخش مقدّمهٔ انگلیسی مراجعه نمایید. [۱۶] (إِلٰهِيّ، به حرمت ملک البحر حضرت خواجه خضر)

reaches your genitalia and after that I will consummate the marriage."' The woman said, 'A piece of cake! I'll do it by all means.' The young man went back to the old man and said, 'She agreed with whatever you had mentioned as a condition.'

{13} The old man said, 'When you place fire into the incense burner then put the snake's head kept in your bag into the fire and tell her to keep it under her genitalia. Be prepared to see what appears, then consummate the marriage.' When the woman put the incense burner near her genitalia, the young man put the snake's head into the incense burner.

{14} To keep a long story short, there was a snake living in the woman's stomach[5]. Whoever visited the city became seduced by the woman's beauty and desired her. Whenever a person was intimate with the woman the snake came out of her stomach and bit the person's penis causing him to die after a couple of days. As such, she took the whole wealth of the deceased as her dowry. This is why she had a lot of money.

{15} The rest of the story. When the young man put the snake's head into the incense burner, its smell reached to the other snake which was living in the stomach of the woman. The snake then became enraged, 'What is another snake doing in my territory?' In this vein, it came out of the woman in order to fight. The young man was, as the old man said, carefully observing and soon killed that snake. That woman looked puzzled and because of her extreme panic she became dizzy and feinted. When she returned to consciousness she bent down to the foot of the young man and rubbed her face on his foot, saying, 'I survived this great calamity due to your grace. Accept me as your servant and I will grant you all my wealth, as you have saved me from the great calamity. What is wealth? I sacrifice my soul and body to you!'

{16} The young man took the woman's hand and brought her to the old man. And both arrived and stood before him. The old man said, 'O young man, I did a few good deeds for you: you were saved from that tree's snake; you were freed from the merchant's trick; and you have been given a beautiful woman with a lot of wealth. What now do you give to me?' The son of Khʷāja Luqmān said, 'I will give you my wife, wealth, and whatever I have.' Then the old man smiled, and said, 'What wealth would help me, I just wanted to see what you would say. When you return to your city convey my best greetings to your father and tell him, "I have met with Khʷāja Khiḍr."'

{17} *O God, by the greatness of Khʷāja Khiḍr (pbuh)*[6] *and Ḥaḍrat Luqmān (pbuh), provide the needs of all seekers and the poor. By Muḥammad and his descendants altogether. [Amen.]*

[5] i.e., womb [6] Also, 'by the greatness of the lord of oceans, Ḥaḍrat Khʷāja Khiḍr'.

در ایمان آوردن بت پرستی با ابراهیم[الف]

{۱} آورده‌اند که کافری بود هفتادسال در بُت‌پرستی گذرانیده بود.[ب] و فرزندی داشت جوان که او را زحمتی پیدا شد. آن مرد کافر هرلحظه در روی فرزندی[۱] خود نگاه می‌کردی و زار زار بگریستی. و گفت «ای فرزندم، می‌ترسم که شاخ جوانی تو پیش‌از من شکستی برسد».[۲] حال پسر را دشوار دید. گفت «بروم و پیش بُتان صِحّت پسرِ خود بخواهم که مدّتی ایشان را به خدای[۳] پرستیده‌ام».[ج]

{۲} چون نزدیک بُتان رسید، پیش هر بتی سرسجده نهاد، گفت «هفتاد سال شما را خدمت کرده‌ام. امروز به حاجتی آمده‌ام که دلبند من به مریضِ[۴] موت گرفتار شده‌است. وی را صِحّت بخشید». پیش هر بتی که حاجت عرض کرد، هیچ جواب نیافت. پشیمان رو به خانه کرد. بر سر راه مسجدی دید که در آن مسلمانان طاعت و بندگی می‌کردند. مَردُ خدای عَزَّوَجَلّ خویش را در خاطر گذرانید که من هم در مسجد روم و از برای شفای فرزند خود از خدای آسمان عَزَّوَجَلّ حاجت خواهم. این فکر بکرد و در مسجد درآمد و سر سجده نهاد، و گفت «إلٰهِيّ، اوصاف کرم تو بسیار شنیده‌ام که لطف تو با همه بالاست. من هم از بهر آشتی بر درِ تو آمده‌ام. و از آن حضرت حاجت می‌خواهم که فرزندُ نزدیک به موت رسیده‌است. او را به لطف خود صِحّت بخش».

[۱] به گمان من «-ی» در انتهای «فرزند» بنابر گویش منطقهٔ کاتب اضافه شده‌است. به هر جهت، مطالعه براین جوانب ارزشمند خواهد بود.
[۲] «شاخ جوانی کسی شکستن» مثلی است رایج در آسیای مرکزی و غرب هندوستان بویژه در افغانستان. این مثل اشاره به «جوان‌مرگی» دارد. برای مطالعهٔ بیشتر مراجعه شود به عبدالله افغانی‌نویس، لغات عامیانهٔ فارسي افغانستان (بلخ: مؤسسه تحقیقات و انتشارات بلخ، ۱۹۹۰)، ۳۶۸.
[۳] به خدایی. [۴] مرض.

[الف] در ایمان آوردن بُت پرست با پسر [ب] آورده‌اند که مردی بود کافر، هفتادسال در بُت‌پرستی عمر تلف کرده‌بود [ج] با مادر او گفت که «هفتادسال است که من این بُت را به خدای پرستیده‌ام. امروز از برای شفای فرزند شفیع آورم. شاید که صِحّت یابد».

CHAPTER 17

On the coming to faith of an idolater through Abraham

{1} It is reported that there was an unbeliever who had worshipped idols for seventy years. He had a young child who was afflicted by illness. The unbeliever began to cry whenever he looked at his child's face. He said, 'O my child, I am afraid that you die quiet early and much earlier than me.' He saw his son's situation worsen. He pondered, 'I should go and ask the idols about my son's health, as I have been worshipping them as God.'

{2} When he arrived near the idols, he prostrated before every one of them, and said, 'I have been serving you for seventy years. I am here today with a request; because my darling son is struggling with a terminal disease. Heal him!' He got no response when he prostrated before every idol. Full of regret, he returned home. Halfway, he noticed a mosque wherein Muslims worshipped and gave thanks. The man remembered his God and thought he would also go to the mosque and pray for his son's healing from the Lord of the Heavens. He thought about this and entered the mosque, prostrated, and said, 'O God, I have heard about your kind attributions, your ultimate kindness with everybody, and I have come to draw close to You. My son is close to death and I want to request from Your Highness that you heal him from Your kindness.'

{۳} درزمانْ از عالمِ غیب آوازی شنید که «برو! که فرزند تو را صِحّت بخشیدیم». بُت پرست شادمان شد. امّا شرمنده شد و سر فرود افکند. با خود گفت «ای نفْس، دیدی لطف او را که فِي الحال اجابت فرمود». پسر سر از بالین برداشت و گفت «ای مادر، پدرم کجاست؟» مادر گفت «چون حال تو را دشوار دید با من گفت که «می‌روم تا از بُتان خود شفای فرزند بخواهم». پسر گفت «ای مادر، آدمی به همه‌حال عاجز است. چون زحمتی می‌رسد عاجزتر می‌گردد. بُتان که ساخته آدمی عاجزند؛ پس، بُتْ سازندهٔ خود را چگونه صِحّت تواند داد؟ و مرا که صِحّت داد؟ آفریدگاری که مرا آفریده است و [او] آفریدگار جملهٔ جهانیان است». این‌قدر[۵] با مادر بگفت و در طلب پدر روی به جانب بُتخانه کرد.

{۴} پدر را در بُتخانه ندید و بازگشت. دید پدر در صحن مسجد سر به شکستگی افکنده، می‌نالد. فرزند پیشتر شد و گفت «ای پدر، درگاه حقّ سُبحانَه و تَعالَی را مَگذار[۶] که در یک‌ساعت[۷] التماسِ تو مرا صِحّت بخشید». چون روی گردانید فرزند را تندرست دید. او را شوق حضرت سُبحانَه و تَعالَی زیاده گشت. به های‌های می‌گریست و گفت «ای خالق من، هفتادسال از تو بیگانه بودم و هرچه کردم در مخالفت تو کردم. و چون از حضرت تو التماس کردم، عداوت هفتادسالهٔ من در میان ندیدی؛ فِي الحال مرا اجابت فرمودی. پس، وای بر من که از همچون خدایی بیگانه باشم!» درزمانْ با فرزند خود کلمه عرض کردند و گفتند «لَآ إِلٰهَ إِلَّا اللّٰه، مُحَمَّدٌ رَسُولُ اللّٰه» و در دین حضرت پیغمبر ﷺ درآمد.

{۵} نظیر دیگر. چون زلیخا شنید[د] که بعداز هشتاد سال یوسف پیغمبر علیه‌السلام به پدر رسید، با خود گفت که «فراقِ جمال یوسف علیه‌السلام مرا رسید چون من از خدای تَعالَی بیگانه بودم؛ هم جوانی و هم چشم برباد دادم و هم مملکت مصر. و فُرقَت[۸] او به پدر، یعقوب، رسید. و مهتر یعقوب علیه‌السلام یگانهٔ حضرت حقّ تَعالَی بود، و چشم او هم در گریه به‌جهت یوسف به بادرفته بود. و حقّ تَعالَی باز فرزند دلبند به او باز رسانید و چشمش باز روشن شد».

{۶} همین‌قدر شکستگی در خاطر وی بگذشت که فرمان رسید «ای یوسف علیه‌السلام، چیست که سوختهٔ محبّتِ خودْ زلیخا را پُرسش نمی‌کنی؟ او را دریاب که در محبّت تو چگونه‌است». یوسف علیه‌السلام فرمود که ندا کنند که «فردا سواری[ه] خواهد بود؛ جملهٔ لشگر سوار شوند». این ندا به گوش زلیخا رسید که شاهِ مصر، یوسف علیه‌السلام، صباح[۹] سوار خواهد شد. کنیزک را گفت «چشم من به فراق جمال او برفت.[و] چوبی به دست من ده تا بر سر راه او بروم و ایستاده شوم. اگرچه من او را نمی‌بینم، باری او مرا ببیند و بداند که همان

[۵] همین‌اندازه. همین‌مقدار. [۶] رها مکن. [۷] چشم برهم زدن. خیلی سریع، در اندک زمان ممکن. [۸] فصل و جدایی، دوری.
[۹] اینکه مراد «صباح» به معنی «بامداد و صبح» یا «صبا» به معنی «فردا»، که در بسیاری از گویش‌های پارسی رایج است، باشد جای تحلیل دارد.

[د] چون زلیخا دید که [ه] شکاری [و] نابینا شد

{3} In the meantime, the man heard a voice from the unseen world that said, 'Go, as We have healed your son.' The idol-worshipper was happy, but he also hung his head in shame. He pondered, 'O my despotic soul, did you notice how His grace immediately responded to my request!' The son, having recovered immediately, asked, 'O mother, where is my father?' The mother said, 'When he found your health worsening, he told me, "I will go to request from the idols that he be healed."' The son said, 'O mother, the human being is always weak. Once a problem emerges, he becomes weaker. Idols that are handmade by human beings are powerless, so how can they heal their own makers?! And who has healed me?! That God who has created me and is the Creator of the whole universe.' He said this to his mother and left for the temple to seek his father.

{4} He could not find his father in the temple. The son returned. He saw that his father was crying in the mosque courtyard while being ashamed. The son moved close [to the father] and said, 'O father, do not leave the Throne of God, as your entreaty immediately brought me to health.' When the father turned, he saw his son healthy. Upon seeing this, his love of God increased, and he sobbed and said, 'O my Creator! I have been away from you for seventy years, and whatever I have done was against You. But as soon as I demanded from Your Highness, You did not take into account my seventy-year enmity but rather quickly responded to my request. Shame on me that I would want to be away from such a God!' At that moment, he and his son both professed the faith and recited, 'There is not god but God, and Muḥammad is the Messenger of God' and accordingly converted to the religion of the Prophet (pbuh).

{5} Another story. When Zulaykhā heard that the Prophet Joseph had reached his father after eighty years, she pondered, 'Being separated from the beautiful face of Joseph pervaded my existence, because I was away from God; I have lost my youthfulness as well as my eyes and Egypt. And such separation also happened to [Joseph's] father, Jacob. And His Eminence Jacob (pbuh) was the peerless servant of God. And he had lost his sight on account of his mourning for Joseph. And God returned his darling son to him and his eyes were again sighted.'

{6} She [i.e., Zulaykhā] was frequently reminded of her mistakes and disability, until a command arrived: 'O Joseph (pbuh), what is happening that you do not recall your broken-hearted Zulaykhā? Find her and see what has happened to her due to her love for you.' Joseph (pbuh) issued a call, 'Tomorrow there will be a parade and the whole army will mount their horses. Zulaykhā heard about this order from the king of Egypt, Joseph (pbuh), that the army will ride tomorrow. Zulaykhā said to herself, 'My sight have been lost because of his beauty. Take a stick so that I may go in front of him and stay there. Although I cannot see him he may see me and know that I am still lovesick and bereft.' She said this and went to the riding path. In the morning, Joseph

آواره و شیدای اوست». این بگفت و بر سر راه شد. علی الصباح[۱۰] یوسف را گفتند که «ای شاه، زلیخا بر راهِ گذر ایستاده». یوسف فرمود که «هر فوجی[۱۱] که نزدیک او رسد، از او پرسد که یوسف میان ما هست یا نه؟»

{۷} فوج می‌آمد و می‌پرسید؛ [زلیخا] می‌گفت «یوسفِ من میان شما نیست». تا آنکه فوج یوسف رسید، و نظر یوسف بر زلیخا افتاد. اسب را نزدیک او راند، و گفت «ای زلیخا، هیچ می‌دانی یوسف تو کجا است؟» زلیخا گفت «یوسف من هم تویی». مهتر یوسف گفت «از کجا دانستی که منم؟» گفت «ای یوسف، هر فوجی که نزدیک من آمدی آواز پای اسبان ایشان بر زمین برآمدی، و چون اسب تو نزدیک من آمد آواز سمّ اسب تو از دل من برآمد. دانستم که یوسفِ من تویی». مهتر یوسف را طاقت نماند، و گفت «ای زلیخا، هنوز از من چه می‌خواهی؟ جوانی که داشتی به باد دادی، و چشمِ بینایی که داشتی برفت و جملهٔ اعضای تو ضعیف گشته‌است. هنوز آتش محبّت تو فرونشسته؟»

{۸} زلیخا گفت «ای یوسف، سرِ تازیانه که در دست داری به من ده». مهتر یوسف سر تازیانه به دست زلیخا داد. زلیخا سر تازیانه بگرفت، و برسینهٔ خود بنهاد، و گفت «ای سینهٔ من که در آتش محبّت یوسف افروخته گشته! شراره از خود بیرون افکن». دیدند که دودی با آتش از دهان زلیخا بیرون آمد و سر تازیانه را بگرفت و به دستهٔ تازیانه رسید. مهتر یوسف از خوفِ آتش تازیانه را از دست انداخت. زلیخا گفت «ای یوسف، تو مرا محبّت خود ملامت می‌کردی. امّا ذرّه آتش مرا تحمّل نیاوردی. منِ بیچارهٔ دلِ خون‌شده را بنگر که سال‌ها آتش محبّت تو را در سینهٔ خود افروخته است».[۱۲]

{۹} نظیر دیگر. آورده‌اند که همچنین فردای قیامت أَمَنَّا بِهِ وَصَدَّقنا مؤمنان را فرمان شود که «بر پل صراط بگذرید». چون گذشتن گیرند،[۱۳] چپ و راست پل صراط را آتش دوزخ گرفته باشد. همه را در گذشتن وحشتی شود. فرمان ربّ العزّت دررسد که «ای مؤمنان، هیچ از آتش دوزخ مترسید که ما به لطف خود سینهٔ هریکی از شما را آتش محبّت خود بنهادیم، که شراره از آن افکنید و مقابل آتش دوزخ بیارید». في الحال ز سینه هر مؤمنی آتش محبّت الهی جدا گردد و نظر آتش دوزخ بر آتش مؤمنان افتد. چند فرسنگ زمین آتش دوزخ در گریز شود، و به زبان حال بگوید که «ای مؤمنان، زود بگذرید. مبادا که آتش شما آتشِ دوزخ را ناچیز گرداند که من از بهر کفّار آفریده شده‌ام». مؤمنان گویند «ای آتش دوزخ، چرا می‌گریزی و تاب آتش ما نمی‌آری؟ یکی بنگر که این آتش را در دنیا سال‌ها چگونه در سینه خویش داشتیم».

{۱۰} همچنین محبّت از دل تو خیزد و دل تو نظرگاه الهی است. گفته‌اند که جملهٔ جهان در پیش آسمانِ اوّل همچنان است که حلقه در بیابان کشیده، و آسمان اوّل در پیش آسمان دوم همچنان است که حلقه در بیابانی کشیده. بدین طریق هفت آسمان در پیش کرسی؛ و هفت آسمان و هفت زمین در پیش دل بندهٔ مؤمن همچنان

[۱۰] اصطلاح «علی الصباح» به معنی بامدادان و صبحگاه در اشعار سعدی و حافظ نیز دیده می‌شود. [۱۱] لشگر.
[۱۲] در برخی نسخ گفتگوی بین یوسف و زلیخا وجود ندارد، و داستان بدین ترتیب تمام می‌شود «باقی حکایت مشهور است».
[۱۳] در حال گذر باشند.

was informed, 'O king! Zulaykhā is waiting on the route.' Joseph said, 'Every trooper that reaches her must ask whether Joseph is present or not.'

{7} Various troops reached her and asked the question. She replied, 'My Joseph, the darling, is not among you.' When Joseph's troop reached her Joseph saw Zulaykhā. He moved his horse near her, and asked, 'O Zulaykhā, do you know where your Joseph is?' She replied, 'You are my Joseph!' His Eminence Joseph asked, 'How did you realise?' She said, 'O Joseph, when every troop of horsemen passed me I heard the sound of hooves on the ground; when your horse got close to me I heard the sound of hooves in my heart. Thus, I realised that you are my Joseph.' His Eminence Joseph could bear it no more and said, 'O Zulaykhā, what do you still want from me!? You lost your youthfulness, your eyesight has gone, and your body is weak. Yet, your flame of love still burns!'

{8} Zulaykhā said, 'O Joseph, pass on to me the whip's popper that is in your hand.' His Eminence Joseph passed the whip's popper to Zulaykhā [while keeping hold of its handle]. She took the whip's popper and held it on her chest. Then she said, 'O my breast that has been burnt in the fire of love for Joseph! Rise from the ashes and show your flame.' All could see that smoke with fire came from Zulaykhā's mouth and burned the whip's popper to its handle. His Eminence Joseph, being startled and afraid of the fire, dropped the whip. Zulaykhā said, 'O Joseph, you blamed me because of my love for you. However, you could not tolerate a spark from my [love] fire. Behold me, poor and broken-hearted, who has kept such fire of love alight in her heart for years.'

{9} Another story. It is reported that on the Day of Judgement, in which we believe, the believers are asked 'to pass the Ṣirāṭ bridge.' They start to cross over it, while the Ṣirāṭ bridge is surrounded left and right by hellfire. All are frightened. The command of the Lord of Honour is received, 'O believers, do not be afraid of the hellfire, as we have, due to Our kindness, filled your breasts with Our fire of love, such that a spark of it can simply confront the whole fire of hell.' Accordingly, the fire of God's love will emerge from every believers' breast and the hellfire will see the fire of the believers. The hellfire will flee to a faraway place and explain its condition: 'O believers, cross as quickly as possible, lest your fire diminishes the hellfire which I have created for infidels and disbelievers.' The believers will say, 'O hellfire, why do you flee and why can you not tolerate our fire? Just imagine how we held this fire in our breasts for years in the world.'

{10} Love emerges from your heart and your heart is the vision of God. It is said that the entire universe as compared to the first heaven resembles a ring in a vast desert, and the first heaven is also like a ring in a vast desert. As such, there are seven heavens before the Throne. And the seven heavens and Earth before the heart of the believing servant is like a ring in a desert. If your heart has not fallen in love with God, you will

است که حلقه در بیابانی. اگر دل تو در عشق محبّت حقّ نبودی، هر روزی سیصد وشصت بار به نظر عنایت خود تو را مخصوص نگردانید. باش تا فردای قیامت عزّت خود بدانی.

{۱۱} نظیر دیگر. چون لیلی در جهان نماند، این خبر به مجنون رسید و تحیّر کرد. مجنون راه شهر لیلی گرفت. چون نزدیک شهر لیلی رسید، دختری چند دید[۱۴] که با همدیگر بازی می‌کردند. از ایشان پرسید می‌دانید که «لیلیِ مرا کجا دفن کرده‌اند؟» دخترکی از میان ایشان جواب داد، و گفت «ای مجنون، سال‌ها غوغای عشق و لاف محبّتِ لیلی در جهان افکندی. امّا دانستم که کمالِ عشقْ در تو نبوده. اگر عشقِ تو را کمال بودی، هرگز تربتِ دوستْ از غیر نمی‌پرسیدی.» ازاین سخنْ مجنون در حیرت شد. و باز دختر گفت «در چه فکر مانده‌ای؟ در گورستان رو! از هر گوری که بوی محبّت آید بدان که تربتِ دوست تو همان است». چون مجنون سخن آن دختر شنید گریه کرد و با خود گفت «ای مجنون، سال‌ها در آتش محبّت بسوختی، امّا کمالِ عشق آن بود که این دختر گفت». روی به گورستان کرد. و به هر قبری که می‌گذشت بوی می‌کرد. تا گذرش بر گورِ لیلی افتاد. درزمانْ بویِ محبّت در مشام مجنون رسید. دانست که تُربت لیلی است. تربت را در کنار گرفته و دمی چند برآورد و جان به حق سبحانه وتعالی تسلیم کرد.

{۱۲} بیت: نخواهم زیستن بی‌تو، تنِ بی‌جان چه کارآید؛ محال است این که بی لیلی، دمی مجنون بیاساید

{۱۳} إلٰهِيّ، به حرمتِ عاشقانِ دیدارْ پاکْ که دولت محبّت دیدار خود را روزی گردانی، من بیچاره و کاتب را [روزی] گردانی. به حقّ محمّد وآله أَجْمَعِين.

[۱۴] چندی دختر دید.

not have been made special by his graceful glance for three hundred and sixty times per day. Wait until you witness your true dignity on the Day of Judgement.

{11} Another story. When Laylī died, the news reached Majnūn, who was shocked. Majnūn went towards the city where Laylī lived. Near the city, he saw a couple of young girls playing together. He asked them, 'Do you know where they have buried my Laylī?' A young girl from among them answered, and said, 'O Majnūn, for years you have been in turmoil through your love of Laylī yet bluffing the whole time. I now understand that you have not experienced true love. If your love had reached perfection you would never have asked the site of your love's grave from others!' Majnūn was again shocked by this answer. The girl continued, 'What are you thinking of? Go to the cemetery. The grave from which the smell of affection emanates, you will then realise is your love's grave.' When Majnūn heard the girl's advice he cried and pondered, 'O Majnūn! You have been burning in love's fire for years! But the perfection of love is what the girl has just said.' He went towards the cemetery. He smelled [the air] upon reaching every single grave. Until he arrived at Laylī's grave. In the meantime, the smell of love reached his olfactory senses. He understood that it was the grave of Laylī. Then, he hugged the grave, drew a deep breath, and passed his soul unto God.

{12} Poem: I do not want to live without you, what could be the benefit of a lifeless body; It is impossible for Majnūn to find comfort for a moment without Laylī

{13} *O God, by the dignity of the pure lovers beholding You, grant the blessing of You beholding me, a humble pauper and the author of this work. By Muḥammad and his family altogether. [Amen.]*

حکایتِ سلطان ابراهیم ادهم قُدِّس سِرُّه[الف]

{۱} آورده‌اند که چون سلطان ابراهیم ادهم مملکت و پادشاهی را ترک کرد، جامهٔ ژنده دربرکرد و به طلب مولی تَعَالَی بیرون شد. مدّتی در راه مسافرت کردی. شبی نزولِ ایشان به شهر هارون الرشید افتاد. امیر عَسَس[1] در شهر می‌گشت و سلطان به او خورد. عَسَس دست و گردن سلطان بست که «تو دزدی» و نگاه داشت.

{۲} صباح،[2] امیر عَسَس کیفیت حال با هارون الرشید عرض گفت «که دگر شب عجب دزدی گرفتار شده‌است. حکم چه می‌شود؟» هارون الرشید فرمود که «پیش ما بیارید».[ب] سلطان ابراهیم ادهم را آوردند. هارون الرشید از طعام خوردن فارغ شده بود، و پالوده[ج] می‌خورد. بالا نگه کرد و نظرش به جمال سلطان افتاد. در ضمیر خاطر خلیفه بگذشت که «از چنین رویی چگونه دزدی آید». باز خلیفه اندیشه کرد «مرا فردای قیامت این حجّت نباشد. ازجهت کار او خود تفحّص کنم».

{۳} آنگاه خلیفه رو به سلطان کرد و گفت «مگر تو دزدی و الّا نیمه شب چرا بیرون آمدی؟» سلطان گفت که «من در طلب مولی تَعَالَی بیرون آمده‌بودم». امیرعَسَس را طاقت نماند؛[3] پس بر روی سلطان سیلی زد، و گفت «خلیفه چیز دیگری می‌پرسد و تو جواب دیگر می‌گویی؟» خلیفه تند شد بر عَسَس و گفت «من از او هرچه پرسیدم او مرا جواب داد. تو چرا بی‌ادبی کردی؟»[د] خلیفه فرمود بَدلِ[4] یک سیلی، عَسَس را ده سیلی بزنند. خلیفه از پیش خود طَبَق پالوده برگرفت و به سلطان داد.

{۴} امیرعَسَس را می‌زدند. سلطان خندید. خلیفه پرسید که «ای درویش، او را می زنند تو چرا در

[1] نگهبان شب یا شبگرد. این لقب، پست یا عنوانِ شغلی در دیگر آثار قرون گذشته دیده می‌شود: مختارنامه، تذْکِرَة المُلُوك، جَوامِع الحِکَایَات وَلَوَامِعُ الرِوَایَاتْ، ابومسلم نامه و همچنین داستان‌ها و روایات نظامی گنجه، عطّار نیشابوری، سعدی شیرازی و مولوی.
[2] بامداد. [3] از کوره در رفت. [4] در عوض.

[الف] قَدَّسَ اللّٰه سِرّه [ب] خلیفه فرمود که او را بیارید [ج] حلوا پالوده [د] «تو را که فرمود که او را در پیش من سیلی بزنی؟»

CHAPTER 18

The story of Sultan Ibrāhīm Adham, may his grave be sanctified

{1} It is reported that when Sultan Ibrāhīm Adham left his kingdom as well as his kingship, he put on a patched cloak and went out for the sake of the Lord. He travelled for a while. One night he arrived in the city of Hārūn al-Rashīd. While the chief night guard was checking the city, the sultan faced him. The chief night guard tied up the hands and neck of the sultan claiming 'you were a thief' and he held him captive.

{2} In the morning, the chief night guard recounted the incident to Hārūn al-Rashīd saying, 'What a thief was arrested last night! What should we do with him?' Hārūn al-Rashīd said, 'Bring him in to us.' They brought Sultan Ibrāhīm Adham. Hārūn al-Rashīd had just finished his food and was eating his *pālūda*.[1] He looked up and saw the sultan's face. The caliph[2] pondered, 'How is it possible that one with such a face becomes a thief!' Then he thought to himself, 'This would not be a proper contention for the Day of Judgement. I must investigate his case myself.'

{3} The caliph looked at the sultan and said, 'You were around during the night. Are not you a thief?' The sultan said, 'I have been out seeking for the Lord.' The chief night guard became furious. He then slapped the sultan's face and said, 'The caliph asked you another question, and have you answered differently?' The caliph angrily told the chief night guard, 'Whatever I asked him, he answered me. Why did you not follow the courtesy?' The caliph asked his people to start to slap the chief night guard ten times, as a payoff for his one slap. The caliph, then, took the tray of *pālūda* and passed it on to the sultan.

{4} The chief night guard was still being beaten. Sultan was then laughing. The caliph asked, 'O dervish, they are beating him. Why are you laughing?' The sultan said,

[1] Persian sorbet, also used in Arab countries; lit., something refined [2] i.e., Hārūn

خنده شده‌ای؟» سلطان گفت «این بیچاره به فرمودهٔ شما جست‌وجو می‌کند. و من در جست‌وجوی پروردگار خود می‌گردم. مرا در طلب مولی پالوده می‌دهند، و او را چون به فرمان تو جست‌وجو می‌کرده می‌زنند!» خلیفه گفت «چیزی نافرموده در حقّ شما گستاخی کرده بود، جزای خود یافت». آنگاه خلیفه گفت «این پالوده که دادم بخور». سلطان گفت «من از این احتراز کرده‌ام. نخواهم خورد». خلیفه گفت «چرا؟» سلطان گفت «از دو حال بیرون نیست: یا پالوده است و یا آلوده است». خلیفه گفت «پالوده چیست و آلوده چه باشد؟»

{۵} سلطان گفت «اگر یک دانه از وجه[۵] حرام درین افتاده است جمله آلوده است و نشاید خورد. و اگر از وجه حلال است ما از چنین لذّت دنی[۶] دل برگرفته‌ایم». خلیفه گفت «تو را از این تهمت دزدی که کرده گرفته‌اند امان می‌دهیم، به شرط آنکه چندگاه مصاحب[۷] ما باشی».

{۶} سلطان گفت «ای خلیفه، به یک شرط پیش تو باشم. اگر در خدمت تو گستاخی کنم با من چه کنی؟»[°] خلیفه دست به تیغ برد و آن را گرفت، و گفت که «سر از تن تو جدا کنم». سلطان گفت «ای خلیفه، هنوز گناه نکرده به گفتن این سخن سر از تن جدا می‌کنی، پس در صحبت تو چگونه توان بود؟ من در خدمت معبود خود چرا نباشم که اگر روزی هزار بار گناه کنم، چون گویم بد کردم او به لطف و کرم خود ببخشد».

{۷} خلیفه گفت «پس اینجا نخواهی بود؟» سلطان گفت «نخواهم بود». خلیفه گفت «چیزی از من جهت زاد و راحله[۸] قبول کن». سلطان گفت «ای خلیفه، وقتی من چیزی بخواهم و قبول کنم که در خزانهٔ حق ﷻ آن‌را اندک بینم». خلیفه گفت «ای بلند همّتِ خوش لقا، مرا بگو تو کیستی؟» سلطان گفت «من پادشاه بلخ بودم. و نام من ابراهیم ادهم است.[۹] در طلب مولیِ خود جمله چیزها در باختم که شاید الله تبارک و تعالی مِنِ شکسته را قبولِ حضرت خویش گرداند». آنگه هارون الرشید برخاست و سلطان را در کنار گرفت، و گریه بسیار کرد. و گفت «معذور می‌دارید که من شما را نشناخته‌ام. باری، اَلْحَمْدُ لله که به دیدار مبارک شما مشرّف گشتم». و بعد با اعزاز[۱۰] و احترام سلطان را به درود کرد.

{۸} سلطان روی به یمن کرد. خلق یمن می‌شنیدند که پادشاه بلخ از بهر مولی خود مملکت پادشاهی درباخته، به طلب مولی بیرون آمده است، و از صغار و کبار[۱۱] یمن به استقبال او بیرون آمده‌است. و به یکدیگر می‌گفتند «رَویم و روی کسی ببینیم که او از جمله چیزهای عالم گذشته و در طلب مولی بیرون آمده. و به دیدار او مشرّف شویم».

[۵] مال یا پول. [۶] پَست و فرومایه. [۷] یار و همصحبت. [۸] توشهٔ سفر.
[۹] در برخی نسخ ابراهیم ادهم خود را معرّفی نمی‌کند. [۱۰] اکرام. [۱۱] کوچک و بزرگ.

[°] اگر بر قوم تو دست درازی کنم تو با من چه کنی؟

'This poor man's job is to investigate on your authority. I investigate how to find God. Interestingly, I am served *pālūda*, while he is punished because he just follows your order and interrogates!' The caliph said, 'He did a wrong thing and not what had been ordered. He is now being punished accordingly.' Then the caliph said, 'Now eat this *pālūda* which I have offered you.' The sultan said, 'I have avoided eating this, and will not eat it.' The caliph asked, 'Why?' The sultan replied, 'This is either refined (*pālūda*) or impure (*ālūda*).' The caliph said, 'What is the difference between refined and impure?'

{5} The sultan said, 'If it is made from unlawful wealth, then it is totally impure and forbidden to eat it. And if it is made from lawful wealth, then we have already forsaken such inferior pleasures.'The caliph said, 'We will protect you from this accusation of theft on the condition that you stay with us for a while.'

{6} The sultan said, 'O caliph, I will be your companion on one condition. If I do something impertinent before you, what will you then do with me?' The caliph took his swor, grabbed him, and said, 'I will behead you now.' The sultan said, 'O caliph, I have not yet done anything wrong, but just because of this question, you want to cut my head off. How is it possible to stay in your company?! Why do I not, therefore, stay in the service of my God; if I commit sins a thousand times every day, and then repent, He will forgive me with his grace and kindness.'

{7} The caliph said, 'So, you will not stay here?' The sultan replied, 'No, I will not be staying.' The caliph said, 'But accept something from me as your travel provision.' The sultan said, 'O caliph, I will demand and accept something if I seldom find it in God's treasury.' The caliph said, 'O graceful person, tell me who you are!' The sultan replied, 'I was the ruler of Balkh and my name is Ibrāhīm Adham. I have relinquished many possessions in seeking my Lord, hoping that God will accept me, a humble peasant, before His presence.' At that moment, Hārūn al-Rashīd stood up, embraced the sultan, and cried many tears, saying, 'Forgive me that I did not recognize you! Truly! Praise be to God that I am honoured to meet you in person.' Later on, with a lot of respect, he said farewell to the sultan.

{8} The sultan moved towards Yemen. The people of Yemen had learned that the king of Balkh had forsaken his kingdom for the sake of his Lord and to instead wander around searching for Him. The people of Yemen, both young and old, went to welcome the sultan. They were saying to each other, 'Let's go and see the face[3] of the one who has left all his material wealth to seek the Lord. We will surely be honoured to meet him.'

[3] i.e., meet him

{۹} و یک منزل مانده بود که به شهر درآید که شخصی از جانب شهر می‌آمد. و به سلطان ابراهیم گفت که «امروز جملۀ خلایق یمن، از وضیع[۱۲] و شریف، شوریده[۱۳] به استقبال سلطان ابراهیم ادهم می‌آیند». سلطان این سخن شنید در خاطر گذراند «ای ابراهیم، کار تو به جایی رسیده که جملۀ خلق از بهر تو سرگردان شده‌اند.» باز با نفْس خود مجادله آغاز کرد و گفت «ای نفْس! گمانِ فاسد بر خود می‌بری. باش تا عبرت خویش از این جا برگیری».

{۱۰} سلطان از قافله جدا شد و تنها رو به یمن کرد. دید خَلقْ فوج‌فوج از پیش می‌آیند. تا فوجی نزدیک سلطان رسید از او پرسیدند که «ای درویش،[د] از سلطان ابراهیم ادهم هیچ خبر داری چند دور است؟» سلطان گفت «حکایت او از چه می‌پرسید که او مردِ دیوانۀ سرگردانِ کار خود است». ایشان ندانستند که سلطان همین است. گفتند که «این سخن ما را جواب نیست. ما از تو خبر و نشان سلطان می‌پرسیم. و تو با اهانت او را سخن می‌گویی؟» این بگفتند و چندان او را مشت و چوب زدند که سلطان بیهوش شد. سلطان بعداز زمان به حال آمد و بر نفْس خود گفت «دیروز در بزرگی خود فکر می‌کردی؟ ای نفْس، آن بزرگی نبود؛ بلکه حشمت و عظمت آن جهانْ امروز در تو پیدا شد. امروز در نظرِ همه خوار گشتی». بعداز آن ایشان دانستند که سلطان همان بود که ایشان رنجاندند.[۱۴]

{۱۱} الغرض. تا روزی گذر سلطان ابراهیم بر بازاری افتاد. دید که مردی انجیر و خرما می‌فروشد. و مدّت سی‌سال بود که او ترک مملکت کرده بود، و گاه‌گاهی دلش بر انجیر و خرما کشیدی. چون دید که هر دو را یک‌جا می‌فروشد دل سلطان مایل شد، و به مرد گفت «نعلین کهنۀ من بستان، و انجیر و خرما بده». انجیر فروش[ز] گفت «بدین کهنه چَرمی خرما و انجیر نفروشم». چون سلطان این سخن بشنید روی به بیابان نهاد.

{۱۲} مردی نزدیک انجیر فروش نشسته بود، گفت «هیچ می‌دانی که او پادشاه بلخ است که ترک عالم کرده و خود را چنین می‌دارد. پُرطَبَقی خرما و انجیر نزد او بَر. هر چه او بخورد هریک را دیناری به تو دهم». انجیر فروش طَبَقی از خرما و انجیر پُر کرد، برداشته از عقبِ سلطان دوان شد. نزدیک رسید. آواز کرد که «ای درویش، زمانی ایستاده شو که از برای تو انجیر و خرما آورده‌ام». سلطان پس[۱۵] نگاه کرد و جواب داد که «أَنَا لَا أبیع الدّین بِالتَّمْر وَالتِینْ،[۱۶] یعنی اکنون نمی‌ستانم از انجیر و خرما[ی] تو و نمی‌فروشم دین خود را». چون از سلطان چنین شنید بازگشت.

[۱۲] غیر شریف، فقیر و پست. [۱۳] به‌طریق هیجان زده هجوم آوردن. [۱۴] شبیه این پاراگراف در تَذْکِرَة الأَولِیَاء عطّار، ولی با اندک تفاوت، دیده می‌شود. این قسمت در متن منسوب به عطّار کوتاه‌تر است. دیگر اینکه، براساس تَذْکِرَة الأَولِیَاء، سلطان ابراهیم ادهم راهی مکّه است، و وی خود را «زندیق» معرّفی می‌کند. در صورتیکه در نسخه‌های «درّالمجالس» وی راهی یمن است و خود را «دیوانه» معرفی می‌کند. در رابطه با متن عطّار، تذکرة الاولیاء، مقدّمه، تصحیح و تعلیقات، محمّد رضا شفیعی کدکنی (تهران: چشمه، ۱۳۹۷/۲۰۱۸)، ج ۱، ص ۱۱۰.

[۱۵] پشت سر. [۱۶] چنین اذکاری در «مَجَالِسْ السَنَانِیَة» هم مشهود است.

[د] ای بنده [ز] خرما فروش

{9} There was only one rest hall to stay before the sultan reaches the city. A fellow came from the city and told Sultan Ibrāhīm Adham, 'Today, all the people of Yemen from, both lowly and noble, are excited and are coming to welcome Sultan Ibrāhīm Adham.' The sultan heard this statement, and thought to himself, 'O Ibrāhīm, you reached such a point that all the people have departed because of you!' He began struggling within himself and said, 'O tempted self! This is a corrupt and unsound thought. Wait and see how you can take a lesson from this moment.'

{10} The sultan left the caravan and went alone towards the city. He noticed that people were coming in groups. When a group of people reached him they asked, 'O dervish, do you know anything about Sultan Ibrāhīm? How far is he [from here]?' The sultan said, 'Why are you asking about him and found him important, as he is a mad wanderer on his own mission?' The people did not realise that this man was the sultan himself. They responded, 'What you are telling us is not the answer we want. We are asking you for any news about the sultan. And you responded with an insult?!' They said this and beat him with fists and batons until the sultan became unconscious. After a while the sultan regained consciousness and asked his tempted self, 'Did you believe in your significance and greatness? O tempted self! It was not greatness! You have today realised the grandeur and greatness of the other world. Today, you are humiliated before everyone.' The people later realised that they had beaten the sultan.[4]

{11} Returning to the story. Sultan Ibrāhīm came across a bazaar one day. He noticed a man selling figs and dates. It had been thirty years since he had left his kingdom and court and sometimes he missed figs and dates. When he saw that both were sold in one place he became interested and told the seller, 'Take these old sandals and give me figs and dates.' The man who was selling the figs said, 'I will not sell dates and figs in exchange for taking this old leather.' When the sultan heard this he left to go to the desert.

{12} There was a man near the seller who said, 'Did you know that he was the king of Balkh who renounced the world to live like this. Take a tray full of dates and figs to him. Whatever he eats, I will give you a dinar for each.' The seller filled a tray with dates and figs and went after the sultan. When he got close he called out, 'O dervish, wait a second as I have brought figs and dates for you.' The sultan looked back and answered, 'I do not sell my faith for dates and figs', meaning that I will not now buy your figs and dates and will not sell my religion. The seller returned when he heard this from the sultan.

[4] One may find similarities between this paragraph and the one outlined in ʿAṭṭār's *Tadhkirat al-Awliyāʾ*. However, the latter is shorter and shows the journey of Ibrāhīm Adham towards Mecca, and that he introduces himself as a '*zindīq*'.

{۱۳} و سلطان رو به صحرا کرد و چپ و راست صحرا نظر کرد. کسی را ندید. وقتِ سلطان خوش شد و مناجات می‌کرد و می‌گفت: «مَولايْ مَولايْ ذِكْرُكَ تَمْرِي وحَلوايّ، ای مولای من، انجیر و خرمای دنیا چه کنم که ذکر تو بر من خرما و حلوا گشته است». و باز آغاز کرد «مَولاي مَولاي ذِكْرُكَ تَمْرِي وحَلوايّ. یعنی ای خدای من، انجیر و خرمای دنیا چه کنم که ذکر تو انجیر و خرمای من گشته». باز آغاز کرد که «مَولاي مَولاي ذِكْرُكَ كرَمِي وبُستانِي، یعنی ای پروردگار من، اگر چه در دنیا باغ و بستان ندارم، ذکر تو باغ و بستان من است که در ایشان میوه‌های گوناگون باشد». باز ثنای دیگر آغاز کرد که « مَولاي مَولاي ذِكْرُكَ غَرِيب وَ إنَّك غريبٌ وَالغريبُ لا ألِفُ إلاّ بِالْغَرِيبُ [...] لاَأُرِيدُ إلاّ ذِكْرُكَ،[ح] یعنی تو در جهان غریبی،[۱۷] و غریب در جهان الفت نگیرد مگر با غریب». چون سلطان این مناجات تمام کرد، جان به حق سُبْحَانَهُ وَتَعَالَى سپرد.

{۱۴} إلهِيّ، به حرمت سلطان ابراهیم ادهم رحمة الله علیه،[ط] گیرِ دل[۱۸] من و کاتب این قصّه را با جمیع مؤمنان از محبّت دنیا دور گردانی و طلب آن جهان گردانی. به حقّ محمّد وآله أجمعین.

[۱۷] به احتمال زیاد اشاره دارد به اینکه کسی در جهان خدا را به‌درستی نمی‌شناگوفتاری.

[ح] «مَولاي ذِكْرُكَ غَرِيب وَ إنَّك غَرِيبٌ وَالغَرِيبُ لَايالِفُ إلاّ بِالغَرِيب إلَىٰ الْمَولاي فِي ذِكْرُكَ»

[ط] إلهِيّ، به حرمت سرحلقهٔ صوفیانْ سلطان ابراهیم ادهم رحمة الله علیه

{13} And the sultan proceeded towards the desert. He looked to the left and right of the desert. He witnessed no one. He felt tranquil and began to pray, 'My Lord! My Lord! Supplicating to You is my delicacy. O my Lord, what I need from the figs and dates of the world is not for them to be my delicacies! Meaning that remembering God is my delight.' Again, he began to say, 'O my Lord! O my Lord! You are my orchard and garden, meaning that although I have no orchard and garden in this world, remembrance of God is my garden and orchard in which there are various fruits.' Subsequently, the sultan began praising again, 'O my Lord, the mention of You is beyond words, and you are indeed lonely and the lonely one is not matched except with a lonely one. He does not want anything but your remembrance, meaning that You are lonely in this world[5] and the Unique One does not befriend anyone in this world but another lonely one.' After the sultan finished this supplication he submitted his soul to God.

{14} *O God, by Sultan Ibrāhīm Adham, God's mercy be upon him, alleviate my heart as well as that of the scribe of this story along with all believers who engage with the love of the world, and [then engage us with] seeking the other world. By Muḥammad and his family altogether. [Amen.]*

[5] i.e., nobody knows God properly

حکایتِ مرد سخی و زن بخیل

{۱} آورده‌اند دختری بود مسلمه،[1] روزی به خدمت حضرت محمّد ﷺ آمد گریه کنان. حضرت گفت «چرا گریه می‌کنی؟» دختر گفت «یا رسول الله، مادر و پدر من وفات کرده‌اند، و من به فراق ایشان روزگار به سر می‌بردم. امشب مادر و پدر به خواب دیدم که گویا قیامت قایم شده است و خلق اوّلین و آخرین را در عرصات قیامت حاضره کرده‌اند. و شوری از هر جانب برآمده و در عرصات قیامت به‌جهت مادر و پدر می‌دَوَم. ناگاه گذر من به سوی دوزخ افتاد. دیدم مادر من مبتلا گشته و آتش دوزخ گردبه‌گرد برآمده، و بر دست راستِ مادرِ من پاره جامهٔ کهنه و بر دستِ چپ پنبه و از هر دو جانب آتش به این جامه و پنبه دفع می‌کند.[الف] گفتم «یا مادر، چه حالت است؟ از شومی چه چیز چنین شده است؟»

{۲} [«] مادر گفت «ای دختر، من به‌غایت نیک کردار بودم و در رضای پدر تو بودم. امّا بخیل بودم که به جز جامهٔ کهنه و پنبه چیزی دیگر به کسی نداده‌ام. و امروز به دست من همان داده‌اند، که آتش دوزخ بدان دفع می‌کنم. امّا از تَف[2] آتشِ دوزخ درون من خشک شده و بی‌آب گشته‌است». دیگر پرسیدم «ای مادر، پدرم کجاست؟» گفت «ای دختر، پدر تو در دنیا سخی بود. و [در] مقام جوان‌مردان بهشت است. او را در بهشت، و در راستای عرش، طلب کن».

[1] در برخی نسخ این جمله وجود ندارد. بلکه چنین آورده‌اند: مرد سخی بود و او را زنی بخیل بود. و دخترکی داشت. ناگاه مادر و پدر او فوت شد. همان شب مادر در خوابِ دختر آمد که در دوزخ می‌سوزد و او از خواب بیدار شد و نعره‌کنان به در مسجد مبارک پیغمبر ؑ آمد.

[2] حرارت.

[الف] «یا رسول الله، عجب حالتی. دیدم که در دست راست مادر من پاره [ای] از جامهٔ کهنه داده‌اند و در دست چپ مادر من پارهٔ پنبه داده‌اند. این هر دو در آتش می‌سوخت. امّا اگر از دستِ راستِ او آتش آمدی، آن را به پاره جامه دفع کردی و اگر از دست چپِ او آتش آمدی آن را به پنبه دفع کردی».

CHAPTER 19

The story of the generous husband and the miserly wife

{1} It is reported that there was a Muslim girl. One day she came to the Prophet (pbuh) while crying. The Prophet asked, 'Why are you crying?' The girl responded, 'O Messenger of God, my mother and father have died. I am lonely these days. I dreamed of mother and father last night, the Day of Judgement had commenced and the whole community of people, from the first to last, were present. There was chaos everywhere, and I ran to my mother and father on the Resurrection Plain. Suddenly, I noticed the hellfire, and I found my mother in trouble – the hellfire had surrounded her! There was a piece of old cloth in my mother's right hand, and there was cotton in her left hand, and she tried to stop the fire coming from both sides with this piece of cloth and cotton. I asked her, "O mother, what has happened to you? What inauspicious event has brought this upon you?"

{2} My mother replied, "O my daughter, I was extremely well mannered and your father was satisfied with me. However, I was miserly as I never gave anything to people except old cloths and cotton. And today, they have given me these two by which I must try to stop the hellfire. The heat of the hellfire has dehydrated my insides!" I also asked, "O mother, where is my father?" She said, "O daughter, your father was generous in the world and paradise is the place of generosity. Seek him in paradise, along with the Throne."

{۳} [«] آنگه به جانب عرش روان شدم. گذر من به حوض کوثر افتاد. دیدم پدر من بر لب حوض کوثر نشسته. و شما را دیدم نشسته اید. و یاران شما نشسته‌اند. و پدر من قدح[۳] آب پر کرده به دست یاران شما می‌دهد، و شما گرفته می‌خورید.[ب] چون پدر خود را بدین مرتبه دیدم گفتم «ای پدر، خداوند تَعَالَى تو را به این مرتبه رسانیده و مادرم در دوزخ به عذاب مبتلا و بی‌آب مانده. یک قدح آب به دست من ده تا به‌جهت مادر خود ببرم». پدر گفت «ای جگر گوشهٔ من، خداوند تَعَالَى حوض کوثر را بر دوزخیان حرام کرده است».

{۴} [«] گفتم «ای پدر، اگر یک قدح آب نمی‌دهی باری اندکی آب بر دست من ریز». پدر گفت «کف دست پیش من آر» . بردم و قدری آب به دست من ریخت. آب را گرفته به سرعت تمام پیش مادر خود رفتم. و گفتم «ای مادر دهن[۴] خود را وا کن». چون دهن باز کرد، آب کوثر را در دهن مادر ریختم. همان ساعت فرشته بانگ بزد که «آب حوض کوثر بر دوزخیان حرام است و تو آب را در دهن ناپاک انداختی. خدای تَعَالَى دست تو خشک گرداند».[۵] از هیبت او بیدار شدم، و نظر بر دست خود کردم؛ خشک شده بود. احوال خواب را این بود که بر شما عرض کردم. یا رسول اللّٰه، بر من رحمتی کنید که بسیار عاجزم و نفقه از این دست پیدا می‌کردم. دعا کنید تا دست من گیران[۶] شود».»

{۵} بر دست صدرِ پدرِ عالم محمّد مُصْطَفَى ﷺ عصای[۷] بود.[۸] به دختر داد و دعا کرد و گفت «إِلٰهِيّ، اگر چنین است که این دختر می‌گوید، و فردای قیامت این چنین خواهد بود، و خواب این ضعیفه راست است، چنانچه دست این دختر در نخست بود چنان گردان». فِي الحَال دست دختر درست شد .

{۶} الغرض.[۹] آورده‌اند که مردی به غایت بخیل بود. تا کار او به جایی رسیده بود که اگر کسی به فقیری چیزی داد او را سه روز دردسر بودی. او را دختری بود. هر روز یک نان دادی. چنانچه یک روز نانی به دست دختر داد و خود از بهر کاری بیرون شد. درویشی بر در خانهٔ آن مردِ بخیل آمده و گفت «از بهر رضا خدای تَعَالَى و رسول خدای عَزَّوَجَلَّ کسی باشد به من چیزی دهد که بسیار گرسنه‌ام؟». دختر با خود گفت «نان که امروز پدر داده‌است از بهر رضای خدای تَعَالَى بدهم. و امروز گرسنه مانم».[ج] نان را به درویش داد. درویش بِستَد[ن][۱۰] و پیشِ درْ نشسته به نان خوردن مشغول شد.

[۳] سبو. [۴] دهان. [۵] «دست خشک شدن» اشاره به بی‌تحرّکی و بی‌حسّی دست دارد. [۶] فعّال و گیرا. [۷] عصایی.

[۸] در تعدادی نسخ، سؤال پایانی دختر از پیامبر و برخورد پیامبر اندکی متفاوت است «یا رسول اللّٰه، اکنون آمدم که تا به خدمت شما عرضه دارم». أَنَس بنْ مَالِك رَضِيَ اللّٰهُ عَنْهُ را رسول گفت «عصای مرا بدان عجوزه بده». عصا را به دست عجوزه بداد. رسول اللّٰه [...] گفت «اگر همچنین است که این دخترک می‌گوید، و فردای قیامت خواهد بود[...]».) [۹] نظیر دیگر؟ [۱۰] بِستَدَن به معنی «گرفتن» به‌کار رفته‌است. این واژه در اشعار فردوسی، عنصری، فرّخی سیستانی و همچنین در تاریخ سیستان و تاریخ بیهقی دیده می‌شود.

[ب] («أَمیر المُؤمِنین عَلی کَرَّمَ اللّٰهُ وَجْهَه قدحی شراب بهشت در دست دارد و به مؤمنان امّت می‌دهد. و پدر من در آن میان است. چون پدر را دیدم گفتم «ای پدر، خدای تَعَالَى تو را بدین سعادت مشرّف گردانید و مادرم در دوزخ مبتلا مانده است». [ج] خود امروز صبر بکنم

{3} "I went towards the Throne. I came across the pool of Kawthar. There, I noticed that my father was sitting on edge of the Kawthar pool and I saw you sitting there, too. Your Companions were present. My father filled a jug of water and passed it to your Companion, and you also took it and drank from it. Upon noticing that my father had such a high status I said, "O father, God has elevated you to such a rank, while my mother is troubled in the hellfire and is thirsty. Give me a bowl of water so that I can take it to her." Father said, "O my darling, God has prohibited the Kawthar pond for the inhabitants of hell."

{4} I said, "O father, if you do not give me a bowl of water, at least pour a small amount of water into my hand." Father said, "Bring your palm to me." I did so and he poured a small amount of water into it. I took the water and went to my mother as quickly as possible and I said, "O mother, open your mouth." When she opened her mouth, I poured the Kawthar water into my mother's mouth. At the same time an angel announced, "The water of Kawthar is prohibited for the inhabitants of hell and you have poured water into the mouth of an impure person. God will disable your hand." Given this fear, I woke up and looked at my hand. It was already disabled. I have told you all the details of my dream. O Messenger of God, have mercy upon me as I am quite weak and I need to be able to gain money and alimony with this hand. Pray that this hand is healed.'

{5} There was a rod in the Prophet's hand. He passed it to the girl and said, 'O God, if this is what the girl wants, and this is what is going to happen on the Day of Judgement, and the dream of this woman is sound, then make the girl's hand as what it was on its first day.' Right after this, the girl's hand was healed.

{6} Another story. It is reported that a man was extremely miserly to the extent that if someone gave something to the poor he would have a headache for three days. He had a daughter to whom he passed one loaf of bread per day. One day after giving a loaf to his daughter he went out to work. A dervish came to the door of that miserly man and said, 'For the sake of God and the Messenger of God, is there anybody who can give me something as I am extremely hungry?' The girl pondered, 'I will give the bread that father has given to me today for the sake of God and I will remain hungry today.' She gave the bread to the dervish. The dervish took the bread and started to eat it at the door.

{۷} آن مرد بخیل باز آمد[۱۱]. دید مردی نزدیک درخانهٔ او نان می‌خورد. چهرهٔ او متغیّر شد،[۱۲] و به خشم از او پرسید که نان به او که داد. درویش اشارت به خانهٔ او کرد.[د] پدر دانست که دختر داده باشد. از روی غصّه و غضب به خانه درآمد و گفت «درویش را تو نان داده‌ای؟» دختر گفت «نان خود را به درویش داده‌ام». مرد بخیل گفت «من هیچ وقتی به کسی چیزی نداده‌ام، و تو برخلاف من نان به درویش می‌دهی. اگر تو دختر من می‌بودی، مخالفت من تو کار نمی‌کردی». این سخن بگفت، و دست آن بیچاره را بگرفت و از شهر بیرون برد و به بیابان برد. آنگه پرسید «به کدام دست نان داده بودی؟» دخترک گفت «به دست راست». آن ظالم بخیل فی‌الحال کارد کشید و آن دست از بندش جدا کرد، و آن بی‌گناه را هم در آن بیابان تنها گذاشت.

{۸} آن مظلومه دست‌درد کردی و تنهایی در وحشت آوردی. روی جانب آسمان کردی، و گفت «إِلٰهِیّ، دیدی پدر از بهرِ نان دادن با من چه کرد؟ اکنون نمی‌دانم که لطف تو با من بیچاره چه خواهد کرد. إِلٰهِیّ، می‌دانی که پدرْ ناحق مرا معیوب کرد، و دوای درد مظلومان جز تو کسی ندهد». هنوز درین مناجات بود که ناگاه پادشاهی درآن دیار، از لشگر خود جدا افتاده بود،[ه] به سر وقت او رسانید.

{۹} و نظر پادشاه بر روی دختر افتاد. گفت تو کیستی و درین بیابان چه می‌کنی؟ دختر گفت «من کنیزک الله تَعَالَی هستم».[۱۳] پادشاه گفت «چگونه درین مقام رسیدی و دستت را که بریده است؟» گفت «حکم خدای تَعَالَی عَزَّوَجَلَّ رفته بود که مرا بی‌دست کردند، و درین بیابان رساند و من صبر کردم و راضی به قَضَاء الله شدم که هرچه خواهد آن کُند». پادشاه چون از وی چنین شنید، رحم کرد و گفت «ای دختر، من در جهان هیچ دختر ندارم. امّا دختر من تو باشی و مرا یک پسر است. حقّ سُبْحَانَهُ وَتَعَالَى مرا در حقّ تو چنان مهربان کرده‌است که تو را از پسر خود دوست‌تر می‌دارم. و من تو را در نکاح پسر خود دارم».

{۱۰} پادشاه محفه طلبید و دختر را در محفه نشاند و به خانه آورد. پسر را طلبید[و] و گفت «ای فرزند، امروز در شکارْ دختری را دیدم؛ غریب و به‌غایت خوب‌خُلق.[ز] و با او گفتم «تو دختر منی و تو را در نکاح پسر خود درآرم»؛ اکنون آورده‌ام». پسر گفت «هر چه رضای پدر باشد من راضیم». پادشاه قاضی را طلبید. نکاح بست. چون عقد شد پادشاه به خازن گفت «هر جواهر که در خزانه خوب و زیبا است بیار». رفت بیاورد.

{۱۱} و پادشاه خود مُقبَل[۱۴] شده دختر را بیاراست، به‌غیر دست راست. پادشاه روی به دختر کرد، و گفت «آنچه از دست می‌آمد تقصیر نکردم. امّا دست درست کردن نَتَوانم که آن قدرت خداوند تَعَالَی است». آنگه پادشاه خادمان را گفت «این دختر را نزد پسر من برید و هر چه پسر من با او بگوید آن را بیارید و بر

[۱۱] بازگشت. [۱۲] متغیّر شدن اشاره به برآشفتن دارد. [۱۳] این پاسخ در برخی نسخ موجود نیست. [۱۴] بر اساس دهخدا، واژهٔ مُقبَل به معنی «پیش آمده و روی آورده به هر چیزی» به کار می‌رود، و در آثار بیهقی نیز دیده شده است. احتمالا اشاره به «پیش قدمی» هم دارد.

[د] درویش گفت «از این خانه عجوزه به من داد» [ه] که در شکار بود [و] آنگاه پادشاه با خود اندیشید که «اگر توقّف کنم شاید که پسر من از بی‌دستی این دختر معلوم کند. مبادا که به نکاح او راضی نشود! هنوز وی را معلوم نشده باشد که من این دختر را در نکاح او درآورم». [ز] صاحب جمال

{7} The miserly man returned. He noticed a man sitting near his front door eating bread. His face blazed and he asked angrily who had given him bread. The dervish indicated to the man's house. The father realised that his daughter had given the bread. Being sad and angry, he entered the house and said, 'Did you give the dervish bread?'His daughter said, 'I have given him my own bread!' The miserly man said, 'I have never given anything to anybody, and you, unlike me, give bread to a dervish! If you were truly my daughter you would not do this against my wishes.' He said this and took the hand of the poor girl and led her out of the town into the desert. Then he asked her, 'With which hand did you give the bread?' The poor daughter said, 'With my right hand.' The miserly oppressor immediately took his knife and cut the hand from its joint, and then he left the poor girl alone in the desert.

{8} The wretched girl was in pain and was scared of being alone. She looked up to the sky and said, 'O God, You witnessed what father did to me because of bread! I do not now know how Your mercy would help poor me. O God, You wisely know that father has unjustly maimed me, and no one except You is able to help the oppressed.' While praying, a king – who was apart from his army – arrived upon her suddenly as decreed by God.

{9} The king saw the girl. He asked, 'Who are you? And what are you doing in this desert?' The girl said, 'I am the slave of God.' The king asked, 'How did you come to this place and what has happened to your hand?' She replied, 'As God decreed, they have made me without a hand, and God sent me to this desert and I was patient and satisfied with whatever God's decree brings upon me,[1] as He does whatever He wishes.' When the king heard this from her he took pitty on her and said, 'O girl, I have no daughter in this world. But you be my daughter. I do have a son. God has made me especially kind to you so that I love you more than my own son. And I will marry you with my son.'

{10} The king sought a howdah and put the girl into it and brought her home. He called his son and said, 'O my son, I found a girl during hunting today; alone and quite well mannered, and I said to her that "you are like my daughter and that I will marry you to my son." I have now brought her here.' The son said, 'Whatever my father is satisfied with, I am satisfied with, too.' The king sought the notary. He married them. When they were married the king ordered the treasurer, 'Bring every beautiful gem from the treasury.' He went and brought them.

{11} The king himself stepped forward and made up the girl, except her right hand. He looked at the girl and said, 'I did not fail in doing as much as I could for

[1] Translation based on William Wright, *Grammar of the Arabic Language* (London: MS. Department of British Museum, 1862), vol. 2, 81.

من عرضه دارید». خادمان دختر را برداشته بُردند. حقّ سُبْحَانَهُ وَتَعَالَىٰ در دلِ پادشاه آن نوعِ مهر و شفقّتی انداخته بود نسبت به آن دختر که طاقت نیاورد. از عقب دختر روان شد که «مبادا پسرمن چیزی گوید نسبت به عیبِ دست و دلِ دختر شکسته شود. باری، پسر خود را بگویم بی‌عیب خداست، دگر هرکه هست از عیب خالی نیست».[۱۵] پادشاه آمد و در پسِ در استاده، از درزِ[۱۶] در نگاه می‌کرد.

{۱۲} پادشاه‌زاده رو به دختر کرد، و گفت «مرا آن بَرگی[۱۷] بده». چون او دست راست نداشت، به دست چپ داد. پادشاه‌زاده گفت «پدر من ازجهت من زنی کرده است که تمام عمر خود برگی نخورده است و دست راست را از چپ نداند». چون دختر این سخن شنید شکسته‌دل شد و چشم پُرآب کرد، و رو به جانب آسمان کرد و گفت «ای راست کنندهٔ عیبِ معیوبان، اگر این دستِ من ازجهت رضای تو بریده شده‌است، خودْ دستِ منِ ضعیف را به قدرت خود می‌توانی درست کردن، تا از روی شوهر شرمنده نباشم». درین سخن بود که ناگاه از گوشهٔ خانه آواز شنید که «دست از چادر بیرون کن» .چون دست بیرون کشید دست درست شده بدید و شوهر را به دست راست برگ داد.

{۱۳} چون پادشاه این را بدید که دست درست شد، طاقت نماند؛ از در درآمد و دختر را در کنار گرفت و بوسید[۱۸] و پرسید «به حرمت آن خدای عَزَّوَجَلَّ که دستِ راستِ تو درست گردانید که واقعهٔ گذشتهٔ خود را با من بگوی». دختر به تمام عرض کرد و [گفت] «همچون تو پادشاهی را به سر وقت من رسانید؛ مهربان و مشفقِ من گردانید تا معلوم اهل عالم بوده باشد که هر کاری که از بهر رضای حقّ سُبْحَانَهُ وَتَعَالَىٰ بکنند هرگز ضایع نشود».[۱۹]

{۱۴} حکایت دیگر بشنو. پادشاهی بخیل بود، و حکم کرده بود که «هرکه در شهرِ من نان به درویشی دهد دست‌ها بزنند و از شهر بیرون کنند». تا کار فقیران به جایی رسید که از گرسنگی می‌مردند. و هر فقیری که مُردْ رَسنی در پای او کرده، از شهر بیرون انداختی. تا روزی فقیری را طاقت نماند. فریاد برآورد که «ای مسلمانان، از بهر رضای پادشاه نان نمی‌دهید؟ باری برای رضای خدای عَزَّوَجَلَّ بدهید تا بوی کنیم؛ باشد که بوی نان به مشام ما برسد و ضعف ما باری تسکین یابد».

{۱۵} در آن شهر عورتی مسلمه، چون آواز درویش شنید که این نوع فریاد می‌کند، در خاطر گذرانید که «دو قُرص جوین[۲۰] دارم. به این درویش دهم، و رضای خدای تَعَالَی حاصل کنم. اگر پادشاه بشنود هر چه خواهد کند». برخاست و دو قرص جوین به درویش داد. مخبران[۲۱] خبر به پادشاه بردند که «در فلان محلات عورتی نان به درویش داد». پادشاه فرمود تا هر دو دستش را ببُرند و از شهر بیرون کنند. آن ضعیفهٔ بیچاره را هر دو

[۱۵] در برخی نسخ این خادمان هستند که در دفاع از دختر ایفای نقش می‌کنند. [۱۶] شکافِ در. [۱۷] براساس دهخدا، واژه «برگ» اشاره دارد به « نوعی کباب تهیّه شده از قطعه‌های گوشت گوسفندی یا گوساله» که در مراسم‌های مختلف تهیّه می‌شود.
[۱۸] عمل بوسیدن عروس توسط پادشاه در برخی نسخ موجود نیست. [۱۹] در نسخهٔ دانشگاه تهران، و در حاشیهٔ این داستان، چنین نوشته شده‌است «هُوَ العَزیز؛ تنگ چشم از نعمت عالم نخواهد گشت سیر؛ پُر نمی‌گردد به دریا کاسهٔ چشم حباب»؛ بیت منسوب به ناصرعلی سرهندی که در سدهٔ یازده هجری قمری می‌زیسته است. [۲۰] دو عدد نان جو. [۲۱] خبررسانان.

you. However, I cannot fix your severed hand as this is only possible through God's power.' Then, the king called his servants and said, 'Take this girl to my son. And let me know everything my son tells her.' The servants took the girl. God had placed such a special affection and kindness for that girl in the king's heart that the king could not bear it. [As such] he went after the girl, thinking, 'If my son mentions about her hand the girl's heart will be broken. I will tell my son that flawlessness is only God, no one else is free from blemish.' The king arrived and stood behind the door watching inside through a peephole.

{12} The prince looked at the girl and said, 'Pass me some meat.' As she did not have her right hand, she passed it with her left hand. The prince, then, said, 'My father has married me with a woman who has never eaten meat and does not know the difference between her right and left hand.' When the girl heard this she became heartbroken and cried and looked at the sky and said, 'O Fixer of the Defective, if my hand has been cut off for the sake of Your satisfaction, You can also fix my hand by Your own power, so I will not be embarrassed before my husband.' While saying this, she heard a voice from the corner of the house saying, 'Pull your hand out of the veil.' When she pulled her hand out she noticed the hand was mended and then passed meat to her husband with her right hand.

{13} When the king witnessed that the hand had been mended he could wait no longer and entered the room, embraced the girl, and kissed her. He asked, 'Given that God has fixed your right hand, tell me about your past and what has happened.' The girl told the whole story and said, 'God sent me such a king as you. He made the king be kind to me so that it can be said to the whole world that everything which is done for the sake of God will never be overlooked.'

{14} Here is another story. There was a miserly king, and he had made a decree, 'Whoever gives bread to a dervish in my city will have his hands cut off and be banished.' All the poor people were dying because of hunger. When a pauper died his leg was ties and he was dragged out of the city. The one day a pauper could tolerate it no longer. He loudly called out, 'O Muslims! Do you desist from giving bread in order to please the king? Give for the sake of God or at least so we can smell the bread. Perhaps with smelling bread our hunger will be relieved.'

{15} There was a Muslim woman in that city. When she heard how a dervish had protested, she thought, 'I have two loaves of barley bread and I will give them to the dervish to please God. If the king hears about this it does not matter what he does.' She went out and gave two loaves of barley bread to the dervish. Informants gave the king this news, 'In this district of your territory a woman gave bread to a dervish.' The king ordered both hands of the woman to be cut off and that she be banished. They cut off the two hands of that poor woman. She had an infant son in a cradle. They

دستش از بند جدا کردند، و پسری در گهواره داشت، از گهواره دَر کردند و گردنِ او بستند، و از شهر بیرون کردند.

{۱۶} آن مظلومه را چهار درد پیش آمد: اوّل: یکی در دست‌ها؛ دوم: عذاب فرزند؛ سوم: از خانه جدا افتاده؛ چهارم مشقّت غربت و تنهایی بیابان.

{۱۷} القصّه. تشنه شد. دربیابان می‌گشت شاید آبی یابد.[۲۲] حق سُبحانَهُ وتَعالیٰ حوض را در نظر او بیاورد. چون نزدیک حوض رفت تا آب خورد دست نداشت که آب خورد. سرنگون کرد[۲۳] تا به دهن آب خورد. بچّه از کتف او در آب افتاد و غرق شد؛ نتوانست به درآوردن. بر درد افزود. در کنار حوض استاده شد، و گفت «رَضَینا بِقَضائِك وَصَبَرنا عَلی بلائِك؛ یعنی راضی شدم به قضای تو، و صبر کردم بر بلای تو».

{۱۸} درین سخن بود که دو جوان صاحب‌جمال[ج] بر سر او رسیدند. آن عورت نظر در جمال ایشان کرد، دید جمله بیابان از پرتو نورِ جمالِ ایشان منوّر شد. به‌مجرّد آنکه نظر در جمال ایشان کرد، دردِ دست و غصّه فرزند را فراموش کرد.[۲۴] ایشان پرسیدند «تو کیستی و در کنار آب چه می‌خواهی؟» عورت گفت «فرزند دلبندم درین آب غرق شده است». یکی از این جوانان دست در آب کرد و فرزند او را سلامت بیرون آورد و به مادرش داد. چون مادر دست دراز کرد که فرزند خود را بگیرد دید که دست ندارد. جوان پرسید که «دست‌های تو را که[۲۵] بریده؟» گفت پادشاه دنیا بریده‌است. جوان گفت «چون کاری بهر پادشاهِ حقیقی کرده بودی، هم‌او نیکو می‌کند». این بگفت و از پیش عورت غایب شد. و همان لحظه بیامدند و هر دو پنجهٔ[۲۶] بریدهٔ او را بیاوردند، و عورت را گفتند «هر دو دست خود بیرون کن». چون هر دو دست بیرون کرد، ایشان هر دو پنجهٔ او را به دو دست او بنهادند. حق سُبحانَهُ وتَعالیٰ هر دو دستش درست گردانید، و جوانان از پیش او روان شدند.

{۱۹} عورت بدوید و دست در دامن ایشان کرد که «شما چه کسانید که در حقّ من این چنین احسانی نمودید؟» ایشان گفتند «ما هر دو دستگیران دین و دنیای توئیم.[۲۷] و ما هر دوتن را که بدین خوبی می‌بینی، دو قرص جوین توئیم که حق سُبحانَهُ وتَعالیٰ بدین صورت نزد تو فرستاده است.[۲۸] چنانکه امروز تو را در دنیا به‌کار آمده‌ایم در عقبی هم دستگیر تو خواهیم بود».

{۲۰} إلٰهِيّ، همهٔ مؤمنان را توفیق سخاوت روزی کن، و در زیر عَلَم صاحب سخاوتان[۲۹] جایی دهی، و از دست أَمیر المُؤمِنین علی کَرَّمَ اللهُ وَجْهه شربت کوثری روزی گردانی. به حقّ محمّد وآله أجمعین.

[۲۲] مراد از «شاید آبی یابد» همان «تا آبی یابد» است. [۲۳] «سر نگون کردن» به «پایین آوردن سر» اشاره دارد.
[۲۴] این عبارت در برخی نسخ موجود نیست. [۲۵] چه کسی. [۲۶] «پنجه» واژه‌ای است که در اکثر متون اسلامی به زبان‌های مختلف، از جمله مالایی، دیده می‌شود. [۲۷] توییم؛ تو هستیم. [۲۸] تشبیه نان جو به جوان در برخی نسخ موجود نیست.
[۲۹] سخاوتمندان.

[ج] صاحب‌دل

took him out of the cradle and placed him upon her neck and sent them out of town.

{16} Four painful things oppressed this woman: first, the severance of her hands; second, the teasing of her infant son; third, being in exile away from home; and four, hardship and loneliness in the desert.

{17} The rest of the story. She was thirsty and looked for water in the desert. God brought to her attention a pond. When she reached the pond, in order to drink water, she had no hand to do so. She brought her head down to drink water with her mouth. At this moment, the child felt from her shoulder into the water and drowned. She was not able to rescue the child. Her pain increased. She stood next to the pond and said, 'We are satisfied with what You decreed and are patient upon the trials You imposed, meaning that I was satisfied with God's decision and patient in misfortune.'

{18} While speaking thus, two young and handsome men came to her. She saw their faces and realised that the whole desert has been illuminated by the light of their faces. As soon as she looked upon their faces, she forgot the pain of her hand and the loss of her child. They asked her, 'Who are you and what are you doing near water?' The woman replied, 'My darling child has drowned in this water.' One of the young men put his hand into the water and brought out the child, safe and sound, and passed him on to his mother. When the mother wanted to hold her child she realised that she did not have a hand. The young man asked her, 'Who has cut off your hands?' She replied, 'The worldly king has cut them off.' The young man said, 'As you have done a good job for the sake of the actual King, He will make them good.' The young man said this, and disappeared before the woman. Soon both men returned and brought both her severed hands and told the woman to, 'Bring both your arms out.' When she brought her arms out they placed the hands back on her arms. God healed both of her hands and the young men left her.

{19} The woman ran after them and dragged at their cloaks asking, 'Who are you that bestowed this kindness upon me?' They replied, 'We are both helpers of your religion and your world. And that you see both of us in such beauty is because we are your two loaves of barley bread that God has sent to you in this [human] guise. As we have helped you today in this world, we will help you in the other world too.

{20} *O God, grant all believers the quality of being generous, and place them under the standard of generous lords, and provide the sorbet of Kawthar from the hand of ʿAlī, may God ennoble his person. By Muḥammad and his family altogether. [Amen.]*

حکایتِ آزر بُت تراش

{۱} آورده‌اند که روزی مهتر ابراهیم علیه‌السلام نزدیک بُتخانه پدر بیامد. دید بُتان را پیشِ خود داشته و پیش ایشان سر به سجده می‌برد. حضرت ابراهیم را طاقت نماند، و گفت «ای پدر، مرا در کار تو عجب می‌آید! از برایِ که بُتان ساخته تو اند[1] و پیشِ ساخته‌گانِ خود سر سجده می‌بری؟ و آن خدای را چرا سجده نمی‌کنی که تو را بیافریده است، و چشم بینا و گوش شنوا و زبان گویا و پای روان[2] داده است؛ و هر عضوی را به عضوی بیاراسته است؟ پس حضرت نگارندهٔ[3] خود را گذاشته این بُتان را سجده می‌کنی؟»

{۲} آزر گفت «ای ابراهیم، اگر سخنْ تو راست بگویی، بگو این بُتان در حقّ پروردگار تو و به رسالت پیغمبری تو گواهی دهند. درین زمان من هم به خدای تو ایمان آرم». چون از پدر این سخن شنید، ابراهیم روی به بُتان کرد[4] و گفت «ای بُتان، به عزّت آن خدای که او قدرت بر همه چیزها دارد، و می‌تواند که شما را با من در سخن آرد، اکنون به وحدانیّت حق عزّوجلّ سبحانه و تعالی و بر رسالت پیغمبری من گواهی دهید». جملهٔ بُتان آغاز کردند که «لآ إِلهَ إِلَّا اللهُ، إِبْراهیم خَلیل الله».[5] چون پدر چنین شنید حیران ماند، و گفت «ای ابراهیم، من توفیق کلمه گفتن نمی‌یابم. اما این بُتان را به تو بخشیدم».

{۳} مهتر ابراهیم دید که پدر رغبت به ایمان آوردن نمی‌کند. همهٔ بُتان را جمع کرد و تبر برداشت تا همه را بشکند، که جبرئیل علیه‌السلام رسید و دست ابراهیم علیه‌السلام گرفت. [جبرئیل] گفت «یا ابراهیم، فرمان می‌شود که همین لحظه این بُتان به وحدانیّت ما و رسالت پیغمبری تو گواهی دادند. نخواهم که تو ایشان را بشکنی».

[1] تو هستند. [2] دوان؟ [3] نقّاش و صورتگر.

[4] در برخی نسخ ابراهیم ابتدا روی به آسمان می‌کند و با خدا صحبت می‌کند، و سپس به بُتان روی می‌آورد.

[5] در برخی نسخ بُتان چنین گویند «لآ إِلهَ إِلَّا اللهُ، مُحَمَّدٌ رَسُولُ اللهِ، إِبرَاهِیمُ خَلِیلِ اللهِ». این عبارت در رسالات صوفیه به زبان‌های متفاوت وجود دارد. از جمله در نقشبندیه (مجموعة أوراد وأحزاب الطريقة النقشبندية)؛ همچنین، در «داستان‌های هزار و یک شب» (متن عربی) و «دلائل نبوت محمدی و شمائل فتوت احمدی» (نسخهٔ ترکی استانبولی) Suppl. Turc. 181 در کتابخانهٔ ملّی فرانسه دیده می‌شود.

The story of Āzar, the idol-maker

{1} It is reported that one day Abraham (pbuh) came to his father's[1] temple. There he saw that he had idols before him and that he prostrated before them. Without waiting, Prophet Abraham said, 'O father, I am surprised by what you do. Because the idols are handmade and you prostrate before them! Why do you not prostrate before the God who has created you and provided you with a sighted eye, a hearing ear, a fluent tongue, feet with which you walk, and who has paired every limb with another so beautifully? You have forsaken the one who breathed life into you in order to prostrate before these idols?'

{2} Āzar said, 'O Abraham, if you are right, then ask these idols to testify as to your God and your prophecy. If they do so then I will have faith in your God.' When he heard this from his father, Abraham looked at the idols and said, 'O idols, by the glory of the God who has control over everything and can enable you to speak with me, now testify to the unity of God and upon my prophecy.' All the idols began to recite, 'There is no god but God, Abraham is the friend of God.'[2] When the father heard this his jaw dropped and he said, 'O Abraham, I will not declare faith but I will forgive these idols because of you.'[3]

{3} His Eminence Abraham noticed that his father was not interested in converting to his faith, so he gathered all the idols together and picked up an axe in order to break them. However, in the meantime, Gabriel (pbuh) arrived and took hold of the hand of Abraham (pbuh). Gabriel said, 'O Abraham, as it was commanded, these idols have now testified upon Our unity and your prophecy. I do not want you to break them down.'

[1] i.e., Āzar's [2] Such a profession to faith is found in the Ottoman Turkish *Delail-i nubuwwe-i Muhammedi we şema'il-i futuwwe-i Ahmedi*, textual resources of the Naqshbandiyya order, and in *One Thousand and One Nights*. [3] They are up to you.

{۴} پس از این مؤمنان را بشارت عظیم است، زیرا که بُتان یک بار اقرار به وحدانیّت خدای عَزَّوَجَلَّ و به رسالت ابراهیم عَلَيْهِ السَّلَامُ کردند، خدای تَعَالَیٰ عَزَّوَجَلَّ نخواست که بشکنند. پس مؤمنان همیشه محبّت الهی در دل دارند و به پیغمبری اقرار دارند. هر زمان به سعادت این کلمه[الف] مشرّف گردند، اگر از عذاب قیامت نجات یابند عجب نباشد. در کارهای خداوند هیچ‌کس چون و چرا نمی‌پرسد «یَفْعَلُ اللّٰهُ مَا یَشَاءُ بِقُدْرَتِهِ وَ یَحْکُمُ مَا یُرِیدُ بِعِزَّتِهِ،[۶] آن‌را که خداوند نجات دهد با کردارهای اندک، و آن‌را که نخواهد، کردارهای او حبط کند».

{۵} آورده‌اند که در عهد دولت موسیٰ کلیم الله صَلَوَاتُ اللّٰه زاهدی بود که چهارصد سال خدای را بندگی کرده و همیشه اوقات به عبادت گذرانیده. و در آن شهر فاسقی بود که هفتاد سال به جز فسق و فجور کار دیگری نکردی. اتّفاقاً قضای[۷] هر دو در یک روز رسید. شوری در بنی اسرائیل افتاد که زاهد از جهان رفت. خلق همه جمیع شدند. پیش حضرت موسیٰ عَلَيْهِ السَّلَامُ آمدند و گفتند «فلانی را که نیک کردار بود امروز وفات یافته. اکنون ما جمع آمده‌ایم تا پسِ جنازه او قدم زنیم تا از برکت او ما همه آمرزیده شویم و بازگردیم». بازگفتند «ای پیغمبرِ عَزَّوَجَلَّ، امروز یک فاسق هم نقل کرده‌است که تمام عمر خود به غیر از فسق و فجور کار دیگر نکرده‌است».[ب]

{۶} چون قوم مهتر موسیٰ عَلَيْهِ السَّلَامُ حکایت فاسق و زاهد را تمام کردند، حضرت موسیٰ عَلَيْهِ السَّلَامُ خواست تا با امّت بر سر زاهد برود، که جبرئیل عَلَيْهِ السَّلَامُ دررسید و گفت «ای موسیٰ، فرمان شده که قوم خود را بگو تا رسنی برند و در پای زاهد بندند و کشاله‌کنان از شهر بیرون آرند، و در مزبله[۸] اندازند. و فرمان شده که بر سر آن گنه‌کار حاضر شوید و نزدِ خودْ او را غسل دهند و بر جنازهٔ او با امّتان خود نماز گویند و با جنازه او بروید و او را به دست خود دفن کنید».

{۷} موسیٰ عَلَيْهِ السَّلَامُ روی سوی امّت خود کرد، و گفت «جبرئیل فرمان چنین رسانیده». مردم در حیرت ماندند. بعده، گفتند «مگر بر عکس می‌شود؟» بازگفتند «ای پیغمبر خدای عَزَّوَجَلَّ، آنچه از این مرد دیده بودیم به شما عرض کردیم. باقی احوالِ دلِ هریکی خداوند تَعَالَیٰ داند». مهتر موسیٰ عَلَيْهِ السَّلَامُ گفت «ما بنده‌ایم و در کارها مجال دم زدن نیست. آنچه فرمان شد همان کنیم». جبرئیل عَلَيْهِ السَّلَامُ رفت و باز بیامد و گفت «ای موسیٰ عَلَيْهِ السَّلَامُ، امّت تو راست می‌گویند که زاهد نیک کردار بود و فاسق بدکردار بود. امّا ایشان به ظاهرْ بیش ندانند و باطنْ

[۶] دعایی است منسوب به پیامبراسلام که توصیه شده که پیش‌از خوابیدن سه مرتبه خوانده شود. گفته می‌شود که ثواب آن برابر با هزار رکعت نماز است. برای مطالعهٔ بیشتر در مورد فضیلتِ این عبارت دعایی مراجعه کنید به: جمعی از نویسندگان، دانشنامه امام علی (تهران: سازمان انتشارات پژوهشگاه فرهنگ و اندیشه اسلامی، ۱۳۸۳/۲۰۰۴) ج ۱، ص ۳۲۹.
[۷] زمان موت.
[۸] زباله‌دان.

[الف] «لآ إِلٰهَ إِلَّا اللّٰه، مُحَمَّدٌ رَسُولُ اللّٰه»
[ب] اگر در راه گذری پیش می‌آمدی في الحال روی از وی گردانیدیم که مبادا شومی فسق او بر ما اثر کند

{4} There is a great lesson in this for believers. Because the idols confessed to the unity of God and the prophecy of Abraham (pbuh), God did not want them to be broken. So, believers should always have divine love in their hearts and bear witness to prophecy. When they are honoured with this phrase[4], then there will be no surprise if they are saved from the torments of the Day of Judgement. No one should ever question God's acts. God does whatever He wants to do with His power, and governs whatever He wants with His self-glory. God will save whom He desires even owing to a few good deeds. Whomsoever He desires not to save then their good deeds will be of no consequence.

{5} It is reported that during the time of Moses, the Interlocutor of God (pbuh), there was a pious man who was always found worshipping and he had worshipped God for four hundred years. There was an impious man in the city who did nothing but commit sin and wickedness. By chance, they died on the same day. There was a huge discussion among the Children of Israel saying, 'The pious man has passed away. We have now gathered to walk after his corpse, so we may be forgiven and repent due to his blessing.' They also said, 'O Prophet of God, one impious man has also died today, who did nothing except commit sin and wickedness during his whole life.'

{6} When the people of His Eminence Moses (pbuh) finished telling the story of the impious man and the story of the pious man, Prophet Moses (pbuh) prepared to accompany his people and join the funeral procession of the pious man when Gabriel (pbuh) arrived and said, 'O Moses, it is commanded that you tell your people to take a rope and tie the pious man's legs, drag him out of town, and throw him on the rubbish dump. It is also commanded that you attend to the corpse of the impious man and wash him before you and pray upon his corpse with your people and walk alongside his corpse and bury him with your own hands.'

{7} Moses (pbuh) looked to his people and said, 'Gabriel has commanded thus!' The people were surprised. Then, they said, 'How is it possible that the reverse must happen?!' Again, they said, 'O Prophet of God, we told you whatever we had seen from this impious man. Only God knows the rest of their past.' His Eminence Moses (pbuh) said, 'We are servants, and in fulfilling tasks there is no time to dispute. Whatever has been ordered, we follow accordingly.' Gabriel (pbuh) left there and returned with a message from God, 'O Moses (pbuh), your people tell the truth that the pious man was well mannered and the impious one was bad-mannered. However, they do not know more than their exteriors. Only We know about the interior of people. Once you return from the funeral of the impious servant go to the houses of both the pious and impious men and ask their wives about their words and actions.'

[4] i.e., the declaration of faith

غیرِ ما غیری نداند.[۹] چون از دفن بندهٔ گنه‌کار بازگردی، در خانهٔ زاهد و فاسق بروید و از زن[ج] ایشان بازپرسید که افعال و اقوال ایشان چه بوده‌است».

{۸} به پای زاهد رسنی بستند و از شهر کشاله‌کشان در مزبله انداختند. و فاسق با تعظیم و تکریم بسیار دفن کردند. بعداز آن، حضرت موسیٰ با امّت خود به خانهٔ زاهد آمد و پرسید که «شوهر تو چگونه کسی بود و عمر خود چگونه گذرانیدی؟» زن گفت «ای پیغمبر خدای عَزَّوَجَلَّ، او تمام عمر روزه داشتی، و از شب تا صبح نماز گزاردی، و به یک پای استاده خدای عَزَّوَجَلَّ را بندگی کردی. امّا گاه‌گاهی یک دو سخن هم می‌گفتی». موسیٰ عَلَیهِ‌السَّلَام گفت «بگو آنچه او گفت». زن گفت «گاه‌گاهی می‌گفت که «چهارصد سال برآمده است که من بندگی و طاعت می‌کنم امّا در خاطر من تحقیق[۱۰] نمی‌شود خدای تَعَالَی یکی است؛ یا موسیٰ که دعوی پیغمبری می‌کند برحقّ است یا دروغ؟»». جبرئیل رسید و گفت «ای موسیٰ، کسی در حقّ من و تو چنین بگوید، پس امّت تو در حقّ او چه گویند؟ همه گویند که «او به‌غایت بدبخت و بی‌سعادت بود؛ کسی در حقّ پروردگار خود به شرکت[۱۱] گمان بد برد و پیغمبر را یقین نداند»

{۹} آنگه روی به خانهٔ فاسق کردند. چون به خانهٔ او رسیدند درِ خانهٔ او بسته دیدند. موسیٰ عَلَیهِ‌السَّلَام گفت «در باز کن». از درون خانه آواز آمد که «کیست که در خانهٔ گنه‌کاری می‌کوبد؟» گفتند «در باز کن که پیغمبر خدای تَعَالَی آمده است». زن بشتافت و در باز کرد و گفت «قدمِ پاک در خانهٔ ناپاکی چگونه درآید؟» موسیٰ عَلَیهِ‌السَّلَام گفت «مرا خبر کن که شوهر تو چگونه کسی بود؟» زن گفت «ای پیغمبر خداوند تَعَالَی عَزَّوَجَلَّ، از وی چه می‌پرسید. هر بدی در جهان است در ذات او بود. همیشه به فساد،[د] و زنا، و خمر خوردن، و بدی کردن، و فحش خالی نبودی. ای برگزیدهٔ رحمان، اگر یک کردارِ زشت او را بگویم [به شرح] راست نیاید».[۱۲]

{۱۰} موسیٰ عَلَیهِ‌السَّلَام پرسید «از وی هیچ افعال و اقوال نیک آمده؟» زن گفت «ای پیغمبر خدای تَعَالَی، چون نیم‌شب شدی، از مستی شراب بیدار شدی و رو به جانب قبله کردی و گفتی «إِلٰهِيّ، روز و شب بی‌فرمانی می‌کنم، اگر فردای قیامت بسوزی لایق اینم. اگر بخشی تو حاکمی. اگر من به بدی در میان بندگان تو مشهورم، تو به کرم و مرحمتِ مشهورِ خویش در هجده‌هزار عالم ببخشایی بر کسی که او چیزی ندارد به جز تو پروای غیری ندارد.[ه] اگر چه گناه‌کارم، در خدایی تو شکّی و شبهه‌ای ندارم. و یقین می‌دانم که همیشه هستی و خواهی بود. و پیغمبر موسیٰ عَلَیهِ‌السَّلَام برحقّ و راست است و فرستادهٔ اوست به سوی بندگان». ای پیغمبر! هیچ شبی نبودی که چنین نگفتی».

[۹] این عبارت در برخی نسخ موجود نیست.
[۱۰] راستی. [۱۱] اشاره به قراردادن شریک برای خدا. [۱۲] راست آمدن با «برابری کردن» و یا «هماهنگی یافتن» مترادف است.

[ج] زنان [د] کثافت‌کاری، جماع [ه] که به غیر از تو کسی ندارم

{8} The people tied the pious man's legs with rope and dragged him from the town and threw him onto the rubbish dump. The impious man was buried with full respect. Subsequently, Prophet Moses went along with his people to the house of the pious man and asked, 'What type of man was your husband, and how did he pass his life?' The woman replied, 'O Prophet of God, he was in fast the whole of his life and prayed from night to morning and always arose worshipping God. However, occasionally he would say a few strange words.' Moses (pbuh) said, 'Tell me what he would say.' The woman said, 'Occasionally he would say, "I have been worshipping God for four hundred years, but it is not clear in my mind whether God is truly One or whether Moses, who claims prophecy, is a righteous or an imposter!" Gabriel arrived and conveyed, 'O Moses, as for the one who talks like this about Me and you, what do your people say about him?'The people said of the pious man, 'He was terrible and miserable, the one who thought wrongly, assuming a partner for his God, and who did not believe in God's prophet.'

{9} Then they moved towards the house of the impious man. When they arrived at his door, the door was closed. Moses (pbuh) said, 'Open the door.' A voice from the house said, 'Who is there, beating on the door of a sinful man?' The people said, 'Open the door as the Prophet of God comes here.' The woman ran quickly and opened the door and said, 'How is it possible for a purified step to enter into an impure house!?' Moses (pbuh) said, 'Tell me what kind of a man your husband was?' The woman said, 'O Prophet of God, whom are you asking about his affairs! Whatever evil there is in the world was in his nature. He never left alone womanising, adultery, wine, bad behaviour, nor swearing. O, he who is the select of the Merciful, it will not be fair and short if I want to explain even one of his wrong-doings.'

{10} Moses (pbuh) asked, 'Have any good deeds or words come from him?' The woman said, 'O Prophet of God, once at midnight he woke up still feeling drunk, and turned towards the direction of prayer and said, "O God, I commit sins morning and night, if You burn me on the Day of Judgement, I deserve it, of course. If You forgive, You are the Ruler. If I am well-known for vice among your servants, You would forgive me due to Your kindness and mercy by which you are well known in the eighteen thousand universes. The one who does not have anything will not be afraid of anybody but You. Although I am a sinner, I do not doubt in your divinity. And I believe that You exist always and will be. And Prophet Moses (pbuh) is the right one and is Your messenger to Your servants." O Prophet, there was not a night for which he did not talk like that.'

{۱۱} جبرئیل علیه‌السلام رسید و گفت «ای موسیٰ، فرمان می‌شود کسی که در حقّ ما و تو چنین گوید، تو در حقّ او چه گویی؟» دیگر فرمان شد «ای موسیٰ، که درآن‌ساعت که در حضرت ما چنین شکستگی می‌آورْد، اگر همهٔ گنه‌کاران عالم را درخواست می‌کرد همه را بدو می‌بخشیدیم» تا معلومِ خوانندگان و شنوندگان باشد که بیچارگی و شکستگی در حضرت ما منزلتی تمام دارد و هر که مغرور به دنیا و یا به عمل خود گشت در آن حضرت قرب و قیمتی ندارد.

{۱۲} حکایت. چنین آورده‌اند که روزی جبرئیل علیه‌السلام بیامد نزد حضرت رسالت پناه صلّی‌الله‌علیه‌وسلّم، و گفت «نزدیک فلان زاهد بودم که چهارصد سال برآمده است که عبادت کرده و همیشه مستقبل قبله بنشسته و جان به حق سبحانه‌وتعالیٰ سپرده. و چون قیامت قایم شود خدای تَعَالَی خلق اوّلین و آخرین را حاضر گرداند. آنگاه، ندا دردهد که انبیاء و اولیاء همه به رحمت ما در بهشت درآیند». آن زاهد بگوید «من چهارصد سال بندگی کرده‌ام. اجر این چه می‌دهی؟». فرمان می‌شود که «به رحمت ما در بهشت رو و اجر خود طلب کن».

{۱۳} باز آن زاهد گوید که «تا اجر چهارصد سالهٔ من ندهند، در بهشت نروم». غیرت حضرت الهی درکار شود که «ای فرشتگان، این زاهد را در دوزخ برید». به حکم فرمان فرشتگان عذاب درآیند، و زاهد را به سوی دوزخ روان کنند. میان زاهد و دوزخ هشتادساله[د] راه مانده باشد که گرمی دوزخ در زاهد اثر کند، چنانچه زبانِ زاهد از تشنگی خشک گردد.

{۱۴} آنگه فرمان شود «فرشته، یک قدح آب برگیر و نزدیک زاهد بَر، و چهارصد سال نیکی و عبادت او را خریداری کن». به‌موجبِ فرموده عمل کرد. چون نظر زاهد بر آن قدح آب افتاد به عجز و زاری گفت «این آب مرا قدری بده». فرشته گوید «دویست سال از چهارصد ساله نیکی و عبادت خود را به من بفروش و نیم‌قدح آب بستان». زاهد دویست ساله عبادت را به نیم‌قدح آب بفروخت.

{۱۵} باز قدری راه رفته بود که تشنگی زیاده شد. فرشته با قدحی آب بنمود.[۱۳] زاهد چون آب را دید از فرشته طلب کرد. فرشته گوید که «دویست ساله عبادت را به نیم‌قدح آب بفروش و تمام قدح بستان». في الحال فروشد و قدح آب بستاند و بخورد. آنگاه فرمان شود که «ای زاهد، به چهارصدساله زُهدِ خود می‌نازیدی. آخر بنگر که به یک قدح آب بفروختی». بعده، فرمان شود که «به تو نعمت بینایي، و گویائی، و شنوایي، و گیرایي[۱۴] داده بودیم. امروز یکی از آن به چهارصد ساله عمل وزن کن[ز] تا کدامین زیاده آید».

۱۳ با قدحی آب ظاهر شد\پیش آمد. ۱۴ لامسه.

د هفتاد ساله ز مقابله کن

{11} Gabriel (pbuh) arrived and said, 'O Moses, it is proclaimed, "The one who talks about Us and you like this, what would We say about him?" When he humbled himself before Our presence, the sins of all the sinners of the world would have been forgiven had he requested it.' Readers should know the status of humility with the Lord. Whosoever becomes proud of his deeds shall have no place in the Lord's presence.

{12} A story was reported that one day Gabriel (pbuh) descended upon the Prophet Muḥammad (pbuh) and said, 'I was with that pious man who worshipped for four hundred years and always sat in the direction of prayer and who has just submitted his soul to God. When the Day of Judgement comes to pass and God gathers the first and last of creation, He will proclaim, "All prophets and saints will be in paradise because of Our mercy." That pious man will say, "I was worshipping for four hundred years. What is my reward?" It will be proclaimed, "Go to paradise because of Our mercy and seek your reward."

{13} Then the pious man will say, "I will not step into paradise unless I am given a four-hundred-year reward." Then, divine jealousy is considered, and it will be said, "O angels, take this pious man to hell." On the basis of this order the angels of torment will come out and take the pious man to hell. There will be a distance of eighty years between the pious man and hell yet the heat of the hellfire will affect the pious man so much so that his tongue will become dry with thirst.

{14} Then a command will be made, "O angel, take a bowl of water and go to the pious man, and purchase his four hundred years of goodness and worship." The angel will do accordingly. When the pious man sees the bowl of water he will cry, requesting, "Give me a portion of this water." The angel will say, "Sell two hundred years of your four hundred years of goodness and worship to me and take half of the water." The pious man will exchange two hundred years of worship for half a bowl of water.

{15} Again, after a while, his thirst will increase. The angel with the bowl of water will appear. When the pious man sees the water he will ask the angel for it. The angel will say, "Sell your two hundred years of worship for half a bowl of water and take the bowl, too." He will immediately sell his deeds and take the bowl of water and drink. Then a command will arrive, "O pious man, you were proud of your four hundred years of worship! Now see that you sold it for a bowl of water!" Then a command will arrive, "We had given you the blessings of seeing, speaking, hearing, and touching. Today, be fair and judge, yourself: weigh one of them against your four hundred years of good deeds in order to see which one is heavier."

{۱۶} فرمان آید که «ای فرشتگان، نعمت بینایی یک چشم زاهد را در یک پلّهٔ ترازو نهید و بسنجید». چون وزن کنند، نعمت بینائی او از چهارصد سال کردار او زیاده آید. چون زاهد این را معاینه ببینَد، سر شرمندگی فرو افکنَد. آنگه فرمان شود که «سربردار! که شرمندگان را و مفلسان را خریداریم. اکنون به رحمت ما در بهشت درآیی[۱۵]»».

{۱۷} إلهِيّ، به حرمت نیک‌بختان که شکستگی ایشان مقبولِ حضرتِ پاکِ توست، که این بیچاره را و کاتب این قصّه را با جمیع مسلمانان با ایمان داری. بمِنَّة وکَرَمه.

۱۵ درآیی.

{16} A command will be given, "O angels, put the blessing of sight in one eye of the pious man into the scale and behold it." When they check the scale the weight of his sight will be more than his four hundred years of deeds. The pious man will notice this clearly and he will lower his head in shame. Then a proclamation will be made, "Raise your head! as We welcome the shameful and humble. Now enter into paradise because of Our kindness.'"

{17} *O God, by the dignity of the auspicious people, whose humility is admissible upon Your pure presence, make this humble pauper and the scribe of this story, as well as all Muslims, faithful. By Your unmerited favour and kindness. [Amen.]*

در حکایتِ گفتنِ طوطی نزد سلیمان پیغمبر علیه‌السلام[الف]

{۱} آورده‌اند که مردی در عهد مهتر سلیمان علیه‌السلام طوطی خرید با الحان و نوایی خوش، و در خانه آورد. بعداز آن از نوا کردن باز ماند. هرچند صاحب تلقین می کرد، طوطی به گفتار نیامد. آن مرد طوطی را همراه قفس نزد سلیمان علیه‌السلام آورد و گفت «این طوطی را که چندگاه الحان خوب می کرد، مدّتی شد که هیچ سخن نمی گوید. نزد شما آورده‌ام، که خدای تَعَالَی دانش جمیع زبان‌ها شما را داده است. که پرسید[ش] که چرا از گفتار خود باز مانده؟»

{۲} چون سلیمان از طوطی پرسید، طوطی جواب گفت «ای پیغمبر خدای، ازآن‌روز که از جفت خود جدا شده‌ام، به فراق به آدمی نالیدم، و به الحان خویش در ناله بودم. ناگاه جفت من در هوا بود و آواز من به سَمع[۱] او رسید. از هوا نزد من آمد، و مرا نصیحت کرد که «چندین مَنَال و صبر کن که خدای تَعَالَی صابران را دوست می‌دارد. باشد که زمانْ[۲] ما را با یکدیگر جمع گرداند. اگر خواست او چنین رفته‌است که جمع کند خودنالیدن تو هیچ سود نکند». تا آنکه جفت من چنین گفته است از نوا و زاری بازمانده‌ام».

{۳} سلیمان نبیّ علیه‌السلام رویْ سویِ صاحبِ طوطی کرد، و گفت «مِنْ بَعْد طوطی در خانهٔ تو هیچ سخن نخواهد کرد. امّا به آنچه خریده‌ای زر از من بستان». مرد گفت «با این مبلغ خریده‌ام». سلیمان آن مبلغ را داد و طوطی را از قفس بیرون آورد و بر دست خود بنشاندند و گفت «اکنون بر جفت خود برو». و طوطی پرید. بر سر بام نشست و گفت «ای پیغمبر خدای تَعَالَی، در حقّ من تو لطف و احسان بسیار نمودی. آنچه در ذات من حق سبحانه وتعالی داده‌است، من هم نزد شما عرض کنم».

[۱] گوش. [۲] زمانه؟

[الف] حکایتِ طوطی؛ که مردی به خدمت مهتر سلیمان علیه‌السلام آورده بود و جواب گفتن طوطی

CHAPTER 21

The story of the parrot speaking with the Prophet Solomon (pbuh)

{1} It is reported that a man bought a parrot with a lovely song during the reign of His Eminence Solomon (pbuh) and took it home. The parrot then stopped singing. Whatever the owner tried the parrot sang no more. The man took the parrot in a cage to Solomon (pbuh) and said, 'This parrot which was singing nicely has not sang for some time. I bring it to you so that you might ask it why it does not sing anymore as God has granted you the knowledge of all languages.'

{2} After Solomon asked the parrot this, the parrot responded, 'O Prophet of God, since I was separated from my mate, I moaned because of my loneliness before this human and wailed with my own song. By chance, my mate was flying and heard my song. It came to me from the sky and advised me, "Do not lament too much and be patient as God likes the patient. Let's hope that time will reunite us with each other. If He has already made the decision to reunite us your lamentation will be unnecessary." Since this advice from my mate I stopped singing and lamenting.'

{3} Prophet Solomon (pbuh) looked at the parrot's owner and said, 'From now on, the parrot will not sing in your home. But you may take gold, as compensation for what you have paid for it.' The man said, 'I bought it for such-and-such price.' Solomon compensated the man and took the parrot out of the cage and sat it on his own hand and said, 'Now fly towards your mate.' And the parrot flew. It sat on top of a roof and said, 'O Prophet of God, you were kind and compassionate to me. What God has placed in my nature, I will tell you.'

{۴} مهتر سلیمان فرمود «بگوی که چه چیز است که در ذات تو نهاده‌اند؟» گفت «ای پیغمبر خدای تَعَالَی، هرجا گنجی باشد از نظر من پوشیده نیست و دراین مقام که شما نشسته‌اید چهارحدّ این خانه گنج است و شما را خبر نیست». سلیمان فرمود تا چهار کُنج خانه را کندند. از هر گوشه گنج ظاهر شد. سلیمان فرمود که «این خود معاینه[۳] شد. امّا بگوی که کسی را خدای تَعَالَی این چنین روشنائی داده باشد، او چگونه گرفتار صیّاد شود؟».

{۵} طوطی گفت «وقتی که صیّاد دام نهاد آسان به دام افتادم».[ب] سلیمان فرمود که «در قعر زمین که گنجی باشد بدانی و دام صیّاد که در دو انگشت زمین دفن کرده اند ندانی؟». طوطی گفت «ای پیغمبر خدای عَزَّوَجَلَّ، إِذَا جَاء القَضاء عَمِي البَصَر،[۴] از اخبار معبود به سمع شما رسیده‌است که چون قضای خدای تَعَالَی دررسد، جمله بینایی‌ها پوشیده شود». این بگفت و از سر بام پرواز کرد.

{۶} آورده‌اند که روزی سلیمان نبیّ صَلَوَاتُ اللّٰهِ عَلَيْه را که گذر در صحرا افتاده بود دید که طفلکان در زیر درختی بازی می‌کردند و بر سر درخت مرغی نشسته است و جانب طفلان می‌بیند و می‌خندد. پرسید که «ای مرغ، خنده تو از بهر چیست؟» مرغ گفت «ازجهت نادانی این طفلان مرا خنده می‌آید که به‌جهت من دام نهاده‌اند. و عمر من چهارصد سال است. اگر این طفلان نادان مرا می‌خواهند بازی دهند و بگیرند، از بهر گرفتن من در رنج[۵] می‌دارند». چون پیغمبر خدای از مرغ این سخن شنید روان شد و رفت.

{۷} بعداز مدّتی بازگشت و به آن راه آمد. دید که آن مرغ را طفلان گرفته‌اند و چشم‌های او را دوخته‌اند و منقارش بسته‌اند و پرها کنده و در هر دو پای او قِید[۶] نهاده‌اند. مهتر سلیمان پرسید که «گفتار تو چیزی دگر بود، گرفتاری[۷] از کجا شد؟» مرغ گفت «ای پیغمبر، همان گفتارم مرا درین بلا انداخت. چون شما از سرْوقت من برفتید دیدم که حلّهٔ جهان را آتش گرفته‌است. با خودم گفتم که «مگر در آشیان من آتش نیست» و خواستم[۸] در آشیان درآیم تا از آتش خلاص شوم. چون درآمدم در دام طفلان گرفتار شدم. هم‌دران محل ندایی شنیدم که «مَا شَاء اللّٰه كَان وَ مَا لَمْ يَشأْ لَمْ يَكُنْ،[۹] خواست هیچ یکی نشود مگر خواست اللّٰه تَبَارَكَ وَتَعَالَی».

{۸} إِلٰهِيّ، به عزّت آنهایی که رضا به قضای تو از سَرِ صِدق داده‌اند، که جمیع مؤمنان را بر آن داری[۱۰] که رضای تو در آن است، و بر من شکسته و کاتب این قصّه رحمت کنی. بِمِنَّةٍ وَكَرَمه.[۱۱]

[۳] مشاهده. [۴] منسوب به ابن عباس. شکل دیگری از این روایت چنین است «إِذَا جَاء القَضاء ذهب البَصَر».
[۵] احتمالا به رنجه به معنای «معذّب ساختن» اشاره دارد. [۶] بند و ریسمان. [۷] اسارت. [۸] مصمّم شدن.
[۹] حدیثی است که در بسیاری از کتب ادعیه و علوم دینی به کار می رود. [۱۰] «بر آن داشتن» اشاره دارد به «اعتقاد داشتن، معتقد بودن، عزم داشتن». به دهخدا رجوع شود. [۱۱] در نسخهٔ کتابخانهٔ دانشگاه تهران، بیتی در حاشیهٔ صفحه نگاشته شده‌است که شبیه بیتی منسوب به شاطر عبّاس صبوحی است «مرجان لب لعل تو مرجان مرا قوت یاقوت نهم نام لعل تو یاقوت؛ دو چشمت همچون بادام است، بادام است...»

[ب] به‌جهت دانه گرفتار شدم

{4} His Eminence Solomon asked, 'Tell me the thing which has been put in your nature?' [The parrot] said, 'O Prophet of God, wherever there is a treasure, it is not overlooked by my eyes, and in this residence wherein you are placed, there is treasure in its four corners, and you are unaware.' Solomon ordered the four corners of his residence to be dug up. From every corner, a treasure emerged. Solomon said, 'This is now observed. But now tell me how has the one who has been given such an illumination by God fallen prey to the hunter?'

{5} The parrot said, 'The hunter had put traps down, and I was easily caught.' Solomon said, 'Of a treasure in the depths of the ground you are aware, but of the hunter's trap which is placed in the ground no more than two fingers deep you are unaware!' The parrot said, 'O Prophet of God, "when destiny arrives, the eyes become blind."[1] You have heard from tradition that when the divine decree arrives, all sorts of sightedness will be covered.' The parrot said this and flew from the top of the roof.

{6} It is reported that Prophet Solomon (pbuh) was passing the desert one day. He noticed children playing under a tree. And a bird was seated on top of the tree. The bird looked upon the children and laughed. Solomon asked, 'O bird, why are you laughing?' The bird said, 'I am laughing because of these children's naivety, as they have made a trap for me. And I am four hundred years old![2] If these foolish children want to play with me and catch me, they are just bothering themselves for the sake of me.' When the Prophet of God heard this from the bird he continued on his business.

{7} After a while, he returned. He noticed that the bird had been taken by the children who sewed its eyes, tied its beak, cut off its feathers, and chained its feet. His Eminence Solomon asked, 'You had said something else, how did you end up in captivity?' The bird said, 'O Prophet, it was the statement of mine that put me into this captivity. After you left me I noticed that there was a huge fire. I thought to myself, 'There should be no fire in my nest.' I decided to enter into my nest in order to be safe from the fire. When I entered, I fell into the children's trap. I heard a voice there that said it, "Whatever God willed happened, and what He did not will, it did not happen", meaning that no one's will occurs but that of God.'

{8} *O God, by those who are faithfully satisfied with what You have decreed for them, lead believers to where Your satisfaction lies. And have mercy upon me, a humble pauper, and the scribe of this story. By Your unmerited favour and kindness. [Amen.]*

[1] Based on a tradition ascribed to Ibn ʿAbbās: *idhā jāʾa al-qaḍā dhahab al-baṣar.*

[2] i.e., well-experienced

حکایتِ خواجه حسن بصری رحمة الله علیه

{۱} آورده‌اند که خواجه حسن بصری رَحْمَةُ اللّٰه عَلَیه در تلاوت کلام مجید[۱] زمانی مشغول بود. چون درین محلّ رسید که سَلَامٌ عَلَیْکُمْ طِبْتُمْ فَادْخُلُوهَا خَالِدِینَ،[۲] گفت «إِلٰهِيّ، بیچاره حسن آرزو دارد که پیشرو قوم بهشتیان باشد تا رضوان بهشت[۳] مرا پیش آید».[۴] از عالم غیب ندا شنید که «آرزوی این دولت پیش‌از تو دگری برد». حسن بصری گفت «إِلٰهِيّ، آن کدام بندهٔ توست که بدین سعادت خواهد رسید؟» ندای دیگر شنید که «ای حسن، پیرزنی است که بدین خلعت[۵] او خواهد رسید». خواجه حسن گفت «خداوند! آن پیرزن کجاست؟» ندایی دگر شنید که «در فلان محلّ می‌باشد». خواجه حسن با خود گفت «بروم تا سعادت ملاقات او دریابم».

{۲} چون خواجه حسن به خانهٔ او رسید در بزَد. از درون خانه آوازی شنید که گفت «کیست که درِ خانهٔ شکسته‌گان می‌کوبد؟» جواب داد «منم حسن بصری». زن بیامد، و در باز کرد. خواجه درآمد، دید «دیگی بر دیگ‌دان[۶] نهاده و فرود آن آتش می‌سوزد». خواجه گفت «ای خواهر، تو را که خبر کرد، یا از کرامت دانستی که مهمان تو خواهم بود؟» زن گفت «از آمدن تو مرا کسی خبر نکرده. امّا این خونِ جگرِ منست که بر آتش دان نهاده‌ام».

{۳} شیخ حسن پرسید که «واقعه چیست که به‌جهت خون جگر دیگ برنشانده‌ای؟» زن گفت «امروز سه‌روز شد که طفلان من چیزی نخورده‌اند. امروز برای تسلّی خاطر ایشان دیگی بر آتش نهاده‌ام. و امشب از

[۱] قرآن مجید. [۲] آیهٔ ۷۳ سورهٔ زمر. [۳] دربان و یا نگهبان بهشت. به دهخدا رجوع شود.
[۴] «پیش‌آمدن» اشاره به نزدیک‌آمدن، و ارتباط معنایی با «به پیشوازآمدن» و «استقبال کردن» دارد.
[۵] پاداش. [۶] اجاق.

CHAPTER 22

The story of Khʷāja Ḥasan Baṣrī God's mercy be upon him

{1} It is reported that Khʷāja Ḥasan Baṣrī, may God's mercy be upon him, was reciting the Glorious Qurʾān. When he arrived at the verse 'Peace be upon you! You have done well, so come in, to stay forever' (Q. 39:73), he pondered, 'O God, this humble pauper Ḥasan has a desire to be the leading inhabitant of paradise, so surely the guard of paradise will welcome me.' He then heard a voice from the unseen world saying, 'This desire for such dignity and blessing has already been made by someone else.' Ḥasan Baṣrī said, 'O God, who is this servant of Yours, who has already received this blessing?' He heard a voice say, 'O Ḥasan! There is an old woman who will get this reward.' Khʷāja Ḥasan said, 'O God, where is that old woman?' He heard another voice saying to him that she is in such-and-such place. Khʷāja Ḥasan said to himself, 'I should go to be blessed through meeting her.'

{2} When Khʷāja Ḥasan arrived at her house, he knocked on the door. A voice emanated from the house, 'Who is the one knocking on the door of the heartbroken?' [He] responded, 'It is me, Ḥasan Baṣrī.' The woman came and opened the door. Khʷāja entered, and saw that she had put a pot in the oven, a fire burning beneath it.' Khʷāja said, 'O sister, who has told you [about me], or did you learn that I am to be your guest because of your ennoblement[1].' The woman said, 'No one has told me about your arrival. But this is nothing, but the blood of my liver[2] that is in the oven.'

{3} Shaykh Ḥasan asked, 'What has happened that makes you describe the content of the pot like this?' The woman said, 'Today is the third day on which my children have not eaten anything. Today, I have put on [an empty] pot just to relieve

[1] i.e., lofty status [2] i.e., grief

خوف خدای عَزَّوَجَلَّ چندان گریسته‌ام که دیگ از آبِ چشم من پر شده‌است. و فرزندان را تسلّی می‌دهم که «خاطرجمع دارید که درین دیگ از برای شما چیزی می‌پزم»»

{۴} چون خواجه حسن بصری از وی این حکایت شنید گفت «راست فرموده‌است پیغمبرِ عَزَّوَجَلَّ که بهشت رایگان نیست. چون تو در راهِ دوستْ خود را چنین می‌سوزی، خوشی و خرّمی تو را باد که من در تلاوت قرآن چون بدین آیت رسیدم که سَلَامٌ عَلَيْكُمْ طِبْتُمْ فَادْخُلُوهَا خَالِدِينَ،[۷] این آرزو کردم که «چه نیک می‌بود که سَرِ[۸] بهشتیان من بودمی تا بدین آیت مغفرت مشرّف شوم». ندا شنیدم که «ای حسن، خاموش باش که این آیت نصیب بیوه‌زنی شده‌است». گفتم «إِلٰهِيّ، فرمان بده تا من ملاقات آن نیک‌بخت حاصل کنم». به حکم فرمان اکنون شرف ملاقات تو حاصل آمد».

{۵} زن گفت «ای خواجه حسن بصری، این‌زمانْ که بشارت دادی قدری خاطر من ساکن شد»[۹]. و سپس گفت «ای خواجه بنشنین». و خود برخاست، و دو رکعت نماز گذارد و سر سجده نهاد، و گفت «إِلٰهِيّ، غایبِ[۱۰] سرِّ من پوشیده بود. اکنون سرِّ مرا بر حسن بگشادی. مرا از این جهان عزیز گردان». این بگفت و هم درین سجده بود که جان به حقّ سُبْحَانَهُ وَتَعَالَىٰ سپرد.

{۶} نقلست که عبدالله مبارك رَحْمَةُ اللهِ عَلَيه به خانهٔ کعبه می‌رفت. آوازی شنید بر اطراف و جوانب ملاحظه کرد. زنی را دید که پیراهن گلیم بر سرکشیده و نعلین کهنه در پای کرده. چون بدید دانست که رَه گم کرده است. خواست که او را راه نماید. گفتم «ای عورت، مگر تو راه گم کرده‌ای؟» جواب داد «مَنْ يَهْدِهِ اللّٰهُ فَلاَ مُضِلَّ لَه،[۱۱] یعنی کسی که راه-نماینده[۱۲] خداوند تَعَالَى باشد، او راه گم نکند». پرسیدم «از کجا آیی؟» گفت «بِسْمِ اللّٰهِ الرَّحْمٰنِ الرَّحِيمِ، سُبْحَانَ الَّذِي أَسْرَىٰ بِعَبْدِهِ لَيْلاً مِنَ الْمَسْجِدِ الْحَرَامِ إِلَى الْمَسْجِدِ الْأَقْصَى الَّذِي بَارَكْنَا».[۱۳] دانستم که می‌گوید که «از بیت المقدسم».[۱۴] گفتم «کجا خواهی رفت؟» گفت «بِسْمِ اللّٰهِ الرَّحْمٰنِ الرَّحِيمِ، وَلِلّٰهِ عَلَى النَّاسِ حِجُّ الْبَيْتِ مَنِ اسْتَطَاعَ إِلَيْهِ سَبِيلاً».[۱۵] دانستم که «می‌گوید به حجّ خواهم رفت». با من شتری بود گفتم «پاره راه برین شتر نشین و من شتر را بخوابانیدم[۱۶]». گفت «بِسْمِ اللّٰهِ الرَّحْمٰنِ الرَّحِيمِ، قُل لِلْمُؤْمِنِينَ يَغُضُّوا مِنْ أَبْصَارِهِمْ».[۱۷] دانستم که می‌گوید «تو چشم را پوش تا من بر شتر نشینم». من روی خود بگردانیدم. چون بر شتر نشست گفت «بِسْمِ اللّٰهِ الرَّحْمٰنِ الرَّحِيمِ، سُبْحَانَ الَّذِي سَخَّرَ لَنَا هَذَا وَمَا كُنَّا لَهُ مُقْرِنِينَ».[۱۸] دانستم بر شتر نشست و خداوند تَعَالَى را شکر و حمد می‌گوید. بعداز آن گفتم «اگر بگویی تو را قدری طعام بدهم». [گفت] «بِسْمِ اللّٰهِ الرَّحْمٰنِ الرَّحِيمِ، وَمَا جَعَلْنَاهُمْ جَسَدًا لا يَأْكُلُونَ الطَّعَامَ».[۱۹] دانستم که می‌خواهد؛ قدری طعام دادم. دیگر گفتم «آب

[۷] آیهٔ ۷۳ سورهٔ زمر. [۸] پیشرو. [۹] حالا خاطرم اندکی التیام یافت. [۱۰] ناپیدا.

[۱۱] به «کتاب النکاح در سنن نسائی» رجوع شود. این عبارت دعایی باآیهٔ ۱۷۸ سورهٔ اعراف نیز مرتبط می‌باشد.

[۱۲] راهنما. [۱۳] آیهٔ ۱ سورهٔ إسراء. [۱۴] اورشلیم. [۱۵] آیهٔ ۹۷ سورهٔ آل عمران. [۱۶] مهیّا کردن شتر تا بر آن سوار شوند.

[۱۷] آیهٔ ۳۰ سورهٔ نور؛ سوره‌ای است که بر اساس روایات اسلامی خواندن آن به زنان توصیه شده‌است.

[۱۸] آیهٔ ۱۳ سورهٔ زخرف. [۱۹] آیهٔ ۸ سورهٔ انبیاء.

their concerns. And I have cried overnight, so much so that the pot is filled with my tears. And I have soothed my children by saying that I am cooking something in the pot for them.'

{4} When Khʷāja Ḥasan Baṣrī heard her story, he said, 'It is true that the Prophet of God has said that paradise is not [given to people] freely. As you sacrifice yourselfing like this for the sake of God, much blessing and joy will be your lot as I have come across this verse while reciting the Qurʾān: "Peace be upon you! You have done well, so come in, to stay forever" (Q. 39:73) and I wished "to be the leader of the inhabitants of paradise and be blessed with forgiveness." Then I heard a voice say, "O Ḥasan, be silent as the virtue of this verse has been bestowed for a widow. Then I said, "O God, may it be that I reach the blessed one." On the basis of His decree I am now blessed with meeting you in person.'

{5} The woman said, 'O Khʷāja Ḥasan Baṣrī, now that you have conveyed this good news, my concerns are somewhat relieved.' She then said, 'O Khʷāja, take a seat.' And she stood up and performed a two-unit prayer and prostrated and said, 'O God, my secret was hidden. But You have now uncovered it for Ḥasan. Dignify me in this world. While being in prostration, she submitted her soul to God.[3]

{6} It is reported that ʿAbdallāh Mubārak, may God's mercy be upon him, was going to the Kaʿba. He heard a voice and looked around. He noticed a woman who was wearing old clothes and old sandals. When he saw this he realised that she was lost. He wanted to help her find her way. I [ʿAbdallāh Mubārak] said, 'O woman, have you lost your way?' She answered, 'Whomsoever God guides will never be led astray',[4] meaning that the one whose Guide is God, will not lose the way. I asked her, 'Where do you come from?' [She] said, 'In the Name of God, the Compassionate, the Merciful. Glory be to the one who took His servant by night from the Sacred Mosque to the Farthest Mosque. We have blessed [...]' (Q. 17:1). So, I figured that she was saying that she is from Jerusalem. I told her, 'Where are you heading?' She said, 'In the Name of God, the Compassionate, the Merciful. Pilgrimage to the House is a duty owed to Allah by all who can make their way to it.' (Q. 3:97). I realised that she was saying that she is travelling to perform the hajj. I had a camel with me. I told her, 'Take a seat on the camel for part of the way.' And I got down from the camel to enable her to sit. She said, 'In the Name of God, the Compassionate, the Merciful. Tell the believing men to lower their gaze and be modest' (Q. 24:30). I understood that she was asking me to avert my gaze until she was seated on the camel so I turned my face away. When she sat on the camel she said, 'In the Name of God, the Compassionate, the Merciful.

[3] i.e., she passed away [4] A supplicatory phrase, also found in Islamic traditional works, e.g., Nasāʾī's *Kitāb al-Nikāḥ* which is related to Q. 7:178.

دهم؟» گفت «بِسۡمِ اللَّهِ الرَّحۡمَٰنِ الرَّحِيمِ، وَجَعَلۡنَا مِنَ الۡمَاءِ كُلَّ شَيۡءٍ حَيٍّ».[۲۰] دانستم که آب می‌خواهد؛ آب دادم.

{۷} نزدیک قبیله رسیدم. نظر در آن قبیله کرد و گفت «بِسۡمِ اللَّهِ الرَّحۡمَٰنِ الرَّحِيمِ، أَنَّمَا أَمۡوَالُكُمۡ وَأَوۡلَادُكُمۡ فِتۡنَةٌ».[۲۱] دانستم که می‌گوید «در این قبلیه فرزندان دارم». دیدم دو جوان از آن قبیله بیرون آمدند. یکی را نام یحییٰ و دیگری را نام عیسیٰ.[۲۲] و سر در قدم مادر نهادند. مادر چون فرزندان را دید گفت «بِسۡمِ اللَّهِ الرَّحۡمَٰنِ الرَّحِيمِ، الۡحَمۡدُ لِلَّهِ الَّذِي أَذۡهَبَ عَنَّا الۡحَزَنَ».[۲۳] دانستم در ملاقات فرزندان شکر می‌گوید خدای تَعَالَی را.

{۸} پرسیدم که «این عورت شما را چه می‌شود؟»[الف] گفتند «مدّت سی سال است به جز قرآن چیزی ذکر نگفته است. و اگر حاجت به چیزی شود به قرآن ما را معلوم کند». آنگه خواستم روان شوم. گفتم «ای مادر، نام تو چیست؟» گفت «بِسۡمِ اللَّهِ الرَّحۡمَٰنِ الرَّحِيمِ، رَاضِيَةً مَرۡضِيَّةً»[۲۴] دانستم که راضیه نام دارد. گفتم می‌روم. روی به فرزندان کرد و گفت «بِسۡمِ اللَّهِ الرَّحۡمَٰنِ الرَّحِيمِ، وَتَزَوَّدُوا فَإِنَّ خَيۡرَ الزَّادِ التَّقۡوَىٰ،[۲۵] یعنی این مرد را توشه دهند. فرزندان او برفتند، و خرما آوردند ،و به من دادند. و من روان شدم.هرکه خود را در راه خدای تَعَالَی چنین بدارد به درجات عالی رسد.

{۹} نظیر دیگر. آورده‌اند که چون سبحانه وتَعَالَی جنّات عدن را بیافرید، جبرئیل را فرمود که «جنّات عدن مرا تماشا کن که بهر بندگان خود چگونه آفریده‌ام». به حکم فرمان، جبرئیل علیه السلام در تماشای بهشت شد. کوشکی[۲۶] دید هریک‌دانه مروراید با هفتاد هزار در، هر دری با یاقوت و لعل و زَبَرجَد مُرَصَّع، و از هر دری تا در دیگر پانصدساله راه باشد. و پیش هر دری، هفتادهزار شهرستان، و در هر شهرستان[۲۷] هفتادهزار قبّه، و در هرقبّه هفتادهزار تخت، و بر هرتختی هفتاد هزار بستر، و بر سر هر بستری حُورٌ عِین نشسته، و در پیش هر حور، هفتادهزار حور دیگر به خدمت استاده.

[۲۰] آیهٔ ۳۰ سورهٔ انبیاء. [۲۱] آیهٔ ۲۸ سورهٔ انفال. [۲۲] در برخی نسخ اشاره‌ای به نام فرزندان نشده است.
[۲۳] آیهٔ ۳۴ سورهٔ فاطر. [۲۴] آیهٔ ۲۸ سورهٔ فجر. [۲۵] آیهٔ ۱۹۷ سورهٔ بقره. [۲۶] عمارت، قصر.
[۲۷] احتمالا به معنی «حاکم نشین» نیز می‌باشد.

[الف] پرسیدم که مادر شما فارسی حرف نمی‌گوید؟

Highly Exalted is the one who has subjected this to us, and in no way could we have done it by ourselves' (Q. 43:13). So, I understood that she was seated on the camel, and praising God. Then I said, 'If you say, I will bring you some food.' [She responded] 'In the Name of God, the Compassionate, the Merciful. We did not give them bodies that ate no food, nor were they immortal.' (Q. 21:8). I understood that she was hungry so I gave her some food. Then I asked, 'Shall I give you water?' She replied, 'In the Name of God, the Compassionate, the Merciful. We made every living thing of water' (Q. 21:30). I understood that she is thirsty so I gave her water.

{7} I arrived near a tribe. She saw the tribe and said, 'In the Name of God, the Compassionate, the Merciful. Indeed, your wealth and your children are but a means of trial' (Q. 8:28). I realised that she was saying that she had children in the tribe. I saw that two young men came from the clan. The name of one of them was Yaḥyā, and the other was ʿĪsā. And they put their heads on their mother's lap. When she saw her children, she said, 'In the Name of God, the Compassionate, the Merciful. Praise be to God, who has separated us from all sorrow' (Q. 35:34). I understood that she was giving praise because of seeing her children.

{8} I asked, 'Who is this woman to you?' They said, 'It has been thirty years since she has not uttered anything but the Qurʾān. And if we demand something, she will indicate to us with alluding to Qurʾānic phrases.' Then I wanted to make a move and leave. I asked, 'O mother, what is your name?' She said, 'In the Name of God, the Compassionate, the Merciful. Return to your Lord well pleased (*rāḍiyya*) and well pleasing (*marḍiyya*)' (Q. 89:28). I realised that her name is, Rāḍiyya (Well-pleased). I said, 'I will go now.' She looked upon her children and said, 'In the Name of God, the Compassionate, the Merciful. So, make provision for yourselves; for the best provision is to ward off evil' (Q. 2:197), meaning, 'Give this man provisions'. The children went and brought dates and gave them to me, and I left. Whosoever makes himself like this in the path of God, will reach high rank.

{9} Another story. It is reported that when God created the Garden of Eden, He said to Gabriel, 'Behold the Garden of Eden that I have created for My servants.' Gabriel looked upon the paradise. He saw a castle of pearls and with seventy thousand gates, each gate adorned with ruby, garnet, and peridot; the distance between one gate and the other being five hundred years. And before every gate, there were seventy thousand plots, and in every plot of land there were seventy thousand domes, and in every dome there were seventy thousand throne beds, and on every throne bed seventy thousand beds, and sitting above every bed was a heavenly cherub, and before every cherub there were more than seventy thousand cherubs to serve.

{۱۰} تا حوری از تخت خود برآید و روان شود. آن هفتادهزار حور از پس‌وپیش او روان شوند، و بر دست هریکی طَبَقی از نور ریاحین،[۲۸] و بر دست راست او هفتادهزار حور دیگر روان گشته، و بر دست هریکی پیرایه‌های[۲۹] گوناگون باشد. و بر دست چپ نیز همین نوع با خلعت‌ها و اطلس‌ها روان گشته؛[ب] همدرین زمان نظر این حور بر جمال جبرئیل علیه‌السلام افتاد. در خنده درآمد. سیمای حور گشاده گشت و هردو لب او از یکدیگر جدا گردید. نوری از دندان آن حور پیدا شد که جبرئیل علیه‌السلام با حاملانِ عرش سر سجده نهادند.[۳۰] خیال کردند که این نور تجلّی الهی است. آن حور گفت با ایشان که «سر بردارید که این نور تجلّی دیدار حقّ نیست. این نور دندان من است که حقّ تَعَالَی مرا ازبرای بندگان خود آفریده‌است».

{۱۱} مهتر جبرئیل گوید «إِلٰهِيّ، او کدام نیک‌بخت بندهٔ توست که با این سعادت و دولت خواهد رسید؟» ندا شنید «وَأَمَّا مَنْ خَافَ مَقَامَ رَبِّهِ وَنَهَى النَّفْسَ عَنِ الْهَوَى؛ فَإِنَّ الْجَنَّةَ هِيَ الْمَأْوَى،[۳۱] هرکه نفس خود را از بهر رضای حقّ تَعَالَی باز دارد او بدین مرتبی رسید.

{۱۲} إِلٰهِيّ، من شکسته را و کاتب این قصّه را با جمیع مؤمنان شایستهٔ جنّتِ رضوان الله گردانی. بِمَنِّهٖ وَكَمَال كَرَمه.

۲۸ جمع «ریحان» و به معنی «گل و گیاه خوش بو» به کار می‌رود. ۲۹ زینت و زیور.
۳۰ این مطلب می‌تواند به آیهٔ ۷ سورهٔ غافر، و آیهٔ ۱۷ سورهٔ الحاقّة اشاره داشته باشد.
۳۱ آیات ۴۰ تا ۴۱ سورهٔ نازعات.

ب و بر چپ او هفتاد هزار حلّه‌های سندس و اطلس روان گشته

{10} When one cherub would leave her bed and throne, those seventy thousand cherubs would move behind and before her, and in each of their hands would be a tray of light replete with sweet-smelling herbs. And to the cherub's right would move seventy thousand cherubs with various ornaments on their hands. And to her left would be garments and silks. At that moment, the cherub noticed Gabriel's face (pbuh). She smiled. Her face widened and her lips parted. A light shone from the cherub's tooth before which Gabriel (pbuh) and those who carried the Throne prostrated.[5] They assumed that it was the light of theophany. That cherub said to them, 'Raise your heads. This is not the light of theophany by which one may witness God. This is just the light of my tooth, as God has created me for the sake of His servants.'

{11} His Eminence Gabriel asked, 'O God, who is the auspicious servant of yours, who will receive such blessing and dignity?' A voice proclaimed, 'Anyone who feared meeting his Lord and restrained himself from base desires; Paradise will certainly be their home.' (Q. 79:40–41), meaning, whoever restrains his desires for the sake of God's satisfaction, will achieve this status.

{12} *O God, may You qualify me, a humble pauper, and the scribe of this story, and other Muslims for paradise. By Your unmerited favour and kindness. [Amen.]*

[5] This may refer to Q. 40:7 and Q. 69:17.

حکایتِ خواهشِ شیطان مردود که فردا بر امّت پیغمبر دعوی کند[1، الف]

{۱}   آورده‌اند که چون قیامت قایم شود حقّ سُبحانَهُ وَتَعالیٰ چندان کرم و لطف در باب امّت محمّد[ب] رسول الله صَلَّی‌اللهُ‌عَلَیهِ‌وَسَلَّم کند که این دشمن قدیم در حسد آید، و چنگ در دامن گنه‌کاران زند و بگوید «إلهي، آن کسانی که در دنیا نیک فرمان‌برداری من کرده‌اند امروز ایشان را برابر من در دوزخ فرست. زیرا که من هفتادهزار سال تو را بندگی کرده‌ام و به یک بی‌فرمانی مرا از درگاه خود براندی. و ایشان هر روز چندین بی‌فرمانی تو کرده‌اند. ایشان سزاوار دوزخند،[2] و من ایشان را نمی‌گذارم تا با خود در دوزخ برم».

{۲}   فرمان شود که «ای ملعون، اگرچه ایشان به تنْ فرمان‌برداری تو کرده‌اند، امّا به دل تو را دشمن می‌داشتند. اگرچه به تنْ بی‌فرمانی من کرده‌اند، امّا به دل مرا دوست می‌داشتند. و دیگر به هرعضوی اگر گناه کرده‌اند، امّا در محلّ من که خدایم قدم‌استوار مانده‌اند. و در زبان، به ما غیری را الله نگفته‌اند. و به دل هم همین استوار داشته‌اند. پس دل را به ما سپرده‌اند و نفس خبیث را به تو. دیگر ای معلون، اگر بنده کسی گناه کند، جواب آن دعوی را از خواجهٔ او پرسند. و امروز تو بر بندگان من دعوی می‌کنی. اگر ازجهت شرع و معامله به تو می‌رسد با خود ببر. و اگر به‌جهت شرع نبود به تو نرسد؛ خود با بندگان ما کاری نداری».

[1] همچون داستان اوّل که در آن خدا به دفاع از بندگانش می‌پردازد، این داستان نیز گفت‌وگویی است بین خدا و شیطان که براساس داستان‌های ثبت شده در کتب اسلامی ارائه می‌شود.
[2] دوزخ هستند.

[الف] حکایتِ شیطان مردود لعین بدبخت علیه اللعنة
[ب] در حقّ محمّدیان

CHAPTER 23

The story of the request of the outcast Satan who harassed the nation of the Prophet Muḥammad

{1} It is reported that when the Day of Judgement happens God will show so much affection and kindness to the community of Muḥammad to the extent that this age-old enemy will become jealous and will drag at the cloaks of sinners with his claws and will say, 'O God, those who have truly obeyed me in the world, now send them to hell before me, because I worshipped you for seventy thousand years and You rejected me from Your Throne just because of one disobedience. Yet these people disobeyed You several times every day. They deserve hell and I will not leave them until I take them with me to hell.'

{2} A proclamation will be made, 'O accursed one! Although they have been obeying you with their body, they considered you as their enemy within their hearts. If they have been disobedient with their bodies, they loved me with their hearts. And if they have physically committed sin with their limbs, in the place where I dwell[1] they stood the test.[2] And they did not verbally call anyone else, 'Allah.' And this is what they have cemented in their hearts. As such, they have given their heart to Us, and the devil's soul to you. Moreover, O accursed one! If someone's servant makes a mistake, a claim will be made on his master. But today you claim against My servants!? If it would legally be fair then you could have taken them but if it would not be fair so you may not take them. You have no claim to Our servants!'

[1] i.e., the heart [2] They stood their ground and did not deny me.

{۳} آنگاه فرمان شود که «ای فرشتگان، در عرصات دو منبر نصب کنید. و امام اعظم[۳] و امام شافعی حاضر گردانید». آنگاه، فرمان شود که «هردو بر منبر برآیند، و بگویند که شمایان در دنیا چه حکم کرده بودید». ایشان گویند که «إِلٰهِيّ، در کدام باب گوییم؟» فرمان شود که «در باب غَصب».

{۴} امام اعظم گوید که «یا ربّ، من حکم کرده‌بودم که اگر شخصی زمین یکی را به غَصب بگیرد، و درآن زمین زراعت کند، چون خَصم[۴] پیدا شود، و ببیند که زمین او را مزروع گردانیده‌است و به دعوی پیش من آیند، من حکم کنم که آنچه در آن زمین کاشته ببر، و زمین را به صاحبش تسلیم کن». فرمان رَبِّ الْعَالَمِيْنْ در رسد که «امروز ما همان کنیم حکم که امام اعظمِ ما فرموده‌است».

{۵} بعداز آن فرمان در رسد که «ای ملعون، تو می‌دانی که ایشان بندگان من‌اند. تو آمدی و تخم معصیت در دل‌های ایشان کاشتی و هر بدی که از تخم معصیت تو حاصل شده‌است در گردن تو بار کنیم، و دل‌های ایشان ازآن من است. بندهٔ خود را به دارالسلام[۵] می‌برم».

{۶} باز فرمان رَبِّ الْعَالَمِيْنْ دررسد که «ای امام شافعی، تو چه حکم کرده‌ای؟» درین باب گفت «حکم کرده بودم که[۶] یکی زمینِ یکی را در تصرّف خود درآورد به غَصب و زراعت کرد. خصم چون دید که زمین را دیگری زراعت کرده‌است. و در دعوی پیش من آمدند. فرمودم[۷] که «اینچنین کسی را عبرت باید داد تا حقّ کسی را در تصرّف خود نیاورد». بعده، هرچه درآن زمین کاشته باشد، کارَنده[۸] بَرَد و زمین را به صاحبش تسلیم نماید». فرمان شود که «ما هم امروز همان حکم کنیم که شافعیِ ما فرموده‌است».

{۷} حقّ سُبْحَانَهُ وَتَعَالَىٰ گوید که «ای شیطان مردود، چون تخم معصیت بر زمین دل‌های بندگان ما به غَصب کاشتی، برداریم و در گردن تو بار کنیم و در دوزخ فرستیم و بندگان خود را پاک و پاکیزه کرده در جنّت درآریم».

{۸} دیگر فرمان شود که «ای مردود بدبخت، حضرت ما امروز همان کنیم که یوسف با برادران خود کرد». قصّهٔ یوسف عَلَيْهِ السَّلَام با برادران این بود که چون قحط به کنعان افتاد، یوسف فرمود «هرکه از کنعان بهرغلّه به مصر آید او را پیش من آرید». خبر آوردند که «قافله از کنعان آمد». یوسف فرمود «همهٔ مردم[۹] را بیارند». چون بیاوردند نظر در صورت ایشان کرد، و بشناخت که همه برادران اویند که در حقّ او جفا کرده بودند؛ او را بی هیچ گناهی در چاه انداخته بودند.

{۹} با جمله برادران پرسید «شما فرزندان کیستید؟» گفتند که «ما فرزندان یعقوب پیغمبریم». یوسف پرسید «حضرت یعقوب چند فرزندان دارد؟» گفتند «دوازده فرزند دارد و از این جملهٔ فرزندان یکی غایب است». یوسف گفت «آنکه غایب است او را چه نام بود؟» گفتند که «یوسف نام داشت». گفت «او

[۳] ابوحنیفه یکی از مؤسسین مکتب فقه حنفی است. [۴] مالک، طرف شخص. به عمید مراجعه شود.
[۵] در سنّت اسلامی «دارالسلام» به عنوان یکی از صفات و نام‌های بهشت به کار می‌رود. [۶] دربارهٔ اینکه.
[۷] فرمان دادم؛ حکم کردم. [۸] زارع. [۹] کاروان.

{3} Then a command will be given: 'O angels, set up two pulpits on the Resurrection Plain. And bring the Imam Aʿẓam [i.e., Abū Ḥanīfa] and Imam Shāfiʿī.' Then it will be commanded of them, 'Sit on the pulpits and ask how did you issue legal edicts in the world.' They will say, 'O God, about which book of the law should we talk?' It will be commanded, 'Regarding the section of usurpation.'

{4} Imam Aʿẓam will say, 'O God, I had issued a decree about when one usurps another's land and farms on that land. If the owner arrives and sees that his land has been cultivated, then they come to me to make a claim, I would rule that the usurper take whatever they farmed on the land and submit the land back to its owner.' The command of the Lord of the Worlds will be, 'Today, We pronounce on what Imam Aʿẓam has ruled upon.'

{5} Then another command will be given [to Satan], 'O accursed one! You know that they are My servants. You came and planted the seeds of transgression in their hearts, and We will hang upon your neck whatever evil emerged from those seeds, and their hearts belong to Me. I will take my servant to the Abode of Peace[3]!'

{6} Again, the Lord of the Worlds will ask, 'O Imam Shāfiʿī, what did you rule?' He will say, 'I had ruled upon a case when one usurped the land of another and began farming. When the owner saw that the other had began farming he came to me to lodge a claim and for restitution. I ruled that the harm for the victim should be minimized, and a lesson should be given to the usurper. The one who planted the seeds may take whatever has been farmed on the land but the land must be given back to its owner.' A proclamation will be made, 'Today, We pronounce as Our Imam Shāfiʿī stated.'

{7} God will say, 'O rejected Satan, as you have illicitly planted the seeds of transgression in the hearts of our servants, We take them and hang them around your neck and send you to hell to purify and cleanse Our servants before taking them into paradise.'

{8} Then a proclamation will be made, 'O the inauspicious rejected one of Our presence, today We do [with our servants] what Joseph did for his brothers. The story of Joseph (pbuh) with his brothers is that when famine emerged in Canaan, Joseph said, "Bring to me whoever comes to Egypt from Canaan for the sake of grain." News was given that 'a caravan from Canaan had arrived.' Joseph ordered that all their people should be brought before him. When they had been brought before him he looked at their faces and realised that they were all his brothers who had treated him with cruelty. They had thrown him into a well even though he did no wrong.

{9} He asked all his brothers, "You are the children of whom?" They replied, "We are the children of Jacob, the prophet." Joseph asked them, "How many children did

[3] i.e., paradise

چگونه غایب شد؟» یکی گفت که «او را گرگ خورده». و دیگری گفت «اثر دیوانگی داشت».[ج] چون ایشان چنین گفتند یوسف گفت «اگر او را ببینید، شناسید؟» گفتند «آری، بشناسیم».

{۱۰} مهتر یوسف برقع از روی برگفت. ایشان چون جمال مهتر یوسف را بدیدند درزمانْ همه شناختند و بیهوش شدند، و بر زمین افتادند. بعداز ساعتی سربرآوردند که «ای یوسف، امروز انتقام آن جفاها که در حقّ تو کرده بودیم خواهی کشید؟» این بگفتند و باز بر زمین بیفتادند که از خود خبر نداشتند. یوسف علیه‌السلام از تخت بدوید و نزدیک ایشان آمد و نزدیکان خود را گفت «ایشان را خدمت کنید». و خاطرجوئیدن[۱۰] ایشان کرد که «ای برادران! خاطرجمع دارید. به عزّت آن خدای که جزء آن خدای دیگری نیست که من جفاهای شما را در خاطر نیاوردم و به جای جفا وفا کنم». بعداز آن فرمود «تا خلعت‌های قیمتی بیارند و همه را پوشانیدند. و عذرخواهی بسیار می‌کردند؛ برادران ایشان شرمنده شدند».

{۱۱} «پس ای شیطان مردود، چنانچه یوسف ما را، که برادران از دست و زبان رنجانیدن او به کرمْ مُجازی[۱۱] عفو و احسان کرد، من که أَرحَم الرّاحِمین ایشانم، و از هزار پدر و مادر مشفق‌ترم، پس مرا اُولی است که در حقّ ایشان احسان و لطف کنم».

{۱۲} «دیگر ای ملعون مردود، بشنو آن روز که یوسف به پدر خویش رسید». بعداز ملاقات یوسف گفت «ای پدر، به درگاه حقّ سبحانه و تعالی نذر کرده بودم که چون به پدر برسم، چندهزار برده، که در زمان پادشاهی خریده‌ام، ایشان‌را آزاد کنم. فرمود که «خریده‌گان[۱۲] مرا بیارید». کسان[۱۳] یوسف برفتند و همه را بیاوردند. مهتر یعقوب در ایشان نگاه کرد همه معیوب بودند.[د] مهتر یوسف علیه‌السلام گفت که «جمله[۱۴] را آزاد کردم از مال خود». و هریکی را جامه و دینار داد و گفت «شما از من خشنود باشید».

{۱۳} آنگاه، مهتر یعقوب پرسید که «ای فرزند، همه‌کس بندهٔ بی‌عیب می‌خرند. تمام این‌ها به صد عیب آراسته‌اند».[ه] گفت «آری، به واسطهٔ دل شکستگی ایشان [را] خریدم که به خود می‌گفتند که «ما را با این عیب که خواهد خرید؟» «دیگر آنکه چون چشم من به جمال مبارک شما مشرّف گشت، دست دعا به درگاه حقّ سبحانه و تعالی برداریم تا به کرم خود همه را شفا دهند». چون دعا و مناجات کردند همه صِحّت یافتند.[۱۵] و در خدمت پدر همه را آزاد کرد.

[۱۰] دل بدست آوردن؛ دلجویی؟

[۱۱] «مُجازی» به «جزا دهنده و پاداش دهنده» اشاره دارد. این لفظ در «جوامع الحکایات» عوفی نیز به کار رفته است.

[۱۲] «خریده‌گان» یا «خریدگان» اشاره دارد به «درم خریده» به معنای «بنده، برده و غلام». به دهخدا رجوع شود.

[۱۳] خدمت‌گزاران. [۱۴] همگی. [۱۵] دعای یوسف و یعقوب برای صِحّت و سلامتی بردگان در برخی نسخ موجود نیست.

[ج] و برادر دیگر گفت که او در چاه افتاد [د] بعضی شَل و بعضی لَنگ و بعضی زحمتی [ه] یعقوب پرسید که «ای فرزند، هیچ‌کس کالای عیب دار نخرد. چندین بنده‌گان با عیب را چرا خریدی؟»

the Prophet Jacob have?" They said, "He has twelve children and from these twelve, one of them is absent." Joseph asked, "What was the name of the one who is absent?" They said, "His name was Joseph." Joseph said, "How did he become absent?" One of them said, "He was eaten by a wolf." Another one said, "He seemed to be mad." When they said this, Joseph said, "Would you recognise him, if you saw him?" They said, "Yes, we would"

{10} His Eminence Joseph removed the veil from his face. As soon as they saw the beautiful face of His Eminence Joseph, they all recognised it and became unconscious and fell to the ground. After a couple of hours, they raised their heads, saying, "O Joseph, will you take revenge for what we have done to you?" They said this and again fell to the ground, unconscious. Joseph (pbuh) ran down from [his] throne and came to them and told his servants, "Serve these people." He calmed them, saying, "O brothers, do not worry." By the dignity of God, that except Him there is no god, I do not remember your cruelty but treat you with fairness instead of cruelty." Then, he started to bring fine garments and clothes them. They pardoned; the brothers became ashamed.

{11} 'So, O rejected Satan, the way that Our Joseph, who was offended by his brothers' words and deeds, forgave them and respected them by showing kindness, I, the One who is the most Merciful of the merciful, and am a thousand times kinder than their fathers and mothers, it is more suitable that I show affection and kindness to them.

{12} 'Also, O rejected and accursed one, hear another story about when Joseph reached his father! After their meeting, Joseph said, "O father, I made a vow to God that when I reach my father, I will release several thousand slaves whom I had bought during my kingship." He ordered, "Bring me my slaves." Joseph's entourage went and brought all of them. His Eminence Jacob looked at them. All of them were lame. His Eminence Joseph (pbuh) said, "I freed all of them and gave each of them garments and money." And he said to them, "May you be satisfied with me."

{13} His Eminence Jacob expressed his concern, "O my son, anybody would buy a fit and healthy slave but these are all replete with physical defects!" Joseph replied, "Yes, I bought them as they were all heartbroken and they told themselves that 'nobody else would purchase us with such defects'" and Joseph said to his father, "As my eyes are blessed with seeing you in person, let us lift our hands to implore that he heals them out of His kindness." They prayed and they were all healed. And he released all of them before his father.

{۱۴} «ای شیطان بدبخت، یوسف علیه‌السلام چندین معیوبان را بر روی پدر آزاد کرد. امروز امّت محمّد به درگاه عالم معبود با گناه آمده‌اند. جمله را از برای روی حضرت محمّد مصطفی صلی‌الله‌علیه‌وسلم از آتش دوزخ آزاد گردانیدم».

{۱۵} آنگه فرمان شود که «ای فرشتگان، این مدّعی بندگان مرا به دوزخ برید». و فرشتگان با غل و زنجیر در گردن به سوی دوزخ کشیدند. فرشتگان هرچند زور کنند او از جای خود نجنبد. فرشتگان در حیرت افتند و بگویند «إلٰهِيّ، در این چه حکمت است؟ از تو هیچ پوشیده نیست که این ملعون به زورِ خود از جای نمی‌جنبد». فرمان شود که «آن‌روز که ما این ملعون را از درِ خود رانده بودیم، و طوق لعنت در گردن او افکنده بودیم، این گرانی[۱۶] طوق لعنت است. طوق لعنت از گردن او دور کنید و تفرّج[۱۷] کنید».[و]

{۱۶} آنگاه، سگی از قعر دوزخ برآید و گردن[ز] شیطان را بگیرد، چنانچه گربه موش را گیرد، و در قعر دوزخ غوطه خورد.[۱۸] دیگر، اهل بشارت می‌گویند که «شیطان ملعون را حقّ تَعَالَی از درِ خود براند و طوق لعنتْ در گردن او پوشانید، و فرشتگان نتوانستند که او از جای بجنبانند. مؤمن که طوق معرفت الهی در گردن دارد اگر به سلامت به دارالسلام حضرتِ حقّ رسد هیچ عجیب نباشد».[ح]

{۱۷} إلٰهِيّ، همهٔ مؤمنان را با ایمان داری، و ازغارت کردن شیطان در حفظ و امان خود نگاه‌داری. بِمِنَّة وَكَمَالِ كَرَمه.

[۱۶] سنگینی، ثقل، نیروی جاذبه. [۱۷] سیر و تماشا کردن.
[۱۸] شباهت با قسمت پایانی داستان سی‌ویک (طولانی) پیرامون مرگ یزید وجود دارد.

[و] درحال فرشتگان آن طوق لعنت از گردن او بکشند. آنگاه فرمان شود که «ای فرشتگان، شما دور شوید». ایشان دور شوند. [ز] گلوی شیطان بگرفت [ح] هیچ دشواری نباشد

{14} 'O wretched Satan, Joseph (pbuh) released a number of disabled slaves for the sake of and before his father. Today, the community of Muḥammad, being sinful, came to the Throne of God. I released all of them from hell because of Muḥammad, the chosen Prophet.'

{15} A command will be made, 'O angels, take this claimant[4] against my servants to hell.' And the angels will try to drag him in chains and shackles towards hell. But whatever the angels try he will not move even a bit. The angels will be surprised and will ask, 'O God, what is happening? Nothing is hidden from You, as this accursed one is too strong to move.' A proclamation will be made, 'The day on which We rejected this accursed one from Our presence, We hung the collar of curses on his neck. It is the weight of the collar of curses that cannot be shifted. Remove the collar of curses from his neck and then stand clear and observe.'

{16} Then a dog came out from the depths of hell to grab Satan's neck, resembling a cat taking a mouse, and he became immersed in the hellfire.[5] Also, the people of glad tidings say, 'Once the accursed Satan whom God turned away from His door, was made to wear the collar of curses, the angels were not able to move him. When the believer wears the collar of divine knowledge on his neck and he sees that he reaches God's paradise safely, he should not be surprised.'

{17} *O God, make all believers faithful and keep them safe from Satan's ambush. By Your unmerited favour and kindness. [Amen.]*

[4] i.e., Satan

[5] Similar to the ending part of the chapter, thirty-on (long version), related to the death of Yazīd.

حکایتِ پادشاه نیشاپور با مظلومی

{۱} آورده‌اند که در عهد پادشاه نیشاپور رهزنان در راه‌ها دزدی می‌کردند. خبر به پادشاه رسید که «در فلان محل دزدان راه می‌زنند». پادشاه جماعتی را تعیین کردند که در کمین‌گاه ایشان بایستند، ایشان را به دست آرند.[۱] لشگریان برفتند. دزدان در آن موضع به دستِ کسانِ پادشاه گرفتار شدن. و ایشان ده نفر بودند. به حضرت پادشاه عریضه فرستاند که «ده دزد گرفته‌ایم». فرمودند که «هر ده نفر را بیارند». از قضا در راه یک دزد گریخت. ملازمان ترسیدند که «ما ده کس نوشته فرستادیم. جواب این یکی را چه گوییم؟» باهم مشورت کردند که «شخصی از راه گذار بگیریم تا عدالت شود».[الف]

{۲} جوانی به مزدوری می‌رفت. او را گرفتند و در میان دزدان درآوردند و بر پادشاه عرض کردند. پادشاه فرمود به زندان برند. این جوان مزدور در حیرت افتاد که «این چه حالت است که مرا پیش آمد، و احوال خود به که گویم که او سخن مرا استوار دارد؟[ب] هیچ بِهْ[۲] ازالآن نیست که به درگاه حق سُبْحَانَهُ وَتَعَالَىٰ روم که هیچ چیز از او پوشیده نیست و ناظر احوال من اوست و راستی و بی‌گناهی مرا می‌داند». به زندان‌بان گفت «مرا قدری آب ده تا وضو سازم». زندان‌بان به جوان آب داد، و او وضو ساخت، و نماز کرد،[ج] و دست به مناجات قَاضِي الْحَاجَات[۳] برداشت و گفت «ای پروردگار من، تو می‌دانی که روشن و ظاهر است که من بی‌گناهم، و به تهمت مرا گرفته‌اند و در زندان کرده‌اند. اگر پادشاهِ دنیا واقعهٔ من نمی‌داند، تو که پادشاهِ حقیقی[۴] می‌دانی. ای چارهٔ بیچاره‌گان و ای فریادرس فریادخواهان،[۵] مرا ازاین زندان خلاصی ده».

[۱] دستگیر کردن. [۲] بهتر. [۳] از صفات خداوند در سنّت اسلامی. [۴] حقیقی هستی. [۵] عباراتی همچون «فریادخواه»، که در اشعار فارسی هم دیده می‌شود، در سنگ قبرهای پارسی در جزیره سوماترا بویژه در منطقه باروس، که متعلّق به قرن نهم هجری قمری یا پانزدهم

[الف] مشورت کردند که یک نفر از راه گذر بگیریم و بر وی تهمت دردی نهیم ، تا ده نفر شوند [ب] این کیفیت را پیش که گویم که هیچ کس باور نمی دارد . [ج] دو رکعت نماز گذارد

CHAPTER 24

The story of the King of Nishapur's treatment of the oppressed

{1} It is reported that during the reign of the King of Nishapur bandits were active on the highways. News reached the king that in Nishapur bandits were carrying out attacks on the roads. The king dispatched a brigade to ambush and surround them. The brigade went and the bandits were arrested. They numbered ten people. The brigade sent a message to the king saying, 'We have taken ten bandits.' He ordered that they bring all ten people to him. Strangely, one of the bandits escaped in the middle of the journey. The brigade was scared, saying, 'We sent a message saying that we have ten people. What should we say now?' They consulted among themselves and determined, 'We should take a passer-by to make up the shortfall'.

{2} A young man was on his way to work. They took him and put him among the bandits and presented them all before the king. The king commanded that they be sent to jail. The young man taken hostage was surprised: 'What is this that has happened to me, and to whom should I speak about it, one who can take my statement into account? Nothing is better than to go to the presence of God, as nothing is hidden from His eyes, and He is the witness of my condition and knows about my integrity and impeccability.' He asked the prison officer, 'Provide me with a small amount of water with which I can perform ablution.' The officer gave water to the young man and the young man performed ablution and prayed. Lifting his hands imploringly before the Provider of Needs the young man said, 'O my God, You know how transparent and obvious it is that I am not guilty and they have wrongly taken me and put me in jail. The worldly king does not know what has happened to me, but You, who are the Real King, know about it. O Redeemer of the poor and Guardian of those who ask for help, release me from this jail!'

{۳} پادشاه بر تخت خود خوابیده بود. فرمان شد که «ای فرشتگان، بروید و تخت پادشاه گردانید[۶]». به‌موجبِ فرموده، تخت پادشاه را گردانیدند و از تخت جدا شده افتاد و بیهوش شد. بعداز زمانی به خود آمد و به نزدیگان گفت «این با من که کرد؟» هرچند تفحّص کردند هیچ نبود. باز در خواب شد. فرشتگان باز تخت را گردانیدند. پادشاه بیفتاد. پادشاه در حیرت بمانْد و بر تخت نشست. و باز در خواب رفت و باز از تخت انداخت. برخاست و نشست و با خود گفت که «این حرکتِ دیو یا پری خواهد بود». کلمهٔ سبحان الله را بخواند و برخود دمید. دیگر بار بخسبید.[۷] بار دیگر فرمان رسید که «تخت را سرنگون ساز». آن فرشته به همان طریق او را از تخت بیفکند.

{۴} پادشاه را هیبتی در کار شد.[۸] بگریزید و به نزدیکان خود گفت که «این حرکتِ دیو نیست. مگر آنکه من در حقّ کسی ناحقّ کرده‌ام». او به درگاه خدای تَعَالَی در ناله درآمده «از بهر او مرا این چنین می نمایند». هم از این جهت گفته‌اند که آنچه مردم را رسد در گریبان خود فرو نظر کنند که «مرا از کدام شومیّت رسید».

{۵} القصّه. پادشاه خواص[۹] خود را فرمود که «در بندخانه[۱۰] را تفحّص کنند»؛ «آن‌گه از زندان‌بانان بپرسید که پادشاه می‌فرماید «ازجهت من بر کسی ظلمی رسیده است؟»» به‌موجبِ فرموده رفته، تفحّص کردند. زندان‌بان گفت «میان این بندیان جوانی طهارت کرده نماز گذارْد و مناجات کرد و گفت «مرا به تهمت در زندان کرده‌اند». خواص برگشته آمدند و گفتند. پادشاه عرض فرمودند که «رفته جوان را بیارید».

{۶} رفتند و آن جوان را بیاوردند. پادشاه فرمود «در حقّ تو چگونه ظلم رفته است؟» گفت «مرا با نُه نفر دیگر به تهمتِ دزدی پیش تو بیاوردند. تو هیچ نپرسیدی و تفحّص نکردی که «چگونه گرفتار شدی» و به زندان فرستادی. و من میانِ ایشان[۱۱] نبودم. و از دزدان یکی گریخته بود. به عوضِ او مرا گرفته آورده‌اند. و من بیچاره راهِ میان ایشان ندانستم و کسی نداشتم به جز حق سُبْحَانَهُ وَتَعَالَى؛ زاری و نیاز به درگاه او بردم».

میلادی است، به چشم می‌خورد. مقاله‌ای در مورد این سنگ قبر با اشعاری منسوب به فردوسی به زودی منتشر خواهد شد:
Daneshgar and Feener, "'Discovering a Hidden Miraculous Grave' (forthcoming).

۶ سرنگون کردن. ۷ بار دیگر خوابید. ۸ ترسید و دلهره داشت. ۹ ملازمان و مقربان. ۱۰ بازداشت‌گاه؛ زندان.
۱۱ یکی از ایشان.

{3} The king was asleep on his throne. It was commanded thus: 'O angels, go and shake the king's bed.' Accordingly, they shook the king's throne and he thrown from his throne, falling off and becoming unconscious. After a while, he woke up and asked his courtiers, 'Who did this to me?' Despite investigation, nothing was found. Again, he went to sleep. Angels, again, shook his bed. The king fell down. He was shocked and sat on his bed. And again, he slept and again he fell from the bed. The king stood, then he sat and pondered, 'This could only have been done by either a demon or a fairy.' He recited the phrase, 'Glory be to God' and blew upon himself. Again, he slept. Again, a command was given, 'Shake the bed!' The angel, as before, did shake the bed and fell him down.

{4} The king was afraid. He ran away from there and told his courtiers, 'This is not the act of a demon. I must have done something unwarranted against someone.' He began to wail in the presence of God, saying 'this has happened to me because of him'. On this subject, it is frequently said that a person should look for the cause of a misfortune in his own innermost mind[1] and ask himself: 'for what reason has a misfortune happened to me?'

{5} Returning to the story. The king asked his courtiers to seek and investigate the jail, 'Then say to the prison warden that the king asks, "Has anybody been oppressed because of me?"' On the basis of the king's order, they went to investigate. The prison warden said, 'Among these prisoners a young man performed ablution and said prayers and lifted his hand beseechingly and said, "They put me in jail on an accusation".' The courtiers returned and told the king about this. The king said, 'Go and bring this young man.'

{6} They went and brought that young man. The king said, 'How was this oppression imposed upon you?' He said, 'They brought me with nine other people and falsly accused me of banditing. You never asked me, and never investigated 'how did they arrest me', and sent me to jail. This is despite the fact that I was not among them. One of the bandits had escaped. Instead of him, they took me. And I, the poor victim, knew nothing about the affair and had no one but God; I took to wailing and placed a demand upon His Throne.'

[1] self

{۷} چون پادشاه این قصّه از وی شنید، به پای برخاست و آن جوان را در کنار گرفت، و عذری بسیار خواست و گفت «ای جوان، سه حاجت به تو دارم. یکی آنکه این خطای که در حقّ تو رفته ببخشی؛ و دگر ده هزار دینار از من قبول کنی؛ و دگر آن که اگر تو را حاجتی به چیزی باشد، بر من بیایی و حاجتی که باشد بگویی». جوان چون این سخن از پادشاه شنید در گریه شد و به پادشاه گفت «دو حاجت شما را قبول کردم و یکی را قبول ندارم. آنکه گفتی که خطائی واقع شده ببخش، بخشیدم. و ده هزار دینار را قبول کردم. امّا آنکه می‌گویی که «به چیزی حاجتی باشد پیش من بیا» هرگز نیایم. ای پادشاه تو منصف شو! کسانِ تو تهمتی کردند، مرا گرفته آوردند. اگر من پیشِ جملهٔ جهانیان می‌رفتم و ایشان را واسطه می‌ساختم در خلاصی خود، تو قبول نمی‌کردی. من به معبود خود نالیدم، سه نوبت تخت تو را بر زمین طپانید. پس وای بر من که از چنان حضرتی روی بتابم،[۱۲] و مقصود خود از غیری حاصل کنم».[۱۳] چون پادشاه از جوان این سخن شنید در دست و پای او افتاد، و صد هزار آفرین و تحسین کرد.

{۸} إلٰهِيّ، من بیچاره را و کاتب این قصّه را با جمیع مؤمنان در دمِ آخر با ایمان بَری. بِمِنَّة وکَرَمه.

[۱۲] برتابیدن؟ [۱۳] عبارت پایانی در برخی نسخ وجود ندارد.

{7} When the king heard this story from him, he stood up and hugged the young man and pardoned him, and said, 'O young man. I have three requests from you. First, that you forgive what has wrongly been imposed upon you. Second, that you accept my ten thousand dinars. And, third, that whenever you need anything, come to me and make your request.' The young man heard this statement from the king and began to cry and told the king, 'I will accept two of your requests and not accept one of them. You said to forgive what has happened. I forgive. And I will accept ten thousand dinars. But when you say, "Whenever you are in need of something, come to me" I will never do. O king, you judge the situation yourself. Your people condemned me. They took me and brought me to you. If I had gone to everyone in the universe and asked them to mediate for me regarding my release, you would not have accepted them. I wailed to my God, He then shook your throne three times. So, shame on me if I turned away from this Your Highness and achieve my request through someone else! When the king heard this from the young man he fell on his hands and knees and praised him one hundred times.

{8} *O God, take me, a humble pauper, and the scribe of this story, along with all believers in a state of faith. [Amen.]*

حکایتِ خواجه ربیع حسام
با دختر خود سؤال و جواب کردن[۱]

{۱} آورده‌اند که خواجه ربیع از خوف باری تَعَالَی روزوشب آسایش و آرام نگرفتی.[الف] و دختر خواجه ربیع از خواجه پرسید که «ای بابا، چیست که شب و روز آرام نمی‌گیری؟» خواجه گفت «ای فرزند، مرا روزی و شبی در پیش است. غم آن می‌خورم که آن‌روز و آن‌شب بر من آسان نشود». دختر گفت «آن کدام شب‌وروز است؟» خواجه فرمود که «دختر، آن‌شبِ اوّلِ گورست. و آن‌روز پنجاه‌هزار سال حشر قیامت است».[ب] دختر گفت «پدر، شنیده‌ام که حساب خانه با حساب بازار راست نیاید،[۲] پس حساب دنیا با حساب آخرت چون راست آید». خواجه این سخن از دختر شنید نعره زد و بیهوش شد و برزمین افتاد.

{۲} بعداز آن که بهوش آمد گفت «ای دختر، تیری برجانم زدی که تا قیامت درد آن نرود. و مرهم آن همان کنی که چون من وفات کنم برخاک قَبر من سربرهنه کنی[۳] و در حضرت خداوند سبحانه وتَعَالَی گویی «إلٰهِیّ، بی‌پدرشدگان به درگاه تو قدری دارند. من آمده‌ام که در گور به پدرِ من رحمت کنی». آن‌قدر[۴] با دختر بگفت و جان به حقّ تَعَالَی سپرد. و دختر بر سر قَبر پدر آمد و خواست سر برهنه کند که ندایی شنید که «ای دختر، سر بپوش که چون پدر تو غم اندیشهٔ گور در جهان داشت، بی‌اندیشه گردانیدم و به مقصود برسانیدم، و او را هرآینه[۵] نجات دادیم».

[۱] این داستان بعدها در کتاب جامع التمثیل محمّدعلی حبله‌رودی در قرن یازدهم هجری‌قمری بازنویسی شده‌است. [۲] اشاره به «شمار خانه با بازار راست نیاید» دارد. و «راست آمدن» به معنی هماهنگ شدن و سازگاری یافتن به کار می‌رود. به دهخدا مراجعه شود. من در این گمان هستم که آیا این اصطلاح می‌تواند به ناترازی «دخل و خرج» خانه اشاره داشته باشد.
[۳] به شیوَن و زاری بیش‌از حدّ اشاره دارد. [۴] آن جملات. [۵] بدون شک، به‌درستی.

[الف] کم خُفتی [ب] ای فرزند آن‌شب، شبِ نخستین گور است، و آن‌روز قیامت است که در ازای وی پنجاه‌هزارسال راه است

CHAPTER 25

The story of Khʷāja Rabīᶜ Ḥusām

with his daughter – the question and the answer[1]

{1} It is reported that Khʷāja Rabīᶜ had not been comfortable in either the day or night for the fear of God. And the daughter of Khʷāja Rabīᶜ asked him, 'O father, what is the reason that you do not relax in either the night or day?' Khʷāja replied, 'O my child, there is a day and night before me of which I am concerned. I am worried that day and night will not go smoothly for me.' The daughter said, 'What is it that frightens you by night and day?' Khʷāja replied, 'Daughter! The night that scares me is the first night after my death. And the day that scares me is the Day of Judgement which lasts for fifty thousand years.' The daughter asked, 'O father, I have heard that the real costs of goods does not compare with their market value;[2] so how can the account of the world be comparable with that of the hereafter?' Upon hearing this from the girl Khʷāja screamed, became unconscious, and fell to the ground.

{2} After he woke up, he said, 'O girl, you shot an arrow through my heart whose pain will not be removed until the Day of Judgement. And as to recover the wound,[3] tear off your headscarf at my graveside after I die,[4] and say before God, "O God, orphans have a particular status before You. I am here asking for Your sincere mercy upon my father in the grave."' Khʷāja said this and submitted his soul to God. When the daughter was at the grave of her father and was about to remove her headscarf she heard a voice: 'O girl, cover your head [and do not worry]! Owing to the extent to which your father

[1] This story is also found in the *Jāmiᶜ al-Tamthīl* of Muḥammad-ᶜAlī Ḥablarūdī in the seventeenth century CE. [2] i.e., these two accounts are not comparable; it may also refer to the difference between one's income and expenses. [3] i.e., heal the pain [4] A reference to hysterical mourning.

{۳} خلیفهٔ شهر مریدِ خواجه ربیع بود.[ج] آن‌روز که خواجه نقل کرده بود خلیفه در شهر نبود. چون به شهر آمد شنید که خواجه به رحمت حق سُبحَانَهُ وتَعَالَىٰ پیوسته و به سرعت تمام آمد که به جنازه بَرخورَد.[۶] رسید ولی جنازه را دفن کرده بودند. فرمود که گور را باز کنند که «من یک‌بارِ دیگر به دیدار او مشرّف گردم». چون تربت باز کردند دید که خواجه ربیع در قَبر نیست.[۷] تربت او پوشیدند و گفت «به خانهٔ خواجه پرسم که واقعه چیست». چون به خانه آمدند و در زدند. دختر آواز داد که «کیست که در خانهٔ بی‌پدری می کوبد؟»

{۴} گفتند که «خلیفه بر درآمده‌است». گفت «مگر پدر را در گور نیافته‌است؟» ایشان گفتند «چگونه دانستی که در گور نیافتیم؟» [دختر] فرمود که «پدر من همیشه غم گور و غم آخرت خوردی و دائم گفتی «رَبِّ لَا تَذَرْنِي فَرْدًا وَأَنتَ خَيْرُ الْوَارِثِينَ»[۸] و همیشه گفتی «إِلٰهِيَ، به حرمت این آیت کلام ربّانی که مرا در گور تنها نگذاری». پس، ای برادر، خدای تَعَالَیٰ دعای دوستان خود را هرگز رد نکند». چون خلیفه چنین شنید گریه‌کنان بازگشت. پس، بدان ای برادر، ندای مرگ هرروز می‌شنوی، و تو امروز بدین دنیای فانی چنان مشغول گشتی که گویی با مُردن کاری نداری. چون وقت آمد، قدم بر قدم برداری نخواهند گذاشت!

{۵} نظیر دیگر. روزی چهاریار[۹] رَضِيَ اللهُ عَنْهم أَجْمَعين در خدمت محمّد مصطفی صَلَّى اللهُ عَلَيْهِ وَسَلَّمَ نشسته بودند که «یا رسول الله، شما را بر حیات خود چه مقدار اعتماد است؟» فرمود که «ای یاران، اوّل شمایان گویید». اوّل أَمیر المُؤمِنین ابوبکر صدّیق گفت «اگر نماز پیشین[۱۰] گذارم امید ندارم که به نماز دیگر[۱۱] برسم». بعداز آن أَمیر المُؤمِنین عمر گفت «اگر نماز دیگر گذارم امید ندارم به نماز شام رسم». أَمیر المُؤمِنین عثمان و أَمیر المُؤمِنین علی رَضِيَ اللهُ عَنْهم أَجْمَعين مطابق و موافق این فرمودند.[د]

{۶} آنگاه حضرت رسالت پناه فرمودند که «اگر محمّد نماز بامداد گذارد چون به دست راست سلام دهد، امید ندارد که برآرد که به دست چپ سلام دهد». آنگه فرمودند که «چون وقت موت برادرم یوسف رسید، از در خانه به درون خانه نگذاشتند تا ملاقات زلیخا کند؛ در بالای اسب جان داد. دیگر وقت موت برادرم سلیمان دررسید، بر عصا[۱۲] تکیه کرده بود. مَلَكُ الْمَوْت نشستن مهلت نداد؛ تکیه بر چوب جان بداد. چون وقت موت بی‌بی مریم[ه] رَضِيَ اللهُ عَنْهَا دررسید، مهتر عیسیٰ عَلَيْهِ السَّلَام از برای افطار ایشان چیزی موجود می‌کرد. چون نزدیک مادر آمد دید که جان به حقّ سپرده بود».[۱۳] پس ای برادر به همه حال این حیات را وفایی و بقایی نیست. این‌جهت گفته‌اند که «هر زمان موت یاد می‌باید کرد، و عبرت از گور باید گرفت».[۱۴]

[۶] رسیدن. [۷] چنین داستان‌ها در مورد درجات عالی و معراج صوفیان اندک نیست. جای خالی مطالعات ادبی و تطبیقی در مورد مفهوم معراج در مسیحیت و تصوّف حس می‌شود. [۸] آیهٔ ۸۹ سورهٔ انبیاء. [۹] خلفاءراشدین. [۱۰] نماز ظهر. [۱۱] نماز عصر.

[۱۲] (بر تخته چوب). در برگ ۱۲۸ نسخهٔ ۱۲۲۲ تاجیکستان، چنین ذکر شده است که یوسف بر عصا تکیه کرده است.

[۱۳] در برخی نسخ داستان درگذشت مریم، مادر عیسیٰ، موجود نیست. [۱۴] در برگ ۱۲۹ نسخهٔ ۱۲۲۲ تاجیکستان، شعری منسوب به

[ج] و خواجه خلیفه داشت [د] عمر گفت «یا رسول الله، اگر من با شما نماز شام گذارم، امید ندارم نمازِ خفتن فرصت دهد یا ندهد [...]». علی گفت «یا پیغمبر خدای، اگر من با شما نمازِ خفتن گذارم امید ندارم که نمازِ بامداد گذارم یا نه». [ه] امّ المؤمنین

worried himself into the grave, we removed the concerns from his mind and gave him what he desired and, indeed, saved him.

{3} The caliph of the town was a disciple of Khʷāja Rabīʿ. On the day that Khʷāja died the caliph was not in town. When he reached the town and heard that Khʷāja had died he went as quickly as possible to see the corpse. However, the body was already buried. He gave an order to exhume the body, so, 'I can be blessed through seeing him again'. When they opened the grave, he noticed that Khʷāja Rabīʿ was not in the grave.[5] They then recovered his grave and [the caliph] said, 'I will ask from the household of Khʷāja what has happened!' Then they went to the house and knocked on the door. The girl called out, 'Who is knocking on the door of an orphan?'

{4} It was said, 'The caliph has come to the door.' She said, 'Did he not find my father in the grave?' They said, 'How did you know that we did not find him in the grave?' She said, 'My father was always concerned about the grave and the hereafter, and would always recite, "Lord! Leave me not solitary[6]. You are the Best Inheritor' (Q. 21:89); and he was always saying, 'O God, by this heavenly verse[7] do not leave me in the grave alone.' O my brother, God never denies His friend's request!' When the caliph heard this, he returned, crying.So, be aware my brother that you should hear the voice of death every day and yet you are engaged with this mortal world so much so that it is as if that you will never die. When the time arrives, even if you want to take but one step away, you will not be allowed to do so.

{5} Another story. One day, four Companions, peace be upon all of them, sat with Prophet Muḥammad (pbuh). They asked, 'O Messenger of God, how long do you think you will live?' The Prophet said, 'O Companions, you say first.' First, the Commander of Believers Abū Bakr Ṣiddīq said, 'When I perform the midday prayer, I am not expectant of performing the next prayer [i.e., the afternoon prayer].' Then, the Commander of Believers ʿUmar said, 'When I perform the afternoon prayer, I am not expectant of performing the dusk prayer.' The commanders of believers ʿUthmān and ʿAlī, peace be upon both of them, said similarly.

{6} At that moment, the Prophet said, 'When Muḥammad performs morning prayer, and offers greetings of peace to the right, he does not expect to complete his greeting so that he can offer greetings of peace to the left.' Then, he said, 'When the moment of death of my brother, Joseph arrived, it did not allow him to enter through the door of the house and meet Zulaykhā; he died when he was still on horseback. Accordingly, when the moment of death of my brother Solomon arrived, he died while

[5] Such episodes on the ascension of saints are found in various Sufi sources. And it is worthy to conduct a comparative analysis between the descriptions outlined in Christian and Muslim Sufi literature.

[6] i.e. without any issue [7] i.e., Q. 21:89

{۷} حکایت. آورده‌اند که هرروز فرشته در چند محلّ ندا می‌کند؛ در خانهٔ کعبه، در روضهٔ حضرت رسول، در بیت المقدس، در گورستان، و در بازارها. ندای اوّل که در خانهٔ کعبه است فرشته می‌گوید «آن‌کسی که از فریضهٔ خدای تَعَالَی روی گردانیده‌است، از رحمت خدای تَعَالَی بی‌نصیب گردد»؛ و در روضهٔ پیامبر فرشته می‌گوید «هر که نماز را گذاشته و نگذارده[۱۵]، از سنّت‌های پیغمبر بازمانده فردای قیامت از شفاعت او محروم ماند»؛ در بیت المقدس ندا می‌کنند که «وای بر آن کسی که دست برمال زده‌اند. اگر نود ونه دانه از وجه حلال است و یک دانه از وجه حرام، آن یک‌دانه جمله[۱۶] را آلوده گرداند. اگر از این وجه جامه سازد، تا آن زمان که آن جامه در بردارد هیچ عبادت او قبول نگردد»؛ و ندایی دیگر در بازارها می‌کنند «وای برآن کسانی که امروز کم می‌دهند و زیاده می‌ستانند. وقتِ مردن از ایمان باز مانید»؛ و ندایی دیگر در گورستان می‌کند که «ای آن کسانی که امروز به حیات دنیا مغرور گشته‌اید. و مقام شما تا صبح قیامت گوراست».

{۸} و گور از دو حال خالی نیست. یا روضه‌ای است از روضه‌های جنّت، یا کنده‌ای[۱۷] است از کنده‌های دوزخ و مقام تنگ و تاریک است؛ بی مونس و با وحشت هم مقامِ مور و مار و کژدمان[۱۸] است. و هر که در وی درآید، روی آفتاب و ماهتاب را نبیند و خورندهٔ گوشت و پوست است و بُرّندهٔ استخوان‌هاست . پس گور صندوق عمل بنده است.

{۹} اکنون بیارایید خیرِخویش را با عمل نیکو، و چون جواب داده باشید مُبشّر و بشیر در حقّ تو دعا کنند و بازگردند. هم‌در آن‌ساعت کردارهای نیک شما به صورت خوب هریکی نزدیک تو آیند، وگویند که «ما مونسان توییم و با تو خواهیم بود تا قیامت». مؤمن جانب خانهٔ خود در بهشت معاینه می‌کند. و دیگر آنکه چون مردم بمیرند از خانه تا گور، جان نزدیک پرّه‌بینی[۱۹] ایشان استاده‌باشد. به‌مجرّد آنکه به گورستان برسد اهلِ گورستان استقبال کنند و بگویند که «از دنیا چگونه آمده‌ای؟ اگر عمل نیک آورده‌ای، خوشی و خرّمی باد تو را که کردارهای نیک تو جمله مونس تو خواهد شد، و روضه‌ای از روضه‌های بهشت بر روی تو خواهند گشاد. و اگر غافلْ با گناه آمده‌ای، همان [گناهان] مار و مور و کژدمان شوند و تو را می‌گزند. و نیز کردارهای بدْ تو را به صورت زشتی گردانند، و تو هر چه که روی از وی گردانی، او در نظر تو استاده شود، و دری از دوزخ گشایند تا بوی‌های گندهٔ[۲۰] دوزخ به مشام تو رسد».

سعدی شیرازی اضافه شده است. بیت ابتدایی آن چنین است: «سکندر که بر عالم حکم داشت؛ در آن دم که می‌رفت عالم گذاشت». اشعار دیگری همچون «آن کیست که دل نهادُ فارغ بنشست، پنداشت که مهلت و تأخیری هست؛ گو خیمه مزن که میخ می‌باید کند؛ گو بار منه که رخت می‌باید بست».

[۱۵] رها کرده و ادا نموده.

[۱۶] همه؛ کلّ.

[۱۷] هم به‌صورت «کَنده» به معنی گودال، و هم بصورت «کُنده» به معنی قطعه چوب و هیزم (در نسخهٔ برلین) به کار می‌رود.

[۱۸] عقرب‌ها.

[۱۹] پردهٔ بینی.

[۲۰] گنده بوی.

he was leaning on his cane. The Angel of Death did not allow him to sit; while leaning on his cane, he died. When the moment of death of Lady Mary (pbuh) had arrived His Eminence Jesus (pbuh) had made something for breaking the fast. When he came to his mother he saw that his mother had already sent her soul to God.' As such, O brother, at every level this worldly life is neither faithful nor everlasting. This is why it is said, 'Always be reminded of death and why lessons should be learned from the grave.'

{7} A new story. It is reported that the angel will call on several places every day: the house of God [i.e., the mosques], the shrine of the Messenger [in Medina], Jerusalem, the cemeteries, and the markets. [Regarding] the first call which is in the house of God, an angel will say, 'Then one who has refused what is obligated [i.e., to recite prayers], he will be deprived of the mercy of God. And an angel will say in the shrine of the Prophet, 'The one who left his prayers aside, and did not perform them, he will lag behind the prophetic traditions, and he will be deprived from his intercession upon the Day of Judgement.' It will be proclaimed in Jerusalem, 'Shame on the one who has taken property. If ninety-nine parts of wealth are lawful and just one part is unlawful, that single part makes the whole wealth unlawful. If one uses this wealth to sew a garment, none of his worship will be accepted so long as he wears this garment.' And another call will be made in the markets, 'Shame on those who sell short measures and demand full measures; at the moment of death they will die without faith'. And another call will be made in the cemeteries, 'O those who are today proud of living in this world, your place will be the grave until the morning of the Day of Judgement.'

{8} And the grave's condition will be one of these two states: either it will be as one of the gardens of paradise, or one of the dark and confined hellish pits. [Regarding the latter] Frightened and without companion, the inhabitant of the grave are only ant, snake, and scorpion. And whoever goes there, will not see the Sun and Moon, and there the flesh and skin of body is eaten and the bone is crushed and broken.' The grave is indeed the chest of the servant's deeds in the world.

{9} Now, glorify your goodness by doing rightful deeds, and if you do so, the bearer of glad tidings will pray for you and then return. Soon after that, your good deeds will transform into beautiful faces and come to you saying, 'We are your companions and will stay with you until the Day of Judgement.' And the believer will be able to imagine his place in paradise [while being still in the grave]. When a person dies and as they are taken to the grave his spirit will still linger at the tip of his nose. As soon as the body reaches the cemetery, the dwellers of the cemetery will welcome it, and say, 'How did you come from the world? If you brought good deeds, you will have happiness and many blessings as your good deeds would become your companions, and a garden from the heavenly gardens will open before you. And if you came burdened with sin, those snakes, ants, and scorpions will

{۱۰} اکنون، ای برادر مؤمن، حیات را غنیمت دان و به کار حقّ تَعَالَی مشغول باش. زیرا که مهمان دنیا بیش نیستی و بدین جاهِ فانی مغرور نباید بود. و نظر در اوّل و آخر کار خود باید کرد. آن روز که به دنیا آمدی، در گریه بودی، و نزدیکان تو از بهر آمدن تو شادی می‌کردند. و چون آخرِ کار تو به مُردن رسد، نزدیکان تو از بهر تو در گریه باشند. باید که تو در آن وقت به خنده از این عالم بروی.

{۱۱} و اگر سؤال کنند که «در وقت مردن خنده چیست که در آن وقت بنده را چند چیز پیش آید. اوّل آن که جان عزیز جدا شود. دوم مهتر عزرائیل قصد جان تو کند. و شیطان عَلَيْه اللَعْنَة طمع ایمان کند، و خوف عاقبت در کار شود. و کشتی عمُر در غرقاب[۲۱] فنا افتد [...] و درآن زمان به خاطر بنده بگذرد «اکنون وقت آن رسید که بازگشت به سوی خداوند باشد؛ امّا بدین روسیاهی[۲۲] در حضرت ذوالجلال پاک چگونه خواهم رفت؟» جواب این است که «چون بنده این اندیشه پیش‌آید، خداوند مشفق جلَّت قُدْرَتُه به کرمِ لطف ندا کند که «لَا تَخَفْ وَلَا تَحْزَنْ،[۲۳] یعنی ای بنده مترس، هیچ نگران مباش». چون این بشنود دل پریشان شدهٔ بنده سامان گیرد».

{۱۲} باز حقّ سُبْحَانَهُ وَتَعَالَى ندای دیگر از روی مرحمت درکار بنده کند که «قُلْ يَا عِبَادِيَ الَّذِينَ أَسْرَفُوا عَلَى أَنْفُسِهِمْ لا تَقْنَطُوا مِنْ رَحْمَةِ اللَّهِ إِنَّ اللَّهَ يَغْفِرُ الذُّنُوبَ جَمِيعًا إِنَّهُ هُوَ الْغَفُورُ الرَّحِيمُ،[۲۴] یعنی ای بنده، اگر تو اسراف کرده‌ای بر نفسِ خویش، نومید مباش از رحمت ما؛ مایی که آمرزندهٔ جمیع گناهان تو [ایم]». پس بنده گوید «که خداوندِ من به لطف و کرم مرا بیامرزید»، و دل از خان و مال و اهل‌وعیال برگیرد. امّا چنانکه سال‌ها با تن خوی گرفته‌است نخواهد که از تن بیرون آید.

{۱۳} حقّ تَعَالَی ندای دیگر کند که «يَا أَيَّتُهَا النَّفْسُ الْمُطْمَئِنَّةُ ارْجِعِي إِلَى رَبِّكِ رَاضِيَةً مَرْضِيَّةً، فَادْخُلِي فِي عِبَادِي، وَادْخُلِي جَنَّتِي،[۲۵] یعنی، ای نفس! آرمیده‌باش وبازگرد به سوی ربّ خویش که او راضی است از تو. چون بنده را حقّ تَعَالَی [...] چون نوزاد شادی کنان جان دهد، و چون جان بنده از قالب بیرون شود، به زبانِ حال[۲۶] گوید که «چه نیک بودی که پیش‌از این می‌مردم تا زودتر با این دولت می‌رسیدم»».

[۲۱] گرداب، و اشاره به «به هلاکت رسیدن» دارد. [۲۲] گنه‌کار و شرمنده. [۲۳] آیهٔ ۳۳ سورهٔ عنکبوت.
[۲۴] آیهٔ ۵۳ سورهٔ زمر. [۲۵] آیات ۲۷ تا ۳۰ سورهٔ فجر. [۲۶] بیان کننده وضع و وضعیت شخص.

be your companions and will eat you. Your bad deeds will convert to ugly faces, and however you try to turn away from them, they will come to your attention, and one door from hell will open to you so that the stench of hell will reach you.'

{10} Now, O faithful brother, take advantage of life and be engaged with God's affairs. Because you will not be the guest of the world for long and should not be proud of this mortal place. And one should take into account the first and last deeds. The day on which you were born into this world, you were crying, and your relatives were happy because of your arrival. And when, finally, you die, your relatives will cry for you. You should smile at that moment that you leave this world.

{11} And they may ask why one smiles during the moment of death, when something will occur to the servant. First, the gentle soul is taken. Second, His Eminence ʿIzrāʾīl is determined to take the soul, and Satan, may he be cursed, is determined to take the faith. And the fear of destiny rises. And the ship of life falls into a whirlpool of decadence [...] and at that time it comes to the servant's attention that 'now is the time to return to God.' But the servant asks, 'How should I go with such a blackened face[8] in the pure presence of the Possessor of Glory?' This is the response: when the servant ponders this he will realise that the kind God, exalted is His power, says, "Do not fear nor grieve (Q. 29:33), meaning, O servant do not fear, do not worry!" On hearing this, the turbulent heart of the servant becomes calm.'

{12} Then, God, in His mercy, makes another announcement for the sake of the servant, '...My servants who have harmed yourselves by your own excess, do not despair of God's mercy. God forgives all sins: He is truly the most Forgiving, the most Merciful' (Q. 39:53), meaning, 'O my servant, if you harm yourself by exceeding the limits, do not despair of Our mercy; We are the Forgiver of all of your sins.' The servant will respond, 'My God will forgive me with His kindness and mercy', so he will be prepared to leave his feasting, wealth, household, and wife behind. Nonetheless, as he has been used to his physical body for years, he will not want to leave his body.

{13} God will make another statement, 'O soul at peace: return to your Lord well pleased and well pleasing; go in among My servants; and enter into My garden (Q. 89: 27–30), meaning, O soul be calm and go back to your Lord who is now satisfied with you [...]. God introduces a soul into the servant, like a cheerful infant (?), and when the servant's soul leaves its body, he says about his feelings, "It would have been good if I had died earlier so I could reach this felicity earlier".'

[8] i.e., feeling ashamed

{۱۴} ای برادر مؤمن، خداوندی که با تو چنین است عجب که تو از وی غافلی و غافل باشی، و روی از وی بگردانی و به دنیای فانی روی آوری که جایگاه تو نیست. زیرا که از مادر متولّد شدی و بدین مقام فانی رسیدی. في الحال در گوش تو بانگ نماز بگفتند و چون بمُردی در جنازه[۲۷] کنند. آنگاه صلاة جنازه[۲۸] گویند. پس حیاتی که میان بانگ نماز و صلاة باشد بدین مقدار چه دل‌بندی؟ و مرگ از شَه‌رَگِ[۲۹] گردن تو به تو نزدیک‌تر است.

{۱۵} و مَلَكُ الْمَوْت در هرساعتی هفتادنظر می‌کند که تا تقاضای جان بنده کند. مردی را گویند که هفتاد سال زیست. چون وقت موت نزدیک رسید، مردمان از بهر پرسیدن او رفتند. و گفتند که «حال تو چیست؟» گفت «چه می‌پرسید که هفتادسال در جهان زیستم، و به جان‌کندن در تکاپوی دنیا بودم. اکنون جان می‌دهم از این بی‌وفا خاکدان.[۳۰] دنیای بی‌وفا این بود که به من برسید». ای برادر، چون تو را درین مقام نخواهند گذاشت، باید که غم آن مقام باقی خوری که وَالْبَاقِيَاتُ الصَّالِحَات.[۳۱]

{۱۶} إِلٰهِيّ، من بیچاره را با جمیع مؤمنان توفیق نیک کرداران عطا کنی، و به نیکان رسانی. بِمِنَّة وَكَرَمه[۳۲]

[۲۷] تابوت. [۲۸] نماز میّت. [۲۹] در اکثر نسخ خطی به‌صورت «شهرگ» نگاشته شده است.
[۳۰] «کهنه خاکدان» اشاره به «دنیا» دارد. هرچند «خاکدان» به معنای «مزبله» نیز به‌کار می‌رود. در نسخهٔ برلین (وفا این بود که به من رسید)
[۳۱] آیهٔ ۴۶ سورهٔ کهف. [۳۲] پاراگراف پایانی در برخی نسخ موجود نیست.

{14} O faithful brother, it is strange that you are aware of this God who particularly likes you, yet you remain unaware, and turn away from Him and become interested in the fleeting world which is not your ultimate abode. You were born from your mother and came to this temporary abode. Right after your birth, they recited a call to prayer in your ears, and once you die they will put you into a coffin then perform the funeral prayer. As such, why should you favour of a short life between a call for prayer and the performance of prayer? And death is as close to you as your artery is to your neck.
{15} And the Angel of Death searches seventy times every hour in order to seek the life of a servant. There is an account about a man who lived for seventy years. When the moment of death arrived, people went to him to see his state. And they asked him, 'How are you feeling?' He replied, 'Do not ask me as I have been living in this world for seventy years and have struggled to make a living. And I am now about to die and leave this unfaithful earthly world. It was the unfaithful world that deceived me.' O brother, as you will not stay in this place forever, you should now be concerned with your place in the hereafter, "But it is the good deeds that endure" (Q. 18:46).

{16} *O God, provide me, a humble pauper, and the true believers with the success that has already reached the good doers, and associate me with good doers. By Your unmerited favour and kindness. [Amen.]*

حکایتِ خواجه سفیان ثوری با شیطان مردود عَلَیه اللَعْنَة

{۱} آورده‌اند که روزی خواجه سفیان ثوری را با شیطان ملاقات افتاد. گفت «ای شیطان، مرا در کار تو عجب می‌آید و از کردار تو در حیرتم. زیرا که شنیده‌ام و در اخبار نوشته دیده‌ام که در هر آسمانی هفت‌هزارسال خدای را بندگی کرده‌ای. در هفت طبق[۱] زمین یک وجب جای نمانده که تو سجده نکرده‌باشی. خدای تعَالَی را آخر بی‌فرمانی کردی و عصیان ورزیدی؟» شیطان گفت «ای سفیان، تو نیز محَبِّ حق سُبحانَهُ وتعَالَی یی و چرا این سخن می‌گویی، زیرا که محَبّ قدر محبّت نیکو می‌داند. امّا ای سفیان، مرا از تو سؤال است جواب آن را با من بگو». سفیان گفت «بگوی».

{۲} شیطان گفت «در محبّت محَبّ غیری را شریک نمی‌باید ساخت. واقعهٔ من همین بود. چون فرمان شد که «می‌خواهیم که خلیفه[الف] پیدا کنم که در راستان[۲] دوستانِ ما[ب] باشد و از وی بنده‌زادگان پیدا گردانم که ایشان نیز دوستان ما باشند». چون ندای آفرینش آدم علیه‌السلام در آسمان‌ها و زمین‌ها دردادند، مرا غیرت در کار شد. که من با فرشتگان دیگر التماس کردیم که «إلهِيّ، با وجود ما این خاکیان را چرا پیدا می‌گردانی؟» فرمان شد که «دَم درکشید، آنچه ما می‌دانیم شمایان نمی‌دانید».

[۱] طبقه؛ شاید به «هفت‌اقلیم» اشاره دارد. [۲] صادقان و نیکوکاران.

[الف] خلیفه خلیفه [ب] محبّت درگاه ما باشد

CHAPTER 26

The story of Khʷāja Sufyān Thawrī with the outcast Satan, God's curse be upon him

{1} It is reported that Khʷāja Sufyān Thawrī had met Satan one day. He said, 'O Satan, I am really surprised by your work and shocked with your behaviour, because I have heard and read in the reports that you had worshipped God in each heaven for seven thousand years. And there is no place on each of the seven spheres of the Earth that you had not prostrated. Finally, you disobeyed God and rebelled?!' Satan said, 'O Sufyān, why do you, as a beloved in the presence of God, ask this question? You know well that beloved is grateful that he is loved! O Sufyān, let me ask you a question and hear your answer.' Sufyān said, 'Go ahead, ask the question'.

{2} Satan said, 'Within the love of a beloved, another's love should not be shared, right?. This also happened to me. When God commanded, "We want to appoint a guardian who will become Our righteous friend, and from him We will create servants; who will also become Our friends." Once the creation of Adam (pbuh) was announced in the heavens and Earth, I held a grudge. Thus, I along with other angels asked, "O God, when you have us why do You create these earthly beings?' A command arrived: "Silence! We know what you know not."'

{۳} الغرض. چون مهتر آدم را ﷺ آفرید،[۳] مرا با جملهٔ فرشتگان فرمان شد که «بروید، شما را در حقّ آدم سخنی گفته بودم که چون او را پیدا کنم سجده کنید». در من رشک آمد و رشک محبّت الهی زیاده شد. گفتم «إِلٰهِيّ، لایق سجده جز تو غیری را نباشد و من غیری را سجده نکنم»».

{۴} چون او[ج] این سخن بگفت خواجه را جوابِ شیطان فراهم نیامد، و ساکت بماند. از گوشهٔ خانه آوازی آمد که «ای خواجه سفیان، چرا خاموش ماندهای؟ این مدّعی کذّاب را جواب نمی‌گویی؟ بگو مُحِبّ کسی باشد که گفته‌ی محبوب بشنود و از سخن او تجاوز نکند. اگر تو را فرمودیم که آدم را سجده کن، در حقیقت سجدهٔ ما را است نه آدم را؛ مقصود از این سجده اطاعت و فرمان بُرداری بود. به‌جای نیاوردی، ازاین جهت تو را از درِ خود راندیم. و داغ لعنت بر جبین ناپاک تو نهادیم که تا قیامت در لعنت باشی. پس، ای ملعون، چنانچه تو را فرمودیم که آدم را سجده کن، این خاکیان را فرمان دادیم که در کعبه و مسجد سجده کنید. ایشان هیچ نگفتند که «کعبه و مسجد از سنگ و کاه است، پس سنگ و کاه را چگونه سجده کنیم که تو را در میان نمی‌بینیم. امّا، در حقیقت، سجده بر پروردگار است نه بر سنگ و کاه». فرمان مولا برین است تا رو به کعبه کنیم و به مسجد رویم.

{۵} بیت: معنی به‌صورت است اگر سجده می‌کنی؛ آن سجده بر خداست نه بر خانهٔ خدا[۴]

{۶} و پروردگار خود را حاضر و ناظر دانیم». چون شیطان این ندا شنید سیاه شد و از پیش خواجه سفیان ثوری برفت[د].

{۷} الغرض. روزی أَمیر المُؤمِنین عمر خطاب رضي الله عنه در کعبه بود. دید که شیطان نزدیک حرم استاده، گریه می‌کند. گفت «ای ملعون و راندهٔ حضرت سبحانه وتَعَالَی، در مقامِ پاک چه کنی؟» شیطان را سخن امیر سخت آمد[۵] و غَرش[۶] درکار شد، و گفت «ای عمر، بر من عتابِ چه می‌کنی و یک نظر در خود نمی‌کنی که تو چه بودی و من که بودم؟ من در ملاء اعلاء[۷] خدای عزّ وجلّ سُبُّوحٌ قُدُّوسٌ می‌گفتم، و تو در بتکده پیش بُتان سجده می‌کردی. اکنون، مرا ببینی[ه] و شکر می‌گویی که خدای بیگانه را یگانه کند و یگانه را بیگانه کند؟» چون أَمیر المُؤمِنین عمر رضي الله عنه از شیطان این سخن بشنید هیچ جوابش یاد نیامد.

[۳] همچنین: چون مهتر آدم ﷺ را آفرید. [۴] این بیت در برخی نسخ موجود نیست. [۵] ناگوار، ناخوشایند، دشوار آمدن.
[۶] خشم و غضب. به‌صورت «غرّش» هم می‌توان خواند. [۷] اشاره به بِالْمَلَإِ الْأَعْلَىٰ درآیهٔ ۶۹ سورهٔ ص دارد.

[ج] شیطان [د] از پیش خواجه سفیان رحمة الله علیه غایب شد [ه] بوبین

{3} To return to the story. 'When His Eminence Adam was created noble, I and all the angels were commanded, 'Go! I informed you about Adam; that when I created him, you must prostrate before him.' I felt resentment inside me and became jealous for God's love. I said, "O God, no one deserves prostration except you, and I will not prostrate to anyone else."'

{4} When Satan declared this, Khʷāja was unable to provide an answer for Satan and he remained silent. A voice was heard from the corner of the house saying, 'O Khʷāja Sufyān, why are you silent? Do you not answer this deceitful adversary? Tell him that the lover is the one who listens to what the beloved says, and does not contradict the beloved's instruction. If We ordered you to prostrate before Adam, that prostration is indeed for Us, not for Adam. The purpose of this prostration is obedience and subjugation. You did not do it. As such, We rejected you from Our presence. And labelled your unclean forehead with a curse in order that you remain blighted until the Day of Judgement. So, accursed one, since We ordered you to prostrate before Adam, We also ordered these earthly beings to prostrate in the Kaʿba and in the mosque. They did not say, "The Kaʿba and mosque are made of stone and straw and how can we prostrate upon stone and straw if we cannot find You there?!" In fact, [this] prostration is for God, not upon the stone and straw. The order of the Lord is to look towards the direction of prayer and go to the mosque, that's all.

{5} Poem: The intention of the prostration before acrolith is to worship; That
prostration is for God not for God's house

{6} And we consider Our God as the Present and the Beholder.' When Satan heard this he became embarrassed and left the presence of Khʷāja Sufyān Thawrī.

{7} A new story. The Commander of Believers, ʿUmar Khaṭṭāb (pbuh) was in the Kaʿba where he saw Satan standing before the shrine, crying. [ʿUmar] said, 'O accursed one and one rejected by God, what are you doing in the sanctuary?' Satan was annoyed with the words of the Commander and said with anger, 'O ʿUmar, you remonstrate with me and do not look at yourself and who you were and who was I! I used to say [addressing God], 'You are free from defects and pure' in 'The exalted assembly [of angels]' (Q. 38:69), and you were in the temple prostrating before idols. Now you see me and praise God for turning an opponent[1] into an intimate, and for turning an intimate[2] into an opponent?!' When the Commander of Believers ʿUmar (pbuh) heard this from Satan, he could not think of any response.

[1] i.e., ʿUmar [2] i.e., Satan

{۸} همان‌ساعت ندا شنید که «ای عمر، چرا جوابش نمی‌گویی که خدای تَعَالَی به علم قدیم خود دانسته‌است که یگانه کیست و بیگانه کیست؟ اگر بیگانه را چندگاه بیگانه داشت، آخر ختم کار وی بر یگانگی گشت، و بیگانه را صدهزار سال یگانه کرد و آخر او بیگانه گشت».

{۹} بیت: از لطف تو هیچ بنده نومید نشد　　مقبول تو جز مقبل جاوید نشد
لطفت به کدام ذرّه پیوست دمی　　کان ذرّه به از هزار خورشید نشد[۸]

{۱۰} آورده‌اند جوانی بود تباه کار، دایم الاوقات گفتی[۹] «کجائی ای شیطان، که آرزوی ملاقات بسیار دارم». شیطان با خود گفت که «در وسواس من این جوان چندین بدی می‌کند. چون به ظاهرملاقات کنم شاید که چنگ در ایمان زنم». شیطان به‌صورت آدمی پیش آمد. جوان پرسید «تو کیستی؟» شیطان گفت «من آن کسم که هر روز تو یاد می‌کردی. امروز پیش تو بدین صورت آمده‌ام که این‌چنین دوست[۱۰] را به ظاهر می‌باید دید».

{۱۱} جوان گفت «تو شیطانی؟»[۱۱] گفت «آری». جوان دریافت که دشمن قدیم است. بخندید و گفت «هیچ می‌دانی که تو را چرا یاد می‌کردم؟» شیطان گفت «هیچ معلوم نکردم[۱۲] که مقصود از ملاقات چیست؟» جوان گفت «مطلوب من از تو سؤالی بود. ازجهت آن از زبان من فراموش نشدی». شیطان گفت «اکنون برتو آمده‌ام، بپرس آنچه می‌پرسی».

{۱۲} جوان گفت «تو را در خاطر چه افتاد که سجده نکردی؟» گفت «ای جوان، تو منصف باشی آدم را چگونه سجده کنم که او از خاک آفریده شد و من از نور؟» جوان گفت «مرا منصف کردی. انصاف آن باشد که با تو کنم». جوان آب‌دهن بر روی شیطان انداخت، و گفت «ای ملعون، اگر آن‌روز از بهر سجده آدم انکار و شرم کردی، امروز چیست که راه‌زنی فرزندان آدم می‌کنی که ما را در خواب صورت [زیبا] پیش می‌آری؟ از سجدهٔ آدم علیه‌السلام کسی که انکار کند او پیش فرزند آدم از این بابت چگونه دم زند؟» شیطان گفت «ای گنه‌کار، من به طمع تو آمده بودم. امّا تو چنان تیری برجانم زدی که تا قیامت از خاطرم نرود».

۸ این ابیات به مولانا و همچنین ابوسعید ابوالخیر نسبت داده شده‌اند. کارل هرمان اته این ابیات را متعلّق به ابوسعید ابوالخیر می‌داند. با این وجود در «تاریخ یمینی» و «جامع التواریخ» نیز به این ابیات اشاره شده است. رجوع شود به *Sitzungsberichte der philosophisch -philologischen und historischen Classe der k. b. Akademie der Wissenschaften zu München* (München: Akademie der Wissenschaften zu München, 1897), 155.
در نسخهٔ برلین، برگ ۱۰۳، این ابیات چنین نگاشته شده‌است «از لطف تو هیچ بنده نومید نشد، مقبول تو جز مقبل جاوید نشد؛ لطفی به کلام ذرّه پیوسته دمی، کان ذرّه به از هزار خورشید نشد، یک ذرّه عنایت توؤ بنده نواز، بهتر زهزار سال و تسبیح و نماز»

۹ همیشه می‌گفت.　۱۰ چنین دوستی را.　۱۱ این سؤال مطرح شده توسط جوان در برخی نسخ موجود نیست.　۱۲ درنیافتم.

{8} At that moment, a voice was heard: 'O ʿUmar, why do you not answer him that God knew, based on His eternal knowledge, who would be friend and who would be foe. If He kept someone as an opponent for a while, he would overall be considered an intimate in the end. However, God considered the opponent as an intimate for one hundred thousand years, but he became an opponent in the end.'

{9} Poem: No one would be disappointed by Your grace, whoever has been graced by You, has won eternal salvation; Which atom was once favoured by you, such an atom would not shine more gloriously than a thousand suns.[3]

{10} It is said that there was a young man committing sins, who was always saying, 'Where are you Satan, I wish to meet you in person?' Satan pondered, 'This young man tempts me a lot. If I meet him in person then maybe I can attack his faith.' Satan came close to the boy in human form. The young man asked, 'Who are you?' Satan said, 'I am the one that you have been talking about every day. I have come to you today in this guise, as one should meet a friend in this way.

{11} The young man asked, 'Are you Satan?' He replied, 'Yes.' The young man realised that this was the eternal enemy. He smiled and said, 'Do you know why I called you?' Satan said, 'I do not know what is the purpose of this meeting?!' The young man said, 'My intention was to ask you a question. As such, you were not forgotten from my mind and tongue'. Satan said, 'Now I come to you. Ask what you want to ask'.

{12} The young man said, 'What do you think made you not prostrate?' He responded, 'Be fair, young man; how can I prostrate before Adam who is made of soil while I am made of fire?!' The young man said, 'Okay! You have asked me to judge it fairly, and fair is what I want to do.' The young man spat in Satan's face and said, 'O accursed one, if you had refused to prostrate before Adam on that day, why do you plunder Adam's children, and seduce us with a beautiful face. The one who had already denied prostrating before Adam, how can he actually talk about his reason before Adam's children?' Satan said, 'O sinful one, I came here to grab your soul. But you have shot an arrow through me that I will not forget until the Day of Judgement.'

[3] These couplets are ascribed to both Rūmī and Abū Saʿīd Abū al-Khayr. Carl Hermann Ethé, nonetheless, ascribed them to Abū Saʿīd Abū al-Khayr alone. The couplets are also found in *Tārīkh-i Yamīnī* and *Jāmiʿ al-Tawārīkh*. See *Sitzungsberichte der philosophisch-philologischen und historischen Classe der k. b. Akademie der Wissenschaften zu München*, p. 155.

{۱۳} پس، ای برادر مؤمن، از جهت ایمان همهٔ مؤمنان یکی‌اند؛ خواه صالح و خواه طالح.[۱۳] و همهٔ مؤمنان چراغ محبّت الهی‌اند. پس چراغ افروختهٔ الهی را شیطان کِی تواند که بی‌نور گرداند؟

{۱۴} بیت: چراغی را که ایزد برفروزد، هرآن کو تُف کند ریشش بسوزد[۱۴]

{۱۵} إلهِيّ، من شکسته را با جمیع مؤمنان از مکر شیطان در پناهِ عصمت خود نگاه‌داری. بِمِنَّة وَکَرَمه.

[۱۳] بدکردار؛ در برخی نسخ به «فاسق» اشاره شده‌است.

[۱۴] همچنین «چراغی را که ایزد برفروزد؛ هرآنکس پُف کند ریشش بسوزد»؛ در برخی نسخ، مصرع دوم تغییر کرده «چراغی را که ایزد برفروزد؛ چنان افتد که هرگز برنخیزد». مصرع دوم بیت اخیر نیز در انوار سهیلی واعظ کاشفی دیده می‌شود «هرآن کهتر که با مهتر ستیزد؛ چنان افتد که هرگز برنخیزد». بیت موجود در «درّالمجالس» در کتب دیگر همچون اکبرنامه، مسخرالبلاد تاریخ شیبانیه، تاریخ رشیدی، و غیره موجود است. با این وجود، در نسخهٔ برلین، برگ ۱۰۴، چنین نوشته شده است «چراغی را که ایزد افروخته، دشمن حقیقی اگر دَم زند، دهنش سوخته».

{13} So, O faithful brother! All believers are the same in terms of being faithful; whether righteous or sinful. And all believers are the light of divine love. As such, Satan cannot dim the divine ignited light.

{14} Poem: The light which is ignited by God, whoever wants to spit on it; his
beard will instead be burnt.[4]

{15} *O God, protect me, a humble pauper, and all other believers with your protection. By Your unmerited favour and kindness. [Amen.]*

[4] This couplet is also found in *Akbar-nāma, Tārīkh-i Rashīdī, Tārīkh-i Shaybāniyya*, etc.

حکایتِ حسن نوری رحمة الله[1]

{۱} آورده‌اند که خواجه حسن نوری رحمة الله علیه دائم به ذکر بودی و زمانی از ذکر دوست خالی نبودی. و بزرگی ایشان منتشر گشته بود. تا روزی دو کس[الف] هم‌اتّفاق کردند که «ساعتی به خدمت خواجه رویم تا سعادت دین و دنیا حاصل آید». در راه نزدیک خواجه حسن دو گربه با یکدیگر در سخن آمدند[ب] که «امروز خواجه حسن نوری در جهان نماند». ایشان هر دو از گفتار گربه تعجّب کردند و گفتند «إِنَّا لِلَّهِ وَإِنَّا إِلَيْهِ رَاجِعُونَ». و بهم گفتند «اگر دولت دیدار روزی نشد، باری رفته قبر[ج] ایشان را زیارت کنیم».

{۲} بر در خانقاه خواجه آمدند، و دست بر در زدند. خواجه آواز شنید از خانقاه بیرون آمد. آن جوانان پرسیدند «شما کیستید؟» گفت «منم حسن نوری». چون آن هر دوتن خواجه را در حیات دیدند، نعره‌ای زدند و بیهوش گشتند. بعداز زمانی بهوش آمدند. خواجه پرسید که «شما چه کسانید و سبب بیهوشی شما چه بود؟» فرمودند که «به زیارت شما می‌آمدیم، در یک دکّان دو گربه حکایت می‌کردند که «امروز خواجه حسن در جهان نماند». گفتیم چون ایشان به جوار رحمت الهی پیوستند، باری خاکِ پاکِ ایشان را زیارت کنیم. چون به در خانقاه رسیدیم و شما را در حال حیات یافتیم وحشت زندگانیِ شما در کار شد، که مُرده چگونه زنده شود، و از آن جهت بی‌خود گشتیم».

{۳} خواجه چون این سخن از ایشان شنید زار گریست و گفت «گربه راست می‌گوید. امروز، یک‌زمانی از ذکر و فکر دوست فراموش بودم. ندا در جمیع عالم ملکوت دادند که «امروز خواجه حسن در جهان نماند که از یاد دوست غافل گشت» و حضرت رسالت پناهی صلی الله علیه وسلم فرموده‌اند که «چون مردم از یاد کردن حق سبحانه وتعالی غافل می‌شوند، در آسمان و زمین ندا می‌کند که «فُلان ابن فُلان بمُرد که یادِ مولا را فراموش کرد»».

[الف] دو جوان [ب] در میان شهر دیدند که دو گربه در دکّانی با یکدیگر در سخن در آمده‌اند [ج] خاک گور

CHAPTER 27

The story of Khʷāja Ḥasan Nūrī, may God's mercy be upon him

{1} It is reported that Khʷāja Ḥasan Nūrī, may God's mercy be upon him, was always praying and never forgot his Friend[1]. And the news regarding his nobleness was widely known. Two men decided 'to visit Khʷāja for a couple of moments to be blessed in the worldly and religious affairs.' On the way to Khʷāja Ḥasan's house two cats were speaking together, 'Khʷāja Ḥasan has left the world today.' The two men were shocked by what the cats said. They recited, 'Surely to God we belong and to Him we will return' (Q. 2:156) and they said to one another, 'If we are not to have the honour of visiting him today, then we will visit his grave.'

{2} They went to the retreat house (*khānqāh*) of Khʷāja and knocked on the door. Khʷāja heard the knock and came to the door. The young men said to him, 'Who are you?' He said, 'I am Ḥasan Nūrī'. When these two men found Khʷāja alive they gased and fainted. After a while, they woke up. Khʷāja asked them, 'Who are you and why did you faint?' They said, 'We were coming to visit you and two cats were talking about a Khʷāja Ḥasan who left the world today. We thought if he died today then we can visit his grave. When we arrived at the retreat house and found you alive we were shocked – how can the dead be living?! For this reson we fainted.'

{3} When Khʷāja heard the story he said, 'The cats were right. I was for a brief moment inattentive to the remembrance of my Friend. An announcement was made throughout the highest kingdom, "Khʷāja Ḥasan will no longer be in the world as he neglected to remember his Friend".' [Khʷāja Ḥasan continued to relate the heavenly announcement], '...and as the Prophet (pbuh) stated, "When people stray from remembering God, a call will be announced in heaven and on Earth that 'so-and-so

[1] i.e., God

{۴} هرکه یک لحظه از ذکر حقّ غافل گردد حکم مرده دارد. و مردگان هیچ آرزو ندارند مگر آنکه «در دنیا رویم و یک‌بار نام حقّ تَعَالَی بر زبان رانیم». امّا، ایشان را این آرزو هیچ سود نداشت زیرا که هرکه در حالِ حیاتِ خود توشهٔ آخرت برگرفت و کاری کرد، واگر نه[۱] بعداز مردن ندامت و پیشمانی سود ندارد.

{۵} الغرض. حکایت در ذکر خواجه حسن نوری رحمة الله علیه بود. [بشنو] روزی در خاطر ایشان شوق خانهٔ کعبه غلبه کرد. و تنها روی به راه نهاد. تا روزی در بیابان رسیدند و تشنه شدند. خواجه در اطراف جانب و خود نظر کرد. ناگاه از دور درخت در نظر آمد. گفت «آنجا روم شاید آب یابم». چون نزدیک درخت آمدند، دیدند که چاه آبست. گفت «اگر دلو[۲] و رسن[۳] بودی مقصود حاصل شدی».

{۶} درین سخن بود که رمه آهوان پیدا شدند؛ بر سر چاه رسیدند. رو به قبله کردند و سرهای خویش را بالا کشیدند و دو چشم سوی آسمان کردند. بعداز آن نظر در چاه کردند. درزمانْ آب از عمقْ بالا آمد، و آهوان به سیراب خوردند و بازگشتند. خواجه خواست که آب خورد، آب در عمق رفت. و خواجه بشورید و گفت «إِلٰهِيّ، از بهرِ وحوشِ بیابانْ آب ازعمقِ چاه بر لبِ چاه آوردی. چون نوبت حسن شد آب به قعر چاه بردی؟» ندایی از عالم غیب شنید که «ای حسن، تو منتظر دلو و رسن بودی، و آهوان هیچ اندیشه نکردند مگر به لطف و کرم ما، هرآینه به مقصود بارز رسیدند. و تو دل به دلو و رسن نهادی؛ بی‌آب ماندی. پس چندان باید صبر کرد تا دلو و رسن پیدا شود».

{۷} چون خواجه این ندای عتاب شنید، تشنگی از وی رفت و رو به راه نهاد. تا روزی جوانی را ملاقات کرد. جوان گفت «السَّلَامُ عَلَيْكُمْ! ای خواجه نوری». جواب سلام داد و گفت «ای جوان، درین بیابان نام من به تو که گفت؟» جوان گفت «ای خواجه، هر که جز حقّ انس بر غیری نگیرد، حقّ تَعَالَی او را آشنای بر همه چیزها گرداند». آنگاه جوان گفت «ای خواجه، هیچ می‌دانی که مقصود از ملاقات چیست؟» خواجه گفت «نمی‌دانم،» جوان گفت «مقصود آنست که یک زمان اینجا باشی تا من جان دهم و تو مرا در خاک دفن کنی». آنگه خواجه گفت «ای جوان، از کجا این سخن می‌گوئی که این سرّ کس ندانسته؟»[د] جوان گفت «ای خواجه، حقّ سُبْحَانَهُ وَتَعَالَى بر بندهٔ خود الهام می‌کند[ه] که از مقام زندان دنیای فانی به مقام جاوید برس. پس مرا معلوم گشته که به حضرت ربّ خود خواهم رفت».

{۸} آنگاه جوان کلمه آغاز کرد، و جان به حقّ تَعَالَی سپرد. خواجه قَبر او را بکافت.[۴] خواجه تلقین کرد و نماز گذارد و در قَبر کرد. خواجه در گریه شد و گفت «إِلٰهِيّ، غریبی به غربت در بیابان جان بداد. برین رحمت کن». جوانِ مُرده در خنده آمد. خواجه در حیرت ماند. گفت «ای جوان، اگر زنده‌ای در گور نرو، و اگر مرده‌ای این خنده از کجاست؟» مُرده در خنده آمد و گفت «ای خواجه، نشنیده‌ای چنانچه فرموده‌اند «أَولِيَاء

۱ وگرنه. ۲ سطل. ۳ طناب. ۴ بشکافت.

د «ای جوان از کجا این سخن می‌گویی که این حالت را پیغمبران ندانسته‌اند وهیچ‌کس نداند» ه خدای تَعَالَی ندای «الرَّحیل» می‌کند

the son of such-and-such has just died because he forgot to remember his Friend'."'

{4} Whoever strays from remembering God is considered dead. And the dead have no desire except to return to the world and invoke the name of God one more time. But this wish will not help them, because someone can only prepare for the hereafter during his lifetime and do something for the sake it. Regret will not help after death!

{5} Return to our story. This story is about Khʷāja Ḥasan Nūrī, may God's mercy be upon him. One day, a desire to visit the Kaʿba surged within him. He set off on the journey to visit the Kaʿba alone. At one point he found himself in the desert and became thirsty. Khʷāja looked around. Suddenly, a tree in the distance came to his attention. He said, 'I should go there, perhaps I can find water'. When he reached the tree, he noticed that there was a water well. He said, 'If there was a bucket and rope, I could reach the water.'

{6} While pondering this, a herd of deer arrived. They went towards the water well. The deer turned towards the direction of prayer and held their heads up to look at the sky. Later, they looked down to the well. The water came up from the depths of the well and the deer fully quenched their thirst and left. Khʷāja went to drink water but the water had gone down into the well. Khʷāja became upset and said, 'O God, You brought the water up from the depths of the well for the sake of animals, but now, when it is Ḥasan's turn, You sent the water back down!?' He heard a voice from the unseen world: 'O Ḥasan, you were waiting for a bucket and a rope, while the deer did not think about anything but Our kindness and mercy, as such, they soon achieved their goal. You relied upon the bucket and the rope and so you were without water. You should wait until you find a bucket and rope!'

{7} When Khʷāja heard this exclamation, he forgot his thirst and continued his journey, until he came across a young man.The young man said, 'Peace be upon you, O Khʷāja Nūrī!' Khʷāja replied to [the greeting] and said, 'O young man, who in this desert told you my name?' The young man replied, 'O Khʷāja, the one who chooses no friend but God, God will make him known everywhere.' Then the young man said, 'O Khʷāja, do you know about the purpose of our meeting?' Khʷāja said, 'I do not know.' The young man said, 'The purpose is that you stay here for a while, until I die, and you bury me.' Then Khʷāja said, 'O young man, how do you know this as no one knows this secret[2]?' The young man said, 'O Khʷāja, God inspired his servant to move from the prison of the temporary world to an everlasting place. As such, it is apparent to me that I am about to go to my own Lord.'

{8} Then the young man professed his faith and submitted his soul to God. Khʷāja dug his grave, conducted the burial rites, performed the funeral prayer, and

[2] i.e., the time of their death

اللهِ لَا يَمُوتُونَ وَلَكِن يَنْتَقِلُونَ مِن دارٍ إلى دار،[۵] یعنی که اولیای خدای تَعَالَی عَزَّوَجَلَّ نمرده‌اند بلکه از دار فنا به دار بقا خرامیده‌اند». خواجه این حال بدید و قَبر او بپوشید و رو به راه نهاده. طالبان خدای عَزَّوَجَلَّ[د] در ذکر و فکر دوست و اندیشه آنچنان مستغرقند.

{۹} بیت:[ذ] جانا دل عارفان عالم ریش است، زان یک منزل که جمله را در پیش است؛ با تیغ اجل بریده در طشت فنا، زین غم سر صد هزار زیرک بیش است[۶]

{۱۰} حکایت. سلطان بایزید[۷] را پرسیدند که «هر روز چه حالست که شما را روی مبارک پژمردگی می‌آرد و زردتر شده؟» جواب داد که «ای مردمان، بردلی که اندیشهٔ چهار چیز بگذرد او را چگونه قرار باشد، و ثمرهٔ روی او چگونه گُلِ خوشی بار آرد؟» گفتند «ای بزرگِ دین، آن چهار چیز کدام است؟»

{۱۱} گفت «آن‌روز که نبی آدم آفریده شد و حقّ تَعَالَی جملهٔ ذرائر[۸] را، که فرزندان آدم بودند، از پشت آدم عَلَيْهِ السَّلَام جدا گردانید و ندا کرد «أَلَسْتُ بِرَبِّكُمْ»[۹] همه گفتند که «قَالُوا بَلَى»،[۱۰] مگر روح‌های کافران که ندا قبول نکردند. هیچ از آن روز باز معلوم بایزید نشد که روحِ بایزید میان روح مؤمنان بود یا میانِ روح کافران. دوم آنکه زمانی که وقت نزول آدم می‌شود، فرشته الحان می کند که «إلهِيّ، بندهٔ تو از دایرهٔ شکم مادر به دنیا آید. چه فرمان می‌دهی؟» طغرای[۱۱] سعادت برجبین او بنویسم، یا علامت بدبختی کشیم. که هیچ معلوم بایزید نشد که نام بایزید در شکم مادر نیک‌بخت نوشته شده است یا بدبخت». پیغمبر صَلَّى اللَّهُ عَلَيْهِ وَسَلَّمَ می‌فرمایند «السعیدُ مَنْ سَعِدَ في بطنِ أُمّهِ والشقيُّ مَنْ شَقِيَ في بطنِ أُمِّهِ». و سوم آنکه چون موت بنده می‌رسد عزرائیل می گوید که «إلهِيّ، بنده تو از دار فنا به دار بقا رحلت می‌کند. جان او را با ایمان برگیرم یا بی‌ایمان؟» اکنون سعادت أُولَئِكَ كَتَبَ فِي قُلُوبِهِمُ الْإِيمَانَ[۱۲] که[۱۳] را دهند، و از دولت ایمان که را محروم گردانند؟ چون نوبت به بایزید رسد چه معامله پیش آید. چهارم چون قیامت شود خلق اوّلین و آخرین را در عرصات حاضر گردانند. در عرصات فرمان شود که «فَرِيقٌ فِي الْجَنَّةِ وَفَرِيقٌ فِي السَّعِيرِ،[۱۴] جدا کنید گروهی را به سوی بهشت برند و گروهی را بسوی دوزخ». بایزید داخل کدام باشد؟»»

[۵] این عبارت در برخی متون وابسته به فرقهٔ «بریلویه» در هند و آسیای جنوبی یافت می‌شود. قسمت پایانی عبارت عربی « وَلَكِن يَنْتَقِلُونَ مِن دارٍ إلى دار» نیز بر برخی سنگ قبرها در جهان مالایا-اندونزی حکاکی شده‌است.

[۶] این بیت در مرصاد العِباد نجم الدین الرازی نیز دیده می‌شود. در برخی نسخ مثل دانشگاه تهران و برلین شعر متفاوتی ذکر شده «جان همه عاقلان از این غم ریش است، زان منزل و این ره همه را در پیش است؛ از هیبت آن دو راه خون شد دل من، تا خود ز کدام ره بُوَد منزل من».

[۷] در نسخهٔ برلین به شکل «بازید» نگاشته شده است. [۸] اولاد و ذریّه. [۹] آیهٔ ۱۷۲ سورهٔ اعراف.

[۱۰] ادامه آیهٔ ۱۷۲ سورهٔ اعراف. [۱۱] خط، فرمان، حکم و نشانه. [۱۲] آیهٔ ۲۲ سورهٔ مجادله. [۱۳] چه کسی.

[۱۴] آیهٔ ۷ سورهٔ شورا.

[د] طالبان مولی که دوستان حقّ سُبْحَانَهُ وَتَعَالَى اند [ذ] رباعی

put him into the grave. Khwāja began to wail and said, 'O God, a lonely person died in the desert. You must have mercy upon him.' The young man smiled. Khwāja was shocked, and said, 'O young man, if you are alive, do not go to the grave, and if you are dead, what is this smile?' The dead man smiled and said, 'O Khwāja, did you not hear, 'God's friends will not die, they just move from one place to another', meaning that the friends of God are not dead, but will move from the temporary world to the everlasting one. Khwāja witnessed this and covered his grave and continued the journey. This is the way that the seekers of God are immersed in invoking, remembering, and thinking of the Friend.

{9} Poem: Dear one, the heart of the gnostics of the world is in turbulence, due to the final place which is ahead of them; it has been cut with the death blade in the vessel of mortality, lined with the head of one hundred thousand sages owing to this grief.

{10} Story. Sultan Bāyazīd had been asked, 'Why does your face become more faded and withered every day?' [He] responded, 'O people, when the heart of a man is always thinking about four things, how would it be possible for it to relax and his face become as fresh as a flower?' [They] asked, 'O the preeminent master of religion, what are those four things?'

{11} [He] replied, 'That day on which Prophet Adam was created and God released every being and particle – which were Adam's descendants – from the loin of Adam and asked, "Am I not your Lord?" (Q. 7:172), and all responded like this, "They replied, 'Yes, You are!'" (Q. 7:172), apart from the spirits of the infidels who did not accept the call. Since that day, it has not been clear to Bāyazīd whether his spirit is among the believers' spirits or those of the infidels. Second, when the time of human birth arrives, the angel raises the question, "O God, Your servant is about to go into world from the mother's womb. What do You command? Should I write down a blissful command on his forehead or draw a sign of misfortune?" It is not yet clear to Bāyazīd whether the name of Bāyazīd has been registered as blissful or miserable in his mother's womb. The Prophet (pbuh) said, "Blessed is the one who is blissful from his mother's womb, and miserable is the one who is wretched from his mother's womb." Third, when the servant's moment of death arrives, ʿIzrāʾīl says, "O God, Your servant travels from the mortal world to the immortal one. Shall I take his soul as faithful or unfaithful?" It is said, "For those who, God has instilled faith in their hearts and strengthened them with a spirit from Him" (Q. 58:22) – so, whom will receive grace and whom will be denied the bounty of faith? What will be bestowed when Bāyazīd's turn arrives? Fourth, when the Day of Judgement dawns the first and last beings will be present in

{۱۲} دیگر بزرگی می گوید «چگونه خوشی کند فرزند آدم که چندین عقاب در پیش دارد: اوّل جان دادن، دوم خوف ایمان که در آن دم چه معامله پیش آید،[ح] سوم منکر و نکیر، چهارم گور تنگ وتاریک،[۱۵] پنجم آنکه سر از گور برکَند پنجاه هزارسال راه روز حشر قیامت در پیش است، که از هیبت آن روز پیغمبران عاجزند. ششم آنکه نامهٔ کردار بر دست راست دهند یا بر دست چپ، نَعُوذُ بِالله. هفتم، ترازوی اعمال در پیش است که اعمال را بسنجند. هشتم، گذشتن از پل صراط که سی‌هزارسال راه‌درازی اوست که از موی باریک‌تر و از تیغ تیزتر».

{۱۳} امّا، نیک‌بختان را فردای قیامت از این عقبه‌های[۱۶] دشوار نجات خواهند داد. زیرا که امروز[۱۷] اندیشهٔ آن روز می گفتند. هرآینه، فردای ایشان را بی‌اندیشه گردانند. و هرکه امروز اندیشهٔ آن روز نکند، بعداز مُردن جمله اندیشه‌ها را پیش او آرند.

{۱۴} إِلٰهِيّ، همهٔ مؤمنان را به دولت دین و دنیا برسان، و اندیشهٔ آن چنان روزی کن. بِمِنَّة وَكَمَال كَرَمه.

[۱۵] این مورد در برخی نسخ موجود نیست. [۱۶] راه دشوار. [۱۷] در این دنیا.

[ح] قیامت که در آخر چه معامله پیش آرند

the Resurrection Plain. A proclamation will be made on the Resurrection Plain, "'A group will be in paradise and another in the blazing fire' (Q. 42:7), separate them, send a group to paradise and the other group to hell." To which will Bāyazīd enter?'

{12} Another eminent person has asked, 'How can Adam's child be cheerful when he has several torments ahead of himself? First, death. Second, whether his faith will withstand scrutiny at the moment of death. Third, Munkar and Nakīr. Fourth, the constricted and dark grave. Fifth, when he arises from the grave there will be a fifty thousand year long road to reach the Resurrection Day, a formidable day which will make even the prophets weak. Sixth, whether the book of deeds will be placed in the right hand or the left hand – from the latter we seek refuge in God! Seven, that there will be a scale with which they will measure our deeds. Eight, crossing the Ṣirāṭ bridge which is thirty thousand years long yet thinner than a strand of hair and sharper than a blade.'

{13} The prosperous will be saved from these difficulties due to their being ever mindful of the Judgement Day. Their tomorrow will be free of concern. Whoever does not think about the Judgement Day, he will be subsumed by concern after death!

{14} *O God, provide every believer with the honour of following the religion and of being blessed in the world. And grant us attentiveness as mentioned above. By Your unmerited favour and kindness! [Amen.]*

حکایتِ شیخ برسیسا

که چگونه بود، و چه کسی بود، و سبب چه بود که ایمان کم کرد، و مؤمن را از آن هُشیار باید بُود؟[1]

{۱} آورده‌اند که شیخ برسیسا کسی بود که هیچ چیز از او پوشیده نبود، و در نظر او از عرش تا تحت الثری[2] هیچ حجاب نبودی. و بیماران و کوران از هرجا[الف] که می‌آمدند بر در صومعهٔ شیخ می‌نشستند. چون نظر شیخ برایشان می‌افتاد صحّت می‌یافتند و هر حاجت که کسی داشتی به مقصود خود رسیدندی.

{۲} تا روزی پادشاه را مهمّی پیش آمد. لشگرهای خود را آراسته می‌کرد و در آن شهر دو برادر و یک خواهر بی‌مادر و پدر بودند، و کسی نداشتند که بر آن اعتمادی بوده باشد. و فرمان پادشاه برین بود که هیچ مرد درین شهر نماند. هر دو برادر دانستند که «ما را برابر پادشاه می‌باید رفت و خواهر ما تنهاست. او را به که مانده و رویم؟» به خاطر گذراندند که «هیچ‌کس بِهْ از شیخ برسیسا نیست. خواهر را نزدیک شیخ بگذاریم». آمدند بر در صومعهٔ شیخ عرض کردند، و قصّه به تمامی تقریر کردند. شیخ برسیسا حُجره تعیین کرد و او را برخود گرفت،

[1] در برخی نسخ شیوهٔ نگارش «برسیسا» به «برصیصا» تغییر می‌کند. در نسخهٔ ۱۸۹۰ ایندیا آفیس، که در کتابخانهٔ بریتانیا نگهداری می شود به‌صورت «شیخ برصیّا» ثبت شده است. در ۵-۲۹۴۴۶ کتابخانهٔ مجمع اسلامی «پیرسا»؛ در برلین «پرسیا». بنابر سنّت اسلامی، این داستان مرتبط است با آیهٔ ۱۶ سورهٔ حشر «كَمَثَلِ الشَّيْطَانِ إِذْ قَالَ لِلْإِنسَانِ اكْفُرْ فَلَمَّا كَفَرَ قَالَ إِنِّي بَرِيءٌ مِّنكَ إِنِّي أَخَافُ اللَّهَ رَبَّ الْعَالَمِينَ». یکی از اوّلین تفاسیر شناخته شده، تفسیر مقاتل بن سلیمان، در دو جا به نام برصیصا\برسیسا اشاره دارد؛ یکی در ذیل تفسیر سورهٔ مائده، و دیگری در ذیل آیهٔ ۱۶ سورهٔ حشر. بااین‌وجود، بیشترین ارجاع تفسیری به این داستان مرتبط است به آیه‌ای در سورهٔ حشر، و اینکه در اکثر تفاسیر وی به عنوان «راهبی از بنی اسرائیل» یا «قوم یهود» معرّفی می‌شود. به‌گمان من، داستان درّالمجالس شباهت زیادی با آنچه در کشف الاسرار رشیدالدین میبدی ارائه شده دارد. نگاه کنید به رشید الدین میبدی، کشف الاسرار وعدة الابرار، ج ۱۰. صص ۵۵-۵۴. براساس برگ ۱۳۹ نسخهٔ ۱۲۲۲ تاجیکستان، شعری به نقش «منفی» زنان در گمراه نمودن«مردان مؤمن» اشاره دارد: «باعورا را جدا زایمان زن کرد، برسیسا را دشمن پند [...] زن کرد؛ از زن شده سینهٔ حسن زهرآلود؛ [...] زن کرد».

[2] زیر زمین.

[الف] از اقالیم عالم

The story of Shaykh Barsīsā

who he was, what type of person he was, and the reason that he lost his faith – believers should take heed![1]

{1} It is reported that Shaykh Barsīsā was a person from whom nothing was hidden; there was no veil before his eyes from the lofty heavens to the depths of the Earth. And the sick and the blind came to his retreat (*khānqāh*) from all around. As soon as the shaykh looked upon them, they would be healed, and whatever request was made, it would be granted.

{2} One day, when the king had a major event, his army was lined up. And there were two orphan brothers and one sister who had no guardian. The order of the king was, 'No male should remain in town'.[2] The brothers said to themselves, 'We need to go into the king's service. Our sister will be alone. To whom shall we entrust her before we go?' They pondered and then said, 'No one is better than Shaykh Barsīsā. We should take our sister to him.' They went to the shaykh's retreat and explained the whole story. Shaykh Barsīsā found living quarters for the girl, welcomed her, and said, 'Bring her to this chamber.' The brothers brought their sister and paid for her upkeep. They bid farewell and went to the king.

[1] This story might be related to Q. 59:16 – '[They are] like Satan when he lures someone to disbelieve. Then after they have done so, he will say [on Judgement Day], "I have absolutely nothing to do with you. I truly fear God – the Lord of all worlds".' A large number of Qur'ānic commentaries include notes about Barsīsā and his fate. *Tafsīr Muqātil*, one of the oldest known commentaries, mentions Barsīsā in its commentary on Q. 5 and Q. 59. Also, there is much similarity between the story in *Durr al-Majālis* and Maybudī's commentrary in his *Tafsīr*, vol. 10, 54–55.

[2] i.e., they must join the ranks of the army

و گفت «در حجره در آرید». برادران خواهر خود را آوردند و آنچه نفقه او می‌شد دادند، وداع کردند، و پیش پادشاه رفتند.

{۳} بعداز دو سه روز به خاطر شیخ گذشت که بروم از حال دختر خبر گیرم. چون شیخ بر در حُجره آمد، دیدی که دختر در نماز است. و شعاع جمال آن دختر شعله می‌زند. چون نظر شیخ بر دختر افتاد، چشم‌پوشیده برگشت. شیطان ملعون بدبخت محلِّ وسواس دید، گفت «ای شیخ، یک نظر در جمال این دختر دار، و از چنین جمال چشم را فرو نباید». به وسوسهٔ شیطان چشم باز کرد، و باز نظر به سوی دختر کرد. به صدهزار دل[۳] شیفتهٔ روی دختر گشت، و به مقام عادت خود در صومعه برآمد و تحریمه[۴] نماز بست. چون دلبسته دگری بود،[ب] در نماز نمی‌دانست چه می‌خواند.

{۴} شب درآمد به خیال جمال او. باز قصد حُجرهٔ او کرد. دید که دختر در نماز است. پیش‌تر شد، و گفت «ای غارت کنندهٔ دل برسیسا! خود را در نماز بازدار که دل مرا به غارت برده‌ای».[ج] آن دخترک مظلومه حیران ماند که این چه حال است! آنگه برسیسا برخاست، و دست دختر بگرفت و جانب خود کشید، و به زور پلیدکاری با وی کرد. چند روز و شب با دختر در حُجره بود. چون مدّتی برین گذشت، دختر را حَمل[۵] پدید آمد. و شیطان را وقت خوش شد. گفت «ای شیخ برسیسا، سال‌ها دعوی زهد و تقوی نمودی. چون این افعال تو ظاهر گردد، زبان طعن بر تو دراز کنند و تو را کسی چه گوید؟ و دفع حمل[۶] چه می‌کنی؟ و از بهر دفع این کار تدبیر باید کرد».

{۵} برسیسا در فکر شد که «آوازهٔ بزرگی من در عالم و اقالیم پر شده‌است. چون این افعال ظاهر گردد هرکسی مرا ملامت کند». شیطان گفت «شیخ تدبیری بِه[۷] از این نیست که این دختر را بکُشی تا افعال تو پوشیده بماند». سخن شیطان در دل او جای گرفت، و گفت «خوب می‌گوید». نیمه شب گذشته بود که شیخ برسیسا کاردی گرفت و نزدیک دختر آمد. دختر خواب بود. سر او را از تن جدا کرد. و هم در آن حُجره گور بکند و دفن کرد.

{۶} بعداز چندروز، برادران همراه پادشاه بیامدند، و در آن حُجره که خواهر را گذاشته بودند، درآمدند. خواهر را ندیدند. گفتند نزد شیخ رفته تفحّص کنیم. چون از شیخ پرسیدند گفت «در بندگی خدای تَعَالَی مشغول بودم که خواهر شما وفات یافت». به‌مجرّد شنیدن گریان و فریاد کنان بازگشتند. شیطان لعین وقت را خوش یافت. به صورت مردِ پیری پیش آمد، و گفت «هیچ می‌دانید که خواهر شما را چه کرد؟» گفتند «نمی دانیم». شیطان گفت «شیخ به خواهر شما میل بد کرد و به زور ناکردنی کرد. و او را حمل شد[۸] و ترسید که فردا فضیحت شود. ترس آنکه رسوا بشود همدرین حجره دفن کرد. و من حاضر شدم.[د] خواستم که فریاد کنم ترسیدم که مرا هم بکشد».

[۳] یک دل نه صد دل عاشق شدن. [۴] تحرمه. بنابر عمید، این واژه اشاره به تکبیری که بعداز نیّت نماز می‌گویند دارد که طبق آن شخص، کلام یا امر دیگری که مربوط به نماز نباشد را بر خود حرام می‌کند. [۵] دختر باردار شد. [۶] سقط جنین.
[۷] بهتر. [۸] باردار شد.

[ب] چون دل او بستهٔ خم ابروی دیگری شده بود [ج] «ای غارت کنندهٔ دل برسیسا! خود را از اقامت رکوع و سجود بازدار که دل مرا به غارت برده‌ای»

{3} After two or three days the shaykh thought that he should see how the girl was doing. When the shaykh arrived near the living quarters of the girl he noticed that she was praying and that she appeared most beautiful. When the shaykh saw the girl he lowered his gaze and turned away. The accursed miserable Satan had found a weakness. [Satan] said, 'O Shaykh, one look upon the beautiful face of the girl and one cannot desist from seeing her beauty.' Due to Satan's temptation, he opened his eyes and again looked at the girl. He fell deeply in love with her. Shaykh Barsīsā went back to his place of prayer in the retreat and commence his prayer with the phrase 'God is Great', yet he was now in love with other than God and he did not know what he was saying in her prayers.

{4} During the night, he decided to visit her quarters in order to see her face. He noticed that the girl was praying. He went a bit closer and said, 'O the one who has stolen the heart of Barsīsā, stop praying as you have stolen my heart!' The poor girl was shocked, 'What is going on!' Barsīsā took the girl's hand and pulled her close to him before violating her. He remained with the girl in her living quarters for several days and nights. After some time passed, the girl became pregnant. Here, Satan became excited. Satan said, 'O Shaykh Barsīsā, you have been claiming piety and have been pious for many years. When what you have done becomes apparent the people will begin to mock you and what will they call you? And how will you conceal the pregnancy? What do you want to do to abort this pregnancy. You should do something, anyway!'

{5} Barsīsā pondered, 'I enjoy a respected status. When people learn about my affairs they will vilify me.' Satan said, 'Shaykh, nothing is better than killing this girl, so that your affair remains secret.' Satan's idea made sense to him and he said to himself, 'He is right.' After midnight, Shaykh Barsīsā took a knife and went to the girl. The girl was in bed. He cut off her head. And dug a grave in her living quarters and buried her.

{6} After a few days, her brothers returned along with the king, and went to the living quarters where they had already sent their sister. They did not find her there. They said, 'We will go to the shaykh in order to investigate.' When they asked the shaykh, he replied, 'I was busy worshipping God, when your sister passed away.' As they heard this, they returned, crying and wailing. The accursed Satan found an opportune moment. Satan, embodied in the form of an old man, said [to the two brothers], 'Do you know what he did to your sister?' They replied, 'No we do not know'. Satan said, 'The shaykh had a lustful inclination towards your sister and violated her. She became pregnant and he was scared of the shame. Due to fear of being scandalised he buried her in her living quarters. I wanted to say something but I was scared that he would kill me too.'

{۷} برادران چنین شنیدند در حجره درآمدند و زمین شکافتند. خواهر را خون آلود برآوردند و نزد پادشاه بردند، و واقعه را عرض کردند که «ما به همراهی پادشاه رفته بودیم، و خواهر خود را اعتماد بر شیخ برسیسا کردیم و در نزدیک او گذاشتیم. آخر او در حقّ خواهر ما چنین ظلمی کرده‌است». پادشاه در غضب شد، و در این کار حیران بماند. فرمود شیخ برسیسا را بر دار کشید .

{۸} شیخ را پای دار آوردند.[ه] شیطان همراه آمده بود. در آن وقت شیطان نزدیک برسیسا آمد، و گفت «ای برسیسا، می‌خواهی تو را خلاص سازم؟» برسیسا گفت «آری». شیطان گفت «روی از قبله بگردان، و یک بار مرا سجده کن؛ درزمانْ خلاصی یابی». في الحال، شیخ برسیسا روی از قبله بگردانید و سجده کرد، و جان بداد و بی ایمان رفت.[و]

{۹} پس، ای برادران مؤمن، از همچنین دشمنی غافل نباید بود، و از مکر او ایمن نباید نشست. چون آدمی را دو دشمن است. یکی ظاهر و دیگری باطن. اگر دشمن ظاهر برتو دست یابد، تو را از حیات منقطع گرداند. امّا سعادت با تو باقی ماند و باشد و از تشهد برانگیخته شدی.[ز] امّا، نَعُوذُ بِاللهِ مِنْهَا، اگر دشمن باطن به تو دست یابد تو را از سعادت ایمان محروم گرداند تا ابد به دوزخ مبتلا گرداند.

{۱۰} و دشمن باطن شیطان است که در سیصد و شصت رگ تو می‌گردد. پس پناه به حضرت حقّ تَعَالَی می‌باید گرفت. و «أَعُوذُ بِاللهِ مِنَ الشَّيْطَانِ الرَّجِيمِ» را دَه کرّت[ح] می‌باید خواندن و بر خود می‌باید دمید تا در حفظ و امانِ خداوند تَعَالَی باشی، زیرا که بر پدر تو آدم عليه‌السلام در بهشت چه وسوسه‌ها کرد تا دانهٔ گندم را، که خدای تَعَالَی از وی نهی کرده‌بود، بخورد. و از جوار رحمت حقّ تَعَالَی محروم گشت، و به زندان دنیا آمد. تا امروز فرزندان او در محنت و بلای دنیا مبتلا شدند.[۹]

{۱۱} بیت: مادر و بابای ما را آن حسود، تاج و پیرایه به چالاکی ربود[۱۰]؛ کردشان آنجا برهنه و زار و
خوار، سال‌ها بگریست آدم زارزار

{۱۲} بعداز آن، حرکت دیگر بر فرزندان آدم آورد. اگر خواستِ لطف کریم بر بندگان نبودی، جمله به زیر زمین ناچیز می‌گشتند. اکنون مکر آن بدبخت را بشنو که [با تو] چه انگیخته بود.

[۹] این پاراگراف در برخی نسخ موجود نیست. [۱۰] در فرهنگ لغات و تعبیرات مثنوی از جوهرین، مادر کنایه از «نفس» است.

[د] من مهمان او بودم [ه] جلّادان خونریز او را بر دار بکردند [و] في الحال، روی از قبله بگردانید و شیطان را سجده کرد. چون مقصود شیطان، دشمن قدیم، حاصل شد از میان برفت. آنگاه، جلّادان برسیسا را بر دار کردند. هم جان بداد و هم ایمان به باد داد. [ز] اگر دشمن ظاهر بر تو دست یابد، تو را از حیات دنیا منقطع سازد. امّا سعادت شهادت بر تو باقی بود و میان شهیدان برانگیخته گردی
[ح] دو کرّت؛ دو سه کرّت

{7} The brothers heard this and then went to the place and dug out the grave. They exhumed their sister's blood-soaked body and took her to the king and explained the whole story: 'We were accompanying Your Excellency and we entrusted our sister to Shaykh Barsīsā. However, he did this crime to our sister.' The king became angry and was shocked. He ordered, 'Hang Shaykh Barsīsā!'

{8} The shaykh was brought forward to be hanged. Satan was also there. At that moment, Satan went to the shaykh and said, 'O Barsīsā, would you like me to release you?' Barsīsā said, 'Yes!' Satan said, 'Turn away from the direction of prayer and prostrate once to me. Thus, you will be quickly released.' Upon hearing this, Shaykh Barsīsā turned away from the direction of prayer, prostrated, and died, and left the world as a disbeliever.

{9} So, O faithful brother, do not underestimate such an enemy and do not feel secure from his trickery! There are two enemies for a human being. One is the apparent one, and the other one is internal. If the apparent enemy gets you, he will kill you. However, grace and blessing of martyrdom will not leave you and [...]. However, seek refuge in God from her, if the inner enemy overcomes, she will lead you astray from faith and put you in hell forever.

{10} And the inner enemy is Satan who seeks you in your 360 vessels, so one should seek refuge in God. And the phrase, 'I seek refuge in God against the rejected Satan' should be recited ten times and one should blow around oneself in order to be under the protection of God. Satan tempted your father, Adam (pubh) in paradise to eat wheat, something which was forbidden to him by God. And he fell away from God's mercy. And he came to the prison of the world. And now his children are still affected by the pain and misery of the world.

{11} Poem: That jealous one, stole the crown and embellishment of our father
and mother with agility; made them naked and weak and humiliated,
for which cried Adam for years.

{12} Later on, Satan did another thing against the children of Adam. If it were not for the kindness and graceful will of God, all humans on Earth would be destroyed. Now hear about the trickery of the wretched one and what he did against you.

{۱۳} گاوی که حقّ سُبْحَانَهُ وَتَعَالَی جهان[ط] را بر شاخ او داشته است، [شیطان] نزد او رفت و گفت «ای گاو، چرا بار جهان و جهانیان قبول و بر سر خویش گرفته‌ای؟ جهان را از سر بفشان و در چراگاه به فراغت مشغول شو». گاو را معقول افتاد. خواست تا جهان را از سر خود بفشاند.[11] خدای تَعَالَی، که دانای اسرار نهانیست،[12] به لطف و عنایت خود فرمان کرد و پشه را فرستاد که «به گاو بگو «اگر تو جهان را از سر خود جدا کنی، من چونان نیش زنم که تو هلاک شوی»». چون گاو این سخن شنید از هیبت پشه دو چشمان فرو کرده و برجای خود مانده‌است.[13]

{۱۴} امّا، روایت دگر آنست که چون شیطان گاو را تلقین کرد، فِي الحال جهان را از شاخ خود بگردانید. خدای تَعَالَی پشه را فرمان داد[ی] که «نزد گاو برو که او بی‌فرمانی کرده است و زمین را از سر خود بگردانیده. پس تو او را نیش زن». پشه به حکم و فرمان خدای تَعَالَی نزدیک گاو شد و یک نیش زد در دماغ گاو، که گاو بر جای بغلطید و چند هزارسال از خود خبر نداشت.[14] چو سُبْحَانَهُ وَتَعَالَی گاو را بهوش آورد، گاو برخاست و نظر بالا کرد که جهان چگونه شده باشد. دید که جهان بر قرار خود معلّق مانده‌است.

{۱۵} گاو در حیرت ماند. فرمان حضرت رَبِّ الْعَالَمِينْ دررسید که «ای گاو، تو پنداشتی که قیامِ جهان به تو وابسته است، و اگر قرارِ جهان به تو بودی آسمان را به غیرستون معلّق که داشتی؟[15] امّا چون تو بی‌فرمانی کردی، تا قیام قیامت بارِ همهٔ جهان برسر تو باشد».[16]

{۱۶} الغرض. دشمنی این ملعون[17] بسیار است. در گور نیز با تو خواهد آمد. چون نکیر و منکر هر دو فرشته بگویند «مَن ربّكَ؟» او بنده را به سوی خود اشارت کند. بنده دریابد که این همان بدبخت است که در وقت جان دادن چنگ در ایمان او زده بود. فِي الحال گوید «ربّ من کسی است که مرا می‌میراند و باز زنده خواهد گردانید». آنگاه شیطانْ سیاه‌روی شده، باز گردد.

{۱۷} آورده‌اند که چون فردای قیامت شود فرمان شود که میمنه[18] و میسره[19] راست کنند، و هر طایفه را بیارند. جوق‌جوق[20] یک‌جا ایستاده کنند. میمنه دست راست عرش باشد، و میسره دست چپ عرش باشد. آنگه فرمان شود که «ای فرشتگان، علَم‌های آتشین از دوزخ بیرون آرید و یکی بر دست شیطان دهید و کفّار را زیر علَمِ او بدارید». و علَم آتشینی به دست فرعون دهند. جمله دعوی کنندگان که او را به خدایی پرستیده‌اند

[11] ریختن. [12] نهان است. [13] اشاره دارد به مفهوم «کیوثاء» و «ثور کیوثا» [14] بیهوش شد. [15] اشاره به آیهٔ ۱۰ سورهٔ لقمان دارد: خَلَقَ السَّمَاوَاتِ بِغَيْرِ عَمَدٍ تَرَوْنَهَا. [16] هرچند در متون گوناگون غیر اسلامی و بویژه اسلامی (تفسیری، کلامی، علوم غریبه، و جغرافیا) اشاره به داستان گاو و حمل جهان دیده می‌شود. امّا، گمان من این است که این داستان شاید ریشه در آسیای جنوبی و جنوب شرقی دارد. چنانچه در ادبیات عامیانه برمه، جایی که احشام، فیل‌ها و پرندگان، نقش پررنگی ایفا می‌کنند تعابیر مشابه برای حیوانات به کار می‌رود. [17] اشاره به داستان دشمنی شیطان با خدا و انسان دارد. [18] جبهٔ راست لشگر. به دهخدا مراجعه شود. [19] جبهٔ چپ لشگر. به دهخدا مراجعه شود. [20] دسته و گروه.

[ط] زمین [ی] پند کرده

{13} Satan went to a bull, on which God had placed the planet Earth on top of its horn,[3] and said to the bull, 'O bull, why do you bear the Earth and its inhabitants on your head? Drop the world from you head and enjoy being in the pasture.' This seemed reasonable to the bull and it wanted to drop the Earth from its head. God, who knows all secrets, commanded with kindness and grace, that a mosquito be sent to the bull, "saying, 'If you drop the Earth from your head, I will kill you with my sting.'" When the bull heard this, it was scared of the mosquito and remained still.

{14} However, another story is that when Satan tempted the bull, the bull then dropped the world from its horn. God commanded that the mosquito go to the disobedient bull and sting it. On the basis of God's decree, the mosquito went to the bull and stung the bull's nose, by which the bull fell down unconscious for several thousand years. When God awoke the bull, it stood and looked up [at its horn] to see what had happened to the Earth. The bull noticed that the Earth remained stable in space.

{15} The bull was surprised. The command of the Lord of the Worlds arrived, 'O bull, did you think that the maintenance of the Earth was dependent upon you? And if you were going to be the stabiliser of the world, why were the heavens founded without pillars? But as you disobeyed, you will carry the whole weight of the world until the Resurrection Day.

{16} Return to the story. The enmity of the accursed one is serious and he will even be with you in the grave. Once Nakīr and Munkar, both angels, say, 'Who is your Lord?' Satan prompts the servant himself. The servant would realise that this is exactly the same miserable one who also attacked his faith at the moment of death. The servant will say, 'My Lord is the one who will make me die and bring me back.' Then Satan will become embarrassed and recede.

{17} It is reported that after the Day of Judgement, a command will be given for the right-hand and left-hand throngs to be lined up. And every clan will be lined up there, group by group. The right-hand army will be to the right of the Throne and the left-hand army will be to the left of the Throne. Then a command will be given: 'O angels, bring blazing standards from hell, and pass one of them to Satan's hand and put all infidels under his standard. And give another blazing standard to Pharaoh. All those who worshipped him and considered him God will be under his standard. And

[3] Referring to Kuyūthā, a fictional bull whose names were outlined in Asian and Islamic classical texts. The planet Earth on the bull's horn or a huge fish or whale may be a reference to the *ḥadīth al-ḥūt* or partially to the 'Behemoth' of the Book of Job. For more, see Sayyid Sulaymān Mūsawī and Muḥammad Ibrāhīm Rawshan Ḍamīr, 'Tahlil-i Sanadi wa Muhtawā' ī-yi "Ḥadīth-i Ḥūt" ba Tawajjuh bih pishīna Tārīkhī ān', *Hadith Pazhūhī* 12/23 (2020), 119–136. One may also wonder whether the whole story of this fictional bull was originally taken from some South and South-East Asian sources.

زیر علَم او باشند. و علَم دیگر به دست قابیل بدهند. جملهٔ خونیان را در زیر علَم او حاضر گردانند. و علَم دگر بر دست ابوجهل دهند. جملهٔ شراب‌خواران زیر علَم او حاضر گردند. علَم دیگر بر دست شیخ برسیسا دهند. جملهٔ زناکنندگان بر علَم او باشند. هر گروهی را جمع کنند در میسره.

{۱۸} آنگاه فرمان شود که «میمنه را راست سازید و علَم‌ها از بهشت بیرون آرید. و علَم‌های نور از بهشت بیرون آرید». اوّل علَم صِدْق بر دست أَمیر المُؤمِنین ابابکر صدّیق دهند. جملهٔ صدّیقان زیر علَم او باشند. و علَم عدل بر دست أَمیر المُؤمِنین عُمَر خطّاب دهند. جملهٔ عادلان زیر علَم او باشند. و علَم شرم و حیاء بر دست أَمیر المُؤمِنین عثمان دهند. جملهٔ حیاء کنندگان[ک] در زیر علَم او باشند. و علَم سخاوت و شجاعت و مروّت[۲۱] بر دست أَمیر المُؤمِنین علی بن ابی طالب کَرَّمَ اللهُ وَجْهَه دهند. چون سخیان و شجاعان و صاحب‌مروّتان در زیر علَم او باشند. و علَم مظلومان بر دست أَمیر المُؤمِنین حسن دهند. جملهٔ مظلومان زیر علَم او باشند. و علَم شهادت بر دست أَمیر المُؤمِنین حسین دهند.[۲۲] جملهٔ شهیدان در زیر علَم او باشند. همچنان هریک گروهی را به گروهی دیگر بپیوندند.

{۱۹} گنه‌کاران استاده مانند؛ [خطاب به آن‌ها] گویند «هرکس به گروهی پیوسته. شما چرا بی‌گروه مانده‌اید؟» گویند «إِلٰهِيّ، ما تقصیر کنندگانیم. ازگناه خود فرو مانده‌ایم». فرمان شود که «شما به گروه رحمت ما درآیید». آنگه اللّٰه تَعَالَی رحمت، بر راستای عرش بنگرد و بگوید که «هؤلاء إِلَى الْجَنَّةِ وَلَا أُبَالِي، وهؤلاء إِلَى النَّارِ وَلَا أُبَالِي،[۲۳] یعنی آنچه بر دست راست عرش است در بهشت فرستیم و از کسی باک نداریم، و آنچه بر دست چپ عرش‌اند به دوزخ فرستیم و از کسی باک نداریم».

{۲۰} و فرمان شود که «فرزندان شیطان را جمع کنید». فرمان شود که «این گنه‌کاران را بر پل صراط برید و بر بَدلِ هریک گناه‌کاری یکی شیاطین را در دوزخ اندازید، و بندگان گنه‌کار ما را سلامت بر پل صراط بگذرانید و در بهشت برید». شیطان ملعون، که دشمن قدیم است، با روی سیاه و حال تباه نومید شود و در دوزخ برود.

{۲۱} إِلٰهِيّ، به حرمت کرم یُمنی[۲۴] خویش که من بیچاره را و کاتب این قصّه را با جمیع مؤمنان از شرّ شیطان نگه داری. بِمِنَّة وَكَرَمه.

[۲۱] در برخی نسخ صفت شجاعت و مروّت ذکر نمی‌شود، بلکه تنها سخاوت مطرح می‌شود. [۲۲] در برخی نسخ علَم شهادت را بر دست أَمیر المُؤمِنین حمزه رضی الله عنه می‌دهند. [۲۳] اشاره دارد به حدیثی که در مشکوة المصابیح به چشم می‌خورد: «فَقَالَ لِلَّذِي فِي يَمِينِهِ إِلَى الْجَنَّةِ وَلَا أُبَالِي وَقَالَ لِلَّذي فِي كَفه الْيُسْرَى إِلَى النَّارِ وَلَا أُبَالِي» [۲۴] «سمت راست»: اشاره به «فرستادن افراد در\از سمت راست به بهشت» دارد.

[ک] اهل حیاء

another standard will be given to the hand of Cain. All the bloodthirsty will be under his standard. And another standard will be given to Abū Jahl. All wine drinkers will be under his standard. Another standard will be given to Barsīsā. All adulterers will be under his standard. All these groups will be lined up on the left.'

{18} Then a command will be given 'to line up the right-hand throng and bring luminous standards from paradise.' The standard of integrity will be given to the Commander of Believers Abū Bakr Ṣiddīq. All righteous people will be under his standard. And the standard of justice will be given to the Commander of Believers ʿUmar Khaṭṭāb. All the just will be under his standard. And the standard of modesty will be given to the Commander of Believers ʿUthmān. All modest people will be under his standard. And the standard of generosity, courage, and chivalry will be given to the Commander of Believers ʿAlī b. Abī Ṭālib, may God ennoble his countenance. All the generous, courageous, and chivalrous will be under his standard. And the standard of the oppressed will be given to the Commander of Believers Ḥasan. All oppressed people will be under his standard. The standard of martyrdom will be given to the Commander of Believers Ḥusayn. All martyrs will be under his standard. All groups will be accordingly gathered.

{19} The sinful will still remain. It will be said, 'Everyone joins a particular group. Why did you remain ungrouped?' They will say, 'O God, we are those who have been neglected and are sinner. We have been left behind due to our sin.' A command will be given, 'You will come into the group of Our mercy.' Then the merciful God looked upon the right-hand throng and said, 'This group to paradise and I do not care, and this group to hell and I do not care', meaning that those who on the right side of the Throne will be sent to paradise and God fears nobody, and those who are on the left side of the Throne will be sent to hell and God is afraid of nobody.'

{20} [In so doing] another command will be given, 'Gather the children of Satan.' And it will be commanded, 'Move these [abovesaid] sinners to the Ṣirāṭ bridge. As an exchange, throw off a devil instead of each of these sinners, ensure our sinful servants cross safely over the Ṣirāṭ bridge, and take them to paradise.' The accursed Satan, who is an eternal enemy, will be disappointed and ashamed and he will go to hell.

{21} *O God, protect me, a humble pauper, and the scribe of this story, and all believers from Satan's evil by the grace of Your right-hand. By Your unmerited favour and kindness. [Amen.]*

در فضیلتِ ماه مبارک رمضان

{۱} حضرت محمّد مصطفی ﷺ فرمودند که «روزه مر حضرت خدای تَعَالَی است و اجر روزه داران حق سُبْحَانَهُ وَتَعَالَى خود می‌دهد». و پروردگار جهان و جهانیان روزه را به خود نسبت می‌کند و او می‌داند که اجر آن خواهد داد؛ قال الله تَعَالَی «الصِيَام لِي وَأَنا أجزي بِه».[1] خدای تَعَالَی را فرشته‌ای است که به عدد ستارگان آسمان چشم‌ها دارد. فرمان شود این فرشته را که «آنچه از ابتدای عالم تا انتهای عالم آفریده‌ایم در شمار بیار». درزمانْ در شمار بیارد و بگوید که چه مقدار است. فرمان شود که «ثواب روزه داران ماه رمضان را هم در شمار بیار». چند هزارسال آن فرشته در شمار باشد نتْواند که ثواب یک روزه‌دار شمار آرد؛ عاجز شود. آنگه فرشته گوید «اجر روزه‌دارْ تو را به کرم خود اضافت کرده‌ای. من در شمار نمی‌توانم آورد».

{۲} دیگر. چون ماه رمضان شود فرمان شود که «ای جبرئیل، در بهشت درا[2] و یک قدح آب طهور بردار. در روضهٔ رسول برو و بگو «ای محمّد، ماه رمضان رسیده‌است. تو هم موافق امّت خود آب طهور بخور»». پیغمبر عَلَیْه وَسَلَّم گوید «ای أخی جبرئیل، به غیر امّت خود شربت چگونه خورم که هنوز جهان باقیست؟» فرمان شود که «تو بخور تا سعادت آب طهور و سعادت پس خوردهٔ تو نصیب امّت تو گردد». رسول پاره بخورد، و قدح بر دست مهتر جبرئیل داد و گفت «ای برادر، چگونه بی امّت این شربت مرا گوارا گردد؟» آنگه فرمان شود «ای جبرئیل، آنچه در قدحست در کوزه‌های روزه‌داران انداز تا ثواب آب طهور، که پس خوردهٔ حضرت محمّد مصطفی است، روزی ایشان شود. هرکه از این آب طهور خورَد آتش دوزخ بر وی حرام گردد».

{۳} چون ماه رمضان المبارك می‌رسد، فرمان می‌شود که «ای فرشتگان، و ای حوران! درهای بهشت باز کنید» و مالک دوزخ را فرمان شود که «درهای دوزخ را بربندید». تا سی روز هفت‌دربسته گردد؛ چون

[1] اشاره دارد به حدیثی شناخته شده که در بسیاری از کتب دینی از جمله سنن النسائی دیده می‌شود «قَالَ اللَّهُ عَزَّوَجَلَّ كُلُّ عَمَلِ ابْنِ آدَمَ لَهُ إِلاَّ الصِّيَامَ هُوَ لِي وَأَنَا أَجْزِي بِهِ وَالَّذِي نَفْسُ مُحَمَّدٍ بِيَدِهِ لَخِلْفَةُ فَمِ الصَّائِمِ أَطْيَبُ عِنْدَ اللَّهِ مِنْ رِيحِ الْمِسْكِ»

[2] درآی.

CHAPTER 29

On the virtue of the holy month of Ramadan

{1} Prophet Muḥammad (pbuh) said, 'Fasting is for God and the reward of the fasters will be given by God.' And the God of the world and beings ascribes fasting to Himself, and He knows that it will result in blessings. God said, 'Fast for Me and I will reward it.' God has an angel who has eyes as many as the stars of the sky. This angel is ordered to count whatever is created from the beginning until the end of the universe. The angel counts quickly and says the particular number. A command is given [to the angel] to also count the rewards of the fasters of Ramadan. The angel was busy counting for several years, however, could not count the rewards for one particular faster. The angel stopped. Then the angel addressed God and said, 'You have, Yourself, allocated the rewards of your faster on the basis of your kindness. I cannot calculate them.'

{2} Another story. When the month of Ramadan arrives, a divine command is made, 'O Gabriel, go to paradise and take a bowl of pure water. Then go to the place of the Messenger and say, "O Muḥammad, the month of Ramadan has begun. May you, along with your community, drink pure water."' The Prophet (pbuh) will say, 'O brother Gabriel, how can I drink without my own community as the world is still turning?' It will be proclaimed, 'Drink, until the grace of the pure water as well as the grace of that left over reaches your community.' The Messenger drank a little and passed the bowl back to Gabriel, saying, 'O brother, how can this drink be pleasant to me without my community?' Then a command was given, 'O Gabriel, whatever is left over in the bowl, pour it into the pitchers of the fasters so the blessing of the pure water, which remains from the Prophet Muḥammad, will be shared with them. Whoever drinks from this pure water, hellfire will be prohibited to them.'

{3} When the holy month of Ramadan arrives, a command is made, 'O angels and O cherubs, open the gates of heaven!' The guardian of hell is ordered to close hell's

هشت درِ بهشت گشاده گردد. و هرروز در هر دری صد هزار عاصی جافی که نام ایشان در دوزخ نبشسته اند دَرآد،[۳] و از آتش دوزخ نجات یابد. و در روز عید[۴] آنچه در تمام ماه از آتش خلاص یافته‌اند، مقدار دگر خلاص شود. دگر فرمان شود «ای جبرئیل، ندا بر گورستان‌ها رسان «خوشی و خرّمی بر[۵] شما را باد که ماه مبارک رمضان رسید. در هیچ گور عذاب نشود و قبرها پر نور گردد».

{۴} الغرض. چون قیامت قایم شود، حقّ تَعَالَی ماه رمضان را به صورت یوسف علیه السلام[الف] به زیر عرش حاضر گرداند و خدای تَعَالَی را سجده کند. فرمان شود «ای ماه رمضان، امروز وقت سجده نیست. وقت کرم و اخلاص است. بخواه از حضرت ما هرچه می‌خواهی». ماه رمضان بگوید «یا ربّ، تو می‌بینی که امّت محمّد در این وقت برهنه خواسته‌اند. فرمان ده تا تن ایشان را بپوشند». فرمان شود «ای فرشتگان، تن‌های ایشان را بپوشانید». هریکی هفتاد هزار حلّه بپوشانند.

{۵} باز، ماه مبارک گوید «سرهای ایشان برهنه است». فرمان شود «ای فرشتگان رفته از بهشت هفتاد هزار تاج بیارند و بر سر امّتان محمّد صلی الله علیه و سلم نهند». باز ماه رمضان التماس می‌کند که «یا ربّ، ایشان پیاده‌اند. تاج با مَرکَب خوب نماید». فرمان شود که «ای فرشتگان، به نام هریکی هفتادهزار بُراق از بهشت بیرون آرید». باز ماه مبارک گوید «یا ربّ، مؤمنان از گور گرسنه و تشنه برخاسته‌اند. تو به کرم خویش ایشان را سیراب و سیر طعام گردان». فرمان شود که «ای فرشتگان، گاوی که جهان را بر او نگاه می‌داشتیم در هفتم زمین است بیارند.[۶] و او را بریان کنند و پیش هریک هفتاد خوان بنهند. تا امّتان هرچه خواهند بخورند».

{۶} باز ماه گوید «یا ربّ، یک التماس دیگر دارم». فرمان شود «بگو». گوید «یا ربّ، آنچه در حقّ محمّدیان از تو خواستم به کرم اجابت فرمودی. فرمان بده تا به سوی بهشت ره‌بَری ایشان کنم». فرمان شود که «تو پیش رو تا جملهٔ روزه‌داران در عقب تو روند، و [آنها را] به دارالسلام بهشت رسان. آنگه فرمان شود «هر مؤمنی را هفتاد هزار فرشته از دست راست و هفتاد هزار از دست چپ و هفتاد هزار در عقب بانگ طرقو در پیش گیرند».

{۷} چون بدین دولت و مرتبه امّت خاتم المرسلین در عرصات پیدا شوند، صد وبیست وچهار هزار پیغمبر در مرتبهٔ محمّدیان حیران بمانند و گویند «به کدام عمل ایشان را چنین نواخته‌اند؟» و فرشتگان گویند «روزه‌داران ماهِ رمضان امّت محمّداند؛ چنین عنایت از پروردگار خود یافته‌اند. تأسّف خورند و گویند کاشکی[۷] ما هم از امّت محمّد می بودیم».[۸]

[۳] درآید. [۴] عید فطر. [۵] استفاده از «بر» در این مورد نیاز نیست.
[۶] برای اطّلاعات بیشتر در مورد این گاو به داستان «برسیسا» در همین مجموعه مراجعه شود.
[۷] ایکاش. [۸] این عبارت در برخی نسخ نیست.

[الف] به صورت خوب

gates; its seven gates will be closed for thirty days, while the eight gates of paradise will be open. Every day, the names of a hundred thousand sinners, whose names are recorded in hell, will be erased and saved from the hellish fire. And to the extent that people are saved from hell during the month of Ramadan, the same number will be released on the day of Eid[1]. Also, another command is given, 'O Gabriel, announce at the graveyards, "Good tidings! The month of Ramadan has arrived. The torment in the graves will stop and tombs will be illuminated."'

{4} Continue the story. When the Day of Judgement begins, the Ramadan moon (or: crescent) will appear on the Throne in the form of Joseph[2] and will prostrate before God. A command will be given, 'O month of Ramadan, today is not the time for prostration. Today is the time of kindness and loyalty. Ask from Our presence, whatever you want.' The month of Ramadan will say, 'O Lord, You see that the community of Muḥammad has now risen naked. Give an order to cover their bodies.' A command will be given, 'O angels, cover their bodies.' Every angel will cover them with seventy thousand garments.

{5} Then the holy month will say, 'Their heads are bare.' Another divine command will be given, 'O angels, go and bring seventy thousand crowns from paradise and put them on Muḥammad's community.' Then, the month of Ramadan will again request, 'O Lord, they are on foot. Their having crowns should be matched by them having something to ride.' A command arrives, 'O angels, bring out seventy thousand Burāqs for each of them from paradise.' Again, the month of Ramadan will say, 'O Lord, the believers have risen from the grave while being hungry and thirsty. By Your kindness and grace, satiate them with water and food.' A command will be given, 'O angels, bring the bull, on whose horn we have set the world and which is in the seventh Earth. Grill it and serve it on seventy tables so the community may eat whatever it desires.'

{6} Then the month of Ramadan will say, 'O Lord, I have another request.' God will say, 'Ask.' [The month of Ramadan] will say, 'O Lord, You kindly provided what I have already demanded from you for the followers of Muḥammad. Allow me to lead them towards paradise.' A divine command will be given, 'You may move ahead until all fasters have come after you and have reached in paradise, the Abode of Peace.' Then another command will be given, 'Surround every believer with seventy thousand angels on the right-hand side, seventy thousand on the left, and seventy thousand to the rear saying, "Make way!"'

{7} When the community of the Last Prophet arrive at the Resurrection Plain in a blessed state of grace, the one hundred and twenty-four thousand prophets will be surprised about the status of Muḥammad's followers and will ask, 'Due to which

[1] i.e., Eid al-Fitr [2] i.e., with a beautiful face

{۸} الغرض. چون بندگان خدای تَعَالَی با ماه رمضان در بهشت رسند گویند «سَلامٌ عَلَیْکُمْ طِبْتُمْ فَادْخُلُوها خالِدِين،[۹] یعنی سلامتی ما بر شما که به مقام جاوید بهشت رسیدید». چون تمام مؤمنان در بهشت درآیند ماه مبارک رمضان گوید «الوِداع الوِداع. باز می‌گردم و شما را اکنون به من حاجتی نماند و به مقصود ابد رسیدید».

{۹} پس، ای برادران، از این نوع دولت یزدانی چرا محروم بمانی؟ باید که درحقّ این ماه مبارک رمضان آنچه شرطست نیکو به‌جا آری. چنانچه گفته‌اند «روزه در چشم و زبان و گوش و دست و پای است»، یعنی چیزی را که نباید دید نبینی، و چیزی را که نباید گفت نگوئی، چیزی را که نباید شنید نشنوی، و چیزی را که نباید گرفت نگیری، و جایی که نباید رفت نروی. غرض که در هر عضوی روزه است. بسیار کسی باشند که روزه دارند و گرسنگی خورند، و از ثواب روزه محروم‌اند.

{۱۰} حکایت. أَمیر المُؤمِنین امام المتّقین علي بن أبي طالب رَضِيَ اللهُ عَنْهُ بعداز وفات سیّد عالم، صدر و بدر اولاد آدم، محمّد مصطفی ﷺ نماز عید گزارده به خانه آمد، و در راه بیهوش شد. خبر به خاتون قیامت بی‌بی فاطمهٔ زهرا آوردند. چون حضرت رسالت‌پناهی در حیات خود گفته بود که «ای فرزندِ جگرگوش،[۱۰] فاطمه! بعداز وفات من چون علی بیهوش شود باید که دستار[۱۱] من بر سر علی بنهند تا بهوش آید». فاطمه رَضِيَ اللهُ عَنْهَا عمامه حضرت را برداشت و در هودج نشست، و خود را نزد أَمیر المُؤمِنین علی رساند. و عمامه حضرت را بر سر ایشان نهاد. درزمانْ بهوش آمدند. یاران پرسیدند که «سبب بیهوشی چه بود؟» فرمودند که «چون از نماز عید بازگشتم در خاطرم گذشته که «ای علی! سی روزه داشتی هیچ می‌دانی که قبول گردند یا نه؟» از هیبت آن بیهوش شدم».

ای برادر، پاکان علم[۱۲] چنین بودند. من و تو کجائیم؟ نظر بر افعال خود باید کرد تا حال چگونه[۱۳] کرد.

{۱۱} حکایت دیگرِ ماه مبارک رمضان. که حضرت رسالت پناهی با أَمیر المُؤمِنین عثمان گفت که «به‌جهت افطار به خانهٔ تو می‌آیم». بسیار خوشحال و خرّم گشت، و با خود گفت «ای عثمان، هیچ می‌دانی قدمِ که[۱۴] به خانهٔ تو می‌آید؟ یعنی عرش به گَردِ نعلین او مشرّف گشت. و تو را هم شکرانهٔ آن قدم باید گردد». در عقب حضرت خواجهٔ عالم برفت و گام‌های ایشان را بشمرد. و از درِ[۱۵] مسجد حضرت تا در خانهٔ خود سیصدوشصت گام شد. فرمود که «سیصد و شصت برده آورند». فرمودند که «ای أَمیر المُؤمِنین عثمان، اینها را از بهر چه آورده‌ای؟» گفت «ای نبي الله، شکرانهٔ قدم پاک تو در خانهٔ چاکرِ خود که بهر گامِ شما یک برده آزاد کنم. اکنون، این سیصدوشصت بنده بر بَدَلِ سیصدوشصت قدم مبارک شما از مُلک خود آزاد کردم». بعداز آن، انواع طعام خوب پیش آوردند و به یاران خود تناول فرموده‌اند. چون از طعام فارغ شدند دعا کرده‌اند. و یاران بازگشتند.

[۹] آیهٔ ۷۳ سورهٔ زمر. [۱۰] جگرگوشه. [۱۱] عمامه. [۱۲] اذکیاء. [۱۳] چنین. [۱۴] چه‌کسی. [۱۵] درب.

of their deeds have they been rewarded like this?' The angels will say, 'These are the people from the community of Muḥammad who kept the fast of Ramadan, and for which they have received such favour from God.' They said with sorrow, 'We wish we were from Muḥammad's community.'

{8} Returning to the story. When the servants of God arrive in paradise, it will be said to them, 'Peace be upon you! You have done well, so come in, to stay forever' (Q. 39:73), meaning that peace be upon you as you have reached an immortal status. When all believers had arrived in paradise safely, the holy month of Ramadan said, 'Farewell! I will return but you do not now need me; you have reached the final goal.'

{9} O brothers, do not miss this divine blessing. You should carry out whatever has to be done in this month. It has been said, 'Fasting is performed by the eye, tongue, ear, hand, and foot', meaning, 'Do not see the thing which should not be seen; do not say the thing which should not be said; do not hear the thing which should not be heard; do not touch the thing which should not be touched, and do not go where you should not go.' This point is that every single limb fasts; there are many people who fast and starve, while not being given the reward of fasting.

{10} Another story. The Commander of Believers ʿAlī (pbuh), the Imam of pious believers, performed the Eid prayer after the death of the Master of the world and of the chidren of Adam, Prophet Muḥammad (pbuh). He fainted while returning home. Fāṭima Zahrā, the Lady of the Day of Judgement informed about this issue. On this subject, the Prophet told her during his life that 'O my darling, Fāṭima! Whenever ʿAlī fainted while I am not alive, place my turban on his head in order to recover his consciousness'. Fāṭima took the Prophet's turban and sat in her howdah, and moved towards ʿAlī. Then she put the turban on ʿAlī's head so he woke up promptly. The Companions asked 'what was the reason of unconsciousness?' ʿAlī replied 'while returning home after the Eid prayer, I pondered "O ʿAlī! You already fasted for thirty-days. Are you sure whether they will be accepted!" I was scared of my own thought and lost consciousness.' O brother! This is the manner of intelligent believers. Where are we and what do we do? We should review our deeds in order to act accordingly.

{11} This is another story about the holy month of Ramadan in which the Prophet (pbuh) spoke with ʿUthmān, saying, 'I will come to your house to break fast.' He was so happy and excited and pondered, 'O ʿUthmān! Are you aware of whom is coming to your house? The one for whom the Throne has been blessed with the dust of his sandals. And you will also be blessed with his step.' He went after the Master of the World[3] to count his steps; from the doorway of the Prophet's mosque to his house was 360 steps. ʿUthmān ordered for 360 slaves to be brought. The Prophet said, 'O

[3] i.e., the Prophet

{۱۲} در خاطر أَمیر المُؤمِنین علی رَضِیَ اللهُ عَنهُ گذشت که «یک داماد توئی و یک داماد عثمان؛ چندین خدمت و تملّق کرد، و در خانهٔ تو نان جوین از برای فرزندان نیست، و من چگونه رسول علیه السلام را ضیافت بکنم؟» درین تفکّر به خانه آمد.

{۱۳} نظر خاتون قیامت برایشان افتاد. پرسید که «چه می‌شود که تو را نگران می‌بینم؟» امیر هیچ نگفت. فاطمه گفت «جان من فدای تو باد، چرا سخن نمی‌گویی؟» امیر با زن نگفت. فاطمه گفت «مگر از برای معاش ما نگرانی؟ هیچ غم مخور که فقرُ فخرِ بابایِ منست». فاطمه را طاقت نماند. گفت «به آن خدای تَعَالَی که می‌فرماید «اگر به جز ذات من سجده بر غیری روا بودی، می‌فرمودم زنان را تا پیش شوهران خود سجده می‌کردند» اکنون یا علی بگو چه چیز تو را در غم آورده؟» امیر گفت «یا فاطمه، پیغمبر صَلَّى اللهُ عَلَيهِ وَسَلَّم را عثمان به افطار به خانهٔ خود بُرد و بَدلِ هر گامِ حضرت برده آزاد کرد، و انواع نعمت پَسِ[۱۶] سیّد المرسلین و یاران کشید. در خاطرم گذشت «یک داماد آنست و یک داماد منم». او چندین ضیافت کند و در خانهٔ من نان جوین هم نباشد که فرزندان من سیر خورند».

{۱۴} فاطمه رَضِیَ اللهُ عَنهَا گفت «آه! یا علی، می‌خواهی دولت فقر مرا ظاهر گردانی؟ شما هم پیغمبر را با دوچندان یاران که در خانهٔ عثمان رَضِیَ اللهُ عَنهُ رفته بودند بیار تا افطار کنند». امیر گفت «در خانه هیچ چیز نیست». فاطمه گفت «یا علی، اگر أَمیر المُؤمِنین عثمان پیغمبر را با قوَّتِ مال خود طلبیده، من به قوَّتِ آفریدگار خود می‌طلبم». امیر گفت «از کرم آفریدگار عجب نیست». فاطمه با امیر گفت «برو پیغمبر را با یاران خبر کن».

{۱۵} حضرت امیر نزد صدر و بدر عالم رفت، و گفت «یا رسول الله، آن‌قدر یاران که در خانهٔ برادرم عثمان بود و چندانِ[۱۷] او امروز از بهر افطار به خانهٔ من بیارید». سیّد عالم فرمود «یا علی! احوال خانهٔ تو را نیکو می‌دانم. از کجا این‌قدر خَلق را مهمانی کنی؟» گفت «یا رسول الله، دختر شما به‌جهت افطار می‌طلبد». گفت «یا علی، غم جانان من بر دلم بازمی‌کنی». آنگه خواجهٔ عالم فرمود «یا بلال، صحابهٔ مرا خبر کن تا از بهر افطار بیایند». چون وقت افطار نزدیک رسید. فاطمه امیر را گفته بود «حضرت را با یاران بیار، معه[۱۸] فرزند و هرکسی بوده باشد». حضرت سیّد عالم فرمود «یا علی، پیش روان‌شو به خانه که ما هم آمدیم».

[۱۶] پیش. [۱۷] آن اندازه؛ همان اندازه بیشتر. [۱۸] به همراه ایشان.

Commander of Believers ʿUthmān, why did you bring them here?' He said, 'O Prophet of God, I will release a slave in exchange for every single step of yours, due to the grace of your purified steps coming to the house of this humble minion. These 360 slaves will be released from my property in exchange for your 360 sacred steps.' Later on, they were offered various types of food and ate alongside the Companions. When they had finished, they began to pray. And the Companions returned.

{12} The Commander of Believers ʿAlī, said to himself, 'One [of Muḥammad's] son-in-law is you, and the other son-in-law is ʿUthmān. He has been excessively served and praised, while there is not even oat bread for your children at home. How can I host the Messenger of God?' He went home while thinking about this.

{13} The Lady of the Day of Judgement[4] saw him, and asked, 'What has happened that I see you so worried?' The Commander[5] did not say anything. Fāṭima said, 'O the one for whom I sacrifice my soul, why don't you speak?' The Commander still did not speak to his wife. Fāṭima said, 'Are you worried about our livelihood? Do not worry as poverty is the pride of my dad.' Fāṭima could not wait anymore. She said, 'By the One God, who says, "If it were not that prostration was only for Me, I would have ordered all women to prostrate before their husbands", O ʿAlī tell me now what has made you sad?' The Commander said, 'O Fāṭima, ʿUthmān took the Prophet (pbuh) to break fast in his house, released slaves in exchange for every single step of the Prophet, and served the Prophet and the Companions with various foods. What a difference, I thought, that "one of his son-in-laws is him[6] and the other one is me!" He hosted like this, while I do not even have oat bread at home with which my children can be fed.'

{14} Fāṭima (pbuh) said, 'Ah! O ʿAlī, would you like to observe the grace of my poverty? Invite the Prophet and double the number of Companions who visited ʿUthmān's house to break their fast.' The Commander said, 'There is nothing at home.' Fāṭima said, 'O ʿAlī, if the Commander of Believers ʿUthmān has hosted the Prophet as the result of his wealth, I would then invite him as the result of my devotion to God.' The Commander said, 'There is no question of God's kindness.' Fāṭima said to the Commander, 'Go and let the Prophet and his Companions know about our intention.'

{15} The Commander went to the Prophet and said, 'O Messenger of God, bring whoever was in the house of my brother, ʿUthmān, and even more to my house for breaking the fast.' The Master of the Worlds asked, 'I am fully aware of your living conditions. How do you want to host such a number of people?' He replied, 'O Messenger of God, your daughter has decided this for the sake of breaking the fast.' The Prophet said, 'O ʿAlī, are you telling me about the concerns of my dearest?' Then the Master of the Worlds said, 'O Bilal, inform my Companions to come for breaking

[4] i.e., Fāṭima [5] i.e., ʿAlī [6] i.e., ʿUthmān

{۱۶} چون امیر درآمد به خانه دید حضرت فاطمه درون حُجره سر سجده نهاده، به درگاه حقّ سُبْحَانَهُ وَتَعَالَى التماس می‌کرد و می‌گفت «إِلٰهِيْ، عثمانْ پیغمبرِ تو را به قوّتِ جاه و مال خود طلبیده. من به اعتماد عظمت جاه و کرم تو پیغمبر تو را از برای افطار طلبیدم. اکنون تو مرا از روی علی و پدر شرمنده مکن». امیر بر حُجره آمد، و پیش حضرت فاطمه قرار گرفت. امیر گفت سر بردار از سجده. چون سر برداشت خوانِ[۱۹] غیب را پیش خود دید.

{۱۷} گفت «یا علی، حضرت تشریف آوردند؟» فرمود «آری». گفت «آبْ بَر تا دست بشویند». چون دست شستند حضرت امیر در حُجره درآمد تا خوان را بیرون آرد. با فاطمه گفت «یارانْ بسیارْ و جوانْ!»[۲۰] فاطمه گفت «یا علی، مگر شما در فلان جنگ همراه رسول نبودید که در بیابان آب پیدا نبود، و تمام لشگر از تشنگی هلاک گشته بودند. یاران پیش حضرت سیّد عالم آمدند که «از تشنگی همهٔ مایان[۲۱] هلاک خواهیم گشت». حضرت رسالت پناهی فرمودند که «آب پیدا کرده، بیارید». تفحّص بسیار کرده در مطهّره[۲۲] قدری آب یافتند. آن‌را در کاسه کردند و پیش حضرت آوردند. ایشان هر پنج انگشت مبارک خود را در آن کاسه کردند. از هر انگشت چشمه‌ای آب روان شد و همه‌کس سیراب شدند و شتران نیز سیراب شدند. یاعلی تو هم این خوان را پیش بابای من ببر و بگویید «سیّدا، فاطمهٔ تو می‌گوید «دست مبارک خود درین خوان کنید، و بگویید که آنقدر وسیع شود که همه‌کس طعام آن جهان به فراغت بخورد»»».

{۱۸} حضرت امیر التماس فاطمه را گفت. حضرت سیّد عالم دست در خوان زد، و گفت «ای خوان، چنان وسیع شو که همهٔ یاران هستند و نعمت آن جهان به مراد بخورند». خوان چنان وسیع شد، به قدرت حقّ سُبْحَانَهُ وَتَعَالَى، که همهٔ یاران و فرزندان و هرکسی بود به فراغت طعام خوردند. و طعام بسیار زیاده آمد که به فقرا و مساکین دادند.

{۱۹} چون از طعام خوردن فارغ شدند، مهتر جبرئیل صَلَوَاتُ اللّٰهِ عَلَيْه بیامد و دربان شد. استاده بود که نظر مبارک حضرت خواجهٔ عالم بر بندهٔ رَبِّ الْعَالَمِيْن افتاد. گفت «ای برادر جبرئیل، بهر چه آمده‌ای؟» گفت «ای پیغمبر خدای، منِ چاکرْ چاکرِ نبوّت توأم و مژده به‌جهت فاطمه و علی و امّتان گنه‌کار تو آورده‌ام تا دل مبارک شما را شاد گردانم. اکنون، حق سُبْحَانَهُ وَتَعَالَى می‌فرماید که «اگر عثمان بعد هر گامِ شما برده آزاد گردانید ما هم بدل هر گامی، که از مسجد تا اینجا سی‌صد و چند گام باشد، هفتادهزار عاصیِ جافی که نام ایشان در دوزخ، از بهرعقوبت، نوشته‌اند از آتش دوزخ آزاده گردانیم».

[۱۹] سفره، طعام. [۲۰] اشاره به اشتها و هیجان زیاد برای خوردن طعام دارد.

[۲۱] همه، ما؛ همچنین می‌تواند برگرفته از «معیان» به معنای «آب و کاه جوینده قوم را [...]. آنکه آب و کاه برای قوم می‌جوید» به کار رود. به دهخدا مراجعه شود. [۲۲] ظرف آبی که با آن وضو سازند. به دهخدا مراجعه شود.

the fast, when its time comes.' Fāṭima had asked ʿAlī 'to bring the Prophet along with his Companions, their children, and whoever else.' The Master of the Worlds said, 'O ʿAlī, you go home, and we will come after you!'

{16} When the Commander entered the house, he noticed that Fāṭima was prostrated in her room. She was beseeching God, 'O God, ʿUthmān had invited Your prophet on the basis of his wealth. In this vein, I invited Your prophet to break fast just because of the greatness of Your power and kindness. Do not embarrass me before ʿAlī and my father.' The Commander entered the chamber and sat next to Fāṭima. He said, 'Lift up your head from prostration.' When she lifted her head, she noticed a table spread coming from the Unseen.

{17} She said, 'O ʿAlī, did the Prophet come?' ʿAlī said, 'Yes.' Fāṭima said, 'Take water for them in order to wash their hands.' When they had washed their hands, the Commander returned to the room in order to take the spread of food. He told Fāṭima, 'There are many Companions and they are all young.'[7] Fāṭima said, 'O ʿAlī, did you not go along with the Prophet in that battle during which the whole army were thirsty and there was no water to be found in the desert? The Companions went to the Master of the Worlds, telling him, "We are about to die of thirst." The Prophet replied, "Seek and bring a small amount of water." They searched everywhere and found a drop of water from the wudu basin. They poured it into a bowl and brought it to the Prophet. He put his five sacred fingers into that bowl. A spring of water flew out of each finger and all were quenched, as were the camels. O ʿAlī, take this spread to my father and say to him, "O Master, your Fāṭima requests that you put your sacred hand onto this food in order for it to be as plentiful as possible so that everybody can eat from the food of the other world."'

{18} The Commander followed Fāṭima's request. The Master of the Worlds put his hand over the spread of food and said, 'O spread, become as plentiful as possible for the Companions, so they enjoy eating the food of the other world with joy and gratitude.' The spread became plentiful by God's power, to the extent that all Companions, children, and whoever was there could eat in comfort, and a lot of food was left that they gave to the poor and the beggars.

{19} When they finished eating, His Eminence Gabriel (pbuh) arrived and stood there as a doorkeeper, and the Prophet saw this servant of the Lord of the Universe. The Prophet said, 'O brother Gabriel, what are you doing here?' Gabriel said, 'O Prophet of God, I, your yes man and inferior, am the messenger of your prophecy and brought good news for Fāṭima, ʿAlī, and your sinful community in order to make you happy. God says, "If ʿUthmān released slaves in exchange for every single step of yours, We

[7] i.e., they are ready to eat!

{۲۰} نظیر دیگر. چه حکمت بود که خدای تَعَالَی روزهٔ ماه مبارک رمضان را به امّت صدر بدر عالم فرض[۲۳] گردانید. ای برادر، بدانید چون بنده در دنیا دوستان خود را به خانهٔ خود جهت مهمانی طلب می‌کند. و پیش‌از آن خبر می‌دهد تا ایشان فکر طعام خانهٔ خود نکند[ب] که دوست در خانهٔ خود انواع نعمت موجود و مهیّا کرده‌است. پس ما به کرم خویش در شأن شما گفته بودیم «يُحِبُّهُمْ وَيُحِبُّونَه»،[۲۴] یعنی ما دوست شما و شما دوست ما». پس امروزتان خبر می‌کنم که «از بهر شما مهمانی‌خانهٔ بهشت آراسته‌ام، و شما در ماه مبارک رمضان گرسنه و تشنه باشید تا نعمت جاوید بهشت شما را بدهیم».

{۲۱} دیگر، «ای بندگان، شما کلمهٔ توحید به صِدقِ دل گفته‌اید. بهشت بر شما واجب گردانید. امّا از سر تا قدم خود را به گناه آلوده کردید. ما به لطف و کرم خود گفته‌ایم وچه حکمت کرده‌ایم که گرسنگی و تشنگی ماه رمضان در میان آوردیم، تا آتش گرسنگی و تشنگی روزه گناهان شما را نابود[ج] گرداند، و از عذاب آتش دوزخ رسته[۲۵] باشند».

{۲۲} إِلٰهِيّ، به کرم کریمی خویش و احسان لطف قدیم خویش که توفیق روزهٔ ماه رمضانِ مِنِ بیچاره را و کاتب این قصّه را با جمیع مؤمنان روزی گردانی. بِمِنَّةً وَكَرَمه.

[۲۳] فریضه؛ واجب. [۲۴] آیهٔ ۵۴ سورهٔ مائده. [۲۵] رها؛ در امان.

[ب] تا ایشان طعام خانهٔ خود نخورند [ج] ناچیز

also release from the hellfire seventy thousand of the sinning and damned whose names are listed in hell for punishment, in exchange for every single step you take, which is three hundred or so from the mosque to here.'"

{20} Another story. What was the reason that God made fasting obligatory for the community of Muḥammad during Ramadan? O brother, when people invite friends to their house for a meal, they inform their friends in advance not to eat beforehand. We,[8] due to Our kindness, say, 'Who love Him and are loved by Him' (Q. 5:54), meaning that God is your friend and you are His friend. I[9] tell you today that 'I have prepared for you a feast in a palace of paradise in that you will stay hungry and thirsty during the holy month of Ramadan until We grant you Our immortal heavenly favour.'

{21} Also, 'O believers who purely professed your faith. Paradise is for you. However, you have covered yourself in sin from top to toe. By Our kindness and grace, We have decreed thirst and starving during the month of Ramadan so that the starving and thirst from fasting may destroy your sins, and save you from hellfire.'

{22} *O God, by Your kindness and your eternal grace that provides me, the humble pauper, and the scribe of this story, and all other believers with the chance of fasting during the month of Ramadan. By Your unmerited favour and kindness. [Amen.]*

[8] i.e., God [9] i.e., God

در حکایتِ خانهٔ کعبة الله[1]

{۱} در خبر است که «مؤمن باید تا زنده باشد نیّت زیارت خانهٔ کعبه کرده باشد، و فراموش نکند زیرا که مؤمن را حجّ فرض است و آن خانه را حضرت حق سبحانه و تعالی به خود اضافت کرده‌است. و مؤمنان را به سوی این خانه می‌خواند؛ هر که در آن خانه درآید ایمن گردد. یعنی روز قیامت از آتش دوزخ رسته گردد». هر سال سی‌صدهزار حاجی به کعبه می‌رسند[الف] و اگر یکی از این کم می‌شود فرشتگان را فرمان می‌شود که «به جای ایشان شما بروید و ثواب خود بر امّت محمّد بدهید که ایشان از سبب عیال و نفقه نرسیده‌اند». برای برادر مؤمن، از برکت و عظمت آن خانه، هر سال چندین هزار کس از مردان و زنان آمرزیده و ساکن و شایان بهشت می‌گردند.

{۲} فردا[ی] قیامت أَمَنَّا وَصدقنا، کعبه را در عرصات قیامت حاضر گردانند. کعبه گوید «إِلٰهِيّ، از تو می‌خواهم که از ابتدای عالم تا انتهای عالم هر که به زیارت من رسیده‌است، ایشان را به من بخشی». فرمان شود که «جمله را به تو بخشیدم». چندین هزار مردان و زنان[ب] خود را به سراپرده‌های آستان کعبه برند.[1] آنگاه کعبه در هوا رود و از جملهٔ عُقاب‌ها و از پل صراط بگذرد و به در بهشت[ج] رسد. پس، ای بردار مؤمن، اگر توانی در عظمت چنین خانهٔ شفیع برس.[2]

{۳} نظیر دیگر. نقلست که حاتم اصمّ را داعیهٔ[3] خانهٔ کعبه شد.[4] به زن گفت «ای عورت، نفقهٔ تو در

[1] اشاره دارد به اشتیاق افراد برای آمرزیده شدن. [2] در نسخهٔ دانشگاه تهران بیتی در حاشیه نوشته شده است «ای دوست اگر جان طلبی بتو بخشم، وز جان چه عزیزست بگو آن به تو بخشم». [3] قصد. [4] نام و داستان‌های متفاوتی از حاتم اصمّ در بوستان سعدی و کشف المحجوب هجویری و بخش‌هایی از حکایتِ سفیان ثوری در تذکرة الاولیاء عطّار، و تفسیر کشف الاسرار رشید الدین میبدی دیده می‌شود. امّا شباهت قابل توجّهی بین این داستان و روایت سنایی، شاعر اهل غزنه، وجود دارد.

[الف] هرسال شش لک و هفتاد هزار حاجی در کعبه می رسد [ب] چندین لک در لک از مردان و زنان [ج] دارالسلام

CHAPTER 30

The story of the Kaʿba

{1} It is traditionally held that 'a believer must intend to visit the Kaʿba so long as he lives, and must not forget, because the hajj is an Islamic fundamental and God named it after Himself. And God calls believers to this house. whoever comes to this house will be safe. Meaning that he will be saved from hellfire.' Three hundred thousand pilgrims visit the Kaʿba annually. And if this number decreases, angels are ordered 'to replace those who couldn't attend and grant the reward to the community of Muḥammad who did not manage to attend because of their responsibilities to their families.' For the sake of a faithful brother, several thousand people, including men and women, are forgiven everywhere because of the holiness of that house, and they will be settled and deserve to be in paradise.

{2} On the Day of Judgement, we believe on and testify, Kaʿba will be present in the Resurrection Plain. The Kaʿba will say, 'O God, I want from You to forgive whoever came to visit me from the beginning until the end of the world.' A response will be given, 'I have forgiven all of them because of you.' Several thousand men and women go to the court of the Kaʿba. Then, the Kaʿba flies and passes every eagle as well as the Ṣirāṭ bridge and arrives at the gates of paradise.[1] So, faithful brother, try to understand the greatness of this intermediary house as much as you can.

{3} Another story. It is reported that Ḥātim al-Aṣamm[2] decided to visit the Kaʿba.[3] He said to his wife, 'O wife, it is my responsibility to cover your expenses. And I intend to visit the Kaʿba. How much will your expenses be while I am travelling?' His

[1] i.e., to support the believers [2] lit., 'Ḥātim the Deaf Person' [3] The name of Ḥātim al-Aṣamm is found in the *Būstān* of Saʿdī, as well as *Kashf al-Maḥjūb*, parts of *Tadhkirat al-Awliyāʾ*, and the *Tafsīr* of Rashīd al-Dīn Maybudī. Further similarities are found in the poems of Sanāʾī.

ذِمّه[۵] من است. و مرا آرزوی خانه کعبه می‌شود. و در رفتن‌وآمدنِ من تو را چقدر نفقه بس کند؟» زن او عارفه بود،[د] گفت «ای شوهر، مرا معلوم کن که چندگاه خواهم زیست». مرد گفت «ای زن، من ندانم از حیات و ممات تو». گفت «ای شوهر، هرکسی که حیات و ممات من می‌داند او متکفّل رزق من است. تا آنگه که زنده‌ام مرا بی‌رزق نگذارد».

{۴} خواجه این سخن از آن عورت بشنید، خوش‌دل شد و وداع کرد. و ره به راه کعبه نهاد. تا روزی در بیابان جوانی را دید که لَبّیك‌گویان می‌رفت، و هیچ زاد و راحله و علامت‌راه بَر وی ندید. گفت «ای جوان، کجا می‌روی؟» جوان گفت «به خانۀ کعبه می‌روم».[ه] خواجه گفت «نزد تو هیچ زاد و راحله نمی‌بینم، چگونه خواهی رفت؟» جوان گفت «ای خواجه، آفریدگاری که آسمان و زمین را بی‌علامتی می دارد، می‌تواند که بنده خود را بی‌زاد و راحله به خانۀ خود رساند». جوان این بگفت و از قافله جدا شده رفت.

{۵} خواجه چون به کعبه رسید، پیش‌از همه جوان را در طواف کعبه بدید. خواجه در فکر شد که «حق سُبحانَهُ وتَعالیٰ در جهان وحوش و طیور را در بیابان بی رزق نمی‌گذارد، و بندۀ خود را کِی بی‌رزق گذارد؟»

{۶} بیت: از لطف توست در دل حاجی هوای حجّ، ورنه که را محال که رنج سفر کشد[۶]

{۷} پس، ای برادر مؤمن، دوستان خدای تَعَالَی جان و تن و مال درباخته‌اند، و رضای مولا حاصل کرده‌اند. چنانچه مهتر ابراهیم خلیل الله صَلَواتُ اللهِ عَلَیْه چون از عمارت خانۀ کعبه فارغ شد، جبرئیل عليه‌السلام در حضرت پروردگار التماس کرد که «إلٰهِيّ، مرا فرمان ده تا ابراهیم، پیغمبر تو،[و] را بیازمایم که در محبّت به تو چگونه محبّت و دوستی دارد». فرمان شد که «برو و بیازمای».

{۸} جبرئیل عليه‌السلام به کعبه بیامد، و در پنهانی آغاز کرد «یا الله». ابراهیم پیغمبر عليه‌السلام چون نامِ الله شنید، در جنبش آمد و گفت «ای گویندۀ نامِ الله، دیگر بار نام دوست من بگو». جبرئیل عليه‌السلام پنهانی گفت «هدیۀ نام دوست درمیان‌آر[۷] تا بار دیگر بگویم». گفت «آن‌قدر شتران و گوسفندان و گاوان که دارم به تو می‌دهم، و هر مال که دارم». بار دیگر بگو. باز جبرئیل پنهانی گفت «یا الله». شوق نامِ الله در دل ایشان زیادت شد و گفت «ای ستایندۀ نامِ محبوبِ من، باز بگو». جبرئیل عليه‌السلام گفت «شکرانۀ نام دوست درمیان‌دار تا دیگر بگویم». ابراهیم عليه‌السلام گفت «هرچه در ملک خود دارم در ملک تو گردانیدم». باز جبرئیل عليه‌السلام گفت «یا الله». ابراهیم عليه‌السلام شوق نامِ الله زیادت شد. گفت «ای گویندۀ نام دوست من، باز بگو تا بشنوم». جبرئیل عليه‌السلام گفت «هرچه داشتی دادی، اکنون چه داری که هدیۀ نامِ دوست در میان آری تا باز گویم؟»

[۵] برعهده. [۶] در برخی نسخ این بیت موجود نیست. [۷] درمیان‌دار.

[د] عارف حضرت حق بود [ه] به خانۀ دوست می‌روم [و] بندۀ تو

wife was a wise gnostic. She said, 'O husband, tell me how long I will live?' The man replied, 'O wife, I do not know about your life and death.' [She] said, 'O husband, the One who knows about my life and death, He is in charge of my expenses. As long as I am alive, He will not leave me without means.'

{4} As Khʷāja [Ḥātim] heard this from his wife he happily bid farewell and set off to visit the Kaʿba. One day, on his journey, he noticed a young man in the desert who was saying, 'Labbayk – here I am!' The young man had no bag nor provisions or anything else which suggested that he was travelling. He asked him, 'Where are you going?' The young man said, 'To the Kaʿba.' Khʷāja said, 'I notice that you have no travel bag or provisions! How will you get there?' The young man said, 'O Khʷāja, the God who holds the heaven and Earth without any obvious sign can also send his servant to His house without any travel bag or provisions.' The young man said this and left the caravan.

{5} When Khʷāja arrived at the Kaʿba, the first person who came to his attention was that young man, circumambulating the Kaʿba. Khʷāja pondered, 'The God who does not leave animals and birds hungry in the desert, how can He leave His servant without any provision?!'

{6} Poem: By Your grace, the pilgrim is prompted to go to the hajj; otherwise,
who does not know about the journey's difficulties

{7} So, O faithful brother, the friends of God have forsaken their souls, body, and property to meet the Friend's satisfaction. When Abraham, the friend of God, finished building the Kaʿba, Gabriel (pbuh) asked God, 'O God, give me permission to test Abraham, Your prophet, to see to what extent he shows affection for Your Love.' A command was given, 'Go and check!'

{8} Gabriel (pbuh) went to the Kaʿba and quietly whispered, 'O Allah!' When Abraham heard the name of 'Allah' he became excited and said, 'O caller of the name "Allah", repeat the name of my friend once again.'Gabriel (pbuh) whispered, 'So offer something for the name of the Friend, and I will repeat it.' Abraham said, 'Whatever camels, sheep, and cows are in my possession, as well as whatever wealth I have, I will give them to you. Just say it again.' Again, Gabriel quietly said, 'O Allah!' Abraham's interest in the name 'Allah' increased and he said, 'O you who praise my beloved, repeat it again!'Gabriel (pbuh) said, 'Give an offering for the sake of the Friend so I will repeat it again.' Abraham said, 'Whatever property I have will become your property.' Again, Gabriel (pbuh) said, 'O Allah!' Abraham's (pbuh) interest in the name 'Allah' became more intense, and he said, 'O caller, say the name of my Friend for me to hear!' Gabriel (pbuh) said, 'you already offered whatever you had. What do you have to offer now

ابراهیم علیه‌السلام گفت «جان و تن دارم؛ می‌دهم». جبرئیل علیه‌السلام گفت «مرحبا مرحبا، خوشی و خرّمی جان پاک تو را باد». به نام آمد که منم جبرئیل علیه‌السلام، و گفت که «از بهر امتحان محبّتِ نامِ الله آمده بودم».

{۹} آری، ای برادرِ مؤمن، دوستان در شنیدن نام حق سبحانه وتعالی جان و تن درباخته‌اند، تا رضای مولا حاصل کرده‌اند. و تو امروز از بهر متاع دنیای مُردارِ فانی چنان مغرور و مشغول گشتی که گویی با مردگان کاری نداری. و نظر بر احوال و کردار خود باید کرد تا چه[۸] حال پیش آید.

{۱۰} نظیر دیگر. چون نمرود مردود دست و پای حضرت ابراهیم علیه‌السلام را در غل و زنجیر کشید، و در منجنیق درآورد و در میان آتش انداخت، جمیع فرشتگان گفتند «إلهيّ، ما را از آسمان در دار دنیا فرست و دستوری بده تا تماشای بندهٔ تو کنیم که نمرود مردود با وی چه می کند». و مهتر جبرئیل علیه‌السلام گفت «إلهيّ، بر بندهٔ تو وقت تنگست. اگر فرمان شود او را یاری کنیم و بیازمایم که چگونه محبّت دارد». فرمان شد «برو و بیازما».

{۱۱} جبرئیل علیه‌السلام نزد ابراهیم علیه‌السلام شد، و گفت «ای ابراهیم، اکنون در آتش نمرود می‌باید رفت. اگر گویی در حقّ تو یاری کنم». ابراهیم گفت «ای جبرئیل امین، تو منصف باش. از عرش تا تَحْتَ ٱلثَّرَىٰ جملهٔ مخلوقات خدای تَعَالَى عاجزند. تو منصف باش که تو عاجزی و از عاجز چه یاری خواهد بود؟ حقّ سبحانه وتعالی حاضر و ناظر است. و از احوال من خداوند تَعَالَى مطّلع است. چه حاجت است که از تو یاری خواهم». جملهٔ فرشتگان انصاف دادند و آفرین گفتند.

{۱۲} نظیر دیگر. چون ابراهیم علیه‌السلام خانهٔ کعبه را تمام کرد، در خواب دید که شکرانهٔ این خانه را قربانی بده. چون از خواب بیدار شد فرمود تا سیصدوشصت گوسفند بر در خانهٔ کعبه قربانی کردند و به خلق خدای تَعَالَى دادند. باز در خواب نمودند که «بهتر از این قربانی بده». چون بیدار شد فرمود سیصدوشصت شتر را به در کعبه قربانی کردند، و به فقرا دادند. بار سیوم[۹] ندا شنید که «هرچه غیر از من دوست می‌داری همان راه بده». ابراهیم علیه‌السلام گفت «إلهيّ، من جگرگوشهٔ خود، اسماعیل، را دوست می‌دارم». فرمان رسید که «همان را قربانی بده».

{۱۳} نزد بی‌بی هاجر رضی‌الله‌عنها آمد و گفت «سر و پای و جامهٔ اسماعیلِ مرا بشوی که او را به خانهٔ دوستی می‌برم». بی‌بی هاجر في الحال سر و پای و جامهٔ او را بشست. و از بس که فرزند خود را دوست می‌داشت، آب بر اعضای او می‌ریخت، و هر عضوی را که می‌شست می گفت «إلهيّ، فرزند مرا به قدرت خود آفریده؛ جمیع مادران و پدران را به لطف خود مهربان کرده‌ای. اگر چه فرزندم با پدر می‌رود، امّا این ضعیف‌تر به تو می‌سپارد؛ سلامت ببر و سلامت به من رسان».

[۸] چنین. [۹] سوم.

so I will repeat it again'. Abraham continued, 'I will give my soul and body; the only things remained.' Gabriel (pbuh) said, 'May you be joyous and happy, O pure soul!' Then introduced himself, 'I am Gabriel (pbuh) and I had come in order to test your love of the name "Allah".'

{9} O my faithful brother, friends have lost body and soul in order to hear the name of God and so they can please the Friend. While you are proud of yourself in the temporary world of carnal desires, seemingly you do not deal with the dead. And one should look and check their behaviour in order to achieve such level now and in the future.

{10} Another story. When the rejected Nimrod chained the hands and feet of the Prophet Abraham (pbuh) and placed him in a catapult and threw him in the fire, all the angels said, 'O God, send us from heaven to the world and allow us to observe your servant and what the rejected Nimrod will do with him.' And His Eminence Gabriel (pbuh) said, 'O God, Your servant's time is pressing. If You permit, we would assist him and [also] test how much love he has?' A command arrived, 'Go and test.'

{11} Gabriel (pbuh) went to Abraham (pbuh) and said, 'O Abraham, now you will go into the Nimrod's fire. If you ask [from me], I will help you.' Abraham said, 'O faithful Gabriel, be fair! From the Throne to whatever is underground, God's creatures are impotent. Be fair! As you are impotent, too, how will you be able to assist? God is Present and the Beholder. And God is aware of my situation. Why should I ask for help from you?' All angels confirmed the reasoning and approved it.

{12} Another story. When Abraham's (pbuh) visit to the Kaʿba had finished, he dreamed, 'For the grace of this house, sacrifice something.' When he woke up, he ordered 360 sheep to be sacrificed before the Kaʿba, and to be distributed among the people of God. Later, he also dreamed, 'Sacrifice something better than this.' When he woke up, he ordered the sacrifice of 360 camels before the Kaʿba and for them to be given to the poor. He heard a voice for the third time saying, 'Whatever you like except Me, sacrifice it.' Abraham (pbuh) said, 'O God, I love my dearest, Ishmael.' A command arrived, 'Sacrifice him.'

{13} [Abraham] went to Hagar (pbuh) and said, 'Wash the head and legs[4] of Ishmael and dress him as I will take him to a friend's house.' Lady Hagar then washed his head and legs and dressed him. As much as she loved her child, when she poured water on his body, and washed every single limb, she said, 'O God, You have created my child with Your own power, and You have made all mothers and fathers kind. Although my child goes with his father, this weak one[5], put him in Your custody. Take him safely and bring him back safely.'

[4] i.e., whole body [5] i.e., Hagar

{۱۴} گفته‌اند «چه حکمت بود که مهتر اسماعیل را از زیر کارد خلاصی دادند، و کارد بر أَمیر المُؤمِنین حسین رَضِیَ‌اللهُ‌عَنهُ روان شد». زیرا که مهتر اسماعیل مادر در حیات داشت، درزمانْ دعای مادر در میان درآمد، نجات دادند، و أَمیر المُؤمِنین حسین مادر نداشت و پدر نداشت. تا بدانی، ای برادر مؤمن، که هم‌ازاین[10] گفته‌اند که مادر و پدر بر سر فرزند نعمتی است بزرگ.[11]

{۱۵} حضرت ابراهیم کارد و رسن گرفته، از خانه برآمد. بی‌بی هاجر گفت «ای پیغمبر خدای تَعَالَی، کارد و رسن از برای چه می‌بری؟» گفت «ای هاجر، مرا دوستی که به مهمانی طلبیده است کریم‌صفت است. شاید از بهرِ اسماعیلِ من گوسفندی دهد. بدین رسن بربندیم». گفت «اگر رسن بهر بستن گوسفند می‌بری، کارد از برای چه می‌بری؟» فرمود «اگر گوسفند آورده نشود، بدین کارد بسمل کرده بیارم». چون از خانه فرزند را گرفته درآمد، شیطان ملعون نزد بی‌بی هاجر آمد، و گفت «می‌دانی پسر تو را کجای می‌برد و کارد و رسن را از بهر چه می‌برد؟» هاجر گفت «نمی‌دانم. مرا گفته‌است که در خانهٔ دوستی می روند به ضیافت. شیطان گفت «با تو حیله کرده‌است. امّا با آن رسن دست و پای اسماعیل را بندد و کارد در حلق او راند».

{۱۶} هاجر فرمود که «هیچ پدری در حقّ فرزند خود چنین نکرده‌است، و پدرْ اسماعیل را بسیاربسیار دوست می‌دارد. ازبهر چه بکشد؟» شیطان گفت «او را فرمان رسیده که چنین کن». بی‌بی هاجر گفت که «مگر تو شیطانْ ملعونی. اگر به حکم و فرمان خدای تَعَالَی بسمل می‌کند جان فرزند و جان من فدای فرمان او». شیطان بدبخت دید که این مکر پیش نرفت با خود گفت «مگر این مکر به اسماعیل کنم که جان‌دادن سخت است».

{۱۷} فِي الحال نزد اسماعیل شد و گفت «با پدر کجا می‌روی که خون تو خواهد ریخت؟» گفت «پدر من در حقّ من مشفق است. خون من چگونه ریزد». گفت «او را خدای تَعَالَی فرموده است که با تو چنین کند». گفت «تو شیطان ملعونی که مرا از راه می‌بری. اگر حکم خدای تَعَالَی شده‌است، زهی سعادت من که خون من در راه مولا ریخته شود». این سخن بگفت و در عقب پدر دوید و فریاد کرد «ای بابا، مردی مرا تشویش می‌دهد». ابراهیم گفت «ای جان پدر، سنگ بزن که سنگ را هم باید به سنگ زدن». تا امروز سنّت ایشان در میان امّت محمّد صَلَّی‌اللهُ‌عَلَیهِ‌وَسَلَّمَ مانده است. که هرکس آنجای رسد سنگ پرتاب می کند.

{۱۸} الغرض. چون به مقام قربانی رسیدند رو به جانب فرزند کرد، و گفت «ای فرزند و ای جگرگوشهٔ پدر، مرا خواب نمودند که تو را در راه دوست قربانی کنم». اسماعیل اگرچه خُرد بود، امّا علوّهمّت بنگر؛ آغاز کرد که «ای پدر، تو پیغمبر خدای تَعَالَی هستی. خواب شما هرگز دروغ نباشد. زودباش! آنچه شما را درحقّ من فرموده بکن که إنشاءالله تَعَالَی مرا یکی از صابران یابی. دگر ای پدر، یک جان من چه باشد که اگر هزارجان بوده باشد فدا کنم. دگر، ای پدر، در قربانی کردن تقصیر نکنی که فخرِ تو فخرِ من باشد».

[10] به این دلیل. [11] این پاراگراف در برخی نسخ موجود نیست.

{14} It is asked 'why His Eminence Ishmael was spared from the knife while the knife worked for the Commander of Believers Ḥusayn (pbuh)? Because His Eminence Ishmael's mother was alive, and her protection prayer functioned and saved him, while the Commander of Believers Ḥusayn had not mother nor father!' So, O faithful brother, you will now realise that this is why mothers and fathers bestow great favour upon their children.

{15} Prophet Abraham picked up a knife and rope and left the house. Lady Hagar said, 'O Prophet of God, why do you take a knife and rope?' He said, 'O Hagar, the friend of mine who has invited me to the party is so kind. Perhaps, he wants to offer a sheep to my Ishmael. We should take the sheep with this rope.' She said, 'If the rope is for tying the sheep, why do you take the knife?' He replied, 'If the sheep cannot be taken, we may sacrifice it with this knife, and take it.' As soon as he took his child and went out of the house, the accursed Satan went to Lady Hagar and said, 'Do you really know where he has taken your son? And why did he take a knife and rope?' Hagar said, 'I do not know! He told me that he will go to a friend's house for a party.' Satan said, 'He tricked you. He wants to tie Ishmael's hands and legs with that rope and cut his throat with the knife.'

{16} Hagar said, 'No father has ever done this to his child. And the father loves Ishmael so much. Why should he kill him?' Satan said, 'He is ordered to do so.' Lady Hagar said, 'You, Satan, are truly accursed. If he must be sacrificed in the name and decree of God, my child's life as well as mine would be sacrificed at His command.' The miserable Satan understood that this trick did not work. Then Satan pondered, 'I should try this trick on Ishmael, as being killed is not easy!'

{17} Soon, Satan went to Ishmael and said, 'Where are you going with your father as he will kill you?!' Ishmael said, 'My father is kind to me. Why should he kill me?' Satan said, 'He is ordered by God to do this to you.' Ishmael said, 'Ha! You are the accursed Satan who wants to lead me astray from the [straight] path. If this has been decreed upon me by God, what a pleasure it is of mine that my blood is poured in the path of the Friend.' Ishmael said this and ran after his father and called out, 'O father, a man is disturbing me.' Abraham said, 'O beloved of your father, throw a stone, as the stone should be hit by stone.' Their tradition[6] has been practised among the community of Muḥammad until today. So, whoever goes there throws a stone.

{18} Returning to the story. When they[7] reached the place of sacrifice, Abraham looked at his child and said, 'O child and the darling of your father, I have dreamed[8] of sacrificing you in the Friend's path.' Although Ishmael was a child, he looked like a high-minded person. He began to say, 'O father, you are the prophet of God. Your

[6] i.e., stone throwing [7] i.e., Abraham and Ishmael [8] i.e., I was inspired

{۱۹} زهی پدری که در فرمان خدای تَعَالَی از سر فرزند خواسته، و زهی پسری که از سر جان خواسته. چون مهتر ابراهیم پسر را در راه خدای تَعَالَی چُست‌وچالاک دید در خاطر شُکر بکرد. آنگاه، مهتر اسماعیل بر پدر آغاز کرد که پدر دگر چند وصیّت دارم. ابراهیم گفت «ای جان پدر، بگو چه وصیّت داری». گفت «چون از من فارغ شوی و باز گردی باید که دعا و بندگی من به حضرت والده رسانیده، و بگویید «چه کنم ای مادر، ندانستم که مرا سفر قیامت پیش خواهد آمد، وگرنه عذرخواهی شما می‌کردم، و مرا در خاطر این بود که خدمت شما بسیار کنم. امّا چه کنم که حیات من خدای تَعَالَی همین‌قدر کرده‌بود». دیگر که ای پدر، مادرم را بگویی که «در قضای حضرت إِلٰهِيّ رضا باید داد، و نخواهم که از بهر من گریه و ندامت کنی که فردای قیامت شرمندهٔ حضرت مولا گردی». دگر، «ای مادر، این دنیا فانیست. بر کسی وفا ندارد. بازگشت همه به سوی حضرت خداوند است؛ جَلَّ جَلَالُهُ». دگر، ای پدر، چون مادر را نگران و گریان بینی، باید که به وعدهٔ حق سُبْحَانَهُ وَتَعَالَى خبر دهی که «او به مقصود ابد رسید، تو نیز صبر کنی تا بدان مقام جاوید برسی»».

{۲۰} آنگه گفت «ای پدر، التماس دارم - که جان دادن دشوار است - باید که دست و پای مرا ببندی تا دست و پای نزنم، و عاصی نشوم و قطرات خون بر جامه و اندام شما نرسد، که در حیاتْ دلِ پاک شما از من آلوده شود. و دیگر، چشم من بربندی تا نظرم در روی مبارک شما نیفتند و چشم من با چشم شما چهار نشود، و مهر پدری پیدا نشود وقت کارد راندن، و در کارِ حق سُبْحَانَهُ وَتَعَالَى تقصیری نشود. دیگر، ای پدر، مرا در روی گردانی[ز] و از قفای[۱۲] من کارد برانی که در سجده حق سُبْحَانَهُ وَتَعَالَى عَزَّ وَجَلَّ جان داده باشم».[۱۳]

{۲۱} القصّه. هر چه پسر گفت پدر قبول کرد. آنگه، کارد بر گلوی مبارک براند و گفت «بِسم الله وَاللهُ اکبَر». دید که کارد هیچ کار نمی‌کند. تیزی برگشت و کُند شد؛ دریافت که «مگر کارد کندست». بر سنگ مالید، و تیز کرد و باز براند. هرچند قصد کرد پوست نیز بریده نشد. باز براند. هرچند قصد کرد، پوست نیز بریده نشد. باز در مقام تیز کردن شد. و هرچند قصد کرد که بِبُرَّد نَبُرّید. و دست را قوّت نماند.

[۱۲] بر پشت؛ شباهت به داستان شمر و بریدن سر حسین بن علی از پشت سر دارد.
[۱۳] یادآور سربریدن حسین توسط شمر در دشت کربلا است. به داستان سی‌ویک مراجعه شود.

[ز] بغلطانی

dream would never be false. Do not wait. Do whatever you are ordered to do with me as, 'God willing' you would find me patient. Also, O my father, what use would be my life alone. If I had a thousand lives I would sacrifice them. Also, O my father, do not fail in sacrificing me, as your pride is mine also.'

{19} What a father who gives his son's head at the command of God, and what a son who has fully dedicated his soul. When His Eminence Abraham found his son like a sharp person in the path of God, he became thankful. Then His Eminence Ishmael said to his father, 'Father, I have a number of bequests. Abraham said, 'O dearest one, tell me about your last will.' Ishmael said, 'Once you have finished with me and returned, you should convey my greetings and dependency to her excellency, mother and tell her [on behalf of me], 'What could I have done O mother, as I did not know that I was heading off to the Day of Judgement,[9] therefore, I apologise to you, and I was thinking that I would always serve you. However, I cannot do anything as God had determined for me to live until now.' O father, also tell my mother, 'To be happy with what God has decreed, and I do not want her to cry and be filled with remorse for me, as you will then be embarrassed before the Friend's presence on the Day of Judgement.' Also [tell her that], 'O mother, this world is mortal. It is not faithful to anyone. Everyone returns to God, Almighty.' O father, if you also find my mother sad and tearful, you should tell her about God's promises, 'He[10] reached the ultimate goal, if you[11] are also patient, you will also reach that immortal place'.'

{20} Then he said, 'O father, I have a request as dying is difficult; will you tie my hands and legs so I will not have the staggers, and not be defiant, and that blood drops will not spill on your clothes and body, so that your purified heart becomes dirty by me in this world. And also close my eyes[12] so I will not see your sacred face, and my eyes will not lock with yours, leading to paternal affection, while cutting my throat with the knife and so you will not fail in the divine task. O father, also turn my face down and cut me from the back, so I will be in prostration to God while dying.'[13]

{21} Returning to the story. The father accepted whatever the son said. Then he put the knife on the sacred throat [of Ishmael] and said, 'In the Name of God, and God is the Greatest.' He noticed that the knife did not cut. The edge of the blade was dull. He thought, 'Perhaps the knife is blunt.' He rubbed it on stone and sharpened it and tried it again. Whatever he tried, the skin would not cut. Again, he tried. Still the skin would not cut. Again he sharpened the blade. And whenever he tried to cut, it did not work and his hand became weak.

[9] i.e., I was about to die [10] i.e., Ishmael [11] i.e., Hagar [12] i.e., cover my eyes

[13] resembling the killing episode of Ḥusayn, Muḥammad's grandson, in Karbala. See chapter thirty-one.

{۲۲} به‌غصّه کارد بر زمین زد، و کارد آغاز کرد «الغیاث الغیاث،[۱۴] یعنی، ای خلیل الله، تو می گویی بِبُرّ، و رحمان[۱۵] می گوید مبُرّ! من گفتهٔ رَحیم[۱۶] بشنوم یا گفتهٔ تو؟» همین‌وقت پیکِ حضرتِ رَبِّ العَالمین، مهتر جبرئیل علیه‌السلام، رسید و گوسفندی هدیه بیاورد، و گفت «این هدیه را حق سبحانه وتعالی به شما فرستاده‌است. بدل اسماعیل قربانی کنی». دیگر فرمان می‌شود که «فردای قیامت امّتان تو و امّتان محمّد صلی الله علیه وسلم قربانی خواهند کرد، و به حجّ خواهند رفت». چون حضرت ابراهیم علیه‌السلام هدیه بدید شاد شد. یعنی هم پسر یافته و هم رضای مولا حاصل کرد. و شیطان ملعون[ح] تماشا می کرد.

{۲۳} چون گوسفند را قربانی کرد، و گوشت ها را برداشت و دست پسر گرفته متوّجه خانه شد. به خانه آمد و واقعه را به بی‌بی هاجر گفت. ایشان گفت «چون شما از خانه بیرون رفتید، شیطان آمد و گفت «فرمان حق سبحانه وتعالی شده که فرزند تو را قربانی کند». من در کار صبر کردم. حقّ سبحانه وتعالی فرزند مرا از زیر کارد امان داد، و سلامت باز به من رسانید».

{۲۴} إلهِيّ، جملهٔ مؤمنان را، از مردان و زنان، با منِ شکستهٔ کاتبِ این قصّه از زیارت خانهٔ کعبه و ثواب آن روزی کنی، و به سعادت خانه مشرّف گردانی. به حقّ محمّد وآله أجمعین.

[۱۴] پناه جستن. [۱۵] یکی از صفات خداوند. [۱۶] یکی از صفات خداوند.

[ح] سیاه‌روی

{22} Feeling sad, he put down the knife. The knife began to cry, 'Help, help!' Meaning, 'O friend of God,[14] you say, 'Cut it', while the Merciful[15] says, 'Do not cut it.' Shall I follow the will of the Merciful or that of yours?' In the meantime, the Messenger of the Lord of the Worlds, His Eminence Gabriel (pbuh) arrived and brought a sheep as a gift, and said, 'This offering is from God to you. Sacrifice it in exchange for Ishmael.' The command also comes, 'Your community as well as that of Muḥammad (pbuh) will continue this tradition[16] and go to hajj.' Prophet Abraham (pbuh) was happy when he saw the gift. Because now he had his son and was able to meet the satisfaction of the Friend. And the accursed Satan could only view this and not do anything!

{23} When he sacrificed the sheep, he took the meat, and holding his son's hand moved towards home. He arrived home and told the story to Lady Hagar. She said, 'When you left the house, Satan came and said, 'It is God's command that your son be sacrificed.' I tried to be patient. As such, God saved my son from the knife, and brought him back to me safely.'

{24} *O God, provide me, the poor scribe of this story, and all believers including men and women with the chance of visiting the House of Kaʿba and its rewards. By Muḥammad and all his family. [Amen.]*

[14] i.e., Abraham [15] i.e., God [16] i.e., sacrifice sheep (or camel)

در مقتل أَمیر المُؤمِنین حسن و حسین رَضِیَ اللهُ عَنهُمَا[1]

(نسخهٔ کوتاه)

{۱}	آورده‌اند که چون معاویه در جهان نماند جای او را یزید به کید[2] گرفت و آن بدبخت ملعون را به‌خاطر افتاد که أَمیر المُؤمِنین حسن و حسین را به مکر از میان بردارد و وقوّت ایشان را از یکدیگر بشکند. تا روزی پیره‌زنی پیش زن أَمیر المُؤمِنین حسن فرستاد و گفت «برو پیغام من به زن أَمیر المُؤمِنین حسن برسان و بگو «دولتِ فرزندان أَمیر المُؤمِنین علی به آخر رسید. و امروز دولت به من است. تو حسن را زهر ده تا من تو را نکاح خود آرم و بر همهٔ حرم‌ها[3] تو مسلّط باشی»».

{۲}	این بی‌عقل نادان بدین فریب مغرورگشت. و در آن روز گرمای سخت بود. و امیر روزه می‌داشت. وقتِ افطار زَهْر در پیاله آب کرد و به امیر داد و امیر او را بخورد. شکمِ خالی فِی الحال زَهْر درکار شد و هفتاد پرکاله[4] از جگر ایشان بیفتاد و خون از حلق می‌ریخت. فرمود «برادرم حسین را بیارید».

{۳}	چون بیامد و حال برادر خود را بدید گریان شد و گفت «ای برادر، بگو این دشمنی را که کرده است؟» گفت «من از خانه‌دانی[5]‌ام که از آن خانه‌دان غمّازی[6] نیامده‌است. خداوند تَعَالَی نصیب ما این کرده بود و صحبت من این است که دست شفقّت از فرزندان من باز نداری که یتیمان شکسته‌دل می‌باشند. و بعداز نقل[7]

[1] در نسخهٔ ۱۲۲۲ تاجیکستان، داستان‌ها، اشعار و روایات متفاوتی پیرامون حسن و حسین در حواشی نگاشته شده‌است.
[2] ترفندوحیله. [3] همسران و زنان دربار. [4] همچنین «پرگاله» به معنی «پاره‌ای از چیزی». به فرهنگ عمید رجوع شود.
[5] نگارش متفاوت واژه «خاندان» است. [6] سخن چینی. لفظ غمّازی در مقدمة الادب زمخشری و اشعار مولانا دیده می‌شود. به دهخدا رجوع شود.
[7] مرگ و رحلت.

CHAPTER 31A

The story of the killing of the commanders of believers Ḥasan and Ḥusayn (pbuh)

[Short Version]

{1} It is reported that when Muʿāwiya died, Yazīd took his place with trickery, and that miserable accursed one decided to destroy the commanders of believers Ḥasan and Ḥusayn, also with deception, and separate them from each other. One day he sent an old woman to the wife of the Commander of Believers Ḥasan, 'Go tell the wife of the Commander of Believers Ḥasan, "The rule and power of the children of the Commander of Believers ʿAlī has ended. And today the rule and power belong to me. You must poison Ḥasan and I will then marry you and you will be foremost in my harem.'

{2} This unwise and feeble-minded person became absorbed by the plot. The weather was hot that day. And the Commander[1] was fasting. As he was breaking his fast she poured poison in a bowl of water and passed it to him to drink. As his stomach was empty, the poison quickly took effect and he was sick, his liver was torn into seventy pieces, and blood oozed out of his throat. Ḥasan said, 'Bring me my brother, Ḥusayn.'

{3} When Ḥusayn came and saw his brother's situation, he cried and said, 'O brother, tell me who did this to you?!' Ḥasan said, 'I come from a family in which gossip is not advised. God had decreed this upon me, so what I am telling you is not to withhold your kindness from my children, as orphans are heartbroken, and bury my

[1] i.e., Ḥasan

مرا در روضهٔ حرم برید، تا از برکت پیغمبر ﷺ خدای تَعَالَی بر من رحمت کند». دگر سخن چند به امام گفت، و کلمه عرض کرد و جان به حق ﷻ سپرد. شوری در مدینه خاست[۸] که «یادگار حضرت پیغمبر از میان ما برفت».

{۴} یک پای جُوازه[۹] را أَمیر المُؤمِنین حسین گرفت، دوم محمّد حنفیّه گرفت و خواستند به حظیرهٔ حضرت رسول برند. یزیدِ بدبخت[۱۰] به امیر مدینه نوشت که «نگذارید حسن را در حظیرهٔ رسول دفن کنند». کسانِ امیرِ مدینه[۱۱] آمدند و نگذاشتند که در حظیره دارند. أَمیر المُؤمِنین حسین خواست تا جنگ کند. عبدالله مسعود درآمد و گفت «ای یادگار حضرت رسول ﷺ، دشمنان قصد کرده؛ مبادا که آفتی پدید آید. هرجا که أَمیر المُؤمِنین حسن رضی الله عنه دفن کنند رحمت خدای بر اوست». آنگه به گورستان غریبان[۱۲] بردند. زن أَمیر المُؤمِنین حسن بر یزید لعین کس فرستاد که «کی مرا در نکاح در می‌آری؟» یزید گفت که «با فرزند صدر بدرعالم چنین کردی؛ با من وفا نکنی». آن نادانِ بی سعادتْ پادشاهی را به باد داد و هم به مقصود نرسید.

{۵} نظیر دیگر. و عداوت یزید لعین ازجهت زن أَمیر المُؤمِنین حسین بود. روزی یزید بدبخت پیش معاویه نشسته بود. معاویه به یزید گفت «من چندین رنج و مشقّت دیدم و خلافت به دست آوردم. از بهر تو هر آرزو که اراده کردی میسّر شد. دگر هیچ آرزو در خاطرت هست که به تو رسانم؟» گفت «ای پدر، عبدالله زبیر زنی صاحب جمال دارد. و آرزوی من آنست که او مرا باشد». روز دیگر معاویه عبدالله زبیر را طلب کرد و خلوت کرد و گفت «تو پسرعموی پیغمبری. در حقّ تو می‌خواهم که لطف و احسان کنم و دختر خود را به تو دهم و ولایت مصر را به تو ارزانی دارم .عبدالله بدین چیزها فریفته کرد و از راه بُرد».تا روزی دگر او را بخواند و گفت «دختر می‌دهیم امّا دختر می‌گوید من از جمال افتاده‌ام. اگر عبدالله آن زن را طلاق گوید او را بخواهم». عبدالله زبیر را ولایت مصر در خاطر افتاد، في الحال زن را طلاق داد.

{۶} معاویه عبدالله را طلب کرد و گفت «دختر من می گوید که «مرا جمال نیست. و این زن را که طلاق گفت ازجهت ولایت مصر بود. و چون ولایت مصر از دست وی برود او مرا نیز طلاق گوید»». چون عبدالله این سخن شنید غمناک بازگشت.

{۷} بعداز آن، معاویه موسیٰ اشعری را طلب کرد. او مردی عالم و پارسا بود. گفت «نَزدِ زنِ عبدالله

[۸] برخاست. [۹] احتمالا «جُوازه» صورت بدنویسی شده از «جنازه» به معنای «تابوت» است. به هرروی، واژهٔ «جُوازه» از «گُوازه» به معنی «تکه چوبی که با آن راه می روند یا حیوانات را می رانند می باشد». علاوه بر دهخدا، رجوع شود به John Richardson, *A Dictionary, Persian, Arabic, and English with a Dissertation on the Languages, Literature, and Manners of Eastern Nations*, Revised and Improved by Charles Wilkins; a New Edition, Considerably Enlarged by Francis Johnson (London: J. L. Cox, 1829), 1244.

[۱۰] این ترکیب به شکل مستقیم وارد ادبیات مالایی شده است. در قدیمی‌ترین نسخهٔ مالایی موجود از «داستان شهادت حسن و حسین» در کتابخانهٔ دانشگاه کیمبریج به شمارهٔ Ll.6.5 ، این ترکیب به‌صورت «یزید چلاک» (*Yazid calaka*) دیده می‌شود که به گمان من برگرفته از واژهٔ ترکی-پارسی «چلاق» به معنای «عاجز و ناتوان» است. [۱۱] مراد همان «مأموران حکومتی» شهر مدینه است.

[۱۲] (غریبانش)؛ اشاره دارد به اینکه وی را «غریبانه بردند».

body in the shrine of the Prophet after my death, so God will bestow mercy upon me due to the greatness of the Prophet.' He said a few more words to Ḥusayn, and professed the faith and submitted his soul to God. A commotion raged across the city of Medina and the people said, 'One of the last vestiges of the Prophet has left us.'

{4} [After the body had been prepared for burial] one side of the coffin was taken by the Commander of Believers Ḥusayn, the other by Muḥammad Ḥanafiyya, and they moved it to the shrine of the Prophet. The wretched Yazīd had written to the ruler of Medina commanding that 'Ḥasan should not be allowed to be buried in the shrine of the Messenger.' Agents of the governor of Medina arrived and prevented Ḥasan from being taken into the shrine. The Commander of Believers Ḥusayn wanted to fight with them, but was interrupted by ʿAbdallāh Masʿūd who said, 'O inheritor of the Messenger (pbuh), the enemies are determined, be careful [and be patient?] not to get hurt. Wherever the Commander of Believers Ḥasan is buried, God's mercy will be upon him.' Then they took him to the cemetery of strangers[2]. The wife of the Commander of Believers Ḥasan, now sent a messenger to the accursed Yazīd asking, 'When will you marry me?' Yazīd replied, 'You have done this with the descendant of the Prophet, how can you be faithful to me?' That unwise and ill-fated woman lost the loyalty of king and did not achieve her goal.

{5} Another story. Nonetheless, the enmity of the accursed Yazīd towards the Commander of Believers Ḥusayn was because of Ḥusayn's wife. The miserable Yazīd was sitting next to Muʿāwiya one day. Muʿāwiya said to Yazīd, 'I gained the caliphate after many difficulties. And whatever you wanted, I provided it to you. Is there anything else you wish me to give you?' Yazīd said, 'O father, ʿAbdallāh Zubayr has a pretty wife and I wish to have her.' Later on, Muʿāwiya asked ʿAbdallāh Zubayr to meet with him to talk privately. He said, 'You are the cousin of the Prophet. I want to do you a favour and give my daughter to you as well as the sovereignty of Egypt.' He succeeded in deceiving ʿAbdallāh with these promises and lead him astray. Later on, Muʿāwiya again asked for ʿAbdallāh Zubayr and told him, 'I would give you my daughter. However, she says that she is not beautiful anymore. If ʿAbdallāh divorces his wife, then I will marry him.' ʿAbdallāh Zubayr, thinking of sovereignty over Egypt, divorced his wife.

{6} [On yet another occasion] Muʿāwiya asked for ʿAbdallāh and said to him, 'My daughter now says, "I am not beautiful and he divorced his beautiful wife just because of Egypt. So, if he loses the sovereignty of Egypt, then he will divorce me, too."' When ʿAbdallāh heard this, he became sad.

{7} Later on, Muʿāwiya asked for Mūsā Ashʿarī who was a wise and pious man. He said to him, 'Go to the [ex-] wife of Zubayr and propose to her on behalf of the filthy

2 Or: like a stranger. He is now buried in al-Baqīʿ Cemetery in Medina in Saudi Arabia.

زبیر برو و او را از جهت یزید پلید[۱۳] بخواه». موسیٰ اشعری روان شد. در راه به قاسم ابن عباس رسید و «گفت کجا می‌روی؟» [موسیٰ اشعری] گفت «پیغام پسر معاویه به‌جهت زن عبدالله زبیر می‌برم». قاسم گفت «پیغام من هم بگو». چون پیش رفت با أَمیر المُؤمِنین حسین رضي الله عنه ملاقات شد. گفت «کجا می‌روی؟» [موسیٰ اشعری] فرمود «به‌جهت یزید بر زن عبدالله زبیر می‌برم». حسین گفت «پیغام من هم بگو».

{۸} القصّه. چون موسیٰ اشعری نزد زن آمد، در جمال او نظر کرد از حال رفت. بعداز آن که به حال آمد گفت «چهار پیغام به تو آوردم». [زن عبدالله زبیر] گفت «بگو». [موسیٰ اشعری] فرمود که «اوّل پیغام خود، بعداز آن پیغام یزید، دگر قاسم، چهارم پیغام أَمیر المُؤمِنین حسین رضي الله عنه». زن گفت «ای موسیٰ، تو پیر و من جوان، نیابد باقی. مصلحت هر سه کس در دست تو دادم». موسیٰ گفت «اگر ولایت و ملک خواهی، یزید را بخواه. و اگر جمال و اصل می‌خواهی قاسم را قبول کن. و اگر دنیا و آخرت می‌خواهی حسین را بخواه».[۱۴] درزمانْ گفت «نکاح من به أَمیر المُؤمِنین حسین رضي الله عنه بخوان تا طمع دیگران از من بریده شود. و من در خاندان پیغمبر ﷺ درآیم».

{۹} بعداز نکاح، موسیٰ اشعری نزدیک رفت و کیفیت بگفت. معاویه گفت «ای موسیٰ، به صد حیله و مکر او را از عبدالله جدا کردم. تو به یک‌ساعت کار زیر و زبر کردی،» یزید بدبخت را از این حال خبر شد. سوگند خورد «هرگاه مُلک[الف] پدر مرا دست دهد سر حسین را از تن جدا گردانم». آن بدبخت این بگفت و رسول خدای را بر خود خصم گردانید. امّا او چه بدبختی بود که اینها تواند کرد؟ حکم واجِب الوُجود بدین رفته بود.

{۱۰} نظیر دیگر. روزی که سیّد عالم محمّد مُصْطَفَی ﷺ نشسته بود، معاویه بیامد. حضرت فرمودند «ای معاویه، از پشت تو پسری پیدا شود که قاتل حسن و حسین من باشد». معاویه گفت «ای سیّد عالم در جهان فرزندی ندارم و بعداز این سوگند می‌خورم که گِرد هیچ عورت نگردم تا مرا فرزند نشود». شبی معاویه از خواب برخاست که بول کند. چون بول کرد استنجا[۱۵] به دیوار می‌کرد. کژدم نیش بر سر آلت آورد و دردِ بی‌قرار[۱۶] گرفت. حکما فرمودند «تا نزدیکی با زنی نکنی زهر آلت تو پریده و برطرف نشود».[۱۷] معاویه بیامد و با زن نزدیکی کرد. هم در آن ساعت یزید پلید در شکم مادر قرار گرفت، تا بدانی ای برادرِ مؤمن که حکم حق سبحانه وتعالی

[۱۳] در برخی نسخ صفت «منفور» برای یزید به کار رفته است.

[۱۴] این بخش از گفت و گو بین موسیٰ اشعری و همسر عبدالله زبیر در قسمت طولانی‌تر داستان به وضوح دیده نمی‌شود.

[۱۵] اصطلاحیست فقهی به معنی پاک کردن محل ادرار و مدفوع با آب، کلوخ، یا غیره. به فرهنگ عمید مراجعه شود.

[۱۶] درد شدید.

[۱۷] داستان خلقت یزید در نسخهٔ طولانی و همچنین نسخ مالایی وجود دارد. برای بیش از نیم قرن باور پژوهشگران (همچون Brakel و Bragisnky) این بود که این قسمت از داستان خلقت یزید، برای مبرّا ساختن معاویه از دخالت در «شرارت» یزید، نوآوری اقوام مالایی و اندونزیایی بوده است. در مقاله‌ای در سال ۲۰۱۸ به نقد گفتارهای این دو بزرگوار پرداختم و درّالمجالس را به عنوان منشاء اصلی این داستان معرّفی کردم. Majid Daneshgar, ‘New Evidence on the Origin of the *Hikayat Muhammad Hanafiyyah*’, *Archipel* 96 (2018): 69–102.

[الف] ملک بغداد

Yazīd.' Mūsā Ashʿarī went out. He reached Qāsim the son of ʿAbbās mid-way, who asked him, 'Where are you going?' Mūsā Ashʿarī replied, 'I am conveying a proposal from Muʿāwiya's son to the ex-wife of ʿAbdallāh Zubayr.' Qāsim then said, 'Propose to her for me, too.' After a couple more steps, he met the Commander of Believers Ḥusayn (pbuh). He asked, 'Where are you going?' Mūsā Ashʿarī replied, 'I am conveying a proposal from Yazīd to the ex-wife of ʿAbdallāh Zubayr.' Ḥusayn said, 'Tell her about my proposal, too.'

{8} The rest of the story. When Mūsā Ashʿarī went to the lady he looked upon her beauty and fainted. When he regained consciousness, he said, 'I have four proposals for you.' She said, 'Tell me.' He said, 'The first is mine, then that of Yazīd, then that of Qāsim, and the fourth that of the Commander of Believers Ḥusayn (pbuh).' The lady said, 'O Mūsā, you are old while I am young; our marriage would not last long. You tell me which of the other three is more qualified.' Mūsā Ashʿarī said, 'If you seek authority and power, choose Yazīd. If you wish to have beauty and dignity accept Qāsim, and if you want both the world and the hereafter, choose Ḥusayn.' She soon replied, 'Marry me with the Commander of Believers Ḥusayn so others will not desire me anymore and so that I may be counted among the descendants of the Prophet (pbuh).'

{9} After the marriage, Mūsā Ashʿarī went back and told the story. Muʿāwiya said, 'O Mūsā, I had separated her from ʿAbdallāh Zubayr with much trickery and you rapidly ruined my plan!' The wretched Yazīd heard about this event and said to himself, 'As soon as my father's sovereignty reaches me, I will behead Ḥusayn.' The miserable wretch said this and his adversary became the Prophet. But how was this pathetic being able to do this? It was the decree of the Necessary Being.

{10} Another story. Once upon a time, the Master of the World, Muḥammad (pbuh) was sitting down when Muʿāwiya arrived. The Prophet said, 'O Muʿāwiya, a son will come out of your loins who will be the killer of Ḥasan and Ḥusayn.' Muʿāwiya said, 'O Master of the World, I have no children in the world and I promised that I would not marry any woman in order not to have a child.' Muʿāwiya woke one night to urinate. After urinating, he cleaned himself with the wall. A scorpion bit the head of his penis and it was excruciatingly painful. Wise people said, 'It will not heal unless you have intercourse with a woman so that the poison will flow out of your penis.' Muʿāwiya then had intercourse with a woman. The filthy Yazīd was conceived in the mother's womb. Be aware, O faithful brother, that the divine decree will be achieved and calamities will befall God's friends. The worst sufferings were imposed upon the prophets, then slightly less upon the friends of God, and a lesser suffering upon the believers. Ones' dignity [in the eye of God] is based on the suffering imposed upon him.

[...] می‌رسد و بلاها به دوستان خود نصیب کرد. سخت ترین رنج‌ها بر انبیاء بود و از آن کمتر اولیاء را بود و مؤمنان را از آن کمتر بود. قدر و قُرب همه به رنج اندراست.

{۱۱} بیت: سعدیا گر همّتی داری منال از جور یار، تا جهان بودست جور یار بر یار آمدست[۱۸]

{۱۲} و حضرت پیغمبر ما از همهٔ دوستان نزدیک تر است و سخت‌ترین بلاها نصیب حضرت محمّد رسول الله ﷺ بود. در دنیا خوش‌دلی کم داشت و از کفّار و منافقان در تن مبارک او چه رنج‌ها رسید.[۱۹] و ازجهت أَمیر المُؤمِنین حسن و حسین چند کرّت دل مبارک ایشان از خوشی به ناخوشی مبدّل شد. و برادر مؤمن به متابعت صدر و بدر عالم خوش‌دلی نطلبد.[۲۰]

{۱۳} چون روز تولّد أَمیر المُؤمِنین حسن و حسین شد، جبرئیل آمد و گفت «یا رسول الله، در خانهٔ دختر شما پسر زاده شده». پیغمبر برخاست و به خانهٔ دختر آمد. و أَمیر المُؤمِنین حسین را در کنار گرفت و در گوش او بانگ نماز گفتند که[۲۱] فرشتگان از خداوند رخصت خواستند و ازجهتِ مبارک‌بادِ پیغمبر علیه‌السلام آمدند. فرشته بر پرّ[۲۲] جبرئیل نشسته نزدیک رسول رسید. پیغمبر علیه‌السلام نگاه کرد، دید که هردو بازوی فرشته سوخته است. پیغمبر علیه‌السلام پرسید که «ای برادر جبرئیل، حکمت چیست که آن فرشته را در بازوی خود نشانده آورده‌ای؟»

{۱۴} جبرئیل گفت «یا نبي اَللّٰه، این فرشته در جمیع عمر خود یک‌بار در فرمان خدای تَعَالَی تقصیر کرده. از شومی آن گناه هر دو بازوی این فرشته سوخته گشته. اکنون از خدای تَعَالَی التماس کرده است که «مرا نزدیک پیغمبر خدای بوبرید[ب]» تا تو را مبارک باد کند و مرا فرمان شده است که «او را نزدیک محمّد ببر و بگو که هر دو دست حسین[۲۳] بر هر دو بازوی فرشته نهد، نیکو شود»».

[۱۸] برگرفته از دیوان غزلیّات سعدی شیرازی است. در برخی نسخ این بیت موجود نیست. امّا در برگ ۱۵۶ نسخهٔ ۱۲۲۲ تاجیکستان چنین آمده است: «سعدی قلم بسختی رفتست و نیکبختی، تا هر چه پیش آید گردن بنه قضا را؛ سعدیا گر همتی داری منال از جور یار، تا جهان باقیست جور یار بر یار آمدست». [۱۹] چه رنج‌ها که نرسید. [۲۰] این باور مبنی بر به همراه داشتن حزن و خوش‌دل نبودن در دنیا همچنان در بین پیروان مکتب تشیّع رایج است. بنابر باور شیعه غمناک بودن برای خدا و اولیاء او، بویژه حسن و حسین، لازمهٔ رسیدن به سعادت دنیوی و اخروی است. [۲۱] در آن لحظه. [۲۲] اشاره به «بال» دارد. [۲۳] براساس اکثر نسخ مالایی، هر دو دست حسن و حسین بر بازوان فرشته قرار می‌گیرد.

[ب] ببرید

{11} Poem: O Saʿdī, do not complain of the friend's maltreatment; the friend's harshness has always been imposed upon the friend for as long as the world has been.[3]

{12} Our Prophet is closer [to God] than all other friends. The worst difficulties were imposed upon Prophet Muḥammad (pbuh). He had few cheerful moments. So much was his suffering at the hands of the infidels and hypocrites! Regarding the commanders of believers Ḥasan and Ḥusayn, the Prophet's heart-felt feelings changed from happiness to sadness several times. In this vein, O faithful brother, and in following the Prophet, being heartily happy would not work.[4]

{13} On the birthday of the commanders of believers Ḥasan and Ḥusayn, Gabriel arrived and said, 'O Messenger of God, a son has been born in the house from your daughter.' The Prophet stood up and went to his daughter's house, and embraced the Commander of Believers Ḥusayn and whispered to call to prayer in his ear. Angels had permission from God to go and congratulate the Prophet. An angel sitting on Gabriel's wing came to the Messenger. The Prophet (pbuh) looked and noticed that both wings of the angel were burnt. The Prophet (pbuh) asked, 'O brother Gabriel, what is the reason that you have brought this angel on your wing?'

{14} Gabriel responded, 'O Prophet of God, this angel has only once failed in following the order of God. Due to that transgression both of his wings have been burnt. He has asked to for permission from God to "bring me" to congratulate you. I have been commanded "to bring him to you and ask you to put both Ḥusayn's hands on the two wings of the angel so that they may be healed.'

[3] Based on Saʿdī's *Dīwān*. [4] Being unhappy for the sake of Ḥasan and Ḥusayn in this world is a common belief among Shīʿī believers.

{۱۵} پیغمبر علیه‌السلام هر دو دست أَمیر المُؤمِنین حسین را بر هر دو بازوی وی فرود آورد. هر دو بازوی فرشته نیکو شد و درزمانْ این فرشته در هوا پرید. حضرت پیغمبر بسیار شادمان گشت که «از برکتِ فرزند من فرشته نیکو شد». حضرت نظر بر روی جبرئیل کرد. او را غمناک دید. پرسید «چرا غمناکی؟» گفت «یا رسول الله، این فرشته که در هوا شده است به جز یک بار دیگر در دنیا نیاید، مگر آن‌روز که این فرزند تو را شهید کنند.[ج] آن‌گه این فرشته التماس کند که «یا ربّ، مرا در دنیا فرست تا ماتم او بدارم».[د] چون حضرت پیغمبر صلی‌الله‌علیه‌وسلم این خبر شنید ملول گشت.

{۱۶} نظیر دیگر. روزی پیک حضرت «ربّ العالَمین»، جبرئیل، به صورت دحیه کلبی[۲۴] به خدمت صدر و بدر عالم آمد. و أَمیر المُؤمِنین حسن و حسین به کنار حضرت نشسته بودند. چون مهتر جبرئیل علیه‌السلام در نظر أَمیر المُؤمِنین حسین درآمد از کنار حضرت برخاست و در کنار جبرئیل علیه‌السلام نشست. و جانب هر دو آستین جبرئیل می‌دید. جبرئیل از صدر و بدر عالم پرسید که «حسین در آستین من چه می‌خواهد؟» سیّد کائنات گفت «ای برادر، تو نزد من به صورت دحیه کلبی آمده و هربار دحیه کلبی می‌آید به‌جهت ایشان تحفه می‌آرد. بدان خیال آستین تو می‌بیند».

{۱۷} جبرئیل علیه‌السلام گفت «رفته[۲۵] تا از حضرت پروردگار التماس کنم تا از برای ایشان چیزی بیارم». رفت و از بهشت دو انار بیاورد. و یکی به حسن و دیگر به حسین دادند. ایشان خوشدل شدند و انار می‌خورند.[۲۶] دل حضرت صدر و بدر عالم شادان شد. جبرئیل علیه‌السلام گفت «یا رسول الله حسن و حسین را دوست می‌داری؟» گفت «بلی، یا أَخی جبرئیل؛ «أَوْلادُنا أَكْبادُنا، یعنی فرزندان ما جگرگوش‌های مایند». رشته سبز در گردن مبارک حسین بسته بودند.[۲۷] و اثر آن خطی بر گلوی او ظاهر شده بود. آن خط را جبرئیل علیه‌السلام می‌دید و می‌گریست و سر خود را می‌جنبانید. حضرت پرسیدند «ای برادر، گردن فرزندم چه نگاه می‌کنی؟» گفت «یا رسول الله، روزی باشد که در دشت کربلا بدین خط شمشیر رود». چون این خبر شنیدند گریان شدند.

{۱۸} نظیر دیگر. روزی پیغمبر علیه‌السلام از نماز عید بازگشته بود و در خانهٔ فاطمه زهرا رضی‌الله‌عنها درآمد. دید که فاطمه غمگین نشسته است و آب در دیده می‌گرداند.[۲۸] پرسیدند «ای جگرگوشه، چرا آب در دید می‌گردانی؟» فاطمه گفت «یا رسول الله، امروز روزعید است. و جامهٔ حسن و حسین کهنه است و چرکین؛ و ایشان می‌گویند که «ما را جامهٔ خوب بده». ازجهت ایشان خاطر قرار نمی‌گیرد و آب در دیده می‌آید». پیغمبر صلی‌الله‌علیه‌وسلم فرمود «ای فاطمه، در حُجرهٔ خود درآی و هر چه بینی بیرون آر». فاطمه گفت «یا پدر بزرگوا، در

[۲۴] دحیة الكلبي. یکی دیگر از نشانه‌های ترجمهٔ مستقیم این داستان به زبان مالایی این است که نام این صحابهٔ پیامبر به‌صورت فارسی آمده است. به احتمال زیاد اکثر داستان‌های صحابه در ادبیات مالایی ریشهٔ فارسی دارند.
[۲۵] هم اکنون می‌روم. [۲۶] در برخی نسخ، جبرئیل انار را فقط به حسین می دهد.
[۲۷] اشاره به رنگ «سبز» رشته در برخی نسخ دیده نمی‌شود. [۲۸] غمگین همراه با بغض.

[ج] مگر آن که این فرزند تو را بکشند [د] تا ماتم بر سر تربت او بدارم

{15} The Prophet (pbuh) put both hands of the Commander of Believers Ḥusayn on the wings of the angel. Both wings healed and the angel quickly flew to the sky. The Prophet was happy, saying, 'Due to the blessing of my child, this angel was healed.' The Prophet looked upon Gabriel. He found Gabriel sad. The Prophet asked him, 'Why are you sad?' Gabriel said, 'O Messenger of God, this angel which is flying, will only come once more into the world; the day on which your child will be martyred. This angel has begged, "O Lord, send me to the world so I can mourn for him.[5]"' When the Prophet (pbuh) heard this, he became upset.

{16} Another story. Once upon a time, the emissary of the Lord of the World, Gabriel, came to the Prophet in the form of [the Companion] Diḥya Kalbī.[6] Also, the commanders of believers Ḥasan and Ḥusayn were next to the Prophet. When the Commander of Believers Ḥusayn saw His Eminence Gabriel (pbuh), he left the Prophet and sat next to Gabriel (pbuh). And he searched both of Gabriel's sleeves. Gabriel asked the Prophet, 'What is he looking for in my sleeves?' The Master of the Worlds said, 'O brother, you came to me in the form of Diḥya al-Kalbī. Whenever Diḥya al-Kalbī comes, he brings a gift for them. He is searching your sleeves because of this habit.'

{17} Gabriel said, 'Let me go, and ask God to give me something for them.' He went and brought two pomegranates from paradise. He gave one of them to Ḥasan and the other to Ḥusayn. They became excited and began to eat the pomegranates. The Prophet felt happy. Gabriel (pbuh) said, 'O Messenger of God, do you love Ḥasan and Ḥusayn?' He replied, 'Yes, O my brother Gabriel; our children are our darlings.' A green cotton thread was tied around the blessed neck of Ḥusayn and its trace was apparent on his throat. Gabriel (pbuh) saw the line and cried, shaking his head. The Prophet asked him, 'O brother, what do you look at on my child's neck?' He said, 'O Messenger of God, a day will arrive on which a sword touches upon this line in the plain of Karbala.' When Muḥammad heard this news he began to cry.

{18} Another story. Once upon a time, the Prophet (pbuh) returned from Eid prayers and went to the house of Fāṭima Zahrā (pbuh). He found Fāṭima sad with her eyes full of tears. He asked, 'O darling, why are you crying?' Fāṭima said, 'O Messenger of God, today is the day of Eid, and the clothes of Ḥasan and Ḥusayn are old and dirty, and they ask for nice clothes. Because of them I am upset and my eyes are tearful.' The Prophet (pbuh) said, 'O Fāṭima, go to your room and bring whatever you can see.' Fāṭima said, 'O honourable father, I have nothing in my room.' The Messenger of God said, 'Go into your room and then behold the power of God.' When she entered into

[5] i.e., Ḥusayn [6] In Arabic: Diḥya al-Kalbī. Another reason that demonstrates the influence of Persian on Malay Muslim literature is the existence of non-Arabic forms of early Muslim names (i.e., without '*al-*') in most of their stories.

حُجرهٔ من چیزی نیست». رسول علیه‌السلام گفت «تو در آر و قدرت حق سبحانه و تعالی را تماشا کن».[ه] چون در حُجره درآمد طَبَقی سیمین[۲۹] دید، دو قبّهٔ زرّین بالا نهاده. از آن بیرون آورد و پیش حضرت نهاده. سر آن را برداشتند و دو حلّه سفید بود. یکی به حسن دادند و ایشان[۳۰] فرمودند که «ما را جامهٔ رنگین می باید.» پیغمبر ﷺ گفت «فاطمه قدری آب در جا[۳۱] کرده بیارید».[و] فاطمه در ظرفِ آب کرده بیاورد و حضرت هر دو حلّه را در آب انداخت. از أَمیر المُؤمِنین حسن پرسید «تو را چه رنگ می‌باید؟» حسن گفت «سبز». [پیامبر] در آب کرده جامهٔ سبز بیرون آورده به او دادند. بعداز آن، از أَمیر المُؤمِنین حسین پرسیدند «تو را چه رنگ می‌باید؟» گفت «مرا سرخ». دست در آب کرده جامهٔ سرخ بیرون آورده به او دادند. هر دو برادران خوشحال شده جامه پوشیدند و در نظر مبارک[۳۲] زیبا می نمودند؛ بر روی ایشان می‌دیدند و شاد می‌شدند.

{۱۹} جبرئیل علیه‌السلام آمد و گفت «یا رسول الله، چنانچه جامهٔ تن ایشان زیبا است؛ حسن را زهر دهند، جملهٔ اندام او سبز گردد، و جملهٔ اندام حسین به خونِ حلق سرخ گردد». چون صدر و بدر عالم خبر شنید از جبرئیل پرسید «کشندگان فرزندانم چه کسانی باشند؟» جبرئیل علیه‌السلام گفت «هم[۳۳] در آن امّتان تو باشند». فرمودند «من در حیات باشم؟» گفت «نه». گفتند «پدر ایشان در حیات باشد؟» [جبرئیل] گفت «نه». گفتند «مادر ایشان باشد؟» گفت «نباشد». گفتند «أَمیر المُؤمِنین ابوبکر و أَمیر المُؤمِنین عمر و أَمیر المُؤمِنین عثمان باشند؟»[۳۴] گفت «نباشند». [پیامبر] فرمودند «تعزیت فرزندان عزیز من که دارد؟» گفت «جانوران بیابان و مرغان هوا و امّتان وفادار تو ماتم بر آرند. هرسال که دههٔ عاشورا[ز] درآید زارزار بگریند. به موافقت ایشان روزه دارند. و تعزیت فرزندان تو به جای آرند».[۳۵]

{۲۰} آمدیم به سر حکایت. چون معاویه از دنیا برفت و خلافت به یزید پلید رسید، نامه در مدینه فرستاد و بر ولید بن عتبه عتاب کرد که «أَمیر المُؤمِنین حسین را در بیعت من بخوان». ولید نامه برگفت و در مسجد خواجهٔ عالم در آمد و نالان زد. أَمیر المُؤمِنین حسین درآمد. نامه پیش أَمیر المُؤمِنین حسین نهاد تا امیر آن را بخواند. در خشم درآمد و فرمود که «من در بیعت او چگونه درآیم که او از اهل دوزخ است».

{۲۱} باز یزید پلید معلونِ روسیاه مکتوب دگر فرستاد که «ای ولید، هرگاه او بیعت من قبول نکند باید که سر او را بریده نزد من فرستی». چون ولید بن عتبه عتاب شنید در مکر و حیله شد که أَمیر المُؤمِنین حسین را گرفته هلاک کنند. امیر به او گفت «در تدبیر کشتن من چه شده‌ای که جدّ من مرا خبر کرده است

[۲۹] سینی نقره‌ای یا نقره‌ای رنگ. [۳۰] فرزندان. [۳۱] آبدان. [۳۲] در نظر پیامبر. [۳۳] همه.

[۳۴] در برخی نسخ سؤالی در مورد نقش فاطمه و ابوبکر و عمر مطرح نمی شود. [۳۵] درنسخهٔ طلعتِ قاهره، برگ ۱۱۵، یک بیت شعر (یا ضرب المثل) وجود دارد «درین عالم کسی بیغام نباشد، اگر باشد بنی آدم نباشد». این شعر در پایان «شرح الهارونية في التصريف» به شمارهٔ XI.-L. S. Cod. G در کتابخانهٔ ماربورگ آلمان دیده می‌شود «درین عالم کسی بی غم نباشد، اگر باشد بنی آدم نباشد».

[ه] گفت «یا پدر بزرگوار، در حُجره من چیزی نیست». رسول الله علیه‌السلام گفت «مرا جبرئیل خبر کرده است چیزی باشد». [و] «یا فاطمه، قدح آب پُر کن و بیار». [ز] ماه عاشورا

the room she noticed a silver tray on which there were two golden containers. She took them out and put them before the Prophet. They lifted the lids and found two white garments there. They gave one of them to Ḥasan and he said, 'Make it colourful'. The Prophet (pbuh) said, 'Fāṭima, pour a drop of water into the container and bring it in.' Fāṭima poured water into the container and brought it. And Prophet put both garments into the water. He asked the Commander of Believers Ḥasan, 'What colour do you prefer?' Ḥasan said, 'Green.' The Prophet put his hand into the water and brought out a green garment and passed it to Ḥasan. Subsequently, he asked the Commander of Believers Ḥusayn, 'What colour do you prefer to have?' Husayn said, 'I want red.' The Prophet put his hand into water and brought out the red garment and passed it on to him. Both brothers were excited and wore their clothes. They both looked happy and smart. Prophet enjoying seeing them happy.

{19} Gabriel (pbuh) arrived and said, 'O Messenger of God, the clothes look nice on them. However, Ḥasan will be poisoned and all his body will become green and the whole of Ḥusayn's body will become red.' When the Prophet heard this news he asked Gabriel, 'Who will be the killers of my children?' Gabriel (pbuh) said, 'They will be from your own community.' The Prophet said, 'Will I be alive?' He replied, 'No'. The Prophet asked, 'Will their father be alive?' Gabriel replied, 'No'. The Prophet said, 'What about their mother?' Gabriel said, 'No'. They said, 'Will the Commander of Believers Abū Bakr, or the Commander of Believers ʿUmar, or the Commander of Believers ʿUthmān be there?' Gabriel said, 'No'. The Prophet said, 'So, who will mourn for my sweet children?' Gabriel said, 'Desert animals, sky birds, and the faithful members of your community will mourn them. They will cry over the day of ʿĀshūrāʾ every year. In this way, they will fast and will mourn for your children.'

{20} We return to rest of the story. When Muʿāwiya died, and his caliphate reached the filthy Yazīd, he sent a letter to Medina, and strictly commanded Walīd the son of ʿUtba (henceforth: Walīd b. ʿUtba), 'Persuade Ḥusayn, the Commander of Believers, to pledge to me his allegiance.' Walīd took the letter and went to the mosque of the Master of the World and called to him. The Commander of Believers Ḥusayn came out. He put the letter before the Commander of Believers Ḥusayn for him to read. Ḥusayn became angry and said, 'How can I pledge allegiance to him as he is from hell!?'

{21} Again, the filthy, accursed, and shameful Yazīd sent another letter, 'O Walīd, if he does not accept to pledge allegiance, you must cut off his head and bring it to me.' When Walīd the son of ʿUtba read this statement he thought of some ways in which he could capture and kill the Commander of Believers Ḥusayn. Ḥusayn said to him, 'How is it that you are thinking about killing me as my grandfather has warned me about this in advance and that the wretched Yazīd is from hell!?' Then Walīd said, 'It is better that you leave this town.' Meanwhile, another letter to the Commander of Believers

که یزید پلید از اهل نار[۳۶] است». آنگاه ولید گفت «شما از این شهر سفر اختیار کنید».[۳۷] درین وقت از کوفه مکتوب به أَمیر المُؤمِنین حسین آمد که «البتّه اینجا تشریف ارزانی فرمایید که ما همه با تو بیعت می‌کنیم. و تو را از دل و جان دوست می داریم و یاری می‌دهیم».

{۲۲} چون نامه بخوانْد نزد جدّه اُمّ‌سَلَمَه بیامد و گفت «ای مادر، در حقّ من چه صواب می‌بینی که دشمنان قصد کشتن من کرده‌اند؟ اگر مصلحت دانی به کوفه روم». اُمّ‌سَلَمَه گفت «ای فرزند، تو را معلوم است که شهید شدن تو نزدیک شده و آن روز نزدیک رسید که حقّ سُبحانَهُ وَتَعالیٰ زمین را به خون تو و خون فرزندان تو کرامت کرده است». پس اُمّ‌سَلَمَه برخاست و در حُجره آمد و شیشه بیرون آورد و چندان گریست که بیهوش گشت. امیر فرمود «ای مادر چه گریه می‌کنی؟» گفت «ای فرزند، تو خُرد بودی و در کنار سیّدالمرسلین محمّد مُصْطَفَى صَلَّى اللهُ عَلَيْهِ وَسَلَّم بازی می‌کردی که جبرئیل عَلَيْهِ السَّلَام در رسید، و حضرت محمّد مُصْطَفَى صَلَّى اللهُ عَلَيْهِ وَسَلَّم تو را به من داد و خود به جبرئیل مشغول شد. چون از جبرئیل فارغ شد تو را از من گرفت و به روی مبارک تو بوسه می‌داد. جبرئیل پرسید «یا رسول الله، تو این فرزند را دوست می‌داری؟» فرمودند «آری. بسیار دوست میدارم». جبرئیل گفت «امّتان تو این فرزند را چنان بکشند که قصّاب گوسفند را کُشد. دیگر اگر بگویی خاک آن زمین را بیارم که حسین بدان کشته خواهد شد». جبرئیل در دشت کربلا برفت و قدری خاک بیاورد و گفت «یا نبي الله، هرگاه که این خاک به رنگ خون گردد، بدانی که کشتن حسین نزدیک رسید». سیّد عالم عَلَيْهِ السَّلَام مرا بخواند و گفت «ای اُمّ‌سَلَمَه، این خاک در شیشه نگاه‌دار و هرسال می‌دیده باش. هرگاه به رنگ سرخ ببینی، بدانی که شهادت حسین نزدیک رسیده است». من امروز در شیشه نظر کردم و به رنگ خون آمد»».

{۲۳} چون أَمیر المُؤمِنین حسین این خبر شنید گریه‌کنان از خانه بیرون آمد، و در روضهٔ صدر و بدر رفت و زیارت کرد و گفت «یا جدّا، امّتان تو قصد کشتن من کردند». تربت جدّ در کنار گرفته بود که در خواب رفت و روی جهان‌آرای جدّ خود محمّد مُصْطَفَى صَلَّى اللهُ عَلَيْهِ وَسَلَّم در خواب دید و فرشتگان و روحانیان و کرّوبیان[۳۸] و جبرئیل و میکائیل و اسرافیل و عزرائیل عَلَيْهِمُ السَّلَام نزد پیغمبر آمدند. چون چشم مبارک جدّ بر حسین افتاد وی را در کنار گرفت و گفت «ای فرزند، می‌دانم که دشمنان در حقّ تو بدی می‌کنند. امّا فردای قیامت ایشان را از شفاعت من نصیب نیست. و تو را نزد حقّ سُبحانَهُ وَتَعالیٰ درجهٔ شهادت داده‌اند. و بدان نرسی تا شهید نگردی. و دیگر ای فرزند، بهشت را از بهر آمدن تو آراسته‌اند، و من با مادر و پدر تو بر خوانِ کَرَمْ آماده شده‌ایم. زود بیا تا به کرامت اَبَد برسی. ای فرزند، بدین درجات نرسی تا شربت شهادت بخشی. پیغمبر صَلَّى اللهُ عَلَيْهِ وَسَلَّم دست مبارک برداشت و دعا کرد و دعا آن است «بِسْمِ اللهِ الرَّحْمَٰنِ الرَّحِيمِ، عَلَى الحُسَينِ صَبْرًا وأعظَمْ أَجْراً، معنی آن است که ای خدای، حسین مرا در صبر دار و در صبر کردن ثوابش ده»». و از خواب درزمانْ بیدار گشت و بر اهل

[۳۶] اهل جهنّم. [۳۷] شما را از این شهر می‌باید رفت. [۳۸] فرشتگان مقرّب درگاه الهی. واژه «کرّوبیان» در اشعار سعدی، خاقانی و حافظ دیده می‌شود.

Ḥusayn arrived from Kufa saying, 'Of course, you are wholeheartedly invited to come here as we all want to pledge our allegiance to you. And we are totally in favour of you and will assist you.'

{22} When he read this letter, he went to his grandmother, Umm Salama, and said, 'O Mother, what would be your advice as the enemies have planned to kill me. If it seems right to you, then I will go to Kufa.' Umm Salama said, 'O my son, it is apparent that the time of your martyrdom is getting closer and the day is about to come in which God will bless the Earth with the blood of you and your children.' Then Umma Salama got up and went to her room and brought out a glass receptacle. She cried to the extent that she became unconscious. The Commander said, 'O mother, why are you crying?' She said, 'O my son, you were still a child and were playing next to the Prophet (pbuh). Then Gabriel arrived and Prophet Muḥammad (pbuh) gave you to me and he was engaged with Gabriel. When he finished with Gabriel, he took you back from me and kissed your face. Gabriel asked, "O Messenger of God, do you like this child?" The Prophet said, "Yes, I love him very much." Gabriel said, "Your community will kill him like a slaughterman kills sheep. Also, if you want I will bring the soil of that land on which Ḥusayn will be killed." Then Gabriel went to the plain of Karbala and brought back a handful of soil, and said, "O Prophet of God, when the colour of this soil turns red, you should know that the moment of killing Ḥusayn is imminent". The Master of the World called me and said, "O Umm Salama, hold this soil in this glass receptacle and check it every year. Whenever you notice the colour turns red, be aware that the moment of martyrdom of Ḥusayn is imminent." And I have now checked the bottle and it has turned a bloody colour.'

{23} When the Commander of Believers Ḥusayn heard this, he came out of the house, crying, and went to visit the shrine of the Prophet, saying, 'O grandfather, your community aims to kill me.' Then he embraced the grave of his grandfather and fell asleep, dreaming of his grandfather's face by which the world is illumined. Muḥammad (pbuh) and all the angels, spiritual beings, and archangels were around the Prophet together with Gabriel and Michael, Seraphiel, and ʿIzrāʾīl (pbuh). When the Prophet's blessed eye noticed Ḥusayn, he hugged him and said, 'O my son, I know how the enemies make trouble for you. However, they will not receive my intercession on the Day of Judgement. And you have been bestowed the level of martyr before God. And you will not achieve this rank until your martyrdom. And, also, my son, paradise has been prepared for your coming and I, along with you mother and father are prepared to receive you in glory. Come soon in order to gain the everlasting blessing. O son, you will not achieve this rank if you do not drink from the cup of martyrdom.' The Prophet (pbuh) lifted his sacred hand in supplication and prayed. And the prayer was, 'In the name of God, the Compassionate, the Merciful, grant patience to Ḥusayn, and

بیت خود این خواب بگفت. جمله در گریه شدند. زیرا که از صدر و بدر عالم همین فرزند یادگار مانده بود.

{۲۴} باز کوفیان نامه دگر فرستادند که زودتر تشریف بیارید. أَمیر المُؤمِنین حسین مسلم بن عقیل را به کوفه فرستاد. یزیدِ پلیدِ ملعون را خبر شد. عبدالله زیاد[۳۹] را حکم کرد تا راه مسلم عقیل را پیشِ راه بگیرد. و باز یزید پلید شنید که أَمیر المُؤمِنین حسین خود به کوفه بیرون آمده است.

{۲۵} باز عبدالله زیاد را گفت «برو با ده هزار سوار و آب فرات بگیر». چون لشگر أَمیر المُؤمِنین در آب فرات رسیدند پرسیدند که «این کدام زمین است؟» گفتند «این را دشت کربلا گویند». درزمانْ شتر حضرت امیر در آن زمین نشست. هرچند أَمیر المُؤمِنین حسین سعی کرد شتر برنخاست. آنگه گفت «رَضِینَا بِقَضاءِ اللهِ تَعَالَی». بعداز آن گفت «ای یاران، بدانید که دراین زمین شهادت من خواهد بود».

{۲۶} از یاران چوبی به‌جهت خیمه می‌برید.[ح] همین که تبر بر درخت زد، خون از درخت ظاهر شد و بر هر درختی که تبر زدی خون جدا گشتی. آن شخص به خدمت أَمیر المُؤمِنین حسین بیامد و حال گفت. أَمیر المُؤمِنین حسین آغاز کرد که «این همان مقام است که جدّم خبر داده بود که شهادت تو بدان مقام خواهد بود که چنین علامت از درخت ظاهر گردد».[۴۰]

{۲۷} و هرگاه که روان می‌شدند خود را باز در آن مقام می‌دیدند.[۴۱] هفت شبانه‌روز در آن بیابان به گرسنگی و تشنگی گذشت. خلق از صغار و کبار[۴۲] از بی‌آبی هلاک می‌شدند. و عمرسعد نام مردی بود از لشگر یزید بدبخت؛ در لب آب فرات فرود آمده بود. کسی را نزد أَمیر المُؤمِنین حسین فرستاد که یزید ملعون ما را چنین گفته که «به هیچ چیز مشغول نگردی تا آنکه حسین را نزد من نیاری». أَمیر المُؤمِنین حسین گفت «مگر شما نمی‌دانید که من کیستم؟ و پدر من که بود و جدّ من کیست؟» گفتند «پدر تو علی مرتضی است. و مادر تو فاطمهٔ زهرا و جدّ تو حضرت محمّد مُصْطَفَی ﷺ». أَمیر المُؤمِنین حسین گفت «اگر چنین می‌دانید پس چرا میان به کین[۴۳] من بسته‌اید، و فردای قیامت پیش حضرت صمدّیت چه جواب خواهید داد؟ و بر روی حضرت رسالت‌پناه چگونه نِگرید؟» جواب دادند «از این باک نداریم و می‌خواهیم تو را در بیعت یزید درآریم». امیر فرمود «وای بر شما باد. هرگز دخترزادهٔ[ط] حضرت رسالت‌پناهی تابع ظالمِ دوزخ نشود. اگر این اندیشه دارید والله که بدین اندیشه نرسید. امّا آنچه خداوند تَعَالَی عَزَّوَجَلَّ خواهد همان خواهد شد. شما را می‌گویم

[۳۹] عبیدالله بن زیاد. [۴۰] بیان بروز علائم شهادت حسین بن علی در دشت کربلا در متون متأخّر بیشتر دیده می‌شود. امّا همچنان از ویژگی‌های قابل توجّه درّالمجالس اشاره‌ای قصّه‌گونه به خروج خون از درختان به دلیل شهادت حسین است. باوری که همچنان در برخی مجامع عمومی (به ویژه در ایران و آسیای جنوبی) وجود دارد. گونهٔ دیگر آن در محرّق القلوب نراقی دیده می‌شود: «نقل کرده‌اند که در بعضی بلاد روم صورت شیریست از سنگ و در همهٔ سال چون روز عاشورا شود از دو چشم آن شیر دو چشمهٔ خون جاری می‌شود و تا شب منقطع نمی‌شود. و مردمی که در آن حوالی سکنی دارند در آنجا جمع می‌شوند و تعزیهٔ اهل بیت می‌دارند». نراقی، محرّق القلوب، نسخهٔ کتابخانهٔ مجلس ۵۷۰۰، برگ ۱۶۷. [۴۱] چنین عبارتی پیرامون سردرگمی و راه‌به‌جایی نداشتن در داستان «بلعم باعور» و در مورد قوم موسیٰ نیز دیده می‌شود. [۴۲] کوچک و بزرگ. [۴۳] جنگ، خصومت، کینه.

[ح] شخصی برای چوب رفته بود تبری برد [ط] نبیره

give him a huge reward for this patience', meaning, 'O God, make my Ḥusayn patient, and reward him for this patience.' At that moment, Ḥusayn woke up and narrated this dream to his household. All began to cry. Because he was the last vestige of the Prophet remaining in the world.

{24} The people of Kufa wrote another letter, again saying, 'Please come as soon as possible.' The Commander of Believers sent Muslim son of ʿAqīl to Kufa. The filthy, accursed Yazīd learned about this. He ordered ʿAbdallāh Ziyād[7] to block Muslim ʿAqīl. And the filthy Yazīd heard again that the Commander of Believers Ḥusayn had himself left for Kufa.

{25} Yazīd, again, ordered ʿAbdallāh Ziyād, 'Go with ten thousand horsemen and block the Euphrates river.' When the troop of the Commander of Believers Ḥusayn came near the Euphrates river, they asked, 'What is this place known as?' They were told, 'Here is the plain of Karbala.' Upon hearing this the Commander's camel sat down. Whatever the Commander of Believers Ḥusayn tried the camel would not rise. Then he said, 'I am satisfied with God's decree.' Later on, he said, 'O Companions, be aware that this land is the place of my martyrdom.'

{26} One of the Companions was cutting wood to make tents. As soon as he hit the tree with an axe, blood issued from the tree; and flowed down touching every single tree.[8] The man came to the Commander of Believers Ḥusayn and told him about this. The Commander of Believers Ḥusayn said, 'This is exactly the place my grandfather has talked about when he said that my martyrdom will happen in a place where such a sign appears from the trees.'

{27} Wherever they went, they again found themselves in the same land.[9] They spent seven hungry and thirsty days in the desert. All members of the camp, young and old, were about to die of thirst. And there was a man from the army of the miserable Yazīd, named ʿUmar Saʿd who had settled next to the river. He sent an emissary to the Commander of Believers Ḥusayn to say, 'The filthy Yazīd has ordered us not to do anything else until we take you to him.' The Commander of Believers said, 'Do you not know who I am? Who my father was? Who my grandfather was?' They said, 'Your

[7] ʿUbaydallāh b. Ziyād. [8] *Durr al-Majālis* is one of the earliest sources in Islamic literature in which natural elements are engaged with the death of Ḥusayn. In recent Shīʿī literature, too, one may find such references as the pouring of blood out of a tree on the tenth day of Muharram, a belief which is still popular among some Shīʿī communities in Iran and South Asia. Shīʿī sources like *Muḥarriq al-qulūb* (f. 167, Ms. 5700 in the Parliamentary Library of Iran) also includes another form of reference to the way nature is engaged with the death of Ḥusayn: 'it is reported that in the territory of Rūm (highly likely, Turkey?), there is a statue of a lion made of stone. Every year on the day of ʿĀshūrāʾ, blood issued and flowed down from its eyes non-stop until the night. And the local people gather around it in order to commemorate the *ahl al-bayt*'. [9] A similar episode is found in the story of 'Balʿam Bāʿūr'.

که مرا راه دهید تا به شهر مسلمانان رویم، و یا آب دهید تا اهل بیت هلاک نگردند». گفتند «ای حسین، امروز سگان و خوکان[۴۴] را آب دهیم و شما را آب ندهیم». خاک بر دهن ایشان.[۴۵]

{۲۸} پس أَمیر المُؤمِنین گفت «بارخدایا، نزد تو ظاهر و روشن است. بلایی برین دشمنان فرست «یا غیاث المستغیثین، ای فریادرس فریادخواهان»». چون مناجات تمام کرد، پس از لشگر یزید حُرّ نامِ مردی بود، از فوج ایشان جدا شد و نزد امیر بیامد. استغفارگویان گفت «ای سرور و اولاد آدم، اگر من می‌دانستم که این خلق را با شما دشمن است، من هرگز نمی‌آمدم. امیر فرمود «چه نام داری؟» گفت «حرُّ [بن] یزید». فرمودند «ای حُرّ، حرام گردانید خدای تَعَالَی آتش دوزخ را بر تو». حُرّ گفت «فرمان ده که با دشمنان تو کارزار کنم و در رضای حقّ ﷻ شهید گردم». این سخن بگفت سلاح بر خود استوار کرد و متوجّه[۴۶] جنگ شد. در اوّل حمله چهار کس را به دوزخ فرستاد. بعداز آن چندان حرب کرد که قوّت نماند و شربت شهادت بدو[۴۷] برسید. اوّل کس که به مرتبه شهادت رسید حُرّ بن یزید بود.

{۲۹} بعداز آن انصاری-نام یاری بود با مادر خود. از صف امیر جدا شد بر دشمنان به حرب پیوست و بسیار کسان را به دوزخ فرستاد و این مناجات می گفت «یُقاتِلُ بَینَ یَدَي إبنِ رَسُولِ اللهِ حَتّي تَدخُلُ فِي شِفاعَتِه». عُمر سعد از لشگر یزید بیرون آمد و با جوان در جنگ شد. بعده، خود هم شربت شهادت چشید. و مادر سر پسر را در کنار گرفت، و خاک از روی او پاک می کرد و در رویش بوسه می‌داد و می گفت «رحمت باد ای فرزند، نیکوکاری کردی که سر خود را در راه فرزند پیغمبر باختی و به مقصود ابد رسیدی». آنگه مادرش بانگ بر عمر سعد بزد که «استاده شو! تا انصاف فرزند خود را از تو بسْتانم که جگرگوشهٔ مرا بکشتی، ودل مرا کباب کردی. اکنون با تو جنگ می کنم، تا خدای تَعَالَی هر چه خواهد آن کند». این سخن بگفت و حمله بر عمر کرد. و چنان بر سر او گرز زد که سرش بشکست[ی] و از پشت اسب بیفتاد و بیهوش شد. این زن به جانب لشگر خود بازگشت. چون چشم أَمیر المُؤمِنین حسین بر آن افتاد گفت «رحمت باد، دل‌شاد کردی ای مادر. برو در میان اهل بیت نشین که جنگ بر زنان نیامده است».[۴۸]

[۴۴] اشاره به حیواناتی که در اسلام ناپاک محسوب می‌شوند. [۴۵] این نفرین در بسیاری از نسخ موجود نیست. امّا در داستان مالایی ترجمه تحت اللفظی آن دیده می‌شود. [۴۶] روی آورد. [۴۷] به او. [۴۸] داستان مادر انصار ی در نسخهٔ طولانی متفاوت است.

[ی] که سر او پاره پاره گشت

father was ʿAlī Murtaḍā, and your mother was Fāṭima Zahrāʾ, and your grandfather was Prophet Muḥammad (pbuh).' The Commander of Believers said, 'If you know this, why did you agree to be hostile towards me? What will you say before the Everlasting Lord on the Day of Judgement? And how will you face the Prophet?' They responded, 'We do not fear this and we only want you to pledge your allegiance to Yazīd.' The Commander said, 'Shame on you! The grandchild of the Prophet will never follow the devilish oppressor. Do not delude yourselves, by God, you will not gain my allegiance. But whatever God wants, will happen. I would ask you to give me a path to reach the city of Muslims, or give me water so that the descendants of the Prophet (*ahl al-bayt*) will not die.' They said – may they be choked [by God] – 'O Ḥusayn, we will water dogs and pigs today, but not you.'

{28} Then, the Commander of Believers said, 'O God, it[10] is obvious and clear to You; send a disaster upon these enemies, O the Helper of those who seek help, O the One who assists the needy!' After he finished praying, a man from the army of Yazīd, known as Ḥurr, was separated from his soldiers and came to the Commander Ḥusayn. While seeking forgiveness, he said, 'O my master, and the descendant of Adam, if I knew that these people would be hostile to you, I would never have accompanied them.' The Commander said, 'What is your name?' He said, 'Ḥurr b. Yazīd.' Ḥusayn said, 'O Ḥurr, God has saved you from hellfire.' Ḥurr said, 'Allow me to fight your enemies and be martyred for the sake of God's pleasure.' He said this, equipped himself, and went to the battlefield. During his first attack, he sent four people to hell. Then, he fought until he was left with no power and [ultimately] drank from the cup of martyrdom. The first one who reached the level of martyr was Ḥurr the son of Yazīd.

{29} After that was a man named Anṣārī, who was with his mother. He left the troop of the Commander to fight the enemy and sent many people to hell, while supplicating, 'He fights before the son of the Messenger of God until he becomes qualified for the Messenger's and/or his son's intercession.' ʿUmar Saʿd emerged from his troops and fought with the young man. Then, the young man drank from the cup of martyrdom.[11] And the mother held the head of her son and removed dust from his face and kissed his face and said, 'May God's mercy be upon you, my son! You performed well in losing your head for the sake of the Prophet's children and reaching the ultimate goal.' Then his mother shouted at ʿUmar Saʿd, 'Stay there until I take revenge for my child on you, as you killed my dearest and broke my hear! Now, I will fight you and reside myself to whatever God desires to do.' She made this statement and attacked ʿUmar. And she hit his head with a bludgeon so forcefully that his head was broken and he fell from his horse and became unconscious. The woman returned to her camp.

[10] i.e., our oppression [11] i.e. he was killed

{۳۰} یک‌یک از لشگر أَمیر المُؤمِنین بیرون می‌شدند و جنگ می‌کردند، کفّار[۴۹] می‌کشتند و شهید می‌شدند. چنانچه خون در زمین روان گشت و هشتاد و سه تن[ک] از لشگر امیر به شهادت رسیدند. پس أَمیر المُؤمِنین قاسم بن حسن، برادرزادهٔ أَمیر المُؤمِنین حسین، گفت «یا عَمّ بزرگوار، دستوری باشد که با دشمنان غزا[۵۰] کنم؟» أَمیر المُؤمِنین گفت «تو خُردی و یادگار برادر منی» . پای عمو بوسید و دستوری خواست. آنگه هر دو یکدیگر را کنار گرفتند و وداع قیامت می‌کردند. و قاسم رو به معرکه کرد و چنان کارزار بکرد که هفتاد کسان به دوزخ فرستاد. چندین کسان در هلاکت افتادند. آنگاه از لشگر یزید مردی با هیبت برآمد و قاسم بن حسن را شهید گردانید.[۵۱] و اسبِ خالی گریزان به‌جانب لشگرگاه امیر آمد. چون اسب را خالی دیدند از مردان و زنان فریاد برآمد. گویی آن روز قایم شده بود. بعداز زمانی أَمیرالمُؤمِنین حسین اهل‌بیت را شکسته‌خاطر دید. ایشان را دلداری می‌داد، و می‌گفت «آنچه حق سُبحانَهُ وَتَعالیٰ اراده کرد[ه] چنان خواهد شد».[ل]

{۳۱} آنگاه أَمیر المُؤمِنین حسین را پسری بود که او را علی اکبر می‌گفتند. گفت «ای پدر، امروز هفت روز است که مادرم را پسری شده است. شیر خشک شده است. مرا دستوری ده تا آب فرات بیارم که مادرم با طفل از تشنگی هلاک نگردد. یا آب آرم یا من هم شربت شهادت بچشم». أَمیر المُؤمِنین حسین چون سخن شنید گریان شد. گفت «ای جان پدر، بیا بابای خود را کنار گیر». بیامد و کنار گرفت و با پدر وداع کرد و بیرون آمد. امیر چشم جانب او بست و می‌گفت «اللّهم قَد خَرَجَ الّذي وَجهَهُ کَوَجهِ جَدّي رسول الله ﷺ، معنی چنین باشد که بار خدایا، بیرون آمد کسی که روی او همچو روی محمّد مُصطَفَی است و هرگاه آرزوی جدّم شدی، آن فرزند بدیدی و خرسند گشتمی. اکنون بار خدایا او روی به دشمنان کرده است، نصرتش بخش». علی اکبر به دشمنان رسید گفت «منم از خاندان مصطفیٰ، اگر ما را آب نمی‌دهید طفلان بی‌گناه هلاک می‌شوند و راه دهید تا قدری آب از بهر ایشان بریم». جواب دادند که «امروز سگان و خوکان را آب دهیم و دشمنان را آب ندهیم». علی اکبر چون شنید غلغلهٔ[۵۲] تکبیر برآورد و چنان حمله بکرد که صد وهفتاد کس را به دوزخ فرستاد. و نزد پدر بیامد و گفت «ای پدر، ازجهت تشنگی و گرسنگی سلاح بر من گران گشته است. اگر حلق من تَر گردد دمار از دشمنان برآرم.[۵۳] امّا ای پدر، بخواه از خداوند تَعالَی عَزَّوَجَلَّ که تشنگی از من برود». أَمیر المُؤمِنین چشم پرآب کرد و روی به آسمان کرد و دعا می‌گفت، هیچ مستجاب نمی‌بیند. آنگاه گفت «ای جگر گوشهٔ پدر، دعا اجابت نمی‌شود که جدّم ما را ازجهت امّت خود درباخته است». علی اکبر چون این سخن از پدر شنید مشتاق نوش[م] شهادت گشت. تاخت و چندان حرب کرد که دویست نفر را به دوزخ فرستاد، و در حملهٔ دگر پنجاه نفر

[۴۹] اینکه دشمنان حسین به عنوان «کافر» و «غیرمسلمان» شناخته می‌شوند احتمالا بیشتر رنگ و بوی شیعی دارد و دربین جمع کثیری از مسلمان معاصر سنّی مذهب به چشم نمی‌خورد. [۵۰] جنگ. [۵۱] در برخی نسخ به این اشاره می‌شود که: او از تشنگی نیز بی‌تاب شده بود. [۵۲] فریاد. [۵۳] «دمار درآوردن» اشاره دارد به «هلاک نمودن» دارد.

[ک] هفتاد و سه تن [ل] «جدّ من مرا در حضرت خداوند تَعالَی درباخته است، و فدای امّت خود گردانیده. اکنون هیچ‌کس خود را در رنج ندارد که هرچه آمد بر من آمد» [م] شهد و شیرینی

When the Commander of Believers Ḥusayn saw her, he said, 'May mercy be upon you! You have made all happy. O mother! Go next to my household in the camp as it is not proper for women to fight.'[12]

{30} One by one they emerged from the army of the Commander of Believers and fought. They killed the infidels and became martyred and much blood flowed on the Earth![13] And eighty-three people from the army of the Commander were martyred. Then, the Commander of Believers Qāsim, son of Ḥasan and the nephew of the Commander of Believers Ḥusayn, said, 'O my honourable uncle. It would be necessary for me to fight the enemies, right?' The Commander of Believers Ḥusayn said, 'You are young and the last vestige of my brother.' Qāsim kissed the foot of his uncle and requested permission. Then they hugged each other and bid farewell until the Day of Judgement. Qāsim went to the battlefield and he fought so fervently that he sent seventy people to hell. Many people were killed. Then a huge strong man from the army of Yazīd appeared and martyred Qāsim, the son of Ḥasan. A riderless horse ran towards the army of the Commander of Believers Ḥusayn. When the camp saw the horse without its rider wailing arose among the men and women; it was as if the Day of Resurrection had commenced![14] The Commander of Believers found his camp upset. He showed them great sympathy and said to them, 'Whatever God decrees will come to pass.'

{31} The Commander of Believers Ḥusayn had also a son who was known as ʿAlī Akbar. He said, 'O father, today is the seventh day since my mother gave birth to a son. Her milk has dried up. Allow me to bring water from the Euphrates so my mother, as well as the infant, will not die of thirst. I will either bring water or will drink from the cup of martyrdom.' The Commander of Believers cried when he heard this. He said, 'O beloved of your father, come and hug your father.' He came and bid farewell to his father and left. The Commander closed his eyes and said, 'O God, the one whose face is the same as the face of my grandfather, the Messenger of God (pbuh), just went out!' meaning, 'O God, the one whose face is similar to the face of Muḥammad has just left, and whenever I missed my grandfather, I would look upon the face of this child and become cheerful. O God, he has now moved towards the enemy; assist him!' ʿAlī Akbar faced the enemies and said, 'I am from the descendants of the Select One [i.e., Muḥammad]. As you do not give us water, innocent infants are about to die. Show us the way to take some water for them.' They said, 'We water dogs and pigs today, but not our enemies.' As ʿAlī Akbar heard this, he shouted, 'God is Greatest!' and he attacked so

[12] This episode is different from the one outlined in the long version of the same story.

[13] Listing the enemies of Ḥusayn as 'infidels', 'disbelievers' or 'non-Muslims' reflects upon the Shīʿī approach of the story.

[14] i.e., the people were experiencing emotional turbulences

را بینداخت. آنگاه مردی از لشگر یزید بیرون آمد، و علی اکبر با وی درآویخت و علی اکبر را شهید کرد. چون از پشت اسب جدا شد به پدر آواز کرد «اینک جدّ من، حضرت محمّد مُصْطَفَی ﷺ، به من شربتی داد که هرگز آن را خوشتر و شیرین‌تر نباشد. ای پدر بشتاب تا به شربت طهور برسی». این بگفت و جان به حق سُبْحَانَهُ وَتَعَالَىٰ سپرد.

{۳۲} چون امیر فرزند خود را دید که شهید شد، به چشم گریان و دل بِریان‌مانند نزد مادرِ علی اکبر آمد. چون به مادر خبر شد که فرزند شهید گشت، گریه‌کنان نزدیک أَمیر المُؤمِنین حسین بیامد، و برادر شیرخوارهٔ او را بیاورد و گفت «علی اکبر شهید شد. جان مرا بسوخت. و دل مرا کباب کرد. و این کودک شیرخواره هلاک خواهد شد. اگر توانی یک قدح آب مرا ده تا این طفل هلاک نیفتد». چون أَمیر المُؤمِنین حسین خُردِ شیرخواره را بدید، لرزه بر اندام او افتاد، و این کودک را پیش سینهٔ خود بگرفت و به جانب آب روان شد. نزدیک آب دشمنی بود. سنگ بر امیر انداخت. آن سنگ بر کودک خورد. هم[۵۴] در کنار پدر جان بداد.

{۳۳} و از سنگر امیر حسین، علی اصغر مانده بود. از خیمه برآمد و گفت «ای پدر، رخصت بده تا با دشمنان تو کارزار کنم و چنان حرب کنم که نزد تو شربت شهادت یابم و به جدّ خود برسم». پدر گفت «ای جان فرزند، نسل من بریده می‌شود. بر خواجهٔ عالم چه گویم؟ و تو یادرگار منی».آنگاه امّ کلثوم دست علی اصغر بگرفت و در خیمه برد. و أَمیر المُؤمِنین حسین اهل بیت خود را وداع کرد و جامهٔ حضرت پیغمبر ﷺ پوشید و دستار ایشان را بر سر بست و علی اصغر را در کنار گرفت، و وداع کرد و به خدای تَعَالَی سپرد. و گفت «ای فرزند، بعداز شهادتِ من نخواهم که با دشمنان حرب کنی تا از اولاد من در جهان فرزندی مانده باشد».[۵۵] و اهل بیت وداع کرد و فریاد از اهل بیت بر آمد و می گفتند «ای فرزند یادگار رسول، تو بودی اکنون بی تو شویم».[۵۶]

[۵۴] همان‌جا.

[۵۵] این عبارت مرتبط است به «نسب‌نامه» های شیعی که نشان دادن امامت (وخلافت) در بین نسل امامان اولویت دارد. در همین راستا: Majid Daneshgar, ‘A Persian Treatise on the Genealogy of Shīʿa Imāms from Jerusalem,’ *Dabir* 9/2 (2024): 3–15.

[۵۶] در حواشی نسخهٔ ۱۲۲۲ تاجیکستان شعری منسوب به واعظ کاشفی بعدها اضافه شده است « اینك آمد نوبت مِن الوِداع، الوداع ای عترت من الوداع». برای استفادهٔ شعر در ادبیات قرن نوزدهم مراجعه شود به: واعظ کاشفی، گنج شهیدان منظوم؛ روضة الشهداء (هندوستان: بی‌جا. ۱۸۷۶)، ص. ۲۵۵.

forcefully that he sent 170 people to hell. And he returned to his father and said, 'Given the thirst and starvation, I cannot bear the weapon's weight anymore! If my thirst is quenched but a little I will be able to kill the enemies. But O father, ask God for me not to feel the thirst, as I am so thirsty.' The Commander of Believers' eyes became tearful and he looked at the sky and prayed! He did not hear any response. Then he said, 'O beloved of the father, my request has not been accepted as my grandfather abandoned us because of his community!'[15] Once ʿAlī Akbar heard this, he became eager for the sweetness of martyrdom. He galloped and fought until he sent 200 people to hell, and in another fight, he felled fifty more. Then a man emerged from Yazīd's army and ʿAlī Akbar fought with him and became martyred. When he fell from his horse, he called to his father, 'Just now, my forefather, Muḥammad (pbuh), gave me a drink which is no more pleasant and sweeter than that. O father, do not wait any longer so you can also receive this drink.' He said this and submitted his soul to God.

{32} When the Commander saw his son martyred, with a tearful eye and broken heart he went to the mother of ʿAlī Akbar. When she heard that her son had been martyred, she went to the Commander of Believers, crying, and took ʿAlī Akbar's infant brother and said, "ʿAlī Akbar has been martyred and my heart has broken. And this infant will be killed soon. If you can provide me with a bowl of water this infant will not die.' When the Commander of Believers saw the newborn baby his body began to shake. He held the baby to his chest and went towards the river. Nearby the water was an enemy. He threw a stone towards the Commander but it hit the infant. The infant died while being in the father's embrace.

{33} ʿAlī Asghar was the only one remaining in the tent of the Commander Ḥusayn. He came out of the tent and said, 'O father, allow me to fight your enemies so that I may drink from the cup of martyrdom and reach my grandfather.' The father said, 'O dearest child, my descendant will then be cut down! What shall I say to the Master of the World[16]? You are my legacy!' Then Umm Kulthūm came and led ʿAlī Asghar by the hand into the tent. And the Commander of Believers Ḥusayn bid farewell to the descendants of the Prophet and put on the garment as well as the turban of the Prophet (pbuh) and hugged ʿAlī Asghar, bid farewell, and entrusted him to God. He said, 'O my child, after my martyrdom, I do not want you to fight with the enemies because then there should be a generation from my children on Earth.'[17] He bid farewell to the descendants of the Prophet, and they wailed, 'O last vestige of the Messenger, you were here, but now we will be without you.'

[15] Or, according to some copies, 'the prophet (pbuh) has sacrificed me in the presence of God and for the sake of his community.' [16] i.e., the Prophet [17] Regarding Shīʿa Imāms' geneaology and literature, see: Majid Daneshgar, 'A Persian Treatise on the Genealogy of Shīʿa Imāms from Jerusalem'.

{۳۴} درین سخن بودند که فوجی از دشمنان پیدا شدند. أَمیر المُؤمِنین تنگ اسب را محکم کرد، و بر نشست و حمله بر دشمنان کرد. در حملهٔ اوّل میسره بر میمنه زد و دویست کس را به دوزخ فرستاد. و تشنگی و گرسنگی به مرتبه [ای] رسید که قوّت نمانده بود. زیرا که هفت‌روز شده بود که طعام و آب نخورده بود. زمانی ایستاده شد تا قرار گیرد. از قضای خدای تَعَالَی دشمنی در کمین بود، تیری فرستاد و بر امیر رسید.[ن] آنگاه أَمیر المُؤمِنین حسین نظر سوی آسمان کرد و گفت «بار خدایا، دشمنان تو قصد کشتن من کرده‌اند و از تو نمی‌ترسند. و از پیغمبر تو شرم نمی‌دارند. تو داناتری بر همهٔ چیزها. قدرت داری که انصاف من در دنیا و آخرت از ایشان بستانی». این‌قدر بگفت و باز حمله کرد و کس بسیار به دوزخ فرستاد. چنانچه جمیع اندام مبارک مجروح گشته بود. از پشت اسب بر زمین افتاد و بگفت «بِسمِ اللّٰه وَعَلَى مِلَّةِ رَسُولِ اللّٰه».[۵۷]

{۳۵} چندین هزار مردان لشگر یزید ایستاده بودند. هیچ‌کس را زَهرهٔ آن نبود که گِرد أَمیر المُؤمِنین حسین گردد. از هیبت آن شیرزاده هریکی بر جای خود مانده بودند. آنگه شمر ملعونِ روسیاهِ ازل تا ابد[۵۸] نزد امیر رسید تا سر مبارک جدا کند. هرچند کرد تیغ هیچ کار نمی‌کرد.[۵۹] امیر گفت «ای ملعون، در گلوی من تیغ کار نخواهد کرد. زیرا که بوسه‌گه جدّ منست. دیگر ای شمر ملعون تو سینهٔ خود بازکن که کشندهٔ مرا جدّ من نشان داده است». شمر بدبخت سینهٔ خود گشاد و چون امیر در سینه نگاه کرد و گفت «صَدق جَدّي یا رسول اللّٰه؛ راست فرموده بود پیغمبر خدای که کشندهٔ تو را در سینه پیسی باشد»؛[۶۰] «شمر بدبخت از قفا تیغ بزن». آن ملعون همچنان بکرد. محاسن مبارک او به دست گرفت و سر ازتن جدا کرد. درآن ساعت عرش و کرسی و لوح و قلم و بهشت و دوزخ و آسمان و زمین و آفتاب و مهتاب، و جملهٔ ستارگان در لرزه درآمدند، و گریان شدند، و روشنائی آفتاب و ماهتاب مغلوب شده بود. و سنگ و کلوخ در گریه شدند و آهوان بیابان بچّه‌گان را شیر[۶۱] ندادند.

{۳۶} سر را بردند و تن مبارک ایشان هم در آن محل افتاده بود؛ چون ماه چهارده می‌تافت. و مرغان هوا و جانوران صحرا و فرشتگان به زاری و فغان آمدند. اسب أَمیر المُؤمِنین حسین گریخته در خیمه‌گاه امیر رسید. چون اهل بیت اسب دیدند خون از جگر باریدند و غریو برخاست. علی اصغر گفت «من بی پدر شدم» و اهل بیت صدر و بدر عالم در زاری شدند.

[۵۷] عبارتی است که گاهی در حین قرار دادن جنازه در گور ذکر می‌شود.

[۵۸] براساس برگ ۳۷۰ نسخهٔ ۱۲۲۲ تاجیکستان: «شمر لعینِ خارجی».

[۵۹] شباهت به داستان سر بریدن اسماعیل دارد.

[۶۰] این پیشگویی نبوی در مورد قاتل حسین در اکثر متون تاریخی دینی مرتبط با واقعهٔ کربلا دیده می‌شود. نمونهٔ کمتر شناخته شدهٔ آن کتاب «محرّق القلوب» نراقی است. همچنین، در برگ ۳۷۱ نسخهٔ ۱۲۲۲ تاجیکستان چنین ذکر شده است «صدق رسول اللّٰه نسانه که گفته بودی درین کافر دیدم که سینهٔ سگ دارد». تشبیه برجستگی نوک سینهٔ شمر به برجستگی نوک سینهٔ سگ در برخی ترجمه‌های مالایی این داستان وجود دارد.

[۶۱] شاید اشاره دارد به نوعی روزهٔ ماتم که از برای حسین گرفته می‌شود.

[ن] بر گلوی أَمیر المُؤمِنین حسین برسید

{34} In the meantime, a group of enemies emerged. The Commander of Believers tightened the horse's saddle and mounted, launching an attack upon the enemies. On his first surge he attacked from left and right and sent 200 people to hell. His thirst and starvation intensified to the extent that he had no power left as he had not eaten food nor drunk water for seven days. He rested a while to recover. As decreed by God, a hidden enemy shot an arrow and hit the Commander. Then the Commander of Believers Ḥusayn looked at the sky and said, 'O God, your enemy aims to kill and they do not fear You and they do not feel ashamed before Your prophet. You are All-Seeing! You are able to take my revenge from them in this world and in the hereafter!' He said this and attacked again and sent many people to hell. His entire body was left wounded. He fell from his horse and said, 'In the Name of God and according to the religion of the Messenger of God.'

{35} Several thousand men from the army of Yazīd stood there. No one dared to approach the Commander of Believers. They all froze, given the grand status of the son of the bravest.[18] Then, the accursed Shamir, shameful from beginning to end, went to the Commander in order to cut off his sacred head. Whatever he tried, the knife did not cut.[19] The Commander said, 'O cursed one, the knife will not cut my throat, because this place has been kissed by my grandfather. Moreover, O accursed Shamir uncover your chest as my grandfather has given me [physical] details of my killer.' The accursed Shamir uncovered his chest and when the Commander looked upon his chest he said, 'My grandfather, the Messenger of God, was correct. He had said correctly, "Your killer will have the sign of leprosy on his chest."[20] O miserable Shamir, slaughter from the back.' The accursed one did so accordingly. Shamir held the blessed beard and beheaded him. At that moment, the Throne, the Seat, the Plate, the Pen, paradise and hell, the heavens and Earth, the Sun and Moon, and all stars began to shake and cried and the illumination of the Sun and the Moon became blurred. And the stones and sands cried and the deer of the desert did not suckle their young.

{36} They took the head and left his sacred body in that place; it was shining like the full moon and the birds in the sky and the desert animals together with the angels began to cry and wail. The horse of the Commander of Believers Ḥusayn ran away and arrived in the camp of the Commander. When the descendants of the Prophet saw the horse, they began to weep and a commotion was heard. ʿAlī Asghar said, 'I am fatherless' and the descendants of the Prophet began wailing.

[18] Lion, i.e., ʿAlī. [19] This reminds the story of Abraham and Ishmael, and the first one's attempt to behead the latter. But the knife did not work. [20] In the Persian Manuscript N. 1222, it has been mentioned that 'Shamir had the nipples of a dog', which is similar to the Malay episode in some versions.

{۳۷} نقل است از امام جعفر صادق رضی‌الله‌عنه[۶۲] که می گفت «آن روزی که در مکّه بودم که أَمیر المُؤمِنین شهادت یافت.[۶۳] در طواف خانهٔ کعبه آوازی شنیدم که مردی می گفت «یا ربّ مرا بیامرز». باز می گفت «یا ربّ بر من رحمت کن. دانم که نکنی». پنداشتم به زبان او مغلطه می‌رود. نزدیک او شدم. دیدم که شخصی مردودٌ روسیاه گشته زارزارمی گرید. بدو گفتم «چرا چنین می گریی و می نالی که جای ناامیدی نیست. و ازجهت خدای تَعَالَی ناامید مباش». گفت «ای خواجه، نا امید از آنم که رحمت نکردم. و بر اولاد رسول الله و برأَمیر المُؤمِنین حسین جفا کردم. گفت رکابدار أَمیر المُؤمِنین حسین بودم. و دههٔ ماه محرّم بود؛ روز عاشورا که أَمیر المُؤمِنین حسین شهید شد. و در اِزار بندِ أَمیر المُؤمِنین حسین گوهر قیمتی خراج ولایتی بود. مرا طمع آن بر سر افتاد که ازبند أَمیر المُؤمِنین بستانم که در جمیع عمر مرا با فرزندان بسنده باشد. چون نزدیک حسین شدم خواستم تا اِزار بند باز کنم دیدم که به دست راست محکم گرفته است. شیطان در خاطر تلقین کرد «دست، دستِ راست بِبُر و بِستان». کارد کشیدم و بر دست أَمیر المُؤمِنین حسین راندم و جدا کردم. باز خواستم تا اِزار بند کشم. باز دوم دست گرفت. دست دوم را هم بریدم. هم درآن ساعت آوازی شنیدم که «ای ناجوانمرد بدبخت، از دستی که از وی عطاها یافتی، بر وی تو نبخشیدی و از خدای نترسیدی، و فردای قیامت از روی پیغمبر شرم نداری». از بیم آن آواز بیهوش گشتم. چون بهوش باز آمدم لرزه در اندام من افتاد. خواستم که از آن‌جا بیرون آیم. پایم کار نمی کرد. به هزار حیله چند قدم پیشتر شدم. ساعتی برآمد که فوجی از فرشتگان فرود آمدند و بساطی از نور گسترانیدند. در نورِآن بساطْ جهانی منوّر گشت و فرشتگان گِرد بساط شدند، و تن أَمیر المُؤمِنین حسین را به مُشک و زعفرانُ گلاب شستند. حقّ سُبحانَهُ وتَعَالَی هودج در تعزیت أَمیر المُؤمِنین حسین در آن بساط فرستاد. در یک هودج مهتر آدم و حوا، در هودج دوم مهتر نوح، در سوم مهتر ابراهیم و بی‌بی ساره بود، و در چهارم هودج پیغمبر ما صلی‌الله‌علیه‌وسلم بود؛ نزدیک أَمیر المُؤمِنین حسین آمدند. تن را کنار گرفت. آنگاه پیغمبر پرسید «ای جگر گوشهٔ جدّت، دست‌های تو را که بریده؟» أَمیر المُؤمِنین حسین گفت «رکابدار من بریده است». پس پیغمبر[س] دست او بگرفت در بساط گاه آورد و بنشاند. هم درآن میان محافه[۶۴] حضرت بی‌بی فاطمه

[۶۲] در برخی نسخ از او با نام جعفرصادق (بدون اشاره به امام بودن وی) یاد شده است.

[۶۳] در برخی نسخ (مثل دانشگاه تهران)، جعفر صادق تنها راوی داستان است و خود وی در مکّه حاضر نبوده است. در دیگر آثار مرتبط با قتل حسین تحت تاثیر ادبیات مکتب تشیّع، تعداد این روایات دوچندان می‌شود. مثلاً جعفر صادق به عنوان راوی برخی از اتفاقات دشت کربلا در ذیل باب شانزدهم کتاب «محرّق القلوب» اثر نراقی معرّفی می‌شود. همچنین در نسخه‌ای چنین ذکر می‌شود «به روایت حضرت جعفر صادق (ع)، هیچ زنی روغن به بدن نمالید، و سرمه به چشم نکشید و گیسوان شانه نکرد تا اینکه سرِ عبدالله را به‌جهت حضرت امام زین العابدین (ع) آوردند و پیوسته در مصیبت آن بزرگوار گریان بودند»: برگ ۱۲۴ نسخهٔ «مقتل» ۱۷۸۰۳ مجلس شورای اسلامی ایران. همچنین اشاره به شخصی روسیاه را می‌توان در داستان «عُتبة الغلام» در «تذکرة الاولیاء» عطّار (ویراست شفیعی کدکنی، ص ۷۴) دید. هرچند سیاه بودن روی شخصی که دست حسین را قطع کرده است احتمالا با گزارشی از تاریخ طبری در ارتباط است: آنجا که نام افرادی که بر سر جنازهٔ حسین حضور دارند ذکر می‌شود. مثلاً، «الأسْود» از قبیلهٔ «بنو أود» را نام می‌برد. او ربایندهٔ کفش‌ها یا سندل‌های حسین معرّفی شده‌است. در داستان محمّد حنفیّه مالایی، وی ناستال\نستال (Nastala) نام دارد. به نسخهٔ Ll.6.5 کیمبریج مراجعه نمایید.

[۶۴] هودج.

[س] نوح

{37} It is reported from Imam Jaʿfar Ṣādiq (pbuh), 'The day on which I was in Mecca, was the day on which the Commander of Believers was martyred [years before].[21] While circumambulating the Kaʿba, I heard the voice of a man saying, "O Lord, forgive me". Then he said again, "O Lord, bestow mercy upon me! Although I know You will not." I sensed that something was wrong with his statement. I moved close to him. I noticed that he had the rejected blackened face of a man who is crying.[22] I asked him, "Why are you crying and wailing like this as here is not the place to lose hope. And do not lose hope in God." He said, "O Khʷāja! I am hopeful of God as I did not show mercy to others. And I inflicted wrong upon the children of the Messenger of God." He said, "I was the servant of the Commander of the Believers Ḥusayn. And it was the first day of the month of Muharram; the day of ʿĀshūrāʾ on which the Commander of Believers was martyred. And there was a valuable gem in the belt of the Commander of Believers Ḥusayn. Greed overtook me and it came to my mind to take the gem from the belt of the Commander of Believers so that I could support myself and my children during my life. When I went closer to Ḥusayn and tried to open the belt, I noticed that he held me tightly with his right hand. Satan tempted me to cut off the hand and take it. I took out my blade and cut off the hand of Ḥusayn. Again, I wanted to take the belt. He took my hand for the second time. I cut off his other hand too. Right after this, I heard a voice saying, 'O miserable scoundrel, you did not lay mercy upon his hand, the hand by which you were given kindness; did you not fear God and do you not feel ashamed of facing the Prophet on the Day of Judgement?' I fainted out of fear. When I woke up, my body began to shake. I wanted to flee from there but my legs would not carry me. With much effort, I managed to move forward a little. After a while, a group of angels descended and bathed the Earth with light; by which the world was illuminated and the

[21] In some copies, like the one in the Library of the University of Tehran, Jaʿfar al-Ṣādiq is only the narrator of the story and he was not in Mecca, which is also found in further stories and *maqtal* literature after the sixteenth century. *Muḥarriq al-qulūb* (chapter sixteen, Ms. 5700 in the Parliamentary Library of Iran) introduces Jaʿfar al-Ṣādiq as the reporter of the incident of Karbala). Another manuscript (Ms. 17803, f. 124) in the Parliamentary Library of Iran also referred to this point.

[22] References to a blackened face are found at many places in classical Islamic literature. The most well known reference can be found in the chapter of ʿUtba Ghulām in ʿAṭṭar's *Tadhkirat al-Awliyāʾ*. Nevertheless, perhaps the evocation in *Durr al-Majālis* of this trope for the man who cut the hands of Ḥusayn in order to steal from his corpse follows the account in *Tārīkh al-Ṭabarī* in which it is said 'al-Aswad' (lit., 'the black') from the clan of Awd approached the corpse of Ḥusayn to steal from him. 'The body of al-Ḥusayn was plundered as it was. Baḥr b. Kaʿb took his trousers. Qays b. al-Ashʿath took his cloak. It was silken, and he was afterward called Qays of the cloak. One of Banū Awd called al-Aswad took his sandals, and one of the Banū Nahshal b. Dārim took his sword. Later it came into the possession of the family of Ḥabīb b. Budayl.' See al-Ṭabarī, *The History of al-Ṭabarī (the Caliphate of Yazīd b. Muʿāwiyah)*, trans. I. K. A. Howard (New York: State University of New York Press, 1990), vol. 14, 161.

زهرا از هوا پیدا شده و فرشتگان[ع] و روحانیان انبوه برابر محافه جامه‌های ماتم پوشیده چون قبّه‌ای نزدیک حسین رسید خود را از قبّه بیرون انداخت و تن حسین را کنار گرفت و می گفت «ای نور دیدهٔ من و ای جگر گوشهٔ من، این چه بی‌رحمتی بود که با تو کردند». آنگاه روی سوی آسمان کرد و گفت «إِلٰهِيّ، دلبند مرا بکشتند و از تو نترسیدند و از پیغمبر تو باک نداشتند و زیادت نیز دستها بریدند. فردای قیامت انصاف من بِستانی». هم درین میان أَمیر المُؤمِنین علی کَرَّمَ اللّٰهُ وَجْهَه با فرشتگان زاری‌کنان و خروشان در رسیدند و تن فرزند خود را در کنار گرفت و می گفت «ای غریبُ کشتهٔ من، چه توان کرد که ربِّ جلیل در حقّ تو حکم کرده‌است که غریب کشته گردی. اگر مرا حیات بودی به جای تو جویبار خون روان بکردمی». بعده، گفت «دستهای تو که برید؟» نظر به من کرد و بگفت که «او بریده است». أَمیر المُؤمِنین علی نظر به سوی من کرد و گفت «خدای تَعَالَی به تو عفو نکند. چنانچه در حقّ فرزند من رحم نکردی[ف]». نزدیک پیغمبر شدم و التماس کردم که «این خطا از من عفو فرمایید». رسول عليه‌السلام بر رویم طپانچه[۶۵] زد و گفت «خدای تَعَالَی برتو هرگز رحمت نکند»».چون آن مرد این حکایت بر امام جعفرصادق رضی‌الله‌عنه بگفت، امام در گریه شد.

{۳۸} بعد از کشتن أَمیر المُؤمِنین در بارگاه[۶۶] درآمدند و خلق را بگرفتند؛ جمله سی‌تن باقی مانده بودند. شمر ملعون شادان سر مبارک امیر را پیش سردار لشگر یزید بیاورد و گفت «اینک سرِ بهترینِ قوم آورده‌ام». سردار لشگر دست به تیغ برد و سر شمر ملعون را از تن جدا کرد، و گفت «چون دانستی که سر بهترین قوم است، چرا سر بریدی؟ اکنون سزای تو این بود». و سردار لشگر دوستدار خاندان پیغمبر بود. امّا از خوف یزید ملعون ظاهر نمی کرد.[۶۷]

[۶۵] سیلی بر صورت زدن. [۶۶] خیمهٔ پادشاهی که اشاره به خیمهٔ حسین بن‌علی دارد.

[۶۷] داستان کشته شدن شمر در نسخهٔ کوتاه با نسخهٔ طولانی، که تطابق بیشتری با نسخ مالایی دارد، متفاوت است. همچنین، پنهان کردن احساسات و عواطف نسبت به اهل بیت می‌تواند اشاره به فرهنگی سیاسی-استراتژیک داشته باشد که در بین شیعیان باعنوان «تقیّه» شناخته می‌شود.

[ع] حوران [ف] نکردیی

angels surrounded the light and washed the body of the Commander of Believers with musk, saffron, and rose water. God sent howdahs to that magnified light of mourning for the Commander of Believers Ḥusayn. In one howdah was Adam and Eve, in the second one was Noah, in the third was Abraham and Lady Sarah, and in the fourth howdah was our Prophet (pbuh); all came close to the body of the Commander of Believers Ḥusayn and embraced the body. Then the Prophet asked, 'O beloved of your father, who has cut off your hands?' The Commander of Believers said, 'My servant has cut them off.' Then the Prophet took the hand of the servant, and brought him to sit in the gathering. In the meantime, the howdah of Lady Fāṭima Zahrā appeared in the sky and many angels and spiritual beings put on mourning clothes. She, like a dome, moved close to Ḥusayn and threw herself onto the body of Ḥusayn and said, 'O light of my eyes, and my darling! What is this unmerciful act that they did to you?!' Then she looked at the sky and said, 'O God, they have killed my darling and they did not fear You nor Your prophet, and moreover, they cut his hands off; take revenge on the Day of Judgement!' In the meantime, the Commander of Believers ʿAlī, may God ennoble his face, arrived with angels, while crying intensely. He held the body of his son and said, 'O my lonely murdered son! What can one do as the glorious God had decreed this upon you that you be killed alone? If I were alive, I would have flowed rivers of blood for you.' Then he said, 'Who has cut off your hands off?' He looked to me and said, 'He has cut them off.' The Commander of Believers ʿAlī looked at me and said, 'God will not forgive you, as you showed no mercy to my son.' I moved close to the Prophet and requested forgiveness for this mistake of mine. The Messenger of God (pbuh) hit my face and said, 'God will never have mercy upon you'."' When that man explained this story to Imam Jaʿfar Ṣādiq (pbuh), the Imam cried.

{38} After the killing of the Commander of Believers, they went to the camp and surrounded the people there. There were, overall, thirty people left. The accursed Shamir, while being cheerful, put the sacred head of the Commander [i.e., Ḥusayn] before the head of Yazīd's army and said, 'I have now brought the head of the best of the people.' The head of the army took a sword and beheaded the accursed Shamir, saying, 'If you knew that this is the head of the best of people, why did you cut it off? This is your penalty!' The head of the army was a devotee of the Prophet's household yet he was not able to express his feelings as he was afraid of the accursed Yazīd.[23]

[23] This killing episode of Shamir is different from the one mentioned in the long version of this story. Also, that the head of the army did not express his feelings about the Prophets' household may refer to a political-strategic Shīʿī concept known as *taqiyyah* ('precautionary concealment').

{۳۹} و فرمان یزید پلید مردود رسید که «هرکه از کسان أَمیر المُؤمِنین حسین مانده است بیارید». و بیشترعورت بودند. هریکی را پیاده بیارند، سرْبرهنه روان کردند. و در منزلی فرود آمدند. ساکن آن مقام راهب بود. چون لشگر یزید ملعون را دید پرسید «به چه کار رفته بودید؟» ایشان گفتند «ما لشگر یزیدیم و از برای حسین، دخترزادهٔ پیغمبر،[۶۸] رفته بودیم. اکنون سرحسین را می‌بریم». راهب ترسا[۶۹] چون این بشنید گفت «امشب مهمان من باشید». ایشان قبول کردند. راهب ایشان را طعام‌ها خوب کَشید و شراب نیز آورد و گفت «سر حسین را بدهید تا نیکو نگاه دارم و سؤالی از این سر کنم». سر را به راهب بدادند و راهب سر را به خانهٔ[۷۰] خود آورد.

{۴۰} دید که نوری از سر مبارک ایشان جدا شده به سوی آسمان می‌رود و می‌آید و تمام عالم منوّر گشته. راهب در تعجّب بماند. برخاست و سرمبارک امیر را به گلاب و کافور[۷۱] بشست. و به زانوی ادب پیش سر نشست، و گفت «ای سیّد السادات، به حرمت جدّ خود که با من به سخن درآیی که دین جدّ تو کدام دین است، تا من هم بدان دین درآیم». در حال، به زبان فصیح، سرِ بریده آواز برآمد[۷۲] که «لآ إِلٰهَ إِلَّا اللهُ، مُحَمَّدٌ رَسُولُ اللهِ». راهب برخاست و از روی صدْق[۷۳] پیش سرمبارک امام مسلمان شد و همهٔ شب نخفت؛ به‌خدمت پیش سراستاده بود.

{۴۱} چون وقت رفتن آن جماعت شد سر را از راهب طلب کردند. راهب گفت «سر ندهم تا سر خود را فدای این سر کنم. این خاک بر سر شما است؛[۷۴] کسی که بندهٔ حق سبحانه و تعالی باشد سرِ فرزند رسول چنین نکند که شما کرده اید؟ و او پیغمبر برحقّ[۷۵] بوده باشد و شما امّت او باشید؟! و از مهتر عیسیٰ علیه السلام هم خری مانده بود، قوم او آن را به زور گرفتند که این خر از پیغمبر ما یادگار است. شما بد گرفتارید[۷۶] که با جگرگوشهٔ پیغمبر علیه السلام چنین بی رحمی کرده‌اید». این سخن بگفت و با ایشان در مقام جنگ شد و سیزده کسی را بکشت، و راهب نومسلمان شربت شهادت نوش کرد. و سر راهب با سر امیر همراه به دمشق بردند.

[۶۸] این که بر «دخترزادهٔ پیغمبر» تاکید شده است می‌تواند به مباحث قرآنی معطوف شود که آیا پیامبر اسلام «پسرزاده‌ای» هم داشته، همان موضوعی که پیش‌تر موضوع بحث دیوید پاورز در کتاب «زید» بود. چنانچه پاورز نشان داده، أسامة فرزند زید بن محمد بن عبدالله (سپس: زید بن حارثة) بسیار مورد لطف پیامبر اسلام بوده است. [۶۹] مسیحی. هرچند گاهی ترسا به‌معنی «راهب» هم به‌کار می‌رود. [۷۰] حُجره. [۷۱] در برخی نسخ کافور ذکر نمی‌شود. [۷۲] به زبان آمد. [۷۳] صادقانه. [۷۴] اشاره دارد به «شرم بر شما باد» و یا «چه ذلیل و حقیر هستند کسانی که...» [۷۵] راستین و حقیقی. [۷۶] مبتلا شدن و گمراه شدن.

{39} An order from Yazīd was received, 'Bring whoever remained from the family of the Commander of Believers Ḥusayn.' They were mostly women. They moved them on foot, while being unveiled. Eventually, they arrived at a place[24] whose resident was a monk. When he saw the army of the accursed Yazīd, he said, 'For what reason had you gone [to war]?' They said, 'We are from the army of Yazīd and went after Ḥusayn, the son of Muḥammad's daughter.[25] And now we have taken the head of Ḥusayn for ourselves.' When the Christian monk heard this, he said, 'Be my guest tonight.' They accepted the offer. The monk provided them with good food and also brought wine, and said to them, 'Give me the head of Ḥusayn, so I may take good care of it, and ask a question of this head.' They gave the head to the monk and the monk took it to his own quarters.

{40} He noticed that a light radiated to the sky from the sacred head and the whole world was illuminated. The monk was surprised. He raised and washed the sacred head of the Commander with rose water and camphor. And he sat before the head respectfully, and said, 'O master of masters, by your grandfather, speak with me telling me what is the religion of your grandfather, so I may convert to it.' Then a voice came out of the head, saying in eloquent language, 'There is no god but God, and Muḥammad is the Messenger of God.' The monk rose up before the sacred head of the Imam and converted to Islam with integrity, and he did not sleep overnight, as he was consciously at the service of the head.

{41} When the army was about to leave, they asked the monk to give the head back. The monk said, 'I will not give you the head, until I sacrifice my own head for the sake of this head! Shame on you! What will you do with the head of the grandchild of the Messenger who is the servant of God? Such a rightful Prophet! And you are members of his community?! When a donkey survived His Eminence Jesus (pbuh), his community struggled to save it, as they said that the donkey is the only vestige surviving their prophet. You have truly strayed as you have committed such savagery upon the beloved of the Prophet (pbuh).' He said this and fought with them and killed thirteen people, and the newly-converted monk drank from the cup of martyrdom[26] and they took to Damascus the head of the monk as well as that of the Commander.

[24] i.e., caravanserai [25] Highlightling the role of Ḥusayn, as Muḥammad's maternal grandchild, may draw our attentions to what David S. Powers indicated in his book, *Zayd*, about the importance of Zayd's son, Usāma, in the presence of Muḥammad. For more, see: David S. Powers, *Zayd* (Philadelphia: University of Pennsylvania Press, 2014). [26] i.e. was martyred

{۴۲} چون یزید ملعون شنید که سر أَمیر المُؤمِنین حسین را می‌آرند شادمان شد. و به غم ابد مبتلا شد.[۷۷] فرمود تا طبل شادی بکوبند. مرد مسلمانی صاحب دمشق این واقعهٔ خاندان شنید، گریان شد و بیهوش گشت. چون بهوش آمد بیرون شهر رفت دید که اهل‌بیت را سرِ برهنه و پابرهنه و پیاده می‌آرند. نزدیک ایشان رفت و گفت «وای بر کسی که بر اهل خاندان نبوّت چنین کند». چون اهل بیت این مرد را مهربان دیدند پرسیدند که «تو کیستی؟» گفت «دوستدار اهل بیت نبوّت». بازپرسیدند که «چه نام داری؟» گفت «صالح». فرمودند «ای صالح، ما را فریادرس که چند روز شد که آب نخورده‌ایم». برفت و مَشک آب بیاورد و همه سیراب کرد. باز فرمودند «یا صالح، سرهای ما برهنه است و نظر ظالمان و نامحرمان بر ما می‌افتد. پوشیده گردان». دستار از سر برداشت و پاره کرد هرکدام را پاره می‌داد. چنانچه سرهای همه پوشیده شد و صالح را دعا کردند و گفتند «یا صالح، حاجتی دگر نیز داریم. سر امیر المؤمنین حسین را با شهیدان دگر از عقب می‌آرند. از ایشان شفاعت کن تا سرهای شهیدان در پیش ما روند. ما را از عقب برند تا نظر هرکسی بر ما نیفتد». صالح نزد ایشان رفت و همچنان کردند.

{۴۳} چون به شهر رسید. یزید لعین رو سیاه فرمود «فرزندان حسین را که مانده‌اند پیش آرید و دگران را به زندان». علی‌اصغر و زینب را در پیشِ یزیدِ ملعونِ روسیاه آوردند. یزید از غایت شادی و خرّمی نشسته، طعام زهر و مار می خورد.[۷۸] علی اصغر را بگفت «چگونه سختی و بلا به شما رسید؟» جواب گفت «مَا أَصَابَ مِن مُّصِيبَةٍ إِلَّا بِإِذْنِ اللَّهِ، هیچ‌کس را مصیبتی نرسد مگر به فرمان خدای تَعَالَی». روی سوی زینب کرد و گفت «از مدینه خرمای خوب آوردند. ای دختر تو می‌خوری؟» بی‌بی زینب چند روز چیزی نخورده بود گفت «آری می‌خورم». دست انداخت.[۷۹] سر امیر پیش او نهاده بود و گفت «ای زینب خرما را بخور». بی‌بی زینب چون سر پدر [sic] بدید شناخت[۸۰]. در گریه شد. برادر و خواهر هر دو می‌گریستند. و یزید بدبخت چون بید[۸۱] در دست داشت بر لب و دندان مبارک أَمیر المُؤمِنین حسین می‌زد.

{۴۴} غلامِ یزیدِ مردود استاده بود و گفت «ای یزید لعین، چوب بر دندان مبارک ایشان مزن که حضرت مُصْطَفَی ﷺ بسیار دیده‌ام که بدین لب و دندان بوسه داده‌اند». یزید لعین گفت «من نیز از آن دشمنی می‌زنم». چون غلام این سخن از یزید پلید شنید دست به تیغ برد امّا قضای باری تَعَالَی برآن بود که تیغ به آن لعین نرسید. غوغا برخاست. غلام چهل نفر را به دوزخ فرستاد. آنگه خود شربت شهادت نوشید.

۷۷ در برخی نسخ این عبارت وجود ندارد. ۷۸ زهرمار کردن؛ کوفت کردن.

۷۹ می‌خواست که خرما بردارد. هرچند، در ابتدا گمان من این بود که اشاره دارد به اینکه یزید وی را دست‌انداخته است.

۸۰ هرچند زینب خواهر حسین بوده است. ۸۱ شاخه چوبی؛ شاخه درخت.

{42} The accursed Yazīd was happy when he heard that they were bringing the head of the Commander of Believers Ḥusayn. And he became ill and a loser for ever more. He commanded for drums to be beaten in joy. A Muslim man coming from[27] Damascus heard this story of the Prophet's descendants. He cried and fainted. When he regained consciousness he went out of the town and saw that they brought the Prophet's descendants unveiled and walking barefooted. He went to them and said, 'Shame on the one who did this upon the descendants of the Prophet.' When the descendants of the Prophet came across this compassionate man, they asked him, 'Who are you?' He said, 'I am a devotee of the Prophet's descendants.' They also asked, 'What is your name?' He said, 'Ṣāliḥ.' They said, 'O Ṣāliḥ, please help us as we have not drunk water for a couple of days.' He fetched a waterskin and all of them copiously drank water. They said, 'O Ṣāliḥ, our heads are unveiled and oppressors and strangers can see us. Cover us!' He took the turban from his head and tore it into several pieces, and gave each of them a piece of it. As such, they were all veiled, and they prayed for Ṣāliḥ and said, 'O Ṣāliḥ, we have another request from you as they are moving the head of the Commander of Believers Ḥusayn, as well as those of other martyrs from behind; ask them to bring the martyrs' heads forward and to send us back so that no one will gaze upon us.' Ṣāliḥ did as requested.

{43} They arrived in the town. The accursed and shameful Yazīd said, 'Bring those children of Ḥusayn who have survived and put the rest in jail.' They brought both ʿAlī Asghar and Zaynab before the filthy, accursed, and shameful Yazīd. While being extremely happy and excited, Yazīd was eating food, and they hoped the food would turn to an unpleasant dish like snake's venom. He asked ʿAlī Asghar, 'How did you suffer?' He responded, 'No one was affected by calamity unless it was decreed by God', meaning that one will not experience difficulty unless it is ordered by God. Yazīd looked at Zaynab and said, 'They brought fresh dates from Medina. O girl, do you wish to eat them?' Lady Zaynab, who had not eaten anything for days, said, 'Yes, I will eat them.' Then she wanted to grab some [fresh dates]. Yazīd put the head of the Commander[28] before her, instead of fresh dates, and said, 'O Zaynab, now eat the dates!' When Lady Zaynab saw the head she recognised it as her father's[29] head (sic). She cried. Both brother and sister were crying. And the accursed Yazīd hit the sacred teeth and lips of the Commander of Believers Ḥusayn with a stick.

{44} The servant of the wretched Yazīd was there and said, 'O accursed Yazīd, do not hit his sacred teeth with this stick as I have already seen several times that the Prophet (pbuh) kissed those lips and teeth.' The accursed Yazīd said, 'I am hitting

[27] Or: passing through [28] i.e., Ḥusayn

[29] In most copies, Ḥusayn is not introduced as Zaynab's brother.

{۴۵} و مادام که یزید پلید ملعون روسیاه بود هرگز خوشدل نبود و فردای قیامت درعرصه میان خلق اوّلین و آخرین زرد روی و رو سیاه گردد و از شفاعت حضرت پیغمبر ﷺ بی‌نصیب گردد.[۸۲]

{۴۶} إلٰهِیّ، به حرمت حسن رضا و حسین شهید دشت کربلا و به حرمت دوستان خاندان اهل نبوّت که جان و تن در باخته‌اند از ثواب ایشان من بیچاره را و کاتب این کتاب را با جمله مؤمنان روزی گردانی، و زبان ما را به ذکر خود و به یاد خود مشغول داری.[۸۳]

[۸۲] تنها در برگ ۱۶۵ نسخهٔ تاجیکستان است که روایتی طولانی از شیوهٔ مرگ یزید بیان می‌شود: «و در وقت بیمار شدن و مردن یزید لعین را هرچند که معالجه می‌کردند هیچ بِه نمی‌شد. تا آنکه طبیبی بود ترسا به نزد یزید آوردند تا بیماری یزید را معالجه کند. آن طبیب گفت که «این بیماری را علاج نمی‌شود تا آنکه گفت ابریشم‌های رشته بیاوردند». و بر سر هر رشتهٔ ابریشم از جگر گوسفند جگربندی بست. و یزید را گفت که «این جگرها را فروبَر تا علامت رنج خود بینی». چون یزید جگربندها را خورد بعداز زمانی طبیب گفت «سرهای رشته‌ها را بکشید از درون یزید لعین». آن جگر بندها بیرون آمد و در هر جگربندی کژدمانِ بسیار و مارانْ چسبیده می‌خوردند. پس آن طبیب گفت که «این کژدمان و ماران را دیدی که بر هر جگربندی هفتاد کژدم و ماران چسبیده بودند.» چون یزید لعین آن را بدید گفت «اینها چه کژدمانند؟» آن طبیب گفت «هر که با فرزندان رسول علیه‌السلام دشمنی کند و ایشان‌را بکشد حال او چنین باشد، و چنین جان بدهد، و به حال سگ بمیرد. و درون تو از این کژدمان و ماران بسیارند و درون تو را و جگرهای تو را میِ‌خوردند و روده‌های تو را پاره‌پاره می‌سازند. و هرگز علاج این بیماری نتوان کرد، و خدا تَعَالَی بدین مرض مبتلا کرده است». و آخر به حالِ سگ یزید لعین جان داد و از درون یزید لعین جگر بندها پاره پاره می‌شد و در روی کژدمان چسبیده بیرون می افتد و آخر یزید لعین به دروخ پرآتش رفت، و در دنیا با این حال جان داد و در آتش دوزخ تا ابد الابدین خواهد بود. و هرکس که از خوارجیان باشند به دوزخ خواهند بودند. إلٰهِیّ، به حرمت حسن رضا و حسین مظلوم دشت کربلا و به حرمت خاندان مصطفا ﷺ که جمیع دوستان و محبّان و مومنان را بیامرزی. بمِنَّة وكرمه يَا أَرْحَمُ الرَّاحِمِينْ. نظم. «اگر گویی که بر من جور رفتست؛ نظر بر کشتگان کربلا کن. اگر گویی که من درویش حالم؛ نظر در خاندان مُصْطَفَی کن».

[۸۳] در برخی نسخ دعای دیگری اضافه می‌شود. به‌طور مثال «در صبح و شام از غیبت و بهتان و دروغ و از جمیع [...] در حفظ و امان خود نگاه داری و در هیچ وقت [...] خود از ما عاصیان بدکردار نامهٔ سیاه روزگار تباه باز نگیری. و به حرمت حبیب خود، محمّد رسول الله که ما را از ناظران جمال خود گردانی، و از این دنیای غدّار ناپایدار بیرون نبری، الاّ آمرزیده و گناهان عفو کرده، و خصمان راضی کرده. إلٰهِیّ، چون نصرت طلب دادی و امیدوار ساختی به غایت بی غایت که ما را نومید نگردانی « يَا إِله العَالَمِين يَا خَيرالناصِرِين، بِفَضلِك وَكَرَمِك يَا أَرْحَمُ الرَّاحِمِينْ وَصَلّي اللّهُ عَلى خَيرِ خَلقِه محمّد وَآلِه أَجمَعين»».

them out of hostility.' When the servant heard this from the filthy Yazīd, he took out his sword! However, it was God's decree that he could not hit Yazīd with his sword. A loud commotion broke out. The servant sent forty people to hell. Then he himself drank from the cup of martyrdom.[30]

{45} As long as the filthy, accursed, and shameful Yazīd was alive, he did not experience joy. And he will be shamed with a blackened face among the first and last beings on the Resurrection Plain of the Day of Judgement, and he will be excluded from the Prophet's (pbuh) intercession.'

{46} *O God, by Ḥasan, the satisfied one, and by Ḥusayn, the martyr of the plain of Karbala, and by friends of the descendants of the Prophet who devoted their soul and body, provide me, the humble pauper, and the scribe of this story, and all believers with their reward, and may You always involve us in invoking and remembering you. [Amen.]*

[30] He was martyred

در مقتل أَمیر المُؤمِنین امام حسن و حسین رَضِيَ اللّٰه عَنْهما

(نسخهٔ طولانی)

{۱} آوردند قوله تَعَالَی «وَلَا تَقُولُوا لِمَن يُقْتَلُ فِي سَبِيلِ اللَّهِ أَمْوَاتٌ بَلْ أَحْيَاءٌ وَلٰكِن لَّا تَشْعُرُونَ،[۱] یعنی می‌گوید هرکسی را که کشته شوند در راه خدای تَعَالَی، که مرده‌اند لیکن شما ندانید».[۲] پیش‌از نزول این آیه شهیدِ آن را مژده می‌خوانند. أَمیر المُؤمِنین عُمر خطّاب رَضِيَ اللّٰهُ عَنْهُ دعا کرد. گفته شد تکرّمی[۳] در حقّ کنندگانِ در راه خود برد که این فرمان شد که «کشتگان در راه ما را مُرده مگویید که ایشان زنده اند. هر که شهید را مُرده گوید بزه‌کار شود». نیز این آیت[۴] [...] رسول صَلَّى اللّٰهُ عَلَيْهِ وَسَلَّمَ فرمود «لِمَن مات فِي سبيل اللّٰه»[۵] و شیخ حمید الدّین[۶] فرمود «هر که از برای دوست کشته نشد اگرچه بسمل کنی مُردارش زیستن[۷] و کشته شدن برای خدای تَعَالَی می‌باید».[۸]

{۲} مردی کشته شد. خبر او بر رسول صَلَّى اللّٰهُ عَلَيْهِ وَسَلَّمَ [رسید]. چشم پر آب کرد که از [بهرِ؟] دوست آن مرده

[۱] آیهٔ ۱۵۴ سورهٔ بقره. [۲] قسمت پایانی را می‌توان چنین خواند «... لیکن شما ندانید که مرده‌اند». «ندانید» اشاره به «مپندارید» دارد.
[۳] اظهار کرم نمودن. [۴] علاوه بر این آیه؟ [۵] روایات زیادی منسوب به پیامبر اسلام در مورد مفهوم شهید، شهادت و کیفیت «شهید شدن» در کتب دینی مسلمانان موجود است. [۶] به احتمال زیاد اشاره به صوفی نامدار خواجه حمیدالدین ناگوری متوفای ۶۷۳ قمری برابر با ۱۲۷۴ میلادی دارد. [۷] همچون مردهٔ متحرّک بودن است.
[۸] «کشته شدن برای خدای تَعَالَی می‌باید» اشاره دارد به اینکه «سزاوار است که انسان در راه حقّ زیست کرده و جان دهد».

The story of the killing of the commanders of believers Ḥasan and Ḥusayn (pbuh)

[Long Version]

{1} It is reported that God said, 'Never say that those martyred in the cause of God are dead – in fact, they are alive! But you do not perceive it' (Q. 2:154), meaning that whoever is killed in the path of God, do not consider them dead. Before revealing this verse, its particular martyr was informed. The Commander of Believers ʿUmar Khaṭṭāb (pbuh) prayed, 'God has shown affection regarding those who act in His path with this verse: "Never say that those martyred in the cause of God are dead – in fact, they are alive!" Whoever calls a martyr "dead" sins.' The Messenger also mentioned the verse, 'For those who are dead in the cause of God…' [?] and Shaykh Ḥamīd al-Dīn[1] also said, 'Whoever does not die for the cause of the Friend [i.e., God], they look like the walking dead – although being slaughtered in a halal path – and death in the cause of God is the ultimate goal.'

{2} A man was killed. The news was heard by the Messenger (pbuh). His eyes became tearful, and he said, 'He died for the cause of the Friend.' The Companions also began to cry. They said, 'How does he come, O Messenger of God.' He said, 'His

[1] of Nagaur

است. گریه در اصحا[ب] افتاد. گفتند که «چرا؟ یا رسول الله» گفت «جگر او به دوستی پروردگار خود سوخته بود[۹] و تن او با اشتیاق مولا نظار[۱۰] شده بود».

{۳} در حکایت. مهتر عالم ﷺ بر سرِ مرده‌ای رسید که [می] گریست. رسول الله ﷺ گفت «گریه برای چیست؟» او گفت «از آن سبب که در راه خدای تَعَالَی کشته نشدم؛ من سر نباختم».[۱۱] رسول علیه‌السلام فرمود «اجرك الله واَتَّصِل من ألف شهید، زیرا که تو کشتهٔ ایشانی.» قوله تَعَالَی «بَلْ أَحْيَاءٌ»[۱۲] و سبب چیست که ایشان را زنده گویند. نزدیک بعضی نام ایشان در جهان باقی می‌ماند که «فلان چنین غزا کرد و همچنین شهادت یافت». و نزدیک بعضی ایشان زنده‌اند[۱۳]؛ نزدیک خدای تَعَالَی. چنانچه گفته اند «بَلْ أَحْيَاءٌ عِندَ رَبِّهِمْ يُرْزَقُونَ؛ فَرِحِينَ بِمَا آتَاهُمُ اللَّهُ مِن فَضْلِهِ[۱۴] و نزدیک بعضی، از آن سبب[۱۵] زنده خوانند که طاعت که در حیات می‌کردند، آن‌قدر[۱۶] ثواب[۱۷] هر روز می‌یابند.

{۴} درجهٔ شهادت کسی را روزی کنند که او را دوست دارند. و درجهٔ شهادت را خدای تَعَالَی بلند گردانیده چون حضرت رسالت پناه ﷺ را نیز شهادت روزی کردند به‌سبب زهر دادن. و آن چنان بود که عورتی زال [بر] مهتر عالم آمد. گفت «یا رسول الله، برای تو مهمانی کردم». رسول ﷺ دست مخست.[۱۸] و یک مرد با رسول بود. آن مرد سابقه کرد،[۱۹] قدری گوشت از آن در دهن کرد. بر زمین افتاد.[۲۰] رسول ﷺ چون لقمه خورد[۲۱] و دست در دوم لقمه دراز کرد گوشت بریان شده در سخن آمد و گفت «یا رسول الله، لَا تَأْكُلْ مِنِّي فَإِنِّي مَسْمُومَة».[۲۲] و آن مرد نقل کرد رسول الله علیه‌السلام را خدای تَعَالَی نگاه داشت.[۲۳]

{۵} زهر را فرمان شد «در پاشنهٔ پایْ باش که وجودِ همیشه در زحمت بودی». هم درینْ تا سَروقْتِ وفاتْ حقّ تَعَالَی زهر را در وجود مهتر عالم بِجُنباند و از آن سبب شهید شد. و أَمیر المُؤمِنین ابوبکر صدیق رضی‌الله‌عنه را مار گزیده بود و وقت مُردن آن زهر در کار شد. و أَمیر المُؤمِنین عُمر را نیز کارد زدند. و أَمیر المُؤمِنین عثمان را غوغا کردند و کشتند. و أَمیر المُؤمِنین علی را در نماز کشتند، و امام حسن و حسین را نیز بدشت کربلا شهید کردند.

{۶} و بدآنکه میان ابناء أَمیر المُؤمِنین علی و معاویه و یزید عداوت اصلی و فرعی بود. و عداوت اصلی این است که شیطان برابر مهتر آدم علیه‌السلام بود و همچنان صالحان و این عداوت بسیار است. چنانچه قابیل هابیل را

[۹] اشاره به «عاشق دل سوخته» دارد. [۱۰] هرچند «نظار» به معنی «منتظر بودن» می‌آید، ولی به احتمال زیاد این یک خطای نوشتاری برای کلمه «نزار» یعنی «لاغر و ضعیف» است. [۱۱] «جان فدا کردن» [۱۲] آیهٔ ۱۶۹ سورهٔ آل عمران. [۱۳] نز دیک ایشان بعضی زنده‌اند. [۱۴] آیات ۱۶۹ و ۱۷۰ سورهٔ آل عمران. [۱۵] بدان دلیل. [۱۶] همان‌قدر. [۱۷] ثواب شهادت؟

[۱۸] اشاره به زخمی و یا مجروح شدن دست پیامبر دارد. [۱۹] پیش‌دستی کردن یا زودتر اقدام کردن. [۲۰] جان داد.

[۲۱] او هم بدین طریق لقمه برداشت. [۲۲] این حدیث در کتب شیعی و سنّی دیده می‌شود. اما واضح‌ترین اشاره را می‌توان در مناقب علی ابن ابی طالب اثر ابن عاشور یافت. همچنین برگ ۱۲۲ و ۱۲۳ نسخهٔ ۱۷۳ در آکلند شامل چنین تعابیری است: «جابر رضی‌الله‌عنه می گوید که «روزی یک یهودی گوسفند زهرآلوده‌ای بریان کرد پیش سید علیه‌السلام . او را خواست که برآن دست زند. گوسفند بریان گفت «من زهر آلوده ام، از من مخور.»». [۲۳] در برگ ۱۲۳ نسخهٔ ۱۷۳ کتابخانهٔ آکلند، داستان گوسفند بریان شدهٔ زهر آلود چنین ادامه می‌یابد «سید علیه‌السلام او [آن یهودی] را گفت «تو این را به چه سبب زهر زدی؟» او گفت «برای امتحان تو. اگر پیغمبر آخرالزمان بخوری و تو را زهر اثر نکند، من ایمان آرم». در نسخ مالایی (مثلا Wall 72 در کتابخانهٔ جاکارتا) این قسمت طولانی تر است، و بحث‌هایی در مورد همسران پیامبر، تعداد آنها و نقش خدیجه (به جاوی: خاتجه) مطرح می‌شود.

heart[2] was burnt for the love of God. And his body was already thin and weak for the sake of the Friend.'

{3} A story. The Eminence of the Universe (pbuh) came across someone dead, who began to cry. The Messenger of God (pbuh) asked him, 'Why are you crying?' He said, 'As I was not killed in the cause of God. I did not sacrifice myself!' The Messenger of God (pbuh) said, 'God will reward you and you will join the one thousand martyrs as you are one of the dead in their path.' God has said, "In fact, they are alive" (Q. 3:169).' And what is the reason that they are called "alive"? The name of some of them remained in the world as 'those who fought and were martyred.' And they are alive before God. As it is said that they are indeed alive with their Lord and well provided for – rejoicing in what God has bestowed upon them of His bounty (Q. 3:169–170). And some are called alive as they were subordinated in the world, for which they are rewarded every day.

{4} The rank of martyr is given to the one who is loved. And God has elevated the level of martyrdom, as the Prophet (pbuh) was also provisioned to be martyred, through poisoning. It happened when a white-haired widow came to the Prophet. She said, 'O Messenger of God, I have arranged for a gathering in your honour.' The Messenger's (pbuh) hand was injured. A man was accompanying the Messenger, who was the first to help the Prophet to eat. But the morsel fell down. The Messenger of God (pbuh) took a bite and was about to take a second bite when the grilled meat began to speak: 'O Messenger of God, do not eat me as I am poisonous.' And the narrator of the incident said that God protected the Messenger of God.[3]

{5} The poison [in the Prophet's body] was ordered, 'Stay put in the heel, for you were always annoying!' It stayed there until it moved at the Prophet's moment of death. As such, the Prophet was martyred. And the Commander of Believers Abū Bakr Ṣiddiq (pbuh) was bitten by a snake and the poison was the cause of death. And the Commander of Believers ʿUmar was stabbed by dragger. And the Commander of Believers ʿUthmān was killed during a riot. And the Commander of Believers ʿAlī was killed while praying, and Imam Ḥasan and Ḥusayn were killed on the plain of Karbala.

{6} And be aware that there were primary and secondary causes for the enmity between the children of the Commander of Believers ʿAlī, on the one hand, and Muʿāwiya and Yazīd, on the other. The main cause of primary enmity was that Satan confronted Adam (pbuh) as well as the righteous, and this is a common form of enmity.

[2] lit., 'liver' [3] In the Auckland copy (GMS-173, ff. 122–123), it says that Jābir narrated, 'Once upon a time, a Jew grilled a poisonous lamb in order to serve the Prophet. When the Prophet went to eat it the grilled lamb said, "I am poisonous, do not take a bite from me." Then the Prophet asked the Jew about his plan, "Why did you make it poisonous?" Then the Jew replied, "I just wanted to test whether you are really the Prophet of the end of time; if the poison did not work, then I would accept Islam."'

بکشت و فرزندان مهتر یعقوب برادر یوسف [...] بدآن‌که در خانهٔ عبد مناف دو پسر به یک شکم آمده بود یکی را نام معاش بود و یکی را نام امیر؛[۲۴] هر دو با یکدیگر چسبیده بودند که از مادر بیامدند و پدر ایشان را جدا کرد. اثر آن تیغ میان ایشان افتاد. معاش را پسر شد عبدالمطلب و امیر را پسر شد حرب. میان ایشان هم تیغ شد. و عبدالمطلب را پسر شد [ابوطالب]. ابوطالب را پسر شد علی رضی‌الله‌عنه و ابوسفیان [از جانب حرب] را پسر شد معاویه، میان ایشان تیغ شد، علی رضی‌الله‌عنه را پسر شد حسن و حسین رضی‌الله‌عنهم، و معاویه را پسر شد به یزید. و یزید قصد ایشان کرد و عداوت فرعی این است.

{۷} و آنچنان بود که معاویه رضی‌الله‌عنه را موت نزدیک شد. چشم پر آب کرد. و گفتند «ای معاویه، گریهٔ این چیست؟»[۲۵] گفت «مرا همین یک پسر بُوَد و مراد او ندهم[۲۶] و کار خیر ایشان بکند و از شادیِ فرزندانِ خود چشم روشن کند».[۲۷]

{۸} الغرض. معاویه یزید را جهد بسیار نمود. یزید بیرون آمد و دوستان را جمع کرد، و گفت «ای یاران، کدام دختر خوب ترست؟» همه گفتند که «ای خلیفه، هیچ زنی در جهان خوب‌تر نیست از شهربانو و او زن عبدالله زبیر است. اگر حیله کنی عبدالله زبیر آن را طلاق دهد. هیچ زن از آن خوب‌تر نیست». یزید از زبان معاویه جانب عبدالله زبیر مکتوب نوشت که «ما را با تو کاری است باید که زود بر من آیی».

{۹} چون مکتوب بر عبدالله زبیر رسید، عبدالله فی الحال برخاست. از مدینه در دمشق درآمد. عبدالله زبیر را یزید بسیار نواخت‌دوست[۲۸]، و بر[۲۹] معاویه بر دو محافه[۳۰] کنند. یزید گفت «ای معاویه، مرا بر عبدالله زبیر وصیّت کن تا بعداز تو روی از من نگرداند؛ این مهتر قوم است». معاویه گفت «ای عبدالله زبیر، تو [...][۳۱] باید که بعداز من از یزید رو نگردانی». عبدالله بیعت با یزید کرد.

[۲۴] داستان برادران دوقلو در خانهٔ عبد مناف به صورت های مختلف در کتب روایی و تاریخی بیان شده است. امّا در تاریخ طبری بخش‌های مختلفی به این دو برادر اختصاص داده شده و دیگر اینکه نام آن دو «هاشم» و «عبد شمس» بوده است، و همچنین انگشت یکی بر پیشانی دیگری چسبیده بوده است. توضیحات بیشتر در بخش ترجمهٔ انگلیسی وجود دارد. [۲۵] این گریه از بهر چیست؟ [۲۶] ندادم.

[۲۷] در برخی نسخ مقتلِ تحت تاثیر ادبیات شیعی وصیّت معاویه متفاوت است. مثلا در برگ ۶ از نسخهٔ ۱۷۸۰۳ مجلس شورای اسلامی چنین آمده است «بدآنکه کیفیت این قصّه‌ها را علمای ما رضوان الله علیهم مختلف ایراد نموده‌اند. به آنچه اعاظم علمای شیعه ایراده کرده‌اند اکتفا می نماید. شیخ ابن بابویه به سند معتبر از حضرت امام زین العابدین (ع) روایت کرده است که «چون هنگام رحلت معاویه به دارالبوار رسید، فرزند شقاوت‌مند خود یزید را طلبید و نزدیک خود نشانید و گفت «ای فرزند، بدان که من برای تو گردن کشان جهان را ذلیل و مُنقاد گردانیدم و جمیع بلاد را به حیطه تصرّف تو در آوردم و جهان‌داری و اسباب ملک و شهریاری را برای تو مهیّا ساختم. لا کن از سه نفر برای اجلال تو می‌ترسم و می‌دانم که مخالفت تو خواهند کرد. توانائی و قدرت ایشان زیاده از تو است. اوّل عبدالله پسر خطّاب، دوم عبدالله پسر زبیر، سوم حسین‌ابن علی (ع) [...]»». در این داستان، عبدالله زبیر «مانند شیری در کمین طعمه خود باشد و شب و روز چون روباه به مکر و حیله مشغول خواهد بود که دولت تو را تباه کند، اگر بر او دست بیابی، بندهای او را از هم جدا بکن» که کاملا با تصویر وی در «درّالمجالس» متفاوت است.

[۲۸] در اصل اشاره به «نواخته دوست» یعنی «دوستُ او را نواخته باشد» دارد. همچنین به گفتهٔ دهخدا این عبارت در کتاب «حبیب السیر» دیده می شود. به صورت «دوست‌نواز» و «دوست‌پرست» هم به کار می‌رود. [۲۹] پهلو، در کنار.

[۳۰] «محفه» که در اینجا اشاره به «تخت» دارد. [۳۱] عبارتی شبیه «تو فرزند منی» که احتمالا نادرست است. هرچند خطاب قرار دادن عبدالله زبیر به عنوان فرزندِ معاویه می‌تواند دلالت بر اصطلاح «عزیزکرده» داشته باشد.

As Cain killed Abel and as the children of His Eminence Jacob took their brother Joseph [...]. Be aware that twin boys were born in the house of ʿAbd al-Manāf. One of them was Maʿāsh and the other was known as Amīr. They were conjoined at birth and their father separated them from each other by sword?.[4] This had influence on their relationship! Maʿāsh's son was ʿAbd al-Muṭṭalib and Amīr's son was Ḥarb. These two fought with each other, too. And ʿAbd al-Muṭṭalib had a son [named Abū Ṭālib]. Abū Ṭālib had a son named ʿAlī (pbuh), and Abū Sufyān[5] had a son named Muʿāwiya. These two also fought with each other. ʿAlī (pbuh) had sons named Ḥasan and Ḥusayn (pbuh) and Muʿāwiya had a son named Yazīd. And Yazīd was determined to kill them, and this is, in fact, the secondary cause of enmity.

{7} And when Muʿāwiya (pbuh) was about to die, he cried, and people asked him, 'O Muʿāwiya, why are you crying?' He said, 'I have only this son, and I have not done anything, as he should marry and by the happiness of his children make him happy.'

{8} Returning to the story. Muʿāwiya greatly encouraged Yazīd [to marry]. Yazīd went out and gathered his friends and said, 'O brethren, which girl is more suitable [for me]?' They all said, 'O caliph, no woman in the world is better than Shahrbānū who is now the wife of ʿAbdallāh Zubayr. If you make a plan for ʿAbdallāh Zubayr to divorce her, then no woman would be better than her.' Yazīd, on behalf of Muʿāwiya, wrote a letter to ʿAbdallāh Zubayr saying, 'We need to talk and you should come here as soon as possible.'

{9} When ʿAbdallāh Zubayr received the letter he went without delay from Medina to Damascus. Yazīd warmly welcomed ʿAbdallāh Zubayr and sat him on a seat next to Muʿāwiya. Yazīd said, 'O Muʿāwiya, recommend that ʿAbdallāh Zubayr not shun me after your death; he is the chief of his people.' Muʿāwiya said, 'O ʿAbdallāh Zubayr, you should [...] not reject Yazīd after me.' ʿAbdallāh pledged his allegiance to Yazīd.

[4] There are various reports about this twin brother in Islamic literature. However, according to al-Ṭabarī, their names were Hāshim and ʿAbd Shams. 'It is said that Hāshim and ʿAbd Shams were twins and that one was born before the other with one of his fingers stuck to his twin's forehead; when his finger was separated blood flowed; people regarded this as an omen and said, 'There will be blood between them'. After his father's death Hāshim succeeded to the office of providing food and drink.' Al-Ṭabarī, *The History of al-Ṭabarī (Muhammad at Mecca)*, trans. W. Montgomery Watt (Albany: State University of New York Press, 1988), vol. 6, 17.

[5] from Ḥarb

{۱۰} دوم روز یزید بر عبدالله گفت «می‌خواهم که تو را خواهر به‌زنی خاکنام که تو مردی با جمعیّتِ بسیارْ مهتر قومی». عبدالله زبیر شاد شد. یزید گفت که «شب ساخته شو که امشب کار خیر است. و ده هزار دینار سرخ یزید عبدالله را داد بر وجه طَبَقْ تا ساخته شود».[۳۲] عبدالله ساخته شد و یزید در خانهٔ خود جمعیّت کرد. چون شب شد عبدالله نیز با جماعت خود آمد شادمان نشسته؛ یزید درون خانه رفته، باز آمد و گفت «خواهر من می‌گوید که «من شنیدم که او زنی صاحب جمال دارد. نبودن او با من چگونه خواهد ساخت»». هرکسی دنبال عبدالله شد[۳۳] که «او را طلاق ده و دختر خلیفه می‌بایستی [که] تمام مُلک برای تو خواهد بود». چندان او را ترغیب کردند [که] عبدالله زن را في الحال طلاق گفت. یزید باز درون خانه رفته و بیرون آمد و گفت «خواهر من می‌گوید «کسی که آن‌چنان زن صاحب جمال را گذاشت، مرا این‌چنین شوهر نباید»». یزید گفت که «ای عبدالله، من چه کنم که او بالغ است و وکیل نفسِ خود است. از راه شرع مرا بر او دسترسی نیست». عبدالله را همان ده هزار دینار مانْد و زن به باد داد و خجل شد و به جانب خانه بازگشت. این خبر بر زن او رسید. هرچند که عبدالله رسالت کرد[۳۴] که «باز تحلیل کنم»[۳۵] زن او را قبول نکرد.

{۱۱} و این مکر یزید بود. و بعضی [که] بر معاویه اضافه می‌کنند بزهکار می‌شوند. زیرا آنکه معاویه از کبار صحابه بود و کاتب وحی بود. و رسول ﷺ گفت «هرکس به ذکر نیک یاد کند اصحاب من را، او را است بهشت» پس هر که معاویه را به بدی یاد کند او بزه‌کار شود.[۳۶] و رسول ﷺ فرمود «أَنَا مَدینَةُ العِلمِ وَعَلِيٌّ بَابُهَا»، و آن جنگ[۳۷] بر طریق اجتهاد بود و مجتهد در خطا بزه‌کار نشود.[۳۸]

{۱۲} الغرض. بعداز وفاتِ معاویه یزید را به خلافت پادشاهی نشاندند، و [او] موسیٰ اشعری را به شهربانو به رسالت فرستاد برای مناکحتِ خود. چون موسیٰ اشعری در مدینه رسید اوّل به زیارت مهتر عالم ﷺ درآمد. امام حسین و عبدالله عمر رضی الله عنهما آنجا نشسته بودند. بر ایشان سلام داد. پرسیدند «ای ابوموسیٰ، به چه مراسلت[۳۹] آمدی؟» گفت «مرا یزید بر شهربانو فرستاد». امام حسین گفت «اگر او را قبول نکند ازجهت من نیز رسالت دهی». عبدالله عمر نیز رسالت داد و ابوموسیٰ را حجاب نشاند[۴۰] و به جانب شهر بانو روان شد.

[۳۲] مهیّا شدن. شاید به معنای «مست نمودن» هم باشد: سرخوش شدن از سر نوشیدن شراب؟

[۳۳] «دنبال شدن» اشاره به «پیگیر بودن» دارد.

[۳۴] پیغام رساندن.

[۳۵] در فقه و احکام نکاح، «تحلیل» اشاره به «حلال نمودن دارد». فقها نظرهای متفاوتی داشته و دارند، امّا بطورکلّی اشاره به عقدی دارد که به آغاز دوبارهٔ رابطهٔ زناشویی و زندگی زوج سه‌طلاقه ختم خواهد شد.

[۳۶] دخیل نکردن معاویه در قتل حسن و حسین به ادبیات آسیای مرکزی و جهان مالایا هم راه یافته است. مردم اندونزی گاهی اوقات به نقل قولی منسوب به نورالدین رانیری، عالم گجراتی ساکن آچه در سوماترا اکتفا می‌کرده‌اند. به بخش انگلیسی مراجعه نمایید.

[۳۷] کشمکش.

[۳۸] اشاره به جدایی سنّی و شیعه دارد و اینکه حدیث پیامبر در مورد علي بن أبي طالب پیرامون تفاوت و «برتری» مرتبط با «اجتهاد شرعی» است.

[۳۹] ارسال پیغام یا نامه.

[۴۰] اشاره دارد به «او را مهیّا ساخت؛ هم از نظر ظاهر و هم از نظر مَرکب». در ترجمهٔ آلمانی دیوان حافظ «در حجاب بودن\شدن» به معنای schleier یعنی «پوشیده بودن» نیز می‌آید
Ḥāfiẓ, *Der Diwan des grossen lyrischen Dichters Hafis im persischen Original herausgegeben, ins deutsche metrisch übersetzt und mit Anmerkungen versehen*, von Vincenz Rosenzweig Ritter von Schwannau (Wien: Druck und Verlag der K. K. Hof-und Staatsdruckerei, 1858), I: 257.

{10} On another day, Yazīd said to ʿAbdallāh, 'I want to betroth my sister to you, as you are the chief of a large clan.' ʿAbdallāh Zubayr was so happy. Yazīd said to him, 'Be ready tonight as there will be a feast.' And Yazīd put ten thousand red dinars on a tray and passed it to ʿAbdallāh.ʿAbdallāh prepared himself. Yazīd brought people to his palace. That night, ʿAbdallāh came along with his clan and sat cheerfully [in Yazīd's palace]. Yazīd went to his quarters and returned. Yazīd said, 'My sister says, "I heard that he has a pretty wife. How can he be with me without her?"' The people urged ʿAbdallāh, 'Divorce her, as you should take the daughter of the caliph [i.e., Muʿāwiya] and then all his power will reach you.' With their encouragement ʿAbdallāh quickly divorced his wife. Yazīd went to his quarters again and returned. He said this time, 'My sister says, "The one who leaves such a pretty wife, he deserves not to be my husband?" Yazīd said, 'O ʿAbdallāh, what can I do as she is mature and is her own guardian. Legally speaking, I cannot force her.' ʿAbdallāh was left with those ten thousand dinars and he lost his wife. He was embarrassed and he returned home. The news reached his wife. ʿAbdallāh sent messages to re-solemnise the remarriage but she did not accept.

{11} And all this was a ruse of Yazīd. And those who ascribe this to Muʿāwiya are sinful. Muʿāwiya was among the great Companions and was a scribe of the revelation. And the Messenger (pbuh) said, 'Whoever remembers my Companions kindly, their place will be in paradise.' Accordingly, whoever remembers Muʿāwiya disrespectfully, they will be sinful. And the Messenger (pbuh) said, 'I am the city of knowledge and ʿAlī is its gate.' Their conflict [of ʿAlī and Muʿāwiya] was about legal reasoning, and so the one who was incorrect will not have sinned.

{12} Returning to the story. After the death of Muʿāwiya, Yazīd was chosen as caliph. And he sent Mūsā Ashʿarī, as his representative, to Shahrbānū for the purpose of marriage. When Mūsā Ashʿarī arrived in Medina, he first visited the tomb of the Eminence of the World (pbuh). Imam Ḥusayn and ʿAbdallāh ʿUmar (PBUT) were there. Mūsā greeted them. They asked, 'What message are you conveying?' He said, 'Yazīd sent me regarding Shahrbānū.' Imam Ḥusayn said, 'If she does not accept Yazīd, then convey to her my message. ʿAbdallāh ʿUmar said the same and he dressed and prepared himself [and also saddled and loaded his animal]. He went towards Shahrbānū.

{۱۳} شهربانو چادری در میان بست و پرسید «به چه مصلحت آمدی؟» گفت که «مرا یزید بر تو فرستاد که تو را به زنی کند. و چون در روضهٔ رسول ﷺ رسیدم امام حسین و عبدالله عمر نشسته دیدم. [درخواست] ایشان نیز بر تو آوردم. هرکه را خواهی قبول کن». شهربانو گفت «تو پیرمردی و سببِ پیری تو را نخواهم. و وکالت خود را بتو سپردم. و مرا از این سه کس گویی». گفت «اگر دنیا می‌خواهی یزید را بخواهی؛ [...] عبدالله عمر را بخواهی، و اگر دین و دنیا خواهی امام حسین را بخواه». شهربانو گفت «امام حسین را بخواه». شهربانو گفت «امام حسین را رسان و بگو که «شُکر هر خدای را که مرا به کنیزگی قبول فرمودی. دیگر می‌خواهم که فردای قیامت در صف محمّد مُصْطَفَی و خدیجهٔ کبری و فاطمهٔ زهرا و علیّ مرتضی[...]»». ابوموسیٰ بازگشت و امام را خبر داد و خود در شام رفت. امام حسین شهربانو را نکاح کرد و در خانهٔ خود در آورد.

{۱۴} الغرض. معاویه را موت قریب رسید. یزید را طلب کرد و در برابر مهتر قومِ ایشان. قوم او را بیعت دادند، و خود بر منبر سوار شد و گفت «ای مسلمانان من از دنیا بیرون خواهم رفت و بر شما وصیّت می‌کنم که[41] حرمت فرزندان رسول الله ﷺ؛ شنیدم[42] «هر که گرامی دارد فرزندان مرا گرامی دارد او را خدای تَعَالَی». بعده، پسر را طلبید و گفت «ای یزید، خلافت به تو سپردم و برابر هرکسی تو را بیعت دادم، و برچند کس زندگانی نیکو کنی. یکی عبدالرحمان ابوبکر رضي الله عنه؛ و برابر ابن‌مسعود و عبدالله عمر، و خدمت فرزندان رسول ﷺ حسن و حسین رضي الله عنهما نیکویی کنی که ایشان از کار حضرت رسول ﷺ مانده. و از ایشان نترسی که ایشان را غرض خلافت نیست. و هر بار که مدینه رَوی در رکاب ایشان پیروی کن که من بسیار دیده‌ام که ایشان بر هر دو کتف مبارک [پیامبر] بودندی. ای پسر، یک روز پیغمبر ﷺ در خانهٔ بی بی فاطمه در آمد و من نیز با حضرت بودم. فاطمه را در گریه دیدم. آن حضرت گفت «ای جان بابا، برای چه می گریی؟»[43] گفت «یا رسول الله، فرزندان تو جایی رفته‌اند برای بازی و تا غایت نیامدند. و ایّام گرم است نباید که ایشان را تشنگی زحمت دهد». رسول الله ﷺ از خانه بیرون آمد و ابوبکر صدّیق را نیز برابر رسول بود تا هر سه نفر رفتیم و گِرد مدینه گشتیم. مردی گوسفندان می‌چرانید از او پرسیدیم. او گفت «من دیدم دو کودک نورانی بدین جانب رفتند». رسول ﷺ بدان نشانِ آن مرد روان شدند. چون پیشتر رفتیم، امام حسن و حسین را در زیر درخت آن را که[44] یافتیم. چون نزدیک رفتیم، رسول ﷺ را جبرئیل سلام داد و فرمودند «عليك السلام يا أخي جبرئيل». نشناختم که یاد کنندهٔ ایشان را جبرئیل بوَد.[45] رسول ﷺ آهسته آمد پای مبارک حسن در کنار گرفت و پای مبارک حسین را ابوبکر صدّیق در کنار گرفت»».

[41] به؟ [42] از پیامبر. [43] «مَا يُبكيك يا فاطمة؟»: حافظ أبي الحسن علي بن محمّد الواسطي، مناقب أمير المؤمنين علي بن أبي طالب رضي الله عنه، تحقيق وتعليق: أبي عبد الرحمن تركي بن عبد الله الوادعي (صنعا: دارالآثار ۱۴۲۴/۲۰۰۳)، ۱۹۷.

[44] شاید مراد «آنگه» می‌باشد. [45] احتمال اینکه این جمله نیز از زبان پیامبر بیان شده باشد هم وجود دارد.

{13} Shahrbānū raised a veil [between herself and Mūsā Ashʿarī] and asked him, 'Why did you come here?' He said, 'Yazīd has sent me as his representative to propose to you in marriage. And when I entered the shrine of the Messenger (pbuh), Imam Ḥusayn and ʿAbdallāh ʿUmar were there. I am informing you of their intention to marry you, too. Accept whoever you like.' Shahrbānū said, 'You are an old man and I do not desire you due to your age. But I do give you my authority. And tell me about the three.' He said, 'If you want to have the world, then marry Yazīd; if [...] then marry ʿAbdallāh ʿUmar. And if you want both religion and the world, then marry Imam Ḥusayn.' Shahrbānū said, 'I choose Imam Ḥusayn. Convey my message to Imam Ḥusayn that all praise is for God as you have accepted me to be your bondwoman. I want to be in the line of Muḥammad Muṣṭafā, Khadīja Kubrā, Fāṭima Zahrā and ʿAlī Murtaḍā [...].' Abū Mūsā returned and informed the Imam of her decision and then he went to Damascus. Imam Ḥusayn married Shahrbānū and brought her into his house.

{14} Returning to the story. Muʿāwiya was on the verge of death. He asked Yazīd to come before the chief of their clan. The people of the clan pledged allegiance, then Muʿāwiya ascended his pulpit and said, 'O Muslims, I will soon die and I recommend you to respect the children of the Messenger of God (pbuh) as I have heard him say, "Whoever respects my children, God will respect them".' Then Muʿāwiya called Yazīd to speak with him. He said, 'O Yazīd, I entrusted power to you before people even pledged their allegiance. You should be kind to a number of people. The first of them is ʿAbd al-Raḥmān Abū Bakr (pbuh), then Ibn Masʿūd, and then ʿAbdallāh ʿUmar, and also be kind to the children of the Messenger (pbuh), Ḥasan and Ḥusayn (pbuh) as they are the last vestiges[6] of the Prophet (pbuh). And do not be scared of them as they do not aim to become caliphs. And whenever you visit Medina you should follow them as I noticed many times that they both sat on the sacred shoulders [of the Prophet]. O son! The Prophet (pbuh) came to the house of Lady Fāṭima one day and I was accompanying him. I saw that Fāṭima was crying. The Prophet asked her, "O darling, why are you crying?" She said, "O Messenger of God, your grandchildren have been out playing for a long time and it is hot and they will be thirsty." The Messenger of God (pbuh) left the house and Abū Bakr Ṣiddīq was before the Prophet. And the three of us went to look for them around Medina. We inquired from a shepherd there. He said, "I saw that two gleaming boys were going that way." The Messenger of God (pbuh) followed the direction shown by the shepherd. After a few more steps we found Imams Ḥasan and Ḥusayn under a tree. When we approached them, the Messenger (pbuh) greeted Gabriel and said, "Peace be upon you, O brother Gabriel." At that time did not I recognise that he was Gabriel. The Messenger (pbuh) approached slowly and hugged

[6] offspring?

{۱۵} معاویه گفت «ای پسر، من دیدم که بر کف پای حسن و حسین رَضِيَ اللهُ عَنْهُ ما بوسه داد، و جبرئیل عليه السلام همچنان یاد می‌کرد و امام حسین دست مبارک خود بر ریش مبارک می‌گیرد، و طپانچه بر روی رخسارهٔ رسول ﷺ بر طریق بازی می‌زد. و می‌گفت که «ما گرسنه شدیم طعام بیار». رسول ﷺ گفت «ای جانِ بابا، در خانه می‌رویم و طعام پیش خواهم آورد». في الحال جبرئیل عليه السلام در رسید و فرمان از حضرت عزّت رسانید که «ای احمد،[۴۶] چرا برای ایشان از درگاه من نخواهی؟» في الحال طعام از هوا پیدا شد و پیش هر دو فرود آمد. ایشان هر دو می‌خوردند و ما نظاره می‌کردیم. هر بار که نان می‌شکستند باز درست می‌شد. بعداز خوردن طعام آب طلبیدند، رسول الله ﷺ انگشت مبارک خود در تنهٔ آن درخت خلانید.[۴۷] به فرمان خدای تَعَالَی از آن سوراخ آبِ سردِ صاف برآمد و از آن آب خوردند. امام حسین را ابوبکر صدّیق بر کتف خود نشاند و امام حسن را رسول ﷺ. و بعدها به جانب خانه روان شدیم. رسول ﷺ گفت «نِعْمَ الحَامِلَانْ وَنِعْمَ المَحْمُولَانْ»».[۴۸]

{۱۶} [معاویه گفت] «پس، ای پسر، اگر ایشان را رنجانی در دوزخ رفتی». یزید گفت «همه وصیّت تو قبول کردم جز این وصیّت». معاویه تفت شد[۴۹] و گفت «عبدالله را طلب کنید». عبدالله حاضر آمد، و [معاویه] گفت «ای عبدالله، در مدینه رو و امام حسن و حسین را به حیله بیار تا من خلافت بدیشان سپارم». و مکتوب به امام حسن و حسین نوشته. چون عبدالله یک منزل رفت معاویه جان به حقّ تسلیم کرد. و بعضی گفتند که زهرش داد[ند].

{۱۷} چون معاویه از این عالم رفت، [یزید] به نوشته عبدالله را بازگردانید و ولایت مدینه بر عتبه ولید[۵۰] داد. عتبه با شصت هزار سوار در مدینه آمد. و ازجهت یزید هرکسی را بیعت کردن. امّا بعضی شهرها بر یزید بیعت نکردند، چنانچه خوارزم و بغداد و هر فرودستان.[۵۱] و گفتند که «جایی که فرزندان حضرت رسول باشند، ما تو را به خلافت قبول نکنیم، و تو را رسول عليه السلام لعنت کرده است آن زمان که در پشت پدر بود».

{۱۸} و چنان آمده است که یک روز رسول ﷺ بر اسب سوار بود. معاویه رکاب آن حضرت ﷺ می‌گرفت. رسول عليه السلام گفت «دور شو از من که مرا از پشت تو بوی خون می‌آید. لعنت خدای بر آن کس باد که در پشت آنست». معاویه دور شد و گفت «یا رسول الله، مرا کیفیت آن سخن روشن کن». آن حضرت

[۴۶] یکی از القاب پیامبر. [۴۷] «خلانیدن» اشاره به داخل نمودن، یا فشار دادن دارد.

[۴۸] اصطلاحی است باکاربردهای متفاوت. در این متن می‌تواند به‌صورت «بهترینِ حمل کننده‌ها و بهترین بارها» خوانده شود. از سماح ممدوح، نویسنده و مترجم صاحب‌قلم مصری، بابت راهنمایی‌های ارزشمندش سپاسگزارم. این قسمت در یکی از بنیادی‌ترین کتب پیشامدرن حدیثی شیعه «بِحَارُ ٱلأَنْوَارُ» در ذیل «تاريخ أَمير المُؤمِنين» ذکر شده‌است، و نقش ابوبکر با جبرئیل به عنوان حاملِ حسین جابجا می‌شود و «حَمل النبي صَلّى اللهُ عَلَيْهَ وَآلِهِ الحُسَن وحَمل جبْرَئيلُ الحُسَيْنْ [...]». در برخی کتب مربوطه با ادبیات مقتل الحسینِ تحت تاثیر قرائت شیعی این جابه‌جایی بیشتر به چشم می‌خورد: العلامة المجلسي، بحار الأنوار، ج ۳۷، ص ۹۰. [۴۹] عصبانی شد.

[۵۰] در اصل « ولید بن عتبه» است. در نسخهٔ گنج بخش نام وی به صورت «عتبه ولید» و «عطبه ولید» نوشته می‌شود.

[۵۱] اگر صحیح خوانده باشم، واژهٔ «فرودست» اشاره به بنگال و آسیای جنوبی دارد. و اگر چنین باشد، بعید نیست که نویسنده و یا کاتب که تبار آسیایی داشته می‌خواسته خود را از بیعت با «یزیدیان» مبرّا سازد.

the sacred leg of Ḥasan and the sacred leg of Ḥusayn was hugged by Abū Bakr Ṣiddīq'.

{15} Muʿāwiya continued, 'O son! I saw myself that the Prophet kissed the feet of Ḥasan and Ḥusayn (pbuh), and that Gabriel (pbuh) did the same. And Imam Ḥusayn took the sacred beard of the Prophet with his sacred hands and playfully slapped the face of the Messenger (pbuh), and said, "We are hungry. Bring us some food." The Messenger (pbuh) said, "O darling, we will go home and I will take food there." In the meantime, Gabriel (pbuh) arrived and brought a message from the Lord of Majesty, "O Ahmad,[7] why did you not ask from My presence?!" Soon food came down from heaven, and was served before both of them. They both ate while we watched them. As much as they consumed the bread, the bread was replaced by God's power. After eating food, they wanted water. The Messenger pushed his sacred finger into the trunk of a tree. By God's power, fresh pure water came out and they drank from it. 'Abū Bakr Ṣiddīq put Imam Ḥusayn on his shoulder and the Messenger (pbuh) did the same with Imam Ḥasan. Later on, they went home. The Messenger of God (pbuh) said "The best holder and the best portable".[8]

{16} [Muʿāwiya said] 'So, O son, if you make them suffer, you will be in hell.' Yazīd said, 'I accept all your recommendations but this one.' Muʿāwiya became angry and asked for ʿAbdallāh. He arrived and [Muʿāwiya] told him, 'O ʿAbdallāh, go to Medina and try your best to bring Imams Ḥasan and Ḥusayn so I can entrust the caliphate to them', and he wrote a letter for Imams Ḥasan and Ḥusayn. When ʿAbdallāh had passed but a short distance Muʿāwiya submitted his soul to God. Some have said that he was poisoned.[9]

{17} As soon as Muʿāwiya left this world, Yazīd wrote a letter to ʿAbdallāh asking him to return. And he entrusted the rule of Medina to Walīd b. ʿUtba. The latter entered Medina with sixty thousand cavalrymen. And they forced everyone to pledge allegiance to Yazīd. However, in some places, such as Khwarazm, Baghdad, and South Asia, including Bengal.[10] They did not pledge allegiance and they said, 'As long as the children of the Messenger remain, we do not accept you as our caliph. And you were already cursed by the Messenger (pbuh) when you were still in your father's loins.'

{18} And it is reported that the Prophet was riding a horse. And Muʿāwiya was taking the stirrup. The Messenger of God said, 'Get away from me as I can smell blood

[7] One of the Prophet's nicknames, meaning 'most highly adored'.

[8] Thanks to Samah Mmdoh, a distinguished Egyptian translator and author, for her assistance to translate this part. It should be noted that in some Shiʿi sources (e.g., *Biḥār al-Anwār*), Abū Bakr's role, as a carrier, is replaced by Gabriel, the angel. To check the reference, see the Persian side of the text.

[9] Based on the story's beginning part, he should have been martyred.

[10] The term used for Bengal is '*furūdast*' which literally means 'the lower part'. However, it is known in classical literature as 'Bengal'.

فرمود «از پشت تو فرزندی زاید که فرزندان من به ناحقّ کُشد». معاویه گفت «که زن نمی کنم». از این سبب زن نکردی تا به تقدیر الله تَعَالَی کژدم آویخته شد. طبیبان گفتند «علاج آن به زن کن تا نیکو شوی». دردِ او غالب شد. کنیزکی داشت که طعام پختی برایش، بر او علاج کرد. به فرمان خدای تَعَالَی از آن علاج یزید در شکم آن کنیزک ماند. گویند که معاویه گفت که «سقط خود [...]» پس کسی را که رسول ﷺ در پشت پدر لعنت کرده باشد، ما را نشاید که طاعت او قبول کنیم.

{۱۹} و قول اهل سنت و جماعت این است که یزید را لعنت نکند که همین صحیح است.

{۲۰} الغرض. یزید قصد کشتن امامین کرد. و مکتوب بر والی مدینه، که عتبه بن ولید بود، نوشت که «امام حسن و حسین را بکشی». عتبه ولید جواب نوشت که من ایشان را کشتن نتْوانم که اهل مدینه همهٔ آنها را دوست می‌دارند. اگر من ایشان را بکشم در حال ایشان مرا بکشند». یزید فرمان فرستاد «اگر ایشان را بکشی در حقّ تو چندان لطف و خدمت کنم و حُرمت دهم که آن را پایان نباشد، و اگر نکنی سر از تن جدا کنم. این زمان در مدینه کیست که از وی میترسی؟»

{۲۱} چون شب شد عتبه پنهان بر امام حسن و حسین درآمد و خدمت کرد، و دست بسته ایستاد شد و گریستن گرفت. سیدزادگان گفتند که «عتبه چرا گریه می کنی؟» مکتوب یزید پیش ایشان انداخت و هر دو برادران خواندند و چشم پر آب کردند. عتبه گفت «ای مخدومزادگان، من درین [؟] است شما را بدی نخواهم» – و بعضی گویند که دشمن ایشان را فریب می‌داد؛ و گفت «شما شب از اینجا بروید و قلع[۵۲] بگیرید». چون چندین ماه گذشت یزید مکتوب دیگر فرستاد که «ای عتبه، مرا معلوم شده که دوستدارِ پسران علی رضی الله عنه هستی. ساخته باش، امروز یا فردا سر از تن جدا می کنم و اگر خیریّت خود می‌خواهی پسران علی را به هر حیله که دانی و توانی ایشان را بکش».

{۲۲} عتبه چاره ندید. قصد کشتن ایشان کرد. و عورتی بود در مدینه ساحره نام مهم؛[۵۳] او را طلب کرد. پیش او هزار دینار سرخ نهاد. گفت «ای مهم، چنان گوش[۵۴] که پسران علی هلاک شوند». آن زن بدبخت چون زر دید فریفته شد و زر را پسندید و در خانه برد. و یک غلوله[۵۵] دارو کرد و در او زهر تعبیه کرد. و نزد زن امام حسن که قُطّامه بود آمد. و امام حسن زنان بسیار داشت و رها می کرده بود. گویند که هفتاد و دو تن زن کرده و به روایتی دویست تا. یک روز أمیر المُؤمِنین علی رضی الله عنه بر منبر آمد و گفت «ای قریشیان، مهاجران و انصار، امام حسن را دختر خود ندهید که او دختران شما را طلاق دهد». مردی از مهتران قبیلهٔ بنی سُلیم، مسعود نام بود، او گفت «ای أمیر المُؤمِنین علی، اگر مرا هفتاد دختران باشند و پسر تو، نکاح آن را شرف خود دانم و سعادت از این تصوّر کنم که ایشان فرزندان رسول اند و نور دیدهٔ فاطمه و جگر گوشه‌گان». حضرت علی رضی الله عنه برین

[۵۲] پناه گرفتن به‌ویژه در کوه. [۵۳] دلّالهٔ زنان است و کار ساز. [۵۴] به دقّت گوش دادن و به خاطر سپردن. شاید هم اشاره به «کوش» به معنی «کوشیدن» دارد. [۵۵] گلوله؛ گلوله ای خمیری. این واژه در آثاری که در خراسان بزرگ و آسیای میانه نگاشته می‌شده اند، همچون ذخیرهٔ خوارزمشاهی، دیده می شود.

from your loins. May God's curse be upon the one who is in your loins.' Muʿāwiya stood back and said, 'O Messenger of God, please enlighten me?' The Prophet said, 'There will be a child from your loins who will unjustly kill my grandchildren.' Muʿāwiya said, 'Then I will not marry!' As such, he did not marry until upon God's decree he was affected by a scorpion. Doctors advised him to heal himself by means of intercourse. His pain increased. He had a bondwoman who used to cook food for him. So he lay with her. By God's order, and through this necessary treatment, Yazīd was made in the bondwoman's womb. It is even said that Muʿāwiya demanded the embryo "be terminated [...]" however, the one who the Prophet cursed while still being in his father's loins, we should not accept his rulership.

{19} The position of the Ahl al-Sunna wa-l-Jamāʿa is correct, specifically, that Yazīd should not be cursed.

{20} Returning to the story. Yazīd was determined to kill both Imams. And he wrote a letter to the ruler of Medina, Walīd b. ʿUtba, ordering him, 'Kill Imams Ḥasan and Ḥusayn'. Walīd b. Utbah answered, 'I cannot kill them as all the people of Medina love them. If I kill them, then the people would kill me straight away.' Yazīd made a promise, 'If you kill them, I would do a lot of favours for you and respect you so much so that you would know no end, and if you do not kill them, I will behead you. Now who is it in Medina that you are afraid of?'

{21} At night, Walīd b. ʿUtba went to Imams Ḥasan and Ḥusayn and bowed to them, and respectfully stood before them and began to cry. The Masters asked, 'Why are you crying Walīd b. ʿUtba?' He showed them Yazīd's letter. Both brothers read the text and their eyes became tearful. Walīd b. ʿUtba said, 'O Masters, I do not wish you ill!' And some reports say that the enemies deceived him. And he told them, 'Seek a safe haven for a while.' After a couple of months, Yazīd sent another letter to Walīd b. ʿUtba saying, 'O Walīd b. ʿUtba, I am informed that you love ʿAlī's (pbuh) sons. Prepare to be beheaded either today or tomorrow. If you want the best for yourself, kill the sons of ʿAlī with all the trickery that you can muster.'

{22} Walīd b. ʿUtba was left with no choice. Thus, he became determined to kill them. He asked for a witch, known as Ṣāḥira, in Medina who was also a matchmaker. He gave her 1,000 red dinars and said, 'O matchmaker, follow carefully and kill the sons of ʿAlī.' The desperate lady was enticed as soon as she saw the money, which she accepted and took home. She prepared a pill filled with poison. She then went to the wife of Imam Ḥasan, whose name was Quṭṭāma. Imam Ḥasan had taken and left many wives. It is said that he had seventy-two wives, and according to some reports two hundred. One day, the Commander of Believers ʿAlī (pbuh) ascended the pulpit and said, 'O people of Quraysh, Emigrants, and Helpers, do not give your daughters to Imam Ḥasan as he would divorce your daughters.' One of the chiefs of the Banī Sulaym

خوش شدند و گفتند «اگر دربان بهشت من باشم تو را اوّل درآورم». آواز آمد، چنانچه حاضران شنیدند، «که تو دربان بهشت مایی». روزی امام حسن را پرسیدند که «مقصود چه داری که زن می کنی و می گذاری؟» امام گفت که «از آن حضرت[۵۶] شنیدم که «از یکی فرزندان[۵۷] مرا زن باشد که خاصیت آن زن بهشت باشد»».[۵۸]

{۲۳} الغرض. چون آن زال بر زن امام حسن آمد و گفت که «امام با تو محبّت دارد یا نه؟» گفت «بسیار شفقّت است که به‌غیر من کوزهٔ آب هم نمی‌خورد و اگر خواب کنم». آنگاه آن زال گفت «پس چرا برابر فلان رسالت کرده است؟» که بانو غمناک شد، گریستن گرفت. آن زال گفت «من یک دارویی دارم اگر آن را برابر دهن خوب بسابی[۵۹] و او را در آب یا طعام بدهی، بر تو هرگز زنی دیگر نکند». و [زال] بدین سوگند خورد. که بانو گفت «زود باش بیار». زال بدبخت آن غلوله کشید و به دست او داد و خود بازگشت.

{۲۴} که بانو في الحال شربت کرد و آن غلوله در وی گداخت. و امام حسن و حسین را در شکار رفته بودند و ایّام تابستان بود. امام حسن در خانهٔ خود آمد که بانو ایستاده شد. پایزار[۶۰] از موزهٔ[۶۱] پای او ستاندند و در خآنگاه[۶۲] غلطید. بعداز ساعت آب طلبیده. بانو گفت «یا امام، شربتی ساخته‌ام که اگر بگویی بیارم». که بانو في الحال آورد و آن شربت بنوشید. بلکه شعله آتش بود. به‌مجرّد نوشیدن شربت شوری در وجود مبارک افتاد. امام حسن پسر خود قاسم را گفت که «ای نور دیدهٔ من، برادرم طلبیده بیاور، و [...] کاهلی نکند. بگوی که «ای برادر، بیا تا وداعِ قیامت کنم و ساعتی روی یکدیگر ببینم»». قاسم رضي الله عنه گریه کنان دوید تا رفت.

{۲۵} چون امام حسین رضي الله عنه چنان دید بجست و گفت «ای جان بابا، برای چه گریه می کنی؟ مگر تو را أَمیر المُؤمِنین حسن سبب تَعَلّم [...]» گفت «ای مخدوم، و ای صاحب من، تو را بابای من طلبید». گفت «گریه چیست؟» گفت «بابای من شربت خورده است و به طریق ماهی که بی‌آب می‌غلطد همان‌طور می‌غلطد». امام حسین گریه کنان و حیران و پابرهنه به جانب خانهٔ امام حسن دوید.

{۲۶} چون امیر را چنان حال دید نعره بزد. خود را بر أَمیر المُؤمِنین حسن [...] کرد. هر دو برادران کنار گرفتند.[۶۳] امام حسین گفت «ای مخدوم من و ای مشفق من، تو را چه شد؟» امام حسن فرمود «[قد] قُرُبَ الأَجَل وَٱنْقَطع الْأَمَل».[۶۴] که بانو خواست که احوال بگوید. امام حسن چشم گشاد کرده[۶۵] و گفت «إسْكُتِي وَلاتتكلّمِي. پردهٔ کسی مگشای (؟). از میان پای من دور شو». امام حسن گفت «ای برادر، وصیّت دارم. بشنو». گفت «در عبادت خدای تَعَالَی مشغول باش و دل به دنیا نبندی و از سبب کسی که حال من چنین شده است او را نرنجانی که من اوّل او را شفاعت خواهم کرد. و به زیارت من بسیار آیی و نظر شفقّت از ابوالقاسم

[۵۶] پیامبر. [۵۷] حسن و حسین. [۵۸] اشاره به «داستان زید و زینب بِنْتِ‌جحش» دارد. در نهایت، زینب و زید از یکدیگر جدا می‌شوند و زینب به نکاح پیامبر در می‌آید. [۵۹] اشاره دارد به اعمالی که در علوم غریبه و خفیه رایج است و از آن طریق فرد بر مادّه ای\جسمی ذکر و یا وردی را به منظوری خاص فوت می‌نماید. [۶۰] پای افزار و پاپوش. [۶۱] چکمه. واژهٔ «موزه» از طریق این داستان در ادبیات کلاسیک مالایی وارد شده است. [۶۲] سرای خانه. [۶۳] یکدیگر را در آغوش گرفتند.
[۶۴] همچنین، در موسوعة امام علی به این عبارت اشاره شده است. [۶۵] علاوه بر «گشودن چشم» اشاره به «ابراز خشم» نیز دارد.

was Masʿūd. He said, 'O Commander of Believers, ʿAlī, if I had seventy daughters and only your son [i.e., as a suitor], then I would be honoured to marry them with him, and I could only imagine such a blessing as he is the grandson of the Messenger and darling and sweetheart of Fāṭima.' ʿAlī (pbuh) was touched. He said, 'If I were the gatekeeper of paradise, I would bring you in first.' A voice was heard, and others also heard it, saying, 'You are the gatekeeper of Our paradise.' One day Imam Ḥasan was asked, 'Why do you marry women and then leave them?' The Imam said, 'I heard from that excellent person,[11] "One of my children will have a wife who is heavenly-natured".'[12]

{23} Returning to the story. The witch came to Imam Ḥasan's wife and asked her, 'Does the Imam love you?' She replied, 'He is so kind that he does not drink water without me or if I am in bed.' Then the witch said, 'If so, why did he propose to someone else while being with you?' The lady became upset and cried. The witch said, 'I have a drug that you can grind before your mouth[13] and give to him with either food or drink. Then he would never marry another women while being with you.' And she swore that she told the truth. Immediately, the lady said, 'Give it to me quickly!' The deceitful witch took out the pill and passed it on to her and then returned.

{24} The lady, in the meantime, made a drink and dissolve in it the pill. Imams Ḥasan and Ḥusayn were out hunting as it was summer. Imam Ḥasan returned home and his wife was waiting there to serve him. She took his upper shaft and boots, and he lay down in the house. After some moments, he asked for water. The lady said, 'O Imam, I have prepared a drink. If you want, I can bring it for you.' So, the lady brought the sherbet and the Imam drank. It felt like drinking a flame. As soon as he drank the drink his sacred body felt uncomfortable. Imam Ḥasan told his son Qāsim, 'O dear one, go and bring my brother and tell him not to wait. Tell him, "O brother, come to say a final goodbye until the Day of Judgement, so that we can see each other for a moment."' Qāsim (pbuh) ran out, crying.

{25} When Imam Ḥusayn (pbuh) saw him, he quickly stood up and said to him, 'O dear one, why are you crying? Did not the Commander of Believers Ḥasan [send you] to study?!' He said, 'O my lord and master, my father wants to meet you now.' [Imam Ḥusayn] said, 'Why are you crying then?' He said, 'My father drank a drink which caused him to writhe in pain.' Imam Ḥusayn cried and was shocked and ran barefoot towards the house of Imam Ḥasan.

{26} When he saw the Commander in that situation, he screamed and then [went closer to] the Commander of Believers Ḥasan, and both brothers embraced. Imam Ḥusayn said, 'O my master, and my support, what has happened to you?' Imam Ḥasan

[11] i.e., the Prophet [12] It may refer to the wife of Zayd, the adopted son of Muḥammad. Her name was Zaynab bint Jaḥsh. [13] [while invoking supplication and talismanic words] (?)

دریغ نداری». أَمیر المُؤمِنین حسین گفت «ای مخدوم من و ای قوّت پشت من، سلام بر رسول و خدیجه و علی و فاطمه رضی‌الله‌عنها برسانی و بگویی «منِ بیچارهٔ غریب تنها ماندم». این‌چنین وصیّت کرد و از دار فنا به دار بقا رحلت نمود. قالوا «إنّا لله وإنّا إليهِ رَاجعُون»[۶۶] به تاریخ دهم از محرّم سنة تِسْعَةَ خَمْسین[۶۷] بود. و آن زال بدبخت هم درین روز مُرد و به دوزخ رسید.

{۲۷} عتبه ولید جانب یزید مکتوب نوشت. یزید شاد شد و برای عتبه جامهٔ ابریشم فرستاد[ه] و بر او نوشته که «این زمان [...]». امیر حسین در روضهٔ رسول الله ﷺ برای زیارت رفته بود. همان‌جا در خواب رفت و مهتر عالم، خدیجه، و علی و فاطمه در خواب دید و همه[۶۸] گفتند که «ای فرزند، زودتر در اینجا بیا» که مشتاق شد. چون بیدار شد در فکر افتاد که تعبیر این خواب چه باشد.

{۲۸} عتبه ولید بر امام حسین گفته فرستاد که «ای مخدوم‌زادهٔ من، یزید بر من هر بار می‌نویسد برای بیعت شما. منِ بنده چه کنم؟» امام حسین برابر محبّان مشورت کرد که «چه اتفاق کنیم؟» همه گفتند «ای مخدوم‌زاده، هر طرف فرمان‌ها بنویسیم[۶۹]؛ همه از دست وی به تنگ آمده، همه کسان توجّه به شما خواهند کرد». و امام حسین فرمود که «من دنیا را پی پشت زده‌ام و دست از وی بر داشته‌ام؛ به حکم حدیث «الدُّنيَا جِيفَةٌ وَطَالِبُها كَلَابٌ»[۷۰] او را ترک کرده‌ام. مرا نیک باشد که گِردِ این کار نَگَردم. و امّا مرا یک صواب افتد که من از مدینه ترک گیرم و سکونت مکّه اختیار کنم. و مکّه را هیچ‌کس فتح نکرده است مگر پیغمبر رسول ﷺ را». اتّفاق هم برین کردند.

{۲۹} و امیر حسین در خانه آمده. اُمّ سَلَمَه رضی‌الله‌عنها زنده بود. چون اُمّ سَلَمَه سوی امیر حسین دید گفت «ای نور دیدهٔ من، تو را غمناک می‌بینم و روی تو زرد شده». گفت «ای سیّده، چه کنم و چگونه غمناک نشوم. از برادر حسن تنها مانده‌ام و یزید دنبال باشد، و من می‌خواهم که از مدینه ترک گیرم و در مکّه روم». اُمّ سَلَمَه دوید و درون حُجْره در آمد و گفت که «ای نور دیدهٔ من، قاروره[۷۱] این است که مرا رسول ﷺ داده بود. و آن خاک از دشت کربلا آمده، و مرا گفته «هرگاه این خاک خون خواهد شد بدانید که موت امیرحسین را نزدیک آمده باشد». پس ای جانِ من، این قاروره را پُر خون شد». امیر حسین رضی‌الله‌عنه را گفت که «رسول الله ﷺ حکایت کرد که «روزی أَمیر المُؤمِنین حسن و تو تخته‌ها نوشته بردید[۷۲] پیش استاد خود معاویه‌ابن ابوسفیان. و امیر حسن می‌گفتی که «خط من نیکو است؟» معاویه گفت «شما هر دو نیکو می‌نویسید». تو گفتی «البتّه خواهد بود». معاویه گفت «نمی‌دانم بر امیر عثمان رو». امیر عثمان بر امیر عمَر فرستاد و امیر عمَر

[۶۶] آیهٔ ۱۵۶ سورهٔ بقره. [۶۷] ۵۹ هجری قمری. هرچند براساس منابع شیعه، حسن بن علی به ماه صفر سال ۵۰ هجری قمری از دنیا رفته است.
[۶۸] هم. [۶۹] بفرستیم؟ [۷۰] «دنیا همچون لاشه‌ای است و خواستار آن همچون سگی». برخی این حدیث را به پیامبر و برخی شیعیان آن را به علی بن ابی طالب نسبت می‌دهند. در نسخ مالایی، به ویژه در حکایت ابوساعید(ابوسعید) ابوالخیر، مانند آنچه که در برگ ۲۱ نسخهٔ سواس لندن آمده به پیامبر نسبت داده شده است. [۷۱] برای انجام آزمایش طبّی ادرار استفاده می‌شده است. این واژه می‌تواند کاربرد استعاره‌ای نیز داشته باشد. به «دفتر چهارم» مثنوی مولوی و همچنین «تذکرة الاولیاء» ذیل «ذکر سفیان ثوری» نیز مراجعه شود.
[۷۲] در آکلند ۱۷۰ به‌صورت «بودو» نوشته شده است.

said, 'Yes, when death arrives, it breaks hope.' The wife [of Ḥasan] wanted to check on him. Imam Ḥasan became angry and said, 'Be quiet and do not speak, do not say anything and get away from here.' Imam Ḥasan said, 'I have a will before death...listen!' He said, 'Be always worshipping God and do not rely on this world, and do not punish the one who did this to me, as I will intercede her first. And visit my grave frequently and do not forget to be kind to Abū al-Qāsim [i.e., Ḥasan's son].' The Commander of Believers Ḥusayn said, 'O supportive master of mine, convey my greetings to the Messenger, Khadīja, ʿAlī, and Fāṭima (pbuh) and tell them that I, the humble pauper, will be alone.' He finished making his will and then proceeded to leave the temporary world for the everlasting one. 'Indeed we belong to God, and indeed to Him we will return' (Q. 2:156). It happened on the tenth of Muḥarram, the year fifty-nine.[14] And the unfortunate witch also died on that day and went to hell.

{27} Walīd b. ʿUtba sent a letter about this to Yazīd who was happy and sent a garment of silk to Walīd b. ʿUtba. He told him that [...]. The Commander Ḥusayn had been to visit the shrine of the Messenger (pbuh). He slept there and dreamed of the Eminence of the Universe [i.e., the Prophet], Khadīja, ʿAlī, and Fāṭima and they all told him, 'O darling, come here very soon'; so Ḥusayn became impatient. When he woke up, he pondered, 'What could be the interpretation of this dream?'

{28} Walīd b. ʿUtba sent a message to Imam Ḥusayn, 'O my master, Yazīd has frequently sent me letters to take your pledge. What shall I, as his servant, do?' Imam Ḥusayn consulted with his close companions, asking them 'What should we decide?' All said, 'O master, we can send out letters to different places; all are fed up with Yazīd (?) and all are inclined towards you.' Imam Ḥusayn said, 'I have left the world behind, on the basis of the narration, "The world is a carcass and its seeker is like a dog." I left it. It is better for me not to engage with it. But the best way for me is to leave Medina and reside in Mecca. Mecca has not been conquered by anyone else but by the Prophet (pbuh).' They all agreed.

{29} And the Commander Ḥusayn came in to the house. Umm Salama (pbuh) was still alive. When Umm Salama saw the face of the Commander Ḥusayn, she said, 'O darling, I found you sad and your face is pale.' He said, 'O Lady, what can I do and why should I not be sad? I am separated from my brother Ḥasan, and Yazīd is after me. I want to leave Medina and settle in Mecca.' Umm Salama [then] ran inside her room and said, 'O my darlings, this is the glass receptacle given to me by the Prophet (pbuh). And the soil in it is from the plain of Karbala. And he [i.e., the Prophet] told me that when the soil becomes like blood the death of Ḥusayn is close. My darling the bottle is now full of blood!' She told the the Commander Ḥusayn (pbuh) about an account told

[14] Although according to traditional sources, he died in the year 50 AH.

بر امیر ابوبکر فرستاد و أَمیر المُؤمِنین ابوبکر نزد رسول ﷺ فرستاد. آن‌حضرت فرمود «ای فرزندان من، در اصل نوشتن نمی‌دانم، فرق کردنِ من چه دانم.»[۷۳] و تو گفتی که «جبرئیل ؑ را بنما». مهتر جبرئیل ؑ در رسید او گفت «یا رسول الله، هر دو خوب نوشته‌اند. حقّ تَعَالَی تو را مبارک[باد] می‌دهد[۷۴] که فرزندان تو نوشتن آموختند».

{۳۰} [جبرئیل] یاقوت سرخ و زمرّد سبز برای ریختن بر تخته‌ها آورد. یاقوت سرخ بر تختهٔ تو حسین ریخته و زمرّد سبز بر تختهٔ حسن ریخته. رسول ﷺ شاد شد و سر سجده نهاد «الله مرا با یاقوت چه کار، در حقّ فرزندان من لطف داری. به حرمت ایشان، عاصیِ امّتِ من ببخشای». فرمان رسید که «به شمار هر موی که بر تن امام حسن و حسین‌اند هزارگان[۷۵] عاصی از امّت تو بخشیدم». رسول ﷺ شاد شدند، و جبرئیل ؑ در گریه شد. رسول ﷺ گفت «ای اخی جبرئیل، در این روزِ شادی تو را چه غم؟»

{۳۱} گفت «یا رسول الله، شفقّت تو که بر امّت داری و بی شفقتی امّت تو که بر فرزندان است. از آن گریه می‌آید که یکی را به زهر خواهند کشت، چنانچه دل و جگر او پرکاله خواهد شد و از دهن بیرون خواهد افتاد، و از أَمیر المُؤمِنین حسین رضی الله عنه که در دشت کربلا خواهند کشت و زبان ایشان از تشنگی خشک خواهد شد و حلق او را خواهند برید و آن نشانی یاقوت سرخ است که من آوردم».

{۳۲} رسول ﷺ در گریه شد و در خاندان آن حضرت ماتم گشت. فرمودند «یا أخي جبرئیل، من آنجا خواهم بود؟» گفت «نه». گفت «علی خواهد بود؟» گفت «نه». گفت «ابوبکر خواهد بود؟» گفت «نه». گفت «عمر خواهد بود؟» گفت «نه». گفت «عثمان خواهد بود؟» گفت «نه». رسول ﷺ فرمود «وای حسن وای حسینا. وای غربیان، وای یتیمان، وای مظلومان».[۷۶] گفت «یا جبرئیل، قدری خاک از دشت کربلا بیار». جبرئیل ؑ رفته از آن خاک آورده. رسول ﷺ در قاروره انداخت و به من داد و گفت «ای أُمّ سَلَمَه، این د[ست] تو خواهد [بود] چون این خاک خون خواهد شد وقت مرگ امام حسین نزدیک رسیده». پس ای فرزند چون آن شده است، ساخته باشید»».

[۷۳] تفاوت آنها را نمی‌دانم. [۷۴] تهنیت گفتن. [۷۵] هزاران. [۷۶] عبارت عاطفی «وای حسن وای حسین» در ادبیات مالایی و داستان محمّد حنفیّه به‌وضوح و گاهاً به شیوهٔ «واه حسن واه حسین» دیده می‌شود. مراجعه کنید به نسخهٔ Ll.6.5 در کیمبریج.

to her by the Messenger of God (pbuh), 'One day the Commander of Believers Ḥasan and you were holding writing slates, and you went before your instructor, Muʿāwiya the son of Abū Sufyān. And the Commander Ḥasan asked, "Is my handwriting beautiful?" Muʿāwiya replied, "You both write beautifully." Then you said, "Of course". Muʿāwiya said, "I do not know, go to the Commander ʿUthmān." The Commander ʿUthmān sent them to the Commander ʿUmar and the Commander ʿUmar sent them to the Commander Abū Bakr and the Commander Abū Bakr sent them to the Messenger of God (pbuh).' The Prophet continued, 'I said, "O my grandchildren, I do not actually know how to write and have no idea about the differences!" and you said, "Ask Gabriel (pbuh)". His Eminence Gabriel arrived saying, "O Messenger of God, both of them have written nicely. God congratulates you as your grandchildren have learned to write."'

{30} [Gabriel] had brought a red ruby and a green emerald to colour the writing slates. The red ruby was for Ḥusayn and the green emerald for Ḥasan. The Messenger (pbuh) prostrated cheerfully, saying, 'God, how I am honoured by this ruby. You have bestowed grace upon my grandchildren. Through them, You forgive the arrogant people of my community.'It was proclaimed that as many transgressors from the community as the hairs on the bodies of Imams Ḥasan and Ḥusayn would be forgiven. The Messenger (pbuh) was happy, and Gabriel began to cry. The Messenger (pbuh) said, 'O brother Gabriel, why are you sad on this pleasant day?'

{31} Gabriel said, 'O Messenger of God, for your kindness to your community and the unkindness of your community to your grandchildren. I am crying as one of them[15] will be killed by poison, his stomach and liver will reach his mouth. And the Commander of Believers Ḥusayn (pbuh) will be killed on the plain of Karbala. He will be thirsty and they will cut his throat and the sign of this is the red ruby that I have brought.'

{32} The Messenger (pbuh) began to cry and the family of the Prophet was full of sadness. He said, 'O brother Gabriel, will I be there?' Gabriel said, 'No'. The Prophet asked, 'What about ʿAlī?' Gabriel said, 'No'. The Prophet asked, 'What about Abū Bakr?' Gabriel said, 'No'. The Prophet asked, 'What about ʿUmar?' Gabriel said, 'No'. The Prophet asked, 'What about, ʿUthmān?' Gabriel said, 'No'. The Messenger (pbuh) said, 'Poor Ḥasan. Poor Ḥusayn. Poor Homeless. Poor Orphans. Poor Wretched!' The Prophet continued, 'O Gabriel, bring some soil form the plain of Karbala.' Gabriel went and brought soil. The Messenger (pbuh) poured it into a glass receptacle and gave it to me,[16] and said, 'O Umm Salama, it will be with you until the soil becomes bloody, then it means that Imam Ḥusayn's moment of death will be close.' As such, O darling, it has now happened. Be ready!

[15] i.e., Ḥasan [16] i.e., Umm Salama

{ ۳۳ } امام حسین وداع کرده، ساخته شد و از مدینه چهارهزار سوار با أَمیر المُؤمِنین روان شدند. و استقبال کردند با غزار[۷۷] و با اکرام آوردند [...] .چون در روضه برای زیارت وداع رفت آواز شنید «یا قُرَّةَ عَینِي عَجِّل إلینَا فیأتون إلی لِقائك رسول ﷺ». وداع کرد و در مدینه گویا قیامت قایم شد. گویند «مدینه» سه بار بدین سختی رفته است: یکی در وفات رسول ﷺ؛ دوم در شهادت حسن رَضِيَ اللهُ عَنهُ؛ سوم بیرون آمدن حسین رَضِيَ اللهُ عَنهُ از مدینه.

{ ۳۴ } چون امیر حسین در مکّه رسید، از آن چهار هزار سوار هفتاد و دو نفر ماند. که اهل مکّه را خبر شد که امیر حسین بن علی رَضِيَ اللهُ عَنهُ [رسید]. [آنها گفتند] «همه شادند در جهان؛ وطن شما مکّه است[۷۸] و در مدینه غریب بودید. و این مقامی است که جز تو هیچ‌کس را فتح نشده، و اینجا همه چاکران و خدمتکاران جدّ تواند[۷۹]. یزید بدبخت نتْواند که شما را زیان رساند».

{ ۳۵ } عتبه بن ولید مکتوب به یزید نوشت که «أَمیر المُؤمِنین حسین رَضِيَ اللهُ عَنهُ در مکّه قرار گرفت». چون این خبر به یزید رسید، في الحال بر عمادِ[۸۰] پادشاه کوفه مکتوب نوشت که «حیله بکن و امیر حسین را از مکّه بیرون آر، که با من دوستی داری وگرنه البتّه سر از تن جدا خواهم کرد». عمادِ کوفی[۸۱] بر امیر حسین رَضِيَ اللهُ عَنهُ عرضه داشت نوشت «که ای مخدوم‌زاده ، چون مدینه گذاشتی باید که هم مکّه را بگذاری که در مکّه تنگی، قحط طعام است، و ما خدمتکاران پدر شماییم. باید که با ما بیای و من هشت‌هزار و چند پیاده دارم تا سر بر تن ما باشد.[۸۲] یزید طرف شما دیدنْ نتْواند». مکتوب به أَمیر المُؤمِنین حسین رَضِيَ اللهُ عَنهُ برسید. شاد شد و اتّفاق کرد بر کوفه.

{ ۳۶ } مکّیان گفتند «ای فرزند رسول، بر کوفیان باور ندارید که الکُوفِي لَا یُوفِي؛ مثل قدیم است.[۸۳] فامّا[۸۴] این شهر حرام است. هرکه در پناه این شهر[۸۵] افتد کسی او را زیان رسانیدن نتواند». هرچه که ایشان گریستند و زاری کردند، قبول نکردند. مسلم عقیل از پیش خود جانب عماد کوفی با چهل هزار سوار فرستاد. مسلم عقیل چون نزدیک رسید، عماد با چهل هزار سوار و پیاده استقبال کرد و با غزار و اکرام او را بر تخت نشاند و خود بسته ایستاد شد. مسلم عقیل مکتوب به أَمیر المُؤمِنین حسین رَضِيَ اللهُ عَنهُ فرستاد که «از دل و جان غلامی شما قبول کرده». چون این مکتوب با أَمیر المُؤمِنین حسین رَضِيَ اللهُ عَنهُ رسید شاد شد.

{ ۳۷ } عماد کوفه به یزید نوشته که «عذر من [...]، مسلم عقیل آمده. امیر حسین رَضِيَ اللهُ عَنهُ امروز یا فردا می‌آید». یزید بدبخت از بهر آن کرده (؟) را طلب کرد و گفت که «ساخته باشید برای کشتن پسر علی». اوّل کسی که خواستْ شمر بن جوشن جهودی بود. برابر او ده هزار سوار؛ دوم برادر او برخاست بر او سیزده هزار سوار بودند و این هر دو برادر همراه یزید لعین بودند. گفتند «اگر دو هزار مسلمان برابر من باشند مرا فتح نشود».

۷۷ نیکی. ۷۸ همین‌طور می‌توان چنین خواند «همه شادند. در جهانْ وطنِ شما مکّه است...». ۷۹ تو هستند.
۸۰ فرمانده و مقام عالی رتبه نظامی. ۸۱ فرماندهٔ اهل کوفه. ۸۲ محافظت کردن. ۸۳ اشاره به این دارد که کوفیان مردمی وفادار و قابل اعتماد نیستند. این جمله در برخی منابع به عبدالله بن مطیع منسوب شده است. ۸۴ از طرفی. ۸۵ شهر مکّه.

{33} Imam Ḥusayn bid farewell. He was prepared and four thousand cavalrymen moved out along with the Commander of Believers and received his instruction warmly [to go to Mecca]. When he went to the shrine [of the Prophet] to say farewell, he heard a voice saying, 'O darling, hasten, come to us, as the Messenger (pbuh) will come to meet you!' He bid farewell. It was tumultuous in Medina. It is said that Medina went through such turbulence only three times. First, when the Messenger (pbuh) died; second, after the martyrdom of Ḥasan (pbuh); and third, when Ḥusayn (pbuh) left Medina.

{34} When the Commander Ḥusayn arrived in Mecca, only seventy-two cavalrymen were left from the four thousand. The people of Mecca were informed upon the arrival of Commander Ḥusayn (pbuh). [They said], 'All the people of the world are happy now! Mecca is your homeland, you were alone in Medina! This is the place which has never been conquered. All the people of Mecca are devotees of your ancestor. The desperate Yazīd cannot hurt you here.

{35} Walīd b. ʿUtba sent a letter to Yazīd, 'The Commander of Believers Ḥusayn (pbuh) is settled in Mecca.' When Yazīd received this news, he immediately wrote a letter to the governor of Kufa, commanding, 'If you have any loyalty then devise a scheme to get the Commander Ḥusayn out of Mecca, otherwise, I will behead you.' The governor of Kufa wrote a letter to Commander Ḥusayn (pbuh) saying, 'O my master, as you have left Medina, you should also leave Mecca, as there is poverty and lack of food, and we are the servants of your father. You should come with us and I have eight thousand or so infantrymen who would protect us. Yazīd cannot touch you.' The letter reached the Commander of Believers Ḥusayn (pbuh). He was satisfied and decided to go to Kufa.

{36} The people of Mecca said, 'O grandchild of the Messenger, do not trust the people of Kufa as the people of Kufa are not faithful as always. And the nature of this city[17] is inviolable. Whoever takes shelter in this city, no one will ever be able to hurt him.' Howsoever they cried and wailed, he did not accept. He sent Muslim ʿAqīl in advance with forty thousand cavalrymen to the governor of Kufa. When Muslim ʿAqīl arrived, the governor of Kufa welcomed him with forty thousand cavalry and infantrymen and sat him on a seat. Respectfully, the governor stood politely ready to be of service. Muslim ʿAqīl then wrote a letter to the Commander of Believers (pbuh), 'They have wholeheartedly accepted to serve you.' When this letter reached the Commander of Believers Ḥusayn, he became cheerful.

{37} The governor of Kufa then wrote a letter to Yazīd saying, 'Forgive me, [...] Muslim ʿAqīl is here. The Commander Ḥusayn (pbuh) will come today or tomorrow.' In this regard, the desperate Yazīd asked for [...] and told them to be ready to kill the

[17] i.e., Mecca

یزیدْ عبدالله زیاد[۸۶] را طلب کرد. او را گفت «تو را نیز هم افتاد». او قبول کرد و برابر او بیست هزار سوار ساخته شد. دوم عبدالله عمر بود، طلب کرد و او گفت «نتوانم که مقابل فرزندان رسول الله ﷺ شوم». یزید در غصّه شد و گفت «بزنید و سر از تن جدا کنید». چون یزید تفت شد[عبدالله عمر] گفت «ای یزید، شب را مشورت کنم». عبدالله عمر در خانه آمد. زن او فاطمه نام بود. گفت «ای نادان، چرا شباشب[۸۷] [...] تا غایت در بهشت رسیدید. در بهشت مشورت [...]، و زنهار این کار اختیار نکنی و الّا در روز قیامت از روی رسول ﷺ شرمنده مانی، و اگر این کار اختیار خواهی کرد مرا طلاق دِه، نشویم[۸۸]». چون روز شد عبدالله عمر پیش یزید رفت، في الحال جامه داد، او را با بیست هزار سوار روان کرد.

{۳۸} چون در کوفه رسیدند عماد بر مسلم عقیل آمد و گفت «ای فرزندان، شما همراه شوید و ایشان سوار شدند». مسلم با یاران از دروازه بیرون آمدند. کوفیان دروازه بستند و گفتند «اینک مسلم عقیل و شما دانید». برابر مسلم عقیل چهار هزار سوار و چند پیاده بودند تا همه شهید شدند. مسلم تنها ماند و اسب او هم تیغ خورده بود، افتاد. و مسلم پیاده شد و تشنگی بر وی غالب شد. مسلم عقیل گفت «کسی هست مسلمان که منِ غریب را آبی خوراند؟» حبشی[۸۹] بود مشک پر آب کرد و آورد. مسلم را آب خورانید و باقی را بر خود ریخت چنانچه سرد شد. وی روی سوی حبشی کرد و گفت «بيَّض الله وَجْهك»[۹۰] درحال رویش سپید گشت و سیاهی از روی او به کُلّ رفت. حبشی گفت «یا أَمیر المُؤمِنین، من نیز پیش تو شهید خواهم شد». آن حبشی کارزار کرد و هفت تن را بکشت. بعدها شهادت یافت.

{۳۹} و از آنجا أَمیر المُؤمِنین حسین رضي الله عنه با چندین هزار سوار روان شدند چون که از مکّه آمدند شب همه گریختند. باقی هفتاد و دو تن و دو سوار ماندند. أَمیر المُؤمِنین حسین رضي الله عنه فرمود «چون در کوفه خواهم رسید سواران بسیار بیشتر بوَد». أَمیر المُؤمِنین حسین رضي الله عنه منزل به منزل می‌آمد تا شب غرّة[۹۱] ماهِ محرّم نزدیک نماز شام در دشت کربلا رسید و اسب أَمیر المُؤمِنین پیشتر نمی‌جنبید. امیر گفت «دشت کربلا»؛ گفت «پناه می‌خواهم از خدای تَعَالَی از کربلا این جای ریختن خون ماست. و این جای کشته شدن یاران است. و این جای یتیم شدن فرزندان من است. و این جای بیوه شدن عروسان من است. و این جای رسیدن من است به دوستان خود».

[۸۶] عبیدالله بن زیاد. [۸۷] شبانه. [۸۸] این‌که بایستی به‌صورت «نشوییم» (احتمالا اشاره به زن و شوهری) یا «نشویم» (اشاره به «زن و شوهر نشویم») خوانده شود نیاز به بررسی بیشتر دارد. [۸۹] اشاره به رنگ سیاه پوست بدن فرد دارد.

[۹۰] در برخی منابع غیر مرتبط با داستان امام حسن و حسین این عبارت دیده می‌شود. و غالبا عبارت طولانی‌تری است «بيَّض الله وجهك وكثرالله خيرك»، به معنای «خداوند تورا روسفید\سفیدروی نماید، و خیر و ثواب تو را دوچندان کند». [۹۱] اوّل ماه.

son of ʿAlī. The first one who was determined was the Jewish Shamir b. Jawshan, with ten thousand cavalrymen. The second one was his brother with thirteen thousand cavalrymen. These two brothers were with the accursed Yazīd. They said, 'If there will be two thousand Muslims against us, then we cannot defeat them.' So, Yazīd asked ʿUbaydallāh the son of Ziyād 'to join the fray.' He accepted and twenty thousand cavalrymen lined up before him. Then he asked for ʿAbdallāh ʿUmar. And he said, 'I cannot confront the children of the Messenger of God (pbuh).' Yazīd became upset and ordered: 'Hit and behead him.' When he saw Yazīd angry, he said, 'O Yazīd, I will talk this over tonight.' ʿAbdallāh ʿUmar returned home. His wife was Fāṭima. His wife said, 'Are you crazy that at night [...] to finally reach paradise. Consulting about being in paradise [...]. And if you do this, you will be ashamed before the Messenger (pbuh) on the Day of Judgement. And if you want to do it, then you must divorce me; we will not be suited to each other.' In the morning, ʿAbdallāh ʿUmar returned to Yazīd. He dressed him in uniform and sent him with twenty thousand cavalrymen.

{38} When they arrived in Kufa, the governor of Kufa came to ʿAqīl and said, 'O Children, come along, and they did so.' Muslim and his companions entered through the gate. The people of Kufa closed the gates and said, 'This is Muslim ʿAqīl and you know what to do.' Four thousand cavalrymen and some infantrymen lined up with Muslim ʿAqīl but all were martyred. Muslim remained alone and his horse was slashed by the swords. Muslim dismounted the horse and he was thirsty. Muslim ʿAqīl said, 'Is there any Muslim believer who will give me, a lonely one, water?' An Ethiopian was there, who filled a waterskin with water and brought it forward to quench Muslim's thirst. Then Muslim poured the rest of the water on his body. Muslim looked at the Ethiopian and said, 'May God whiten and shed light on your face.' Immediately, his faced turned white and blackness left him. The Ethiopian said, 'O Commander of Believers, I will also become a martyr with you.' The Ethiopian fought and killed seven people. Then he was martyred.

{39} And the Commander of Believers Ḥusayn (pbuh) as well as several thousand cavalrymen moved on. As soon as they left Mecca they all fled from his side during the night. All that remained were seventy-two people and two cavalrymen. The Commander of Believers (pbuh) said, 'When we arrive in Kufa, there will be more cavalry for us.' The Commander of Believers (pbuh) took the route, making some stops, until on the first night of the month of Muharram around the time of the night prayer, he arrived on the plain of Karbala. And the horse of the Commander of Believers would move no further. The Commander said, 'The plain of Karbala'; he continued, 'I seek refuge in God from Karbala which is the site where our blood will be shed. And here is where our companions will be killed, and where my children will become orphans, and where my brides will become widows, and from where I will reach my friends.'

{۴۰} و این قدر بگفت و نیزه بر زمین زد. و از اسب فرود آمد و چند نفر برای آب وضو کردن جانب آب فرات رفتند. چه بینند که لشگر فرود آمده و گِرد آبِ فرات گرفته‌اند. یاران امام حسین پرسیدند که «برای چه آمدید؟» گفتند «برای کشتن امام حسین». گفتند «زهی، یزید لعین برای کشتن فرزندان رسول ﷺ لشگر فرستاد». این سخن گفتند و بازگشتند. و این خبر به أَمیر المُؤمِنین رسانیدند.

{۴۱} أَمیر المُؤمِنین شباشب گرد خندق درانید و عورتان را در میان خندق نشانید. چون روز شد أَمیر المُؤمِنین حسین با هفتاد دو نفر و دو کودک: ابوالقاسم بن‌حسین رَضِيَ ٱللَّٰهُ عَنْهُ، دوم علی اکبر بن‌حسین [...]. اوّل از لشگر بیرون آمد جوانی که نام او حُرّ بود. از اینجا أَمیر المُؤمِنین حسین رَضِيَ ٱللَّٰهُ عَنْهُ بیرون آمد و گفت «ای حُرّ آن‌روز فراموش کردی که یکی بازی می کردیم. امروز چگونه شد که با کارزار من پیش آمدی؟» چون حرّ این سخن از أَمیر المُؤمِنین حسین رَضِيَ ٱللَّٰهُ عَنْهُ شنید نعره بزد و از اسب فرود آمد؛ در پای أَمیر المُؤمِنین افتاد و گِرد سر او میگشت و گفت «ای مخدوم‌زاده، پیش تو اوّل من جان نثارکنم». أَمیر المُؤمِنین حسین رَضِيَ ٱللَّٰهُ عَنْهُ او را درکنار گرفت و اوّل بار سوار شد. چون شیر گرسنه حمله کرد و هفتاد نفر را بکشت و در حمله دوم پنجاه نفر را بکشت. پس بسیار لشگر یزید براو حمله کردند و یک نیزه در شانهٔ او رسید؛ بیهوش شدن. أَمیر المُؤمِنین حسین رَضِيَ ٱللَّٰهُ عَنْهُ رسید و از اسب فرود آمد و گفت ثبتك الله[۹۲] و جان به حقّ تسلیم کرد. پس أَمیر المُؤمِنین او را در کنار گرفت و بر پیشانی او بوسه داد و دفن کرد.

{۴۲} دوم از لشگر أَمیرالمؤمنین حسین رَضِيَ ٱللَّٰهُ عَنْهُ عبدالله عمر بیرون آمد. و آن جوانی بود خوب‌رویِ شجاع. تکبیر گفت و حمله کرد و چندان بار در لشگر خارجیان خود را انداخت و بس کسی از لشگر یزید به دوزخ فرستاد خود شهادت یافت. سوم از لشگر أَمیر المُؤمِنین خالد بن نصر بیرون آمد. و سه بار حمله کرد. یکصد و دو نفر بکشت و او هم شهید شد. چهارم از لشگر أَمیر المُؤمِنین مسعود بن سعد جوانی بود صالح‌روی. در قدم أَمیر المُؤمِنین نهاد و وداع کرد و حمله نمود و سیصد نفر را بکشت.

{۴۳} شمر ملعون نعره زد که «ای نامردان، شما را چه شد». و خود حمله کرد چند تیر در وجود مبارک او[۹۳] رسید و بی [...] شد و هفتاد بار دو[۹۴] گفت «رجعتُ الی الله و [...] باب الله» و جان به حقّ تسلیم کرد. پنجم از لشگر أَمیر المُؤمِنین عَبدالرَحمٰن وافی بیرون آمد. چون فیلِ مست[۹۵] در لشگر افتاد بسیار کس را کشت و شهید شد. ششم از لشگر أَمیر المُؤمِنین قاسم عمر [زاده] بیرون آمد میمنه و میسره[۹۶] برهم زد. چندان کشت که دست او مانده شد.[۹۷] و بعدها دوهزار مرد بر وی حمله کردند چنانچه شهید ساختند. نفر هفتم از لشگر أَمیر المُؤمِنین خالد بیرون آمد، و او عالِم و حافظ بود. و از تشنگی زبان او نجنبید. حمله کرد و شهید شد

[۹۲] اشاره به آیهٔ ۲۷ سورهٔ ابراهیم دارد. [۹۳] مسعود بن سعد. [۹۴] هفتاد و دو بار.

[۹۵] قدرتمند، جنون زده و افسار گسیخته. اصطلاح «فیل مست» در ادبیات پارسی هندوستان و آسیای مرکزی به وفور دیده می‌شود. به کتاب اکبرنامه رجوع کنید. [۹۶] هرآنچه در سمت راست و چپ بود. [۹۷] دیگر توان نداشت و خسته شد.

{40} After saying this, he hit the ground with a spear. And he dismounted his horse and with some people went to the River Euphrates for ablution. They noticed that an army had arrived there, surrounding the River Euphrates. Imam Ḥusayn's companions asked them, 'Why are you here?' They said, 'We are here in order to kill Ḥusayn.' They said, 'O Really! The accursed Yazīd has sent an army to kill the children of the Messenger (pbuh)!' They said this and returned. The companions relayed this news to the Commander of Believers [i.e., Ḥusayn].

{41} The Commander of Believers dug a trench overnight and placed the women in it. In the morning, the Commander of Believers Ḥusayn as well as seventy-two people and two children – Abū al-Qāsim b. Ḥusayn (pbuh) and ʿAlī Akbar b. Ḥusayn [...]. The first coming from the army [of Yazīd] was a young man named Ḥurr. From [the other side], the Commander of Believers Ḥusayn (pbuh) came out and said, 'O Ḥurr, do you forget the time when we played together? What has happened, that you came to fight me today?' When Ḥurr heard this from the Commander of Believers Ḥusayn (pbuh), he screamed and dismounted his horse, falling at the feet of the Commander of Believers. He said, 'O master! I will first sacrifice my life before you.' The Commander of Believers (pbuh) embraced him. For the first time, he rode his horse and attacked like a hungry lion, killing seventy people. During his second attack, he killed fifty more. Then a large division of Yazīd's army attacked him and a spear went through his shoulder, and he became unconscious. The Commander of Believers Ḥusayn (pbuh) arrived and dismounted, saying, 'May God keep you steadfast',[18] and he submitted his soul to God. The Commander of Believers embraced him, kissed his forehead, and buried him.

{42} The second soldier from the troop of the Commander of Believers Ḥusayn (pbuh) was ʿAbdallāh ʿUmar. He was a handsome and brave boy. He chanted, 'God is great' and attacked and became so engaged with the enemy soldiers that he sent many of Yazīd's troops to hell, before becoming martyred himself.The third soldier from the troop of the Commander of Believers was Khālid b. Naṣr. He attacked three times, and killed two people, and then he was martyred himself. The fourth from the troop of the Commander of Believers was Masʿūd, the son of Saʿd, who seemed righteous. He first went to the Commander of Believers to bid farewell and then attacked and killed 300 people.

{43} The accursed Shamir shouted [to his soldiers] 'You fools! What's wrong with you!?' and then he himself attacked and some arrows hit the blessed Masʿūd and he became [...] and seventy-two times said, 'I returned to God, I have reached to the door of God' (?), and he finally submitted his soul to God. The fifth from the troop of the Commander of Believers was ʿAbd al-Raḥmān Wāfī. He attacked the enemy army

[18] Based on Q. 14:27

و چون سر او جدا کردند و بُریدند گفت «أباعبدلله، و رجعتُ الی الله إِنَّا لله وَإِنَّا إِلَیهِ رَاجِعُونَ». بعد سورهٔ «[ال]رحمان» تمام خواند.[۹۸]

{۴۴} هشتم عبدالله دحیه کلبی از لشگر أَمیر المُؤمِنین بیرون آمد، و شبانی بود. چون أَمیر المُؤمِنین حسین در دشت کربلا رسید و درآن میدان این مرد گوسفندان می‌چرانید مادر خود را آمده گفت که «ای مادر، اگر بگویی من نیز همواره أَمیر المُؤمِنین حسین را یاری کنم و شهید شوم». مادر گفت «زهی سعادت.» گوسفندان به راه حقّ تَعَالَی داد و برابر مادر سرِ[۹۹] أَمیر المُؤمِنین حسین آمد. مادرش گفت «ای فرزند رسول، فرزند خود را آوردم تا پیش تو جان دهد». امام حسین رضي الله عنه او را بسیار نواخت. چون جوان حمله کرد به زخمِ نیزه بسیار تَن از خارجیان هلاک کرد. تا هفتاد تن را بکشت و بر مادر آمد و گفت «ای مادر، من تشنه‌ام.» [مادر] گفت «حوران شربت در دست کرده استاده‌اند؛ برو به زودی شهید شو». بازگشت. از یزیدیان پنجاه نفر را بکشت. یزیدیان حمله کردند و سر از تن جدا کردن و جانب مادرش انداختند. مادرش سر را بوسید. پس آن زمان کمر محکم بسته[۱۰۰] و چوبی بر دست کرد. أَمیر المُؤمِنین بر سر او رسید. او را گفت «باز گرد که کار تو نیست». گفت «ای فرزند رسول، از برای خدای تَعَالَی مرا بگذار تا از این صحبت[۱۰۱] پس نمانم». امیر حسین رضي الله عنه بگریست و او را بگذاشت. آن زن چندی آنها را بکشت و خود هم شهید شد.

{۴۵} نهم از لشگر أَمیر المُؤمِنین دو[۱۰۲] برادران بودند یکی زبیر علی و طلح [علی]، و جعفر علی.

ابن زبیر از مادر تنها بود. چون بیرون شد أَمیر المُؤمِنین گفت «ای برادر، تو دل مادر منوّر کن که او را هیچ فرزندی نیست». مادر او نعره بزد و گفت «ای أَمیر المُؤمِنین حسین»؛ [مادر] برادری در کنار گرفت و زارزار می‌گریست.[۱۰۳] بیرون آمد و شعر گفت و حمله کرد و از ایشان کشید و شهید شد.

[۹۸] قرائت سورهٔ الرحمان پیش از جان‌باختن اشاره به حدیثی منسوب به امام ششم شیعیان، جعفرصادق، دارد. بنابر این حدیث که در کتاب ثَواب الأَعْمال وَعِقاب الأَعْمال از ابن‌بابویه آمده، اگر فردی که سورهٔ الرحمان را می‌خواند پس از رسیدن به آیه ۷۷ این سوره ابراز شکر کند که «لابِشَيْءٍ مِنْ آلائِکَ رَبِّ أُکَذِّبُ، یعنی یا خدا! من هیچ یک از نعمت‌های پروردگار را انکار نخواهم کرد»، چه در شب بمیرد چه در روز مرگ وی شهادت محسوب می‌شود: «أَبِي ره قَالَ حَدَّثَنِي سَعْدُ بْنُ عَبْدِ اللَّهِ عَنْ يَعْقُوبَ بْنِ يَزِيدَ عَنِ ابْنِ أَبِي عُمَيْرٍ عَنْ هِشَامٍ أَوْ بَعْضِ أَصْحَابِنَا عَمَّنْ حَدَّثَهُ عَنْ أَبِي عَبْدِ اللَّهِ ع قَالَ: مَنْ قَرَأَ سُورَةَ الرَّحْمَنِ فَقَالَ عِنْدَ كُلِّ فَبِأَيِّ آلاءِ رَبِّكُمَا تُكَذِّبانِ لَا بِشَيْءٍ مِنْ آلَائِكَ رَبِّ أُكَذِّبُ فَإِنْ قَرَأَهَا لَيْلاً ثُمَّ مَاتَ مَاتَ شَهِيداً وَإِنْ قَرَأَهَا نَهَاراً ثُمَّ مَاتَ مَاتَ شَهِيداً.» ابن‌بابویه، ثَواب الأَعْمال وَعِقاب الأَعْمال (قم: دار الشريف الرضي للنشر، ۱۹۸۶/۱۴۰۶)، ۱۱۶–۱۱۷. این نکته به درک بهتر ما از تاثیر ادبیات شیعی در توسعه و گسترش ادبیات فارسی در جای‌جای آسیا کمک خواهد کرد.

[۹۹] نزد.

[۱۰۰] اشاره به مهیّا شدن برای نبرد دارد.

[۱۰۱] در متون قدیمی «صحبت» به معنای «یاری» و «یاری رسانیدن» به کار می رفته است. گاهی هم به‌صورت «صُحْبت» خوانده می‌شود.

[۱۰۲] احتمالا می بایستی «سه برادران» نگاشته می‌شده است.

[۱۰۳] شاید بتوان خوانش و ترجمهٔ بهتری از این عبارت ارائه داد.

like an angry and powerful elephant. He killed many and was martyred. The sixth from the troop of the Commander of Believers was Qāsim ʿUmar who came out and attacked the right and left flanks of the enemy army. He killed so many that his hand became numb [from wielding his sword]. Then two thousand men attacked him and killed him thereafter. The seventh one from the troop of the Commander of Believers was Khālid. He was a scholar as well as a memoriser of the Qurʾān. He was so thirsty he could not open his mouth. He attacked and was martyred. When they went to cut off his head, he exclaimed, "ʿAbā ʿAbdallāh![19] I returned to my God! "Indeed we belong to God, and indeed to Him we will return" (Q. 2:156).' Then he recited *Sūrat al-Raḥmān* (Q. 55) from memory.[20]

{44} The eighth one from the troop of the Commander of Believers was ʿAbdallāh Diḥya al-Kalbī. He was a shepherd. When the Commander of Believers Ḥusayn arrived on the plain of Karbala, this man was pasturing sheep, and he went to his mother saying, 'O mother, allow me to assist the Commander of Believers Ḥusayn and become martyred.' His mother replied, 'What an honour!' He put the flock of sheep in the path of God, and along with his mother went to the Commander of Believers Ḥusayn. His mother said, 'O grandson of the Messenger, I brought my own son to be sacrificed for you.' Imam Ḥusayn (pbuh) treated him kindly. When the young man attacked with a spear he wounded and killed many of the enemy. He killed seventy people and returned to his mother, and said to her, 'O mother, I am thirsty.' She said, 'Heavenly cherubs and nymphs wait for you with refreshing drinks. Go and be martyred quickly!' He returned. He killed fifty of Yazīd's people. The people of Yazīd then attacked and beheaded him, and threw his head towards his mother. The mother kissed the head. Then she stalwartly prepared herself to fight and picked up a stick. The Commander of Believers went to her side and said, 'Return, as this is not your job.' She said, 'O grandson of the Messenger of God, allow me for the sake of God not to be left out of this assistance and companionship.' The Commander of Believers (pbuh) cried and allowed her to do so. The woman killed some of them and she became martyred.

{45} The ninth from the troop of the Commander of Believers were three brothers.[21] One of them was Zubayr ʿAlī and the others were Ṭalḥa [ʿAlī] and Jaʿfar ʿAlī. The son of Zubayr[22], was the last vestige of his mother. When he went out, the Commander

[19] i.e., the *kunya* of Ḥusayn. [20] Reciting Q. 55 before death may be related to a report ascribed to the sixth Imam of Shīʿa, Jaʿfar al-Ṣādiq, in the book of *Thawāb al-Aʿmāl wa-ʿIqāb al-Aʿmāl* by the Persian Shīʿī thinker, Ibn al-Babāwayh (d. c. 991 CE). Through this report, one will die like a martyer if they recite it and invoke a specific supplication after Q. 55:77. For more see, the Persian side of the text. This may invite readers to think about the contribution of Shīʿī elements in circulation of Persianate materials across Asia. [21] The scribe mistakenly indicates that they were two brothers. [22] i.e., ibn Zubair

{۴۶} دهم طلحه علی بیرون آمد، شعر گفت و حمله کرد. و چندان بِکُشت که فریاد از لشگر یزیدیان برخاست.[۱۰۴] بر [...] شهید شد.

{۴۷} یازدهم جعفر بیرون آمد. أَمیر المُؤمِنین حسین او را در کنار گرفت و زارزار بگریست. جعفر بیرون شد و شعر گفت و حمله کرد. بسیار هلاک کرد. که او مجروح شد و شهید گشت.

{۴۸} پس هیچ مردی نزدیک أَمیر المُؤمِنین حسین رضی‌الله‌عنه نماند مگر دو کودک. یکی قاسم پسر أَمیر المُؤمِنین حسن رضی‌الله‌عنه، دوم علی اکبر پسر أَمیر المُؤمِنین حسین رضی‌الله‌عنه. از پَس پُشت فریاد کرد که «امشب آیید [...] شب عاشورا است». امشب باز گردند تا یکی عبادت کرده [...] و [...] دو کودکان [...]. أَمیر المُؤمِنین حسین با دو کودک بازگشت و شب عاشورا گذشت.

{۴۹} بعداز نماز بامداد، أَمیر المُؤمِنین، برادرزاده، و پسر خود برابر خیلخانهٔ[۱۰۵] خود وداع کردند و بیرون آمدند. و چندگام زدند. مادر قاسم، و مادر علی اکبر فریاد کردند که «ای نور دیده‌گان، یک‌بار بازگردید تا روی مبارک شما ببینم». هر دو بازگشتند و در پای مادران افتند[۱۰۶] و زارزار بگریستند و وداع کرده بیرون آمدند. چون در میدان رسیدند قاسم از اسب فرود آمد، گفت «ای مخدوم من، و ای مهربان من، کجا می‌روی شما؟ باشید تا من جان خود را زیر قدم تو نثار کنم». أَمیر المُؤمِنین حسین رضی‌الله‌عنه او را در کنار گرفت و گفت «ای جان من، پدر تو مرا وصیّتی کرده بود که «نظر شفقّت از پسر من دریغ نداری». چگونه روا دارم که پیش من کشته شوی؟» گفت «این جان دادن من شفقّت باشد که مرا تنها نگذاری و برابر خود سوی بهشت بری». أَمیر المُؤمِنین رخسارهٔ او بوسیده و زارزار بگریست و اجازه داد. قاسم قدم بوس[۱۰۷] او کرد و اسب‌دوان بر مادر رفت و گام مادر را بوسید و در کنار گرفت. بعده،[۱۰۸] در میدان رفت. این شعر بگفت و مانند شیر[۱۰۹] حمله کرد و بیست نفر را بکشت و شهید شد.

{۵۰} چون امام حسین خواست که بیرون آید،[۱۱۰] پسر أَمیر المُؤمِنین، علی اکبر، دوید و عنان اسب پدر بگرفت و گفت «بابا کجا می‌روی؟» امام حسین او را در کنار گرفت و گفت «ای جان پدر، تو خُرد هستی». گفت «ای بابا، به غیر تو جان چه کار آید و برادران من به بهشت رسیدن، به غیر آنها من در دنیا چه کنم؟ به حقّ محمّد رسول الله مرا اجازه ده». أَمیر المُؤمِنین گفت «چون من بمیرم بعداز آن تیغ زنی». گفت «ای بابا، من روا ندارم کشته ببینم». چون الحاج[۱۱۱] بسیار کرد او را هم اجازه داد. علی اکبرِ شیر مشابهت به حضرت رسول بود. مقابله اِستاد[ه] شد. عبیدالله زیاد گفت که «ای فرزند رسول، برای خدای تَعَالَی برقع از روی دور کن تا تو را ببینم که مرا بسیار اشتیاق بر جمال محمّد مُصْطَفَی صلی‌الله‌علیه‌وسلم شده است». علی اکبر برقع از روی دور کرد. همهٔ یزیدیان روی او را دیدند و در گریه شدند، و از هر طرف نعره و گریه خواست. شمر گفت «این مسلمانان چندین کسان

[۱۰۴] اشاره به درماندەشدن لشگر یزید دارد. [۱۰۵] خاندان. [۱۰۶] افتادند. [۱۰۷] پای بوس. [۱۰۸] پس‌از آن.

[۱۰۹] در اکثر آثار ادبی مالایی پیش‌از قرن ۱۹ میلادی، واژهٔ پارسی «شیر» به «هریمو» (harimau) یا همان «ببر» ترجمه شده است.

[۱۱۰] در اینجا «بیرون آمدن» دلالت بر «سرکشی کردن» دارد. [۱۱۱] جبر نمودن.

of Believers stated, 'O brother, illuminate the heart of your mother as she does not have any more children.' The mother exclaimed, 'O Commander of Believers Ḥusayn!' and she hugged [Ḥusayn] like her brother and cried uncontrollably.[23] He went out to face the army, chanted combat verses[24], and attacked. After killing many people he was injured and martyred.

{46} The tenth was Ṭalḥa ʿAlī. He came out, chanted combat verses, and attacked. He killed so many, to the extent that Yazīd's army screamed vociferously and were confused. [...] and he was finally martyred.

{47} The eleventh one to emerge was Jaʿfar. The Commander of Believers embraced him and cried uncontrollably. Jaʿfar went out and chanted combat verses and attacked. He killed many, and was injured, and then became martyred.

{48} As such, no more men were around the Commander of Believers Ḥusayn (pbuh), just two young boys, Qāsim the son of the Commander of Believers Ḥasan (pbuh), and the second one, ʿAlī Akbar the son of the Commander of Believers Ḥusayn (pbuh). From the back a voice called out, 'Come [back] tonight, [...] tonight is the night of ʿĀshūrāʾ [i.e., the tenth day].' They returned at night and one [...] worship and [...] both children [...]. The Commander of Believers returned with two children and the night of the tenth day passed.

{49} After the dawn prayer, the Commander of Believers, his nephew, and his son bid farewell before their camp and left. After just a few steps, the mother of Qāsim and the mother of ʿAlī Akbar each exclaimed, 'O darlings, turn back once more so I can see your faces!' They both returned and fell down at the feet of their mothers and cried pitifully. They bid farewell and left. When they arrived at the battlefield, Qāsim dismounted his horse. He said, 'O sir, and O kind relative of mine, where [and why] are you going? Stay here until I sacrifice my life for you.' The Commander of Believers Ḥusayn (pbuh) hugged him and said, 'O dear one, your father[25] shared his final will with me, "Do not forget to show kindness to my son." How can I bear to see you killed before me?' He said, 'This death is exactly a sort of kindness as you are not going to leave me behind, but bring me into paradise along with yourself.' The Commander of Believers kissed his face and cried uncontrollably and gave him permission [to fight]. Qāsim kissed his foot and rode to his mother and kissed and embraced her foot. He then moved towards the battlefield. He chanted and attacked like a lion and killed twenty people and became martyred himself.

{50} Imam Ḥusayn wanted to see what had happened. One of the son's of the Commander of Believers, ʿAlī Akbar, ran and took hold of the bridle of his father's horse and said, 'Where are you going father?' Imam Ḥusayn hugged him and said,

[23] Perhaps, this sentence can be translated differently. [24] i.e., *rajaz* [25] i.e., Ḥasan

را چرا کشتند؟» این بگفت و لشگر حمله کرد و علی اکبر نیز حمله کرد و دویست نفر بکشت. و أَمیر المُؤمِنین حسین زبان خود را در دهن او بداد. و گفت[۱۱۲] «ای بابا، زبان تو نیز خشک شده، آبی بده». و گفت «یَا أبي العَطَش»؛ از تشنگی بنالید. أَمیر المُؤمِنین حسین گفت «ای جان بابا، همین‌زمان با[۱۱۳] آب بهشت خواهی رسید». بازگشت و حمله کرد و سیصد نفر را بکشت. شهید شد. بعداز شهادت آواز کرد: «یا أبي! وَجَدْتُ مَا وَعدت عَجِل إلینا حتّی نَشْرب الآن».

{۵۱} و گوید که أَمیر المُؤمِنین را یک خُرد کودکِ دیگر محمود نام، و از تشنگی هلاک می‌شد. او را در کنار آوردند. أَمیر المُؤمِنین حسین را دادند و او در کنار کرد و نزدیک آب فرات رفت و گفت «ای برادران، اگر ما گناه کردیم ما را آب ندهند. فامّا این خردک[۱۱۴] چه گناه کرده است که او را آب نمی‌دهید؟». یک بدبخت تیر کشید و چنان زد که در سینه آن کودک رسید و هم در کنار امام حسین رَضِيَ اللهُ عَنْهُ شهادت یافت. امیر نعره زد و او را بر مادر رسانید. مادر او گفت «آب خورانیدی؟» گفت «خورانیدم، آب بهشت». بیچاره مادر چه بیند[۱۱۵] پسر هلاک شده و شهادت یافت.

{۵۲} در تمام حرم گویا که قیامت قایم شده. آوردند که شب عاشورا، شهربانو، فاطمه رَضِيَ اللهُ عَنْهَا را در خواب دید که دامنی در کمر بسته و جارو بر دست کرده، میدان را پاک می‌کرد و سنگ ریزه‌ها دور می‌کرد و گفت «مخدوم، این چه کار است که تو می‌کنی؟» گفت «فردا نور دیدهٔ من امام حسین رَضِيَ اللهُ عَنْهُ در اینجا شهید خواهد شد. این میدان را پاک می‌کنم تا بر وجود مبارک او آسیبی نرسد»».

[۱۱۲] علی اکبر بگفت(؟) [۱۱۳] به. [۱۱۴] صغیر کردن «خُرد» از لحاظ ادبی قابل توجّه است.
[۱۱۵] یعنی اینکه: بیچاره مادر چه دید!

'O dear one, you are still young.' He said, 'O father, how will life make sense without you, and all my brothers are already in paradise. What shall I do without them in the world? By Muḥammad, the Messenger of God, allow me [to fight]!' The Commander of Believers said, 'When I die then you may fight.' He replied, 'O father, I would not like to see you dead.' Due to his excessive insistence, Ḥusayn permitted him. ʿAlī Akbar, the lion, looked like the Prophet. He lined up [before the enemy]. ʿUbaydallāh Ziyād said, 'O grandchildren of the Messenger, remove the veil from you face for the sake of God so I can see your face, as I have always yearned to see the face of Muḥammad (pbuh).' ʿAlī Akbar removed the veil. All the people of Yazīd saw his face and began to cry, and screaming could be heard from every corner. Shamir said, 'How come these Muslims have killed so many of us.' He said this and the army [of Yazīd] attacked, and ʿAlī Akbar counterattacked and killed 200 people. The Commander of Believers Ḥusayn, put his own tongue into his mouth [i.e., ʿAlī Akbar's] and said, 'O father, your tongue is also dry, give me water.' And he said, 'O father, thirst!' – complaining of his thirst. The Commander of Believers Ḥusayn said, 'O dear one, you will soon reach the water of paradise.' He returned and attacked and killed 300 people. Then he was martyred. After martyrdom he said, 'O father, I found what you promised, it came towards us quickly so we drink it now.'

{51} And it is said that the Commander of Believers had another child, a newborn named Maḥmūd; he was about to die of thirst. He was brought next to the Commander of Believers Ḥusayn, and he embraced him and went near the River Euphrates. He said, 'O brothers, if we are guilty then do not give us water. But what is the sin of this newborn that you do not give him water!?' A depraved man shot an arrow into the newborn's chest, causing him to be martyred while being in the arms of Imam Ḥusayn. The Commander screamed and took him to his mother. His mother said, 'Did you give him water to drink?' He said, ' I gave him a drink, but with the water of paradise.' The poor mother understood what had happened; the newborn son had been killed and martyred.

{52} It seems that the turbulence of the Day of Judgement had arisen all around.[26] It is said that on the night of the tenth of Muḥarram,[27] Shahrbānū dreamed of Fāṭima (pbuh) tightening her belt and taking a broom to sweep the battlefield and move away stones. She said, 'O Lady, why are you doing this?' She replied, 'My darling, Imam Ḥusayn (pbuh) will be killed here tomorrow. I am cleaning this battlefield in order that his sacred body is not hurt.'

[26] i.e. chaos was everwhere [27] i.e., ʿĀshūrāʾ

{۵۳} بعده، امام حسین تنها ماند و آفتاب به غایت گرم بود و راه آب بر وی بسته شده و فرزندان را درونه[۱۱۶] می‌سوخت. امام حسین رَضِيَ اللهُ عَنْهُ در خیمه آمد. اهل پرده خود را وداع کرد، و عمامهٔ محمّد مُصْطَفَی ﷺ بر سر نهاد، و ذوالفقار پدر را بر دست گرفت. به سوی میدان خرامید و آواز داد که «ای قوم [از] خدای تَعَالَی شرم دارید؛ «مَنْ عَرَّفَنِی فَقَد عَرَّفَنِی وَمَنْ لَمْ يَعْرِفْنِي فَإِنَّ ابْنَ الْمُرْتَضَى وَجَدِّي مُحَمَّد الْمُصْطَفَىٰ ﷺ وَأُمِّي فَاطِمَةُ زهرا و منم حسین».[۱۱۷] این کلمات بگفت و در میدان در آمد. غلغله در ملکوت افتاد و وحوش و طیور گریه درگشاد. و این شعر گفت و استاده ماند. یزیدیان گفتند «چرا استاده شده؟ مگر ترسیدی؟» گفت «از شرم. اوّل نمی‌کنم.[۱۱۸] نباید که فردای قیامت از رسول ﷺ شرمنده بمانم که گوید «چرا امّت من کشتی»». یزیدیان حمله کردند. أَمیر المُؤمِنین نیز حمله کردی چنانچه شیر گرسنه در گوسفندان درآید. همچنان در آمدند و سیصد نفر از آنها هلاک کردند، و در دوزخ فرستاد.

{۵۴} باز بسوی خیمه آمدند و یکان یکان فرزندان خود را وداع کرد. و ساعتی در خواب شد. جمال جهان آرای سید کائنات در خواب دید. فرمود «ای حسین من، و ای[۱۱۹] جگرگوشهٔ من، فردا بر آن حوض کوثر با یکدیگر آب خواهیم خورد. فاطمهٔ زهرا خواهی دید، جامهٔ ماتمی پوشیده و پدر خود علی نیز خواهی دید». أَمیر المُؤمِنین چون این حال دید از اشتیاق جمال عزیزان تقاضای دل بجنبانید.[۱۲۰] أَمیر المُؤمِنین حسین دیده گشاد، وضو کرد، و فرزندان را دیگربار وداع کرد و گریست. و همهٔ اهل خانه گریستند. و بعضی زنان راه بیوگی آمد. بعضی را درد یتیمی رسید.

{۵۵} چون بامداد طبل های جنگی بکوفتند و صف‌ها کشیدند و هفت روز گذشته بود که آب نچشیده بودند. اهل نزدیک امام حسین آمدند و گفتند «یا أَمیر المُؤمِنین، از تشنگی هلاک شدیم. یکی کوزه آب بده». أَمیر المُؤمِنین حسین اسب را زین کردند. أَمیر المُؤمِنین مشک به فتراک[۱۲۱] بست و سوار شد. چون یزیدیان دیدند که امام حسین سوار شد، نزدیک آب آمدند و همه گرد آب فرات حلقه کردند و آب ندادند. پس [...][۱۲۲] أَمیر المُؤمِنین حسین ابن المرتضی و امّی فاطمة الزَهْرَا وَجَدِّي مُحَمَّد المُصْطَفَىٰ ﷺ. قال «الظالمون عرفنا».

{۵۶} پس أَمیر المُؤمِنین حسین رَضِيَ اللهُ عَنْهُ گفت «یک کوزهٔ آب بدهید که جگر من می‌سوزد و فرزندان من تشنه شدند. که هفتم روز است که آب نخوردند». آن بدبختان جواب دادند که «ما تو را آب ندهم». امام حسین فرمود «اگر آب دهید شما [را] برابر خود در بهشت برم و خون را دعوی نکنم؛ مرا پاره آب دهید».

[۱۱۶] اندرون.

[۱۱۷] چنین ترکیب‌های عربی و فارسی در یک جمله را می‌توان در داستان‌های مالایی همچون حکایت امیرحمزه دید. رجوع کنید به Daneshgar, Majid, 'Persianate Aspects of the Malay-Indonesian World: Some Rare Manuscripts in the Leiden University Library', *Dabir* 8 (2021) 51–78.

[۱۱۸] من اوّل تیغ نزنم. [۱۱۹] حتی به‌صورت «وای» خوانده می‌شود.

[۱۲۰] می‌تواند با «دل جنبانیدن\دل جنباندن» به معنی «عجله کردن» بیاید.

[۱۲۱] تسمه. [۱۲۲] گفت(؟)

{53} Then, Imam Ḥusayn was alone and the weather was sweltering and he had no access to water and children were burning from inside. Imam Ḥusayn (pbuh) entered the tent. He bid farewell to his family there, and wore the turban of Muḥammad (pbuh), and took the Dhū al-Faqār[28] of his father. He moved towards the battlefield and chanted, 'O people, be ashamed of God. Those who knew me, they know, and those who do not know me, I am the son of Murtaḍā [i.e., ʿAlī], my grandfather is Muḥammad (pbuh) and my mother is Zahrāʾ, and I am Ḥusayn!' Upon saying these words he stepped onto the battlefield. The universe convulsed and animals and birds began to cry. Ḥusayn chanted and stood [to fight]. The people of Yazīd said, 'Why did you stop there? Are you afraid?' He said, 'I feel inhibited, I will not start! I should not on the Day of Judgement be ashamed before the Messenger of God asking me, "Why did you kill my community?"' The people of Yazīd then attacked. The Commander of Believers attacked, like a hungry lion moving towards a flock of sheep. He did so and killed 300 people and sent them to hell.

{54} He returned to his camp and bid farewell to each of his children and slept for a while. He dreamed of the beautiful face of the Master of the Worlds. He said, 'O my Ḥusayn, and my beloved, tomorrow we will drink water together from the pool of Kawthar. You will see Fāṭima Zahrāʾ wearing mourning dress and your father, ʿAlī, as well.' The Commander of Believers observed this scene, and became excited in anticipation. The Commander of Believers opened his eyes, performed ablution, and bid farewell to his children once more, he cried and all of the camp began to cry; some women felt as if they were being widowed themselves. Some of them even felt the pain of being orphaned.

{55} In the morning, drums were beaten and the troop lined up, not having had a drink of water for seven days. The descendants of the Prophet came to Imam Ḥusayn and said, 'O Commander of Believers, we are dying of thirst; bring a jug of water.' The Commander of Believers Ḥusayn saddled his horse. He hooked the waterskin to the saddle and rode off. When the people of Yazīd noticed that Imam Ḥusayn rode the horse, they approached the River Euphrates and surrounded it; and did not give him water [...] the Commander of Believers said, 'I am Ḥusayn the son of Murtaḍā, my mother is Fāṭima al-Zahrāʾ, and my grandfather is Muḥammad (pbuh).' He added, 'we knew the oppressors!'

{56} The Commander of Believers (pbuh) said, 'Give us a jug of water as our livers are burning and my children are thirsty too. This is the seventh day that they have no water. Those blighted ones answered that they would not give him water. Imam Ḥusayn said, 'If you give me water, I will take you to paradise with me and will not

[28] Name of the infamous and fabled sword of Imam ʿAlī.

ایشان ندادند[۱۲۳] و أَمیر المُؤمِنین بار دیگر حمله کردند و در میان آب فرات در آمد. خواست تا آب خورد در حال فرزندانش یاد آمد گفت «اه! فرزندم علی اکبر از من آب طلبیده بود. من چگونه بخورم». أَمیر المُؤمِنین حمله کرد. هفتصد چند نفر را بکشت. بعده چندان تیر در وجود مبارک او رسید که جای ناخن گشاد[۱۲۴] نبود. و امام حسین بی‌تاب شد و بر زمین افتاد و تمام لشگر یزید گرداگرد أَمیر المُؤمِنین حسین شدند.

{۵۷} شمر بدبخت بر سینهٔ مبارک نشسته و کارد بر حلقش راند. هرچند که زور می‌کرد کار نمی‌کرد.[۱۲۵] امام حسین گفت که «ای بدبخت، در [بر] حلقِ من محمّد مُصْطَفَی ﷺ چندبار بوسه داده. چگونه بُریدن می‌خواهی؟» امام حسین رضي الله عنه گفت «ای شمر، وصیّت دارم؛ اگر به‌جا آری فردای قیامت تو را برابر من خود در بهشت برم». شمر گفت «بگو». امام حسین گفت «یکی آنکه کوزهٔ آب ده که تشنه‌ام و دوم سینهٔ خود باز کن و سوم پس قفا[۱۲۶] افکن تا من در سجده باشم». آن بدبخت سینه را باز کرد. داغ برص[۱۲۷] بر سینهٔ او بود. امام حسین گفت «صِدق شنیدم از جدّ خود محمّد مُصْطَفَی ﷺ که کُشندهٔ حسین کسی باشد که داغ برص بر سینهٔ او باشد». و امام حسین را پس قفا افکند و سرش ببرید. و روحش در مرغزار[۱۲۸] بهشت رفت. عرش و کرسی در لرزه آمدند. مرغان هوا و ماهیان دریا و درّندگان بیابان و جملهٔ وحوش و طیور برای أَمیر المُؤمِنین بگریستند. و سی[۱۲۹] روز تاریکی شده بود چنانچه کسی را نمی‌دیدی. بعد [بی‌بدنْ] سر او یک سیپاره[۱۳۰] کلام الله خوانده بود.

{۵۸} باز از قصّه بیان کنم.[۱۳۱] چون أَمیر المُؤمِنین از اسب افتاد، اسب نعره زد. خود را از ایشان خلاصی رهانید و [پای] خود را بر زمین زدن[۱۳۲] گرفت، و سوی آن بدبختان حمله کرد. با دو دست و زخم دندان[۱۳۳]

[۱۲۳] در متن اصلی «بدادند» ذکر شده است که احتمال یک اشتباه نوشتاری است. [۱۲۴] احتمالا اشاره دارد به «خدشه وارد شدن» و «زخمی‌شدن». به این بیت از ابوالقاسم حبیب اللّهی (نوید) نگاه کنید: « هزاران سنگ با دندان شکستن؛ هزاران عقده با ناخن گشادن». نتوانستم منبع اصلی شعر «نوید» را بیابم.

[۱۲۵] یادآور داستان اسماعیل است که هرچه ابراهیم تلاش می‌کرد تیزی در کار نمی‌شد. [۱۲۶] پشت گردن، پس گردن. [۱۲۷] جذام.

[۱۲۸] چمن زار. [۱۲۹] کلمهٔ «سی» در اینجا اشاره به «مانند» و «مثل» دارد. به دهخدا مراجعه شود؛ «همچون روز تاریکی شده بود».

[۱۳۰] «سپاره» به معنی «یک بخش از سی بخش قرآن» است. [۱۳۱] این عبارت و یا «القصّه» معادل دیگری برای «الغرض» است.

[۱۳۲] به نشانهٔ خشم پا بر زمین کوفتن. [۱۳۳] اصطلاحی جهان‌شمول و مهم که در گلستان سعدی نیز دیده می‌شود «زخم دندان دشمنی بتر ست». اکثر ترجمه‌های گلستان به زبان انگلیسی این اصطلاح را به‌صورت wound of enemy/foe تعبیر کرده‌اند که درست به نظر نمی‌رسد. مراد از «زخم دندان» همان زخم کشنده و ضربهٔ سهمگین است. این اصطلاح در زبان‌های گوناگون از جمله ترکی هم به کار می‌رفته است. در این راستا، توماس روبوک (Thomas Roebuck)، علی‌رغم ارائهٔ یک ترجمهٔ تحت اللفظی، به درستی این اشعار و مثل‌های سعدی را در ذیل اصطلاحات و امثال شرقی (oriental proverbs) قرار داده است. شایان ذکر است که خوانش دقیق‌تر از این اصطلاح را می‌توان در ترجمهٔ گروهی از پژوهشگران انگلیسی در قرن نوزدهم از حکایت «شتر و خار» در بهارستان جامی یافت. نگاه کنید به:
Roebuck, *A Collection of Proverbs*, 257; Editors, *The Flower of Persian Literature, Containing Extracts from the Most Celebrated Authors, in Prose and Verse, with a Translation Into English Being Intended as a Companion to Sir William Jones's Persian Grammar to which is Prefixed an Essay on the Language and Literature of Persian.* (London: printed by S. Rousseau at the Arabic and Persian Press, 1804), 205.

proceed to fight against you regarding the bloodshed; just give me a little sip of water.' They did not give him any and the Commander of Believers attacked once more and went to the river. He wanted to drink water then he remembered his children, 'Ah! My son ʿAlī Akbar demanded water from me! How can I drink it now?' The Commander of Believers attacked again. He killed 700 or so. Later on, his sacred body was speared by so many arrows that there was no place left to be struck. Imam Ḥusayn became restless and powerless and fell to the ground, and the whole army of Yazīd surrounded the Commander of Believers Ḥusayn.

{57} The despicable Shamir sat on the sacred chest of Ḥusayn and put a butcher's knife to his throat. Whenever he tried to cut it, it did not cut.[29] Imam Ḥusayn said to him, 'O accursed! Muḥammad (pbuh) has kissed my throat several times. Why do you want to cut it?' Imam Ḥusayn (pbuh) added, 'O Shamir, I have a final suggestion that if you accept, I will take you with me to paradise on the Day of Judgement.' Shamir said, 'Tell me.' Imam Ḥusayn said, 'First, you give me a jug of water as I am extremely thirsty and, second, show your chest and turn me over to cut from the nape of the neck so that I will be in prostration.' The ill-omened Shamir showed his chest. His chest was traced with leprous sores. Imam Ḥusayn said, 'Verily, I heard from my grandfather Muḥammad (pbuh) that my killer's breast would be traced with leprous sores.' Then he turned Imam Ḥusayn over and cut off his head. His soul went to the grasslands of paradise. The Throne and the Seat shook. The birds in the sky, the fish in the oceans, the desert predators, and all animals and birds began to cry for the Commander of Believers. And the day appeared dark, no one was able to see anyone else clearly. Then his head began to recite one part of the Word of God.[30]

{58} Returning to the story. When the Commander of Believers fell from his horse, the horse made a loud neigh, released itself from them[31] and angrily pounded the ground with its leg and attacked them. The horse manages to kill 300 people[32] with its two front legs and strong and poisonous teeth and these oppressors were defeated. The horse was seriously injured and it returned feebly to the corpse of the Commander of Believers Ḥusayn (pbuh) before itself falling down. When the horse realised that they[33] were approaching, it moved towards the house, whinnying as it got closer. And Ḥusayn's camp heard the sound of the horse. Umm Kulthūm said, 'My son has returned', Shahrbānū said, 'my lord arrived', and ʿAlī Aṣghar and the girls said, 'Father has arrived.' When they found the horse injured, and without rider, the poor women suddenly removed their scarves and ran out of the tent and screamed and hugged the

[29] It reminds the story of Abraham and Ishmael, when the knife did not work. [30] i.e., the Qurʾān

[31] i.e., the surrounding troops of Yazīd's army [32] In some copies, the horse kills 600 people.

[33] i.e., the descendants of the Prophet (?)

سیصد[الف] نفر میان ایشان بکشت و ایشانِ گُرداش[۱۳۴] باختند. و آن اسب چندان زخم خورده که بی‌طاقت بازگشت برتن أَمیر المُؤمِنین حسین رَضِيَ اللهُ عَنْهُ و خود را بر زمین زد. چون دید که ایشان نزدیک وی آمدند بنالید (؟)، و روی سوی جانب خانه کرد و بانگ و فریاد کنان می‌آمد، و اهل بیت أَمیر المُؤمِنین حسین آواز اسب شنیدند. امّ کلثوم گفت که «فرزند من آمد»، و شهربانو گفت که «شاهِ من آمد» و علی اصغر و دختران گفتند «بابا[ی] من آمد». چون اسب را خالی دیدند و زخم‌های خورده، عوراتِ بیچاره یک‌بارگی سر برهنه کرده و از خیمه بیرون آمدند و فریاد برآوردند و اسب در کنار گرفتند و علی اصغر [..] دو گریه کرده آمدند و گفت «ای اسب! بابائی من[۱۳۵] چه کردی؟ و پدرم را گذاشته آمدی؟ ما را غریب کردی و یتیم و بیچاره کردی» و چندان سر بر زمین زدند که بیهوش شدند. چون اسبِ بیچاره این حال دید، خود را بر زمین چنان زد که هلاک شد، و خون از چشم و بینی او بیرون آمد، و هر دو دختر و پسر اسب را در کنار گرفتند و می‌گریستند و اسب را در خاک کردند.

{۵۹} پس، ای امّتان،[۱۳۶] وفاداران، امروز آب از چشم بیارید[۱۳۷] تا فردا[ی] قیامت از شفاعت محمّد رسول الله صَلَّى اللهُ عَلَيْهِ وَسَلَّمَ محروم نمانید.

{۶۰} موسیٰ اشعری می‌گوید که «مردی زخم خورده میان کشتگان افتاده بود. می‌دیدید که حوران بهشت طَبَق‌های نور و شراب طهور بر دست کرده، هریکی را می‌دادند. می‌گویند که «این شوهر ماست و دیگر حوری می‌گوید این شوهر من است، هریکی به شوهری می‌گرفتند».

{۶۱} جعفر بن صادق[۱۳۸] رَضِيَ اللهُ عَنْهُ می‌گوید «من آن روز در مکّه بودم که أَمیر المُؤمِنین شهادت یافته از طواف کعبه آوازی شنیدم که مردی می‌گفت «باری بر من رحمت کن». نزدیک او شدم، چه‌بینم که شخصی نیم‌رو سیاه گشته و زاری می‌کرد. گفتم «چرا چنین می‌نالی که این جای ناامیدی نیست؟ و از جهت خدای تَعَالَیٰ نا امید مباش». گفت «ای خدایا، ناامید از آنم که رحمت نکردم بر اولاد رسول صَلَّى اللهُ عَلَيْهِ وَسَلَّمَ». جعفر صادق گفت «مرا بگو آن چه بود». گفت «من رکابدار امام حسین بودم. دهم ماه محرّم روز عاشورا امام حسین بن علی شهید شد. در ازار بند ایشان گوهر قیمتی خراج ولایت بود. طمع آن در من افتاد که آن را از بند أَمیر المُؤمِنین بستانم که مرا باقی عمر پسند باشد. چون نزدیک امام حسین رسیدم خواستم تا شلوار از بند باز کنم دیدم که به دست چپ محکم گرفت. شیطان در خاطر من تلقین کرد که «دست ببُر». کارد کشیدم و بر بند دست راندم و جدا گردانیدم. باز خواستم تا از بند بگشایم با دوم دست گرفت. همدران ساعت آوازی شنیدم که «ای ناجوانمرد، چرا بر وی نبخشیدی و از خدای نترسیدی؟ فردا[ی] قیامت از روی پیغمبر شرم نداشتی؟ از بیم آن آواز بیهوش [...]».

[۱۳۴] از واژه «گُرداس» به معنی «ستمگر» است. [۱۳۵] بابای من. [۱۳۶] امّت. [۱۳۷] روان سازید. [۱۳۸] گمان رایج این است که این شکلی از اشتباه نگارشی از نام جعفر صادق، ششمین امام شیعیان، است. در نسخهٔ کوتاه این داستان به بررسی این موضوع پرداخته‌ام.

[الف] ششصد

horse, and ʿAlī Aṣghar and [...] both cried and said, 'O horse, what did you do with my father?[34] You returned leaving father alone? Have you made us lonely, orphaned, and poor?' They wailed and hit their heads on the ground so much so that they became unconscious. When the poor horse saw this scene, it fell down so hard it died, and blood gushed from its eyes and nose, and both the girl and son embraced the horse and cried as they buried it.

{59} So, O Muslim community, O faithful followers, try to cry today in order not to be omitted from Muḥammad's (pbuh) intercession on the Day of Judgement.

{60} Mūsā Ashʿarī said, 'A wounded fellow was among those killed. He noticed that heavenly cherubs brought trays of light and purified wine, passing them to everyone killed, while saying, "This is my husband", they each took one as a husband.'

{61} Jaʿfar the son of Ṣādiq[35] (pbuh), says, 'I was in Mecca the day the Commander of Believers was martyred. I heard the voice of a man around the Kaʿba saying, "Anyway, bestow Your mercy upon me." I approached him. What I saw was a man whose face was half blackened and he was wailing. I asked him, "Why are you crying like this, as here is not the place of despair." He said, "O God! I am ashamed as I was not merciful with the children of the Messenger (pbuh)."' Jaʿfar Ṣādiq said, 'Tell me what has happened?' He said, 'I was the camel-driver of Imam Ḥusayn. Imam Ḥusayn the son of ʿAlī was martyred on the tenth of Muharram [i.e., ʿĀshūrāʾ]. There was a gemstone in his belt. I was tempted to take it from the belt of the Commander of Believers as it could suffice me for the rest of my life. I approached Imam Ḥusayn and wanted to loosen his trousers from the belt then I noticed my hand was taken by his left hand. Satan tempted me to severe the hand. I took a butcher's knife and cut the hand, severing it. Then I went to open the belt but my hand was taken again, but this time with his right hand. I heard a voice saying, "O faithless one, why were you not kind to him and did not fear God? Were you not afraid [and ashamed] of the Prophet on the Day of Judgement?" Being very scared as the voice rang out, I [...] fell into a swoon.

[34] i.e., where is my father [35] i.e. Jaʿfar al-Ṣādiq

{۶۲} بازآمدم[۱۳۹] لرزه در اندام من افتاد. چون خواستم که از آنجا بیرون شوم، پایم کار نمی‌کرد. به‌حیل[۱۴۰] چند قدم بیشتر شدم. ساعتی بود دید[م] که فوج فرشتگان آمد، بساط نورانی گستردند و از نو آن بساط جهان منوّر شد. أَمیر المُؤمِنین حسین را به مشک و زعفران شستند. حقّ تَعَالَی چهار هودج را فرستاد. با یک هودج مهتر آدم و حوا، و در دوم هودج مهتر نوح بود، و در سوم هودج مهتر ابراهیم و بی‌بی سارا، و در چهارم هودج پیغمبر ما محمّد رسول الله ﷺ بود. نزدیک تن أَمیر المُؤمِنین شدند و تن را گرفتند.

{۶۳} آنگاه پرسیدند که «ای جگر گوشهٔ من، دست‌های تو را که برید؟» امام گفت «رکابدار من بریده». پس نوح پیغمبر دست[۱۴۱] از بساط‌گاه آورده و بنشاند. هم درین محل فاطمه رضی الله عنها از هوا پیدا شد و فرشتگانِ انبوه برابر محافه[۱۴۲] جامه‌های ماتم پوشیده نزدیک امام حسین رسیدند و بی‌بی فاطمه خود را از محافه بیرون انداخت[۱۴۳] و تن امام حسین را در کنار گرفت، و می‌گفت «که ای نور دیدهٔ من و ای جگر گوشهٔ من،[۱۴۴] و ای اسیرگشتهٔ من، این چه بی‌رحمتی بود که با تو کردند». آنگاه رویِ سوی آسمان کرد و گفت «إِلٰهِيّ، بندهٔ تو را کشتند و از تو نترسیدند. و از پیغمبر تو باک نداشتند که زیاده از آن دستها بریدند. فردا[ی] قیامت انصاف فرزندان من بستانی». و درین میان، علی مرتضی با فرشتگان زاری‌کنان رسید. تن فرزند را در کنار گرفت و می‌گفت «ای غریب کشتهٔ من، چه توان کرد که ربّ جلیل در حقّ تو چنین حکم کرده که کشته گردی. اگر مرا حیات بود به جای تو جوی‌های خون روان کردمی». بعداز آن گفت «دستان تو را که برید؟» نظر به من کرد گفت «که خدای تَعَالَی از تو عفو نکند چنانچه در حقّ فرزند غریب من رحم نکردی». بعده، نزدیک پیغمبر ﷺ شدم و التماس کردم که خطا عفو فرمایند. رسول ﷺ بر روی من طپانچه[۱۴۵] زد و گفت «خدای تَعَالَی هرگز بر تو رحم نکند»».

{۶۴} [...][۱۴۶] «چون آمدید این سر امشب مرا بدهند و فردا سر شما را خواهم داد». ایشان آن سر را به او دادند. راهب آن سر پاک را در خانهٔ خود برد و طشت بیاورد و گلاب نیز آورد و آن سر نیکو شست و گفت «ای سر، برای خدای تَعَالَی که تو را آفریده است بگو که تو سرِ کیستی؟» سر درحالْ در جنبش درآمد و به آواز خوش گفت و زبان گشاد «أَنَا رَأْس الْحُسَيْنْ بِنْ عَلِيّ الْمُرْتَضَىٰ، أَنَا الغَرِيبْ وأَنَا اليَتِيمْ وَأَنَا المَقْتُولِ دشت

[۱۳۹] بهوش آمدم. [۱۴۰] به هر ترفندی که بود. [۱۴۱] مراد همان «پنجه» است که نماد دست قطع شدهٔ حسین است. هرچند در ادبیات عاشوراییِ ایرانی گاهی به عنوان «دست عبّاس» شناخته می‌شود. در مراسم ویژهٔ شهادت امامان حسن و حسین در سوماترا با عنوان تابوت، که تحت تاثیر حکایات محمّد حنفیّه است، از پنجه یا *Jari Jari* استفاده می‌شود، چنانچه در مراسم عاشورا در ایران و هند نیز از آن استفاده می‌شود. در مورد نمادها و موسیقی مرتبط با مراسم تابوت در سوماترا:
Margaret Kartomi, *Musical Journeys in Sumatra* (Illinois: University of Illinois Press, 2012), 85.

[۱۴۲] هودج. [۱۴۳] با سرعت خارج شد. [۱۴۴] دوست داشتنی و عزیز. [۱۴۵] سیلی.

[۱۴۶] داستان ناگهان تغییر می‌کند و بخش قبلی در مورد رکابدار حسین بن علی ناتمام رها می‌شود.

{62} 'When I woke up, my body was shaking. I wanted to leave but my legs did not help. Hardly able to scramble, I took a few steps. After a few moments, I found a group of angels bearing a carpet of light and through its light the whole world was illuminated. They washed the Commander of Believers Ḥusayn with musk and saffron. God sent down four howdahs. The first howdah carried Their Eminences Adam and Eve, the second howdah His Eminence Noah, the third howdah Their Eminences Abraham and Lady Sarah, and in the fourth one our Prophet Muḥammad (pbuh). They all approached the corpse of the Commander of Believers and embraced it.

{63} 'Then they asked, "O dearest one, who cut off your hands?" The Imam replied, "My camel-driver did so." In this vein, the Prophet Noah brought out a hand from his possessions and implanted it.[36] Fāṭima descended from the sky in her howdah with many angels and wearing mourning clothes. She arrived next to Imam Ḥusayn and promptly descended from the howdah to embrace the corpse of Imam Ḥusayn to say "O my dear! O my darling! O my poor son held captive! Who did this aggression to you?" Then she looked at the sky and said, "O God, they killed Your servant, and they were not afraid of You nor Your prophet, as they went further and cut his hands off. Take revenge for my sons on the Day of Judgement!" 'At that moment, ʿAlī Murtaḍā came along with angels while lamenting, "O my murdered son killed lonely! What can one do as the Majestic Lord has decreed that you be killed. If I were alive, I would have flowed streams of blood instead of you." Then he asked, "Who cut your hands off?" He looked at me and said, "God does not forgive you as you were hostile to my lonely son." 'Then I approached the Prophet (pbuh) and asked him to forgive my sin. The Messenger (pbuh) slapped my face and said, "God does not bestow mercy upon you".' [...]

{64} [...] 'as you arrived, give me the head tonight, and I will give you the head back tomorrow.' They[37] gave him the head. The monk took the sacred head into his house, brought a basin as well as rose water with which he gently washed the head. He said, 'O head, by the God who has created you, tell me to whom do you belong?' The head moved, opened its mouth, and in a pleasant voice said, 'I am the head of Ḥusayn son of ʿAlī Murtaḍā, I am the lonely one and the orphan one and the one killed on the plain of Karbala. My grandfather is Muḥammad (pbuh) and my mother is Fāṭima Zahrāʾ.'[38] When the monk heard this he raised his index finger and professed faith, and became faithful.

[36] It refers to "panja" (Malay: Jari-jari) a common metal or wooden symbol used in Muharram to commomorate the killing of Ḥasan and Ḥusayn in Indonesia (Sumatra). For more, see: Margaret Kartomi, *Musical Journeys in Sumatra* (Illinois: University of Illinois Press, 2012) [37] i.e., Yazīd's army

[38] The existence of frequent allusions to the maternal bond between Fāṭima and Ḥusayn is worthy of attention.

کربلا. جدّم محمّد مُصطَفَى ﷺ واُمّي فاطمهٔ زهرا».[۱۴۷] چون راهب این شنید انگشت[۱۴۸] برآورد و کلمهٔ شهادت گفت و ایمان آورد.

{۶۵} آن راهب هفت پسران داشت. هر هفت مسلمان شدند و همه تعزیت کردند. چون صبح بدمید، [سر] أَمیر المُؤمِنین [را] خواستند. راهب پسری را طلب کرد و گفت «این زمان پاکیزه مسلمان شدید. این بهترین خلق [...] است. چگونه روا داریم که سر أَمیر المُؤمِنین حسین بر سرنیزه کرد یزید». پسر بزرگ گفت «ای پدر، سر من ببر، ایشان را بده». راهب سر پسر ببرید و ایشان را داد. و ایشان شناختند و گفتند «این سر امام حسین نیست». آن راهب همچنین تا شش پسر را بکشت و فرستاد. ایشان قبول نکردند. هفتم پسرش بود، او گفت «ای پدر، [...] توقّف کن که وضو سازم و دو رکعت نماز بگذارم». [در نماز گفت] «خدای تَعَالَی، روی [و] سَر من چون روی و سَر امام حسین کند».[۱۴۹] و همچنین گردانید. راهب سر پسر خود را برید که هیچ فرق نمانده و هر دو را برابر داشته[...]. آن سر به ایشان داد، قبول کردند و گفتند که این سر أَمیر المُؤمِنین حسین است. سر را بر نیزه کردند. بعده، راهب کسان خود را فرستاد و جامه‌هایی به ایشان داد تا تن أَمیر المُؤمِنین حسین را از دشت کربلا آورند. چون در کربلا رسیدند، شب تاریک بود؛ بدیدند که تن أَمیر المُؤمِنین میان دیگران چون نور می‌شتافت. شناخته از کربلا آوردند. راهبِ کورِ أَمیر المُؤمِنین، دمیان[۱۵۰] هفت پسران کرد. چون آن بدبختان سر أَمیر المُؤمِنین حسین را بردند، یزید لعین شاد شد.

{۶۶} باز از سر قصّه بیان کنم. آن روز که أَمیر المُؤمِنین شهادت یافت با او هفتاد دو نفر در دشت کربلا نیز شهادت بودند. غلام قدیم (؟) أَمیر المُؤمِنین رضی الله عنه بود. رسول ﷺ پیوسته بر [...] می برد[۱۵۱] أَمیر المُؤمِنین حسین رضی الله عنه؛ آن غلام را رنج رسیده بود، [در] دشت کربلا [...] برأَمیر المُؤمِنین حسین رضی الله عنه گشاده بود. و آن جا به‌جهت راه کوفه [...] أَمیر المُؤمِنین علی بود. چون غلام در کوفه آمد در آنجا نماند. در مکّه در آمد. شادیانهٔ[۱۵۲] یزید می‌زدند. و آن غلام در مدینه درآمد. آنجا هم شادیانهٔ یزید زدند؛ «آنجا بروم که جای حمزه[۱۵۳] خلیفهٔ پهلوانِ آخرالزمان و شیر پاک عالم است. و در شهر بامیان[۱۵۴] همان‌جا بروم». چنانچه سه ماه راه رود، قطع کرد و در شهر بامیان رفت. به نزدیک آن درخت بود و زیر آن درخت مردمان نشسته بود و آن غلام نزدیک مردمان رفت و پرسید که «اینجا خلیفه کیست؟» ایشان گفتند که «شیر پاک عالم، پهلوان

[۱۴۷] ارجاعات مکرّر به رابطهٔ مادر-فرزندی فاطمه و حسین قابل تأمّل است.

[۱۴۸] اشاره به «انگشت شهادت» یا «انگشت اشاره» دارد.

[۱۴۹] اشاره دارد به داستانی قرآنی در مورد کشته شدن بَدَلِ عیسیٰ به جای شخص عیسیٰ که درآیهٔ ۱۵۷ سورهٔ نساء مطرح شده است.

[۱۵۰] اشاره به «خون ریختن» دارد. [۱۵۱] در برخی نسخ «می بود» است. [۱۵۲] پایکوبی و شادمانی.

[۱۵۳] علاوه براینکه به معنای «شیر» به‌کار می‌رود، نشانگر دلیری و شباهت داشتن وی به حمزه عموی پیامبر است.

[۱۵۴] شهری با نام بانیان در نزدیکی شهرستان فسا وجود دارد. امّا با ویژگی های داستان محمّد حنفیّه همخوانی ندارد. به احتمال زیاد اشاره به منطقهٔ بامیان در افغانستان کنونی دارد. در نسخه‌های دیگری که شامل این داستان هستند اسامی شهرهای متفاوت ذکر شده است.

{65} The monk had seven sons. All seven converted to Islam and all mourned. In the morning, [Yazīd's people] asked for the Commander of Believers.[39] The monk, in the meantime, asked for one of his sons and said, 'You are now purely converted to Islam. He[40] is the best of people. How can we allow Yazīd to put the head of the Commander of Believers on a spear?' The oldest son said, 'O father, pass my head on to them, instead.' The monk passed the head of his son on to them. They recognised it and said to the monk, 'This is not the head of Imam Ḥusayn.' The monk killed six sons and sent their heads. They[41] did not accept them. His seventh son said, 'O father, wait until I make ablution and perform a two-unit prayer.' [While praying, the son said], 'O God, make my face resemble that of Ḥusayn.'[42] God brought this about. The monk beheaded his son which was in no way different to the other head when compared. He gave them this head and they accepted it, and said, 'This is the head of the Commander of Believers Ḥusayn.' They put the head on a spear. Then the monk sent his friends to go to the plain of Karbala with garments and bring back the corpse of the Commander of Believers Ḥusayn. They arrived in Karbala at night. They noticed that the body of the Commander of Believers was moving quickly like a light. They recognised the body and brought it back from Karbala. The monk, being blinded by the Commander of Believers,[43] slaughtered his seven sons. When those people of ill-faith took the head of the Commander of Believers Ḥusayn, the accursed Yazīd became cheerful.

{66} Now I shall tell the rest of the story. The day on which the Commander of Believers was martyred, seventy-two people were also martyred with him on the plain of Karbala. The former servant of the Commander of Believers was also there[44] and was always [along with] the Messenger while […] visiting the Commander of Believers. He had suffered greatly and was released by the Commander of Believers on the plain of Karbala […]. From there he moved towards Kufa […] of the Commander of Believers ʿAlī. When the servant arrived in Kufa, he did not stop but moved onward to Mecca. There were people partaking in Yazīd's feast. The servant arrived in Medina. There was also a feast of Yazīd. [The servant asked himself] 'Should I go to where the lion, the brave caliph of the end of time and the most gallant knight of the universe is located?' He set off for the city of Bamyan. It took him three months to get there. After taking a shorter route he arrived in the city of Bamyan. A tree was close by and people were under the tree; the servant went to the people asking, 'Who is the caliph here?' They

[39] i.e., his head [40] i.e., Ḥusayn [41] i.e., Yazīd's soldiers [42] Referring to an Islamised Biblical narrative depicted in Q. 4:157, where 'another was made to resemble him to them'. For more about this verse and its biblical aspects, see: Gabriel Said Reynolds, *The Qur'an and the Bible: Text and Commentary* (New Haven and London: Yale University Press, 2018), 180-181. [43] i.e., in favor of Ḥusayn
[44] i.e., on the plain of Karbala

آخرالزمان أَمیر المُؤمِنین محمّد حنفیّه[ب] رضی الله عنه [است] که جملهٔ پادشاهان عالم را از او وحشت است». آن غلام کاغذ سفیدخط گشود نبشته (؟) و خود جامه‌های کبود پوشیده درون شهر درآمد و پرسید که «امیر شهر کجاست و کدام وقت باز می‌دهد». گفتند «بر[و] دربانی نیست، هرکه می‌رود او را در حضور خود می‌طلبد و هر کیفیت که باشد». از وی زبانی پر شد.[۱۵۵]

{۶۷} آن غلام درون سرای درآمد و جامه‌ها پاره‌پاره کرده، دست بر زمین زد و خاک بر سر خود انداخت و فریاد برآورد؛ غلطیدن گرفت. و محمّد حنفیّه را از طپیبدن[۱۵۶] او غایت سرآمد و گفت که «کاغذ از دست او ستانید و بر من بیارید». چون محمّد حنفیّه کاغذ گشاد و بخواند. تمام کیفیت و اخبار برادران خود و برادرزادگان شنید. أَمیر المُؤمِنین محمّد حنفیّه رضی الله عنه تاج که بر سر داشت بر زمین زد و جامه بر تن داشت پاره پاره کرد و خود را بر زمین زد[۱۵۷] و چنانچه قرار نداشت. بعداز آن فرمود که «اسباب و خزانه تمام بیرون آورده و لشگر سپاه را ساخته کنید و خیمه‌ها و بارگاه در صحرا زنید». و فرمود که دوات و قلم بیارید و مکتوب به جانب مسیّب کاقه[۱۵۸] نوشت و در عراق فرستاد.

{۶۸} و چنان نوشت که «ای برادران، حالْ خاندان رسول الله ﷺ اسیر و در بند افتادند. اگر آن [...] الان بیایید یاری کند خوب است. من می‌روم شاید که آنان را از بند رها کنیم که مملکت تمام یزید گرفت». و یک مکتوب برابر داشته، در شهر نجف فرستاد که «ای برادران بیایید و در مدینه بپیوندید و احوال خاندان رسول ﷺ به بینید[۱۵۹] که چون شده است». و یک مکتوب بر برادران خود نوشته و یک مکتوب بر طوغان[۱۶۰] ترک، امیر تبریز نوشته «ای بهادران،[۱۶۱] در حدّ مدینه بیایید». و یک مکتوب به طرف عمر علی، طالب علی و عقیل علی نوشته در شام فرستاد که «ای برادران، بودیم پیش پدر خود، پیش سرور عالم محمّد مُصطَفیٰ ﷺ.[۱۶۲] دست‌ها بسته اِستاد میشدم. و از مادرْ برادرانِ سرورِ ما بودند: یکی امام حسن، دوم امام حسین رضی الله عنهما. به یاد داریم».

[۱۵۵] بنابر دهخدا « زبان پر بودن . [زَ پ ُ دَ] (مص مرکب)... از سخنی؛ آن سخن را فراوان گفتن». [۱۵۶] بی‌قراری.

[۱۵۷] بی قراری از شدّت ناراحتی. [۱۵۸] به‌صورت «مشی» نیز نوشته شده است. اشاره به مسیّب بن قعقاع دارد، فردی که نامش در آثار روایی و داستانی در مورد واقعهٔ کربلا ذکر شده است. همچنین داستان هایی پیرامون وی و دیگر شخصیت های خون‌خواه حسین همچون «مسیّب نامه» وجود دارد. در نسخهٔ مالایی با نام «مشی کاقه»، «مَسیب کا کا» و یا «موسب ققا» شناخته می شود. در داستان‌های «مسیّب نامه» و «ابومسلم نامه» اشاراتی به نقش محمّد حنفیّه و اتّفاقاتی که برای او افتاده است می‌شود در «درّالمجالس» نیز یافت می‌شود. شباهت‌های ساختاری و محتوایی بین فصل سی و یکم «درّالمجالس» و داستان‌ها و روایت‌های دیگر پیرامون کشته شدن حسن و حسین شایسته بررّسی بیشتر در آینده است. برای داستان‌های مرتبط و ادبیات مربوطه نگاه کنید به: ابوطاهر طرسوسی، ابومسلم نامه، به کوشش حسین اسماعیلی (تهران: معین، قطره، انجمن ایران شناسی فرانسه در ایران، ۱۳۸۰/۲۰۰۱) ج. ۱، ص ۱۷-۱۹۸؛ داستان کلیات کتاب مسیب نامه: شامل بهترین روایات و اخبار و جنگهای واقعی باقتله حضرت سیدالشهداء و کشته شدن آنها بدست آن نامدار وفادار (تهران: شرکت سهامی چاپ و انتشارات کتب ایران، بی تاریخ)؛ و محمّد بقای وارس بخاری، حماسه مسیّب نامه: پیش درآمد ابومسلم نامه، روایت بزرگ آسیای میانه، تصحیح و تحقیق دکتر میلاد جعفرپور، سه جلد (تهران: انتشارات دکتر محمود افشار، ۱۳۹۸/۲۰۱۹) [۱۵۹] ببینید. [۱۶۰] توغان. [۱۶۱] دلیران.

[۱۶۲] امّا براساس آنچه در «روضة الشهداء» اثر واعظ کاشفی ارائه شده است، همهٔ این افراد از جمله عمر علی، طالب علی و عقیل علی کشته می‌شوند و نقشی در کنار محمّد حنفیّه ایفا نمی‌کنند.

[ب] محمّد حنیفه

replied, 'The most gallant knight of the universe, the brave one of the end of time, the Commander of Believers Muḥammad Ḥanafiyya, of whom all kings of the world are afraid. The servant took out a sheet of white paper and sat to write, and then he wore black dress and entered the city and asked where the ruler of the city was and when one could meet him. They said, 'There is no guard there, whoever enters in, whatever their disposition, he would welcome in his presence'; he began to tell about the tragic story.

{67} The servant entered the court and tore off his garment, took soil from the ground, and poured it upon his own head, screamed, and fell on the ground. Muḥammad Ḥanafiyya was unhappy with his restlessness and ordered, 'Take the letter from him, and bring it to me.' Muḥammad Ḥanafiyya opened the letter and read it carefully. And he read fully the details and the incidents that had befallen his brothers as well as his nephews. The Commander of Believers Muḥammad Ḥanafiyya threw the crown on his head to the ground and tore his dress and became restless and tormented. Then he ordered, 'Prepare all weapons, equip the army, and set up tents and camps in the desert.' And he ordered, 'Bring an inkwell and pen and write a letter to Musayyib Qaʿqāʿ[45] and send it to Iraq.'

{68} In the letter he mentioned, 'O brothers, the descendants of the Messenger are now captured and imprisoned. Being able [...] to assist, would be good. I will go with the hope of releasing them from slavery and being imprisoned, as all territories are under Yazīd's control.' And another similar letter was sent to the city of Najaf, 'O brothers, come and join me in Medina and see the current condition of the descendants of the Messenger and what has happened to them.' And a letter was sent to his brothers and a letter sent to Tughān Turk, the ruler of Tabriz, 'O the chivalrous ones, come close to [the borders of] Medina.' And another letter was sent to, ʿUmar ʿAlī, Ṭālib ʿAlī, and ʿAqīl ʿAlī and sent out to Sham, 'We are brothers sharing the same father, and we were politely and respectfully at the service of the Master of the Worlds, Muḥammad, and from our mother's side, our brothers and masters are first Imam Ḥasan and second Imam Ḥusayn. We remember them!'

[45] Mashi bi-Kaqah

{۶۹} و خود محمّد حنفیّه با دوازده‌هزار سوار به جانب مدینه روان شدند. چون محمّد حنفیّه رضی‌الله‌عنه نزدیک مدینه رسید و روضهٔ رسول الله ﷺ بدید پیاده شد، و زاری و عاجزی کردن گرفته که «یا رسول الله، با اولاد تو این چنین یزید لعین کرد». محمّد حنفیّه در آنجا خواب آمد. در خواب دید رسول الله ﷺ گفت «ای فرزندان،[۱۶۳] او را بکش که من با تو هستم و هیچ خطا و آفت و نکبتی بر تو نخواهد رسید، و تو را فتح و نصرت خواهد شد». محمّد حنفیّه گفت «یا رسول الله، روزی هجده برادران در شهرها و قلعه ها می‌رفتیم و می گرفتیم، امروز مرا هم تنها آمده و طائفهٔ خارجیان همه را گرفتند».

{۷۰} القصّه. محمّد حنفیّه طبل های جنگی بکوفت و غوغا در مدینه افتاد. و اندرون مسجد دو [تن] نشسته بودند. یکی عتبه ولید دوم مروان.[۱۶۴] چون ایشان آواز طبل‌ها شندید چند کس را دوانیدند که «خبر بیارید که این چیست و در میان چون ایشان کیست؟» گفتند «[...] ازجهت یزید». محمّد حنفیّه مروان را گفته فرستاد که «فرزند رسول ﷺ را به مکر کُشتی و در دشت کربلا کشانیدی. اگر مردانگی دارید بنمائید[۱۶۵] و بیائید».

{۷۱} سی هزار نفر جمع شدند و صف‌ها راست کردند. عتبه ولید و مروان در قلب[۱۶۶] استادند در میان یزیدیان؛ فوج ها راست کردند. و محمّد حنفیّه رضی‌الله‌عنه با هشتاد هزار سوار بود، چهارهزار [sic][۱۶۷] سوار در میمنه و چهارهزار [sic] سوار در میسره استادند. نقیبان بانگ کردند که «هریکی برای محبّت خاندان رسول ﷺ با خارجیان کارزار کند و برابر ایشان تیغ زند ولایت و خلعت ایمان او را عطا شود». محمّد حنفیّه رضی‌الله‌عنه گفت «ای برادران و ای دوستان، از برای محبّت خاندان رسول ﷺ و برای دوستی امام حسن و حسین رضی‌الله‌عنهما کسی بیرون آید». یکی از لشگر محمّد حنفیّه، آعجش نام[۱۶۸] بیرون آمد و یکی از لشگر یزید بیرون آمد. هر دو نیزه به دست آمدند. آعجش نام، هجده‌هزار خارجیان دیگر را در دوزخ فرستاد. عبته ولید گفت «این نیکو [نیست]، یک نفر از لشگر أَمیر المُؤمِنین محمّد حنفیّه رضی‌الله‌عنه چندین نفر خارجیان کشَت.» دیگر هیچ خارجیان پیش‌آورد نیامد.

{۷۲} مروان پلید گفت «ایشان دوازده‌هزار سوارند و ما سی‌هزار سواریم. همه یکبارگی حمله کردند، شور [و] غوغا برخاست؛ گویند که حشر شد. أَمیر المُؤمِنین محمّد حنفیّه را تیغ صمصام[۱۶۹] در حمایل[۱۷۰] دست کشیده بر دست کرده در افتاد، چنانچه شیرِ گرسنه در میان گوسفندان درآید. همچنان أَمیر المُؤمِنین محمّد حنفیّه از لشگر خارجیان می‌کشت، عتبه ولید و مروان عرض داشته بر یزید نوشته و گفتند که «آن پهلوان غازی[۱۷۱] پنجاه‌وپنجاه[۱۷۲] گرز داشت و سیصد و پنجاه و پنج مَن[۱۷۳] گرز بر دست می‌کرد». عرضه بر یزید لعین در دمشق رسید. روی او زرد شد. چون برگ درخت بلرزید و گفت که «مرا خبر نبود که این‌چنین خصمی و پهلوانی بر

[۱۶۳] ای فرزند؟ [۱۶۴] ولید بن مروان. [۱۶۵] خود را نشان دهید. [۱۶۶] میانه، وسط.

[۱۶۷] اگر «هشتاد هزار سوار» درست بوده باشد بایستی به دو گروه «چهل هزار سواری» تقسیم شوند.

[۱۶۸] احتمالا نوشتار اشتباهی از «اعجس» است. [۱۶۹] شمشیر تیز و برنده. [۱۷۰] آویزان کرده. [۱۷۱] مجاهد و جنگجو.

[۱۷۲] احتمالا اشاره به «پنجاه و پنج دارد»، و یا اشاره به «صد» دارد. و یا اصطلاحی است که دلالت به فراوانی وسایل رزم دارد.

[۱۷۳] هر «مَن» برابر با «سه کیلوگرم» می باشد.

{69} And Muḥammad Ḥanafiyya, himself, went towards Medina with twelve thousand cavalrymen. As soon as Muḥammad Ḥanafiyya approached Medina and noticed the tomb of the Messenger, he got off his horse and began to cry and wail, 'O Messenger of God, this is what the accursed Yazīd did to your children!' There, Muḥammad Ḥanafiyya fell asleep. He dreamed that the Messenger said, 'O my children, kill him as I will be with you and no loss, trial, or calamity will befall you, and you will be the ones who gain victory and who are victorious.' Muḥammad Ḥanafiyya said, 'O Messenger of God, we, eighteen brothers, used to go into cities and castles to conquer them, however, I am now alone and foreigners[46] have taken everyone.'

{70} Returning to the story. Muḥammad Ḥanafiyya beat drums and Medina was mobbed. Two people were in the mosque. One of them was Walīd b. ʿUtba, and the second was [Walīd] Marwān. When they heard the drums beating they sent messengers, 'Go and see what is going on and who is there.' They said, 'All are against Yazīd.' Muḥammad Ḥanafiyya sent an envoy saying, 'You killed the grandchildren of the Messenger of God through deception, and sent them to the plain of Karbala. If you are manly, show yourself and come out.'

{71} Thirty thousand people gathered and lined up. With Walīd b. ʿUtba and Marwān placed at the centre of the people of Yazīd, the soldiers marched out to the militants. Muḥammad Ḥanafiyya proceeded with eighty thousand cavalrymen, four thousand to the right and four thousand to the left [*sic*]. Senior officers announced, 'Whoever fights with foreigners for the love of the descendants of the Prophet, overcoming them with his sword, he will be granted the reward and devotion of faith.' Muḥammad Ḥanafiyya then said, 'O brothers and O friends, one may come forward for the love of the Messenger's descendants and the love of Imam Ḥasan and Imam Ḥusayn.' One named Aʿjash came forth from the troop of Muḥammad Ḥanafiyya, and one from Yazīd's army. Both moved forward holding spears. Aʿjash sent eighteen thousand foreigners to hell. Walīd ʿUtba said, 'This is not fair! That one from the troop of the Commander of Believers Muḥammad Ḥanafiyya killed such a large number of foreigners.' No one from the army of foreigners took a step forward.

{72} The filthy Marwān said, 'They have twelve thousand cavalrymen while we have thirty thousand.' Then all the people rushed forth and rioted. It is said it looked like the Resurrection. The Commander of Believers Muḥammad Ḥanafiyya took out the sharp sword of his father girdled around his shoulder and began to fight, like a hungry lion hurling into a flock of sheep. The Commander of Believers was still killing the army of foreigners. Walīd ʿUtba and Marwān noticed [the threat] and sent a message to

[46] The term "foreigner" is often used to address infidels and those who do not follow Ḥusayn and his followers.

سر امام حسین رَضِیَ اللهُ عَنْهُ بود». عمر سعد و عبیدالله زیاد گفت[ند] که «این[۱۷۴] برادرانِ بهترِ او هنوز نیامدند. این زمان[۱۷۵] او بی پشت[۱۷۶] است».

{۷۳} یزید گفت «من نیکو می‌دانم که أَمیر المُؤمِنین محمّد حنفیّه پهلوان عالم است و شیرپاک آخرالزمان است». بعده یزید گفت «کدام یاران با او یار خواهد شد؟» آن گفت «یکی مسیب کاقه پسر أَمیر المُؤمِنین علی کَرَّم الله وَجْهه، دوم طوغان ترکِ پادشاه، سوم ابراهیم، پسران علی: عمر و طالب و عقیل». بعده، یزید گفت «هریکی از شما بر هریکی سرلشکر شوید». عبیدالله زیاد گفت «جانب مسیّب کاقه من می‌شوم» و عمر سعد گفت «من جانب ابراهیم اشتر[۱۷۷] می‌شوم»، و شمر ملعون گفت «من جانب پسران علی می‌شوم». بعده، یزید پنجاه هزار برابر عبدالله زیاد داد، و چهل هزار سوار برابر عمر سعد داد و سیصد هزار سوار شمر ملعون را داد. و هریکی را برابر ایشان روان کرد و به طرف مروان، که در مدینه بود، سر و پا[۱۷۸] یک لک[۱۷۹] سوار فرستاد که با محمّد حنفیّه جنگ کن. و محمّد حنفیّه در مدینه برابر خارجیان جنگ می‌کرد. و ایشان را می‌کشت. و محمّد حنفیّه با دوگان‌نفر[۱۸۰] جنگ می‌کرد که از پس پشت [...] می‌خواست [...] ندا گفتند که یزید[...] به طرف مروان یک لک سوار مدد فرستاد. بعده، محمّد حنفیّه گفت که «جنگ دوگان نفر چه شود»[۱۸۱]. تیغ صمصام از حمایل کشید و حمله کرد و در میان یک لک سوار درآمد و تیغ می‌زد. چندان خارجیان بکشت که عدد آن را شما نبود و جوی خون روان شده.

{۷۴} أَمیر المُؤمِنین محمّد حنفیّه رَضِیَ اللهُ عَنْهُ مکتوب و قاصدان که بر مسیّب کاقه و ابراهیم اشتر و بر پسران علی و بر طوغان ترک فرستاده بود، آن قاصدان آن مکتوبات بر ایشان رسانیدند و هریکی ساخته با لشگر ایشان را [...] ملاقی شدند و هریک در جنگ در آمدند. فتح ربّانی و نصرت یزدانی به حال یاران محمّد حنفیّه [...] و لشگر خارجیان [را] زیر دست آوردند.[۱۸۲] چنانچه مشی\مسیّب کاقه سعد را گرفته، و پسران علی شمر ملعون را گرفته و غل و زنجیر در گردن ایشان کردند. مسیّب کاقه سی هزار سوار خارجیان را در تیغ آورد. و سی هزار سوار را زنده گرفتند و عمر [سعد] و شمر ملعون را دست پسِ پشتْ بسته برنگون‌سر[۱۸۳] کردند و جانب مدینه روان شدند و بر محمّد حنفیّه آوردند. محمّد حنفیّه مشی\مسیّب کاقه را در کنار گرفته و مسلمانان شاد شدند و شمر ملعون را به دار آویختند و تیرباران کردند. ناگاه به فرمان خدای تَعَالَی آتش آمد و شمر ملعون سوخت و مسلمانان را فتح شد.

{۷۵} محمّد حنفیّه در روضهٔ [پیامبر] آمد و زیارت کرده و در خانهٔ خود آمد. و یاران در خانه‌های قدیم

[۱۷۴] آن. [۱۷۵] در حال حاضر. [۱۷۶] بی پشتوانه. [۱۷۷] در داستان مالایی به‌صورت «ابراهیم عستر» نوشته می‌شود، که احتمالا تاثیر پذیرفته از تغییر رسم الخط هندی-سانسکریت به جاوی است. نمونه بارز در برگ ۱۴۱ از MSS Malay B.6 کتابخانهٔ بریتانیا دیده می‌شود. [۱۷۸] اوّل و آخر، به طور کلّی. [۱۷۹] صدهزار. [۱۸۰] چندین نفر. [۱۸۱] ترجمهٔ این قسمت دشوار است. احتمالا اشاره به جنگ تن‌به‌تن یا دوئل دارد. [۱۸۲] در اینجا، «زیر دست آوردن» به صورت «زیر آوردن» و به معنی «شکست دادن» و یا «مغلوب ساختن» به‌کار می‌رود. [۱۸۳] نگونسار، وارونه. همچنین به معنی «پشت رو» به کار می رود.

Yazīd saying, 'The chivalrous warrior has fifty [or so] staffs and holds a staff weighing a tonne.' The message reached Yazīd in Damascus; his colour paled; he shook like a withered leaf, and said, 'I was not aware that such a revenger and warrior would come after Imam Ḥusayn. ʿUmar Saʿd and ʿUbaydallāh Ziyād said, 'His other brothers who are [much] better have not yet arrived. He is still alone!'

{73} Yazīd said, 'I truly know that the Commander of Believers Muḥammad Ḥanafiyya is a chivalrous warrior of the universe and of the end times.' Then Yazīd said, 'Who are those who would join him?' They said, 'One of them is Musayyib Qaʿqāʿ, the son of the Commander of Believers ʿAlī, may God ennoble his face, second is Tughān Turk, the king, third is Ibrāhīm and the sons of ʿAlī, ʿUmar and Ṭālib and ʿAqīl.' Then Yazīd said, 'Each of you confront each of them with an army.' ʿUbaydallāh said, 'I will go for Musayyib [b.] Qaʿqāʿ. And ʿUmar Saʿd said, 'I will go for Ibrāhīm Ashtar'. Shamir, the accursed one, said, 'I will go towards the sons of ʿAlī.' Then Yazīd gave fifty thousand men to ʿUbaydallāh Ziyād, and forty thousand cavalrymen to ʿUmar Saʿd, and 300 cavalrymen to the accursed Shamir, and sent overall 100,000 people to Marwān, who was in Medina in order to fight Muḥammad Ḥanafiyya. And Muḥammad Ḥanafiyya fought and killed foreigners in Medina. And Muḥammad Ḥanafiyya fought with groups, that from the back [...] said [...] that Yazīd has sent 100,000 auxiliary forces for Marwān. Then Muḥammad Ḥanafiyya said, 'What about the duel?' He unsheathed a sharp sword from its scabbard and attacked, hurling himself into the army of 100,000. He killed many foreigners, whose number cannot be counted, and their blood flowed.

{74} The Commander of Believers Muḥammad Ḥanafiyya's letters and emissaries were sent to Musayyib [b.] Qaʿqāʿ and Ibrāhīm Ashtar and to the sons of ʿAlī as well as to Tughān Turk, and each of them got ready with their own army [...] visited, and each were engaged in battle.Divine victory and assistance was [...] bestowed upon the companions of Muḥammad Ḥanafiyya, and they defeated the army of foreigners. Musayyib [b.] Qaʿqāʿ captured Saʿd, and the son of ʿAlī took the accursed Shamir and chained his neck. Musayyib [b.] Qaʿqāʿ killed thirty thousand foreigner cavalrymen, and captured thirty thousand of their number alive, and they tied the hands of ʿUmar [Saʿd] and the accursed Shamir behind their backs and hung them upside down and they moved towards Medina and brought them before Muḥammad Ḥanafiyya. Muḥammad Ḥanafiyya hugged Musayyib [b.] Qaʿqāʿ and the Muslims became cheerful and hanged the accursed Shamir and then shot him. In the meantime, through God's decree, a fire came about by which the accursed Shamir was burned, and the Muslims saw an aperture[47].

{75} Muḥammad Ḥanafiyya went to the tomb [of the Prophet] and then returned

[47] i.e. good omen

خود آمدند. و جاسوسان را جانب دمشق فرستاد تا خبر بیارند. جاسوسان خبر آوردند که خاقان چین برابر یک لک و چهل هزار سوار می‌آید و هر دو [؟] پادشاه برای یاری دادن می‌آیند. أَمیر المُؤمِنین محمّد حنفیّه رضی‌الله‌عنه با یاران مشورت کردند که «چگونه باید کرد؟» مشی\مسیّب کاقه گفت «مرا چهل هزار سوار بده که قاچین[۱۸۴] را من می‌دانم». مسیّب کاقه و عمر علی با چهل هزار سوار مقابله خاقان شدند. و طوغان ترک و ارسلان[۱۸۵] ترک با چهل هزار سوار مقابلۀ حبشی شدند. و أَمیر المُؤمِنین محمّد حنفیّه رضی‌الله‌عنه جانب دمشق روان شدند. و یزید را ده لک سوار بود و با آنها در میدان در آمدند و جنگ می‌کردند؛ و دوپاس روز تیغ رفته.

{۷۶} محمّد حنفیّه تنها در حرب آمدند و آنجا که محمّد حنفیّه بود هشت لک [سوار] و دویست فیل بودند که گردیگرد[۱۸۶] کردند. پسِ پشت[۱۸۷] محمّد حنفیّه طالب علی بود. محمّد حنفیّه چندان را کشت که عدد آن را نبود و توده بر توده افتاد، و جوی‌هایی خون روان شدند. لشگر یزید پراکنده شد. بعده، یزید گفت که «فیلان را گرد کنید». غیص-شیر نامِ فیل بود و چون آن فیل نعره زد، بعده (؟) بر زمین زد.[۱۸۸] و یک امرای جانب یزید بود، او یزید را گفت «خود نمودار کن»؛[۱۸۹] ابوطالب علی پسِ پشت محمّد حنفیّه بود. یک فیل میان ایشان درآمد و هر دو را جدا کرد. چون هر دو جدا شدند، محمّد حنفیّه تیغ بر فیل زد کستوان[۱۹۰] و [...] را یزید تیغ برکشید و بر فیل زد.[۱۹۱] ناگاه عرصۀ شیر فیلان[۱۹۲] از پسِ پشت محمّد حنفیّه پیدا شدند. و کمنداندازان[۱۹۳] در کمر و گردن محمّد حنفیّه انداخته به‌جانب خود می‌کشیدند. آنگاه از اسب افتاد. یزیدیان دیدند و آن شیر مبارز را بگرفتند.

۱۸۴ کلمات مشابه در کردی و ترکی استانبولی وجود دارد که معنای آنها با محتوای متن فعلی تطابق ندارد. اگر اشکال نوشتاری از جانب کاتب و کاتبان را در نظر نگیریم، «قاچین» می‌تواند به «قاچیون» یا *catchioun* خاندانی در مغولستان و ترکستان مرتبط باشد. در برخی آثار تاریخی به زبان فارسی، همچون «تاریخ جهانگشای جوینی»، و «جوامع التواریخ» به نام «قاچیون» اشاره شده است. همچنین، به اثر ذیل مراجعه نمایید Abraham Constantin Mouradgea d'Ohsson, *Histoire des Mongols, depuis Tchinguiz-Khan jusqu'à Timour Bey ou Tamerlan* (Amsterdam: Frederik Muller, 1852), II: p. 6.

۱۸۵ در برخی نسخ به‌صورت «سیلان» که همان Ceylon یا سریلانکا است، و یا حتی «سَیَلان» و «سَیلان» خوانده می شود.

۱۸۶ گِردگرد، حلقه زدند. ۱۸۷ پشت سر، در عقب. ۱۸۸ هم اشاره به محکم کوفتن بر زمین دارد، و هم شکست دادن دشمن.

۱۸۹ معانی بسیار زیادی برای «نمودار کردن» وجود دارد. به احتمال زیاد، در اینجا اشاره به «طرح نقشه» دارد. در لمعات فخرالدین عراقی معانی مختلف استعمال شده است. ۱۹۰ اشاره به «بَرگُستوان» دارد. بنابر دهخدا «در گرشاسب نامه بجای برگستوان، کستوان آمده است» که اشاره به « پوشش اسب و پیل در جنگ» دارد. این کلمه در ادبیات ترکی عثمانی نیز کاربرد داشته است. با این وجود معادل ترکی آن «ات دونی» است. رجوع نمایید به برگ ۲۰ از Cod. Pers. 309 در کتابخانۀ باوریا در شهر مونیخ. ۱۹۱ به علت ناخوانا بودن این قسمت، اطمینان کافی از درک و ترجمۀ صحیح این قسمت ندارم. شاید به عملکرد فرمانده‌هان جنگ برای مقابله با دشمن اشاره دارد؛ نشان بالابردن شمشیر و ضربه زدن با آن به اسب یا فیل و سپس شروع و ادامه حمله. ۱۹۲ این اصطلاح نیز به‌صورت «فیل فیلان» به معنی بهترین و ممتازترین فیل‌ها در نبرد با هندی‌ها و حاکمان دهلی (دارالملک یا پایتخت هندوستان) به‌کار رفته است. مراجعه کنید به مطلع السعدین و مجمع البحرین اثر سمرقندی، برگ ۲۸۰، نسخۀ ۷۴۶۹۵، کتابخانۀ مجلس شورای اسلامی ایران. ۱۹۳ افرادی که کمند یا طناب بلندی را برای شکار حیوان یا اسیر کردن انسان پرتاب می کنند.

home and his companions and friends went to their own homes. They sent spies to Damascus to bring news. They reported, 'The emperor [Khaqān] of China, along with 140,000 cavalrymen were coming and that both [?] emperors are coming to assist.' The Commander of Believers Muḥammad Ḥanafiyya consulted with his companions and friends, 'What shall we do?' Musayyib [b.] Qaʿqāʿ said, 'Give me forty thousand cavalrymen as I well know Catchioun [?]. Musayyib [b.] Qaʿqāʿ and ʿUmar ʿAlī along with forty thousand cavalrymen confronted the Chinese emperor. And Tughān Turk and Arsalān Turk along with forty thousand cavalrymen confronted the Abyssinians. The Commander of Believers Muḥammad Ḥanafiyya went towards Damascus. Yazīd owned one million cavalrymen and he stepped onto the battlefield with them and they began to fight. It took them two days to fight with each other with swords.

{76} Muḥammad Ḥanafiyya remained alone in the battle and he was surrounded by 800,000 [cavalrymen] and 200 elephants. Ṭālib ʿAlī was behind Muḥammad Ḥanafiyya. Muḥammad Ḥanafiyya killed so many that the dead could not be counted, and the dead had fallen in a heap upon each other, and a stream of blood flowed. The army of Yazīd was scattered. Then Yazīd said 'to bring and gather all elephants.' There was an elephant named Ghayṣ-shīr that trumpeted and proved its strength. And one of Yazīd's ministers who was next to Yazīd, told him, 'It is time for you to make a plan[48].' Abū Ṭālib, the son of ʿAlī, was behind Muḥammad Ḥanafiyya. An elephant intervened and separated them from each other. As they were separated, Muḥammad Ḥanafiyya hit the elephant, but its armour [...] Yazīd [?] also raised his sword and hit the elephant. In the meantime, a wide area covered by elephants appeared behind Muḥammad Ḥanafiyya and lasso-throwers ensnared a rope around the waist and neck of Muḥammad Ḥanafiyya and dragged him towards themselves. Then he fell off his horse.

[48] Or: show yourself?

{۷۷} و طالب علی سر برهنه[۱۹۴] جانب میدان روان شدند و مشی\مسیّب کاقه و عمرعلی و طوغان ترک و ارسلان ترک و ابراهیم اشتر بشارت قلبی[۱۹۵] کردند. و دیدند که گردی خاست؛ طالب علی سر برهنه کرده گریان می‌آید و در میان خاک غلطیدن گرفت که «شیر زادهٔ پاک عالم به باد دادم». ایشان پرسید که «چگونه حال بود؟». قصّهٔ حال بگفت.

{۷۸} بعده، ایشان گفتند که «عمرعلی را سردار لشگر کنیم». هرچند که گفته اند [...] گفت «اگر سرلشگر تو باشی ما پراکنده نشویم». همچنان جانب دمشق روان شدند. و در آنجا که محمّد حنفیّه را گرفتند پیش یزید بردند. یزید گفت «اینکه مملکت مرا پراکنده[۱۹۶] کرد!» جلّاد را طلبید که «محمّد حنفية را پوست بکش». درزمانْ وزیر تبریزی مسلمان بود و دوستدار رسول ﷺ بود. در خاطر اندیشید که «بهتر است که اینچنین شاه‌زاده را نکشتند. اگر ما کشته شویم فدای خاک پاک باشم». وزیر افسوس کرد[۱۹۷] که «ای پادشاه، محمّد حنفیّه را برادران شیرپاک و مبارز دارد. بفرما تا نگاه دارند. اگر آنها بر ما بیایند با ایشان جنگ کنیم و اگر ایشان را برانیم می‌توانیم کشت. اگر با ایشان نتوانیم اوّل [او را] بدیشان بدهیم و حدّی در میان بندیم».

{۷۹} و زبیر فرمود که «محمّد حنفیّه را نگاه داشتند». مسیّب کاقه و عمرعلی و طوغان ترک و ارسلان ترک و ابراهیم اشتر و طالب علی رِضْوان اللهِ عَلَيْهِمْ أَجْمَعِين در دمشق در آمدند. و طبل جنگ بکوفتند که «ای یزید!». یکی را جانب یزید فرستاد[ند]. گفتند «ای یزید، محمّد حنفیّه را گرفتی دیگر رسم جنگ باز از سر قایم شد.[۱۹۸] چند روز با لشگر یزیدیان جنگ کردند. بعده، امرای یزید مشورت کردند که «محمّد حنفیّه را چرا زنده می‌گذاری؟! تا آن‌زمان که او زنده است جنگ قایم خواهد بود». یزید لعین فرمود که «جانب برآمدن آفتاب که دروازهٔ دمشق است در این کوه هیزم بُریده خرمن کنید تا دشمنان محمّد حنفیّه او را با بیست هزار مردم سوزند». درزمانْ نام وزیر، که دوستدار خاندان رسول بود، عرضه داشت نوشته، غلام خود را طلبیده و پانصد تنگ نقد او را داد و گفت «این نوشته بر مشی\مسیّب کاقه برسان و بگو که یزید چنین مشورت کرده که فردا محمّد حنفیّه را برای سوختن در وقت برآمدن آفتاب به طرف دروازه مکّه جانب دمشق است خواهد برد».

{۸۰} و ایشان در آن شب غم‌زده نشسته بودند. ناگاه غلام برایشان آمد و نوشته از بر زبان بر [...] و قصّهٔ ایشان گفت. مسیّب کاقه هزار سوار بر ابراهیم اشتر داد و گفت «برو و پسِ پشت کوه کمین شو که هر (؟) امان[۱۹۹] وزیر نشانی کرده بود»؛[۲۰۰] «هروقت رود، من خبر خواهم کرد، شما درآیید». یزید پلید، محمّد حنفیّه را،

[۱۹۴] بدون پوشش یا سرتراشیده. در داستان مالایی، علی اکبر یا عمرعلی با دیدن این صحنه، موهای سر خود را می‌تراشد و برای عقب نشینی به جای پرچم بر عَلَم می‌بندد.
'Setelah Umar Ali melihat Muhammad Hanafiyyah tertangkap, maka Umar Alipun memenggal rambutnya, maka diikatkannya pada panjipanjinya maka Umar Alipun surutlah.' See Brakel, 1975, p. 257.

[۱۹۵] اشاره به «تباشیر» دارد. [۱۹۶] نابسامان. [۱۹۷] احتمالا اشاره به تظاهر به افسوس خوردن و در عین حال کنایه آمیز بودن دارد. در فرهنگ معین «افسوس کردن» به معنی «مسخره کردن» آمده است. [۱۹۸] برقرار و ثابت بودن.

[۱۹۹] هر زمان؟ واضح نیست. [۲۰۰] جای امن پشت کوه که توسط وزیر مشخّص شده بود.

{77} And Ṭālib ʿAlī made himself bareheaded and retreated. And Musayyib [b.] Qaʿqāʿ and ʿUmar ʿAlī and Tughān Turk, and Arsalān Turk and Ibrāhīm Ashtar had thoughts of good news, and noticed stirred up dust and that a bareheaded Ṭālib ʿAlī was coming. He threw himself on the ground, saying, 'I lost the most chivalrous person of the universe.' They asked 'what had happened?' He said what had happened.

{78} Then they said that they would appoint ʿUmar ʿAlī as the major general of the army. They said jointly that 'if you would be the major general of their army, then they would not be scattered.' They then moved towards Damascus where they took and brought Muḥammad Ḥanafiyya before Yazīd. Yazīd said, 'He is the one who caused chaos in my affairs.' He summoned for an executioner to, 'Rid me of him!' There was a vizier from Tabriz who was a [sincere] Muslim and a lover of the Messenger. He said to himself, 'It would not be appropriate to kill the prince like this, although if I were killed, that would be for the sake of a pure motive.' The vizier said, with a sneer, 'O king, Muḥammad Ḥanafiyya has chivalrous brothers. Order them to stop [and not to kill him]. If his brothers attack, we will fight with them. If we were able to push them back, then we would be able to kill him. If we cannot defeat them, then we would pass him on to them and make a boundary between our regions.'

{79} And Zubayr said, 'They kept Muḥammad Ḥanafiyya alive.' Musayyib [b.] Qaʿqāʿ, ʿUmar ʿAlī, Tughān Turk, Arsalān Turk, Ibrāhīm Ashtar, and Ṭālib ʿAlī, may God be pleased with them all, arrived in Damascus. They began to beat drums of war, 'O Yazīd!' They sent someone to Yazīd telling him, 'O Yazīd, you have captured Muḥammad Hanafiyya, but the principles of fighting and battling are still the same.' They[49] fought with the army of Yazīd for a couple of days. Then the commanders of Yazīd discussed the issue, 'Why do you keep Muḥammad Ḥanafiyya alive?! As long as he is alive, the battle will continue.' The accursed Yazīd gave the order, 'To cut and gather firewood on the slope of the mountain where the Sun rises and there is also the gate of Damascus', where the enemies of Muḥammad Ḥanafiyya would kill him along with twenty thousand people. At that moment, the aforementioned vizier[50] began to write a letter. He called for his servant and gave him 500 dinars He said, 'Pass this letter to Musayyib [b.] Qaʿqāʿ and tell him, "Yazīd has agreed to take Muḥammad Ḥanafiyya to the Damascus gate towards the direction of Mecca tomorrow morning at sunrise in order to burn him."'

{80} They[51] stayed together on that sorrowful night. In the meantime, the emissary arrived and told them about the letter as well as the entire story. Musayyib [b.] Qaʿqāʿ gave a thousand cavalrymen to Ibrāhīm Ashtar and said, 'Go and hide behind the

49 i.e., Muḥammad Ḥanafiyya's brothers

50 *or*, the one who was called Wazīr

51 i.e., the brothers

عقیل را، با بیست هزار مردم مسلمان برای سوختن کشانید جانب پس پشت کوه بند[۲۰۱] روان کردند. از دروازه یک فرسنگ رفتند. نزدیک کوه بندیان را آوردند و گرداگرد ایشان هیزم ازجهت سوختن داشتند، و [...] بالای ایشان نیز هیزم ازجهت سوختن داشتند. انداختند، می‌خواستند تا آتش اندازند. درزمانْ وزیر دود آتش کرد چنانچه دودی خواست[۲۰۲] ابراهیم اشتر کمین‌گاه بود با شانزده‌هزار لشگر درآمدند و لشگر یزید را گرد کردند و پشتارهٔ هیزم بیرون کشیدند و مسلمانان چنانچه محمّد حنفیّه را، عقیل را و بیست هزار مرد مسلمان، بیرون آوردند.[۲۰۳] یزید بدبخت که در آنجا بود گریخت و در دمشق آمد.

{۸۱} ایشان شاهزادگان را سوار کردند و آن لشگر خود را نیز سوار کردند. جانب خیمه‌های خود آمدند. به کَرَمِ الله تَعَالَی ایشان را فتح شد. أَمیر المُؤمِنین محمّد حنفیّه در آن شب محمّد رسول الله ﷺ را در خواب دید؛ و سر محمّد حنفیّه را در کنار گرفت و بوسید و گفت که «حکم لم یزل برین بود. فامّا، بعداز این تو را فتح [...] خواهد بود. گفت بازوی خود را بطلب و بیار. گفت آنجا چهل فیلان را کشته بودی. گفت آنجا برو بازو بند خود به أَمیر المُؤمِنین بداد و آنجا قدرت خدای تَعَالَی ببینی».[۲۰۴] محمّد حنفیّه خود آنجا رفت چه بیند که آن بازوی افتاده است چنانچه ماه در ستارگان می درخشید آن بازوی برداشته آورد. چنانچه رسول الله ﷺ فرمود، همچنانکه به فرمان بود محمّد حنفیّه زین اسب محکم کرد و در گوش اسب گفت که «ای اسب، امروز کاری افتاد اگر مرا یاری کنی به فرمان خدای تَعَالَی و با دشمنان امیر حسین تیغ بازی کنم». اسب خدمت کرد و سر خود را فرود آورد. محمّد حنفیّه حمله کرد و سلام خدای تَعَالَی را گفت، و سوی میمنه و میسره حمله کرد. چندان یزیدیان را کشت که اسب او تا گوش در خون شد و جوی‌های خون روان شدند. همان ساعت [...] دیدن آن لشگر کسی را طاقت نماند.

[۲۰۱] کلمهٔ «بند روان کردن» اشاره دارد به انتقال افراد با دست‌های بسته در پشت سر یکدیگر؛ امّا اگر «بند» اسم خاصی برای «کوه» باشد، در این‌صورت دلالت بر نام «کوه‌بند» در افغانستان دارد. [۲۰۲] به احتمال زیاد دلالت دارد به علامت دادن به برادران و اصحاب محمّد حنفیّه که در آن حوالی مخفی شده بودند. [۲۰۳] سناریوی مرتبط به تلاش یزید مبنی بر سوزاندن محمد حنفیّه و سپس رهایی او از آتش احتمالا الهام گرفته از داستان نمرود و ابراهیم است. همچنین، گروگان گرفتن محمّد حنفیّه و رهایی وی در برخی از بخش‌های «مسیّب نامه» دیده می شود.

[۲۰۴] در نسخهٔ مالایی بدین نکته اشاره می‌شود که محمّد حنفیّه پیشتر دست خود را در نبرد از دست داده است و بدین دلیل نمی‌تواند به جنگ یزیدیان برود. همچنین، در نسخهٔ کامل داستان در گنج‌بخش پاکستان به شمارهٔ ۱۴۹۸-۰۰۱ رؤیای محمّد حنفیّه چنین ذکر شده است «[۵۱۴] در آن شب امام محمّد حنفیّه در خواب رفت. حضرت رسالت پناه محمّد مُصْطَفَی ﷺ جلوهٔ جهان آرا نمود و سر و روی امام را بوسه زد و گفت که «ای فرزند، رضای قادر لایزال چنین رفته بود. بعداز این تو را فتح و نصرت خواهد بود. برو پنجهٔ خود را بیار و بر بازوی خود بند تا به قدرت پروردگار باز پنجهٔ تو درست خواهد شد». محمّد حنفیّه عرض نمود که «یا رسول الله، پنجهٔ خود را کجا یابم؟» [۵۱۵] گفت که «پنجهٔ نور در مقامی که چهل فیل بر زمین زده بودی» ناگهان از خواب برخاست و یک نفر را فرستاد و نشانه‌ای که حضرت به او نموده بود به او بِنُمود. آن پنجهٔ مبارک در آن‌جا بود؛ یافته بیاورد. و چنانچه پیغمبر ﷺ فرمود همچونان کرد. في الحال، دست مبارک همچنان شد که بود. شکر یزدان پاک به‌جا آورده، تنگ اسب خود محکم کشیده در گوش اسب خود گفت که «ای اسب، ما را با تو کار است، اگر از جناب باری تَعَالَی مددی آید تا در صف دشمنانِ حسن و حسین [رویم]»».

mountain', whose safety was confirmed by the vizier, 'Wherever they go, I will send signals and you can attack.' The filthy Yazīd brought out Muḥammad Ḥanafiyya as well as ʿAqīl and twenty thousand chained people to burn and moved towards the back of the mountain. After going one *pārsang*[52] from the gate, they brought the chained people near the mountain where they had gathered firewood to burn them; and also [...] had firewood above and [...] them. They made a fire, and wanted to burn them. At that moment, the vizier made smoke from the fire. As soon as the smoke rose, Ibrāhīm Ashtar, who was hidden there, attacked with his army of sixty thousand and surrounded the army of Yazīd, and dragged away the pile of firewood and the Muslims, then, rescued Muḥammad Ḥanafiyya, ʿAqīl, and twenty thousand Muslim men. The miserable Yazīd ran away and fled to Damascus.

{81} They[53] picked up the princes, and he set up his army. They moved towards their own campsite. By God's predetermined grace, they were granted an opening. The Commander of Believers Muḥammad Ḥanafiyya dreamed of Muḥammad, the Messenger of God, at night; [he] hugged Muḥammad Ḥanafiyya, kissed him, and said, 'This was a predetermined decree. From now, you will always conquer.' He said, 'Call and bring your arm.'[54] He said, 'A blessed arm allowed you to kill forty elephants.' Suddenly, he woke up and sent for someone and gave him all the signs, those given by the Prophet about the hand. That blessed hand was there, he found it and brought it back. And whatever the Prophet mentioned, Muḥammad Ḥanafiyya did. The blessed hand resembled its original shape. He praised God, and fastened his horse's saddle, and said in its ear, 'O horse, we require your help today, with God's help we will break through the troop of Ḥasan and Ḥusayn.'[55] The horse bowed and lowered its head. Muḥammad Ḥanafiyya attacked and greeted God and lunged towards the right and left flanks of the army. He killed many of Yazīd's people, to the extent that blood rose up to his horse's ear, and streams of blood flowed. At that moment, no one was able to beat that army.

[52] c. six kilometres [53] i.e., Muḥammad Ḥanafiyya's associates [54] In the complete story of the Auckland version, GMS-173, it is mentioned as 'arm' (*bāzū*), while in the complete Ganjbakhsh story, it is 'hand' (*panja*). [55] According to the Malay version, also partially indicated in the Ganjbakhsh version 001-1498, Muḥammad Ḥanafiyya lost his hand in the battle, through which the Prophet recommended him to bring it and fastened it to his shoulder. Muḥammad Ḥanafiyya replied, 'O Envoy of God! The family of the Prophet is still in prison, without me being able to free them, because one of my arms has been cut off!' Thereupon the Prophet advised him to have his arm searched for and to fasten it to his shoulder [...]'. See Brakel, *Hikayat Muhammad Hanafiyyah*, 75. However, our translation of Muḥammad Ḥanafiyya's dream is based on the complete story of Auckland and Ganjbakhsh manuscripts.

{۸۲} چه ببیند که علم‌های سبز و سرخ، سفید و زرد و سیاه پیدا شدند. چون یزید لعین آن لشگر بدید زَهره، او تنگ شد و طاقت آن لشگر نیاورد. محمّد حنفیّه رضی الله عنه چون شیر شیران در میدان درآمد. لشگر یزید چون رمه، گوسفندان [...] بود. یزید لعین چون لشگر منصور بدید بگریخت، که لشگر محمّد حنفیّه رضی الله عنه در عقب لشگر یزید درآمدند، و محمّد حنفیّه منادی فرمود که «هر که از یزیدیان بیابد بکشد و زنده نگذارد. هرکدام از یزیدیان در مسجد در آید او را رها کنید». محمّد حنفیّه همه را بگذاشت به دنبال یزید؛ یزید بگریخته در قصر آمد. چون محمّد حنفیّه را دید از اسب فرود آمد و در طشت‌خانه درآمد و میان پلیدی غوطه خورد. محمّد حنفیّه رضی الله عنه فرمود تا آتش گردانند. و بعضی گویند که سنگ[۲۰۵] سیاه شد گردبگرد[۲۰۶] کوه قاف بگردد تا روز قیامت نَشُسته[۲۰۷] خواهد بود.

{۸۳} بعداز آن فتح شد و علی اصغر در دمشق و امام زین العابدین را شام به خلافت نشانید و خود به سلامت و سعادت در شهر بامیان بازگشت.

{۸۴} إلٰهِيّ، به حرمت حسن و رضای حسین، شهید دشت کربلا، و به حرمت این شهیدان که به دوستی خاندان نبوّت جان و تن در باخته‌اند ثواب ایشان منِ بیچاره را با جمیع مؤمنان روزی گردانی. به حقّ محمّد وآله أجْمَعین. بمِنَّه وفَضْله وکَرمه. تمّت تمام شد.

[۲۰۵] سگ؟ [۲۰۶] گرداگرد. [۲۰۷] بعید می‌دانم که به‌صورت «نَشِسته» خوانده شود.

{82} They[56] noticed that the green and red, white and yellow and black flags appeared. When the accursed Yazīd noticed this, he was frightened and could not confront that army. Muḥammad Ḥanafiyya entered in like a brave lion. The army of Yazīd like the flock of sheep [...]. When the accursed Yazīd found their army victorious, he fled. And the army of Muḥammad Ḥanafiyya pursued the army of Yazīd. Muḥammad Ḥanafiyya announced, 'Kill whoever you find from the people of Yazīd – do not spare anyone! But leave those who take refuge in mosques.' Muḥammad Ḥanafiyya left all his people and went after Yazīd. Yazīd fled to the palace. When he saw Muḥammad Ḥanafiyya, he got off his horse and hid in the toilet, becoming covered in filth. Muḥammad Ḥanafiyya ordered a fire to be lit [around him], and some say that Yazīd became like a black stone and would run around the mountain of Qāf,[57] and be unclean until the Day of Judgement.

{83} Then they were conquered and Muḥammad Ḥanafiyya appointed as rulers ʿAlī Aṣghar in Damascus and Imam Zayn al-ʿĀbidīn in Sham. And he himself returned safely to the city of Bamyan.

{84} *O God, by the honor of Ḥasan and by the acquiescence of Ḥusayn, the martyr of Karbala; and by the dignity of these martyrs who lost their souls and bodies for the love of the Prophet's descendants; may You provision for me, the poor, and all believers, their rewards; by Muḥammad, his whole family, and by Your unmerited virtue, favour, and kindness. Amen.*

[56] i.e., the soldiers of Yazīd

[57] or: perhaps, he became part of the mountain of Qāf.

حکایتِ سلطان ابوسعید ابوالخیر
که حقّ مرید بر پیر[1] چیست و حقّ پیر بر مرید چیست

{۱} آورده‌اند که سلطان ابوسعید را در مرتبهٔ کودکی به دبیرستان[2] فرستادند. تا روزی درویشی به دبیرستان درآمد، و کُنجی گرفته خرقهٔ خود کشیده پیوند می‌زد. نظر سلطان بر آن درویش افتاد و دید که بر سر درویش آفتاب می‌تابد. سلطان ابوسعید تخته در کنار داشت با آن تخته بر سر درویش سایه بکرد. درویش نظر بالا بکرد و دید که کودکی با تخته سایه کرده ایستاده است. دل درویش خوش شد و گفت «ای کودک، درین خرقه دو بخیه به نام تو می‌زنم. یکی از بهر دولت این جهان و دوم از برای سعادت آن جهان». و هر روز سلطان ابوسعید ابوالخیر را هم در کودکی کار به نظام می‌شد و روز به روز زیادت می‌شد؛ به جایی رسید که محل پای-در-رکاب-نهادیِ بارگاهِ آن از سُندُس[3] نصب می‌کردند و طناب‌های ابریشمین و میخ‌های زرّین بودی.
{۲} تا روزی شخصی از سلطان پرسید «پدر تو بوالخیر هزار دینار زر از من قرض گرفته بود. او از جهان وفات یافت و حقّ من در گردن پدر تو مانده است. و تو امروز به جاه و دولت رسیده‌ای، قرض پدر خود از گردن فرو دار». سلطان ابوسعید گفت «از قرض پدر من هم خبر دارم که پدر من گرفته بود. امّا چند روز مهلت بده تا از وجه فتوح[4] غیب ادا کنم». آن مرد سلطان را مهلت بداد و خود بازگشت.

[1] کلمه «پیر» در ادبیات صوفیانه به عنوان «مرشد» معنی می‌شود. این نکته قابل ذکر است که بنابر کتب لغت ترکی عثمانی «مرشد» معادل رایجی بوده که توسط ترک‌زبانان برای ترجمهٔ «پیر» استفاده می‌شده است. برای اطّلاعات بیشتر به برگ ۲، از Cod. Pers. 309 در کتابخانهٔ باوریا شهر مونیخ رجوع نمایید. این نسخه یک فرهنگ لغت و قواعد «صرفیه» فارسی-ترکی عثمانی است «فارسیده کلمه اوانده کلن با اکثر تعدیه ایچوندی». [2] مکتب. [3] پارچهٔ ابریشمی زربافت. [4] صندوق مالی ویژهٔ دراویش.

CHAPTER 32

The story of our sovereign-master Abu Saʿīd Abū al-Khayr

regarding the right of the disciple upon the spiritual master, and the right of the spiritual master upon the disciple

{1} It is reported that Sultan Abū Saʿīd Abū al-Khayr was sent to school in his childhood. A dervish came to the school one day and sat in a corner and began to sew his cloak. Sultan saw the dervish and that the Sun was shining on his head. Sultan Abū Saʿīd made a sunshade by placing a wooden board over his head. The dervish looked up and saw that a child had made a shadow by means of a wooden board. This made the dervish happy and he said, 'O child, while sewing this cloak, I shall dedicate two of its knots to you; one for the sake of blessings in this world, and the second for felicity in the other world.' From then on, Sultan Abū Saʿīd Abū al-Khayr's affairs went smoothly throughout his childhood and his circumstances improved day after day. He flourished to the extent that the stirrup of his horse, where he put his foot, was covered in silky golden fabric, the reins were made of silks, and the nails [in the horse's hooves] of gold.

{2} One day a man came to Sultan and said, 'Abū al-Khayr, your father had borrowed one thousand dinars from me. He died and he did not return it. And you now have high status and wealth, so you must pay your father's debt.' Sultan Abū Saʿīd said, 'I am aware of my father's debt. But give me a few days so I can repay it from the special dervish treasury.' The man then gave him a deadline, and retreated.

{۳} اهل سلطان چهل مرید بودند و در صفّه نشسته و هریک مرید در پایان صفّه نگاه‌بانی نعلین مردمان کردی. بعداز چند روز نظر سلطان بر آن مرید افتاد و او را به نزدیک خود طلبید و گفت «درغزنی برو» . به‌مجرّدی که از زبان پیر این سخن [...] هم زاد و هم راحله نطلبید و نگفت که «به چه کار می‌فرستی»؛ در ساعت خدمت بکرد، روی به غزنی نهاد و بعداز چند روز آن مرید به غزنی رسید.

{۴} و در خاطر آن مرد گذشت که «من روزی از زبان پیر خود شنیده بودم که چون مردم قصد شهری کند به شب در نیاید». این فکر بکرد و پیش دروازه غزنی بخفت. هم در آن شب سلطان محمود غزنی را به خواب نمودند که «مردی از مریدان سلطان ابوسعید برتو آمده است و او را دریاب». سلطان محمود از خواب بیدار گشت و نزدیکان خود را فرمود که «به سوی دروازه بروید و آینده‌ای[۵] از پیش سلطان ابوسعید آمده است؛ او را پیش من آرید» .

{۵} کسان پیش دروازه آمدند و دیدند که مردی نزدیک دروازه خفته است. او را از خواب بیدار کردند و پیش سلطان محمود آوردند. سلطان پرسید که «تو کیستی؟» گفت «من یکی از مریدان سلطان ابوسعید ابوالخیرم». سلطان گفت «به چه کار آمده‌ای؟» گفت «من هیچ نمی‌دانم که مقصود فرستادن بهر چه کار بود». سلطان محمود خادمان خود را فرمود که «سه روز او را مهمان داری کنید و بعداز سه روز او را پیش من بیارید». همچنان کردند.

{۶} چون سه روز گذشت پیش سلطان بردند. سلطان محمود فرمود که «هزار دینار بیارید و صد دینار زر علی حِدَه[۶] کرده بیارید». کسان سلطان به حکم و فرمان هزار و صد دینار بیاوردند. سلطان گفت «ای مرد، چون به خدمت پیر برسی هزار دینار به ایشان بداری و صد دینار مزدپای[۷] توست. این صد دینار بگیر و در میان بربند و به سوی پیر خود باز گرد».

{۷} آن مرد چنان کرد و رُخ به شهر خود نهاد. تا روزی در اثنای راه در نظر او کوهی نمود. و چون در آن کوه برنشست. و فرود آن کوه شهرستانی دید که در آن میوه‌های گوناگون و چشمه‌ها و شتران و گوسفندان می‌چرند. و پیشتر شد و قصری بدید به غایت بی نظیر و در بالای آن قصر دختر جهودی با جمال بر دریچه نشسته. به‌مجرّدی که نظر درویش به آن دختر افتاد شیفتهٔ وصال او شد. تا وقت شام در پیش قصر چشم درهوا مانده بود، و هر بار که دختر نظر بر وی کردی دیدی که مردی دو چشم به قصر او نهاده و نظارهٔ جمال او می‌کند.

{۸} دریافت که این مرد عاشق جمال او گشته و دایهٔ خود را طلب کرد و گفت «این مرد که به سوی من نگاه کرده، ایستاده است، به نزدیک او برو و بگو که «مقصود چه داری که زیر قصر ایستاده‌ای؟» اگر او بگوید که «من عاشق اویم پس او را بگو که «هرکه خواهد که با این دختر نزدیکی کند هزار دینار زر بدهد، و اگر صحبت کند شکرانهٔ آن صد دینار درمیان آرد»».

[۵] کسی که از جایی بیاید. [۶] جداگانه. [۷] احتمالا اشاره به پای‌مزد به معنای «مزد» است. به فرهنگ معین مراجعه شود.

{3} The Sultan's entourage numbered forty; they sat in a chamber, and were all his disciples. One, at the end of the chamber, was guarding people's sandals [that they removed upon entering the chamber]. After a few days, Sultan looked at the disciple, telling him to go to Ghaznī. As soon as he heard this from his *pīr*[1], he obeyed and went towards Ghaznī, without even asking for provisions, nor did he ask the reason. He arrived in Ghaznī a few days later.

{4} The man pondered, 'I heard from my *pīr* one day that if people are going to visit a city, they must not enter at night.' With this teaching in mind he slept behind the gate of the city of Ghaznī. The same night, Sultan Maḥmūd of Ghaznī was sent a message in his dream , 'A disciple of Sultan Abū Saʿīd has come to you, and you should find him.' Sultan Maḥmūd woke up and told his courtiers, 'Go to the gate and bring the emissary of Sultan Bū Saʿīd to me.'

{5} The courtiers went to the gate and noticed that a man was sleeping nearby. They woke him and took him to Sultan Maḥmūd. Sultan Maḥmūd asked, 'Who are you?' He replied, 'I am one of the disciples of Sultan Abū Saʿīd Abū al-Khayr.' Sultan Maḥmūd said, 'Why have you come here?' He said, 'I actually do not know the reason for coming here!' Sultan Maḥmūd asked his servants to host him for three days, and added, 'Bring him to me after three days.' They did so.

{6} After the third day, they brought him to Sultan Maḥmūd. He said, 'Bring 1,000 dinars as well as another 100 golden dinars.' The courtiers of the Sultan brought 1,000 dinars as well as 100 golden dinars, accordingly. Sultan said, 'O man, when you return to the *pīr*, give him 1,000 dinars, and the 100 dinars is your wage; take the 100 dinars and keep them inside your belt and return to your *pīr*.'

{7} The man did so and set off for his own city. On the way he noticed a mountain so he went and sat on it. He saw a small city at the bottom of the mountain in which there were various fruits and springs, and camels and sheep were grazing. He moved a little closer and saw an extremely beautiful palace, on top of it and before a window, a pretty Jewish girl was seated. As soon the dervish saw the girl, he fell in love with her. He stared at her until night. And whenever the girl looked at the man, she noticed that he gazed at the palace and looked at her beauty.

{8} She understood that the man loved her beauty. She summoned her house-maid and said, 'The man that is looking at me, over there. Go and ask him, "What do you want, that you have stayed before the palace?" If he responds, "I love her", then you should tell him, "Whoever wants to lay with this girl, should pay 1,000 dinars, and if he wants only to speak with her, he should offer 100 dinars for that opportunity".'

[1] i.e., spiritual master

{۹} چون دایه بیامد پرسید «چه مطلوب داری که همهٔ روز نظر بالا می کنی؟» گفت «چه کنم که صاحب این قصر دلم را به غارت برده‌است». دایه گفت «اگر مطلوب بستر او داری هزار دینار زر بده، و اگر می‌خواهی که هم‌سخن شَوی صد دینار بده تا میسّر گردد». آن مرد چون این سخن از دایه شنید خوش‌دل شد و هزار دینار که در کمر داشت پیش آورد. آن‌گه صد دینار خود را بگشاد و پیش دایه نهاد و گفت «هزار دینار او را بده و صد دینار شکرانهٔ تو که مرا بدین مژده بشارت دادی».

{۱۰} دایه در قصر درآمد. هزار دینار پیش دختر نهاد و صد دینار را هم در نظر دختر نهاد. پس دایه را گفت که «عیش‌گاه بیارآی و او را بالای قصر بیار». دایه خواب‌گاه و اسبابِ عیش موجود کرد، و نزد آن جوان آمد و او را بالای قصر برآورد.

{۱۱} بعداز زمانی در پس او بغلطید و جوان را کنار گرفت و خواست دست بر ابزار بند او زند و با وی جمیع آید. في الحال دیوار قصر از میان دوپاره شد. دستی پدید آمد و در رخسارهٔ آن مرد طپانچه بزد که هر دوتن از هیبت آن طپانچه بیهوش شدند. بعداز آن که بهوش آمد در خاطر آن مرد گذشت که «اگر جان از بهر چنین دل‌ربایی برود، گو برود». و دیگر بار کنارش گرفت، و خواست تا دست بر بند اِزار بیندازد که جمع شود. بار دیگر دیوار بشکافت و دستی پدید آمد و بار دوم بر رخسارهٔ او طپانچه بزد.

{۱۲} دختر از هیبت آن از کنارش برجست و گفت «زود بگوی که دین تو کدام است؟» او گفت «دین مسلمانی دارم، و پیر من سلطان ابوسعید ابوالخیراست». دختر گفت «پیر تو حاضر است که تو را از کار بدِ ناشایسته باز می‌دارد». آن‌گه دختر دایه را گفت «هزار دینار با صد دینار خود بیاور». دایه بیاورد. و دختر گفت «این زرهای خود را بر میان بند و رو به شهر پیرخود گیر که مرا نیز ولایتِ او سرگردانیده. دلم به این شارستان[۸] قرار نمی گیرد».

{۱۳} القصّه. مرد زر برداشت و روی به راه کرد. چون به خدمت سلطان رسید هزار دینار را با صد دینار پیش پیر نهاد، و چهل مریدِ اهل صفّه این درویش را تحسین کردند. و سلطان جانب روی مرید و دینار می‌دید و تبسّم می‌کرد. این مرید را طاقت نماند، خدمت کرد[۹] و استاده شد و گفت «ای خواجه، یک سؤال دارم». خواجه گفت «بگو چه سؤال داری» [گفت] «مرا معلوم نیست که حقّ پیر بر مرید چیست و حقّ مرید بر پیر چیست؟» سلطان فرمود «حقّ ما بر تو این بود که تو را به غزنی فرستادیم. تو هیچ نگفتی و زاد و راحله طلب نکردی. و حقّ تو بر ما این بود که تو را از کار ناشایست باز آوریم و دو طپانچه از بهر ادب بزدیم». چون این معنی از زبان پیر شنید سر شرمندگی فرو انداخت.

[۸] ولایت و شهرستان. [۹] شاید «خدمت کردن» اشاره به «تعظیم کردن» داشته باشد. به فرهنگ خداپرستی رجوع شود.

{9} The housemaid went and asked, 'What do you want, as you've looked at the palace all the day?' He said, 'I cannot help it for the mistress of this palace has stolen my heart!' The housemaid said, 'If you want to lay with her, you should offer 1,000 dinars and if you want only to speak with her [and have good moments] you should then offer 100 dinars.' When the man heard this from the housemaid, he became excited and brought out the 1,000 dinars from his belt. Then he took out his own 100 dinars and passed it on to the housemaid. He told her, 'Give her these 1,000 dinars and take the 100 dinars for yourself, as you brought this good news!'

{10} The housemaid returned to the palace. She put one thousand dinars before the girl and also showed her the 100 dinars. The girl asked of the housemaid, 'Prepare and beautify the bed and bring him to the palace.' The housemaid made the bed and prepared everything for the purposes of pleasure, then went to the young man and took him to the palace.

{11} After a while the girl lay next to the young man, embraced him, and was about to open his belt when the palace's wall collapsed. A hand emerged and slapped the face of that man. As they were scared, they both fainted. When the man came round, he thought, 'If I am going to die for the sake of such a temptress then let it be!' and he hugged her again and tried to take off his belt himself in order to have his way with her. The wall collapsed further, and a hand emerged once more and slapped his face again.

{12} Witnessing the scene, the girl jumped up from the man and asked, 'come on, tell me your religion!' He said, 'I am a Muslim. And my *pīr* is Sultan Abū Saʿīd Abū al-Khayr.' The girl said, 'Your *pīr* is present here, and he wants to prevent you from an unlawful deed.' Then the girl said to her housemaid, 'Bring those 1,000 dinars with your own 100.' The housemaid brought them. And the girl said, 'Take your own golden coins in your belt and go back to your *pīr*'s city, as I am also a follower of his sainthood. My heart will not be settled in this town anymore.'

{13} Returning to the story. The man took the coins and began his journey. When he arrived before Sultan Abū Saʿīd, he gave him the 1,000 dinars as well as the other 100 dinars and all forty disciples of the chamber applauded him. Sultan Abū Saʿīd was looking at the disciple as well as the dinars, and he smiled. The man could bear the tension no longer. He bowed and politely said, 'O Khʷāja, I have a question.' Khʷāja said, 'Tell me, what is your question.' The man said, 'It is not yet clear to me what is the right of the *pīr* upon his disciple and what is the right of the disciple upon the *pīr*?' Sultan replied, 'Our demand upon you was to send you to Ghaznī. You did not ask any questions and did not demand any provision for the journey. And your right was about our duty; to abstain from sin. To prevent you from committing sin, your face was slapped twice for the sake of *adab*.' When he heard the insinuation of the *pīr*, he hung head in shame.

{۱۴} باز سلطان فرمود «خاطر جمع‌دار[۱۰] که آن زن را از خدای عَزَّوَجَلَّ درخواستیم که از کفر به اسلام بازآید. امّا آن قصر و باغ و شتران و گوسفندان که دیدی همه را می‌فروشد تا شکرانهٔ ایمان خویش در راه خدای تَعَالَی دربازد، و به من ارادت آرد. و من او را به نکاحِ زنی به تو خواهم داد».

{۱۵} چون مرید این شنید خوش‌دل و خندان شد. بعداز چند روز دیدند که دختر به خدمت سلطان رسید و به شرف ایمان مشرّف شد. و تمام اسباب که آورده بودند همه را در راه حق سُبْحَانَهُ وَتَعَالَى داد و ارادت به سلطان گفت. و سلطان به نکاحِ او را به همان درویش بداد. و حضرت سلطان عقدِ ایشان بخواند و تسلیمِ مرید بکرد.

{۱۶} چون شب شد هر دو یک‌جا خُفتیدند. و چون روز شد دیدند که هر دو جان به حق سُبْحَانَهُ وَتَعَالَى سپردند. و خبر به سلطان ابوسعید رسانیدند. سلطان فرمودند که «هر دو را پیش روضهٔ من دفن کنند که هر که به زیارت من آید اوّل زیارت ایشان کنند، بعداز آن زیارت من کنند».

{۱۷} پس مرید را باید که اعتماد کلّی بر پیر خود بندد، و پیر را شاید که در کدورت[۱۱] مرید چنان صیقل دهد که مصفّا شود. امّا اگر در پیر کدورت باشد، مرید هرگز صفا نیابد و شرمندهٔ حضرت مولی شود.

{۱۸} إِلٰهِيّ، جملهٔ پیران را در راه راست مستقیم دار، و جملهٔ مریدان را به مراد دینی و دنیایی رسانی. و سؤال منکر و نکیر بر زبان ما جاری گردانی. او [را] با ایمان برانگیزانی و ازسیاه‌رویی در پناه عصمت خویشتن نگاه‌داری. بِمِنَّة وَكَرَمه.

[۱۰] خیال راحت داشتن، نگران نبودن. [۱۱] ناپاکی.

{14} Again, Sultan Abū Saʿīd said, 'Do not worry, because we asked God to convert that woman from infidelity to Islam. As a consequence, she is selling the palace, garden, camels, and sheep that you saw, for the sake of God and to bless her faith. And she will become my loyal disciple. And I will marry her to you, as your wife.'

{15} The disciple was so happy upon hearing this. After a few days the girl came before Sultan and converted to the faith, and he saw whatever provisions and supplies she had placed in the path of God to become the Sultan's loyal disciple. And Sultan married her to that dervish, and His Excellency the Sultan, himself, conducted their contract of matrimony, and gave the girl to the disciple.

{16} That night they both slept in one bed. In the morning, the people noticed that they had both died. They informed Sultan Abū Saʿīd about this. Sultan said, 'Bury both of them next to my tomb so whoever visits my tomb, will visit their graves first, and then come to visit mine.'

{17} Thus, a disciple should fully trust the *pīr*, and the *pīr* may warn his disciple to purify himself when he is about to transgress. However, if the *pīr* is impure, the disciple can never be purified and will be ashamed in the presence of the Friend.

{18} *O God, guide all* pīrs *on the straight path, and provide all disciples with religious and worldly goals. Help us to answer the questions of Munkar and Nakīr. Raise us faithfully and protect us under Your infallibility from being ashamed. By Your unmerited favour and kindness. [Amen.]*

حکایتِ اهل بهشت

که به دیدار حق سبحانه وتعالی مشرّف خواهند شد و آخرین از امّت محمّد مُصطَفی صلی الله علیه وسلم که از دوزخ بیرون آید

{۱} آورده‌اند که آخرین کسی که از دوزخ بیرون آرند بعداز چهل هزارسال است.[الف] امّا عظمت گنه‌کاران امّت محمّد بشنو. تا آنگاه که او در دوزخ باشد، درین مدّت دیدار خدای تَعَالَی را هیچ پیغمبری، اولیائی و از اهل بهشت نبیند. تا آنکه امّت محمّد در بهشت درنیاید. زهی[۱] کرم و لطف حق سبحانه وتعالی که با این امّت افتاده است. از بهر گناه‌کاری که بعداز چهل هزارسال از دوزخ خواهند کشید[۲] دیدار خود به دیگران نمی نُماید. امّا، زهی[۳] غفلت آدمِ خاکی که قدر خود نمی‌داند که به چه سبب آفریده شده‌است و مَلك[۴] عَلَّام[۵] با تو چه سرّهایی دارد و تو خود از آن رو می گردانی.

{۲} بیت: مشتاق توام با همه جوری و جفایی، محبوب منی با همه جرمی و خطایی[۶]

[۱] در این‌جا «زهی» از ادات تحسین محسوب می‌شود. [۲] بیرون خواهند کشید. [۳] در این‌جا «زهی» از ادات تاسف محسوب می‌شود. [۴] نامی از نام های خدا. [۵] علیم. [۶] از غزلیّات سعدی. این بیت در تفسیر «حدائق الحقائق، قسمت سورهٔ یوسف» منسوب به معین الدین فراهی هروی از قرن نهم و دهم هجری قمری به‌کار رفته است. شایان ذکر است که، چنانچه پیشتر نشان دادم، این تفسیر در اوایل قرن هفدهم میلادی در آچه-اندونزی به زبان مالایی ترجمه شده است. این نسخه در مجموعهٔ ارپنیوس به شمارهٔ CUL.MS. Dd.5.37 در کتابخانهٔ دانشگاه کیمبریج قرار دارد. مراجعه نمایید به
Majid Daneshgar, 'Translating Persian Tafsir in Aceh: The Oldest Malay "Story of Joseph" at Cambridge

[الف] آورده‌اند که آخرین کسی که از دوزخ بیرون آرند بعداز [هفتاد] هزار سال و به روایتی بعداز سی\چهل هزار سال بیرون آرند

CHAPTER 33

The story of the inhabitants of paradise

who will be blessed with a meeting with God, and the last person from the community of Muḥammad to leave hell

{1} It is reported that the last person will leave hell after forty thousand years.[1] Now hear about the exalted dignity of the sinful community of Muḥammad. As long as one [sinful member of Muḥammad's community] remains in hell, no prophets, saints, or inhabitants of paradise will be able to see a vision of God. Not until the whole community of Muḥammad enters paradise. What a favour and kindness God has bestowed upon this community! He will not show Himself to others for the sake of one sinner who will remain in hell for forty thousand years. The earthly human being, neglected, does not know his dignity: why he has actually been created and of the type of divine secrets the All-Knowing God is aware, and from whom you, yourself, turn away.

{2} Poem: I am keen to visit You with all my maltreatment and oppression;
You are still my beloved despite all sins and failures.[2]

[1] Some manuscripts say 'after seventy thousand years'.

[2] Ascribed to Saʿdī, based on his *ghazaliyyāt*.

{۳} آن گنه‌کار در دوزخ الله تَعَالَی را بدین نام یاد کند «یَا حَنَّان یَا مَنَّان». چون ارادت حقّ سبحانه و تعالی در حقّ او چنین رفته‌است به آخر رسد و بعداز چهل‌هزارسال[ب] باز لطف می‌کند، و آواز ذکر در گوش مهتر جبرئیل علیه السلام می‌رساند. جبرئیل گوید که «إِلٰهِيّ، یکی از بندگان امّت محمّد ﷺ[ج] توست که در دوزخ مانده‌است او را به من ببخش، زیرا که من خادم اهل نبوّتم تا یکی از محمّدیان را دستگیر باشم». فرمان شود که «او را به تو بخشیدم. برو او را از دوزخ بیرون آر».

{۴} جبرئیل به حکم و فرمان برلب دوزخ آید. مالک دوزخ[7] را مهتر جبرئیل فرمان حضرت ذوالجلال رساند که «یکی از امّت محمّد علیه السلام در دوزخ مانده‌است، او را بیرون آر». مالک در دوزخ دررود و در وادی‌های دوزخ او را نیابد. بعداز هزارسال مالک به مقام خود آید و بگوید «ای جبرئیل،[د] ازجهت خود هرچند تفحّص کردم و هزارسال در طلب او بودم نیافتم».

{۵} جبرئیل علیه السلام باز زیر عرش آید و مناجات کند که «إِلٰهِيّ، تو می‌دانی که مالک می‌گوید که هزارسال در طلب وی بود و نیافت». جبرئیل را باز فرمان شود که «مالک را بگو که در فلان وادی دوزخ چاهی است و در آن چاه صندوقی و در آن صندوق ماری و در دهان آن مار آسیایی[8] و در میان آسیا آویزان است».

{۶} جبرئیل این فرمان بر مالک باز رساند. مالک در آن وادی در رَود. چاهی بلند و در آن چاه صندوقی نهاده و در میان صندوق ماری[ه] نشسته و در دهن آن مار آسیایی[9] از آتش می‌گردد و او در میان آن آتش می‌سوزد و نام خدای تَعَالَی به زبان می‌راند.

{۷} مالک نزدیک مار شود و بگوید «ای مار، امانتی که از بهر عذاب در تو نهاده‌اند، آن را بیرون افکن،» مار آن بنده را فِي الحال از دهن جدا کند. مالک دست او را بگیرد و بیرون آرد و تسلیم مهتر جبرئیل کرد. مهتر جبرئیل او را گرفته به سوی بهشت روان شد.

{۸} بنده قدری راه رود و از جبرئیل سؤال کند که «ای فرشته خوب‌لقا،[10] مرا کجا می‌بری؟» جبرئیل گوید که «تو را خدای تَعَالَی در بهشت فرستاده است و از دوزخ بیرون آورده». به‌مجرّد شنیدن نام بهشت این بنده غمناک شود و سر فرو اندازد. مهتر جبرئیل نظر بر روی او افکند و از حال او عجب ماند و بگوید «چرا سر فرود کردی و

University Library', *Cambridge University Library Special Collections Blog*: https://specialcollections-blog.lib.cam.ac.uk/?p=26005

[7] فرشته‌ای که اداره‌کنندهٔ امورات دوزخ است. در گذشته گاهی واژهٔ «مالک» به معنای «نگهبان جهنّم» به کار می‌رفته است.

[8] آسیاب. [9] واژهٔ «آسیا» به معنی «خرد کننده» در بسیاری از اشعار فارسی منسوب به فردوسی و ناصرخسرو دیده می‌شود. همچنین به معنای «دندان» به کار می‌رود. [10] «خوب‌لقا» به معنی «خوش‌سیما» و «خوش‌چهره» به کار می‌رود. توصیف چهرهٔ فرشته در این داستان قابل تامّل است.

[ب] چندین هزار سال [ج] یکی از امّتان حبیب تو [د] جبرائیل [ه] مار آتشین

{3} In hell, the sinner remembers God with the retort, 'O All-Loving! O All-Kind!' As God has always paid kind attention to the sinner, [this period] will end after forty thousand years, He will show affection to him; and the sound of their remembrance of God will be heard by Gabriel. Gabriel will say, 'O God, this is one of the sinners from the community of Your Muḥammad who is in hell, forgive him because of me, as I am the servant of the prophetic circle in order to help one of the Muḥammadans.' A divine proclamation will be made: 'I forgave him because of you. Go and bring him out of hell.'

{4} Following the divine command, Gabriel will go to the edge of hell and inform the guardian of hell [an angel known as Mālik] about God's command, 'One of the community of Muḥammad is still in hell, bring him out!' The guardian will search hell but will not find him anywhere. After a thousand years, the guardian will return and say, 'O Gabriel, I investigated thoroughly and searched for him for a thousand years, but I could not find him.'

{5} Gabriel (pbuh) will sit under the Throne and begin to pray, 'O God, You know that the guardian of hell says that he could not find him,[3] after 1,000 years of searching.' Gabriel will again be asked, 'Tell the guardian of hell that there is a well in such-and-such place of hell, inside which is a chest and in that chest there is a snake and in the snake's mouth a fiery mill wheel is rotating; and he is right there

{6} Gabriel passed on this message to the guardian of hell. The guardian went arrived in that region. He noticed a deep well, inside which was a chest and thee was a snake there, and in the snake's mouth a fiery mill wheel is rotating. The servant is burning in the fire, while invoking God.

{7} The guardian went to the snake and commanded, "O snake, throw out the prisoner who has been put in your mouth for the sake of torment!"' The snake soon released the servant from its mouth. The guardian took his hand and brought him out and took him to His Eminence Gabriel. His Eminence Gabriel took him and moved towards heaven.

{8} After taking a few steps, the servant asked Gabriel, 'O beautiful angel, where do you take me?' Gabriel said, 'God is sending you to paradise and taking you from hell.' On hearing the word 'paradise', the servant became sad and hung his head. His Eminence Gabriel looked at him, wonderingly, and asked, 'Why do you hang your head and why are you unhappy after hearing the name of and the good news about paradise?' The servant says, 'O angel, I have a question for you, and if your response pleases me, then I will enter paradise, otherwise, I will have nothing to do with paradise; I prefer to choose hell.'

[3] i.e., the sinful Muḥammadan

از شنیدن نام[د] بهشت شاد نمی‌شوی؟» آن بنده گوید «ای فرشته، مرا نزد تو سؤالیست[11] که اگر جواب آن سبب تسلّی خاطر گردد، از تو بشنوم و در بهشت می‌روم، وگرنه با بهشت مرا کاری نیست؛ همین دوزخ اختیار کردم».

{۹} جبرئیل را از گفتار او عجب آید و بگوید «آن کدام سؤال است که می‌کنی؟» گوید «مرا خبر کن که دیدار حقّ بهشتیان را نصیب شده است یا نه؟ اگر دیدار نور تجلّی برای اهل بهشت نشده است خود مرا ببر، و اگرنه خود مرا بازگردان و با مالک دوزخ بسپار، که مقصود از بهشت دیدار حقّ است. چون نصیب دیگران شده باشد، مرا سوختن بهتر از به بهشت رفتن».

{۱۰} جبرئیل گوید «احسنت! ای امّت بلند همّت محمّد.[ذ] خدای تَعَالَی تو به علم قدیم خود دانست که در این چهل هزارسال از بهر تو دیدار خود به کسی ننموده است. و مهتر موسیٰ دیدار معبود درخواست می‌کند[ح] که فرموده بود « إِلٰهِيّ، من دیدار تو در دنیا درخواست کرده بودم. فرمودی که در دنیای فانی دیدار باقی نتوان دید، چون در بهشت ما برسی آنگه دیدار ما را ببینی. اکنون در بهشت درآوردی. دیدار خود بنمایی که اشتیاق از حدّ گذشته و بی‌طاقت شده است». موسیٰ کلیم الله را با جمیع عاشقان فرمان شود که «صبر کنید که درین حکمت الهی است»».

{۱۱} جبرئیل علیه السلام گوید «امروز حکمت الهی ما معلوم شد. تو ای بنده خاطر خود را جمع دار. آنگه که تو در بهشت درآیی، تجلّی دیدار حقّ به بهشتیان شود». بدین بشارتِ جبرئیل دل آن بنده خوش شود و به‌سوی جنّت روان شود.

{۱۲} باز قدری راه رفته باشد که در خاطر رسید که «چندین هزارسال در دوزخ بودم. بهشتیان در قصرها و منزل‌های بهشت قرار گرفته باشند. بهرِ من مقام کجا مانده باشد؟» همان‌زمانْ فرمان حضرت ربّ العَالمین دررسد که «ای بنده، آنچه در خاطر تو گذشت ازعلم قدیم ما پوشیده نیست. اگر تو را مُلک چهار پادشاه دنیا در بهشت بدهیم از ما خرسند باشی؟» بنده گوید «إِلٰهِيّ، بدین راضی و خرسند گردم». فرمان شود که «ای بنده، در بهشت درآی که ما ده‌چندان مُلک دنیا بدهیم».

{۱۳} الغرض. چون آن بنده در بهشت درآید و هیچ گوینده کلمهٔ «لَآ إِلٰهَ إِلَّا اللهُ، مُحَمَّدٌ رَسُولُ اللهِ»[12] در دوزخ نماند مگر کافران، آن‌گاه فرمان شود که بهشت را سرپوش کنند. و مقنعهٔ نور الهی به بهشت درکشند.[ط] بعداز آن فرمان شود که «ای فرشتگان، سرپوشِ طبق[13] عذاب بر روی دوزخ مُهر کنند». هر هفت دوزخ را باد دَرکات[14] در لرزه افتد و امید کفّار از بهشت بریده شود. و بداند که مقام جاوید ما همین است.

[11] سؤالی است. [12] هیچ مسلمانی. [13] پوشش و ظرف بزرگ.
[14] به معنی «منازل دوزخ» که در مقابل کلمه «درجات» به معنی «مراتب بهشت» به کار می‌رود.

[د] مژده \ بشارت [ذ] احسنت احسنت ای امّت بلند همّت [ح] مهتر موسیٰ و دیگر پیغمبران و اولیایان درخواست می‌کنند [ط] مقنعه‌ای از نور الهی در بهشت کشیده شود

{9} Gabriel will be surprised and will say, 'What is the question you have?' He will say, 'Tell me whether or not God's vision has been granted to the inhabitants of paradise? If God's theophanic manifestation has not yet been granted to the people of paradise, then you may take me in, otherwise, you, yourself, must send me back and pass me on to the guardian of hell, as the purpose of being in paradise is only for a vision of God. If it has already been granted to others, burning is much better for me than going to paradise.'

{10} Gabriel will say, 'Bravo! O determined community of Muḥammad! Your God, based on His eternal knowledge, has not granted His vision to anyone else in these forty thousand years, just because of you.' And His Eminence Moses will ask for God's vision, saying, 'O God, I had requested Your vision in the world. You said, "The everlasting vision cannot happen in the temporary world, once you enter Our paradise, then you will visit Us." [Moses will continue,] 'Now You have brought me to paradise, manifest Yourself, as I cannot wait anymore.' Moses, with whom God spoke, as well as other believers, will be commanded, 'Be patient, as there is a divine wisdom behind this."'

{11} Gabriel (pbuh) will arrive to say, 'Today the divine wisdom will be manifest. You, O servant, worry not. As soon as you enter paradise, God's theophanic manifestation will be possible for the people of paradise.' The servant will be happy on account of the good news brought by Gabriel and will move towards paradise.

{12} Again, after a while, he will reflect, 'As I have been a thousand years in hell, the people in paradise will already be placed in heavenly palaces and houses. Where, then, should my place be?!' A proclamation from the Lord of the Worlds will be made, 'O servant, what has come into your mind is not hidden from Our eternal knowledge. Will you be happy with Us if we grant you a kingdom as large as the kingdom of four kings on Earth?' The servant will say, 'O God, I will be happy and satisfied!' A divine command will be given, 'O servant, go to paradise as We give you ten times more than the worldly kingdom.'

{13} To return to the story. When the servant arrived in paradise, and no one remained in hell from the people who used to say, 'There is no god, but God; Muḥammad is the Messenger of God'[4], except the infidels, then a command will be given to fully cover paradise, and illuminate it with divine light. Another command will also be given, 'O angels, seal hell with a seal made of torment.' A tornado will shake all the seven layers of hell and the infidels will be disappointed to not be in paradise, and they will know that they are in their permanent abode.

[4] i.e., the Muslims

{۱۴} آنگه فرمان شود «ای فرشتگان، اکنون تحفه‌ها از حضرت ما برگیرید و برای بندگان ما برید». بر دست هر فرشته طَبَقی بدهند و در آن طبق سیبی باشد و بر قصرها رسند. و ایستاده شوند و از نگهبانان قصر پرسند که «مالک بهشت به چه مشغول است؟» جواب گویند که «درعیش نعیمِ ما حوران به فراغت گشته‌اند».[ی]

{۱۵} فرشتگان بازگردند و بگویند «الهی، نگهبانان بهشت چنین می گویند». فرمان شود «بر درِ بندگان ما باشید تا وقتی باز شود. چون شما را بخوانند آنگاه تحفهٔ حضرت عزّت ما را پیش دارید». به‌موجبِ فرموده فرشتگان بر در قصرهای بهشت باشند. چندان که نگهبانان از روی ایشان شرمنده شوند و نزد خادمان آیند و گویند «مدّت چهل‌هزارسال برآمد که فرشتگان از پیش حضرت حق سُبْحَانَهُ وَتَعَالَىٰ تحفه‌ها بر دست گرفته بر دَرْ استاده‌اند. خادمان نزد غِلمان شوند و بگویند که فرشته از نزد باری تَعَالَى عَزَّوَجَلَّ تحفه بر دست گرفته استاده‌اند. و غِلمانِ وِلْدَانٌ[۱۵] را خبر کنند، و وِلْدَانٌ حوران را خبر دهند و حوران نزد سیّدهٔ زن دنیا شوند و گویند که «فرشته‌ای با تحفه‌ای از پروردگار گرفته استاده است». سیّده گوید «ای ملک اهل بهشت، فرشتگان به حکم خدای تَعَالَى مدّت چهل [هزار] سال است که تحفه بر دست گرفته استاده‌اند»».

{۱۶} به‌موجبِ فرموده این تحفه را بر دست استاده آورند. چون فرشتگان نزدیک رسند، تحفه‌ای که از خدای عَزَّوَجَلَّ آورده باشند آن را پیش دارند؛ و مالک سرپوشِ طبق باز کند. در میان آن سیبی بیند. آن سیب را بوی کند.[ک] مشام او معطّر کند.[ل] و فرحی در وجود او پیدا گردد و با خود گوید که در بوی کردن سیب چندین فرحی در من رسید، تا در خوردن این چه لذّت باشد .آن سیب را دو پاره کند. حوری از آن سیب پیدا گردد. دگر هرگز مثل آن حوری ندیده باشد. طاقت نماند، دست جانب او دراز کند. آن حور گوید «شتاب مکن؛ من ازآنِ توام. امّا این نوشته را که حضرت ربّ غفور به تو آورده مطالعه کن».

{۱۷} حور پاره حریری بر او بدهد. بنده آن را گرفته مطالعه کند. در سطر اوّل نوشته اند که «هذا المکتوب إِلَى المَلِكِ الحَيِّ الَّذِي لايَمُوت، این نوشته است از ملکی که او را مرگ روا نی». و در سطر دوم نوشته پیدا گردد که «وَمِنَ المَلِكِ الحَيِّ الَّذِي لا يَزُوُلُ مُلكِه وَإِلَى المَلِكِ الَّذِي لا يَزُوُلُ بمُلكِه،[۱۶] این نوشته‌است از ملکی که ملک او را زوال نه، و به سوی ملکی که ملک او را زوال نه». و در سطر سوم نوشته پیدا گردد که «یا

[۱۵] این قسمت مرتبط با بخش‌هایی از سورهٔ طور (آیات ۲۳ تا ۲۵) و سورهٔ انسان (آیهٔ ۱۹) می‌باشد. همچنین، قرار گرفتن اسامی غلمان و ولدان و حوران در برخی کتب عربی و فارسی داستانی و روایی دیده می‌شود. برخی از بخش‌های این داستان در مورد مشغول بودن بندگان با\\به فرشتگان و نعمات بهشتی در کتاب «المجالس» عثمان بن حسن بن احمد الخویوي دیده می‌شود. این کتاب با عنوان «درّة الناصحین في الوعظ والإرشاد» و یا «درة الواعظین في تفسیر آیات وأحادیث تحفة الواعظین» در هند منتشر شد. در شهر آستانه نیز به عنوان «مجالس» و در مطبعة میمنه شهر مکّه با عنوان «درّة الناصحین» منتشر شده است. این واژه را به دلیل موزون بودن با تنوین و به شکل «وِلْدَانٌ» به‌کار برده‌ام.

[۱۶] برخی از این اذکار در شرحهای «سِفر دانیال» ذکر شده است.

[ی] جواب گویند که در عیش و نعیم با خود مشغول است

[ک] آن سیب را بر دست گیرد و بوی کند

[ل] چنان بوی از سیب جدا گردد که مشام او را معطّر کند

{14} Then a command will be given, 'O angels, now take gems and gifts from Us and pass them on to the servants.' A tray will be given to every single angel on top of which there will be an apple and they will reach the palaces and ready to serve. And they will ask the guards of paradise, 'What are the dwellers of paradise doing?' In response it will be said, 'Being pleased with Our blissful paradise, they are enjoying the cherubs.'

{15} The angels will return and tell God how the guards of paradise responded, and will add, 'When they needed You, You put before them gifts from us.' As such, the angels will go toward the heavenly palaces. Ultimately, the guards will feel embarrassed and will come to the servants in paradise and they will say, 'It has been for forty thousand years that these angels have waited to bestow God's gifts!' The servants will go to the handsome lads dwelling in paradise and will say, 'Angels have come bearing God's gifts.' The handsome lads will inform the eternal youths[5] and the eternal youths will inform the cherubs and the cherubs will approach the Lady of the World and tell her, 'Angels with gifts from God stayed there.' The Lady will say, 'O residents of paradise, the angels, following God's decree, have gifts for which they have waited forty [thousand] years.'

{16} Upon hearing this [from the Lady], they will begin to bring the gifts. When the angels arrive, they will present the gifts given by God; the tray's cover will be removed by the custodian of the palace. An apple will lie there. The custodian will smell the apple and it will have a fine scent. Joy will fill his body and he will say to himself, 'Just smelling it makes me joyful, let alone how enjoyable it would be to eat it.' The custodian will cut the apple in half. A cherub will emerge from it: no one will have seen a cherub like this before. With unbearable longing, the custodian will try to reach the cherub but the cherub will say, 'Do not rush! I belong to you, but first read the letter sent by the Forgiver Lord.'

{17} The cherub will give a piece of silk to the custodian of the palace. The servant will begin to read it. The first written line will say, 'This is from a living God who is undying.' The second line, 'From a living God whose kingdom will not decay and to a living God whose kingdom will not decay.'[6] In the third line, 'O my servant, you have been so busy with cherubs and palaces that you have not remembered Us, indeed, I look forward to visiting you',[7] meaning, 'You have been so occupied with cherubs and palaces, you have forgotten Us. Are you one of the forgetful?'[God will ask,] 'Did We not fulfil whatever We promised to you?' The servants say, 'That promise was fulfilled through Your kindness.' Then the servants will say to God, 'O God, You granted us

[5] This part is related to Q. 52:23–25, Q. 76:19. [6] Such invocations and notes are also found in commentary on the Book of Daniel. [7] This is also found in the commentaries on al-Kalābādhī's *al-Taʿāruf li-Madhhab Ahl al-Taṣawwuf*.

عَبدي إشتَغلَّتَ بالحُورِ والقُصُورِ ونَسِيت لِقَاءَنَا فأنِّي مُشتَاقٌ إلَى لِقَائك،[۱۷] یعنی: ای بنده، چنان مشغول گشتی در حور و قصور که از ما یاد هم نمی‌کنی مگر فراموش کنندگان دیرینه‌اید شما»؛ «امّا هر وعده که به شما کرده بودیم وفا شد یا نه؟» بندگان گویند «آن وعده به کرم تو وفا شد». آن‌گه هر وعده [؟] به حضرت ذوالجلال عرض دارند «إلٰهِيّ، در دنیا همانا رزق ما دادی، اگر گناه کردیم. چون به آخر رسیدی ملك‌الموت قصد جان کرد و ملعونِ شیطان چنگ در ایمان زد. در آن وقت در کار خود حیران گشتیم. فرمان فرستادی که «ای فرشتهٔ قابض ارواح، جان بندهٔ ما را به‌سختی نَسْتانی و از شیطان مردود در حفظ و امان خود نگاه داشتی». و چون در گور دفن کردند سؤال منکر و نکیر بر ما آسان کردی، و گور که مقام[۱۸] تنگ و تاریک است فرمودی تا روضهٔ رضوان کنند. چون سر از نقاب تُراب[۱۹] برگیریم از هول قیامت در زیر عرش جای ما کردی، و چون نامه‌های کردار ما گران گشت فرمودی تا نامه به دست راست ما دادند و بگویند «بنشینید و نخوانید».

{۱۸} و چون وقت گذشتن پل صراط شد، سی‌هزار سال راه از موی باریک تر و از تیغ تیزتر، به لطف خود آسان کردی و در بهشت درآوردی و حیات ابدی دادی که آن را سیری نباشد، و تندرستی دادی که آن را هرگز بیمارگی نباشد،[۴] و ملک ابدِ آبادْ روزی گردانیدی. کنون ما را در حضرت تو چه وعده‌ها مانده است؟»

{۱۹} فرمان شود که «بزرگترین وعده‌ها هنوز باقی مانده‌است». مؤمنان گویند «یا رَبّ، آن کدام وعده است؟» فرمان رسید که «وعدهٔ دیدار خود در دنیا به شما کرده بودم که به شما روزی خواهم کرد. اکنون آن وعده را وفا کنم». چون بندگان این مژدهٔ پروردگار خود بشنوند جمله عیشِ بهشت را ترک دهند و از قصرها بیرون آیند.

{۲۰} و حضرت داود پیغمبر ﷺ را فرمان شود که «نغمهٔ داودی[۲۰] خویش برگیرد و امّت محمّد رسول الله ﷺ با تو نغمه درآیند». هریکی را همچون مهتر داود الحان بَرکَشَنْد، و هریکی را جمالِ یوسف ﷺ دهند تا همه حمد و ثنای حق سبحانه وتعالی عزّوجلّ گویند و مشتاق شوق رحمان از قصرها بیرون آیند.

{۲۱} و از غلغلهٔ شوقِ محمّدیانْ جملهٔ در و دیوارِ بهشت و انهار و اشجار در نوای الحان درآیند تا مؤمنان به «دارالجلال»[۲۱] برسند. حق سبحانه وتعالی مقامی در بهشت آفریده است که آن را «دارالجلال» گویند و هفتادهزار سال راه مسافتِ اوست. جمله مؤمنان در آن مقام جمیع شوند و به دیدار حق سبحانه وتعالی عزّوجلّ مشرّف گشتند. آن‌گه فرمان شود که «ای فرشتگان، جام شراب برگیرید و ایشان را بخورانید. چندان شراب خوردند که فرشتگان از خادمی

[۱۷] در شرح «التعرف لمذهب التصوف» نیز آمده است. همچنین بخشی از آن در «درّة الناصحین» و «حدائق الحقائق، قسمت سورهٔ یوسف» آمده است. [۱۸] مکان و جایگاه. [۱۹] خاک قبر. [۲۰] الحان داودی. همچنین با عنوان «حلق داودی» شناخته می‌شود.

[۲۱] بنابر قول بیضاوی و به استناد روایت ابن عباس «دارالجلال یکی از هشت بهشتی است که تمام بخش‌های آن مملو از نور است: «(إِنَّ لَهُم جَنّاتٌ) أی بان لهم بساتین کثیرة جمع جنة و هی ثمان. قال ابن عباس رضی الله عنه وهی دارالجلال ودار القرار ودار السلام وجنة عدن وجنة المأوی وجنة الفردوس وجنة الخلد وجنة نعیم. قال دار الجلال کلّها من النور مدائنها وقصورها وبیوتها وشرفها وأبوابها ودرجها وغرفها [...]».حسن بن ام سینان، المجالس السینانی. بی م. ۱۸۴۴. ص ۱۶.

[۴] و جوانی دادی که آن را پیری نباشد

provisions in this world, although we committed sins. When we neared the end of our life, and the Angel of Death wanted to take our soul, and the accursed Satan wanted to grab our faith, we felt desperate. You, then, proclaimed, "O the angel who takes the souls, do not take the soul of my servants harshly, and protect my servants [and the soul] from the rejected Satan." And once they put us in the grave, You facilitated the interrogation of Munkar and Nakīr upon us, and You ordered that the grave, a place which is tight and dark, be transformed into a garden of paradise. When we rose from the grave, You protected us under the Throne from fear of the Day of Judgement, and when our record of deeds grew heavier [in terms of sins], You ordered for it to be given to our right hand, saying, "Easy! no need to read it."

{18} And upon crossing the Ṣirāṭ bridge – a thirty-thousand year long road thinner than a strand of hair and sharper than a blade – You made it easy and brought us into paradise, and granted us an immortality in which one will never be jaded, and granted us health, with no pestilence, as well as a prosperous everlasting kingdom! So what could have been left except for us to be fulfilled in Your presence?!'

{19} A proclamation will be made, 'The greatest promises are still coming.' The believers will say, 'O Lord, what are those promises?' It will be proclaimed, 'We had promised you in the world to provide you with Our vision. Now I want to fulfil that promise.' When the servants hear this good news from their God, they will all leave the pleasure of paradise behind and came out of their palaces.

{20} And Prophet David will be ordered 'to sing melodically and this will prompt the community of Muḥammad (pbuh) to start singing with him, too.' Each of them will sing beautiflly like David, and each of them will be given the beauty of Joseph (pbuh), and all will praise and thank God; they will leave their palaces for the sake of the Merciful.

{21} Given the large number of Muḥammadans who will be impatiently excited, all the gates and walls of paradise, as well as rivers and trees, will begin to sing until the believers arrive in the Glorious Abode. God has made a place in paradise called the Glorious Abode,[8] and there is a seventy-thousand year long road to reach there. All believers will gather there and will be awarded with God's vision. Then a command will be given, 'O angels, bring glasses of wine for them to drink.' They will drink wine until the angels become exhausted from all the serving. They will not become drunk and the angels will all be surprised by this. It will be proclaimed, 'O angels, why did you stop, as they will not become drunk, because they are hopeful of Our vision. They will not be drunk until they see Our beauty. Go away, so they can be awarded Our vision and be drunk on that.'

[8] *Dār al-Jalāl*

مانده شوند. از شراب خوردن مست نگردند و فرشته‌ها در حیرت افتند». فرمان شود که «ای فرشته‌ها، چه مانده‌اید که ایشان هرگز مست نگردند، چون امید لطفِ دیدارِ ما برایشان رسید. تا آنکه جمال ما نبینند هرگز مست نشوند. اکنون شما از میان دور شوید تا ایشان به شرف دیدار ما مشرّف و مست گردند».

{۲۲} بعداز آن حقّ سُبْحَانَهُ وَتَعَالَىٰ عَزَّوَجَلَّ با بندگان خود هم سخن شود که «ای دوستانِ حضرت ما، در دنیا وعدهٔ دیدار کرده بودیم، و مکتوب کلام خود ازجهت شما به سوی پیغمبر شما فرستادیم - یعنی قرآن - و در آن وعده بدین رفته بود که «وَسَقَاهُمْ رَبُّهُمْ شَرَابًا طَهُورًا،[۲۲] پس وعده به شما کنم و جام شرابِ به‌غیرِواسطه برآید، و نزدیک لب و دهن همهٔ خلق برسد پروار کنان؛ و هم درآن نوش قدحِ جامِ اوّل غلغلهٔ محبّت به شوق برآرند.

{۲۳} هم درین محلّ ملک المشایخ[۲۳] شیخ سعدی شیرازی فرموده: «قدح چون دور ما باشد به هشیاران مجلس ده، مرا بگذار تا حیران بماند چشم بر ساقی؛ نه حسنت آخری دارد نه سعدی را سخن پایان، بمیرد تشنه مستسقی و دریا همچنان باقی».[۲۴،ن]

{۲۴} آنگاه پردهٔ حجابِ قدرتْ از میان دور شود تا دیدار تجلّی همچون و هیچ‌گونهٔ مولی ببینند. به‌مجرّد آنکه تجلّی دیدار معبود برایشان تابَد تا هشتاد هزارسال مست دواله[۲۵] معبود خود چنان شود که از خویشتن هم یاد نیارند. بعداز هشتاد هزارسال جبرئیل را فرمان شود که ایشان را نداکند تا به بهشت باز گردند. بگویند «إِلٰهِيّ، دیدار خود به ما سیراب نما». فرمان شود «هیچ می‌دانید که دیدارما چه مقدار دیده‌اید؟» گویند «الهی، به قیاس یک روز و یک شب دیده‌ایم». فرمان شود که «به عزّت و جلال ما که هشتادهزار سال برآمده‌است که مست و مدهوش دیدار ما بودید. اکنون به مقام‌های خود باز گردید که جُفتان و حورانِ شما منتظرِ شمایند».

{۲۵} درین باب، افتخار آل طه ویس، سیّد جلال الدین بخاری[۲۶] قَدَّسَ اللّٰه رُوحه العزیز می‌فرمایند: «دریغا جمالش سیری ندیدم، من مست و مدهوش دیوانه بودم؛ نبودم لایق دیدار لیکن، بکرد لطف تو شایان دیدار».[۲۷]

{۲۶} إِلٰهِيّ، به کرم کریمی خویش و احسان قدیم خویش در حقّ من بیچارهٔ شکسته و کاتبِ درآن مجلس را با جمیع مؤمنان گلستان بهشت و دیدار خود کرامت کنی، و به شرف دیدار پاک خود مشرّف گردانی. بِمِنَّةٍ وَكَمَال كَرَمه.

[۲۲] آیهٔ ۲۱ سورهٔ انسان. [۲۳] در برخی نسخ درّالمجالس، سعدی با عنوان «شیخ الشعراء» معرّفی شده است. به مقدّمه رجوع فرمایید. [۲۴] همچنین، بنابر برگ ۱۴۹ نسخهٔ برلین «نه صنعت آخرین دارد نه سعدیرا سخن پایان؛ بمیرد تشنه مستسقی و دریا همچنان باقی». این ابیات براساس دیوان اشعار سعدی است. [۲۵] احتمالا، بنابر دهخدا، به معنی « داروی خوشبوی» به کار می‌رود. به گمانم به معنی «عطر» نیز به کار می‌رود. [۲۶] با این وجود، در بسیاری از نسخ به‌صورت «سید جلال الدین» ذکر شده است. برای توضیحات بیشتر به مقدّمه رجوع نمایید. [۲۷] شبیه بیتی منسوب به امیر خسرو دهلوی است: «دریغا، خیالش به سیری ندیدم؛ که شوریده و مست و دیوانه بودم».

[ن] «قدح چون دور من گردد به هشیاران مجلس ده، مرا بگذار تا حیران بمانم چشم بر ساقی؛ نه حسنت آخری دارد نه سعدی را سخن پایان، بمیرد تشنه مستسقی لب دریای رحمانی».

{22} Then, God will begin to speak with His servants, 'O friends of Our presence, We had already promised you Our vision in the world. And We gave Our word, the Qur'ān, for you from your prophet, in which the promise was, "Their Lord will give them a purifying drink" (Q. 76:21). As such, I fulfil this promise and the glass of wine will come to the lips and mouths of all of you without mediator and instantly; it will be nourishing.' And as soon as they drink the first glass, their sounds of happiness will be heard loudly.

{23} On this subject, the lord of the saints,[9] Shaykh Saʿdī Shīrāzī, states: *If the glass is going to be around us, pass it on to the sober in the party, just leave me alone to gaze at the Captain; Neither Your beauty, nor the speech of Saʿdī will have an end; Ultimately, the thirsty will die thirsty while the ocean is still full.*[10]

{24} Then the veil of power will be removed in order to experience the unique theophanic manifestation: the vision of God. As soon as the theophanic manifestation illuminates them, they will be drunk on the fragrance of their God for eighty thousand years such that they will not remember themselves. After eighty thousand years, Gabriel will be commanded, 'Call them back to paradise.' They would reply, 'O God, saturate us with Your vision.' A command will be given, 'Did you realise how long you have been visiting Us?' They say, 'O God, we visited You as long as a day and a night.' It will be proclaimed, 'By Our glory and dignity, it has been eight thousand years that you have been drunk and engrossed by Our vision. Now get back to your palaces because your mates and cherubs are waiting for you.'

{25} In this regard, the pride of the Prophet, Sayyid Jalāl al-Dīn Bukhārī, may God sanctify his revered spirit, says, *Alas, I could not fully see His beauty, as I was drunk, engrossed, and mad; I was not actually qualified for the vision, however, due to Your kindness, I was able.*

{26} *O God, by Your kindness and Your eternal love, may You show kindness to me, the humble pauper, and the scribe in the gathering; and all believers in the garden of paradise; provide us with Your vision. By Your unmerited favour and kindness. [Amen.]*

[9] Also known as the Lord of Poets. See the Introduction.

[10] Found in Saʿdī's *dīwān*.

در کیفیتِ بلعم باعور[1]

{۱}	آورده اند که در میان بنی اسرائیل زاهدی بود مُسْتَجَاب اَلدَّعْوَة، هر تیری که از کمانِ بیانِ او بیرون آمدن بی خطا در نشانه رسیدن. همهٔ اهل شهر در کَنف[2] حمایت او بودند. هر دعایی که کردن، البتّه رد نشدن. بعداز سالی از صومعهٔ خود بیرون آمدی تا خلق روی او بدیدی.

{۲}	او در زمان مهتر موسیٰ علیه‌السلام بود. مهتر موسیٰ را اتفاق افتاد که آن شهر را از جهت بنی اسرائیل خراب گرداند. لشگری ترتیب داده بیرون آمد. چند منزل که سوی آن شهر رفت، خلقِ بنی اسرائیل جمع آمدند. پیش بلعم باعور رفتند. عرضه داشتند که «مهتر موسیٰ قصد ما کرده است؛ تو به درگاه حضرت باری تَعَالَی یاری‌دِهِ دلُ دعا کن که «مهتر موسیٰ به این جانب[3] نیاید تا خلق ما متفرّق نشوند»». بلعم باعور گفت «او پیغمبر خداست، دعای من در حقّ او مستجاب نشود». هرچند التماس بیشتر می‌کردند او احتراز می‌کرد.

{۳}	و چون خلق دیدند که «سخن ما قبول نمی‌کند» زنان خویش را پیش زن او فرستادند که «تو بلعم باعور را بر آن دار که در این باب دعایی بکند». به [چنین] گفتار زن هم قبول نکرد. آخر [...] دنیایی او را بفریفتند، [و] او قبول کرد. بر بلعم مزاحم شد که «دعا کنْ که[4] خلقِ اینجای با ما زندگانی کرده‌اند». او قبول نمی‌کرد.

{۴}	روزی زن و شوهر در خلوت‌گاه غلطیده بودند. هرچند بلعم فرصت طلبید زن گفت «اگر تو قبول سازی و دعا کنی که مهتر موسیٰ درین شهر نیاید در بستر تو بیایم». بیچاره آدمی چون به حکم نصِّ بربستهٔ

[1] به‌گمان من این داستان برگرفته از مثنوی معنوی مولانا است. شاید بتوان گفت که به دلیل اختصاص حجم اندکی به نقش جبرئیل در ساختار این داستان، و نوع جمله بندی‌های متفاوتش، این قسمت از مجموعهٔ دیگری گرفته شده باشد. بنابر منابع اسلامی، داستان بلعم باعور یا باعورا با آیات ۱۷۵ و ۱۷۶ سورهٔ اعراف مرتبط است.	[2] پناه و حمایت.	[3] به این طرف؛ به این جهت.	[4] برای اینکه.

CHAPTER 34

Regarding Balᶜam Bāᶜūr[1]

{1} It is reported that there was a saint among the the Children of Israel, one whose prayers were always answered. His prayers, like every arrow from his bow, would hit its target without fail. He supported everyone in his city, whatever they requested, and their requests were never rejected. After many years, he came out of his hermitage and people saw his face.

{2} He lived during the times of His Eminence Moses (pbuh). It so happened that His Eminence Moses came to destroy the city of the Children of Israel. He prepared an army and moved towards it. After going some way and nearing the city, the people of the Children of Israel gathered. They went to Balᶜam Bāᶜūr and told him, 'His Eminence Moses is coming for us. Pray upon the presence of God who is the Helper of the heart that "His Eminence Moses does not come here, so our nation will not be scattered."' Balᶜam Bāᶜūr said, 'He is the prophet of God, and my request regarding him will not be answered.' However, much the people begged him, he refused their demand.

{3} When the people noticed that 'he would not accept our request', they then sent their wives to his wife, asking her 'to convince Balᶜam Bāᶜūr to pray for us.' The wife also did not accept their request. Finally, they deceived her with worldly [guile?]. She agreed and went to Balᶜam Bāᶜūr, telling him, 'Pray! as these people have been living and commuting with us.' Yet, Balᶜam Bāᶜūr did not accept to pray.

{4} One day, the wife and husband were in bed. Balᶜam wanted to be intimate and start having intercourse but his wife said, 'If you accept to pray that His Eminence Moses does not come to this city then I will be intimate with you.' Unfortunate is always

[1] This might have been influenced by Rūmī's *Masnavī*. The structure is a bit different from other parts of *Durr al-Majālis* and Gabriel plays less of a role in it. As such, it might have been taken from other sources. It is said that this story is based on Muslim commentaries on Q. 7:175–176.

نفْس و شهوت است. به ضرورت قبول کرد. بعداز مُلاعَبَه[5]، چون از زناشوهری فارغ شدند، بلعم دست به دعا برداشت گفت «إلهِيّ، مهتر موسیٰ را همان‌جا بدار تا این‌جانب نیاید».

{۵} حق سُبحانَهُ وتَعالیٰ مهترموسیٰ را در آن زمین بسته گردانید. هر روز کوچ کردی؛ باز لشگر از مقامی که کوچ می‌کردند وقت فرود آمدنْ خود را باز هم در آن مقام می‌دید. چندگاه برین گذشت، درماندند. مهتر موسیٰ در حضرتِ بی‌نیاز بنالید، و دست به دعا برآورد گفت «راه نمی‌دانم، چارهٔ این چیست و چه حالیست؟» وحی آمد که «یا موسیٰ، زاهدیست در میان آن قومْ بلعم نام دارد؛ در حقّ تو دعا کرد». موسیٰ التماس التجا[6] کرد که «إلهِيّ، آنچه در وی خلاصه است برگیر». ایمان از دل[7] سلب شد.

{۶} قول دیگر آنست که چون او دعا کرد در حقّ موسیٰ مستجاب شد. زبان بلعم باعور بیرون ماند باز[8] در کام نرفت. به طریق زبان سگ بیرون افتاد. چون دید که زبان گِرد[9] نمی‌آید آغاز کرد که «اگر من می‌دانستم که آخر درحال با من چنین خواهی کرد من چندین سال تو را نمی‌پرستیدم». از این سبب کافر شد.

{۷} گفته اند فردای قیامت پوست بلعم با سگ اصحاب کهف پوشانند و در بهشت برند. حکمت چه بود؟

{۸} آورده اند که چون جُستهٔ[10] مهتر آدم مرتّب شد، شیطان آمد به‌جهت دیدن. چون دید آب و آتش و خاک و باد، هر یکی را مخالف یکدیگر دید. گفت «چیزی نیست». بر جسه[11] آدم خون انداخت، به جای ناف افتاد. جبرئیل را فرمان شد که «این‌قدر گِل از مهتر آدم برگیر نزد من بیار که کار دارم». از خون شیطان پلید و گِل پاک آدم سگ اصحاب کهف را پیدا کردند.

{۹} آورده اند که دقیانوس نام پادشاهی بود. این هفت تن از ظلم وی گریختند. با شبانی ملاقی[12] شدند. سگی همراه او بود هرچند او را زدند آن سگ از ایشان جدا نمی‌شد. تا به حدّی زدند که دست و پای مجروح شد. سگ به فرمان خدای تَعَالَی با ایشان به سخن درآمد و گفت «کجا می‌روید؟» گفتند «به طلب خدای تَعَالَی که دارنده [و] آفرینندهٔ آسمان و زمین است». گفت «مرا چرا می‌زنید؟» گفت «از جنس [...]» گفت «پیش وی که می‌روید او از جنس شماست؟ در محبّتْ جنس شرط نیست».

[5] عشق بازی؛ بازی کردن مرد و زن با یکدیگر. [6] پناه گرفتن. [7] دل بلعم. [8] دیگر بار.
[9] ممکن است در برخی گویش ها به‌صورت «گَرد» نیز خوانده شود. [10] جثة. [11] این‌که خطای نگارشی واژه «جثه\جثة» است و یا براساس گویشی در مناطق شمال شرقی ایران و نواحی غربی هند نوشته شده است نیاز به بررّسی دقیق‌تر دارد. [12] روبه رو؛ رو در رو.

human, as he is, according to the divine decree, enslaved by lust! He had to accept his wife's request. Once they had finished being intimate, Balʿam lifted his hands imploring, 'O God, stop His Eminence Moses from coming in this direction.' \

{5} God stopped Moses where he stood. They[2] moved every day but whenever they stopped they found themselves no further. Some time passed like this, and they became flustered. His Eminence Moses wailed in the presence of the Everlasting Refuge and lifted his hands beseeching, 'I do not know the way, how can I figure out where I am and what has happened?' A revelation was sent down, 'O Moses, there is a saint among that nation whose name is Balʿam. He has prayed against you.' Moses cast himself on God's mercy saying, 'O God, take from him whatever by which he is known.' Faith was removed from Balʿam's heart.

{6} Another report says that when Balʿam prayed regarding Moses, it was accepted. But when Balʿam Bāʿūr's tongue moved [because of praying] it did not go back to his mouth, and it hung like the tongue of a dog. When he noticed that his tongue did not go back to normal, he said, '[O God] if I had known that you would do this to me, I would never have worshipped you for such a long time.' He became an infidel.

{7} It is said that the body/skin of Balʿam would be covered by the/by that of the dog of the Seven Sleepers, and then brought to paradise. What is the reason and the story?

{8} It is reported that when the body of Adam was fully formed Satan came to see the result. There, Satan saw that water, fire, soil, and wind were in disagreement. He 'found time' to place a drop of blood on his navel. Gabriel was ordered, 'Go and take some clay from His Eminence Adam's body and bring it to me, as I want to do sometihng.' From the filthy Satan's blood and the clean clay of Adam, the dog of the Seven Sleepers was created.

{9} It is reported that Daqyānūs (Decius) was the name of a king. Seven people ran away from his tyranny. They met a shepherd. There was a dog with him. Even if they beat the dog several times it would not go away. They hit the dog so much its paws and legs were injured. By God's command, the dog began to speak with them asking, 'Where are you going?' They said, 'We are going to find God who is the Possessor and Creator of the heavens and the Earth.' The dog asked, 'Why did you hit me?' They said, 'You are different [?].' [The Dog] said, 'The one to whom you are going, is He similar to you in terms of nature and essence?! Race and/or species type does not matter in love.'

[2] i.e., Moses' army

{۱۰} چون این جواب از او شنیدند او را در میان خود راه دادند. چون لشگر پادشاه دقیانوس رسید ایشان در غار خزیدند و نامِ آن غار کهف بود. هفتصدسال در میان غار بودند. هربار فرشتگان می‌آمدند آدمیان را پهلوِ به پهلو می کردند از [...] امّا بر سگ دست نمی زدند. به قدرت خدای تَعَالَی پهلو به پهلو می گردید؛ از کمالِ محبّتْ این درجه یافت.

{۱۱} بیت[۱۳]: سگ اصحاب کهف روزی چند، پی نیکان گرفت و مردم شد[۱۴] [...][۱۵]

[۱۳] در نسخهٔ لایدن ۵۶۵ واژهٔ «نظم» به‌کار رفته است. [۱۴] این بیت در گلستان سعدی نیز وجود دارد. [۱۵] در انتها این متن به این داستان اضافه می شود «چون کشتهٔ دوست را دینِ دوست بود، پس خوب‌تر از کشته شدن کاری نیست. هم از این در مجاز نظر باید کرد. صاحب نظر که ببیند بر روی خوب رویان، در باطنش حقیقت ظاهر مجاز باشد. و بعضی بر روی خوب نگریستن خطا می‌دانند. امّا نزدیک عاشقانِ محقّق و محبّانِ صادق خطا نیست. چه تهمت می‌نهی در پاک‌چشمان، که حیران مانده در صنع خدابند\خداوند»

{10} When they heard this answer from the dog, they welcomed it among themselves. When the army of the king Daqyānūs arrived, they ran to a cave, and the name of the cave was, 'Kahf.' They stayed in there for seven hundred years. Angels visited the humans regularly to turn them side-to-side [...] but they did not touch the dog. The dog was turned side-to-side by God's power. It received such a high status owing to its perfect love.

{11} Poem: The dog of the Seven Sleepers followed the path of the righteous
for some time and became one of the humans.[3]

[3] Found in Saʿdī's *Gulistān*. This chapter appears to end abruptly and there is no supplication as with other chapters.

موسیٰ[1] نامه

{۱} بِسْمِ اللّٰهِ الرَّحْمٰنِ الرَّحِيمِ، الحَمْدُ لله رَبِّ العَالَمِينَ وَالعَاقِبَةُ لِلْمُتَّقِينَ وَصَلوٰات وَٱلسَلامُ عَلی رَسُولِه محمد وَآلِهِ وَأَصحَابِه أجمَعين.[1]

{۲} باب در حديث موسیٰ علیه‌السلام که حضرت حقّ تولّی کرده و [موسیٰ] بی‌واسطه جواب شنیده. چنین آورده‌اند که خدای عزّوجلّ خواست که با مهتر موسیٰ سخن گوید. به یک‌بار[2] امر ربّانی و وحی سبحانی نازل شد که «ای موسیٰ، [...] قلب خود را از دوستی و شغل دنیا منزّه گردان و خمیر[3] خود را از جمیع [...] ناپایدار بَرکن تا به تو نور تجلّی ما ظاهر گردد. بعداز آن لسان خود را از تکلّمات[4] مخلوقات محفوظ دار. تن خود را مطهّر ساز که من می‌خواهم بی‌کام[5] و بی‌زبان به تو سخن گویم».[6]

{۳} چون این ندا از حضرت بی‌چون[7] به گوش مهتر موسیٰ دررسید، به‌جهت شکرانهٔ این عطا، موسیٰ چهل‌روز متّصل در لَیل وَنَهار روزه داشتی و چهل‌شب قیام نمودی، و حمد و تسبیح به جای آوردی. بعداز آن به فرمان ذُوالجَلال و قادرِ پُرکمال و آن حَيِّ لایَزَال وآن جَبّارِ بی‌مَثال از زیرعرش آوازی پدید آمد که «ای کوه‌ها سر برآورید[8] که حق سبحانه‌وتعالی می‌خواهد که با مهتر موسیٰ در بالای یک کوه از کوه‌های دنیا سخن گوید».

[1] شروع این داستان با چنین عبارت دعایی احتمالا مرتبط است به آیهٔ ۱۲۸ سورهٔ اعراف، در مورد موسیٰ و قوم وی، که بخش پایانی آن « وَالعَاقِبَةُ لِلْمُتَّقِينَ» در این عبارت نیز دیده می‌شود. [2] ناگهان. [3] خمیره به معنای سرشت و طبیعت. [4] گفتگوها و سخن‌ها. به دهخدا مراجعه شود. [5] دهان. [6] استفاده از عبارت موزون «بی‌کام» و «بی‌زبان» بایستی براساس شعری از مولانا باشد: « دل چشم گشت جمله چو چشمم به دل بگفت؛ بی‌کام و بی‌زبان عجب وصف‌های تو » [7] بی‌همتا. صفات «بی‌همتایی» و «بی‌مثالی» برای پروردگار به وفور در ادبیات بایبلی (یهودی و مسیحی) دیده می‌شود. در مقابل آن، منابع اسلامی جنبهٔ «احدیّت و یکی بودن» که متفاوت از «بی مانندی» است را بیش از حدّ پررنگ می‌نمایند. برای اشارهٔ بایبلی به «بی‌همتایی» به اشعیا ۴۰:۲۵ مراجعه نمایید. [8] برخیزید.

CHAPTER 35

The tale of Moses

{1} In the Name of God, the Most Compassionate, Most Merciful. All praise is for God, Lord of the worlds, and the final outcome belongs to the righteous. And blessing and peace upon His messenger, Muḥammad and his family and Companions.[1]

{2} A chapter regarding a report on Moses (pbuh) with whom God sought friendship, and Moses heard a response directly from God. It is said that God wanted to speak with His Eminence Moses. Suddenly, a divine order and sublime revelation was revealed: 'O Moses [...] release your heart from engaging with the world and part your nature from all that is unstable [...] in order that Our theophany emerges upon you. Keep away from conversing with people; purify your body as I want to speak with you without mouth and tongue.'[2]

{3} When this proclamation from the Incomparable God[3] was heard by His Eminence Moses, he began to fast for forty consecutive days and nights and to rise to his feet for forty nights and praise God, on account of this honour. Later, on the command of the Lord of Majesty, the Perfect Omnipotence, the Eternal Life, and the

[1] Beginning this story with this supplicatory setence is probably related to its partial inclusion of Q. 7:128 about Moses and his people. [2] This phrase (viz., without mouth [or: palate] and tongue) should have been written based on one of the poems of Rūmī "the whole heart of mine shifted itself into the eye, and then the eyes of mine turned to the heart of mine, and pointed out; Your wonderous beautiful attributions without mouth and tongue'. The German translation of this couplet is worthy of attention: *Es hat das Herz sich ganz zum Aug' umstaltet, Als einst mein Aug's zum Herzen sich gewandt; und frug, wie ohne Gaum-und Zungenband, es deinen holden Zauber wohl entfaltet?* For more, see: Ǧalāl-ad-Dīn Rūmī, *Auswahl aus den Diwanen des grössten mystischen Dichters Persiens Mewlana Dschelaleddin Rumi*. Von Vincenz von Rosenzweig (Wien: Mechitaristen-Congregations-Buchhandlung, 1838), 186–187. [3] The 'incomparability' of God, as an adjective and attribution, is more often found in Biblical literature (e.g., Isaiah 40:25).

{۴} جمیع کوه‌ها سربرآوردند. هر کدام با یکدیگر مذکور می‌نمودند که «از همه بلندتر منم. اگر الله تعَالَی با موسیٰ درسخن آید بر سر من خواهد گفت». به خلافُ کوهِ طورِ سینا از تواضع و شکستگی سر برنداشت، و گفت «من باشم که نزرک[۹] این تمنّا[۱۰] بزرگ به خاطر قرار بدهم». چون کوه طور در حضرت باری تعَالَی خود را معدوم[۱۱] پنداشت، چون این شکستگی در کوه طور مشاهده نمود، فرمان شد «ای موسیٰ، بر سر کوه طور سینا بِرَوی که من با تو راز گویم[۱۲] که کوه طور سینا به حضرت ما عجز و شکستگی آورده است».

{۵} مهتر موسیٰ با هفتاد مرد از بنی اسرائیل گرفته روان شده، چون نزدیک کوه طور رسید مهتر موسیٰ با یاران بنی اسرائیل گفت «شمایان همین‌جا باشید تا من به کوه طورِ سینا برآیم. آنچه از حضرت حمدیّت شنوم با شما معلوم سازم».

{۶} مهتر موسیٰ عليه‌السلام نعلین از پای خود کشید و بالای کوه طور سینا بر آمد و به نماز مشغول شد. دو رکعت نماز ادا نمودند و هر رکعتی «فاتحة الکتاب» یک‌بار و سورهٔ «إخْلاص» سه‌بار بخوانْد. بعداز آن به حضرت حمدیّت استاد. و به قدرت خویش خواند آوازی به گوشِ مهتر موسیٰ «امروز بی‌واسطه سخن بشنو». همان‌زمانْ موسیٰ سر بر زمین نهاد. فرمان قهّاری در رسید که «ای موسیٰ، سر بردار که وقتِ گفتنِ راز است و آنچه سؤال کنی جواب بی‌واسطه شنوی».

{۷} موسیٰ گفت «خداوندا، تو داناتری و از تو هیچ چیز پوشیده نیست؟» فرمان شد که «یا موسیٰ، از من چگونه پوشیده باشد، اگر مورچه در زیر چاه تاریک بگردد آنچه او بگوید مرا معلوم است». موسیٰ گفت «خداواندا، تو دانائی». ناگاه آواز «لبّیك» بر موسیٰ عليه‌السلام دررسید. موسیٰ بیهوش باز آمد. فرمان شد که «ای موسیٰ، چرا بیهوش شدی؟» موسیٰ گفت «إلٰهِيّ، تو به کرم و الطاف خود مرا لبّیك گفتی. از خود بی‌خود شدم».

{۸} فرمان شد که «ای موسیٰ، چون بندهٔ خود را دوست دارم او را به‌نام خوانم و او مرا نیز به‌نام خواند. به درستی او جواب لبّیك برآن بنده بگویم. ای موسیٰ، می‌دانی که بی‌ترجمه[۱۳] چرا با تو سخن گفتم؟» موسیٰ گفت «خداوندا تو دانایی». فرمان شد که «ای موسیٰ، از همه چیز تو را با تواضع دیدم. از آن جهت تو را برگزیدم و با تو سخن گفتم».

{۹} مهتر موسیٰ گفت «یا رَبّ، ابلیس لعین بیامد مرا وسوسه کرد، و گفت «ای موسیٰ آنکه با تو سخن می‌گوید خدای تو نیست. اگر خدای تو بَرحقّ است بگوی تا روی خود را با تو نماید». إلٰهِيّ، رَبِّ أَرِنِي أَنْظُرْ إِلَيْكَ،[۱۴] ای پروردگارِ من، مرا روی خود بنمای». چون موسیٰ عليه‌السلام این سخن بگفت آفتاب و ماه و ستارگان و کوه‌ها و زمین‌ها و درختان در لرزه شدند و ملائکه‌های هفت آسمان و زمین و دیوان و پریان و کلّ پرنده و چرنده[۱۵] گفتند «یا موسیٰ، سخن به اندازهٔ قدرِ خود بگوی و بسیار بی‌ادبی مکن. و تو بزرگیِ حضرت عزّوجلّ را

[۹] خُرد و کوچک. [۱۰] آرزو. [۱۱] نیست و فانی. [۱۲] سخن با کسی پوشیده گفتن.
[۱۳] در حاشیهٔ برگ ۱۱۴نسخهٔ ۱۷۰ آکلند چنین نوشته شده است: [«ترجمه یعنی «ادب»].
[۱۴] آیهٔ ۱۴۳ سورهٔ اعراف. [۱۵] تمام حیوانات.

Incomparable All-Compeller, a voice came from the Throne, 'O mountains, arise! God wants to speak with His Eminence Moses on top of one of the Earth's mountains.'

{4} All the mountains rose. They began to vie with each other, 'I am the highest one; if God wants to speak with Moses, He will do it on my top.' In humility and modesty, Mount Sinai did not rise but said, 'I am too inferior to even think of such a great honour.' When Mount Sinai considered itself as nothing and inferior to enter the presence of God, and as God witnessed such humility in Mount Sinai, a command was given, 'O Moses, go to the summit of Mount Sinai where I can speak with you privately, as Mount Sinai has displayed its weakness and humility before Us.'

{5} His Eminence Moses, along with seventy men from the Children of Israel, came out. When they arrived near Mount Sinai, His Eminence Moses ordered his companions from the Children of Israel, 'You stay here until I go to the top of the Mount Sinai. Whatever I hear from God the Glorious I will inform you.'

{6} His Eminence Moses (pbuh) took off his sandals and ascended Mount Sinai and began to pray. He performed a two-unit prayer; in each unit he recited the Qurʾānic chapters *al-Fātiḥa* (Q. 1) once and *al-Ikhlāṣ* (Q. 112) three times. Then he stood before the Almighty. God announced Himself: 'His Eminence Moses, today hear directly.' Right after this, Moses prostrated on the earth. A command was given, 'O Moses, lift your head as this is the time to speak privately, and you will receive a direct response for every one of your questions.'

{7} Moses said, 'O God, You are the All-Wise and nothing is hidden to You.' A proclamation was made, 'O Moses, do you wonder how nothing is hidden from Me? If an ant moves in a dark well, whatever it says is clear to me.' Moses said, 'O God, You are the Omniscient One.' Immediately, a response was given, 'Yes, I am the One'. Moses fainted. It was asked, 'O Moses, why did you faint?' Moses replied, 'O God, You answered my question with your kindness and grace, so I fainted.'

{8} It was again proclaimed, 'O Moses, as I love my servant, I would call him by name, so he will call Me by name. Therefore, I sincerely respond to that servant with my own confirmation, "I hear you!" O Moses, do you know why I speak to you with such explicit clarity?' Moses said, 'O God, You are the Omniscient One!'[4] It was proclaimed, 'O Moses, I found you with a modest disposition. This is why I have chosen to speak with you.'

{9} His Eminence Moses said, 'O Lord, the accursed Satan came to tempt me and said, "O Moses, the one who is speaking with you is not your God. If your God is true, then ask Him to appear before you." O God, "My Lord! Reveal Yourself to me so I may observe You" (Q. 7:143).' As Moses (pbuh) made this statement, the entire Sun,

[4] i.e., 'You know better than I!'

نیک نشناختی؟» چون موسیٰ این سخن بشنید از هوش برفت و در زمین سرافکند. حقّ تَعَالَی به کرم و لطف قدیم خود ندا درداد که «ای موسیٰ، برخیز به طریق ضعیفان».

{۱۰} به حکمِ فرمان از زمین برخاست. بیچاره‌وار گفت «یا رَبّ، سخن از نادانی خود گفتم. بعداز این در حضرت تو گستاخی نکنم». فرمان شد «ای موسیٰ، به گفتهٔ ابلیس این محنت[۱۶] دیدی». جبرئیل را فرمان شد که «به نزدیک موسیٰ برو. دست راست بر سینهٔ موسیٰ بنه و دست چپ را بر کتف موسیٰ بگذار[۱۷] تا قدرت ما را مشاهده کند». بعداز آن مهتر جبرئیل فرمان به جای آورد تا قوّت برداشت سؤال جواب در نهان او پدید آمد. چون حقّ تَعَالَی از نور خود به مقدار سوفار سوزن[۱۸] بر کوه طورِسینا انداخت، کوه طور سینا پاره‌پاره گردید.[۱۹] موسیٰ سه شبانه‌روز نیز بیهوش افتاد. سُرمه که در چشم می‌کشند هم ازآن کوه است. هر که ازآن سرمه در چشم کَشَد روشنائی چشم را افزون کند.

{۱۱} چون موسیٰ عَلَيْهِ السَّلَام بهوش باز آمد سر از زمین برداشت. روی او همچوماه تابان شده بود. موسیٰ گفت «إِلٰهِيّ، بر منِ ضعیف چیزی بیاموز که به حضرت تو نزدیک‌تر شوم که شایستهٔ خدمت تو گردم تا رضای تو را به‌دست آورم». فرمان شد «ای موسیٰ، بگو «لَآ إِلٰهَ إِلَّا اللهُ، مُحَمَّدٌ رَسُولُ اللهِ»». باز گفت «ای موسیٰ، اگر آسمان‌ها و زمین‌ها و آنچه در وی است، همه را در یک پلّهٔ[الف] ترازو نهند و این کلمه را در یک پلّه گذارند، هموَرانی کلمه گران آید؛ و من از آن بنده راضی و شاکر باشم و بهشت جای آن سخن باشد».

{۱۲} باز فرمان شد «ای موسیٰ، اگر می‌خواهی که به حضرت ما نزدیک شوی چنانکه از سیاهی چشم و سفیدی هنوز نزدیک‌تر باشم؟» موسیٰ گفت «بلی،[۲۰] یا رَبّ». فرمان شد «ای موسیٰ، درود بر محمّد مُصْطَفَی صَلَّى اللهُ عَلَيْهِ وَسَلَّمَ بفرست». چون موسیٰ عَلَيْهِ السَّلَام نام محمّد بشنید [...] از دست موسیٰ بیفتاد. موسیٰ گفت «إِلٰهِيّ، محمّد کیست که نام او بگویم به حضرت تو؛ از برکت آن نام نزدیک شوم؟» فرمان شد که «ای موسیٰ، اگر محمّد و امّت او نبودی، دنیا و معیشت‌های بهشت، دوزخ، آسمان و زمین و آفتاب و ماه و کواکب، روز و شب و آنچه که هست را از نعمت‌های گوناگون نیافریدی، و اگر دوستی و فضل محمّد نبودی تو را با آتش دوزخ انداختمی. و اگر ابراهیم خلیل من نبودی زیر معصیت بدادی.[۲۱] ای موسیٰ، به عزّت جلالیّت من که در بهشت هیچ درختی و کوشکی نیافریدی؛ و ای موسیٰ، آنچه به قدرت خود آفریده‌ام از برکت این کلمه «لَآ إِلٰهَ إِلَّا اللهُ، مُحَمَّدٌ رَسُولُ اللهِ» است که در نهاد هر کدام پرتو تجلّی دارد. چنانچه در بهشت و دوزخ، در آفتاب و ماه و ستاره‌ها و عرش و کرسی و لوح

[۱۶] هرچند «محنت» به معنای گرفتاری به کار می‌رود امّا در اینجا شاید دلالت بر «آزمایش» دارد. به فرهنگ «خداپرستی» مراجعه شود.
[۱۷] در حاشیهٔ برگ ۱۱۴ آکلند ۱۷۰ چنین نوشته شده است: [«بگذ[ا]ر» یعنی «رخ»]؛ احتمالا «رخ» همان‌صورت عربی‌شدهٔ کلمه هندی (रखना) است که در پنجابی (ਰੱਖੇ) و بنگالی (রাখা) هم دیده می‌شود. [۱۸] سوراخ سوزن. [۱۹] اشاره به متلاشی شدن و سوخته شدن کوه دارد. این عبارت دلیلی است برای به‌وجود آمدن «سرمه» از این کوه که در سطر بعدی به آن اشاره شده‌است. [۲۰] در حاشیهٔ آکلند ۱۷۰ چنین نوشته شده است [بلی یعنی سیچ] [۲۱] این جمله واضح نیست.

[الف] پلیه

Moon, stars, mountains, land mass, and trees began to shake, and all the angels of the seven heavens and Earth, the demons, the fairies and all birds and grazing animals said, 'O Moses, behave yourself and do not speak impolitely; and you have not realised the greatness of the Exalted'. When Moses heard this he fainted and fell down. God, due to His eternal kindness and grace, called to him: 'O Moses, arise like a humiliated one[5]'.

{10} Given this order, Moses rose. He began to wail, while being humble, saying 'O Lord, what I said was due to my ignorance. I would never wish to be impertinent in Your presence'. A command came, 'O Moses, this happened to you due to following the Satan's word.' Gabriel [then] was ordered, 'Go close to Moses, and put your right hand on his chest, and hold your left hand on Moses' shoulder until he witnesses Our power.' His Eminence Gabriel followed the order of God, enabling Moses to continue to question. The Mount of Sinai was burnt, and split once God began to shine a little light of Himself on it. Then Moses fainted for three days. The traditional mascara[6] is also taken from this Mount. Anyone applying this special mascara will have an enhanced vision.

{11} When Moses woke up and lifted his head, his face began to shine like a full Moon. Moses said, 'O my God, instruct me, such an inferior person, to get closer to You, so I can deserve to be at Your service, and meet Your satisfaction'. A proclamation was made, 'O Moses, say, 'There is no god, but God; Muḥammad is the Messenger of God.' Then God continued, 'O Moses, if one puts whatever is in the heavens, Earth, and all their contents on one pan of the scale, and puts this phrase into the other pan, the phrase's weight will be heavier; so I am happy and thankful for that person; and paradise is the right place for this phrase.'

{12} Again, a proclamation was made, 'O Moses, do you want to get close to Our presence, even closer than the pupil of the eye to the white of the eye?' Moses responded, 'Yes, O Lord'. A command was made, 'O Moses, send your blessing and peace upon Muḥammad (pbuh)'. When Moses (pbuh) heard the name of Muḥammad, [...] fell down from Moses' hand. Moses asked, 'O God, who is Muḥammad whose name I should mention in Your presence so that I will get closer to you due to the grace of his name?' God said, 'O Moses, if it was not for Muḥammad and his community, I would not have created the world, heavenly livelihood, hell, heaven, the Earth, Sun, Moon, planets, day, night, and all sorts of bounties. And if it were not for Muḥammad's friendship and virtue I would have you sent to hell, and if there were no Abraham, the friend of God, you would have committed sin [?]. O Moses, by My dignity and majesty, I would not have made trees nor palaces in paradise, and O Moses, whatever I have created through My power, all is because of the glory of this phrase, "There is

[5] i.e., like a weakling [6] Kohl or surma

و قلم و آنچه آفریده‌ام همه به دوستی محمّد است. ای آنکه گفتی «محمّد کیست؟» همان‌زمانْ تخت‌ها[۲۲] از تو برفت و اگر محمّد را هم‌چو خود از دست اندازی[۲۳] این نور که چنین در تو نهاده‌ام از تو مفارقت کند».

{۱۳} بعداز آن موسیٰ باز گفت «خداوندا، محمّد را دوست می‌داری یا مرا؟» فرمان شد که «ای موسیٰ، محمّد حبیب من است و تو کلیم منی. پس حبیب خوب تر است از کلیم». موسیٰ گفت «خداوندا، بی‌ترجمه با من سخن گفتی، چگونه محمّد را بر من فاضل اندازی؟» فرمان از حضرت حمدیّت در رسید که «ای موسیٰ، چون با تو سخن در کوه طورِسینا کردم و چون وقت برسد با محمّد سخن به مقام علّیّن[۲۴] را گویم و من با محمّد نزدیک‌ترم از سیاهی و سفیدی چشم. ای موسیٰ، هر که بر محمّد شک آرد کافر گردد و جای او را در دوزخ سازم و نام مسلمانی از لوح او پاک گردانم. ای موسیٰ، اگر محمّد نبودی یک قطره باران از آسمان بر زمین نیامدی و برگ گیاه نرستی.[۲۵] اگر محمّد امّتان و عبادت‌کنندگان را او نبودی دیگر و هر آنکه بودی عاصی شدی درحال هلاک شدندی. اگر شکر گویان محمّد نبودی، آسمان و کوه‌ها تمام بسوختی. دیگر [اگر] راست گویندگان[۲۶] امّت محمّد نبودی، گناه‌کاران جمله هلاک شدندی. و اگر توبه‌کنندگان امّت محمّد نبودی، دروغ‌گویان را در دوزخ انداختمی».

{۱۴} موسیٰ گفت «خداوندا، از من پیش‌تر سخن با که گفتی و بعداز من با که گویی؟» فرمان حضرت عزّت دررسید که «ای موسیٰ، اوّل سخن با آدم صفي الله عليه‌السلام، بعده، به محمّد مُصْطَفَی عليه‌السلام گویم و بشنوم». موسیٰ گفت «خداوندا، امّت محمّد را دوست داری یا بنی اسرائیل را؟» فرمان شد که «امّت محمّد را دوست دارم از جملهٔ پیغمبران دیگر». موسیٰ گفت «یا ربّ، فضلای امّت محمّد را دوست داری یا علمای بنی اسرائیل را؟» فرمان آمد «یا موسیٰ، فضلای امّت محمّد را افضل است از علمای بنی اسرائیل؛ من ایشان را دوست دارم».

{۱۵} فرمان شد که «ای موسیٰ، به درستیِ محمّد، دَه خصلتْ امّتِ محمّد را داده ام». موسیٰ گفت «یا رَبّ، آن خصلت کدام است تا بنی اسرائیل را بیاموزم؟» فرمان شد «ای موسیٰ، اوّل نماز، دوم روزه، سوم حجّ، چهارم زکات، پنجم ریاضت، ششم عاشورا، هفتم روز جمعه، هشتم نماز با جماعت، نهم عیدین، دهم امر معروف و نهی از منکر بر ایشان عطا کرده ام».[۲۷]

[۲۲] مراد آن «لوح» است یا «تخت‌های بهشتی». [۲۳] این جمله خیلی واضح نیست. [۲۴] اعلی و بهشت برین.
[۲۵] جوانه زدن و روییدن. [۲۶] کسی که سخن به راستی و درستی گوید. [۲۷] تقسیم کردن خصلت مسلمانان به ده قسمت و اینکه عاشورا و ریاضت در بین آن است می‌تواند اشاره به مفهومی داشته باشد که من آن را «صوفیان عاشورایی» می‌نامم. شاید دلیل رواج همزمان عاشورا و تصوّف در آسیای مرکزی، هندوستان جنوب‌شرق آسیا همین متن باشد. برخی از این تقسیم‌بندی‌ها بین خوجه‌ها و بهره‌ها در هند و شرق آفریقا دیده می‌شود.

no god, but God; Muḥammad is the Messenger of God" whose essence is the light of Our illumination. And whatever I have created – paradise, hell, the Sun, the Moon, stars, the Throne, the Seat, the Plate, the Pen, and so on and so forth – is just because of Muḥammad's companionship. O he who asked, "Who is Muḥammad?", when you asked this, all Plates[7] were taken from you, and if you underestimate Muḥammad, the light which I have founded in your nature will leave you.'

{13} Then, Moses said, 'O God, do you like Muḥammad or I?' God said, 'O Moses, Muḥammad is My friend and you are My converser. As such, friend is better than converser.' Moses said, 'O God, You have spoken with me directly. How do you prefer Muḥammad to me?' God said, 'O Moses, if I am speaking with you on Mount Sinai, then I will speak with Muḥammad in the highest paradise when the time arrives. I am closer to Muḥammad than the closeness of the pupil of the eye to the white of the eye. O Moses, whoever has doubt in Muḥammad, he will become an infidel and I'll make his place in hell and the name of, 'Muslim' will be removed from his record. O Moses, if there were no Muḥammad, a drop of rain would not even touch the ground and the plant's leaf would not even bud. If there were no Muḥammad, all communities and worshippers would be turbulent and all would totally perish. Without admirers of Muḥammad, the heavens and all mountains would have been burnt. If there were no righteous people of Muḥammad, all the sinful would have perished, and if there were no penitents in Muḥammad's community, We would have put all liars into hell.'

{14} Moses said, 'O God, who did You talk to before me and who will You talk to after me?' God said, 'O Moses, I conversed first of all with Adam, God's chosen one (pbuh), and later on with Muḥammad, also God's chosen one (pbuh).' Moses said, 'O God, do you like Muḥammad's community or the Children of Israel?' God said, 'I like Muḥammad's community more than the communities of other prophets.' Moses said, 'O Lord, do you like the elites of Muḥammad's community or the scholars of the Children of Israel?' God said, 'O Moses, the elites of Muḥammad's community are superior to the scholars of the Children of Israel; I like them.'

{15} God said, 'O Moses, I have given Muḥammad's community ten special qualities, because of Muḥammad's faithfulness.' Moses then said, 'O Lord, what are these qualities so I can instruct the Children of Israel about them?' God said, 'O Moses, I have granted them, first, prayer; second, fasting; third, pilgrimage; fourth, almsgiving; fifth, mortification; sixth, ʿĀshūrā; seventh, Friday; eighth, congregational prayer; ninth, the two Eids; tenth, commending good and forbidding evil.'

[7] Or: heavenly thrones?

{۱۶} موسیٰ گفت «یا رَبّ، ریازت[۲۸] بهشت چیست؟» فرمان شد که «ای موسیٰ، علمای امّت محمّد باشند. چنانچه در مجلس‌اند[۲۹] بزرگان دین جمع باشند، کلمات حقّانی و صفات من از زبان علماء بشنوند و بدان عمل کنند و مشغول باشند و از آنجا برخیزند، هیچ گناه در وجود ایشان نباشد و از خوف دوزخ ترسان باشند و از درآمدنِ بهشت امیدوار باشند».

{۱۷} موسیٰ گفت «خداوندا، امّت محمّد گناه کنند و عاصی شوند؟» فرمان شد «ای موسیٰ، اگر گناه‌کار یک بار کلمه طیّبه لآ إِلٰهَ إِلَّا اللهُ، مُحَمَّدٌ رَسُولُ اللهِ بر زبان رانند خشم من فرونشیند و من بر ایشان بَخشم. ای موسیٰ، زمین را مسجد[۳۰] ایشان ساختم و یک نیک ایشان را [...] مبدّل کرده، مقبولِ درگاه خود ساختم. ای موسیٰ، اگر بنی اسرائیل یک گناه کنند به پیشانی[۳۱] ایشان فرشته‌ها نبوسند، و سزای ایشان این باشد. و این سَنَخ[۳۲] از امّت محمّد برگرفتم تا در میان خلق حشر نشوند. ای موسیٰ، اگر امّت محمّد دو رکعت نمازِ وقتِ بَرآمدِ آفتاب[۳۳] بگذارد به هر رکعتی زیادت کنم در رزقْ بر آن بنده. و چون سایَه بکرد[۳۴] و چهار رکعت نماز بگذارد[۳۵] از بهر رکعتی در اعمال آن بنویسند و هفتاد امان از دوزخ به آن بنده بدهم. و چهار رکعت به وقتِ فرو رفتنِ آفتاب ایشان را فرمودم.[۳۶] چون ادا کنند ثوابِ همه نیکانِ عالَم به آن بنده بدهم. و چون آفتاب فرو نشیند سه رکعت نمازِ شام به آن فرمودم.[۳۷] چون ادا کنند ثواب به آن بنده بدهم. و چون سرخی از سفیدی فرو شود، چهار رکعت نماز خفتن بگذارند[۳۸] و سختی جان کندن از ایشان بردارم؛ جان آن را به آسانی برگیرم.

{۱۸} درسالْ یک‌ماه روزه فرمودم. نامِ آن ماه رمضان گذاشتم، و چون روزه دارند گناهان ایشان را بیامرزم. و ایشان را غُسل جَنابَت فرمودم تا هر قطره آبی که از وجود ایشان بچکید فرشتگانی بیافریدم که مر تسبیح را به همان بنده بخشم.[۳۹] ای موسیٰ، دعای ایشان را مستجاب کردم. ای موسیٰ، ایشان را حجّ فرمودم تا هرگام که در راه خانهٔ کعبه بزنند امانی از آتش دوزخ برایشان رحم کنم، و امّت محمّد را در آخرالزمان آفریدم. و عمر ایشان را کوتاه گردانیدم و لیکن پیش از امّتانِ پیغمبرانْ امّتِ محمّد را در بهشتِ عَنبرْسِرِشْتْ[۴۰] فرستم. ای موسیٰ، این همه از کرامت محمّد است ﷺ. چون عُمر ایشان به چهل برسد بی‌قراری و دیوانه‌گی از ایشان بردارم. و چون

[۲۸] زیارت؟ریاست؟ [۲۹] احتمالا این عبارت توسط کاتب اضافه شده و خطاب به افرادی است که در جمع وی حضور دارند.

[۳۰] اشاره به عبادت‌گاه و محلّی برای پیشانی دارد. [۳۱] پیشانی اشاره به «سجده‌گاه» دارد. چنانچه مسجَد به معنای «پیشانی» نیز می‌تواند به‌کار رود. [۳۲] تباه شدن. [۳۳] نماز صبح. [۳۴] اگر اشاره به «سایه کردن» داشته باشد می‌تواند به‌صورت «زمانی که سایه ازجهت آفتاب پدید می‌آید» درک شود. امّا اینکه این کلمه به‌صورت «سایه بگرد» باید خوانده شود به تحقیق نیاز دارد.

[۳۵] نماز ظهر. [۳۶] نماز عصر. [۳۷] نماز مغرب. [۳۸] نماز عشاء. [۳۹] چنین تصویری در کتاب «مفتاح الفلاح» از بهاء الدین محمّد بن حسین العاملی و ترجمهٔ علی بن طیفور بسطامی به چشم می خورد. [۴۰] «عَنبرْسِرِشْتْ» به معنای آمیخته با عنبر است. و اصطلاح «بهشتِ عَنبرْسِرِشْتْ» در آثار تاریخی از جمله «تاریخ بخارا»، و همچنین اشعار نظامی و فرّخی به چشم می‌خورد. به دهخدا مراجعه شود. همچنین، بنابر کتاب «برهان قاطع» چاپ کلکته ۱۲۳۳ هجری قمری برابر با ۱۸۱۸ میلادی، عبارت «بهشتِ عَنبرْسِرِشْتْ» مترادف «سرای جاوید»، «جنّةُ المأوی» و «رضوان‌کده» است. این عبارت در اشعار و ادبیات ترکی عثمانی و هندوستانی نیز دیده می‌شود.

{16} Moses asked, 'O Lord, how can one reside in[8] paradise?' God said, 'O Moses, they will be the community of Muḥammad. When they are at gatherings, they will be considered as the nobles of religion, they listen to righteous words and My attributions from the scholars' mouths, and they will act upon their words and engage with them forever, and once they leave the gatherings, nothing from sin will be in their nature, and they will be afraid of hell, and be hopeful of entering paradise.'

{17} Moses said, 'O God, does Muḥammad's community commit sin and will it disobey?' God said, 'O Moses, if the sinful only state the blessed phrase "There is no god, but God; Muḥammad is the Messenger of God", My wrath will be abated, and I will forgive them. O Moses, I have prepared the Earth to be their place of worship, and changed one of their good deeds to [...], and accepted it in My own presence. O Moses, if the Children of Israel commits one sin, angels will not kiss their foreheads, and this is their penalty. And I have taken such decay from the community of Muḥammad, they will not be resurrected among the people [i.e., so that their failure is not noticed]. O Moses, if one from the community of Muḥammad performs a two-unit dawn prayer, I would increase the provision of the praying servant. And if one performs a four-unit prayer when the Sun makes shade [i.e., afternoon prayer], they [i.e., angels] would write good things for each unit and I would give seventy refuge from hell, and I would tell them to perform a four-unit prayer at the moment of sunset. If they do so, I will grant a reward to all the righteous people of the world, and when the Sun disappears, I will order them to perform a three-unit disk prayer. If they perform it accordingly, I will grant them a reward. And when the redness leaves the sky's whiteness, they should perform a four-unit evening prayer, and I will take the harshness of the moment of death from them, and take their souls with ease.

{18} 'I have ordered them to fast for a month every year. I have named that month as Ramadan. And when they fast, I will forgive their sins. And I have ordered them to perform ablution after sexual intercourse, so in exchange for every drop of water dripping from their bodies, the glorifying of God[9] will be given back to them by special angels I have Myself created. O Moses, I have answered the requests. O Moses, I have obliged them to perform hajj and in exchange for their every single step in the sanctuary of the Kaʿba, I will grant that a quarter of them are saved from hellfire, and I have created the community of Muḥammad at the end of time.'And I have given them a short life span, as such the community of Muḥammad will enter the Garden of Abode earlier than the community of other prophets. O Moses, all these are because of Muḥammad's (pbuh) blessing. When they reach forty, I will take from them restiveness and madness. And when they reach fifty, I will purify them from sins. And when they

[8] Or: visit? [9] i.e., its reward

به پنجاه رسد از گناه پاک گردند. و چون به شصت رسد نیکی ایشان را زیادت کنم. و چون به هفتاد برسد دوستی دنیا از دل ایشان محو[41] سازم و قلم عفو بر ایشان کشم».

{۱۹} موسیٰ گفت «خداوندا، امّت محمّد پارساترند یا بنی اسرائیل؟» فرمان شد که «ای موسیٰ، امّت محمّد پارساترند». بعداز آن موسیٰ گفت «إلهيّ، امّتان محمّد کجا باشند؟» فرمان حضرت حمدیّت در رسید که «ای موسیٰ، می‌خواهی که آواز[42] امّتان محمّد را بشنوی؟» گفت «بلی، یا رَبّ،» به فرمانِ قدرتِ [بیانِ] «كُنْ فَيَكونُ»[43]، از بالای عرش آواز آمد که «یا امّتان!» ایشان از صُلبِ پدران و از رَحِمِ مادران[44] جواب دادند که «لبّيك اللّهم لبّيك، لبيك لا شريكَ له» . فرمان شد که «ای موسیٰ، آواز امّت محمّد است ﷺ. و چون عُمر ایشان به آخر رسد برایشان رحمت کنم». موسیٰ عليه السلام گفت «خداوندا، آوازِ حضرتِ ذوالجلالِ تو رسید وسلام تو بود که رسانید. و مرا در قیامت حشر کن». حقّ تَعَالَی جواب داد که «ای موسیٰ، همچنان کنم».

{۲۰} موسیٰ گفت «خداوندا، مسئله چند در تورات نوشته دیده‌ام. می‌خواهم که از تو سؤال کنم». ندا از حضرت رَبِّ العَالَمِين دررسید که «ای موسیٰ، میان من و تو هیچ حجاب نیست؛ هرچه به خاطر داری سؤال کن». موسیٰ گفت «خداوندا، تو کریمی که سخن همچو من بندهٔ ضعیف را در حضرت خود قبول کردی اکنون سؤال کنم». در بیانِ مایلْ[45] موسیٰ عليه السلام گفت «یا رَبّ، در تورات که فرستاده است قومی را می‌بینم که طاعت و عبادت در دل‌های ایشان همچون آفتاب می‌تابد. و ایشان را از امّتِ من گردان». فرمان شد که «ای موسیٰ، این کرامت [امّت] محمّد باشد». موسیٰ گفت «یا رَبّ، این درجه به چه عمل یافته‌اند؟» فرمان شد «به فاقِه[46] و گرسنگی».

{۲۱} موسیٰ گفت «یا رَبّ، در تورات می‌بینم که قومی با کافران غزا کنند. ایشان را از امّتِ من گردان». فرمان شد که «این هم از امّت محمّد است».

{۲۲} عليه السلام موسیٰ گفت «در تورات می‌بینم که قومی که در دل خود اندیشهٔ خیر و نیکی بکنند هنوز به وقوع نیامده باشد که ثواب نیکی در دیوان اعمال ایشان نویسند و اگر در دل بدی پذیرند تا نکنند[47] ننویسند. و ایشان را از امّت من گردان». فرمان شد که «این هم از امّت محمّد است».

{۲۳} باز موسیٰ گفت «یا رَبّ، قومی را می‌بینم که روزه برایشان واجب است و بعضی روزه ندارند و تو بر ایشان می‌بخشی. آنها را از امّت من گردان». فرمان رسید که «این نیز از امّت محمّدند».

[41] در حاشیهٔ برگ ۱۱۷ آ کلند ۱۷۰ در مورد کلمهٔ «محو» نوشته‌ای شبیه «[...]اعوکا» دیده می‌شود. احتمالا شکل عربی‌شدهٔ واژهٔ مالایالم (മങ്ങുക) یا هندی (फीका) است.
[42] اخبار و صفات.
[43] آیهٔ ۱۱۷ سورهٔ بقره؛ آیات ۴۷ و ۵۹ سورهٔ آل عمران؛ آیهٔ ۷۳ سورهٔ انعام؛ آیهٔ ۴۰ سورهٔ نحل؛ آیهٔ ۳۵ سورهٔ مریم؛ آیهٔ ۸۲ سورهٔ یس؛ آیهٔ ۶۸ سورهٔ غافر.
[44] اشاره به آیهٔ ۷ سورهٔ طارق دارد «يَخْرُجُ مِنْ بَيْنِ الصُّلْبِ وَ التَّرائِبِ»؛ هرچند معنای «ترائب» به عنوان «رَحِم» کاربرد رایجی ندارد.
[45] یافتن معنای دقیق این کلمه نیاز به بررسی بیشتر دارد. احتمالا اشاره به اشتیاق و یا پرسش‌گری خاضعانه دارد.
[46] تنگدستی.
[47] انجام ندهند.

arrive at sixty I will increase their goodness and when they reach seventy, I will remove the love of the world from their heart and forgive them.'

{19} Moses asked, 'O God, between the community of Muḥammad and the Children of Israel, which is the more pious?' God said, 'O Moses, the community of Muḥammad is more pious.' Then, Moses asked, 'O God, where is the community of Muḥammad?' God said, 'O Moses, would you like to hear the attributions of Muḥammad's community?' Moses said, 'Yes, O Lord!' Following the command of the One who says '"Be!" And it is' (Q. 2:117; 3:47; 3:59; 6:73; etc.), a call from the top of the Throne was made, 'O People!' They[10] responded to the call from the loins of their fathers and wombs of their mothers, 'Here I am, O God, here I am. Here I am, You have no partner'. God said, 'O Moses, this is the attribution of the community of Muḥammad (pbuh). And when they draw close to death I will bestow mercy upon them.' Moses (pbuh) said, 'O God, the Proclamation of Your Lord of Majesty was heard and it [the Proclamation of Your Lord] passed on Your greeting. And resurrect me on the Day of Judgement'. God responded, 'O Moses, I will do so'.

{20} Moses said, 'O God, I have a couple of questions from the written Torah that I want to ask of You.' A voice from the Lord of the Worlds came, 'O Moses, there will be no veil between I and you; ask whatever comes to your mind!' Moses said, 'O God, as You are the One who agreed to hear the poor servant, in Your presence, then I will ask now.' Moses (pbuh) gently asked, 'O Lord, in the revealed Torah, I came across a people whose hearts are illuminated by obedience and worship. Place them in my community!' God said, 'O Moses, this is the blessing of Muḥammad's community.' Moses asked, 'O Lord, how did they achieve this status?' God said, 'Through poverty and starvation'.

{21} Moses asked, 'O Lord, I read in the Torah that a number of people battle with infidels. Place them in my community!' God said, 'These are also from Muḥammad's community.'

{22} Moses (pbuh) asked, 'I read in the Torah that a community will have members whose minds are replete with goodness and righteousness but which has not yet been created; the reward of their forthcoming goodness is written in their record of deeds [in advance] and if they are [even] inclined to badness, it will not be written in their record of deeds until they commit the sin. Place them in my community!' God said, 'These are also from Muḥammad's community.'

{23} Moses said, 'O God, I can see a community which is obliged to fast. Some of them did not fast but You still forgive them. Place them in my community!' God said, 'They are also from the community of Muḥammad'.

[10] i.e., Muḥammad's community

{۲۴} باز موسیٰ گفت «یا رَبّ، در تورات نوشته می‌بینم که قومی از نیکوکارانِ کعبه شفاعتِ گنه‌کاران کنند. ایشان را از امّت من گردان». فرمان شد «این درجه نیز بر امّتان محمّد باشد».

{۲۵} موسیٰ گفت «یا رَبّ، در تورات می‌بینم که قومی را بر بُراق سوار خواهی کرد. ایشان را از امّت من گردان». فرمان شد که «این هم از امّت محمّد عليه‌السلام است».

{۲۶} موسیٰ گفت «یا رَبّ، به چه عمل این درجهٔ امّت کردی؟ فرمان شد که [...]».[۴۸]

{۲۷} موسیٰ گفت «خداوندا، در تورات می‌بینم که قومی از گور برخیزند بی‌حساب در بهشت در آیند. ایشان را از امّت من گردان». فرمان شد که «از امّت محمّد است». موسیٰ گفت «یا رَبّ، به چه عمل این درجه به امّت کردی؟» فرمان شد که «ایشان را در آخرالزمان آفریدم، و در جهان مرا یاد می‌کنند، و فرموده‌های مرا به جای می‌آرند که کسی واقف به جزء من نمی‌شود. و من کرده‌های ایشان را آشکار می‌کنم».

{۲۸} موسیٰ گفت «یا رَبّ، در تورات می‌بینم که همهٔ چیزها از کرامت محمّد عليه‌السلام است. بار خدایا مرا نیز از امّت محمّد عليه‌السلام گردان تا از شفاعت بهره[۴۹] برم». فرمان شد «یا موسیٰ، چنان که تو گفتی خواهم کرد».

{۲۹} باز موسیٰ عليه‌السلام گفت «یا رَبّ، کدام بندهٔ تو پارساتر است و کدام بندهٔ تو عالِم‌تر است؟» فرمان شد که «ای موسیٰ، پارسا آن است که در هیچ حال مرا فراموش نکند؛ خواه در راحتُ خواه در محنت. و عالِم آن است که از عِلمی که می‌دانند عَملی زیاده کنند. یعنی عبادت را بیش از پیش کنند».

{۳۰} موسیٰ گفت «یا رَبّ، کدام بندهٔ تو قوی‌تر است؟» فرمان شد که «مسلمانان و آن کسانی که هوای نفس را بِکُشند و خلاف نَفْس کارکنند».

{۳۱} موسیٰ گفت «یا رَبّ، بنده‌ای که در حضرت تو عزیزتر است کدام است؟» فرمان شد «آن کسانی که به تواضع باشند و عالمان را دوست دارند».

{۳۲} باز موسیٰ گفت «یا رَبّ، کدام بندهٔ تو رحم‌دل است؟» فرمان شد «آن کسانی که شب بیدار باشند و به ذکر من مشغول شوند رحم در دل آنها افکنم و ظلم از دل‌های آنها بردارم».

{۳۳} موسیٰ گفت «یا رَبّ، کدام بندهٔ تو باعبادت‌تر است؟» فرمان شد «آن کسانی که مؤمنان را دوست دارند و خدمتِ عالِمان بکنند، و منافقان را دشمن بدانند».

{۳۴} باز موسیٰ گفت «یا رَبّ، کدام بنده تو بدکردار تر است؟» فرمان شد «آن کسانی که همسایه‌گان را برنجانند بی‌گناه».

{۳۵} موسیٰ گفت «یا رَبّ،کدام بندهٔ تو بدبخت‌تر است؟» فرمان شد «آن کسانی که آخرت را به دنیا بدل کنند».

[۴۸] این قسمت از سؤال موسیٰ دوبار و بدون پاسخ تکرار می‌شود.

[۴۹] در حاشیهٔ برگ ۱۱۸ آ کلند ۱۷۰ چنین نوشته شده است «[بهر یعنی امید حاصل]»

{24} Again, Moses said, 'O Lord, I saw a line in the Torah that a community from the Kaʿba that performs good deeds will make intercession for the sinful. Place them in my community!' God said, 'This status has been already granted to the community of Muḥammad.'

{25} Moses said, 'O Lord, I read inYour Torah that You give a Burāq to a community. Place these people in my community!' God said, 'These are also from the community of Muḥammad (pbuh).'

{26} Moses asked, 'O Lord, how did they reach such a status?' God said, '[...]'.

{27} Moses said, 'O God, I read in the Torah that a community will rise from the grave and will enter paradise promptly, without being investigated. Place them in my community!' God said, 'They are from the community of Muḥammad.' Moses asked, 'O Lord, how did You give them this level?' God said, 'I have created them in the end times and they remember Me in the world and they follow my commands, and no one is aware of their deeds except Me, and I only show up their deeds.'

{28} Moses said, 'O Lord, I read in the Torah that everything is because of Muḥammad's (pbuh) blessing. O God, please make me one of Muḥammad's (pbuh) community so I can benefit from the intercession!' God said, 'O Moses, I will do as you request'.

{29} Again Moses (pbuh) said, 'O Lord, which of your servants is more pious and which one is more knowledgeable?' God said, 'O Moses, the pious are the one who never forget me, either in comfort or in hardship. And knowledgeable are the ones who learn from science and understand and practise it. It is these that worship me more and more'.

{30} Moses asked, 'O Lord, which of Your servants is strongest?' God said, 'Muslims and those who pacify the despotic soul and move in contrast to self-temptation.'

{31} Moses asked, 'O Lord, who are the most precious servants in Your presence?' God said, 'Those who are modest and are like scholars.'

{32} Then, Moses asked, 'O Lord, which of Your servants are gracious?' God said, 'Those who are awake at night to remember Me, I will put kindness in their hearts and remove oppression and tyranny from their hearts.'

{33} Again, Moses asked, 'O Lord, which of Your servants are the most worshipful?' God said, 'Those who befriend believers, serve the scholars, and are the enemies and rejecters of hypocrites.'

{34} Again, Moses asked, 'O Lord, which of Your servants are most ungracious?' God said, 'Those who annoy their neighbours without reason.

{35} Moses asked, 'O Lord, which of Your servants are the most misfortunate?' God said, 'Those who take the world instead of the hereafter.'

{۳۶} موسیٰ گفت «یا رَبّ، کدام بندهٔ تو صادق‌تر است؟» فرمان شد «آن کسانی که سخن چین کنند».[ب]

{۳۷} باز موسیٰ گفت «یا رَبّ، کدام بندهٔ تو سیاه‌دل تر است؟» فرمان شد «آن کسانی که حلال و حرام را نشناسند».

{۳۸} باز موسیٰ گفت «یا رَبّ، کدام بندهٔ تو بخیل است؟» فرمان شد «آن کسانی که به برادر مؤمن بخل ورزد و از معیشت خود به مؤمنان بهره نکند».

{۳۹} باز موسیٰ گفت «یا رَبّ، کدام خلق نیک‌کردار باشد؟» فرمان شد «آن کسانی که زبان خود را از بدگفتن نگاه دارد».

{۴۰} موسیٰ گفت «یا رَبّ، کدام بندهٔ تو فرمان‌بردار است و از بندهٔ خود به کدام عمل راضی شوی؟» فرمان شد «هر که بر رضایی من[۵۰] باشد و فرمودهٔ مرا به جای آرد، و یتیمان را گرامی[۵۱] بدارد. من از آن کسان راضیم».

[سؤال پرسیدن خدا از موسیٰ]

{۴۱} [خداوند] در بیانِ مناجات[۵۲] موسیٰ گفت «ای موسیٰ، می‌خواهی که تو را نزدیک خود بخواهم؟» گفت «بلی، یا رَبّ». فرمان شد که «ای موسیٰ، سایل را محروم مگردان و حمد من بسیار بگوی تا محبّتِ دوستی من از زبان انتقاد[ج] کرده به دل قرار گیرد. اگر چنانچه زبانِ تو تکلّم کند، امّا دل همیشه در گرو باشد تا از همهٔ گناهان پاک شوی قُربِ من به تو حاصل گردد».

{۴۲} باز فرمان شد «یا موسیٰ، می‌خواهی که دعای تو مستجاب شود؟» موسیٰ گفت «یا رَبّ می‌خواهم». فرمان شد که «دَستِ خود را از گرفتن چیز حرام، دهن خود را از خوردن حرام نگاه‌دار».

{۴۳} باز گفت «یا موسیٰ، می‌خواهی که تو را پیش‌از همهٔ خلق به بهشت ببرم؟» موسیٰ گفت «بلی، یا رَبّ». گفت «حاجت درماندگان را برآری».

{۴۴} باز گفت «یا موسیٰ، می‌خواهی که روزی هفتادبار به نَظَرِ رَحمَتْ به سوی تو بنگرم؟» موسیٰ گفت «بلی، یا رَبّ». فرمان شد که «با یتیمان مُشفِق باشی چنان که پدران با فرزندان کنند».

[۵۰] رضای من. [۵۱] در حاشیهٔ برگ ۱۱۸ آ کلند ۱۷۰ چنین نوشته شده است [گرامی یعنی بزرگ] [۵۲] واژهٔ «مناجات» با تاکید بر «گفتگو» بیشتر کاربرد فارسی دارد؛ در ادبیات مالایی-اندونزیایی به‌صورت «Musa Munajat» یا «Musa-nama» دیده می‌شود.

[ب] آن کسانی که سخن چینی نکنند [ج] انتقال

{36} Moses asked, 'O Lord, which of Your servants is most [dis]honest?' God said, 'The talebearers.'

{37} Moses asked, 'O Lord, which of Your servants have the most blackened hearts?' God said, 'Those who do not know the permissible from the impermissible.'

{38} Again, Moses asked, 'O Lord, which of Your servants are miserly?' God said, 'Those who hold a grudge against their Muslim brothers and do not offer believers from their provisions.'

{39} Again, Moses asked, 'O Lord, which of Your servants are most righteous?' God said, 'Those who abstain from saying bad words.'

{40} Moses asked, 'O Lord, which of Your servants are more obedient and with which of Your servant's deeds will You be satisfied?' God said, 'Those who act for My satisfaction and practice My command and respect orphans, I will be satisfied with them.'

GOD THEN ASKED QUESTIONS FROM MOSES

{41} [God] asked 'O Moses, would you like Me to bring you close to Myself? Moses said, 'Yes, O Lord!'God said, 'Do not let the beggar down and praise Me a lot until the love of My friendship moves from the tongue to the heart. Although your tongue praises, your heart will always be on hold and dependent, only when it will be cleansed from all sins, will you experience My closeness.'

{42} Again, God asked, 'O Moses, do you want your request and prayer to be answered?' Moses said: 'O Lord, indeed I do!' God said, 'Do not take impermissible things in your hand, do not eat impermissible things with your mouth.'

{43} Again, God asked, 'O Moses, do you want me to take you to paradise earlier than others?' Moses said, 'Yes, O Lord!' God said, 'You must provide for the needs of the helpless.'

{44} Again, God asked, 'O Moses, do you want Me to look mercifully upon you seventy times every day?' Moses said, 'Yes, my Lord!' God said, 'Be kind with orphans as much as fathers are to their children.'

{۴۵} باز گفت «یا موسیٰ، می‌خواهی که روز قیامت از تشنگی نجات یابی؟» موسیٰ گفت «بلی، یا رَبّ». فرمان شد که «مسلمانان را خوار مدار و تشنه‌گان را آب بده. گرسنگان را طعام ده و برهنه‌گان را کهنه و نو بده».

{۴۶} فرمان شد که «ای موسیٰ، می‌خواهی که پایهٔ نیکی تو گران کنم؟» موسیٰ گفت «بلی، یا رَبّ». فرمان شد که «با خلق نیکویی کن و سخاوت پیشه‌گیر».

{۴۷} باز گفت «ای موسیٰ، می‌خواهی که سؤال منکر و نکیر بر تو آسان گردانم؟» موسیٰ گفت «بلی، یا رَبّ». فرمان شد که «آنکه بر مسلمان بهتان نکنی و با عالمان صحبت بداری».

{۴۸} گفت «ای موسیٰ، می‌خواهی که حساب قیامت را آسان سازم؟» موسیٰ گفت «بلی، یا رَبّ». فرمان شد که «بعداز حجّ شصت [؟] بار «أستَغفر اللّٰه ولِوالدَي وَبِجَميع [؟] المُؤمِنين وَالمُؤمِنَات وَالمُسلِمِين وَالمُسلِمات الأحياء مِنهُم وَالأموات إنَّكَ مُجيب الدَعَوات وَرافِع الدَرَجَاة بِرحمَتِك يَا أرْحَم الرّاحِمِينْ »[۵۳] [بخوان؟]

سؤالات موسیٰ از خدا

در بیان جوابِ سؤال

{۴۹} موسیٰ علیه‌السلام گفت «یا رَبّ، آن کسانی که علم بسیار خوانَد جزای او چه باشد؟» فرمان شد که «رحمت خود بر آن بنده افکنم».

{۵۰} موسیٰ گفت «یا رَبّ، آن کسانی که شب نمازگزارند جزای او چیست؟» فرمان شد که «روزی آن بنده را منوّر گردانم و بساطِ[۵۴] بهشت به او روزی گردانم که دائم [است]».

{۵۱} موسیٰ گفت «یا رَبّ، هر که همه‌شان را (؟) که مؤمن باشند دوست دارد، جزای آن چیست؟» فرمان شد که در «عُمر او برکت کنم و دعای او را مستجاب کنم».

{۵۲} موسیٰ گفت «یا رَبّ، آنکه در حقّ مادر و پدر نیکی کند و خدمت به جای آرد جزای او چیست؟» فرمان شد که «گناهان آن بنده را بیامرزم».

{۵۳} موسیٰ گفت «یا رَبّ، آنکه کلمهٔ لآ إلٰهَ إلَّا اللّٰه، مُحَمَّدٌ رَسُولُ اللّٰه بسیار گوید جزای او چیست؟» فرمان شد که «بیامرزم هرچند که عاصی و گناه‌کار باشد. و هزار بلا از تَنِ او دفع کنم و رزق او را فراوان کنم».

{۵۴} موسیٰ گفت «یا رَبّ، آن که غُسلِ روزِ جمعه کُند جزای او چیست؟» فرمان شد که «فَلَه[۵۵] گناه از نامهٔ اعمال او بردارم [...] در گور او روضه باز کنم».

[۵۳] اشاره دارد به این دعا: «اللهم اغفر لي ولوالدي ولجميع المؤمنين والمؤمنات، والمسلمين والمسلمات الأحياء منهم والأموات [...]»

[۵۴] در حاشیه برگ ۱۱۹ آکلند ۱۷۰ [و بساط یعنی بهشت ...سایا...]

[۵۵] حجم زیاد و یک جا.

{45} Again, God asked, 'O Moses, would you like to be saved from thirst on the Day of Judgement?' Moses said, 'Yes, O Lord!' God said, 'Do not humiliate Muslims and provide the thirsty people with water. Provide the hungry people with food and clothe the naked with old or new garments.'

{46} God asked, 'O Moses, do you want Me to increase the balance of your goodness?' Moses said, 'Yes, O Lord!' God said, 'Be nice with people and be generous.'

{47} Again, God asked, 'O Moses, would you like Me to help you pass Munkar and Nakīr's interrogation with ease?' Moses said, 'Yes, my Lord!' God said, 'Do not curse Muslims and do converse with scholars.'

{48} God asked, 'O Moses, do you want me to make your reckoning on the Day of Judgement easy?' Moses said, 'Yes, O Lord!' God said, 'After hajj [...] the supplication, 'Forgive me God, my parents, and all male and female believers, and all male and female Muslims, whether alive or dead, as You are the One who answers the requests and who is the Elevator of ranks, by Your mercy, O the most Merciful of the merciful.'

THE QUESTIONS OF MOSES FROM GOD

On Divine Responses to Questions

{49} Moses (pbuh) asked, 'O Lord, what is the reward of the one who gathers a lot of knowledge?' God said, 'I bestow My mercy upon that servant.'

{50} Moses asked, 'O Lord, what is the reward of one who prays at night?' God said, 'I will illuminate the provision of that servant and provide them with a heavenly spread, which is everlasting.'

{51} Moses asked, 'O Lord, what is the reward of the one who likes all believers?' God said, 'I will increase his longevity, and respond to his requests.'

{52} Moses asked, 'O Lord, what is the reward of the one who is good with his mother and father and serves them?' God said, 'I will forgive his sins.'

{53} Moses asked, 'O Lord, what is the reward of the one who says a lot, "There is no god but God; Muḥammad is the Messenger of God"?' God said, 'I will forgive whatever he did that was disobedient and sinful. And I will ward off a thousand calamities and disasters from his body and increase his provision.'

{54} Moses asked, 'O Lord, what is the reward of the one who performs the ritual Friday ablution?' God said, 'I remove many sins from his record of deeds, and make his grave like a garden.'

{55} Moses asked, 'O Lord, what is the reward of the one who visits the sick?' God said, 'O Moses, in exchange for every single step he takes towards visiting the

{۵۵} موسیٰ گفت «یا رَبّ، آن کس که بیمار پُرسَد جزای چه باشد؟» فرمان شد که «یا موسیٰ، هر قدمی که به پرسش بیمار نهد هزار نیکی در نامۀ اعمال او بنویسند، و هزار بدی از اعمال او بردارم».

{۵۶} مهتر موسیٰ گفت «یا رَبّ، شخصی که مُرده را کَفن بدهد جزای او چیست؟» فرمان شد از حضرت العِزّتُ که «ای موسیٰ، آن بنده را حُلّه‌های بهشت پوشانم».

{۵۷} مهتر موسیٰ گفت «یا رَبّ، آن کس که پای جنازه بردارد جزای او چه باشد؟» فرمان شد که «ای موسیٰ، در هر قدمی که در پای جنازه رود ثواب آخرت و ثواب آزاد کردن بنده به کس بدهم».

{۵۸} موسیٰ گفت «یا رَبّ، آن کس که مسجد بنا کند جزای او چه باشد؟» فرمان شد که «ای موسیٰ، در بهشت کوشکی از برای آن بنده بنا کنم که برابر دنیا باشد».

{۵۹} مهتر موسیٰ گفت «یا رَبّ، شخصی که برهنه‌گان را بپوشاند جزای او چه باشد؟» فرمان شود که «از استبرق[۵۶] حوله‌هایِ بهشتی آن بنده را پوشانم».

{۶۰} باز مهتر موسیٰ گفت «خداوندا، آن کسی که همسایه‌گان را گرامی دارد جزای او چیست؟» فرمان شود که «آن بنده را به لطف خود بدی‌های او را محو کنم. و در خواب دیدار خود را نمایم».

{۶۱} مهتر موسیٰ گفت «خداوندا، آن کسانی که از ترسِ تو آب از دیدگان[۵۷] بریزند جزای آن چه باشد؟» فرمان شود که «گناهان بنده را عفو کنم و بَعدِ دو قَطرِهِ آبِ دیده، فرشته‌ها تا روز قیامت نیکی در نامۀ اعمال او ثبت گردانند».

{۶۲} باز موسیٰ گفت «یا رَبّ، آنکه مهمان را عزیز دارد جزای او چه باشد؟» فرمان شود که «مغفرتِ آمرزش در حقّ او زیاده کنم».

{۶۳} موسیٰ گفت «یا رَبّ، آنکه قرآن بخواند جزای او چیست؟» فرمان شود که «آن بنده را از پل صراط آسان گذاریم و هرکه را شَفیع شود بخشم».

{۶۴} باز موسیٰ گفت «یا رَبّ، آنکه مردمان را از معصیت باز دارد جزای او چیست؟» فرمان شود «یا موسیٰ، مرا از روی او شرم آید، او را در قیامت عذاب نکنم».

{۶۵} موسیٰ گفت «یا رَبّ، آنکه محتاج را دست گیرد و او را مَمنون[۵۸] سازد جزای او چه باشد؟» فرمان شود که دل او را از پلیدی‌های دنیا پاک گردانم».

{۶۶} موسیٰ گفت «یا رَبّ، آنکه مَردمان را بد گوید و زشت‌زبانْ[۵۹] باشد جزای او چه بوَد؟» فرمان شود «یا موسیٰ، به عدد هر مویِ در سرو تن او باشد ملائکه‌ها از برای او لعنت فرستند».

۵۶ در حاشیۀ برگ ۱۲۰ آ کلند ۱۷۰ چنین آمده: [استبرق یعنی پوشاک بهشت]. همچنین به معنی پارچۀ ابریشمی و زیبا به‌کار می‌رود.

۵۷ دیده‌گان. ۵۸ در حاشیۀ برگ ۱۲۰ آ کلند ۱۷۰ [ممنون یعنی امیّد]. ۵۹ بد زبان و فحّاش.

sick, a thousand good deeds will be written in his record, and a thousand vices will be removed.'

{56} His Eminence Moses asked, 'O Lord, what is the reward of the one who shrouds the dead?' the glorious God said, 'I will dress him with heavenly clothes.'

{57} His Eminence Moses asked, 'O Lord, what is the reward of the one who carries the coffin of the dead?' God said, 'O Moses, in exchange for every single step taken with the coffin I will grant him the reward of the hereafter as well as the reward of releasing slaves.'

{58} Moses asked, 'O Lord, what is the reward of the one who builds a mosque?' God said, 'O Moses, I will build a palace for him in paradise as large as the world.'

{59} His Eminence Moses asked, 'O Lord, what is the reward of the one who covers the naked poor?' God said, 'I will cover him with dresses made of silk and gold.'

{60} Again, His Eminence Moses asked, 'O God, what is the reward of the one who respects his neighbours?' God said, 'I will remove the badness of the servant through My grace, and will grant him My vision in a dream.'

{61} His Eminence Moses asked, 'O God, what is the reward of the one who cries from fear of You?' God said, 'I will forgive his sins and after two tear drops, angels will write goodness in his record of deeds until the Day of Judgement.'

{62} Again, Moses asked, 'O Lord, what is the reward of the one who respects the guests?' God said, 'I will forgive him more.'

{63} Moses asked, 'O Lord, what is the reward of the one who recites the Qurʾān?' God said, 'I will ease the crossing of that servant over the Ṣirāṭ bridge and when he intercedes on behalf of others to have their sins forgiven, I will accept and forgive them.'

{64} Then Moses asked, 'O Lord, what is the reward of the one who forbids people from committing indecency?' God said, 'O Moses, I will be ashamed to punish him on the Day of Judgement.'

{65} Moses asked, 'O Lord, what is the reward of the one who assists the needy, providing them with favour?' God said, 'I will purify his heart from worldly impurities.'

{66} Moses asked, 'O Lord, what is the punishment of the one who is foul-mouthed?' God said, 'O Moses, angels will call curses upon him as much as every strand of hair on his head and body.'

{۶۷} موسیٰ گفت «یا رَبّ، آنکه خود را نیکو دارد درمیانِ خَلق جزای او چه بوَد؟ فرمان شود «یا موسیٰ، نام وی را در دیوانِ[۶۰] گناه‌کاران ننویسم».

{۶۸} باز موسیٰ گفت «یا رَبّ، آنکه به [دوبنده؟] نیکوئی کند جزای او چه بوَد؟» فرمان شود «من که خداوندم در مرده و زندهٔ او رحمت فرستم».

{۶۹} موسیٰ گفت «یا رَبّ، آنکه در آبِ سَرد وضوء کند جزای او چیست؟» فرمان شود که «تا نماز را ادا کردن ملائکه رحمت از برای او آمرزش خواهند و دعای خیر در حقّ او بکنند».

{۷۰} باز موسیٰ گفت «یا رَبّ، آنکه به دعای خیرْ مسلمانان را یاد کند جزای او چه باشد؟» فرمان شود «ثواب هفتاد رکعت نماز یابد».

{۷۱} موسیٰ گفت «یا رَبّ، آنکه برادر مؤمن را دوست دارد جزای او چه باشد؟» فرمان شد که «او را از آتش دوزخ آزاد گردانم».

{۷۲} موسیٰ گفت «یا رَبّ، آن که در وقتِ نمازِ خودش حاضر شود جزای او چیست؟» فرمان شد که «به عدد هر مویی که در تن او باشد به آن کس نیکی کرامت کنم».

{۷۳} موسیٰ گفت «یا رَبّ، آنکه تشنه را آب دهد جزای او چیست؟» فرمان شد «او را از حرارتِ گرمیِ قیامت نگاه دارم و از آتش دوزخ آزادی نصیب کنم».

{۷۴} موسیٰ گفت «یا رَبّ، آن‌کس که سوگند به دروغ خورد جزای او چه باشد؟» فرمان شود که «رزق او را کم کنم و برکت او ستانم».

{۷۵} موسیٰ گفت «یا رَبّ، آن‌کس که غیبت کسی را بگوید جزای او چیست؟» فرمان شد «او آنچه در دنیا نیکی کرده باشد ثواب آن را از پلهٔ او بردارم و به کس دیگر بدهم».

{۷۶} مهتر موسیٰ گفت «یا رَبّ، اگر کسی همسایگان را برنجاند جزای او چه باشد؟» فرمان شود که «عمل‌های نیک او را محو کنم و دری از آتش دوزخ بر وی باز کنم».

{۷۷} موسیٰ گفت «یا رَبّ، آنکه مال یتیمان خَرِف‌خوی[۶۱] سازد جزای او چه باشد؟» فرمان شد «دعای او را هرگز قبول نکنم».

{۷۸} موسیٰ گفت «یا رَبّ، آن‌کس که از مر اِتبان[۶۲] مُفلس پرهیز کند و مُشفق نباشد جزای او چه باشد؟» فرمان شد که «کوتاهی در عمر ادا کنم و روزی او تنگ سازم و نماز و حجّ او را قبول نکنم».

{۷۹} مهتر موسیٰ گفت «یا رَبّ، آن‌کس که مالِ بیوه‌گان خورَد جزای او چه باشد؟» فرمان آید که «هر روز آفتاب و ماه برآید برآن بنده لعنت کنند و شکم آن بنده را پُرِ آتشِ دوزخ گردانم و زهراب[۶۳] مار و کژدم بر آن کس خوردن دهم».

۶۰ دفتر.
۶۱ کم‌توان. همچنین به‌صورت «خِرِف» هم به‌کار می‌رود.
۶۲ برگرفته از واژهٔ تبن به معنی «به فرزندی پذیرفتن» و «پرورش دادن» است.
۶۳ آب زهرآلود، ادرار.

{67} Moses asked, 'O Lord, what is the reward of the one who refines himself among the people?' God said, 'O Moses, I will not write his name in the record of the sinners.'

{68} Again, Moses asked, 'O Lord, what is the reward of the one who acts nicely with [...]?' God said, 'I, as God, will send him mercy whether dead or alive.'

{69} Moses asked, 'O Lord, what is the reward of the one who takes ablution in cold water?' God said, 'As soon as he performs prayer, the angels of mercy will demand forgiveness for them and pray for them.'

{70} Again, Moses asked, 'O Lord, what is the reward of the one who remembers and supports Muslims with kind and pure prayers?' God said, 'He will achieve the reward of seventy units of prayer.'

{71} Moses asked, 'O Lord, what is the reward of the one who loves and respects his Muslim brothers?' God said, 'I will release him from hellfire.'

{72} Moses asked, 'O Lord, what is the reward of the one who rises to say his prayers on time?' God said, 'I will grant him blessings as much as the hairs on his body.'

{73} Moses asked, 'O Lord, what is the reward of the one who gives water to the thirsty?' God said, 'I will protect him from the heat of the Day of Judgement and release him from hellfire.'

{74} Moses asked, 'O Lord, what is the punishment of the one who gives false testimony?' God said, 'I will reduce his provision and remove blessings from him.'

{75} Moses asked, 'O Lord, what is the punishment of the one who gossips about people?' God said, 'Whatever he did good in the world, its reward will be taken from his scales and will be given to someone else.'

{76} His Eminence Moses asked, 'O Lord, what is the punishment of the one who annoys his neighbour?' God said, 'I will remove his good acts and open the door to hellfire for him.'

{77} Moses asked, 'O Lord, what is the punishment of the one who profits from lunatic[11] orphans?' God said, 'I will never accept his requests.'

{78} Moses asked, 'O Lord, what is the punishment of the one who refuses to support the destitute and who is not kind?' God said, 'I will reduce his longevity and his provision and will not accept his prayers and pilgrimage.'

{79} His Eminence Moses asked, 'O Lord, what is the punishment of the one who amasses wealth from the wealth of orphans?' God said, 'Whenever the Sun and Moon rise, they will curse that servant and I will fill the stomach of the servant with fire and make him drink the poison[12] of snakes and scorpions.'

[11] also, handicapped [12] also, urine

{۸۰} موسیٰ گفت «یا رَبّ، آن کس که تو را کمتر یاد کند جزای آن چه بوَد؟» فرمان شد «من نیز رزق او را کم کنم و برکت از دانگانهٔ[۶۴] او بردارم»

{۸۱} باز موسیٰ گفت «یا رَبّ، آن کس که زنا کند جزای او چه باشد؟» فرمان شود که «پیراهنی از آتش دوزخ در بَرِ او پوشانم».

{۸۲} موسیٰ گفت «یا رَبّ، آن کس که حقّ عَبْد[۶۵] کَنَد جزای او چه بوَد؟» فرمان رسد که «تمام گناهان بندگان را عفو کنم. امّا حقّ عبد را نبخشم تا شود (...) در عقوبت آخرت گرفتار باشد».

{۸۳} موسیٰ گفت «یا رَبّ، آن کس که امانت را خیانت کند جزای او چه باشد؟» فرمان شود که «ای موسیٰ، هرگاه آن بنده به درگاه ما حاجت خواهد، من که خداوندم هزار لعنت بدو فرستم».

{۸۴} موسیٰ گفت «یا رَبّ، آن کس که بر مسلمانان غزا کند جزای او چه باشد؟» فرمان شود که «ای موسیٰ، جای آن قوم را در سجّین[۶۶] سازم که همیشه به قعر آتشِ من می‌سوخته باشند».

{۸۵} باز موسیٰ گفت «یا رَبّ، آن کس غلّه به نیّت گرانی بِخَرَد، تا آنکه چون گران شود بفروشد، جزای او چه باشد؟» فرمان شود «آنچه در دنیا نکویی کرده باشد به بدی مبدّل گردانم».

{۸۶} باز موسیٰ گفت «یا رَبّ، آن کس که عِلم و عَالِمان را به چشمِ حقارت بیند جزای آن چه باشد؟» فرمان شود «آن کس کافر گردد و هر که کافران را عزیز دارد، من که پروردگار اویم، از او بی‌زار باشم».

{۸۷} باز موسیٰ گفت «یا رَبّ، آن کسانی که سخن‌چینی کنند جزای آنها چه باشد؟» فرمان شود «فرشتگان رحمت از او بی‌زار شوند».

{۸۸} باز موسیٰ گفت «یا رَبّ، زنانی که خلاف شوهر کار کنند جزای آنها چه باشد؟» فرمان شود «یا موسیٰ، نیکی‌های آن‌ها را به شوهران بدهم».

{۸۹} باز موسیٰ گفت «یا رَبّ، کسی که حقّ مزدور نگاه دارد جزای او چه باشد؟» فرمان شود «یا موسیٰ، فردای قیامت «أمَنَّا وَصدَّقنا [...]من که خداوندم، حضرت او باشم».[۶۷]

در بیان مسائل

{۹۰} مهتر موسیٰ گفت «یا رَبّ، می‌خواهم که در حضرتِ تو چند سؤال کنم امّا می ترسم». فرمان شد که «ای موسیٰ، قدحی پُرآب کن و به حضرتِ ما بیا تا قدرت ما را مشاهده کنی». موسیٰ قدح پر آب کرد و بر کفِ دست گرفت و بایستاد. حق سُبحانَهُ وَتَعَالیٰ خود را برابر موسیٰ گماشت. قدح از دست موسیٰ بیفتاد و بشکست و

[۶۴] اشاره به سُفره و خزانه نیز دارد. همچنین «دُنگ» [۶۵] غلام و برده.
[۶۶] «جایی در دوزخ» یا «زندان»؛ به عمید مراجعه شود. [۶۷] مفهوم مشخصی ندارد.

{80} Moses asked, 'O Lord, what is the punishment of the one who remembers you less?' God said, 'I, in return, will reduce his provision and remove My blessing from his previous deeds.'

{81} Again, Moses asked, 'O Lord, what is the punishment of the one who commits adultery?' God said, 'I will put a compress[13] from hellfire on him.'

{82} Moses asked, 'O Lord, what is the punishment of the one who violates the rights of slaves?' God said, 'I forgive every sin of the servant. However, I will not forgive violating the slaves' rights so [...] he will be in torment in the hereafter.'

{83} Moses asked, 'O Lord, what is the punishment of the one who is not maintain trust?' God said, 'O Moses, whenever that servant demands something from us, I, as God, will send down a curse upon him.'

{84} Moses asked, 'O Lord, what is the punishment of the one who fights with Muslims?' God said, 'O Moses, I will imprison him [in hell], and he will always burn at the bottom of My fire.'

{85} Again, Moses asked, 'O Lord, what is the punishment of the one who purchases grain for hoarding and sells it once the price increases?' God said, 'Whatever good he did in the world, I will convert it to vice.'

{86} Again, Moses asked, 'O Lord, what is the punishment for the one who underestimates and who belittles scholarship and the scholars?' God said, 'This fellow will become an infidel and whoever respects infidels, I, as God, will refuse them.'

{87} Again, Moses asked, 'O Lord, what is the punishment of a talebearer?' God said, 'The angels of mercy will be hesitant towards them and refuse them.'

{88} Again, Moses asked, 'O Lord, what is the punishment of the woman who acts against her husband's desires?' God said, 'O Moses, I will pass on her goodness to her husband.'

{89} Again, Moses asked, 'O Lord, what is the punishment of the one who holds the wage of the worker?' God said, 'O Moses, I, who is God, will be Exalted above them on the Day of Judgement [...].'

On the clarification of questions

{90} His Eminence Moses said, 'O Lord, I want to ask a number of questions of Your Excellency, but I am afraid!' God said, 'O Moses, fill a cup full with water and bring it to Our presence in order to behold Our power.' Moses filled a cup with water and held it in the palm of his hands, and stayed there [calmly]. God placed Himself before Moses. The

[13] garment

آب نیز بریخت. فرمان شد «ای موسیٰ، به عزّت جلالیّتِ من که اگر یک طَرفَة العَینی[۶۸] از خلق غافل شوم، عرش و کرسی و لوح و قلم و آسمان و زمین و آنچه هست همه درهم شود».

{۹۱} موسیٰ گفت «یا رَبّ، خوردنی و پوشیدنیِ تو از چیست؟» فرمان شد که «خوردن من صبر کردن است در غمِ بندگان. یعنی غمِ جملهٔ خلایق می‌خورم روزی[؟][۶۹] می‌رسانم. پوشیدن من عظمت است».

{۹۲} موسیٰ گفت «یا رَبّ، از مشرق تا به مغرب چگونه می‌بینی؟» فرمان شد که «در نظر من چنان است که دانه در کَفِ دست موسیٰ».

{۹۳} باز موسیٰ گفت «یا رَبّ، چگونه روا داری که ظالم بر مظلوم ظلم کند؟ تو می‌بینی!» فرمان شد که «سخاوت ظالم را بر مظلوم دهم و ظلم کننده را بدبخت گردانم. جای او در دوزخ باشد و من خَصمِ او باشم».

{۹۴} باز موسیٰ گفت «یا رَبّ، اندیشه‌ای که در دلِ بندگان گذرد چگونه دانی؟» فرمان شد که «بندگان بند قدرت منست[۷۰] چنانچه ستارگان در آسمان معلّق باشد. هرآن بنده که نیّت بد[۷۱] در دل می‌کند، دل آن بنده را همچون ابر سیاه تاریک می‌گردانم».[۷۲]

{۹۵} باز موسیٰ گفت «یا رَبّ، پیش‌از آنکه آسمان‌ها و زمین‌ها نبود تو کجا می‌بودی؟» فرمان شد که «ای موسیٰ، در بالای دَری؛ آن دَر پانصدسال راه است [؟]».

{۹۶} باز موسیٰ گفت «یا رَبّ، پیش‌از آنکه دَر نبود تو کجا می‌بودی؟» فرمان شد که «ای موسیٰ، اگر رحمت من بر تو قرین (نبودی) تو را بر آتش دوزخ هلاک گردانیدمی. و اگر دوستی ابراهیم خلیل من نبودی بر تو معصیت افکندی». چون موسیٰ عتاب شنید از دست برفت و بهوش آمد. باز گفت «یا رَبّ، بر منِ ضعیف چَشم گرفتی؟»[۷۳] فرمان شد «ای موسیٰ از برای آنکه سخن به غایت عظیم گفتی».

{۹۷} موسیٰ گفت «یا رَبّ، بد کردم که به حضرتِ پاکِ تو بی‌ادبی کردم». فرمان حضرتِ حمدیّت دررسید که «موسیٰ، یک نظر کرده (بر) آن مروارید که از هیبت خدای تَعَالَی گداخته و آب شدی؛ ای موسیٰ، یک نظر در آب کردم به جوش آمد و موج برآورد و از کَفِ آن آبْ زمین را بیافریدیم، و از دودْ[۷۴] آسمان‌ها آفریدم و ستاره‌گان پیدا گردانیدم. تمام باب‌ها در بیت المقدس است. چون روز قیامت شود [...] از آن باب [ها] سنگِ سفید پیدا گردانم که سفیدتر از نقرهٔ خامْ باشد و بزرگی آن سنگ هَم چَنْد[۷۵] دنیا باشد، و هر شهرستان (؟) را هزاران سال عباد (؟) کنند. و از جملهٔ ایشانْ یکی عاصی شود. همه را بر هم زنم و ناچیز گردانم».[۷۶]

{۹۸} موسیٰ گفت «یا رَبّ، گناه یکی کند، چگونه همه را هلاک کنی؟» فرمان شد که «یا موسیٰ، به

[۶۸] یک لحظهٔ کوتاه، یک‌آن. [۶۹] اینکه آیا این واژه «زی»، «زیّ» و یا «روزی» است مشخّص نیست. [۷۰] من هستند.
[۷۱] به جای «نیّت بد» به «نیّت نیک» اشاره شده‌است. [۷۲] منظور این عبارت واضح نیست آیا اشاره به ابر باران‌زا دارد، آلودگی را می‌زادید و نشانهٔ نیکویی است؛ یا مراد ابر سیاهی است که نشانهٔ تاریک بودن و عذاب است. [۷۳] به احتمال بسیار زیاد اشاره به «چشم زهره گرفتن» دارد که به عنوان «نگاه خیره و غضب آلود کردن به کسی» به‌کار می‌رود. به معین مراجعه شود. [۷۴] بخار. [۷۵] برابر.
[۷۶] چنین تصویری از آفرینش را می‌توان در نسخهٔ فارسی-مالایی ۵۶۵۶ لایدن که پیشتر در جاوا (اندونزی) بوده است مشاهده نمود. نگاه کنید به Daneshgar, ‘Persianate Fiqh in Indonesia’.

cup of water fell from Moses' hands and broke, and the water poured out. God said, 'O Moses, by My Glory and Majesty that if I do not notice[14] the people for a very short moment, the whole Throne, Seat, Plate, Pen, Heaven, Earth, and whatever else will be dishevelled.'

{91} Moses asked, 'O Lord, what do You eat and wear?' God said, 'My food is being patient in grieving for the people. It means that I grieve for all people and provide for them. And greatness is what I wear.'

{92} Moses asked, 'O Lord, how do You see from the East to the West?' God said, 'like the way you see a seed in the palm of your hand, Moses.'

{93} Again, Moses asked, 'O Lord, why and how do You allow an oppressor to oppress the oppressed? You can see that, right!' God said, 'I give the generosity of the oppressor to the oppressed, and I topple the oppressor; their place will be in hell for ever and I will claim against them and be their adversary.'

{94} Again, Moses asked, 'O Lord, how do You know what the servants think about?' God said, 'The servants are subject to, and dependent upon, My power, like the way stars are suspended in the sky. As soon as a bad intention enters the servant's heart, I will make the heart of the servant like a dark cloud.'

{95} Again, Moses asked, 'O Lord, where were You before the heavens and the Earth?' God answered, 'O Moses, I was above a gate; that gate is 500 years away [?].'

{96} Again, Moses asked, 'O Lord, where were You before the gate was created?' God said, 'O Moses, I would have punished you with hellfire if My mercy was not upon you. And if there was not the friendship of the Friend of Mine, Abraham, I would have rebelled against you.'When Moses was rebuked, he fainted. When he came round, he again said, 'O Lord, why did You look upon me with wrath and anger?' God said, 'O Moses, because you did not know your limitations.'[15]

{97} Moses said, 'O Lord, I did wrong to disrespect Your pure majesty.' God said, 'O Moses, have a look at the pearl which has been melted down due to the fear of God. 'O Moses, I briefly looked upon the water, and made the water boil and foam. And I made the Earth from the water's foam, and I made the heavens from its vapour and created stars in it. 'All gates are in Jerusalem. On the Day of Judgement, I make a white stone from these gates, which is whiter than the purest silver, and its size is as large as the world; provisions are [complete for] obedient worshippers for a thousand years.[16] And if one of them disobeys, I will make everything unsettled and void.'[17]

{98} Moses said, 'O Lord, one commits a sin and You make all perish?' God said,

[14] i.e., look after [15] Perhaps, referring to biting off more than one can chew. [16] 'There are provisions for obedient worshipers for a thousand years. [17] This description is, to some extent, similar to the one in the Persian-Malay manuscript Or. 5656, collected in Banten, Indonesia, now parts of the Leiden University Library. About this manuscript, see: Daneshgar, 'Persianate Fiqh in Indonesia'.

زیر درخت بنشین». موسیٰ به فرمان به زیرِ درخت نشست. به فرمان خدای عَزَّوَجَلَّ هزار مورچه به پای مبارک مهتر موسیٰ برآمدند. و یک مورچه‌ای پای ایشان را بگزید. از خواب به خشم بیدار شد و دست فراز گردید آن مورچه‌گان بمالید. جملهٔ مورچه‌گان را هلاک کرد. بعداز آن موسیٰ برخاست و وضو ساخت. دو رکعت نماز گذارید. فرمان حقّ تَعَالَیٰ شد که «ای موسیٰ، یک مورچه گناه کرده. بدل یک گناه‌کار جملهٔ مورچه‌گان را هلاک کردی؟» موسیٰ شرمنده باشد. آن‌گاه از حق سُبْحَانَهُ وَتَعَالَىٰ بی‌واسطه ندا آمد که «ای موسیٰ، من که خداوندم اگر بنده به قصدُ گناه کند من رحمتِ خود از آن بنده بردارم».

{۹۹} باز موسیٰ گفت «یا رَبّ، بهشت و حوض کوثر از برای [که...]؟» فرمان شد که «از برای محمّد آخرالزمان و امّتان او».

{۱۰۰} موسیٰ گفت «یا رَبّ، مرا چیزی بیاموز تا بدان فخر کنم». فرمان شد که «ای موسیٰ، هر روز پنجاه بار بگو «الحمدُ لله عَلَیٰ کُلّ حَال، لآ إِلٰهَ إِلَّا اللهُ ٱلمَلِكُ ٱلحَقّ ٱليَقِين». بعد فرشتگان آسمان و زمین ثواب تو را بدهند». موسیٰ گفت «یا رَبّ، چنین کنم».

{۱۰۱} باز فرمان شد که «ای موسیٰ، هر روز پنجاه بار «سُبحَان ٱلمِيزان وَٱلحَمْدُلله أَكْبَر لَه ٱلميزان»[۷۷] چنان است که گویا جملهٔ درویشان را صدقه داده باشی».

در بیان وصیّت کردنِ موسیٰ عَلَيْهِ السَّلَامُ

{۱۰۲} گفت «یا ربِّ نصیحت کن». فرمان شد که «ای موسیٰ، دروغ گویی دشمن من است و دروغ گفتن کار ملعون است».

{۱۰۳} موسیٰ گفت «یا ربّ، رحمت زیادت کن». فرمان شد که «ای موسیٰ، کِبر نکنی که کِبرکنندگان شایسته نباشند. و هرکه کِبر کند او را به آتش دوزخ مبتلا گردانم».

{۱۰۴} مهتر موسیٰ گفت «یا ربّ، رحمت خود زیادت کن». فرمان شد «ای موسیٰ مهمان را عزیز بداری».

{۱۰۵} موسیٰ گفت «یا ربّ، مهمان تو کیست؟» گفت «آن که حاضر شد و او را کس نشناسد و چون غایب شود او را کس نپرسد. آن‌کس مهمان من است».

{۱۰۶} موسیٰ گفت «یا ربّ، همسایهٔ تو کیست؟» فرمان شد «آن‌کس که شب گرسنه خواب رود؛ از کس چیزی طمع نکند».

{۱۰۷} مهتر موسیٰ گفت «یا ربّ، رحمت زیادت بکن». فرمان شد «ای موسیٰ، همنشین مرا گرامی دار».

۷۷ احتمالا اشاره به «وَٱلْحَمْدُ للهِ تملأ المیزان، وَسُبْحَانَ الله وَٱلْحَمْدُ للهِ تملآن يَعني تملأ المِيزَان» دارد.

'O Moses, sit under the tree.' Moses did so and sat under the tree at God's command. Through the divine order, a thousand ants moved up the blessed leg of Moses. One of them bit his leg. Moses, woke up, became angry, and with his hand he crushed the ants. He killed all the ants. He then got up, performed ablution, and then offered a two-unit prayer. God said, 'O Moses, only one ant did wrong, but you killed all of them in exchange for that one mistake!' Moses was ashamed. Then a direct voice arrived from God, 'O Moses, I, as God, will take my mercy away from a servant who commits sins deliberately.'

{99} Again, Moses asked, 'O Lord, for whom is paradise and the pool of Kawthar created?' God said, 'For Muḥammad at the end of time and his community.'

{100} Moses said, 'O Lord, teach me something of which I can be proud.' God said, 'O Moses, repeat this phrase fifty times every day, "All praise is for God in every situation; there is no god but God, the Righteous Lord of certainty." Then, the angels of heaven and Earth will give you your reward.' Moses said, 'O Lord, I will do so!'

{101} Again God said, 'O Moses, repeat this phrase fifty times each day, "Glory be to the Divine Balance and all praise is for God who is the Balance." It will be as if you have given alms to all the dervishes.'

On Instructing Moses (pbuh)

{102} [Moses] said, 'O Lord, give me some advice.' God said, 'O Moses, lying is my enemy and telling a lie is the act of accursed ones.'

{103} Moses said, 'O Lord, increase Your benevolence.'[18] God said, 'O Moses, do not be arrogant, as arrogance is not admirable. And whoever is arrogant I will put into the hellfire.'

{104} His Eminence Moses said, 'O Lord, more!' God said, 'O Moses, welcome the guest.'

{105} Moses asked, 'O Lord, who is Your guest?' God said, 'The one who presents while no one knows them, and the one who disappears while no one asks [about] them. This person is My guest.'

{106} Moses asked, 'O Lord, who is Your neighbour?' God said, 'The one who goes home at night while starving, and is not covetous and open-mouthed of others[19]

[18] i.e., kindly tell me more [19] i.e., waiting for other people to feed him.

{۱۰۸} موسیٰ گفت «یا ربّ، همنشین تو کیست؟» فرمان شد «ای موسیٰ، آن‌کس که در مسجد بانگ نماز[۷۸] به آواز فصیح گوید».

{۱۰۹} باز موسیٰ گفت «یا ربّ، رحمت زیادت کن». فرمان شد که «مسکینانِ بی‌نوایان را طعام بده و نزدیک ایشان [باش؟] [هرکه؟] بر تو ظلم کند تو به آن‌کس نیکی کن تا ثواب هفتاد هزار پیغمبران مرسل و ثواب ملائکه‌های مقرّب در دیوان اعمال تو ثابت گردانم. ای موسیٰ، به درویشان رحم [کن. چون رحم] من برایشان است. بعداز آن موسیٰ ﷺ صحبت به درویشان داشتی تا از همهٔ بلاها ایمن شدی».

{۱۱۰} گفت «ای موسیٰ، بگو «شَهِدَ اللَّهُ أَنَّهُ لَا إِلَٰهَ إِلَّا هُوَ وَالْمَلَائِكَةُ وَأُولُو الْعِلْمِ قَائِمًا بِالْقِسْطِ لَا إِلَٰهَ إِلَّا هُوَ الْعَزِيزُ الْحَكِيمُ»[۷۹]. بعده، آیة الکرسي[۸۰] تمام بخواند تا ثواب زاهدان و عابدان تو را بدهم».

{۱۱۱} باز موسیٰ گفت «یا ربّ، اوّل که‌را آفریدی؟» فرمان شد که «اوّل نورِ محمّد[۸۱] را آفریدم».

{۱۱۲} موسیٰ گفت «یا ربّ، طاعت تو [اوّل] که کرده‌است؟» فرمان شد که «ای موسیٰ، اوّل طاعت بر من روحِ محمّد کرده‌است و هفتصد هزارسال به خدمت من بایستاد و از آن سبب رحمت خود بر وی نثار کردم. سپس، سجدهٔ سر نهاد. طهارت بر وی واجب کرد[م]. بعده، سر از سجده برداشت و سجدهٔ دوم کرد. چون پرتویی از قدرت خود بر او نثار کردم و پنج وقت نماز هر روز بر ایشان فریضه کردم. به‌جهت [؟] آن نماز موجبِ تندرستی و شایان جنّت باشد. و روحِ محمّد را در پیش خود داشتم تا در آخرالزمان او را بیافرینم که بعداز محمّد پیغمبرِ دیگری نخواهد به وجود آمد. که او را ختمِ پیغمبران گردانیده‌ام.

در بیانِ سؤال

{۱۱۳} موسیٰ گفت «یا ربّ، می‌خواهم از حضرت تو چند سخن پرسم امّا می‌ترسم که بر من خشم کنی». فرمانِ بی‌چون دررسید که «ای موسیٰ آنچه می‌دانی بگوی».

{۱۱۴} موسیٰ گفت «یا ربّ، تو از کی باز خدائی؟» فرمان شد که «ای موسیٰ، اگر رحمت من بر تو نبودی تو را هلاک دوزخ کردمی».

{۱۱۵} موسیٰ گفت «یا ربّ، تو عفو کن و رحمت زیاده کن». فرمان شد که «ای موسیٰ، خدایی مرا نهایت نیست. اوّل [و] آخر نیست. لیکن پیش‌از آن که عرش و کرسی و لوح و قلم و آسمان و زمین نیافریده بودم، هشتاد هزار شهرستان آفریده‌ام و بلای یکدیگر نهادم. و هر شهرستانی پنجْ همچون دنیا است و تمام او را از

[۷۸] اذان گوید. [۷۹] آیهٔ ۱۸ سورهٔ آل عمران. [۸۰] آیهٔ ۲۵۵ سورهٔ بقره.
[۸۱] در قسمت پایانی و در بخش «نورنامه» به تلفّظ این واژه اشاره شده است.

{107} His Eminence Moses said, 'O Lord, tell me more!' God said, 'O Moses, always respect my company.'

{108} Moses said, 'O Lord, who is Your company?' God said, 'O Moses, the one who eloquently calls to prayer in the mosque.'

{109} Again, Moses said, 'O Lord, tell me more!' God said, 'Feed the poor and the weak and be with them. Whoever is unfair to you, treat them nicely for which I will register a reward of seventy thousand Messengers as well as the rewards of My favoured-angels in the record of your deeds. O Moses, be kind with dervish as my mercy is upon them. O Moses (pbuh) be accompanied by dervishes so you will be protected from all sorts of disaster.'

{110} God said, 'O Moses recite, "God bears witness that there is no god but Him, as do the angels and those who have knowledge. He upholds justice. There is no god but Him, the Almighty, the All-Wise" (Q. 3:18). Then recite the Verse of the Thorne (Q. 2:255) in order to give you the reward of every saint and worshipper.'

{111} Again, Moses said, 'O Lord, who did You first create?' God said, 'First, I made the light of Muḥammad.'

{112} Moses said, 'O Lord, who was the first to obey You?' God said, 'O Moses, the first to obey Me was the soul of Muḥammad and it served me for seven hundred years for which I bestowed My mercy upon him. So, the soul of Muḥammad prostrated. I gave ablution and purification to him. Then, he lifted his head from prostration and prostrated for a second time. Then, I granted the radiance of My own power upon him and obliged him to perform prayer five times a day. As such, praying leads to health and to paradise. And I kept the soul of Muḥammad close to Me in order to create him in the End Times, that no more prophets would come after Muḥammad. As I have made him the Seal of the Prophets.'

Raising Questions

{113} Moses said, 'O Lord, I want to ask You a number of questions. But I am afraid.' The command of the Incomparable one arrived, 'O Moses, ask what you want to know!'

{114} Moses asked, 'Since when have You been God?' God said, 'O Moses, if My mercy was not upon you, I would have made you perish in hell.'

{115} Moses said, 'O Lord, forgive me, and [instruct me] a little more.' God said, 'O Moses, there will be no end to My divinity. It does not have a beginning and an end. However, before I created the Throne, the Seat, the Plate, the Pen, the Heaven and the Earth, I had created eighty thousand provinces and made them the bedevil and envy

دانهٔ خشخش[۸۲] پُر کردم. و یک مرغ نیز بیافریدم. و گفتم «ای مرغ، این روزی توست، بخور». چون تمام شود جان تو را قَبْض کنم. و آن مرغ از ترسِ جانْ هر روز یک دانه می‌خورْد. تا به یک‌ماه یک‌دانه خوردن گرفت. تا به یک سال یک دانه خوردن گرفته. چون به آخر رسید یک دانه مانده بود و آن دانه را در منقارِ خود گرفته بود تا هزار سال، و از ترس جان فرو نمی‌بُرد. آخر نَفْس غالب شد و فرو برد و جان او را قبض کردم. بعداز آن هشتاد مَرد آفریدم. هریکی را هزار سال عمر دادم و هریکی آفریدم. آخر همه را فنا کردم. بعداز آن هشتاد، مَرد[ی] آفریدم، نام او را آدَمْ نهادم. و او پدرِ اِبْلیس بود. بعداز آن مَردِ دیگری آفریدم نام او را نیز آدَمْ نهادم، و او را پنجاه‌هزار سال عمر دادم. بعداز آن ده‌هزار مَرد دیگر آفریدم و عمر هریک را ده‌هزار سال کردم. بعداز آن پدر شما «آدَم صَفِي» را بیافریدم. ای موسیٰ هیچ می‌دانی که حساب این چند می‌شود؟»

{۱۱۶} هوشِ مهتر موسیٰ برفت، و چون بهوش آمد گفت «سُبْحَانَكَ قَبَلَ اليك وأنا المؤمنين».[۸۳]

{۱۱۷} موسیٰ گفت «یا ربّ، مرا فخر است و تو را فخر نیست». فرمان شد که «ای موسیٰ، فخر تو چیست؟» موسیٰ گفت «یا ربّ، فخر من آن است که تو خدای منی و تو را خدائی نیست که بدان فخر کنی». فرمان شد که «ای موسیٰ راست گفتی. به عزّت و جلالیت من و قدرت باکمالِ من که مرا بندگانند که به نظرِ رحمتْ به‌سوی ایشان می‌نگرم».

{۱۱۸} موسیٰ گفت «یا ربّ، به چه عمل این درجه یافته‌اند؟» فرمان شد که «ای موسیٰ، تا زنده‌اند به غیر از من کسی را یاد نمی‌کنند».

{۱۱۹} موسیٰ گفت «یا ربّ، آن قومی که گمراه شود؟ [...]» فرمان شد که «آن عدّه[۸۴] گاو داشتند بر زبان آمدند و گفتند «یا ربّ، فَتْح ما در این گاو کن»، چنان کردم».

{۱۲۰} موسیٰ گفت «یا ربّ، این‌همه خواستِ تو است». [فرمان شد] «يَفْعَلُ مَا يَشَاءُ[۸۵] وَيَهدي مَن يَشاء[۸۶] وَأنتَ اِلَيْنا وَغَفرلَنا وارْحَمْنا وَأَنتَ (؟) لِلْكَافِرِين عَذَابٌ أَلِيم(؟)»

دنبالهٔ مسائل

{۱۲۱} مهتر موسیٰ عليه‌السلام گفت «یا ربّ، گروهی اکراهی گناه کرده بود جزای[۸۷] آنها چیست؟» فرمان شد

[۸۲] رسم الخط خشخش، و همچنین استفاده از آن نشان می‌دهد که این متن در ابتدا بایستی در آسیای مرکزی یا جنوبی و مناطق نزدیک آن نوشته شده باشد. شکل نوشتاری دیگر آن «خشخاش» است که نزدیک به رسم الخط پشتو می‌باشد. مراجعه کنید به ویراست جدید: عبدالله افغانی نویس، افغان قاموس: فارسی به پشتو (کابل: ۲۰۰۷) ، ۵۶۹. در داستان‌های مالایی پیرامون آفرینش از «دانهٔ خردل» به‌جای «خشخش» استفاده شده‌است.

[۸۳] اشاره به آیهٔ ۱۴۳ سورهٔ اعراف دارد.

[۸۴] همچنین به‌صورت «آن‌ها دَه گاو داشتند» هم خوانده می‌شود.

[۸۵] اشاره به آیهٔ ۴۰ سورهٔ آل عمران دارد.

[۸۶] اشاره به آیهٔ ۲۵ سورهٔ یونس دارد.

[۸۷] به صورت «خبر» نیز خوانده می‌شود.

of each other and every province was five times bigger than the world, and I filled it with poppy seeds.[20] And then I created a bird. And I said, "O bird, this is your food. Eat it! When it is finished, I will take your soul." And the bird only ate one seed for the sake of its life. The bird ate one seed every day for a month. Then it did so for one year. When only one seed remained, the bird held the last poppy seed between its beak for one thousand years and did not eat it for the sake of its life. At last, self-temptation was overcome and it ate the seed and I took its life. 'Then I created eighty men. I granted each of them a life of a thousand years, I created them and I made them all perish. After those eighty, I created a man and I named him Adam. And he was the father of Iblīs [i.e., Satan]. After that, I created another man and I named him Adam, too, and granted him fifty thousand years. Subsequently, I created ten thousand more people and granted each of them ten thousand years. Then, I created your father, the chosen Adam. O Moses, are you able to fathom this?'

{116} His Eminence Moses fainted and when he regained consciousness, he said, 'Glory be to You! To You I get close! I am [the first] to believe!'[21]

{117} Moses continued, 'O Lord, I am honoured but You are not honoured!' God said, 'O Moses, what is your honour?' Moses said, 'O Lord, my honour is that You are my God and there is no higher god than You in whom to be proud.' God said, 'O Moses, you are right. By My Glory and Majesty and My Perfect Power I have [such] servants upon whom I look mercifully.'

{118} Moses said, 'O Lord, how did they achieve such status?' God said, 'O Moses, they did not remember anyone else as long as they were alive.'

{119} Moses said, 'O Lord, the community who strayed [...]?' God said, 'They had a cow. They began to say, 'O Lord, ease our problems with this cow', and I did so!'

{120} Moses said, 'O Lord, all is just because of Your will!' [God said,] 'God does what He wills (Q. 3:40), guides whom He wills (Q. 10:25), and You forgive us, and You are [...] for the disbelievers is a painful punishment. [?]'

Other questions

{121} His Eminence Moses (pbuh) said, 'O Lord, what are the rewards of the community that is reluctant to commit sin?'[22] God said, 'They are angels.' There were twelve thousand Jews [?], and for every Jew, and every Jew [...] to the extent of human beings, fairies, animals, birds, livestock, raindrops, and desert sands and with the number of

[20] In Malay literature, it is *Biji Sawi* ('mustard seed'). [21] This may refer to Q. 7:143. [22] Based on the original text, this can also be read as 'What is the punishment of the community who commits sins?'

که «ملائکه‌ها بودند.[۸۸] دوازده هزار سبطی[۸۹] و هر سبطی [...] به عدد آدمیان و پریان و جانوران و پرندگان و چهارپایان و قطرات باران و ریگ بیابان و به عدد یأجوج و مأجوج و دوازده هزار چندین هزار که در حساب نیامد. موسیٰ گفت «یا ربِّ، «سُبحَانَكَ مَا أَعْظَمُ يَا قَوْمك»».[۹۰]

{۱۲۲} موسیٰ گفت «یا ربّ، درازی میکائیل چند است؟» فرمان شد که «سیصد برابر دنیا است».

{۱۲۳} باز موسیٰ گفت «یا ربّ، درازی عزرائیل چند است؟» فرمان شد که «هفتاد هزارسال راه است».

{۱۲۴} موسیٰ گفت «یا ربّ، القاسم [؟] چیست؟» فرمان شد که «ای موسیٰ، اسبانند که بزرگی هر کدام دو چندانِ این دنیا است».

{۱۲۵} موسیٰ گفت «یا ربّ، تو را با این اسبان چه حاجت است؟» فرمان شد که «ای موسیٰ، شکم‌های آن‌ها پُر است از رحمت که بر امّتانِ گناهکارانِ محمّد نثار کنم. و این اسبان خُفته می‌خیزند و آب [دریا] حیوانْ می‌خوراند و این دریا، دریای رحمت است. که هفتاد اسبان یکی را به دنیا فرستم؛ هریکِ هفتادُ اسبان دنیا فرو کَشیَد و در شکم این‌ها ناپدید[۹۱] شوند».

{۱۲۶} باز مهتر موسیٰ گفت «یا ربّ، مرا عرش خود بنمائی؟» فرمان شد که «ای موسیٰ، نتوانی دید چرا که محمل‌های[۹۲] اسبان است».

{۱۲۷} موسیٰ خود نظر کرده؛ سربرآورد، بیهوش شد. افتاد. و چون بهوش باز آمد گفت «سُبحَانَكَ أَعْظَم بِقُدْرَة ذِكْر [...]»

{۱۲۸} بعداز آن موسیٰ گفت «یا ربّ، مردی را دیدم زیر عرش، دو پای او در بهشت بود،» فرمان شد که «ای موسیٰ، آن مردی است [از] بنی اسرائیل».

{۱۲۹} موسیٰ گفت «یا ربّ، از کجا چنین درجه یافته است؟» فرمان شد که «این مرد از غیبت گفتن و ربا خوردن ترک کرده است. از آن جهت او را برگزیدم».

{۱۳۰} موسیٰ گفت «یا ربّ، در زیر عرش قصر دیدم از زرِ سرخِ بزرگ». [فرمان شد] «آن قصرها پر از رحمتند. چون روز قیامت أَمَنَّا وَصدَّقنا همه را بر امّتان محمّد نثار کنم».

{۱۳۱} موسیٰ گفت «یا ربّ، مرا نیز از امّت محمّد گردان».

{۱۳۲} باز موسیٰ گفت «یا ربّ، مر آنجا بوَد در آنجا مرا یاد کُند». [فرمان] شد «ای موسیٰ، به هر حال[۹۳] مرا یاد کن و هرکه مرا بخواهد به من نزدیک شود و من نیز او را یاد کنم و بزرگ دانم».

[۸۸] می‌توان این عبارت را بدین شکل نوشت «مهتر موسیٰ علیه‌السلام گفت «یا ربّ، گروهی که اکراه گناه کرده، خبر\جزای آنها چیست؟» فرمان شد که «ملائکه‌ها بودند». [۸۹] در حاشیهٔ برگ ۱۲۵ آکلند ۱۷۰ آمده [سبطی یعنی تولی] . هرچند معنای دقیق این واژه\عبارت مشخص نیست. به احتمال زیاد واژهٔ «سبطی» مرتبط است با آیهٔ ۸۴ سورهٔ آل عمران؛ ارتباط این واژه با «سبط اللاويين» ارزش بررسی بیشتر دارد.
[۹۰] ویرایش دقیق‌تر این عبارت به زمان بیشتری نیاز دارد. [۹۱] در حاشیهٔ برگ ۱۲۵ آکلند ۱۷۰ چنین نوشته شده است [پدید شود معلوم پری\برین زمین]. با این وجود معنی این جمله مشخص نیست. [۹۲] تخت روان، هودج. [۹۳] در هر حال.

Gog and Magog, and twelve thousand and several thousand that cannot be calculated.[23] Moses said, 'O Lord, Glory be to You, how great are Your people?'

{122} And Moses said, 'O Lord, how tall is Michael?' God said, 'Three hundred times bigger than the world.'

{123} Again Moses said, 'O Lord, how long is ʿIzrāʾīl?' God said, 'He is as long as a seventy-thousand year road.'

{124} Moses said, 'O Lord, what are al-Qāsim [?] ?' God said, 'O Moses, they are horses whose size is twice that of the world.'

{125} Moses said, 'O Lord, how do they fulfil Your need?' God said, 'O Moses, their bellies are full of mercy and grace and I will devote it to the sinful from the community of Muḥammad. These horses move while asleep and drink from the sea, and this sea is the sea of mercy. From these seventy horses, I will send one towards the world; each of these horses [may] swallow the world that will be placed in their bellies.'

{126} Again, His Eminence Moses said, 'O Lord, could You show me Your Throne?' God said, 'O Moses, can you not see it as it is the howdah of the horses.'

{127} Moses wanted to look at it himself. He raised his head to see. He became unconscious. When he woke up, he said, 'Glory be to God, the Greatest [...].'

{128} Then, Moses said, 'O Lord, I saw a man below the Throne whose two legs were in paradise.' God said, 'O Moses, that man is someone from the Children of Israel.'

{129} Moses said, 'O Lord, how did he get this rank?' God said, 'He abandoned gossip and usury. This is why I have chosen him.'

{130} Moses said, 'O Lord, I have noticed a huge palace made of red gold under the Throne.' [God said,] 'Those palaces are replete with mercy. I will devote them to the community of Muḥammad on the Day of Judgement' (*in which we believe*).

{131} Moses said, 'O Lord, place me in the community of Muḥammad!'

{132} Again, Moses said, 'O Lord, wherever possible, remember me!' God replied, 'O Moses, remember Me whenever and wherever you are. And whoever wants Me, they get close to Me; I also remember them and bless them.'

[23] This rendition needs further research

{۱۳۳} موسیٰ گفت «یا ربّ، چون مرگ بر سر من آید منکر و نکیر پرسند، چه گویم؟» فرمان شد که «درین حال گور را یاد کن که گوشت اندام تو را کِرمان[۹۴] خواهند خورد تا کبر از سَر بِرَود. و دامنِ عبادت کننده‌گان را دوست می‌دارم. اگر رحمت برسد صبر کن تا به درجهٔ اعلی برسانم».

{۱۳۴} چون سخن به آخر رسید، مهتر موسیٰ از کوه طور سینا فروز آمد. نزدیک علمای بنی اسرائیل رفته و روی موسیٰ علیه‌السلام همچون ماه شب چهارده[د] تابان شده بود که هیچ کس را تابِ دیدنِ مهتر موسیٰ علیه‌السلام نبود. و بُرقع بر روی خود افکنده بود و همهٔ خلق را دعوت می‌کرد.

{۱۳۵} إِلٰهِيّ، به حرمت محمّد مُصْطَفَی صلی الله علیه و سلم منِ ضعیف را از شفاعت اولی نصیب گردانی. بِمِنَّة وَكَرَمه وَآلِه. بِرَحْمَتِكَ يَا أَرْحَمَ ٱلرّحِمين. بانالی[۹۵] موسیٰ علیه‌السلام بالتوفیق شد. تمام شد. این «موسیٰ نامه» تمام شدی بود.

[۹۴] کرم‌ها. [۹۵] « نالیدن. به‌صورت مزید مؤخر به دنبال اسم و صفت آید». به دهخدا مراجعه شود.

[د] چارده

{133} Moses said, 'O Lord, when I die, what shall I say upon Munkar and Nakīr's interrogation?' God said, 'Remind yourself of the grave where worms will eat the flesh of your body so the arrogance will be erased. I love my worshippers' invocations. If mercy comes, be patient until you reach the highest level.'

{134} When the conversation ended, His Eminence Moses came down from Mount Sinai. He went to the scholars and elders of the Children of Israel. And the face of Moses (pbuh) was illuminated like the full moon, so much that no one could bear to see it. He removed the veil from his face and invited all people [to God].

{135} *O God, by Muḥammad (pbuh) that provides me with the sublime intercession. By Your unmerited favour and kindness. By Your mercy, O most Merciful of those who have mercy. 'The Lamentation' of Moses has been successful. It has been completed. The Mūsā-nāma has been finished. [Amen.]*

حکایتِ پادشاه شام

{۱} [...] را روایت می کند کَعْبُ الْأَحبَارْ رَضِيَ اللهُ عَنْهُ که رسول صَلَّى اللهُ عَلَيْهِ وَسَلَّمَ گفت «روزی مهتر عیسیٰ عَلَيْهِ السَّلَامُ در بیابان می‌رفت و در وادی‌های[1] شام[2] یک کاسهٔ سَرِ آدمی اُفتاده بدید. به غایت سفید بود پس بِگُرِفْت و تعجّب بمانْد».[3] گفت «خداوند، به عزّت خدایِ عیسیٰ[4] این کاسهٔ سر آدمی را گویا گردان تا با من سخن گوید و آنچه از وی پرسم جواب گوید». پس وحی آمد و گفت «ای روح الله، بپرس آنچه خواهی تا تو را جواب گوید».

{۲} پس مهتر عیسیٰ گفت «ای گوشت و پوستِ از استخوان فرو شده،[5] با من به سخن درآی». از کاسهٔ سر آدمی آواز برآمد. به زبانِ فصیح گفت «یا روح الله، بپرس آنچه خواهی تا تو را جواب [دهم] به فرمان خدای تَعَالَى عَزَّ وَجَلَّ». عیسیٰ پیغمبر آغاز کرد و گفت «نام چه داری؟» گفت «جمجمه پادشاه بود». [عیسیٰ] گفت «مردی بودی یا زن؟» گفت «مردی بودم».[6] [عیسیٰ] گفت «جوانمرد بودی یا بخیل؟» گفت «جوانمرد». گفت «نیک‌بخت بودم و چهارصد سال عُمرِ من بود و پادشاه دوازده هزار فرسنگ زمینی بودم. یا روح الله، روزی من بیرون آمده بودم. نهصدهزار غلام صف آراسته گِرد[7] می‌بودند و چهارصدهزار غلام دیگر بر دست چپ من بودند. هریکی را جامه‌های ابریشم سفیدِ یک‌رنگ پوشیده و اسبان تازی و زین‌های زرّین و تنگ‌های ابریشمی؛ بر سر هر غلامی تاجی مرصّع به جواهر و یاقوت نهاده و دوازده هزارغلام دیگر عمود[8] زرّین بر گردن نهاده پیش می‌رفتند».

[1] بیابان. واژهٔ «وادی» در حالت اضافی به معنی «گورستان» به کار می رود، همچون گورستان «وادي السلام» که در نجف-عراق واقع است.
[2] در نسخهٔ مالایی ۱۰۹ جاکارتا برگ ۱، کلمهٔ «شام» با الف کوتاه و به صورت «شَم» نوشته شده است، که شیوهٔ نگارشی مشابهی در ادبیات جاوی در طی قرون گذشته بوده است. [3] متعجّب شد. [4] به گمانم این یک عبارت تاکیدی است و دلالت دارد بر وجههٔ اسلامی عیسیٰ، که برخلاف باور رایج مسیحیّت، این متن عیسیٰ را به عنوان «فرزند» پروردگار معرّفی نمی کند. [5] ناپدید و نابود شده. در نسخهٔ «قصص القرآن» کتابخانهٔ ملّی ایران ۵-۲۵۰۴۵، این عبارت چنین آمده است: عیسیٰ گفت «یا استخوان ریزیده و یا پوست پوسیده، با من سخن بگو». [6] در نسخهٔ ۵-۲۳۷۹۶ کتابخانهٔ ملّی ایران برگ ۲۸۷، سوال عیسیٰ چنین مطرح می شود «بازگو که نرینه بودی یا مادینه؟ سعیدی بودی یا شقی؟ توانگر بودی یا درویش؟ خوب بودی یا زشت؟ سخی بودی یا بخیل؟»
[7] «گِرد» به معنای «اطراف و پیرامون»؛ و «گُرد» به معنای «پهلوان» است. [8] گرز.

CHAPTER 36

The story of the King of the Levant

{1} Kaʿb al-Aḥbār (pbuh) reports that the Messenger (pbuh) said that 'once upon a time, His Eminence Jesus (pbuh) was crossing a desert. And there was a human skull there in the Levant. It was extremely white. Jesus held it and wondered. He said, "God, by the Glory of the God of Jesus[1] make this human skull speak with me and answer whatever I ask of him." Then a revelation was sent, "O Spirit of God, ask what you want and the skull will answer."

{2} His Eminence Jesus said, "O, the one whose bones have neither flesh nor skin, talk to me!" A voice from the human skull, using eloquent language said, "O Spirit of God, ask what you want and I will answer you by God's will." The Prophet Jesus asked the first question, "What is your name?" He said, "King Jumjuma." Jesus asked, "Were you male or female?" He said, "I was a man". Jesus asked, "Were you generous or miserly?" He said, "I was generous". The skull continued, "I was happy and I had lived for four hundred years and my kingdom spanned twelve thousand *parsangs*. O Spirit of God, one day I went out. Nine hundred thousand slaves were lined up around me, and another four hundred thousand slaves were lined up on my left-hand side. I clothed each of them with white silky garments, and provided them with Arabian horses that had golden saddles fastened with silk. I placed a crown adorned with gems and rubies on the head of every slave, and another twelve thousand slaves marched, holding bludgeons of metal on their shoulders.

[1] This may be related to Muslim belief that calls not Jesus as the Son of God.

{۳} «من پادشاه گردن‌کَش بودم و هیچ خصمی دشمن سپر[...] نیامدی. هر طرف که نظر می‌کردم هزیمت شدی و پیش من کسی نایستادی. و تخت از زرِ سرخ[۹] بودی و گوهرها مرصّع، قیمتِ بسیار و بی‌شمار بود. و من زیبا روی بودم. هرکه روی من بدیدی غم و اندوه از بدن او به دررفته و هر که مرا دوست گرفتی از دیدن من خوشی شدی. و من نان‌ده[۱۰] بودم. هر که را گرسنه دیدمی چندانش بدادمی که در همهٔ عمر او [را] بَسَند بودی، و هر برهنه را که دیدمی جامه‌های نو پوشانیدمی. و غریب دوست[۱۱] بودم و مسکینان و ضعیفان را دوست می‌داشتم. و هر سائل را که من می‌دیدمی و بر من آمدی او را محروم نگذاشتم، و هر که از من چیزی خواستی بر او خشمگین نَشُدمی بلکه شاد شُدَمی. و چون شب شدی در شهر بِگَشتَمی و هرجا که درویش محتاج را بِدیدمی بر خود آوردمی و غذا بسیار خواستَمی. وقت نان خوردن طبل کوفتندی و ندا کردندی و هزار دینار هریکی را دادمی».

{۴} آنگاه حضرت عیسیٰ علیه‌السلام بگریست و بر او رحم آمد. حضرت عیسیٰ گفت «ای جمجمه، چندگاه است و مُردن تو چگونه بود و مَلَكُ الْمَوْت را چگونه دیدی؟» آنگاه کاسهٔ سر گفت ««یا روح الله، هفت هزارسال از مُردن است و سبب مُردن این بود که روزی من از کُوشکْ بیرون آمدم. عَزم به شکارگاه با لشگر گران، و دنبال صدی اسب براندم. وقتْ گرم[۱۲] بود و سرِ مَنْ درد گرفت. بازگشتم و [به] پرده‌سرا[۱۳] آمدم. ساعت بود[۱۴] که صفرای[۱۵] من اثر کرد و خادمان و خدمتکاران و ندیمان و بردگان بیامدند و هر ولایت و شهری بر من دارو کردند.[۱۶] و لیکن هیچ سود نکرد، بلکه هر روز زیادتر می‌شد. چون روز پنج شد زبان سیاه شد و دست و پای من سپید گشت و مرا مرگ نزدیک‌تر آمد. فرزندان و غلامان و خدمت‌کاران بیامدند و موی‌هایِ کندیدن[۱۷] گرفتند، و بر من می‌گریستند. آواز ایشان در گوش من افتاد.[۱۸] خواستم تا ایشان را منع کنم زبان من کار نکرد. آواز برنمی‌آمد. پس مَلَكُ الْمَوْت در رسید و همهٔ لذّت‌های دنیا بر من زَهر گشت. یا روح الله، از تلخی جان‌کندن چه گویم؟»

{۵} روح الله گفت «ای جمجمه، مَلَكُ المَوْت را چگونه دیدی و صف لشکر او چگونه است؟» گفت «مَلَكُ الْمَوْت را شش روی دیدم».[۱۹] گفت «کدام جانب؟» گفت «جانب دست [راست]، دوم روی به جانب دست چپ، سوم روی به جانبِ سر، چهارم جائی که روی آدمی است و یک رو به جانب پشت و یک رو به جانب زنخ». حضرت عیسیٰ گفت «یا جمجمه، دانی که کدام روی گران[۲۰] نُماید؟» گفت «اوّل

[۹] بنابر باوری «زرِ سرخ» همان «طلای زرد» است که در مقابل با «زرِ سفید» یا «نقره» به کار می رود. بحث هایی در مورد ارتباط «زرِ سرخ و مس» نیز مطرح می شود. [۱۰] «کریم و بخشنده». [۱۱] غریب نواز. [۱۲] وقت گرما، و اشاره به ظهر دارد.

[۱۳] سراپرده و خیمه. [۱۴] بعداز زمانی. [۱۵] اشاره به شروع بیماری، همچنین زرد و صفراوی شدن وی دارد.

[۱۶] درمان نمودن. [۱۷] اشاره به مویه و زاری دارد. [۱۸] احتمالا اشاره به انزجار وی از ناله های دیگران دارد.

[۱۹] در نسخهٔ «قصص القرآن» کتابخانهٔ ملّی ایران این توصیف چنین نوشته شده است «مَلَكُ الْمَوْت درآمد، چماق در دست گرفته و طاس شربت مرگ آورده. او را دیدم به صورت سهمناک. سر او به آسمان دیدم و پای او به زمین هفتم و بر سر وی رویها (؟) دیدم، عظیم سهمناک».

[۲۰] «گران نماید» یعنی عظیم، دشوار و تحمّل ناپذیر بودن. از جهتی، «کران نماید» یعنی به پایان رسانیدن.

{3} "I was an obstreperous king and there was no enemy able to confront me [...]. Wherever I moved, their army experienced disaster and no one was able to engage nor deal with me. And my thrones were made of red gold adorned with valuable gems. And I was a handsome man. Whoever saw my face, their grief was removed, and whoever was in my company enjoyed seeing my face. And I was generous and a philanthropist.[2] Whoever was hungry came to my attention, I gave them provision, sufficient for the rest of their life. And I dressed whoever was naked with new clothes. And I was hospitable and befriended beggars and the weak. And I never ignored a beggar whom I saw or came to me, and when one requested something from me, I did not become angry but become happy. And at night I wandered in the city and brought poor dervishes to sit around me and asked for them to be served abundant food. While eating food, we used to beat drums and call people to come and we would give each of them one thousand dinars".

{4} Then Prophet Jesus (pbuh) cried and took pity on him. Prophet Jesus asked, 'O Jumjuma, how long have you been dead, and how did you die and how did you find the Angel of Death?' Then the skull said, 'O Spirit of God, it has been seven thousand years since I died. The reason for my death is that I left the palace one day in order to hunt along with a large troop of soldiers. And I ran after a hundred horses. It was in the heat of day and I succumbed to a headache. I returned to the camp. After a while, I became queasy and ill. All servants, maidservants, companions, and slaves attended and people from every province and city tried to treat me. However, nothing worked, and my situation worsened day by day. On the fifth day, my tongue became black and my hands and legs became white[3] and death neared. My children, slaves, and servants and maidservants came and began to moan and cried for me immsensly. I heard their voices. I wanted to stop them but my tongue did not help. I could not make a sound. Then, the Angel of Death arrived and all the joys of my life turned to poison. O Spirit of God, what shall I say about the pain and bitterness of dying?'

{5} The Spirit of God asked, "O Jumjuma, how did you find the Angel of Death, and how was his army?" He said, "I saw the Angel of Death from six sides [*or*, with six faces].' Jesus said, 'What are those sides/faces?" He said, "From the right-hand side, from the left-hand side, from the head, from the face, from the rear, and from the chin." Prophet Jesus asked, "Which of these sides was most devastating?" He said, "The one from the right takes the life of the people in the Orient [?]. And the one on the left side will take the life of vicious people. The one from the head takes the life of the prophets and the righteous; seeing that face comes with happiness, health, and no grief as it is the best of the faces. As it is right there to take the soul of the community

[2] Or a "breadwinner"? [3] i.e. pale

روی آنکه به جانب راست دارد؛ جان‌های اهلِ مشرق[۲۱] (؟) ستاند. و آن روی که جانب چپ دارد جان‌های اهل فسق ستاند. و رویی که بر سر دارد جان‌های پیغمبران و صدّیقان ستاند. هرآن روی ببیند دوست، شادی و تندرست و بی غم باشد که آن روی أحسَنُ الوُجُوه است. که راست است جان‌های امّت محمّد مُصْطَفَی ﷺ ستاند. و خوشی و خنکی[۲۲] باد هر آن کس را که مشرف دارد بر او ایمان. و آن رویی که پشت است دست سیاه دارد. و امّت محمّد مُصْطَفَی ﷺ، پیغمبرِ آخرِ زمان خواهد بود؛ آن امّت باشد از همهٔ امّتان بهتر. و خداوند عَزَّوَجَلَّ گفت خَيْرَ أُمَّة.[۲۳] و آنْ روح[۲۴] راحت هر که را رو نماید هرگز غم نیاید.[۲۵] و آن روی که زیر زنخ است بدترین روی ها است. بدان رویْ جان‌های منافقان ستاند».

{۶} گفت «یا روح الله، لشگر مَلَك الْمَوْت را دیدم. بی‌مقیاس و بی‌اندازه و بی‌شمار، و هیچ‌کس را به دیدار ایشان طاقت نماند، و دندان ایشان چون تنهٔ درخت خرما باشد. و موهای ایشان بر سر ایستاده.[۲۶] و چشم های ایشان چون آتشی می‌زند و سخنْ شنیدنِ ایشانْ[۲۷] هیچ‌کس را طاقت نماند. دسته‌عمودهای آتشین هریکی را، و هریک به ابهّت. چون بدیدم خواستم که فریاد کنم تا ایشان را بپرسم. آنگاه ایشان در دهان من شدند و زبان من بگرفتند و استوار کردند. از گفتنِ سخن بازماندم. و هم تن من آتش گرفت چنانکه ماهی زنده را بریان کنند و یا از زنده‌ها گوشت بُرند. هرچند که گفتم مرا فرصت دهد تا آنچه در مُلْکِ ما است صدقه کنم و توشه آخرت برم، گرز بر سر زدند چنانچه گردنم بشکست. اگر چنین بدانستمی در عمر خود یک لحمه[۲۸] و لحظه از ذکر حقّ تَعَالَی غافل نبودم. گفت[م] «ای فرشتگان، همهٔ عیال و فرزندان به شما بخشیدم». گفتند «خیر! است و نیست»[۲۹]؛ از همهٔ چیزهایْ معزول کردند.[الف] [آنها گفتند] «اگر پیش از این می‌بخشیدی تو را سود داشتی. درین وقت تو را هیچ سود ندارد. قال تعالی فَإِذَا جَاءَ أَجَلُهُمْ لَا يَسْتَأْخِرُونَ سَاعَةً وَلَا يَسْتَقْدِمُونَ،[۳۰] آنچه داشتی خیرات دیگران شد. فرمان تو این است». پس روحِ مرا به دشواری قبض کردند».

{۷} «چون به گورستان نهادند منکر [و] نکیر حاضر آمدند و گفتند «یا عبد الله، برخیز و آنچه در دنیا کردی از کردارهای خود بنویس». گفتم «کاغذ و قلم ندارم». گفتند «انگشتِ تو قلم، و دهانِ تو دوات، و کفنِ تو کاغذ است» و از من نویسانیدند.[۳۱] بعده، برفتند. بعداز آن دو فرشتهٔ دیگر آمدند. شکم‌هایی چون تنهٔ درخت خرما. و زمین را پاره‌پاره کردند و عمودهایی بر دست گرفته و هیچ شفقّت و رحمت در ایشان نبود. گفتند

[۲۱] در برخی منابع، «مشرق» به عنوان «مکان الصلاة» معرّفی می‌شود. به دهخدا مراجعه شود.

[۲۲] سعادت. [۲۳] آیهٔ ۱۱۰ سورهٔ آل عمران. [۲۴] احتمالا «روی»

[۲۵] معنای این جمله مشخص نیست. اینکه «روح راحت» به چه معنا است نیاز به بررسی بیشتر دارد.

[۲۶] هم دلالت بر بی نظمی و ژولیدگی دارد و هم بر بالابودن جهت مو-که تصویری متضاد با دندان های بلند را ارائه می دهد.

[۲۷] سخن ایشان را شنیدن. [۲۸] اندک زمان. [۲۹] «هست و نیست» به معنی دارایی. [۳۰] آیهٔ ۳۴ سورهٔ اعراف.

[۳۱] یا «نویساندن» به معنی «به نوشتن واداشتن» است.

[الف] خیر. است-تو-نیست. از همه چیزهایی معزول کردند.

of Muḥammad (pbuh). And how lucky and blissful is the one who is blessed with faith. And the one from the rear has a black hand. And the community of Muḥammad (pbuh), whose prophet is the prophet of the end times, and that community is the best of all communities. And God said about them that they are, "The best community" (Q. 3:110). And if the spirit/side (?) of comfort is bestowed upon everyone it brings no grief. And the one from the chin is the worst one, by which the soul of hypocrites are taken."

{6} [Jumjuma] said, "O Spirit of God, I saw the army of the Angel of Death. It was unmeasurable, unlimited and no one is capable of seeing them. Their teeth look like the trunks of palm trees. Their hairs are upright on their heads. And their eyes blaze and no one is able to tolerate their speech. Each of them holds an igneous bludgeon, which is huge. When I saw this, I wanted to call out to them loudly and ask from them. But they entered into my mouth and took my tongue and braced it. As such, I could not speak anymore. And my body began to burn like a living fish which is grilled or like flesh when it is cut from a living body. Whatever I said to try to placate them, and I would have given freely whatever was in my power and prepare a provision for the Day of Judgement, they instead hit my head with their bludgeons until my neck broke. If I had known what would happen to me I would never have forgotten to remember God for a single moment. I told them, 'O angels, I will give you all my wives and children.' They said straightforward 'No! we get all your possessions' and took me away from everything. [They said] 'If you had offered them before [your death], then that would have been helpful. Now they do not help and [such offerings] do not have any benefit. Almighty God says, 'When their time arrives, they can neither delay it for a moment, nor can they advance it.' (Q. 7:34), Whatever you left behind are benefactions for others. This is the command for you."They, in this way, took my soul with difficulty.'

{7} 'Once they placed me in the graveyard, Munkar and Nakīr arrived and commanded, "O servant of God, arise and write whatever you have done in the world." I told them I do not have paper and pen. They said, "Your finger is your pen, your mouth is your inkwell, and your shroud is your paper", and they forced me to write. Then they left me and were gone. After this, two other angels came in. Their bellies resembled the trunk of a palm tree. They ripped the ground, held bludgeons and there was no sign of affection nor mercy in them. They said, 'Stand up, servant of God!' They asked, "Who is your God?" When I saw them, I lost consciousness and the power of reasoning and all I knew was forgotten, and I answered, 'You are my God.' They arose, and they hit me with their bludgeons so strongly for which I was plunged into the ground. O Spirit of God, the interrogation of Munkar and Nakīr is extremely difficult.'

«برخیز ای بنده خدای!». باز گفتند «مَن رَبّك، خدای تو کیست؟ چون ایشان را بدیدم هوش و عقل از من برفت و فراموش شد. گفتم که «شما خداوندم[ی] » برخاستند و باز عمودها بر سر من زدند چنانچه در زمین فرو شدم؛ یا روح الله، سوال منکر و نکیر به غایت دشوار است».

{۸} الغرض. «چون ایشان بدیدم آنچه از عمر لذّت داشتم فراموش کردم. یا روح الله، آن فرشتگان باز پرسیدند که «مَن رَبّك، خدای تو کیست؟» باز گفتم که «شما خدای من‌اید[۳۲]». باز عمودها بر سر من زدند. یا روح الله، فرزند آدم، از عالِم و جاهل و پادشاه و وزیر، اگر بدانند که پیش من چه خواهد بود، در همهٔ عُمر از عبادت و ثنا غافل نباشد و هرگز بر کسی ظلم نکند. و در هیچ شادی نخندد؛ فرزندِ آدم در پیشْ چنین عذاب و مشقّت دارد، و او به‌جهت دنیا فانی می‌رود[۳۳]».

{۹} حضرت عیسیٰ علیه‌السلام بسیار گریست. جمجمه پادشاه گفت «یا «روح الله، چنان بزدند که در زمین فرو شدم. گفتند درشکم من آمده «کینه از تو بکشیم»[۳۴]. و باز مرا از زمین کشیدند و سرنگون عذاب می‌کردند. پس آن دو فرشته که کردار من نویسانیده بودند مرا برداشتند و برابر عرش و کرسی داشتند. آنجا راحت یافتم».

{۱۰} حضرت عیسیٰ علیه‌السلام گفت «درعرش چه دیدی و از فرشتگان چه پرسیدی؟» گفت «کرسی دیدم. اوّل کرسی مهتر آدم علیه‌السلام. دوم کرسی مهتر ابراهیم خلیل الله علیه‌السلام. سوم کرسی مهتر موسیٰ علیه‌السلام. چهارم کرسی مهتر عیسیٰ علیه‌السلام. پنجم کرسی محمّد مُصْطَفَى صلی‌الله‌علیه‌وسلم. فرمان آمد مالک را که مرا به دوزخ برند و پاره‌پاره کردند و باز دُرست گشتم و در چاه انداختند. بعداز آن از دوزخ خلاص شدم.

{۱۱} یا روح الله، خدای تَعَالَى گفت إِنَّا لَا نُضِيعُ أَجْرَ مَنْ أَحْسَنَ عَمَلاً[۳۵]. از حضرت آفریدگار ندا آمد که بندهٔ من بسیار نیکی کرده و صدقهٔ بسیار داده است و از خواهندگان هیچ دریغ نداشته. نیکی از وی ضایع نکنم»».

{۱۲} آنگاه حضرت عیسیٰ علیه‌السلام گفت «در وقت کدام پیغمبر بودی؟» گفت «در وقت الیاس پیغمبر بودم». [عیسیٰ پرسید] «و این چندین عذاب‌ها که[۳۶] بود؟» [جمجمه گفت] «به‌سبب آن بود که در آن وقت یکی گاو بود. سُرُون[۳۷] های سُرخ مُلَمَّع[۳۸] و تاج مُرَصَّع و گوهر و یاقوت. به‌جهت سُرُون های او کردند و من نیز فریضه[۳۹] برآن گاو.[۴۰] و این همه عذاب از سبب آن دیدم».

{۱۳} حضرت عیسیٰ گفت «ای جمجمه، می‌خواهی که بار دیگر مرگ باشد؟» گفت «چندین عذابِ جان کندن که من دیدم طاقت ندارم». عیسیٰ علیه‌السلام گفت «ای جمجمه، تو در آن وقت از دین گردیده بودی.

[۳۲] من هستید. [۳۳] ویرایش و ترجمهٔ قسمت آخر این جمله نیاز به زمان بیشتری دارد. [۳۴] «کینه کشیدن» اشاره به «انتقام گرفتن» دارد. این اصطلاح در ابیات ناصر خسرو و خاقانی به چشم می‌خورد. همچنین، به دهخدا مراجعه شود. [۳۵] آیهٔ ۳۰ سورهٔ کهف.
[۳۶] چه؟ [۳۷] شاخ. واژهٔ «سرون» در اشعار فردوسی، فرّخی، منوچهری و نظامی به چشم دیده می‌شود. به دهخدا مراجعه شود.
[۳۸] رنگارنگ. [۳۹] فریفته؟ [۴۰] احتمالا اشاره به نمازگزاردن بر حیوان دارد، و اینکه این متن در فضایی تدوین گشته که «گاو» به عنوان یک حیوان مقدس به شمار می‌رفته است. تاثیرپذیری از ادبیات بابلی و همچنین ادبیات هندویی جای تامّل دارد.

{8} Returning to the story. 'When I noticed them, I forgot whatever joy I had during my lifetime. O Spirit of God, those angels asked again, "Who is your God?" Again, I said, "You are my God." They hit me with their bludgeons one more time. O Spirit of God, the children of Adam, including the thinker, the ignorant, the king, the vizier, if they knew that what was ahead of me, they would never have forgotten to worship and invoke and would never have oppressed anyone. And not to laugh at parties as the children of Adam have such difficult moments ahead of them, after this mortal world (?) .

{9} Prophet Jesus (pbuh) cried a lot. The King Jumjuma said, 'O Spirit of God, they [angels] hit me so hard I fell down and plunged into the ground. They said they will enter my stomach "to take revenge." Then they picked me off the earth[4] and hung me upside down to punish me. And those two angels, who forced me to write about my deeds, then took me and put me next to the Throne and the Seat. There, I became free and comfortable.'

{10} Prophet Jesus (pbuh) asked, 'What did you see at the Throne and what did you ask from the angels?' He said, 'I saw the Seat. First, the Seat of His Eminence Adam (pbuh). Second, the Seat of His Eminence Abraham, the friend of God. Third, the Seat of His Eminence Moses (pbuh). Fourth, the Seat of His Eminence Jesus (pbuh). Fifth, the Seat of Muḥammad (pbuh). The gatekeeper of hell was ordered to take me to hell and they ripped me and reshaped me again and put me into a well. Then I was released from hell.'

{11} 'O Spirit of God, God said, "Indeed, We will not allow the reward to be lost of any who did well in deeds" (Q. 18:30). A proclamation arrived from the Creator, "My servant did good and offered charity and did not reject the requests of the needy. We do not deprive them from goodness."'

{12} Prophet Jesus (pbuh) said, 'You lived during the life of which Prophet?' He said, 'It was during the period of Prophet Elias.' [Jesus said,] 'And what was the reason for such torment?' He said, 'There was a cow at that time, with red and colourful horns and adorned with a crown of pearls and rubies. They killed the cow for its horns and I prayed over the corpse (?). And I was tormented because of that.'

{13} Prophet Jesus asked, 'O Jumjuma, would you like to experience dying once again?' He said, 'As I have experienced such hardship at the moment of dying, I have no more toleration for it.' Prophet Jesus (pbuh) said, 'O Jumjuma, at that time[5] you were not religious. When you revive, should you convert to my faith?' He said, 'I agree, if this works and is better. O Prophet of God, ask for me to be resurrected!'

[4] *or*, dragged me [5] that you saw such difficulties

چون زنده شوی به من گردی؟» گفت «نیکو و بهتر باشد. ای پیغمبر خدای دعا کن که من زنده شوم».

{۱۴} پس مهتر عیسیٰ سر سجده نهاد و دعا کرد و گفت «خداوندا و پروردگارا، به قدرت خویش جمجمه زنده گردان.» درحال و در همون[۴۱] ساعت زنده شد. و چون مهتر عیسیٰ روح اللّٰه را بدید در حال،[۴۲] درحال گفت «لآ إِلٰهَ إِلَّا اللّٰه، عیسیٰ رُوحِ اللّٰه»[۴۳]. بعداز آن هفتادِ دیگر بزیست،[۴۴] و قصّه این که تمام شد.

{۱۵} إِلٰهِيّ، به حرمت کرم عمیم خویش که جمیع مسلمانان را بر حکم خویش صابر و راضی گردان. بِجُودكَ بِجَلالك وكَرَمك وفَضْلك ورحمتك يَا أَرْحَمَ ٱلرّاحِمين. تمّت تمام.

[۴۱] یا «همان» [۴۲] مشاهدهٔ حضوری. [۴۳] در نسخهٔ «قصص القرآن» در کتابخانهٔ ملّی ایران، که هویّت صاحب اثر و نویسندهٔ آن مشخص نیست، و در برخی نسخه‌های مالايي و جاوه‌ای این داستان عبارت «أشهد أن لا إله الاّ اللّٰه و أن عیسیٰ رسول اللّٰه» در همان ابتدای فصل و به عنوان اوّلین جمله از زبان جمجمه بیان می‌شود. [۴۴] نسخهٔ عربی «قصّهٔ جمجمه» برگ ۷۷ در موزه و کتابخانهٔ ملک در تهران، اشاره به زیست جمجمه برای «چهل سال دیگر» دارد «فَعَاشَت تِلكَ الجُمجُمَه اَربَعینَ سِنَة». در نسخهٔ «قصص القرآن» کتابخانهٔ ملّی ایران، وی پس از رستاخیز به مدّت «هشت سال» زندگی می کند.

{14} His Eminence Jesus prostrated and prayed and said, 'O God, by your power make the skull alive.' Immediately, the skull became alive. And when it saw His Eminence Jesus, the Spirit of God, he immediately said, 'There is no god, but God, Jesus is the Spirit of God.' After this, he lived for seventy years and this story ended.

{15} *O God, by the dignity of your comprehensive grace that makes all Muslims patient and satisfied upon Your decree. By Your generosity, greatness, kindness, unmerited favour, and mercy, O the most Merciful of the merciful! Amen.*

پایان

«نورنامه»

این نورنامۀ حضرت رسول الله عَلَيۡهِ وَسَلَّمۡ

{۱} بِسۡمِ ٱللَّهِ ٱلرَّحۡمَٰنِ ٱلرَّحِيمِ ٱلۡحَمۡدُ لِلَّهِ رَبِّ ٱلۡعَٰلَمِينَ[۱] والعاقبةُ لِلۡمُتَّقِين.[۲] وَالصَّلاةُ وَالسَّلام عَلى رَسُولِه مُحَمَّد وَآله وَأَصۡحَابِه أَجۡمَعِينۡ.

{۲} نقل است که حضرت بی بی فاطمه رَضِيَ ٱللَّهُ عَنۡهَا یک روز پرسیدن که «یا رسول الله، شما بزرگتری یا جبرئیل عَلَيۡهِ ٱلسَّلَامُ؟» رسول الله صَلَّى ٱللَّهُ عَلَيۡهِ وَسَلَّمَ در فکر بودند که جبرئیل عَلَيۡهِ ٱلسَّلَامُ درآنۡ آمد و گفت «یا رسول الله، شما بزرگترید. امّا عمر من دراز [تر] است». پس[۳] رسول الله عَلَيۡهِ ٱلسَّلَامُ گفت «یا أخي جبرئیل، چه چیز یاد دارید؟» جبرئیل عَلَيۡهِ ٱلسَّلَامُ گفت «یا رسول الله، خدای تَعَالَی یک ستاره را آفریده است و بعداز هفتاد هزارسال بیرون می‌آید و بعداز آن غروب می‌شود. من او را هفتاد بار دیدم». رسول الله صَلَّى ٱللَّهُ عَلَيۡهِ وَسَلَّمَ گفت «او ستاره از نور من است؟» جبرئیل عَلَيۡهِ ٱلسَّلَامُ گفت «من نمی‌دانم».

{۳} پس رسول الله علیه وسلّم گفت «یا أخي جبرئیل، اگر آن ستاره ببینی بشناسی؟» جبرئیل گفت «بشناسم». پس رسول الله عَلَيۡهِ ٱلسَّلَامُ دست مبارک از سر بالا کرد. جبرئیل عَلَيۡهِ ٱلسَّلَامُ شناخت و گفت «أَمَنَّا وَصدَّقنا یا رسول الله». پس رسول الله صَلَّى ٱللَّهُ عَلَيۡهِ وَسَلَّمَ گفت «یا أخي جبرئیل، پیش‌از آن ستاره پنجاه [...] و چهار هزار سال اوّل نور من آفریده شد به حکم خداوند عَزَّ وَجَلَّ».

[۱] آیات ۱ و ۲ سورۀ فاتحه و همچنین عبارتی با مضمون دعا. [۲] آیۀ ۸۳ سورۀ قصص.
[۳] «پس» به جای «سپس» استفاده شده است.

Nūr-nāma

THIS IS THE *NŪR-NĀMA* OF THE MESSENGER (PBUH)

{1} In the Name of God, the most Compassionate, the most Merciful; all praise is for God, the Lord of the Worlds [Q. 1:1–2]; and the good end is for the righteous [Q. 28:83]; blessings and peace be upon the Messenger of God Muḥammad and all his Family and Companions.

{2} It is reported that the Lady Fāṭima asked a question one day: 'O Messenger of God, who is older, you or Gabriel?' The Messenger was pondering when Gabriel arrived and said, 'O Messenger of God, you are greater but I am more advanced in age.' Then, the Messenger of God said, 'O brother Gabriel, what do you remember?' Gabriel said, 'O Messenger of God, God has created one star which comes out after seventy thousand years and then goes down. I have seen it seventy times.' The Messenger of God said, 'That star is made of my light.' Gabriel replied, 'I have no idea'.

{3} In this regard, the Messenger of God said, 'O brother Gabriel, would you recognise the star if you saw it again?' Gabriel said, 'I will indeed recognise it!' Then the Messenger of God raised his hand up to his head. Gabriel recognised this and said, 'We believe, we affirm the truth, O Messenger of God!' Then the Messenger of God said, 'O brother Gabriel, before this star, the first fifty[...]four thousand years, it was my light which was created by the decree of the Almighty God.'

{۴} دیگر گفت «یا أخي جبرئیل، بشنوید تا پیش [از] شما حکایت می‌کنم. شما یاد گیرید صفتِ آفرینش[۴]». پس رسول ﷺ گفت «أَوَّل مَا خَلَقَ اللّٰه تعالی نُوري».[۵] چنین می‌فرماید آن خلاصهٔ[۶] موجودات و برگزیدهٔ مخلوقات، یعنی محمّد مُصْطَفَی ﷺ «اوّل چیزی که حضرت حق سبحانه وتعالی آفریده نور من بود».

{۵} در ابتدای پیدا کردن، سر سجده نهاد و فرمان آمد که «نورِ حبیبِ من و ای برگزیدهٔ من، مقصودِ من و مطلوبِ من توی و از محبّت تو هفت دریا آفریده‌ام. اوّل دریای علم. دوم دریای حلم[۷]، سوم دریای حیاء، چهارم دریای عقل، پنجم دریای فقر، ششم دریای نعمت، هفتم نور [...]. در هر دریائی نور مرا به فرمان خدای عزّ وجلّ هفتاد و هفت هزارسال.[۸]

{۶} فرمان حق سبحانه وتعالی در رسید که «ای نور حضرت حبیبِ من و ای نورِ برگزیدهٔ من، برخیز و خود را بجنبان». چون نور من خود را بجنباند از او صد و بیست چهار قطره صلب نبوّت پیدا شد. بعداز آن دو قطره آب از چشم راستِ نور من چکید. از قطرهٔ اوّل مهتر جبرئیل آفریده شد و از قطرهٔ دوم میکائیل آفریده شد. باز دو قطره آب از چشم چپِ نور من بچکید. از قطرهٔ اول اسرافیل آفریده شد؛ دوم قطره عزرائیل آفریده شد. باز دو قطره آب از سوراخ گوش راستِ نور من بچکید. اوّل قطره لوح آفریده شد، و از قطرهٔ دوم قلم آفریده شد. باز دو قطره آب ازگوش چپِ نور من بچکید. از قطرهٔ اوّل عرش آفریده شد، و از دوم قطره کرسی آفریده شد. باز هشت قطره آب از سوراخ بینيِ نور من بچکید. از آن هشت بهشت آفریده شد. باز دو قطره آب از میان دو شانهٔ نور من بچکید. از قطرهٔ او آفتاب آفریده شد، و از قطرهٔ دوم ماهتاب آفریده شد. باز پنج قطره آب از دست راست نور من بچکید. از قطرهٔ اوّل سِدْرَةِ الْمُنْتَهَی آفریده شد، و از قطرهٔ دوم درخت طوبی، و از قطرهٔ سوم حوض کوثر، و از قطرهٔ چهارم جان پیغمبران، و از قطرهٔ پنجم آدم صفي الله صَلَوَاتُ اللّٰهِ والسَّلَام آفریده شد.

[۴] در نسخهٔ ۱۷۰ آ کلند به شکل «آفرین نش» نوشته شده است.

[۵] عبارتی رایج که در اکثر منابع عربی، فارسی، ترکی، ترکی استانبولی و مالایی-اندونزیایی دیده می‌شود. نمونهٔ دیگر آن چنین است: «اوّل ما خلق اللّٰه نوري، اوّل ما خلق اللّٰه روحي، اوّل ما خلق اللّٰه العَقل، اوّل ما خلق اللّٰه القَلم»: Gustav Flügel, Die Arabischen, *Persischen und Türkischen Handschriften der Kaiserlich-königlichen Hofbibliothek zu Wien im auAuftrage der vorgesetzten K. K. behörde geordnet und beschrieben* (Wien: K. K. Hof- und Staatsdruckerei, 1867) I: 470.

[۶] برگزیده. [۷] شکیبایی. [۸] در نسخهٔ دیگری از «نور نامه» به شمارهٔ ۱۷۳ آ کلند به خط شیخ داود (کاتب درّالمجالس؛ نسخه آ کلند ۱۷۰)، داستان به شرح ذیل آغاز می‌شود (صص ۲-۴): «اوّل چیزی که خدای تَعَالَی بیافرید نور من بود. پس نور من حقّ تَعَالَی را سجده کرد. پس فرمان شد «ای نور حبیبِ من، از محبّت تو دَه دریا آفریدم. پس اوّل دریای علم، دوم دریای حلم، سوم دریای عشق، چهارم دریای خوف، پنجم دریای عمل، ششم دریای صبر، هفتم دریای شکر، هشتم دریای عقل، نهم دریای فقر، دهم دریای رحمت». پس پیغمبر فرمود ﷺ [فرمود] «در هر دریایی نور من ده هزار سال مانده. پس فرمان شد که بیرون آئی و خود را بجنبان»».

{4} Then he continued, 'O brother Gabriel, now listen to the story before your time, so you will learn about the form of creation.' Then the Messenger said, 'The first thing created by God was my light.' This is what the chosen Muḥammad said 'The first thing that God created was my light.

{5} Immediately after its creation, my light prostrated and God proclaimed, "O the Light of my Friend and O the chosen one! My purpose and goal is you, and I have created seven oceans from you. First, the ocean of knowledge; second, the ocean of tolerance; third, the ocean of chastity; fourth, the ocean of intellect; fifth, the ocean of poverty; sixth, the ocean of blessing; seventh, the light [...]. In every ocean, by God's decree, my light is for seventy-seven thousand years."[1]

{6} God commanded, "O Light of My friend and O Light of My chosen one, get out [from the oceans] and shake yourself!" 'When my light began to shake itself, 124,000 drops from the loins of prophets appeared. Later on, two drops of water dripped from the right eye of my light. His Eminence Gabriel was created from the first drop of light and Michael was created from the second drop. Then two other drops of water dripped from the left eye of my light. Isrāfīl was created from the first drop, and ʿIzrāʾīl was created from the second drop.'Then, two drops of water dripped from the canal of the right ear of my light. The Plate was created from the first drop and the Pen was created from the second. Then two other drops dripped from the canal of the left ear of my light. The Throne was created from the first and the Seat from the second drop. Then eight drops dripped from the nostril of my light. The Eight Paradises were made of the eight drops. Then two more drops of water came between the shoulders. Of my light the Sun was created from the first drop, and the Moon was created from the second drop. 'Then five drops of water dripped from the right hand of my light. The Lote Tree [in the seventh paradise] came from the first drop and the Ṭūbā Tree from the second drop and the Kawthar pool from the third drop and the Soul of Prophets was created from the forth drop and the chosen Adam (pbuh) was created from the fifth drop.

[1] In another version of the *Nūr-nāma* (GMS-173, ff. 2–4) held in the Auckland Libraries, also copied by the scribe of *Durr al-Majālis* (GMS-170), the creation story is as follows. 'The first thing that God had created was my light. Then, my light prostrated before God. Then a proclamation was made, "O the light of My friend, I have created ten oceans due to your passion: first, the ocean of science; second, the ocean of tolerance; third, the ocean of love; fourth, the ocean of fear; fifth, the ocean of action; sixth, the ocean of patience; seventh, the ocean of praise; eighth, the ocean of intellect; ninth, the ocean of poverty; tenth, the ocean of mercy'. Then the Prophet stated, "My light used to be in all of these oceans for ten thousand years. Then my light was ordered to come out of the water and shake itself down."'

{۷} باز چهار قطره آب از دست چپ نور من بچکید. اوّل باد، دوم خاک، سوم آب، چهارم آتش آفریده شد. آنگاه فرمان حقّ تَعَالَی در رسید که «نور حبیبِ منْ و ای برگزیدهٔ من، چهارم چیز آفریده‌ام. از این چهار چیز کدام اختیار می‌کنی تا پیغمبری تو را بر حقّ آشکارا کنم؟»[۹]

{۸} پس نورِمحمّد[۱۰] باد را گفت «السَّلَامُ عَلَيْكُمْ یا باد». جواب سلام باز داد. نورِمحمد گفت «ای باد تو در دنیا چه خواهی کرد؟» باد گفت «هر چه مراد من باشد». نورِمحمّد گفت »یا باد، در خود بنگر که چه عیب داری». باد گفت «ای نورِمحمّد، چه عیب دارم؟» نورِمحمّد گفت «تو بنده گریزپائی». باد گفت «ای نورِمحمّد، مگر تو بی عیب هستی؟» نورِمحمّد گفت «بی عیب خداست. بنده پرعیب است». بعداز آن این کلمهٔ شهادت به زبان راند که «أَشْهَدُ أَنْ لَآ إِلٰهَ إِلَّا اللّٰهُ وَحْدَهُ لا شَرِيكَ لَهُ وَأَشْهَدُ أَنَّ مُحَمَّداً عَبْدُهُ وَرَسولُه». باد در دینِ محمّد آمد، پیغمبری قبول کرد و حلقهٔ بندگی در گوش کرد.

{۹} باز نورِمحمّد آب را آواز داد: «السَّلَامُ عَلَيْكَ یا آب». آب گفت «عَلَيْكُمْ السَلَام یا نورِمحمّد». نورِمحمّد گفت «یا آب، تو در دنیا چه خواهی کرد؟» آب گفت «آنچه مراد منست آن کنم». نورِمحمّد گفت «ای آب، تو در خود بنگر که چه عیب داری». آب گفت «چه عیب دارم؟» نورِمحمّد گفت «ای آب، خدای تَعَالَی بندگان را خواهد آفرید تا جملهٔ ناپاکان از تو پاک شوند. تو را آفتاب پاک شونده [است]». آب گفت «ای نورِمحمّد، مگر تو بی عیب هستی؟» نورِمحمّد گفت «که بی عیب خدا است. بنده پر عیب است». بعداز آن آب نیز ایمان آورد و کلمهٔ شهادت به زبان راند و در دین مسلمانی درآمد. حلقهٔ بندگی در گوش کرد.

{۱۰} نورِمحمّد آتش را گفت «السَّلَامُ عَلَيْكَ یا آتش». گفت «عَلَيْكَ السَلَام یا نورِمحمّد». نورِمحمّد گفت «ای آتش، تو در دنیا چه خواهی کرد؟» آتش گفت «آنچه مراد منست». آن نورِمحمّد گفت «ای آتش، تو در خود بنگر که عیب داری،». آتش گفت که «چه عیب دارم؟» نورِمحمّد گفت «کشندهٔ تو آب است، و قوّت [تو] باد است». آتش گفت «ای نورِمحمّد، مگر تو بی عیبی؟» نورِمحمّد گفت «أستغفرالله، بی عیب خداست. بنده پر عیب است». آتش نیز مسلمان شد و کلمهٔ شهادت بر زبان راند و حلقهٔ بندگی محمّد عَلَيْهِ ٱلصَّلَوٰةُ وَٱلسَّلَمُ در گوش کرد.

[۹] بخشی از این داستان در «مجموع الخانی في بحر المعانی» که دربردارندهٔ فتاوی و ارجاعات فقهی می‌باشد موجود، است. این نسخهٔ پارسی از «مجموع الخانی» در کتابخانهٔ دانشگاه لایدن به شمارهٔ ۵۶۵۸، توسط هرخرونیه، از بَنْتِن در اندونزی به‌دست آمده و حاوی دست نوشته‌هایی به زبان مالایی است. در همین مورد مراجعه شود به: Majid Daneshgar, 'Persianate *Fiqh* in Indonesia'.

[۱۰] همچنین به شکل «نورُ محمّد» نیز خوانده می شود، چنانچه که در ادبیات مالایی رایج است.

{7} Then four drops of water dripped from the left-hand of my light. First, wind; second, soil; third, water; and fourth, fire were created from them. Then God's command arrived: "O Light of my friend and O the chosen of mine! I have created four things. Which of these four would you like to choose, after which I can truly demonstrate your prophecy?"

{8} Then the Light of Muḥammad greeted the wind and said, 'Peace be upon you, O Wind!' The wind replied to the greeting. The Light of Muḥammad asked, 'O Wind, what will you do in the world?' The Wind replied, 'Whatever I wish.' The Light of Muḥammad said, 'O Wind, behold yourself and tell me what is your point of weakness?' The Wind asked, 'O Light of Muḥammad, what is my point of weakness?' The Light of Muḥammad said, 'You are elusive and evasive.' The Wind said to the Light of Muḥammad, 'Are you without a point of weakness?' The Light of Muḥammad said, 'The perfect and flawless is God. The servant is always full of flaws.' After this, the Wind expressed the profession of faith, 'I testify that there is no god but God, Who has no partner; and I testify that Muḥammad is His servant and His Messenger.' The Wind converted to the religion of Muḥammad, accepted his prophecy and put a ring of bondage to its ear.

{9} The Light of Muḥammad then said, 'Peace be upon you, O Water!' The Water said, 'Peace be upon you, O Light of Muḥammad!' The Light of Muḥammad said, 'O Water, what will you do in the world?' The Water said, 'Whatever I wish.' The Light of Muḥammad said, 'O Water, behold yourself and tell me what is your point of weakness?' The Water asked, 'What is my point of weakness?' The Light of Muḥammad said, 'O Water, God will create servants and all that is unclean will be clean by means of you. However, it is the Sun that cleans you.' The Water said, 'O Light of Muḥammad, are you without a point of weakness?' The Light of Muḥammad said, 'The perfect and flawless is God. The servant is always full of flaws.' Then, the water converted to the faith, too, and expressed the profession of faith and became a Muslim. It also put a ring of bondage to its ear.

{10} The Light of Muḥammad said to the Fire, 'Peace be upon you, O Fire!' [The Fire] said, 'Peace be upon you, O Light of Muḥammad!' The Light of Muḥammad said, 'O Fire, what will you do in the world?' The Fire said, 'Whatever I wish.' The Light of Muḥammad said, 'O Fire, behold yourself and tell me what is your point of weakness?' The Fire asked, 'What is my point of weakness?' The Light of Muḥammad responded, 'Your are extinguished by water and wind strengthens you.' The Fire said, 'O Light of Muḥammad, are you without a point of weakness?' The Light of Muḥammad said, 'I seek the forgiveness of God; the perfect and flawless is God. The servant is always full of flaws.' The Fire also became a Muslim and expressed the profession of faith and embraced the ring of servitude to Muḥammad.

{۱۱} بعداز آن نورِ محمّد گفت خاک را «السَّلَامُ عَلَيْكَ ای خاک». خاک بر زبان حال گفت «عَلَيْكَ السَّلَام یا نورِ محمّد». نورِ محمّد گفت «ای خاک تو در دنیا چه خواهی کارمی کنی؟» خاک گفت «مَنِ بنده را مراد خود چه‌کار می‌آید». خاک کلمهٔ شهادت گفت و در دین محمّد درآمد و مسلمان شد و حلقهٔ بندگی ختم الرسالت علیه أفْضَل الصَلاة در گوش کرد. پس نورِ محمّد خاک را در کنار گرفته و گفت «اوّل و آخر تو را اختیار کردم».

{۱۲} وهیچ بندهٔ خدا از این أربع[11] عناصر خالی نیست. آنها که بادی‌اند متکبّرانند، و آنها که آتشی‌اند ظالمانند، و آنها که آبی‌اند جوانمردانند، و آنها که خاکی‌اند مسکینانند.[12] نورِ محمّد خاک را قبول کرد. حقّ تَعَالَی می فرماید که «بعضی را از آتش آفریده‌ام. هم به آب می‌پرورم و باز به آب هلاک می‌کنم، و بعضی را از آب آفریده‌ام. هم به آب می‌پرورم و به آب هلاک کنم، و بعضی را از باد آفریده‌ام و به باد می‌پرورم و به باد هلاک کنم، و بعضی را از خاک آفریده‌ام و به خاک پرورم و در خاک هلاک کنم».[13]

{۱۳} پس حقّ تَعَالَی چنین فرماید که «سر مبارک آن حضرت را از برکت آفریده‌ام و روی مبارک آن حضرت را از تجلّی آفریده‌ام، و بینی مبارک محمّد را از عنبر بهشت آفریده‌ام، و دو چشم مبارک محمّد مُصْطَفَی را [از] حیاء آفریده‌ام، و هر دو لب مبارک رسول الله را [از] تسبیح آفریده‌ام، و زبان مبارک سرور انبیاء را از ذکر خود[14] آفریده‌ام، و دندان مبارک ﷺ را از نور آفریده‌ام، و دل مبارک سیّدالمرسلین از اخلاص[ی] آفریده‌ام، و دو بازوی مبارک حضرت سرور کائنات را از قوت[15] آفریده‌ام، و گوش مبارک ختم الرسالت را از مشک جنّت آفریده‌ام، و حلق مبارک ختم النبی را از عسلِ جنّت آفریده‌ام، و موی مبارک از خشبوها و گل‌های جنّت آفریده‌ام، و قد مبارک رسول رَبِّ العَالَمِیْنَ را از بهر عبادت آفریده‌ام».

{۱۴} در حدیث آمده است «هرکه این نورنامه را بخواند و خود بشنود یا آنکه با خود نگاه دارد و حقّ تَعَالَی آن بنده را از بلا دو جهانی محفوظ دارد. هر محلّ که آن بنده را اجل فرا رسد وقت جان کندن برو آسان باشد و فرشته های رحمت نامهٔ اعمال او به دست راست بدهند. حقّ تَعَالَی جمیع گناهان او را به کرم خویش بخشد و وجود او را در گور کِرمان نخورند و استخوان او پوسیده نگردد، و ایمان وی را حقّ سبحانه ازغارت شیطان نگاه دارد و ثواب چهار کتاب یابد: اوّل ثواب تورات موسیٰ علیه السلام، دوم ثواب انجیل که بر عیسیٰ علیه السلام فرود آمده بود، سوم ثواب زبور که بر داود علیه السلام فرود آمده بود، چهارم ثواب فرقان که بر حضرت محمّد مُصْطَفَی ﷺ نازل شده بود. حقّ تَعَالَی گناهان آن بنده و گناهان آبا و اجداد اولاد و فرزندان او را بیامرزد و بر ایشان رحمت کناد».

{۱۵} هر که این نورنامه را بخواند با اعتقاد درست و اگر خواندن نداند دیگری را بدهد و بفرماید که بخواند، خود بشنود، از زبان بدگویان و سخن‌چینان و منافقان در امان بماند. و از بلاهای دو جهانی و از زلزله،

[11] چهار. [12] گمان من این است که ارتباط معناداری بین این چنین عبارات در «درّالمجالس» و مکتب «خاکساریه» وجود دارد.
[13] ارتباط خاکی بودن و اهمّیّت آن نزد خدا در فصل‌های مختلف این کتاب مطرح شده، موضوعی است که احتمالا به اندیشه و طریقت قلندریه و خاکساریه مرتبط باشد. خوش‌باد روزگاری که با شاهرخ راعی در فرایبورگِ آلمان در مورد آن صحبت نمودم. این موضوع در آینده‌ای نه چندان دور مورد بررسی بیشتر قرار خواهد گرفت. [14] خدا. [15] فیض خداوند.

{11} Then the Light of Muḥammad said to the Soil, 'Peace be upon you, O Soil!' The Soil spoke and said, 'Peace be upon you, O Light of Muḥammad!' The Light of Muḥammad said, 'O Soil, what will you do in the world?' The Soil said, 'What can be done by a servant like me and how?' The Soil then expressed the profession of faith and came to the religion of Muḥammad and became a Muslim and embraced the ring of servitude of the Seal of the Prophets, upon whom is the best of blessings. Then the Light of Muḥammad hugged the soil and said, 'I only choose you'.

{12} And none of the servants of God are void of these four elements. Those who are like wind are arrogant. Those who are like fire are oppressive. Those who are like water are chivalrous. And those who are like soil are humiliate and poor. The Light of Muḥammad accepted the soil. God said, 'I made some from the fire, bred them with water, and killed them with water. And I made some from water, bred them with water, and killed them again with water. And I made some from wind, and bred them with wind, and killed them with wind. And I made some from soil, bred them with soil, and killed them in soil.'

{13} Also, God said, 'I created the sacred head of the Prophet from the blessing, and his sacred face from the theophany; and the sacred nose of Muḥammad from the heavenly amber; and the two sacred eyes of Muḥammad from chastity; and both sacred lips of the Messenger of God from My praising; and the sacred tongue of the Master of the Worlds from My own invocation; and the sacred tooth of the Messenger, peace be upon him, from the Light; and the sacred heart of the Master of the emissaries from loyalty; and the two sacred arms of the Master of the Worlds from divine grace; and the sacred ear of the Seal of apostleship from the heavenly musk; and the sacred throat of the Seal of prophecy from the heavenly honey; and the sacred hair from the heavenly fragrance and flowers; and the sacred height [i.e., body] of the Messenger of the Lord of the Worlds for worshipping.'

{14} It has been mentioned in a tradition (*ḥadīth*) that whoever reads this *Nūr-nāma* and/or listens to it and/or carries it with them, God will protect them from the calamity of both worlds. And whenever the death of the servant approaches, the dying moment will be easy for them, and the angels of mercy will pass his record of deeds to his right hand. God will forgive all his sins by His kindness. And his body will not be eaten by worms in the grave and his bones will not rot. And God will protect his faith from Satan's plundering. And he will be given the reward of the Four Books: first, the reward of the Torah of Moses; second, the reward of the Gospels (Injīl) revealed to Jesus; third the reward of the Psalms (Zabūr) revealed to David; and fourth, the reward of the Criterion (Furqān) revealed to Muḥammad. God will forgive the sins of the servant, as well as the sins of their ancestors and descendants and bestow mercy upon them.

{15} Whoever reads this *Nūr-nāma* with firm belief, and if they cannot read, give

قحطی محفوظ ماند و ثواب قاریان و شهیدان یابد و از فتنهٔ دجّال کورچشمِ لعین در امان باشد و در زُمرهٔ[۱۶] نیک‌بختان استاده شود.

{۱۶} حقّ تَعَالَی می فرماید که «هر که این نورنامه را بخواند از من حاجت طلبد. اگر من حاجت وی را روا نگردانم خدایِ وی نباشم». هر که شب جمعه این نورنامه را بخواند یک‌بار یا که بشنود، ثواب هزار و سیصد پیغمبران مرسل یابد و در آن شب آن بنده را فرشتگان حمد و ثنا گویند. چنانچه هم کَر [؟] و بیان آرزو کنند که کاشکی این ثواب به ما نصیب شدی.

{۱۷} نقلست از امام محمّد غزالی رَحْمَةُ اللهِ عَلَيْهِ که «نهصد و نود نسخه بود معتبر؛ روزی در کتابخانهٔ خود سفتهٔ این نسخه را یافت و مطالعه کرد. بسیار وی را خوش آمد. نیّت کرد که این نسخه را به سلطان محمود غزنوی ببرد. از این معنی سلطان آگاه شد. یازده روز راه استقبال وی رفته. چنانکه در آن روز خلق بسیار بود از ترک و عجم و تاجیک و عرب و از بنده و از همه حاضر بودند. این نورنامه را دیدند و شنیدند که بسیار فضیلتِ دارد. همه خوشحال گشتند.

{۱۸} چون محمود نسخه را زیارت کرد به شکرانهٔ این نسخه هزار گوسفند و صد شتر قربانی کرد. و علما و فضلا و اهالی[۱۷] و موالی[۱۸] مکّه [را؟] مهمانی نمودند، و زر[۱۹] بسیار نثار کرد و این نسخه را حِرزِ جان[۲۰] خود ساخت. همان شب در واقعه[۲۱] دید که حضرت رسالت پناه ﷺ با پانصد هزار صلب نبوت تشریف فرمودن و از حضرت عزّت جَلَّ وَعَلَا در حقّ سلطان دعا کرد؛ ایشان خواست [...] که خطاب احدی در رسید که «سلطان محمود را بیامرزیدم و گناهان صغیره و کبیره او را عفو کردم. چنانکه نورنامه را عزیز داشت من در دنیا و آخرت عزیز گردانیدم و درهای بهشت بر وی گشادم».

{۱۹} بعداز آن به شکرانه این خواب، دوازده هزارغلامِ حلقه به گوش آزاد کرد و هزار مدرسه بنا نمود و اهالی و موالی شهر را خلعت داد و بر رعیت مهربان شد.

[۱۶] دسته، گروه، جماعت. [۱۷] مردمان. [۱۸] سروران و بزرگان. [۱۹] سکّه و پول. [۲۰] حِرزِجان «تعویذی است که برای حفظ روح از صدمات ارواح پلید و دیوان می بستند». به دهخدا مراجعه شود. [۲۱] خواب و رؤیا.

it to someone else asking them to read it and they themselves listen to it, then they will be protected from abusive and talebearing people and hypocrites. And they will be kept far from the calamities of the two worlds and from earthquakes and famine. And they will be granted the reward of the Qurʾān reciters as well as the reward of the martyrs. And they will be protected from the sedition and temptation of the blind accursed Antichrist[2]. And they will be placed among the auspicious.

{16} God said, 'I would not be God if I did not answer the request of the one who has read this *Nūr-nāma* and requested from Me. Whoever recites this *Nūr-nāma* on the eve of Friday once, or listens to it, will be granted the reward of one thousand and three hundred prophets and they will be praised by angels on that night, and every person – whether deaf or speaking – will say, "I wish that such rewards were for me!"'

{17} It is reported by Imam Muḥammad Ghazālī that there were 990 verified versions [of the *Nūr-nāma*]. One day, he found a version of it in his library and studied it. He enjoyed it immensely. He decided to take this copy to Sultan Maḥmūd Ghaznawī. The sultan learned about this [i.e., the intention of Ghazālī]. He walked in the path of the Ghazālī for eleven days to welcome him; the day on which there was a large crowd including Turks, non-Arabs (*ʿajams*), Tajiks, Arabs, slaves and others. They noticed the *Nūr-nāma* and heard that it possesses a lot of blessings. All became happy.

{18} When Maḥmūd saw the copy he slaughtered one thousand sheep and camels due to its blessing and he hosted scholars, knowledgeable people, and senior chiefs of Mecca and he paid a fortune [for Imam Ghazālī's copy of the *Nūr-nāma*] and he used it as his protective amulet. That same night, he dreamed that the Prophet came along with five hundred prophetic loins and hearts and prayed for the sultan before the presence of God. He did so [...] and the proclamation of the Divine Oneness was heard, 'I forgive Sultan Maḥmūd of all his minor and major sins. He respected *Nūr-nāma*, I have then cherished him in the world and the hereafter and opened the gate of paradise to him.'

{19} Then, as a sign of gratitude for this dream, he released twelve thousand ear-ringed slaves, established one thousand schools, dressed the people and senior chiefs of the city, and showed kindness to the common people.

[2] Dajjāl

{۲۰} و هر بنده که این نسخهٔ نورنامه را مُدام بخواند از رنج جمیع بیماری و درد اندام و علّت باد قولنج و بواسیر و سرخ باد[22] و سفید باد[23] و هر علّتی که در وجود آدمی باشد از آن نجات یابد. یا شافي [یا] الله، [...] رسول الله ﷺ والله أعلم بالصواب.

{۲۱} این کتاب درّالمجالس نوشته شده است.[24]

[22] بیماری «سرخ باد» در اکثر جوامع اسلامی رایج بوده است. در بین ترکان عثمانی با عنوان «قیزل یل» شناخته می‌شده است. نگاه کنید به برگ ۱۵ از نسخهٔ Cod. Pers. 309 در کتابخانهٔ باوریا شهر مونیخ. در ادبیات مالایی هم به این بیماری با نام عربی «الریح الأحمر» اشاره شده است. به نسخهٔ Add.3789 در کیمبریج مراجعه نمایید.

[23] دعای ویژه‌ای برای هریک از این بیماری‌ها وجود دارد. دعای سرخ باد عموماً در کنار دیگر ادعیهٔ اسلامی مثل دعای مولای، دعای هیکل سبع، دعای جنّ و دیو، و دعای سلطان محمود غزنوی نوشته می‌شده‌است.

Wilhelm Pertsch, *Die orientalischen Handschriften der Herzoglichen Bibliothek zu Gotha* (Gotha: FRIEDR . ANDR. PERTHES, 1880), II: 90.

[24] در آکلند ۱۷۰ این متن با جملات اضافی تمام می‌شود «چون در تمام سال پنج روزی هشت ثواب هزارروزه باشد، اوّل روزه بیست و هفت شهر رجب. اگر که شب معراج است. دوم روزهٔ بیست و پنج شهر ذی قعده که سبب بناء کعبه است. سیّوم روزهٔ هشتم شهر ذی حجّ که کعبهٔ شریف تبار گشت. چهارم روز بیست دویّم شهر محرّم الحرام چون جبرئیل علیه‌السلام برابر محمّد رسول الله ﷺ امامت کردند. پنج روزهٔ دوازدهم شهر ربیع الاوّل رسول الله علیه‌السلام رحلت فرمودند».

{20} And every servant who regularly reads this copy of the *Nūr-nāma* will be protected from all sorts of disease, body pain, spasm, haemorrhoids, erysipelas, and the origin of all diseases in the human body.[3] *O Healer, [O] God [...] the Messenger of God, peace be upon him, and God Knows the right thing.*

{21} This book *Durr al-Majālis* has been completed!

[3] In Islamic medical and occult literature, there are specific supplications for specific diseases. For a list, see Wilhelm Pertsch, *Die orientalischen Handschriften der Herzoglichen Bibliothek zu Gotha* (Gotha: Friedr. Andr. Perthes, 1880), vol. 2, 90.

فهرست فصول

List of the Chapters

باب نوزدهم: حکایتِ مرد سخی و زن بخیل

باب بیستم: حکایتِ آزر بت‌تراش

باب بیست و یکم: حکایتِ طوطی به حضرت سلیمان بن داود علیه السلام

باب بیست و دوم: حکایتِ آرزوی خواجه حسن بصری

باب بیست و سوم: حکایتِ خواهش شیطان مردود که فردا بر امّت پیغمبر دعوی خواهد کرد

باب بیست و چهارم: حکایتِ پادشاه نیشاپور با مظلومی

باب بیست و پنجم: حکایتِ ربیع حسام، قدس الله ثراه، با دختر خود، و سؤال‌وجواب به خدمت پدر

باب بیست و ششم: حکایتِ خواجه سفیان ثوری با شیطان مردود عَلَیْه اللَعْنَة

باب بیست و هفتم: حکایتِ خواجه حسن نوری – رحمة الله علیه

باب بیست و هشتم: حکایتِ شیخ برسیسا که چگونه بود، و چه کسی بود، و سبب چه بود که ایمان کم کرد، و مؤمن را از آن هُشیار باید بُود؟

باب بیست و نهم: در فضیلتِ ماه مبارک رمضان.

باب سی‌ام: حکایتِ خانهٔ کعبة الله

باب سی و یکم (الف): مقتل أَمیر المُؤمِنین امام حسن و حسین شهید کربلا رضی الله عنهما [نسخهٔ کوتاه]

باب سی و یکم (ب): مقتل أَمیر المُؤمِنین امام حسن و حسین شهید کربلا رضی الله عنهما [نسخهٔ طولانی]

باب سی و دوم: حکایتِ سلطان ابوسعید ابوالخیر که حقّ مرید بر پیر چیست و حقّ پیر بر مرید چیست؟

باب سی و سوم: حکایتِ اهل بهشت که به دیدار حقّ سبحانه و تعالی مشرّف خواهند شد و آخرین از امّت محمّد مصطفی صلی الله علیه و سلم که از دوزخ بیرون آید

باب سی و چهارم: در کیفیتِ بلعم باعور

باب سی و پنجم: موسیٰ‌نامه

باب سی و ششم: حکایتِ پادشاه شام

پایان: نورنامه

Chapter 19: The story of the generous husband and the miserly wife
Chapter 20: The story of Āzar, the idol-maker
Chapter 21: The story of the parrot speaking with the Prophet Solomon (pbuh)
Chapter 22: The story of Khʷāja Ḥasan Baṣrī God's mercy be upon him
Chapter 23: The story of the request of the outcast Satan who harassed the nation of the Prophet Muḥammad
Chapter 24: The story of the King of Nishapur's treatment of the oppressed
Chapter 25: The story of Khʷāja Rabīʿ Ḥusām; with his daughter – the question and the answer
Chapter 26: The story of Khʷāja Sufyān Thawrī with the outcast Satan, God's curse be upon him
Chapter 27: The story of Khʷāja Ḥasan Nūrī, may God's mercy be upon him
Chapter 28: The story of Shaykh Barsīsā; who he was, what type of person he was, and the reason that he lost his faith – believers should take heed!
Chapter 29: On the virtue of the holy month of Ramadan
Chapter 30: The story of the Kaʿba
Chapter 31: The story of the killing of the commanders of believers Ḥasan and Ḥusayn (pbuh) [including short (a) and long (b) versions]
Chapter 32: The story of our sovereign-master Abu Saʿīd Abū al-Khayr; regarding the right of the disciple upon the spiritual master, and the right of the spiritual master upon the disciple
Chapter 33: The story of the inhabitants of paradise; who will be blessed with a meeting with God, and the last person from the community of Muḥammad to leave hell
Chapter 34: Regarding Balʿam Bāʿūr
Chapter 35: The tale of Moses
Chapter 36: The story of the King of the Levant
Epilogue: *Nūr-nāma*

PART C

APPENDICES

Appendices

by Majid Daneshgar

In these appendices I list some available manuscripts of *Durr al-Majālis* – region by region – giving details where appropriate. Most of the known manuscript copies of *Durr al-Majālis* have been examined by myself for the preparation of this volume. Some copies located in Iran and Pakistan were not made accessible despite attempts.

Durr al-Majālis clearly made inroads to different parts of the Muslim world very rapidly. Not only did it continue to be copied and translated until the mid-fourteenth/twentieth century, it was also printed from the late thirteenth/nineteenth century onwards. Most manuscripts and printed volumes were based on the shorter and more common version with only thirty-three chapters that does not include the longer version of the Karbala saga (*Hikayat Muhammad Hanafiyya*), the Tale of Moses (*Munājāt-nāma*), the Tale of Jesus and King Jumjuma, or the *Nūr-nāma*. The editors of early printed copies admit to only basing their editions on a few manuscript copies.

A Description of Select Persian-Language Manuscripts

1. IRAN

There are several manuscripts of *Durr al-Majālis* held in private and public libraries in Iran. Apart from those in the National Library of Iran (six copies) or the Parliamentary Library (three copies), others are found in the University of Tehran Library (one copy), Imam Sadiq University Library (one copy), Ferdowsi University of Mashhad (one copy), the Mausoleum of Ṣafī al-Dīn Ardabīlī (one copy) (now the Iranology Foundation), the Āyatullāh Marʿashī Najafī Library, Qum (two copies), as well as in the Āstān Quds Raḍawī Library, Mashhad and its subdivisions in other cities like Yazd (sixteen copies, some of them not yet catalogued) and the Mirāth-i Maktūb collection in Qum (one copy). Most of these copies are similar in terms of length and content and they were all completed after the twelfth/eighteenth century. Some copies in the Āstān Quds Raḍawī Library appear alongside anonymous treatises about the Day of Judgement and the Antichrist but which nevertheless can be identified based on another copy preserved in the Iranian National Library (see 5–33429).

University of Tehran Library

No. 8047

Copied by Khʷāja Shāh Muḥammad b. Khʷāja Muḥammad Ṭāhir Laylakī (?) in Ṣafar. The owner of the manuscript was ʿAbd al-Qādir who received it as a gift on 2 Jumādā al-Thānī 1246/18 November 1830. A reference is made to a Shaykh Ḥamīdullāh, who perhaps was in the possession of the book in Rajab 1287/1870. Given the numbering style, this manuscript may have been produced by someone with a Hindustani background. With thirty-three chapters the manuscript is bound with another treatise on the story of a deer, its hunter, and Muḥammad, as well as a poetic supplication (*munājāt*) about Muḥammad, his ascension, and prophecy. One of its couplets reads as follows (f. 167),

سلیمان اگر داشت خاتم چه سود؛ که ختم نبوّت به نام تو بود

What could be the benefit of Solomon's having a signet ring (viz., seal)
while the seal of prophecy was coined with your name [O Muḥammad].

The Mausoleum of Shaykh Ṣafī al-Dīn Ardabīlī (now in Iranology Foundation)

33 (408)

In this copy, the author is noted as Sayf al-Muẓaffar b. Burhān. This manuscript can be considered as one of the important copies and it is a copy I paid close attention to while editing the text. The name of the scribe, who copied the work in Persian *nastaʿlīq* in 985/c.1577, is given as Pāyanda Nā-murād (?). This version includes thirty-three chapters and was in the possession of Mīr-Mahdī Ḥisārī whose seal is seen on folio 2, coming with a recommendation to perform ablution and recite a supplication from Awḥad al-Dīn Kirmānī.

This manuscript was originally housed in the mausoleum (*buqʿa*) of Ṣafī al-Dīn Ardabīlī in Ardabil, Iran. The collection of this mausoleum is mainly owed to the patronage of the Safawid kings of Persia which is no surprise given that Ṣafī al-Dīn Ardabīlī (735/1334) is considered as the eponymous ancestor of the dynasty. Its collection was, according to a note attached to the manuscript, plundered by Russian armies during World War II. This manuscript is now kept in the National Library of Russia (no. 222), but the Iranian government archived scanned copies in the 1990s.

The main body of the story is accompanied with other material such as different occult, legal, theological, and mystical treatises and poems. It addresses the virtues of reading historical works on prophets and prescribes a healing formula with magical square, or *jadwal*. The additional material also includes statements from ʿAlī b. Abī Ṭālib, Imam Samarqandī, Khʷāja Imām Muḥammad Shukrī, Khʷāja Muḥammad ʿAlī Ḥakīm Tirmidhī, and from the Prophet Muḥammad, as well as supplications and suchlike. There is a section on inauspicious days (*ayyām-i naḥs*), which is explained by references to Prophet Moses who mentioned that there are twenty-four major inauspicious days in the year; the fate of one who is born or taken ill on one of these days is suggested (f. 11). There are instructions on how to identify the Night of Decree (*laylat al-qadr*) by Abū al-Ḥasan Kharaqānī. A supplicatory formula known as the Prayer of the Crazy Dog (*duʿā-yi sag-i dīwāna*) is prescribed for one bitten by a stray dog. A chapter on Nawrūz, the Persian new year, is ascribed to Ḥakīm Tirmidhī. Instructions for ritual purification (*ṭahāra*) are also given in both Arabic and Persian. The back of the folio includes references to legal issues relating to the corpse and poems of Rumi copied by someone known as 'Muḥammad Qūshchī' (also Qusci) and dated 1026/c.1617, suggesting that he was from the northwestern Iran.

The Parliamentary Library, Iran

14248

It is a very important Persian manuscript due to its circulation among Tamil Muslims. The scribe is not known but the text could have been produced between the eleventh/seventeenth and twelfth/eighteenth centuries in India. On f. 120, a note in the *nastaʿlīq* script says, 'the book was purchased in Maḥmūd-Bandar', referring to present-day Parangippettai, Tamil Nadu. Also apparent are Tamil texts written with Arabic script (Arwī) and some minor Urdu notes.

This manuscript (ff. 1–119) demonstrates the Sufi leanings of the scribe, as the term *ilāhī* ('O my God') is repeated three times on different occasions (e.g., f. 119).[1] A treatise of nineteen chapters, titled *Rāḥat al-Qulūb* (The Ease of Hearts), is also included in the manuscript. This work deals with Islamic theology and eschatology, as does *Durr al-Majālis* itself. Another work in the manuscript is a story titled *Ḥikāyat-i Qiṣṣa-yi Abū Shaḥma, farzand-i Amīr al-Muʾminīn ʿUmar Khaṭṭāb* (The Tale of Abū Shaḥma, the son of the Commander of Believers ʿUmar Khaṭṭāb),[2] the content of which can be related to the Malay *Hikayat Abu Syahma*. Other elements of the manuscript include a tradition in Arabic from Ibn ʿAbbās about hell, punishment, and the afterlife (f. 156); a tradition in Persian also from Ibn ʿAbbās about five important days in the year upon which one is recommended to fast (ff. 156–157); Arabic and Arwī references to those who leave praying (f. 158); a short note on abbreviated forms of prophets' scriptures (f. 158); Arabic supplications (ff. 158–160); an Arwī supplication (f. 160); Arabic treatises on Islamic law (*sharīʿa*) and faith (*īmān*) (ff. 160–162); a Persian treatise based on

[1] For details of its ownership and initial pages, see my previous reference.
[2] According to Islamic traditions Abū Shaḥma was a Jew.

al-Manār al-Musāfirīn (The Travellers' Milestone) about the significance of Islamic law (ff. 163–165 without my revision).

شریعت بجای تخم است و طریقت بجای شاخ و برک و حقیقت بجای کل است و حقیقت الحقیقت بجای میوه.
پس اکر تخم نباشد، شاخ و برک و کل و میوه کجا ظاهر شوند.

> The Law (*sharīʿa*) is like a seed, and the Path (*ṭarīqa*) is like the branches and leaves, and the Reality (*ḥaqīqa*) like a flower, and the *ḥaqīqat al-ḥaqīqat* (the Truth of the Reality) like a fruit. If there is no seed, how may the branch and leaves and flower and fruit appear?

Also, we find an Arabic treatise about the one who refrains from prayer (f. 167); an Arabic treatise on the importance of prayer (167–169); a *wafat-nāma* of Muḥammad (170–177); the treatise of *Ḥayrat al-Fiqh* (178–180); a short exegetical note on the Qurʾānic term *kalāla* (one who dies without leaving parents or children) based on the commentary of Sarājī, the *Tafsīr-i Ḥusaynī* of Kāshifī, *Tafsīr al-Bayḍāwī*, *Tafsīr al-Jalālayn*, and *Tafsīr Baḥr al-Mawwāj* (f. 180); An Arwī and Arabic treatise on living beings (ff. 182–185); an Arabic tradition from Ibn ʿAbbās (f. 186). It also includes a table (Table 2) with abbreviations of holy scriptures.

Faʿim: The Arabic *Furqān* [i.e., Qurʾān] of Muḥammad	فَعِمْ: فرقان عربی محمد
Tuʿamm: the Hebrew Torah of Moses	تُعَمّ: تورات عبری موسی
Zayd: The Greek Psalms of David	زَيْدْ: زبور یونانی داود
Isʿa: The Syriac Gospel of Jesus	إسَعْ: انجیل سریانی عیسی

Table 2. Abbreviations of Holy Scripture Titles.

Iranian National Library

5–22341

This incomplete version has been registered as *Qiṣṣa-yi Anbiyāʾ* (The Tale of Prophets). The manuscript shows minor interlinear translations for Arabic notes and a few additional Persian phrases and terms, and marginal translations of Qurʾānic verses. Some of the names seen on folio 258 suggest that it was produced in India.

5–7992

This manuscript bears the date 1280/c.1863; drawings can be seen on folio 303; a marginal note on folio 369 includes a Dari expression popular in Afghanistan.

عالم تمام گشتم دلبر نیافتم؛ هرکس برای مطلب خود دلبری کند
هیچ، هیچ شدم زلف [...]

5–21172

This is an incomplete copy bound copy with the *Faqr-nāma* of Muḥammad and a commentary of the thirtieth part of the Qurʾān ('Juzʾ ʿAmma') copied by a 'Mawlānā Lāla' from Jummūn (present-day Jammu) of Kashmir.[3]

5–27641

Apart from marginalia and corrigenda (ff. 61, 109), the initial pages of this manuscript show numbers and prices, and the word 'Rupee' is seen (f. 5), suggesting its circulation in South Asia.

5–9182

Scribe unknown but the name of Muḥammad Muʾmin-jān and the Afghani date of 10 Ḥūt 1318, corresponding to 1 March 1940, are seen. The presence of this manuscript in Afghanistan in the mid-fourteenth/twentieth century clearly suggests its subject matter would have been of interest.

5–22910

Replete with marginalia, corrigenda, drawings, signs, and different handwriting by someone not competent in Persian. The beginning is slightly different from other copies, and chapter thirty-one, usually known as *The Killing Story of Ḥasan and Ḥusayn*, is titled *On the Killing of Ḥasan* (*Dar Maqtal-i Ḥasan*).

5–7341

The forename of the scribe who copied the manuscript in Lahore on 8 Ṣafar 1194/14 February 1780 is given as Muḥammad. The last part of his name is not legible. He ends the manuscript as follows (f. 151):

[3] Jammu also used to be known as Dār al-Amān (the Abode of Security). See Chas. J. Rodgers, *Catalogue of the Coins of the Indian Museum* (Calcutta: Printed by order of the Trustees of the Indian Museum, 1895), vol. 3, 121.

نسخهٔ متبرکهٔ درمجالس
The blessed manuscript *Durr-i Majālis*

5–28575
An incomplete manuscript from South or Central Asia. Fl. 337 includes some magical and intuitional codes, along with a Persian note 'Mullā Muḥammad Qāsim-jān has come and gone'. Fl. 334 also has a marginal note indicating the date of production as 1215/1800–01.

5–6465
An incomplete manuscript finished on 'An auspicious day, the eleventh of the month of [...]' (f. 269). Some seals are apparent although feint and illegible. Fl. 270 includes the name of Muḥammad Muʿaẓẓam Bahādur-Pādshāh, obviously referring to the Mughal emperor, Bahādur Shāh I (1643–1712). Also, the Persian stamp of Anjuman-i Taraqqī-yi Urdū, Jāmiʿ Masjid, Dihlī, can be seen, referring to one of the important cultural associations for preserving Urdu literature. A few names and dates can be seen: Mīrzā Rustam Beig/Bayg 1221/1806–7 or Mīrzā Suhrāb Bayg 1291/1874–5, Mīrzā Afrāsiyāb Bayg (1903), Mīrzā Jamshīd Bayg, Mīrzā Changīz (1925).

5–33429
The manuscript was copied by ʿAbbās ʿAlī b. ʿAbd al-Qādir, a resident of Machīlī-Bandar, referring to Machilipatnam in the Krishna District of India. After the text of *Durr-i Majālis* (ff. 1–254), there is an eschatological and theological treatise by Faqīr b. Ḥusām al-Dīn, known as 'ʿAnqā' (?) about 'Imam Mahdī the Owner of the End Time, the Day of Judgement, Dajjāl, Gog and Magog, and Beast of the Earth' (ff. 255–282). The name refers to the famous Indian scholar, Ḥusām al-Dīn al-Muttaqī al-Hindī (888–975/1472–1567). In this treatise, he describes the forty main signs that single the appearance of the Antichrist and the Mahdī.[4] The manuscript ends with a glossary of words used in the treatise and their meanings (ff. 283–288).

5–29446
An incomplete copy, originally belonging to the Iranian Ahl al-Bayt Assembly. It does not introduce the author or the title. The opening page includes the term *ghazal mawlūd sharīf* (lyrics for the Noble Birthday), perhaps a South Asian (or Afghani)

4 This treatise, deserving of further research, might be the origin of some Southeast Asian eschatological beliefs and texts.

reference to the birthday of Muḥammad.[5] Fl.1 has marginal handwriting in Urdu introducing the manuscript as '*Kitāb Durr al-Majālis*' with different accounts. It has been catalogued as a *maqtal* in the National Library of Iran.

5-34451

The scribe is known as Shaykh Muḥammad b. Shaykh Saʿdullāh who completed the text during the reign of the Mughal emperor Awrangzib (ʿĀlamgīr I; r. 1658–1707).

Āstān Quds Raḍawī

8784

The manuscript was copied in 1305/1887–8 by General Amīr Aḥmad Khān, who was the Afghan envoy in Kolkata (formerly, Calcutta) and father of Durrani envoy Wali Ahmad Khan. The copy was made during the reign of ʿAbd al-Raḥmān Khān (r. 1880–1901).[6]

Āyatullāh Marʿashī Najafī Library

10680

Including thirty-three chapters, this work was copied by Mīrzā Muḥammad Diyūbandī in 1253/c.1837.

2. TURKEY

A thorough search suggests that among the publicly accessible libraries of Turkey only two copies of *Durr al-Majālis* are held in the country. Both manuscripts are said to be in the possession of the Istanbul University Library, however, only one of the manuscripts could be located. The number of copies of *Durr al-Majālis* in Turkey may be higher if private collections are taken into consideration.

[5] Whether it had influence on Malay Maulid ceremony deserves to be examined in the future.

[6] For more on history of Afghanistan and its emir, see Shah Mahmoud Hanifi, *Connecting Histories in Afghanistan: Market Relations and State Formation on a Colonial Frontier* (Sandford: Stanford University Press, 2011): http://www.gutenberg-e.org/hanifi/chapter4.html. Short profile about the manuscripts can be found from: https://library.razavi.ir/en

Istanbul University Central Library

813
This copy is dated 6 Shawwal 1286/9 January 1870 and bears the name Sharaf b. Ḥusayn al-Marḥūm Qara-Qālpāq (Karakalpak). It includes both Persian and Ottoman Turkish notes.[7]

3. EGYPT

Despite indications to the contrary, only one copy of *Durr al-Majālis* could be found in Egypt, in the Talaat Library of Cairo. Another copy from Cairo is now kept in Munich.

Talaat Library, Cairo

53
This manuscript was copied by Ḥusayn b. Sayfullāh Yamliḥā b. Raḥmān-Qulī in 1825 and was transported to Egypt from Istanbul. Fl.1 shows a marginal note in red mentioning the owner of the manuscript as 'Yamliḥā b. Raḥmān-Qulī'. The manuscript includes interlinear and marginal translations and notes in Turkish. Russian handwriting and Turkish notes on the first folio are also apparent.

4. KASHMIR

Manuscripts of *Durr al-Majālis* from Kashmir could only be found in the Oriental Research Library of Srinagar (three copies). They are either copies of the main work, or are parts of its chapters that were reproduced independently.

Oriental Research Library of Srinagar

2940
Titled as *Dūrd al-Majālis*, this is a disordered and incomplete manuscript. The name of the scribe is not mentioned. On folio 54 the name of Kh^{w}āja Muḥyi al-Dīn is seen.

[7] My thanks go to Onur Yıldırım for providing this information.

Some chapters of this copy end with the phrase '*niẓām shud; tamām shud kār-i man*' (I am done with this manuscript), suggesting that some chapters were read independently (e.g., f. 31). Numbers written in Urdu are found (f. 31). Poetic verses in broken Persian, often ascribed to Saʿdī, and dealing with 'praise of [heavenly] wine' and 'in censure of Satan' are seen.

بده ساقیان آبِ آتش لباس
کسی را که شیطان بود پیشوا
کجا بازگردد به راه خداه[8]

863

This short treatise is titled as *Qiṣṣa-yi Wafāt-i Ḥaḍrat Fāṭima* (The Death Story of Lady Fāṭima), in reference to the daughter of Muḥammad. The work was written based on the eleventh chapter of *Durr al-Majālis* dealing with her death and her recommendations to her husband, ʿAlī. It was copied by Bābā Asadullāh[9] of Kashmir in 12 Shawwāl 1282/28 February 1866. Final pages including astrological and magical formula and rhythmic occult phrases are seen.

2030

This is a two-treatise collection. The first one (ff. 1–4) is an anonymous work on the virtues of *Sūrat al-Fātiḥa* (Q. 1), whose genre and content is similar to chapter thirty-five of *Durr al-Majālis*, where Moses wonders how to find the 'straight path', to which the answer is 'through the Qurʾān of Muḥammad'. Also, the qualities and features of the scriptures of David, Moses, and Jesus are compared with that of Muḥammad. Such forms of Islamisation of biblical prophets, through which they are informed of their deficiency in comparison to the Prophet of Islam, is a recurring theme in *Durr al-Majālis*. As for the second treatise, *Sharḥ-i Sūrat al-Fātiḥa*, it is a detailed commentary that highlights the particularities of Islamic eschatology as outlined in *Qiyāmat-nāma* (Book of the Day of Judgement). This treatise (ff. 5–45) was written based on the views of a 'Shaykh Muʿīn', perhaps referring to Muʿīn al-Dīn Muḥammad Amīn al-Farāḥī al-Harawī (also known as Muʿīn-i Miskīn; d. 907/1501–02), who was

[8] Regarding the application of these verses in India, see Sorabshaw Byramji Doctor, *Second Book of Persian to which are Added the Pandnáma of Shaikh Saádi and the Gulistán, Chapter I., together with Vocabularies and Short Notes* (Surat: Printed at the Irish Presbyterian Mission Press, by W. Raymond, 1880, 2nd ed.), 61.

[9] Perhaps, by Asadullāh Shāh Kashmīrī.

the author of *Tārīkh-i Mūsāwī* a work which collects Muslim legends about Moses.[10] Every part of the chapter is divided into a *majlis*, that is, a religious gathering or assembly, suggesting the pedagogical context of the manuscript. Details about the Day of Judgement in this work correlate with what has been described in the chapters of *Durr al-Majālis*, suggesting a direct influence of *Durr al-Majālis* on the text. This work was copied by ʿAbd al-Raḥmān b. Amīr Muḥammad Saʿīd b. Mīr-Muḥammad Ṣādiq b. Mīr-ʿAbdullāh b. Mīr-ʿAbd al-Ghaffār al-Bukhārī, known as 'al-ʿAllāma al-ʿAṣr' (the Polymath of the Era) on 20 Rabīʿ al-Awwal of 1094/19 March 1683.

5. INDIA

There are several *Durr al-Majālis* manuscripts in Indian libraries. They are found in Khanqah Mujeebia Library and Khudabaksh Oriental Public Library (six copies), Andhra Pradesh Government's Oriental Manuscripts Library and Research Institute (8 copies, one of which is the Urdu translation), Bombay University Library (one copy), Indian Council for Cultural Relations (two copies), Rampur Reza Library (three copies), Tippo Sultan of Mysore (one copy), Mulla Firuz Library (one copy), former Fort William College (two copies), Hazrat Pir Mohammed Shah Dargah Library (two copies), Dargah Alia Mahdaviya Library (one copy), Idāra-yi Adabiyyāt-i Urdū-yi Ḥaydarābād (one copy), Aligarh University Library (one copy), Asiatic Society of Bengal (three copies), and some more in the collection of the India Office which is now in the possession of the British Library in London.

Hazrat Pir Mohammed Shah Dargah Library

1395

Introducing the main author as Ẓafar Lutihārī and the manuscript as *Durr-i Majālis al-Anām*, this is an incomplete copy of thirty chapters, but the name of the owner is given as ʿAbd al-Raḥīm. The first page bears an inscription, written in a different hand: 'This book *Durr al-Majālis* has been written about the miracles of the Prophet Muḥammad and other prophets'.

[10] For more, see Wladimir Ivanow, *Concise Descriptive Catalogue of the Persian Manuscripts in the Collection of the Asiatic Society of Bengal* (Calcutta: The Baptist Mission Press, 1924), 139.

1396
This incomplete copy ends with the unfinished story about splitting the Moon. This manuscript was copied by Shaykh Iḥsān Muḥammad son of Shaykh Nūr Muḥammad Anṣārī from Bari, India. He copied the text for his friend Laʿl Muḥammad, which may refer to a person of the same name who lived in Pulton Bazzar in the late twelfth/eighteenth century.[11] This manuscript begins with a note from *Mirʾat al-Asrār* of ʿAbd al-Raḥmān Chishtī and refers to Najm al-Dīn Kubrā about the way ʿAlī b. Abī Ṭālib's caliphate reached subsequent generations through Imam Ḥasan, Imam Ḥusayn, and then Khoja Kumayl and Khoja Ḥasan Baṣrī.

Idāra-yi Adabiyyāt-i Urdū-yi Ḥaydarābād[12]

311
This is a well-written manuscript copied by Jaʿfar Bayg Naṣrullāh in 1088/1677–88. Aligarh University Library

452
The scribe introduces himself as ʿAbd al-Raḥīm b. ʿAbd al-Raḥmān Samarqandī, from Ganji (?), who copied the text in 1062/1652–3.

Indian Council for Cultural Relations

M82
This manuscript was copied by Shaykh Abū Layth Chishtī from Lucknow in the Kingship of India. He copied it for the sake of bestowing courage on the ruling classes, completing his effort on 27 Ramaḍān 1080/18 February 1670.

M84
The name of the author mentioned in this manuscript, given as Kh^{w}āja Yaʿqūb Muṣliḥ Sayf Ẓafar Bihārī, is quite different to that mentioned in other copies. The manuscript was copied by Ladī-khān.

11 See: Charles Stewart (trans.), *Original Persian Letters, and Other Documents, with Fac-Similes* (London: William Nicol, 1825), 28–29.

12 On the manuscript and printed volumes, see Muḥammad Akbaruddīn Ṣiddīqī, *Fihrist-i matbu'at-i kutubkhanah-yi Idarah-yi Adabiyat-i Urdu* (Dakan: Idārah-yi Adabiyāt-i Urdū, Ḥaidarābād, 1963).

6. PAKISTAN

In terms of manuscript copies of *Durr al-Majālis*, the libraries of Pakistan are able to rival the rich and important collections of Iran, India, and Russia. Although the largest collection of *Durr al-Majālis* manuscripts is found in the Ganjbakhsh (nine copies), other copies can be located in the Punjab University of Lahore (two copies), the Punjab University Azer Collection (four copies), the Punjab University Shirani Collection (five copies), Darul-Ulum-i-Sarhad Peshawar (one copy), the Basirpur Library (one copy), and the National Archives of Pakistan (one copy).

Ganjbakhsh

PAK-001–1180

This version of *Durr al-Majālis* (ff. 1–185) includes thirty-two chapters. The well-written copy was produced by Miān Khudā-Baksh in 1888, perhaps the famous Punjabi scholar, Miān Muḥammad Bakhsh (1830–1907). The text is followed with another treatise in Arabic (ff. 186–188) on theological and legal issues, in which references to *Tafsīr al-Jalālayn*, statements of Abī Layth, and *Fatāwā al-Zāhidī*, can be found.

PAK-001–1043

The author's name is mentioned as Sayf Ẓafar Pūrtahārī. This copy (ff. 44–304) ends with the story of Balʿam Bāʿūrā and the 'dog' of the People of the Cave. The scribe was ʿUmar Bāfanda from India who copied the text on 14 Rabīʿ al-Thānī 1212/6 October 1797. The manuscript ends with a table (*jadwal*) about the physical features of Muḥammad (e.g., long arms, hairless body) (f. 309), also related to the occultic supplication of *muhr-i nabuwwat*, and an instruction on how to seek an omen (*istikhāra*) by invoking ʿAbd al-Qādir Jīlānī's name (f. 310).

PAK-001–1498

The author's name is mentioned as Sayf Ẓafar Pūtuvārī. The preface is different from other copies, indicating topics which are usually outlined in the *miʿrāj-nāma* of the Prophet. This copy includes the complete *Story of the Killing of Ḥasan and Ḥusayn* and the rise of their half-brother, Muḥammad Ḥanafiyya. It was copied by Muḥammad Sharīf son of Mullā Quraysh Akhundzāda.

PAK-001–0770

This manuscript is an incomplete version of *Durr al-Majālis* (ff. 6–321). The scribe is unknown. The text was apparently completed in 1092/c.1681, which would make it the oldest known copy of *Durr al-Majālis* in the Ganjbakhsh collection. Initial (ff. 1–5) and final folios (ff. 322–324) cover different theological arguments and are written in another hand.

PAK-001-1471

This manuscript is an incomplete copy of *Durr al-Majālis* that includes interesting information about the circulation of Persian texts in Kashgar, China. It clearly suggests that not only were Chinese Muslims translating Persian texts into Turkish but they also reproduced them in the original Persian. This copy (ff. 1–503) was written by Mullā Muḥammad Rāzīq from Kashgar in 1257/c.1841 (see my discussion above). It begins with the middle part of chapter three and includes marginal notes in Persian and Arabic from the *Lubāb al-ḥadīth* of, perhaps, al-Suyūṭī.[13] Also, the *Durr al-Majālis* section dealing with the Pharaoh's secret conversation with God about his forthcoming encounter with Moses, is glossed with marginal points (without my revision).

در تفسیر امام جعفر عمر رحمته (sic) اللّٰه علیه میکوید که هر بره‌کتی که در توریٰت و انجیل و زبور بودست، آن بره‌کت [در] قرآن است. و هر برکتی که [در] قرآن است، آن برکت [در] فاتحه است. و هر بره‌کتیکه فاتحت [دارد] آن بارکت بِسْمِ اللّٰهِ الرَّحْمٰنِ الرَّحِیمِ ست. هر که با [ا]خلاص بکوید که توریٰت انجیل زبور فرقان خواندن او را ثواب بدید. در تفسیرعمدة میکوید که جون[۱۴]کودک بر معلّم [...]

> In the commentary of Imam Jaʿfar ʿUmar (?), may God's mercy be upon him, it is said that 'all forms of grace found in the Torah, Gospels, and Psalms, are already in the Qurʾān. And whatever the grace of the Qurʾān is, it can be found in *al-Fātiḥa* [Q. 1]. And whatever the grace from al-Fātiḥa is, it can be found in the phrase 'In the Name of God, the Compassionate, the Merciful'. Whoever recites it with a pure heart, they will be granted the grace of the Torah, Gospels, Psalms, and Criterion (*al-Furqān*). In the commentary of ʿUmdat [by Ibn Kathīr?] it says that when a child went to his teacher [. . .]. (f. 11)

Such references to *Sūrat al-Fātiḥa* prove that the loftiness of the Qurʾān is highlighted in other copies of *Durr al-Majālis*. This suggests a global understanding of the virtues (*faḍāʾil*) of the Qurʾān and its verses through other religious and literary texts and the contribution of Persian sources in shaping a transregional understanding of Islamic values and concepts. The ending material (ff. 504–510) is in Arabic and Turkish starting

[13] Although Nawawi of Banten has also produced a work with the same title.

[14] It has been written with *jīm*.

with a Turkish translation of the Verse of the Throne (*āyat al-kursī*) with marginal Persian, Arabic, and Turkish supplicatory phrases. One supplication is about the attributes of Muḥammad and uses the phrase '*shāh*' (king), a title which is also found in some Malay texts (e.g., *Hikayat Samun*) that introduce him as the 'King of Medina'.[15] A Turkish version of supplications and talismanic phrases to ward off disasters and body pain is also seen.

PAK-001–1666

This manuscript, of unknown provenance, includes an incomplete copy of *Durr al-Majālis*. The main folios (ff. 3–116) are written in different hands. The end matter (ff. 117–132) includes a *Qiyāmat-nāma* that mentions the signs of the Day of Judgement and the Dajjāl.

PAK-001–1506

This manuscript, of unknown provenance, is an incomplete copy of *Durr al-Majālis* that includes marginal points written in different hands. Perhaps some of the notes are in the hand of the original possessor, apparently, Ghulām or Ghulam Qadīrī. The final folio bears different dates and phrases, suggesting the text was owned by different people at various times.

PAK-001–2123

This manuscript includes an incomplete copy of *Durr al-Majālis* (ff. 1–147). Fl. 152v includes a note written in blue-coloured pencil mentioning the name of the book as *Durr-i Majālis*. This copy includes other treatises, like a *tawallud-nāma* on the creation of Muḥammad (ff. 147v–149), a *faqr-nāma* on the mystical ways of poverty expressed by Muḥammad (ff. 150–154), the admonitions of Muḥammad to his daughter Fāṭima (ff. 155v–158), and also supplications for Laylat al-Raghāʾib (the Night of Wishes) (f. 159) – an auspicious occasion commemorated by Shīʿa – as well as couplets of Jāmī. The significance of mystical teachings is depicted with a simple and concise explanation that in the path of poverty and perfection one should behold five imams and five qiblas (prayer directions). The five imams are body (*tan*), soul (*jān*), heart (*dil*), intellect (*khird*), and action (*fiʿl*). The five qiblas are the prayer niche (*miḥrāb*), Kaʿba, Frequented House (*bayt al-maʿmūr*), the Seat (*kursī*), and the Throne (*ʿarsh*). The term 'Khoja' (*khūcha*; *khʷācha*) is frequently used in these treatises, and the role and status

15 Using the term '*shāh*' is very common in Sufi literature, also used by Indonesian Sufis. See the manuscript, Or. 5658 at Leiden University Library.

of women is frequently discussed. It should be noted that the term "khoja" was also used in the Malay-Indonesian literature, often written as "خوج".

Punjab University Shirani Collection

128

This is a two-section treatise comprising a *tawallud-nāma* and a *wafat-nāma* on the creation and death of Muḥammad as has clearly outlined in *Durr al-Majālis*. This manuscript was copied by Muḥammad ʿĀlamgīr in the third year of the reign of the Mughal ruler Akbar Shah II (r. 1806–37) in India.

137

This is a treatise on the killing of Ḥasan and Ḥusayn titled *Maqtal-nāma* and is obviously the thirty-first chapter of *Durr al-Majālis*.

2273

This manuscript includes selected stories of *Durr al-Majālis* such as those relating to the virtues of the Prophet (pbuh), of Imams Ḥasan and Ḥusayn, and the story of Muḥammad Ḥanīf or Ḥanafiyya.

Punjab University Azer Collection

H-125

This treatise is titled *Qiṣṣa-yi jang kardan-i Imām Ḥanafiyya bā Munāfiqān* (The Battle Story of Imam Ḥanafiyya with Hypocrites). Also, known as *Dāstān-i Muḥammad Ḥanafiyya*, it was copied by Ghul-Ghulām Muḥammad in 1220/1805–6. This story is accompanied by the *Rawḍat al-Shuhadāʾ* of al-Kāshifī.

Lahore University Library

6618

This manuscript was written by Saʿdullāh b. ʿAbdullāh Afghān in the early thirteenth/nineteenth century. It is accompanied by another *majlis*-based work known as *Rushd [*or, *Rāshid] al-Majālis*, a text written to guide Muslims towards the 'right path' by Afghani scholar Mūsā b. Muḥammad Shaywān Afghān. An appendix on theological and eschatological issues advises readers on how to benefit the deceased.

7. EUROPE

Manuscript copies of *Durr al-Majālis* are also found in European collections. Most of these were brought to Europe from Persianate regions and a few from the Arab world. That a given manuscript of *Durr al-Majālis* was copied in an Arab society does, of course, not necessarily mean that the work was widely read by Arabs. However, observing the presence of various copies of the text in different Arabic collections suggests that Arabs were, to some degree, familiar with *Durr al-Majālis.*

The Bayerische Staatsbibliothek houses two copies of *Durr al-Majālis*, one of them brought by Jean-Joseph Marcel (d. 1845) from Cairo, and another which includes a few of its chapters alongside other material. There is also one copy of *Durr al-Majālis* in another German library, the Staatsbibliothek zu Berlin. Other copies in European collections include copies in the Austrian Kaiserlich-Königlichen Hofbibliothek zu Wien (one copy), the British Library, including copies from the India Office (eleven copies), Cambridge University Library (two copies), SOAS (one copy), the Bodleian Library of Oxford University (one copy), the Wellcome Library (one copy), Leiden University Library (four copies), and Uppsala University Library of Sweden (two copies).

Germany

Bayerische Staatsbibliothek (Bavarian State Library)

BSB. Pers. Or.187
This manuscript was brought from Cairo by Marcel. The first folio has a note in Persian.

كتاب الجواهر تاليف بسيف الظفر ابن البرهان

The *Book of Jewels* by Sayf al-Ẓafar b. al-Burhān

It was copied by Ḥasan Muḥammad b. Yadigār Muḥammad Rubāṭ Khājagī. The title of the chapters in this copy are listed somewhat differently from other copies. For instance, chapter seventeen which is usually known as 'On the Coming to Faith of an Idolater Through Abraham' is titled 'On the Coming to Islam of an Idolater Through his Son'. Similarly, chapter twenty-five, usually titled 'The Story of Khʷāja Rabīʿ Ḥusām with his Daughter – the Question and the Answer', is given as 'The Story of Khʷāja Rabīʿ of Jām' (a change also found in O Nov. 331 held in the Uppsala University Library of Sweden). The manuscript ends with a supplication, asking God to bestow His reward upon the author, scribe, and reader of the book and to one who may hear it read to him (f. 161). A mystical phrase also appears at the end of the manuscript.

ای وجود تو اصـــل هر موجود

O You whose existence is the origin of every single existent

BSB. Pers. Or.188

This is an incomplete manuscript copy (only one volume) comprising eighteen chapters that are disordered. For instance, chapter sixteen is titled 'The Story of Khadīja and ʿĀʾisha' but the content relates to what is usually chapter twelve, that is, 'The Story of Mary the Copt, the Servant of Muḥammad' in which the name of two other wives of Muḥammad, that is, Ḥafṣa and ʿĀʾisha, are mentioned. Besides being disordered, some of the chapter titles are also different to those found in most copies. The manuscript ends with the story of the teeth of Muḥammad.

This copy of *Durr al-Majālis* was produced by Faqīr [?] ʿAlī for Muḥammad Khayrātī [Bihishtī] son of Muḥammad Kālī of Bakirganj (Backergunge), Bengal on 7 Dhī Ḥajja 1201/20 September 1787. The manuscript ends with a common supplication.

خدایا بیامرز این هرسه را، مصنّف نویسنده خواننده را

O God, forgive all these three; the author, the scribe, and the reader!

BSB. Pers. Or.193

This manuscript features a collection of mystical treatises and stories, as listed below. Items (d), (g), (j), (m), and (n) show the strong influence of *Durr al-Majālis.*

(a) Poems about the regions of the world (f. 2) through which Hindustan's greatness is compared to the Occident, Turkistan, Rome, Khurasan, and other lands and oceans.

تمام روی زمین است بیست‌وپنج هزار
از آن چهار فرنگست و پنج ترکستان
شش است روم و خراسان و جانب برّ وبحر
چه ده‌هزار بماند تمام هندوستان

The size of the Earth's surface is twenty-five thousand,
Four thousands of it is for Europe (?) and five thousands for Turkistan
Six thousands for Rūm, Khorasan and the seashores
The remaining ten thousands for the land of India

(b) Quotations from Khʷāja ʿAbdullāh Anṣārī (f. 2) on the end times.

از خواجه عبدالله انصاری منقولست «نشانهٔ قیامت سه چیز است: باران بسیار، نبات کم؛ علماء بسیار، فقهای کم؛ امراء بسیار، انصاف کم»

According to Khwāja ʿAbdullāh Anṣārī 'the three signs of the coming of the Day of Judgement are: a lot of rain and few plants (low fertility), many scholars and few just jurists, many rulers and lack of justice.

(c) A short treatise for the preparation of travellers intending long journeys, for example, advice on clothing and food (ff. 2–8).
(d) An incomplete story about the shape and face of the world on the Day of Judgement. The world will appear as an old lady with blackened eyes and devilish teeth. Beforehand people would have killed one another and sewn discord for the sake of the world (f. 9).
(e) The Tale of the Derwish and Khʷāja (f. 9).
(f) The story of Bahrām Shāh in the garden of pomegranates (f. 10).
(g) Moses's conversation with a naked man as well as with God (f. 11).
(h) A story of a sinner and the Prophet (f. 12).
(i) A story on Sultan Maḥmūd, 'the bird of paradise' (*humā*), and his servant Āyaz/Ayaz (f. 13).
(j) The dialogue of Moses with the Angel of Death and his final conversation with his household (f. 14).
(k) A story on Jesus and his mother which includes a narrative of the death of Mary and the involvement of the Angel of Death (f. 15).
(l) An account of Moses and Khiḍr and their coming to learn about Muḥammad and 'his knowledgeable and brave successor, ʿAlī' (f. 16).
(m) The conversation of Jesus with a dead body in a cemetery (f. 20).
(n) The story of an oppressive king who forbade people from helping poor dervishes.

Staatsbibliothek zu Berlin

Ms.Or.Fol.3112

A complete and well-written copy. It was copied by Muḥammad Ẓafar on 15 Shawwal 1078/29 March 1668. This copy was received by the owner (for two rupees) on 16 Rajab of the year 2 or 1125/8 August 1713 during the reign/period of Muḥammad Ḥasan Sulṭān of Ghakhar (f. 1).

United Kingdom

Wellcome Library

No. 348
This manuscript copy of *Durr al-Majālis* includes thirty-five chapters. The unknown scribe calls it a 'blessed' (*mutabarrika*) work.

British Library (originally from the India Office)

Add.8149
This copy contains the Killing Story of Ḥasan, then Ḥusayn and the rise of their half-brother. It was produced in Murshidabad of Bengal in 1721. This version was examined by both van Ronkel and Brakel while completing their comparative studies on the Malay tale of Karbala.

Delhi Persian 917
This is a manuscript in two parts. The first part (ff. 1v–92r) is *Durr al-Majālis*. This concise treatise introduces the author as Sayf al-Ẓafar Būtuhādī (f. 3).
The copying of this manuscript was finished on 27 Rajab 1230/5 July 1815 which is said to be in the ninth year of the rule of Muḥammad Akbar II, suggesting that the text was produced in India. The second part (ff. 93–188r) is a treatise of numerous chapters, starting with a chapter on the genealogy, creation, and death of Muḥammad. Other chapters cover his daughter Fāṭima, his son-in-law ʿAlī, and then the life and death of Ḥasan, then Ḥusayn and his army in Karbala, and then an account of the Ḥusayn's killer, al-Shamir (ff. 182v–186v). The style, structure, and content of the second treatise are influenced by Kāshifī's *Rawḍat al-Shuhadāʾ* and Mullā Muḥammad Mahdī Narāqī's (d. 1209/1795–6) *Muḥarriq al-Qulūb* in which the life and death story of Ḥasan and Ḥusayn are narrated in *different* and *separate* chapters and based on Islamic traditional and mystical references and quotations.

SOAS

No. 46429

This copy of *Durr al-Majālis* was in the possession of James O'Kinealy (1837–1903), an imperial officer in Bengal, which was later donated to the London School of Oriental and African Studies (SOAS). It demonstrates that non-Persian speakers, probably Malay residents of Bengal, were practising the Persian language. For more, see my discussion in the introduction.

The Netherlands

Leiden University Library

Or.565

A number of features suggest that this manuscript is one of the most important manuscript copies of *Durr al-Majālis*. To begin with, it is one of the oldest known copies scribed by Muḥammad Amīn b. Muḥammad ʿAlī in Ṣafar 973/September 1565. Moreover, it includes thirty-four chapters, ending with the story of Balʿam Bāʿūr and the 'dog' of the People of the Cave. This particular copy clearly changed hands between Shīʿī and Sunnī owners. On several occasions the name of ʿAlī b. Abī Ṭālib, the first Imam of Shīʿa, was scratched out and replaced in gold ink with the names of Abū Bakr or ʿUmar. Also, a tag with these names in gold ink has been pasted over a portion of text with the name of ʿAlī. It appears, therefore, that the original copy was written by a Shīʿī. For example, chapter 7 begins with mention of the first man accepting Islam at the hands of Muḥammad. According to almost every available copy of *Durr al-Majālis*, the Commander of Believers Abū Bakr was the first. However, this particular copy mentions ʿAlī (f. 31). A tag with the name of Abū Bakr has been used to conceal the name of ʿAlī.

The question of who first accepted the religion of Islam was a topic of controversy among Sunnīs and Shīʿīs. According to Sunnī accounts, Abū Bakr was the first who converted to Islam. Conversely, Shīʿīs insist ʿAlī was the first to accept Islam from the Prophet. This sectarian controversy is manifested in this particular manuscript. The manuscript was most likely written by someone of a Shīʿī inclination but later revised, or censored, by a Sunnī who did not welcome the way the scribe probably changed the original story of *Durr al-Majālis*.

Or.565 includes Turkish handwriting and calligraphy and was collected by Levinus Warner (d. c.1665). He collected most of his materials from Istanbul where he stayed from 1645 until his death. Interestingly, other available copies of *Durr al-Majālis* in the Leiden University Library (e.g., Or.877) with the stamps or embossed stamps of Warner were also collected from Turkey and all featuring various marginal or minor Turkish notes and texts. Perhaps the manuscript Or.565 was produced by a Shīʿī, either in Istanbul or elsewhere, and was later checked for errors by a Sunnī believer.

Soviet Union Collections

Various Persian copies of *Durr al-Majālis* can be found scattered in the territories of the former Soviet Union. They were mostly bought or catalogued before the 1980s. Collections holding copies of *Durr al-Majālis* include the National Academy of Sciences of Tajikistan (five copies), the Rudaki Library of Tajikistan (two copies), the Collection of Abu Reyhon Beruni Institute of Oriental Studies, Academy of Sciences of Uzbekistan, Tashkent (overall fourteen copies)[16] and the Institute of Oriental Studies of the Russian Academy of Sciences (thirty-one copies). Most of these manuscripts present the same content as other copies. Interesting features include the names given of scribes, notes on how the text was used in *madrasas* (see the introduction above), the style of calligraphy, and the dedications to kings. Some copies of this collection were also written in Bukhara calligraphic style.

Academy of Sciences of Tajikistan

1222
This work was copied on 6 Dhū al-Qaʿda 858/28 October 1454 by Muḥammad b. Dūst Muḥammad al-Bukhārī. The manuscript is replete with marginalia (written in different hands) that are often related to the theme of the chapter. In contrast to almost all known copies, this manuscript includes several poems by Abū Saʿīd Abū al-Khayr (f. 40), Rūmī, that is, 'Mawlawī' (f. 74, ff. 129–130), and marginal couplets ascribed to Jāmī (f. 162) and Ibn Yamīn (f. 162), and so forth. The manuscript's marginalia with particular references to Shīʿa Imams suggest that the manuscript was in the possession of Shīʿī believers.

16 Some copies are registered in both the Academy of Science and the Oriental Institute of Uzbekistan, and some are now not in their own library. As such, the total number of *Durr al-Majālis* manuscripts in Tashkent is fourteen.

5988
This has been copied by someone known as 'Kh^{w}āja' in 1252/c.1836, using a Central Asian calligraphic style.

5996
This golden-framed copy was produced for Muḥammad Raḥīm Khān II of Khiva (1847–1910), who was interested in reproducing and translating Persian works. Using the Khadiv calligraphic style, this copy was written by Mullā Ḥabībullāh Mullā ʿAbd al-Salām al-Khānqāhī in Ramaḍān 1320/late December 1902.

8. NORTH AMERICA

There are a few Persian copies of *Durr al-Majālis* in Canada and the United States. These are held in the McGill University Library (two copies), Michigan University Library (two copies), Princeton University Library (including one microfilm from the Soviet Union's Institute Vostokovedeniia), and the Free Library of Philadelphia (one copy).

Canada

McGill University Library

MS BW IVANOW 0100
Some chapters of this manuscript are shorter than in other copies. The preface is significantly shorter and does not include the book's title nor the author's name. However, the colophon does give the the title of the work as *Durr al-Majālis*. The account of Muḥammad Ḥanafiyya's revenge on Yazīd for the killing of Ḥasan and Ḥusayn is slightly shorter than other complete copies held in New Zealand and Pakistan. This manuscript was copied by Shaykh Raḥmatullāh b. Salīm Anṣārī, a resident of the village of Nūr-Saray, in India on 18 Jumādā al-Thānī 1077/16 December 1666.

MS BW IVANOW 0101
This is an incomplete and undated manuscript, in broken Persian, and featuring interlinear and marginal corrections. The owner introduces himself as Ḥāfiẓ

Muḥamamd Dāʾim son of Shaykh Maḥmūd and resident of the village Arol, India.[17]

United States of America

Free Library of Philadelphia

RBD LEWIS O 189

This manuscript was produced by Mawlānā ʿUmar b. Dūst Muḥammad in order that his children should be instructed with Islamic teachings in Ramadan 1307/1890. The original author of this work is introduced as Ẓafar Bihārī. The text includes marginal commentaries and Islamic traditions. The colophon, using Arabic numerals written in an Urdu style, suggest the South Asian origin of the text.

Special Collections Library, University of Michigan

Isl. Ms. 853

This manuscript was collected from Amritsar in the Punjab State of India in 1888. It is a collection of notes and treatises in two main parts but also with additional notes. The first part begins with a popular Shīʿī supplication dedicated to the first Imam, *Nād-i ʿAlī* (Invoking ʿAlī) (f. 4). Then there is a poetic version of *Durr al-Majālis*, known as *Jang-nāma* in Punjabi (ff. 5–232), originally by Ḥāmida (Ḥāmida Shāha ʿAbbāsī) and copied in the region of Amīnpūr in c.1253/1838. Fl. 233 includes a few elegiac poems on the death of 'Shah Ḥusayn' who is the 'darling of ʿAlī and Fāṭima'. Then there is a supplication to be recited after the call to prayer (f. 234; without my revision).

اللّهُمَّ رَبَّ هَذِهِ الدّعْوَةِ التّامَّة وَالصّلاةِ القَائِمَة آتِ مُحَمَّداً الوَسيلةَ وَالْفَضيلَة وَابْعَثْه مَقاماً مَحموداً الَّذي
وَعَدْتَه إِنَّكَ لا تُخْلِفُ الميعاد

O God, Lord of this perfect call and established prayer. Bestow Muḥammad the intercession and favour, and raise him to the honoured station You have promised him, truly You do not neglect promises.[18]

[17] As far as I am aware there are three villages in India carrying the name of Arol (*arūl*). One in the State of Jharkhand, one in Madhya Pradesh, and another in Gaya, (Bihar) that appears in some historical reports. [18] See *Ḥisn al-Muslim*, 25 (also, see www.sunnah.com)

The main body of the second part is the Persian prose of *Durr al-Majālis* (ff. 236–424). This version, in contrast to most available copies, ends with *The Killing Story of Ḥasan and Ḥusayn*. This one was copied by Muḥammad Baksh(ī) b. Muḥammad ʿAẓīm on 15 Rajab 1233/21 May 1818 in Amīnpūr, Punjab. Also, there is a folio of the Urdu translation of Luke 17:22–25/26.

9. OCEANIA

The copies of *Durr al-Majālis* in Oceania that came to my attention are held in Australia and New Zealand. One abridgement in Persian and Urdu is held in the Melbourne University Special Collections in Australia and there are two manuscript held by the Auckland Libraries of New Zealand.

Australia

Melbourne University Special Collections

b3126838

This manuscript relates the Karbala tragedy in verse. As with other accounts of Ḥusayn's death, this one begins with the creation of Muḥammad and his light (f. 1), the virtues of the twelve Shīʿa Imams (ff. 3–4) and the four rightly-guided caliphs (ff. 4–5), a birth account (*tawallud-nāma*) of Fāṭima (ff. 6–8), and an account of the marriage of Fāṭima and ʿAlī (ff. 8–?). The sections on the birth of Fāṭima and on her marriage with ʿAlī incorporate text from *Durr al-Majālis*. The structure and style of the section on the killing of Ḥusayn resembles Kāshifī's *Rawḍat al-Shuhadāʾ*, a work which is in turn heavily influenced by *Durr al-Majālis*. Perhaps it was commonplace for *Rawḍat al-Shuhadāʾ* and *Durr al-Majālis* to be read alongside each other (cf. Delhi Persian 917, British Library). This manuscript, catalogued as *Jang-nāma-yi Karbalā*, was copied by Ḥāfiẓ Muḥammad, a resident of Panipat, India in the mosque of Shaykhān (?), 18 Ṣafar 1278/1861 (f. 233).

New Zealand

Auckland Libraries

GMS-170

This manuscript comprises two main parts. One part is a shorter version of *Durr al-Majālis* that has thirty-three chapters, of which there is a shorter version of *The Killing Story of Ḥasan and Ḥusayn*. The other part is a longer version of *Durr al-Majālis* with four additional chapters, specifically, the second part of the Ḥasan and Ḥusayn story that includes the rise of Muḥammad Ḥanafiyya; Moses' conversation with God; Jesus' dialogue with King Jumjuma; and a copy of the *Nūr-nāma* of Muḥammad that addresses the profound interest of Maḥmūd of Ghazna. There are two colophons relating to the two parts, both produced by the same scribe, Shaykh Khalīfa Dāwūd Mardikar. The shorter version (ff. 1–112) was completed 18 Dhū al-Ḥijja 1219/20 March 1805. The longer version (ff. 113–162) is dated 10 Muḥarram, and was probably completed in the following year, 1220 AH. After the two versions of *Durr al-Majālis*, short and long, the manuscript includes a short treatise on the Twelve Imams of the Shīʿa (ff. 162–163). Shaykh Dāwūd introduces himself as a resident of Masnabi (Mausambi), highly likely referring to a port city (*bandar*) in Mozambique; it should be noted that this copy was in the possession of George Grey while he was a commander in Africa. Given the apparent affinity of the scribe to twelve Shīʿī Imams, and also his presentation of Jesus as an Islamised messenger in different parts of the manuscript, it would not be farfetched to consider him as a member of an Indian diaspora Shīʿī community such as the Bohra or Khoja communities of Mumbai.[19]

GMS-173

This is a two-treatise collection. The first one, also largely influenced by *Durr al-Majālis* includes the *nūr-nāma* of Muḥammad (ff. 1–11), a *tawallud-nāma* of Muḥammad, the story of splitting the Moon, the death of Khadīja, Najāshī and Muḥammad, *miʿrāj-nāma*, Mary the Copt and her son, a *wafāt-nāma* on the death of Muḥammad by poisoned food,[20] the miracles of Muḥammad, stories about the afterlife of Muḥammad – that Abū Bakr heard that Muḥammad either passed away or ascended (like Jesus) (f. 135). The second part is the Urdu story of Tamīm Anṣārī, the famous Saint of Chennai with some traces of Hindustani. This manuscript was also copied by Shaykh Dāwūd Mardikar and includes two colophons. The first one is dated to Jumādā al-Awwal 1229/

[19] When studying this manuscript, I came across a person from Mumbai who was known as Shaykh Aḥmad son of Shaykh Dāwūd. Shaykh Aḥmad had promoted Shīʿī accounts of the 'massacre' of Karbala (e.g., based on Narāqī's *Muḥarriq al-Qulūb*) in Khojki script. This work is available as a manuscript, MS Indic 2534, in the Houghton Library, Harvard University. About Masnabi (Mausambi) and Mozambique, see Ibrāhim Pūrdāvūd, *Hurmazd-nāma* (Tehran: Anjuman-i Īrān-shināsī, 1952), 89.

[20] *Rawḍat al-Shuhadāʾ* also mentions an attempt on Muḥammad's life by means of poisoned food and that Ḥasan survived poisoned food and drink.

May 1814 (fl. 137), while the second one to 17 Ṣafar 1230/29 January 1815. However, the second colophon suggests that Shaykh Dāwūd was the son of Marḥamullāh [Taʿālā] Miān ʿAbd al-Raḥmān Mardikar.

A Description of Select Translated Copies

Durr al-Majālis has been welcomed in different Muslim contexts. Wherever Muslims were actively contributing to culture, literature, and politics *Durr al-Majālis* was to be found. Its Persian copies were circulated in Turkey, Central Asia, India and many other places. Its reception among various communities is evident, for example, from some Persian copies including [partial] interlinear translations (e.g., the Talaat copy of Cairo) and some including marginal Arabic notes. *Durr al-Majālis* was also widely translated from its original Persian into different languages such as Turkish and Turkic, Bengali, Punjabi, Pushto, Kurdish (Kurmanji), among others.

TURKIC TRANSLATIONS

The Jarring collection of Lund University, Sweden has the largest collection of Turkic copies of *Durr al-Majālis.*

Prove. 91

This manuscript was produced in Kashgar, China. The first part (ff. 1–119) is a Uyghuri Turkish translation of *Durr al-Majālis* written by Mullā Tūkhta Īlmādūz in Kashgar in Muḥarram 1150/May 1737. It is followed by Turkish rhythmic phrases (ff. 120–121) indicating the name of influential mystics in Turkistan (e.g., Najm al-Dīn Kubrā); a *miʿrāj-nāma* of Muḥammad (ff. 122–153); and a Turkish translation of Arabic statements regarding the three caliphs (i.e., ʿUmar, ʿUthmān, and ʿAlī), their characteristics, and virtues.

Prov.108

This manuscript was originally produced by ʿAbd al-Laṭīf Khaṭāyanī (?) who belonged to the region of Khitāy, historically known as Turkistan. This copy of *Durr al-Majālis* (ff. 1–195) was dedicated to the ruler of Khiva, Central Asia, Abū al-Mūẓaffar Muʿīn al-Dīn Khurāzm/Khwārazm Shāh Bahādur Sulṭān. It was copied [from Russian] by Mullā ʿAbd al-Sattār on 21 Dhū al-Qaʿda 1286/22 February 1870. The story is followed by a number of items, as listed below.

A *wafāt-nāma* of Fāṭima dated 1286/1870 (ff. 196–197).

A *wafāt-nāma* of Muḥammad by Mullā ʿAbd al-Sattār on 29 Dhū al-Qaʿda 1286/2 March 1870 (ff. 199–210).

A *qiyāmat-nāma* of Muḥammad that ends with a couplet, 'should you accept my prayer; by the glory of the Arabian Muḥammad' (*ham duʿāʾī marā qabūl kunī; tu bi-ḥaqq-i Muḥammad-i ʿarabī*) and a Turkish phrase, '*Durr al-Majālis* ends here' (*işbu kitab dur li-Majālis'ta durur*) (ff. 212–225).

A private conversation between Moses and God about Muḥammad's community (ff. 226–237).

A religious and historical text about Muḥammad as well as Mirzā Abā-Bakr (perhaps, a ruler or a prince) (ff. 238–247).

A story about commuters/travellers in Isfahan, Aḥmad b. Iṣfahānī, Dūst b. Bakhtiyārī, and Muḥammad Rāzī, perhaps inspired by *Jāmiʿ al-Ḥikāyāt* (ff. 248–260).

An incomplete story about the city of Balkh during the reign of the sultan of Sanjar, based on *Jāmiʿ al-Ḥikāyāt* (ff. 262–272).

Some additional religious couplets about the Prophet, caliphs, Ḥasan and Ḥusayn, and the wishes of the scribe (f. 273).

Prov.342

This contents of this manuscript are as listed below.

A Turkish translation of *Qābus-nāma*, a mirror for princes by Kaykāwūs b. Iskandar b. Qābus b. Wushmgīr from the thirteenth/nineteenth century, dated 17 ʿĀshūr 1235/5 November 1819 (ff. 1–137).

A Turkish version of *Ẓafar-nāma* dated 1211/1796–7 (ff. 141–155).

A *miʿrāj-nāma* of Muḥammad (ff. 158–173).

Another copy of ʿAbd al-Laṭīf Khatāyanī's translation of *Durr al-Majālis* dedicated to Khurāzm/Khwārazm Shāh Bahādur Sulṭān (ff. 174–282).

A *wafāt-nāma* of Muḥammad (ff. 283–292).

A *wafat-nāma* of Fāṭima (ff. 293–294).

A *qiyāmat-nāma* of Muḥammad (ff. 295–307).

A *rāḍī-nāma* about Moses' conversation with God about Muḥammad, his community,

and lofty status (ff. 308–316).
A text dealing with the elevated rank of Muḥammad and Fāṭima and also referring to Mirzā Abā-Bakr and Shāh-Ṭālib Sarmast (?) (ff. 317–323).[1]

Prov. 383
This manuscript begins with praise of Muḥammad and a few notes on the initial pages mentioning that the manuscript is a *jang-nāma* and that it addresses Qāsim Ākhund. The battle tale (ff. 1–222) begins with the return of ʿAlī from battle with the Byzantines and his marriage to a newly-converted woman who becomes the mother of Muḥammad al-Ḥanafiyya. Accounts are presented of the chivalry of ʿAlī and his descendants. Other accounts of battles and conflicts between Muslims and non-Muslims – such as the conflict between Muḥammad and Abū Jahl – are also mentioned. The chivalry of Zirqūm (Zirkum) Shāh is also extolled in Turkish and Tatar and form part of the Uzbek romances.

Vámbéry notes,

> The Heroes are taken out of the Islamic world, as, for instance, in the story of Zirkum Shah, where Ali conquers the last named heathen prince of Persia, in wonderful engagements, which border upon the imaginative, and may be compared to the poems of Ariosto and Bojardi; finally, he converts him to Islam.[2]

Some themes in this manuscript – such as the conflict between Muḥammad and Abū Jahl or some of the things mentioned about Muḥammad Ḥanafiyya – are clearly influenced by *Durr al-Majālis*. The *qiyāmat-nāma* of Muḥammad (ff. 223–228) shows some influence from chapters of *Durr al-Majālis*, especially chapter twenty-five.

The manuscript ends with an account of the death of Ḥasan and Ḥusayn and the cruelty of their enemies (ff. 228–231); a treatise on Imam Zayn al-ʿĀbidīn (ff. 231–235); and also addresses various Sufi figures including Qāḍī ʿAbdullāh and Khʷāja Mahyār (?) Pashmīna-pūsh.

Prov.111
This manuscript begins with some names and dates, perhaps birth or death dates, on its initial pages (e.g., ʿAbd al-Walī Ākhund 1348 Nabī/1929–30). A Turkish phrase *işbu kitab Durr al-Majālis Turki* (this is the Turkish book of *Durr al-Majālis*) and further

[1] 'ʿAlī-Shāh' and 'Ṭālib' form parts of titles in the Khāksāriyya Sufi order.
[2] Arminius Vámbéry, *Sketches of Central Asia: Additional Chapters on My Travels, Adventures, and on the Ethnology of Central Asia* (London: Wm. H. Allen & Co., 1868), 351.

notes on Prophet Jacob are found. A marginal note indicates that the manuscript, referred to as *Durr al-Majālis*, belonged to Mullā Abū al-Khid(?) Khatīb Ākhund Nīn(?) (f. 2).

The text of *Durr al-Majālis* (ff. 3–249) has been directly translated from Persian by Raḥmān Qulī son of Mullā Yāghmūrjī for the benefit of the people of Mongolia. The work has been dedicated to ʿAbd al-Raḥmān Bayg/Beig. Numerous revisions to the text have been made by the scribe who mentions that additional Sunnī and Shīʿī works such as *ʿUyūn al-Riḍā* and *Kanz al-Gharāʾib* were consulted while translating *The Killing Story of Ḥasan and Ḥusayn* (see, e.g., f. 203 and 224) or while addressing the accounts of ʿUmar b. Abū al-Layth Khurāsānī (f. 216), Kamāl Khujandī (f. 248), of *Tamhīd al-Maʿrifa* (f. 248), of al-Thaʿālibī and al-Wāqidī (f. 249)

Some parts of the *Nūr-nāma* have been rendered in poetry (ff. 250–251). Notes in the end matter show the scribe's or owner's calligraphy practice. These calligraphic notes include Persian poems written in the *nastaʿlīq* style and parts of the Qurʾān (e.g., *Sūra Yā-Sīn* and Q. 1). A note written in pencil mentions that the manuscript was read by ʿAbd Walī Ākhund in 1928.

N. 54165

This manuscript is kept in the Āstān Quds Raḍawī collection. It was originally translated by Naqīb b. Jaʿfar and copied by Qurbān b. ʿAlī and dated 1283/c.1867. It has not been possible to physically inspect the manuscript.

A Description of Select South Asian/ Indic-Language Manuscripts

The largest number of Persian copies of *Durr al-Majālis* were produced in India. With its great ethnic and cultural diversity and many cosmopolitan centres and abodes of peace it is unsurprising that it was in India that *Durr al-Majālis* was translated into various local languages. Translations into different South Asian languages were kept in the collections of the Nizam. In this appendix one Bengali and one Punjabi manuscript are considered although Urdu versions of *Durr al-Majālis* are also found in some Indian collections.

A BENGALI TRANSLATION

Interestingly, Sayf Ẓafar's influence is mostly seen in Bengal where various Persian copies were reproduced (now held by SOAS and the British Library). *Durr al-Majālis* work was rendered into Bengali by ʿAbd al-Ḥākīm (c.1008–80/1600–70) from the part of India which is now southeastern Bangladesh.[1] Not only did he produce a Bengali version of *Durr al-Majālis*, but he also reproduced select parts of *Durr al-Majālis* as independent treatises. As I have shown in the introduction, ʿAbd al-Ḥākīm's *Nūr-nāma* of Muḥammad with reference to Maḥmūd of Ghazna and the tale of Muḥammad Ḥanafiyya (known in Bengali as Hāniphāra Laṛāī)[2] after the killing of Ḥasan and Ḥusayn are direct translations from Sayf Ẓafar's magnum opus.

1 D'Hubert, 'ʿAbd al-Ḥakīm', 2–3.
2 Ibid.

No.323

A microfilm of a Bengali manuscript, previously catalogued by the University of Dacca Library as No. 323, is now in my possession. A translation of Sayf Ẓafar's *Durr al-Majālis* titled as *Dulla Majlis*. This manuscript was copied by ʿAbd al-Karīm Khundkar who was born in Arakan in the twelfth/eighteenth century. The *Descriptive Catalogue of Bengali Manuscripts in Munshi Abdul Karim's Collection* provides helpful information about this text and its author.

> [...] translation of a Persian book divided into 33 chapters [...] There was a merchant called Atibar at Bandar village in the state of Rosang. He was pious and charitably disposed. The king of Rosang Marung conferred upon him the title of Sadi Unk meaning good looking influential merchant. Atibar was appointed officer in-charge of the king's Mint. It was under his orders that this author translated Dulla Majlis from the Persian. Earlier he had already written two other works namely *Hazar Masail* and *Tamim Ansari*. The great great grandfather of the author was Ramsul Mian. He was a Customs Officer in the king's service. His son Mohsen [Machan] Ali was an interpreter in the Customs office of the same king. Mohsen Ali's son, Ali Akbar was the father of Abdul Karim, the author. The work was composed in 1200 Hijra [1758 CE] [...].[3]

The suggestion, then, is that insufficient knowledge of Persian among the people of Bengal was perhaps the main reason that prompted the ruler to ask ʿAbd al-Karīm to translate *Durr al-Majālis* into Bengali. This translation would have had special significance in Bengali literature as it was produced during 'the last year of the independent kingdom of Arakan'.[4] The full version of Sayf Ẓafar's *Durr al-Majālis* was translated into Bengali along with other works – also related to parts of *Durr al-Majālis* – like *Mūsā-nāma* by Muḥammad ʿAqīl, *Jang-nāma* by Naṣrullāh Khandkar, *Amīr Ḥamza* by ʿAbd al-Nabī, *Maqtal Ḥusayn* by Muḥammad Khān and *Fāl-nāma*[5] by ʿUmar, among others.[6]

[3] Munshi Abdul Karim and Ahmad Sharif, *Descriptive Catalogue of Bengali Manuscripts in Munshi Abdul Karim's Collection* (Dacca: Asiatic Society of Pakistan, 1961), 215–220.

[4] For a detailed autobiography, see http://www.theartgardenrohingya.com/abdul-karim-khondkar-whos-forefathers-were-engaged-in-state-services-of-roshang/

[5] *Fāl-nāma* is a general title ascribed to divinatory literature across the Muslim world. However, the combination of *fāl* (divination) and *nāma* (book) in one term is peculiarly Persian.

[6] For the full list of Bengali literature in the seventeenth century, see Karim and Sharif, *Descriptive Catalogue of Bengali Manuscripts*, 110–111.

A PUNJABI TRANSLATION

Isl. Ms. 853

This manuscript was originally written by Ḥāmida Shāha ʿAbbāsī in the eleventh/seventeenth century in the Punjab. The manuscript is held by the University of Michigan. Partially written in Punjabi, it is a poetic *jang-nāma* based on *Durr al-Majālis.*

PUSHTO TRANSLATIONS

In a recent Pushto catalogue of Afghan authors, writers, and editors, ʿAbd al-Raʾūf Rāfiqī suggests that fourteen Pushto copies of *Durr al-Majālis* were produced from the early thirteenth/nineteenth century by Afghan scholars.[7] Some of them, such as ʿAbd al-Kabīr, have produced 'metrical versions' of *Durr al-Majālis* and the miracles of Muḥammad.[8]

A few full and partial copies of *Durr al-Majālis* written in Pushto can be found in the Rylands Library, Manchester. These manuscripts, described below, have been catalogued with different numbers: Afghan 4 (or: 138), Afghan 2 (or: 139), Afghan 13b (or: 140), and Afghan 12 (or: 141).[9]

Afghan 4

This manuscript includes the tales of *King Jumjuma*, *Tawallod-nāma* and *Jang-nāma-i Imāmayn Ḥassan wa Ḥusayn*. The stories are all based on Sayf Ẓafar's magnum opus referred to as 'Durr-i Majālis' and they are all rendered in verse. The stories have been adapted by Ghulām Muḥammad Gagyānī around the time of the late twelfth/eighteenth and early thirteenth/nineteenth centuries.

Afghan 2

Also including a *jang-nāma* (see Afghan 4)

Afghan 13b

In addition to the stories of Afghan 4, this manuscript includes a *tawallud-nāma* of Muḥammad.

[7] Blumhardt and MacKenzie, *Catalogue of Pashto Manuscripts*, 90.

[8] Blumhardt and MacKenzie, *Catalogue of Pashto Manuscripts*, 111.

[9] For more details, see ibid., 108–110.

Afghan 12

In addition to the stories of Afghan 4, this manuscript is again *Jang-nāma-i Imāmayn*.

A KURMANJI TRANSLATION

No. ГПБ, курд 40

Minority communities of the Middle East have shown interest in the *Durr al-Majālis* of Sayf Ẓafar. The most important example of such interest is the manuscript catalogued as No. ГПБ, курд 40 in the Institute of the Peoples of Asia of the former USSR Academy of Sciences. The manuscript is a Kurmanji adaptation of *Durr al-Majālis* that was produced at the request of the orientalist Auguste de Jaba/Żaba. The choice of chapters in this manuscript is quite different from many of the available copies of *Durr al-Majālis* in various languages, with some popular chapters removed and other new chapters added. This manuscript, ascribed to Mullā Mūsā Hikkārī and scribed by Mela Mahmût Beyazîdî in the mid-thirteenth/nineteenth century, includes fifty-eight chapters as listed in Table 3.

Chapter No.	No. ГПБ, курд 40	Standard?
1	The story of Shaykh Barsīsa	Yes
2	The story of the parrot	Yes
3	The story of Ghanim	No
4	The story of the generous beggar	Yes
5	The story of King Solomon and the Queen of Sheba	No
6	The story of King Solomon	Yes
7	The cunning wife	Yes
8	The story of King David and the wife of his vizier	No
9	On Jesus	Yes
10	Anūshīrwān the Just	No
11	The wise minister	Yes
12	Solomon and the bird, ʿAnqa	No
13	The merchants and the parrot	No

14	On Alexander the Great	No
15	The story of a woman in a mountain tribe (*ahl-i chīyaʾī*)	No
16	Sultan Bāyazīd and his captivity	No
17	Ḥātim Ṭāʾiy	No
18	The fisherman	Yes
19	On the name of 'Baghdad'	No
20	On Pharaoh	Yes
21	On the dishonest shepherd	No
22	On the siege of Baghdad	No
23	On the love story of Farhād and Shīrīn	No
24	On Avicenna (Авиценне) (?)	No
25	The battle of the Persians with the Indian army	No
26	The story of an Indian prince's adventure	No
27	King Solomon and the old man	No
28	The poor gardener	No
29	Ten robbers	No
30	Anūshīrwān the Just and the wood engraver	No
31	Joseph and Zulaykha	Yes
32	Prophet Job (Ayyūb)	No
33	The pious wife of a merchant	Yes
34	Two rogues	No
35	The wisdom of Pharaoh	No
36	The King Zahhak	No
37	The story of King Solomon	Yes
38	The Turkish cheaters	No
39	On Hafiz Shirazi	No
40	The righteous shaykh	No

41	On Caliph Yazīd	Partial Resemblance
42	The killing story of Ḥusayn	Yes
43	On Maḥmūd of Ghazna	Partial Resemblance
44	On Ḥātim Ṭāʾiy	No
45	The prowess of Rustam	No
46	Solomon and Hishām	No
47	On Genghis Khan's marriage	No
48	Adam and Eve	Yes
49	Prophet Idrīs	No
50	King Nimrod	No
51	On Lot, the Prophet	No
52	The global flood [of Noah]	No
53	On Prophet Jonah	No
54	On King Shaddād	No
55	On Hārūt and Mārūt, the angels	No
56	On the carpenter	No
57	The insidious wife	No
58	The coppersmith	No

Table 3. A list of the chapters in a Kurmanji adaptation of Sayf Ẓafar's *Durr al-Majālis* known as No. ГПБ, курд 40 and a comparison to the chapters standardly found in his work.

It is clear that this Kurmanji abridgement, in addition to *Durr al-Majālis*, was inspired by hagiographic works on the lineage of the prophets as well as other stories. For example, the topic of chapter fifty-five is addressed in al-Qazwīnī's *ʿAjāʾib al-Makhlūqāt.*[10] It should be noted that an edition of this version of *Durr al-Majālis* has been produced by Hêmin Khoshnaw by Soran Univesity, Iraqi Kurdistan, in 2019.

[10] For more details on the description of the manuscript, see Omar Ahmad, 'Molla Musa Hakkari'nin' and Rudenko, Описание курдских рукописей Ленинградских собраний.

APPENDIX D

A Description of Select Printed Volumes

It appears that the first printing of *Durr al-Majālis* was by the Muḥammadī Printing House of Lahore in 1293/1876. This edition was the shorter version of *Durr al-Majālis* and was edited by Maulwī Ghulām Ḥusayn Ṣāḥib, imam of the Gumti Mosque of the Lahore book market/bazaar. The book was printed at the request of three merchants of the Kashmiri market, Faqīrullāh, ʿAbd al-Qādir, and ʿAbd al-ʿAzīz. This print edition does not include the longer version of the story of Ḥasan and Ḥusayn's killing, Moses' conversation with God, the conversation of Jesus and King Jumjuma, or the *nūr-nāma*. Ghulām Ḥusayn Ṣāḥib admits to shortcomings in his edition and requests the cooperation of readers.

[...] امید از ناظران آن که از نسخه های قلمی در آن مقام خود تصحیح نمایند، و برین عاجز خورده نگیرند.
I hope that reviewers revise the text based on manuscript copies available to them and do not blame me for errors. (p. 132)

A second edition of this book was printed in Lahore in 1882 by Qadīrī Press. Other merchants also requested the right to print. Muḥammad ʿAbdullāh known as [Mulk-i] Asīr (?),[1] a merchant of the Kashmiri market of Lahore, paid the printing fees to the Muṣṭafāʾī Printing House in Lahore in 1884. The work was printed along with another treatise titled *Dalīl al-Iḥsān*. The text was rewritten by Muḥammad Ramaḍān ʿAlī, a Lahori copyist in the late thirteenth/nineteenth century.

[1] For the people, carrying the nickname of Asīr in Indian contexts, see the manuscript, Shoults Collection Inc 1853 A, in the Otago University Special Collections, New Zealand.

In these early printed copies of *Durr al-Majālis* the name of the author is written as Sayf Ẓafar Tūtuhārī/Ūtuhārī. A Pushto version was also printed in Afghanistan[2] and then later Tatar Muslims also began to give the work special attention. The community and merchants of Kazan played a crucial role in reprinting Islamic materials in Central Asia as well as in the Soviet Union. The first known attempt to print a Tatar version of *Durr al-Majālis* was by the Imperial University of Kazan in 1898, an edition which was reproduced in 1905 and 1910. A local merchant, Ḥājj Shams al-Dīn b. Ḥusayn al-Qursawī al-Kāzānī, was instrumental in the production of this version. Having a family-based printing house in Kazan, Beraderan Karimilar showed a lot of interest in publishing Tatar translations of religious texts and hagiographic treatises such as the *Story of Prophets* in 1908. This printing house also printed *Durr al-Majālis* in 1909. In these Tatar printed editions, which are all based on the shorter version, the name of the author is recorded as Sayf Ẓafar Bukhārī.[3]

The most recent printed version of *Durr al-Majālis* appears to be the Uzbek translation published by Meros Nashriyyat in Tashkent, Uzbekistan in 1991 and reprinted in 1992. This translation was based on one manuscript copy dated 1267/1850. Apparently, the Tajik version (based on the Uzbek one) was produced by the Oriëno press in Dushanbe in 1992.[4] However, all these copies, despite being rich and valuable, were based on a limited number of manuscripts, and without a critical and philological analysis of the contents.

[2] Manuscripts in Peshawar, 59.

[3] My thanks go to Rashid for providing me with these Tatar versions.

[4] *Durr-ul-majolis Attribution [tahiiai Sharofati Mirzodukht; muharriri mas"ul Muhammadjon Umarov;* sarmuharrir Amriddin Jalolzoda]. Variant title on p. [4] of cover in Arabic script: *Durr al-majālis*, Published in Dushanbe: 'Oriëno', 1992.

Personal Digital Collection

Daneshgar.Durr.1

This manuscript, purchased by myself, was at the outset preserved by a private collector in Iran. It was copied by Muḥammad b. Mullā Aḥmad b. Mullā Ādīna in the village of Jakān, Herat on 23 Jumādā al-Thānī 1306/24 February 1889, 'during the rule of Amīr ʿAbd al-Raḥmān Khān' and in the office of Saʿd al-Dīn Khān. Different handwriting can be detected on the front and back covers, presumably the hands of various owners. The manuscript includes popular supplications for health, safety, and fortune such as 'In the name of the Restorer of Health (*al-Shāfī*); in the name of the All Sufficing (*al-Kāfī*); in the name of the Forgiver (*al-Maʿāfī*)'. The last folios also include couplets and a quatrain (*rubāʿī*) ascribed to Abū Saʿīd Abū al-Khayr.

یا ربّ به رسالت رسول الثقلین؛ یا ربّ به غزا کنندهٔ بدر و حنین
عُصیان مرا دو حِصّه کن در عرصات؛ نیمی به حسن ببخش و نیمی به حسین

O Lord, by the apostleship of the messenger of mankind and of jinn;
O Lord, by the warrior of [the battle of] Badr and Ḥunayn
Divide my disobedience and turbulence into two parts
in the Resurrection Plain;
forgive half for [the sake of] Ḥasan and the other half
for [the sake of] Ḥusayn

Bibliography

FURTHER PRIMARY SOURCES

ʿAmīd, Ḥasan, *Farhang-i Lughat-i ʿAmīd*: www.vajehyab.com

ʿAṭṭār, Farīd al-Dīn, *Tadhkirat al-Awliyāʾ*, ed. Shafīʿī Kadkanī (Tehran: Sukhan, 1397/2018), vols. 2.

al-Balādhurī, *Kitāb Jumal min Ansāb al-Ashrāf, vol. III* (Beirut: Dār al-Fikr, n.d.).

Bukhārī, Aḥmad b. Muḥammad, *Tāj al-Qiṣaṣ*, ed. Sayyid ʿAlī Āl-i Dāwūd (Tehran: Farhangistān-i Adab wa Zabān-i Fārsī, 1387/2009), vol. 1.

Dehkhoda, ʿAlī Akbar, *Lughat-Nāma-yi Dehkhudā:* www.vajehyab.com

Ganjoor, *Durdāni-hā-yi Adab-i Fārsī*: https://ganjoor.net

Favre, Pierre- *Étienne-Lazare, Dictionnaire javanais-français* (Vienna: Imprimerie Imperiale et Royale, 1870).

Ḥisn al-Muslim www.sunnah.com

Maḥbūb al-Albāb fī taʿrīf al-Kutub wa l-Kuttāb (Khoda-Bakhsh Oriental Public Library, 1991).

Muʿīn, Muḥammad, *Farhang-i Muʿīn*: www.vajehyab.com

MS 109, National Library of the Republic of Indonesia.

MS 1327, National Library of Iran.

MS 138, *Collection of Prof. Muḥammad Iqbal Mujaddidi in the Punjab University Library.*

MS 17641, Parliamentary Library of Iran.

MS 17803, Parliamentary Library of Iran.

MS 17811, Parliamentary Library of Iran.

MS 17811, Parliamentary Library of Iran.

MS 18745, Parliamentary Library of Iran.

MS 1890, India Office, the British Library.

MS 213, Emmanuel College Library, University of Cambridge.

MS 37082, SOAS.

MS 5–17454, National Library of Iran.

MS 5–25045 , National Library of Iran.
MS 5–27641, National Library of Iran.
MS 5–28348/2, National Library of Iran.
MS 5–9337, National Library of Iran.
MS 5700, Parliamentary Library of Iran.
MS 813948, Iran National Library.
MS 814239, National Library of Iran.
MS 818174 (5144/1), the National Library of Iran.
MS 879, Parliamentary Library of Iran.
MS Add.3789, Cambridge University Library.
MS Cod. Pers. 184, Bayerische Staatsbibliothek.
MS Cod. Pers. 309, Bayerische Staatsbibliothek.
MS Gg. 6. 40, Cambridge University Library.
MS Indic 2534, Houghton Library, Harvard University.
MS Isl. Ms. 853, Michigan University Library.
MS Jarring Prov. 111, Lund University Library.
MS LJS 425, University of Pennsylvania Library.
MS Ll.6.5, Cambridge University Library.
MS M. 82, Indian Council for Cultural Relations of New Delhi.
MS Malay B.6, British Library/Singapore National Library.
MS Malay B.7 (also John Leyden collection (285), acquired by the India Office.
MS N. 1222, Academy of Sciences of Tajikistan.
MS N. 125, the Wall Collection, National Library of the Republic of Indonesia.
MS N. 72, the Wall Collection, National Library of the Republic of Indonesia.
MS No. 18 of the Raffles collection, Royal Asiatic Society.
MS No.327, Staatsbibliothek zu Berlin.
MS Or. 1744a, Leiden University Library.
MS Or. 5658.
MS Or. fol. 297, Staatsbibliothek zu Berlin.
MS Or.3213, Leiden University Library.
MS Or.3306, Leiden University Library.
MS RAS Raffles Malay 62, Royal Asiatic Collection.
MS Shoults Collection Inc 1853 A, Otago University Special Collections.
MS Suppl. Turc. 181, The Bibliothèque nationale de France.
MS XI. -L. S. Cod. G , Marburg University Library.
MS. 21045, the Parliamentary Library of Iran.
MS. 33429, National Library of Iran.
MS. Dd.5.37, Cambridge University Library.

Nasikhun (ed.), *Hikayat Ceritera Nabi Musa Munadjat* (Yogyakarta: Sunan Kalijaga, 1985).

The Qurʾān: www.quran.com

Sayf Zafar, *Durr-ul-majolis Attribution [tahiiai Sharofati Mirzodukht; muharriri mas"ul Muhammadjon Umarov ; sarmuharrir Amriddin Jalolzoda]*. (Dushanbe: 'Oriëno', 1992).

al-Ṭabarī, *The History of al-Ṭabarī (Muhammad at Mecca)*, translated by W. Montgomery Watt, VI (Albany: State University of New York Press, 1988).

al-Ṭabarī, *The History of al-Ṭabarī (the Caliphate of Yazīd b. Muʿāwiyah)*, translated by I. K. A. Howard, XIX (New York: State University of New York Press, 1990).

al-Ṭabarī, *The History of al-Ṭabarī, General Introduction and from Creation to the Flood*, translated and annotated by Franz Rosenthal, vol. 1 (New York: State University of New York Press, 1989).

al-Thaʿlabī, *ʿArāʾis al-Majālis fī Qiṣaṣ al-Anbiyāʾ*, *Lives of the Prophets*, translated and annotated by William M. Brinner (Leiden, Boston and Köln: Brill, 2002), 52–53.

Vullers, Ioannis Augusti. *Lexicon persico-latinum etymologicum* (Bonnae ad Rhenum: Impensis Adolphi Marci, 1855)

SECONDARY SOURCES

Abdul Karim, Munshi, *Social History of the Muslims in Bengal (Down to A. D. 1538)* (Dacca: The Asiatic Society of Pakistan, 1959).

Abdul Karim, Munshi and Ahmad Sharif, *Descriptive Catalogue of Bengali Manuscripts in Munshi Abdul Karim's Collection, English edition with an introduction by Syed Sajjad Husain* (Dacca: Asiatic Society of Pakistan, 1961).

Abramyan, R., 'Armyanskiy putevoditel' po Indii XII veka' [An Armenian itinerary to twelfth-century India], *Vestnik Matenadarana* 4 (1958), 317–328.

Abū al-Fidāʾ, Ismāʿīl b. ʿAlī, *Géographie d'Aboulféda*, vol. 1: *Introduction générale à la géographie des Orientaux*, ed. M. Reinaud (Paris: Imprimé par Autorisation du Gouvernement a L'imprimerie Nationale, 1846).

Ahmad, Hêmin Omar, 'Molla Musa Hakkari'nin Dürrü'l-Mecalis İsimli Yazma Eseri', *1st International Zap Basin Scholars Symposium* (Hakkari: Hakkari University, 2018).

Ahmed, Shahab, *What is Islam? The Importance of Being Islamic* (Princeton: Princeton University Press, 2016).

Akbaruddīn Ṣiddīqī, Muḥammad, *Fihrist-i matbu'at-i kutubkhanah-yi Idarah-yi Adabiyat-i Urdu* (Dakan: Idārah-yi Adabiyāt-i Urdū, Ḥaidarābād, 1963).

Åkesson, Joyce, *Arabic Morphology and Phonology: Based on the Marāḥ al-arwāḥ by Aḥmad b. ʿAī b. Masʿūd, Vol.1* (Leiden and Boston: Brill, 2001).

Al Ghouz, Abdelkader, *Brokers of Islamic Philosophy in Mamlūk Egypt: Shams ad-Dīn Maḥmūd b. ʿAbd ar-Raḥmān al-Iṣfahānī (d. 1348) as a Case Study in the Transmission of Philosophical Knowledge through Commentary Writing* (Bonn: Annemarie Schimmel Kolleg, 2015).

Ali-de-Unzaga, Umar, 'The Conversation between Moses and God (Munājāt Mūsā) in the Epistles of the Pure Brethren (*Rasāʾil Ikhwān al-Safaʾ*)', *Al-Kitab: La Sacralité du Texte Dans Le Monde de l'Islam; Actes du Symposium International Tenu à Leuven et Louvain-la-Neuve du 29 Mai au 1 Juin 2002*, ed. Daniel De Smet, Godefroyde Callataÿ, and Jan Van Reeth (Brussels, Louvain-la-Neuve; Leuven: Acta Orientalia Belgica, Subsidia III, 2004), 371–387.

Alves, Jorge Dos Santos and Nader Nasiri-Moghaddam, 'Une lettre en persan de 1519 sur la situation à Melaka', *Archipel* 75 (2008), 145–166.

Amanat, Abbas and Assef Ashraf (eds), *The Persianate World: Rethinking a Shared Sphere* (Leiden: Brill, 2018).

Anonymous, untitled, *Journal of the Asiatic Society of Bengal*. Vol. 46 (1877).

Anonymous, *Journal of the Pakistan Historical Society* (1959), 215.

Anonymous, untitled. *Bayaz (Anjuman-i Fārsī)* 4/1–2 (1984): n.p.

Arya, Gholam-Ali and Matthew Melvin-Koushki, 'Bukhārī, Sayyid Jalāl al-Dīn', *Encyclopaedia Islamica Online*, ed. Wilferd Madelung and Farhad Daftary (Leiden: Brill, 2011) https://doi.org/10.1163/1875-9831_isla_COM_05000024

Assmussen, Jes P., *Studies in Judeo-Persian Literature* (Leiden: Brill, 1973).

al-Attas, Syed Muhammad Naquib, Al-Raniri and the Wujudiyyah of 17th Century Acheh, (MA thesis, McGill University, 1962).

al-Attas, Syed Muhammad Naquib, *The Mysticism of Hamzah Fanṣūrī* (Kuala Lumpur: University of Malay Press, 1970).

al-Attas, Syed Muhammad Naquib, *The Oldest Known Malay Manuscript: A Sixteenth Century Malay Translation of the 'Aqa'id of al-Nasafi* (Kuala Lumpur: Department of Publication, University of Malaya, 1988).

Aumer, Joseph, *Die persischen Handschriften der Hof- und. Staatsbibliothek in München* (Munich: Commission der Palm'schen Hofbuchhandlung 1866).

Baried, Baroroh, 'Le Shiʿisme en Indonésie', *Archipel* 15 (1978), 65-84.

Bausani, Alessandro, 'Un manoscritto Persiano-Malese di grammatica Araba del xvi secolo', *Annali dell'Ist. Univ. Orientale di Napoli* 19/29 (1969), 69–98.

Bausani, Alessandro, 'Note sui vocaboli Persiani in Malese-Indonesiano', *Annali dell'Ist. Univ. Orientale di Napoli* 14 (1964), 1–32.

Beale, Thomas W., *The Oriental Biographical Dictionary*, ed. Asiatic Society of Bengal under the supervision of Henry George Keene (Calcutta: J. W. Thomas, Baptist Mission Press, 1881).

Behrend, T. E. (ed.) Perpustakaan Nasional Republik Indonesia. Jakarta: Yayasan Obor Indonesia & EFEO. (Katalog induk naskah-naskah Nusantara; Jil.4, 1998).

Bilmez, Bülent, 'Shemseddin Sami Frashëri (1850–1904): Contributing to the Construction of Albanian and Turkish Identities', *Centre for Advanced Study Sofia* (2011), 1–27.

Blumhardt, James Fuller and D. N. MacKenzie, *Catalogue of Pashto Manuscripts in the Libraries of the British Isles* (London: The Trustees of the British Museum and the Commonwealth Relations Office, 1965).

Bosworth, Clifford E., 'Munādjāt', in *Encyclopaedia of Islam, Second Edition*, ed. P. Bearman, Th. Bianquis, C. E. Bosworth, E. van Donzel, and W. P. Heinrichs. Retrieved 18 June 2021. http://dx.doi.org/10.1163/1573-3912_islam_SIM_5499

Bosworth, Clifford E., 'Sayābidja', in *Encyclopaedia of Islam New Edition Online* (2012): https://doi.org/10.1163/1573-3912_islam_SIM_6676

Bosworth, Clifford E. and M. S. Asimov, *History of Civilizations of Central Asia: The Age of Achievement, A. D. 750 to the End of the Fifteenth Century* (Paris: UNESCO, 1992).

Braginsky, Vladimir, 'Two Eastern Christian Sources on Mediaeval Nusantara', *Bijdragen tot de taal-, land- en volkenkunde/Journal of the Humanities and Social Sciences of Southeast Asia* 154/3 (1998). 367–396.

Braginsky, Vladimir, 'Towards the biography of Hamzah Fanṣūrī. When did Hamzah live? Data from his poems and early European accounts', *Archipel* 57/2 (1999), 135–175.

Braginsky, Vladimir, *The Heritage of Traditional Malay Literature: A Historical Survey of Genres, Writings and Literary Views* (Leiden, KITLV Press, 2005).

Braginsky, Vladimir, 'Jalinan dan Khazanah Kutipan: Terjemaham dari Bahasa Parsi dalam Kesusasteraan Melayu, Khususnya yang berkaitan dengan "Cerita-Cerita Parsi"'. *Sadur: Sejarah Terjamahan di Indonesia dan Malaysia*, ed. Henri Chambert-Loir (Jakarta: Ecole Francaise de Extreme Orient, 2009), 59–117.

Brakel, L. F., 'The Birthplace of Hamzah Fanṣūrī', *Journal of the Malaysian Branch of the Royal Asiatic Society* 42/2 (1969), 206–212.

Brakel, L. F., 'Persian Influence on Malay Literature', *Abr Nahrayn* 9 (1969–1970), 1–16.

Brakel, L. F., *The Story of Muḥammad Ḥanafiyya* (Leiden, Koninklijk Instituut Voor Taal-, Land- en Volkenkunde, 1977).

Brakel, L. F., 'Hamza Fanṣūrī. Notes on: yoga practices, lahir dan zahir, the 'taxallos', punning, a difficult passage in the Kitab al-Muntahi, Hamzah's likely place of birth and Hamza's imagery', *Journal of the Malaysian Branch of the Royal Asiatic Society* 52/1 (1979), 73–98.

Brakel, L. F., *The Hikayat Muhammad Hanafiyyah: A Mediaeval Muslim-Malay Romance* (Berlin: Springer, 1981).

Brakel-Papenhuyzen, Clara, 'The Tale of the Skull: An Islamic Description of Hell in Javanese', *Bijdragen tot de Taal-, Land-en Volkenkunde* 158/1 (2002), 1–19.

Brophy, David, 'A Lingua Franca in Decline? The Place of Persian in Qing China', in *The Persianate World*, ed. Nile Green (California: University of California Press, 2019).

Brown, C. C., 'The Malay Annals', *Journal of the Malayan Branch of the Royal Asiatic Society* 25/2–3 (1952), 6–276.

Browne, Edward G., *A Literary History of Persia*, vol. 3: *The Tartar Dominion (1265–1502)* (Cambridge: Cambridge University Press, 1928).

Browne, Edward G., *Az Saʿdī tā Jāmī*, trans. ʿAlī Aṣghar Ḥikmat (Tehran: Bank Melli Iran Printing House, 1327/1948).

Bulliet, Richard W., 'Naw Bahār and the Survival of Iranian Buddhism', *Iran* 14 (1976), 140–145.

Bustanov, Alfrid, 'Speaking 'Bukharan': The Circulation of Persian Texts in Imperial Russia', *The Persianate World: The Frontiers of a Eurasian Lingua Franca*, ed. Nile Green (Oakland: University of California Press, 2019).

Calmard, Jean, 'Mohammad b. al-Hanafiyya dans la religion populaire, le folklore, les légendes dans le monde turco-persan et indo-persan', *Cahiers d'Asie centrale* 5/6 (1998), 201–220.

Calmard, Jean, 'Popular Literature under the Safavids', in *Society and Culture in the Early Modern Middle East: Studies on Iran in the Safavid Period*, ed. Andrew J. Newman, (Leiden and Boston: Brill, 2003), 316–339.

Carter, Landon, 'Extracts from Diary of Col. Landon Carter', *The William and Mary Quarterly* 13/1 (1904), 45–53.

Colless, Brian E., 'Persian Merchants and Missionaries in Mediaeval Malaya', *Journal of the Malaysian Branch of the Royal Asiatic Society* 2/2 (1969), 10–47.

Cowan, H. K. J., 'A Persian Inscription in North Sumatra', *Tijdschrift voor Indische Taal-, Land- en Volkenkunde* 80/1 (1940), 15–21.

Crawfurd, John, *History of the Indian Archipelago Containing an Account of the Manners, Arts, Language, Religions, Institutions, and Commerce of its Inhabitants* (Edinburgh: Archibald Constable and Co. Edinburgh, 1820), vol. 1.

d'Hubert, Thibaut, 'Persian at the Court or in the Village? The Elusive Presence of Persian in Bengal', in *The Persianate World*, ed. Nile Green (California: University of California Press, 2019).

d'Hubert, Thibaut, ''Abd al-Ḥakīm', *Encyclopaedia of Islam, THREE*, ed. Kate Fleet, Gudrun Krämer, Denis Matringe, John Nawas, and Everett Rowson (Leiden: Brill, 2021), 2–3.

D'hulster, Kristof, 'A 19th-century Chaghatay-Kazakh Version of the Story of Jesus and the Skull', in *Turcologica Upsaliensia, An Illustrated Collection of Essays*, ed. Éva Á. Csató, Gunilla Gren-Eklund, Lars Johanson, Birsel Karakoç (Leiden and Boston, Brill, 2020), 198–208.

Daneshgar, Majid, 'The Study of Persian Shiʿism in the Malay-Indonesian World: A Review of Literature from the Nineteenth Century Onwards', *Journal of Shi'a Islamic Studies* 7/2 (2014), 191–229.

Daneshgar, Majid, 'The Divinatory Role of the Qurʾan in the Malay World', *Indonesia and the Malay World* 44/129 (2016), 123–144.

Daneshgar, Majid, *Middle Eastern and Islamic Manuscripts Sir George Grey Special Collections; Auckland Libraries New Zealand* (Auckland: Auckland Libraries, 2018).

Daneshgar, Majid, 'New Evidence on the Origin of the Hikayat Muhammad Hanafiyyah', *Archipel* 96 (2018), 69–102.

Daneshgar, Majid, 'Pieter J. Veth on the Tabut Feast: Judaic and Persian-Shīʿī Traces of a Tradition in Java', *Berita* (Summer 2020), 4–9.

Daneshgar, Majid, 'Indonesian Manuscripts in Iran', *Indonesia and the Malay World* 49/143 (2021), 126–138.

Daneshgar, Majid, 'Peter G. Riddell, Malay Court Religion, Culture and Language: Interpreting the Qurʾān in 17th Century Aceh', *Der Islam* 98/1 (2021), 293–296.

Daneshgar, Majid, 'Persianate Aspects of the Malay-Indonesian World: Some Rare Manuscripts in the Leiden University Library', *Dabir* 8 (2021) 51–78.

Daneshgar, Majid, 'The Prophet Shaving: Persians and the Origin of the Malay *Hikayat Nabi Bercukur*', *Der Islam* 98/2 (2021), 394–424.

Daneshgar, Majid, 'A Very Old Malay Islamic Manuscript: Carbon Dating and Further Analysis of a Persian-Malay Anthology', *Indonesia and the Malay World* 147 (2022), 161–172.

Daneshgar, Majid, 'An Early "Mirror for Princes" in Southeast Asia: The First Known Malay Translation of Akhlaq-i Mohseni', *Cambridge University Library Special Collection* (2022) https://specialcollections-blog.lib.cam.ac.uk/?p=23968

Daneshgar, Majid, 'An Old Malay Manuscript of *Tafsīr* and *Tajwīd*: Formative Islamic Sciences in Nusantara', in *Malay-Indonesian Islamic Studies: A Festschrift in Honor of Peter G. Riddell*, edited by Majid Daneshgar and Ervan Nurtawab (Leiden: Brill, 2023), 163–181.

Daneshgar, Majid, 'Persianate Fiqh in Indonesia: *Majmuʿih-yi Khani* as a Rare Legal Manuscript in a Cosmopolitan Context', *International Journal of Islam in Asia* 2/2 (2023), 144–169.

Daneshgar, Majid, 'A Persian Treatise on the Genealogy of Shīʿa Imāms from Jerusalem,' *Dabir* 9/2 (2024): 3–15.

Daneshgar, Majid, 'Anthologies of Persian Poetry Inscribed in Indonesia: A Handlist of Rare Manuscripts', *Dabir* 10/1 (2024): 27–48.

Daneshgar, Majid, "Translating Persian Tafsir in Aceh: The Oldest Malay "Story of Joseph" at Cambridge University Library", *Cambridge University Library Special Collections Blog* (2024): https://specialcollections-blog.lib.cam.ac.uk/?p=26005

Daneshgar, Majid, 'The Iranian Diaspora in Southeast Asia: Old Manuscript, New Perspectives', *Leiden Specialcollections Blog* (2024): https://www.leidenspecialcollectionsblog.nl/articles/persians-of-java-re-examining-the-cultural-context-of-indonesia

Daneshgar, Majid and Anthony Tedeschi, *Middle Eastern and Islamic Manuscripts, Alexander Turnbull Library Collections; The National Library of New Zealand* (Wellington: National Library, 2019).

Daneshgar, Majid and Sajjad Rizvi, 'Inscribing Persian in the Arabic Cosmopolis: Case Study of Qur'ānic Exegesis from Khorasan', *Australian Journal of Islamic Studies* 7/1 (2022), 5–28.

Daneshgar, Majid, Gregorius Dwi Kuswanta, Masykur Syafruddin, and R. Michael Feener. 'A 15th-Century Persian Inscription from Bireuen, Aceh: An Early 'Flash'of Sufism before Fanṣūrī in Southeast Asia.' In *Malay-Indonesian Islamic Studies: A Festschrift in Honor of Peter G. Riddell*, edited by Majid Daneshgar and Ervan Nurtawab (Leiden: Brill, 2022), 86–105.

Daneshgar, Majid and R. Michael Feener, "'Discovering a Hidden Miraculous Grave': A Rare Persian Inscription of Ferdowsi's Shāhnāmah from Barus, Indonesia" (forthcoming).

Daneshgar, Majid, 'A Persian Shiʿi Anthology circulating in Patna, Dhaka and Siam in the Seventeenth Century: A Lesser-known Ship of Persians to South-East Asia', In *Iran and Persianate Culture in the Indian Ocean World*, ed. A. C. S. Peacock (London: Bloomsbury, 2025), 249–260.

Devic, L. Marcel, *Dictionnaire étymologique des mots français d'origine orientale (arabe, persan, turc, malais)* (Paris: Imprimerie Nationale, 1876).

DeWeese, Devin, 'Persian and Turkic from Kazan to Tobolsk: Literary Frontiers in Muslim Inner Asia', *The Persianate World*, ed. Nile Green (California: University of California Press, 2019).

Doorenbos, J., *De Geschriften van Hamzah Pansoeri* (PhD thesis, Leiden State University, 1933).

Drewes, G. W. J. and L. F. Brakel, *The Poems of Hamzah Fanṣūrī* (Dordrecht, Netherlands and Cinnaminson, NJ: Foris Publications, 1986).

Eaton, Richard M., *India in the Persianate Age: 1000–1765* (London: Penguin, 2019).

Editors, *The Flower of Persian Literature, Containing Extracts from the Most Celebrated Authors, in Prose and Verse, with a Translation Into English Being Intended as a Companion to Sir William Jones's Persian Grammar to which is Prefixed an Essay on the Language and Literature of Persian.* (London: printed by S. Rousseau at the Arabic and Persian Press, 1804).

Ethé, Carl H., *Neupersische Literatur* (Strassburg: Grundriss der iranischen Philologie Seperat-Abdruck, 1897), vol. 2.

Ethé, Carl H., *Catalogue of Persian Manuscripts in the Library of the India Office* (Oxford: Printed for the India Office, 1903), vol. 1.

Ethé, Carl H., *Tārīkh-i Adabiyyāt-i Fārsī*, trans. Riḍā Zādih Shafaq (Tehran: Bungāh-i Tarjuma wa Nashr-i Kitāb, 1337/1958).

Faḍlullāh Hamadānī, Rashīd al-Dīn, *Tawārīkh: Taʾrīkh-i Mubārak-i Ghazānī*, ed. Muḥammad Rawshan and Muṣṭafā Mūsawī (Tehran: Mirāth-i Maktūb, 1394/2015), vol. 1.

Fang, Liaw Y., *A History of Classical Malay Literature*, trans. Razif Bahari and Harry Aveling (Singapore and Jakarta: Institute of Southeast Asian Studies and Yayasan Pustaka Obor Indonesia, 2013).

Farid, G. S., 'Khatt-i-Bihari, the Indian Style of Arabic Writing', *Indo-Iranica: The Quarterly Organ of the Iran Society* 1–4/29 (1976), 102–112.

Farridnejad, Shervin, 'The Jewish Ḥāfeẓ: Classical New Persian Literature in the Judeo-Persian Garšūni Literary Tradition', *Journal of the Royal Asiatic Society* 31/3 (2021), 515–534.

Fatimi, S. Q., *Islam Comes to Malaysia* (Singapore: Malaysian Sociological Research Institute Ltd. 1963).

Fawcett, Thompson, 'The Rich Manuscripts', *The British Museum Quarterly* (1963), 18–23.

Feener, R. Michael, Patrick Daly, and Anthony Reed (Eds.), *Mapping the Acehnese Past* (Leiden: KITLV Press, 2009).

Feener, R. Michael, "ʿAlid Piety and State-sponsored Spectacle: Tabot Tradition in Bengkulu, Sumatra', In *Shiʿism in South-East Asia: ʿAlid Piety and Sectarian Constructions*, edited by Chiara Formichi and R. Michael Feener (London: C. Hurst & Co. Ltd., 2015), 187–202.

Flügel, Gustav. Die Arabischen, *Persischen und Türkischen Handschriften der Kaiserlich-königlichen Hofbibliothek zu Wien im Auftrage der vorgesetzten K. K. behörde geordnet und beschrieben* (Wien: K. K. Hof- und Staatsdruckerei, 1867), vol. 1.

Ferrand, Gabriel, 'Sayābid̲j̲a', in *Encyclopaedia of Islam First Edition Online* (2012) https://doi.org/10.1163/2214-871X_ei1_SIM_5215

Ferrand, Gabriel, 'Zābag', in *Encyclopaedia of Islam First Edition Online* (2012) https://doi.org/10.1163/2214-871X_ei1_SIM_6039

Fragner, Bert, *Die 'Persophonie': Regionalität, Identität und Sprachkontakt in der Geschichte Asiens* (Berlin: Das Arabische Buch, 1999).

Gaborieau, Marc, 'Légende et culte du saint musulman Ghâzî Miyân au Népal occidental et en Inde du Nord', *Objets et Mondes* 15/3 (1975) 289–310.

Green, Nile (ed.), *The Persianate World: The Frontiers of a Eurasian Lingua Franca* (California: University of California Press, 2019).

Ḥāfiẓ, *Der Diwan des grossen lyrischen Dichters Hafis im persischen Original herausgegeben, ins deutsche metrisch übersetzt und mit Anmerkungen versehen*, von Vincenz Rosenzweig Ritter von Schwannau (Wien:Druck und Verlag der K. K. Hof-und Staatsdruckerei, 1858), vol. 1.

Hajib, N. A. and E. Shahi, *Readings from Persian Prose and Poetry for High Schools* (Surat: I. P. Mission Press, 1899).

Hamid, Ismail, *The Malay Islamic Hikayat* (Bangi: Institut Bahasa, Kesusasteraan dan Kebudayaan Melayu, 1983).

Hanifi, Shah Mahmoud, *Connecting Histories in Afghanistan: Market Relations and State Formation on a Colonial Frontier* (Stanford: Stanford University Press, 2011) http://www.gutenberg-e.org/hanifi/chapter4.html

Hanaoka, Mimi, *Authority and Identity in Mediaeval Islamic Historiography: Persian Histories from the Peripheries* (Cambridge: Cambridge University Press, 2016).

Harun, Jelani bin, Nuruddin al-Raniri's Bustan al-Salatin: A Universal History and Adab Work from Seventeenth Century Aceh (PhD thesis, SOAS, University of London, 1999).

Helfrich, L. W. R. Winter, and D. M. J. Schiff, 'Het Hasan-Hosein of Taboet-feest te Bengkoelen', in *Internationales Archivfür Ethnographie* I (1888), 191–196.

Hervey, D. F. A., 'Valentyn's Account of Malacca (Continued from p. 301 of No. 16 of the Society's Journal)', *Journal of the Straits Branch of the Royal Asiatic Society* 22 (1890), 225–246.

Hodgson, Marshall G. S., *The Venture of Islam* (Chicago: The University of Chicago Press, 1974).

Honorary Secretaries, The (eds), *The Proceedings of the Asiatic Society of Bengal* (Calcutta: Tile Asiatic Society, 1879).

Humāyūn-Farrukh, Rukn al-Dīn, 'Dasta-gulī Taqdīm bi-dustdārān-i Kitāb', *Hunar wa Mardum* 49 (1345/1966), 41–60.

Ḥusayn, Muḥammad Bashīr, *Fihrist-i Makhṭūṭāt-i Shīrānī* (Lahore: Punjab Library, 1968).

Hurgronje, C. Snouck, *De Atjehers* (Leiden and Batavia: E. J. Brill and Landsdrukkerij, 1894), vol. 2.

Hurgronje, C. Snouck. *The Achehnese*, trans. A. W. S. O'Sullivan (Leiden: Brill, 1906).

Hylén, Torsten, Ḥusayn, the Mediator: A structural Analysis of the Karbalā′ drama according to Abū Ja'far Muḥammad b. Jarīr al-Ṭabarī (d. 310/923) (PhD thesis., Uppsala University, 2007).

Ibrahim, Mohammad, *The Ship of Sulaiman*, ed. J. O'Kane (London: Routledge and Kegan Paul, 1972).

Ingenito, Domenico, *Beholding Beauty: Saʿdi of Shiraz and the Aesthetics of Desire in Mediaeval Persian Poetry* (Leiden and Boston: Brill, 2021).

Irani, Ayesha A., Sacred Biography, Translation, and Conversion: The Nabivamsa of Saiyad Sultan and the Making of Bengali Islam, 1600-present (PhD thesis, University of Pennsylvania, 2011), 488–497.

Irani, Ayesha A., *The Muhammad Avatāra: Salvation History, Translation, and the Making of Bengali Islam* (Oxford: Oxford University Press, 2021).

Iṣfahānī, Ṣādiq, *The Geographical Works of Sádik Isfaháni*, trans. J. C. (London, 1832).

Ivanow, Wladimir. *Concise Descriptive Catalogue of the Persian Manuscripts in the Collection of the Asiatic Society of Bengal* (Calcutta: The Baptist Mission Press, 1924).

Jehngoh, A., Arabic Elements in Hikayat Bayan Budiman, the Oldest Classical Malay Text (Lund University, Sweden, 2003).

Jones, Russell, *Loan-words in Indonesian and Malay* (Leiden: KITLV Press, 2007).

Jusuf, Jumsari, Aisyah Ibrahim, Nikmah A. Soenardjo, and Hani'ah (eds), *Sastra Indonesia lama pengaruh Islam* (Jakarta: Pusat Pembinaan dan Pengembangan Bahasa, Departemen Pendidikan dan Kebudayaan, 1984).

Juynboll, H., *Catalogus van de Maleische en Sundaneesche handschriften der Leidsche universiteits-bibliotheek* (Leiden: Brill, 1899).

Kayhān, Masʿūd, *Jughrāfiyyā-yi Mufaṣṣal-i Īrān* (Tehran: Maṭbaʿa Majlis, 1310/1931).

Khan, Aiza, 'The Ottomans in the Arabian Peninsula', *Routledge Handbook of Persian Gulf Politics*, ed. Mehrdad Kamrava (London and New York: Routledge, 2020).

Kartomi, Margaret. *Musical Journeys in Sumatra* (Illinois: University of Illinois Press, 2012).

Khazeni, Arash, *The City and the Wilderness: Indo-Persian Encounters in Southeast Asia* (California: University of California Press, 2020).

Kia, Mana, 'The Necessary Ornaments of Place: Similarity and Alterity in the Persianate Imaginary', *Comparative Islamic Studies* 13/1–2 (2017), 47–73.

Kraemer, H., *Een Javaansche Primbon uitde Zest iende Eeuw* (Leiden: Trap, 1921).

Laffan, Michael, *Finding Java: Muslim Nomenclature of Insular Southeast Asia from Śrivijaya to Snouck Hurgronje* (Singapore: Asia Research Institute, National University of Singapore, 2005) .

Lambourn, Elizabeth, 'From Cambay to Samudera-Pasai and Gresik: The Export of Gujarati Grave Memorials to Sumatra and Java in the Fifteenth Century CE', *Indonesia and the Malay World* 31/90 (2003), 221–289.

Lambourn, Elizabeth, 'The Formation of the Batu Aceh Tradition in Fifteenth-Century Samudera-Pasai', *Indonesia and the Malay World* 32/93 (2004), 188–210.

Lecker, Michael, 'On the Markets of Medina (Yathrib) in Pre-Islamic and Early Islamic Times', *Jerusalem Studies in Arabic and Islam* 8 (1986), 133–147.

Leezenberg, Michiel, 'Between Islamic Learning and Philological Nationalism: Mullah Mahmûdê Bayazîdî's Auto-ethnography of the Kurds', *Die Welt des Islams* 60 (2020), 433–472.

Lewisohn, Leonard, 'Haravī, Amīr Ḥusaynī', *Encyclopaedia of Islam, THREE*, ed. Kate Fleet, Gudrun

Krämer, Denis Matringe, John Nawas, and Everett Rowson. Retrieved 9 May 2024 https://doi.org/10.1163/1573-3912_ei3_COM_25692

Madelung, W., 'Kuraybiyya', *Encyclopaedia of Islam, Second Edition*, ed. P. Bearman, Th. Bianquis, C. E. Bosworth, E. van Donzel, and W. P. Heinrichs. (Leiden: Brill, 1979), vol. 5, 433–434.

Mahdi, Waruno, 'The First Standard Grammar of Malay: George Werndly's 1736 Maleische spraakkunst', *Wacana* 19/2 (2018), 257–290.

Maier, H. M. J., Fragments of Reading: The Malay Hikayat Merong Mahawangsa. (PhD thesis, Leiden University, 1985).

Marcinkowski, Christoph, 'Shiʿism in Thailand from the Ayutthaya Period to the Present', *Shīʿīsm in South East Asia: Alid Piety and Sectarian Constructions*, eds. Chiara Formichi and Michael Feener (Oxford: Oxford University Press, 2015).

Marrison, G. E., 'Persian Influences in Malay Life (1280–1650)', *Journal of the Malayan Branch of the Royal Asiatic Society* 28/1 (1955), 52–69.

Marʿashī Najafī, Sayyid Maḥmūd. *Fihrist-i Nuskha-hā-yi Khaṭṭi-yi Kitāb-khāna-yi Buzurg-i Āyatullāh Marʿashī Najafī* (Qum: Kitāb-khāna-yi Buzurg-i Āyatullāh Marʿashī Najafī, 1383/2004), vol. 1.

Matthee, Rudi. 'Safavid Dynasty', *Encyclopaedia Iranica* (2008):

https://www.iranicaonline.org/articles/safavids

Melvin-Koushki, Matthew, 'Is (Islamic) Occult Science Science?' *Theology and Science* 18/2 (2020), 303–324.

Millie, Julian, 'Three Books on the Literary Tradition of West Java', *Bijdragen tot de Taal-, Land-en Volkenkunde/Journal of the Humanities and Social Sciences of Southeast Asia* 160/2 (2004), 416–423.

Ming, Ding Ch., 'Access to Malay manuscripts', *Bijdragen tot de Taal-, Land- en Volkenkunde/Journal of the Humanities and Social Sciences of Southeast Asia* 143/4 (1987), 425–451.

Morrison, George, *History of Persian Literature from the Beginning of the Islamic Period to the Present Day* (Leiden and Köln: Brill, 1981).

Morrison, Robert Gordon, *Islam and Science: The intellectual Career of Nizam al-Din al-Nisaburi* (London: Routledge, 2007).

Mouradgea d'Ohsson, Abraham Constantin, *Histoire des Mongols, depuis Tchinguiz-Khan jusqu'à Timour Bey ou Tamerlan* (Amsterdam: Frederik Muller, 1852), vol. 2.

Mūsawī, Sayyid Sulaymān and Muḥammad Ibrāhīm Rawshan Ḍamīr, 'Tahlīl-i Sanadī wa Muḥtawāʾī-yi "Ḥadīth-i Hūt" ba tawajjuh bih pīshīna tārīkhī ān', *Ḥadīth Pazhūhī* 12/23 (2020), 119–136.

Nasir-u'd-din Chiragh of Delhi and Hamid Qalandar, *Khair-u'l-Mjaalis*, ed. Khaliq Ahmad Nizami (Aligarh: Department of History, Muslim University, 1959).

al-Nīsābūrī, *Qiṣaṣ al-Anbiyāʾ, Dāstān-hā-yi Payghambarān*, ed. Ḥabīb Yaghmāʾī (Tehran: Shirkat-i Intishārāt-i ʿIlmī wa Farhangī, 1340/1961).

Nīshābūrī, Muḥammad ʿAbdullāh Ḥakīm, *Taʾrīkh-i Nīshābūr*, trans. Muḥammad Ḥusayn Khalīfa Nīshāpūrī, ed. Bahman Karīmī (Tehran: Kitāb-khāna Ibn Sīnā, n.d.).

Nizam Ad-din Awliya, *Morals for the Heart: Conversations of Shaykh Nizam Ad-din Awliya Recorded by*

Amir Hasan Sijzi, trans. Bruce B. Lawrence, introduction by Khaliq Ahmad Nizami (New York and Mahwah: Paulist Press, 1992).

Nūrī-niyyā, Muḥammad Ḥusayn et al., *Fihrist-i Nuskha-hā-yi Khaṭṭī* (Mashhad: Sāzmān-i Kitāb-khāna-hā, Mūza-hā wa Markaz-i Asnād-i Āstān-i Quds-i Raḍawī, 1388/2009).

Orum, Olav G. *ʾUṣṣit il-gumguma, or, 'The Story of the Skull': With Parallel Versions, Translation and Linguistic Analysis of Three 19th-century Judaeo-Arabic Manuscripts from Egypt* (Leiden and Boston: Brill, 2017).

Pāpulī Yazdī, Muḥammad Ḥusayn, *Farhang-i Ābādīhā wa Makān-hā-yi Madhhabī-yi Kishwar* (Mashhad: Bunyād-i Pazhūhish-hā-yi Islāmī-yi Āstān-i Quds-i Raḍawī, 1367/1988).

Peacock, A. C. S. and Annabel Teh Gallop (eds), *From Anatolia to Aceh Ottomans, Turks, and Southeast Asia* (Leiden and Boston: Brill, 2015).

Peacock, A. C. S., 'Notes on Some Persian Documents from Early Modern Southeast Asia', *Sejarah* 27/1 (2018), 81–97.

Peacock, A. C. S., "Jamāl al-Ḥusaynī's *Rawżat al-Aḥbāb* between Herat, Istanbul and Sumatra: The transformations of a Timurid Persian history of the Prophet and early Islam," In *Authorship and Textual Transmission in the Manuscript Age: Contextualising Ideological Variants*, edited by Sacha Alsancakli and Philip Bockholt (Leuven Peeters Publishers, 2023), 21–57.

Pertsch, Wilhelm, *Die orientalischen Handschriften der Herzoglichen Bibliothek zu Gotha* (Gotha: Friedr. Andr. Perthes, 1880), vol. 2.

Pertsch, Wilhelm, *Verzeichniss der persischen Handschriften der Königlichen Bibliothek zu Berlin* (Berlin: A. Asher & Co., 1888), vol. 4.

Petrů, Tomaš, '"Lands below the Winds" as Part of the Persian Cosmopolis: An Inquiry into Linguistic and Cultural Borrowings from the Persianate societies in the Malay World', *Moussons* 27 (2016), 147–161.

Phillott, Douglas C., 'Note on a Shiʿa Imprecation', *Journal and Proceedings of the Asiatic Society of Bengal* 7/10 (1911), 691.

Pelliot, Paul, 'Les plus anciens monuments de l'écriture arabe en Chine', *Journal Asiatique* 11/2 (1913), 177–191 [also, 5–19].

Pertsch, Wilhelm, *Die orientalischen Handschriften der Herzoglichen Bibliothek zu Gotha* (Gotha: FRIEDR . ANDR. PERTHES, 1880), vol. 2.

Pires, Tomé, *Suma Oriental*, 2 vols (London: Hakluyt Society, 1944).

Powers, David S. *Zayd* (Philadelphia: University of Pennsylvania Press, 2014).

Pregill, Michael, Marianna Klar, and Roberto Tottoli, 'Qiṣaṣ al-Anbiyāʾ as Genre and Discourse: From the Qurʾān to Elijah Muhammad', *Mizan: Journal for the Study of Muslim Societies and Civilizations* 2/1 (2017), 1–28.

Pūrdāvūd, Ibrāhim, *Hurmazd-nāma* (Tehran: Anjuman-i Īrān-shināsī, 1952).

Radsehkran, *Gushāyish-nāma* (Lucknow: Nawal Kishore, 1287/1871).

Rāhī, Akhtar, *Tarjuma-hā-yi Mutūn-i Fārsī bih Zabān-hā-yi Pākistānī* (Islamabad: Markaz-i Taḥqīqāt-i Fārsī-yi Īrān va Pākistān, 1986).

Rajāʾī, Aḥmad A., *Yād-dāshtī darbāra Lahjeh Bukharaī/Le Dialecte de Bukhārā* (Mashhad: University of Mashhad, 1342–3/1964).

Ranīn, Ismāʿīl, *Daryā-navardī-yi Īrāniyyān* (Tehran: Jāvīdān, 1356/1977).

Raverty, H. G., 'Account of Upper and Lower Suwat, and the Kohistan, to the Source of the Suwat River; with an Account of the Tribes Inhabiting Those Valleys', *Journal of the Asiatic Society of Bengal* 31 (1862), 227–281.

Redhouse, J. W., *A Lexicon, English and Turkish; Shewing, in Turkish, the Literal, Incidental, Figurative, Colloquial, and Technical Significations of the English Terms, Indicating Their Pronunciation in a New and Systematic Manner and Preceded by a Sketch of English Etymology, to Faculitate to Turkish Students the Acquisition of the English Language* (Constantinople: A. H. Boyajian, 3rd ed., 1884).

Richardson, John, *A Dictionary, Persian, Arabic, and English with a Dissertation on the Languages, Literature, and Manners of Eastern Nations*, Revised and Improved by Charles Wilkins; a New Edition, Considerably Enlarged by Francis Johnson (London: J. L. Cox, 1829).

Ricklefs, Merle C., *A History of Modern Indonesia Since c.1200* (Hampshire: Palgrave, 3rd ed., 2001).

Riddell, Peter G., *Malay Court Religion, Culture and Language Interpreting the Qurʾān in 17th Century Aceh* (Leiden and Boston: Brill, 2017).

Ridderhof, W. H., Nieuw Practisch Maleis-Nederlands Woordenboek (Zutphen: W. J. Thieme & Cie, 1936);

Rieu, Charles, *Catalogue of the Persian Manuscripts in the British Museum* (London, The British Museum, 1881), vol. 2.

Rodgers, Chas. J., *Catalogue of the Coins of the Indian Museum* (Calcutta: Printed by order of the Trustees of the Indian Museum, 1895), vol. 3.

Roebuck, Thomas, *A Collection of Proverbs, and Proverbial Phrases, in the Persian and Hindoostanee Languages* (Calcutta: Printed at the Hindustanee Press, 1824).

Rubin, Uri, 'Muḥammad's Message in Mecca: Warnings, Signs, and Miracles' in *The Cambridge Companion to Muḥammad*, ed. Jonathan E. Brockopp (Cambridge: Cambridge University Press, 2010), 39–60.

Rudenko, M. B., Описание курдских рукописей Ленинградских собраний [Description of the Kurdish Manuscripts from Leningrad Collections] (Moscow: Izdatelstvo Vostochnoi Literatury, 1961).

Rūmī, Ǧalāl-ad-Dīn, *Auswahl aus den Diwanen des grössten mystischen Dichters Persiens Mewlana Dschelaleddin Rumi.* Von Vincenz von Rosenzweig (Wien: Mechitaristen-Congregations-Buchhandlung, 1838).

Sami, Şemseddin, *Kamus-ül Alâm: Tarih ve Coğrafya Lûgati ve Tabir-i Esahhiyle Kâffe-yi Esma-yi Hassa-yi Camidir* (Istanbul: Mihran Matbaası, 1311/1894).

Schippers, Arie, 'Stories about Women in the collections of Nissim ibn Shāhīn, Petrus Alphonsi, and Yosef ibn Zabāra, and their relation to Mediaeval European Narratives', *Frankfurter Judaistische Beiträge* 37 (2012), 123–135.

Semenov, A. A. and Voronovsky, Собрание восточных рукописей Академии наук Узбекской ССР [Collection of Oriental Manuscripts at the Academy of Sciences of the Uzbek SSR] (Tashkent: Издательство: 'Фан' Узбекской ССР, 1967).

Setudeh-Nejad, Shahab, 'Cultural and Cosmological Impact of Iranian Civilization in Vietnam and Peninsular Areas of Southeast Asia,' *Iran Chamber Society*: https://www.iranchamber.com/culture/articles/iranian_cultural_impact_southeastasia.php

Ṣiddīqī, Muḥammad Akbaruddīn, Fihrist-i matbu'at-i kutubkhanah-yi Idarah-yi Adabiyat-i Urdu (Dakan: Idārah-yi Adabiyāt-i Urdū, Ḥaidarābād, 1963).

Sitzungsberichte der philosophisch -philologischen und historischen Classe der k. b. Akademie der Wissenschaften zu München (München: Akademie der Wissenschaften zu München ,1897).

Shafiee, Hasan Ali and Elham Moravej-Salehi, 'Anbarnesa: The Past Tradition, the Future Medicine', *Iran Red Crescent Medical Journal* 17/12 (2015), e29536.

Shahristānī, Shāh ʿAlī Akbar, *Qāmūs-i Lahja Dari-yi Hazāra-gī* (Kabul: University of Kabul, 1358/1980).

Shams, Moḥammad Javad. 'Amīr Ḥusaynī,' *Centre for the Great Islamic Encyclopaedia* (1399/2020) https://www.cgie.org.ir/fa/article/225765/امیر-حسینی

Skilling, Peter, 'The Advent of Theravāda Buddhism to Mainland South-East Asia', *Journal of the International Association of Buddhist Studies* 20/1 (1997), 93–107.

Smith, Paul (trans.), *Hasan Dehlavi: Life and Poems* (Victoria: Book Heaven, 2006).

Doctor, Sorabshaw Byramji, *Second Book of Persian to which are Added the Pandnáma of Shaikh Saádi and the Gulistán, Chapter I., together with Vocabularies and Short Notes* (Surat: Printed at the Irish Presbuterian Mission Press, by W. Raymond, 2nd ed., 1880).

Soriente, Antonia, 'I prestiti persiani in indonesiano: Bausani cinquant'anni dopo', *Iranian Studies in Honour of Adriano V. Rossi*, ed. Sabir Badalkhan, Gian Pietro Basello, and Matteo de Chiara (Naples: Università Degli Studi di Napoli 'L'Orientale'), 971–1031.

Steenbrink, Karel, *Adam Redivivus: Muslim Elaboration of the Adam Saga with Special Reference to the Indonesian Literary Traditions* (Zoetermeer: Meinema, 1998).

Stewart, Charles (trans.), *Original Persian Letters, and Other Documents, with Fac-Similes* (London: Printed for the Author, by William Nicol and Kingsbury, Parbury, Allen, & Co., 1825).

Subrahmanyam, Sanjay, 'Iranians Abroad: Intra-Asian Elite Migration and Early Modern State Formation', *The Journal of Asian Studies* 51/2 (1992), 340–363.

Syed Mustafizur Rahman, Pares Islam, *Islamic Calligraphy in Mediaeval India* (Bangladesh: University Press Limited, 1979).

Tassy, Garcin de, *Histoire de la littérature hindouie et hindoustanie* (Paris: Adolphe Labitte, 2nd ed., 1870).

Tavernier, Jean-Baptiste, *Les six voyages de Jean-Baptiste Tavernier: Ecuyer, Baron D'aubonne, qu'il a fait en Turquie, en Perse et aux Indes, Pendant quarante Ans* (Paris: Gervais Clouzier [etc.] 1676).

Tavernier, Jean-Baptiste, *The Six Voyages of John Baptiste Tavernier*, trans. J. Phillips, 2 vols (London: Printed for R. L. and M. P., 1678).

Todd, Loreto. *Tortoise the Trickster, and Other Folktales from Cameroon* (London: Routledge & Kegan Paul, 1979).

Todd, Loreto. *Muzd-i Khirad*, trans. ʿAlī Khākbāz (Tehran: Daftar-i Nashr-i Farhang-i Islāmī, 1373/1994).

Tottoli, Roberto, *Biblical Prophets in the Qur'an and Muslim Literature* (London: Routledge, 2002).

Thackston, W. McIntosh (trans.). *A Century of Princes: Sources on Timurid History and Art* (London: Aga Khan Program for Islamic Architecture, 1989).

Vámbéry, Arminius, *Sketches of Central Asia: Additional Chapters on My Travels, Adventures, and on the Ethnology of Central Asia* (London: WM. H. Allen & Co., 1868).

Van Ronkel, P. S. 'Account of Six Malay Manuscripts of the Cambridge University Library', *Bijdragen tot de taal-, land-en volkenkunde/Journal of the Humanities and Social Sciences of Southeast Asia* 46/1 (1896), 1–53.

Van Ronkel, P. S., *De Roman van Amīr Hamza* (Leiden: E. J. Brill, 1895).

Van Ronkel, P. S., *Maleis Woordenboek Maleis – Nederlands Nederlands – Malets In de Officiële Maleise Spelling, vierde druk* (The Hague: Batavia G. B. Van Goor Zonen's Uitgeversmij, 1939).

Versteegh, Kees, 'Can a Language be Islamic?', *Eurasian Studies* 18/1 (2020), 5–25.

Veth, Pieter, J., 'Opmerkingen naar aanleiding van het opstel, Hat Hasan-Hosein of Taboetfeest te Benkoelen', *Internationales Archivfür Ethnographie* 1 (1888), 230–233.

Volkov, Denis V., 'Persian Studies and the Military in Late Imperial Russia (1863–1917): State Power in the Service of Knowledge?' *Iranian Studies* 47/6 (2014), 915–932.

Voorhoeve, P., 'Kutaha, Ketah of Misschien Kutah?', *Bijdragen tot de Taal-, Land- en Volkenkunde* 140 (2/3), 333–334.

Werndly, George H., *Maleische Spraakkunst uit de eige schriften der Maleiers opgemacht met eene Voorreden* (Amsterdam: Wetstein, 1736).

Wieringa, Edwin P., 'Does Traditional Islamic Malay Literature contain Shiitic Elements? Alî and Fâtimah in Malay Hikayat Literature', *Studia Islamika* 3/4 (1996), 93–111.

Wieringa, Edwin P., *Catalogue of Malay and Minangkabau Manuscripts in the Library of Leiden University and Other Collections in the Netherlands. Volume One, Comprising the Acquisitions of Malay Manuscripts in Leiden University Library Up to the Year 1896* (Leiden: Legatum Warnerianum in Leiden University Library, 1998).

Wieringa, Edwin P., 'Pegon', *Encyclopaedia of Islam, THREE*, ed. Kate Fleet, Gudrun Krämer, Denis Matringe, John Nawas, and Everett Rowson (Leiden and Boston: Brill, 2021), 139–140.

Winstedt, Richard O., 'Some More Malay Words', *Journal of the Straits Branch of the Royal Asiatic Society* 80 (1919), 135–137.

Winstedt, Richard O., 'Perak the Arrow-Chosen', *Journal of the Straits Branch of the Royal Asiatic Society* 82 (1920), 137.

Winstedt, Richard O., 'The Malay Annals or Sejarah Melayu', *Journal of the Malayan Branch of the Royal Asiatic Society* 16/3 (1938), 1–226.

Winstedt, Richard O., *A History of Classical Malay Literature* (Kuala Lumpur: Oxford University Press, 1969).

Witkam, Jan J., *Inventory of the Oriental Manuscripts in Leiden University Library* (Leiden: Ter Lugt Press, 2007), vols. 2, 4, 14.

Wright, William *Grammar of the Arabic Language: Founded on the German work of Caspari, and edited, with numerous additions and corrections* (London: MS. Department of British Museum, 1862), vol. 2.

Zahidul Husaini, Qazi Muhammad. *Commentators of the Holy Quran*, trans. S. Naseer-ud-Din (Lahore: Ferozsons, 1992).

Zulkifli, The Struggle of the Shīʿīs in Indonesia (PhD thesis, University of Leiden, 2009).

ابن‌بابویه، ثَواب الأَعْمال وَعِقاب الأَعْمال (قم: دار الشريف الرضي للنشر، 1986/۱۴۰۶)

افغانی‌نویس، عبدالله، لغات عامیانهٔ فارسي افغانستان (بلخ: مؤسسه تحقیقات و انتشارات بلخ، 1990).

بقای وارس بخاری، محمّد، حماسه مسیّب نامه: پیش درآمد ابومسلم نامه، روایت بزرگ آسیای میانه، تصحیح و تحقیق دکتر میلاد جعفرپور، سه جلد (تهران: انتشارات دکتر محمود افشار، 2019/۱۳۹۸).

بی‌نام، داستان کلیات کتاب مسیب نامه: شامل بهترین روایات و اخبار و جنگهای واقعی با قتله حضرت سیدالشهداء و کشته شدن آنها بدست آن نامدار وفادار (تهران: شرکت سهامی چاپ و انتشارات کتب ایران، بی تاریخ).

تبریزی، محمّد حسین، برهان قاطع (کلکته: بی‌جا، 1818).

جمعی از نویسندگان، دانشنامه امام علی، ج ۱ (تهران: سازمان انتشارات پژوهشگاه فرهنگ و اندیشه اسلامی، 2004/۱۳۸۳).

حسن بن ام سینان، المجالس السینانی (بی‌جا، ۱۸۴۴).

رازی، نجم الدین، مرصاد العِباد (تهران: مجلس؟ 1933/۱۳۱۲).

سعدی، مشرف الدین مصلح بن عبدالله، گلستان، مقدّمه و تصحیح محمد علی فروغی (تهران: عارف کامل، 2010/۱۳۸۹).

شهرانی، عنایت‌الله، ضرب‌المثل‌های دری افغانستان (تهران: بنیاد موقوفات دکتر محمود افشار، 2003/۱۳۸۲).

طرسوسی، ابوطاهر، ابومسلم نامه، به کوشش حسین اسماعیلی. ج ۱ (تهران: معین، قطره، انجمن ایران شناسی فرانسه در ایران، 2001/۱۳۸۰).

عاملی، بهاء الدین محمّد بن حسین، مفتاح الفلاح، ترجمهٔ علی بن طیفور (تهران:حکمت، 2011/۱۳۹۰).

عطّار، فرید الدین، تذکرة الاولیاء، مقدّمه، تصحیح و تعلیقات، محمّد رضا شفیعی کدکنی. ج 1 (تهران: چشمه، 2018/۱۳۹۷).

محمّد بن محمّد بهاء الدین، مجموعة أوراد وأحزاب الطریقة النقشبندیة (بیروت: ناشرون، 2013).

میبدی، رشید الدین، کشف الأسرار وعدّة الأبرار، به اهتمام علی اصغر حکمت، ج 10 (تهران: امیرکبیر، 1992/۱۳۷۱).

نسفی، عزیزالدین بن محمّد، کشف الحقّائق، ویراست احمد مهدوی دامغانی (تهران: شرکت انتشارات علمی و فرهنگی، 2005/۱۳۸۴).

واعظ کاشفی، حسین، گنج شهیدان منظوم؛ روضة الشهداء (هندوستان، بی‌جا، 1876).

الواسطي، حافظ أبي الحسن علي بن محمّد، مناقب أمیر المؤمنین علي بن أبي طالب رضي الله عنه، تحقیق وتعلیق: أبي عبد الرحمن ترکي بن عبد الله الوادعي (صنعا: دارالآثار 2003/۱۴۲۴).

Index

ʿAbbās ʿAlī b. ʿAbd al-Qādir 622
ʿAbd al-Ḥakīm 64, 65, 647
ʿAbd al-Jamāl 27
ʿAbd al-Laṭīf Khatāyanī 68, 644
ʿAbd al-Majīd b. Ḥajj Ibrāhīm 19
ʿAbd al-Qādir 617
ʿAbd al-Raḥmān b. Amīr Muḥammad Saʿīd b. Mīr-Muḥammad Ṣādiq b. Mīr-ʿAbdullāh b. Mīr-ʿAbd al-Ghaffār al-Bukhārī 626
ʿAbd al-Raḥmān Khān 623, 655
ʿAbd al-Raḥmān Wāfī 493
ʿAbd al-Waḥīd b. Muḥammad Muftī 43
ʿAbdallāh al-Kafīf 117
ʿAbdallāh Zubayr 110, 437, 439, 473, 475
ʿAbdallāh ʿUmar 475, 477, 491, 493
Abū al-Fidāʾ 10n
Abū Bakr (Abu Bakar) 43, 66, 97, 99, 110, 111, 112, 135, 211, 217, 221, 223, 255, 263, 291, 295, 377, 409, 445, 471, 477, 479, 487, 636, 641
Abū Iṣḥāq al-Ḥimyarī al-ʾAḥbār 116
Abū Isḥāq Nīsāpūrī 90
Abū Jaʿfar al-Bāqir 79
Abū Jahl 66, 68, 97, 99, 211–225, 409, 645
Abū al-Khayr, Abū Saʿīd 26, 43, 139, 389, 525–531, 611, 637, 655
Abū al-Qāsim 485, 493
Abū al-Qāsim Maḥmūd Jayhānī 43
Abū Tammām 26
Abyssinia *also* Abyssininan 10, 119, 517
Academy of Sciences of Tajikistan 52, 59, 73, 127, 637, 658
Academy of Sciences of the Uzbek SSR (Uzbikestan) 46, 48, 637, 650, 669
Aceh, Indonesia *see also* Lamrin xxiv, 11, 18, 24–26, 29, 30n, 35, 36, 532
Acehnese 12, 113
Aden 10
Adham, Ibrāhīm b. 39, 43, 95, 101, 137, 321–327
Afghanistan 105–106, 621, 623n, 654
Afghan; Afghani 11, 129, 621–622, 623, 631, 649–650
Mūsā b. Muḥammad Shaywān Afghān 631
Saʿdullāh b. ʿAbdullāh Afghān 631
Afridūn, the ruler 28
ʿAjāʾib al-Makhlūqāt wa Gharāʾib al-Mawjūdāt 90, 652
ʿAjāʾib al-Qiṣaṣ 43
Akhlāq-i Muḥsinī; *see also* Wāʿiẓ Kāshifī 28, 35, 87
Aleppo, Syria 35
Alexander Turnbull Library, New Zealand 47
ʿAlī Akbar 453, 455, 493, 497, 499, 503
ʿAlī Aṣghar 455, 457, 465, 503, 505, 523
ʿAlī b. Aḥmad b. ʿAlī Mahaymī 62
Aligarh University Library, India 626–627
al-ʿAllāma al-ʿAṣr *see* ʿAbd al-Ghaffār al-Bukhārī
Amīr Aḥmad Khān, the General 623
ʿanbar-i niṣārā 77
andarz-nāma 85
Anjuman-i Taraqqī-yi Urdū 622

ʿAnqā 622
Ansāb al-Ashrāf 104
Ant, the insect 285, 379, 553, 577
Anūshīrwān, Khusraw 8, 650–651
Anwār al-Majālis 54
Anwār-i Suhaylī; see also Wāʿiẓ Kāshifī 35, 44
ʿAqīl ʿAlī 111, 511
Arab Iraq 8–9
Arabic Language 55, 672
Arabic Zone 5–6, 72
Arjuna 34
Armenia *see also* Yerevan 11, 16, 47
Arwī *see also* Tamil 619–620
Ashtar, Ibrāhīm 101, 515, 519, 521
ʿĀshūrāʾ 445, 449, 459, 497, 499, 505
Asia Minor 9
Asiatic Journal 117
Asiatic Society of Bengal 66, 626
Āstān Quds Raḍawī Library, Iran 617
ʿAṭṭār, Farīd al-Dīn 5, 26, 45, 51, 61, 84, 118, 119, 197n, 325, 459n
Auguste de Jaba (Żaba) 73, 650
ʿAwfī, Muḥammad 12, 44
Awrangzib 623
Āyatullāh Marʿashī Najafī Library, Iran 617, 623
Āzādbakht, the King 35
Azerbaijan 9
ʿĀʾisha 93–94, 239, 247, 261, 263, 265, 267, 633

Baalbek, Lebanon 11
Baghdad, Iraq 4–5, 167, 479, 651
Bahār, Muḥammad Taqī 96
Bakhtiyār-nāma 44
Bâlâbâd 21–22
Balādhurī, Aḥmad b. Yaḥyā 104
Balkh, Afghanistan 5, 31, 43–44, 323, 325, 644
Balʿam Bāʿūr 126, 128, 139, 157, 449, 545–549, 611, 628, 636
Balʿamī 66
Bamyan Valley, Afghanistan 105–106
Bandar Abbas, Iran 19
Banil Kalle, Pakistan 106
Banten, Indonesia 15, 19, 575n, 629n
Banyaz 106
Barus 11–12n
Bashkurtustan 71
al-Baṣrī, Ḥasan 43, 137, 353–359, 611, 627
Bastāmī, Bāyazīd/Abū Yazīd 39, 55, 89, 143, 397, 399, 651
Batavia, Indonesia 18–19, 27, 66
Bayazîdî, Mullah Mahmûdê 73n
Beale, Thomas William 49–50
Beejanuggur, India 10, 13
Beijing, China 10–11
Bengal 4–5, 10–13, 16, 32, 39, 49, 64–67, 71, 88, 103, 479, 626, 633, 635–636, 647–648
  Bengali xxii, 49, 64–65, 88, 122, 126, 129–130, 643, 647–648
  Balkans-to-Bengal 4, 39
Bhagavad-Gita 34
Bharatas 45
  Mahabharata 45
Bhulua 64
Bībī Ḥanīfa 105
Bible xxi
Biḥār al-Anwār 114, 479n
Bihar State, India 49, 52
Bihārī script (Bahārī) 58
Bombay, India 62, 626
  Bombay University Library, India 626
Brahmin 45
Brunei 6
Buddhist 45, 64, 76n
  Buddhist Southeast Asian mainland 14
  Buddhist traditions 64
Bukhara 3–5, 30, 49, 51–53, 58–59, 70–71, 637
  Bukhārāʾī 49–50n
  Bukhārī (family, Malfūẓāt, etc.) 48, 55, 59
  Jawharī Bukhārī 35
  Uch-i Bukhārī 53–54
Bukhārī, Abū Naṣr Aḥmad
Bukhārī, Darwīsh Muḥammad b. Dūst Muḥammad 59
Bukhārī, Sayyid Jalāl al-Dīn 52–54, 543
Bunīra 104–106
Buqʿa-yi Mīr Muḥammad-i Ḥanafiyya 105
Burma (Myanmar) xxii, 6, 10n, 14–15n, 18, 87
Būstān al-Salāṭīn 35

Byzantium 57

Cairo, Egypt xxii, 5, 72, 624, 632, 643
Calmucks 10
Cambodia 6, 8, 87n
Candi Uleeblang, Indonesia 25
Cape Colony, South Africa xxi
cat 393, 367
Catholic Church 45
Cerita Tabut 37
Cerita Umar Maya 37
Ceritera Akan Raja Jumjuman 118
Ceritera Nabi Allah 'Isa dan Raja Jumjuma 118
Ceylon (Sarandib; Sri Lanka) 10, 13, 92, 155, 516
Chagatai, the language 35n, 71
  Chagatai-dominated Turkic community 68
Chirāgh Dihlawī, Naṣīr al-Dīn Maḥmūd 53
Chishtī, Sufism 53–54, 56
Chishtī, Abū Layth 52, 627
Chishtī, ʿAbd al-Raḥmān 627
Christianity 75, 117
  Christian 12, 76, 117, 281, 283, 285, 287, 289, 377n, 463
  Christian Arabist 27
  Christian literature 78n
  Christian Persian 18
Collection of Prof. Muḥammad Iqbal Mujaddidi in the Punjab University Library 63n, 657
cow 45, 70, 425, 581, 593
Cumania 10

Damascus 5, 111, 463, 465, 473, 477, 515, 517, 519, 521, 523
Dār al-Amān (Abode of Peace/Security) 10, 17, 363, 413, 621
Dargah Alia Mahdaviya Library 626
Dari, the language 59, 621
Dāstān-i Mūsā 114
David, the King and the Prophet 98, 541, 603, 620, 625, 650
Dawlatabad, India 61
Daydūzamī 65
de-Shīʿitisation xvii, 79, 81–83
Deccan 14, 28n, 63
Deccan, Abdullah 50
Delhi Sultanate, India 14, 31, 36, 44n, 55–56, 59, 62
  Delhi (*also* New Delhi) 11, 14, 52n, 62, 128, 635, 640, 658
Denouserin *see also* Tenasserim, Burma 16–17n
Deo Mahal (Dev Mahal; Diwa-Mahall) 10
Devic, L. Marcel 23
devil 78, 90, 155, 157, 361, 409
  bedevil 579
  devilish 89, 451, 634
Dewi Mariah 93
Di bawah angin 21
Dihistānī, Ḥusayn b. Asʿad 42
Dihlawī, Ḥasan 54, 56, 62
  Dihlawī, Ḥasan Sijzī 267n
Diḥya al-Kalbī 107–108, 273, 443, 495
Dīwān-i Ḥāfiẓ 47
Durar Multaqiṭ 62
Durrani 623
Dutch East India Company 19

Eastern Turkistan 4, 57n, 67
Egypt *see* Cairo
Elephant 16, 56, 495, 517, 521
Ethé, Carl Hermann 42–45, 48, 389n
Ethiopia, the Kingdom 261
  Ethiopian 113, 241, 491
Euphrates 493, 499, 501
Eve 43n, 45, 77–79, 89–90, 111, 153, 155, 461, 507, 652

Fanṣūrī, Hamzah 26–29
  Fanṣūriyyān *see also* wujūdiyya 29
Faqīr b. Ḥusām al-Dīn 622
Faqr-nāma 85, 621, 630
Far East 8, 11, 7, 21, 39
Fars, Iran 10
Favre, L'Abbe P. 114–115
fig tree 78, 89–90, 92, 153
Filipino *see also* Philippines xxii
Fiqh 4, 76
  Ḥayrat al-Fiqh 620
Firdawsī, Abū ʾl-Qāsim 11, 26, 31, 101

Fīrūz Shāh Tughlūq, Sulṭān
Forbidden Tree 77
Fort William College 626
Frashëriri, Şemseddin Sami 50
Free Library of Philadelphia, USA 46, 128, 638–639
Fuḍūlī Baghdādī 14
Futuwwat-nāma-yi Salmāniyyān 15

Gagyānī, Ghulām Muḥammad 64, 649
Georgia 11
Gharqad (Baqīᶜ al-Gharqad) 105
Ghazāt-nāma 67
Ghāzī Miyān 106
Ghazna 11
Maḥmūd of Ghazna 64, 106, 122, 124, 641, 647, 652
Ghaznawid Turks 30–31, 106
Gibberish 16
Giovanni de' Marignolli, Italian traveler 12
Golconda, India 16–17n
Greater Khurasan 5, 12
Grey, Sir George xi, xxi, 641
Guilan, Iran 105
Gujarat, India 10, 13–14
Gujarati 29, 31
Gulbarga, India 10
Gulf of Bengal 16
Gulf of Siam 16
Gulistān 5, 42, 47, 73, 549
Gushāyish-nāma 42

Ḥabīb b. Mālik 97
Ḥafṣa 261–267, 633
Hagar 111, 427, 429, 431, 433
Ḥambiya Muḥammad 106
Ḥanīfa Bānū 100
Hāniphāra Laṛāī 65, 647
Ḥarrānī, Ibn Shuᶜba 114
Ḥasan-Ḥusayn-feest 24
Ḥaydar 101
Ḥaydarābād 626–627
Ḥayrat al-Fiqh 620
Hazaras 59
Hazrat Pir Mohammed Shah Dargah Library of Ahmedabad 48
Herat, Afghanistan 5, 11, 14, 31, 55, 82, 655
Hikayat Abu Syahma 619
Hikayat Ali Kawin dengan Fatimah 95
Hikayat Amir Hamza 32–33, 36–37, 101, 648
Hikayat Balᶜam Bāᶜūr see Balᶜam Bāᶜūr
Hikayat Bayan Budiman 34–37, 95
Hikayat Bulan berbelah 37–38, 66, 96–97, 99
Hikayat Bulan Berbelah Dua 38
Hikayat Ceritera Nabi Musa Munadjat 115
Hikayat Fatimah Berswami 37
Hikayat Firawn 90
Ḥikāyat Ghanim 73
Hikayat Hasan dan Husain 37
Ḥikāyat Jumjuma kih dar ᶜAhd-i ᶜĪsā ᶜalayhi al-salām zinda shud 118
Hikayat kejadian Nur Muhammad 37–38, 121–123
Hikayat Lahad 94
Hikayat Maharaja Ali 119
Hikayat Muhammad Hanafiyya (Hanafiah) 31–33, 36–37, 39, 65, 81, 88, 93, 96, 100, 103, 106–107, 112, 199n, 615
Hikayat Musa Munajat dibukit 113
Hikayat Nabi Bercukur 15
Hikayat Nabi dan Iblis 38, 94
Hikayat Nabi dan Orang Miskin 38, 95
Hikayat Nabi Muhammad Mengajar Anaknya Bibi Fatimah 37
Hikayat Nabi Wafat 37–38
Hikayat Nasiha Lukman al-Hakim 95
Hikayat Nur Muhammad xvii, 32, 37–38, 121, 123
Hikayat Pasai 36
Hikayat Raja Jumjuma 96, 116, 118–119, 130
Hikayat Raja Khandak 37–38
Hikayat Raja Lahad 38
Hikayat Raja Pasai 33
Hikayat Tatkal Fatimah Bertanya kepada Dzulfakar 37
Hikayat Wafat Nabi Muhammad 37
Hikayat Wasiat Lukman al-Hakim 95
Ḥikāyat-i Bakhtiyār see also *Bakhtiyār-nāma* 35
Ḥikāyat-i Kalīla wa Dimna 35
Ḥikāyat-i Muḥammad Ḥanafiyya see also

Hikayat Muhammad Hanafiyya 32
Ḥikāyat-i Pādshāh-i Shām 118
Ḥikāyat-i Qiṣṣa-yi Abū Shaḥma, farzand-i Amīr al-Muʾminīn ʿUmar Khaṭṭāb 619
Hindu 4, 7, 30, 36, 45, 50, 64, 76, 106
Hindu temples 31
Hindustan 9, 13, 57
Hindustani xi, xxi, 35, 50–51, 57, 63, 113, 618, 633, 641
Ḥisārī, Mīr-Mahdī 618
Hitopadesha 119
Hormuz *see also* Jarun 8, 9, 13, 16
Hurgronje, Christiaan Snouck 24, 26, 104, 106
Ḥusām al-Dīn al-Muttaqī al-Hindī 622
Ḥusayn b. Seyfullāh Yamliḥā b. Raḥmān-Qulī 72, 624
Ḥusaynī Hirawī, Amīr Sādāt (Amīr Ḥusaynī) 55

Ibn al-Fāriḍ 26
Ibn al-ʿArabī 26, 29
Ibn Baṭṭūṭa 12
Ibn Masʿūd 241, 477
Ibn Sīnā 77
Ibn ʿAbbās 351, 619–620
Imāmzāda-yi Muḥammad-i Ḥanafiyya 105
India Office 44, 47–48, 58, 63, 626, 632, 635, 657–658
Indian Council for Cultural Relations 46, 48, 52, 128, 626–627, 658
Indus 16
Iranology Foundation xii, 617–618
al-ʿIrāqī, Fakhr al-Dīn 26, 62
Isaac 111
Isfahan 5, 14–17, 47, 644
Iṣfāhānī, Abū Nuʿaym 116
Isḥāq b. Bishr 116
ʿiṣma 15
Italian 16
ʿIzrāʾīl 89, 91, 145, 185, 187, 381, 397, 447, 583, 599

Jakarta, Indonesia xxiv, 19
Jalāliyya 53
Jāmī, ʿAbd al-Raḥmān 29, 44, 62, 630, 637
Jāmiʿ al-Ḥikāyāt 22, 644
Jāmiʿ al-ʿUlūm 54
Jāmiʿ Masjid 622
Jang-nāma 63–64, 67, 88, 639, 645, 648–649
Jang-nāma-yi ʿAlī va Muḥammad Ḥanafiyya 101
Jang-nāma-i Imāmayn Ḥassan wa Ḥusayn 649–650
Jang-nāma-yi Karbalā 640
Jang-nāma-yi Muḥammad Ḥanafiyya xvii, 88, 102, 114

Janu Malik 97
Jarring, Gunnar xvii, 67–69, 71, 129, 658
Jarun *see* Hormuz
Java, Indonesia xvi, 10, 12, 18
Javanese xvi, 10, 15, 19–26n, 34, 65, 90–92, 107, 118, 153, 155, 679
Javanese paper 27
Old Javanese 26
Jawi, the script xi, 20–21, 67, 98, 108, 114, 120, 122
Jaʿfar Bayg Naṣrullāh 627
Jaʿfar Ṣādiq 459, 461, 505
Jaʿfar Ṣādiq, Muḥammad 110–111
Jaʿfar ʿAlī 495
Jeddah, Saudi Arabia 10, 78–79
Jethro, the Prophet 92, 130, 137, 173–177
Jewish 18, 43, 104, 113, 117, 169, 491, 527
Jews 581
Judaism 75
Johnson, Mr. 47
Johol, Malaysia 19
Judeo-Arabic literature 42n
Jummūn (Jammu) 621
Junayd-nāma 107
al-Juwayrī 65–66

Kabarol Akirat 87
al-Kāfī 15, 655
Kalāla 620
Kamus-ül alâm 50
Karbala 24, 65, 106–108, 110, 137, 235, 255, 431, 443, 447, 449, 459n, 467, 469, 471, 485, 487, 491, 495, 507, 509, 513, 523, 615, 635, 640–641
Kashf al-Rumūz 22

Kashgar (Qäshqär) 68, 71, 629, 643
Muḥammad Ṣādiq Kāshgarī 68
Kauravas 34
Kaysāniyya 80, 105n
Kazan xiii, 49, 71, 129, 654
Kaʿb al-Aḥbār 117, 587
Kedah *see also* Zamīn Turan 24, 35
Kedah Annal 35
Kedah legend
Khadīja, Prophet's wife 66, 98, 111, 217, 223, 225, 227, 255, 477, 485, 633, 641
Khālid b. Naṣr 493
Khālid b. Walīd 76, 93, 279–289, 137, 609
Khambhat, India 10, 13
Khān Bālīgh 10
Kharaqānī, Abū al-Ḥasan 619
Kharg Island, Iran 105
Khayyām 26
Khiḍr 55, 311, 634
Khirqa 53, 55
Khitāyāy 57
Khiva, Central Asia 68, 70, 638, 644
Khoja Ḥasan Baṣrī 627 *see also* al-Baṣrī
Khoja Kumayl 627
Khoqand 70
Khudabaksh Oriental Public Library 52, 58, 626
Khulāṣa ʿIlm al-Ṣarf 27
Khurasan *see* Greater Khurasan
Khurasanian 12
Khutan 57
Khwāja Niẓām al-Mulk 87
Khwāja Shāh Muḥammad b. Khwāja Muḥammad Ṭāhir Laylakī 617
Khwarāzm Shāh Bahādur Sulṭān, Ibn Abū al-Muẓaffar Muʿīn al-Dīn 644
King Bakti 93
King Mindon 18
King Muḥammad 93
King of Iram 101
Kipchak *see* Cumania
al-Kirmānī, Awḥad al-Dīn 26, 618
Kisah al-anbiyāʾ 90–91
Kisāʾī 65–66
Kitab Ahlu Tafsir 90
Kitāb al-Faraj baʿd al-Shidda 3
Klang, Malaysia 12
Krishna District of India 622
Krut (Lho' Kruet, Krudai, and Daya) 11
Kubrā, Najm al-Dīn 627
Kufa, Iraq 447, 449, 489, 491, 509
Kurdistan, the Iraqi region of 652
Central Kurdistan 24
Kurds 6, 73
Kurmanji, the language xix, 6, 73, 129, 643, 650, 652

Lahore, Pakistan 49, 128–129, 621, 628, 631, 653
Lāla, Mawlānā 621
Lamrin, 11 *see* Aceh
Laos 6
Laylī and Majnūn 51, 209, 319
Levant 4–5n, 8, 11, 73, 118, 128, 139, 587, 611
lion 449n, 457, 493, 497, 499, 501, 509, 513, 523
lion-hearted 105
Lion of God 257
Lisbon, Portugal xxi

Machīlī-Bandar *also* Machilipatnam 622
madrasa 6, 46–47, 62, 71, 637
Mahdī, the Imam 105, 622
Maḥmūd Ghūrī 31
Ghurid Empire 31
Maḥmūd-Bandar, Hindustan 619
Majālis-i tadhkīr 44
Majd al-Dīn Muḥammad al-Ḥusaynī 44
Majlipatan (Masulipatam) 16
Majmaʿ al-Nuqūl 42
Majmūʿih-yi Khānī 15
Makhdūm-i Jahāniyyan 52
Manāqib-i Makhdūm-i Jahāniyyān 54
Makhdūmiyya 53
Malabar, India 10, 13
Malacca (Melakha) 10n, 12–13, 16–18, 33–34, 36, 101, 103
Malaysia xii, xxii, xxiv, 6–7, 12, 15, 19
Maldives 10n
Malfūẓāt 53–55
Malik al-mawt *see* ʿIzrāʾīl

Mālik Dīnār 87, 235, 237
Manār al-Musāfirīn 620
Mansoureh 31
Manṣūr b. Khalaf 42
Maqtal-nāma 42, 63, 631
Marāḥ al-Arwāḥ 27
Marcel, Jean-Joseph 72, 632
Mardin, Turkey 11
Māriya al-Qibṭiya *see* Mary the Copt
Marong Mahawangsa 35 *see also* Kedah Annals
Marwān 111, 513, 515
Mary, mother of Jesus 111, 130
Mary the Copt 93, 137, 199, 261–267, 609, 633–634, 641
Mashīb bi-Kāqah *see* Musayyib Qaʿqaʿ
Mashots Matenadaran Library, Armenia 11
Maṭlaʿ al-Saʿdayn wa Majmaʿ al-Baḥrayn 5n, 9, 13
Mausoleum of Ṣafī al-Dīn Ardabīlī 127, 617–618
Maysan 78n
Māzandarānī, Muḥammad Taqī 14, 87
  Safīna-yi Māzandarānī 87
Mehmed Oğlu Tahir Efendi 72
Meinsma, J. J. 117–118
Mela Mahmût Beyazîdî 73, 650
Mesopotamia 17
Mirāth-i Maktūb collection, Iran 617
Mīrzā Afrāsiyāb Bayg 622
Mīrzā Changīz 622
Mīrzā Jamshīd Bayg 622
Mīrzā Muḥammad Diyūbandī 623
Mīrzā Rustam Beig/Bayg 622
Mīrzā Suhrāb Bayg 622
Mirʾat al-Asrār 627
Mirʾāt al-Muʾminīn 27
Moghul India 14
Mohamadan Histories of India 49
Mojopait (Majapahit) 12
Mombasa, Kenya xxi
Mongol Il-Khan dynasty 14
Mongolia 57, 68, 646
Moresco 16
Moultan (Multan) 11, 31, 49, 52–53, 56, 59
Mount Sinai 84, 113, 137, 179, 185, 293, 553, 557, 585, 609
Mountain of Ceylon 92n
Mountains of Raḍwā 105n
Mozambique xxi, 641
Mufarraḥ al-Qulūb 119
Mughan Turk 112
Muḥammad b. Abū Bakr 110
Muḥammad b. ʿUmar al-Wāqidī 104
Muḥammad Ḥanīfa 100, 126 *see* Muḥammad Ḥanafiyya
Muḥammad Muʿaẓẓam Bahādur-Pādshāh 622
Mukhtār-nāma 107
Mulla Firuz Library 626
Mullā Muḥammad Qāsim-jān 622
Mullā Muḥammad Rāziq 629
Mullā Mūsā Hikkārī 73, 650
Mullā Tūkhta Īlmādūz 70, 643
Munājāt-nāma 41, 82, 615
  Musa Munajat 91, 96, 113, 564n
  Mūsā-nāma 41, 84, 114, 564n, 585, 648
Munkar and Nakīr 121, 399, 531, 541, 567, 591
Murshidabad, Bengal 19, 32, 65, 88, 635
Mūsā Ashʿarī 110, 437, 439, 475, 477, 505
Musayyib Qaʿqaʿ (Mashīb bi-Kāqah) 111, 511, 515
al-Muslim 96
Muslim ʿAlīds 13
Muʾmin-jān, Muḥammad 621

Nabīvaṃśa 65–66
al-Nasafī, Najm al-Dīn 29
al-Nasāʾī 96, 355
Naṣīḥat-nāma 85
Nasikhun, J. 114–115
Nastal (Nastala) 111, 458
National Archives of the Republic of Indonesia 19
National Library of Iran 9, 13, 46, 48, 52, 85, 101, 114, 117–119, 617, 623, 657–658
National Library of Malaysia 19
Nawrūz 619
Nāʾinā Ḥusām al-Dīn 25
Negeri Sembilan, Malaysia 19
Nestorian Christians 12
Nimrod 219, 427, 652
Nimruz Province, Afghanistan 106

Nīshābūrī, Niẓām al-Dīn 61
Nishapur 5, 42
  King of Nishapur *see* Chapter 26
Niẓāmī Ganjawī 51
Noah 98, 111, 265, 461, 507, 652
Nur Muhammad, a person's name 66–67

O'Kinealy, James 66, 636

P. Van der Vorm 27
Panchur *see also* Barus, Indonesia
Pand-nāma 85
Pandavas 34
Pandua 10n
Panggaga Micky 87
Parangippettai 619
Pars 12
Parsees 12
Pasai, Indonesia 12, 25, 31, 36
Pāyanda Nā-murād 618
peacock 79
Pedir Museum, Indonesia 24n
Pegon 20–21
Pegu 16
Peninsula of Malacca *see* Malacca
Pentateuch 113; *see also* Bible
Perak 24
Persian Gulf, Iran 8–9, 17, 20, 105
Persian Safawids 16–17, 107
Persian Shīʿī 14–15, 19, 24, 61, 80, 87, 495n
Persophone 25
Peshawar 31, 628, 654n
Philippines 6, 87
Phillott D. C. 80
Philological and Physical Science Committees of the Asiatic Society of Bengal 66
polygamy 104
Portuguese 12n, 16, 18, 33–34, 103
Prayer of the Crazy Dog (*duʿā-yi sag-i dīwāna*) 619
Pulton Bazzar 627

Qāḍī Shihāb al-Dīn Dawlatābādī al-Dihlawī 62
Qāsim ʿUmar 495
al-Qazwīnī *see* ʿAjāʾib al-Makhlūqāt wa Gharāʾib al-Mawjūdāt
Qing dynasty 70
  Qing officials 70
Qipchaq plain *see* Cumania 10
qiṣaṣ al-anbiyāʾ 39, 42, 66, 88, 92, 113
  Qiṣṣa-yi Anbiyāʾ 620
  Qiṣaṣ al-Anbiyāʾ-i Nayshāpūrī 42
Qiṣṣa-yi Amīr al-Muʿminīn Ḥasan wa Ḥusayn 32; see also *Hikayat Muhammad Hanafiyya*
Qiṣṣa-yi Wafāt-i Ḥaḍrat Fāṭima 625
Qïzïl Chapchak 71
Qum, Iran 617
al-Qummī, Ibn Bābawayh 81
Qurbān Muḥammad Bāy Yār 59
Qūshchī, Muḥammad 619
Quṭbī, Ibrāhīm Aḥmad 52

Rāḍī-nāma 84, 114, 644
Radsehkran and Chayath 42
Rāfiḍī 15
Rāḥat al-Qulūb 619
Raḥmān Qulī b. Mullā Yāghmurjī 68, 646
Rampur Reza Library 626
al-Ranīrī al-Sūratī, Nūr al-Dīn 29–30n, 35, 113
Rawḍat al-Shuhadāʾ 80, 126n, 631, 635, 640–641n; *see* Wāʿiẓ Kāshifī
Rawżat al-Aḥbāb 82n
Reland, Adriaan 23
Rembau *also* Rimbu 19
Rich, Claudius James 47
Rind wa Zahid 14
al-Rūmī, Jalāl al-Dīn 26, 29, 44–45, 52, 61, 293n, 389n, 545, 551n, 619, 637
Rūzbihān Baqlī 26

Saba (Shabat) 12
Safīna-yi Māzandarānī *see* Māzandarānī
Safīna-yi Sulaymanī 14
Sālār Masʿūd 106
Sāliḥ 111
Samanid Empire 30
Samarkand *also* Samarqand 5, 14, 30, 59

Samarqandī, Imam 618
al-Samarqandī, ʿAbd al-Raḥīm b. ʿAbd al-Raḥmān 627
al-Samarqandī, ʿAbd al-Razzāq 9, 56n–57
al-Samhūdī, ʿAlī b. Aḥmad 105
Sanskrit 34–35, 65, 67, 119
Sarah 111, 461, 507
Sarntip 11; *see also* Ceylon
Sasanid 8
Sayābija *also* Zābag 8
Sayyid Muḥammad b. Sayyid Yūsuf Ḥusaynī Shāh Rajū Qattāl *also* Banda Nawāz 62
Saʿdī Shīrāzī 5, 25–26, 34n, 42, 44–45, 47, 51–52, 55, 61–62, 73, 423n, 441, 533, 543, 549, 625
Schröder, Johann Wilhelm 23
Schröder, Nikolaus Wilhelm 23
Secotora 10
Sejarah Melayu 23, 33–36n, 101, 103
Serat Anbiya 90
Serat Raja Kepala 118
serpent 219
Shabistarī, Maḥmūd 26, 29
Shah Abbas II 16
Shahbāz Qalandar 19
Shāhnāma 101; *see also* Firdawsī
Shahr-i Naw, Thailand 10
Shahrbānū 112–113, 473, 475, 477, 499, 503
Shām *see* Levant
Shamir (Shimr) 63, 110, 457, 461, 491, 493, 499, 503, 515
Sharaf b. Ḥusayn al-Marḥūm Qara-Qālpāq (Karakalpak) 624
Shaw, Henry xi, xxi
shaykh al-islām, in Aceh 29
Shaykh Ḥamīdullāh 617
Shaykh Muḥammad b. Shaykh Saʿdullāh 623, 631
Shaykh Niẓām al-Dīn Awliyāʾ 54
Shayth *also* Seth 92
Shirani Collection 42, 628, 631
Shīʿism 14, 24, 36, 80, 82, 105
  Shīʿī Persian 14, 17
Siberia 5, 57n
Sindh 8n, 11, 59n
Singapore 6, 35n, 658
Siraf, Iran 8
Sirāj al-Hidāya 54
Soran, Kurdistan 129, 652
al-Suhrawardī, Shihāb al-Dīn 53
Suhrawardiyya 56
Śukasaptati 34
Sullam al-Anbiya' 48
Suluk Pathak 118
Sunni xvii, 17, 20, 53, 81, 82–83, 107, 126, 130, 636–637, 646
  anti-Sunni sentiment 14
Sūrat al-Raḥmān 495
al-Suyūṭī 27, 629
Syriac 16, 620

al-Ṭabrisī 96
Tabriz, Iran 5, 14, 111, 511, 519
Tabut festival 111
Tadhkirat al-Awliyāʾ 51, 325n, 423n, 459n; *see also* ʿAṭṭār
tafsīr 4, 113, 401n
  Tafsīr al-Bayḍāwī 59, 620
  Tafsīr Baḥr al-Mawwāj 620
  Tafsīr-i Ḥusaynī 620
  Tafsīr al-Jalālayn 628
  Tafsīr Kashf al-Asrār, of Rashīd al-Dīn Maybudī 261n, 401n, 423n
  Tafsīr Majmaʿ al-Bayān 96
  Tafsīr Muqātil 401n
Tāj al-Qiṣaṣ 43
Tāj al-Salāṭīn 35, 87
Talaat Library, Egypt xii, 72, 127, 624
Ṭalḥa ʿAlī 495, 497
Tamil Nadu, India 619
  Tamil (language) 619; *see also* Arwī
  Tamils xxii
Tamīm Ansārī 126, 641, 648
Tanah diatas angin 22
al-Tanūkhī 42
Tapel Adam 90–92n, 153
Tarīḥī, Fakhr al-Dīn 114
Tārīkh-i Mūsāwī 626
Tartus 5
Tashkent, Uzbekistan 129, 637, 654

Tataristan 5, 57n
Tavernier, Jean-Baptiste 16–17n
Ṭawāf 110
Tawallud-nāma 63–64, 114, 126, 630–631, 640–641, 649
Taʾrīkh al-Ṭabarī 90
Tenasserim 10, 14, 16; *see also* Denouserin
Teungku Sareh 25
Thailand xxii, 6, 10, 14–16n
al-Thaʿlabī 65, 77–79
Timurids 14
Tippo Sultan of Mysore 626
al-Tirmidhī 96, 618–619
Transoxiana 10
Ṭūbā Tree 283, 599
Tugha; Tughan Turk 56, 111–112, 511, 515, 517, 519
Tur Sina 113
Turan 4n, 56
Turānshāh, Fakhr al-Dīn 9
Turkey 6, 11, 28, 44, 50n, 72–73, 127, 449, 623, 637, 643
Turkic xiii, xvii, xxii, 49, 56, 67–71, 103n, 114, 129, 643
Turkistan *also* Eastern Turkistan xiv, 4, 5, 10, 24, 57, 67–68, 70, 101, 114, 633–634, 643–644
Ṭūsī, Naṣīr al-Dīn 42n
Ṭūṭī-nāma 34–35n, 44, 95
Twelver Khoja xix

ʿUbaydallāh b.ʿAbdallāh 22
ʿUbaydallāh Ziyād 499, 515
ʿUmar ʿAlī 111, 511, 517, 519
Umm Salama 110, 447, 485, 487
  University of Tehran Library 119, 617
Urdu xix, 63n, 130, 619, 622–623, 625–627, 639–641, 647
ʿUthman, the Caliph 43, 135, 255, 295, 377, 409, 415, 417, 419, 445, 471, 487, 643

Victorian era xix
Vietnam 6, 8

Wafāʾ al-Wafā 105
waḥdat al-wujūd 29
  Wujūdiyya 29n
Wali Ahmad Khan 623
Wāʿiẓ Kāshifī 28, 35, 44, 80, 87, 620, 635, 640

Xinjiang, China xv, 68–70

Yanbu 10
Yarkand 68
Yatīm-nāma 85
Yerevan 11; *see also* Armenia
Yūnus b. Iskandar 68

Zakariyyā, Bahāʾ al-Dīn 52, 56
al-Zamakhsharī 44, 61–62
Zamīn Turan 24; *see also* Kedah
Zanggi 112
Zanzibar *also* Zansibar 10
Zayn al-ʿĀbidīn 107, 523, 645
Zaynab bint ʿAlī 465
Zaynab bint Jaḥsh 483n
Zīfnūn 101
  Zīghanūn *also* Zīghnūn 101
Zindīq 29, 325n
Zirbâd 21–22n
Zoroastrians 12
Zubayr ʿAlī 495, 519
Zulaykha (Zulaykhā) 92, 147, 149, 315, 317, 377, 651
Zuṭṭ 8
Zuzan 24

مغولستان ۶۸، ۵۱۶
مفتاح الفلاح ۵۵۸
مگس انگبین ۲۶۲
ملاّ محمّد رازیق ۷۱
ملیبار ۹
ممبوسا ۶۸۰
منطق الطّیرِ عطاّر ۶۸۰
منکر و نکیر ۳۹۸، ۴۰۶، ۵۳۰، ۵۴۰، ۵۶۶، ۵۸۴، ۵۹۰، ۵۹۲
موزامبیک ۶۸۰
موزۀ پای ۴۸۲
مولانا بنگرید به مثنوی معنوی

ناستال (نستال) ۴۵۸
ناصرعلی سرهندی ۳۳۴
نجف ۵۱۰، ۵۸۶
نراقی ۴۴۸، ۴۵۶، ۴۵۸
نسفی، عزیزالدین بن محمّد ۲۱۴
نظامی گنجوی ۲۱۴
نغمۀ داودی ۵۴۰
حلق داودی ۵۴۰
نقره همچنین زر سفید ۹، ۴۴۴، ۵۸۸
نقرۀ خام ۵۷۴

وادي السلام ۵۸۶
واعظ کاشفی ۳۹۰، ۴۵۴

هارون الرشید ۳۲۰، ۳۲۲
هرات، افغانستان ۶۸۰
هرموز ۹
هکاری همچنین هه کاری\حکاری ۶۸۰

یاقوت ۲۵۴، ۳۵۰، ۳۵۶، ۵۸۶، ۵۹۲
یاقوت سرخ ۴۸۶
یأجوج و مأجوج ۵۸۲
یزیدیان ۴۷۸، ۴۹۴، ۴۹۶، ۵۰۰، ۵۱۲، ۵۱۶، ۵۱۸، ۵۲۰، ۵۲۲
ینبوع ۹

رود نیل ۱۸۰، ۱۸۲، ۱۸۴، ۲۱۸، ۲۸۴

زبرجد ۳۵۶
زبور ۱۲۲، ۶۰۲، ۶۲۹
زبور یونانی ۶۲۰
زرتشتی ۱۶۲
زغن ۱۹۰
زمرّد ۴۸۶
زن لوط ۲۶۴
زن نوح ۲۶۴
زنبور عسل ۲۶۲
زنگبار ۹
زهراب ۵۷۰
زینب بنت علي ۴۶۴
زینب بُنتِ جحش ۴۸۲

سال مرغ ۷۰
سجزی دهلوی، حسن ۲۶۶
سرون ۵۹۲
سعدی شیرازی ۱۴۲، ۳۱۶، ۳۲۰، ۳۷۶، ۴۲۲، ۴۴۰، ۴۴۶، ۵۰۲، ۵۳۲، ۵۴۲، ۵۴۸، ۶۸۰
سفر دانیال ۵۳۸
سقط جنین ۴۰۲
سقوطره ۹
سمرقند ۶۸۰
سمرقندی ۵۱۶
سُندُس ۳۵۸، ۵۲۴
سندیان ۹
سیام (تایلند) ۱۶۶، ۶۸۰
سیلان ۹، ۵۱۶

شجرهٔ گندم ۱۵۲
شمر ۴۳۰، ۴۵۶، ۴۶۰، ۴۸۸، ۴۹۲، ۴۹۶، ۵۰۲، ۵۱۴
شهربانو ۴۷۲، ۴۷۴، ۴۷۶، ۴۹۸، ۵۰۴
شیعیان پارسی زبان ۱۶۶

صفویه ۱۶۶؛ همچنین شیعیان پارسی

طبری ۲۶۰، ۴۵۸، ۴۷۲
تاریخ طبری ۴۵۸، ۴۷۲
تفسیر طبری ۲۶۰
طشت خانه ۵۲۲
طوغان ترک ۵۱۴، ۵۱۶، ۵۱۸

عاشورا ۴۴۴، ۴۴۸، ۴۵۸، ۴۹۶، ۴۹۸، ۵۰۴، ۵۰۶، ۵۵۶
عشور (به ترکی ترکستانی) ۷۰
عاملی، بهاء الدین محمد بن حسین ۵۵۸
عبد شمس ۴۷۲
عبدالله مبارك ۳۵۴
عبدالمطلب ۴۷۲
عبدمناف ۴۷۲
عُتبة الغلام ۴۵۸
عدن ۹
عراق ۵۱۰، ۵۸۶
عراق عجم ۹
عراق عرب ۹
عراقیان ۹
عراقی، فخرالدین ۵۱۶
عنبر سرشت ۵۵۸
عنبرنسارا همچنین عنبر نصارا ۳۱۰
عنصری ۳۳۰
عوفی ۳۶۴

غایط ۲۸۲
غزالی، محمّد ۶۰۴
غزنوی، محمود ۶۰۴، ۶۰۶
غلیواز (غلیواژ، غلیواج، غلیواج، خلواج و خلیواج) ۱۹۰، ۱۹۶

فرّخی سیستانی ۳۰۶، ۳۳۰
فردوستان ۴۷۸

قاچین همچنین قاچیون ۵۱۶
قبچاق، دشت ۹
قدم جای ۲۷۰، ۲۷۲
قشلاق ۵۷
قصص القرآن ۵۸۶، ۵۸۸، ۵۹۴
قلماق ۹
قیصر ۵۸

کاشقر همچنین کاشغر ۷۱-۷۰
کافور ۴۶۲
کالج امانوئل ۲۱۰
کرّوبیان ۴۴۶
کژدم همچنین عقرب ۳۷۸، ۴۳۸، ۴۶۶، ۴۸۰، ۵۷۰
کشف الحقائق ۲۱۴
کنبات ۹
کنعان ۳۶۲
کوفه ۴۴۶، ۴۴۸، ۴۸۸، ۴۹۰، ۵۰۸
کوه عرفات ۱۵۴
کوه قاف ۵۲۲
گجرات ۹
گجراتی ۴۷۴
گلبرگه ۹
گلستانِ سعدی؛ بنگرید به سعدی شیرازی

لمعاتِ عراقی؛ بنگرید به عراقی
لوط بنگرید به زن لوط

ماوراء النهر ۹
ماه عشور بنگرید به عاشورا
مثنوی مولوی (مثنوی معنوی) ۲۹۲، ۴۰۴، ۴۸۴، ۵۴۴
مجنون و لیلی ۲۰۸، ۳۱۸
مجوس ۱۶۲
محرّق القلوب ۴۴۸، ۴۵۸
مرصاد العباد ۳۹۶
مسیّب قعقاع ۵۱۰
مسیّب نامه ۵۱۰
مُشک ۱۵۴، ۲۱۴، ۲۹۴، ۴۵۸، ۵۰۶، ۶۰۲

فهرست

آچه، اندونزی ۴۷۴، ۵۳۲

آذربایجان ۹

آزر ۱۳۶، ۱۵۶؛ بنگرید به باب بیستم

آستانه ۵۳۸

آسیا «دندان؛ خرد کننده» ۵۳۴

آسیای مرکزی یا میانه ۲۱۴، ۳۱۲، ۴۷۴، ۴۸۰، ۵۵۶، ۵۸۰، ۶۸۰

آسیای جنوبی ۱۴۲، ۳۹۶، ۴۰۶، ۴۴۸، ۴۷۸، ۴۹۲، ۵۸۰، ۶۷۸، ۶۸۰

آسیای جنوب شرق ۱۵۲، ۱۶۶، ۴۰۶، ۵۵۶، ۶۷۷، ۶۷۹

آعجش ۵۱۲

آفتاب حرّا ۳۰۶

آکلند، زلاند نو ۴۷۰، ۴۸۴، ۵۵۲، ۵۵۴، ۵۶۰، ۵۶۲، ۵۶۴، ۵۶۶، ۵۶۸، ۵۸۲، ۵۹۸، ۶۰۶، ۶۷۷، ۶۷۸، ۶۷۹

آلت تناسلی زنان ۳۱۰

آلت تناسلی مردان ۲۴۶، ۳۱۰، ۴۳۸

آهو؛ ج. آهوان ۱۶۴، ۳۹۴، ۴۵۶

ابراهیم اشتر ۵۱۴، ۵۱۸، ۵۲۰

ابراهیم عستر ۵۱۴

ابلیس ۵۵۲، ۵۵۴، ۵۸۰

ابن بابویه ۴۷۲، ۴۹۴

ابن عباس ۳۵۰، ۵۴۰

قاسم ابن عباس ۴۳۸

ابن مسعود ۲۴۰، ۲۴۲، ۴۷۶

ابوبکر ۱۳۴، ۲۱۰، ۲۱۶، ۲۲۰، ۲۲۲، ۲۵۴، ۲۶۲، ۲۹۰، ۲۹۴، ۳۷۶، ۴۴۴، ۴۷۰، ۴۷۶، ۴۷۸، ۴۸۶، ۶۷۸

جعفر ابن ابوبکرنصدیق ۱۱۱

ابوجهل ۴۰۸؛ بنگرید به باب هفتم

ابوحنیفه، فقیه ۳۶۲

ابوسفیان ۴۷۲

ابومسلم نامه ۵۱۰

اردبیل ۱۴۴، ۶۸۰

ارسلان ترک۵۱۶، ۵۱۸

اژدها ۹۹، ۲۱۸

استانبول ۶۸۰

ترکی استانبولی (ترکی عثمانی) ۲۱۲، ۳۳۸، ۵۱۶، ۵۹۸

اسرافیل ۱۴۴، ۴۴۶، ۵۹۸

اسماعیل، فرزند ابراهیم ۱۴۶، ۴۲۶، ۴۲۸، ۴۳۰، ۴۳۲، ۴۵۶، ۵۰۲

اسماعیل، فرزند جعفر صادق ۶۲

اشعهٔ جامی ۶۸۰

اصحاب کهف بنگرید به باب سی و چهارم

سگ اصحاب کهف ۱۵۶، ۵۴۶، ۵۴۸

امّ کلثوم ۴۵۴، ۵۰۴

امام اعظم ۳۶۲

امام جعفرصادق ۶۲، ۱۶۰، ۴۵۸، ۴۶۰

امام جعفر عمر ۶۲۹

امر به معروف و نهی از منکر ۵۵۶

امیر حسینی ۱۴۲

امیرعسس ۳۲۰

انجیر ۱۵۲

انجیل ۱۲۲، ۲۹۸، ۶۰۲، ۶۲۹

انجیل سریانی ۶۲۰

اندونزی ۵۳۲، ۵۷۴، ۶۰۰، ۶۷۹؛ همچنین بنگرید به آچه

مالایا-اندونزی ۱۳۲، ۲۱۰، ۳۹۶، ۴۳۸، ۴۷۴، ۵۳۲، ۵۶۴، ۵۹۸، ۶۷۷، ۶۷۸

اهل بیت پیامبر ۲۶۶، ۴۵۰، ۴۵۲، ۴۵۴، ۴۵۶، ۴۶۰، ۴۶۴، ۵۰۴

ایغور، ایغور ۶۸۰

بامیان ۵۰۸، ۵۲۲

باوریا، مونیخ ۲۷۰، ۵۲۴، ۵۱۶، ۶۰۶

بِبُر ۴۹۶

بخارا (تاریخ بخارا) ۵۵۸، ۶۸۰

سید جلال الدین بخاری ۵۴۲

براق ۴۱۲، ۵۶۲

برهان قاطع ۵۵۸، ۶۷۹

بریلویه ۳۹۶

بسمل [کردن]۱۶۴، ۴۲۸، ۴۶۸

بقعهٔ شیخ صفیّ الدین اردبیلی ۶۷۸

نسخهٔ شیخ صفیّ الدین اردبیلی ۱۳۴

بلال ۱۳۶، ۱۵۶، ۴۱۶، ۶۰۸؛ بنگرید به

داستان سی و یکم (نسخهٔ طولانی)، در مورد شهادت حسن و حسین و انتقام محمّد حنفیّه از یزید بن معاویه، براساس این سه نسخه ویرایش و ترجمه شده است. همچنین داستان بلعم باعور که در ادبیات اسلامی هند و بنگال و آسیای جنوب شرقی ریشه دوانده است تنها در گنج‌بخش پاکستان ۰۰۱-۱۰۴۳ و لایدن ۵۶۵ وجود دارد. برخی از قسمت‌های داستان موسیٰ در فصل چهارم براساس آکلند ۱۷۰ و ترجمه‌های ترکی و مالایی درّالمجالس صورت پذیرفته‌است. داستان شناخته شدهٔ شاه-جمجمه در مورد برخورد عیسیٰ با یک جمجمهٔ سپید رنگ، که در اکثر مناطق جهان اسلام بویژه مالایا-اندونزی دیده می‌شود تنها درمتن فارسی آکلند ۱۷۰ یافت می‌شود. نورنامهٔ پیامبر اسلام براساس آکلند ۱۷۰، آکلند ۱۷۳ و نسخهٔ ۸۱۴۹ کتابخانهٔ بریتانیا ویرایش شده است.

- شیوهٔ بهره‌گیری از نسخه‌های اساس و بدل در بخش انگلیسی و به شیوه‌ای مفصّل توضیح داده شده است.
- برای دستیابی به لیست اکثر نسخ خطّی و چاپی درّالمجالس به بخش ضمائم مراجعه شود.

از نظرات کارشناسانهٔ رادمان رسولی مهربانی، دوستی فرهیخته و صبور، پیرامون ویرایش این اثر سپاسگزاری می‌نمایم. از زحمات و حمایت‌های بی‌دریغ اندرو پیکاک، سردبیر محترم، و امیر دستمالچیان، طراح حرفه‌ای و مدیر مرکز ادونت، بسیار سپاسگزارم . دستان محسن فیض‌بخش عزیز را برای حمایت‌های بی‌دریغش در طی سال‌های گذشته به گرمی می‌فشارم.

قدردان خانوادهٔ نازنینم - آذرهمسری باوفا و عاشق، شهد دختری شیرین‌تر از عسل، و مهر پسری چون آفتاب تابان -دیگر دوستان و همکاران خود در اقصی نقاط این جهان پرآشوب هستم. در پایان این اثر را به دکتر یوتا شوریگِ شهرِ فرایبورگِ آلمان، انسانی وارسته، خوش‌صفت و زبان-دان تقدیم می‌کنم.

تنها اینجانب مسئول هرگونه کاستی و خطایی هستم که در این کتاب یافت می‌شود.

مجید دانشگر

از شرقی‌ترین شرق

کیوتو - ژاپن

خرداد ماه ۱۴۰۳

- شیوهٔ نگارش نام «ابوبکر» به‌صورت «ابابکر» که در برخی مناطق آسیای جنوبی وغربی به‌کار می‌رود نیز دیده می‌شود.
- بنابر فضای داستان مربوطه، نامِ عمربن خطّاب گاهاً با آوانویسی «عُمَر» ارائه شده است تا از خوانش اشتباه آن به‌صورت «عُمَر» جلوگیری شود.
- در مواردی که واژهٔ «الهی» به شکل درخواست و در قالب تضرّع به‌کار می‌رفته به‌شیوهٔ «إلٰهِيّ» نگاشته شده‌است.
- اکثر آیات قرآنی بر اساس «الرسم العثماني» نگاشته شده‌اند، و برای سلام و صلوات‌های ویژهٔ پیامبران، امامان و اولیاء الله و برخی عناوین و القاب عربی یکسان‌سازی صورت گرفته است.
- واژهٔ «صلعم» که به‌وفور پس از ذکر نام پیامبر اسلام دیده می‌شود اشاره به عبارت «صَلَّی اللّٰهُ عَلَیْهِ وَسَلَّم» دارد.
- براساس نسخه‌های مورد بررسی، برخی واژگان به شیوه‌های متفاوت نگاشته شده‌اند: زنهار و زینهار؛ رحمت الله و رحمة الله؛ اسب و اسپ.
- «فاطمه زهرا» غالباً و براساس فضای داستان مربوطه به شکل «فاطمهٔ زهرا» نوشته شده است.
- واژهٔ «مولا» به شیوهٔ «مولی» نوشته می‌شود.
- تعداد بسیار زیادی از نسخ خطّی درّالمجالس، خواه به زبان فارسی خواه به زبان‌های دیگر، به شکل‌های متفاوت (کامل یا جزءجزء) در جهان وجود دارد. از اینرو، بهره‌گیری از تنها یک نسخهٔ اساس امری غیرممکن است. متن ویراستی فارسی درّالمجالس براساس مطالعهٔ دقیق نسخ و آثار چاپی متعدّد صورت گرفته است. نسخ خطّی آکلند زلاندنو ۱۷۰، گنج‌بخش پاکستان ۱۴۹۸-۰۰۱ و لایدن ۵۶۵ علاوه بر جامعیّت بیشترین شباهت موضوعی را با داستان‌های بنیادین در ادبیات اسلامی مالایی-اندونزیایی دارا می‌باشند. آنجا که آکلند ۱۷۰ ناقص یا نامفهوم بوده به دو نسخهٔ دیگر رجوع شده است. پس از در نظر گرفتن این سه نسخهٔ حیاتی، و به منظور بالابردن سطح کیفیّت اثر، چهار نسخهٔ دیگر را مورد مطالعهٔ موشکافانه قرار داده‌ام: نسخ ۳۳ بقعهٔ شیخ صفیّ الدین اردبیلی ایران، ۵۳ کتابخانهٔ طلعت مصر، ۸۵۳ کتابخانهٔ دانشگاه میشیگان ایالات متّحدهٔ آمریکا و ۱۲۲۲ بنیاد علوم تاجیکستان. لازم به ذکر است که متن فارسی تولید شده، در نهایت و طیّ چندین سال، با تعداد کثیری از دیگر نسخ خطّی و چاپی درّالمجالس به زبان‌های فارسی، ترکی، پنجابی، بنگالی، پشتو و غیره قیاس شده تا بیش از این بر سنگینی کاستی‌های آن افزوده نشود.
- معادل فارسی برخی از داستان‌های مالایی از جمله داستان محمّد حنفیّه تنها در سه نسخهٔ فارسی درّالمجالس یافت می‌شود (آکلند ۱۷۰، گنج‌بخش ۱۴۹۸-۰۰۱، ایوانف ۰۱۰۰ دانشگاه مک‌گیل کانادا). بدین ترتیب

عامل دیگری که مرا بیش از پیش در تصحیح، ترجمه و معرّفی این کتاب مصمّم ساخت، تأثیرگذاری درّالمجالس بر سرزمین‌های اسلامی منطقهٔ جنوب شرق آسیا بوده است. آنچه سیف ظفر نگاشت اندکی بعد خمیرمایهٔ ادبیات داستانی اسلامی در اندونزی، مالزی، برونئی، فیلیپین و مناطق جنوبی تایلند و برمه شد. آنچه اهمیّت درّالمجالس را بیشتر آشکار می‌کند این است که آموزه‌های اسلامی در این سرزمین‌ها بیشتر از طریق حکایات اسلامی منتقل می‌شدند تا از طریق قرآن، احادیث و رسالات فقهی. و این موضوعی است که کمتر مورد توجّه قرار گرفته‌است. اینکه چگونه مجموعه‌ای از داستان‌های کوتاه و بلند فارسی طی قرون متمادی در ادبیات و اندیشهٔ دینی و سیاسی مردم جنوب شرق آسیا و جهان مالایا-اندونزی تاثیر داشته‌اند رازی است که شاید بتوان پاسخش را از دل اثر سیف ظفر جست.

برای اینکه بتوانم تحلیلی نسبتاً دقیق از ارتباط متن فارسی با متون مشابه آن به زبان مالایی و جاوه‌ای پیش‌روی خوانندگان قرار دهم از نسخه‌های خطّی و کتاب‌های متنوّع به زبان‌های مختلف آسیایی و اروپایی بهره جسته‌ام. با این وجود، بخش اصلی مقدّمهٔ کتاب، شیوهٔ تصحیح و ترجمهٔ متن، لیست نسخه‌های اساس و اهمّیّت آنها و ترجمهٔ درّالمجالس به زبان انگلیسی ارائه شده است. برای نشان دادن ارتباط بین این اثر قدیمی و ادبیات اسلامی مالایی-اندونزیایی از منابع و عبارات مالایی (Malay) و جاوه‌ای (Javanese) استفاده کرده‌ام.

شاید در آینده‌ای نه‌چندان دور ترجمهٔ فارسی آن هم منتشر شود؛ البتّه به شرط حیات و توان.

لازم دیدم پیش‌از آغاز بخش فارسیِ متن درّالمجالس به چند نکته اشاره نمایم:

- شرح و توضیح پاورقیِ بخش فارسی برای علاقه‌مندان ارائه شده است، که لزوماً مرتبط و یا منطبق با پاورقی‌های بخش انگلیسی نمی‌باشد.
- علامت نقل قول مستقیم به این شکل است: «...».
- نقل قول در نقل قول چنین آمده است: «...«...»...».
- شرح فارسی را با اعداد و تصحیح و ویرایش خود را با حروف ابجد نمایش داده‌ام.
- معانی کلمات دشوار براساس فرهنگ لغات دهخدا، معین، عمید، برهان قاطع و برخی آثار شرق‌شناسان ارائه شده است. به لیست منابع مراجعه فرمایند.
- بسیاری از اشعار براساس پایگاه دیجیتال گنجور بازخوانی و بررسی شده‌اند.
- نام نسخه‌های خطّی به شکل کوتاه درج شده است، برای مثال «نسخه خطّی GMS-۱۷۰ کتابخانهٔ آکلند» بیشتر به‌صورت «آکلند ۱۷۰» آمده است.
- قسمت‌های ناخوانا یا قسمت‌های ناتمام در متن اصلی با شکل [...] نشان داده شده‌اند.
- بسیاری از واژگان با آوانویسی کامل ارائه شده‌اند.

پیشگفتار

کتابی که در دست دارید محصول بیش از هفت سال پژوهش و نگارش من در نقاط مختلف جهان است. این بخش از کتاب دربردارندهٔ متن فارسی درّالمجالس از سیف ظفر است. بنابر منابع در دسترس، وی اهل تصوّف بوده است. او از اواخر سدهٔ هفتم تا اواسط سدهٔ هشتم هجری قمری در بخش‌هایی از آسیای مرکزی و آسیای جنوبی می‌زیسته است. سیف ظفر این اثر را، که مشتمل بر داستان‌های روایی-اسلامی متفاوتی است، احتمالا در اواخر عمر خود و در اواسط سدهٔ هشتم هجری قمری برابر با چهاردهم میلادی به رشتهٔ تحریر درآورده است. پس از اتمام این اثر نسخه‌های کوتاه و بلندی از آن در سرتاسر جهان اسلام بازنویسی و همچنین به زبان‌های گوناگون ترجمه شد. چنانچه در بخش انگلیسی این کتاب اشاره کرده‌ام، استقبال گسترده از این اثر، از شرق تا غربِ سرزمین‌های اسلامی، مرا بر آن داشت تا آن را رقیبی شایسته برای آثار شاعران و واعظان نامدار اسلامی برشمارم، چراکه در مدّت زمان کوتاهی مسلمانان زیادی را برآن داشت تا «سر به جیب مراقبت فرو برده و در بحر مکاشفت مستغرق شوند».[1] همچنین، «صیت سخنش در بسیط زمین رفت و رقعهٔ منشآتش را چون کاغذ زر می‌بردند»[2] و از این نظر با گلستانِ سعدی، منطق الطّیرِ عطّار، اشعارِ مولانا، لمعات عراقی، و اشعهٔ جامی مقایسه‌شدنی است.

دست‌نویس سیف ظفر به سرزمین‌های عرب‌زبانی همچون مصر راه یافت. ساکنان هندی الاصل شرق آفریقا، بویژه در بندر موزامبیک و ممبوسا در کنیا، آن را در قرن نوزدهم بازنویسی کرده و در اختیار مسلمانان مهاجر قرار دادند. تعداد زیادی از حاکمان، تجّار، پژوهشگران و عوام در استانبول، اردبیل، هکاری (هه‌کاری\حکاری)، هرات، سمرقند، بخارا، پنجاب، پتنه، تامیل نادو، بنگال و دهاکه، کازان (قازان)، تاشکند، ختن، ایغورِ (اویغور) ترکستان، تناسر و سیام ارادت ویژه‌ای به این اثر داشته‌اند.

[1] چنانکه سعدی در دیباچهٔ گلستان نوشته است.

[2] چنانکه سعدی در دیباچهٔ گلستان نوشته است. از رادمان رسولی مهربانی برای پیشنهاد ارزشمندش سپاسگزارم.

تقدیم به

دکتر یوتا شوریگ

نثر فارسی فرا-مرزی و
شکل‌گیری ادبیات اسلامی مالایی

به همراه مقدّمهٔ انتقادی، شرح و ترجمهٔ انگلیسی

و ویرایش فارسی **دُرّالْمَجالِس**

اثر **سَیف ظَفَر** اواخر سدهٔ هفتم و اواسط سدهٔ هشتم هجری قمری

مجید دانشگر

بنیاد یادمان گیب وانتشارات دانشگاه ادینبرو

EDINBURGH
University Press

THE E J W GIBB
MEMORIAL TRUST

نثر فارسی فرا- مرزی و شکل گیری
ادبیات اسلامی مالایی

www.ingramcontent.com/pod-product-compliance
Lightning Source LLC
Chambersburg PA
CBHW081131131125
35397CB00006B/45